Lecture Notes in Computer Science 9034

Advanced Research in Computing and Software Science

Subline of Lecture Notes in Computer Science

More information about this series at http://www.springer.com/series/7407

Andrew Pitts (Ed.)

Foundations of Software Science and Computation Structures

18th International Conference, FOSSACS 2015
Held as Part of the European Joint Conferences on Theory and Practice of Software, ETAPS 2015
London, UK, April 11–18, 2015
Proceedings

Springer

Editor
Andrew Pitts
University of Cambridge
Cambridge
United Kingdom

ISSN 0302-9743 ISSN 1611-3349 (electronic)
Lecture Notes in Computer Science
ISBN 978-3-662-46677-3 ISBN 978-3-662-46678-0 (eBook)
DOI 10.1007/978-3-662-46678-0

Library of Congress Control Number: 2015934135

LNCS Sublibrary: SL1 – Theoretical Computer Science and General Issues

Springer Heidelberg New York Dordrecht London

Printed on acid-free paper

Springer-Verlag GmbH Berlin Heidelberg is part of Springer Science+Business Media
(www.springer.com)

Foreword

ETAPS 2015 was the 18th instance of the European Joint Conferences on Theory and Practice of Software. ETAPS is an annual federated conference that was established in 1998, and this year consisted of six constituting conferences (CC, ESOP, FASE, FoSSaCS, TACAS, and POST) including five invited speakers and two tutorial speakers. Prior to and after the main conference, numerous satellite workshops took place and attracted many researchers from all over the world.

ETAPS is a confederation of several conferences, each with its own Program Committee and its own Steering Committee (if any). The conferences cover various aspects of software systems, ranging from theoretical foundations to programming language developments, compiler advancements, analysis tools, formal approaches to software engineering, and security. Organizing these conferences into a coherent, highly synchronized conference program enables the participation in an exciting event, having the possibility to meet many researchers working in different directions in the field, and to easily attend talks at different conferences.

The six main conferences together received 544 submissions this year, 152 of which were accepted (including 10 tool demonstration papers), yielding an overall acceptance rate of 27.9%. I thank all authors for their interest in ETAPS, all reviewers for the peer-reviewing process, the PC members for their involvement, and in particular the PC Co-chairs for running this entire intensive process. Last but not least, my congratulations to all authors of the accepted papers!

ETAPS 2015 was greatly enriched by the invited talks by Daniel Licata (Wesleyan University, USA) and Catuscia Palamidessi (Inria Saclay and LIX, France), both unifying speakers, and the conference-specific invited speakers [CC] Keshav Pingali (University of Texas, USA), [FoSSaCS] Frank Pfenning (Carnegie Mellon University, USA), and [TACAS] Wang Yi (Uppsala University, Sweden). Invited tutorials were provided by Daniel Bernstein (Eindhoven University of Technology, the Netherlands and the University of Illinois at Chicago, USA), and Florent Kirchner (CEA, the Alternative Energies and Atomic Energy Commission, France). My sincere thanks to all these speakers for their inspiring talks!

ETAPS 2015 took place in the capital of England, the largest metropolitan area in the UK and the largest urban zone in the European Union by most measures. ETAPS 2015 was organized by the Queen Mary University of London in cooperation with the following associations and societies: ETAPS e.V., EATCS (European Association for Theoretical Computer Science), EAPLS (European Association for Programming Languages and Systems), and EASST (European Association of Software Science and Technology). It was supported by the following sponsors: Semmle, Winton, Facebook, Microsoft Research, and Springer-Verlag.

The organization team comprised:

- General Chairs: Pasquale Malacaria and Nikos Tzevelekos
- Workshops Chair: Paulo Oliva
- Publicity chairs: Michael Tautschnig and Greta Yorsh
- Members: Dino Distefano, Edmund Robinson, and Mehrnoosh Sadrzadeh

The overall planning for ETAPS is the responsibility of the Steering Committee. The ETAPS Steering Committee consists of an Executive Board (EB) and representatives of the individual ETAPS conferences, as well as representatives of EATCS, EAPLS, and EASST. The Executive Board comprises Gilles Barthe (satellite events, Madrid), Holger Hermanns (Saarbrücken), Joost-Pieter Katoen (Chair, Aachen and Twente), Gerald Lüttgen (Treasurer, Bamberg), and Tarmo Uustalu (publicity, Tallinn). Other members of the Steering Committee are: Christel Baier (Dresden), David Basin (Zurich), Giuseppe Castagna (Paris), Marsha Chechik (Toronto), Alexander Egyed (Linz), Riccardo Focardi (Venice), Björn Franke (Edinburgh), Jan Friso Groote (Eindhoven), Reiko Heckel (Leicester), Bart Jacobs (Nijmegen), Paul Klint (Amsterdam), Jens Knoop (Vienna), Christof Löding (Aachen), Ina Schäfer (Braunschweig), Pasquale Malacaria (London), Tiziana Margaria (Limerick), Andrew Myers (Boston), Catuscia Palamidessi (Paris), Frank Piessens (Leuven), Andrew Pitts (Cambridge), Jean-Francois Raskin (Brussels), Don Sannella (Edinburgh), Vladimiro Sassone (Southampton), Perdita Stevens (Edinburgh), Gabriele Taentzer (Marburg), Peter Thiemann (Freiburg), Cesare Tinelli (Iowa City), Luca Vigano (London), Jan Vitek (Boston), Igor Walukiewicz (Bordeaux), Andrzej Wąsowski (Copenhagen), and Lenore Zuck (Chicago).

I sincerely thank all ETAPS SC members for all their hard work to make the 18th edition of ETAPS a success. Moreover, thanks to all speakers, attendants, organizers of the satellite workshops, and to Springer for their support. Finally, many thanks to Pasquale and Nikos and their local organization team for all their efforts enabling ETAPS to take place in London!

January 2015 Joost-Pieter Katoen

Preface

This volume contains the papers presented at the 18th International Conference on Foundations of Software Science and Computation Structures (FoSSaCS 2015) held at Queen Mary University of London, UK, during April 13–16, 2015. FoSSaCS is one of the European Joint Conferences on Theory and Practice of Software (ETAPS). It is dedicated to foundational research with a clear significance for software science and invites submissions on theories and methods to support the analysis, integration, synthesis, transformation, and verification of programs and software systems.

In addition to an invited talk by Frank Pfenning (CMU, USA) on Polarized Substructural Session Types, the contributed papers in the conference ranged over the following topics: semantics of programming languages; categorical models and logics; logical aspects of computational complexity; concurrent, probabilistic and timed systems; automata, games, and verification; modal and temporal logics; type theory, proof theory, and implicit computational complexity.

In response to the call for papers, the Program Committee received a total of 93 submissions. Each submission was reviewed by three or more Program Committee members, aided by sub-reviewers. The committee decided to accept 28 papers. The selection was made after extensive discussion by email, based on originality, quality, and relevance to the scope of FoSSaCS. The quality of the submissions was very high and many deserving papers could not be selected.

I wish to thank all the authors who submitted papers for consideration, the members of the Program Committee for their scholarly efforts and enthusiasm, and all subreviewers who assisted the Program Committee in the evaluation process. I am grateful to the ETAPS 2015 General Chairs, Pasquale Malacaria and Nikos Tzevelekos and their support staff for their assistance. I would also like to thank the ETAPS Steering Committe and particularly its Chair, Joost-Pieter Katoen, for overseeing the complicated process of producing a joint conference. The conference management system EasyChair was used to handle the submissions, to conduct the electronic Program Committee meeting, and to assist with the assembly of this proceedings.

January 2015 Andrew Pitts

Organization

Program Committee

Andreas Abel	Chalmers University of Technology, Sweden
Andrej Bauer	University of Ljubljana, Slovenia
Udi Boker	Interdisciplinary Center Herzliya, Israel
Luis Caires	Universidade Nova de Lisboa, Portugal
Krishnendu Chatterjee	Institute of Science and Technology, Austria
Thomas Colcombet	Université Paris Diderot, France
Andrea Corradini	Università di Pisa, Italy
Ugo Dal Lago	Università di Bologna, Italy
Maribel Fernandez	King's College London, UK
Daniel Hirschkoff	École Normale Supérieure de Lyon, France
Radha Jagadeesan	DePaul University, USA
Sławomir Lasota	University of Warsaw, Poland
Ranko Lazic	University of Warwick, UK
Paul Levy	University of Birmingham, UK
Daniel Licata	Wesleyan University, USA
Dirk Pattinson	Australian National University, Australia
Nir Piterman	University of Leicester, UK
Andrew Pitts	University of Cambridge, UK
Ulrich Schöpp	Ludwig-Maximilians-Universität München, Germany
Alexandra Silva	Radboud Universiteit Nijmegen, The Netherlands
Alex Simpson	University of Edinburgh, UK
Lutz Strassburger	Inria Saclay-Ile de France, France
Thomas Streicher	Technische Universität Darmstadt, Germany
Ashish Tiwari	SRI International, USA
Daniele Varacca	University Paris-Est Créteil Val de Marne, France

Additional Reviewers

Abdulla, Parosh
Adams, Robin
Ahmed, Amal
Al-Humaimeedy, Abeer
Almagor, Shaull
Aminof, Benjamin
Aubert, Clément
Avanzini, Martin
Avni, Guy
Baldan, Paolo
Basilico, Nicola
Ben-Amram, Amir
Berdine, Josh
Berger, Ulrich
Berwanger, Dietmar
Blot, Valentin

Blumensath, Achim
Bonchi, Filippo
Brenguier, Romain
Brotherston, James
Bruni, Roberto
Bujorianu, Manuela
Cadilhac, Michaël
Carayol, Arnaud
Castellani, Ilaria
Clairambault, Pierre
Clemente, Lorenzo
Crafa, Silvia
Crubillé, Raphaëlle
Das, Anupam
de Carvalho, Daniel
Degorre, Aldric
Demri, Stéphane
Di Gianantonio, Pietro
Fearnley, John
Feret, Jerome
Figueira, Diego
Fijalkow, Nathanaël
French, Tim
Gadducci, Fabio
Ganty, Pierre
Gascon, Adria
Gebler, Daniel
Geerarts, Gilles
Gheerbrant, Amelie
Goncharov, Sergey
Gorla, Daniele
Guenot, Nicolas
Haase, Christoph
Hasuo, Ichiro
Heckel, Reiko
Hermida, Claudio
Hidaka, Soichiro
Hofman, Piotr
Hofman, Piotrek
Horn, Florian
Hunter, Paul
Huschenbett, Martin
Hyon, Emmanuel
Hüttel, Hans
Ibsen-Jensen, Rasmus
Iliev, Petar
Ilik, Danko
Ivan, Szabolcs
Jongmans, Sung-Shik T.Q.
Jurdzinski, Marcin
Kaiser, Lukasz
Keimel, Klaus
Kiefer, Stefan
Klin, Bartek
Klueppelholz, Sascha
Kontchakov, Roman
Kopczynski, Eryk
Koutavas, Vasileios
Kretinsky, Jan
Krishnaswami, Neelakantan
Kucera, Antonin
Kuperberg, Denis
Kupke, Clemens
Kurz, Alexander
Kuznets, Roman
König, Barbara
Laird, James
Lamarche, Francois
Lanese, Ivan
Lang, Martin
Lange, Julien
Lenglet, Sergueï
Lenisa, Marina
Lumsdaine, Peter Lefanu
Maieli, Roberto
Majumdar, Rupak
Maletti, Andreas
Manuel, Amaldev
Mardare, Radu
Marion, Jean-Yves
Martini, Simone
Matthes, Ralph
McCusker, Guy
Meel, Kuldeep S.
Mehner, Stefan
Meier, Arne
Melgratti, Hernan
Milius, Stefan
Mimram, Samuel
Miranda-Perea, Favio E.
Montanari, Ugo
Mostrous, Dimitris

Murano, Aniello
Murawski, Andrzej
Møgelberg, Rasmus Ejlers
Novakovic, Novak
Novotný, Petr
Obdrzalek, Jan
Otop, Jan
Oualhadj, Youssouf
Pagani, Michele
Parys, Paweł
Pavlogiannis, Andreas
Pelz, Elisabeth
Perelli, Giuseppe
Pous, Damien
Pretnar, Matija
Radhakrishna, Arjun
Ramsay, Steven
Rathke, Julian
Rehof, Jakob
Riba, Colin
Rogalewicz, Adam
Rot, Jurriaan
Rukhaia, Mikheil
Salvati, Sylvain
Sangnier, Arnaud
Schröder, Lutz
Shehtman, Valentin
Skrzypczak, Michał
Skvortsov, Dmitrij
Sobocinski, Pawel
Sreejith, A.V.
Staton, Sam
Stefani, Jean-Bernard
Szreter, Maciej
Tabareau, Nicolas
Terui, Kazushige
Totzke, Patrick
Trivedi, Ashutosh
Tzevelekos, Nikos
Urzyczyn, Pawel
Valencia, Frank
van Bakel, Steffen
Velner, Yaron
Vezzosi, Andrea
Vignudelli, Valeria
Villard, Jules
Vollmer, Heribert
Widder, Josef
Wojtczak, Dominik
Wolper, Pierre
Worrell, James
Yang, Fan
Zanasi, Fabio
Zielonka, Wieslaw
Zuleger, Florian

Contents

Invited Talk

Semantics of Programming Languages I

Categorical Models and Logics

Modal and Temporal Logics

Concurrent, Probabilistic and Timed Systems

Semantics of Programming Languages II

Automata, Games, Verification

Logical Aspects of Computational Complexity

Type Theory, Proof Theory and Implicit Computational Complexity

Invited Talk

Polarized Substructural Session Types

Frank Pfenning[1] and Dennis Griffith[2]

[1] Carnegie Mellon University, Pittsburgh, PA 15213, USA
fp@cs.cmu.edu
[2] University of Illinois at Urbana-Champaign, Urbana, IL 61801, USA
dgriffi3@illinois.edu

Abstract. The deep connection between session-typed concurrency and linear logic is embodied in the language SILL that integrates functional and message-passing concurrent programming. The exacting nature of linear typing provides strong guarantees, such as global progress, absence of deadlock, and race freedom, but it also requires explicit resource management by the programmer. This burden is alleviated in an affine type system where resources need not be used, relying on a simple form of garbage collection.

In this paper we show how to effectively support both linear and affine typing in a single language, in addition to the already present unrestricted (intuitionistic) types. The approach, based on Benton's adjoint construction, suggests that the usual distinction between synchronous and asynchronous communication can be viewed through the lens of modal logic. We show how polarizing the propositions into positive and negative connectives allows us to elegantly express synchronization in the type instead of encoding it by extra-logical means.

1 Introduction

Session types prescribe the communication behavior of concurrent message-passing processes [13,14]. Anticipated with some analogies for some time [11,23], session types have recently been placed upon the firm foundation of linear logic via a Curry-Howard interpretation of linear propositions as types, proofs as processes, and cut reduction as communication. Variations apply for both intuitionistic [5,6] and classical [24] linear logic. This has enabled the application of proof-theoretic techniques in this domain, for example, developing logical relations [17], corecursion [22], and parametricity and behavioral polymorphism [4]. It has also given rise to the design of SILL, a modular extension of an underlying functional language with session-typed concurrency [21].

Practical experience with a SILL prototype has led to a number of new questions. For example, should the type system really be *linear*, where all resources must be fully accounted for by the programmer, or should it be *affine*[16], where resources may be reclaimed by a form of garbage collection? Another question concerns the underlying model of communication: should it be synchronous or asynchronous? The proof theory does not provide a definitive answer to this question, supporting both. The purpose of this paper is to show that we can

A. Pitts (Ed.): FOSSACS 2015, LNCS 9034, pp. 3–22, 2015.
DOI: 10.1007/978-3-662-46678-0_1

have our cake and eat it, too, in both cases. First, we combine linear and affine types in an elegant and proof-theoretically justified way, slightly reformulating unrestricted types along the way. Second, we show how to support synchronous and asynchronous communication patterns in a single language, again taking our inspiration from proof theory.

The central idea behind the first step is to generalize Benton's LNL [3] in the spirit of Reed's adjoint logic [18]. This stratifies the propositions into linear, affine, and unrestricted ones, with modal operators *shifting* between the strata. For example, the familiar exponential of linear logic $!A$ is decomposed into two shifting modalities, one going from A (which is linear) into the unrestricted layer, and one going from the unrestricted layer back to the linear one. Similar modalities connect the linear and affine layers of the language.

The main idea behind the second step is to *polarize* the presentation of linear logic [15], segregating positive (sending) connectives from negative (receiving) connectives. Surprisingly, the two sublanguages of propositions can be connected by new versions of the shift modalities, fully consistent with the adjoint construction, leading to a pleasantly coherent language.

In the rest of this note we walk through these steps, taking small liberties with previously published notations for the sake of consistency.

2 Linear Logic and Session Types

We give here only the briefest review of linear logic and its deep connection to session types. The interested reader is referred to [5,6,21] for further background.

The key idea of linear logic [12] is to view logical propositions as resources: they must be used exactly once in a proof. We adopt the intuitionistic version [2], which is defined via a *linear hypothetical judgment* [8]

$$A_1, \ldots, A_n \vdash A$$

where the hypotheses $A_1, \ldots, A_n$ must be used exactly once in the proof of the conclusion A. We do not care about the order of the assumptions, treating them like a multiset, and use Δ to denote such a multiset. The judgmental rules (sometimes called structural rules) explain the meaning of the hypothetical judgment itself and are independent of any particular propositions. In a sequent calculus, there are two such rules: cut, which states that if we can prove A we are justified to use A as a resource, and identity, which says that we can use a resource A to prove A.

$$\frac{\Delta \vdash A \quad \Delta', A \vdash C}{\Delta, \Delta' \vdash C}\ \mathsf{cut} \qquad\qquad \frac{}{A \vdash A}\ \mathsf{id}$$

Under the Curry-Howard isomorphism for intuitionistic logic, propositions are related to types, proofs to programs, and proof reduction to computation. Here, linear logic propositions are related to session types, proofs to concurrent programs, and cut reduction in proofs to computation. For this correspondence, each hypothesis is labeled by a *channel* (rather than a variable). In addition, we also label the conclusion by a channel. This is because, unlike functional programming, we do not reduce a process to a value but we interact with it. For such interaction to take place in the concurrent setting, we need a channel to communicate along.

$$x_1{:}A_1, \ldots, x_n{:}A_n \vdash P :: (x : A)$$

Here, $x_1, \ldots, x_n$ and x are distinct channels, and $A_1, \ldots, A_n$ and A are their respective session types. We say that process P *provides* A along channel x and *uses* channels $x_1, \ldots, x_n$.

The rule of cut now is a form of *process composition*, connecting a client (here Q) to a provider (here P).

$$\frac{\Delta \vdash P_x :: (x : A) \quad \Delta, x{:}A \vdash Q_x :: (z : C)}{\Delta, \Delta' \vdash (x \leftarrow P_x \ ; Q_x) :: (z : C)}\ \mathsf{cut}$$

We use syntactic forms for processes, rather than π-calculus terms, to emphasize the interpretation of proofs as programs. Because every (well-typed) process P offers a session along exactly one channel, and each channel is provided by exactly one process, we can think of channels as unique process identifiers. Under this interpretation, suggested by the intuitionistic formulation of linear logic, we can see that the cut rule *spawns* P as a new process. More precisely, the process identified by z executing $(x \leftarrow P_x \ ; Q_x)$ creates a fresh channel a, spawns a process executing P_a that provides session A along a, and continues as Q_a. Because a is fresh, this channel will be a private channel between P_a and Q_a.

We can express this in a *substructural operational semantics* [19] which is based on *multiset rewriting* [7]. The notation is again borrowed from linear logic, but it should not be confused with the use of linear logic propositions as session types.

$$\mathsf{cut} : \mathsf{proc}_c(x \leftarrow P_x \ ; Q_x) \multimap \{\exists a.\ \mathsf{proc}_a(P_a) \otimes \mathsf{proc}_c(Q_a)\}$$

In this formalization $\mathsf{proc}_c(P)$ is the state of a process executing program P, offering along channel c. The multiplicative conjunction ($\otimes$) combines processes in the same state, linear implication ($\multimap$) expresses a state transition from left to right, and the existential quantification corresponds to generation of a fresh channel. The curly braces $\{\cdots\}$ indicate a monad which essentially forces the rule above to be interpreted as a multiset rewriting rule.

The identity rule instead *forwards* between its client and the process that it uses, which must be of the same type.

$$\frac{}{y{:}A \vdash (x \leftarrow y) :: x : A}\ \mathsf{id}$$

There are several ways to describe this action operationally. A straightforward one globally identifies the channels x and y, while the forwarding process itself terminates.

$$\mathsf{id} : \mathsf{proc}_c(c \leftarrow d) \multimap \{c = d\}$$

This could be implemented in the substrate of the network or operating system. Or it could be implemented more explicitly by sending a message along c asking the client to use d for subsequent interactions. For now, we abstract over such lower level details.

Assigning process expressions to each rule of linear logic yields the following interpretation of propositions.

$$
\begin{array}{rll}
A, B, C ::= & \mathbf{1} & \text{send } \mathsf{end} \text{ and terminate} \\
\mid & A \otimes B & \text{send channel of type } A \text{ and continue as } B \\
\mid & A \oplus B & \text{send } \mathsf{inl} \text{ or } \mathsf{inr} \text{ and continue as } A \text{ or } B\text{, respectively} \\
\mid & \tau \wedge B & \text{send value } v \text{ of type } \tau \text{ and continue as } B \\
\mid & A \multimap B & \text{receive channel of type } A \\
\mid & A \,\&\, B & \text{receive } \mathsf{inl} \text{ or } \mathsf{inr} \text{ and continue as } A \text{ or } B\text{, respectively} \\
\mid & \tau \supset B & \text{receive value } V \text{ of type } \tau \text{ and continue as } B
\end{array}
$$

Here, we wrote $\tau \wedge B$ as a special case of $\exists x{:}\tau.\, B$ where x does not appear in B, and $\tau \supset B$ is a special case of $\forall x{:}\tau.\, B$. The syntactic simplification is justified because in this paper we do not consider propositions that depend on terms.

Below is a summary of the process expressions, with the sending construct followed by the matching receiving construct. For the purpose of the examples we generalize the binary choice constructs $A \,\&\, B$ and $A \oplus B$ to n-ary choice $\&\{lab_i : A_i\}_i$ and $\oplus\{lab_i : A_i\}_i$, respectively. We have as a special case $A \,\&\, B = \&\{\mathsf{inl} : A, \mathsf{inr} : B\}$ and $A \oplus B = \oplus\{\mathsf{inl} : A, \mathsf{inr} : B\}$.

$$
\begin{array}{rll}
P, Q, R ::= & x \leftarrow P_x \,;\, Q_x & \mathsf{cut} \;\; \text{(spawn)} \\
\mid & c \leftarrow d & \mathsf{id} \;\; \text{(forward)} \\
\mid & \mathsf{close}\; c \mid \mathsf{wait}\; c & \mathbf{1} \\
\mid & \mathsf{send}\; c\; (y \leftarrow P_y) \,;\, Q \mid x \leftarrow \mathsf{recv}\; c \,;\, R_x & A \otimes B, A \multimap B \\
\mid & \mathsf{send}\; c\; d & \text{derived form } A \otimes B,\; A \multimap B \\
\mid & \mathsf{send}\; c\; M \,;\, P \mid n \leftarrow \mathsf{recv}\; c \,;\, Q_n & A \wedge B, A \supset B \\
\mid & c.lab \,;\, P \mid \mathsf{case}\; c\; \{lab_i \rightarrow Q_i\}_i & \&\{lab_i : A_i\}_i, \oplus\{lab_i : A_i\}_i
\end{array}
$$

As a running example in this paper we will use variations of an implementation of polymorphic queues. We begin with the purely linear version. The interface specifies that a queue presents an external choice between enqueue and dequeue operations. When the client selects to enqueue, we input a channel of type A (to be stored in the queue), and recurse. When the client selects to dequeue, we either indicate that the queue is empty and terminate, or we indicate that there is some element in the queue, send the first element (removing it in the process), and recurse. The "recursion" here is an instance of an *equirecursive session type* [10]; some logical underpinnings are available for *coinductive types* [22]. We also use polymorphism intuitively; a formal development can be found in [4].

First, the specification of the queue interface.

$$\mathsf{queue}\, A = \&\{\mathsf{enq} : A \multimap \mathsf{queue}\, A, \mathsf{deq} : \oplus\{\mathsf{none} : \mathbf{1}, \mathsf{some} : A \otimes \mathsf{queue}\, A\}\}$$

We implement queues with two forms of recursive processes, *empty* for the empty queue and *elem* for a process holding exactly one element. For processes with

$$x_1{:}A_1, \ldots, x_n{:}A_n \vdash P :: (x : A)$$

we write $P : \{A \leftarrow A_1, \ldots, A_n\}$ to specify its typing and $x \leftarrow P \leftarrow x_1, \ldots, x_n$ to provide its interface.

```
empty : {queue A}

c ← empty =
  case c of
  | enq → x ← recv c ;
          e ← empty ;
          c ← elem ← x, e
  | deq → c.none ;
          close c
```

```
elem : {queue A ← A, queue A}

c ← elem ← x, d =
  case c of
  | enq → y ← recv c ;
          d.enq ; send d y ;
          c ← elem ← x, d
  | deq → c.some ;
          send c x ;
          c ← d
```

From the perspective of the client, this implementation has constant time enqueue and dequeue operations. For dequeue this is obvious. For enqueue, the process at the front of the queue passes the element down the queue and is immediately available to serve another request while the element travels to the end of the queue.

3 Categorical Truth

The linear logic proposition $!A$ allows A to be used arbitrarily often in a proof—it functions as an unrestricted resource. In the intuitionistic reconstruction of linear logic [8], $!A$ internalizes a *categorical judgment.* We say that A is *valid* if it is true, and its proof does not depend on any assumptions about the truth of other propositions. Since we are working with a linear hypothetical judgment, this means that the proof of A does not depend on any resources. We further allow hypotheses Γ that are assumed to be valid (rather than merely true), and these are allowed in a proof A *valid*.

$$\Gamma \,;\, \Delta \vdash C$$

The meaning of validity is captured in the following two judgmental rules, where '$\cdot$' stands for an empty context:

$$\frac{\Gamma \,;\, \cdot \vdash A \quad (\Gamma, A) \,;\, \Delta \vdash C}{\Gamma \,;\, \Delta \vdash C}\ \mathsf{cut!} \qquad \frac{(\Gamma, A) \,;\, \Delta, A \vdash C}{(\Gamma, A) \,;\, \Delta \vdash C}\ \mathsf{copy}$$

The first, cut!, states that we are justified in assuming that A is valid if we can prove it without using any resources. The second, copy, states that we are justified in assuming a copy of the resource A if A is known to be valid. All the purely linear rules are generalized by adding an unrestricted context Γ which is propagated to all premises.

How do we think of these in terms of processes? We introduce a new form of channel, called a *shared channel* (denoted by u, w) which can be used arbitrarily often in a client, and by arbitrarily many clients. It is offered by a *persistent process*. Operationally, a persistent process offering along $w : A$ inputs a fresh linear channel c and spawns a new process P that offers A along c.

We have the following typing rules, first at the level of judgments.

$$\frac{\Gamma, u{:}A \,;\, \Delta, x{:}A \vdash P_x :: (z{:}C)}{\Gamma, u{:}A \,;\, \Delta \vdash (x \leftarrow \mathsf{send}\ u \,;\, P_x) :: (z{:}C)}\ \mathsf{copy}$$

$$\frac{\Gamma \,;\, \cdot \vdash P_y :: (y{:}A) \quad \Gamma, u{:}A \,;\, \Delta \vdash Q_u :: (z{:}C)}{\Gamma \,;\, \Delta \vdash (u \leftarrow !(y \leftarrow \mathsf{recv}\ u \,;\, P_y) \,;\, Q_u) :: (z{:}C)}\ \mathsf{cut!}$$

The copy rule has a slightly strange process expression,

$$x \leftarrow \mathsf{send}\ u \,;\, P_x$$

It expresses that we send a *new* channel x along u. The continuation P refers to x so it can communicate along this new channel. This pattern will be common for sending fresh channels in a variety of constructs in this paper.

We see that the cut! rule incorporates two steps: creating a new shared channel u and then immediately receiving a linear channel y along u. There is no simple way to avoid this, since P in the first premise offers along a linear channel y. We will see alternatives in later sections.

In the operational semantics we write $!\mathsf{proc}_w(P)$ for a persistent process, offering along shared channel w. In the language of substructural specification, $!\mathsf{proc}_w(P)$ on the left-hand side of a rule means that it has to match a persistent proposition. We therefore do not need to repeat it on the right-hand side: it will continue to appear in the state. In this notation, the operational semantics is as follows:

$$\begin{aligned}\mathsf{copy} : \ & !\mathsf{proc}_w(y \leftarrow \mathsf{recv}\ w \,;\, P_y) \otimes \mathsf{proc}_c(x \leftarrow \mathsf{send}\ w \,;\, Q_x) \\ & \multimap \{\exists a.\ \mathsf{proc}_a(P_a) \otimes \mathsf{proc}_c(Q_a)\}\end{aligned}$$

$$\begin{aligned}\mathsf{cut!} \ : \ & \mathsf{proc}_c(u \leftarrow !(y \leftarrow \mathsf{recv}\ u \,;\, P_y) \,;\, Q_u) \\ & \multimap \{\exists w.\ !\mathsf{proc}_w(y \leftarrow \mathsf{recv}\ w \,;\, P_y) \otimes \mathsf{proc}_c(Q_w)\}\end{aligned}$$

The validity judgment realized by persistent processes offering along unrestricted channels can be internalized as a proposition $!A$ with the following rules. Note that the linear context must be empty in the !R rule, since validity is a categorical judgment. Allowing dependence on linear channels would violate their linearity.

$$\frac{\Gamma \,;\, \cdot \vdash P_y :: (y{:}A)}{\Gamma \,;\, \cdot \vdash (u \leftarrow \mathsf{send}\ x \,;\, !(y \leftarrow \mathsf{recv}\ u \,;\, P_y)) :: (x{:}!A)}\ !\mathsf{R}$$

$$\frac{\Gamma, u{:}A \,;\, \Delta \vdash Q_u :: (z{:}C)}{\Gamma \,;\, \Delta, x{:}!A \vdash (u \leftarrow \mathsf{recv}\ x \,;\, Q_u) :: (z{:}C)}\ !\mathsf{L}$$

Again the !R rule combines two steps: sending a new persistent channel u along x and then receiving a linear channel y along u. Operationally:

$$\begin{aligned}\mathsf{bang} : \mathsf{proc}_c(u \leftarrow \mathsf{recv}\ a\ ;\ Q_u) \otimes \mathsf{proc}_a(u \leftarrow \mathsf{send}\ a\ ;\ !(y \leftarrow \mathsf{recv}\ u\ ;\ P_y))\\ \multimap \{\exists w.\ \mathsf{proc}_c(Q_w) \otimes !\mathsf{proc}_w(y \leftarrow \mathsf{recv}\ w\ ;\ P_y)\}\end{aligned}$$

As expected, the persistent process spawned by the bang computation rule has exactly the same form as the one spawned by cut!, because a linear cut for a proposition $!A$ becomes a persistent cut for a proposition A.

Let's analyze the two-step rule in more detail.

$$\frac{\Gamma\ ;\ \cdot \vdash P_y :: (y{:}A)}{\Gamma\ ;\ \cdot \vdash (u \leftarrow \mathsf{send}\ x\ !(y \leftarrow \mathsf{recv}\ u\ ;\ P_y)) :: (x{:}!A)}\ !\mathsf{R}$$

The judgment A *valid* (corresponding to an unrestricted hypothesis $u{:}A$) is elided on the right-hand side: we jump directly from the truth of $!A$ to the truth of A. Writing it out as an intermediate step appears entirely reasonable. We do not even mention the linear hypotheses in the intermediate step, since the validity of A depends only on assumptions of validity in Γ.

$$\frac{\dfrac{\Gamma\ ;\ \cdot \vdash P_y :: (y{:}A)}{\Gamma \vdash (y \leftarrow \mathsf{recv}\ u\ ;\ P_y) :: (u{:}A)}\ \mathsf{valid}}{\Gamma\ ;\ \cdot \vdash (u \leftarrow \mathsf{send}\ x\ ;\ !(y \leftarrow \mathsf{recv}\ u\ ;\ P_y)) :: (x{:}!A)}\ !\mathsf{R}$$

We emphasize that $!A$ is positive (in the sense of polarized logic), so it corresponds to a send, while $A\,\mathsf{valid}$ is negative as a judgment, so it correspond to a receive. In the next section we elevate this from a judgmental to a first-class logical step.

Revisiting the example, recall that if we are the client of a channel $c : \mathsf{queue}\, A$, we must use this channel. This means we have to explicitly dequeue all its elements. In fact, we have to explicitly consume each of the elements as well, since they are also linear. However, if we know that each element in the queue is in fact unrestricted, we can destroy it recursively with the following program.

```
destroy : {1 ← queue (!A)}

c ← destroy ← q =
  q.deq ;
  case q of
  | none → wait q ; close c
  | some → x ← recv q ;        % obtain element x
           u ← recv x ;        % receive shared channel u, using x
           c ← destroy ← q     % recurse, ignoring u
```

4 Adjoint Logic

Adjoint logic is based on the idea that instead of a modality like $!A$ that remains within a given language of propositions, we have two mutually dependent languages and *two* modalities going back and forth between them. For this to make sense, the operators have to satisfy certain properties that pertain to the semantics of the two languages. We have in fact three language layers, which we call *linear propositions* A_L, *affine propositions* A_F, and *unrestricted propositions* A_U. They are characterized by the structural properties they satisfy: linear propositions are subject to none (they must be used exactly once), affine proposition can be weakened (they can be used at most once), and unrestricted propositions can be contracted and weakened (they can be used arbitrarily often). The order of propositions in the context matters for none of them. The hierarchy of structural properties is reflected in a hierarchy of modes of truth:

$$\mathsf{U} > \mathsf{F} > \mathsf{L}$$

U is *stronger* than F in the sense that unrestricted hypotheses can be used to prove affine conclusions, but not vice versa, and similarly for the other relations. Contexts Ψ combine assumptions with all modes. We write $\geq$ for the reflexive and transitive closure of $>$ and define

$$\Psi \geq k \quad \text{if } m \geq k \text{ for every } B_m \text{ in } \Psi$$

and

$$\Psi \vdash A_k \qquad \text{presupposes } \Psi \geq k$$

We use the notation $\uparrow_k^m A_k$ for an operator going from mode k *up* to mode m, and $\downarrow_k^m A_m$ for an operator going *down* from mode m to mode k. In both cases we presuppose $m > k$.

Taking this approach we obtain the following language:

$$\begin{array}{lll}
\text{Modes} & m, k, r & ::= \mathsf{U} \mid \mathsf{F} \mid \mathsf{L} \\
\text{Propositions} & A_m, B_m & ::= \mathbf{1}_m \mid A_m \otimes_m B_m \mid A_m \oplus_m B_m \mid \tau \wedge_m B_m \\
 & & \quad \mid A_m \multimap_m B_m \mid A_m \mathbin{\&}_m B_m \mid \tau \supset_m B_m \\
 & & \quad \mid \uparrow_k^m A_k \qquad (m > k) \\
 & & \quad \mid \downarrow_m^r A_r \qquad (r > m)
\end{array}$$

Because both $!A$ and A are linear propositions, the exponential $!A$ decomposes into two modalities:

$$!A = \downarrow_\mathsf{L}^\mathsf{U} \uparrow_\mathsf{L}^\mathsf{U} A_\mathsf{L}$$

Because linear and affine propositions behave essentially the same way except that affine channels need not be used, we reuse all the same syntax (both for propositions and for process expressions) at these two layers. Unrestricted propositions would behave quite differently in ways that are outside the scope of this note, so we specify that there are no unrestricted propositions besides $\uparrow_\mathsf{L}^\mathsf{U} A_\mathsf{L}$ and $\uparrow_\mathsf{F}^\mathsf{U} A_\mathsf{F}$.

In the following logical rules we always presuppose that the sequent in the conclusion is well-formed and add enough conditions to verify the presupposition in the premises.

$$\frac{\Psi \vdash A_k}{\Psi \vdash \uparrow_k^m A_k} \uparrow\mathsf{R} \qquad \frac{k \geq r \quad \Psi, A_k \vdash C_r}{\Psi, \uparrow_k^m A_k \vdash C_r} \uparrow\mathsf{L}$$

$$\frac{\Psi_{\geq m} \vdash A_m}{\Psi \vdash \downarrow_k^m A_m} \downarrow\mathsf{R} \qquad \frac{\Psi, A_m \vdash C_r}{\Psi, \downarrow_k^m A_m \vdash C_r} \downarrow\mathsf{L}$$

Here $\Psi_{\geq m}$ is the restriction of Ψ to propositions A_k with $k \geq m$. The rule does not apply if this would erase a linear proposition A_{L} since only affine and unrestricted propositions are subject to weakening.

The rules with no condition on the modes are invertible, while the others are not invertible. This means $\uparrow A$ is *negative* while $\downarrow A$ is *positive* (in the terminology of polarized logic [15]). We already noted that processes offering a negative type receive, while processes offering a positive type send. But what do we send or receive? Thinking of channels as intrinsically linear, affine, or shared suggests that we should send and receive fresh channels of different modes. Following this reasoning we obtain:

$$\frac{\Psi \vdash P_{x_k} :: (x_k{:}A_k)}{\Psi \vdash (x_k \leftarrow \mathsf{recv}\, x_m \;;\; P_{x_k}) :: (x_m{:}\uparrow_k^m A_k)} \uparrow\mathsf{R}$$

$$\frac{k \geq r \quad \Psi, x_k{:}A_k \vdash Q_{x_k} :: (z_r{:}C_r)}{\Psi, x_m{:}\uparrow_k^m A_k \vdash (x_k \leftarrow \mathsf{send}\, x_m \;;\; Q_{x_k}) :: (z_r{:}C_r)} \uparrow\mathsf{L}$$

For clarity, we annotate each channel with its mode, although it may not be strictly necessary. Operationally:

$$\begin{aligned} \mathsf{up}_k^m : {} & \mathsf{proc}_{a_r}(x_k \leftarrow \mathsf{send}\, c_m \;;\; Q_{x_k}) \otimes \mathsf{proc}_{c_m}(y_k \leftarrow \mathsf{recv}\, c_m \;;\; P_{y_k}) \\ & \multimap \{\exists c_k.\ \mathsf{proc}_{a_r}(Q_{c_k}) \otimes \mathsf{proc}_{c_k}(P_{c_k})\} \end{aligned}$$

And for the other modality:

$$\frac{\Psi \geq m \quad \Psi \vdash Q_{x_m} :: (x_m{:}A_m)}{\Psi \vdash (x_m \leftarrow \mathsf{send}\, x_k \;;\; Q_{x_m}) :: (x_k{:}\downarrow_k^m A_m)} \downarrow\mathsf{R}$$

$$\frac{\Psi, x_m{:}A_m \vdash P_{x_m} :: (z_r{:}C_r)}{\Psi, x_k{:}\downarrow_k^m A_m \vdash (x_m \leftarrow \mathsf{recv}\, x_k \;;\; P_{x_m}) :: (z_r{:}C_r)} \downarrow\mathsf{L}$$

Operationally:

$$\begin{aligned} \mathsf{down}_k^m : {} & \mathsf{proc}_{a_r}(y_m \leftarrow \mathsf{recv}\, c_k \;;\; P_{y_m}) \otimes \mathsf{proc}_{c_k}(x_m \leftarrow \mathsf{send}\, c_k \;;\; Q_{x_m}) \\ & \multimap \{\exists c_m.\ \mathsf{proc}_{a_r}(P_{c_m}) \otimes \mathsf{proc}_{c_m}(Q_{c_m})\} \end{aligned}$$

Since processes offering along unrestricted channels are persistent, we use here the (admittedly dangerous) notational convention that all processes offering along unrestricted channels c_{U} are implicitly marked persistent. In particular, we should read $\mathsf{up}_k^{\mathsf{U}}$ and $\mathsf{down}_k^{\mathsf{U}}$ as

$$\begin{aligned}
\mathsf{up}_k^{\mathsf{U}} \ &: \mathsf{proc}_{a_r}(x_k \leftarrow \mathsf{send}\ c_{\mathsf{U}} \ ; Q_{x_k}) \otimes !\mathsf{proc}_{c_{\mathsf{U}}}(x_k \leftarrow \mathsf{recv}\ c_{\mathsf{U}} \ ; P_{x_k}) \\
&\quad \multimap \{\exists c_k.\ \mathsf{proc}_{a_r}(Q_{c_k}) \otimes \mathsf{proc}_{c_k}(P_{c_k})\}
\end{aligned}$$

$$\begin{aligned}
\mathsf{down}_k^{\mathsf{U}} &: \mathsf{proc}_{a_r}(x_{\mathsf{U}} \leftarrow \mathsf{recv}\ c_k \ ; P_{x_{\mathsf{U}}}) \otimes \mathsf{proc}_{c_k}(x_{\mathsf{U}} \leftarrow \mathsf{send}\ c_k \ ; Q_{x_{\mathsf{U}}}) \\
&\quad \multimap \{\exists c_{\mathsf{U}}.\ \mathsf{proc}_{a_r}(P_{c_{\mathsf{U}}}) \otimes !\mathsf{proc}_{c_{\mathsf{U}}}(Q_{c_{\mathsf{U}}})\}
\end{aligned}$$

At this point we have achieved that every logical connective, including the up and down modalities, correspond to exactly one matching send and receive action. Moreover, as we can check, the compound rules for $!A$ decompose into individual steps.

Returning to our example, we can now specify that our queue is supposed to be affine, that is, that we can decide to ignore it. We annotate defined types and type variables with their mode (U, F, or L), but we overload the logical connectives since their meanings, when defined, are consistent. The elements of an affine queue should also be affine. If we make them linear, as in

$$\begin{aligned}
\mathsf{queue}_{\mathsf{F}}\ A_{\mathsf{L}} = \&\{\ &\mathsf{enq} : {\uparrow}_{\mathsf{L}}^{\mathsf{F}} A_{\mathsf{L}} \multimap \mathsf{queue}_{\mathsf{F}}\ A_{\mathsf{L}}, \\
&\mathsf{deq} : \{\mathsf{none} : \mathbf{1}, \mathsf{some} : {\uparrow}_{\mathsf{L}}^{\mathsf{F}} A_{\mathsf{L}} \otimes \mathsf{queue}_{\mathsf{F}}\ A_{\mathsf{L}}\}\ \}
\end{aligned}$$

then we could never use $x : {\uparrow}_{\mathsf{L}}^{\mathsf{F}} A_{\mathsf{L}}$ in a process offering an affine service (rule ${\uparrow}L$) since $\mathsf{L} \not\geq \mathsf{F}$. So instead we should define an affine queue as

$$\begin{aligned}
\mathsf{queue}_{\mathsf{F}}\ A_{\mathsf{F}} = \&\{\ &\mathsf{enq} : A_{\mathsf{F}} \multimap \mathsf{queue}_{\mathsf{F}}\ A_{\mathsf{F}}, \\
&\mathsf{deq} : \{\mathsf{none} : \mathbf{1}, \mathsf{some} : A_{\mathsf{F}} \otimes \mathsf{queue}_{\mathsf{F}}\ A_{\mathsf{F}}\}\ \}
\end{aligned}$$

so that all types in the definition (including A_{F}) are affine. Now we no longer need to explicitly destroy a queue, we can just abandon it and the runtime system will deallocate it by a form of garbage collection.

If we want to enforce a linear discipline, destroying a queue with linear elements will have to rely on a consumer for the elements of the queue. This consumer must be unrestricted because it is used for each element. Channels are linear by default, so in the example we only annotate affine and unrestricted channels with their mode.

$$\mathit{destroy} : \{\mathbf{1} \leftarrow \mathsf{queue}_{\mathsf{L}}\ A_{\mathsf{L}}, {\uparrow}_{\mathsf{L}}^{\mathsf{U}}(A_{\mathsf{L}} \multimap \mathbf{1})\}$$

$$\begin{array}{lll}
\multicolumn{3}{l}{c \leftarrow \mathit{destroy} \leftarrow q, u_{\mathsf{U}} =} \\
\quad q.\mathsf{deq}\ ; & & \\
\quad \mathsf{case}\ q\ \mathsf{of} & & \\
\quad \mid \mathsf{none} \rightarrow \mathsf{wait}\ q\ ; \mathsf{close}\ c & & \\
\quad \mid \mathsf{some} \rightarrow x \leftarrow \mathsf{recv}\ q\ ; & & \\
\qquad\qquad\quad d \leftarrow \mathsf{send}\ u_{\mathsf{U}}\ ; & & \%\ \mathit{obtain\ instance}\ d\ \mathit{of}\ u_{\mathsf{U}} \\
\qquad\qquad\quad \mathsf{send}\ d\ x\ ; \mathsf{wait}\ d\ ; & & \%\ \mathit{use}\ d\ \mathit{to\ consume}\ x \\
\qquad\qquad\quad c \leftarrow \mathit{destroy} \leftarrow q, u_{\mathsf{U}} & & \%\ \mathit{recurse,\ reusing}\ u_{\mathsf{U}}
\end{array}$$

5 Polarized Logic

We now take a step in a different direction by introducing asynchronous communication, postponing discussion of the modalities for now. In asynchronous communication each linear channel contains a message queue [11], which can be related directly to the proof system via continuation channels [9]. Sending adds to the queue on one end and receiving takes from the other. Because session-based communication goes in both directions, the queue switches direction at certain times. Moreover, the queue must maintain some information on the direction of the queue so that a process that performs a send followed by a receive does not incorrectly read its own message. Fortunately, session typing guarantees that there is no send/receive mismatch.

A simple way to maintain the direction of a queue is to set a flag when enqueuing a message. We write just q when the direction of q does not matter, and $\overleftarrow{q}$ and $\overrightarrow{q}$ for the two directions. Our convention is that $\overleftarrow{q}$ corresponds to messages from a provider to its client, and $\overrightarrow{q}$ for messages from a client to the provider. The reasons for this convention is that in $\mathsf{proc}_c(P)$, the channel c is to the left of P, which is in turn derived from $c \leftarrow P$ for a process expression P offering a service along c.

We have a predicate $\mathsf{queue}(c, q, d)$ for a queue q connecting a process Q using c with one providing d. Here are two example rules for sending and receiving data values.

$$\begin{aligned} \mathsf{and\_s} : \mathsf{queue}(c, q, d) \otimes \mathsf{proc}_d(\mathsf{send}\ d\ v\ ;\ P) \\ \multimap \{\mathsf{queue}(c, \overleftarrow{q \cdot v}, d) \otimes \mathsf{proc}_d(P)\} \\ \mathsf{and\_r} : \mathsf{proc}_c(x \leftarrow \mathsf{recv}\ c\ ;\ Q_x) \otimes \mathsf{queue}(c, \overleftarrow{v \cdot q}, d) \\ \multimap \{\mathsf{proc}_c(Q_v) \otimes \mathsf{queue}(c, q, d)\} \end{aligned}$$

We see some difficulty in the second rule, where the direction of q is unclear. It should be $\overleftarrow{q}$ unless q is empty, it which case it is unknown. This ambiguity is also present in forwarding.

$$\begin{aligned} \mathsf{fwd} : \mathsf{queue}(c, p, d) \otimes \mathsf{proc}_d(d \leftarrow e) \otimes \mathsf{queue}(d, q, e) \\ \multimap \{\mathsf{queue}(c, p \cdot q, e)\} \end{aligned}$$

We won't go into detail why there are some difficulties implementing this, but we see that there are multiple possibilities for p and q pointing left, right, or being empty.

Next we note that the *polarity* of each connective determines the direction of communication. From the perspective of the service provider, if we have $P ::$ $(x{:}A)$ for a *positive* A then the action of P along x will be a send, if A is *negative* it will be receive. Intuitively this is because the right rules for negative connectives are invertible and therefore carry no information: any information has to come from the outside. Conversely, the right rules for positive connectives involve some choice and can therefore communicate the essence of that information. We can make this explicit by *polarizing* the logic, dividing the propositions into positive and negative propositions with explicit *shift* operators connecting them. Omitting other modalities, the syntax of polarized logic is:

$$\begin{array}{llll}
\text{Positive propositions} & A^+, B^+ ::= & \mathbf{1} & \text{send end and terminate} \\
 & \mid & A^+ \otimes B^+ & \text{send channel of type } A^+ \\
 & \mid & A^+ \oplus B^+ & \text{send inl or inr} \\
 & \mid & \tau \wedge B^+ & \text{send value of type } \tau \\
 & \mid & {\downarrow}A^- & \text{send shift, then receive} \\
\text{Negative propositions} & A^-, B^- ::= & A^+ \multimap B^- & \text{receive channel of type } A^+ \\
 & \mid & A^- \mathbin{\&} B^- & \text{receive inl or inr} \\
 & \mid & \tau \supset B^- & \text{receive value of type } \tau \\
 & \mid & {\uparrow}A^+ & \text{receive shift, then send}
\end{array}$$

Note that a process that sends along a channel will continue to do so until it sends a shift and then it starts receiving. Conversely, a process that receives continues to do so until it receives a shift after which it starts sending. The new constructs are:

$$\begin{array}{lll}
P, Q, R ::= & \mathsf{send}\ c\ \mathsf{shift}\ ;\ P & \text{send shift, then receive along } c \text{ in } P \\
\mid & \mathsf{shift} \leftarrow \mathsf{recv}\ c\ ;\ Q & \text{receive shift, then send along } c \text{ in } Q
\end{array}$$

We have already annotated the shifts with their expected operational semantics. Queues now always have a definite direction and there can be no further messages following a shift. We write m for messages other than shift, such as data values, labels, and channels and treat $\cdot$ as an associative concatenation operator with the empty queue as its unit.

$$\begin{array}{lll}
\text{Queue filled by provider} & \overleftarrow{q} ::= \overleftarrow{\cdot} \mid \overleftarrow{m \cdot q} \mid \overleftarrow{\mathsf{end}} \mid \overleftarrow{\mathsf{shift}} \\
\text{Queue filled by client} & \overrightarrow{q} ::= \overrightarrow{\mathsf{shift}} \mid \overrightarrow{q \cdot m} \mid \overrightarrow{\cdot}
\end{array}$$

In the polarized setting, we just need to initialize the direction correctly when a new channel is created, after which the direction is maintained correctly throughout. When receiving, the direction needs to be checked. When sending, the direction will always be correct by invariant.

$$\begin{array}{l}
\mathsf{and_s} : \mathsf{queue}(c, \overleftarrow{q}, d) \otimes \mathsf{proc}_d(\mathsf{send}\ d\ v\ ;\ P) \\
\quad \multimap \{\mathsf{queue}(c, \overleftarrow{q \cdot v}, d) \otimes \mathsf{proc}_d(P)\} \\
\mathsf{and_r} : \mathsf{proc}_c(n \leftarrow \mathsf{recv}\ c\ ;\ Q_n) \otimes \mathsf{queue}(c, \overleftarrow{v \cdot q}, d) \\
\quad \multimap \{\mathsf{proc}_c(Q_v) \otimes \mathsf{queue}(c, \overleftarrow{q}, d)\}
\end{array}$$

The shift reverses direction when received.

$$\begin{array}{l}
\mathsf{shift_s} : \mathsf{queue}(c, \overleftarrow{q}, d) \otimes \mathsf{proc}_d(\mathsf{send}\ d\ \mathsf{shift}\ ;\ P) \\
\quad \multimap \{\mathsf{queue}(c, \overleftarrow{q \cdot \mathsf{shift}}, d) \otimes \mathsf{proc}_d(P)\} \\
\mathsf{shift_r} : \mathsf{proc}_a(\mathsf{shift} \leftarrow \mathsf{recv}\ c\ ;\ Q) \otimes \mathsf{queue}(c, \overleftarrow{\mathsf{shift}}, d) \\
\quad \multimap \{\mathsf{proc}_a(Q) \otimes \mathsf{queue}(c, \overrightarrow{\cdot}, d)\}
\end{array}$$

There are symmetric rules for $\overrightarrow{\mathsf{shift}}$, which we elide here.

In our running example, the natural polarization would interpret *queue* as a negative type, since it offers an external choice. We have to switch to positive when we send a response to the dequeue request, and then switch again before we recurse. The type parameter A is most naturally positive, since both occurrences in the type are in fact positive.

$$\begin{aligned}\mathsf{queue}^-\ A^+ = \&\{\ &\mathsf{enq} : A^+ \multimap \mathsf{queue}^-\ A^+,\\ &\mathsf{deq} : \uparrow \oplus \{\mathsf{none} : \mathbf{1}, \mathsf{some} : A^+ \otimes \downarrow \mathsf{queue}^-\ A^+\}\ \}\end{aligned}$$

The code requires some minimal changes: we have to insert three shift operators.

```
empty : {queue⁻ A⁺}
c ← empty =
  case c of
  | enq → x ← recv c ;
          e ← empty ;
          c ← elem ← x, e
  | deq → shift ← recv c ;
          c.none ;
          close c
```

```
elem : {queue⁻ A⁺ ← A⁺, queue⁻ A⁺}
c ← elem ← x, d =
  case c of
  | enq → y ← recv c ;
          d.enq ; send d y ;
          c ← elem ← x, d
  | deq → shift ← recv c ;     % shift c to send
          c.some ; send c x ;
          send c shift ;       % shift c to recv
          c ← d
```

6 Recovering Synchronous Communication

We obtain maximally asynchronous communication by inserting shifts in a bare (unpolarized) session type only where necessary.

$$\begin{array}{lll}
(1)^+ & = 1 & \\
(A \otimes B)^+ & = (A)^+ \otimes (B)^+ & \\
(A \oplus B)^+ & = (A)^+ \oplus (B)^+ & \\
(\tau \wedge B)^+ & = \tau \wedge (B)^+ & \\
(A)^+ & = \downarrow(A)^- & \text{for other propositions } A \\
(A \multimap B)^- & = (A)^+ \multimap (B)^- & \\
(A \& B)^- & = (A)^- \& (B)^- & \\
(\tau \supset B)^- & = \tau \supset (B)^- & \\
(A)^- & = \uparrow(A)^+ & \text{for other propositions } A
\end{array}$$

As a provider, we can send asynchronously at a positive session type until we shift explicitly to perform an input because we are now at a negative proposition. A client behaves dually.

In order to simulate synchronous communication, we insert additional shifts to prevent two consecutive send operations on the same channel. Here, the down shift after a send switches to a mode where we wait for an acknowledgment, which is implicit in the next receive. If this is another shift, it acts as a pure acknowledgment, otherwise it is already the next message.

$$
\begin{array}{lll}
(1)^+ & = 1 & \\
(A \otimes B)^+ & = (A)^+ \otimes {\downarrow}(B)^- & \\
(A \oplus B)^+ & = {\downarrow}(A)^- \oplus {\downarrow}(B)^- & \\
(\tau \wedge B)^+ & = \tau \wedge {\downarrow}(B)^- & \\
(A)^+ & = {\downarrow}(A)^- & \text{for other propositions } A \\
(A \multimap B)^- & = (A)^+ \multimap {\uparrow}(B)^+ & \\
(A \,\&\, B)^- & = {\uparrow}(A)^+ \,\&\, {\uparrow}(B)^+ & \\
(\tau \supset B)^- & = \tau \supset {\uparrow}(B)^+ & \\
(A)^- & = {\uparrow}(A)^+ & \text{for other propositions } A
\end{array}
$$

If we want to bound the size of message queues then we can insert shift in session types which would otherwise allow an unbounded number of consecutive sends.

In our running example, a client of a queue can perform an unbounded number of enqueue operations in the asynchronous operational semantics before the queue implementation must react. This is because this portion of the queue type is entirely negative. In order to force synchronization, we can change the type of the enqueue operation before we recurse.

$$
\begin{array}{l}
\mathsf{queue}^- \, A^+ = \&\{ \; \mathsf{enq} : A^+ \multimap {\uparrow}{\downarrow}\mathsf{queue}^- \, A^+, \\
\qquad\qquad\qquad\quad \mathsf{deq} : {\uparrow}\oplus\{\mathsf{none} : \mathbf{1}, \mathsf{some} : A^+ \otimes {\downarrow}\mathsf{queue}^- \, A^+\} \; \}
\end{array}
$$

Now the maximal size of the queue will be 3 in one direction ($\mathsf{shift} \cdot x \cdot \mathsf{enq}$) and also 3 in the other direction ($\mathsf{some} \cdot x \cdot \mathsf{shift}$). In a slightly different language, boundedness calculations for queues in asynchronous session-typed communication can be found in [11], so we do not repeat a more formal analysis here.

7 Synthesis in Polarized Adjoint Logic

Now we are ready to combine the ideas from adjoint logic in Sec. 4 with polarization in Sec. 5. Amazingly, they are fully consistent. The two differences to the polarized presentation are that (a) the modalities go between positive and negative propositions (already anticipated by the fact that $\downarrow$ is positive and $\uparrow$ is negative), and (b) the modalities ${\downarrow}_k^m A$ and ${\uparrow}_k^m$ allow $m \geq k$ rather than presupposing $m > k$ as before. We no longer index the connectives, overloading their meaning at the different layers.

$$
\begin{array}{lrll}
\text{Pos. propositions } A_m^+, B_m^+ & ::= & \mathbf{1} & \text{send } \mathsf{end} \text{ and terminate} \\
& \mid & A_m^+ \otimes B_m^+ & \text{send channel of type } A_m^+ \\
& \mid & A_m^+ \oplus B_m^+ & \text{send } \mathsf{inl} \text{ or } \mathsf{inr} \\
& \mid & \tau \wedge B_m^+ & \text{send value of type } \tau \\
& \mid & {\downarrow}_m^r A_r^- & (r \geq m), \text{send } \mathsf{shift}, \text{ then receive} \\
\text{Neg. propositions } A_m^-, B_m^- & ::= & A_m^+ \multimap B_m^- & \text{receive channel of type } A_m^+ \\
& \mid & A_m^- \,\&\, B_m^- & \text{receive } \mathsf{inl} \text{ or } \mathsf{inr} \\
& \mid & \tau \supset B_m^- & \text{receive value of type } \tau \\
& \mid & {\uparrow}_k^m A_k^+ & (m \geq k), \text{receive } \mathsf{shift}, \text{ then send}
\end{array}
$$

A shift staying at the same level just changes the polarity but is otherwise not subject to any restrictions. We can see this from the rules, now annotated with a polarity: if $m = k$ in $\uparrow$L, then $k \geq r$ by presupposition since $(\Psi, \uparrow_k^m A_k^+) \geq r$. Similarly, in $\downarrow$R, $\Psi \geq m$ by presupposition if $m = k$.

$$\frac{\Psi \vdash A_k^+}{\Psi \vdash \uparrow_k^m A_k^+}\ \uparrow\mathsf{R} \qquad \frac{k \geq r \quad \Psi, A_k^+ \vdash C_r}{\Psi, \uparrow_k^m A_k^+ \vdash C_r}\ \uparrow\mathsf{L}$$

$$\frac{\Psi_{\geq m} \vdash A_m^-}{\Psi \vdash \downarrow_k^m A_m^-}\ \downarrow\mathsf{R} \qquad \frac{\Psi, A_m^- \vdash C_r}{\Psi, \downarrow_k^m A_m^- \vdash C_r}\ \downarrow\mathsf{L}$$

Adding process expressions in a straightforward manner generalizes the shift to carry a fresh channel because there may now be a change in modes associated with the shift. We have the following new syntax

$$\begin{array}{lll} P, Q ::= & \mathsf{shift}\ x_k \leftarrow \mathsf{send}\ c_m\ ;\ P_{x_k} & \text{send fresh shift } x_k\text{, then recv. along } x_k \text{ in } P \\ \mid & \mathsf{shift}\ x_k \leftarrow \mathsf{recv}\ c_m\ ;\ Q_{x_k} & \text{receive shift } x_k\text{, then send along } x_k \text{ in } Q \end{array}$$

and the modified rules

$$\frac{\Psi \vdash P_{x_k} :: (x_k{:}A_k^+)}{\Psi \vdash (\mathsf{shift}\ x_k \leftarrow \mathsf{recv}\ x_m\ ;\ P_{x_k}) :: (x_m{:}\uparrow_k^m A_k^+)}\ \uparrow\mathsf{R}$$

$$\frac{k \geq r \quad \Psi, x_k{:}A_k^+ \vdash Q_{x_k} :: (z_r{:}C_r)}{\Psi, x_m{:}\uparrow_k^m A_k^+ \vdash (\mathsf{shift}\ x_k \leftarrow \mathsf{send}\ x_m\ ;\ Q_{x_k}) :: (z_r{:}C_r)}\ \uparrow\mathsf{L}$$

$$\frac{\Psi_{\geq m} \vdash Q_{x_m} :: (x_m{:}A_m^-)}{\Psi \vdash (\mathsf{shift}\ x_m \leftarrow \mathsf{send}\ x_k\ ;\ Q_{x_m}) :: (x_k{:}\downarrow_k^m A_m^-)}\ \downarrow\mathsf{R}$$

$$\frac{\Psi, x_m{:}A_m^- \vdash P_{x_m} :: (z_r{:}C_r)}{\Psi, x_k{:}\downarrow_k^m A_m^- \vdash (\mathsf{shift}\ x_m \leftarrow \mathsf{recv}\ x_k\ ;\ P_{x_m}) :: (z_r{:}C_r)}\ \downarrow\mathsf{L}$$

Operationally:

$$\begin{array}{ll} \mathsf{up}_k^m\mathsf{\_s} & : \mathsf{proc}_{a_r}(\mathsf{shift}\ x_k \leftarrow \mathsf{send}\ c_m\ ;\ Q_{x_k}) \otimes \mathsf{queue}(c_m, \overrightarrow{q}, d_m) \\ & \quad \multimap \{\exists c_k.\ \exists d_k.\ \mathsf{proc}_{a_r}(Q_{c_k}) \otimes \mathsf{queue}(c_k, \overrightarrow{\mathsf{shift}\ d_k \cdot q}, d_m)\} \\ \mathsf{up}_k^m\mathsf{\_r} & : \mathsf{queue}(c_k, \overrightarrow{\mathsf{shift}\ d_k}, d_m) \otimes \mathsf{proc}_{d_m}(\mathsf{shift}\ x_k \leftarrow \mathsf{recv}\ d_m\ ;\ P_{x_k}) \\ & \quad \multimap \{\mathsf{queue}(c_k, \overleftarrow{\cdot}, d_k) \otimes \mathsf{proc}_{d_k}(P_{d_k})\} \\ \mathsf{down}_k^m\mathsf{\_s} & : \mathsf{queue}(c_k, \overleftarrow{q}, d_k) \otimes \mathsf{proc}_{d_k}(\mathsf{shift}\ x_m \leftarrow \mathsf{send}\ d_k\ ;\ Q_{x_m}) \\ & \quad \multimap \{\exists c_m.\ \exists d_m.\ \mathsf{queue}(c_k, \overleftarrow{q \cdot \mathsf{shift}\ c_m}, d_m) \otimes \mathsf{proc}_{d_m}(Q_{d_m})\} \\ \mathsf{down}_k^m\mathsf{\_r} & : \mathsf{proc}_{a_r}(\mathsf{shift}\ x_m \leftarrow \mathsf{recv}\ c_k\ ;\ P_{x_m}) \otimes \mathsf{queue}(c_k, \overleftarrow{\mathsf{shift}\ c_m}, d_m) \\ & \quad \multimap \{\mathsf{proc}_{a_r}(P_{c_m}) \otimes \mathsf{queue}(c_m, \overrightarrow{\cdot}, d_m)\} \end{array}$$

As pointed out in Sec. 4, we have to assume that processes that offer along an unrestricted channel c_{U} are persistent. Also, this formulation introduces a new channel even when $m = k$, a slight redundancy best avoided in the syntax and semantics of a real implementation. Even when going between linear and affine channels, creating new channels might be avoided in favor of just changing some channel property.

Returning to forwarding, the earlier agnostic formulation will work more elegantly, since both queues to be appended are guaranteed to go into the same direction.

$$\begin{aligned}\mathsf{fwd} : \mathsf{queue}(c, p, d) \otimes \mathsf{proc}_d(d \leftarrow e) \otimes \mathsf{queue}(d, q, e)\\ \multimap \{\mathsf{queue}(c, p \cdot q, e)\}\end{aligned}$$

If implementation or other considerations suggest forwarding as an explicit message, we can also implement this, taking advantage of the direction information that is always available. Here we write $x \leftarrow \mathsf{recv}\ c$ as a generic receive operation along channel c, which is turned into a receive along the forwarded channel e.

$$\begin{aligned}\mathsf{fwd\_s} : \mathsf{queue}(c, \overleftarrow{p}, d) \otimes \mathsf{proc}_d(d \leftarrow e)\\ \multimap \{\mathsf{queue}(c, \overleftarrow{p \cdot \mathsf{fwd}}, e)\}\end{aligned}$$

$$\begin{aligned}\mathsf{fwd\_r} : \mathsf{proc}_a(x \leftarrow \mathsf{recv}\ c\ ;\ P_x) \otimes \mathsf{queue}(c, \overleftarrow{\mathsf{fwd}}, e)\\ \multimap \{\mathsf{proc}_a(x \leftarrow \mathsf{recv}\ e\ ;\ P_x)\}\end{aligned}$$

We elide the symmetric version of the rules pointing to the right. The reason we would forward in the direction of the current communication is so that send remains fully asynchronous and does not have to check if a forwarding message may be present on the channel.

Once again rewriting the linear version of the example, forcing synchronization.

$$\begin{aligned}\mathsf{queue}^- A^+ = \&\{\ & \mathsf{enq} : A^+ \multimap \uparrow\downarrow\mathsf{queue}^- A^+,\\ & \mathsf{deq} : \uparrow\oplus\{\mathsf{none} : \mathbf{1}, \mathsf{some} : A^+ \otimes \downarrow\mathsf{queue}^- A^+\}\ \}\end{aligned}$$

```
empty : {queue⁻ A⁺}

c ← empty =
  case c of
  | enq → x ← recv c ;
          shift c ← recv c
          shift c ← send c
          e ← empty ;
          c ← elem ← x, e
  | deq → shift c ← recv c
          c.none ;
          close c
```

```
elem : {queue⁻ A⁺ ← A⁺, queue⁻ A⁺}

c ← elem ← x, d =
  case c of
  | enq → y ← recv c ;
          shift c ← recv c ;   % shift to send
          shift c ← send c ;   % send ack
          d.enq ; send d y ;
          shift d ← send d ;   % shift to recv
          shift d ← recv d ;   % recv ack
          c ← elem ← x, d
  | deq → shift c ← recv c ;   % shift to send
          c.some ; send c x ;
          shift c ← send c ;   % shift to recv
          c ← d
```

And destroying a linear queue with affine elements:

```
destroy : {1 ← queue (↓^F_L A_F)}

c ← destroy ← q =
  q.deq ;
  shift q ← send q ;          % shift to recv
  case q of
  | none → wait q ; close c
  | some → x ← recv q ;           % obtain element x
           shift a_F ← recv x ;   % obtain affine a_F, consuming x
           shift q ← send q ;     % shift to recv
           c ← destroy ← q        % recurse, ignoring a_F
```

8 Sequent Calculus for Polarized Adjoint Logic

We summarize the sequent calculus rules for polarized adjoint logic in Fig. 1, omitting the uninteresting rules for existential and universal quantification. However, we have added in atomic propositions p_m^+ and p_m^- (corresponding to session type variables) and removed the stipulation that the only unrestricted propositions are $\uparrow_m^{\mathsf{U}} A_m^+$, thereby making our theorem slightly more general at the expense of a nonstandard notation for intuitionistic connectives such as $A_{\mathsf{U}} \multimap_{\mathsf{U}} B_{\mathsf{U}}$ for $A \supset B$.

We have the following theorem.

Theorem 1.

1. *Cut is admissible in the system without cut.*
2. *Identity is admissible for arbitrary propositions in the system with the identity restricted to atomic propositions and without cut.*

Proof. The admissibility of cut follows by a nested structural induction, first on the cut formula A, second simultaneously on the proofs of the left and right premise. We liberally use a lemma which states that we can weaken a proof with affine and unrestricted hypotheses without changing its structure and we exploit the transitivity of $\geq$. See [8,18] for analogous proofs.

The admissibility of identity at A follows by a simple structural induction on the proposition A, exploiting the reflexivity of $\geq$ in one critical case. □

A simple corollary is *cut elimination*, stating that every provable sequent has a cut-free proof. Cut elimination of the logic is the central reason why the session-typed processes assigned to these rules satisfy the by now expected properties of *session fidelity* (processes are guaranteed to follow the behavior prescribed by the session type) and *global progress* (a closed process network of type $c_0 : \mathbf{1}$ can either take a step will send end along c_0). In addition, we also have *productivity* (processes will eventually perform the action prescribed by the session type) and *termination* if recursive processes are appropriately restricted. The proofs of these properties closely follow those in the literature for related systems [6,22,20], so we do not formally state or prove them here.

$$
\begin{array}{lll}
m, k, r & ::= \mathsf{U} \mid \mathsf{F} \mid \mathsf{L} \quad \text{with } \mathsf{U} > \mathsf{F} > \mathsf{L} & \\
A^+_m, B^+_m & ::= p^+_m \mid \mathbf{1}_m \mid A^+_m \otimes_m B^+_m \mid A^+_m \oplus_m B^+_m \mid {\downarrow}^r_m A^-_r & (r \geq m) \\
A^-_m, B^-_m & ::= p^-_m \mid A^+_m \multimap_m B^-_m \mid A^-_m \,\&_m\, B^-_m \mid {\uparrow}^m_k A^+_k & (m \geq k) \\
A_m, B_m, C_m & ::= A^+_m \mid A^-_m &
\end{array}
$$

$$
\frac{\Psi \geq \mathsf{F}}{\Psi, A_m \vdash A_m}\ \mathsf{id}
\qquad
\frac{\Psi \geq m \geq r \quad \Psi \vdash A_m \quad \Psi', A_m \vdash C_r}{\Psi, \Psi' \vdash C_r}\ \mathsf{cut}
$$

$$
\frac{\Psi \vdash A^+_k}{\Psi \vdash {\uparrow}^m_k A^+_k}\ {\uparrow}\mathsf{R}
\qquad
\frac{k \geq r \quad \Psi, A^+_k \vdash C_r}{\Psi, {\uparrow}^m_k A^+_k \vdash C_r}\ {\uparrow}\mathsf{L}
$$

$$
\frac{\Psi_{\geq m} \vdash A^-_m}{\Psi \vdash {\downarrow}^m_k A^-_m}\ {\downarrow}\mathsf{R}
\qquad
\frac{\Psi, A^-_m \vdash C_r}{\Psi, {\downarrow}^m_k A^-_m \vdash C_r}\ {\downarrow}\mathsf{L}
$$

$$
\frac{\Psi \geq \mathsf{F}}{\Psi \vdash \mathbf{1}_m}\ \mathbf{1}R
\qquad
\frac{\Psi \vdash C_r}{\Psi, \mathbf{1}_m \vdash C_r}\ \mathbf{1}L
$$

$$
\frac{\Psi \vdash A^+_m \quad \Psi' \vdash B^+_m}{\Psi, \Psi' \vdash A^+_m \otimes_m B^+_m}\ \otimes R
\qquad
\frac{\Psi, A^+_m, B^+_m \vdash C_r}{\Psi, A^+_m \otimes_m B^+_m \vdash C_r}\ \otimes L
$$

$$
\frac{\Psi, A^+_m \vdash B^-_m}{\Psi \vdash A^+_m \multimap_m B^-_m}\ {\multimap} R
\qquad
\frac{\Psi \geq m \quad \Psi \vdash A^+_m \quad \Psi', B^-_m \vdash C_r}{\Psi, \Psi', A^+_m \multimap_m B^-_m \vdash C_r}\ {\multimap} L
$$

$$
\frac{\Psi \vdash A^-_m \quad \Psi \vdash B^-_m}{\Psi \vdash A^-_m \,\&_m\, B^-_m}\ \& R
\qquad
\frac{\Psi, A^-_m \vdash C_r}{\Psi, A^-_m \,\&_m\, B^-_m \vdash C_r}\ \& L_1
\qquad
\frac{\Psi, B^-_m \vdash C_r}{\Psi, A^-_m \,\&_m\, B^-_m \vdash C_r}\ \& L_2
$$

$$
\frac{\Psi \vdash A^+_m}{\Psi \vdash A^+_m \oplus_m B^+_m}\ \oplus R_1
\qquad
\frac{\Psi \vdash B^+_m}{\Psi \vdash A^+_m \oplus_m B^+_m}\ \oplus R_2
\qquad
\frac{\Psi, A^+_m \vdash C_r \quad \Psi, B^+_m \vdash C_r}{\Psi, A^+_m \oplus_m B^+_m \vdash C_r}\ \oplus L
$$

All judgments $\Psi \vdash A_m$ presuppose $\Psi \geq m$.
Ψ, Ψ' allows contraction of unrestricted A_{U} shared between Ψ and Ψ'

Fig. 1. Polarized Adjoint Logic

9 Conclusion

We have developed a language which uniformly integrates linear, affine, and unrestricted types, allowing the programmer to vary the degree of precision with which resources are managed. At the same time, the programmer has fine-grained control over which communications are synchronous or asynchronous, and these decisions are reflected in the type in a logically motivated manner.

On the pragmatic side, we should decide to what extent the constructs here are exposed to the programmer or inferred during type checking, and develop a concise and intuitive concrete syntax for those that are explicitly available in types and process expressions.

Finally, our language is polarized, but deductions are not focused [1]. This is perhaps somewhat unexpected since the two are closely connected and historically tied to each other. It suggests that some further benefits from proof-theoretic concepts are still to be discovered, continuing the current line of investigation into the foundation of session-typed concurrency.

Acknowledgments. This material is based upon work supported by the National Science Foundation under Grant No. CNS-1423168 and by the Department of Energy under Grant No. SNL 1488651. The authors would like to acknowledge helpful discussions with Stephanie Balzer, Luís Caires, Henry DeYoung, Hannah Gommerstadt, Elsa Gunter, Limin Jia, Rokhini Prabhu, Bernardo Toninho, and Max Willsey.

References

1. Andreoli, J.M.: Logic programming with focusing proofs in linear logic. Journal of Logic and Computation 2(3), 197–347 (1992)
2. Barber, A.: Dual intuitionistic linear logic. Tech. Rep. ECS-LFCS-96-347, Department of Computer Science, University of Edinburgh (September 1996)
3. Benton, N.: A mixed linear and non-linear logic: Proofs, terms and models. In: Pacholski, L., Tiuryn, J. (eds.) CSL 1994. LNCS, vol. 933, pp. 121–135. Springer, Heidelberg (1995), an extended version appears as Technical Report UCAM-CL-TR-352, University of Cambridge
4. Caires, L., Pérez, J.A., Pfenning, F., Toninho, B.: Behavioral polymorphism and parametricity in session-based communication. In: Felleisen, M., Gardner, P. (eds.) ESOP 2013. LNCS, vol. 7792, pp. 330–349. Springer, Heidelberg (2013)
5. Caires, L., Pfenning, F.: Session types as intuitionistic linear propositions. In: Gastin, P., Laroussinie, F. (eds.) CONCUR 2010. LNCS, vol. 6269, pp. 222–236. Springer, Heidelberg (2010)
6. Caires, L., Pfenning, F., Toninho, B.: Linear logic propositions as session types. Mathematical Structures in Computer Science (2013) (to appear) Special Issue on Behavioural Types
7. Cervesato, I., Scedrov, A.: Relating state-based and process-based concurrency through linear logic. Information and Computation 207(10), 1044–1077 (2009)
8. Chang, B.Y.E., Chaudhuri, K., Pfenning, F.: A judgmental analysis of linear logic. Tech. Rep. CMU-CS-03-131R, Carnegie Mellon University, Department of Computer Science (December 2003)
9. DeYoung, H., Caires, L., Pfenning, F., Toninho, B.: Cut reduction in linear logic as asynchronous session-typed communication. In: Cégielski, P., Durand, A. (eds.) Proceedings of the 21st Conference on Computer Science Logic, CSL 2012, Leibniz International Proceedings in Informatics, Fontainebleau, France, pp. 228–242 (September 2012)
10. Gay, S.J., Hole, M.: Subtyping for session types in the π-calculus. Acta Informatica 42(2-3), 191–225 (2005)
11. Gay, S.J., Vasconcelos, V.T.: Linear type theory for asynchronous session types. Journal of Functional Programming 20(1), 19–50 (2010)
12. Girard, J.Y.: Linear logic. Theoretical Computer Science 50, 1–102 (1987)

13. Honda, K.: Types for dyadic interaction. In: Best, E. (ed.) CONCUR 1993. LNCS, vol. 715, pp. 509–523. Springer, Heidelberg (1993)
14. Honda, K., Vasconcelos, V.T., Kubo, M.: Language primitives and type discipline for structured communication-based programming. In: Hankin, C. (ed.) ESOP 1998. LNCS, vol. 1381, pp. 122–138. Springer, Heidelberg (1998)
15. Laurent, O.: Polarized proof-nets: Proof-nets for LC. In: Girard, J.-Y. (ed.) TLCA 1999. LNCS, vol. 1581, pp. 213–227. Springer, Heidelberg (1999)
16. Mostrous, D., Vasconcelos, V.: Affine sessions. In: Kühn, E., Pugliese, R. (eds.) COORDINATION 2014. LNCS, vol. 8459, pp. 115–130. Springer, Heidelberg (2014)
17. Pérez, J.A., Caires, L., Pfenning, F., Toninho, B.: Linear logical relations and observational equivalences for session-based concurrency. Information and Computation 239, 254–302 (2014)
18. Reed, J.: A judgmental deconstruction of modal logic (2009) (unpublished manuscript)
19. Simmons, R.J.: Substructural Logical Specifications. Ph.D. thesis, Carnegie Mellon University, available as Technical Report CMU-CS-12-142 (November 2012)
20. Toninho, B.: A Logical Foundation for Session-based Concurrent Computation. Ph.D. thesis, Carnegie Mellon University and New University of Lisbon (2015) (in preparation)
21. Toninho, B., Caires, L., Pfenning, F.: Higher-order processes, functions, and sessions: A monadic integration. In: Felleisen, M., Gardner, P. (eds.) ESOP 2013. LNCS, vol. 7792, pp. 350–369. Springer, Heidelberg (2013)
22. Toninho, B., Caires, L., Pfenning, F.: Corecursion and non-divergence in session-typed processes. In: Proceedings of the 9th International Symposium on Trustworthy Global Computing (TGC 2014), Rome, Italy (September 2014) (to appear)
23. Vasconcelos, V.T.: Fundamentals of session types. Information and Computation 217, 52–70 (2012)
24. Wadler, P.: Propositions as sessions. In: Proceedings of the 17th International Conference on Functional Programming, ICFP 2012, pp. 273–286. ACM Press, Copenhagen (2012)

Semantics of Programming Languages I

Synthesis of Strategies and the Hoare Logic of Angelic Nondeterminism*

Konstantinos Mamouras

Cornell University
mamouras@cs.cornell.edu

Abstract. We study a propositional variant of Hoare logic that can be used for reasoning about programs that exhibit both angelic and demonic nondeterminism. We work in an uninterpreted setting, where the meaning of the atomic actions is specified axiomatically using hypotheses of a certain form. Our logical formalism is entirely compositional and it subsumes the non-compositional formalism of safety games on finite graphs. We present sound and complete Hoare-style (partial-correctness) calculi that are useful for establishing Hoare assertions, as well as for synthesizing implementations. The computational complexity of the Hoare theory of dual nondeterminism is investigated using operational models, and it is shown that the theory is complete for exponential time.

1 Introduction

One source of demonic nondeterminism in a program is its interaction with the environment (e.g., user input, thread scheduling, etc.), which is not under the control of the program. Even in the absence of such "real" nondeterminacy, we may use demonic nondeterminism to represent abstraction and partial knowledge of the state of a computation. Angelic nondeterminism, on the other hand, is used to express nondeterminacy that is under the control of the program. For example, we use angelic nondeterminism when implementation details are left underspecified, but we control how they can be resolved in order to achieve the desired result. The process of resolving these implementation details amounts to *synthesizing* a fully specified program. The term *dual nondeterminism* is used to refer to the combination of angelic and demonic nondeterminism.

In order to reason about dual nondeterminism, one first needs to have a semantic model of how programs with angelic and demonic choices compute. One semantic model that has been used extensively uses a class of mathematical objects that are called monotonic predicate transformers [1] (based on Dijkstra's predicate transformer semantics [4,11]). An equivalent denotational model that is based on binary relations was introduced in [13] (up-closed multirelations) and further investigated in [10]. These relations have an intuitive interpretation as two-round games between the angel and the demon.

* Part of the present work was done while visiting Radboud University Nijmegen.

A. Pitts (Ed.): FOSSACS 2015, LNCS 9034, pp. 25–40, 2015.
DOI: 10.1007/978-3-662-46678-0_2

We are interested here in verifying properties of programs that can be expressed as Hoare assertions [5], that is, formulas of the form $\{p\}f\{q\}$, where f is the program text and p, q denote predicates on the state space, called precondition and postcondition respectively. The formula $\{p\}f\{q\}$ asserts, informally, that starting from any state satisfying the precondition p, the angel has a strategy so that whatever the demon does, the final state of the computation of f (assuming termination) satisfies the postcondition q. This describes a notion of partial correctness, because in the case of divergence (non-termination) the angel wins vacuously. Our language for programs and preconditions/postconditions involves abstract test symbols $p, q, r, \ldots$ and abstract action symbols $a, b, \ldots$ with no fixed interpretation. We constrain their meaning with extra hypotheses: we consider a finite set Φ of Boolean axioms for the tests, and a finite set Ψ of axioms of the form $\{p\}a\{q\}$ for the action letters. So, we typically assert implications of the form $\Phi, \Psi \Rightarrow \{p\}f\{q\}$, which we call *simple Hoare implications.* We want to design a formal system that allows the derivation of the valid Hoare implications. One important desideratum for such a formal system is to also provide us with program text that corresponds to the winning strategy of the angel. Then, the system can be used for the deductive synthesis of programs that satisfy their Hoare specifications.

There has been previous work on deductive methods to reduce angelic nondeterminism and synthesize winning strategies for the angel. The work [2], which is based on ideas of the refinement calculus [1,11], explores a total-correctness Hoare-style calculus to reason about angelic nondeterminism. The analysis is in the first-order interpreted setting, and no completeness or relative completeness results are discussed.

Of particular relevance is the line of work that concerns two-player infinite games played on finite graphs [14]. Such games are useful for analyzing (nonterminating) reactive programs. One of the players represents the "environment", and the other player is the "controller". Computing the strategies that witness the winning regions of the two players amounts to synthesizing an appropriate implementation for the controller. The formalism of games on finite graphs is very convenient for developing an algorithmic theory of synthesis. However, the formalism is non-succinct and, additionally, it is inherently non-compositional. An important class of properties for these games are the so called *safety* properties, which assert that something bad never happens. For such properties, we see that a fully compositional formalism involving usual (terminating) programs and partial-correctness properties suffices.

Our Contribution. We consider a propositionally abstracted language for programs with demonic and angelic choices. Our results are the following:

- We present a sound and *unconditionally* complete calculus for the weak Hoare theory of dual nondeterminism (over the class of all interpretations). We also consider a restricted class of interpretations, where the atomic actions are non-angelic, and we extend our calculus so that it is complete for the Hoare theory of this smaller class (called strong Hoare theory). The proofs of these results rely on the construction of free models.

- We show that (for the free models) the denotational semantics is equivalent to the intended operational semantics. Using this result, we prove that the strong Hoare theory of dual nondeterminism is EXPTIME-complete.
- We consider an extension of our Hoare-style calculus with annotations that denote the winning strategies of the angel. We thus obtain a sound and complete deductive system for the synthesis of angelic strategies.
- Our formalism is shown to subsume that of safety games on finite graphs, hence it provides a compositional method for reasoning about safety in reactive systems. The language of dually nondeterministic program schemes is exponentially more succinct than explicitly represented game graphs, and it is arguably a more natural language for describing algorithms and protocols.

Due to lack of space all proofs will be given in a full version of the paper [9].

2 Preliminaries

In this section we give some preliminary definitions regarding while program schemes with the additional construct $\sqcap$ of demonic nondeterministic choice. First, we present the syntax of these abstract while programs. Then, we give the standard denotational semantics for them, which is based on binary relations.

We consider a two-sorted algebraic language. There is the sort of *tests* and the sort of *programs*. The tests are built up from *atomic tests* and the constants true and false, using the usual Boolean operations: $\neg$ (negation), $\wedge$ (conjunction), and $\vee$ (disjunction). We use the letters $p, q, r, \ldots$ to range over arbitrary tests.

The base programs are the *atomic programs* $a, b, c, \ldots$ (also called *atomic actions*), as well as the constants id (*skip*) and $\bot$ (*diverge*). The programs are constructed using the operations ; (*sequential composition*), if (*conditional*), while (*iteration*), and $\sqcap$ (*demonic nondeterministic choice*). We write $f, g, h, \ldots$ to range over arbitrary programs. So, the programs are given by the grammar:

$$f, g ::= \text{actions } a, b, \ldots \mid \mathsf{id} \mid \bot \mid f; g \mid \mathsf{if}\, p\, \mathsf{then}\, f\, \mathsf{else}\, g \mid \mathsf{while}\, p\, \mathsf{do}\, f \mid f \sqcap g.$$

We also write $p[f, g]$ instead of $\mathsf{if}\, p\, \mathsf{then}\, f\, \mathsf{else}\, g$, and $\mathsf{W}pf$ instead of $\mathsf{while}\, p\, \mathsf{do}\, f$.

We will present the standard denotational semantics of nondeterministic while schemes. Every test is interpreted as a unary predicate on the state space, and every program is interpreted as a binary relation on the state space.

Definition 1 (Nondeterministic Functions & Operations). For a set A, we write $\wp A$ for the *powerset* of A. For sets A and B, we say that a function of type $\phi : A \to \wp B$ is a *nondeterministic function* from A to B. We write $\phi : a \mapsto b$ to mean that $b \in \phi(a)$. We think informally that such a function describes only one kind of nondeterminism (for our purposes here, demonic nondeterminism).

The operations of *(Kleisli) composition* ;, *conditional* $(-)[-,-]$, *binary (nondeterministic) choice* $+$, *arbitrary choice* $\sum$, *identity* 1, *zero* 0, and *iteration* $(\mathbf{wh} - \mathbf{do} -)$ are defined as follows:

$$\phi; \psi \triangleq \lambda x \in A.\ \bigcup_{y \in \phi(x)} \psi(y) : A \to \wp C, \text{ for } \phi : A \to \wp B,\ \psi : B \to \wp C$$

$$P[\phi, \psi] \triangleq (\phi \cap (P \times \wp B)) \cup (\psi \cap ({\sim}P \times \wp B)), \text{ for } \phi, \psi : A \to \wp B,\ P \subseteq A$$
$$\phi + \psi \triangleq \lambda x \in A.\ \phi(x) \cup \psi(y) : A \to \wp B, \text{ where } \phi, \psi : A \to \wp B$$
$$\textstyle\sum_i \phi_i \triangleq \lambda x \in A.\ \bigcup_i \phi_i(x) : A \to \wp B, \text{ where } \phi_i : A \to \wp B$$
$$1_A \triangleq \lambda x \in A.\ \{x\} : A \to \wp A \quad \text{and} \quad 0_{AB} \triangleq \lambda x \in A.\ \emptyset : A \to \wp B$$
$$\mathbf{wh}\, P\, \mathbf{do}\, \phi \triangleq \textstyle\sum_{n \geq 0} W_n : A \to \wp A, \text{ where } \phi : A \to \wp A \text{ and } P \subseteq A$$
$$W_0 \triangleq P[0_{AA}, 1_A] \quad \text{and} \quad W_{n+1} \triangleq P[\phi; W_n, 1_A]$$

where ${\sim}P = A \setminus P$ above denotes the complement of P w.r.t. A. From the definition of the conditional, we see that $P[\phi, \psi](x)$ is equal to $\phi(x)$ when $x \in P$, and equal to $\psi(x)$ when $x \notin P$.

Definition 2 (Nondeterministic Interpretation). An interpretation of the language of nondeterministic while program schemes consists of a nonempty set S, called the *state space*, and an *interpretation function* R. For a program term f, its *interpretation* $R(f) : S \to \wp S$ is a nondeterministic function on S.

The interpretation $R(p)$ of a test p is a unary predicate on S, i.e., $R(p) \subseteq S$. R specifies the meaning of every atomic test, and it extends as follows:

$$R(\mathsf{true}) = S \qquad R(\neg p) = {\sim}R(p) \qquad R(p \wedge q) = R(p) \cap R(q)$$
$$R(\mathsf{false}) = \emptyset \qquad\qquad R(p \vee q) = R(p) \cup R(q)$$

where $\sim$ is the operation of complementation w.r.t. S, that is, ${\sim}A = S \setminus A$. Moreover, the interpretation function R specifies the meaning $R(a) : S \to \wp S$ of every atomic program. We extend the interpretation to all program terms:

$$R(\mathsf{id}) = 1_S \qquad R(f; g) = R(f); R(g) \qquad R(p[f, g]) = R(p)[R(f), R(g)]$$
$$R(\bot) = 0_{SS} \qquad R(f \sqcap g) = R(f) + R(g) \qquad R(\mathsf{w}pf) = \mathbf{wh}\, R(p)\, \mathbf{do}\, R(f)$$

Our definition agrees with the standard relational semantics of while schemes.

3 Angelic and Demonic Nondeterminism

We extend the syntax of nondeterministic while program schemes with the additional construct $\sqcup$ of *angelic (nondeterministic) choice*. So, the grammar for the program terms now becomes:

$$f, g ::= \text{actions } a, b, \ldots \mid \mathsf{id} \mid \bot \mid f; g \mid p[f, g] \mid \mathsf{w}pf \mid f \sqcap g \mid f \sqcup g.$$

We call these program terms *while game schemes*, because they can be considered to be descriptions of games between the angel (who controls the angelic choices) and the demon (who controls the demonic choices). Informally, the angel tries to satisfy the specification, while the demon attempts to falsify it.

We present a relational denotational semantics for while game schemes with abstract atomic actions. A nonempty set S represents the abstract state space, and every test is interpreted as a unary predicate on the state space. Every program term is interpreted as a binary relation from S to $\wp S$.

Consider such a binary relation $f \subseteq S \times \wp S$, which should be thought of as the extension of a game program scheme. Informally, the pair (u, X) is supposed to belong to f when the following holds: if the program starts at state u, then the angel has a strategy so that whatever the demon does, the final state (supposing that the program terminates) satisfies the predicate X.

The binary relation $f \subseteq S \times \wp S$ encodes both the choices of the angel and the demon, and it can be understood as a two-round game. The angel moves first, and then the demon makes the final move. The options that are available to the angel are given by multiple pairs (u, X_1), (u, X_2), and so on. So, when the game starts at state u, the angel first chooses either X_1, or X_2, or any of the other available options. Suppose that the angel first chooses X_i, where (u, X_i) is in f. Then, during the second round, the demon chooses some final state $v \in X_i$.

When (u, X) is in f, we understand this as meaning that that the angel can guarantee the predicate X when we start at u. So, we should expect that the angel also guarantees any predicate that is weaker than X.

Definition 3 (Game Functions). For nonempty sets A and B, we say that $f \subseteq A \times \wp B$ is a *game function* from A to B, denoted $f : A \rightsquigarrow B$, if it satifies:

1. The set f is *closed upwards*: $(u, X) \in f$ and $X \subseteq Y \subseteq B \implies (u, Y) \in f$.
2. For every $u \in A$ there is some $X \subseteq B$ with $(u, X) \in f$.

Given Condition (1), we can equivalently require that $(u, B) \in f$ for every $u \in A$, instead of having Condition (2).

Let $f : A \rightsquigarrow B$ be a game function. The *options* of the angel at $u \in A$, which we denote by $f(u)$, is the set $f(u) := \{X \subseteq B \mid (u, X) \in f\}$. In other words, $f(u)$ is the set of all predicates that the angel can guarantee from u.

We say that a game function $f : A \rightsquigarrow B$ is *non-angelic* if for every $u \in A$ there is some $X \subseteq B$ so that $f(u) = \{Y \subseteq B \mid X \subseteq Y\}$. It is easy to see that this $X \subseteq B$ is unique, because the equality $\{Y \subseteq B \mid X_1 \subseteq Y\} = \{Y \subseteq B \mid X_2 \subseteq Y\}$ implies that $X_1 = X_2$. Essentially, the definition says that the angel always has exactly one minimal choice: for every $u \in A$ there is exactly one minimal predicate X that the angel can guarantee.

Definition 4 (Lifting & Non-angelic Game Functions). When $f : A \rightsquigarrow B$ is a non-angelic game function, there is essentially only demonic nondeterminism. So, the same information can be provided by a nondeterministic function $A \to \wp B$. Indeed, we see easily that $f : A \rightsquigarrow B$ is non-angelic iff there exists some function $\phi : A \to \wp B$ so that $f = \mathsf{lift}\,\phi$, where

$$\mathsf{lift}\,\phi \triangleq \{(u, Y) \mid u \in A,\ \phi(u) \subseteq Y\} : A \rightsquigarrow B$$

defines the *lifting operation* lift. The definition says that for every $u \in A$ and $Y \subseteq B$: $(u, Y) \in \mathsf{lift}\,\phi$ iff $\phi(u) \subseteq Y$.

Definition 5 (Operations on Game Functions). We define a binary *composition* operation for game functions, whose typing rule and definition are:

$$\frac{f : A \rightsquigarrow B \quad g : B \rightsquigarrow C}{f;g : A \rightsquigarrow C} \qquad \begin{array}{r}(u,Z) \in (f;g) \Leftrightarrow \text{there is } Y \subseteq B \text{ s.t. } (u,Y) \in f,\\ \text{and } (v,Z) \in g \text{ for every } v \in Y.\end{array}$$

The *(semantic) conditional operation* is given as follows:

$$P[f,g] \triangleq \big(f \cap (P \times \wp B)\big) \cup \big(g \cap ({\sim}P \times \wp B)\big), \text{ for } f,g : A \rightsquigarrow B \text{ and } P \subseteq A,$$

where ${\sim}P = A \setminus P$ is the complement of P w.r.t. A. The *angelic choice* operation $\sqcup$ for game functions is defined by:

$$f \sqcup g \triangleq f \cup g, \text{ where } f,g : A \rightsquigarrow B.$$

As expected, the angelic choice operation increases the options available to the angel. Now, we define the *demonic choice* operation $\sqcap$ for game functions as:

$$f \sqcap g \triangleq \{(u, X \cup Y) \mid (u,X) \in f,\ (u,Y) \in g\}, \text{ where } f,g : A \rightsquigarrow B.$$

So, demonic choice increases the options of the demon. The above definition is equivalent to $f \sqcap g = f \cap g$. The *identity function* $\mathbb{1}_A : A \rightsquigarrow A$ is defined by

$$\mathbb{1}_A \triangleq \{(u,X) \mid u \in A \text{ and } u \in X\}.$$

So, $\mathbb{1}_A$ is the smallest game function that contains $(u,\{u\})$ for every $u \in A$. Informally, this definition says that on input u, the angel guarantees output u in the identity game. The *diverging* game function $\mathbb{0}_{AB} : A \rightsquigarrow B$ is given by

$$\mathbb{0}_{AB} \triangleq \{(u,X) \mid u \in A \text{ and } X \subseteq B\} = A \times \wp B.$$

The intuition for the definition of $\mathbb{0}_{AB}$ is that when the program diverges, the demon cannot lead the game to an error state, therefore the angel can guarantee anything. This describes a notion of partial correctness. Finally, the *(semantic) while operation* ($\mathbf{wh} - \mathbf{do} -$) has the following typing rule and definition:

$$\frac{P \subseteq A \qquad f : A \rightsquigarrow A}{\mathbf{wh}\, P\, \mathbf{do}\, f \triangleq \bigcap_{\kappa \in \mathbf{Ord}} W_\kappa : A \rightsquigarrow A} \qquad \begin{aligned} W_0 &= P[\mathbb{0}_{AA}, \mathbb{1}_A] \\ W_{\kappa+1} &= P[f;W_\kappa, \mathbb{1}_A] \\ W_\lambda &= \textstyle\bigcap_{\kappa<\lambda} W_\kappa, \text{ limit ordinal } \lambda \end{aligned}$$

The sets $W_0 \supseteq W_1 \supseteq W_2 \supseteq \cdots \supseteq W_\kappa \supseteq \cdots$ form a decreasing chain. That is, $\kappa \leq \lambda$ implies $W_\kappa \supseteq W_\lambda$, for any ordinals κ and λ.

We note that the above definition gives the while operation as a greatest fixpoint. This is not surprising, because the semantics we consider is meant to be useful for reasoning about *safety properties*. As we will see, this definition agrees with the standard least fixpoint definition of while loops when there is only one kind of nondeterminism (Lemma 6). More importantly, we will prove that our definition is *exactly right*, becauses it agrees with the intended operational semantics of dual nondeterminism (Proposition 28).

Lemma 6 **(lift Commutes with the Operations).** Let ϕ and ψ be nondeterministic functions, and P be a predicate. Then, the following hold:

$$\begin{array}{lll} \mathsf{lift}\, 0_{AB} = \mathbb{0}_{AB} & \mathsf{lift}(\phi;\psi) = (\mathsf{lift}\,\phi);(\mathsf{lift}\,\psi) & \mathsf{lift}(P[\phi,\psi]) = P[\,\mathsf{lift}\,\phi, \mathsf{lift}\,\psi] \\ \mathsf{lift}\, 1_A = \mathbb{1}_A & \mathsf{lift}(\phi+\psi) = (\mathsf{lift}\,\phi) \sqcap (\mathsf{lift}\,\psi) & \mathsf{lift}(\mathbf{wh}\, P\, \mathbf{do}\, \phi) = \mathbf{wh}\, P\, \mathbf{do}\, (\mathsf{lift}\,\phi) \end{array}$$

Essentially, the lemma says that the game function operations are a generalization of the nondeterministic function operations.

For a nondeterministic function $\phi : A \to \wp B$ and a game function $f : A \leadsto B$, we say that ϕ *implements* f if $\mathsf{lift}\,\phi \subseteq f$. So, ϕ implements f when it resolves (in some possible way) the angelic nondeterminism of f.

Definition 7 (Game Interpretation of Programs). As in the case of nondeterministic program schemes (Definition 2), an interpretation of the language of while game schemes consists of a nonempty *state space* S and an *interpretation function* I. For a program term f, its *interpretation* $I(f) : S \leadsto S$ is a game function on S. The function I specifies the meaning of every atomic test, and extends to all tests in the obvious way. Moreover, I specifies the meaning $I(a) : S \leadsto S$ of every atomic action. It extends as: $I(\mathsf{id}) = \mathbb{1}_S$, $I(\bot) = \mathbb{0}_{SS}$, and

$$\begin{array}{lll} I(f;g) = I(f);I(g) & I(f \sqcup g) = I(f) \sqcup I(g) & I(p[f,g]) = I(p)\,[I(f), I(g)] \\ & I(f \sqcap g) = I(f) \sqcap I(g) & I(\mathsf{w}pf) = \mathbf{wh}\, I(p)\, \mathbf{do}\, I(f) \end{array}$$

We say that the game interpretation I *lifts* the nondeterministic interpretation R if they have the same state space, and additionally: (i) $I(p) = R(p)$ for every atomic test p, and (ii) $I(a) = \mathsf{lift}\, R(a)$ for every atomic program a. We also say that I *is the lifting of* R.

4 Hoare Formulas and Their Meaning

In this section, we present formulas that are used to specify programs. The basic formulas are called Hoare assertions, and we also consider assertions under certain hypotheses of a simple form (Hoare implications).

Definition 8 (Tests and Entailment). Let I be an interpretation of tests. For a test p and a state $u \in S$, we write $I, u \models p$ when $u \in I(p)$. We read this as: "the state u satisfies p (under I)". When $I, u \models p$ for every state $u \in S$, we say that I *satisfies* p, and we write $I \models p$. For a set Φ of tests, the interpretation I *satisfies* Φ if it satisfies every test in Φ. We then write $I \models \Phi$. Finally, we say that Φ *entails* p, denoted $\Phi \models p$, if $I \models \Phi$ implies $I \models p$ for every I.

Definition 9 (Hoare Assertions). An expression $\{p\}f\{q\}$, where p and q are tests and f is a program term, is called a *Hoare assertion*. The test p is called the *precondition* and the test q is called the *postcondition* of the assertion. Informally, the formula $\{p\}f\{q\}$ says that when the program f starts at a state satisfying the predicate p, then the angel has a strategy so that whatever the demon does, the final state (upon termination) satisfies the predicate q. The Hoare assertion $\{p\}a\{q\}$, where a is an atomic program, is called a *simple Hoare assertion.* More formally, consider an interpretation I. We say that I *satisfies* $\{p\}f\{q\}$, and we write $I \models \{p\}f\{q\}$, when the following holds for every state $u \in S$: $I, u \models p$ implies that $(u, I(q)) \in I(f)$.

Definition 10 (Simple Hoare Implications). Let Φ be a finite set of tests, and Ψ be a finite set of simple Hoare assertions. We call the expression

$$\Phi, \Psi \Rightarrow \{p\}f\{q\}$$

a *simple Hoare implication.* The tests in Φ and the simple assertions in Ψ are the *hypotheses* of the implication, and the Hoare assertion $\{p\}f\{q\}$ is the *conclusion.*

Let I be an interpretation of tests and actions. We say that I *satisfies* the implication $\Phi, \Psi \Rightarrow \{p\}f\{q\}$, which we denote by $I \models \Phi, \Psi \Rightarrow \{p\}f\{q\}$, when the following holds: If the interpretation I satisfies every test in Φ and every assertion in Ψ, then I satisfies the assertion $\{p\}f\{q\}$. An implication $\Phi, \Psi \Rightarrow \{p\}f\{q\}$ is *valid*, denoted $\Phi, \Psi \models \{p\}f\{q\}$, if every interpretation satisfies it. The set of all valid Hoare implications forms the *weak Hoare theory* of while game schemes.

Definition 11 (Boolean Atoms & Φ-consistency). Suppose that we have fixed a finite set of atomic tests. For an atomic test p, the expressions p and $\neg p$ are called *literals* for p (*positive* and *negative* respectively). Fix an enumeration $p_1, p_2, \ldots, p_k$ of the atomic tests. A *Boolean atom* (or simply *atom*) is an expression $\ell_1 \ell_2 \cdots \ell_k$, where every ℓ_i is a literal for p_i. We use lowercase letters $\alpha, \beta, \gamma, \ldots$ from the beginning of the Greek alphabet to range over atoms. An atom is essentially a conjunction of literals, and it can also be thought of as a propositional truth assignment. We write $\alpha \leq p$ to mean that the atom α satisfies the test p. We denote by At the set of all atoms.

Assume that Φ is a finite set of tests. We say that an atom α is *Φ-consistent* if $\alpha \leq p$ for every test p in Φ. We write At_Φ for the set of all Φ-consistent atoms.

Definition 12 (The Free Test Interpretation). Let Φ be a finite set of tests. We define the interpretation I_Φ on tests, which is called the *free test interpretation* w.r.t. Φ. The state space is the set At_Φ of Φ-consistent atoms, and every test is interpreted as a unary predicate on At_Φ. For an atomic test p, define $I_\Phi(p) := \{\alpha \in \mathsf{At}_\Phi \mid \alpha \leq p\}$ to be the set of Φ-consistent atoms that satisfy p.

An easy induction on the structure of tests proves that for every (atomic or composite) test p, $I_\Phi(p)$ is equal to the set of Φ-consistent atoms that satisfy p.

Note 13 (Complete Boolean Calculus). We assume that we have a complete Boolean calculus, with which we derive judgments $\Phi \vdash p$, where Φ is a finite set of tests and p is a test. This means that the statements $\Phi \models p$, $I_\Phi \models p$, $I_\Phi(p) = \mathsf{At}_\Phi$, and $\Phi \vdash p$ are all equivalent. Moreover, $I_\Phi(p) \subseteq I_\Phi(q)$ iff $\Phi \vdash p \rightarrow q$.

5 A Hoare Calculus for While Game Schemes

In this section we propose a Hoare-style calculus (Table 1), which is used for deriving simple Hoare implications that involve while game schemes. As we will show, the calculus of Table 1 is sound and complete for the weak Hoare theory of while game schemes. Establishing soundness is a relatively straightforward result. The most interesting part is the soundness of the (loop) rule for while loops. The observation is that the loop invariant defines a "safe region" of the game, and the angel has a strategy to keep a play within this region.

Table 1. *Game Hoare Logic*: A sound and complete Hoare-style calculus for while program schemes with angelic and demonic nondeterministic choice

$$\frac{\{p\}a\{q\} \text{ in } \Psi}{\Phi, \Psi \vdash \{p\}a\{q\}}\ (\mathsf{hyp}) \qquad \frac{}{\Phi, \Psi \vdash \{p\}\mathsf{id}\{p\}}\ (\mathsf{skip}) \qquad \frac{}{\Phi, \Psi \vdash \{p\}\bot\{q\}}\ (\mathsf{dvrg})$$

$$\frac{\Phi, \Psi \vdash \{p\}f\{q\} \quad \Phi, \Psi \vdash \{q\}g\{r\}}{\Phi, \Psi \vdash \{p\}f;g\{r\}}\ (\mathsf{seq}) \qquad \frac{\Phi, \Psi \vdash \{q \wedge p\}f\{r\} \quad \Phi, \Psi \vdash \{q \wedge \neg p\}g\{r\}}{\Phi, \Psi \vdash \{q\}\mathsf{if}\, p\, \mathsf{then}\, f\, \mathsf{else}\, g\{r\}}\ (\mathsf{cond})$$

$$\frac{\Phi, \Psi \vdash \{r \wedge p\}f\{r\}}{\Phi, \Psi \vdash \{r\}\mathsf{while}\, p\, \mathsf{do}\, f\{r \wedge \neg p\}}\ (\mathsf{loop})$$

$$\frac{\Phi, \Psi \vdash \{p\}f_i\{q\}}{\Phi, \Psi \vdash \{p\}f_1 \sqcup f_2\{q\}}\ (\mathsf{ang}_i) \qquad \frac{\Phi, \Psi \vdash \{p\}f\{q\} \quad \Phi, \Psi \vdash \{p\}g\{q\}}{\Phi, \Psi \vdash \{p\}f \sqcap g\{q\}}\ (\mathsf{dem})$$

$$\frac{\Phi \vdash p' \to p \quad \Phi, \Psi \vdash \{p\}f\{q\} \quad \Phi \vdash q \to q'}{\Phi, \Psi \vdash \{p'\}f\{q'\}}\ (\mathsf{weak})$$

$$\frac{\Phi, \Psi \vdash \{p_1\}f\{q\} \quad \Phi, \Psi \vdash \{p_2\}f\{q\}}{\Phi, \Psi \vdash \{p_1 \vee p_2\}f\{q\}}\ (\mathsf{join}) \qquad \begin{array}{ll} \Phi, \Psi \vdash \{\mathsf{false}\}f\{q\} & (\mathsf{join}_0) \\ \Phi, \Psi \vdash \{p\}f\{\mathsf{true}\} & (\mathsf{meet}_0) \end{array}$$

Theorem 14 (Soundness). The Hoare calculus of Table 1 is sound.

5.1 First Completeness Theorem: Weak Hoare Theory

We will now prove the completeness of the Hoare calculus of Table 1 with respect to the class of all interpretations. This means that we consider arbitrary interpretations of the atomic programs $a, b, \ldots$ as game functions. So, the deductive system of Table 1 is complete for the weak Hoare theory of while game schemes. Note that this is an *unconditional* completeness result (no extra assumptions), not a relative completeness theorem [3].

Definition 15 (The Free Game Interpretation). Let Φ be a finite set of tests, and Ψ be a finite set of simple Hoare assertions. We define the *free game interpretation* $I_{\Phi\Psi}$ (w.r.t. Φ and Ψ) to have At_Φ as state space, and to interpret the tests as I_Φ (the free test interpretation w.r.t. Φ, see Definition 12) does. Moreover, the interpretation $I_{\Phi\Psi}(a) : \mathsf{At}_\Phi \rightsquigarrow \mathsf{At}_\Phi$ of the atomic action a is given by: for every Φ-consistent atom α,

- $(\alpha, \mathsf{At}_\Phi) \in I_{\Phi\Psi}(a)$, and for every subset $X \subsetneq \mathsf{At}_\Phi$,
- $(\alpha, X) \in I_{\Phi\Psi}(a)$ iff there exists $\{p\}a\{q\} \in \Psi$ s.t. $\alpha \leq p$ and $I_\Phi(q) \subseteq X$.

Lemma 16. Let Φ be a finite set of tests, and Ψ be a finite set of simple Hoare assertions. The free game interpretation $I_{\Phi\Psi}$ satisfies all formulas in Φ and Ψ.

Theorem 17 (Completeness). Let Φ be a finite set of tests, and Ψ be a finite set of simple Hoare assertions. For every program term f and every Φ-consistent atom α, $(\alpha, X) \in I_{\Phi\Psi}(f)$ implies that $\Phi, \Psi \vdash \{\alpha\}f\{\bigvee X\}$.

Corollary 18 (Completeness). Let Φ be a finite set of tests, and Ψ be a finite set of simple Hoare assertions. For every program f, the following are equivalent:
(1) $\Phi, \Psi \models \{p\}f\{q\}$.
(2) For every Φ-consistent $\alpha \leq p$, the pair $(\alpha, I_\Phi(q))$ is in $I_{\Phi\Psi}(f)$.
(3) $\Phi, \Psi \vdash \{p\}f\{q\}$.

Corollary 18 gives us a decision procedure for the weak Hoare theory of dual nondeterminism. Given a Hoare implication $\Phi, \Psi \Rightarrow \{p\}f\{q\}$, we simply have to compute the free interpretation $I_{\Phi\Psi}(f) \subseteq \mathsf{At}_\Phi \times \wp\mathsf{At}_\Phi$, which is a finite object. Observe that $I_{\Phi\Psi}(f)$ is of doubly exponential size. We will see later that, with some more work, we can devise a faster algorithm of exponential complexity.

5.2 Second Completeness Theorem: Strong Hoare Theory

The completeness theorem of Section 5.1 concerns the theory generated by the class of all interpretations, that is, when the atomic programs are allowed to be interpreted as any game function. However, for most realistic applications the atomic actions $a, b, \ldots$ correspond to computational operations (e.g., variable assignments $x := t$, etc.) that involve no angelic nondeterministic choice. This leads us to consider a strictly smaller class of interpretations, and thus the question is raised of whether this smaller class has the same Hoare theory.

Definition 19 (Validity Over a Class of Interpretations). We fix a language with atomic tests and atomic actions. Let $\mathcal{C}$ be a class of interpretations of the atomic symbols (extending to all tests and programs in the usual way). We say that a Hoare implication $\Phi, \Psi \Rightarrow \{p\}f\{q\}$ is *valid in* $\mathcal{C}$ (or $\mathcal{C}$*-valid*) if every interpretation I in $\mathcal{C}$ satisfies the implication. We then write $\Phi, \Psi \models_{\mathcal{C}} \{p\}f\{q\}$. The set of all $\mathcal{C}$-validities is called the *Hoare theory of* $\mathcal{C}$.

Let *All* be the class of all interpretations. Observe that an implication is valid iff it is valid in *All*. Now, let *Dem* $\subseteq$ *All* be the strict subclass of interpretations where the atomic actions are interpreted as non-angelic game functions.

Lemma 20 (Soundness). The rule (meet) of Table 2, where a is an atomic action, is sound for the class *Dem* of interpretations.

Lemma 20 also establishes that the Hoare theory of *Dem* is different from the Hoare theory of *All*. Strictly more implications hold, when we restrict attention to the interpretations of *Dem*. For example, consider the set of hypotheses Ψ,

Table 2. A rule that is sound when the atomic actions are interpretated as non-angelic game functions. That is, (meet) is sound for the class *Dem*.

$$\frac{\Phi, \Psi \vdash \{p\}a\{q_1\} \qquad \Phi, \Psi \vdash \{p\}a\{q_2\}}{\Phi, \Psi \vdash \{p\}a\{q_1 \wedge q_2\}} \;(a\text{-}\mathsf{meet})$$

which consists of the two simple assertions $\{p\}a\{q\}$ and $\{p\}a\{r\}$, where p, q, r are distinct atomic tests. Observe that the implication $\Psi \Rightarrow \{p\}a\{q \wedge r\}$ is valid in *Dem* (by Lemma 20), but it is not valid in *All* (by virtue of Corollary 18).

Definition 21 (The Free Non-angelic Interpretation). Let Φ be a finite set of tests, and Ψ be a finite set of simple Hoare assertions. For an atomic action a, define the nondeterministic interpretation $R_{\Phi\Psi}(a) : \mathsf{At}_\Phi \to \wp\mathsf{At}_\Phi$ as

$$R_{\Phi\Psi}(a)(\alpha) \triangleq \{\beta \in \mathsf{At}_\Phi \mid \text{for every } \{p\}a\{q\} \in \Psi \text{ with } \alpha \leq p, \text{ we have } \beta \leq q\}.$$

We define the *free non-angelic interpretation* $J_{\Phi\Psi}$ (w.r.t. Φ and Ψ) to have At_Φ as state space, and to interpret the tests as I_Φ (the free test interpretation w.r.t. Φ, see Definition 12) does. Moreover, the interpretation $J_{\Phi\Psi}(a) : \mathsf{At}_\Phi \rightsquigarrow \mathsf{At}_\Phi$ of the atomic action a is given by $J_{\Phi\Psi}(a) := \mathsf{lift}\, R_{\Phi\Psi}(a)$.

Lemma 22. Let Φ be a finite set of tests, and Ψ be a finite set of simple Hoare assertions. The free non-angelic interpretation $J_{\Phi\Psi}$ satisfies both Φ and Ψ.

Recall that we used the symbol $\vdash$ in Section 5 to denote provability in the Hoare-style system of Table 1. Now, we will use the symbol $\vdash_d$ to denote provability in the Hoare-style system that extends the calculus of Table 1 with the additional rule (meet) shown in Table 2.

Theorem 23 (Completeness). Let Φ be a finite set of tests, and Ψ be a finite set of simple Hoare assertions. For every program term f and every Φ-consistent atom α, $(\alpha, Y) \in J_{\Phi\Psi}(f)$ implies that $\Phi, \Psi \vdash_d \{\alpha\}f\{\bigvee Y\}$.

Corollary 24 (Completeness). Let Φ and Ψ be finite sets of tests and simple Hoare assertions respectively. For every program f, the following are equivalent:

(1) $\Phi, \Psi \models_{Dem} \{p\}f\{q\}$.
(2) For every Φ-consistent $\alpha \leq p$, the pair $(\alpha, I_\Phi(q))$ is in $J_{\Phi\Psi}(f)$.
(3) $\Phi, \Psi \vdash_d \{p\}f\{q\}$.

The results of this section imply that the Hoare theory of the class *Dem*, which we also call the *strong Hoare theory* of while game schemes, can be reduced to the weak Hoare theory of the class *All*. Let $\Phi, \Psi \Rightarrow \{p\}f\{q\}$ be an arbitrary Hoare implication. W.l.o.g. the axioms in Ψ are of the form $\{\alpha\}a\{q\}$, where α is an atom and a is an atomic action. Now, define Ψ' to be the set of hypotheses that results from Ψ by replacing the axioms $\{\alpha\}a\{q_i\}$ involving α, a by a single axiom $\{\alpha\}a\{\bigwedge_i q_i\}$. The crucial observation is that the interpretation $J_{\Phi\Psi}$ is the same as $I_{\Phi\Psi'}$. Using our two completeness results of Corollary 18 and Corollary 24, it follows that $\Phi, \Psi \vdash_d \{p\}f\{q\}$ iff $\Phi, \Psi' \vdash \{p\}f\{q\}$.

6 Operational Model and Complexity

In this section we investigate the computational complexity of the strong Hoare theory of while game schemes. We prove that this theory is complete for exponential time. In order to obtain the EXPTIME upper bound, we consider a standard operational model that corresponds to the free game interpretation. We establish that our denotational semantics coincides in a precise sense to the operational semantics. The operational model is a safety game on a finite graph, and we can decide validity by computing the winning regions of the players. The lower bound of EXPTIME-hardness is obtained with a reduction from alternating Turing machines with polynomially bounded tapes.

First, we restrict slightly the syntax of program terms by eliminating the diverging $\bot$ program, and by forbidding compositions $(f;g);h$ that associate to the left. These are not really limitations, because $\bot$ is semantically equivalent to the infinite loop $\mathsf{while\,true\,do\,id}$, and $(f;g);h$ is equivalent to $f;(g;h)$. We define the syntactic categories *factor* and *term* with the following grammars:

$$\text{factor } e ::= a \mid \mathsf{id} \mid p[f,g] \mid \mathsf{w}pf \mid f \sqcup g \mid f \sqcap g \qquad\qquad \text{terms } f,g ::= e \mid e;f$$

A term according to the above definition is a nonempty list of factors. We write @ for the concatenation of terms: $e@g = e;g$ and $(e;f)@g = e;(f@g)$.

Definition 25 (Closure & the $\rightarrow$ Relation on Terms). We define the *closure* function $C(\cdot)$ that sends a term to a finite set of terms.

$$C(a) = \{a, \mathsf{id}\} \quad C(\mathsf{w}pf) = \{\mathsf{w}pf, \mathsf{id}\} \cup C(f)@\mathsf{w}pf \quad C(e;f) = C(e)@f \cup C(f)$$
$$C(\mathsf{id}) = \{\mathsf{id}\} \quad C(f \oplus g) = \{f \oplus g\} \cup C(f) \cup C(g)$$

where $(- \oplus -)$ is any of the constructors $(- \sqcup -)$, $(- \sqcap -)$, or $p[-,-]$. We define the relation $\rightarrow$ on terms as follows:

$$a \rightarrow \mathsf{id} \qquad \mathsf{w}pf \rightarrow f@\mathsf{w}pf,\ \mathsf{id} \qquad f \oplus g \rightarrow f,\ g \qquad \mathsf{id};h \rightarrow h$$
$$a;h \rightarrow h \quad \mathsf{w}pf;h \rightarrow f@(\mathsf{w}pf);h,\ \mathsf{id};h \quad (f \oplus g);h \rightarrow f@h,\ g@h$$

We write $\rightarrow^*$ for the reflexive transitive closure of $\rightarrow$. The definition of $\rightarrow$ says, in particular, that id has no successor. The while loop $\mathsf{w}pf$ has exactly two successors, namely $f@\mathsf{w}pf$ and id.

Lemma 26 (Closure & Reachability). Let f be a program term. The cardinality of $C(f)$ is linear in the size $|f|$ of f, in fact, $|C(f)| \leq 2|f|$. Moreover, $C(f)$ is equal to the set $\{f' \mid f \rightarrow^* f'\}$ of terms that are reachable from f via $\rightarrow$.

Definition 27 (Operational Model). Fix a finite set Φ of tests, and a finite set Ψ of simple Hoare assertions. W.l.o.g. we assume that Ψ contains exactly one assertion $\{\alpha\}a\{q\}$ for every atomic program a and every Φ-consistent atom α.

Table 3. The operational model that corresponds to the free game interpretation $I_{\Phi\Psi}$

$$
\begin{array}{ll}
\multicolumn{2}{c}{(\alpha, a) \rightarrow (I_\Phi(q), \mathsf{id}), \text{ where } \{\alpha\}a\{q\} \in \Psi} \\
\multicolumn{2}{c}{(\alpha, a; h) \rightarrow (I_\Phi(q), \mathsf{id}; h), \text{ where } \{\alpha\}a\{q\} \in \Psi} \\
(\alpha, \mathsf{id}) \rightarrow & (\alpha, \mathsf{id}; h) \rightarrow (\alpha, h) \\
(\alpha, p[f, g]) \rightarrow (\alpha, f), \text{ if } \alpha \leq p & (\alpha, p[f, g]; h) \rightarrow (a, f@h), \text{ if } \alpha \leq p \\
(\alpha, p[f, g]) \rightarrow (\alpha, g), \text{ if } \alpha \leq \neg p & (\alpha, p[f, g]; h) \rightarrow (a, g@h), \text{ if } \alpha \leq \neg p \\
(\alpha, \mathsf{W}pf) \rightarrow (\alpha, f@\mathsf{W}pf), \text{ if } \alpha \leq p & (\alpha, (\mathsf{W}pf); h) \rightarrow (\alpha, f@(\mathsf{W}pf); h), \text{ if } \alpha \leq p \\
(\alpha, \mathsf{W}pf) \rightarrow (\alpha, \mathsf{id}), \text{ if } \alpha \leq \neg p & (\alpha, (\mathsf{W}pf); h) \rightarrow (\alpha, \mathsf{id}; h), \text{ if } \alpha \leq \neg p \\
(\alpha, f \sqcup g) \rightarrow (\alpha, f),\ (\alpha, g) & (\alpha, (f \sqcup g); h) \rightarrow (\alpha, f@h),\ (\alpha, g@h) \\
(\alpha, f \sqcap g) \rightarrow (\alpha, f),\ (\alpha, g) & (\alpha, (f \sqcap g); h) \rightarrow (\alpha, f@h),\ (\alpha, g@h) \\
\multicolumn{2}{c}{(X, f) \rightarrow (\alpha, f), \text{ where } \alpha \in X \subseteq \mathsf{At}_\Phi}
\end{array}
$$

Let f be a program term, and $E \subseteq \mathsf{At}_\Phi$ be a set of *error atoms*. We define the *operational model* for Φ, Ψ, f, E, denoted $G_{\Phi\Psi}(f, E)$, to be the safety game

$$G_{\Phi\Psi}(f, E) = (V, V_0, V_1, \rightarrow, E \times \{\mathsf{id}\}),$$

where $V = (\mathsf{At}_\Phi \times C(f)) \cup \bigcup_{\{\alpha\}a\{q\} \in \Psi} (I_\Phi(q) \times C(f))$ and the transition relation $\rightarrow$ is defined in Table 3.

- The 0-vertices $V_0 \subseteq V$ consist of the pairs of the form $(\alpha, f \sqcup g)$, as well as (α, a) and $(\alpha, a; h)$ for atomic program a.
- The 1-vertices $V_1 \subseteq V$ consist of the pairs $(\alpha, f \sqcap g)$, as well as (X, f) where $X \subseteq \mathsf{At}_\Phi$ is equal to some $I_\Phi(q)$ with $\{\alpha\}a\{q\} \in \Psi$.

The terminal vertices are the pairs (α, id), and the error vertices are $E \times \{\mathsf{id}\}$.

Proposition 28 (Operational & Denotational Semantics). Let Φ be a finite set of tests, Ψ be a finite set of simple Hoare assertions, f be a program term, $\alpha \in \mathsf{At}_\Phi$, and $X \subseteq \mathsf{At}_\Phi$. Then, $(\alpha, X) \in I_{\Phi\Psi}(f)$ iff Player 0 has a winning strategy from the vertex (α, f) in the safety game $G_{\Phi\Psi}(f, {\sim}X)$, where ${\sim}X = \mathsf{At}_\Phi \setminus X$.

Theorem 29 (Complexity Upper & Lower Bound). The strong Hoare theory (over the class *Dem*) of while game schemes is EXPTIME-complete.

It is an immediate corollary of the above theorem that the weak Hoare theory (over the class *All*) can also be decided in exponential time.

7 A Complete Hoare-Style Calculus for Synthesis

We introduce in Table 4 a Hoare-style calculus which can be used for the deductive synthesis of $\sqcup$-free programs that satisfy a Hoare specification. It is based on the complete calculus for the Hoare theory of the class *Dem*, which contains interpretations assigning non-angelic game functions (Def. 3) to the atomic programs (Table 1 with extra rule of a-meet of Table 2). The main differences are:

Table 4. A sound and complete Hoare-style calculus for the synthesis of programs

$$\frac{\{p\}a\{q\} \text{ in } \Psi}{\Phi, \Psi \vdash a : \{p\}a\{q\}}\ (\mathsf{hyp}) \qquad \frac{}{\Phi, \Psi \vdash \mathsf{id} : \{p\}\mathsf{id}\{p\}}\ (\mathsf{skip}) \qquad \frac{}{\Phi, \Psi \vdash \bot : \{p\}\bot\{q\}}\ (\mathsf{dvrg})$$

$$\frac{\Phi, \Psi \vdash \phi : \{p\}f\{q\} \quad \Phi, \Psi \vdash \psi : \{q\}g\{r\}}{\Phi, \Psi \vdash \phi;\psi : \{p\}f;g\{r\}}\ (\mathsf{seq}) \qquad \frac{\Phi, \Psi \vdash \phi : \{q \wedge p\}f\{r\} \quad \Phi, \Psi \vdash \psi : \{q \wedge \neg p\}g\{r\}}{\Phi, \Psi \vdash p[\phi, \psi] : \{q\}\mathsf{if}\ p\ \mathsf{then}\ f\ \mathsf{else}\ g\{r\}}\ (\mathsf{cond})$$

$$\frac{\Phi, \Psi \vdash \phi : \{r \wedge p\}f\{r\}}{\Phi, \Psi \vdash \mathsf{W}p\phi : \{r\}\mathsf{while}\ p\ \mathsf{do}\ f\{r \wedge \neg p\}}\ (\mathsf{loop})$$

$$\frac{\Phi, \Psi \vdash \phi : \{p\}f_i\{q\}}{\Phi, \Psi \vdash \phi : \{p\}f_1 \sqcup f_2\{q\}}\ (\mathsf{ang}_i) \qquad \frac{\Phi, \Psi \vdash \phi : \{p\}f\{q\} \quad \Phi, \Psi \vdash \psi : \{p\}g\{q\}}{\Phi, \Psi \vdash \phi \sqcap \psi : \{p\}f \sqcap g\{q\}}\ (\mathsf{dem})$$

$$\frac{\Phi \vdash p' \to p \quad \Phi, \Psi \vdash \phi : \{p\}f\{q\} \quad \Phi \vdash q \to q'}{\Phi, \Psi \vdash \phi : \{p'\}f\{q'\}}\ (\mathsf{weak})$$

$$\frac{\Phi, \Psi \vdash \phi_1 : \{p_1\}f\{q\} \quad \Phi, \Psi \vdash \phi_2 : \{p_2\}f\{q\}}{\Phi, \Psi \vdash p_1[\phi_1, \phi_2] : \{p_1 \vee p_2\}f\{q\}}\ (\mathsf{join}) \qquad \begin{array}{c}(a\text{-}\mathsf{join}_0)\\ \Phi, \Psi \vdash a : \{\mathsf{false}\}a\{q\}\end{array}$$

$$\frac{\Phi, \Psi \vdash a : \{p\}a\{q_1\} \quad \Phi, \Psi \vdash a : \{p\}a\{q_2\}}{\Phi, \Psi \vdash a : \{p\}a\{q_1 \wedge q_2\}}\ (a\text{-}\mathsf{meet}) \qquad \begin{array}{c}(a\text{-}\mathsf{meet}_0)\\ \Phi, \Psi \vdash a : \{p\}a\{\mathsf{true}\}\end{array}$$

$$\frac{\Phi, \Psi \vdash \phi : \{p_1\}f\{q\} \quad \Phi, \Psi \vdash \phi : \{p_2\}f\{q\}}{\Phi, \Psi \vdash \phi : \{p_1 \vee p_2\}f\{q\}}\ (\mathsf{join}') \qquad \frac{\Phi, \Psi \vdash \phi_1 : \{p \wedge r\}f\{q\} \quad \Phi, \Psi \vdash \phi_2 : \{p \wedge \neg r\}f\{q\}}{\Phi, \Psi \vdash r[\phi_1, \phi_2] : \{p\}f\{q\}}\ (\mathsf{join}'')$$

(i) The rules join_0 and meet_0 (of Table 1) have been weakened into the rules a-join_0 and a-meet_0 (this is inconsequential).

(ii) Every conclusion $\{p\}f\{q\}$ is decorated with a $\sqcup$-free program term ϕ, which satisfies the specification $\{p\}\phi\{q\}$ and implements a winning strategy for the angel in the safety game described by the assertion $\{p\}f\{q\}$.

Another difference that deserves mention is the introduction in Table 4 of two new variants (join') and (join'') of the rule (join). These rules are not necessary for completeness and they can be omitted without breaking our theorems, but they are useful from a practical viewpoint. The new rules (join') and (join'') are sound, and they allow useful shortcuts in the synthesis of $\sqcup$-free programs.

Theorem 30 (Soundness). Suppose that a judgment $\Phi, \Psi \vdash \phi : \{p\}f\{q\}$ is derivable using the Hoare-style calculus of Table 4. The following hold:

1. Every game interpretation I in *Dem* satisfies the formula $\Phi, \Psi \Rightarrow \{p\}f\{q\}$.
2. Every nondeterministic interpretation R satisfies $\Phi, \Psi \Rightarrow \{p\}\phi\{q\}$.
3. Let R be a nondeterministic interpretation, and I be the game interpretation that lifts R (see Definition 7). Then, $\mathsf{lift}\, R(\phi) \subseteq I(f)$.

Part (3) of the theorem says that $R(\phi)$ implements $I(f)$ when I lifts R.

Theorem 31 (Completeness). Let Φ and Ψ be finite sets of tests and simple Hoare assertions respectively, and f be a program s.t. $\Phi, \Psi \models_{Dem} \{p\}f\{q\}$. Then, there exists a $\sqcup$-free program ϕ such that $\Phi, \Psi \vdash \phi : \{p\}f\{q\}$.

Finally, we will see that solving safety games on finite graphs can be reduced to deciding the *Dem*-validity of a Hoare implication involving a while game scheme that simulates the safety game. This reduction thus gives us a compositional deductive way of designing winning strategies for safety games. Let $G = (V_0, V_1, R, E)$ be a safety game. For every vertex $u \in V = V_0 \cup V_1$, introduce an atomic test p_u, which asserts that the token is currently on the vertex u. We take Φ to contain the axioms $\bigvee_{u \in V} p_u$ and $\neg(p_u \wedge p_v)$ for all $u, v \in V$ with $u \neq v$. The axioms of Φ say that the token is on exactly one vertex. So, we can identify the set At_Φ of Φ-consistent atoms with the set $\{p_u \mid u \in V\}$. For every vertex $u \in V$, we introduce an atomic action $u!$, which moves the token to the vertex u. So, we take Ψ to contain the axioms $\{\mathsf{true}\}u!\{p_u\}$ for every $u \in V$. To emphasize that Φ and Ψ depend on G, let us denote them by Φ_G and Ψ_G respectively. For an arbitrary vertex $u \in V$, define the program term (take transition from u) to be equal to $\bigsqcup_{v \in uR} v!$ if $u \in V_0$, and equal to $\bigsqcap_{v \in uR} v!$ if $u \in V_1$. Now, we put

$$
\begin{aligned}
f_G = \mathsf{while}\,(\textstyle\bigvee\{p_u \mid u \in V \setminus E\})\,\mathsf{do}\\
&\mathsf{if}\ p_u\ \mathsf{then}\ (\text{take transition from } u)\\
&\quad\cdots\\
&\mathsf{else\ if}\ p_w\ \mathsf{then}\ (\text{take transition from } w)
\end{aligned}
$$

which describes how the safety game is played. A play stops as soon as an error vertex is encountered.

Theorem 32 (Safety Games). Let $G = (V_0, V_1, R, E)$ be a finite safety game. Player 0 has a winning strategy from $u \in V_0 \cup V_1$ iff $\Phi_G, \Psi_G \vdash \{p_u\} f_G \{\mathsf{false}\}$.

8 Discussion and Conclusion

At a technical level, the present work is closely related to the line of work on the propositional fragment of Hoare logic, called *Propositional Hoare Logic* or PHL [6]. In [8,7], a propositional variant of Hoare logic for mutually recursive programs is investigated. The present work differs from both [6,8] in considering the combination of angelic and demonic nondeterminism, which presents significant new challenges for obtaining completeness and decision procedures.

An extension of Propositional Dynamic Logic, called *Game Logic* [12], is also relevant to our work. We note that there are no completeness results for full Game Logic, and that the theory we consider is *not* a fragment of Game Logic. Even though hypotheses-free Hoare assertions $\{p\}f\{q\}$ can be encoded in Dynamic Logic as partial correctness formulas $p \to [f]q$, there is no direct mechanism for encoding the hypotheses of an implication $\Phi, \Psi \Rightarrow \{p\}f\{q\}$ (which would correspond to some kind of global consequence relation in Dynamic Logic).

We have considered here the weak (over the class *All*) and the strong (over the class *Dem*) Hoare theories of dual nondeterminism, and we have obtained sound and unconditionally complete Hoare-style calculi for both of them. We have also shown that they can be both be decided in exponential time, and that the strong

Hoare theory is EXPTIME-hard. Finally, we have extended our proof system so that it constructs program terms for the strategies of the angel, thus obtaining a sound and complete calculus for synthesis.

References

1. Back, R.-J., Wright, J.: Refinement Calculus: A Systematic Introduction. Springer, Heidelberg (1998)
2. Celiku, O., Wright, J.v.: Implementing angelic nondeterminism. In: Tenth Asia-Pacific Software Engineering Conference, pp. 176–185 (2003)
3. Cook, S.A.: Soundness and completeness of an axiom system for program verification. SIAM Journal on Computing 7(1), 70–90 (1978)
4. Dijkstra, E.W.: Guarded commands, nondeterminacy and formal derivation of programs. Communications of the ACM 18(8), 453–457 (1975)
5. Hoare, C.A.R.: An axiomatic basis for computer programming. Communications of the ACM 12(10), 576–580 (1969)
6. Kozen, D.: On Hoare logic and Kleene algebra with tests. ACM Transactions on Computational Logic 1(1), 60–76 (2000)
7. Mamouras, K.: The Hoare logic of deterministic and nondeterministic monadic recursion schemes (2014) (manuscript)
8. Mamouras, K.: On the Hoare theory of monadic recursion schemes. In: Proceedings of CSL-LICS (2014)
9. Mamouras, K.: Synthesis of strategies using the Hoare logic of angelic and demonic nondeterminism (2015) (in preparation)
10. Martin, C.E., Curtis, S.A., Rewitzky, I.: Modelling nondeterminism. In: Mathematics of Program Construction, pp. 228–251 (2004)
11. Morgan, C.: Programming From Specifications. Prentice-Hall (1998)
12. Pauly, M., Parikh, R.: Game logic — An overview. Studia Logica 75(2), 165–182 (2003)
13. Rewitzky, I.: Binary multirelations. In: de Swart, H., Orłowska, E., Schmidt, G., Roubens, M. (eds.) TARSKI. LNCS, vol. 2929, pp. 256–271. Springer, Heidelberg (2003)
14. Thomas, W.: On the synthesis of strategies in infinite games. In: Mayr, E.W., Puech, C. (eds.) STACS 1995. LNCS, vol. 900, pp. 1–13. Springer, Heidelberg (1995)

An Infinitary Model of Linear Logic

Charles Grellois and Paul-André Melliès

Université Paris Diderot, Sorbonne Paris Cité, Laboratoire Preuves, Programmes, Systèmes, Paris, France
{grellois,mellies}@pps.univ-paris-diderot.fr

Abstract. In this paper, we construct an infinitary variant of the relational model of linear logic, where the exponential modality is interpreted as the set of finite or countable multisets. We explain how to interpret in this model the fixpoint operator **Y** as a Conway operator alternatively defined in an inductive or a coinductive way. We then extend the relational semantics with a notion of color or priority in the sense of parity games. This extension enables us to define a new fixpoint operator **Y** combining both inductive and coinductive policies. We conclude the paper by mentionning a connection between the resulting model of λ-calculus with recursion and higher-order model-checking.

Keywords: Linear logic, relational semantics, fixpoint operators, induction and coinduction, parity conditions, higher-order model-checking.

1 Introduction

In many respects, denotational semantics started in the late 1960's with Dana Scott's introduction of domains and the fundamental intuition that λ-terms should be interpreted as *continuous* rather than general functions between domains. This seminal insight has been so influential in the history of our discipline that it remains deeply rooted in the foundations of denotational semantics more than fourty-five years later. In the case of linear logic, this inclination for continuity means that the interpretation of the exponential modality

$$A \quad \mapsto \quad !\,A$$

is *finitary* in most denotational semantics of linear logic. This finitary nature of the exponential modality is tightly connected to continuity because this modality regulates the linear decomposition of the intuitionistic implication:

$$A \Rightarrow B \quad = \quad !\,A \multimap B.$$

Typically, in the qualitative and quantitative coherence space semantics of linear logic, the coherence space $!\,A$ is either defined as the coherence space $!A$ of *finite* cliques (in the qualitative semantics) or of *finite* multi-cliques (in the quantitative semantics) of the original coherence space A. This finiteness condition on the cliques $\{a_1, \ldots, a_n\}$ or multi-cliques $[a_1, \ldots, a_n]$ of the coherence space $!A$

A. Pitts (Ed.): FOSSACS 2015, LNCS 9034, pp. 41–55, 2015.
DOI: 10.1007/978-3-662-46678-0_3

captures the computational intuition that, in order to reach a given position b of the coherence space B, every proof or program

$$f \quad : \quad !A \multimap B$$

will only explore a *finite* number of copies of the hypothesis A, and reach at the end of the computation a specific position a_i in each copy of the coherence space A. In other words, the finitary nature of the interpretation of $!A$ is just an alternative and very concrete way to express in these traditional models of linear logic the continuity of proofs and programs.

In this paper, we would like to revisit this well-established semantic tradition and accomodate another equally well-established tradition, coming this time from verification and model-checking. We find especially important to address and to clarify an apparent antagonism between the two traditions. Model-checking is generally interested in infinitary (typically ω-regular) inductive and coinductive behaviours of programs which lie obviously far beyond the scope of Scott continuity. For that reason, we introduce a variant of the relational semantics of linear logic where the exponential modality, noted in this context

$$A \quad \mapsto \quad \lightning A$$

is defined as the set of *finite* or *countable* multisets of the set A. From this follows that a proof or a program

$$A \Rightarrow B \quad = \quad \lightning A \multimap B.$$

is allowed in the resulting infinitary semantics to explore a possibly countable number of copies of his hypothesis A in order to reach a position in B. By relaxing the continuity principle, this mild alteration of the original relational semantics paves the way to a fruitful interaction between linear logic and model-checking. This link between linear logic and model-checking is supported by the somewhat unexpected observation that the binary relation

$$Y(f) \quad : \quad !X \quad \longrightarrow \quad A$$

defining the fixpoint $\mathbf{Y}(f)$ associated to a morphism

$$f \quad : \quad !X \otimes !A \quad \longrightarrow \quad A$$

in the familiar (and thus finitary) relational semantics of linear logic is defined by performing a series of explorations of the infinite binary tree

comb =

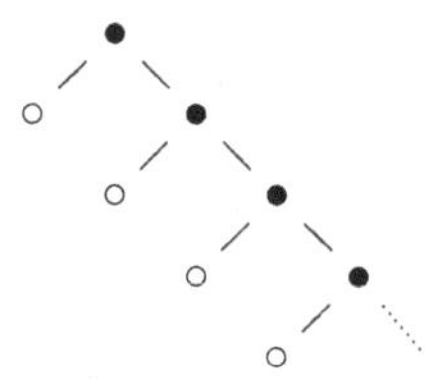

by an alternating tree automaton $\langle\, \Sigma\, ,\, Q\, ,\, \delta_f\, \rangle$ on the alphabet $\Sigma = \{\bullet, \circ\}$ defined by the binary relation f. The key idea is to define the set of states of the automaton as $Q = A \uplus X$ and to associate a transition

$$\delta_f(\bullet, a) \quad = \quad (\, x_1 \wedge \cdots \wedge x_k \,,\, a_1 \wedge \cdots \wedge a_n \,)$$

of the automaton to any element $(([x_1, \ldots, x_k], [a_1, \ldots, a_n]), a)$ of the binary relation f, where the x_i's are elements of X and the a_i's are elements of A ; and to let the symbol $\circ$ accept any state $x \in X$. Then, it appears that the traditional definition of the fixpoint operator $\mathbf{Y}(f)$ as a binary relation $!X \to A$ may be derived from the construction of run-trees of the tree-automaton $\langle\, \Sigma \,,\, Q \,,\, \delta_f \,\rangle$ on the infinitary tree **comb**. More precisely, the binary relation $Y(f)$ contains all the elements $([x_1, \ldots, x_k], a)$ such that there exists a finite run-tree (called *witness*) of the tree automaton $\langle\, \Sigma \,,\, Q \,,\, \delta_f \,\rangle$ accepting the state a with the multi-set of states $[x_1, \ldots, x_k]$ collected at the leaves $\circ$. As far as we know, this automata-theoretic account of the traditional construction of the fixpoint operator $\mathbf{Y}(f)$ in the relational semantics of linear logic is a new insight of the present paper, which we carefully develop in §4.

Once this healthy bridge between linear logic and tree automata theory identified, it makes sense to study variations of the relational semantics inspired by verification. This is precisely the path we follow here by replacing the finitary interpretation $!A$ of the exponential modality by the finite-or-countable one $\lightning A$. This alteration enables us to define an inductive as well as a coinductive fixpoint operator $\mathbf{Y}$ in the resulting infinitary relational semantics. The two fixpoint operators only differ in the acceptance condition applied to the run-tree *witness*. We carry on in this direction, and introduce a *coloured* variant of the relational semantics, designed in such a way that the tree automaton $\langle\, \Sigma \,,\, Q \,,\, \delta_f \,\rangle$ associated to a morphism $f : !X \otimes !A \to A$ defines a parity tree automaton. This leads us to the definition of an inductive-coinductive fixpoint operator $\mathbf{Y}$ tightly connected to the current investigations on higher-order model-checking.

Related Works. The present paper is part of a wider research project devoted to the relationship between linear logic, denotational semantics and higher-order model-checking. The idea developed here of shifting from the traditional finitary relational semantics of linear logic to infinitary variants is far from new. The closest to our work in this respect is probably the work by Miquel [12] where stable but non-continuous functions between coherence spaces are considered. However, our motivations are different, since we focus here on the case of a modality $!A$ defined by finite-or-countable multisets in A, which is indeed crucial for higher-order model-checking, but is not considered by Miquel. In another closely related line of work, Carraro, Ehrhard and Salibra [5] formulate a general and possibly infinitary construction of the exponential modality $A \mapsto !A$ in the relational model of linear logic. However, the authors make the extra finiteness assumption in [5] that the support of a possibly infinite multiset in $!A$ is necessarily finite. Seen from that prospect, one purpose of our work is precisely to relax this finiteness condition which appears to be too restrictive for our semantic account of higher-order model-checking based on linear logic. In a series of recent works, Salvati and Walukiewicz [15] [16] have exhibited a nice and promising connection between higher-order model checking and finite models of the simply-typed

λ-calculus. In particular, they establish the decidability of weak MSO properties of higher-order recursion schemes by using purely semantic methods. In comparison, we construct here a cartesian-closed category of sets and coloured relations (rather than finite domains) where ω-regular properties of higher-order recursion schemes (and more generally of λY-terms) may be interpreted semantically thanks to a colour modality. In a similar direction, Ong and Tsukada [22] have recently constructed a cartesian-closed category of infinitary games and strategies with similar connections to higher-order model-checking. Coming back to linear logic, we would like to mention the works by Baelde [1] and Montelatici [13] who developed infinitary variants (either inductive-coinductive or recursive) of linear logic, with an emphasis on the syntactic rather than semantic side. In a recent paper working like we do here at the converging point of linear logic and automata theory, Terui [21] uses a qualitative variant of the relational semantics of linear logic where formulas are interpreted as partial orders and proofs as downward sets in order to establish a series of striking results on the complexity of normalization of simply-typed λ-terms. Finally, an important related question which we leave untouched here is the comparison between our work and the categorical reconstruction of parity games achieved by Santocanale [17,18] using the notion of bicomplete category, see also his more recent work with Fortier [6].

Plan of the Paper. We start by recalling in §2 the traditional relational model of linear logic. Then, after recalling in §3 the definition of a Conway fixpoint operator in a Seely category, we construct in §4 such a Conway operator for the relational semantics. We then introduce in §5 our infinitary variant of the relational semantics, and illustrate its expressive power in §6 by defining two different Conway fixpoint operators. Then, we define in §7 a coloured modality for the relational semantics, and construct in §8 a Conway fixpoint operator in that framework. We finally conclude in §9.

2 The Relational Model of Linear Logic

In order to be reasonably self-contained, we briefly recall the relational model of linear logic. The category *Rel* is defined as the category with finite or countable sets as objects, and with binary relations between A and B as morphisms $A \to B$. The category *Rel* is symmetric monoidal closed, with tensor product defined as (set-theoretic) cartesian product, and tensorial unit defined as singleton:

$$A \otimes B = A \times B \qquad\qquad 1 = \{\star\}.$$

Its internal hom (also called linear implication) $X \multimap Y$ simply defined as $X \otimes Y$. Since the object $\bot = 1 = \{\star\}$ is dualizing, the category *Rel* is moreover $*$-autonomous. The category *Rel* has also finite products defined as

$$A\&B \quad = \quad \{(1,a) \mid a \in A\} \cup \{(2,b) \mid b \in B\}$$

with the empty set as terminal object $\top$. As in any category with finite products, there is a diagonal morphism $\Delta_A : A \to A \,\&\, A$ for every object A, defined as

$$\Delta_A \quad = \quad \{(a,\, (i,\, a)) \mid i \in \{1,\, 2\} \text{ and } a \in A\}$$

Note that the category *Rel* has finite sums as well, since the negation $A^\perp = A \multimap \perp$ of any object A is isomorphic to the object A itself. All this makes *Rel* a model of multiplicative additive linear logic. In order to establish that it defines a model of propositional linear logic, we find convenient to check that it satisfies the axioms of a Seely category, as originally axiomatized by Seely [19] and then revisited by Bierman [2], see the survey [11] for details. To that purpose, recall that a *finite multiset* over a set A is a (set-theoretic) function $w : A \to \mathbb{N}$ with finite support, where the support of w is the set of elements of A whose image is not equal to 0. The functor $! : Rel \to Rel$ is defined as

$$\begin{array}{rcl} !A & = & \mathcal{M}_{fin}(A) \\ !f & = & \{([a_1, \cdots, a_n], [b_1, \cdots, b_n]) \mid \forall i, (a_i, b_i) \in f\} \end{array}$$

The comultiplication and counit of the comonad are defined as the digging and dereliction morphisms below:

$$\begin{array}{rcl} \mathbf{dig}_A & = & \{(w_1 + \cdots + w_k, [w_1, \cdots, w_k]) \mid \forall i, w_i \in !A\} \in Rel(!A, !!A) \\ \mathbf{der}_A & = & \{([a], a) \mid a \in A\} \in Rel(!A, A) \end{array}$$

In order to define a Seely category, one also needs the family of isomorphisms

$$\begin{array}{rcccc} m^0 & : & 1 & \longrightarrow & !\top \\ m^2_{A,B} & : & !A \otimes !B & \longrightarrow & !(A \& B) \end{array}$$

which are defined as $m^0 = \{(\star, [])\}$ and

$$m^2_{A,B} = \{(([a_1, \cdots, a_m], [b_1, \cdots, b_n]), [(1, a_1), \cdots, (1, a_m), (2, b_1), \cdots, (2, b_n)])\}$$

One then carefully checks that the coherence diagrams expected of a Seely category commute. From this follows that

Property 1. The category *Rel* together with the finite multiset interpretation of the exponential modality ! defines a model of propositional linear logic.

3 Fixpoint Operators in Models of Linear Logic

We want to extend linear logic with a fixpoint rule:

$$\frac{!X \otimes !A \vdash A}{!X \vdash A}\ fix$$

In order to interpret it in a Seely category, we need a parametrized fixpoint operator, defined below as a family of functions

$$\mathbf{Y}_{X,A} : \mathscr{C}(!X \otimes !A, A) \longrightarrow \mathscr{C}(!X, A)$$

parametrized by X, A and satisfying two elementary conditions, mentioned for instance by Simpson and Plotkin in [20].

- **Naturality:** for any $g : !X \multimap Z$ and $f : !Z \otimes !A \multimap A$, the diagram:

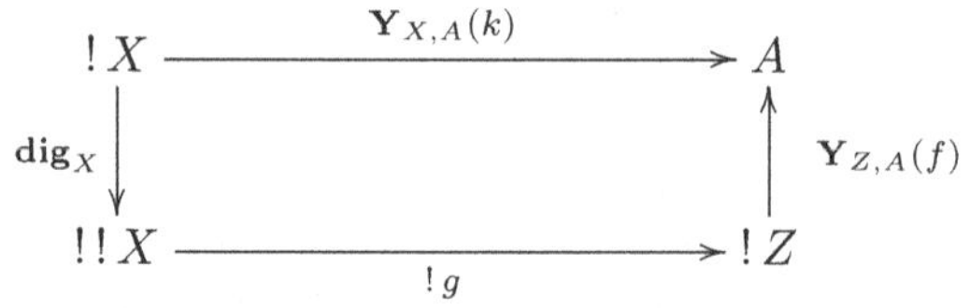

  commutes, where the morphism $k : !X \otimes !A \multimap A$ in the upper part of the diagram is defined as the composite

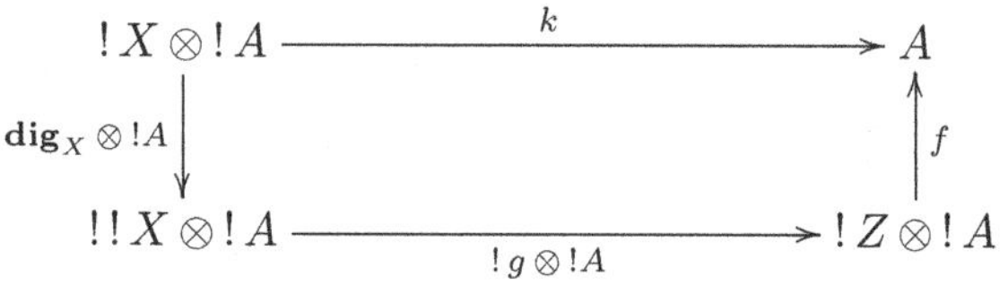

- **Parametrized fixpoint property:** for any $f : !X \otimes !A \multimap A$, the following diagram commutes:

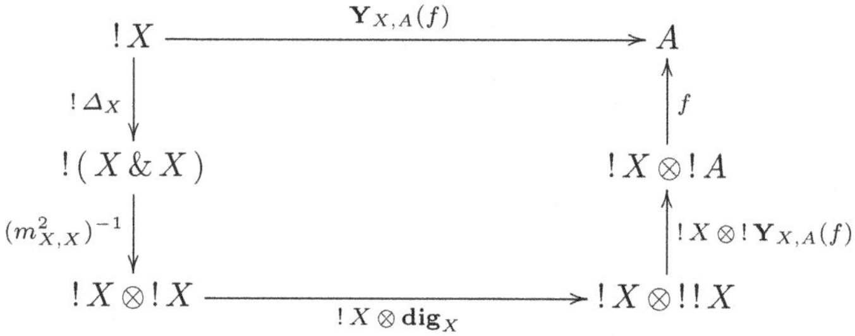

These two equations are fundamental but they do not reflect all the equational properties of the fixpoint operator in domain theory. For that reason, Bloom and Esik introduced the notion of *Conway theory* in their seminal work on iteration theories [3,4]. This notion was then rediscovered and adapted to cartesian categories by Hasegawa [8], by Hyland and by Simpson and Plotkin [20]. Hasegawa and Hyland moreover independently established a nice correspondence between the resulting notion of *Conway fixpoint operator* and the notion of trace operator introduced a few years earlier by Joyal, Street and Verity [9]. Here, we adapt in the most straightforward way this notion of Conway fixpoint operator to the specific setting of Seely categories. Before going any further, we find useful to introduce the following notation: for every pair of morphisms

$$f : !X \otimes !B \multimap A \quad \text{and} \quad g : !X \otimes !A \multimap B$$

we write $f \star g : !X \otimes !A \multimap A$ for the composite:

$$
\begin{array}{ccc}
!X \otimes !A & \xrightarrow{\quad f \star g \quad} & A \\
\Big\downarrow {\scriptstyle !\Delta_X \otimes !A} & & \Big\uparrow {\scriptstyle f} \\
!(X \& X) \otimes !A & & !X \otimes !B \\
\Big\downarrow {\scriptstyle (m^2_{X,X})^{-1} \otimes !A} & & \Big\uparrow {\scriptstyle !X \otimes !g} \\
!X \otimes !X \otimes !A & & !X \otimes !(!X \otimes !A) \\
\Big\downarrow {\scriptstyle !X \otimes m^2_{X,A}} & & \Big\uparrow {\scriptstyle !X \otimes !(m^2_{X,A})^{-1}} \\
!X \otimes !(X \& A) & \xrightarrow[\quad !X \otimes \mathbf{dig}_{X \& A} \quad]{} & !X \otimes !!(X \& A)
\end{array}
$$

A Conway operator is then defined as a parametrized fixpoint operator satisfying the two additional properties below:

- **Parametrized dinaturality:** for any $f \, : !X \otimes !B \multimap A$ and $g \, : !X \otimes !A \multimap B$, the following diagram commutes:

$$
\begin{array}{ccc}
!X & \xrightarrow{\quad \mathbf{Y}_{X,A}(f \star g) \quad} & A \\
\Big\downarrow {\scriptstyle !\Delta_X} & & \Big\uparrow {\scriptstyle f} \\
!(X \& X) & & !X \otimes !B \\
\Big\downarrow {\scriptstyle (m^2_{X,X})^{-1}} & & \Big\uparrow {\scriptstyle !X \otimes !\mathbf{Y}_{X,B}(g \star f)} \\
!X \otimes !X & \xrightarrow[\quad !X \otimes \mathbf{dig}_X \quad]{} & !X \otimes !!X
\end{array}
$$

- **Diagonal property:** for every morphism $f \, : !X \otimes !A \otimes !A \multimap A$,

$$
\mathbf{Y}_{X,A}\,(\,(m^2_{X,A})^{-1} \circ \mathbf{Y}_{X\&A,A}\,(\,f \circ (\,(m^2_{X,A})^{-1} \otimes !A\,)\,)\,) \tag{1}
$$

belongs to $!X \multimap A$, since

$$
!(X \& A) \otimes !A \xrightarrow{(m^2_{X,A})^{-1} \otimes !A} !X \otimes !A \otimes !A \xrightarrow{\quad f \quad} A
$$

is sent by $\mathbf{Y}_{X\&A,A}$ to a morphism of $!(X \& A) \multimap A$, so that

$$
(m^2_{X,A})^{-1} \circ \mathbf{Y}_{X\&A,A}\,(\,f \circ (\,(m^2_{X,A})^{-1} \otimes !A\,) \; : !X \otimes !A \multimap A
$$

to which the fixpoint operator $\mathbf{Y}_{X,A}$ can be applied, giving the morphism (1) of $!X \multimap A$. This morphism is required to coincide with the morphism $\mathbf{Y}_{X,A}(k)$, where the morphism $k : !X \otimes !A \to A$ is defined as the composite

$$
\begin{array}{ccc}
!X \otimes !A & \xrightarrow{\quad k \quad} & A \\
\Big\downarrow {\scriptstyle !X \otimes !\Delta_A} & & \Big\uparrow {\scriptstyle f} \\
!X \otimes !(A \& A) & \xrightarrow[\quad !X \otimes (m^2_{A,A})^{-1} \quad]{} & !X \otimes !A \otimes !A
\end{array}
$$

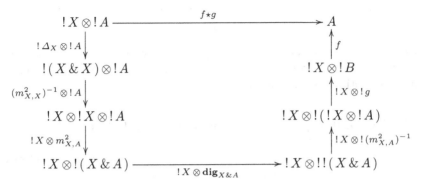

Just as expected, we recover in that way the familiar notion of Conway fixpoint operator as formulated in any cartesian category by Hasegawa, Hyland, Simpson and Plotkin:

Property 2. A Conway operator in a Seely category is the same thing as a Conway operator (in the sense of [8,20]) in the cartesian closed category associated to the exponential modality by the Kleisli construction.

4 A Fixpoint Operator in the Relational Semantics

The relational model of linear logic can be equipped with a natural parameterized fixpoint operator $\mathbf{Y}$ which transports any binary relation

$$f \quad : \quad !X \otimes !A \quad \multimap \quad A$$

to the binary relation

$$\mathbf{Y}_{X,A}(f) \quad : \quad !X \multimap A$$

defined in the following way:

$$\mathbf{Y}_{X,A}(f) \;=\; \{\, (w,a) \mid \exists \mathit{witness} \in \mathbf{run\text{-}tree}(f,a) \text{ with } w = \mathbf{leaves}(\mathit{witness}) \text{ and } \mathit{witness} \text{ is accepting} \,\} \tag{2}$$

where $\mathbf{run\text{-}tree}(f,a)$ is the set of "run-trees" defined as trees with nodes labelled by elements of the set $X \uplus A$ and such that:

- the root of the tree is labelled by a,
- the inner nodes are labelled by elements of the set A,
- the leaves are labelled by elements of the set $X \uplus A$,
- and for every node labelled by an element $b \in A$:
  - if b is an inner node, and letting $a_1, \cdots, a_n$ denote the labels of its children belonging to A and $x_1, \cdots, x_m$ the labels belonging to X:

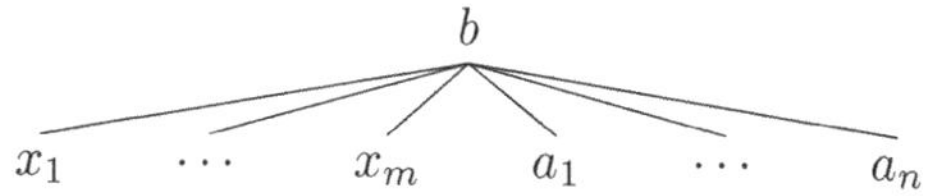

    then $([(1,x_1), \cdots, (1,x_m), (2,a_1), \cdots, (2,a_n)], b) \in f$
  - if b is a leaf, then $([], b) \in f$.

and where $\mathbf{leaves}(\mathit{witness})$ is the multiset obtained by enumerating the labels of the leaves of the run-tree *witness*. Recall that multisets account for the number of occurences of an element, so that $\mathbf{leaves}(\mathit{witness})$ has the same number of elements as there are leaves in the run-tree *witness*. Moreover, $\mathbf{leaves}(\mathit{witness})$ is independent of the enumeration of the leaves, since multisets can be understood as abelian versions of lists. Finally, we declare that a run-tree is *accepting* when it is a finite tree.

Property 3. The fixpoint operator $\mathbf{Y}$ is a Conway operator on Rel.

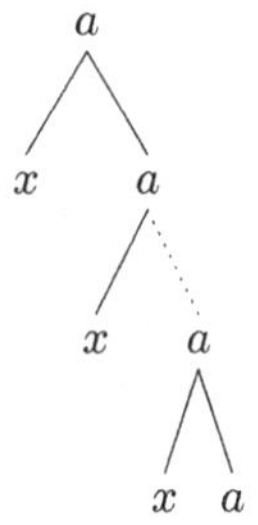

Fig. 1. An accepting run-tree

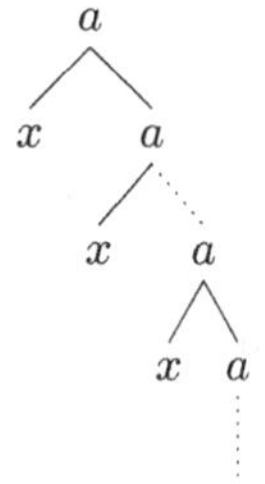

Fig. 2. A non-accepting run-tree

Example 1. Suppose that

$$f \quad = \quad \{([], a)\} \cup \{([a, x], a)\}$$

where $A = \{a\}$ and $X = \{x\}$. Denote by $\mathcal{M}_n$ the finite multiset containing the element x with multiplicity n. Then, for every $n \in \mathbb{N}$, we have that $(\mathcal{M}_n, a) \in \mathbf{Y}_{X,A}(f)$ since $(\mathcal{M}_n, a)$ can be obtained from the $\{a, x\}$-labelled witness run-tree of Figure 1, which has $n+1$ internal occurrences of the element a, and n occurrences of the element x at the leaves. The witness tree is finite, so that it is accepted. Now, consider the relation

$$g \quad = \quad \{([a], a)\} \cup \{([a, x], a)\}$$

In that case, $(\mathcal{M}_n, a)$ is not an element of $\mathbf{Y}_{X,A}(g)$ for any $n \in \mathbb{N}$ because all run-trees are necessarily infinite, as depicted in Figure 2, and thus, none is accepting. As a consequence, $\mathbf{Y}_{X,A}(g)$ is the empty relation.

The terminology which we have chosen for the definition of $\mathbf{Y}$ is obviously automata-theoretic. In fact, as we already mentioned in the introduction, this definition may be formulated as an exploration of the infinitary tree **comb** on the ranked alphabet $\Sigma = \{\bullet : 2, \circ : 0\}$ by an alternating tree automaton associated to the binary relation $f : !X \otimes !A \multimap A$. Indeed, given an element $a \in A$, consider the alternating tree automata $\mathcal{A}_{f,a} = \langle \Sigma, X \uplus A, \delta, a\rangle$ where, for $b \in A$ and $x \in X$:

$$\delta(b, \bullet) = \bigvee_{(([x_1, \cdots, x_n), [a_1, \cdots, a_m]), b) \in f} ((1, x_1) \wedge \cdots \wedge (1, x_n) \wedge (2, a_1) \wedge \cdots \wedge (2, a_m))$$

$$\delta(x, \bullet) \;=\; \bot \qquad \delta(x, \circ) \;=\; \top \qquad \delta(b, \circ) \;=\; \begin{cases} \top & \text{if } ([], b) \in f \\ \bot & \text{else} \end{cases}$$

Note that we allow here the use of an infinite non-deterministic choice operator $\bigvee$ in formulas describing transitions, but only with *finite* alternation. Now, our point is that **run-tree**(f, a) coincides with the set of run-trees of the alternating automaton $\mathcal{A}_{f,a}$ over the infinite tree **comb** depicted in the Introduction. Notice that only finite run-trees are accepting: this requires that for some $b \in A$ the transition $\delta(b, \bullet)$ contains the alternating choice $\top$, in which the exploration of the infinite branch of **comb** stops and produces an accepting run-tree. This requires in particular the existence of some $b \in A$ such that $([], b) \in f$.

5 Infinitary Exponentials

Now that we established a link with tree automata theory, it is tempting to relax the finiteness acceptance condition on run-trees applied in the previous section. To that purpose, however, we need to relax the usual assumption that the formulas of linear logic are interpreted as finite or countable sets. Suppose indeed that we want to interpret the exponential modality

$$\lightning A$$

as the set of finite or countable multisets, where a countable multiset of elements of A is defined as a function

$$A \longrightarrow \overline{\mathbb{N}}$$

with finite or countable support. Quite obviously, the set

$$\lightning \mathbb{N}$$

has the cardinality of the reals $2^{\aleph_0}$. We thus need to go beyond the traditionally countable relational interpretations of linear logic. However, we may suppose that every set A interpreting a formula has a cardinality below or equal $2^{\aleph_0}$. In order to understand why, it is useful to reformulate the elements of $\lightning A$ as finite or infinite words of elements of A modulo an appropriate notion of equivalence of finite or infinite words up to permutation of letters. Given a finite word u and a finite or infinite word w, we write

$$u \sqsubseteq w$$

when there exists a finite prefix v of w such that u is a prefix of v modulo permutation of letter. We write

$$w_1 \simeq w_2 \overset{def}{\Longleftrightarrow} \forall u \in A^*, \quad u \sqsubseteq w_1 \Longleftrightarrow u \sqsubseteq w_2$$

where A^* denotes the set of finite words on the alphabet A.

Proposition 1. *There is a one-to-one relationship between the elements of $\lightning A$ and the finite or infinite words on the alphabet A modulo the equivalence relation $\simeq$.*

This means in particular that for every set A, there is a surjection from the set $A^\infty = A^* \uplus A^\omega$ of finite or infinite words on the alphabet A to the set $\lightning A$ of finite or countable multisets. An element of the equivalence class associated to a multiset is called a *representation* of this multiset. Notice that if a set A has cardinality at most $2^{\aleph_0}$, the set A^∞ is itself bounded by $2^{\aleph_0}$, since $(2^{\aleph_0})^{\aleph_0} = 2^{\aleph_0 \times \aleph_0} = 2^{\aleph_0}$. This property leads us to define the following extension of *Rel*:

Definition 1. *The category $\underline{Rel}$ has the sets A, B of cardinality at most $2^{\aleph_0}$ as objects, and binary relations $f \subseteq A \times B$ between A and B as morphisms $A \to B$.*

Since a binary relation between two sets A and B is a subset of $A \times B$, the cardinality of a binary relation in $\underline{Rel}$ is also bounded by $2^{\aleph_0}$. Note that the hom-set $\underline{Rel}(A, B)$ is in general of higher cardinality than $2^{\aleph_0}$, yet it is bounded by the cardinality of the powerset of the reals. It is immediate to establish that:

Property 4. The category $\underline{Rel}$ is $*$-autonomous and has finite products. As such, it provides a model of multiplicative additive linear logic.

There remains to show that the finite-or-countable multiset construction $\lightning$ defines a categorical interpretation of the exponential modality of linear logic. Again, just as in the finitary case, we find convenient to check that $\underline{Rel}$ together with the finite-or-countable multiset interpretation $\lightning$ satisfy the axioms of a Seely category. In that specific formulation of a model of linear logic, the first property to check is that:

Property 5. The finite-or-countable multiset construction $\lightning$ defines a comonad on the category $\underline{Rel}$.

The counit of the comonad is defined as the binary relation

$$\mathbf{der}_A \quad : \quad \lightning A \quad \longrightarrow \quad A$$

which relates $[a]$ to a for every element a of the set A. In order to define its comultiplication, we need first to extend the notion of sum of multisets to the infinitary case, which we do in the obvious way, by extending the binary sum of $\mathbb{N}$ to possibly infinite sums in its completion $\overline{\mathbb{N}}$. In order to unify the notation for finite-or-countable multisets with the one for finite multisets used in Section 2, we find convenient to denote by $[a_1, a_2, \cdots]$ the countable multiset admitting the representation $a_1 a_2 \cdots$

We are now ready to describe the comultiplication

$$\mathbf{dig}_A \quad : \quad \lightning A \quad \to \quad \lightning \lightning A$$

of the comonad $\lightning$ as a straightforward generalization of the finite case:

$$\begin{array}{rcl}\mathbf{dig}_A & = & \{(w_1 + \cdots + w_k,\ [w_1, \cdots, w_k]) \mid \forall i \in \{1, \cdots n\},\ w_i \in \lightning A\} \\ & & \cup\ \{(w_1 + \cdots + w_k + \cdots,\ [w_1, \cdots, w_k, \cdots]) \mid \forall i \in \mathbb{N},\ w_i \in \lightning A\}\end{array}$$

One then defines the isomorphism

$$m^0 \ = \ \{(\star, [\,])\} \quad : \quad 1 \quad \longrightarrow \quad \lightning \top \tag{3}$$

and the family of isomorphisms

$$m^2_{A,B} \quad : \quad \lightning A \otimes \lightning B \quad \longrightarrow \quad \lightning (A \& B) \tag{4}$$

indexed by the objects A, B of the category $\underline{Rel}$ which relates every pair (w_A, w_B) of the set $\lightning A \otimes \lightning B$ with the finite-or-countable multiset

$$(\{1\} \times w_A) + (\{2\} \times w_B) \quad \in \quad \lightning (A \& B)$$

where the operation $\{1\} \times w_A$ maps the finite-or-countable multiset $w_A = [a_1, a_2, \ldots]$ of elements of A to the finite-or-countable multiset $[(1, a_1), (1, a_2), \ldots]$ of $\lightning (A \& B)$. We define $\{2\} \times w_B$ similarly. We check carefully that

Property 6. The comonad $\lightning$ on the category $\underline{Rel}$ together with the isomorphisms (3) and (4) satisfy the coherence axioms of a Seely category – see [11].

In other words, this comonad $\lightning$ over the category $\underline{Rel}$ induces a new and infinitary model of propositional linear logic. The next section is devoted to the definition of two different fixpoint operators living inside this new model.

6 Inductive and Coinductive Fixpoint Operators

In the infinitary relational semantics, a binary relation

$$f \ : \ \lightning A \multimap B$$

may require a countable multiset w of elements (or positions) of the input set A in order to reach a position b of the output set B. For that reason, we need to generalize the notion of alternating tree automata to *finite-or-countable alternating tree automata*, a variant in which formulas defining transitions use of a possibly countable alternation operator $\bigwedge$ and of a possibly countable non-deterministic choice operator $\bigvee$. The generalization of the family of automata $\mathcal{A}_{f,a}$ of §4 leads to a new definition of the set **run-tree**(f, a), in which witness trees may have internal nodes of countable arity. A first important observation is the following result:

Property 7. Given $f \ : \ \lightning A \otimes \lightning X \multimap A$, $a \in A$, and $witness \in$ **run-tree**(f, a), the multiset **leaves**$(witness)$ is finite or countable.

An important consequence of this observation is that the definition of the Conway operator $\mathbf{Y}$ given in Equation (2) can be very simply adapted to the finite-or-countable interpretation of the exponential modality $\lightning$ in the Seely category $\underline{Rel}$. Moreover, in this infinitary model of linear logic, we can give more elaborate acceptation conditions, among which two are canonical:

- considering that any run-tree is accepting, one defines the *coinductive* fixpoint on the model, which is the greatest fixpoint over $\underline{Rel}$.
- on the other hand, by accepting only trees without infinite branches, we obtain the *inductive* interpretation of the fixpoint, which is the least fixpoint operator over $\underline{Rel}$.

It is easy to see that the two fixpoint operators are different: recall Example 1, and observe that the binary relation g is also a relation in the infinitary semantics. It turns out that its inductive fixpoint is the empty relation, while its coinductive fixpoint coincides with the relation

$$\{\mathcal{M}_n, a) \mid \forall n \in \mathbb{N}\} \ \cup \ \{([x, \ x, \ \cdots], a)\}$$

In this coinductive interpretation, the run-tree obtained by using infinitely $([x, a], a)$ and never $([a], a)$ is accepting and is the witness tree generating $\{([x, \ x, \ \cdots], a)\}$.

Property 8. The inductive and coinductive fixpoint operators over the infinitary relational model of linear logic are Conway operators on this Seely category.

7 The Coloured Exponential Modality

In their semantic study of the parity conditions used in higher-order model-checking, and more specifically in the work by Kobayashi and Ong [10], the authors have recently discovered [7] that these parity conditions are secretly regulated by the existence of a comonad $\Box$ which can be interpreted in the relational semantics of linear logic as

$$\Box\, A \quad = \quad Col \times A$$

where $Col = \{1, \ldots, N\}$ is a finite set of integers called *colours*. The colours (or priorities) are introduced in order to regulate the fixpoint discipline: in the immediate scope of an even colour, fixpoints should be interpreted coinductively, and inductively in the immediate scope of an odd colour. It is worth mentioning that the comonad $\Box$ has its comultiplication defined by the maximum operator in order to track the maximum colour encountered during a computation:

$$\begin{array}{rlcrcl} \delta_A = & \{(max(c_1, c_2), a), (c_1, (c_2, a))) \mid c_1, c_2 \in Col, a \in A\} & : & \Box A & \multimap & \Box\Box A \\ \varepsilon_A = & \{(1, a), a) \mid a \in A\} & : & \Box A & \multimap & A \end{array}$$

whereas the counit is defined using the minimum colour 1. The resulting comonad is symmetric monoidal and also satisfies the following key property:

Property 9. There exists a distributive law $\lambda : \lightning\, \Box \rightarrow \Box\, \lightning$ between comonads.

A fundamental consequence is that the two comonads can be composed into a single comonad $\boldsymbol{\lightning}$ defined as follows:

$$\boldsymbol{\lightning} \quad = \quad \lightning \circ \Box$$

The resulting *infinitary* and *coloured* relational semantics of linear logic is obtained from the category <u>*Rel*</u> equipped with the composite comonad $\boldsymbol{\lightning}$.

Theorem 1. *The category* <u>*Rel*</u> *together with the comonad* $\boldsymbol{\lightning}$ *defines a Seely category and thus a model of propositional linear logic.*

8 The Inductive-Coinductive Fixpoint Operator Y

We combine the results of the previous sections in order to define a fixpoint operator **Y** over the infinitary coloured relational model, which generalizes both the inductive and the coinductive fixpoint operators. Note that in this infinitary and coloured framework, we wish to define a fixpoint operator **Y** which transports a binary relation

$$f \quad : \quad \boldsymbol{\lightning} X \otimes \boldsymbol{\lightning} A \multimap A$$

into a binary relation

$$\mathbf{Y}_{X,A}(f) \quad : \quad \boldsymbol{\lightning} X \multimap A.$$

To that purpose, notice that the definition given in §4 of the set $\textbf{run-tree}(f, a)$ of run-trees extends immediately to this new coloured setting, since the only change is in the set of labellings. Again, accepting all run-trees would lead to the coinductive fixpoint, while accepting only run-trees whose branches are finite would lead to the inductive fixpoint. We now define our acceptance condition for run-trees in the expected way, directly inspired by the notion of alternating parity tree automaton. Consider a run-tree *witness*, and remark that its nodes are labelled with elements of $(\,Col \times A\,) \cup (\,Col \times X\,)$. We call the colour of a node the first element of its label. Coloured acceptance is then defined as follows:

- a finite branch is accepting,
- an infinite branch is accepting precisely when the greatest colour appearing infinitely often in the labels of its nodes is even.
- a run-tree is accepting precisely when all its branches are accepting.

Note that a run-tree whose nodes are all of an even colour will be accepted independently of its depth, as in the coinductive interpretation, while a run-tree labelled only with odd colours will be accepted precisely when it is finite, just as in the inductive interpretation. We call the fixpoint operator associated with the notion of coloured acceptation the inductive-coinductive fixpoint operator over the infinitary coloured relational model.

Theorem 2. *The inductive-coinductive fixpoint operator* $\boldsymbol{Y}$ *defined over the infinitary coloured relational semantics of linear logic is a Conway operator.*

9 Conclusion

In this article, we introduced an infinitary variant of the familiar relational semantics of linear logic. We then established that this infinitary model accomodates an inductive as well as a coinductive Conway operator $\mathbf{Y}$. This propelled us to define a coloured relational semantics and to define an inductive-coinductive fixpoint operator based on a parity acceptance condition. The authors proved recently [7] that a recursion scheme can be interpreted in this model in such a way that its denotation contains the initial state of an alternating parity automaton if and only if the tree it produces satisifies the MSO property associated to the automaton. A crucial point related to the work by Salvati and Walukiewicz [14] is the fact that a tree satisfies a given MSO property if and only if any suitable representation as an infinite tree of a λY-term generating it also does. We are thus convinced that this infinitary and coloured variant of the relational semantics of linear logic will play an important and clarifying role in the denotational and compositional study of higher-order model-checking.

References

1. Baelde, D.: Least and greatest fixed points in linear logic. ACM Trans. Comput. Log. 13(1), 2 (2012)
2. Bierman, G.M.: What is a categorical model of intuitionistic linear logic? In: Dezani-Ciancaglini, M., Plotkin, G. (eds.) TLCA 1995. LNCS, vol. 902, pp. 78–93. Springer, Heidelberg (1995)
3. Bloom, S.L., Ésik, Z.: Iteration theories: the equational logic of iterative processes. EATCS monographs on theoretical computer science. Springer (1993)
4. Bloom, S.L., Ésik, Z.: Fixed-point operations on ccc's. part i. Theoretical Computer Science 155(1), 1–38 (1996)

5. Carraro, A., Ehrhard, T., Salibra, A.: Exponentials with infinite multiplicities. In: Dawar, A., Veith, H. (eds.) CSL 2010. LNCS, vol. 6247, pp. 170–184. Springer, Heidelberg (2010)
6. Fortier, J., Santocanale, L.: Cuts for circular proofs: semantics and cut-elimination. In: Rocca, S.R.D. (ed.) CSL. LIPIcs, vol. 23, pp. 248–262. Schloss Dagstuhl - Leibniz-Zentrum fuer Informatik (2013)
7. Grellois, C., Melliès, P.-A.: Tensorial logic with colours and higher-order model checking (submitted, 2015), http://arxiv.org/abs/1501.04789
8. Hasegawa, M.: Models of Sharing Graphs: A Categorical Semantics of Let and Letrec. Distinguished dissertations series, vol. 1192. Springer (1999)
9. Joyal, A., Street, R., Verity, D.: Traced monoidal categories. Mathematical Proceedings of the Cambridge Philosophical Society 119, 447–468 (1996)
10. Kobayashi, N., Luke Ong, C.-H.: A type system equivalent to the modal mu-calculus model checking of higher-order recursion schemes. In: LICS, pp. 179–188. IEEE Computer Society (2009)
11. Melliès, P.-A.: Categorical semantics of linear logic. In: Interactive models of computation and program behaviour, pp. 1–196 (2009)
12. Miquel, A.: Le calcul des constructions implicites: syntaxe et sémantique. PhD thesis, Université Paris 7 (2001)
13. Montelatici, R.: Polarized proof nets with cycles and fixpoints semantics. In: Hofmann, M.O. (ed.) TLCA 2003. LNCS, vol. 2701, pp. 256–270. Springer, Heidelberg (2003)
14. Salvati, S., Walukiewicz, I.: Evaluation is msol-compatible. In: Seth, A., Vishnoi, N.K. (eds.) FSTTCS. LIPIcs, vol. 24, pp. 103–114. Schloss Dagstuhl - Leibniz-Zentrum fuer Informatik (2013)
15. Salvati, S., Walukiewicz, I.: Using models to model-check recursive schemes. In: Hasegawa, M. (ed.) TLCA 2013. LNCS, vol. 7941, pp. 189–204. Springer, Heidelberg (2013)
16. Salvati, S., Walukiewicz, I.: Typing weak MSOL properties (September 2014)
17. Santocanale, L.: A calculus of circular proofs and its categorical semantics. In: Nielsen, M., Engberg, U. (eds.) FOSSACS 2002. LNCS, vol. 2303, pp. 357–371. Springer, Heidelberg (2002)
18. Santocanale, L.: μ-bicomplete categories and parity games. ITA 36(2), 195–227 (2002)
19. Seely, R.A.G.: Linear logic, *-autonomous categories and cofree coalgebras. In: Categories in Computer Science and Logic, pp. 371–382. American Mathematical Society (1989)
20. Simpson, A.K., Plotkin, G.D.: Complete axioms for categorical fixed-point operators. In: LICS 2000, USA, June 26-29, pp. 30–41. IEEE Computer Society (2000)
21. Terui, K.: Semantic evaluation, intersection types and complexity of simply typed lambda calculus. In: Tiwari, A. (ed.) RTA. LIPIcs, vol. 15, pp. 323–338. Schloss Dagstuhl - Leibniz-Zentrum fuer Informatik (2012)
22. Tsukada, T., Luke Ong, C.-H.: Compositional higher-order model checking via ω-regular games over böhm trees. In: Henzinger, T.A., Miller, D. (eds.) CSL-LICS 2014, Vienna, Austria, July 14-18, p. 78. ACM (2014)

Game Semantics and Normalization by Evaluation

Pierre Clairambault[1] and Peter Dybjer[2]

[1] CNRS, ENS Lyon, Inria, UCBL, Université de Lyon, Lyon, France
[2] Chalmers Tekniska Högskola, Gothenburg, Sweden

Abstract. We show that Hyland and Ong's game semantics for PCF can be presented using normalization by evaluation (nbe). We use the bijective correspondence between innocent well-bracketed strategies and PCF Böhm trees, and show how operations on PCF Böhm trees, such as composition, can be computed lazily and simply by nbe. The usual equations characteristic of games follow from the nbe construction without reference to low-level game-theoretic machinery. As an illustration, we give a Haskell program computing the application of innocent strategies.

1 Introduction

In game semantics [17,3] types are interpreted as games between two players (Player/Opponent), and programs as strategies for Player. Combinators for programs become operations on strategies that can be quite complex. Composition of strategies for instance, involves an intricate mechanism of parallel interaction plus hiding *à la* CCS. The proof that they satisfy required equations is typically lengthy and non-trivial. In Hyland and Ong's game semantics of PCF [17] in particular, strategies interpreting programs are *innocent*: recall that a strategy is a set of admissible plays for Player, and is innocent when Player's action only depends on a subset of the play called the *P-view*. So innocent strategies are specified – and often defined as – a set of P-views (the *view functions*). Composing two such strategies involves computing the full set of plays of both strategies, composing these using parallel interaction plus hiding, and computing the P-views of the compound strategy. These computations are quite complex.

Several authors have tried to give more direct or elegant presentations of innocent strategies and their composition. Quite early, Curien gave syntactic representations of innocent strategies as *abstract Böhm trees* [10] and gave an abstract machine (the VAM) to compose them – this machinery is also quite involved. Amadio and Curien [5] reason about innocent strategies for PCF syntactically as *PCF Böhm trees* and compose them via infinitary rewriting. Finally and more recently, Harmer, Hyland and Melliès gave an elegant categorical reconstruction of innocent strategies from a basic category of simple games [16]. The resulting algorithm to compose strategies is however still quite involved.

In the present paper we provide yet another presentation of the innocent game semantics for PCF. Like Amadio and Curien we represent strategies as

A. Pitts (Ed.): FOSSACS 2015, LNCS 9034, pp. 56–70, 2015.
DOI: 10.1007/978-3-662-46678-0_4

PCF Böhm trees. However, we use normalization by evaluation (nbe) [6] rather than infinitary rewriting. As Aehlig and Joachimski [4] showed, nbe can be used for computing the potentially partial and infinite Böhm trees of the untyped lambda calculus, and not only for computing normal forms. To this end they used lazy evaluation for computing the finite approximations of the Böhm tree.

We here adapt the nbe technique to PCF Böhm trees. To compute an operation on terms (PCF Böhm trees, strategies), we first evaluate them in a non-standard semantic domain where we then perform the corresponding semantic operation. Finally, the result is read back to the resulting PCF Böhm tree. For example, composition of PCF Böhm trees is performed by ordinary function composition in the semantic domain.

Finally note that our construction and its soundness are independent of the standard presentation of game semantics. The fact that our model agrees with the standard presentation of the innocent model for PCF follows from high-level reasons that use the soundness, adequacy and definability properties of game semantics. In particular, our contribution does not (and does not aim to) give insights into the low-level combinatorics of innocent interaction.

Related work. The first author and Murawski [9] use nbe to generate representations of innocent strategies in boolean PCF by higher-order recursion schemes. They exploit the fact that booleans can be replaced by their Church encoding. In contrast we consider here PCF with a datatype for lazy natural numbers, which is infinite. Thus our proof requires different techniques and is significantly more complex. Our approach is not particular to natural numbers and should smoothly extend to McCusker's games for recursive types [18].

Our non-standard semantic domain is similar to those used for previous work on untyped nbe [15,14], where semantic elements can be thought of as infinitary terms in higher order abstract syntax (hoas). We define a semantic domain for PCF Böhm trees in hoas, and show how to compute semantic operations in such a way that certain commuting conversions are executed. This is a key difference to the semantic domain used for normalizing terms in Gödel system T [1], which does not include these commuting conversions. We remark that although this approach to nbe initially was used for untyped nbe, it can also be used to advantage for typed languages. For example, it was a crucial step in devising nbe for dependent type theory [2] to use a similar semantic domain of untyped normal forms in hoas.

Plan of the paper. The rest of the paper is organized as follows. In Section 2 we introduce the syntax and reduction rules of PCF and our notion of model. We recall some notions from Hyland-Ong game semantics including the notions of innocent strategy and PCF Böhm tree. We also write a Haskell program for application of PCF Böhm trees using nbe. In Section 3 we provide a domain interpretation of the non-standard model used in the Haskell program. We prove that the interpretation function preserves all syntactic conversions of PCF, and that the interpretation of a term is identical to its PCF Böhm tree. In Section 4 we use these results to reconstruct the game model of PCF from nbe.

2 PCF, Innocent Strategies, and PCF Böhm Trees

2.1 PCF

Our version of PCF is close to Plotkin's original [20], except that we consider *lazy* (rather than *flat*) natural numbers. (Ultimately, we are interested in the connection between game semantics and Martin-Löf's meaning explanations [13], which are based on lazy evaluation of the terms of intuitionistic type theory.) Nothing in our approach is particular to natural numbers and we believe the approach extends to a more general setting of recursive types.

Types and terms. The **types** of PCF are generated by the type N of natural numbers, and function types $A \to B$. A **context** is a list of types denoted by Γ, Δ. The empty context is []. We define the set of **raw** terms by the following grammar, where $n \in \mathbb{N}$ is a natural number.

$$a, b, c ::= \underline{n} \mid \mathrm{app}\, a\, b \mid \lambda\, a \mid 0 \mid \mathrm{suc}\, a \mid \mathrm{case}\, a\, b\, c \mid \mathrm{fix}\, a \mid \Omega$$

Note that we use *de Bruijn indices*: the variable $\underline{n}$ refers to (if it exists) the first λ encountered after crossing n occurrences of λ when going up the syntax tree from the variable to the root. We include the non-terminating program Ω. Terms are assigned types using standard typing rules, displayed in Figure 1.

$$\frac{}{A_{n-1}, \ldots, A_0 \vdash \underline{i} : A_i} \qquad \frac{\Gamma \vdash b : A \to B \qquad \Gamma \vdash a : A}{\Gamma \vdash \mathrm{app}\, b\, a : B} \qquad \frac{\Gamma, A \vdash b : B}{\Gamma \vdash \lambda b : A \to B} \qquad \frac{}{\Gamma \vdash 0 : \mathrm{N}}$$

$$\frac{\Gamma \vdash a : \mathrm{N} \qquad \Gamma \vdash b : A \qquad \Gamma, \mathrm{N} \vdash c : A}{\Gamma \vdash \mathrm{case}\, a\, b\, c : A} \qquad \frac{\Gamma \vdash a : \mathrm{N}}{\Gamma \vdash \mathrm{suc}\, a : \mathrm{N}} \qquad \frac{\Gamma, A \vdash c : A}{\Gamma \vdash \mathrm{fix}\, c : A} \qquad \frac{}{\Gamma \vdash \Omega : \mathrm{N}}$$

Fig. 1. Typing rules for PCF

Substitution. A **substitution** is a sequence of terms, written $\Gamma \vdash \langle a_{n-1}, \ldots, a_0 \rangle : A_{n-1}, \ldots, A_0$ if for all $0 \leq i \leq n-1$ we have $\Gamma \vdash a_i : A_i$. For $|\Gamma| = n$ we define abbreviations $\mathrm{id}_\Gamma = \langle \underline{n-1}, \ldots, \underline{0} \rangle$, $\mathrm{p}_{\Gamma,A} = \langle \underline{n}, \ldots, \underline{1} \rangle$ and $\mathrm{q}_{\Gamma,A} = \underline{0}$. We have $\Gamma \vdash \mathrm{id}_\Gamma : \Gamma$ and $\Gamma, A \vdash \mathrm{p}_{\Gamma,A} : \Gamma$. We will often just write id, p, and q.

$$\begin{array}{rll}
(\mathrm{case}\, a\, b\, c)[\gamma] = \mathrm{case}\, a[\gamma]\, b[\gamma]\, c[\langle \gamma \circ \mathrm{p}, \mathrm{q} \rangle] & (\mathrm{suc}\, a)[\gamma] = \mathrm{suc}\, (a[\gamma]) & 0[\gamma] = 0 \\
(\mathrm{app}\, f\, a)[\gamma] = \mathrm{app}\, (f[\gamma])\, (a[\gamma]) & (\mathrm{fix}\, c)[\gamma] = \mathrm{fix}\, (c[\langle \gamma \circ \mathrm{p}, \mathrm{q} \rangle]) & \Omega[\gamma] = \Omega \\
(\lambda f)[\gamma] = \lambda\, (f[\langle \gamma \circ \mathrm{p}, \mathrm{q} \rangle]) & &
\end{array}$$

Fig. 2. Substitution on term constructors

We define the action $a[\gamma]$ of a substitution $\Delta \vdash \gamma : \Gamma$ on a term $\Gamma \vdash a : A$ by induction on a, with $\underline{i}[\langle a_{n-1}, \ldots, a_0 \rangle] = a_i$ for variables and following the rules of Figure 2 for term constructors. The composition of substitutions is defined by $\langle a_{n-1}, \ldots, a_0 \rangle \circ \gamma = \langle a_{n-1}[\gamma], \ldots, a_0[\gamma] \rangle$. When composing substitutions we will sometimes omit the operator $\circ$ and just use juxtaposition. By abuse of notation, we write $\langle \gamma, a \rangle$ for the sequence obtained by adding a at the end of γ.

$$\begin{array}{rl}
\mathrm{app}\,(\lambda\, a)\, b \rightarrow_{\beta_1} & a[\langle \mathrm{id}, b \rangle] \\
\mathrm{case}\, 0\, b\, c \rightarrow_{\beta_2} & b \\
\mathrm{case}\,(\mathrm{suc}\, a)\, b\, c \rightarrow_{\beta_3} & c[\langle \mathrm{id}, a \rangle] \\
\mathrm{fix}\, f \rightarrow_{\delta} & f[\langle \mathrm{id}, \mathrm{fix}\, f \rangle] \\
\Omega \rightarrow_{\Omega} & \Omega
\end{array}
\qquad
\begin{array}{rl}
c \rightarrow_{\eta_1} & \lambda\,(\mathrm{app}\,(c[\mathrm{p}])\,\mathrm{q}) \\
a \rightarrow_{\eta_2} & \mathrm{case}\, a\, 0\,(\mathrm{suc}\,\mathrm{q}) \\
\mathrm{case}\,(\mathrm{case}\, a\, b\, f)\, b'\, f' \rightarrow_{\gamma_1} & \mathrm{case}\, a\,(\mathrm{case}\, b\, b'\, f) \\
& \quad (\mathrm{case}\, f\,(b'[\mathrm{p}]) \\
& \quad\quad (f'[\langle \mathrm{pp}, \mathrm{q} \rangle])) \\
\mathrm{app}\,(\mathrm{case}\, a\, b\, f)\, c \rightarrow_{\gamma_2} & \mathrm{case}\, a\,(\mathrm{app}\, b\, c)(\mathrm{app}\, f\,(c[\mathrm{p}]))
\end{array}$$

Fig. 3. Reduction rules for PCF

Reduction. We equip PCF with the (context closure of the) reduction rules in Figure 3. The rules are *typed*: a reduction applies when both sides typecheck. We write $\approx$ for **convertibility**, i.e. the contextual equivalence closure of these relations. The two columns of Figure 3 will be treated quite differently in our development. The left hand side contains the *computation* rules which are used for evaluating a closed term of ground type. The right hand side contains η-*expansion* and *commutating conversions*, which are additional rules needed in Section 3.4 for transforming an arbitrary term to its *PCF Böhm tree.*

We will also need *head reduction*. For that, define **head environments** as:

$$H[] ::= [] \mid \mathrm{case}\ H[]\ b\ c \mid \mathrm{app}\ H[]\ b \mid \lambda\ H[]$$

Head reduction $\rightarrow_h$ is $H[\rightarrow_\alpha]$ for $\alpha \in \{\beta_1, \beta_2, \beta_3, \delta, \Omega\}$ a computation rule. Head reduction is deterministic: for each term, at most one head reduction applies. A term a is a **head normal form** if it is $\rightarrow_h$-normal. If $a \rightarrow_h^* a'$ where a' is $\rightarrow_h$-normal, then a' is the **head normal form** of a.

Non-dependent cwfs. Usually a model of PCF is a cartesian closed category with extra structure. We prefer to use a notion of model which separates contexts and types, and thus more closely matches the structure of our syntax. For that we use categories with families (cwfs) [12]. Cwfs provide a notion of model of dependent type theory which is both close to the syntax, and completely algebraic: it can be presented as a generalized algebraic theory in the sense of Cartmell [7].

Since we do not have dependent types we use *non-dependent cwfs*, that is cwfs where the set of types Type(Γ) does not depend on the context Γ.

Definition 1. *A* ***non-dependent cwf*** *consists of a set of* types Type, *plus:*

- *A base category* $\mathbb{C}$. *Its objects represent* contexts *and its morphisms represent* substitutions. *We write* $\Delta \vdash \gamma : \Gamma$ *for a context morphism from* Δ *to* Γ. *The identity is written* $\Gamma \vdash \mathrm{id}_\Gamma : \Gamma$ *and composition is written* $\gamma \circ \delta$, *or just* $\gamma\delta$.

- *A functor* $T : \mathbb{C}^{op} \to \mathbf{Set}^{\mathrm{Type}}$. *For each context* Γ *and type* A *this gives a set* $T(\Gamma)(A)$, *written* $\Gamma \vdash A$, *of terms of type* A *in context* Γ. *We write* $\Gamma \vdash a : A$ *for* $a \in \Gamma \vdash A$. *For* $\gamma : \Delta \to \Gamma$ *a morphism in* $\mathbb{C}$, *then* $T(\gamma)(A) : \Gamma \vdash A \to \Delta \vdash A$ *provides a* substitution *operation, written* $\Delta \vdash a[\gamma] : A$.
- *A* terminal object $[]$ *of* $\mathbb{C}$ *which represents the* empty context *and a terminal morphism* $\langle\rangle : \Delta \to []$ *which represents the* empty substitution.
- *A* context comprehension *which to an object* Γ *in* $\mathbb{C}$ *and a type* $A \in \mathrm{Type}$ *associates an object* $\Gamma{\cdot}A$ *of* $\mathbb{C}$, *a morphism* $\mathrm{p}_{\Gamma,A} : \Gamma{\cdot}A \to \Gamma$ *of* $\mathbb{C}$ *and a term* $\Gamma{\cdot}A \vdash \mathrm{q}_{\Gamma,A} : A$ *such that the following universal property holds: for each object* Δ *in* $\mathbb{C}$, *morphism* $\gamma : \Delta \to \Gamma$, *and term* $a : \Delta \vdash A$, *there is a unique morphism* $\theta = \langle\gamma, a\rangle : \Delta \to \Gamma{\cdot}A$, *such that* $\mathrm{p}_{\Gamma,A} \circ \theta = \gamma$ *and* $\mathrm{q}_{\Gamma,A}[\theta] = a$.

Democratic [8] non-dependent cwfs are equivalent to categories with finite products, but mimic more closely the structure of syntax. To describe the intended models of PCF we equip non-dependent cwfs with more structure, as follows.

Definition 2. *A non-dependent cwf* ***supports*** *PCF, or is a* ***pcf-cwf****, iff it is closed under the types and term constructors of Figure 1 (other than variable) and validates the equations and reduction rules of Figures 2 and 3, which have been chosen to make formal sense in an arbitrary non-dependent cwf as well as in the syntax of PCF. (A de Bruijn variable* $\underline{n}$ *in PCF is interpreted as an iterated projection* $\mathrm{q}[\mathrm{p}^n]$ *and all other syntactic constructs have a direct interpretation.)*

2.2 Innocent Strategies for PCF

We start with a simple operational presentation of the pcf-cwf of *innocent well-bracketed strategies* playing on (arenas for) PCF types.

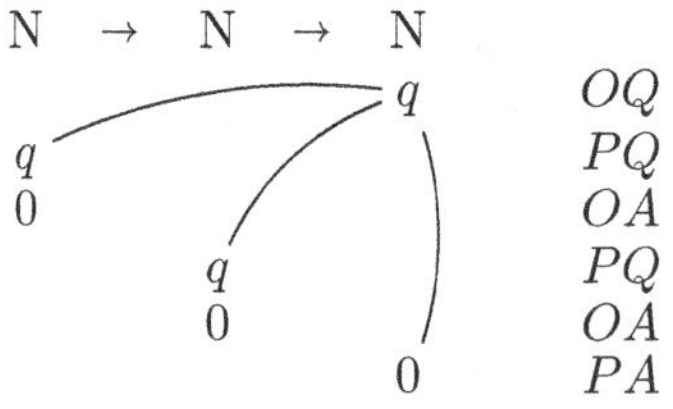

Fig. 4. A play on N → N → N

Game semantics formalize the intuition that a program is a strategy, and that execution is a play of this strategy against its execution environment according to rules determined by the type. For instance, a dialogue of type N → N → N could be that of Figure 4. Moves are either Questions (Q) or Answers (A) by either Player (P) or Opponent (O). Questions correspond to variable calls, and Answers to evaluation to terminating calls. The lines between moves are *justification pointers*: they convey information about *thread indexing* – here they are redundant, but become necessary on higher types. The diagram above should be read as follows: Opponent asks for the output of a function f : N → N → N. This function f (Player) proceeds to interrogate its first argument. This argument is part of the execution environment of f, so it is played by Opponent – if it evaluates to 0, then f evaluates its second argument. If it also evaluates to 0, then f answers 0. A *strategy* is a collection of such interactions, informing the full behaviour of a program under execution.

The dialogue above, considered as a branch of a strategy, can also be represented syntactically by the term $\vdash \lambda\ (\lambda\ (\text{case}\ \underline{1}\ (\text{case}\ \underline{0}\ 0\ \Omega)\ \Omega)) : \mathrm{N} \to \mathrm{N} \to \mathrm{N}$, where the occurrences of Ω indicate parts of the term for which the dialogue above gives no information. In general a dialogue such as the above where *(1)* Opponent moves are *justified* by their immediate predecessor and *(2)* every Answer is justified by the last unanswered Question, can always be represented syntactically as a partial term – such dialogues are usually called *well-bracketed P-views.* In our example, the dialogue is a branch of the strategy for *left-plus* that first evaluates its first argument (and copies lazily each successor), then the second. The strategy for left-plus contains countably many dialogues. As a typical example, we show the dialogue for the computation of 2 + 2 in Figure 5.

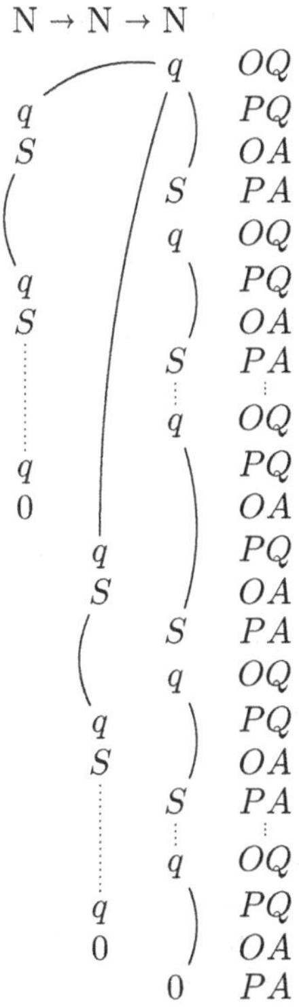

Fig. 5. *left-plus*

Representing these plays syntactically and pasting them together, one obtains the infinitary term $\vdash$ plus : $\mathrm{N} \to \mathrm{N} \to \mathrm{N}$ defined by

$$\begin{aligned} \text{plus} &= \lambda\,(\lambda\,(\text{case}\,\underline{1}\,\text{cc}\,(\text{suc}\,\text{plus}_1))) \\ \text{cc} &= \text{case}\,\underline{0}\,0\,(\text{suc}\,\text{cc}) \\ \text{plus}_n &= \text{case}\,\underline{0}\,(\text{case}\,\underline{n}\,0\,(\text{suc}\,\text{cc}))\,(\text{suc}\,\text{plus}_{n+1}) \end{aligned}$$

Here cc stands for *copycat*, the back-and-forth copying performed by the strategy when evaluating its second argument. Note that the de Bruijn indices grow. Indeed the second argument of case is an abstraction which binds a new variable, so the address of the second argument of f corresponds to larger and larger integers. Alternatively one can say that each Opponent Answer S in the plays provide a possible justifier that has to be crossed before reaching the second argument of f. We call the infinitary term above the *PCF Böhm tree* of *left-plus.*

The ideas above can easily be extended to represent syntactically (as an infinitary term) any *innocent well-bracketed strategy,* i.e. set of well-bracketed P-views on first-order PCF types $\mathrm{N} \to \ldots \to \mathrm{N} \to \mathrm{N}$. In general however, types of PCF have the form $A_{n-1} \to \ldots \to A_0 \to \mathrm{N}$, where each A_i has itself the form $A_{i,p_i-1} \to \ldots \to A_{i,0} \to \mathrm{N}$. In that case the discussion above still applies to the restriction of a strategy to its "first-order sub-type", which provides the backbone of a PCF Böhm tree. However, Player also needs to specify its behaviour should Opponent interrogate any of the arguments $A_{i,j}$ of a Player Question at the root of A_i. For each such Opponent Question, following (co-)inductively the same reasoning, a strategy for Player would inform a new strategy playing on $A_{n-1} \to \ldots \to A_0 \to A_{i,j}$ that can be set as an argument to the variable call matching the Player Question under consideration. This presentation of a strategy is called its *PCF Böhm tree.*

PCF Böhm trees. We now describe the terms obtained by this process. There are two kinds. On the one hand we define the *neutral PCF Böhm trees* which specify one Player Question (a variable call) along with the Player sub-strategies for the *arguments* of this call. On the other hand we define *PCF Böhm trees* wrap neutral PCF Böhm trees in a case statement, specifying the Player sub-strategies to play if Opponent answers 0 or S. We write $\Gamma \vdash_{\mathrm{Ne}} e : A$ if e is a *finite neutral Böhm tree* and $\Gamma \vdash_{\mathrm{Bt}} t : A$ if t is a *finite PCF Böhm trees* of type A in context Γ. They are defined as follows:

$$\frac{}{A_{n-1}, \ldots, A_i, \ldots, A_0 \vdash_{\mathrm{Ne}} \underline{i} : A_i} \qquad \frac{\Gamma \vdash_{\mathrm{Ne}} e : A \to B \quad \Gamma \vdash_{\mathrm{Bt}} t : A}{\Gamma \vdash_{\mathrm{Ne}} \mathrm{app}\, e\, t : B} \qquad \frac{\Gamma, A \vdash_{\mathrm{Bt}} t : B}{\Gamma \vdash_{\mathrm{Bt}} \lambda t : A \to B}$$

$$\frac{\Gamma \vdash_{\mathrm{Bt}} a : \mathrm{N}}{\Gamma \vdash_{\mathrm{Bt}} \mathrm{suc}\, a : \mathrm{N}} \qquad \frac{\Gamma \vdash_{\mathrm{Ne}} e : \mathrm{N} \quad \Gamma \vdash_{\mathrm{Bt}} t : \mathrm{N} \quad \Gamma, \mathrm{N} \vdash_{\mathrm{Bt}} t' : \mathrm{N}}{\Gamma \vdash_{\mathrm{Bt}} \mathrm{case}\, e\, t\, t' : \mathrm{N}} \qquad \frac{}{\Gamma \vdash_{\mathrm{Bt}} \Omega : \mathrm{N}} \qquad \frac{}{\Gamma \vdash_{\mathrm{Bt}} 0 : \mathrm{N}}$$

Fig. 6. Typing rules for finite PCF Böhm trees

These two sets are partially ordered by (the contextual closure of) $\Omega \leq a$ for all a, and their infinitary counterparts are defined as ideals (non-empty downward directed sets) for this order [21] – we will often keep this ideal completion implicit. From now on all PCF Böhm trees are considered infinitary,

The representation process outlined above yields a PCF Böhm tree in this formal sense. Moreover, this PCF Böhm tree is an infinitary PCF term, so can be sent back to a strategy using (by continuity) the usual game-theoretic interpretation of terms. This operation is inverse to the reification process described above, yielding an isomorphism between PCF Böhm trees and innocent strategies. In fact the correspondence is so direct that in the remainder of this paper we will identify them, and simply consider PCF Böhm trees as our representation of innocent strategies.

This correspondence is nothing new – it is one of the fundamental properties of the game model leading to definability: see *eg* Theorem 5.1 in [11]. It is easy to adapt this to lazy PCF. It is implicit in McCusker's definability process for a language with lazy recursive types (see Proposition 5.8 in [18]). We have not spelled out this connection more formally, since it would take too much space to introduce the required game-theoretic machinery.

2.3 Computing Operations on Strategies by nbe

To conclude this section we present (one aspect of) our result: that we can compute operations on innocent well-bracketed strategies, regarded as PCF Böhm trees, by nbe. As an example, a Haskell program that, given two infinite PCF Böhm trees as input, produces lazily the application of one to the other. All other operations of pcf-cwfs can be defined in an analogous way. In the remaining sections we will then show that application, and all the other pcf-cwf operations, satisfy the expected equations, and that we get a pcf-cwf **PCFInn** of PCF-Böhm trees (or innocent, well-bracketed strategies).

The Haskell datatype for representing PCF Böhm trees and types of PCF is:

```
data Tm = ZeroTm | SuccTm Tm | LamTm Tm | CaseTm Tm Tm Tm
        | VarTm Int | AppTm Tm Tm
data Ty = Nat | Arr Ty Ty
```

It should be clear to the reader how inhabitants of `Tm` include representatives for PCF Böhm trees, hence for innocent strategies. The first step is to interpret PCF Böhm trees in a semantic domain `D`, which is a hoas version of `Tm`:

```
data D = ZeroD | SuccD D | LamD (D -> D) | CaseD D D (D -> D)
       | VarD Int | AppD D D
```

We then introduce two semantic operations `appD :: D -> D -> D` for application, and `caseD :: D -> D -> (D -> D) -> D` for case construction.

```
appD (LamD f)       d' = f d'
appD (CaseD e d f) d' = CaseD e (appD d d') (\x -> appD (f x) d')
appD (VarD n)       d' = AppD (VarD n) d'
appD (AppD e d)     d' = AppD (AppD e d) d'

caseD ZeroD          e' f' = e'
caseD (SuccD d)      e' f' = f' d
caseD (CaseD e d f) e' f' = CaseD e (caseD d e' f')
                                   (\x -> caseD (f x) e' f')
caseD (AppD e d)     e' f' = CaseD (AppD e d) e' f'
caseD (VarD i)       e' f' = CaseD (VarD i) e' f'
```

We can interpret a PCF Böhm tree in the semantic domain `D` by the function `eval :: Tm -> [D] -> D`. It takes a term and interprets it in a given environment, encoded as a list of elements of the domain.

```
eval ZeroTm              env = ZeroD
eval (SuccTm t)          env = SuccD (eval t env)
eval (LamTm t)           env = LamD (\x -> eval t (x:env))
eval (CaseTm t1 t2 t3) env = caseD (eval t1 env) (eval t2 env)
                                    (\x -> eval t3 (x:env))
eval (VarTm i)           env = env !! i
eval (AppTm t1 t2)       env = appD (eval t1 env) (eval t2 env)
```

An element of the semantic domain can be read back to a term using the function `readbackD :: Int -> D -> Tm`, defined as follows.

```
readbackD n ZeroD          = ZeroTm
readbackD n (SuccD d)      = SuccTm (readbackD n d)
readbackD n (LamD f)       = LamTm (readbackD (n+1) (f (VarD n)))
readbackD n (CaseD e d f) = CaseTm (readbackD n e) (readbackD n d)
                                (readbackD (n+1) (f (VarD n)))
readbackD n (VarD i)       = VarTm (n-i-1)
readbackD n (AppD e d)     = AppTm (readbackD n e) (readbackD n d)
```

Finally, we obtain `readback :: Int -> ([D] -> D) -> Tm` as

```
readback n f          = readbackD n (f [VarD (n-i-1) | i <- [0..(n-1)]])
```

The application of a PCF Böhm tree (innocent strategy) $\Gamma \vdash_{\mathrm{Bt}} t : A \to B$ to $\Gamma \vdash_{\mathrm{Bt}} t' : A$ with $|\Gamma| = n$ can now be computed lazily as `app n t t'`, where `app :: Int -> Tm -> Tm -> Tm` is defined by

```
app n t t' = readback n (\x -> appD (eval t x) (eval t' x))
```

We will in the following sections prove that this simple definition computes the claimed result. We can define functions for all other pcf-cwf combinators in a similar way, and prove that they satisfy the pcf-cwf-laws. In this way we get a pcf-cwf **PCFInn** which is an alternative nbe-based presentation of the innocent strategies model of PCF – these will come as a by-product of a nbe procedure producing the innocent strategy for a term.

3 The Domain Interpretation

To prove the correctness of the nbe program we use its denotational semantics in Scott domains. We first show that the interpretation function is sound w.r.t. syntactic conversion and computationally adequate. Then we show that the η-expanded interpretation of a term is equal to that of its PCF Böhm tree.

3.1 A Semantic Domain

D and its combinators. The Haskell datatype `D` can be interpreted as a Scott domain D which is the solution of the domain equation given by the constructors:

$$\mathrm{Lam_D} : (\mathrm{D} \to \mathrm{D}) \to \mathrm{D} \qquad \mathrm{Suc_D} : \mathrm{D} \to \mathrm{D} \qquad 0_{\mathrm{D}} : \mathrm{D}$$
$$\mathrm{App_D} : \mathrm{D} \to \mathrm{D} \to \mathrm{D} \qquad \mathrm{Case_D} : \mathrm{D} \to \mathrm{D} \to (\mathrm{D} \to \mathrm{D}) \to \mathrm{D} \qquad \mathrm{Var_D} : \mathrm{N} \to \mathrm{D}$$

We write Ω_{D} for the bottom element. The two semantic operations $\mathrm{app_D} : \mathrm{D} \to \mathrm{D} \to \mathrm{D}$ and $\mathrm{case_D} : \mathrm{D} \to \mathrm{D} \to (\mathrm{D} \to \mathrm{D}) \to \mathrm{D}$ are defined as their Haskell counterparts in Section 2.3.

Interpretation of PCF. Let Tm be the set of elements of the raw syntax of PCF. If E is a set, $[E]$ denotes the set of lists of elements of E. As for substitutions, we write $\langle\rangle$ for the empty list. If $\rho \in [\mathrm{D}]$ and $d \in \mathrm{D}$, we write $\rho :: d$ for the addition of d at the end of ρ[1] Finally, $\rho(i)$ is the i-th element of ρ *starting from the right and from* 0, if it exists, and Ω_{D} otherwise.

The **interpretation of PCF** is defined as a function $[\![-]\!] : \mathrm{Tm} \to [\mathrm{D}] \to D$:

$$\begin{aligned}
[\![\mathrm{fix}\, f]\!]\, \rho &= \textstyle\bigsqcup_{n\in\mathrm{N}}(\lambda d.\, [\![f]\!]\, (\rho :: d))^n(\Omega_{\mathrm{D}}) & [\![\underline{n}]\!]\, \rho &= \rho(n)\\
[\![\mathrm{app}\, s\, t]\!]\, \rho &= \mathrm{app_D}\, ([\![s]\!]\, \rho)\, ([\![t]\!]\, \rho) & [\![\mathrm{suc}\, a]\!]\, \rho &= \mathrm{Suc_D}\, ([\![a]\!]\, \rho)\\
[\![\lambda\, t]\!]\, \rho &= \mathrm{Lam_D}\, (\lambda x.[\![t]\!]\, (\rho :: x)) & [\![\Omega]\!]\, \rho &= \Omega_{\mathrm{D}}\\
[\![\mathrm{case}\, a\, b\, c]\!]\, \rho &= \mathrm{case_D}\, ([\![a]\!]\, \rho)\, ([\![b]\!]\, \rho)\, (\lambda x.\, [\![c]\!]\, (\rho :: x)) & [\![0]\!]\, \rho &= 0_{\mathrm{D}}
\end{aligned}$$

[1] This notational difference from the Haskell program ensures that the order of environments matches that of the context.

It is extended to substitutions $\gamma = \langle a_{n-1}, \ldots, a_0 \rangle$ by $[\![\gamma]\!]\,\rho = \langle [\![a_{n-1}]\!]\,\rho, \ldots, [\![a_0]\!]\,\rho \rangle$.

3.2 Soundness for Conversion

Here, we prove that the interpretation described above is sound with respect to conversion in PCF. Reduction rules of PCF come in three kinds: the *computation rules* ($\beta_1, \beta_2, \beta_3, \delta, \Omega$), the *commutation rules* (γ_1, γ_2) and the *η-expansion rules* (η_1, η_2). Soundness w.r.t. computation rules follows from standard (and simple) verifications, and we verify only the commutation and η-expansion rules.

Commutation rules. The interpretation of PCF validates γ_1 and γ_2.

Lemma 1. *For all $d_1, d_2, d_3 \in \mathrm{D}$ and $f, f_1, f_2 \in \mathrm{D} \to \mathrm{D}$, we have:*

$$\mathrm{app_D}\,(\mathrm{case_D}\,d_1\,d_2\,f)\,d_3 = \mathrm{case_D}\,d_1\,(\mathrm{app_D}\,d_2\,d_3)\,(\lambda x.\,\mathrm{app_D}\,(f\,x)\,d_3)$$
$$\mathrm{case_D}\,(\mathrm{case_D}\,d_1\,d_2\,f_1)\,d_3\,f_2 = \mathrm{case_D}\,d_1\,(\mathrm{case_D}\,d_2\,d_3\,f_2)\,(\lambda x.\,\mathrm{case_D}\,(f_1\,x)\,d_3\,f_2)$$

Proof. We apply Pitts' co-induction principle [19] for proving inequalities in recursively defined domains. The proof proceeds by defining a relation R containing the identity relation on D and all pairs (for $d_1, d_2, d_3 \in \mathrm{D}$ and $f \in \mathrm{D} \to \mathrm{D}$):

$$(\mathrm{app_D}\,(\mathrm{case_D}\,d_1\,d_2\,f)\,d_3, \mathrm{case_D}\,d_1\,(\mathrm{app_D}\,d_2\,d_3)\,(\lambda x.\,\mathrm{app_D}\,(f\,x)\,d_3))$$

Then, R is a bisimulation. For $d_1 = \Omega_\mathrm{D}, \mathrm{Var_D}\,i, \mathrm{App_D}\,d_1'\,d_2', \mathrm{Lam_D}\,f', 0_\mathrm{D}$ or $\mathrm{Suc_D}\,d'$, both sides evaluate to the same, so the bisimulation property is trivial. For $d_1 = \mathrm{Case_D}\,d_1'\,d_2'\,f'$, by direct calculations both sides start with $\mathrm{Case_D}$, followed by arguments related by R. By Pitts' result [19] the equality follows.

η-expansion rules. Note that these cannot be true in general since the interpretation ignores type information. So we define a semantic version of η-expansion:

$$\eta_N\,d = \mathrm{case_D}\,d\,0_\mathrm{D}\,(\lambda x.\,\eta_N\,x) \qquad \eta_{A\to B}\,d = \mathrm{Lam_D}\,(\lambda x.\,\eta_B\,\mathrm{app_D}\,d\,(\eta_A\,x))$$

It extends to environments by $\eta_{[]}\,\rho = []$, $\eta_{\Gamma,A}\,[] = (\eta_\Gamma\,[]) :: \Omega_\mathrm{D}$ and $\eta_{\Gamma,A}\,(\rho :: d) = (\eta_\Gamma\,\rho) :: (\eta_A\,d)$. For $f : [\mathrm{D}] \to \mathrm{D}$ we define $\eta_{\Gamma\vdash A}\,f = \lambda\rho.\,\eta_A\,(f\,(\eta_\Gamma\,\rho))$.

From semantic η-expansion we get a *typed* notion of equality *up to η-expansion* in the domain: for a type A and elements $d, d' \in \mathrm{D}$ we write $d =_A d'$ iff $\eta_A\,d = \eta_A\,d'$. This generalizes to $f =_{\Gamma\vdash A} f'$ in the obvious way. We now prove that *syntactic* η-expansion is validated up to *semantic* η-expansion.

It is easy to see that for $\Gamma \vdash b : A \to B$ we have $[\![b]\!] =_{\Gamma\vdash A\to B} [\![\lambda\,(\mathrm{app}\,b[\mathrm{p}]\,\underline{0})]\!]$ and also to verify the η-rule for N. However, reduction rules are closed under context, so we need to check that typed equality is a congruence.

This relies on the fact that the interpretation of terms cannot distinguish an input from its η-expansion. To prove that we start by defining a realizability predicate on D, by $d \Vdash \mathrm{N}$ for all $d \in \mathrm{D}$, and $d \Vdash A \to B$ iff for all $d' \Vdash A$, *(1)* $\mathrm{app_D}\,d\,d' =_B \mathrm{app_D}\,d\,(\eta_A\,d')$ and *(2)* $\mathrm{app_D}\,d\,d' \Vdash B$. This predicate generalizes to contexts (written $\rho \Vdash \Gamma$) in the obvious way. We observe by induction on A that η-expanded elements of D are realizers: for all $d \in \mathrm{D}$, $\eta_A\, d \Vdash A$. But the interpretation of terms, despite not being η-expanded, also satisfy it. Indeed we prove, by induction on typing judgments, the following adequacy lemma.

Lemma 2. *For $\Gamma \vdash a : A$, $\rho \Vdash \Gamma$, then (1) $[\![a]\!]\,\rho =_A [\![a]\!]\,(\eta_\Gamma\, \rho)$ and (2) $[\![a]\!]\,\rho \Vdash A$.*

It is then immediate that the interpretation of term constructors preserves typed equality. All conversion rules hold up to typed equality in D, which is a congruence w.r.t. the interpretation of terms. Putting it all together we conclude:

Proposition 1 (Soundness). *For $\Gamma \vdash a, a' : A$ with $a \approx a'$, $[\![a]\!] =_{\Gamma \vdash A} [\![a']\!]$.*

3.3 Computational Adequacy

As a step towards our main result, we prove computational adequacy:

Proposition 2. *If $\Gamma \vdash a : A$ and $[\![a]\!] \neq_{\Gamma \vdash A} \Omega_{\mathrm{D}}$ then a has a head normal form.*

First, we reduce the problem to closed terms by noting two properties:

- Firstly, $\Gamma, A \vdash b : B$ has a head normal form iff $\lambda\, b$ has,
- Secondly, $[\![b]\!] =_{\Gamma, A \vdash B} \Omega_{\mathrm{D}}$ iff $[\![\lambda\, b]\!] =_{\Gamma \vdash A \to B} \Omega_{\mathrm{D}}$, as can be checked by a simple calculation.

So we abstract all free variables of a term and reason only on closed terms.

We now aim to prove it for closed terms. The proof has two steps: *(1)* we prove it for closed terms of ground type using logical relations, and *(2)* we deduce it for closed terms of higher-order types. To obtain *(2)* from *(1)* we will need to temporarily enrich the syntax with an *error* constant $*$. This $*$ has all types – we write $\Gamma \vdash_* a : A$ for typing judgments in the extended syntax. We also add two head reductions $\mathrm{app} * a \to_h *$ and $\mathrm{case} * a\, b\, c \to_h *$.

We also need to give an interpretation of $*$ in D. At this point it is tempting to enrich the domain D with a constructor for $*$. Fortunately we can avoid that; indeed the reader can check that setting $[\![*]\!]\,\rho = \mathrm{Case}_{\mathrm{D}}\, \Omega_{\mathrm{D}}\, \Omega_{\mathrm{D}}\, (\lambda x.\, \Omega_{\mathrm{D}}) = *_{\mathrm{D}}$, the interpretation validates the two reduction rules above. Note that the term $*$ is only an auxiliary device used in this section: we will never attempt to apply nbe on a term with error, so this coincidence will be harmless.

Ground type. We first define our logical relations.

Definition 3. *We define a relation $\sim^n_{\mathrm{N}}$ between closed terms $\vdash_* a : \mathrm{N}$ and elements of D by induction on n. First $a \sim^0_{\mathrm{N}} d$ always. Then, $a \sim^{n+1}_{\mathrm{N}} d$ iff either $d = \Omega_D$, or $a \to^*_h 0$ and $d = 0_{\mathrm{D}}$, or $a \to^*_h *$ and $d = *_{\mathrm{D}}$, or finally, if $a \to^*_h \mathrm{suc}\, a'$ and $d = \mathrm{Suc}_{\mathrm{D}}\, d'$ and $a' \sim^n_{\mathrm{N}} d'$. We then define $a \sim_N d$ iff for all $n \in \mathbb{N}$, $a \sim^n_N d$. Finally, $b \sim_{A \to B} d$ iff for any $a \sim_A e$, $\mathrm{app}\, b\, a \sim_B \mathrm{app}_{\mathrm{D}}\, d\, e$.*

This relation is closed under backward head reduction, and satisfies the continuity property that for any ω-chain $(d_i)_{i \in \mathbb{N}}$, if $a \sim_A d_i$ for all i then $a \sim_A \sqcup_i d_i$. The fundamental lemma of logical relations follows by induction on a.

Lemma 3. *For any term $\Gamma \vdash_* a : A$, for any $\delta \sim_\Gamma \rho$, we have $a[\delta] \sim_A [\![a]\!]\,\rho$.*

By definition of $\sim_A$, computational adequacy follows for closed terms of type N.

Higher-order types. Suppose $\vdash a : A_{n-1} \to \ldots \to A_0 \to \mathrm{N} = A$ satisfies $[\![a]\!] \neq_A \Omega_{\mathrm{D}}$. We need to show that a has a head normal form, but our previous analysis only applies to terms of ground type. By hypothesis we know that for $[\![a]\!]$ there are some arguments $d_{n-1}, \ldots, d_0$ making $[\![a]\!]$ non-bottom. However, in order to apply our earlier result for ground type, we need to find syntactic counterparts to $d_{n-1}, \ldots, d_0$ – and there is no reason why those would exist. So instead we replace the d_is with $*_{\mathrm{D}}$, which *does* have a syntactic counterpart.

The core argument is that replacing arguments of $[\![a]\!]$ with $*_{\mathrm{D}}$ only increases chances of convergence. To show that we introduce:

Definition 4. *We define $\lesssim^n_{\mathrm{N}} \subseteq \mathrm{D}^2$ by induction on n. Let $d_1 \lesssim^0_{\mathrm{N}} d_2 \Leftrightarrow \top$ and*

$$d_1 \lesssim^{n+1}_{\mathrm{N}} d_2 \Leftrightarrow \begin{cases} \textit{If } d_1 = d_2 = 0_{\mathrm{D}} \\ \textit{If } d_1 = \mathrm{Suc_D}\, d'_1,\ d_2 = \mathrm{Suc_D}\, d'_2 \textit{ and } d'_1 \lesssim^n_{\mathrm{N}} d'_2 \\ \textit{If } d_1 = \Omega_D \textit{ or } d_2 \geq *_D \end{cases}$$

We set $d_1 \lesssim_{\mathrm{N}} d_2$ iff for all $n \in \mathbb{N}$, $d_1 \lesssim^n_{\mathrm{N}} d_2$. We lift this to all types by stating that $d_1 \lesssim_{A\to B} d_2$ iff for all $d'_1 \lesssim_A d'_2$, $\mathrm{app_D}\, d_1\, d'_1 \lesssim_B \mathrm{app_D}\, d_2\, d'_2$.

This generalizes to a relation on environments $\rho_1 \lesssim_\Gamma \rho_2$, but unlike what the notation suggests, $\lesssim_A$ is *not* an ordering: it is neither reflexive, nor transitive, nor antisymmetric. However, for all A and $d \in \mathrm{D}$ we have $\Omega_{\mathrm{D}} \lesssim_A d \lesssim_A *_{\mathrm{D}}$.

The following fundamental lemma is proved by induction on a.

Lemma 4. *For any term $\Gamma \vdash_* a : A$, for any $\rho_1 \lesssim_\Gamma \rho_2$, $[\![a]\!]\,\rho_1 \lesssim_A [\![a]\!]\,\rho_2$.*

Putting the ingredients above together, we prove the following lemma.

Lemma 5. *For $\vdash_* a : A$, $d \lesssim_A [\![a]\!]$ and $d \neq_A \Omega_{\mathrm{D}}$, a has a head normal form.*

Proof. For N, assume there is $d \lesssim_{\mathrm{N}} [\![a]\!]$ such that $d \neq_{\mathrm{N}} \Omega_{\mathrm{D}}$, so $d \neq \Omega_{\mathrm{D}}$. It follows by definition of $\lesssim_{\mathrm{N}}$ that either $[\![a]\!] = *_D$, or d and $[\![a]\!]$ respectively start both with 0_{D} or both with $\mathrm{Suc_D}$. But by Lemma 3 we have $a \sim_{\mathrm{N}} [\![a]\!]$, so by definition of logical relations, a has a head normal form.

For $A \to B$, take $\vdash_* b : A \to B$ and assume there is $d \lesssim_{A\to B} [\![b]\!]$ such that $d \neq_{A\to B} \Omega_{\mathrm{D}}$. So there is $d' \in D$ such that $\mathrm{app_D}\, d\,(\eta_A\, d') \neq_B \Omega_{\mathrm{D}}$. But we have observed above that $\eta_A\, d' \lesssim_A *_D$. Therefore, by definition of $\lesssim_{A\to B}$, we have:

$$\mathrm{app_D}\, d\,(\eta_A\, d') \lesssim_B \mathrm{app_D}\, [\![b]\!]\, *_D = [\![\mathrm{app}\, b\, *]\!]$$

By induction hypothesis, $\mathrm{app}\, b\, *$ has a head normal form. But head reduction is deterministic, and any potentially infinite head reduction chain on b would transport to $\mathrm{app}\, b\, *$, so b has a head normal form.

Finally, it remains to deduce computational adequacy for closed terms. But for arbitrary $\vdash_* a : A$ such that $[\![a]\!] \neq_A \Omega_{\mathrm{D}}$, by Lemma 4 we have $[\![a]\!] \lesssim_A [\![a]\!]$, so we are in the range of Lemma 5 – therefore, a has a head normal form.

3.4 PCF Böhm Trees Defined by Repeated Head Reduction

In the next section we show how the PCF Böhm tree of a term can be computed by nbe. We also show that the result of this computation coincides with the traditional way of defining a PCF Böhm tree as obtained by repeated head reduction. This definition relies on the following lemma.

Lemma 6. *The system $\{\rightarrow_{\gamma_1}, \rightarrow_{\gamma_2}\}$ of commutations is strongly normalizing.*

Proof. Local confluence follows from a direct analysis of the (two) critical pairs, and one gets a decreasing measure by defining $|a| = 1$ on all leaves of the syntax tree, $|\mathrm{case}\, a\, b\, f| = 2|a| + \max(|b|, |f|)$ and $|\mathrm{app}\, a\, b| = 2|a| + |b|$ and $| - |$ behaves additively on all other constructors.

The PCF Böhm tree of a term. The PCF Böhm tree $\mathrm{BT}(a)$ of a term $\Gamma \vdash a : A$ is defined as follows. If $A = \mathrm{N}$ and a has no head normal form then $\mathrm{BT}(a) = \Omega$. Otherwise we convert a to head normal form and then to $\rightarrow_{\gamma_1,\gamma_2}$-normal form a' by Lemma 6 which is still a head normal form. The only possible cases are:

- $\mathrm{BT}(a) = 0$ if $a' = 0$.
- $\mathrm{BT}(a) = \mathrm{suc}\,\mathrm{BT}(a'')$ if $a' = \mathrm{suc}\, a''$
- $\mathrm{BT}(a) = \mathrm{case}\ (\mathrm{app}\ \underline{i}\ \overrightarrow{\mathrm{BT}(a_j)})\ 0\ (\mathrm{suc}\ \mathrm{BT}(\underline{0}))$ if $a' = \mathrm{app}\,\underline{i}\,\overrightarrow{a_j}$
- $\mathrm{BT}(a) = \mathrm{case}\,(\mathrm{app}\,\underline{i}\,\overrightarrow{\mathrm{BT}(a_j)})\,\mathrm{BT}(b)\,\mathrm{BT}(c)$ if $a' = \mathrm{case}\,(\mathrm{app}\,\underline{i}\,\overrightarrow{a_j})\,b\,c$.

If $A = B \rightarrow C$ then $\mathrm{BT}(a) = \lambda\,\mathrm{BT}(\mathrm{app}\,(a[\mathrm{p}])\,\underline{0})$. ($\mathrm{BT}(a)$ could be more explicitly defined as an ideal of finite approximations, see e.g. [14] for details.)

Together with the earlier results, we get the main result of this section.

Proposition 3. *If $\Gamma \vdash a : A$ then $\Gamma \vdash_{\mathrm{Bt}} \mathrm{BT}(a) : A$ and $\eta_{\Gamma \vdash A}\, [\![a]\!] = [\![\mathrm{BT}(a)]\!]$.*

Proof. As we aim to prove the equality of two elements of D we use again Pitts' method [19] and define the following relation

$$R = \{([\![\mathrm{BT}(a)]\!]\,(\eta_\Gamma\, \rho), \eta_A\,([\![a]\!]\,(\eta_\Gamma\, \rho))) \mid \Gamma \vdash a : A\ \&\ \rho \in [\mathrm{D}]\}$$

and show that it is a bisimulation. Proposition 1 ensures that the conversion steps needed to transform a term to its PCF Böhm tree are sound in the model, Proposition 2 ensures that both sides are Ω_{D} at the same time.

This ends the core of the technical development. The same proof scheme can be used to show that the game interpretation of Section 2.2 validates conversion to PCF Böhm trees. Details can be obtained by adapting McCusker's proof [18].

4 Game Semantics of PCF Based on nbe

Normalization by evaluation. We are now ready to show the correctness of an nbe algorithm which computes innocent strategies for *infinitary terms*. Recall that in Section 2.2 we defined PCF Böhm trees as ideals of finite PCF Böhm trees. The same construction on arbitrary PCF terms yields a notion of infinitary term on which BT and $[\![-]\!]$ automatically extends, along with Proposition 3.

The readback function $\mathrm{R}_n : ([\mathrm{D}] \to \mathrm{D}) \to \mathrm{Tm}$ is the semantic counterpart of the Haskell `readback` function in Section 2.3. The following is proved on finitary terms by a direct induction and extends to PCF Böhm trees by continuity.

Lemma 7. *If $\Gamma \vdash_{\mathrm{Bt}} t : A$ is a PCF Böhm tree with $|\Gamma| = n$, then $\mathrm{R}_n [\![t]\!] = t$.*

We now define an nbe algorithm which maps a PCF term to its PCF Böhm tree, and use this lemma together with Proposition 3 to show its correctness:

Theorem 1. *Let $\Gamma \vdash a : A$ be an (infinitary) PCF term. If $\mathrm{nbe}(a) = \mathrm{R}_n(\eta_{\Gamma \vdash A}[\![a]\!])$, where $|\Gamma| = n$, then $\mathrm{nbe}(a) = \mathrm{BT}(a)$.*

The pcf-cwf of PCF Böhm trees. We conclude this paper by showing how to recover the Hyland-Ong game model of PCF, up to isomorphism of pcf-cwfs. If $d \in \mathrm{D}$, say that d has **(semantic) type** A iff $\eta_A\, d = d$. Likewise a function $f : [\mathrm{D}] \to \mathrm{D}$ has type $\Gamma \vdash A$ iff $\eta_{\Gamma \vdash A}\, f = f$, and a function $\gamma : [\mathrm{D}] \to [\mathrm{D}]$ has type $\Gamma \vdash \Delta$ iff it is obtained by tupling functions of the appropriate types. This generalizes to a pcf-cwf **D** having PCF contexts as objects and functions (resp. elements) of the appropriate type as morphisms (resp. terms).

As a pcf-cwf, **D** supports the interpretation of PCF. But the plain domain interpretation $[\![a]\!]$ (of Section 3) of a PCF Böhm tree $\Gamma \vdash_{\mathrm{Bt}} a : A$ automatically has semantic type $\Gamma \vdash A$, and so is a term in the sense of **D**. Furthermore, this map from PCF Böhm trees to **D** is injective by Theorem 1. Finally, the image of PCF Böhm trees in **D** is closed under all pcf-cwf operations: each of these can be replicated in the infinitary PCF syntax then normalized using nbe, yielding by Theorem 1 and Proposition 3 a PCF Böhm tree whose interpretation matches the result of the corresponding operation in **D**. So, the interpretation of PCF Böhm trees forms a sub-pcf-cwf of **D**, called **PCFInn**, satisfying:

Theorem 2. **PCFInn** *is isomorphic to the pcf-cwf of PCF contexts/types, and innocent well-bracketed strategies between the corresponding arenas.*

If we unfold this definition we get the Haskell program for application in Section 2.3 and similar programs for composition and the other pcf-cwf operations. The pcf-cwf laws for these programs, such as associativity of composition, β, and η, follow from the corresponding laws for their domain interpretation in **D**.

Acknowledgments. The first author acknowledges the support of the French ANR Project RAPIDO, ANR-14-CE25-0007 and the second author of the Swedish VR Frame Programme Types for Proofs and Programs.

References

1. Abel, A.: Normalization by Evaluation: Dependent Types and Impredicativity. Institut für Informatik, Ludwig-Maximilians-Universität München, Habilitation thesis (May 2013)

2. Abel, A., Aehlig, K., Dybjer, P.: Normalization by evaluation for Martin-Löf type theory with one universe. In: 23rd Conference on the Mathematical Foundations of Programming Semantics, MFPS XXIII. Electronic Notes in Theoretical Computer Science, pp. 17–40. Elsevier (2007)
3. Abramsky, S., Jagadeesan, R., Malacaria, P.: Full abstraction for PCF. Inf. Comput. 163(2), 409–470 (2000)
4. Aehlig, K., Joachimski, F.: Operational aspects of untyped normalisation by evaluation. Mathematical Structures in Computer Science 14(4) (2004)
5. Amadio, R., Curien, P.-L.: Domains and lambda-calculi, vol. 46. Cambridge University Press (1998)
6. Berger, U., Schwichtenberg, H.: An inverse to the evaluation functional for typed λ-calculus. In: Proceedings of the 6th Annual IEEE Symposium on Logic in Computer Science, Amsterdam, pp. 203–211 (July 1991)
7. Cartmell, J.: Generalized algebraic theories and contextual categories. Annals of Pure and Applied Logic 32, 209–243 (1986)
8. Clairambault, P., Dybjer, P.: The biequivalence of locally cartesian closed categories and Martin-Löf type theories. Mathematical Structures in Computer Science 24(5) (2013)
9. Clairambault, P., Murawski, A.S.: Böhm trees as higher-order recursive schemes. In: IARCS Annual Conference on Foundations of Software Technology and Theoretical Computer Science, FSTTCS 2013, Guwahati, India, December 12-14, pp. 91–102 (2013)
10. Curien, P.-L.: Abstract Böhm trees. Mathematical Structures in Computer Science 8(6), 559–591 (1998)
11. Curien, P.-L.: Notes on game semantics. From the authors web page (2006)
12. Dybjer, P.: Internal type theory. In: Berardi, S., Coppo, M. (eds.) TYPES 1995. LNCS, vol. 1158, pp. 120–134. Springer, Heidelberg (1996)
13. Dybjer, P.: Program testing and the meaning explanations of intuitionistic type theory. In: Epistemology versus Ontology - Essays on the Philosophy and Foundations of Mathematics in Honour of Per Martin-Löf, pp. 215–241 (2012)
14. Dybjer, P., Kuperberg, D.: Formal neighbourhoods, combinatory Böhm trees, and untyped normalization by evaluation. Ann. Pure Appl. Logic 163(2), 122–131 (2012)
15. Filinski, A., Rohde, H.K.: Denotational aspects of untyped normalization by evaluation. Theor. Inf. and App. 39(3), 423–453 (2005)
16. Harmer, R., Hyland, M., Melliès, P.-A.: Categorical combinators for innocent strategies. In: 22nd IEEE Symposium on Logic in Computer Science, Wroclaw, Poland, Proceedings, pp. 379–388. IEEE Computer Society (2007)
17. Hyland, J.M.E., Luke Ong, C.-H.: On full abstraction for PCF: I, II, and III. Inf. Comput. 163(2), 285–408 (2000)
18. McCusker, G.: Games and full abstraction for FPC. Inf. Comput. 160(1-2), 1–61 (2000)
19. Pitts, A.M.: A co-induction principle for recursively defined domains. Theor. Comput. Sci. 124(2), 195–219 (1994)
20. Plotkin, G.D.: LCF considered as a programming language. Theor. Comput. Sci. 5(3), 223–255 (1977)
21. Plotkin, G.D.: Post-graduate lecture notes in advanced domain theory (incorporating the "Pisa Notes"). Dept. of Computer Science, Univ. of Edinburgh (1981)

Foundations of Differential Dataflow

Martín Abadi, Frank McSherry, and Gordon D. Plotkin[1,2]

[1] Microsoft Research*
[2] LFCS, School of Informatics, University of Edinburgh, UK

Abstract. Differential dataflow is a recent approach to incremental computation that relies on a partially ordered set of differences. In the present paper, we aim to develop its foundations. We define a small programming language whose types are abelian groups equipped with linear inverses, and provide both a standard and a differential denotational semantics. The two semantics coincide in that the differential semantics is the differential of the standard one. Möbius inversion, a well-known idea from combinatorics, permits a systematic treatment of various operators and constructs.

1 Introduction

Differential computation [2] is a recent approach to incremental computation (see, e.g., [1,3]) that relies on partially ordered versions of data. We model partially ordered versions as functions over a partial order, and call them *streams*. In the intended implementations of differential computation, the set of updates required to reconstruct any given version A_t of a stream A is retained in a data structure indexed by the partial order, rather than consolidated into a "current" version. For example, in an iterative algorithm with two nested loops with counters i and j, differential computation may associate a version with each pair (i, j) (with the product partial order on such pairs). Then an implementation may re-use work done at all $(i', j') < (i, j)$ to compute the (i, j)-th version.

Differential dataflow is an instantiation of differential computation in a data-parallel dataflow setting. In such a setting the data used are large collections of records and the fundamental operators are independently applied to disjoint parts of their inputs. Differential computation preserves the sparseness of input differences in the output, as an output can change only if its input has changed. The result can be very concise representations and efficient updates. The Naiad system [4] includes a realization of differential dataflow that supports high-throughput, low-latency computations on frequently updated large datasets.

Differential dataflow aims to avoid redundant computation by replacing the versions of its collection-valued variables with versions of *differences*. These versions may have negative multiplicities, so that a version A_t of a stream A is the

* Most of this work was done while the authors were at Microsoft. M. Abadi is now at Google and the University of California at Santa Cruz.

A. Pitts (Ed.): FOSSACS 2015, LNCS 9034, pp. 71–83, 2015.
DOI: 10.1007/978-3-662-46678-0_5

sum of the differences $(\delta A)_s$ at versions $s \leq t$: $A_t = \sum_{s \leq t} \delta A_s$. This formula resembles those used in incremental computation, where $s, t \in \mathbb{N}$, but permits more general partial orders.

Functions on streams A are replaced by their *differentials*, which operate on the corresponding difference streams δA, and are responsible for producing corresponding output difference streams. In particular, as established in [2], the product partial order $\mathbb{N}^k$ enables very efficient nested iterative differential computation, because each nested iteration can selectively re-use some of the previously computed differences, but is not required to use all of them. Efficiently updating the state of an iterative computation is challenging, and is the main feature of differential dataflow.

In the present paper we aim to develop the foundations of differential dataflow. We show that the use of collections allowing negative multiplicities and product partial orders of the natural numbers are special cases of general differential computation on abelian groups and locally finite partial orders. We demonstrate the relevance and usefulness of Möbius inversion, a well-known idea from combinatorics (see, for example, [5,6]), to understanding and verifying properties of function differentials.

Specifically, we consider the question of finding the differential of a computation given by a program in a small programming language that includes nested iteration. To this end, we define both a standard compositional denotational semantics for the language and a compositional differential one. Our main theorem (Theorem 1 below) states that the two semantics are consistent in that the differential semantics is the differential of the standard semantics.

In Section 2 we lay the mathematical foundations for differential computation. We discuss how abelian groups arise naturally when considering collections with negative multiplicities. We explain Möbius inversion for spaces of functions from partial orders to abelian groups. This leads us to a uniform framework of abelian groups equipped with linear inverses. We then define function differentials, giving some examples. In particular, we derive some formulas for such differentials, previously set out without justification [2].

In Section 3 we consider loops. Two policies for loop egress are mentioned in [2]: exit after a fixed number of iterations and exit on a first repetition. We consider only the first of these, as it is the one used in practice and mathematically simpler: the second would require the use of partial streams.

In Section 4 we present the language and its two semantics, and establish Theorem 1. As noted above, the semantics are denotational, defining what is computed, rather than how; going further, it may be attractive to describe an operational semantics in terms of the propagation of differences in a dataflow graph, somewhat closer to Naiad's implementation.

In Section 5 we discuss the treatment of prioritization, a technique from [2] for nested iterative computations. The treatment in [2] via lexicographic products of partial orders does not correctly support more than one nested loop (despite the suggestion there that it should); further, the treatment of differential aspects is incomplete, and it is not clear how to proceed. We instead propose a simpler rule and show that it correctly achieves the goal of arbitrary prioritized computation.

We conclude in Section 6, and discuss some possible future work.

2 Mathematical Foundations

The mathematical foundations of differential dataflow concern: data organized into abelian groups; version-indexed streams of data and their differentials, which are obtained by Möbius transformation; and stream operations and their differentials, which, in their turn, operate on stream differentials. These three topics are covered in Sections 2.1, 2.2, and 2.3.

2.1 Abelian Groups

Abelian groups play a major role in our theory, arising from negative multiplicities. The set of collections, or multisets, $\mathcal{C}(X)$ over a set X can be defined as the functions $c : X \to \mathbb{N}$ that are 0 almost everywhere. It forms a commutative monoid under multiset union, defined pointwise by: $(c \cup d)(x) = c(x) + d(x)$. The set of multisets $\mathcal{A}(X)$ with possibly negative multiplicities is obtained by replacing $\mathbb{N}$ by $\mathbb{Z}$; it forms an abelian group under pointwise sum.

A function between commutative monoids is *linear* if it preserves finite sums; e.g., selection and aggregation provide linear functions from $\mathcal{C}(X)$ to commutative monoids such as $\mathcal{C}(Y)$ and $\mathbb{N}$. These functions lift to the corresponding groups: every linear $f : \mathcal{C}(X) \to G$, with G an abelian group, has a unique linear extension $\overline{f} : \mathcal{A}(X) \to G$ given by $\overline{f}(c) = \sum_{x \in X} c(x) f(x)$ (omitting the evident map $X \to \mathcal{C}(X)$). These observations exemplify a well-known general construction universally embedding cancellative commutative monoids in abelian groups.

2.2 Versions, Streams, and Möbius Inversion

We work with *locally finite partial orders*, that is, partial orders T such that $\downarrow t =_{\text{def}} \{t' \mid t' \leq t\}$ is finite for all $t \in T$. Examples include finite products of $\mathbb{N}$, as mentioned in the introduction, and the partial order $\mathcal{P}_{\text{fin}}(I)$, of finite subsets of a given set I (perhaps used to model a set of individuals), ordered by subset. We think of functions from T to G as *T-indexed streams of elements of G*.

The *Möbius coefficients* $\mu_T(t', t) \in \mathbb{Z}$, with $t, t' \in T$, are given recursively by:

$$\mu_T(t', t) = \begin{cases} 0 & (t' \not\leq t) \\ 1 & (t' = t) \\ -\sum_{t' \leq r < t} \mu_T(t', r) & (t' < t) \end{cases}$$

For example for $T = \mathbb{N}$ (the natural numbers with their usual ordering), $\mu_{\mathbb{N}}(n', n)$ is 1, if $n' = n$; is -1, if $n' = n-1$; and is 0, otherwise. For $T = \mathcal{P}_{\text{fin}}(I)$, $\mu(W', W)$ is $-1^{\#(W \setminus W')}$, if $W' \subseteq W$; and is 0 otherwise. For product partial orders one has: $\mu_{S \times T}((s', t'), (s, t)) = \mu_S(s', s)\mu_T(t', t)$.

The *Möbius transformation* of a function $f : T \to G$, where G is an abelian group, is given by:

$$\delta_T(f)(t) = \sum_{t' \leq t} \mu_T(t', t) f(t')$$

For example $\delta_{\mathbb{N}}(f)(n) = f(n) - f(n-1)$, if $n > 0$, and $= f(0)$ if $n = 0$.

Defining

$$S_T(f)(t) = \sum_{t' \leq t} f(t')$$

we obtain the famous Möbius inversion formulas:

$$S_T(\delta_T(f)) = f = \delta_T(S_T(f))$$

See, for example, [5,6]. Expanded out, these formulas read:

$$f(t) = \sum_{t' \leq t} \sum_{t'' \leq t'} \mu_T(t'', t') f(t'') \qquad f(t) = \sum_{t' \leq t} \mu_T(t', t) \sum_{t'' \leq t'} f(t'')$$

The collection G^T of all T-indexed streams of elements of G forms an abelian group under pointwise addition. We would further like to iterate this function space construction to obtain the doubly indexed functions mentioned in the introduction; we would also like to consider products of such groups. It is therefore natural to generalize to abelian groups G equipped with linear inverses $G \xrightarrow{\delta_G} G \xrightarrow{S_G} G$. A simple example is any abelian group G, such as $\mathcal{A}(X)$, with $\delta_G = S_G = \mathrm{id}_G$, the identity on G.

For such a G and a locally finite partial order T we define linear inverses $G^T \xrightarrow{\delta_{G^T}} G^T \xrightarrow{S_{G^T}} G^T$ on G^T by setting:

$$\delta_{G^T}(f)(t) = \sum_{t' \leq t} \mu_T(t', t) \delta_G(f(t')) \quad \text{and} \quad S_{G^T}(f)(t) = \sum_{t' \leq t} S_G(f(t'))$$

It is clear that δ_{G^P} and S_{G^P} are linear; we check they are mutually inverse:

$$\begin{aligned}
\delta_{G^P}(S_{G^P}(f))(t) &= \textstyle\sum_{t' \leq t} \mu(t', t) \delta_G(\sum_{t'' \leq t'} S_G(f(t''))) \\
&= \textstyle\sum_{t' \leq t} \sum_{t'' \leq t'} \mu(t', t) \delta_G(S_G(f(t''))) \qquad \text{(as } \delta_G \text{ is linear)} \\
&= \textstyle\sum_{t' \leq t} \mu(t', t) \sum_{t'' \leq t'} f(t'') \\
&= f(t) \qquad \text{(by the Möbius inversion formula)}
\end{aligned}$$

$$\begin{aligned}
S_{G^P}(\delta_{G^P}(f))(t) &= \textstyle\sum_{t' \leq t} S_G(\sum_{t'' \leq t'} \mu(t'', t') \delta_G(f(t''))) \\
&= \textstyle\sum_{t' \leq t} \sum_{t'' \leq t'} \mu(t'', t') S_G(\delta_G(f(t''))) \qquad \text{(as } S_G \text{ is linear)} \\
&= \textstyle\sum_{t' \leq t} \sum_{t'' \leq t'} \mu(t'', t') f(t'') \\
&= f(t) \qquad \text{(by the Möbius inversion formula)}
\end{aligned}$$

Iterating the stream construction enables us to avoid the explicit use of product partial orders, as the group isomorphism $(G^T)^{T'} \cong G^{T \times T'}$ extends to an isomorphism of their linear inverses.

As for products, given two abelian groups G and H with linear inverses δ_G, S_G and δ_H, S_H, we construct linear inverses $\delta_{G \times H}$ and $S_{G \times H}$ for $G \times H$ by setting: $\delta_{G \times H}(c, d) = (\delta_G(c), \delta_H(d))$ and $S_{G \times H}(c, d) = (S_G(c), S_H(d))$. We write π_0 and π_1 for the first and second projections.

2.3 Function Differentials

The *differential* (or *conjugate*) of a function $f : G \to H$ is the function $\delta(f) : G \to H$ where:

$$\delta(f) =_{\text{def}} \delta_H \circ f \circ S_G$$

The definition applies to n-ary functions, e.g., for $f : G \times H \to K$ we have $\delta(f)(c, d) = \delta_K(f(S_G(c), S_H(d)))$. So $\delta(f)(\delta_G(c_1), \delta_H(c_2)) = \delta_K(f(c_1, c_2))$ and compositions of functions can be recast differentially by replacing both streams and functions by their corresponding differentials. Efficient differential implementations were developed in [2] for several important classes of primitive functions (e.g., selection, projection, relational joins).

For any partial order T, a function $f : G \to H$ can be lifted pointwise to a function $f^T : G^T \to H^T$ by setting:

$$f^T(c)_t = f(c_t)$$

The most common case is when $T = \mathbb{N}$, used to lift a function to one whose inputs may vary sequentially, either because it is placed within a loop or because external stimuli may change its inputs. The following proposition relates the differential of a lifted function to its own differential. It justifies some implementations from [2], showing that some lifted linear functions, such as selection and projection, are their own differentials.

Proposition 1. *For any $c \in G^T$ and $t \in T$ we have:*

1.
$$\delta(f^T)(c)_t = \sum_{t' \leq t} \mu(t', t)\delta(f)(\sum_{t'' \leq t'} c_{t''})$$

2. *If, further, f is linear then we have: $\delta(f^T)(c)_t = \delta(f)(c_t)$.*
3. *If, yet further, $\delta(f) = f$ then $\delta(f^T) = f^T$, that is, $\delta(f^T)(c)_t = f(c_t)$.*

Proof. 1. We calculate:

$$\begin{aligned}
\delta(f^T)(c)_t &= \textstyle\sum_{t' \leq t} \mu(t', t)\delta_H(f^T(S_{G^T}(c))_{t'}) \\
&= \textstyle\sum_{t' \leq t} \mu(t', t)\delta_H(f(S_{G^T}(c)_{t'})) \\
&= \textstyle\sum_{t' \leq t} \mu(t', t)\delta_H(f(\sum_{t'' \leq t'} S_G(c)_{t''})) \\
&= \textstyle\sum_{t' \leq t} \mu(t', t)\delta_H(f(S_G(\sum_{t' \leq t'} c_{t''}))) \\
&= \textstyle\sum_{t' \leq t} \mu(t', t)\delta(f)(\sum_{t'' \leq t'} c_{t''})
\end{aligned}$$

2. If f is linear so is $\delta(f)$ and then, continuing the previous calculation:

$$\begin{aligned}
\delta(f^T)(c)_t &= \textstyle\sum_{t' \leq t} \mu(t', t)\delta(f)(\sum_{t'' \leq t'} c_{t''}) \\
&= \textstyle\sum_{t' \leq t} \mu(t', t) \sum_{t'' \leq t'} \delta(f)(c_{t''}) \\
&= \delta(f)(c_t)
\end{aligned}$$

3. This is an immediate consequence of the previous part.

□

For binary functions $f : G \times H \to K$, we define $f^T : G^T \times H^T \to K^T$ by $f^T(c,d)_t = f(c_t, d_t)$. In the case $T = \mathbb{N}$ a straightforward calculation shows that if f is bilinear (i.e., linear in each of its arguments) then:

$$\delta(f^{\mathbb{N}})(c,d)_n = \delta(f)(c_n, \delta(d)_n) + \delta(f)(\delta(c)_n, d_n) - \delta(f)(\delta(c)_n, \delta(d)_n)$$

justifying the implementations in [2] of differentials of lifted bilinear functions such as relational join. The equation generalizes to forests, i.e., those locally finite partial orders whose restriction to any $\downarrow t$ is linear.

The following proposition (proof omitted) applies more generally; Part 2 justifies the implementation of binary function differentials in [2].

Proposition 2. *For any $c \in G^T$, $d \in H^T$, and $t \in T$ we have:*

1. $$\delta(f^T)(c,d)_t = \sum_{t' \le t} \mu(t',t)\delta(f)(\sum_{t'' \le t'} c_{t''}, \sum_{t'' \le t'} d_{t''})$$

2. *If, further, f is bilinear (i.e., linear in each argument separately), and T has binary sups then we have:*

$$\delta(f^T)(c,d)_t = \sum_{\substack{r,\,s \\ r \vee s = t}} \delta(f)(c_r, d_s)$$

3. *If, yet further, $\delta(f) = f$ we have:*

$$\delta(f^T)(c,d)_t = \sum_{\substack{r,\,s \\ r \vee s = t}} f(c_r, d_s)$$

3 Loops

We follow [2] for the differential of an iterative computation, but employ additional formalism to justify the construction, and to be able to generalize it sufficiently to support prioritization correctly. Loops follow the dataflow computation pictured in Figure 1. The Ingress node introduces input to a loop, and is modeled by the function $\texttt{in} : G \to G^{\mathbb{N}}$ where:

$$\texttt{in}(c)_i =_{\mathrm{def}} \begin{cases} c \ (i = 0) \\ 0 \ (i > 0) \end{cases}$$

The Feedback node advances values from one iteration to the next, and is modeled by the function $\texttt{fb} : G^{\mathbb{N}} \to G^{\mathbb{N}}$ where:

$$\texttt{fb}(c)_i =_{\mathrm{def}} \begin{cases} 0 & (i = 0) \\ c_{i-1} & (i > 0) \end{cases}$$

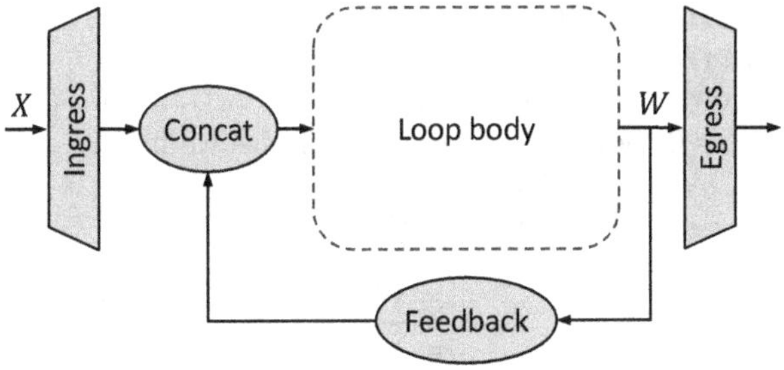

Fig. 1. A loop (reproduced with permission from [2])

The Concat node merges the input and feedback streams, and is modeled by the function $+_{G^T} : G^T \times G^T \to G^T$. The Egress node effects the fixed-iteration-number loop egress policy, returning the value at some kth iteration, and is modeled by the function $\mathtt{out}_k : G^{\mathbb{N}} \to G$ where:

$$\mathtt{out}_k(c) = c_k$$

In addition, the loop body is modeled by a function $f^{\mathbb{N}} : G^{\mathbb{N}} \to G^{\mathbb{N}}$ for a given function f on G.

The loop is intended to output an $\mathbb{N}$-indexed stream $s \in G^{\mathbb{N}}$ at W, starting at $f(c)$, where $c \in G$ is input at X, and then successively output $f^2(c)$, $f^3(c)$, ... It is more convenient, and a little more general, to instead take the output just after Concat, obtaining the sequence $c, f(c), f^2(c), \ldots$. This s is a solution of the fixed-point equation

$$d = \mathtt{in}(c) + \mathtt{fb}(f^{\mathbb{N}}(d)) \tag{1}$$

Indeed it is the unique solution, as one easily checks that the equation is equivalent to the following iteration equations:

$$d_0 = c \qquad d_{n+1} = f(d_n)$$

which recursively determine d. The output of the loop is obtained by applying $\mathtt{out}_k$ to s, and so the whole loop construct computes $f^k(c)$.

The differential version of the loop employs the differential versions of in, fb, and out, so we first check these agree with [2].

Proposition 3. *The differentials of* in, fb, *and* out *satisfy:*

$$\delta(\mathtt{in})(c)_i = \begin{cases} c & (i = 0) \\ -c & (i = 1) \\ 0 & (i \geq 2) \end{cases} \qquad \delta(\mathtt{fb}) = \mathtt{fb} \qquad \delta(\mathtt{out}_k)(c) = \sum_{m \leq k} c_m$$

Proof. 1. We have:

$$\delta(\mathtt{in})(c)(j) = \delta_{G^{\mathbb{N}}}(\mathtt{in}(S_G(c))(j) = \textstyle\sum_{i \leq j} \mu(i,j)\delta_G(\mathtt{in}(S_G(c))(i))$$

Then we see that if $j = 0$, this is $\delta_G(\texttt{in}(S_G(c))(0)) = \delta_G(S_G(c)) = c$; if $j = 1$, this is $\delta_G(\texttt{in}(S_G(c))(1)) - \delta_G(\texttt{in}(S_G(c))(0)) = 0 - c$; and if $j \geq 2$, this is $\delta_G(\texttt{in}(S_G(c))(j)) - \delta_G(\texttt{in}(S_G(c))(j-1)) = 0 - 0$.

2. It suffices to show $\texttt{fb}$ preserves S, i.e., $\texttt{fb}(S_{G^T}(c))_j = S_{G^T}(\texttt{fb}(c))_j$, for all $j \in \mathbb{N}$. In case $j = 0$, both sides are 0. Otherwise we have:

$$\begin{aligned} \texttt{fb}(S_{G^T}(c))_j &= S_{G^T}(c)_{j-1} \\ &= \textstyle\sum_{i \leq j-1} S_G(c_i) \\ &= \textstyle\sum_{1 \leq i \leq j} S_G(c_{i-1}) \\ &= \textstyle\sum_{i \leq j} S_G(\texttt{fb}(c)_i) \\ &= S_{G^T}(\texttt{fb}(c))_j \end{aligned}$$

3. We calculate:

$$\begin{aligned} \delta(\texttt{out}_k)(c) &= \delta_G(\texttt{out}_k(S_{G^T}(c)) \\ &= \delta_G(\texttt{out}_k(m \mapsto \textstyle\sum_{m' \leq m} S_G(c_{m'}))) \\ &= \delta_G(\textstyle\sum_{m \leq k} S_G(c_m)) \\ &= \textstyle\sum_{m \leq k} c_m \end{aligned}$$

□

As the differential version of the loop employs the differential versions of $\texttt{in}$, $\texttt{fb}$, and $+$, one expects $\delta(s)$ to satisfy the following equation:

$$d = \delta(\texttt{in})(\delta(c)) + \texttt{fb}(\delta(f^{\mathbb{N}})(d)) \tag{2}$$

since $+$ and $\texttt{fb}$ are their own differentials. This equation arises if we differentiate Equation 1; more precisely, Equation 1 specifies that d is a fixed-point of F, where $F(d) =_{\text{def}} \texttt{in}(c) + \texttt{fb}(f^{\mathbb{N}}(d))$. One then calculates $\delta(F)$:

$$\begin{aligned} \delta(F)(d) &= \delta(F(S(d))) \\ &= \delta(\texttt{in}(c) + \texttt{fb}(f^{\mathbb{N}}(Sd))) \\ &= \delta(\texttt{in})(\delta(c)) + \texttt{fb}(\delta(f^{\mathbb{N}}(Sd))) \\ &= \delta(\texttt{in})(\delta(c)) + \texttt{fb}(\delta(f^{\mathbb{N}})(\delta(Sd))) \\ &= \delta(\texttt{in})(\delta(c)) + \texttt{fb}(\delta(f^{\mathbb{N}})(d)) \end{aligned}$$

So Equation 2 specifies that $\delta(s)$ is a fixed-point of $\delta(F)$. It is immediate, for any G and $F : G \to G$, that d is a fixed-point of F iff $\delta(d)$ is a fixed-point of $\delta(F)$; so $\delta(s)$ is the unique solution of the second equation. As $s_n = f^n(c)$, differentiating we obtain an explicit formula for $\delta(s)$:

$$\delta(s)_n = \sum_{m \leq n} \mu(m,n)\delta(f)^m(\delta(c))$$

equivalently:

$$\delta(s)_n = \begin{cases} \delta(c) & (n = 0) \\ \delta(f)^n(\delta(c)) - \delta(f)^{n-1}(\delta(c)) & (n > 0) \end{cases}$$

Finally, combining the differential versions of the loop and the egress policy, we find:

$$\begin{aligned} \delta(\texttt{out}_k)(\delta(s)) &= \textstyle\sum_{m \leq k} \delta(s)_m \\ &= \textstyle\sum_{m \leq k} \sum_{l \leq m} \mu(l,m)\delta(f)^l(\delta(c)) \\ &= \delta(f)^k(\delta(c)) \end{aligned}$$

and so the differential of the loop followed by the differential of egress is, as expected, the differential of the kth iteration of the loop body.

4 The Programming Language

The language has expressions e of various types σ, given as follows.

Types

$$\sigma ::= b \mid \sigma \times \tau \mid \texttt{unit} \mid \sigma^+$$

where b varies over a given set of *base types*. Types will denote abelian groups with linear inverses, with σ^+ denoting a group of $\mathbb{N}$-streams.

Expressions

$$\begin{array}{rl} e ::= & x \mid f(e_1, \ldots, e_n) \mid \texttt{let}\ x : \sigma\ \texttt{be}\ e\ \texttt{on}\ e' \mid \\ & 0_\sigma \mid e + e' \mid -e \mid \\ & \langle e, e' \rangle \mid \texttt{fst}(e) \mid \texttt{snd}(e) \mid * \mid \\ & \texttt{iter}\ x : \sigma\ \texttt{to}\ e\ \texttt{on}\ e' \mid \texttt{out}_k(e) \quad (k \in \mathbb{N}) \end{array}$$

where we are given a signature $f : \sigma_1, \ldots, \sigma_n \to \sigma$ of *basic function symbols.* (The basic types and function symbols are the built-ins.) The iteration construct $\texttt{iter}\ x : \sigma\ \texttt{to}\ e\ \texttt{on}\ e'$ produces the stream obtained by iterating the function $\lambda x : \sigma.\, e$, starting from the value produced by e'. The expression $\texttt{out}_k(e)$ produces the kth element of the stream produced by e.

Typing Environments $\Gamma = x_1 : \sigma_1, \ldots, x_n : \sigma_n$ are sequences of variable bindings, with no variable repetition. We give axioms and rules to establish *typing judgments*, which have the form $\Gamma \vdash e : \sigma$.

Typing Axioms and Rules

$$\Gamma \vdash x : \sigma \quad (x : \sigma \in \Gamma)$$

$$\frac{\Gamma \vdash e_i : \sigma_i \ (i = 1, \ldots, n)}{\Gamma \vdash f(e_1, \ldots, e_n) : \sigma} \quad (f : \sigma_1, \ldots, \sigma_n \to \sigma)$$

$$\frac{\Gamma \vdash e : \sigma \quad \Gamma, x : \sigma \vdash e' : \tau}{\Gamma \vdash \texttt{let}\ x : \sigma\ \texttt{be}\ e\ \texttt{on}\ e' : \tau}$$

$$\Gamma \vdash 0_\sigma : \sigma \qquad \frac{\Gamma \vdash e : \sigma \quad \Gamma \vdash e' : \sigma}{\Gamma \vdash e + e' : \sigma} \qquad \frac{\Gamma \vdash e : \sigma}{\Gamma \vdash -e : \sigma}$$

$$\frac{\Gamma \vdash e : \sigma \quad \Gamma \vdash e' : \tau}{\Gamma \vdash \langle e, e' \rangle : \sigma \times \tau} \qquad \frac{\Gamma \vdash e : \sigma \times \tau}{\Gamma \vdash \texttt{fst}(e) : \sigma} \qquad \frac{\Gamma \vdash e : \sigma \times \tau}{\Gamma \vdash \texttt{snd}(e) : \tau}$$

$$\frac{\Gamma, x : \sigma \vdash e : \sigma \qquad \Gamma \vdash e' : \sigma}{\Gamma \vdash \texttt{iter}\ x : \sigma\ \texttt{to}\ e\ \texttt{on}\ e' : \sigma^+} \qquad \frac{\Gamma \vdash e : \sigma^+}{\Gamma \vdash \texttt{out}_k(e) : \sigma}$$

Proposition 4. *(Unique typing) For any environment Γ and expression e, there is at most one type σ such that $\Gamma \vdash e : \sigma$.*

In fact, there will also be a unique derivation of $\Gamma \vdash e : \sigma$.

4.1 Language Semantics

Types Types are modeled by abelian groups with inverses, as described in Section 2. For for each basic type b we assume given an abelian group with inverses $(\mathcal{B}[\![b]\!], \delta_b, S_b)$. The denotational semantics of types is then:

$$\begin{aligned} \mathcal{D}[\![b]\!] &= \mathcal{B}[\![b]\!] \\ \mathcal{D}[\![\sigma \times \tau]\!] &= \mathcal{D}[\![\sigma]\!] \times \mathcal{D}[\![\tau]\!] \\ \mathcal{D}[\![\mathtt{unit}]\!] &= \mathbb{1} \\ \mathcal{D}[\![\sigma^+]\!] &= \mathcal{D}[\![\sigma]\!]^{\mathbb{N}} \end{aligned}$$

Expressions For each basic function symbol $f : \sigma_1, \ldots, \sigma_n \to \sigma$ we assume given a map:

$$\mathcal{B}[\![f]\!] : \mathcal{D}[\![\sigma_1]\!] \times \ldots \times \mathcal{D}[\![\sigma_n]\!] \longrightarrow \mathcal{D}[\![\sigma]\!] \,.$$

We do *not* assume these are linear, multilinear, or preserve the δ's or S's.

Let $\mathcal{D}[\![\Gamma]\!] = \mathcal{D}[\![\sigma_1]\!] \times \ldots \times \mathcal{D}[\![\sigma_n]\!]$ for $\Gamma = x : \sigma_1, \ldots, x_n : \sigma_n$. Then for each $\Gamma \vdash e : \sigma$ we define its semantics with type:

$$\mathcal{D}[\![\Gamma \vdash e : \sigma]\!] : \mathcal{D}[\![\Gamma]\!] \longrightarrow \mathcal{D}[\![\sigma]\!]$$

In case Γ, σ are evident, we may just write $\mathcal{D}[\![e]\!]$.

Definition of $\mathcal{D}$ We define $\mathcal{D}[\![\Gamma \vdash e : \sigma]\!](\alpha) \in \mathcal{D}[\![\sigma]\!]$, for each $\alpha \in \mathcal{D}[\![\Gamma]\!]$ by structural induction on e as follows:

$$\begin{aligned} \mathcal{D}[\![\Gamma \vdash x_i : \sigma_i]\!](\alpha) &= \alpha_i \\ \mathcal{D}[\![\Gamma \vdash f(e_1, \ldots, e_n) : \sigma]\!](\alpha) &= \mathcal{B}[\![f]\!](\mathcal{D}[\![e_1]\!](\alpha), \ldots, \mathcal{D}[\![e_n]\!](\alpha)) \\ \mathcal{D}[\![\Gamma \vdash \mathtt{let}\ x : \sigma\ \mathtt{be}\ e\ \mathtt{on}\ e' : \tau]\!](\alpha) &= \mathcal{D}[\![\Gamma, x : \sigma \vdash e']\!](\alpha, \mathcal{D}[\![e]\!](\alpha)) \\ \mathcal{D}[\![\Gamma \vdash 0_\sigma : \sigma]\!](\alpha) &= 0_{\mathcal{D}[\![\sigma]\!]} \\ \mathcal{D}[\![\Gamma \vdash e + e' : \sigma]\!](\alpha) &= \mathcal{D}[\![e]\!](\alpha) +_{\mathcal{D}[\![\sigma]\!]} \mathcal{D}[\![e']\!](\alpha) \\ \mathcal{D}[\![\Gamma \vdash -e : \sigma]\!](\alpha) &= -_{\mathcal{D}[\![\sigma]\!]}(\mathcal{D}[\![e]\!](\alpha)) \\ \mathcal{D}[\![\Gamma \vdash \langle e, e' \rangle : \sigma \times \tau]\!](\alpha) &= (\mathcal{D}[\![e]\!](\alpha), \mathcal{D}[\![e']\!](\alpha)) \\ \mathcal{D}[\![\Gamma \vdash \mathtt{fst}(e) : \sigma]\!](\alpha) &= \pi_0(\mathcal{D}[\![e]\!](\alpha)) \\ \mathcal{D}[\![\Gamma \vdash \mathtt{snd}(e) : \tau]\!](\alpha) &= \pi_1(\mathcal{D}[\![e]\!](\alpha)) \\ \mathcal{D}[\![\Gamma \vdash * : \mathtt{unit}]\!](\alpha) &= * \\ \mathcal{D}[\![\Gamma \vdash \mathtt{iter}\ x{:}\sigma\ \mathtt{to}\ e\ \mathtt{on}\ e' {:} \sigma^+]\!](\alpha)_n &= (\lambda a{:}\mathcal{D}[\![\sigma]\!].\, \mathcal{D}[\![e]\!](\alpha, a))^n(\mathcal{D}[\![e']\!](\alpha)) \\ \mathcal{D}[\![\Gamma \vdash \mathtt{out}_k(e) : \sigma]\!](\alpha) &= \mathtt{out}_k(\mathcal{D}[\![e]\!](\alpha)) \end{aligned}$$

The semantics of iteration is in accord with the discussion of the solution of Equation 1 for loops.

4.2 Differential Semantics

We next define the differential semantics of our expressions. It has the same form as the ordinary semantics:

$$\mathcal{D}^\delta[\![\Gamma \vdash e : \sigma]\!] : \mathcal{D}[\![\Gamma]\!] \longrightarrow \mathcal{D}[\![\sigma]\!]$$

The semantics of types is not changed from the non-differential case.

First for $f : \sigma_1, \ldots, \sigma_n \to \sigma$ we set

$$\mathcal{B}^\delta[\![f]\!](\alpha_1, \ldots, \alpha_n) = \delta_{\mathcal{D}[\![\sigma]\!]}(\mathcal{B}[\![f]\!](S_{\mathcal{D}[\![\sigma_1]\!]}(\alpha_1), \ldots, S_{\mathcal{D}[\![\sigma_n]\!]}(\alpha_n))$$

Then $\mathcal{D}^\delta$ is defined exactly as for the non-differential case except for iteration and egress where, following the discussion of loops, we set

$$\begin{array}{l}\mathcal{D}^\delta[\![\Gamma \vdash \texttt{iter}\ x : \sigma\ \texttt{to}\ e\ \texttt{on}\ e' : \sigma^+]\!](\alpha)(n) = \\ \qquad \sum_{n' \le n} \mu(n', n)(\lambda a : \mathcal{D}[\![\sigma]\!].\mathcal{D}^\delta[\![e]\!](\alpha, a))^{n'}(\mathcal{D}^\delta[\![e]\!](\alpha)))\end{array}$$

and

$$\mathcal{D}^\delta[\![\Gamma \vdash \texttt{out}_k(e) : \sigma]\!](\alpha) = \sum_{n \le k} \mathcal{D}^\delta[\![e]\!](\alpha)(n)$$

Theorem 1. *(Correctness of differential semantics) Suppose $\Gamma \vdash e : \sigma$. Then:*

$$\mathcal{D}^\delta[\![\Gamma \vdash e : \sigma]\!](\alpha) = \delta_{\mathcal{D}[\![\sigma]\!]}(\mathcal{D}[\![\Gamma \vdash e : \sigma]\!](S_{\mathcal{D}[\![\sigma]\!]}(\alpha)))$$

equivalently:

$$\mathcal{D}^\delta[\![\Gamma \vdash e : \sigma]\!](\delta_{\mathcal{D}[\![\sigma]\!]}(\alpha)) = \delta_{\mathcal{D}[\![\sigma]\!]}(\mathcal{D}[\![\Gamma \vdash e : \sigma]\!](\alpha))$$

Proof. The first of these equivalent statements is proved by structural induction on expressions. We only give the last two cases of the proof.

Iteration:

$$\begin{array}{l}\mathcal{D}^\delta[\![\Gamma \vdash \texttt{iter}\ x : \sigma\ \texttt{to}\ e\ \texttt{on}\ e' : \sigma^+]\!](\alpha)(n) \\ \quad = \sum_{n' \le n} \mu(n', n)(\lambda a : \mathcal{D}[\![\sigma]\!].\, \mathcal{D}^\delta[\![e]\!](\alpha, a))^{n'}(\mathcal{D}^\delta[\![e']\!](\alpha)) \\ \quad = \sum_{n' \le n} \mu(n', n)(\lambda a : \mathcal{D}[\![\sigma]\!].\, \delta(\mathcal{D}[\![e]\!](S\alpha, Sa)))^{n'}(\delta(\mathcal{D}[\![e']\!](S\alpha)))\ \text{(by IH)} \\ \quad = \sum_{n' \le n} \mu(n', n)(\delta \circ (\lambda a : \mathcal{D}[\![\sigma]\!].\, \mathcal{D}[\![e]\!](S\alpha, a)) \circ S)^{n'}(\delta(\mathcal{D}[\![e']\!](S\alpha))) \\ \quad = \sum_{n' \le n} \mu(n', n)\delta((\lambda a : \mathcal{D}[\![\sigma]\!].\, \mathcal{D}[\![e]\!](S\alpha, a))^{n'}(\mathcal{D}[\![e']\!](S\alpha))) \\ \quad = \sum_{n' \le n} \mu(n', n)\delta(\mathcal{D}[\![\texttt{iter}\ x : \sigma\ \texttt{to}\ e\ \texttt{on}\ e']\!](S\alpha)(n')) \\ \quad = \delta(\mathcal{D}[\![\texttt{iter}\ x : \sigma\ \texttt{to}\ e\ \texttt{on}\ e']\!](S\alpha))(n)\end{array}$$

Egress:

$$\begin{array}{rl}\mathcal{D}^\delta[\![\Gamma \vdash \texttt{out}_k(e) : \sigma]\!](\alpha) & = \sum_{n \le k} \mathcal{D}^\delta[\![e]\!](\alpha)(n) \\ & = \sum_{n \le k} \delta(\mathcal{D}[\![e]\!](S\alpha))(n) \quad \text{(by IH)} \\ & = \sum_{n \le k} \sum_{n' \le n} \mu(n', n)\delta(\mathcal{D}[\![e]\!](S\alpha)(n')) \\ & = \delta(\mathcal{D}[\![e]\!](S\alpha)(k)) \\ & = \delta(\mathcal{D}[\![\texttt{out}_k(e)]\!](S\alpha))\end{array}$$

□

A compositional differential semantics satisfying Theorem 1 exists on general grounds[1], as functions $f : G \to H$ over given abelian groups G, H with inverses are in 1-1 correspondence with their conjugates (the conjugate operator has inverse $f \mapsto S_H \circ f \circ \delta_G$). However the direct definition of the differential semantics is remarkably simple and practical.

[1] We thank the anonymous referee who pointed this out.

5 Priorities

In "prioritized iteration" [2], a sequence of fixed-point computations consumes the input values in batches; each batch consists of the set of values assigned a given priority, and each fixed-point computation starts from the result of the previous one, plus all input values in the next batch.

Such computations can be much more efficient than ordinary iterations, but it was left open in [2] how to implement them correctly for anything more complicated than loop bodies with no nested iteration. The proposed notion of time was the lexicographic product of $\mathbb{N}$ with any nested T, i.e., the partial order on $\mathbb{N} \times T$ with:

$$(e, s) \leq (e', s') \equiv (e < e') \vee (e = e' \wedge s \leq s')$$

where a pair (e, s) is thought of as "stage s in epoch e". Unfortunately, the construction in [2] appears incorrect for $T \neq \mathbb{N}$. Moreover, the lexicographic product is not locally finite, so our theory cannot be applied.

It may be that the use of lexicographic products can be rescued. We propose instead to avoid these difficulties by using a simple generalization of iteration where new input can be introduced at each iteration. One use of this generality is prioritized iteration, where elements with priority i are introduced at iteration $i \times k$; this scheme provides exactly k iterations for each priority, before moving to the next priority starting from where the previous priority left off. This is exactly the prioritized iteration strategy from [2] with the fixed-iteration-number loop-egress policy, but cast in a framework where we can verify its correctness.

The generalisation of Equation 1 is:

$$d = c + \mathtt{fb}(f^{\mathbb{N}}(d)) \tag{3}$$

where now c is in $G^{\mathbb{N}}$ (rather than in G, and placed at iteration 0 by `in`). This equation is equivalent to the two iteration equations $d_0 = c_0$ and $d_{n+1} = c_{n+1} + f(d_n)$ and so has a unique solution, say s. Differentiating Equation 3, we obtain:

$$d = \delta(c) + \mathtt{fb}(\delta(f^{\mathbb{N}})(d))$$

By the remark in Section 3 on fixed-points of function differentials, this also has a unique solution, viz. $\delta(s)$. To adapt the language, one simply changes the iteration construct typing rule to:

$$\frac{\Gamma, x : \sigma \vdash e : \sigma \qquad \Gamma \vdash e' : \sigma^+}{\Gamma \vdash \mathtt{iter}\ x : \sigma\ \mathtt{to}\ e\ \mathtt{on}\ e' : \sigma^+}$$

We assume the ingress function is available as a built-in function; other built-in functions can enable the use of priority functions. The semantics of this version of iteration is given by:

$$\mathcal{D}[\![\Gamma \vdash \mathtt{iter}\ x{:}\sigma\ \mathtt{to}\ e\ \mathtt{on}\ e'{:}\sigma^+]\!](\alpha) = \mu d{:}\mathcal{D}[\![\sigma^+]\!].\, \mathcal{D}[\![e']\!](\alpha) + \mathtt{fb}(\mathcal{D}[\![e]\!](\alpha, d))$$

where we are making use of the usual notation for fixed-points; that is justified here by the discussion of Equation 3. The differential semantics has exactly the same form, and Theorem 1 extends.

6 Discussion

We have given mathematical foundations for differential dataflow, which was introduced in [2]. By accounting for differentials using Möbius inversion, we systematically justified various operator and loop differentials discussed there. Using the theory we could also distinguish the difficult case of lexicographic products, and justify an alternative.

Via a schematic language we showed that a differential semantics is the differential of the ordinary semantics, verifying the intuition that to compute the differential of a computation, one only changes how individual operators are computed, but not its overall shape. (We could have given a more concrete language with selection and other such operators, but we felt our approach brought out the underlying ideas more clearly.)

There are some natural possibilities for further work. As mentioned in the introduction, one might formulate a small-step operational semantics that propagates differences in a dataflow graph; one would prove a soundness theorem linking it to the denotational semantics. It would also be interesting to consider the egress policy of exiting on a first repetition, i.e., at the first k such that $c_k = c_{k+1}$, where c is the output stream. As no such k may exist, one is led to consider partial streams, as mentioned in the introduction. This would need a theory of Möbius inversion for partial functions, but would also give the possibility, via standard domain theory, of a general recursion construct, and so of more general loops.

References

1. Bhatotia, P., Wieder, A., Rodrigues, R., Acar, U.A., Pasquin, R.: Incoop: MapReduce for incremental computations. In: Proc. 2nd ACM Symposium on Cloud Computing, 7p. (2011)
2. McSherry, F., Murray, D.G., Isaacs, R., Isard, M.: Differential dataflow. In: Proc. Sixth Biennial Conference on Innovative Data Systems Research (2013), `http://www.cidrdb.org`
3. Mihaylov, S.R., Ives, Z.G., Guha, S.: REX: recursive, delta-based data-centric computation. Proc. VLDB Endowment 5(11), 1280–1291 (2012)
4. Murray, D.G., McSherry, F., Isaacs, R., Isard, M., Barham, P., Abadi, M.: Naiad: a timely dataflow system. In: Proc. ACM SIGOPS 24th. Symposium on Operating Systems Principles, pp. 439–455 (2013)
5. Rota, G.-C.: On the foundations of combinatorial theory I, Theory of Möbius functions. Probability Theory and Related Fields 2(4), 340–368 (1964)
6. Stanley, R.P.: Enumerative Combinatorics, vol. 1. CUP (2011)

Categorical Models and Logics

States of Convex Sets

Bart Jacobs, Bas Westerbaan, and Bram Westerbaan

Institute for Computing and Information Sciences,
Radboud Universiteit Nijmegen, The Netherlands
{bart,bwesterb,awesterb}@cs.ru.nl

Abstract. State spaces in probabilistic and quantum computation are convex sets, that is, Eilenberg–Moore algebras of the distribution monad. This article studies some computationally relevant properties of convex sets. We introduce the term effectus for a category with suitable coproducts (so that predicates, as arrows of the shape $X \to 1 + 1$, form effect modules, and states, arrows of the shape $1 \to X$, form convex sets). One main result is that the category of *cancellative* convex sets is such an effectus. A second result says that the state functor is a "map of effecti". We also define 'normalisation of states' and show how this property is closed related to conditional probability. This is elaborated in an example of probabilistic Bayesian inference.

1 Introduction

The defining property of a convex set X is its closure under convex combinations. This means that for $x, y \in X$ and $\lambda \in [0, 1]$ the convex combination $\lambda x + (1 - \lambda)y$ is also in X. There are some subtle properties that these convex combinations should satisfy, going back to Stone [Sto49]. Here we shall use a more abstract — but equivalent — categorical approach and call an Eilenberg–Moore algebra of the distribution monad $\mathcal{D}$ a convex set.

It is a basic fact that state spaces (*i.e.* sets of states) in probabilistic computation (both discrete and continuous) and in quantum computation are convex sets. Any serious model of such forms of computation will thus involve convex structures. It is within this line of research that the present paper contributes by clarifying several issues in the (computational) theory of convex sets. On a technical level the paper pinpoints (1) the relevance of a property of convex sets called 'cancellation', and (2) a 'normalisation' condition that is crucial for conditional probability and (Bayesian) inference.

These two points may seem strange and obscure. However, they play an important role in an ongoing project [Jac14] to determine the appropriate categorical axiomatisation for probabilistic and quantum logic and computation. Here we introduce the term 'effectus' for such a category. The main technical results of the paper can then be summarised as: the category **CConv** of **cancellative** convex sets is an effectus, and: the state functor Stat: $\mathbf{B} \to \mathbf{CConv}$ from an arbitrary effectus $\mathbf{B}$ to **CConv** is a map of effecti. We illustrate how these results solidify the notion of effectus, and its associated state-and-effect triangle.

A. Pitts (Ed.): FOSSACS 2015, LNCS 9034, pp. 87–101, 2015.
DOI: 10.1007/978-3-662-46678-0_6

We further show that conditional probability and (Bayesian) inference can be described both succinctly and generally via the idea of normalisation of stages.

Convex structures play an important role in mathematics (esp. functional analysis, see *e.g.* [AE80]), and in many application areas like economics. In the context of the axiomatisation of quantum (and probability) theory they are used systematically in for instance [Gud73] or [Fri09, BW11]. This paper fits in the latter line of research. It continues and refines [Jac14], by concentrating on the role of state spaces and their structure as convex sets.

The paper starts by describing background information on (discrete probability) distributions and convex sets. Coproducts + of convex sets play an important role in the sequel, and are analysed in some detail. Subsequently, Section 3 concentrates on a well-known property of convex sets, known as cancellation. We recall how cancellation can be formulated in various ways, and show the equivalence with a joint monicity property that occurs in earlier work on categorical quantum axiomatisation [Jac14]. Section 4 introduces a categorical description of the well-known phenomenon of normalisation in probability. Finally, the resulting abstract description of conditional state in Section 6 is illustrated in a concrete example in Bayesian inference, using probability distributions as states.

2 Preliminaries on Distributions and Convex Sets

For an arbitrary set X we write $\mathcal{D}(X)$ for the set of formal finite convex combinations of elements from X. These elements of $\mathcal{D}(X)$ will be represented in two equivalent ways.

- As formal convex sums $\lambda_1 |x_1\rangle + \cdots + \lambda_n |x_n\rangle$, for $x_i \in X$ and $\lambda_i \in [0,1]$ with $\sum_i \lambda_i = 1$. We use the 'ket' notation $|x\rangle$ in such formal sums to prevent confusion with elements $x \in X$.
- As functions $\varphi\colon X \to [0,1]$ with finite support and $\sum_x \varphi(x) = 1$. The support of φ is the set $\{\, x \in X : \varphi(x) \neq 0 \,\}$.

Elements of $\mathcal{D}(X)$ are also called (discrete probability) distributions over X.

The mapping $X \mapsto \mathcal{D}(X)$ can be made functorial: for $f\colon X \to Y$ we get a function $\mathcal{D}(f)\colon \mathcal{D}(X) \to \mathcal{D}(Y)$ which may be described in two equivalent ways:

$$\mathcal{D}(f)\big(\textstyle\sum_i \lambda_i |x_i\rangle\,\big) = \textstyle\sum_i \lambda_i |f(x_i)\rangle \qquad \text{or} \qquad \mathcal{D}(f)(\varphi)(y) = \textstyle\sum_{x\in f^{-1}(y)} \varphi(x).$$

Moreover, $\mathcal{D}$ is a monad, with unit $\eta\colon X \to \mathcal{D}(X)$ given by $\eta(x) = 1|x\rangle$, and multiplication $\mu\colon \mathcal{D}^2(X) \to \mathcal{D}(X)$ by $\mu(\sum_i \lambda_i |\varphi\rangle\,)(x) = \sum_i \lambda_i \cdot \varphi_i(x)$. This monad is *monoidal* (or sometimes called *commutative*) from which the following result follows by general categorical reasoning (see [Koc71a, Koc71b]).

Proposition 1. *The category* **Conv** $= \mathcal{EM}(\mathcal{D})$ *of Eilenberg–Moore algebras is both complete and cocomplete, and it is symmetric monoidal closed. The tensor unit is the final singleton set* 1*, since* $\mathcal{D}(1) \cong 1$*.* □

We recall that an Eilenberg–Moore algebra (of the monad $\mathcal{D}$) is a map of the form $\gamma\colon \mathcal{D}(X) \to X$ satisfying $\gamma \circ \eta = \mathrm{id}$ and $\gamma \circ \mu = \gamma \circ \mathcal{D}(\gamma)$. A morphism $\big(\mathcal{D}(X) \xrightarrow{\gamma} X\big) \longrightarrow \big(\mathcal{D}(X') \xrightarrow{\gamma'} X'\big)$ in $\mathcal{EM}(\mathcal{D})$ is a map $f\colon X \to X'$ with $f \circ \gamma = \gamma' \circ \mathcal{D}(f)$. An important point is that we identify an algebra with a convex set: the map $\gamma\colon \mathcal{D}(X) \to X$ turns a formal convex combination into an actual element in X. Maps of algebras preserve such convex sums and are commonly called *affine* functions. Therefore we often write **Conv** for the category $\mathcal{EM}(\mathcal{D})$.

Examples 2. *1. Let X be a set. The space $\mathcal{D}(X)$ of formal convex combinations over X is itself a convex set (with structure map $\mu_X\colon \mathcal{D}^2(X) \to \mathcal{D}(X)$). Given a natural number n the space $\mathcal{D}(n+1)$ is (isomorphic to) the n-th* simplex. *E.g., $\mathcal{D}(1)$ contains a single point, and $\mathcal{D}(2)$, $\mathcal{D}(3)$ and $\mathcal{D}(4)$ are pictured right.*

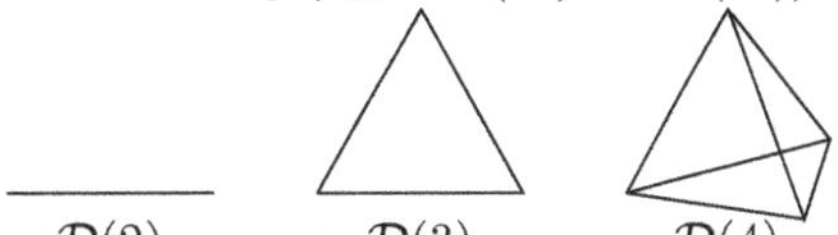

$\mathcal{D}(2)$ $\mathcal{D}(3)$ $\mathcal{D}(4)$

2. Any real vector space V is a convex set with structure map $\gamma\colon \mathcal{D}(V) \to V$ given by, $\gamma(\varphi) = \sum_{v \in V} \varphi(v) \cdot v$, for $\varphi \in \mathcal{D}(V)$. 3. Obviously a convex subset of a convex space is again a convex set. 4. A convex set which is isomorphic to a convex subset of a real vector space is called **representable**. *For every set X the space $\mathcal{D}(X)$ is representable since $\mathcal{D}(X)$ is a subset of the real vector space of functions from X to $\mathbb{R}$.*

In the remainder of this section we concentrate on coproducts of convex sets. Each category of algebras for a monad on **Sets** is cocomplete, by a theorem of Linton, see *e.g.* [BW85, § 9.3, Prop. 4]. This applies in particular to the category **Conv** $= \mathcal{EM}(\mathcal{D})$, see Proposition 1. Hence we know that coproducts $+$ exist in **Conv**, but the problem is that the abstract construction of such coproducts of algebras uses a coequaliser in the category of algebras. Our aim is to get a more concrete description. We proceed by first describing the coproduct $X_\bullet = X + 1$ in **Conv**, where 1 is the final one-element convex set $1 = \{\bullet\}$.

Elements of this 'lift' $X_\bullet = X + 1$ can be thought of as being either λx for $\lambda(0,1]$ and $x \in X$, or the special element $\bullet$. This lift construction will be useful to construct the coproduct of convex sets later on.

Definition 3. *Let X be a convex set, via $\alpha\colon \mathcal{D}(X) \to X$. Define the set*

$$X_\bullet \;=\; \{\, (\lambda, x) \in [0,1] \times (\, X \cup \{\bullet\}\,) \colon\; \lambda = 0 \;\text{ iff }\; x = \bullet \,\}.$$

We will often write $(0, e)$ even when e is an expression that does not make sense. In that case, by $(0, e)$ we mean $(0, \bullet)$. For example, $(0, \frac{1}{0}) = (0, \bullet)$. Given $(\lambda, x) \in X_\bullet$, we call λ the weight *of (λ, x) and denote it as $|(\lambda, x)| = \lambda$.*

Now, we may define a convex structure $\beta\colon \mathcal{D}(X_\bullet) \to X_\bullet$ succinctly:

$$\beta(\, \rho_1 \,|(\lambda_1, x_1)\rangle + \cdots + \rho_n \,|(\lambda_n, x_n)\rangle \,) \;=\; (\, \zeta,\, \alpha(\tfrac{\rho_1 \lambda_1}{\zeta} \,|x_1\rangle + \cdots + \tfrac{\rho_n \lambda_n}{\zeta} \,|x_n\rangle) \,),$$

where $\zeta = \lambda_1 \rho_1 + \cdots + \lambda_n \rho_n$. Given an affine map $f\colon X \to Y$, define $f_\bullet\colon X_\bullet \to Y_\bullet$ by $f_\bullet(\lambda, x) = (\lambda, f(x))$ where $f(\bullet) := \bullet$.

Lemma 4. *This* $(X_\bullet, \beta)$ *is a convex set and it is the coproduct* $X + 1$ *in* **Conv**.

Proof. The equation $\beta \circ \eta = \mathrm{id}$ is easy: for $(x, \lambda) \in X_\bullet$,

$$\beta(\eta(\lambda, x)) = \beta(\,|(\lambda, x)\rangle\,) = (\lambda, \alpha(\tfrac{\lambda}{\lambda}|x\rangle)) = (\lambda, \alpha(|x\rangle)) = (\lambda, x).$$

Verification of the μ-equation is left to the reader. There are obvious coprojections $\kappa_1 \colon X \to X_\bullet$ and $\kappa_2 \colon 1 \to X_\bullet$ given by $\kappa_1(x) = (1, x)$ and $\kappa_2(\bullet) = (0, \bullet)$. Given any convex set Y with $\gamma \colon \mathcal{D}(Y) \to Y$ together with affine maps $c_1 \colon X \to Y$ and $c_2 \colon 1 \to Y$, we can define a unique affine map $h \colon X_\bullet \to Y$ by $h(\lambda, x) = \gamma(\,\lambda\,|c_1(x)\rangle + (1-\lambda)\,|c_2(\bullet)\rangle\,)$. When $x = \bullet$ (and so $\lambda = 0$) we interpret $h(\lambda, x) = \gamma(|c_2(\bullet)\rangle)$. □

This lifted convex set $X_\bullet$ provides a simple description of coproducts.

Proposition 5. *The coproduct of two convex sets* X *and* Y *can be identified with the convex subset of* $X_\bullet \times Y_\bullet$ *of pairs whose weights sum to one. That is:*

$$X + Y \;\cong\; \{\, (x, y) \in X_\bullet \times Y_\bullet \colon\; |x| + |y| = 1 \,\}$$

The convex structure on this subset is inherited from the product $X_\bullet \times Y_\bullet$. *The first coprojection is given by* $\kappa_1(x) = \langle\, (1, x), (0, \bullet)\,\rangle$, *and there is a similar expression for* κ_2. *The cotuple is* $[f, g]((\lambda, x), (\rho, y)) = \lambda f(x) + \rho g(y)$. □

There is a similar description for the coproduct of n convex sets. E.g., for $n = 3$,

$$X + Y + Z = \{\, (x, y, z) \in X_\bullet \times Y_\bullet \times Z_\bullet \colon\; |x| + |y| + |z| = 1 \,\}.$$

From now on we shall use this concrete description for the coproduct $+$ in **Conv**. By the way, the initial object in **Conv** is simply the empty set, $\emptyset$.

3 The Cancellation Property for Convex Sets

The cancellation property that will be defined next plays an important role in the theory of convex sets. This section collects several equivalent descriptions from the literature, and adds one new equivalent property, expressed in terms of 'jointly monicity', see Theorem 8 (4) below. Crucially, this property is part of the axiomatisation proposed in [Jac14], and its equivalence to cancellation is the main contribution of this section.

Definition 6. *Let* X *be a convex set. We call* X ***cancellative*** *provided that for all* $x, y_1, y_2 \in X$ *and* $\lambda \in [0, 1]$ *with* $\lambda \neq 1$ *we have*

$$\lambda x + (1 - \lambda) y_1 = \lambda x + (1 - \lambda) y_2 \qquad \Longrightarrow \qquad y_1 = y_2.$$

We write **CConv** $\hookrightarrow$ **Conv** *for the full subcategory of cancellative convex sets.*

Representable convex sets — subsets of real vector spaces — clearly satisfy this cancellation property. But not all convex sets do.

Examples 7. *1. If we remove from the unit interval* $[0,1]$ *the point* 1 *and replace it by a copy of the unit interval whose points we will denote by* 1_a *for* $a \in [0,1]$, *we get a convex space we will call* $\dashv$ *(pictured right). The convex structure on* $\dashv$ *is such that the inclusion* $a \mapsto 1_a$ *is affine and the quotient* $\dashv \to [0,1]$ *which maps* 1_a *to* 1 *and* $[0,1)$ *on itself is affine. We have* $\frac{1}{2} \cdot 0 + \frac{1}{2} \cdot 1_0 = \frac{1}{2} = \frac{1}{2} \cdot 0 + \frac{1}{2} \cdot 1_1$, *but* $1_0 \neq 1_1$. *Thus* $\dashv$ *is not cancellative and hence not representable.*

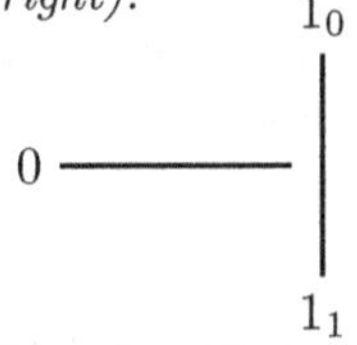

2. A semilattice L *becomes a convex set if we define* $\sum_i \lambda_i x_i = \bigvee_i x_i$ *for all* $x_i \in L$ *and* $\lambda_i \in (0,1]$ *with* $\sum_i \lambda_i = 1$ *(see [Neu70], §4.5). The semilattice* L *is cancellative as convex set if and only if* $x = y$ *for all* $x, y \in L$.

Theorem 8. *For a convex set* X *the following statements are equivalent.*

1. *X is cancellative — see Definition 6;*
2. *X is representable, i.e. isomorphic to a convex subset of a real vector space;*
3. *X is* separated, *in the sense that for all* $x, y \in X$ *if* $f(x) = f(y)$ *for all affine maps* $f\colon X \to \mathbb{R}$, *then* $x = y$;
4. *The two maps* $[\kappa_1, \kappa_2, \kappa_2]$, $[\kappa_2, \kappa_1, \kappa_2]\colon X + X + X \to X + X$ *are jointly monic in* **Conv**.

Proof. (3) $\Longrightarrow$ (2) Let $\mathrm{Aff}(X)$ denote the set of affine maps $X \to \mathbb{R}$, and V the vector space of (all) functions $\mathrm{Aff}(X) \to \mathbb{R}$, with pointwise structure. Let $\eta\colon X \to V$ be given by $\eta(x)(f) = f(x)$. We will prove that η is an injective affine map, making X representable.

Let $x_1, \ldots, x_N \in X$ and $\lambda_1, \ldots, \lambda_N \in [0,1]$ with $\sum_n \lambda_n = 1$ be given, and also $f \in \mathrm{Aff}(X)$ be given. Since f is affine, we get that η is affine too:

$$\begin{aligned}
\eta(\,\lambda_1 x_1 + \cdots + \lambda_N x_N\,)(f) &= f(\,\lambda_1 x_1 + \cdots + \lambda_N x_N\,) \\
&= \lambda_1 f(x_1) + \cdots + \lambda_N f(x_N) \\
&= \lambda_1 \eta(x_1)(f) + \cdots + \lambda_N \eta(x_N)(f) \\
&= (\,\lambda_1 \eta(x_1) + \cdots + \lambda_N \eta(x_N)\,)(f).
\end{aligned}$$

Towards injectivity of η, let $x, y \in X$ with $\eta(x) = \eta(y)$ be given. Then for each $f \in \mathrm{Aff}(X)$ we have $f(x) = \eta(x)(f) = \eta(y)(f) = f(y)$. Thus $x = y$ since X is separated.

(2) $\Longrightarrow$ (3) Since X is representable we may assume X is a convex subset of a real vector space V. Let $x, y \in X$ with $x \neq y$ be given. To show that X is separated we must find an affine map $f\colon X \to \mathbb{R}$ such that $f(x) \neq f(y)$.

Since $x \neq y$, we have that $x - y \neq 0$. By Zorn's lemma there is a maximal linearly independent set $\mathcal{B}$ which contains $x - y$. The set $\mathcal{B}$ spans V for if $v \in V$ is not in the span of $\mathcal{B}$ then $\mathcal{B} \cup \{v\}$ is a linearly independent set and $\mathcal{B}$ is not maximal. Thus $\mathcal{B}$ is a base for V. There is a unique linear map $f\colon \mathcal{B} \to \mathbb{R}$ such that $f(x-y) = 1$ and $f(b) = 0$ for all $b \in \mathcal{B}$ with $b \neq x - y$. Note that $f(x) \neq f(y)$. Let $g\colon X \to \mathbb{R}$ be the restriction of f to X. Then g is an affine map and $g(x) = f(x) \neq f(y) = g(y)$. Hence X is separated.

(2) $\Longrightarrow$ (1) is easy.
(1) $\Longrightarrow$ (2) We give an outline of the proof, but leave the key step to Stone (see [Sto49]). Let V be the real vector space of functions from X to $\mathbb{R}$ with finite support. Recall that $\mathcal{D}(X) = \{f \in V \colon \sum_{x \in X} f(x) = 1\}$. So we have a map $\eta_X \colon X \to \mathcal{D}(X) \subseteq V$. Let I be the linear span of

$$\{\, \eta_X(\gamma(f)) - f \colon\ f \in \mathcal{D}(X) \,\} \tag{1}$$

where $\gamma \colon \mathcal{D}(X) \to X$ is the structure map of X. Let $q \colon V \to V/I$ be the quotient map. Then by definition of I, the map $q \circ \eta_X \colon X \longrightarrow V$ is affine. So to show that X is representable it suffices to show that $q \circ \eta_X$ is injective. Let $x, y \in X$ with $q(\eta_X(x)) = q(\eta_X(y))$ be given. We must show that $x = y$. We have $f := \eta_X(x) - \eta_Y(y) \in I$. So f is a linear combination of elements from the set in (1). By the same syntactic argument as in the proof of Theorem 1 of [Sto49] we get that $f = 0$ since X is cancellative, and thus $x = y$.
(1) $\Longrightarrow$ (4) Write $\nabla_1 = [\kappa_1, \kappa_2, \kappa_2]$ and $\nabla_2 = [\kappa_2, \kappa_1, \kappa_2]$. We will prove that ∇_1 and ∇_2 are jointly injective (and thus jointly monic). Let $a, b \in X + X + X$ with $\nabla_1(a) = \nabla_1(b)$ and $\nabla_2(a) = \nabla_2(b)$ be given. We must show that $a = b$. Write $a \equiv (a_1, a_2, a_3)$ and $b \equiv (b_1, b_2, b_3)$ (see Proposition 5). Then we have

$$\nabla_1(a) \;=\; (\, a_1,\, a_2 \oplus a_3\,), \qquad \nabla_2(a) \;=\; (\, a_2,\, a_1 \oplus a_3\,), \tag{2}$$

where $\oplus$ is the partial binary operation on $X_\bullet$ given by

$$(\lambda, x) \oplus (\mu, y) \;=\; (\, \lambda + \mu,\ \tfrac{\lambda}{\lambda+\mu} x \,+\, \tfrac{\mu}{\lambda+\mu} y\,)$$

when $\lambda + \mu \leq 1$, and undefined otherwise. By the equalities from Statement (2) and similar equalities for $\nabla_1(b)$ and $\nabla_2(b)$, we get $a_1 = b_1$, $a_2 \oplus a_3 = b_2 \oplus b_3$, $a_2 = b_2$, and $a_1 \oplus a_3 = b_1 \oplus b_3$. It remains to be shown that $a_3 = b_3$. It is easy to see that $\oplus$ is cancellative since X is cancellative. Thus $a_1 \oplus a_3 = b_1 \oplus b_3$ and $a_1 = b_1$ give us that $b_1 = b_3$. Thus $a = b$.
(4) $\Longrightarrow$ (1) We assume that $\nabla_1, \nabla_2 \colon X + X + X \to X + X$ (see above) are jointly monic and must prove that X is cancellative. The affine maps from 1 to $X + X + X$ correspond to the (actual) points of $X + X + X$, so it is not hard to see that ∇_1 and ∇_2 are jointly injective. Let $x_1, x_2, y \in X$ and $\lambda \in [0, 1]$ with $\lambda \neq 0$ and $\lambda x_1 + (1 - \lambda) y = \lambda x_2 + (1 - \lambda) y$ be given. We must show that $x_1 = x_2$.

Write $a_i = (\frac{\lambda}{2-\lambda}, x_i)$ and $b = (\frac{1-\lambda}{2-\lambda}, y)$ (where $i \in \{1, 2\}$). Then $a_i, b \in X_\bullet$. Further, $|a_i| + |b| + |b| = 1$, so $v_i := (b, b, a) \in X + X + X$. Note that

$$a_i \oplus b \;=\; (\, \tfrac{1}{2-\lambda},\ \lambda x_i + (1 - \lambda) y \,).$$

So we see that $a_1 \oplus b = a_2 \oplus b$. We have

$$\begin{aligned} \nabla_1(b, b, a_1) \;&=\; (b, b \oplus a_1) \;=\; (b, b \oplus a_2) \;=\; \nabla_1(b, b, a_2), \\ \nabla_2(b, b, a_1) \;&=\; (b, b \oplus a_1) \;=\; (b, b \oplus a_2) \;=\; \nabla_2(b, b, a_2). \end{aligned}$$

Since ∇_1,∇_2 are jointly injective this entails $a_1 = a_2$. Thus $x_1 = x_2$. $\square$

What we call (cancellative) convex sets appear under various different names in the literature. For instance, cancellative convex sets are called convex structures in [Gud77], convex sets in [Ś74], convex spaces of geometric type in [Fri09], and are the topic of the barycentric calculus of [Sto49]. Convex sets are called semiconvex sets in [Ś74, Flo81], and convex spaces in [Fri09]. The fact that every cancellative convex set is representable as a convex subset of a real vector space was proven by Stone, see Theorem 2 of [Sto49]. The description of convex sets as Eilenberg–Moore algebras is probably due to Świrszcz, see §4.1.3 of [Ś74] (see also [Jac10]), but the (quasi)variety of (cancellative) convex sets was already studied by Neumann [Neu70]. The fact that a convex set is cancellative iff it is separated by functionals was also noted by Gudder, see Theorem 3 of [Gud77]. The separation of points (and subsets) by a functional in a non-cancellative convex set has been studied in detail by Flood [Flo81]. The pathological convex set ⊣ (see Ex. 1) appears in [Fri09].

The duality of states and effects in quantum theory, see [HZ12], is formalised categorically in terms of an adjunction between 'effect modules' and convex sets. An effect module is a positive cancellative partial commutative monoid $(E, \ovee, 0)$ with a selected element 1 such that for all a there is a (unique) $a^\perp$ with $a \ovee a^\perp = 1$ *and* with a compatible action of $[0,1]$. By **EMod**, we denote the category of effect modules with maps that preserve partial addition $\ovee$, scalar multiplication and 1. For details on effect modules we refer to [Jac14], but for the record we should note the following.

Proposition 9. *The adjunction* $\mathbf{EMod}^{op} \leftrightarrows \mathbf{Conv}$ *obtained by "homming into* $[0,1]$*" restricts to an adjunction* $\mathbf{EMod}^{op} \leftrightarrows \mathbf{CConv}$. □

4 Normalisation

This section introduces a categorical description of normalisation, and illustrates what it means in several examples. As far as we know, this is new. Roughly, normalisation says that each non-zero substate can be written as a scalar product of a unique state.

Definition 10. *Let* **C** *be a category with finite coproducts* $(+, 0)$ *and a final object* 1. *We call maps* $1 \to X$ ***states*** *on* X, *and maps* $1 \to X + 1$ ***substates***. *We introduce the property* ***normalisation*** *as follows: for each substate* $\sigma\colon 1 \to X + 1$ *with* $\sigma \neq \kappa_2$ *there is a unique state* $\omega\colon 1 \to X$ *such that* $((\omega \circ !) + id) \circ \sigma = \sigma$. *That is, the diagram to the right commutes. The scalar involved is the map* $(! + \mathrm{id}) \circ \sigma\colon 1 \to 1 + 1$. *(The formulation of normalisation can be simplified a bit in the Kleisli category of the lift monad* $(-) + 1$.*)*

$$\begin{array}{ccc} 1 & \xrightarrow{\ \sigma\ } & X+1 \\ {\scriptstyle\sigma}\downarrow & & \uparrow{\scriptstyle\omega+id} \\ X+1 & \xrightarrow[\ !+id\ ]{} & 1+1 \end{array}$$

Examples 11. *We briefly describe what normalisation means in several categories, and refer to [Jac14] for background information about these categories.*

1. *In the Kleisli category* $\mathcal{K}\ell(\mathcal{D})$ *of the distribution monad* $\mathcal{D}$ *a state* $1 \to X$ *is a distribution* $\omega \in \mathcal{D}(X)$*, and a substate* $1 \to X + 1$ *is a* subdistribution $\sigma \in \mathcal{D}_{\leq 1}(X)$*, for which* $\sum_x \sigma(x) \leq 1$*. If such a* σ *is not* κ_2*, that is, if* $r = \sum_x \sigma(x) \in [0,1]$ *is not zero, take* $\omega(x) = \frac{\varphi(x)}{r}$*. Then* $\sum_x \omega(x) = 1$*.*
2. *Let* $\mathbf{Cstar}_{PU}$ *be the category of* C^**-algebras with positive unital maps. We claim that normalisation holds in the opposite category* $\mathbf{Cstar}_{PU}^{op}$*. The opposite is used in this context because* C^**-algebras form a category of predicate transformers, corresponding to computations going in the reverse direction. In* $\mathbf{Cstar}_{PU}^{op}$ *the complex numbers* $\mathbb{C}$ *are final, and coproducts are given by* $\times$*. Thus, let* $\sigma \colon \mathscr{A} \times \mathbb{C} \to \mathbb{C}$ *be a substate on a* C^**-algebra* $\mathscr{A}$*. If* σ *is not the second projection, then* $r := \sigma(1,0) \in [0,1]$ *is non-zero. Hence we define* $\omega \colon \mathscr{A} \to \mathbb{C}$ *as* $\omega(a) = \frac{\sigma(a,0)}{r}$*. Clearly,* ω *is positive, linear and* $\omega(1) = 1$*. (In fact, substates* $\mathscr{A} \times \mathbb{C} \to \mathbb{C}$ *may be identified with* subunital *positive maps* $\omega \colon \mathscr{A} \to \mathbb{C}$*, for which* $0 \leq \omega(1) \leq 1$*. Normalisation rescales such a map* ω *to* $\omega' := \frac{\omega(-)}{\omega(1)}$ *with* $\omega'(1) = 1$*.)*
3. *The same argument can be used in the opposite category* $\mathbf{EMod}^{op}$ *of effect modules. Hence* $\mathbf{EMod}^{op}$ *also satisfies normalisation.*
4. *Normalisation holds both in* **Conv** *and in* **CConv***, that is, it holds for convex and for cancellative convex sets. This is easy to see using the description* $X + 1 = X_\bullet$ *from Lemma 4. Indeed, if* $\sigma \colon 1 \to X_\bullet$ *is not* κ_2*, then writing* $\sigma(\bullet) \equiv (\lambda, a)$ *we have* $\lambda > 0$ *and* $a \neq \bullet$*. Now take as state* $\omega \colon 1 \to X$ *with* $\omega(1) = a$*.*

In the present context we restrict ourselves to effect modules and convex sets over the unit interval $[0,1]$, and not over some arbitrary effect monoid, like in [Jac14]. Normalisation holds for such effect modules over $[0,1]$ because we can do division $\frac{s}{r}$ in $[0,1]$, for $s \leq r$. More generally, it must be axiomatised in effect monoids. That is beyond the scope of the current article.

5 Effecti

The next definition refines the requirements from [Jac14] and introduces the name 'effectus' for the kind of category at hand. The main result is that taking the states of an arbitrary effects yields a functor to cancellative convex sets, which preserves coproducts. This leads to a robust notion, which is illustrated via the state-and-effect triangle associated with an effectus, which now consists of maps of effecti.

Definition 12. *A category* **C** *is called an* ***effectus*** *if:*

1. *it has a final object* 1 *and finite coproducts* $(0, +)$*;*
2. *the following diagrams are pullbacks;*

$$\begin{array}{ccc} A + X & \xrightarrow{id+g} & A + Y \\ {\scriptstyle f+id}\downarrow & & \downarrow{\scriptstyle f+id} \\ B + X & \xrightarrow[id+g]{} & B + Y \end{array} \qquad \begin{array}{ccc} Y & = & Y \\ {\scriptstyle \kappa_1}\downarrow & & \downarrow{\scriptstyle \kappa_1} \\ Y + A & \xrightarrow[id+g]{} & Y + B \end{array}$$

3. the maps $[\kappa_1, \kappa_2, \kappa_2]$, $[\kappa_2, \kappa_1, \kappa_2]\colon\ X + X + X \to X + X$ *are jointly monic.*

An ***effectus with normalisation*** *is an effectus in which normalisation holds — see Definition 10.*

The main examples of effecti with normalisation — see also Examples 11 — include the Kleisli category $\mathcal{K}\ell(\mathcal{D})$ of the distribution monad $\mathcal{D}$ for discrete probality, but also the Kleisli category $\mathcal{K}\ell(\mathcal{G})$ of the Giry monad for continuous probability (which we don't discuss here). In the quantum setting our main example is the opposite $\mathbf{Cstar}_{\mathrm{PU}}^{\mathrm{op}}$ of the category of C^*-algebras, with positive unital maps.

A **predicate** on an object X in an effectus is an arrow $X \to 1 + 1$. A **scalar** is an arrow $1 \to 1+1$. A **state** on X is an arrow $1 \to X$. We write $\mathrm{Pred}(X)$ and $\mathrm{Stat}(X)$ for the collections of predicates and states on X, so that the scalars are in $\mathrm{Pred}(1) = \mathrm{Stat}(1+1)$. We shall say that $\mathbf{C}$ is an effectus *over* $[0,1]$ if the set of scalars $\mathrm{Pred}(1)$ in $\mathbf{C}$ is (isomorphic to) $[0,1]$. This is the case in all previously mentioned effecti, see Examples 11. An n**-test** on X is a map $X \to n \cdot 1$, where $n \cdot 1$ is the n-fold copower $1 + \cdots + 1$.

This paper goes beyond [Jac14] in that it considers not only effecti but also their morphisms. This gives a new perspective, see the proposition about the predicate functor below.

Definition 13. *Let* $\mathbf{C}$, $\mathbf{D}$ *be two effecti. A* ***map of effecti*** $\mathbf{C} \to \mathbf{D}$ *is a functor that preserves the final object and the finite coproducts (and as a consequence, preserves the two pullbacks in Definition 12).*

The next result is proven in [Jac14], without using the terminology of effecti.

Proposition 14. *Let* $\mathbf{C}$ *be an effectus over* $[0,1]$*. The assignment* $X \mapsto \mathrm{Pred}(X)$ *forms a functor* $\mathrm{Pred}\colon \mathbf{C} \to \mathbf{EMod}^{op}$*. This functor is a map of effecti.* □

This motivates us to see if there is a corresponding result for states, *i.e.* whether the assignment $X \mapsto \mathrm{Stat}(X)$ is also a map of effecti. This is where the cancellation and normalisation properties come into play.

Proposition 15. *The category* **CConv** *of cancellative convex sets is an effectus with normalisation.*

Proof. It is clear that the one-point convex set 1 is cancellative. It is also easy to see using the description of the coproduct of convex sets from Proposition 5 that the coproduct in **Conv** of two cancellative convex sets is cancellative. So the coproducts + of **Conv** restrict to **CConv**.

Moreover, the jointly monic property holds in **CConv** by Theorem 8, and normalisation holds by Example 11 (4). What remains is showing that the two diagrams in Definition 12 are pullbacks in **CConv**. For this we use the representation of the coproduct of (cancellative) convex sets of Proposition 5.

To show that the diagram on the left in Definition 12 (2) is a pullback in **CConv** it suffices to show that it is a pullback in **Sets**, so let elements $(a, y) \in$

$A+Y$ and $(b,x) \in B+X$ with $(f+\mathrm{id})(a,y) = (\mathrm{id}+g)(b,x)$ be given. We must show that there is a unique $e \in A+X$ with the following property, called $P(e)$.

$$(\mathrm{id}+g)(e) \;=\; (a,y) \qquad \text{and} \qquad (f+\mathrm{id})(e) \;=\; (b,x) \qquad\qquad (P(e))$$

We claim that $P(a,x)$. For this we must first show that $(a,x) \in A+X$, that is, $|a|+|x| = 1$. Note that since $(f_\bullet(a),y) \equiv (f+\mathrm{id})(a,y) = (\mathrm{id}+g)(b,x) \equiv (b, g_\bullet(x))$ we have $f_\bullet(a) = b$ and $g_\bullet(x) = y$. Then $|a| = |f_\bullet(a)| = |b|$. Further, $|b|+|x| = 1$ since $(b,x) \in B+X$. Thus $|a|+|x| = 1$, and $(a,x) \in A+X$. Now, $(\mathrm{id}+g)(a,x) = (a, g_\bullet(x)) = (a,y)$, and similarly we have $(f+\mathrm{id})(a,x) = (b,x)$. Hence $P(a,x)$.

For uniqueness, suppose that $(a',x') \in A+X$ with $P(a',x')$ is given. We must show that $a = a'$ and $x = x'$. We have $(a,y) = (\mathrm{id}+g)(a',x') = (a', g_\bullet(x'))$ and similarly $(b,x) = (f_\bullet(a'),x')$. Thus $a' = a$ and $x = x'$. Hence the diagram on the left is pullback in **CConv**. A similar reasoning works for the diagram on the right in Definition 12. □

Proposition 16. *Let* $\mathbf{C}$ *be an effectus with normalisation over* $[0,1]$. *The state functor* $\mathrm{Stat}\colon \mathbf{C} \to \mathbf{Conv}$ *preserves coproducts:* $\mathrm{Stat}(X+Y) \cong \mathrm{Stat}(X)+\mathrm{Stat}(Y)$ *for* $X, Y \in \mathbf{C}$.

Proof. For objects $X, Y \in \mathbf{C}$, consider the canonical map:

$$\mathrm{Stat}(X) + \mathrm{Stat}(Y) \xrightarrow{\vartheta := [\,\mathrm{Stat}(\kappa_1),\, \mathrm{Stat}(\kappa_2)\,]} \mathrm{Stat}(X+Y)$$

We have to show that this ϑ is bijective. First, we give a direct expression for ϑ. Let $(x,y) \in \mathrm{Stat}(X)+\mathrm{Stat}(Y)$ be such that $|x|, |y| \in (0,1)$. Then there are a scalar $\lambda\colon 1 \to 1+1$ and states $\hat{x}\colon 1 \to X$ and $\hat{y}\colon 1 \to Y$ such that $(x,y) = \lambda\kappa_1(\hat{x}) + \lambda^\perp\kappa_2(\hat{y})$, where $\lambda^\perp = [\kappa_2,\kappa_1] \circ \lambda = 1-\lambda$. Observe $\vartheta(x,y) = (\hat{x}+\hat{y}) \circ \lambda$.

To prove surjectivity, let $\omega\colon 1 \to X+Y$ be a state. Define a scalar $\lambda = (!+!) \circ \omega\colon 1 \to 1+1$. Define substates $x = (\mathrm{id}+!) \circ \omega\colon 1 \to X+1$ and $y = [\kappa_2 \circ !, \kappa_1] \circ \omega\colon 1 \to Y+1$. For now, suppose that $\lambda \neq \kappa_1$ and $\lambda \neq \kappa_2$, i.e., $x \neq \kappa_2$ and $y \neq \kappa_2$. Then by normalisation, there are states $\hat{x}\colon 1 \to X$ and $\hat{y}\colon 1 \to Y$ such that

$$x = (\hat{x}+\mathrm{id}) \circ (!+\mathrm{id}) \circ x \qquad \text{and} \qquad y = (\hat{y}+\mathrm{id}) \circ (!+\mathrm{id}) \circ y.$$

Define $\sigma := \langle\, (\lambda, \hat{x}),\, (\lambda^\perp, \hat{y})\,\rangle \in \mathrm{Stat}(X)+\mathrm{Stat}(Y)$. We claim that $\vartheta(\sigma) = \omega$. That is, we must show that $(\hat{x}+\hat{y}) \circ \lambda = \omega$. Note that the two maps

$$(\mathrm{id}+!)\colon X+Y \to X+1 \qquad \text{and} \qquad [\kappa_2 \circ !, \kappa_1]\colon X+Y \to Y+1$$

are jointly monic in $\mathbf{C}$ by the pullback diagram on the left in Definition 12 (2). Thus it suffices to show that

$$(\mathrm{id}+!) \circ (\hat{x}+\hat{y}) \circ \lambda \;=\; (\mathrm{id}+!) \circ \omega \equiv x$$
$$\text{and} \qquad [\kappa_2 \circ !, \kappa_1] \circ (\hat{x}+\hat{y}) \circ \lambda \;=\; [\kappa_2 \circ !, \kappa_1] \circ \omega \equiv y$$

We verify the first equality and leave the second equality to the reader.

$$\begin{aligned}
(\mathrm{id}+!) \circ (\hat{x} + \hat{y}) \circ \lambda &= \big(\,(\mathrm{id} \circ \hat{x}) \,+\, (! \circ \hat{y})\,\big) \circ \lambda \\
&= (\hat{x} + \mathrm{id}) \circ \lambda \\
&= (\hat{x} + \mathrm{id}) \circ (! + \mathrm{id}) \circ (\mathrm{id}+!) \circ \omega && \text{by def. of } \lambda \\
&= (\hat{x} + \mathrm{id}) \circ (! + \mathrm{id}) \circ x && \text{by def. of } x \\
&= x && \text{by def. of } \hat{x}
\end{aligned}$$

Suppose $\lambda = \kappa_2$, i.e., $x = \kappa_2$. Then $\lambda^\perp = \kappa_1$, so $y \neq \kappa_2$. Thus there is a unique $\hat{y}$ with $y = (\hat{y} + \mathrm{id}) \circ (! + \mathrm{id}) \circ y = (\hat{y} + \mathrm{id}) \circ \lambda^\perp = (\hat{y} + \mathrm{id}) \circ \kappa_1 = \kappa_1 \circ \hat{y}$. Thus:

$$\begin{aligned}
(\mathrm{id}+!) \circ \kappa_2 \circ \hat{y} &= \kappa_2 \circ ! \circ \hat{y} = \kappa_2 = x = (\mathrm{id}+!) \circ \omega \\
[\kappa_2 \circ !, \kappa_1] \circ \kappa_2 \circ \hat{y} &= \kappa_1 \circ \hat{y} = y = [\kappa_2 \circ !, \kappa_1] \circ \omega.
\end{aligned}$$

By joint monicity of $(\mathrm{id}+!)$ and $[\kappa_2 \circ !, \kappa_1]$ we derive $\omega = \kappa_2 \circ \hat{y} \equiv \vartheta(\kappa_1(\hat{y}))$. The case for $x = \kappa_1$ is similar. Thus ϑ is surjective.

For injectivity, let $(x, y), (x', y') \in \mathrm{Stat}(X) + \mathrm{Stat}(Y)$ with $\vartheta(x, y) = \vartheta(x', y')$ be given. Note that $|x'| = (!+!) \circ \vartheta(x', y') = (!+!) \circ \vartheta(x, y) = |x|$. Assume that $|x| \in (0, 1)$. Then there are $\hat{x}, \hat{x}' \colon 1 \to X$ and $\hat{y}, \hat{y}' \colon 1 \to Y$ such that

$$x = (|x|, \hat{x}); \quad y = (|x|^\perp, \hat{y}); \quad x' = (|x|, \hat{x}') \quad \text{and} \quad y' = (|x|^\perp, \hat{y}').$$

Consequently:

$$\begin{aligned}
(\hat{x} + \mathrm{id}) \circ |x| &= (\mathrm{id}+!) \circ (\hat{x} + \hat{y}) \circ |x| = (\mathrm{id}+!) \circ \vartheta(x, y) = (\mathrm{id}+!) \circ \vartheta(x', y') \\
&= (\mathrm{id}+!) \circ (\hat{x}' + \hat{y}') \circ |x| = (\hat{x}' + \mathrm{id}) \circ |x|.
\end{aligned}$$

It follows that we have two 'normalisations' $\hat{x}, \hat{x}' \colon 1 \to X$ for the substate $\sigma = (\hat{x} + \mathrm{id}) \circ |x| = (\hat{x}' + \mathrm{id}) \circ |x| \colon 1 \to X + 1$:

$$(\hat{x} + \mathrm{id}) \circ (! + \mathrm{id}) \circ \sigma = (\hat{x} + \mathrm{id}) \circ |x| = (\hat{x}' + \mathrm{id}) \circ |x| = (\hat{x}' + \mathrm{id}) \circ (! + \mathrm{id}) \circ \sigma.$$

And thus by the uniqueness in the normalisation assumption, we conclude $\hat{x} = \hat{x}'$. Similarly, $\hat{y} = \hat{y}'$. Hence $(x, y) = (x', y')$. We leave it to the reader to show that $(x, y) = (x', y')$ when $|x| \in \{0, 1\}$. Thus ϑ is injective. □

This preservation of coproducts is an important property for an abstract account of conditional probability, see Section 6 for the discrete case. For C^*-algebras the above result takes the following concrete, familiar form: let ω be a state of the form $\omega \colon \mathscr{A} \times \mathscr{B} \to \mathbb{C}$ — so that ω is a map $1 \to \mathscr{A} + \mathscr{B}$ in $\mathbf{Cstar}_{\mathrm{PU}}^{\mathrm{op}}$. Take $\lambda = \omega(1, 0) \in [0, 1]$. If we exclude the border cases $\lambda = 0$ and $\lambda = 1$, then we can write ω as convex combination $\omega = \lambda(\omega_1 \circ \pi_1) + (1 - \lambda)(\omega_2 \circ \pi_2)$ for states $\omega_1 = \frac{\omega(-,0)}{\lambda} \colon \mathscr{A} \to \mathbb{C}$ and $\omega_2 = \frac{\omega(0,-)}{1-\lambda} \colon \mathscr{B} \to \mathbb{C}$.

Now we obtain the analogue of Proposition 14 for states.

Theorem 17. *Let* $\mathbf{C}$ *be an effectus with normalisation over* $[0, 1]$. *The assignment* $X \mapsto \mathrm{Stat}(X)$ *yields a functor* $\mathrm{Stat} \colon \mathbf{C} \to \mathbf{CConv}$, *which is a map of effecti.*

Proof. Most of this is already clear: the functor Stat preserves $+$ by Proposition 16. It sends the initial object $0 \in \mathbf{C}$ to the set $\mathrm{Stat}(0) = \mathrm{Hom}(1, 0)$. This set must be empty, because otherwise $1 \cong 0$, which trivialises $\mathbf{C}$ and makes it impossible that $\mathbf{C}$ has $[0, 1]$ as its scalars. Also, $\mathrm{Stat}(1) \cong 1$, since there is only one map $1 \to 1$.

What remains to be shown is that each convex set $\mathrm{Stat}(X)$ is cancellative. By Theorem 8 we are done if we can show that the following two maps are jointly monic in the category **Conv**.

$$\mathrm{Stat}(X) + \mathrm{Stat}(X) + \mathrm{Stat}(X) \underset{[\kappa_2,\kappa_1,\kappa_2]}{\overset{[\kappa_1,\kappa_2,\kappa_2]}{\rightrightarrows}} \mathrm{Stat}(X) + \mathrm{Stat}(X)$$

But since the functor $\mathrm{Stat}\colon \mathbf{C} \to \mathbf{Conv}$ preserves coproducts by Proposition 16 this is the same as joint monicity of the maps:

$$\mathrm{Stat}(X + X + X) \underset{\mathrm{Stat}([\kappa_2,\kappa_1,\kappa_2])}{\overset{\mathrm{Stat}([\kappa_1,\kappa_2,\kappa_2])}{\rightrightarrows}} \mathrm{Stat}(X + X)$$

Suppose we have two states $\omega, \omega' \in \mathrm{Stat}(X + X + X)$ with $\mathrm{Stat}([\kappa_1, \kappa_2, \kappa_2])(\omega) = \mathrm{Stat}([\kappa_1, \kappa_2, \kappa_2])(\omega')$ and $\mathrm{Stat}([\kappa_2, \kappa_1, \kappa_2])(\omega) = \mathrm{Stat}([\kappa_2, \kappa_1, \kappa_2])(\omega')$. This means that $\omega, \omega'\colon 1 \to X + X + X$ satisfy $[\kappa_1, \kappa_2, \kappa_2] \circ \omega = [\kappa_1, \kappa_2, \kappa_2] \circ \omega'$ and $[\kappa_2, \kappa_1, \kappa_2] \circ \omega = [\kappa_2, \kappa_1, \kappa_2] \circ \omega'$. By using the joint monicity property in $\mathbf{C}$, see Definition 12 (3), we obtain $\omega = \omega'$. □

The following observation ties things closer together.

Proposition 18. *The adjunction* $\mathbf{EMod}^{op} \leftrightarrows \mathbf{CConv}$ *from Proposition 9 can be understood in terms of maps of effecti:*

- *the one functor* $\mathbf{EMod}(-, [0, 1])\colon \mathbf{EMod}^{op} \to \mathbf{CConv}$ *is the states functor* $\mathrm{Stat} = \mathbf{EMod}^{op}(1, -)$, *since* $[0, 1]$ *is the initial effect module, and thus the final object* 1 *in* $\mathbf{EMod}^{op}$*;*
- *the other functor* $\mathbf{CConv}(-, [0, 1])\colon \mathbf{CConv} \to \mathbf{EMod}^{op}$ *is the predicate functor* $\mathrm{Pred} = \mathbf{CConv}(-, 1 + 1)$, *since the sum* $1 + 1$ *in* $\mathbf{CConv}$ *is* $[0, 1]$. □

The above series of results culminates in the following.

Corollary 19. *Let* $\mathbf{C}$ *be an effectus over* $[0, 1]$*. Then we obtain a "state-and-effect" triangle shown on the right, where all the arrows are maps of effecti. (Arrows need not commute.)*

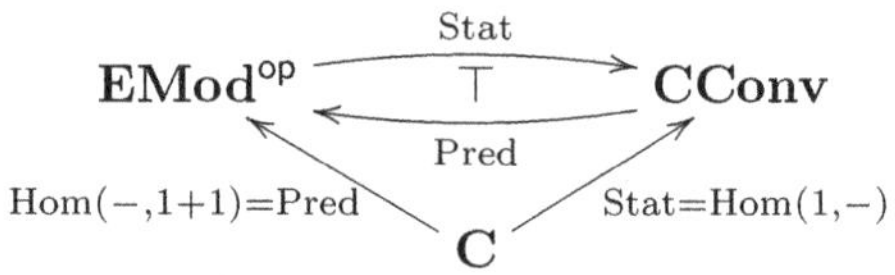

As degenerate cases of the triangle we obtain:

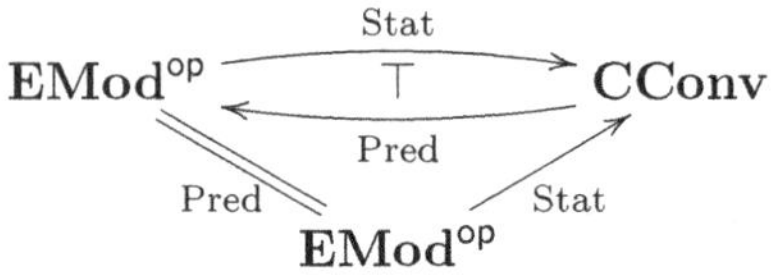

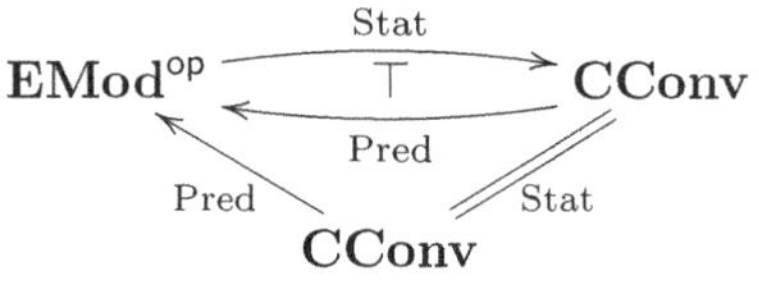

6 Conditional Probability

An essential ingredient of conditional probability is normalisation, *i.e.* rescaling of probabilities: if we throw a dice, then the probability $P(4)$ of getting 4 is $\frac{1}{6}$. But the conditional probability $P(4 \mid \text{even})$ of getting 4 if we already know that the outcome is even, is $\frac{1}{3}$. This $\frac{1}{3}$ is obtained by rescaling of $\frac{1}{6}$, via division by the probability $\frac{1}{2}$ of obtaining an even outcome. Essentially this is the normalisation mechanism of Definition 10, and the resulting coproduct-preservation of the states functor from Proposition 16, as we will illustrate in the current section. Our general approach to conditional probability applies to both probabilistic and quantum systems. We present it in terms of an effectus with so-called 'instruments'. They are described in great detail in [Jac14], but here we repeat the essentials, for the Kleisli category $\mathcal{K}\ell(\mathcal{D})$ of the distribution monad $\mathcal{D}$. In a later, extended version of this paper the quantum case, using the effectus $\mathbf{Cstar}_{\mathrm{PU}}^{\mathrm{op}}$ of C^*-algebras will be included.

Let $\mathbf{C}$ be an arbitrary effectus. Recall its predicate functor $\mathrm{Pred}\colon \mathbf{C} \to \mathbf{EMod}^{\mathrm{op}}$ which takes the maps $X \to 1+1$ as predicates on X. In case $\mathbf{C} = \mathcal{K}\ell(\mathcal{D})$ we have $\mathrm{Pred}(X) = [0,1]^X$, the fuzzy predicates on X. An *n-test* in an effectus is an n-tuple of predicates $p_1, \ldots, p_n \in \mathrm{Pred}(X)$ with $p_1 \otimes \cdots \otimes p_n = 1$. In $\mathcal{K}\ell(\mathcal{D})$ this translates to predicates $p_i \in [0,1]^X$ with $\sum_i p_i(x) = 1$, for each $x \in X$. An *instrument* for an n-test $\vec{p}$ is a map $\mathrm{instr}_{\vec{p}}\colon X \to n \cdot X$ in $\mathbf{C}$, where $n \cdot X = X + \cdots + X$ is the n-fold coproduct. These instruments should satisfy certain requirements, but we skip them here. In $\mathcal{K}\ell(\mathcal{D})$ such an instrument is a map $\mathrm{instr}_{\vec{p}}\colon X \to \mathcal{D}(n \cdot X)$ defined as:

$$\mathrm{instr}_{\vec{p}}(x) \;=\; p_1(x)\,|\kappa_1 x\rangle + \cdots + p_n(x)\,|\kappa_n x\rangle\,.$$

We can now introduce the notion of conditional state, via coproduct-preservation.

Definition 20. *Let* $\mathbf{C}$ *be an effectus (over* $[0,1]$*) with normalisation, and with instruments as sketched above. Let* $\omega \in \mathrm{Stat}(X)$ *be a state, and* $\vec{p} = p_1, \ldots, p_n$ *be an n-test on* X*, of predicates* $p_i \in \mathrm{Pred}(X)$*. By applying the state functor* $\mathrm{Stat}\colon \mathbf{C} \to \mathbf{CConv}$ *we can form the new state:*

$$\omega' \;=\; \mathrm{Stat}\big(\mathrm{instr}_{\vec{p}}\big)(\omega) \in \mathrm{Stat}(n \cdot X) \;\overset{Prop.16}{\cong}\; n \cdot \mathrm{Stat}(X) \;\overset{Prop.5}{\subseteq}\; \textstyle\prod_n \mathrm{Stat}(X).$$

Hence we write this new state ω' *as a convex combination of what we call* ***conditional*** *states on* X*, written as* $\omega|p_i \in \mathrm{Stat}(X)$*. The probabilities* r_i *in this convex combination can be computed as validity probabilities:*

$$r_i \;=\; \omega \models p_i \;=\; p_i \circ \omega\colon 1 \longrightarrow 1+1.$$

When each r_i *is non-zero, there are* n *such conditional states* $\omega|p_i$*.*

From a Bayesian perspective such a conditional state $\omega|p_i$ can be seen as an update of our state of knowledge, resulting from evidence p_i. This will be illustrated next in a discrete probabilistic example of Bayesian inference. It uses the Kleisli category $\mathcal{K}\ell(\mathcal{D})$ as effectus, in which a state $1 \to X$ in $\mathcal{K}\ell(\mathcal{D})$ corresponds to a distribution $\varphi \in \mathcal{D}(X)$. Conditional states, as defined above, appear as conditional distributions, generalising ordinary conditional probabilities.

Example 21. *Suppose, at an archaeological site, we are investigating a tomb of which we know that it must be from the second century AD, that is, somewhere from the time period 100 – 200. We wish to learn its origin more precisely. During excavation we are especially looking for three kinds of objects* $0, 1, 2$*, of which we know the time of use more precisely, in terms of "prior" distributions. This prior knowledge involves a split of the time period 100 – 200 into four equal subperiods* $A = 100 - 125$*,* $B = 125 - 150$*,* $C = 150 - 175$*,* $D = 175 - 200$*. Associated with each object* $i = 0, 1, 2$ *there is a predicate* $p_i \in [0,1]^{\{A,B,C,D\}}$*, which we write as sequence of probabilities of the form:*

$$p_0 = [0.7, 0.5, 0.2, 0.1] \qquad p_1 = [0.2, 0.2, 0.1, 0.1] \qquad p_2 = [0.1, 0.3, 0.7, 0.8].$$

Predicate p_0 *incorporates the prior knowledge that object* 0 *is with probability* 0.7 *from subperiod* A*, with probability* 0.5 *from subperiod* B*, etc. Notice that these three predicates form a 3-test, since* $p_0 \otimes p_1 \otimes p_2 = 1$*. They can be described jointly as a Kleisli map* $\{A, B, C, D\} \to \mathcal{D}(\{0, 1, 2\})$*.*

Inference works as follows. Let our current knowledge about the subperiod of origin of the tomb be given as a distribution $\varphi \in \mathcal{D}(\{A, B, C, D\})$*. We can compute* $\varphi' = \text{instr}_{\vec{p}}(\varphi) \in \mathcal{D}(3 \cdot \{A, B, C, D\})$ *and split* φ' *up into three conditional distributions* $\varphi|p_0, \varphi|p_1, \varphi|p_2 \in \mathcal{D}(\{A, B, C, D\})$*, like in Definition 20. If we find as "evidence" object* i*, then we update our knowledge from* φ *to* $\varphi|p_i$*.*

If we start from a uniform distribution, and find objects $i_1, \ldots, i_n \in \{0, 1, 2\}$*, then we have as inferred distribution (knowledge)* $\varphi|p_{i_1}|p_{i_2}|\cdots|p_{i_n}$*. For instance, the series of findings* $1, 2, 2, 0, 1, 1, 1, 1$ *yields the consecutive distributions shown in figure 21. Hence period* B *is most likely. These distributions are computed by a simple Python program that executes the steps of Definition 20. Interestingly, a change in the order of the objects that are found does not affect the final distribution. This is different in the quantum case, where such commutativity is lacking.*

$$0.25\,|A\rangle + 0.25\,|B\rangle + 0.25\,|C\rangle + 0.25\,|D\rangle$$
$$0.33\,|A\rangle + 0.33\,|B\rangle + 0.17\,|C\rangle + 0.17\,|D\rangle$$
$$0.09\,|A\rangle + 0.26\,|B\rangle + 0.30\,|C\rangle + 0.35\,|D\rangle$$
$$0.02\,|A\rangle + 0.14\,|B\rangle + 0.37\,|C\rangle + 0.48\,|D\rangle$$
$$0.05\,|A\rangle + 0.34\,|B\rangle + 0.37\,|C\rangle + 0.24\,|D\rangle$$
$$0.08\,|A\rangle + 0.49\,|B\rangle + 0.26\,|C\rangle + 0.17\,|D\rangle$$
$$0.10\,|A\rangle + 0.62\,|B\rangle + 0.17\,|C\rangle + 0.11\,|D\rangle$$
$$0.11\,|A\rangle + 0.72\,|B\rangle + 0.10\,|C\rangle + 0.06\,|D\rangle$$
$$0.12\,|A\rangle + 0.79\,|B\rangle + 0.05\,|C\rangle + 0.04\,|D\rangle$$

Fig. 1. Inferred distributions

7 Conclusions

Starting from convex sets, in particular from the cancellation property and a concrete description of coproducts, we have arrived at the notion of effectus as a step towards a categorical axiomatisation of probabilistic and quantum computation. We have proven some 'closure' properties for effecti, among them that the states functor is a map of effecti. The concept of normalisation gave rise to a general notion of conditional state, which we have illustrated in the context of Bayesian inference.

Acknowledgements. We would like to thank Kenta Cho and the anonymous referees for their constructive feedback.

References

[AE80] Asimow, L., Ellis, A.: Convexity Theory and its Applications in Functional Analysis. Academic Press, New York (1980)

[BW85] Barr, M., Wells, C.: Toposes, triples and theories, vol. 278. Springer, New York (1985)

[BW11] Barnum, H., Wilce, A.: Information processing in convex operational theories. In: Coecke, B., Mackie, I., Panangaden, P., Selinger, P. (eds.) Proceedings of QPL/DCM 2008. Elect. Notes in Theor. Comp. Sci, vol. 270(2), pp. 3–15. Elsevier, Amsterdam (2008)

[Flo81] Flood, J.: Semiconvex geometry. Journal of the Australiam Mathematical Society 30, 496–510 (1981)

[Fri09] Fritz, T.: Convex spaces I: Definition and examples. arXiv preprint arXiv:0903.5522 (2009)

[Gud73] Gudder, S.: Convex structures and operational quantum mechanics. Communic. Math. Physics 29(3), 249–264 (1973)

[Gud77] Gudder, S.: Convexity and mixtures. Siam Review 19(2), 221–240 (1977)

[HZ12] Heinosaari, T., Ziman, M.: The mathematical language of quantum theory: from uncertainty to entanglement. AMC 10, 12 (2012)

[Jac10] Jacobs, B.: Convexity, duality and effects. In: Calude, C.S., Sassone, V. (eds.) TCS 2010. IFIP AICT, vol. 323, pp. 1–19. Springer, Heidelberg (2010)

[Jac14] Jacobs, B.: New directions in categorical logic, for classical, probabilistic and quantum logic. arXiv preprint arXiv:1205.3940v3 (2014)

[Koc71a] Kock, A.: Bilinearity and cartesian closed monads. Mathematica Scandinavica 29, 161–174 (1971)

[Koc71b] Kock, A.: Closed categories generated by commutative monads. Journal of the Australian Mathematical Society 12(04), 405–424 (1971)

[Neu70] Neumann, W.D.: On the quasivariety of convex subsets of affine spaces. Archiv der Mathematik 21(1), 11–16 (1970)

[Ś74] Świrszcz, T.: Monadic functors and categories of convex sets. PhD thesis, Polish Academy of Sciences (1974)

[Sto49] Stone, M.: Postulates for the barycentric calculus. Annali di Matematica Pura ed Applicata 29(1), 25–30 (1949)

A Categorical Semantics for Linear Logical Frameworks

Matthijs Vákár

Department of Computer Science,
University of Oxford, Oxford, United Kingdom

Abstract. A type theory is presented that combines (intuitionistic) linear types with type dependency, thus properly generalising both intuitionistic dependent type theory and full linear logic. A syntax and complete categorical semantics are developed, the latter in terms of (strict) indexed symmetric monoidal categories with comprehension. Various optional type formers are treated in a modular way. In particular, we will see that the historically much-debated multiplicative quantifiers and identity types arise naturally from categorical considerations. These new multiplicative connectives are further characterised by several identities relating them to the usual connectives from dependent type theory and linear logic. Finally, one important class of models, given by families with values in some symmetric monoidal category, is investigated in detail.

1 Introduction

Starting from Church's simply typed λ-calculus (or intuitionistic propositional type theory), two extensions in perpendicular directions depart:

- following the Curry-Howard propositions-as-types interpretation *dependent type theory* (DTT) [1] extends the simply typed λ-calculus from a proof-calculus of intuitionistic propositional logic to one for predicate logic;
- *linear logic* [2] gives a more detailed resource sensitive analysis, exposing precisely how many times each assumption is used in proofs.

A combined *linear dependent type theory* is one of the interesting directions to explore to gain a more fine-grained understanding of *homotopy type theory* [3] from a computer science point of view, explaining its flow of information. Indeed, many of the usual settings for computational semantics are naturally linear in character, either because they arise as !-co-Kleisli categories (coherence space and game semantics) or for more fundamental reasons (quantum computation).

Combining dependent types and linear types is a non-trivial task, however, and despite some work by various authors that we shall discuss, the precise relationship between the two systems remains poorly understood. The discrepancy between linear and dependent types is the following.

- The lack of structural rules in *linear type theory* forces us to refer to each variable precisely once - for a sequent $x : A \vdash t : B$, x occurs uniquely in t.
- In *dependent type theory*, types can have free variables - $x : A \vdash B$ type, where x is free in B. Crucially, if $x : A \vdash t : B$, x may also be free in t.

A. Pitts (Ed.): FOSSACS 2015, LNCS 9034, pp. 102–116, 2015.
DOI: 10.1007/978-3-662-46678-0_7

What does it mean for x to occur uniquely in t in a dependent setting? Do we count its occurrence in B? The usual way out, which we shall follow too, is to restrict type dependency on intuitionistic terms. Although this seems very limiting - for instance, we do not obtain an equivalent of the Girard translation, embedding DTT in the resulting system -, it is not clear that there is a reasonable alternative. Moreover, as even this limited scenario has not been studied extensively, we hope that a semantic analysis, which was so far missing entirely, may shed new light on the old mystery of linear type dependency.

Historically, Girard's early work in linear logic already makes movements to extend a linear analysis to predicate logic. Although it talks about first-order quantifiers, the analysis appears to have stayed rather superficial, omitting the identity predicates which, in a way, are what make first-order logic tick. Closely related is that an account of internal quantification, or a linear variant of Martin-Löf's type theory, was missing, let alone a Curry-Howard correspondence.

Later, linear types and dependent types were first combined in a Linear Logical Framework [4], where a syntax was presented that extends a Logical Framework with linear types (that depend on terms of intuitionistic types). This has given rise to a line of work in the computer science community [5–7]. All the work seems to be syntactic in nature, however, and seems to be mostly restricted to the asynchronous fragment in which we only have $\multimap$-, Π-, $\top$-, and $\&$-types. An exception is the Concurrent Logical Framework [8], which treats synchronous connectives resembling our I-, $\otimes$-, Σ-, and $!$-types. An account of additive disjunctions and identity types is missing entirely.

On the other hand, similar ideas, this time at the level of categorical semantics and specific models (from homotopy theory, algebra, and physics), have emerged in the mathematical community [9–12]. In these models, as with Girard, a notion of comprehension was missing and, with that, a notion of identity type. Although, in the past year, some suggestions have been made on the nLab and nForum of possible connections between the syntactic and semantic work, no account of the correspondence was published, as far as the author is aware.

The point of this paper[1] is to close this gap between syntax and semantics and to pave the way for a proper semantic analysis of linear type dependency, treating a range of type formers including the crucial Id-types[2]. Firstly, in section 2, we present a syntax, intuitionistic linear dependent type theory (ILDTT), a natural blend of the dual intuitionistic linear logic (DILL) [15] and dependent type theory (DTT) [16] which generalises both. Secondly, in section 3, we present a complete categorical semantics, an obvious combination of linear/non-linear adjunctions [15] and comprehension categories [17]. Finally, in section 4, an important class of models is studied: families with values in a symmetric monoidal category.

[1] This paper is based on the technical report [13] where proofs and more discussion can be found. Independently, Krishnaswami et al. [14] developed a roughly equivalent syntax and gave an operational rather than a denotational semantics. There, type dependency is added to Benton's LNL calculus, rather than to DILL.

[2] To be precise: extensional Id-types. Intensional Id-types remain a topic of investigation, due to the subtlety of dependent elimination rules in a linear setting.

2 Syntax

We assume the reader has some familiarity with the formal syntax of dependent type theory and linear type theory. In particular, we will not go into syntactic details like α-conversion, name binding, capture-free substitution of a for x in t (write $t[a/x]$), and pre-syntax. Details on all of these topics can be found in [16].

We next present the formal syntax of ILDTT. We start with a presentation of the judgements that will represent the propositions in the language and then discuss its rules of inference: first its structural core, then the logical rules for a series of optional type formers. We conclude this section with a few basic results about the syntax.

Judgements. We adopt a notation $\Delta; \Xi$ for contexts, where Δ is 'an intuitionistic region' and Ξ is 'a linear region', as in DILL [15]. The idea will be that we have an empty context and can extend an existing context $\Delta; \Xi$ with both intuitionistic and linear types that are allowed to depend on Δ.

Our language will express judgements of the following six forms.

ILDTT judgement	**Intended meaning**
$\vdash \Delta; \Xi$ ctxt	$\Delta; \Xi$ is a valid context
$\Delta; \cdot \vdash A$ type	A is a type in (intuitionistic) context Δ
$\Delta; \Xi \vdash a : A$	a is a term of type A in context $\Delta; \Xi$
$\vdash \Delta; \Xi \equiv \Delta'; \Xi'$ ctxt	$\Delta; \Xi$ and $\Delta'; \Xi'$ are judgementally equal contexts
$\Delta; \cdot \vdash A \equiv A'$ type	A and A' are judgementally equal types in (intuitionistic) context Δ
$\Delta; \Xi \vdash a \equiv a' : A$	a and a' are judgementally equal terms of type A in context $\Delta; \Xi$

Fig. 1. Judgements of ILDTT

Structural Rules. We will use the following structural rules, which are essentially the structural rules of dependent type theory where some rules appear in both an intuitionistic and a linear form. We present the rules per group, with their names, from left-to-right, top-to-bottom.

Rules for context formation (C-Emp, Int-C-Ext, Int-C-Ext-Eq, Lin-C-Ext, Lin-C-Ext-Eq):

$$\frac{}{\cdot;\cdot \text{ ctxt}}$$

$$\frac{\vdash \Delta; \Xi \text{ ctxt} \qquad \Delta; \cdot \vdash A \text{ type}}{\vdash \Delta, x : A; \Xi \text{ ctxt}} \qquad \frac{\Delta; \Xi \equiv \Delta'; \Xi' \text{ ctxt} \qquad \Delta; \cdot \vdash A \equiv B \text{ type}}{\vdash \Delta, x : A; \Xi \equiv \Delta', y : B; \Xi' \text{ ctxt}}$$

$$\frac{\vdash \Delta; \Xi \text{ ctxt} \qquad \Delta; \cdot \vdash A \text{ type}}{\vdash \Delta; \Xi, x : A \text{ ctxt}} \qquad \frac{\Delta; \Xi \equiv \Delta'; \Xi' \text{ ctxt} \qquad \Delta; \cdot \vdash A \equiv B \text{ type}}{\vdash \Delta; \Xi, x : A \equiv \Delta'; \Xi', y : B \text{ ctxt}}$$

Variable declaration/axiom rules (Int-Var, Lin-Var):

$$\frac{\Delta, x : A, \Delta'; \cdot \text{ ctxt}}{\Delta, x : A, \Delta'; \cdot \vdash x : A} \qquad \frac{\Delta; x : A \text{ ctxt}}{\Delta; x : A \vdash x : A}$$

Fig. 2. Context formation and variable declaration rules

The standard rules expressing that judgemental equality is an equivalence relation (C-Eq-R, C-Eq-S, C-Eq-T, Ty-Eq-R, Ty-Eq-S, Ty-Eq-T, Tm-Eq-R, Tm-Eq-S, Tm-Eq-T):

$$\frac{\vdash \Delta; \Xi \text{ ctxt}}{\vdash \Delta; \Xi \equiv \Delta; \Xi \text{ ctxt}} \qquad \frac{\vdash \Delta; \Xi \equiv \Delta'; \Xi' \text{ ctxt}}{\vdash \Delta'; \Xi' \equiv \Delta; \Xi \text{ ctxt}}$$

$$\frac{\vdash \Delta; \Xi \equiv \Delta'; \Xi' \text{ ctxt} \qquad \vdash \Delta'; \Xi' \equiv \Delta''; \Xi'' \text{ ctxt}}{\vdash \Delta; \Xi \equiv \Delta''; \Xi'' \text{ ctxt}}$$

$$\frac{\Delta; \Xi \vdash A \text{ type}}{\Delta; \Xi \vdash A \equiv A \text{ type}} \qquad \frac{\Delta; \Xi \vdash A \equiv A' \text{ type}}{\Delta; \Xi \vdash A' \equiv A \text{ type}}$$

$$\frac{\Delta; \Xi \vdash A \equiv A' \text{ type} \qquad \Delta; \Xi \vdash A' \equiv A'' \text{ type}}{\Delta; \Xi \vdash A \equiv A'' \text{ type}}$$

$$\frac{\Delta; \Xi \vdash a : A}{\Delta; \Xi \vdash a \equiv a : A} \qquad \frac{\Delta; \Xi \vdash a \equiv a' : A}{\Delta; \Xi \vdash a' \equiv a : A}$$

$$\frac{\Delta; \Xi \vdash a \equiv a' : A \qquad \Delta; \Xi \vdash a' \equiv a'' : A}{\Delta; \Xi \vdash a \equiv a'' : A}$$

The standard rules relating typing and judgemental equality (Tm-Conv, Ty-Conv):

$$\frac{\Delta; \Xi \vdash a : A \qquad \vdash \Delta; \Xi \equiv \Delta; \Xi' \text{ ctxt} \qquad \Delta; \cdot \vdash A \equiv A' \text{ Type}}{\Delta'; \Xi' \vdash a : A'}$$

$$\frac{\Delta'; \cdot \vdash A \text{ type} \qquad \vdash \Delta; \cdot \equiv \Delta'; \cdot \text{ ctxt}}{\Delta'; \cdot \vdash A \text{ type}}$$

Fig. 3. A few standard rules for judgemental equality

Exchange, weakening, and substitution rules (Int-Weak, Int-Exch, Lin-Exch, Int-Ty-Subst, Int-Ty-Subst-Eq, Int-Tm-Subst, Int-Tm-Subst-Eq, Lin-Tm-Subst, Lin-Tm-Subst-Eq):

$$\frac{\Delta, \Delta'; \Xi \vdash \mathcal{J} \qquad \Delta; \cdot \vdash A \text{ type}}{\Delta, x : A, \Delta'; \Xi \vdash \mathcal{J}}$$

$$\frac{\Delta, x : A, x' : A', \Delta'; \Xi \vdash \mathcal{J}}{\Delta, x' : A', x : A, \Delta'; \Xi \vdash \mathcal{J}} \qquad \frac{\Delta; \Xi, x : A, x' : A', \Xi' \vdash \mathcal{J}}{\Delta; \Xi, x' : A', x : A, \Xi' \vdash \mathcal{J}}$$

(if x is not free in A')

$$\frac{\Delta, x : A, \Delta'; \cdot \vdash B \text{ type} \qquad \Delta; \cdot \vdash a : A}{\Delta, \Delta'[a/x]; \cdot \vdash B[a/x] \text{ type}} \qquad \frac{\Delta, x : A, \Delta'; \cdot \vdash B \equiv B' \text{ type} \qquad \Delta; \cdot \vdash a : A}{\Delta, \Delta'[a/x]; \cdot \vdash B[a/x] \equiv B'[a/x] \text{ type}}$$

$$\frac{\Delta, x : A, \Delta'; \Xi \vdash b : B \qquad \Delta; \cdot \vdash a : A}{\Delta, \Delta'[a/x]; \Xi[a/x] \vdash b[a/x] : B[a/x]} \qquad \frac{\Delta, x : A, \Delta'; \Xi \vdash b \equiv b' : B \qquad \Delta; \cdot \vdash a : A}{\Delta, \Delta'[a/x]; \Xi \vdash b[a/x] \equiv b'[a/x] : B[a/x]}$$

$$\frac{\Delta; \Xi, x : A \vdash b : B \qquad \Delta; \Xi' \vdash a : A}{\Delta; \Xi, \Xi' \vdash b[a/x] : B} \qquad \frac{\Delta; \Xi, x : A \vdash b \equiv b' : B \qquad \Delta; \Xi' \vdash a : A}{\Delta; \Xi, \Xi' \vdash b[a/x] \equiv b'[a/x] : B}$$

Fig. 4. Exchange, weakening, and substitution rules. Here, $\mathcal{J}$ represents a statement of the form B type, $B \equiv B'$, $b : B$, or $b \equiv b' : B$, such that all judgements are well-formed.

Logical Rules. We describe some (optional) type and term formers, for which we give type formation (denoted -F), introduction (-I), elimination (-E), computation rules (-C), and (judgemental) uniqueness principles (-U). We also assume the obvious rules to hold that state that the type formers and term formers respect judgemental equality. Moreover, $\Sigma_{!x:!A}$, $\Pi_{!x:!A}$, $\lambda_{!x:!A}$, and $\lambda_{x:A}$ are name binding operators, binding free occurences of x within their scope.

We demand -U-rules for the various type formers in this paper, as this allows us to give a natural categorical semantics. This includes Id-types: we study extensional identity types. In practice, when building a computational implementation of a type theory like ours, one would probably drop some of these rules to make the system decidable, which would correspond to switching to weak equivalents of the categorical constructions presented here.[3]

$$\frac{\Delta, x : A; \cdot \vdash B \text{ type}}{\Delta; \cdot \vdash \Sigma_{!x:!A} B \text{ type}}$$

$$\frac{\Delta; \cdot \vdash a : A \qquad \Delta; \Xi \vdash b : B[a/x]}{\Delta; \Xi \vdash !a \otimes b : \Sigma_{!x:!A} B}$$

$$\frac{\begin{array}{c}\Delta; \cdot \vdash C \text{ type}\\ \Delta; \Xi \vdash t : \Sigma_{!x:!A} B\\ \Delta, x : A; \Xi', y : B \vdash c : C\end{array}}{\Delta; \Xi, \Xi' \vdash \text{let } t \text{ be } !x \otimes y \text{ in } c : C}$$

$$\frac{\Delta; \Xi \vdash \text{let } !a \otimes b \text{ be } !x \otimes y \text{ in } c : C}{\Delta; \Xi \vdash \text{let } !a \otimes b \text{ be } !x \otimes y \text{ in } c \equiv c[a/x, b/y] : C}$$

$$\frac{\Delta; \Xi \vdash \text{let } t \text{ be } !x \otimes y \text{ in } !x \otimes y : \Sigma_{!x:!A} B}{\Delta; \Xi \vdash \text{let } t \text{ be } !x \otimes y \text{ in } !x \otimes y \equiv t : \Sigma_{!x:!A} B}$$

$$\frac{\Delta, x : A; \cdot \vdash B \text{ type}}{\Delta; \cdot \vdash \Pi_{!x:!A} B \text{ type}}$$

$$\frac{\vdash \Delta; \Xi \text{ ctxt} \qquad \Delta, x : A; \Xi \vdash b : B}{\Delta; \Xi \vdash \lambda_{!x:!A} b : \Pi_{!x:!A} B}$$

$$\frac{\Delta; \cdot \vdash a : A \qquad \Delta; \Xi \vdash f : \Pi_{!x:!A} B}{\Delta; \Xi \vdash f(!a) : B[a/x]}$$

$$\frac{\Delta; \Xi \vdash (\lambda_{!x:!A} b)(!a) : B}{\Delta; \Xi \vdash (\lambda_{!x:!A} b)(!a) \equiv b[a/x] : B[a/x]}$$

$$\frac{\Delta; \Xi \vdash \lambda_{!x:!A} f(!x) : \Pi_{!x:!A} B}{\Delta; \Xi \vdash f \equiv \lambda_{!x:!A} f(!x) : \Pi_{!x:!A} B}$$

$$\frac{\Delta; \cdot \vdash a : A \qquad \Delta; \cdot \vdash a' : A}{\Delta; \cdot \vdash \mathrm{Id}_{!A}(a, a') \text{ type}}$$

$$\frac{\Delta; \cdot \vdash a : A}{\Delta; \cdot \vdash \mathrm{refl}_{!a} : \mathrm{Id}_{!A}(a, a)}$$

$$\frac{\begin{array}{l}\Delta, x : A, x' : A; \cdot \vdash D \text{ type}\\ \Delta, z : A; \Xi \vdash d : D[z/x, z/x']\\ \Delta; \cdot \vdash a : A\\ \Delta; \cdot \vdash a' : A\\ \Delta; \Xi' \vdash p : \mathrm{Id}_{!A}(a, a')\end{array}}{\Delta; \Xi[a/z], \Xi' \vdash \text{let } (a, a', p) \text{ be } (z, z, \mathrm{refl}_{!z}) \text{ in } d : D[a/x, a'/x']}$$

$$\frac{\Delta; \Xi \vdash \text{let } (a, a, \mathrm{refl}_{!a}) \text{ be } (z, z, \mathrm{refl}_{!z}) \text{ in } d : D[a/x, a/x']}{\Delta; \Xi \vdash \text{let } (a, a, \mathrm{refl}_{!a}) \text{ be } (z, z, \mathrm{refl}_{!z}) \text{ in } d \equiv d[a/z] : D[a/x, a/x']}$$

$$\frac{\Delta, x : A, x' : A; \Xi, z : \mathrm{Id}_{!A}(x, x') \vdash \text{let } (x, x', z) \text{ be } (x, x, \mathrm{refl}_{!x}) \text{ in } c[x/x', \mathrm{refl}_{!x}/z] : C}{\Delta, x : A, x' : A; \Xi, z : \mathrm{Id}_{!A}(x, x') \vdash \text{let } (x, x', z) \text{ be } (x, x, \mathrm{refl}_{!x}) \text{ in } c[x/x', \mathrm{refl}_{!x}/z] \equiv c : C}$$

Fig. 5. Rules for linear equivalents of some of the usual type formers from DTT (Σ-F, -I, -E, -C, -U, Π-F, -I, -E, -C, -U, Id-F, -I, -E, -C, -U)

[3] In that case, in DTT, one would usually demand some stronger 'dependent' elimination rules, which would make propositional equivalents of the -U-rules provable, adding some extensionality to the system, while preserving its computational properties. Such rules are problematic in ILDTT, however, both from a syntactic and semantic point of view and a further investigation is warranted here.

$$\frac{}{\Delta;\cdot\vdash I\ \text{type}}\qquad\frac{}{\Delta;\cdot\vdash *:I}\qquad\frac{\Delta;\Xi'\vdash t:I\qquad\Delta;\Xi\vdash a:A}{\Delta;\Xi,\Xi'\vdash \text{let}\ t\ \text{be}\ *\ \text{in}\ a:A}$$

$$\frac{\Delta;\Xi\vdash \text{let}\ *\ \text{be}\ *\ \text{in}\ a:A}{\Delta;\Xi\vdash \text{let}\ *\ \text{be}\ *\ \text{in}\ a\equiv a:A}\qquad\frac{\Delta;\Xi\vdash \text{let}\ t\ \text{be}\ *\ \text{in}\ *:I}{\Delta;\Xi\vdash \text{let}\ t\ \text{be}\ *\ \text{in}\ *\equiv t:I}$$

$$\frac{\Delta;\cdot\vdash A\ \text{type}\qquad\Delta;\cdot\vdash B\ \text{type}}{\Delta;\cdot\vdash A\otimes B\ \text{type}}$$

$$\frac{\Delta;\Xi\vdash a:A\qquad\Delta;\Xi'\vdash b:B}{\Delta;\Xi,\Xi'\vdash a\otimes b:A\otimes B}\qquad\frac{\Delta;\Xi\vdash t:A\otimes B\qquad\Delta;\Xi',x:A,y:B\vdash c:C}{\Delta;\Xi,\Xi'\vdash \text{let}\ t\ \text{be}\ x\otimes y\ \text{in}\ c:C}$$

$$\frac{\Delta;\Xi\vdash \text{let}\ a\otimes b\ \text{be}\ x\otimes y\ \text{in}\ c:C}{\Delta;\Xi\vdash \text{let}\ a\otimes b\ \text{be}\ x\otimes y\ \text{in}\ c\equiv c[a/x,b/y]:C}\qquad\frac{\Delta;\Xi\vdash \text{let}\ t\ \text{be}\ x\otimes y\ \text{in}\ x\otimes y:A\otimes B}{\Delta;\Xi\vdash \text{let}\ t\ \text{be}\ x\otimes y\ \text{in}\ x\otimes y\equiv t:A\otimes B}$$

$$\frac{\Delta;\cdot\vdash A\ \text{type}\qquad\Delta;\cdot\vdash B\ \text{type}}{\Delta;\cdot\vdash A\multimap B\ \text{type}}$$

$$\frac{\Delta;\Xi,x:A\vdash b:B}{\Delta;\Xi\vdash \lambda_{x:A}b:A\multimap B}\qquad\frac{\Delta;\Xi\vdash f:A\multimap B\qquad\Delta;\Xi'\vdash a:A}{\Delta;\Xi,\Xi'\vdash f(a):B}$$

$$\frac{\Delta;\Xi\vdash(\lambda_{x:A}b)(a):B}{\Delta;\Xi\vdash(\lambda_{x:A}b)(a)\equiv b[a/x]:B}\qquad\frac{\Delta;\Xi\vdash \lambda_{x:A}fx:A\multimap B}{\Delta;\Xi\vdash \lambda_{x:A}fx\equiv f:A\multimap B}$$

$$\frac{}{\Delta;\cdot\vdash\top\ \text{type}}\qquad\frac{\Delta;\Xi\ \text{ctxt}}{\Delta;\Xi\vdash\langle\rangle:\top}\qquad\frac{\Delta;\Xi\vdash t:\top}{\Delta;\Xi\vdash t\equiv\langle\rangle:\top}$$

$$\frac{\Delta;\cdot\vdash A\ \text{type}\qquad\Delta;\cdot\vdash B\ \text{type}}{\Delta;\cdot\vdash A\&B\ \text{type}}\qquad\frac{\Delta;\Xi\vdash a:A\qquad\Delta;\Xi\vdash b:B}{\Delta;\Xi\vdash\langle a,b\rangle:A\&B}$$

$$\frac{\Delta;\Xi\vdash t:A\&B}{\Delta;\Xi\vdash \text{fst}(t):A}\qquad\frac{\Delta;\Xi\vdash t:A\&B}{\Delta;\Xi\vdash \text{snd}(t):B}$$

$$\frac{\Delta;\Xi\vdash \text{fst}(\langle a,b\rangle):A}{\Delta;\Xi\vdash \text{fst}(\langle a,b\rangle)\equiv a:A}\qquad\frac{\Delta;\Xi\vdash \text{snd}(\langle a,b\rangle):B}{\Delta;\Xi\vdash \text{snd}(\langle a,b\rangle)\equiv b:B}$$

$$\frac{\Delta;\Xi\vdash\langle\text{fst}(t),\text{snd}(t)\rangle:A\&B}{\Delta;\Xi\vdash\langle\text{fst}(t),\text{snd}(t)\rangle\equiv t:A\&B}$$

$$\frac{}{\Delta;\cdot\vdash 0\ \text{type}}\qquad\frac{\Delta;\Xi\vdash t:0}{\Delta;\Xi,\Xi'\vdash \text{false}(t):B}\qquad\frac{\Delta;\Xi\vdash t:0}{\Delta;\Xi\vdash \text{false}(t)\equiv t:0}$$

$$\frac{\Delta;\cdot\vdash A\ \text{type}\qquad\Delta;\cdot\vdash B\ \text{type}}{\Delta;\cdot\vdash A\oplus B\ \text{type}}$$

$$\frac{\Delta;\Xi\vdash a:A}{\Delta;\Xi\vdash \text{inl}(a):A\oplus B}\qquad\frac{\Delta;\Xi\vdash b:B}{\Delta;\Xi\vdash \text{inr}(b):A\oplus B}$$

$$\frac{\Delta;\Xi,x:A\vdash c:C\qquad\Delta;\Xi,y:B\vdash d:C\qquad\Delta;\Xi'\vdash t:A\oplus B}{\Delta;\Xi,\Xi'\vdash \text{case}\ t\ \text{of}\ \text{inl}(x)\to c\ ||\ \text{inr}(y)\to d:C}$$

$$\frac{\Delta;\Xi,\Xi'\vdash \text{case}\ \text{inl}(a)\ \text{of}\ \text{inl}(x)\to c\ ||\ \text{inr}(y)\to d:C}{\Delta;\Xi,\Xi'\vdash \text{case}\ \text{inl}(a)\ \text{of}\ \text{inl}(x)\to c\ ||\ \text{inr}(y)\to d\equiv c[a/x]:C}$$

$$\frac{\Delta;\Xi,\Xi'\vdash \text{case}\ \text{inr}(b)\ \text{of}\ \text{inl}(x)\to c\ ||\ \text{inr}(y)\to d:C}{\Delta;\Xi,\Xi'\vdash \text{case}\ \text{inr}(b)\ \text{of}\ \text{inl}(x)\to c\ ||\ \text{inr}(y)\to d\equiv d[b/y]:C}$$

$$\frac{\Delta;\Xi,\Xi'\vdash \text{case}\ t\ \text{of}\ \text{inl}(x)\to \text{inl}(x)\ ||\ \text{inr}(y)\to \text{inr}(y):A\oplus B}{\Delta;\Xi,\Xi'\vdash \text{case}\ t\ \text{of}\ \text{inl}(x)\to \text{inl}(x)\ ||\ \text{inr}(y)\to \text{inr}(y)\equiv t:A\oplus B}$$

Fig. 6. Rules for the usual linear type formers in each context (I-F, -I, -E, -C, -U, $\otimes$-F, -I, -E, -C, -U, $\multimap$-F, -I, -E, -C, -U, $\top$-F, -I, -U, &-F, -I, -E1, -E2, -C1, -C2, -U, 0-F, -E, -U, $\oplus$-F, -I1, -I2, -E, -C1, -C2, -U, !-F, -I, -E, -C, -U)

$$\frac{\Delta;\cdot\vdash A\ \text{type}}{\Delta;\cdot\vdash !A\ \text{type}}$$

$$\frac{\Delta;\cdot\vdash a : A}{\Delta;\cdot\vdash !a : !A} \qquad \frac{\Delta;\Xi\vdash t : !A \qquad \Delta, x : A;\Xi'\vdash b : B}{\Delta;\Xi,\Xi'\vdash \text{let } t \text{ be } !x \text{ in } b : B}$$

$$\frac{\Delta;\Xi\vdash \text{let } !a \text{ be } !x \text{ in } b : B}{\Delta;\Xi\vdash \text{let } !a \text{ be } !x \text{ in } b \equiv b[a/x] : B} \qquad \frac{\Delta;\Xi\vdash \text{let } t \text{ be } !x \text{ in } !x : !A}{\Delta;\Xi\vdash \text{let } t \text{ be } !x \text{ in } !x \equiv t : !A}$$

Fig. 6. *(Continued)*

Finally, we add rules that say we have all the possible commuting conversions, which from a syntactic point of view restore the subformula property and from a semantic point of view say that our rules are natural transformations (between hom-functors), which simplifies the categorical semantics significantly. We represent these schematically, following [15]. That is, if $C[-]$ is a linear program context, i.e. a context built without using !, then (abusing notation and dealing with all the let be in -constructors in one go) the following rules hold.

$$\frac{\Delta;\Xi\vdash C[\text{let } a \text{ be } b \text{ in } c] : D}{\Delta;\Xi\vdash C[\text{let } a \text{ be } b \text{ in } c] \equiv \text{let } a \text{ be } b \text{ in } C[c] : D}$$

if $C[-]$ does not bind any free variables in a or b;

$$\frac{\Delta;\Xi\vdash C[\text{false}(t)] : D}{\Delta;\Xi\vdash C[\text{false}(t)] \equiv \text{false}(t) : D}$$

if $C[-]$ does not bind any free variables in t;

$$\frac{\Delta;\Xi\vdash C[\text{case } t \text{ of inl}(x)\to c \mid\mid \text{inr}(y)\to d] : D}{\Delta;\Xi\vdash C[\text{case } t \text{ of inl}(x)\to c \mid\mid \text{inr}(y)\to d] \equiv \text{case } t \text{ of inl}(x)\to C[c] \mid\mid \text{inr}(y)\to C[d] : D}$$

if $C[-]$ does not bind any free variables in t or x or y.

Fig. 7. Commuting conversions

Remark 1. Note that all type formers that are defined context-wise (I, $\otimes$, $\multimap$, $\top$, $\&$, 0, $\oplus$, and !) are automatically preserved under the substitutions from Int-Ty-Subst (up to canonical isomorphism[4]), in the sense that $F(A_1,\ldots,A_n)[a/x]$ is isomorphic to $F(A_1[a/x],\ldots,A_n[a/x])$ for an n-ary type former F. Similarly, for $T = \Sigma$ or Π, we have that $(T_{!y:!B}C)[a/x]$ is isomorphic to $T_{!y:!B[a/x]}C[a/x]$ and $(Id_{!B}(b,b'))[a/x]$ is isomorphic to $Id_{!B[a/x]}(b[a/x],b'[a/x])$. This gives us Beck-Chevalley conditions in the categorical semantics.

Remark 2. The reader can note that the usual formulation of universes for DTT transfers very naturally to ILDTT, giving us a notion of universes for linear types. This allows us to write rules for forming types as rules for forming terms, as usual. We do not choose this approach and define the various type formers in the setting without universes.

[4] By an isomorphism of types $\Delta;\cdot\vdash A$ type and $\Delta;\cdot\vdash B$ type in context Δ, we here mean a pair of terms $\Delta;x : A\vdash f : B$ and $\Delta;y : B\vdash g : A$ together with a pair of judgemental equalities $\Delta;x : A\vdash g[f/y]\equiv x : A$ and $\Delta;y : B\vdash f[g/x]\equiv y : B$.

Some Basic Results. As the focus of this paper is the syntax-semantics correspondence, we will only briefly state a few syntactic results. For some standard metatheoretic properties for (a system equivalent to) the $\multimap, \Pi, \top, \&$-fragment of our syntax, we refer the reader to [4]. Standard techniques and some small adaptations of the system should be enough to extend the results to all of ILDTT.

We will only note the consistency of ILDTT both as a type theory (not, for all $\Delta; \Xi \vdash a, a' : A$, $\Delta; \Xi \vdash a \equiv a' : A$) and as a logic (ILDTT does not prove that every type is inhabited).

Theorem 1 (Consistency). *ILDTT with all its type formers is consistent, both as a type theory and as a logic.*

Proof (sketch). This follows from model-theoretic considerations. Later, in section 3, we shall see that our model theory encompasses that of DTT, for which we have models exhibiting both types of consistency.

To give the reader some intuition for these linear Π- and Σ-types, we suggest the following two interpretations.

Theorem 2 (Π and Σ as Dependent $!(-) \multimap (-)$ and $!(-) \otimes (-)$). *Suppose we have !-types. Let* $\Delta, x : A; \cdot \vdash B$ type, *where x is not free in B. Then,*

1. *$\Pi_{!x:!A} B$ is isomorphic to $!A \multimap B$, if we have Π-types and $\multimap$-types;*
2. *$\Sigma_{!x:!A} B$ is isomorphic to $!A \otimes B$, if we have Σ-types and $\otimes$-types.*

In particular, we have the following stronger version of a special case.

Theorem 3 (! as ΣI). *Suppose we have Σ- and I-types. Let* $\Delta; \cdot \vdash A$ type. *Then, $\Sigma_{!x:!A} I$ satisfies the rules for $!A$. Conversely, if we have !- and I-types, then $!A$ satisfies the rules for $\Sigma_{!x:!A} I$.*

A second interpretation is that Π and Σ generalise $\&$ and $\oplus$. Indeed, the idea is that that (or their infinitary equivalents) is what they reduce to when taken over discrete types. The subtlety in this result is the definition of a discrete type. The same phenomenon is observed in a different context in section 4.

For our purposes, a discrete type is a strong sum of $\top$ (a sum with a dependent -E-rule). Let us for simplicity limit ourselves to the binary case. For us, the discrete type with two elements will be $2 = \top \oplus \top$, where $\oplus$ has a strong/dependent -E-rule (note that this is not our $\oplus$-E). Explicitly, 2 is a type with the following -F-, -I-, and -E-rules (and the obvious -C- and -U-rules):

$$\frac{}{\Delta; \cdot \vdash 2 \text{ type}} \qquad \frac{}{\Delta; \cdot \vdash \mathrm{tt} : 2} \qquad \frac{}{\Delta; \cdot \vdash \mathrm{ff} : 2}$$

$$\frac{\Delta, x : 2; \cdot \vdash A \text{ type} \qquad \Delta; \cdot \vdash t : 2 \qquad \Delta; \Xi \vdash a_{\mathrm{tt}} : A[\mathrm{tt}/x] \qquad \Delta; \Xi \vdash a_{\mathrm{ff}} : A[\mathrm{ff}/x]}{\Delta; \Xi \vdash \text{if } t \text{ then } a_{\mathrm{tt}} \text{ else } a_{\mathrm{ff}} : A[t/x]}$$

Fig. 8. Rules for a discrete type 2, with -C- and -U-rules omitted for reasons of space

Theorem 4 (Π and Σ as Infinitary Non-Discrete $\&$ and $\oplus$). *If we have a discrete type 2 and a type family $\Delta, x : 2; \cdot \vdash A$, then*

1. *$\Pi_{!x:!2} A$ satisfies the rules for $A[\mathrm{tt}/x] \& A[\mathrm{ff}/x]$;*
2. *$\Sigma_{!x:!2} A$ satisfies the rules for $A[\mathrm{tt}/x] \oplus A[\mathrm{ff}/x]$.*

3 Categorical Semantics

We now introduce a notion of categorical model for which soundness and completeness results hold with respect to the syntax of ILDTT in presence of I- and $\otimes$-types[5]. This notion of model will prove to be particularly useful when thinking about various (extensional) type formers.

Definition 1. *By a* strict indexed symmetric monoidal category with comprehension, *we will mean the following data.*

1. *A category $\mathcal{C}$ with a terminal object $\cdot$.*
2. *A strict indexed symmetric monoidal category $\mathcal{L}$ over $\mathcal{C}$, i.e. a contravariant functor $\mathcal{L}$ into the category* SMCat *of (small) symmetric monoidal categories and strong monoidal functors $\mathcal{C}^{op} \xrightarrow{\mathcal{L}} \mathrm{SMCat}$. We will also write $-\{f\} := \mathcal{L}(f)$ for the action of $\mathcal{L}$ on a morphism f of $\mathcal{C}$.*
3. *A* comprehension schema, *i.e. for each $\Delta \in \mathrm{ob}(\mathcal{C})$ and $A \in \mathrm{ob}(\mathcal{L}(\Delta))$ a representation for the functor*

$$x \mapsto \mathcal{L}(\mathrm{dom}(x))(I, A\{x\}) : (\mathcal{C}/\Delta)^{op} \longrightarrow \mathrm{Set}.$$

We will write its representing object[6] $\Delta.A \xrightarrow{\mathbf{p}_{\Delta,A}} \Delta \in \mathrm{ob}(\mathcal{C}/\Delta)$ and universal element $\mathbf{v}_{\Delta,A} \in \mathcal{L}(\Delta.A)(I, A\{\mathbf{p}_{\Delta,A}\})$. We will write $a \mapsto \langle f, a\rangle$ for the isomorphism $\mathcal{L}(\Delta')(I, A\{f\}) \cong \mathcal{C}/\Delta(f, \mathbf{p}_{\Delta,A})$, if $\Delta' \xrightarrow{f} \Delta$.

Remark 3. Note that this notion of model reduces to a standard notion of model for DTT in the case the monoidal structures on the fibre categories are Cartesian: a reformulation of split comprehension categories with 1- and $\times$-types. To get a precise fit with the syntax, the extra demand called "fullness" is usually put on these [17]. The fact that we leave out this last condition precisely allows for non-trivial !-types (i.e. ones such that $!A \not\cong A$) in our models of ILDTT. Every model of DTT is, in particular, a (degenerate) model of ILDTT, though. We will see that the type formers of ILDTT also generalise those of DTT.

Theorem 5 (Soundness). *We can soundly interpret ILDTT with I- and $\otimes$-types in a strict indexed symmetric monoidal category $(\mathcal{C}, \mathcal{L})$ with comprehension.*

Proof (sketch). The idea is that a context $\Delta; \Xi$ will be (inductively) interpreted by a pair of objects $[\![\Delta]\!] \in \mathrm{ob}(\mathcal{C})$, $[\![\Xi]\!] \in \mathrm{ob}(\mathcal{L}([\![\Delta]\!])$, a type A in context $\Delta; \cdot$ by an object $[\![A]\!]$ of $\mathcal{L}([\![\Delta]\!])$, and a term $a : A$ in context $\Delta; \Xi$ by a morphism $[\![\Xi]\!] \xrightarrow{[\![a]\!]} [\![A]\!] \in \mathcal{L}[\![\Delta]\!])$. Generally, the interpretation of the propositional linear type theory in intuitionistic context $\Delta; \cdot$ will happen in $\mathcal{L}(\Delta)$ as would be expected.

The crux is that Int-C-Ext ($[\![\Delta, x : A]\!] := \mathrm{dom}(\mathbf{p}_{[\![\Delta]\!],[\![A]\!]})$), Int-Var ($[\![\Delta, x : A; \cdot \vdash x : A]\!] := \mathbf{v}_{\Delta,A}$), and Int-Subst (by $\mathcal{L}(\langle \mathrm{id}_\Delta, a\rangle)$ are interpreted through the comprehension, as is Int-Weak (through $\mathcal{L}$ of the obvious morphism in $\mathcal{C}$).

Finally, Soundness is a trivial verification.

---

[5] In case we are interested in the case without I- and $\otimes$-types, the semantics easily generalises to strict indexed symmetric multicategories with comprehension.

[6] Really, $\Delta.MA \xrightarrow{\mathbf{p}_{\Delta,MA}} \Delta$ would be a better notation, where we think of $L \dashv M$ as an adjunction inducing !, but it would be very verbose.

Theorem 6 (Completeness). *In fact, this interpretation is complete.*

Proof (sketch). We see this through the construction of a syntactic category.

In fact, we would like to say that the syntax is even an internal language for such categories. This is almost true, can be made entirely true by either putting the restriction on our notion of model that excludes any non-trivial morphisms into objects that are not of the form $\Delta.A$. Alternatively, we can extend the syntax to talk about context morphisms explicitly [18]. Following the DTT tradition, we have opted against the latter.

We will next characterise the categorical description of the various type formers. First, we note the following.

Theorem 7 (Comprehension Functor). *A comprehension schema* $(\mathbf{p}, \mathbf{v})$ *on a strict indexed symmetric monoidal category* $(\mathcal{C}, \mathcal{L})$ *defines a morphism* $\mathcal{L} \xrightarrow{M} \mathcal{I}$ *of indexed categories, where* $\mathcal{I}$ *is the full sub-indexed category of* $\mathcal{C}/-$ *(by making a choice of pullbacks) on the objects of the form* $\mathbf{p}_{\Delta,A}$ *and where* $M_\Delta(A \xrightarrow{a} B) := \mathbf{p}_{\Delta,A} \xrightarrow{\langle \mathbf{p}_{\Delta,A}, a\{\mathbf{p}_{\Delta,A}\} \circ \mathbf{v}_{\Delta,A}\rangle} \mathbf{p}_{\Delta,B}$.

Note that $\mathcal{I}$ is a display map category and hence a model of DTT [17]. We will think of it as the intuitionistic content of $\mathcal{L}$. We will see that the comprehension functor will give us a unique candidate for !-types: $! := LM$, where $L \dashv M$ is a monoidal adjunction. We conclude that, in ILDTT, the !-modality is uniquely determined by the indexing. This is worth noting, because, in propositional linear type theory, we might have many different candidates for !-types.

Theorem 8 (Semantic Type Formers). *For the other type formers, we have the following. A model* $(\mathcal{C}, \mathcal{L}, \mathbf{p}, \mathbf{v})$ *of ILDTT with* I*- and* $\otimes$*-types...*

1. *...supports* Σ*-types iff all the pullback functors* $\mathcal{L}(\mathbf{p}_{\Delta,A})$ *have left adjoints* $\Sigma_{!A}$ *that satisfy the Beck-Chevalley condition in the sense that the canonical map* $\Sigma_{!A\{f\}} \circ \mathcal{L}(\mathbf{q}_{f,A}) \longrightarrow \mathcal{L}(f) \circ \Sigma_{!A}$ *is an iso, where* $\Delta' \xrightarrow{f} \Delta$ *and* $\mathbf{q}_{f,A} := \langle f \circ \mathbf{p}_{\Delta',A\{f\}}, \mathbf{v}_{\Delta',A\{f\}}\rangle$*, and that satisfy Frobenius reciprocity in the sense that the canonical morphism* $\Sigma_{!A}(\Xi'\{\mathbf{p}_{\Delta,A}\} \otimes B) \longrightarrow \Xi' \otimes \Sigma_{!A}B$ *is an isomorphism , for all* $\Xi' \in \mathcal{L}(\Delta)$, $B \in \mathcal{L}(\Delta.A)$ *.*
2. *...supports* Π*-types iff all the pullback functors* $\mathcal{L}(\mathbf{p}_{\Delta,A})$ *have right adjoints* $\Pi_{!A}$ *that satisfy the dual Beck-Chevalley condition for pullbacks of the form* $(*)$*: the canonical* $\mathcal{L}(f) \circ \Pi_{!A} \longrightarrow \Pi_{!A\{f\}} \circ \mathcal{L}(\mathbf{q}_{f,A})$ *is an iso.*
3. *...supports* $\multimap$*-types iff* $\mathcal{L}$ *factors over the category* SMCCat *of symmetric monoidal closed categories and their homomorphisms.*
4. *...supports* $\top$*- and* $\&$*-types iff* $\mathcal{L}$ *factors over the category* SMCCat *of Cartesian categories with symmetric monoidal structure and their homomorphisms.*
5. *...supports* 0*- and* $\oplus$*-types iff* $\mathcal{L}$ *factors over the category* dSMcCCat *of co-Cartesian categories with a distributive symmetric monoidal structure and their homomorphisms.*

6. *...that supports $\multimap$-types, supports !-types iff all the comprehension functors $\mathcal{L}(\Delta) \xrightarrow{M_\Delta} \mathcal{I}(\Delta)$ have a strong monoidal left adjoint $\mathcal{I}(\Delta) \xrightarrow{L_\Delta} \mathcal{L}(\Delta)$ and L_- is a morphism of indexed categories: for all $\Delta' \xrightarrow{f} \Delta \in \mathcal{C}$, $L_{\Delta'}\mathcal{I}(f) = \mathcal{L}(f)L_\Delta$. Then $!_\Delta := L_\Delta \circ M_\Delta$ interprets the comodality ! in context Δ.*
7. *... that supports $\multimap$-types, supports Id-types iff for all $A \in \mathrm{ob}(\mathcal{L}(\Delta))$, we have left adjoints $\mathrm{Id}_{!A} \dashv -\{\mathrm{diag}_{\Delta,A}\}$ that satisfy a Beck-Chevalley condition: $\mathrm{Id}_{!A\{f\}} \circ \mathcal{L}(\mathbf{q}_{f,A}) \longrightarrow \mathcal{L}(\mathbf{q}_{\mathbf{q}_{f,A},A\{\mathbf{p}_{\Delta,A}\}}) \circ \mathrm{Id}_{!A}$ is an iso. Now, $\mathrm{Id}_{!A}(I)$ interprets $\mathrm{Id}_{!A}(x,x')$. Above, $\Delta.A \xrightarrow{\mathrm{diag}_{\Delta,A} := \langle \mathrm{id}_{\Delta.A}, \mathbf{v}_{\Delta,A}\rangle} \Delta.A.A\{\mathbf{p}_{\Delta,A}\}$.*

The semantics of ! suggests an alternative definition for the notion of a comprehension: if we have Σ-types in a strong sense, it is a derived notion!

Theorem 9 (Lawvere Comprehension). *Given a strict indexed monoidal category $(\mathcal{C},\mathcal{L})$ with left adjoints Σ_{Lf} to $\mathcal{L}(f)$ for arbitrary $\Delta' \xrightarrow{f} \Delta \in \mathcal{C}$, then we can define $\mathcal{C}/\Delta \xrightarrow{L_\Delta} \mathcal{L}(\Delta)$ by $L_\Delta(-) := \Sigma_{L_-}I$. In that case, $(\mathcal{C},\mathcal{L})$ has a comprehension schema iff L_Δ has a right adjoint M_Δ (for which then $M_{\Delta'} \circ \mathcal{L}(f) = \mathcal{L}(f) \circ M_\Delta$ for all $\Delta' \xrightarrow{f} \Delta \in \mathcal{C}$). That is, our notion of comprehension generalises that of Lawvere [19]. Finally, if Σ_{Lf} satisfy Frobenius reciprocity and Beck-Chevalley, then $(\mathcal{C},\mathcal{L})$ supports comprehension iff it supports !-types.*

Proof (sketch). This follows trivially if we write out both the representability condition defining a comprehension and the adjointness condition for Σ_f.

We observe the following about the usual intuitionistic type formers in $\mathcal{I}$.

Theorem 10 (Type Formers in $\mathcal{I}$). *$\mathcal{I}$ supports Σ-types iff $\mathrm{ob}(\mathcal{I}) \subset \mathrm{mor}(\mathcal{C})$ is closed under binary compositions. $\mathcal{I}$ supports Id-types iff $\mathrm{ob}(\mathcal{I})$ is closed under post-composition with $\mathrm{diag}_{\Delta,A}$. If $\mathcal{L}$ supports !- and Π-types, then $\mathcal{I}$ supports Π-types. Moreover, type formers in $\mathcal{I}$ relate to those in $\mathcal{L}$ as follows, leaving out the subscripts of the indexed functors $L \dashv M$:*

$$\Sigma_{!A}!B \cong L(\Sigma_{MA}MB) \qquad \mathrm{Id}_{!A}(!B) \cong L\mathrm{Id}_{MA}(MB) \qquad M\Pi_{!B}C \cong \Pi_{MB}MC.$$

Remark 4 (Dependent Seely Isomorphisms?). It is easily seen that $M_\Delta(\top) = \mathrm{id}_\Delta$ and $M_\Delta(A\&B) = M_\Delta(A) \times M_\Delta(B)$, hence $!_\Delta\top = I$ and $!_\Delta(A\&B) = !_\Delta A \otimes !_\Delta B$.

Now, theorem 10 suggests similar Seely isomorphisms for Σ- and Id-types. Indeed, $\mathcal{I}$ supports Σ- respectively Id-types iff we have "additive" Σ- resp. Id-types, that is $\Sigma^\&_A B, \mathrm{Id}^\&_A(B) \in \mathrm{ob}(\mathcal{L})$ s.t.

$$M\Sigma^\&_A B \cong \Sigma_{MA}MB \quad \text{and hence} \quad !\Sigma^\&_A B \cong \Sigma^\otimes_{!A}!B \quad \text{resp.}$$

$$M\mathrm{Id}^\&_A(B) \cong \mathrm{Id}_{MA}(MB) \quad \text{and hence} \quad !\mathrm{Id}^\&_A(B) \cong \mathrm{Id}^\otimes_{!A}(!B),$$

where we write $\Sigma^\otimes$ and $\mathrm{Id}^\otimes$ for the usual multiplicative Σ- and Id-types[7].

We are in this situation and have to consider such additive Σ- and Id-types if $L. \dashv M. : \mathcal{L}(\cdot) \longrightarrow \mathcal{C}$ is the co-Kleisli adjunction of !. See [13] for more discussion.

[7] We call usual Id-types "multiplicative" connectives e.g. since $\mathrm{Id}^\otimes_{!A}(B) \cong \mathrm{Id}^\otimes_{!A}(I) \otimes B$. Similarly, if we have a suitable $\mathrm{Id}^\&_A(\top)$, we can define $\mathrm{Id}^\&_A(B) := \mathrm{Id}^\&_A(\top)\&B$.

4 Some Discrete Models: Monoidal Families

We discuss a simple class of models in terms of families with values in a symmetric monoidal category. On a logical level, what the construction boils down to is starting with a model $\mathcal{V}$ of a linear propositional logic and taking the cofree linear predicate logic on Set with values in this propositional logic. This important example illustrates how Σ- and Π-types can represent infinitary additive disjunctions and conjunctions. The model is discrete in nature, however, and, in that respect, is not representative for ILDTT.

Suppose $\mathcal{V}$ is a symmetric monoidal category. We can then consider a strict Set-indexed category, defined through the following enriched Yoneda embedding $\mathrm{Fam}(\mathcal{V}) := \mathcal{V}^- := \mathrm{SMCat}(-, \mathcal{V})$:

$$\mathrm{Set}^{op} \xrightarrow{\mathrm{Fam}(\mathcal{V})} \mathrm{SMCat} \qquad\qquad S \xrightarrow{f} S' \longmapsto \mathcal{V}^S \xleftarrow{-\circ f} \mathcal{V}^{S'}.$$

Note that this definition naturally extends to a functorial embedding Fam.

Theorem 11 (Families Model ILDTT). *The construction* Fam *adds type dependency on* Set *cofreely, in the sense that it is right adjoint to the forgetful functor* ev_1 *that evaluates a model of linear dependent type theory at the empty context to obtain a model of linear propositional type theory (where* $\mathrm{SMCat}^{\mathrm{Set}^{op}}_{\mathrm{compr}}$ *is the full subcategory of* $\mathrm{SMCat}^{\mathrm{Set}^{op}}$ *on the objects with comprehension):*

$$\mathrm{SMCat} \underset{\mathrm{Fam}}{\overset{\mathrm{ev}_1}{\underset{\hookrightarrow}{\overset{\longleftarrow}{\perp}}}} \mathrm{SMCat}^{\mathrm{Set}^{op}}_{\mathrm{compr}}.$$

Proof (sketch). The comprehension on $\mathrm{Fam}(\mathcal{V})$ is given by the obvious bijection

$$\mathrm{Fam}(\mathcal{V})(S)(I, B\{f\}) \cong \mathrm{prod}_{s \in S} \mathcal{V}(I, B(f(s))) \cong \mathrm{Set}/S'(f, \mathbf{p}_{S',B}),$$

where $\mathbf{p}_{S',B} := \mathrm{coprod}_{s' \in S'} \mathcal{V}(I, B(s')) \xrightarrow{\mathrm{fst}} S'$. The rest of the proof is a straightforward verification, where the adjunction relies on Set being well-pointed.

We express the existence of type formers in $\mathrm{Fam}(\mathcal{V})$ as conditions on $\mathcal{V}$. A characterisation of additive Σ- and Id-types can be found in [13].

Theorem 12 (Type Formers for Families). $\mathcal{V}$ *has small coproducts that distribute over* $\otimes$ *iff* $\mathrm{Fam}(\mathcal{V})$ *supports* Σ*-types. In that case,* $\mathrm{Fam}(\mathcal{V})$ *also supports* 0- *and* $\oplus$*-types (which correspond precisely to finite distributive coproducts).*

$\mathcal{V}$ *has small products iff* $\mathrm{Fam}(\mathcal{V})$ *supports* Π*-types. In that case,* $\mathrm{Fam}(\mathcal{V})$ *also supports* $\top$*- and* &*-types (which correspond precisely to finite products).*

$\mathrm{Fam}(\mathcal{V})$ *supports* $\multimap$*-types iff* $\mathcal{V}$ *is monoidal closed.*

$\mathrm{Fam}(\mathcal{V})$ *supports* !*-types iff* $\mathcal{V}$ *has small coproducts of* I *that are preserved by* $\otimes$ *in the sense that the canonical morphism* $\mathrm{coprod}_S(\Xi' \otimes I) \longrightarrow \Xi' \otimes \mathrm{coprod}_S I$ *is an isomorphism for any* $\Xi' \in \mathrm{ob}\,\mathcal{V}$ *and* $S \in \mathrm{ob}\,\mathrm{Set}$*. In particular, if* $\mathrm{Fam}(\mathcal{V})$ *supports* Σ*-types, then it also supports* !*-types.*

$\mathrm{Fam}(\mathcal{V})$ *supports* Id*-types if* $\mathcal{V}$ *has an initial object. Supposing that* $\mathcal{V}$ *has a terminal object, the only if also holds.*

Proof (sketch). We supply some definitions and leave the rest to the reader.

$\top$-, &-, 0-, and $\oplus$-types are clear as (co)limits are pointwise in a functor category. $\multimap$-types are immediate as well from the previous section. We define $\Sigma_{Lf}(A)(s') := \mathrm{coprod}_{s \in f^{-1}(s')} A(s)$ and $\Pi_{Lf}(A)(s') = \mathrm{prod}_{s \in f^{-1}(s')} A(s)$. Then $\Sigma_{Lf} \dashv -\{f\} \dashv \Pi_{Lf}$. We define $\mathrm{Id}_{!A}(B)(s,a,a') := \begin{cases} B(s,a) \text{ if } a = a' \\ 0 \text{ else} \end{cases}$. Then, $\mathrm{Id}_{!A} \dashv -\{\mathrm{diag}_{S,A}\}$. Beck-Chevalley conditions are taken care of by the fact that subtitution is interpreted as precomposition. Finally, this leads to the definition $!A(s) := \mathrm{coprod}_{\mathcal{V}(I,A(s))} I$, which we can note only depends on $A(s)$.

Remark 5. Note that an obvious way to guarantee distributivity of coproducts over $\otimes$ is by demanding that $\mathcal{V}$ is monoidal closed.

Two simple concrete examples of $\mathcal{V}$ come to mind that accommodate all type formers and illustrate real *linear* type dependency: a category $\mathcal{V} = \mathrm{Vect}_F$ of vector spaces over a field F, with the tensor product, and the category $\mathcal{V} = \mathrm{Set}_*$ of pointed sets, with the smash product. All type formers get their obvious interpretation, but let us consider ! as it is a novelty of ILDTT that it gets uniquely determined by the indexing, while in propositional linear logic we might have several choices. In the first example, ! boils down to the following: $(!B)(s') = \mathrm{coprod}_{\mathrm{Vect}_F(F,B(s'))} F \cong \bigoplus_{B(s')} F$, i.e. taking the vector space freely spanned by all vectors. In the second example, $(!B)(s') = \mathrm{coprod}_{\mathrm{Set}_*(2_*,B(s'))} 2_* = \bigvee_{B(s')} 2_* = B(s') + \{*\}$, i.e. ! freely adds a new basepoint. These models show the following.

Theorem 13 (DTT,DILL$\subsetneq$ ILDTT). *ILDTT is a proper generalisation of DTT and DILL: we have inclusions of the classes of models DTT,DILL$\subsetneq$ILDTT.*

Although this class of models is important, it is clear that it only represents a limited part of the generality of ILDTT. Hence, we are in need of non-Cartsian models that are less discrete in nature, if we are hoping to observe interesting new phenomena arising from the connectives of linear dependent type theory. Some suggestions and work in progress will be discussed in the next section.

5 Conclusions and Future Work

We hope to have convinced the reader that linear dependent types fit very naturally in the landscape of existing type theories and that they admit a well-behaved semantic theory.

We have presented a system, ILDTT, that, on a syntactic level, is a natural blend between (intuitionistic) dependent type theory (DTT) and dual intuitionistic linear logic (DILL). On a semantic level, if one starts with the right notion of model for dependent types, the linear generalisation is obtained through the usual philosophy of passing from Cartesian to symmetric monoidal structures. The resulting notion of a model forms a natural blend between comprehension categories, modelling DTT, and linear-non-linear models of DILL.

It is very pleasing to see that all the syntactically natural rules for type formers are equivalent to their semantic counterparts that would be expected based on the traditions of categorical logic of dependent types and linear types.

In particular, from the point of view of logic, it is interesting to see that the categorical semantics seems to have a preference for multiplicative quantifiers.

Finally, we have shown that, as in the intuitionistic case, we can represent infinitary (additive) disjunctions and conjunctions in linear type theory, through cofree Σ- and Π-types, indexed over Set. In particular, this construction exhibits a family of non-trivial truly linear models of dependent types. Moreover, it shows that ILDTT properly extends both DILL and DTT.

Despite what might be expected from this paper, much of this work has been very semantically motivated, by specific models. In joint work with Samson Abramsky, a model of linear dependent types with comprehension has been constructed in a category of coherence spaces. Apart from the usual type constructors from linear logic, it also supports Σ-, Π-, and Id-types. A detailed account of this model will be made available soon.

In addition to providing a first non-trivial model of such a type system that goes properly beyond DILL and DTT and is semantically motivated, this work served as a stepping stone for a model in a category of games, which we developed together with Radha Jagadeesan and Samson Abramsky. This, in particular, provides a game semantics for dependent type theory.

An indexed category of spectra over topological spaces has been studied as a setting for stable homotopy theory [9, 11]. It has been shown to admit I-, $\otimes$-, $\multimap$-, and Σ-types. The natural candidate for a comprehension adjunction, here, is that between the infinite suspension spectrum and the infinite loop space: $L \dashv M = \Sigma^{\infty} \dashv \Omega^{\infty}$. A detailed examination of the situation and an explanation of the relation with the Goodwillie calculus is desirable. This might fit in with our ultimate objective of a linear analysis of homotopy type theory.

Another fascinating possibility is that of models related to quantum mechanics. Non-dependent linear type theory has found interesting interpretations in quantum computation [20]. The question rises if the extension to dependent linear types has a natural counterpart in physics and could e.g. provide stronger type systems for quantum computing. Also suggestive is Schreiber's work [12], in which it is sketched how linear dependent types can serve as a language to talk about quantum field theory and quantisation in particular.

Finally, there are still plenty of theoretical questions within the type theory. Can we find interesting models with type dependency on the co-Kleisli category of ! and can we make sense of additive Σ- and Id-types, e.g. from the point of view of syntax? Or should we perhaps doubt the canonicity of the Girard translation and accept that dependent types are more naturally modeled in co-Eilenberg-Moore categories? Is there an equivalent of strong/dependent E-rules for ILDTT and how do we model interesting intensional Id-types? Does the Curry-Howard correspondence extend in its full glory: do we have a propositions-as-types interpretation of linear predicate logic in ILDTT? These questions need to be addressed by a combination of research into the formal system and study of specific models. We hope that the general framework we sketched will play its part in connecting all the different sides of the story: from syntax to semantics; from computer science and logic to geometry and physics.

Acknowledgements. My thanks go out to Samson Abramsky and Radha Jagadeesan for the stimulating discussions and to Urs Schreiber for sparking my curiosity for this topic. I am indebted to the anonymous reviewers, whose comments have been very helpful. This research was supported by the EPSRC and the Clarendon Fund.

References

1. Martin-Löf, P.: An intuitionistic theory of types. Twenty-five Years of Constructive Type Theory 36, 127–172 (1998)
2. Girard, J.Y.: Linear logic. Theoretical Computer Science 50(1), 1–101 (1987)
3. Program, T.U.F.: Homotopy Type Theory: Univalent Foundations of Mathematics. Institute for Advanced Study (2013), `http://homotopytypetheory.org/book`
4. Cervesato, I., Pfenning, F.: A linear logical framework. In: LICS 1996. Proceedings, pp. 264–275. IEEE (1996)
5. Dal Lago, U., Gaboardi, M.: Linear dependent types and relative completeness. In: LiCS 2011. Proceeding, pp. 133–142. IEEE (2011)
6. Petit, B., et al.: Linear dependent types in a call-by-value scenario. In: Proceedings of the 14th Symposium on Principles and Practice of Declarative Programming, pp. 115–126. ACM (2012)
7. Gaboardi, M., Haeberlen, A., Hsu, J., Narayan, A., Pierce, B.C.: Linear dependent types for differential privacy. ACM SIGPLAN Notices 48, 357–370 (2013)
8. Watkins, K., Cervesato, I., Pfenning, F., Walker, D.: A concurrent logical framework i: Judgments and properties. Technical report, DTIC Document (2003)
9. May, J.P., Sigurdsson, J.: Parametrized homotopy theory, vol. 132. American Mathematical Soc. (2006)
10. Shulman, M.: Enriched indexed categories. Theory and Applications of Categories 28(21), 616–695 (2013)
11. Ponto, K., Shulman, M.: Duality and traces for indexed monoidal categories. Theory and Applications of Categories 26(23), 582–659 (2012)
12. Schreiber, U.: Quantization via linear homotopy types. arXiv preprint arXiv:1402.7041 (2014)
13. Vákár, M.: Syntax and semantics of linear dependent types. arXiv preprint arXiv:1405.0033 (original preprint from April 2014)
14. Krishnaswami, N.R., Pradic, P., Benton, N.: Integrating dependent and linear types (July 2014), `https://www.mpi-sws.org/~neelk/dlnl-paper.pdf`
15. Barber, A.: Dual intuitionistic linear logic. Technical Report ECS-LFCS-96-347, University of Edinburgh, Edinburgh (1996)
16. Hofmann, M.: Syntax and semantics of dependent types. In: Extensional Constructs in Intensional Type Theory, pp. 13–54. Springer (1997)
17. Jacobs, B.: Comprehension categories and the semantics of type dependency. Theoretical Computer Science 107(2), 169–207 (1993)
18. Pitts, A.M.: Categorical logic. In: Abramsky, S., Gabbay, D.M., Maibaum, T.S.E. (eds.) Handbook of Logic in Computer Science. Algebraic and Logical Structures, vol. 5, pp. 39–128. Oxford University Press (2000)
19. Lawvere, F.W.: Equality in hyperdoctrines and comprehension schema as an adjoint functor. Applications of Categorical Algebra 17, 1–14 (1970)
20. Abramsky, S., Duncan, R.: A categorical quantum logic. Mathematical Structures in Computer Science 16(3), 469–489 (2006), Preprint available at `http://arxiv.org/abs/quant-ph/0512114`

A Completeness Result for Finite λ-bisimulations*

Joost Winter

Faculty of Mathematics, Informatics, and Mechanics, University of Warsaw, Warsaw, Poland

Abstract. We show that finite λ-bisimulations (closely related to bisimulations up to context) are sound and complete for finitely generated λ-bialgebras for distributive laws λ of a monad T on **Set** over an endofunctor F on **Set**, such that F preserves weak pullbacks and finitely generated T-algebras are closed under taking kernel pairs. This result is used to infer the decidability of weighted language equivalence when the underlying semiring is a subsemiring of an effectively presentable Noetherian semiring. These results are closely connected to [ÉM10] and [BMS13], concerned with respectively the decidability and axiomatization of weighted language equivalence w.r.t. Noetherian semirings.

1 Introduction

The notion of bisimulation, originating from the world of process algebra, plays an important role in the field of universal coalgebra: a survey of important results can be found, for example, in [Rut00]. Bisimulation up to techniques, generalizing ordinary bisimulations, have been first considered coalgebraically in [Len99]; later, extensions were given in, for example [PS11], [RBR13], [Pou13], and [RBB$^+$13]. The soundness of various notions of coalgebraic bisimulation up to has been extensively studied; in [BP13], moreover, a completeness result for finite bisimulations up to context (in the setting of NFAs) is presented, together with an efficient algorithm for deciding equivalence. As far as the author is aware, this is so far the only result of this type present in the literature.

Structures that have both an algebraic and coalgebraic structure can often be described as λ-*bialgebras* using *distributive laws*. Introductions to this framework can be found in e.g. [Bar04], [Jac06], and [Kli11]. This framework has been used to formulate the *generalized powerset construction*, considered in [SBBR10], [JSS12], and [SBBR13], providing a category-theoretical generalization of the classical powerset construction.

Weighted automata, introduced in [Sch61], have been extensively studied: surveys can be found in e.g. [Eil76] or [BR11]. An important notion here is that of a *simulation* between automata, which can be used to prove equivalence of weighted automata, studied in for example [BLS06] and [ÉM10]. In [ÉM10], it is shown that weighted language equivalence is decidable over semirings that

* Work supported by the Warsaw Center of Mathematics and Computer Science, and by the Polish National Science Centre (NCN) grant 2012/07/E/ST6/03026.

A. Pitts (Ed.): FOSSACS 2015, LNCS 9034, pp. 117–132, 2015.
DOI: 10.1007/978-3-662-46678-0_8

are Noetherian and effectively presentable, using the notions of simulation and proper semirings. In the Appendix of this paper, we show how these notions relate to the results in this paper, and how some of the results from [ÉM10] can be derived from the main result in this paper.

Co- and bialgebraic treatments to weighted automata, instantiating the framework of λ-bialgebras, are found in e.g. [BBB$^+$12], [BMS13], and [JSS12]. In [BMS13], an (abstract) sound and complete axiomatization is presented for monads and endofunctors satisfying the same conditions as those required for Proposition 7, and subsequently instantiated to a concrete axiomatization for weighted languages over Noetherian semirings. The methods used differ substantially from those used in this paper, but the obtained results are closely related.

After presenting the required preliminaries from the existing literature, in this paper we show that finite λ-bisimulations are, in certain cases, complete already (λ-bisimulations in general are complete whenever the behaviour functor preserves weak pullbacks). From this we derive the decidability of weighted language equivalence over subsemirings of semirings that are Noetherian and effectively presentable. Finally, in an appendix we discuss the relationship between some parts of the coalgebraic and classical, respectively, approaches to weighted automata.

Hence, one of the aims of this paper can be stated as bringing closer together, on a general level, the classical and coalgebraic approaches to weighted automata, and, in particular, relating the results from [BMS13] to those from [ÉM10].

2 Preliminaries

We will, in this section, present the preliminary material required for presenting the main result in the next section. We assume familiar the basic notions of category theory (which can be found in e.g. [Awo10] or [Mac71]), as well as the notions of monoids, semirings, and (left and right) semimodules over a semiring (which can be found in e.g. [BR11]). All of the material presented in this section can be found in existing literature.

Given a category **C** and a monad T on **C**, $\mathbf{C}^T$ denotes the category of Eilenberg-Moore algebras for T. We moreover adopt the convention of using the term *S-module* to refer to *left S-semimodules.*

Some of the results in this paper require the axiom of choice (which can be formulated categorically by stating that (in **Set**) *every epi splits*, i.e. has a right inverse): these results are labelled with the marker (AC).

2.1 Algebras and Congruences

In this subsection, we present the notions of a *finitely generated algebra* and of a *kernel pair*, on a relatively concrete level, sufficient for obtaining the main results later in the paper.[1] Next, we give the definition of a *congruence*, and present a

[1] These are related to *finitely presentable algebras*, which are extensively studied in [AR94]: however, for the results in this paper, this notion is not needed.

result on the existence of coequalizers in $\mathbf{Set}^T$, required for our main result in the next section.

In the (concrete) case where T is a monad on $\mathbf{Set}$, a T-algebra (X, α_X) is called *finitely generated*[2] whenever there is a finite set Y together with a function $i : Y \to X$ such that the unique T-algebra morphism $i^* : (T(Y), \mu_Y) \to (X, \alpha_X)$ extending i is a regular epimorphism.[3] The condition of the epi i^* being regular directly implies that the mapping $U(i^*) : T(Y) \twoheadrightarrow X$ obtained by applying the forgetful functor is an epi in $\mathbf{Set}$, that is, a surjective function. We can moreover, without problems, assume that i itself is an injective function, i.e. a mono, and hence that Y can be regarded as a subset of X.

Given a morphism $f : X \to Y$ in a category with pullbacks, the *kernel pair* is the pullback of f with itself. Because the forgetful functor $U : \mathbf{Set}^T \to \mathbf{Set}$ creates all limits, the carrier of a kernel pair in $\mathbf{Set}^T$ can be described as the set

$$\{(x, y) \mid x, y \in UX \wedge Uf(x) = Uf(y)\}$$

and moreover, its algebra structure is compatible with the product algebra $X \times X$, i.e. the kernel pair is a subalgebra of $X \times X$.

Given an endofunctor T on $\mathbf{Set}$, and algebras (X, α_X) and (Y, α_Y) for this functor, a *congruence* between these algebras is a relation $R \subseteq X \times Y$ such that there is a unique T-algebra structure α_R on R making the following diagram commute:

$$\begin{array}{ccccc} TX & \xleftarrow{T\pi_1} & TR & \xrightarrow{T\pi_2} & TY \\ \downarrow{\scriptstyle \alpha_X} & & \downarrow{\scriptstyle \alpha_R} & & \downarrow{\scriptstyle \alpha_Y} \\ X & \xleftarrow{\pi_1} & R & \xrightarrow{\pi_2} & FY \end{array}$$

We furthermore will need the following result establishing the existence of coequalizers in $\mathbf{Set}^T$:

Proposition 1. *(AC) For any monad T on* **Set***, coequalizers exist in* $\mathbf{Set}^T$ *and are preserved by the forgetful functor.*

Proof. Established in the proof of [BW06, Proposition 9.3.4]. □

2.2 Universal Coalgebra

We will, in this section, consider some elementary and required results from the theory of universal coalgebra. For a more comprehensive reference to the theory, where the results below can also be found, we refer to [Rut00].

Given an endofunctor F on a category $\mathbf{C}$, a F-coalgebra consists of an object X in $\mathbf{C}$, together with a mapping $\delta : X \to TX$. Given two F-coalgebras (X, γ)

[2] This is known to correspond to the more general categorical definition of a finitely generated algebra; see e.g. the remark on `http://ncatlab.org/nlab/show/finitely+generated+object` under 'Definition in concrete categories'.

[3] An morphism is a *regular epimorphism* iff it is the coequalizer of a parallel pair of morphisms, see e.g. [Bor94]

and (Y, δ), a morphism between these coalgebras consists of a morphism $f : X \to Y$ such that the following diagram commutes:

$$\begin{array}{ccc} X & \xrightarrow{f} & Y \\ \gamma \downarrow & & \downarrow \delta \\ FX & \xrightarrow{Ff} & FY \end{array}$$

F-coalgebras and their morphisms form a category, and a terminal object in this category is called a *final coalgebra*. Given a F-coalgebra (X, δ_X), we let $[\![-]\!]_X$ denote the unique mapping into the final coalgebra whenever F has a final coalgebra.

Given two F-coalgebras (X, δ_X) and (Y, δ_Y), a F*-bisimulation* between X and Y is a relation $R \subseteq X \times Y$ such that there is some (not necessarily unique) F-coalgebra structure δ_R on R making the following diagram commute:

$$\begin{array}{ccccc} X & \xleftarrow{\pi_1} & R & \xrightarrow{\pi_2} & Y \\ \delta_X \downarrow & & \delta_R \downarrow & & \downarrow \delta_Y \\ FX & \xleftarrow{F\pi_1} & FR & \xrightarrow{F\pi_2} & FY \end{array}$$

In general, a largest bisimulation between two F-coalgebras always exists, and is denoted by $\sim_{X,Y}$. (We omit the subscripts when no confusion can arise.) Elements $x \in X$ and $y \in Y$ are called *bisimilar* whenever $x \sim_{X,Y} y$, and *behaviourally equivalent* whenever there is some F-coalgebra morphism f such that $f(x) = f(y)$. Whenever a final F-coalgebra exists, the latter condition is equivalent to $[\![x]\!]_X = [\![y]\!]_Y$.

In general, if two elements $x \in X$ and $y \in Y$ in F-coalgebras (X, δ_X) and (Y, δ_Y) are bisimilar, it follows that x and y are behaviourally equivalent (one may refer to this condition as the *soundness* of bisimulation). Under the condition that the functor F preserves *weak pullbacks* (a weak pullback is defined in the same way as a pullback, but without the uniqueness condition), the converse (which may be called the *completeness* of bisimulation) also holds.

2.3 λ-bialgebras

In this section, we will present, on an abstract level, the relevant material from the theory of λ-bialgebras, and the closely related *generalized powerset construction.* Comprehensive introductions to the material presented here can be found in e.g. [Bar04], [Jac06], [Kli11], [SBBR10], and [JSS12]. We will be concerned, in particular, with λ-bialgebras for a distributive law of a monad (T, μ, η) over an endofunctor F, without assuming any additional structure (e.g. that of a copointed functor or comonad) on the behaviour functor F.

Given a monad (T, μ, η) and an endofunctor F on any category $\mathbf{C}$, a *distributive law* of the monad T over F is a natural transformation

$$\lambda : TF \Rightarrow FT$$

such that the two diagrams of natural transformations

$$\begin{array}{ccc} F & \overset{\eta F}{\Longrightarrow} & TF \\ & \underset{F\eta}{\searrow\!\!\searrow} & \Big\Downarrow \lambda \\ & & FT \end{array} \qquad \text{and} \qquad \begin{array}{ccccc} TTF & & \overset{\mu F}{\Longrightarrow} & & TF \\ T\lambda \Big\Downarrow & & & & \Big\Downarrow \lambda \\ TFT & \overset{\lambda T}{\Longrightarrow} & FTT & \overset{F\mu}{\Longrightarrow} & FT \end{array}$$

commute.

Furthermore, given a distributive law $\lambda : TF \Rightarrow FT$, *λ-bialgebra* (X, α, γ) consists of a coalgebra (X, γ) for the functor F together with an algebra (X, α) for the monad T, such that the diagram

$$\begin{array}{ccccc} TX & \xrightarrow{\alpha} & X & \xrightarrow{\gamma} & FX \\ T\gamma \big\downarrow & & & & \big\uparrow F\alpha \\ TFX & & \xrightarrow{\lambda_X} & & FTX \end{array}$$

commutes. Morphisms of λ-algebras are mappings that simultaneously are F-coalgebra morphisms and T-algebra morphisms.

The two following, elementary, lemmata can be found in e.g. [Bar04]:

Lemma 2. *Given a distributive law λ of a monad (T, μ, η) over an endofunctor F and a FT-coalgebra (X, δ), $(TX, \mu_X, \hat{\delta})$ is a λ-bialgebra, with $\hat{\delta}$ given as:*

$$\hat{\delta} = F\mu_X \circ \lambda_{TX} \circ T\delta.$$

Proof. This is the first part of [Bar04, Lemma 4.3.3]. □

Lemma 3. *Given a distributive law λ of a monad (T, μ, η) over an endofunctor F, a λ-bialgebra (Q, α, γ) and an FT-coalgebra (X, δ), if $f : X \to Q$ makes the diagram*

$$\begin{array}{ccc} X & \xrightarrow{f} & Q \\ \delta \big\downarrow & & \big\downarrow \gamma \\ FTX & \xrightarrow{Ff^*} & FQ \end{array}$$

commute (where $f^* : TX \to Q$ is obtained by applying the forgetful functor to the unique T-algebra morphism from (TX, μ_X) to (Q, α) extending f), then f^* is a morphism of λ-bialgebras between $(TX, \mu_X, \hat{\delta})$ and (Q, α, γ).

Proof. See e.g. [Bar04, Lemma 4.3.4]. □

Given two λ-bialgebras (X, α_X, δ_X) and (Y, α_Y, δ_Y), a *λ-bisimulation* between X and Y is a relation $R \subseteq X \times Y$ such that there is some (not necessarily unique) FT-coalgebra structure on R making the following diagram commute:

$$\begin{array}{ccccc} X & \xleftarrow{\pi_1} & R & \xrightarrow{\pi_2} & Y \\ \delta_X \big\downarrow & & \delta_R \big\downarrow & & \big\downarrow \delta_Y \\ FX & \xleftarrow{F\pi_1{}^*} & FTR & \xrightarrow{F\pi_2{}^*} & FY \end{array}$$

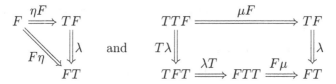

The following proposition establishes the soundness of λ-bisimulations:

Proposition 4. *Given two λ-bialgebras (X, α_X, δ_X) and (Y, α_Y, δ_Y), every λ-bisimulation $R \subseteq X \times Y$ is contained in a bisimulation S (for the functor F).*

Proof. See [Bar04, Corollary 4.3.5].   □

Moreover, the greatest bisimulation on two λ-bialgebras (X, α_X, δ_X) and (Y, α_Y, δ_Y) is a congruence:

Proposition 5. *Given two λ-bialgebras (X, α_X, δ_X) and (Y, α_Y, δ_Y), the relation $\sim_{X,Y}$ is a congruence, and its algebra structure is an Eilenberg-Moore algebra.*

Proof. See [Bar04, Corollary 3.4.22] and [Bar04, Corollary 3.4.23].   □

Any final F-coalgebra can be uniquely extended to a final λ-bialgebra:

Proposition 6. *Given a distributive law $\lambda : TF \Rightarrow FT$ for a functor F that has a final coalgebra (Ω, δ_Ω), there is a unique λ-bialgebra compatible with this final coalgebra, which is a final λ-bialgebra.*

Proof. See [Bar04, Corollary 3.4.19] and the following remark.   □

In this case, we can combine the extension from Lemma 2 with the unique mapping into the final F-coalgebra, obtaining the diagram

$$
\begin{array}{ccccc}
X & \xrightarrow{\eta_X} & TX & \xrightarrow{\ [\![-]\!]\ } & \Omega \\
{\scriptstyle \delta}\downarrow & \nearrow {\scriptstyle \hat{\delta}} & & & \downarrow{\scriptstyle \omega} \\
FTX & & \xrightarrow{F[\![-]\!]} & & F\Omega
\end{array}
$$

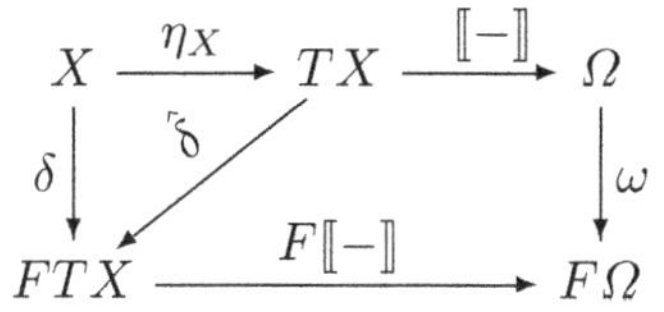

This construction, called the *generalized powerset construction*, is extensively studied in [SBBR10], [SBBR13], and [JSS12].

We finish this section by noting that there is a close relationship between the notion of a λ-bisimulation, and that of a *bisimulation up to context* (see e.g. [RBB$^+$13] for a comprehensive treatment of this notion). Given two λ-bialgebras (X, α_X, δ_X) and (Y, α_Y, δ_Y), a relation $R \subseteq X \times Y$ is called a bisimulation up to context whenever there is some δ_R making the diagram

$$
\begin{array}{ccccc}
X & \xleftarrow{\pi_1} & R & \xrightarrow{\pi_2} & Y \\
{\scriptstyle \delta_X}\downarrow & & \downarrow{\scriptstyle \delta_R} & & \downarrow{\scriptstyle \delta_Y} \\
FX & \xleftarrow{F\pi_1} & Fc(R) & \xrightarrow{F\pi_2} & FY
\end{array}
$$

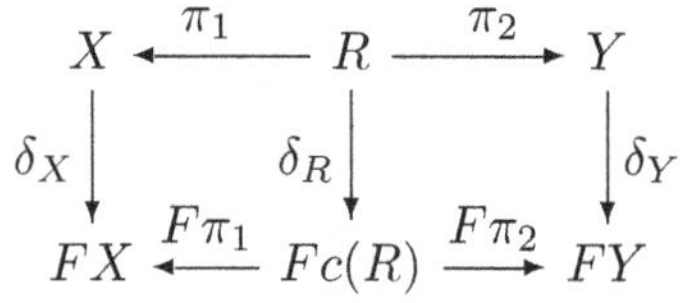

commute, where $c(R) = \langle \alpha_X \circ T\pi_1, \alpha_Y \circ T\pi_2 \rangle(TR) \subseteq X \times Y$. We note that there is a surjection $e : TR \twoheadrightarrow c(R)$, and thus, if δ_R is a witness to R being a λ-bisimulation, it directly follows that $Fe \circ \delta_R$ is a bisimulation up to context. If we assume the axiom of choice, the converse also holds: it now follows that there is some $f : c(R) \to TR$ such that $e \circ f = 1_{c(R)}$, and if δ_R witnesses that R is a bisimulation up to context, then $Ff \circ \delta_R$ witnesses that R is a λ-bisimulation.

2.4 Weighted Automata, Bialgebraically

We now briefly present the bialgebraic approach to weighted automata (over arbitrary semirings S). More comprehensive treatments of this bialgebraic approach can be found in e.g. [BMS13], [BBB+12], and [JSS12].

Here the monad T is instantiated as $\mathrm{Lin}_S(-)$, where $\mathrm{Lin}_S(X)$ is the set

$$\{f : X \to S \mid f \text{ has finite support}\}$$

regarded as representing finite (left) S-linear combinations of elements of X, for any semiring S, and the monadic structure can be specified by

$$\eta_X(x)(y) = \textbf{if } x = y \textbf{ then } 1 \textbf{ else } 0$$

and

$$\mu_X(f)(x) = \sum_{g \in \mathsf{supp}(f)} f(g) \cdot g(x).$$

The category of algebras for this monad is isomorphic to the category of S-modules and (left) S-linear mappings.

Furthermore, the behaviour functor is instantiated as $S \times -^A$. A coalgebra for this functor (or for the functor $S \times T(-)^A$ where T is some monad) is usually represented as a pair of mappings $(o, \delta) : X \to S \times X^A$, with $\delta(x)(a)$ usually represented as x_a (or, in the case of a single alphabet symbol, x'), and called the *a-derivative* of x, and with $o(x)$ referred to as the *output* of x. This notation allows us to conveniently represent these coalgebras as *systems of behavioural differential equations.*

There exists a final coalgebra for this functor, with its carrier given by the set

$$S\langle\langle A\rangle\rangle = (A^* \to S),$$

of formal power series in noncommuting variables, and the coalgebraic structure given by, for any $\sigma \in S\langle\langle A\rangle\rangle$, $o(\sigma) = \sigma(1)$ (with 1 denoting the empty word), and $\sigma_a(w) = \sigma(aw)$.

The distributive law

$$\lambda : \mathrm{Lin}_S(S \times -^A) \Rightarrow S \times \mathrm{Lin}_S(-)^A$$

can be given componentwise by

$$\lambda_X \left(\sum_{i=1}^{n} s_i(o_i, d_i) \right) = \left(\sum_{i=1}^{n} s_i o_i, a \mapsto \sum_{i=1}^{n} s_i d_i(a) \right).$$

We call a λ-bialgebra for this distributive law an *S-linear automaton*. The final bialgebra for this distributive law can be given by adding a pointwise S-module structure to $S\langle\langle A\rangle\rangle$. We regard coalgebras for the functor $S \times \mathrm{Lin}_S(-)^A$ as S-weighted automata, which can be extended into S-linear automata using Lemma 2. The formal power series accepted by a S-weighted automaton is then given by the unique mapping of this S-linear automaton into the final S-linear automaton.

The notion of λ-bisimulation here instantiates to the notion of *bisimulation up to linear combinations*. This condition can be concretely expressed as follows: given S-linear automata (X, o_X, δ_X) and (Y, o_Y, δ_Y), a relation $R \subseteq X \times Y$ is a bisimulation up to linear combinations whenever, for all $(x, y) \in R$, $o_X(x) = o_Y(y)$, and for every alphabet symbol $a \in A$ there is a $n \in \mathbb{N}$, together with elements $x_0, \ldots, x_{n-1} \in X$, $y_0, \ldots, y_{n-1} \in Y$, and scalars $s_0, \ldots, s_{n-1} \in S$, such that for each $i \leq n$, $(x_i, y_i) \in R$, and furthermore, $x_a = \sum_{i=1}^n s_i x_i$ and $y_a = \sum_{i=1}^n s_i y_i$. The latter condition can conveniently be represented using the following notation:

$$x_a = \sum_{i=1}^{n} s_i x_i \;\; \Sigma R \;\; \sum_{i=1}^{n} s_i y_i = y_a$$

3 Main Result

We now are able to state the main result, which can be seen as a *completeness* result for finite λ-bisimulations for distributive laws satisfying the required conditions, similarly to how Proposition 4 can be seen as stating the *soundness* of λ-bisimulations in general.

We first note that, given a λ-bialgebra (X, α, δ), the bisimilarity relation $\sim$ has both a F-coalgebra structure (by the definition of bisimulations), as well as that of an algebra for the monad T (by Proposition 5). Moreover, as a result of Proposition 1, the set $X/\sim$ has the structure of an algebra for the monad T, such that the function $h : X \to X/\sim$ sending each $x \in X$ to its equivalence class w.r.t. $\sim$ is a T-algebra morphism.

Proposition 7. *(AC) Assume:*

1. *T is a monad on* **Set** *such that finitely generated T-algebras are closed under taking kernel pairs.*
2. *F is an endofunctor on* **Set** *that preserves weak pullbacks.*
3. *λ is a distributive law $TF \Rightarrow FT$.*
4. *(X, α_X, δ_X) is a finitely generated λ-bialgebra.*

Then, given two states $x, y \in X$, x and y are behaviourally equivalent if and only if there is a finite λ-bisimulation $R \subseteq X \times X$ with $(x, y) \in R$.

Proof. If such a λ-bisimulation R exists, it immediately follows that R is contained in some bisimulation, and hence, that x and y are behaviourally equivalent.

Conversely, assume that there are $x, y \in X$ that are behaviourally equivalent. Because F preserves weak pullbacks, it directly follows that $x \sim y$. We now start by taking the kernel pair of the morphism $h : X \to X/\sim$. This kernel pair can be given by the set

$$\sim = \{(x, y) \mid Uh(x) = Uh(y)\}$$

with an algebra structure $\alpha_\sim : T(\sim) \to \sim$ such that $(\sim, \alpha_\sim)$ is a subalgebra of the product algebra $(X, \alpha_X) \times (X, \alpha_X)$. Because (X, α_X) is finitely generated, it follows from the first assumption that $(\sim, \alpha_\sim)$ again is finitely generated.

Simultaneously, $\sim$ is the greatest bisimulation on X, i.e., there is some (not necessarily unique) $\delta_\sim$ making the diagram

$$\begin{array}{ccccc} X & \xleftarrow{\pi_1} & \sim & \xrightarrow{\pi_2} & X \\ {\scriptstyle \delta_X}\downarrow & & {\scriptstyle \delta_\sim}\downarrow & & \downarrow{\scriptstyle \delta_X} \\ FX & \xleftarrow{F\pi_1} & F(\sim) & \xrightarrow{F\pi_2} & FX \end{array}$$

commute. (Note that, although $\sim$ is both the carrier of an algebra for the monad T and a F-coalgebra, we have not established that $\sim$ is a λ-bialgebra.)

Because $\sim$ is finitely generated, there is some finite $R \subseteq\sim$ (let i denote the inclusion of R into $\sim$) such that the extension $i^* : T(R) \to\sim$ is a regular epimorphism in $\mathbf{Set}^T$, and hence an epi in $\mathbf{Set}$.

Because the epi i^* splits by the axiom of choice, it has a right inverse j, and we can now construct δ_R as $Fj \circ \delta_\sim \circ i$ to make the diagram

$$\begin{array}{ccc} R & \xrightarrow{i} & \sim \\ {\scriptstyle \delta_R}\downarrow & & \downarrow{\scriptstyle \delta_\sim} \\ FTR & \xrightarrow{F(i^*)} & F(\sim) \end{array}$$

commute. We can furthermore assume that $(x, y) \in R$, simply by adding this single element to the finite set of generators.

We can now conclude that the diagram

$$\begin{array}{ccccc} X & \xleftarrow{\pi_1 \circ i} & R & \xrightarrow{\pi_2 \circ i} & X \\ {\scriptstyle \delta_X}\downarrow & & {\scriptstyle \delta_R}\downarrow & & \downarrow{\scriptstyle \delta_X} \\ FX & \xleftarrow{F(\pi_1 \circ i^*)} & FTR & \xrightarrow{F(\pi_2 \circ i^*)} & FX \end{array} \qquad (1)$$

again commutes.

As i^* and π_1 are both T-algebra morphisms, it now also follows that $\pi_1 \circ i^*$ is an T-algebra morphism extending $\pi_1 \circ i$. Because (TR, μ_R) is a free algebra, it now follows that $\pi_1 \circ i^* = (\pi_1 \circ i)^*$ and $\pi_2 \circ i^* = (\pi_2 \circ i)^*$. Making these substitutions in Diagram (1), we can conclude that R is a λ-bisimulation. □

Remark. If a final coalgebra for the functor F exists, there exists a unique λ-bialgebra structure on this final coalgebra, and hence it is possible to replace the morphism h used in the proof with the unique morphism $[\![-]\!]$ into the final λ-bialgebra, now yielding $\sim$ as the kernel pair of the morphism $[\![-]\!]$. The reliance on the axiom of choice can then be relaxed to the condition that, for finite sets X and arbitrary Y, every epi from TX to Y splits. In particular, this condition is satisfied by the monad $\mathrm{Lin}_S(-)$, as $\mathrm{Lin}_S(X)$ is countable whenever X is finite. As a consequence, in the next section, the decidability result can be established without reliance on the axiom of choice.

4 An Example

In this section, we will present an example illustrating how to prove the equivalence of states in an automaton using finite λ-bisimulation (or concretely, bisimulation up to linear combinations). The example given is a direct adaptation of one of the examples given in [BMS13].

Consider the following $\mathbb{Q}$-weighted automaton (over a singleton alphabet)

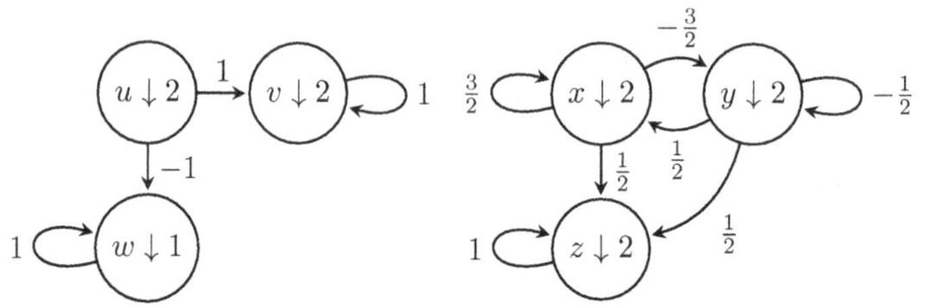

which corresponds to the following system of behavioural differential equations:

$$\begin{aligned} o(u) &= 2 & u' &= v - w & o(x) &= 2 & x' &= \tfrac{3}{2}x - \tfrac{3}{2}y + \tfrac{1}{2}z \\ o(v) &= 2 & v' &= v & o(y) &= 2 & y' &= \tfrac{1}{2}x - \tfrac{1}{2}y + \tfrac{1}{2}z \\ o(w) &= 1 & w' &= w & o(z) &= 2 & z' &= z \end{aligned}$$

Next, consider the following relation:

$$R = \{(u, x), (v, z), (\tfrac{1}{2}v - w, \tfrac{3}{2}x - \tfrac{3}{2}y)\}$$

A proof that R is a bisimulation up to linear combinations is given by

$$\begin{aligned} u' = \tfrac{1}{2}v + (\tfrac{1}{2}v - w) \ &\Sigma R \ \tfrac{1}{2}z + (\tfrac{3}{2}x - \tfrac{3}{2}y) = x' \\ v' = v \ &\Sigma R \ z = z' \\ (\tfrac{1}{2}v - w)' = \tfrac{1}{2}v - w \ &\Sigma R \ \tfrac{3}{2}x - \tfrac{3}{2}y = (\tfrac{3}{2}x - \tfrac{3}{2}y)' \end{aligned}$$

or alternatively by assigning the following weighted automaton structure to R:

$$\begin{aligned} o(u, x) &= 2 & (u, x)' &= \tfrac{1}{2}(v, z) + (\tfrac{1}{2} - w, \tfrac{3}{2}x - \tfrac{3}{2}y) \\ o(v, z) &= 2 & (v, z)' &= (v, z) \\ o(\tfrac{1}{2}v - w, \tfrac{3}{2}x - \tfrac{3}{2}y) &= 0 & (\tfrac{1}{2}v - w, \tfrac{3}{2}x - \tfrac{3}{2}y)' &= (\tfrac{1}{2}v - w, \tfrac{3}{2}x - \tfrac{3}{2}y) \end{aligned}$$

5 Decidability of Weighted Language Equivalence

Following [ÉM10], we call a semiring *Noetherian* whenever any submodule of a finitely generated S-module is again finitely generated. Using the result from Section 3, we can now directly derive a decidability result for equivalence of (states in) weighted automata over Noetherian semirings. We start by noting that, if S is a Noetherian semiring, and X is a finitely generated S-module, Y

is an arbitrary S-module, and $f : X \to Y$ is a S-linear mapping, then the kernel pair of f is a sub-S-module of the finitely generated S-module $X \times X$, and hence again finitely generated. Hence, the monad $\mathrm{Lin}_S(-)$ satisfies the first condition of Proposition 7 whenever S is a Noetherian semiring.

We moreover call, following the definition in [ÉM10], a semiring *effectively presentable*, whenever its carrier can be represented as a recursive subset of $\mathbb{N}$ such that the operations $+$ and $\cdot$ are recursive functions. This condition by itself is enough to establish the semidecidability of non-equivalence.

The results in this section are closely related to the decidability results from [ÉM10]. In the proof of semidecidability of equivalence, the crucial difference is relying on Proposition 7 instead of on a concrete result establishing properness.

The semidecidability of non-behavioural equivalence holds in general for effectively presentable semirings:

Proposition 8. *Given any effectively presentable semiring S, non-behavioural equivalence of states in finitely generated S-linear automata is semidecidable.*

Proof. (See also [ÉM10, Lemma 5.1].) If states x, y in a finitely generated S-linear automaton (X, o, δ) are not equivalent, there is some word $w \in A^*$ such that $o(x_w) \neq o(y_w)$. We can enumerate all words $w \in A^*$ and, because S is effectively presentable, can check for each word whether $o(x_w) = o(y_w)$. If x and y are not equivalent, eventually some word w witnessing this will be found. □

Moreover, if S additionally is a subsemiring of a Noetherian semiring, we can also derive semidecidability of behavioural equivalence (and hence, in combination with the preceding result, decidability) using Proposition 7.

Proposition 9. *Given any semiring S that is a subsemiring of an effectively presentable Noetherian semiring S', behavioural equivalence of states in free finitely generated S-linear automata is semidecidable.*

Proof. We start by noting that we can see any free finitely generated S-linear automaton as a free finitely generated S'-linear automaton (X, o, δ). Because S' is effectively presentable, it is countable, and the set of tuples

$$(R \in \mathcal{P}_\omega(\mathrm{Lin}_S(X) \times \mathrm{Lin}_S(X)), \delta_R : R \to S \times \mathrm{Lin}_S(R))$$

again is countable, giving an enumeration of its elements.

For each element of this set, we can check whether $(x, y) \in R$ and whether (R, δ_R) makes Diagram (1) commute. If $[\![x]\!]_X = [\![y]\!]_X$, a suitable candidate will eventually be found as a result of Proposition 7, so the process will terminate. □

Corollary 10. *Given any semiring S that is a subsemiring of an effectively presentable Noetherian semiring S', behavioural equivalence of states in free finitely generated S-linear automata is decidable.*

6 Further Directions

The results in this paper give rise to several possible directions for future work. One possibility is looking for extensions of the main result to distributive laws of a monad over a functor with additional structure, e.g. that of a copointed functor or a comonad.

As a final observation, we note that it is also possible to use the main result to conclude that certain monads do *not* have the property that finitely generated algebras are closed under taking kernel pairs. A first example follows the approach in [ÉM10], where it is shown that the tropical semiring $\mathbb{T}$ is not Noetherian: likewise, we can show that finitely generated algebras for the monad $\text{Lin}_{\mathbb{T}}(-)$ are not closed under taking kernel pairs, as this would imply decidability and it is known that equivalence of $\mathbb{T}$-weighted automata is not decidable.

A second example of such a negative result can be given by the monad $\mathcal{P}_\omega((- + A)^*)$: because the context-free languages can be characterized using a distributive law of this monad over the functor $2 \times -^A$ ([BHKR13], [WBR13]), and because equivalence of context-free languages is not decidable, it follows that algebras for the monad $\mathcal{P}_\omega((- + A)^*)$ are not closed under taking kernel pairs. (This result can be contrasted to the results in [Cau90] and [CHS95], which establish the decidability of bisimilarity for context-free processes. However, note that bisimulation over determinized systems is equal to language equivalence, which corresponds to the process-algebraic notion of trace equivalence.) A more detailed study of this type of results is left as future work.

Acknowledgements. For helpful suggestions and comments, the author would like to thank Bartek Klin (in particular for the observation that the existence of a final coalgebra is not required for the main result) and Jurriaan Rot (in particular for sharing his observations about the relationship between λ-bisimulation and bisimulation up to context, which have been incorporated into the paper). The author would furthermore like to thank the anonymous reviewers for their constructive comments on the first version of the paper.

References

[AR94] Adámek, J., Rosicky, J.: Locally Presentable and Accessible Categories. Cambridge University Press (1994)

[Awo10] Awodey, S.: Category Theory. Oxford University Press (2010)

[Bar04] Bartels, F.: On Generalized Coinduction and Probabilistic Specification Formats. PhD thesis, Vrije Universiteit Amsterdam (2004)

[BBB+12] Bonchi, F., Bonsangue, M.M., Boreale, M., Rutten, J., Silva, A.: A coalgebraic perspective on linear weighted automata. Information and Computation 211, 77–105 (2012)

[BHKR13] Bonsangue, M.M., Hansen, H.H., Kurz, A., Rot, J.: Presenting distributive laws. In: Heckel, R., Milius, S. (eds.) CALCO 2013. LNCS, vol. 8089, pp. 95–109. Springer, Heidelberg (2013)

[BLS06] Béal, M.-P., Lombardy, S., Sakarovitch, J.: Conjugacy and equivalence of weighted automata and functional transducers. In: Grigoriev, D., Harrison, J., Hirsch, E.A. (eds.) CSR 2006. LNCS, vol. 3967, pp. 58–69. Springer, Heidelberg (2006)

[BMS13] Bonsangue, M.M., Milius, S., Silva, A.: Sound and complete axiomatizations of coalgebraic language equivalence. ACM Transactions on Computational Logic 14(1), 7 (2013)

[Bor94] Borceux, F.: Handbook of Categorical Algebra. Basic category theory, vol. 1. Cambridge University Press (1994)

[BP13] Bonchi, F., Pous, D.: Checking NFA equivalence with bisimulations up to congruence. In: POPL, pp. 457–468. ACM (2013)

[BR11] Berstel, J., Reutenauer, C.: Noncommutative Rational Series with Applications. Cambridge University Press (2011)

[BW06] Barr, M., Wells, C.: Toposes, triples and theories. Reprints in Theory and Applications of Categories 12, 1–287 (2006)

[Cau90] Caucal, D.: Graphes canoniques de graphes algébriques. ITA 24, 339–352 (1990)

[CHS95] Christensen, S., Hüttel, H., Stirling, C.: Bisimulation equivalence is decidable for all context-free processes. Information and Computation 121(2), 143–148 (1995)

[Eil76] Eilenberg, S.: Automata, Languages, and Machines. Academic Press, Inc. (1976)

[ÉM10] Ésik, Z., Maletti, A.: Simulation vs. equivalence. In: Arabnia, H.R., Gravvanis, G.A., Solo, A.M.G. (eds.) FCS, pp. 119–124. CSREA Press (2010)

[HM13] Heckel, R., Milius, S. (eds.): CALCO 2013. LNCS, vol. 8089. Springer, Heidelberg (2013)

[Jac06] Jacobs, B.: A bialgebraic review of deterministic automata, regular expressions and languages. In: Futatsugi, K., Jouannaud, J.-P., Meseguer, J. (eds.)Goguen Festschr 2006. LNCS, vol. 4060, pp. 375–404. Springer, Heidelberg (2006)

[JSS12] Jacobs, B., Silva, A., Sokolova, A.: Trace semantics via determinization. In: Pattinson, D., Schröder, L. (eds.) CMCS 2012. LNCS, vol. 7399, pp. 109–129. Springer, Heidelberg (2012)

[Kli11] Klin, B.: Bialgebras for structural operational semantics: An introduction. Theoretical Computer Science 412(38), 5043–5069 (2011)

[Len99] Lenisa, M.: From set-theoretic coinduction to coalgebraic coinduction: some results, some problems. Electronic Notes in Theoretical Computer Science 19, 2–22 (1999)

[Mac71] MacLane, S.: Categories for the Working Mathematician. Graduate Texts in Mathematics, vol. 5. Springer, New York (1971)

[Pou13] Pous, D.: Coalgebraic up-to techniques. In: Heckel, R., Milius, S. (eds.) CALCO 2013. LNCS, vol. 8089, pp. 34–35. Springer, Heidelberg (2013)

[PS11] Pous, D., Sangiorgi, D.: Enhancements of the coinductive proof method. In: Advanced Topics in Bisimulation and Coinduction. Cambridge University Press (2011)

[RBB+13] Rot, J., Bonchi, F., Bonsangue, M.M., Pous, D., Rutten, J., Silva, A.: Enhanced coalgebraic bisimulation. Submitted to Mathematical Structures in Computer Science (2013)

[RBR13] Rot, J., Bonsangue, M., Rutten, J.: Coalgebraic bisimulation-up-to. In: van Emde Boas, P., Groen, F.C.A., Italiano, G.F., Nawrocki, J., Sack, H.

(eds.) SOFSEM 2013. LNCS, vol. 7741, pp. 369–381. Springer, Heidelberg (2013)

[Rut00] Rutten, J.: Universal coalgebra: A theory of systems. Theoretical Computer Science 249(1), 3–80 (2000)

[SBBR10] Silva, A., Bonchi, F., Bonsangue, M.M., Rutten, J.: Generalizing the powerset construction, coalgebraically. In: Lodaya, K., Mahajan, M. (eds.) FSTTCS. LIPIcs, vol. 8, pp. 272–283. Schloss Dagstuhl—Leibniz-Zentrum für Informatik (2010)

[SBBR13] Silva, A., Bonchi, F., Bonsangue, M., Rutten, J.: Generalizing determinization from automata to coalgebras. Logical Methods in Computer Science 9(1) (2013)

[Sch61] Schützenberger, M.-P.: On the definition of a family of automata. Information and Control 4(2-3), 245–270 (1961)

[WBR13] Winter, J., Bonsangue, M.M., Rutten, J.J.M.M.: Coalgebraic characterizations of context-free languages. Logical Methods in Computer Science 9(3:14) (2013)

A Simulations and Bialgebra Homomorphisms

This appendix is meant to elucidate the relation between the notion of a *simulation*[4], which has been an important tool in the classical theory of weighted automata for proving the equivalence between automata, and the bialgebraic notion of a *homomorphism* between S-linear automata, which plays a similar role in the co- and bialgebraic approach.

To make the correspondence between the two approaches somewhat more straightforward, we give a presentation of classical weighted automata that is symmetric to the traditional one: i.e. in terms of left-linear mappings and matrix multiplication on the left, rather than in terms of right-linear mappings.

A.1 Weighted Automata

In the classical presentation, a (finite) *weighted automaton* of dimension $n \geq 1$ over a finite alphabet A and a semiring S is a triple $\mathcal{A} = (\alpha, M_{a \in A}, \beta)$ where

- $\alpha \in S^{n \times 1}$ is a vector of length n, the initial vector;
- for every $a \in A$, $M_a \in S^{n \times n}$ is the transition matrix for the alphabet symbol a; and
- $\beta \in S^{1 \times n}$ is a vector of length n, the final vector.

The correspondence with the coalgebraic view on automata is now given as follows: we note that we can view every $n \times n$ matrix as a left-linear mapping[5] $\mathrm{Lin}_S(n) \to \mathrm{Lin}_S(n)$ (corresponding to the extension $\hat{\delta}(-, a)$), uniquely determined by a function $n \to \mathrm{Lin}_S(n)$ (corresponding to $\delta(-, a)$), and the final vector can be seen as a left-linear mapping from the left S-module $\mathrm{Lin}_S(n)$ to S itself, seen as a left S-module, again uniquely determined by a function $n \to S$.

[4] Unrelated to simulations as defined in process algebra.

[5] Note that $\mathrm{Lin}_S(n)$ can simply be seen as S^n here.

Ignoring the initial vector α, a traditional weighted automaton can then be seen as a coalgebra as follows:

$$\mathrm{Lin}_S(n) \xrightarrow{(\beta, M)} S \times \mathrm{Lin}_S(n)^A$$

The initial vector α, furthermore, simply is an element of $\mathrm{Lin}_S(n)$, and taking the word derivative of α to a word $w = a_1 \dots a_n$ corresponds to the sequence of matrix multiplications

$$M_{a_n} \dots M_{a_1} \alpha.$$

Finally, the formal power series $\mathcal{L}(\mathcal{A})$ *accepted* by a weighted automaton $\mathcal{A} = (\alpha, M_{a \in A}, \beta)$ can be specified by

$$\mathcal{L}(\mathcal{A})(a_1 \dots a_k) = \beta M_{a_k} \dots M_{a_1} \alpha$$

and by the above construction, it is seen to be equal to the power series $[\![\alpha_w]\!]$, where $[\![-]\!]$ is the usual notion of final coalgebra semantics for the functor $S \times -^A$, with respect to the coalgebra $(\mathrm{Lin}_S(n), \beta, M)$.

A.2 Simulations and Homomorphisms

Given two weighted automata $\mathcal{A} = (\alpha, M, \beta)$ (of dimension m) and $\mathcal{B} = (\gamma, N, \delta)$ (of dimension n), a matrix $Z \in S^{n \times m}$ is called a *simulation* from $\mathcal{A}$ to $\mathcal{B}$ whenever the following equations hold (in the case of the second equation, for all $a \in A$):

$$Z\alpha = \gamma \qquad ZM_a = N_a Z \qquad \beta = \delta Z$$

This definition corresponds to the one given in [ÉM10], with the modification that Z now represents a left-linear mapping, rather than a right-linear mapping.

A basic fact about simulations is that a simulation between weighted automata $\mathcal{A} = (\alpha, M, \beta)$ and $\mathcal{B} = (\gamma, N, \delta)$ in all cases implies equivalence of the weighted languages accepted by these automata, i.e. $\mathcal{L}(\mathcal{A}) = \mathcal{L}(\mathcal{B})$. We will now turn to the connection between this notion of a simulation, and the notion of a homomorphism of coalgebras, from which this equivalence directly follows.

As $S^{n \times m}$ matrices are in bijective correspondence with left-linear mappings from $\mathrm{Lin}_S(m)$ to $\mathrm{Lin}_S(n)$, it directly follows that the second and third condition are equivalent to the condition that the following diagram commutes:

$$\begin{array}{ccc} \mathrm{Lin}_S(m) & \xrightarrow{\quad Z \quad} & \mathrm{Lin}_S(n) \\ \downarrow{\scriptstyle (\beta, M)} & & \downarrow{\scriptstyle (\delta, N)} \\ S \times \mathrm{Lin}_S(m)^A & \xrightarrow{1_S \times Z^A} & S \times \mathrm{Lin}_S(n)^A \end{array}$$

Hence, for finite weighted automata (X, o_X, δ_X) and (Y, o_Y, δ_Y), the classical notion of a simulation between these automata corresponds to the coalgebraic notion of a homomorphism h from the extended automaton $(\mathrm{Lin}_S(X), \hat{o}_X, \hat{\delta}_X)$ to the extended automaton $(\mathrm{Lin}_S(Y), \hat{o}_Y, \hat{\delta}_Y)$, together with two elements $x \in \mathrm{Lin}_S(X)$ and $y \in \mathrm{Lin}_S(Y)$ such that $h(x) = y$.

A.3 Proper Semirings

In [ÉM10], a semiring S is called *proper* whenever, if two automata $\mathcal{A} = (\alpha, M, \beta)$ and $\mathcal{B} = (\gamma, N, \delta)$ are equivalent, i.e. $\mathcal{L}(\mathcal{A}) = \mathcal{L}(\mathcal{B})$, there is a finite sequence of automata $\mathcal{A}_1, \ldots, \mathcal{A}_k$ for some k with $\mathcal{A}_1 = \mathcal{A}$ and $\mathcal{A}_k = \mathcal{B}$, such that for each i with $1 \leq i < k$ there either is a simulation from $\mathcal{A}_i$ to $\mathcal{A}_{i+1}$ or there is a simulation from $\mathcal{A}_{i+1}$ to $\mathcal{A}_i$.

Using the results from Section 3, we can now directly conclude that every Noetherian semiring is proper, as follows: assume we have two S-weighted automata (X, o_X, δ_X) and (Y, o_Y, δ_Y) and elements $x \in \mathrm{Lin}_S(X)$ and $y \in \mathrm{Lin}_S(Y)$ such that $[\![x]\!]_X = [\![y]\!]_Y$ w.r.t. the linear extensions of these automata.

We can first construct a weighted automaton $(X+Y, o_{X+Y}, \delta_{X+Y})$, and it is easy to see that this gives homomorphisms

$$\mathrm{Lin}_S(\kappa_1) : \mathrm{Lin}_S(X) \to \mathrm{Lin}_S(X+Y)$$
$$\mathrm{Lin}_S(\kappa_2) : \mathrm{Lin}_S(Y) \to \mathrm{Lin}_S(X+Y)$$

where $\kappa_1 : X \to X+Y$ and $\kappa_2 : Y \to X+Y$ denote the injections of the coproduct. Instantiating $\mathrm{Lin}_S(X+Y)$ for X in Diagram (1) and Proposition 7, we can now conclude that there are homomorphisms

$$(\pi_1 \circ i)^* : \mathrm{Lin}_S(R) \to \mathrm{Lin}_S(X+Y)$$
$$(\pi_2 \circ i)^* : \mathrm{Lin}_S(R) \to \mathrm{Lin}_S(X+Y)$$

and that $(\kappa_1(x), \kappa_2(y)) \in R$.

It now follows that this gives a chain of simulations of automata, as a result of (a) $\mathrm{Lin}_S(\kappa_1)$ mapping x to $\kappa_1(x)$; (b) $(\pi_1 \circ i)^*$ mapping $(\kappa_1(x), \kappa_2(y))$ to $\kappa_1(x)$; (c) $(\pi_2 \circ i)^*$ mapping $(\kappa_1(x), \kappa_2(y))$ to $\kappa_2(y)$; and (d) $\mathrm{Lin}_S(\kappa_2)$ mapping y to $\kappa_2(y)$.

Hence, we can now conclude that S satisfies the conditions of being proper. This fact is also observed in [ÉM10], using a somewhat different argument, using the properties of Noetherian semirings, rather than the property of monads where kernel pairs of finitely generated objects are finitely generated again.

Sequent Calculus in the Topos of Trees

Ranald Clouston[1] and Rajeev Goré[2]

[1] Department of Computer Science, Aarhus University, Aarhus, Denmark
ranald.clouston@cs.au.dk
[2] Research School of Computer Science, Australian National University, Canberra, Australia
rajeev.gore@anu.edu.au

Abstract. Nakano's "later" modality, inspired by Gödel-Löb provability logic, has been applied in type systems and program logics to capture guarded recursion. Birkedal et al modelled this modality via the internal logic of the topos of trees. We show that the semantics of the propositional fragment of this logic can be given by linear converse-well-founded intuitionistic Kripke frames, so this logic is a marriage of the intuitionistic modal logic KM and the intermediate logic LC. We therefore call this logic KM_{lin}. We give a sound and cut-free complete sequent calculus for KM_{lin} via a strategy that decomposes implication into its static and irreflexive components. Our calculus provides deterministic and terminating backward proof-search, yields decidability of the logic and the coNP-completeness of its validity problem. Our calculus and decision procedure can be restricted to drop linearity and hence capture KM.

1 Introduction

Guarded recursion [11] on an infinite data structure requires that recursive calls be nested beneath constructors. For example, a stream of zeros can be defined with the self-reference guarded by the cons:

```
zeros = 0 : zeros
```

Such equations have *unique* solutions and are *productive*: they compute arbitrarily large prefixes of the infinite structure in finite time, a useful property in lazy programming.

Syntactic checks do not always play well with higher-order functions; the insight of Nakano [27] is that guarded recursion can be enforced through the *type system* via an 'approximation modality' inspired by Gödel-Löb provability logic [7]. We follow Appel et al [1] and call this modality *later*, and use the symbol $\triangleright$. The meaning of $\triangleright\tau$ is roughly 'τ one computation step later'. Type definitions must have their self-reference guarded by later. For example streams of integers, which we perhaps expect to be defined as $Stream \cong \mathbb{Z} \times Stream$, are instead

$$Stream \cong \mathbb{Z} \times \triangleright Stream$$

A. Pitts (Ed.): FOSSACS 2015, LNCS 9034, pp. 133–147, 2015.
DOI: 10.1007/978-3-662-46678-0_9

Nakano showed that versions of Curry's fixed-point combinator **Y**, and Turing's fixed-point combinator likewise, can be typed by the *strong Löb axiom* (see [24])

$$(\triangleright\tau \to \tau) \to \tau \tag{1}$$

Returning to our example, **Y** can be applied to the function

$$\lambda x.\langle 0, x\rangle : \triangleright Stream \to \mathbb{Z} \times \triangleright Stream$$

to define the stream of zeros.

Nakano's modality was popularised by the typing discipline for intermediate and assembly languages of Appel et al [1], where for certain 'necessary' types a 'Löb rule' applies which correlates to the strong Löb axiom (1). The modality has since been applied in a wide range of ways; a non-exhaustive but representative list follows. As a type constructor, $\triangleright$ appears in Rowe's type system for Featherweight Java [30], the kind system of the System F extension FORK [28], and in types for functional reactive programming [22], with applications to graphical user interfaces [21]. As a logical connective, $\triangleright$ was married to separation logic in [19], then to higher-order separation logic in [2], and to *step-indexed* logical relations for reasoning about programming languages with LSLR [13]. Thus Nakano's modality is important in various applications in computer science.

We have so far been coy on precisely what the logic of later is, beyond positing that $\triangleright$ is a modality obeying the strong Löb axiom. Nakano cited Gödel-Löb provability logic as inspiration, but this is a *classical* modal logic with the *weak* Löb axiom $\Box(\Box\tau \to \tau) \to \Box\tau$, whereas we desire intuitionistic implication and the stronger axiom (1). In fact there does exist a tradition of intuitionistic analogues of Gödel-Löb logic [24], of which Nakano seemed mainly unaware; we will see that logic with later can partly be understood through this tradition. In the computer science literature it has been most common to leave proof theory and search implicit and fix some concrete semantics; for example see Appel et al's Kripke semantics of stores [1]. A more abstract and general model can be given via the internal logic of the *topos of trees* $\mathcal{S}$ [4]. This was shown to generalise several previous models for logic with later, such as the ultrametric spaces of [5,22], and provides the basis for a rich theory of dependent types. We hence take the internal logic of $\mathcal{S}$ as a prominent and useful model of logic with later, in which we can study proof theory and proof search.

In this paper we look at the propositional-modal core of the internal logic of $\mathcal{S}$. This fragment will be seen to have semantics in *linear intuitionistic Kripke frames* whose reflexive reduction is *converse-well-founded*. Linear intuitionistic frames are known to be captured by the *intermediate* logic Dummett's LC [8]; the validity of the LC axiom in the topos of trees was first observed by Litak [23]. Intuitionistic frames with converse-well-founded reflexive reduction are captured by the intuitionistic modal logic KM, first called I^{Δ} [26]. Hence the internal propositional modal logic of the topos of trees is semantically exactly their combination, which we call KM_{lin} (Litak [24, Thm. 50] has subsequently confirmed this relationship at the level of Hilbert axioms also).

Our specific contribution is to give a sound and cut-free complete sequent calculus for KM_{lin}, and by restriction for KM also, supporting terminating backwards proof search and hence yielding the decidability and finite model property of these logics. Our sequent calculus also establishes the coNP-completeness of deciding validity in KM_{lin}.

To our knowledge sequent calculi for intuitionistic Gödel-Löb logics, let alone KM or KM_{lin}, have not before been investigated, but such proof systems provide a solid foundation for proving results such as decidability, complexity, and interpolation, and given an appropriate link between calculus and semantics can provide explicit, usually finite, counter-models falsifying given non-theorems.

The main technical novelty of our sequent calculus is that we leverage the fact that the intutionistic accessibility relation is the reflexive closure of the modal relation, by decomposing implication into a static (classical) component and a dynamic 'irreflexive implication' $\twoheadrightarrow$ that looks forward along the modal relation. In fact, this irreflexive implication obviates the need for $\rhd$ entirely, as $\rhd\varphi$ is easily seen to be equivalent to $\top \twoheadrightarrow \varphi$. Semantically the converse of this applies also, as $\varphi \twoheadrightarrow \psi$ is semantically equivalent to $\rhd(\varphi \to \psi)$[1], but the $\twoheadrightarrow$ connective is a necessary part of our calculus. We maintain $\rhd$ as a first-class connective in deference to the computer science applications and logic traditions from which we draw, but note that formulae of the form $\rhd(\varphi \to \psi)$ are common in the literature - see Nakano's $(\to E)$ rule [27], and even more directly Birkedal and Møgelberg's $\circledast$ constructor. We therefore suspect that treating $\twoheadrightarrow$ as a first-class connective could be a conceptually fruitful side-benefit of our work.

Note that for space reasons some proofs appear only in the extended version of this paper [10].

2 From the Topos of Trees to Kripke Frames

In this section we outline the *topos of trees* model and its internal logic, and show that this logic can be described semantically by conditions on intuitionistic Kripke frames. Therefore after this section we discard category theory and proceed with reference to Kripke frames alone.

The topos of trees, written $\mathcal{S}$, is the category of presheaves on the first infinite ordinal ω (with objects $1, 2, \ldots$, rather than starting at 0, in keeping with the relevant literature). Concretely an *object* A is a pair of a family of sets A_i indexed by the positive integers, and a family of *restriction functions* $r_i^A : A_{i+1} \to A_i$ indexed similarly. An *arrow* $f : A \to B$ is a family of functions $f_i : A_i \to B_i$ indexed similarly, subject to *naturality*, i.e. all squares below commute:

$$\begin{array}{ccccccccc}
A_1 & \xleftarrow{a_1} & A_2 & \xleftarrow{a_2} & A_3 & \cdots & A_j & \xleftarrow{a_j} & A_{j+1} \\
\downarrow{\scriptstyle f_1} & & \downarrow{\scriptstyle f_2} & & \downarrow{\scriptstyle f_3} & & \downarrow{\scriptstyle f_j} & & \downarrow{\scriptstyle f_{j+1}} \\
B_1 & \xleftarrow[b_1]{} & B_2 & \xleftarrow[b_2]{} & B_3 & \cdots & B_j & \xleftarrow[b_j]{} & B_{j+1}
\end{array}$$

[1] This in turn is equivalent in KM_{lin} (but is not in KM) to $\rhd\varphi \to \rhd\psi$ [27, Sec. 3].

Two $\mathcal{S}$-objects are of particular interest: the *terminal object* 1 has singletons as component sets and identities as restriction functions; the *subobject classifier* Ω has $\Omega_j = \{0, \ldots, j\}$ and $\omega_j(k) = min(j, k)$. We regard the positive integers as *worlds* and functions $x : 1 \to \Omega$ as *truth values* over these worlds, by considering x true at j iff $x_j = j$. Such an x is constrained by naturality to have one of three forms: $x_j = j$ for all j (*true everywhere*); $x_j = 0$ for all j (*true nowhere*); or given any positive integer k, x_j is k for all $j \geq k$, and is j for all $j \leq k$ (*becomes true at world k, remains true at all lesser worlds*). As such the truth values can be identified with the set $\mathbb{N} \cup \{\infty\}$, where ∞ captures 'true everywhere'.

Formulae of the internal logic of $\mathcal{S}$ are defined as

$$\varphi ::= p \mid \top \mid \bot \mid \varphi \wedge \varphi \mid \varphi \vee \varphi \mid \varphi \to \varphi \mid \varphi \twoheadrightarrow \varphi \mid \rhd\varphi$$

where $p \in \text{Atm}$ is an atomic formula. Negation may be defined as usual as $\varphi \to \bot$. The connective $\twoheadrightarrow$, read as *irreflexive implication*, is not in Birekedal et al [4] but is critical to the sequent calculus of this paper; readers may view $\twoheadrightarrow$ as a second-class connective generated and then disposed of by our proof system, or as a novel first-class connective, as they prefer.

Given a map η from propositional variables $p \in \text{Atm}$ to arrows $\eta(p) : 1 \to \Omega$, and a positive integer j, the Kripke-Joyal forcing semantics for $\mathcal{S}$ are defined by

$\eta, j \Vdash p$	iff $\eta(p)_j = j$
$\eta, j \Vdash \top$	always
$\eta, j \Vdash \bot$	never
$\eta, j \Vdash \varphi \wedge \psi$	iff $\eta, j \Vdash \varphi$ and $\eta, j \Vdash \psi$
$\eta, j \Vdash \varphi \vee \psi$	iff $\eta, j \Vdash \varphi$ or $\eta, j \Vdash \psi$
$\eta, j \Vdash \varphi \to \psi$	iff $\forall k \leq j.\ \eta, k \Vdash \varphi$ implies $\eta, k \Vdash \psi$
$\eta, j \Vdash \varphi \twoheadrightarrow \psi$	iff $\forall k < j.\ \eta, k \Vdash \varphi$ implies $\eta, k \Vdash \psi$
$\eta, j \Vdash \rhd\varphi$	iff $\forall k < j.\ \eta, k \Vdash \varphi$

A formula φ is *valid* if $\eta, j \Vdash \varphi$ for all η, j. Note that $\varphi \twoheadrightarrow \psi$ is equivalent to $\rhd(\varphi \to \psi)$, and $\rhd\varphi$ is equivalent to $\top \twoheadrightarrow \varphi$. While implication $\to$ can be seen as a conjunction of static and irreflexive components:

$$j \Vdash \varphi \to \psi \text{ iff } (j \Vdash \varphi \text{ implies } j \Vdash \psi) \text{ and } j \Vdash \varphi \twoheadrightarrow \psi \tag{2}$$

it is not definable from the other connectives, because we have no static (that is, classical) implication. However our sequent calculus will effectively capture (2).

We now turn to Kripke frame semantics. Kripke semantics for intuitionistic modal logics are usually defined via bi-relational frames $\langle W, R_{\to}, R_{\Box}\rangle$, where $R_{\to}$ and $R_{\Box}$ are binary relations on W, with certain interaction conditions ensuring that modal formulae persist along the intuitionistic relation [33]. However for KM and KM_{lin} the intuitionistic relation is definable in terms of the box relation, and so only the latter relation need be explicitly given to define a frame:

Definition 2.1. *A* frame *is a pair $\langle W, R\rangle$ where W is a non-empty set and R a binary relation on W. A* KM-frame *has R transitive and* converse-well-founded, *i.e. there is no infinite sequence $x_1 R x_2 R x_3 R \cdots$. A* KM_{lin}-frame *is a* KM*-frame with R also* connected, *i.e.* $\forall x, y \in W.\ x = y$ *or* $R(x, y)$ *or* $R(y, x)$.

Converse-well-foundedness implies irreflexivity. Also, KM- and KM_{lin}-frames may be infinite because non-well-founded chains $\cdots Rw_3Rw_2Rw_1$ are permitted.

Given a binary relation R, let $R^=$ be its *reflexive closure*. If $\langle W, R\rangle$ is a KM-frame then $\langle W, R^=\rangle$ is reflexive and transitive so provides frame semantics for intuitionistic logic. In fact frames arising in this way in general satisfy only the theorems of intuitionistic logic, so KM is conservative over intuitionistic logic. In other words, the usual propositional connectives are too coarse to detect the converse well-foundedness of a frame; for that we need $\rhd$ and the strong Löb axiom (1). Similarly the reflexive closure of a KM_{lin}-frame is a *linear* relation and so gives semantics for the logic LC, over which KM_{lin} is conservative.

A *model* $\langle W, R, \vartheta\rangle$ consists of a frame $\langle W, R\rangle$ and a valuation $\vartheta : \text{Atm} \mapsto 2^W$ obeying **persistence**:

$$\text{if } w \in \vartheta(p) \text{ and } wRx \text{ then } x \in \vartheta(p)$$

We hence define KM- and KM_{lin}-models by the relevant frame conditions.

We can now define when a KM- or KM_{lin}-model $M = \langle W, R, \vartheta\rangle$ makes a formula true at a world $w \in W$, with obvious cases $\top, \bot, \wedge, \vee$ omitted:

$$\begin{array}{ll} M, w \Vdash p & \text{iff } w \in \vartheta(p) \\ M, w \Vdash \varphi \to \psi & \text{iff } \forall x.\, wR^=x \text{ and } M, x \Vdash \varphi \text{ implies } M, x \Vdash \psi \\ M, w \Vdash \varphi \twoheadrightarrow \psi & \text{iff } \forall x.\, wRx \text{ and } M, x \Vdash \varphi \text{ implies } M, x \Vdash \psi \\ M, w \Vdash \rhd\varphi & \text{iff } \forall x.\, wRx \text{ implies } M, x \Vdash \varphi \end{array}$$

Thus $\rhd$ is the usual modal box. As usual for intuitionistic logic, we have a monotonicity lemma, provable by induction on the formation of φ:

Lemma 2.2 (Monotonicity). *If $M, w \Vdash \varphi$ and wRv then $M, v \Vdash \varphi$.*

Fixing a class of models (KM- or KM_{lin}-), a formula φ is *valid* if for every world w in every model M we have $M, w \Vdash \varphi$. It is easy to observe that the two semantics presented above coincide, given the right choice of frame conditions:

Theorem 2.3. *Formula φ is valid in the internal logic of $\mathcal{S}$ iff it is KM_{lin}-valid.*

3 The Sequent Calculus SKM_{lin} for KM_{lin}

A *sequent* is an expression of the form $\Gamma \vdash \Delta$ where Γ and Δ are finite, possibly empty, sets of formulae with Γ the *antecedent* and Δ the *succedent*. We write Γ, φ for $\Gamma \cup \{\varphi\}$. Our sequents are "multiple-conclusioned" since the succedent Δ is a finite set rather than a single formula as in "single-conclusioned" sequents.

A sequent *derivation* is a finite tree of sequents where each internal node is obtained from its parents by instantiating a rule. The root of a derivation is the *end-sequent*. A sequent derivation is a *proof* if all the leaves are zero-premise rules. A rule may require extra side-conditions for its (backward) application.

The sequent calculus SKM_{lin} is shown in Fig. 1, where Γ, Δ, Φ, Θ, and Σ, with superscripts and/or subscripts, are finite, possibly empty, sets of formulae.

$$\top R \frac{}{\Gamma \vdash \top, \Delta} \qquad id \frac{}{\Gamma, \varphi \vdash \varphi, \Delta} \qquad \bot L \frac{}{\Gamma, \bot \vdash \Delta}$$

$$\vee L \frac{\Gamma, \varphi \vdash \Delta \qquad \Gamma, \psi \vdash \Delta}{\Gamma, \varphi \vee \psi \vdash \Delta} \qquad \vee R \frac{\Gamma \vdash \varphi, \psi, \Delta}{\Gamma \vdash \varphi \vee \psi, \Delta}$$

$$\wedge L \frac{\Gamma, \varphi, \psi \vdash \Delta}{\Gamma, \varphi \wedge \psi \vdash \Delta} \qquad \wedge R \frac{\Gamma \vdash \varphi, \Delta \qquad \Gamma \vdash \psi, \Delta}{\Gamma \vdash \varphi \wedge \psi, \Delta}$$

$$\to L \frac{\Gamma, \varphi \twoheadrightarrow \psi \vdash \varphi, \Delta \qquad \Gamma, \varphi \twoheadrightarrow \psi, \psi \vdash \Delta}{\Gamma, \varphi \to \psi \vdash \Delta} \qquad \to R \frac{\Gamma, \varphi \vdash \psi, \Delta \qquad \Gamma \vdash \varphi \twoheadrightarrow \psi, \Delta}{\Gamma \vdash \varphi \to \psi, \Delta}$$

$$\text{STEP} \frac{\text{Prem}_1 \quad \cdots \quad \text{Prem}_k \quad \text{Prem}_{k+1} \quad \cdots \quad \text{Prem}_{k+n}}{\Sigma_l, \Theta^{\rhd}, \Gamma^{\twoheadrightarrow} \vdash \Delta^{\twoheadrightarrow}, \Phi^{\rhd}, \Sigma_r} \dagger$$

$$\text{Prem}_{1 \leq i \leq k} \quad = \Sigma_l, \Theta, \Theta^{\rhd}, \Gamma^{\to}, \varphi_i \twoheadrightarrow \psi_i, \varphi_i \vdash \psi_i, \Delta^{\to}_{-i}, \Phi$$
$$\text{Prem}_{k+1 \leq i \leq k+n} = \Sigma_l, \Theta, \Theta^{\rhd}, \Gamma^{\to}, \rhd\phi_{i-k} \vdash \Delta^{\to}, \Phi$$

$\Theta^{\rhd} = \rhd\theta_1, \cdots, \rhd\theta_j$ $\qquad$ $\Theta = \theta_1, \cdots, \theta_j$
$\Gamma^{\twoheadrightarrow} = \{\alpha_1 \twoheadrightarrow \beta_1, \cdots, \alpha_l \twoheadrightarrow \beta_l\}$ $\qquad$ $\Gamma^{\to} = \{\alpha_1 \to \beta_1, \cdots, \alpha_l \to \beta_l\}$
$\Delta^{\twoheadrightarrow} = \{\varphi_1 \twoheadrightarrow \psi_1, \cdots, \varphi_k \twoheadrightarrow \psi_k\}$ $\qquad$ $\Delta^{\to} = \{\varphi_1 \to \psi_1, \cdots, \varphi_k \to \psi_k\}$
$\Delta^{\to}_{-i} = \Delta^{\to} \setminus \{\varphi_i \to \psi_i\}$
$\Phi^{\rhd} = \rhd\phi_1, \cdots, \rhd\phi_n$ $\qquad$ $\Phi = \phi_1, \cdots, \phi_n$

where † means that the conditions C0, C1 and C2 below must hold
(C0) $\Delta^{\twoheadrightarrow} \cup \Phi^{\rhd} \neq \emptyset$
(C1) $\bot \notin \Sigma_l$ and $\top \notin \Sigma_r$ and $(\Sigma_l \cup \Theta^{\rhd} \cup \Gamma^{\twoheadrightarrow}) \cap (\Delta^{\twoheadrightarrow} \cup \Phi^{\rhd} \cup \Sigma_r) = \emptyset$
(C2) Σ_l and Σ_r each contain atomic formulae only

Explanations for the conditions:
(C0) there must be at least one $\rhd$- or $\twoheadrightarrow$-formula in the succedent of the conclusion
(C1) none of the rules $\bot$L, $\top$R, *id* are applicable to the conclusion
(C2) none of the rules $\vee$L, , $\vee$R, $\wedge$L, $\wedge$R, $\to$L, $\to$R are applicable to the conclusion

Fig. 1. Rules for sequent calculus SKM_{lin}

Rules $\top$R, $\bot$L, *id*, $\vee$L, $\vee$R, $\wedge$L, $\wedge$R are standard for a multiple-conclusioned calculus for Int [32]. Rules $\to$L and $\to$R can be seen as branching on a conjunction of static and an irreflexive implication: see equation (2). The occurrence of $\varphi \twoheadrightarrow \psi$ in the right premise of $\to$L is redundant, since ψ implies $\varphi \twoheadrightarrow \psi$, but its presence makes our termination argument simpler.

The rule STEP resembles Sonobe's multi-premise rule for $\to$R in LC [31,12], but its interplay of static and dynamic connectives allows us to capture the converse-well-foundedness of our frames. The reader may like to skip forward to compare it to the rules for KM in Fig. 4, which are simpler because they do not have to deal with linearity. Condition C0 is essential for soundness; C1 and C2 are not, but ensure that the STEP rule is applicable only if no other rules are applicable (upwards), which is necessary for semantic invertibility (Lem. 3.11). Note that the formulae in $\Theta^{\rhd}$ appear intact in the antecedent of every premise.

$$\dfrac{\dfrac{\dfrac{}{(\rhd p \to p) \to p, \rhd p \to p, \rhd p \vdash p}\,\text{mp}}{(\rhd p \to p) \twoheadrightarrow p, \rhd p \twoheadrightarrow p \vdash \rhd p, p}\,\textsc{step} \qquad \dfrac{}{(\rhd p \to p) \twoheadrightarrow p, \rhd p \twoheadrightarrow p, p \vdash p}\,\text{id}}{\dfrac{(\rhd p \to p) \twoheadrightarrow p, \rhd p \to p \vdash p}{\vdash (\rhd p \to p) \twoheadrightarrow p}\,\textsc{step}}\,{\to}\text{L}$$

$$\dfrac{\dfrac{\dfrac{\dfrac{}{\rhd p \to p, \rhd p \vdash p}\,\text{mp}}{\rhd p \twoheadrightarrow p \vdash \rhd p, p}\,\textsc{step} \qquad \dfrac{}{\rhd p \twoheadrightarrow p, p \vdash p}\,\text{id}}{\rhd p \to p \vdash p}\,{\to}\text{L} \qquad \vdash (\rhd p \to p) \twoheadrightarrow p}{\vdash (\rhd p \to p) \to p}\,{\to}\text{R}$$

Fig. 2. SKM_{lin} proof of the strong Löb axiom

$$\dfrac{\dfrac{\dfrac{}{p \twoheadrightarrow q, p, q \vdash p, q}\,\text{id} \qquad \dfrac{\dfrac{}{p \to q, p, q \twoheadrightarrow p, q \vdash p}\,\text{id}}{p \twoheadrightarrow q, p \vdash q, q \twoheadrightarrow p}\,\textsc{step}}{p \twoheadrightarrow q, p \vdash q, q \to p}\,{\to}\text{R} \qquad \dfrac{\text{Symmetric to left}}{q \twoheadrightarrow p, q \vdash p, p \to q}}{\vdash p \twoheadrightarrow q, q \twoheadrightarrow p}\,\textsc{step}$$

$$\dfrac{\dfrac{\dfrac{\dfrac{}{p, q \vdash q, p}\,\text{id} \qquad \dfrac{\dfrac{}{p, q \twoheadrightarrow p, q \vdash p}\,\text{id}}{p \vdash q, q \twoheadrightarrow p}\,\textsc{step}}{p \vdash q, q \to p}\,{\to}\text{R} \qquad \dfrac{\dfrac{\dfrac{}{q, p \twoheadrightarrow q, p \vdash q}\,\text{id}}{q \vdash p, p \twoheadrightarrow q}\,\textsc{step} \qquad \vdash p \twoheadrightarrow q, q \twoheadrightarrow p}{\vdash p \twoheadrightarrow q, q \to p}\,{\to}\text{R}}{\vdash p \to q, q \to p}\,{\to}\text{R}}{\vdash p \to q \vee q \to p}\,\vee\text{R}$$

Fig. 3. SKM_{lin} proof of the LC axiom

This is not essential as Θ implies $\Theta^{\rhd}$, but will simplify our proof of completeness. In constrast the formulae in $\Phi^{\rhd}$ do not appear in the succedent of any premise. Also, the formulae in Σ_r do not appear in the succedent of any premise. So STEP contains two aspects of weakening, but C2 ensures this is not done prematurely.

Figs. 2 and 3 give example proofs, using the following derived rule:

Lemma 3.1. *The Modus Ponens rules* mp *is derivable in* SKM_{lin} *as follows:*

Proof.

$$\dfrac{\dfrac{}{\Gamma, \varphi, \varphi \twoheadrightarrow \psi \vdash \varphi, \psi}\,\text{id} \qquad \dfrac{}{\Gamma, \varphi, \varphi \twoheadrightarrow \psi, \psi \vdash \psi}\,\text{id}}{\Gamma, \varphi, \varphi \to \psi \vdash \psi}\,{\to}\text{L}$$

3.1 Soundness of SKM_{lin}

Given a world w in some model M, and finite sets Γ and Δ of formulae, we write $w \Vdash \Gamma$ if every formula in Γ is true at w in model M and write $w \nVdash \Delta$ if every formula in Δ is not true at w in model M.

A sequent $\Gamma \vdash \Delta$ is **refutable** if there exists a model M and a world w in that model such that $w \Vdash \Gamma$ and $w \nVdash \Delta$. A sequent is **valid** if it is not refutable.

A rule is **sound** if some premise is refutable whenever the conclusion is refutable. A rule is **semantically invertible** if the conclusion is refutable whenever some premise is refutable. Given a model M and a formula φ, a world w is a **refuter** for φ if $M, w \not\Vdash \varphi$. It is a **last refuter** for φ if in addition $M, w \Vdash \rhd\varphi$. An **eventuality** is a formula of the form $\varphi \twoheadrightarrow \psi$ or $\rhd\varphi$ in the succedent of the conclusion of an application of the rule STEP.

Lemma 3.2. *In every model, every formula φ with a refuter has a last refuter.*

Proof. Suppose φ has refuter w in model M, i.e. $M, w \not\Vdash \varphi$. If all R-successors v of w have $v \Vdash \varphi$ then $w \Vdash \rhd\varphi$, and so w is the last refuter we seek. Else pick any successor v such that $M, v \not\Vdash \varphi$ and repeat the argument replacing w with v. By converse well-foundedness this can only be done finitely often before reaching a world with no R-successors, which vacuously satisfies $\rhd\varphi$.

Theorem 3.3 (Soundness). *If $\vdash \varphi$ is* SKM$_{lin}$*-derivable then φ is* KM$_{lin}$*-valid. Proved in extended version [10].*

3.2 Terminating Backward Proof Search

In this section we describe how to systematically find derivations using backward proof search. To this end, we divide the rules into three sets as follows:

Termination Rules: the rules id, $\bot$L, $\top$R
Static Rules: the rules $\to$L, $\to$R, $\vee$L, $\vee$R, $\wedge$L, $\wedge$R
Transitional Rule: STEP.

The proof search strategy below starts at the leaf (end-sequent) $\Gamma_0 \vdash \Delta_0$:

while some rule is applicable to a leaf sequent **do**
  stop: apply any applicable termination rule to that leaf
  saturate: else apply any applicable static rule to that leaf
  transition: else apply the transitional rule to that leaf

The phase where only static rules are applied is called the **saturation** phase. The only non-determinism in our procedure is the choice of static rule when many static rules are applicable, but as we shall see later, any choice suffices. Note that conditions C1 and C2 actually force STEP to have lowest priority.

Let $sf(\varphi)$ be the set of subformulae of φ, including φ itself and let m be the length of φ. Let $cl(\varphi) = sf(\varphi) \cup \{\psi_1 \twoheadrightarrow \psi_2 \mid \psi_1 \to \psi_2 \in sf(\varphi)\}$.

Proposition 3.4. *The (backward) saturation phase terminates for any sequent.*

Proof. Each rule either: removes a connective; or removes a formula completely; or replaces a formula $\varphi \to \psi$ with $\varphi \twoheadrightarrow \psi$ to which no static rule can be applied.

Given our strategy (and condition C1), we know that the conclusion of the STEP rule will never be an instance of id, hence $\varphi \twoheadrightarrow \psi$ or $\rhd\varphi$ is only an eventuality when an occurrence of it does not already appear in the antecedent of the conclusion of the STEP rule in question.

Proposition 3.5. *For all rules, the formulae in the premise succedents are subformulae of formulae in the conclusion, or are $\rightarrow$-formulae created from $\twoheadrightarrow$-formulae in the conclusion succedent: we never create new eventualities upwards.*

Proposition 3.6. *Any application of the rule* STEP *has strictly fewer eventualities in each premise, than in its conclusion.*

Proof. For each premise, an eventuality $\rhd\varphi$ crosses from the succedent of the conclusion to the antecedent of that premise and appears in all higher antecedents, or an eventuality $\varphi \twoheadrightarrow \psi$ from the succedent of the conclusion turns into $\varphi \rightarrow \psi$ in the antecedent of the premise and this $\varphi \rightarrow \psi$ turns back into $\varphi \twoheadrightarrow \psi$ via saturation, meaning that the eventuality ($\rhd\varphi$ or $\varphi \twoheadrightarrow \psi$) cannot reappear in the succedent of some higher *saturated* sequent without creating an instance of *id*.

Theorem 3.7. *Backward proof search terminates.*

Proof. By Prop. 3.4 each saturation phase terminates, so the only way a branch can be infinite is via an infinite number of applications of the STEP rule. But by Prop. 3.6 each such application reduces the number of eventualities of the branch, and by Prop. 3.5, no rule creates new eventualities. Thus we must eventually reach a saturated sequent to which no rule is applicable, or reach an instance of a termination rule. Either way, proof search terminates.

Proposition 3.8. *Given an end-sequent $\Gamma_0 \vdash \Delta_0$, the maximum number of different eventualities is the sum of the lengths of the formula in $\Gamma_0 \cup \Delta_0$.*

Proof. Each eventuality $\rhd\varphi$ is a subformula of the end-sequent, and each eventuality $\varphi \twoheadrightarrow \psi$ is created from a subformula $\varphi \rightarrow \psi$ which is also a subformula of the end-sequent or is a subformula of the end-sequent.

Corollary 3.9. *Any branch of our proof-search procedure for end-sequent $\Gamma_0 \vdash \Delta_0$ contains at most l applications of the* STEP *rule, where l is the sum of the lengths of the formulae in $\Gamma_0 \cup \Delta_0$.*

3.3 Cut-Free Completeness Without Backtracking

The rules of our sequent calculus, when used according to conditions C0, C1, and C2, can be shown to preserve validity upwards as follows.

Lemma 3.10 (Semantic Invertibility). *All static rules are semantically invertible: if some premise is refutable then so is the conclusion. Proved in extended version [10].*

For a given conclusion instance of the STEP rule, we have already seen that conditions C0, C1 and C2 guarantee that there is at least one eventuality in the succedent, that no termination rule is applicable, that the conclusion is saturated, and that no eventuality in the succedent of the conclusion is ignored.

Lemma 3.11. *The rule* STEP *(with* C0, C1 *and* C2*) is semantically invertible.*

Proof. Suppose some premise is refutable. That is,

1. for some $1 \leq i \leq k$ there exists a model $M_1 = \langle W_1, R_1, \vartheta_1 \rangle$ and $w_1 \in W_1$ such that $M_1, w_1 \Vdash \Sigma_l, \Theta, \Theta^{\rhd}, \Gamma^{\rightarrow}, \varphi_i \twoheadrightarrow \psi_i, \varphi_i$ and $M_1, w_1 \nVdash \psi_i, \Delta^{\rightarrow}_{-i}, \Phi$; or
2. for some $k+1 \leq i \leq k+n$ there exists a model $M_2 = \langle W_2, R_2, \vartheta_2 \rangle$ and $w_2 \in W_2$ such that $M_2, w_2 \Vdash \Sigma_l, \Theta, \Theta^{\rhd}, \Gamma^{\rightarrow}, \rhd\phi_{i-k}$ and $M_2, w_2 \nVdash \Delta^{\rightarrow}, \Phi$.

$1 \leq i \leq k$: We must show there is some model M containing a world w_0 such that $M, w_0 \Vdash \Sigma_l, \Theta^{\rhd}, \Gamma^{\twoheadrightarrow}$ and $M, w_0 \nVdash \Delta^{\twoheadrightarrow}, \Phi^{\rhd}, \Sigma_r$. We do this by taking the submodel generated by w_1, adding an extra world w_0 as a predecessor of w_1, letting w_0 reach every world reachable from w_1, and setting every member of Σ_l to be true at w_0.

We formally define M by: $W = \{w \in W_1 \mid w_1 R_1 w\} \cup \{w_0, w_1\}$; $R = \{(v, w) \in R_1 \mid v \in W, w \in W\} \cup \{(w_0, w) \mid w \in W \setminus \{w_0\}\}$; for every atomic formula p and for every $w \in W \setminus \{w_0\}$, let $w \in \vartheta(p)$ iff $w \in \vartheta_1(p)$ and put $w_0 \in \vartheta(p)$ iff $p \in \Sigma_l$.

By simultaneous induction on the size of any formula ξ, it follows that for every world $w \neq w_0$ in W, we have $M_1, w \Vdash \xi$ iff $M, w \Vdash \xi$.

We have $M, w_0 \nVdash \Sigma_r$ by definition (since its intersection with Σ_l is empty). We have $M, w_0 \Vdash \Theta^{\rhd}$ since $M_1, w_1 \Vdash \Theta$ implies $M, w_1 \Vdash \Theta$, and we know that $w_0 R w_1$. Similarly, we have $M, w_0 \Vdash \Gamma^{\twoheadrightarrow}$ since $w_0 R w_1$ and $M_1, w_1 \Vdash \Gamma^{\rightarrow}$. Since $M_1, w_1 \Vdash \varphi_i$ and $M_1, w_1 \nVdash \psi_i$, we must have $M, w_0 \nVdash \varphi_i \twoheadrightarrow \psi_i$ as desired. Together with $M_1, w_1 \nVdash \Delta^{\rightarrow}_{-i}$, we have $M, w_0 \nVdash \Delta^{\twoheadrightarrow}$. Finally, since $M_1, w_1 \nVdash \Phi$, we must have $M, w_0 \nVdash \Phi^{\rhd}$. Collecting everything together, we have $M, w_0 \Vdash \Sigma_l, \Theta^{\rhd}, \Gamma^{\twoheadrightarrow}$ and $M, w_0 \nVdash \Delta^{\twoheadrightarrow}, \Phi^{\rhd}, \Sigma_r$ as desired.

The case $k+1 \leq i \leq k+n$ follows similarly.

Theorem 3.12. *If the sequent* $\vdash \varphi_0$ *is not derivable using the rules of Fig. 1 according to our proof-search strategy then* φ_0 *is not* KM_{lin}*-valid.*

Proof. Suppose $\vdash \varphi_0$ is not derivable using our systematic backward proof search procedure. Thus our procedure gives a finite tree with at least one leaf $\Sigma_l, \Gamma^{\twoheadrightarrow}, \Theta^{\rhd} \vdash \Sigma_r$ obeying both C1 and C2 to which no rules are applicable.

Construct $M_0 = \langle W_0, R_0, \vartheta_0 \rangle$ as follows: let $W_0 = \{w_0\}$; let $R_0 = \emptyset$; and $w_0 \in \vartheta_0(p)$ iff $p \in \Sigma_l$. Clearly, we have $M_0, w_0 \Vdash \Sigma_l$ by definition. Also, $M_0, w_0 \nVdash \Sigma_r$ since its intersection with Σ_l is empty by C1. Every formula $\alpha \twoheadrightarrow \beta \in \Gamma^{\twoheadrightarrow}$ and $\rhd\theta \in \Theta^{\rhd}$ is vacuously true at w_0 in M_0 since w_0 has no strict successors. Thus the leaf sequent $\Sigma_l, \Gamma^{\twoheadrightarrow}, \Theta^{\rhd} \vdash \Sigma_r$ is refuted by w_0 in model M_0. The Invertibility Lemmas 3.10 and 3.11 now imply that $\vdash \varphi_0$ is refutable in some KM_{lin}-model.

Corollary 3.13 (Completeness). *If* φ *is* KM_{lin}*-valid then* $\vdash \varphi$ *is* SKM_{lin}*-derivable.*

Cor. 3.13 guarantees that any sound rule can be added to our calculus without increasing the set of provable end-sequents, including both forms of cut below:

$$\frac{\Gamma \vdash \varphi, \Delta \qquad \Gamma, \varphi \vdash \Delta}{\Gamma \vdash \Delta} \qquad \frac{\Gamma, \vdash \varphi, \Delta \qquad \Gamma', \varphi \vdash \Delta'}{\Gamma, \Gamma' \vdash \Delta, \Delta'}$$

Since all static rules are semantically invertible, any order of rule applications for saturation suffices. Since all rules are invertible we never need backtracking. That is, our strategy straightfowardly yields a *decision procedure*. It also tells us that KM_{lin}, like its parent logics KM and LC, enjoys the finite model property:

Theorem 3.14. *If φ is not KM_{lin}-valid then it is refutable in a rooted (finite) KM_{lin}-model of length at most $l+1$ where l is the length of φ.*

Proof. Suppose that φ is not valid: that is, φ is refuted by some world in some KM_{lin} model. By soundness Thm. 3.3 $\vdash \varphi$ is not derivable using our proof-search strategy. In particular, in any branch, there can be at most l applications of the rule STEP by Cor. 3.9. From such a branch, completeness Thm. 3.12 allows us to construct a model M and a world w which refutes φ. But the model M we constuct in the completeness proof is a rooted (finite) KM_{lin}-model with at most $l+1$ worlds since the only rule that creates new worlds is the (transitional) STEP rule and there are at most l such rule applications in any branch.

Corollary 3.15. *KM_{lin} has the finite model property.*

3.4 Complexity

We first embed classical propositional logic into KM_{lin}.

Lemma 3.16. *If φ is a formula built out of atomic formulae, $\top$ and $\bot$ using only the connectives $\wedge$, $\vee$, $\rightarrow$, and the sequent $\vdash (\varphi \rightarrow \bot) \rightarrow \bot$ is derivable, then φ is a tautology of classical propositional logic.*

Proof. Any derivation in our systematic proof search procedure ends as:

$$\dfrac{\dfrac{\varphi \twoheadrightarrow \bot \vdash \varphi, \bot \qquad \cdots}{\varphi \rightarrow \bot \vdash \bot}\rightarrow\mathrm{L} \qquad \cdots}{\vdash (\varphi \rightarrow \bot) \rightarrow \bot}\rightarrow\mathrm{R}$$

Thus, the sequent $\varphi \twoheadrightarrow \bot \vdash \varphi, \bot$ is derivable.

Soundness Thm. 3.3 then implies that this sequent is valid on all models. In particular, it is valid on the class of single-pointed models $M = \langle W, R, \vartheta \rangle$ where $W = \{w_0\}$ and $R = \emptyset$. The formula $\varphi \twoheadrightarrow \bot$ is true at w_0 vacuously since w_0 has no R-successor. The formula $\bot$ is not true in any model, including this one, hence $M, w_0 \not\Vdash \bot$. Thus $M, w_0 \Vdash \varphi$. That is, φ itself is valid on all single-pointed models. But such a model is just a valuation of classical propositional logic.

Lemma 3.17. *If φ is a formula built out of atomic formulae, $\top$ and $\bot$ using only the connectives $\wedge$, $\vee$, $\rightarrow$, and the sequent $\vdash (\varphi \rightarrow \bot) \rightarrow \bot$ is not derivable, then φ is not a tautology of classical propositional logic.*

Proof. Suppose $\vdash (\varphi \rightarrow \bot) \rightarrow \bot$ is not derivable. Then, by Thm. 3.12, $(\varphi \rightarrow \bot) \rightarrow \bot$ is not KM_{lin}-valid. Thus, there is a finite linear model $M = \langle W, R, \vartheta \rangle$ with root world $w_0 \in W$ such that $M, w_0 \not\Vdash (\varphi \rightarrow \bot) \rightarrow \bot$. Thus there is a world v such that $w_0 R^= v$ and $M, v \Vdash \varphi \rightarrow \bot$, which implies that every $R^=$-succesor

$$\twoheadrightarrow R \frac{\Sigma_l, \Theta, \Theta^{\rhd}, \Gamma^{\twoheadrightarrow}, \varphi \twoheadrightarrow \psi, \varphi \vdash \psi}{\Sigma_l, \Theta^{\rhd}, \Gamma^{\twoheadrightarrow} \vdash \varphi \twoheadrightarrow \psi, \Delta^{\twoheadrightarrow}, \Phi^{\rhd}, \Sigma_r} \ddagger \qquad \rhd\mathrm{R} \frac{\Sigma_l, \Theta, \Theta^{\rhd}, \Gamma^{\twoheadrightarrow}, \rhd\psi \vdash \psi}{\Sigma_l, \Theta^{\rhd}, \Gamma^{\twoheadrightarrow} \vdash \rhd\psi, \Delta^{\twoheadrightarrow}, \Phi^{\rhd}, \Sigma_r} \ddagger$$

where $\ddagger$ means that the following conditions hold:
(C1): $\bot \notin \Sigma_l$ and $\top \notin \Sigma_r$ and the conclusion is not an instance of *id*
(C2): Σ_l and Σ_r contain only atomic formulae (*i.e.* the conclusion is saturated)

Fig. 4. Transitional rules for logic KM

of v, including a world u (say) with no R-successors, makes φ false. But such a final world u is just a valuation of classical propositional logic, thus there is a model of classical propositional logic which makes φ false. That is, φ is not a tautology of classical propositional logic.

Lemma 3.18. *There is a non-deterministic algorithm to test the refutability (non-validity) of the sequent $\vdash \varphi$ in time polynomial in the length of φ. Proved in extended version [10].*

Corollary 3.19. *The validity problem for* KM_{lin} *is coNP-complete.*

Proof. By Lem. 3.16 we can faithfully embed the validity problem for classical propositional logic into KM_{lin}, hence it is at least as hard as checking validity in classical propositional logic (coNP). By Lem. 3.18, we can non-deterministically check non-validity of a given formula in time at most polynomial in its size.

4 Terminating Proof Search for KM

This section turns to logic KM, for which models need not be linear. One might expect that KM, which is conservative over Int, would require single-conclusioned sequents only, but KM-theorems such as the axiom $\rhd\varphi \rightarrow (\varphi \vee (\varphi \rightarrow \psi))$ (see Litak [24]) seem to require multiple conclusions. As such our calculus will resemble that for KM_{lin}. The static rules will be those of KM_{lin}, but the transitional rule STEP of KM_{lin} is now replaced by rules $\twoheadrightarrow R$ and $\rhd$R as shown in Fig. 4.

The backward proof-search strategy is the same as that of Sec. 3.2, except the transitional rule applications now reads as below:

> **transition:** else choose a $\twoheadrightarrow$- or $\rhd$-formula from the succedent and apply $\twoheadrightarrow R$ or $\rhd$R, backtracking over these choices until a derivation is found or all choices of principal formula have been exhausted.

So if the given sequent is $\vdash \Delta^{\twoheadrightarrow}, \Phi^{\rhd}, \Sigma_r$ and $\Delta^{\twoheadrightarrow}$ contains m formulae and $\Phi^{\rhd}$ contains n formulae, then in the worst case we must explore m premise instances of $\twoheadrightarrow R$ and n premise instances of $\rhd$R.

Theorem 4.1. *The rules $\twoheadrightarrow R$ and $\rhd$R are* sound *for the logic* KM. *Proved in extended version [10].*

Termination follows using the same argument as for SKM_{lin}. However the new rules are not semantically invertible, since we have to choose a particular $\twoheadrightarrow$- or $\rhd$-formula from the succedent of the conclusion and discard all others when moving to the premise, yet a different choice may have given a derivation of the conclusion. Thus these rules require the backtracking which is built into the new **transition** part of our proof search strategy.

Lemma 4.2. *If a sequent s obeys the ‡ conditions and every premise instance obtained by applying the rules* $\twoheadrightarrow R$ *and* $\rhd$R *backwards to s is not derivable, then the sequent s is refutable. Proved in extended version [10].*

Corollary 4.3. *If the end-sequent* $\Gamma_0 \vdash \Delta_0$ *is not derivable using backward proof search according to our strategy then* $\Gamma_0 \vdash \Delta_0$ *is refutable.*

Corollary 4.4. *If* φ_0 *is* KM*-valid then* $\vdash \varphi_0$ *is* SKM*-derivable.*

As for KM_{lin}, our proofs yield the finite model property for KM as an immediate consequence, although for KM this is already known [26].

5 Related Work

Ferrrari et al [15] give sequent calculi for intuitionistic logic using a compartment Θ in the antecedents of their sequents $\Theta; \Gamma \vdash \Delta$. This compartment contains formulae that are not necessarily true now, but are true in all strict successors. Fiorino [16] gives a sequent calculus using this compartment for LC. This yields linear depth derivations, albeit requiring a semantic check which is quadratic. Both [15,16] build in aspects of Gödel-Löb logic by allowing (sub)formulae to cross from the succedent of the conclusion into the compartment Θ. Our calculus differs by giving syntactic analogues $\rhd$ and $\twoheadrightarrow$ for these meta-level features, and by requiring no compartments, but it should be possible to adapt these authors' work to design sequent calculi for KM_{lin} with linear depth derivations.

Restall [29] investigates "subintuitionistic logics" where each of the conditions on Kripke frames of reflexivity, transitivity and persistence can be dropped. The logic of our novel connective $\twoheadrightarrow$ can be seen as the logic bka, which lacks reflexivity, but has the additional conditions of linearity and converse well-foundedness, which Restall does not consider. The models studied by Restall all require a root world, and thus they disallow sequences $\cdots x_3 R x_2 R x_1$ which are permitted by KM_{lin}-models. Ishigaki and Kikuchi [20] give "tree-sequent" calculi for the first-order versions of some of these subintuitionistic logics. Thus "tree-sequent" calculi for KM and KM_{lin} are possible, but our calculi require no labels.

Labelled sequent calculi for KM and KM_{lin} are possible by extending the work of Dyckhoff and Negri [14] but termination proofs and complexity results for labelled calculi are significantly harder than our proofs.

Garg et al [17] give labelled sequent calculi for intuitionistic modal logics and general conditions on decidability. Their method relies on a first-order characterisation of the underlying Kripke relations, but converse well-foundedness is not first-order definable. Labelled calculi can handle converse well-founded frames by allowing formulae to "cross" sides as in our calculus, but it is not clear whether the method of Garg et al [17] then applies.

Our complexity results follow directly from our calculi; a possible alternative may be to adapt the polynomial encoding of LC into classical satisfiability [8].

6 Conclusion

We have seen that the internal *propositional* logic of the topos of trees is KM_{lin}. Indeed it may be tempting to think that KM_{lin} is just LC, as both are sound and complete with respect to the class of finite sequences of reflexive points, but note that we cannot express the modality $\rhd$ in terms of the connectives of LC.

Linear frames seem concordant with the *step-indexing* applications of later, based as they are on induction on the natural numbers rather than any branching structure, but seem less natural from a *types* point of view, which tend to build on intuitionistic logic. For a possible type-theoretic intepretation of linearity see Hirai's λ-calculus for LC with applications to 'waitfree' computation [18]. More broadly our work provides a proof-theoretical basis for future research into computational aspects of intuitionistic Gödel-Löb provability logic.

The topos of trees, which generalises some previous models, has itself been generalised as a model of guarded recursion in several ways [4,3,25]. These categories do not all correspond to KM_{lin}; some clearly fail to be linear. The logical content of these general settings may also be worthy of study.

The most immediate application of our proof search algorithm may be to provide automation for program logics that use later [19,2,9]. Support for a richer class of connectives, such as first and higher order quantifiers, would be desirable. We in particular note the 'backwards looking box' used by Bizjak and Birkedal [6] in sheaves over the first uncountable ordinal ω_1, and subsequently in the topos of trees by Clouston et al [9] to reason about coinductive types.

Acknowledgments. We gratefully acknowledge helpful discussions with Lars Birkedal, Stephané Demri, Tadeusz Litak, and Jimmy Thomson, and the comments of the reviewers of this and a previous unsuccessful submission.

References

1. Appel, A.W., Melliès, P.A., Richards, C.D., Vouillon, J.: A very modal model of a modern, major, general type system. In: POPL, pp. 109–122 (2007)
2. Bengtson, J., Jensen, J.B., Sieczkowski, F., Birkedal, L.: Verifying object-oriented programs with higher-order separation logic in Coq. In: van Eekelen, M., Geuvers, H., Schmaltz, J., Wiedijk, F. (eds.) ITP 2011. LNCS, vol. 6898, pp. 22–38. Springer, Heidelberg (2011)
3. Birkedal, L., Møgelberg, R.E.: Intensional type theory with guarded recursive types qua fixed points on universes. In: LICS, pp. 213–222 (2013)
4. Birkedal, L., Møgelberg, R.E., Schwinghammer, J., Støvring, K.: First steps in synthetic guarded domain theory: Step-indexing in the topos of trees. LMCS 8(4) (2012)
5. Birkedal, L., Schwinghammer, J., Støvring, K.: A metric model of lambda calculus with guarded recursion. In: FICS, pp. 19–25 (2010)
6. Bizjak, A., Birkedal, L., Miculan, M.: A model of countable nondeterminism in guarded type theory. In: Dowek, G. (ed.) RTA-TLCA 2014. LNCS, vol. 8560, pp. 108–123. Springer, Heidelberg (2014)
7. Boolos, G.: The logic of provability. CUP (1995)
8. Chagrov, A., Zakharyaschev, M.: Modal Logic. OUP (1997)

9. Clouston, R., Bizjak, A., Grathwohl, H.B., Birkedal, L.: Programming and reasoning with guarded recursion for coinductive types. In: Pitts, A. (ed.) FoSSaCS 2015. LNCS, vol. 9034, pp. 407–421. Springer, Heidelberg (2015)
10. Clouston, R., Goré, R.: Sequent calculus in the topos of trees. arXiv:1501.03293, extended version (2015)
11. Coquand, T.: Infinite objects in type theory. In: Barendregt, H., Nipkow, T. (eds.) TYPES 1993. LNCS, vol. 806, pp. 62–78. Springer, Heidelberg (1994)
12. Corsi, G.: Semantic trees for Dummett's logic LC. Stud. Log. 45(2), 199–206 (1986)
13. Dreyer, D., Ahmed, A., Birkedal, L.: Logical step-indexed logical relations. In: LICS, pp. 71–80 (2009)
14. Dyckhoff, R., Negri, S.: Proof analysis in intermediate logics. Arch. Math. Log. 51(1-2), 71–92 (2012)
15. Ferrari, M., Fiorentini, C., Fiorino, G.: Contraction-free linear depth sequent calculi for intuitionistic propositional logic with the subformula property and minimal depth counter-models. J. Autom. Reason. 51(2), 129–149 (2013)
16. Fiorino, G.: Terminating calculi for propositional Dummett logic with subformula property. J. Autom. Reason. 52(1), 67–97 (2014)
17. Garg, D., Genovese, V., Negri, S.: Countermodels from sequent calculi in multi-modal logics. In: LICS, pp. 315–324 (2012)
18. Hirai, Y.: A lambda calculus for Gödel–Dummett logic capturing waitfreedom. In: Schrijvers, T., Thiemann, P. (eds.) FLOPS 2012. LNCS, vol. 7294, pp. 151–165. Springer, Heidelberg (2012)
19. Hobor, A., Appel, A.W., Nardelli, F.Z.: Oracle semantics for concurrent separation logic. In: Drossopoulou, S. (ed.) ESOP 2008. LNCS, vol. 4960, pp. 353–367. Springer, Heidelberg (2008)
20. Ishigaki, R., Kikuchi, K.: Tree-sequent methods for subintuitionistic predicate logics. In: Olivetti, N. (ed.) TABLEAUX 2007. LNCS (LNAI), vol. 4548, pp. 149–164. Springer, Heidelberg (2007)
21. Krishnaswami, N.R., Benton, N.: A semantic model for graphical user interfaces. In: ICFP, pp. 45–57 (2011)
22. Krishnaswami, N.R., Benton, N.: Ultrametric semantics of reactive programs. In: LICS, pp. 257–266 (2011)
23. Litak, T.: A typing system for the modalized Heyting calculus. In: COS (2013)
24. Litak, T.: Constructive modalities with provability smack, author's cut v. 2.03 (2014) (retrieved from author's website)
25. Milius, S., Litak, T.: Guard your daggers and traces: On the equational properties of guarded (co-) recursion. arXiv:1309.0895 (2013)
26. Muravitsky, A.: Logic KM: A biography. Outstanding Contributions to Logic 4, 155–185 (2014)
27. Nakano, H.: A modality for recursion. In: LICS, pp. 255–266 (2000)
28. Pottier, F.: A typed store-passing translation for general references. In: POPL, pp. 147–158 (2011)
29. Restall, G.: Subintuitionistic logics. NDJFL 34(1), 116–129 (1994)
30. Rowe, R.N.: Semantic Types for Class-based Objects. Ph.D. thesis, Imperial College London (2012)
31. Sonobe, O.: A Gentzen-type formulation of some intermediate propositional logics. J. Tsuda College 7, 7–14 (1975)
32. Troelstra, A., Schwichtenberg, H.: Basic Proof Theory. CUP (1996)
33. Wolter, F., Zakharyaschev, M.: Intuitionistic modal logics. In: Logic and Foundations of Mathematics, pp. 227–238 (1999)

Modal and Temporal Logics

Coalgebraic Trace Semantics via Forgetful Logics

Bartek Klin[1,*] and Jurriaan Rot[2,**]

[1] University of Warsaw
[2] Leiden University, CWI

Abstract. We use modal logic as a framework for coalgebraic trace semantics, and show the flexibility of the approach with concrete examples such as the language semantics of weighted, alternating and tree automata. We provide a sufficient condition under which a logical semantics coincides with the trace semantics obtained via a given determinization construction. Finally, we consider a condition that guarantees the existence of a canonical determinization procedure that is correct with respect to a given logical semantics. That procedure is closely related to Brzozowski's minimization algorithm.

1 Introduction

Coalgebraic methods [22, 11] have been rather successful in modeling branching time behaviour of various kinds of transition systems, with a general notion of bisimulation and final semantics as the main contributions. Coalgebraic modeling of linear time behaviour such as trace semantics of transition systems or language semantics of automata, has also attracted significant attention. However, the emerging picture is considerably more complex: a few approaches have been developed whose scopes and connections are not yet fully understood. Here, we exacerbate the situation by suggesting yet another approach.

To study trace semantics coalgebraically, one usually considers systems whose behaviour type is a composite functor of the form TB or BT, where T represents a branching aspect of behaviour that trace semantics is supposed to "resolve", and B represents the transition aspect that should be recorded in system traces. Typically it is assumed that T is a monad, and its multiplication structure is used to resolve branching. For example, in [21, 9], a distributive law of B over T is used to lift B to the Kleisli category of T, and trace semantics is obtained as final semantics for the lifted functor. Additional assumptions on T are needed for this, so this approach does not work for coalgebras such as weighted automata. On the other hand, in [12, 24] a distributive law of T over B is used to lift B to the Eilenberg-Moore category of T, with trace semantics again obtained as final semantics for the lifted functor. This can be seen as a coalgebraic

* Supported by the Polish National Science Centre (NCN) grant 2012/07/E/ST6/03026.

** Supported by NWO project 612.063.920. This research was carried out during the second author's stay at University of Warsaw, partially supported by WCMCS.

A. Pitts (Ed.): FOSSACS 2015, LNCS 9034, pp. 151–166, 2015.
DOI: 10.1007/978-3-662-46678-0_10

generalization of the powerset determinization procedure for non-deterministic automata. While it applies to many examples, that approach does not work for systems that do not determinize, such as tree automata. A detailed comparison of these two approaches is in [12]. In the recent [17], the entire functor TB (or BT) is embedded in a single monad, which provides some more flexibility. In [8], it is embedded in a more complex functor with a so-called observer.

In this paper, we study trace semantics in terms of modal logic. The basic idea is very simple: we view traces as formulas in suitable modal logics, and trace semantics of a state arises from all formulas that hold for it. A coalgebraic approach to modal logic based on dual adjunctions is by now well developed [20, 15, 13, 16], and we apply it to speak of traces generally. Obviously not every logic counts as a trace logic: assuming a behaviour type of the form BT or TB, we construct logics from arbitrary (but usually expressive) logics for B and special logics for T whose purpose is to resolve branching. We call such logics *forgetful*.

Our approach differs from previous studies in a few ways:

- We do not assume that T is a monad, unless we want to relate our logical approach to ones that do, in particular to determinization constructions.
- Instead of using monad multiplication $\mu\colon TT \Rightarrow T$ to resolve branching, we use a natural transformation $\alpha\colon TG \Rightarrow G$, where G is a contravariant functor that provides the basic infrastructure of logics. In case of nondeterministic systems, T is the covariant powerset functor and G the contravariant powerset, so TT and TG act the same on objects, but they carry significantly different intuitions.
- Trace semantics is obtained not as final semantics of coalgebras, but by initial semantics of algebras. Fundamentally, we view trace semantics as an inductive concept and not a coinductive one akin to bisimulation, although in some well-behaved cases the inductive and coinductive views coincide.
- Thanks to the flexibility of modal logics, we are able to cover examples such as the language semantics of weighted tree automata, that does not quite fit into previously studied approaches, or alternating automata.

The idea of using modal logics for coalgebraic trace semantics is not new; it is visible already in [20]. In [9] it is related to behavioural equivalence, and applied to non-deterministic systems. A generalized notion of relation lifting is used in [5] to obtain infinite trace semantics, and applied in [6] to get canonical linear time logics. In [14], coalgebraic modal logic is combined with the idea of lifting behaviours to Eilenberg-Moore categories, with trace semantics in mind. In [12], a connection to modal logics is sketched from the perspective of coalgebraic determinization procedures. In a sense, this paper describes the same connection from the perspective of logic.

Our main new contribution is the notion of forgetful logic and its ramifications. The basic definitions are provided in Section 3 and some illustrative examples in Section 4. We introduce a systematic way of relating trace semantics to determinization, by giving sufficient conditions for a given determinization procedure, understood in a slightly more general way than in [12], to be correct with respect to a given forgetful logic (Section 6). For instance, this allows showing in a coalgebraic setting that the determinization of alternating automata into non-deterministic automata preserves language semantics.

A correct determinization procedure may not exist in general. In Section 7 we study a situation where a canonical correct determinization procedure exists. It turns out that even in the simple case of non-deterministic automata that procedure is not the classical powerset construction; instead, it relies on a double application of contravariant powerset construction. Interestingly, this is what also happens in Brzozowski's algorithm for automata minimization [4], so as a by-product, we get a new perspective on that algorithm which has recently attracted much attention in the coalgebraic community [1–3].

2 Preliminaries

We assume familiarity with basic notions of category theory (see, e.g., [19]). A coalgebra for a functor $B\colon \mathcal{C} \to \mathcal{C}$ consists of an object X and a map $f\colon X \to BX$. A homomorphism from $f\colon X \to BX$ to $g\colon Y \to BY$ is a map $h\colon X \to Y$ such that $g \circ h = Bh \circ f$. The category of B-coalgebras is denoted $\mathsf{Coalg}(B)$. Algebras for a functor L are defined dually; the category of L-algebras and homomorphisms is denoted $\mathsf{Alg}(L)$.

We list a few examples, where $\mathcal{C} = \mathsf{Set}$, the category of sets and functions. Consider the functor $\mathcal{P}_\omega(A \times -)$, where $\mathcal{P}_\omega$ is the finite powerset functor and A is a fixed set. A coalgebra $f\colon X \to \mathcal{P}_\omega(A \times X)$ is a finitely branching labelled transition system: it maps every state to a finite set of next states. Coalgebras for the functor $(\mathcal{P}_\omega -)^A$ are image-finite labelled transition systems, i.e., the set of next states for every label is finite. When A is finite the two notions coincide. A coalgebra $f\colon X \to \mathcal{P}_\omega(A \times X + 1)$, where $1 = \{*\}$ is a singleton, is a non-deterministic automaton; a state x is accepting whenever $* \in f(x)$.

Consider the functor $BX = 2 \times X^A$, where 2 is a two-element set of truth values. A coalgebra $\langle o, f\rangle\colon X \to BX$ is a deterministic automaton; a state x is accepting if $o(x) = \mathsf{tt}$, and $f(x)$ is the transition function. The composition $B\mathcal{P}_\omega$ yields non-deterministic automata, presented in a different way than above. We shall also consider $B\mathcal{P}_\omega\mathcal{P}_\omega$-coalgebras, which represent a general version of alternating automata.

Let $\mathbb{S}$ be a semiring. Define $\mathcal{M}X = \{\varphi \in \mathbb{S}^X \mid \mathrm{supp}(\varphi) \text{ is finite}\}$ where $\mathrm{supp}(\varphi) = \{x \mid \varphi(x) \neq 0\}$, and $\mathcal{M}(f\colon X \to Y)(\varphi)(y) = \sum_{x \in f^{-1}(y)} \varphi(x)$. A *weighted automaton* is a coalgebra for the functor $\mathcal{M}(A \times - + 1)$. Let Σ be a polynomial functor corresponding to an algebraic signature. A *top-down weighted tree automaton* is a coalgebra for the functor $\mathcal{M}\Sigma$. For $\mathbb{S}$ the Boolean semiring these are *non-deterministic tree automata.* Similar to non-deterministic automata above, one can present weighted automata as coalgebras for $\mathbb{S} \times (\mathcal{M}-)^A$.

We note that $\mathcal{P}_\omega$ is a monad, by taking $\eta_X(x) = \{x\}$ and μ to be union. More generally, the functor $\mathcal{M}$ extends to a monad, by taking $\mu_X(\varphi)(x) = \sum_{\psi \in \mathbb{S}^X} \varphi(\psi) \cdot \psi(x)$. The case of $\mathcal{P}_\omega$ is obtained by taking the Boolean semiring. Notice that the finite support condition is required for μ to be well-defined.

2.1 Contravariant Adjunctions

The basic framework of coalgebraic logic is formed of two categories $\mathcal{C}$, $\mathcal{D}$ connected by functors $F\colon \mathcal{C}^{op} \to \mathcal{D}$ and $G\colon \mathcal{D}^{op} \to \mathcal{C}$ that form an adjunction $F^{op} \dashv G$. For example, one may take $\mathcal{C} = \mathcal{D} = \mathsf{Set}$ and $F = G = 2^{-}$, for 2 a two-element set of logical values. The intuition is that objects of $\mathcal{C}$ are collections of processes, or states, and objects of $\mathcal{D}$ are logical theories.

To avoid cluttering the presentation with too much of the $(-)^{op}$ notation, we opt to treat F and G as *contravariant functors*, i.e., ones that reverse the direction of all arrows (maps), between $\mathcal{C}$ and $\mathcal{D}$. The adjunction then becomes a contravariant adjunction "on the right", meaning that there is a natural bijection

$$\mathcal{C}(X, G\Phi) \cong \mathcal{D}(\Phi, FX) \qquad \text{for } X \in \mathcal{C}, \Phi \in \mathcal{D}.$$

Slightly abusing the notation, we shall denote both sides of this bijection by $(-)^{\flat}$. Applying the bijection to a map is referred to as transposing the map.

In such an adjunction, GF is a monad on $\mathcal{C}$, whose unit we denote by $\iota\colon \mathsf{Id} \Rightarrow GF$, and FG is a monad on $\mathcal{D}$, with unit denoted by $\epsilon\colon \mathsf{Id} \Rightarrow FG$. Both F and G map colimits to limits, by standard preservation results for adjoint functors.

In what follows, the reader need only remember that F and G are contravariant, i.e., they reverse maps and natural transformations. All other functors, except a few that lift F and G to other categories, are standard covariant functors.

3 Forgetful Logics

We begin by recalling an approach to coalgebraic modal logic based on contravariant adjunctions, see, e.g., [15, 13]. Consider categories $\mathcal{C}$, $\mathcal{D}$ and functors F, G as in Section 2.1. Given an endofunctor $B\colon \mathcal{C} \to \mathcal{C}$, a *coalgebraic logic* to be interpreted on B-coalgebras is built of *syntax*, i.e., an endofunctor $L\colon \mathcal{D} \to \mathcal{D}$, and *semantics*, a natural transformation $\rho\colon LF \Rightarrow FB$. We will usually refer to ρ simply as a logic. If an initial L-algebra $a\colon L\Phi \to \Phi$ exists then, for any B-coalgebra $h\colon X \to BX$, the *logical semantics* of ρ on h is a map $s^{\flat}\colon X \to G\Phi$ obtained by transposing the map defined by initiality of a as on the left:

$$\begin{array}{ccc} L\Phi & \xrightarrow{Ls} & LFX \\ & & \downarrow{\scriptstyle \rho_X} \\ \downarrow{\scriptstyle a} & & FBX \\ & & \downarrow{\scriptstyle Fh} \\ \Phi & \xrightarrow[s]{} & FX \end{array} \qquad\qquad \begin{array}{ccc} \mathsf{Coalg}(B) & \xrightarrow{\hat{F}} & \mathsf{Alg}(L) \\ \downarrow & & \downarrow \\ \mathcal{C} & \xrightarrow[F]{} & \mathcal{D} \end{array} \qquad (1)$$

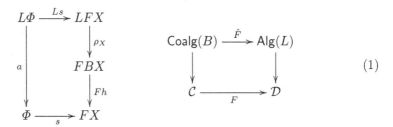

The mapping of a B-coalgebra $h\colon X \to BX$ to an L-algebra $Fh \circ \rho_X\colon LFX \to FX$ determines a contravariant functor $\hat{F}$ that lifts F, i.e., acts as F on carriers, depicted on the right above. This functor has no (contravariant) adjoint in general; later in Section 7 we shall study well-behaved situations when it does. Notice that $\hat{F}$ maps coalgebra homomorphisms to algebra homomorphisms, and indeed the logical semantics factors through coalgebra homomorphisms, i.e., behavioural equivalence implies logical equivalence. The converse holds if ρ is *expressive*, meaning that the logical semantics decomposes as a coalgebra homomorphism followed by a mono.

Example 1. Let $\mathcal{C} = \mathcal{D} = \mathsf{Set}$, $F = G = 2^{-}$, $B = 2 \times -^{A}$ and $L = A \times - + 1$. The initial algebra of L is the set A^* of words over A. We define a logic $\rho\colon LF \Rightarrow FB$ as follows: $\rho_X(*)(o,t) = o$ and $\rho_X(a,\varphi)(o,t) = \varphi(t(a))$. For a coalgebra $\langle o, f\rangle\colon X \to 2 \times X^A$ the logical semantics is a map $s^\flat\colon X \to 2^{A^*}$, yielding the usual language semantics of the automaton: $s^\flat(x)(\varepsilon) = o(x)$ for the empty word ε, and $s^\flat(x)(aw) = s^\flat(f(x)(a))(w)$ for any $a \in A, w \in A^*$.

Note that logical equivalences, understood as kernel relations of logical semantics, are conceptually different from behavioural equivalences typically considered in coalgebra theory, in that they do not arise from finality of coalgebras, but rather from initiality of algebras (albeit in a different category). Fundamentally, logical semantics for coalgebras is defined by induction rather than coinduction. In some particularly well-behaved cases the inductive and coinductive views coincide; we shall study such situations in Section 7.

A logic $\rho\colon LF \Rightarrow FB$ gives rise to its *mate* $\rho^\flat\colon BG \Rightarrow GL$, defined by

$$BG \xRightarrow{\iota BG} GFBG \xRightarrow{G\rho G} GLFG \xRightarrow{GL\epsilon} GL, \tag{2}$$

where ι and ϵ are as in Section 2.1. A routine calculation shows that ρ in turn is the mate of $\rho^\flat$ (with the roles of F, G, ι and ϵ swapped), giving a bijective correspondence between logics and their mates. Some important properties of logics are conveniently stated in terms of their mates; e.g., under mild additional assumptions (see [15]), if the mate is pointwise monic then the logic is expressive.

There is a direct characterization of logical semantic maps in terms of mates, first formulated in [20]. Indeed, by transposing (1) it is easy to check that the logical semantics $s^\flat\colon X \to G\Phi$ on a coalgebra $h\colon X \to BX$ is a unique map that makes the "twisted coalgebra morphism" diagram in (3) commute.

$$\begin{array}{ccc} BX & \xrightarrow{Bs^\flat} & BG\Phi \\ \uparrow & & \downarrow{\scriptstyle \rho^\flat_\Phi} \\ {\scriptstyle h}\,| & & G L\Phi \\ | & & \uparrow{\scriptstyle Ga} \\ X & \xrightarrow[s^\flat]{} & G\Phi. \end{array} \tag{3}$$

Logics for composite functors can often be obtained from logics of their components. Consider functors $B, T\colon \mathcal{C} \to \mathcal{C}$ and logics for them $\rho\colon LF \Rightarrow FB$ and $\alpha\colon NF \Rightarrow FT$, for some functors $L, N\colon \mathcal{D} \to \mathcal{D}$. One can then define logics for the functors TB and BT:

$$\alpha \circledcirc \rho = \alpha B \circ N\rho\colon NLF \Rightarrow FTB, \qquad \rho \circledcirc \alpha = \rho T \circ L\alpha\colon LNF \Rightarrow FBT.$$

It is easy to see that taking the mate of a logic respects this composition operator, i.e., that $(\alpha \circledcirc \rho)^\flat = \alpha^\flat \circledcirc \rho^\flat$. Such compositions of logics appear in [11] and were studied in a slightly more concrete setting in [7, 23].

We shall be interested in the case where the logic for T has a trivial syntax; in other words, where $N = \mathsf{Id}$. Intuitively speaking, we require a logic for T that consists of a single unary operator, which could therefore be elided in a syntactic presentation of logical formulas. The semantics of such an operator is defined by a natural transformation $\alpha\colon F \Rightarrow FT$ or equivalently by its mate $\alpha^\flat : TG \Rightarrow G$. Intuitively, the composite logics $\alpha \circledcirc \rho$ and $\rho \circledcirc \alpha$, when interpreted on TB- and BT-coalgebras respectively disregard, or forget, the aspect of their behaviour related to the functor T, in a manner prescribed by α. We call logics obtained in this fashion *forgetful logics.*

4 Examples

We instantiate the setting of Section 3 and use forgetful logics to obtain trace semantics for several concrete types of coalgebras: non-deterministic automata, transition systems, alternating automata and weighted tree automata.

In the first few examples we let $\mathcal{C} = \mathcal{D} = \mathsf{Set}$ and $F = G = 2^-$, and consider TB or BT-coalgebras, where $T = \mathcal{P}_\omega$ is the finite powerset functor. Our examples involve the logic $\alpha\colon 2^- \Rightarrow 2^{\mathcal{P}_\omega}$ defined by:

$$\alpha_X(\varphi)(S) = \mathsf{tt} \text{ iff } \exists x \in S.\varphi(x) = \mathsf{tt}. \tag{4}$$

This choice of F and G has been studied thoroughly in the field of coalgebraic logic, and our α is an example of the standard notion of predicate lifting [11, 16] corresponding to the so-called diamond modality. Its mate $\alpha^\flat : \mathcal{P}_\omega 2^- \Rightarrow 2^-$ is as follows: $\alpha^\flat_\Phi(S)(w) = \mathsf{tt}$ iff $\exists \varphi \in S.S(w) = \mathsf{tt}$. In all examples below, $\mathcal{P}_\omega$ could be replaced by the full powerset $\mathcal{P}$ without any problems.

Example 2. We define a forgetful logic $\alpha \circledcirc \rho$ for $\mathcal{P}_\omega B$, where $BX = A \times X + 1$; α is as above and ρ is given below in terms of its mate $\rho^\flat : BG \Rightarrow GL$, in such a way that the logical semantics yields the usual language semantics. We let $L = B$, hence A^* carries the structure of an initial L-algebra. As a result, the logical semantics on an automaton will be a map from states to languages (elements of 2^{A^*}). Define $\rho^\flat : A \times 2^- + 1 \Rightarrow 2^{A\times - +1}$ by

$$\rho^\flat_\Phi(*)(t) = \mathsf{tt} \text{ iff } t = * \qquad \rho^\flat_\Phi(a, \varphi)(t) = \mathsf{tt} \text{ iff } t = (a, w) \text{ and } \varphi(w) = \mathsf{tt},$$

for any set Φ. The semantics of the logic $\alpha \circledcirc \rho$ on an automaton $f\colon X \to \mathcal{P}_\omega BX$ is the map $s^\flat$ from (3), and it is easy to calculate that for any $x \in X$:

$$\begin{aligned} s^\flat(x)(\varepsilon) &= \mathsf{tt} \text{ iff } * \in f(x), \\ s^\flat(x)(aw) &= \mathsf{tt} \text{ iff } \exists y \in X.(a, y) \in f(x) \text{ and } s^\flat(y)(w) = \mathsf{tt}, \end{aligned}$$

for ε the empty word, and for all $a \in A$ and $w \in A^*$.

Note that the logic ρ in the above example is expressive. One may expect that given a different expressive logic θ involving the same functors, the forgetful logics $\alpha \circledcirc \rho$ and $\alpha \circledcirc \theta$ yield the same logical equivalences, but this is not the case.

For instance, define $\theta^\flat\colon BG \Rightarrow GL$ as $\theta^\flat_\Phi(*)(t) = \mathtt{tt}$ for all t, and $\theta^\flat_\Phi(a,\varphi) = \rho^\flat_\Phi(a,\varphi)$. This logic is expressive as well (since $\theta^\flat$ is componentwise monic) but in the semantics of the forgetful logic $\alpha \circledcirc \theta$, information on final states is discarded.

Example 3 (Length of words). The initial algebra of $LX = X + 1$ is $\mathbb{N}$, the set of natural numbers. Define a logic for $BX = A \times X + 1$ by its mate $\rho^\flat\colon A \times 2^- + 1 \Rightarrow 2^{-+1}$ as follows: $\rho^\flat_\Phi(*)(t) = \mathtt{tt}$ iff $t = *$, and $\rho^\flat_\Phi(a,\varphi)(t) = \mathtt{tt}$ iff $t = w$ and $\varphi(w) = \mathtt{tt}$. Note that this logic is not expressive. With the above α, we have a logic $\alpha \circledcirc \rho$, and given any $f\colon X \to \mathcal{P}_\omega(A \times X + 1)$, this yields $s^\flat\colon X \to 2^{\mathbb{N}}$ so that $s^\flat(x)(0) = \mathtt{tt}$ iff $* \in f(x)$ and $s^\flat(x)(n+1) = \mathtt{tt}$ iff $\exists a \in A, y \in X$ s.t. $(a,y) \in f(x)$ and $s^\flat(y)(n) = \mathtt{tt}$. Thus, $s^\flat(x)$ is the binary sequence which is tt at position n iff the automaton f accepts a word of length n, starting in state x.

Example 4 (Non-deterministic automata as BT-coalgebras). Consider the functor $BX = 2 \times X^A$. Let $LX = A \times X + 1$, let $\rho^\flat\colon 2 \times (2^-)^A \Rightarrow 2^{A\times -+1}$ be the mate of the logic ρ given in Example 1; explicitly, it is the obvious isomorphism given by manipulating exponents:

$$\rho^\flat_\Phi(o,\varphi)(*) = o \qquad \rho^\flat_\Phi(o,\varphi)(a,w) = \varphi(a)(w) \tag{5}$$

The logical semantics $s^\flat\colon X \to 2^{A^*}$ of $\rho \circledcirc \alpha$ on a coalgebra $\langle o, f\rangle\colon X \to 2 \times \mathcal{P}_\omega(X)^A$ is the usual language semantics: for any $x \in X$ we have $s^\flat(x)(\varepsilon) = o(x)$, and $s^\flat(x)(aw) = \mathtt{tt}$ iff $s^\flat(y)(w) = \mathtt{tt}$ for some $y \in f(x)(a)$.

A minor variation on the above, taking $BX = X^A$ and adapting $\rho^\flat$ appropriately so that $\rho^\flat(t)(*) = \mathtt{tt}$ for any t, yields finite traces of transition systems.

Non-determinism can be resolved differently: in contrast to (4), consider $\beta^\flat\colon \mathcal{P}_\omega 2^- \Rightarrow 2^-$ given by $\beta^\flat_\Phi(S)(x) = \mathtt{tt}$ iff $\forall \varphi \in S. S(x) = \mathtt{tt}$. Similarly to (4), β is a predicate lifting that corresponds to the so-called box modality. The semantics $s^\flat$ induced by the forgetful logic $\rho \circledcirc \beta$ accepts a word if *all* paths end in an accepting state: $s^\flat(x)(\varepsilon) = o(x)$, and $s^\flat(x)(aw) = \mathtt{tt}$ iff $s^\flat(y)(w) = \mathtt{tt}$ for all $y \in f(x)(a)$. We call this the conjunctive semantics. In automata-theoretic terms, this is the language semantics for ($B\mathcal{P}_\omega$-coalgebras understood as) co-nondeterministic automata, i.e., alternating automata with only universal states.

Some non-examples. It is not clear how to use forgetful logics to give a conjunctive semantics to coalgebras for $\mathcal{P}_\omega(A \times X + -)$; simply using β together with ρ from Example 2 does not yield the expected logical semantics. Also, transition systems as $\mathcal{P}_\omega(A \times -)$-coalgebras do not work well; with α as in (4) the logical semantics of a state with no successors is always empty, while it should contain the empty trace.

Example 5 (Alternating automata). Consider $B\mathcal{P}_\omega\mathcal{P}_\omega$-coalgebras with $B = 2 \times -^A$. We give a forgetful logic by combining ρ, α, and β from the previous example (more precisely, the logic is $(\rho \circledcirc \alpha) \circledcirc \beta$); recall that α and β resolve the non-determinism by disjunction and conjunction respectively. Spelling out the details for a coalgebra $\langle o, f\rangle\colon X \to 2 \times (\mathcal{P}_\omega\mathcal{P}_\omega X)^A$ yields, for any $x \in X$: $s^\flat(x)(\varepsilon) = o(x)$ and for any $a \in A$ and $w \in A^*$: $s^\flat(x)(aw) = \mathtt{tt}$ iff there is $S \in f(x)(a)$ such that $s^\flat(y)(w) = \mathtt{tt}$ for all $y \in S$.

Example 6 (Weighted Tree Automata). In this example we let $\mathcal{C} = \mathcal{D} = \mathsf{Set}$ and $F = G = \mathbb{S}^-$ for a semiring $\mathbb{S}$. We consider coalgebras for $\mathcal{M}\Sigma$ (Section 2), where Σ is a polynomial functor corresponding to a signature. The initial algebra of Σ is carried by the set of finite Σ-trees, denoted by $\Sigma^*\emptyset$. Define $\rho\colon \Sigma F \Rightarrow F\Sigma$ by cases on the operators σ in the signature:

$$\rho_X(\sigma(\varphi_1,\ldots,\varphi_n))(\tau(x_1,\ldots,x_m)) = \begin{cases} \prod_{i=1..n}\varphi_i(x_i) & \text{if } \sigma = \tau \\ 0 & \text{otherwise} \end{cases}$$

where n is the arity of σ. Define $\alpha\colon \mathbb{S}^- \Rightarrow \mathbb{S}^{\mathcal{M}}$ by its mate: $\alpha^\flat_\Phi(\varphi)(w) = \sum_{\psi\in\mathbb{S}^\Phi}\varphi(\psi)\cdot\psi(w)$. Notice that α and ρ generalize the logics of Example 2.

Let $s^\flat$ be the logical semantics of $\alpha \circledcirc \rho$ on a weighted tree automaton $f\colon X \to \mathcal{M}\Sigma X$. For any tree $\sigma(t_1,\ldots t_n)$ and any $x \in X$ we have:

$$s^\flat(x)(\sigma(t_1,\ldots,t_n)) = \sum_{x_1,\ldots,x_n\in X} f(x)(\sigma(x_1,\ldots,x_n))\cdot\prod_{i=1..n} s^\flat(x_i)(t_i)$$

As a special case, we obtain for any *weighted automaton* $f\colon X \to \mathcal{M}(A\times X+1)$ a unique map $s^\flat\colon X \to \mathbb{S}^{A^*}$ so that for any $x \in X$, $a \in A$ and $w \in A^*$: $s^\flat(x)(\varepsilon) = f(x)(*)$ and $s^\flat(x)(aw) = \sum_{y\in X} f(x)(a,y)\cdot s^\flat(y)(w)$. For $\mathbb{S}$ the Boolean semiring we get the usual semantics of tree automata: $s^\flat(x)(\sigma(t_1,\ldots,t_n)) = \mathsf{tt}$ iff there are $x_1,\ldots,x_n$ such that $\sigma(x_1,\ldots,x_n) \in f(x)$ and for all $i \le n$: $s^\flat(x_i)(t_i) = \mathsf{tt}$.

Notice that the Σ-algebra $\hat{F}(X,f)$ (see (1)) is a *deterministic bottom-up tree automaton*. It corresponds to the top-down automaton f, in the sense that the semantics $s^\flat$ of f is the transpose of the unique homomorphism $s\colon \Sigma^*\emptyset \to \mathbb{S}^X$ arising by initiality; the latter is the usual semantics of bottom-up tree automata.

5 Forgetful Logics for Monads

In most coalgebraic attempts to trace semantics [5, 8, 12, 14, 17, 21], the functor T, which models the branching aspect of system behaviour, is assumed to be a monad. The basic definition of a forgetful logic is more relaxed in that it allows an arbitrary functor T but one may notice that in all examples in Section 4, T is a monad.

In coalgebraic approaches cited above, the structure of T is resolved using monad multiplication $\mu\colon TT \Rightarrow T$. Forgetful logics use transformations $\alpha\colon F \Rightarrow FT$ with their mates $\alpha^\flat\colon TG \Rightarrow T$ for the same purpose. If T is a monad, it will be useful to assume a few basic axioms analogous to those of monad multiplication:

Definition 1. *Let (T,η,μ) be a monad. A natural transformation $\alpha^\flat\colon TG \Rightarrow G$ is a (T)-*action *(on G) if $\alpha^\flat \circ \eta G = \mathsf{id}$ and $\alpha^\flat \circ T\alpha^\flat = \alpha^\flat \circ \mu G$, i.e., if each component of $\alpha^\flat$ is an Eilenberg-Moore algebra for T.*

Just as monads generalize monoids, monad actions on functors generalize monoid actions on sets. We shall use properties of monad actions to relate forgetful logics to the determinization constructions of [12] in Section 6. It is easy to check by hand that in all examples in Section 4, $\alpha^\flat$ is an action, but it also follows from the following considerations.

In some well-structured cases, one can search for a suitable α by looking at T-algebras in $\mathcal{C}$. We mention it only briefly and not explain the details, as it will not be directly used in the following.

If $\mathcal{C}$ has products, then for any object $V \in \mathcal{C}$ there is a contravariant adjunction as in Section 2.1, where: $\mathcal{D} = \mathsf{Set}$, $F = \mathcal{C}(-, V)$ and $G = V^-$, where V^X denotes the X-fold product of V in $\mathcal{C}$. (This adjunction was studied in [18] for the purpose of combining distributive laws.) By the Yoneda Lemma, natural transformations $\alpha\colon F \Rightarrow FT$ are in bijective correspondence with algebras $g\colon TV \to V$. Routine calculation shows that the mate $\alpha^\flat$ is a T-action if and only if the corresponding g is an Eilenberg-Moore algebra for T.

Alternatively, one may assume that $\mathcal{C} = \mathcal{D}$ is a symmetric monoidal closed category and $F = G = V^-$ is the internal hom-functor based on an object $V \in \mathcal{C}$. (This adjunction was studied in [15] in the context of coalgebraic modal logic.) If, additionally, the functor T is strong, then every algebra $g\colon TV \to V$ gives rise to $\alpha\colon F \Rightarrow FT$, whose components $\alpha_X\colon V^X \to V^{TX}$ are given by transposing:

$$TX \otimes V^X \xrightarrow{\text{strength}} T(X \otimes V^X) \xrightarrow{T(\text{application})} TV \xrightarrow{g} V$$

If T is a strong monad and g is an E-M algebra for T then $\alpha^\flat$ is a T-action.

If $\mathcal{C} = \mathcal{D} = \mathsf{Set}$ then both these constructions apply (and coincide). All examples in Section 4 fit in this special case. In this situation more can be said [12, 11]: the resulting contravariant adjunction can be factored through the category of Eilenberg-Moore algebras for T.

6 Determinization

The classical powerset construction turns a non-deterministic automaton into a deterministic one, with states of the former interpreted as singleton states in the latter. More generally, a determinization procedure of coalgebras involves a change of state space. We define it as follows:

Definition 2. *For a functor T, a (T)-*determinization procedure *of H-coalgebras consists of a natural transformation $\eta\colon \mathsf{Id} \Rightarrow T$, a functor K and a lifting of T:*

$$\begin{array}{ccc}
\mathsf{Coalg}(H) & \xrightarrow{\bar{T}} & \mathsf{Coalg}(K) \\
\downarrow & & \downarrow \\
\mathcal{C} & \xrightarrow{T} & \mathcal{C}
\end{array}$$

We will mostly focus on cases where $H = TB$ or $H = BT$, but in Section 7 we will consider situations where T is not directly related to H.

The classical powerset construction is *correct*, in the sense that the language semantics of a state x in a non-deterministic automaton coincides with the final semantics (the accepted language) of the singleton of x in the determinized automaton. At the coalgebraic level, we capture trace semantics by a forgetful logic. Then, a determinization procedure is correct if logical equivalence on the original system coincides with behavioural equivalence on the determinized system along η:

Definition 3. *A determinization procedure* $(\bar{T}, \eta)$ *of* H*-coalgebras is* correct *wrt. a logic for* H *if for any* H*-coalgebra* (X, f) *with logical semantics* $s^\flat$*:*

1. $s^\flat$ *factors through* $h \circ \eta_X$*, for any* K*-coalgebra homomorphism* h *from* $\bar{T}(X, f)$*.*
2. *there exists a* K*-coalgebra homomorphism* h *from* $\bar{T}(X, f)$ *and a mono* m *so that* $s^\flat = m \circ h \circ \eta_X$*.*

The first condition states that behavioural equivalence on the determinized system implies logical equivalence on the original system; the second condition states the converse.

In [12] a more specific kind of determinization was studied, arising from a natural transformation $\kappa\colon TB \Rightarrow KT$ and a monad (T, η, μ). A determinization procedure T^κ for TB-coalgebras maps any $f\colon X \to TBX$ to

$$T^\kappa(X, f) = (TX \xrightarrow{Tf} TTBX \xrightarrow{\mu_{BX}} TBX \xrightarrow{\kappa_X} KTX) \tag{6}$$

It is easy to see that this construction respects homomorphisms, so that this indeed yields a lifting. For examples see, e.g., [12] and the end of this section.

The same type of natural transformation can be used to determinize BT-coalgebras, by mapping any $f\colon X \to BTX$ to

$$T_\kappa(X, f) = (TX \xrightarrow{Tf} TBTX \xrightarrow{\kappa_{TX}} KTTX \xrightarrow{K\mu_X} KTX) \tag{7}$$

This is considered in [24, 12] for the case where $B = K$ and κ is a distributive law of monad over functor. Again, this conforms to Definition 2.

The following gives a sufficient condition for the logical semantics on TB or BT-coalgebras to coincide with a logical semantics on determinized K-coalgebras.

Theorem 1. *Suppose* (T, η, μ) *is a monad and there are* α, ρ, κ *as above and* $\theta\colon LF \Rightarrow FK$ *so that* $\alpha^\flat$ *is an action and the following diagram commutes:*

$$\begin{array}{ccccc} TBG & \xRightarrow{T\rho^\flat} & TGL & \xRightarrow{\alpha^\flat L} & GL \\ \Downarrow{\scriptstyle \kappa G} & & & & \| \\ KTG & \xRightarrow{K\alpha^\flat} & KG & \xRightarrow{\theta^\flat} & GL. \end{array}$$

Let $s^\flat$ *be the semantics of* $\alpha \circledcirc \rho$ *on some coalgebra* $f\colon X \to TBX$*, and let* $s^\flat_\theta$ *be the semantics of* θ *on* $T^\kappa(X, f)$ *(see (6)). Then* $s^\flat = s^\flat_\theta \circ \eta_X$*.*

The same holds for the determinization procedure T_κ *(see (7)) for* BT*-coalgebras and the logic* $\rho \circledcirc \alpha$*.*

This can be connected to behavioural equivalence if θ is expressive:

Corollary 1. *Let* (T, η, μ), α, ρ, θ *and* κ *be as in Theorem 1, and suppose that* θ *is an expressive logic. Then the determinization procedure* T^κ *of* TB*-coalgebras* (6) *is correct with respect to* $\alpha \circledcirc \rho$, *and the determinization procedure* T_κ *of* BT*-coalgebras* (7) *is correct with respect to* $\rho \circledcirc \alpha$.

To illustrate all this, we show that the determinization of weighted automata as given in [12] is correct with respect to weighted language equivalence. (There is no such result for tree automata, as they do not determinize.)

Example 7. Fix a semiring $\mathbb{S}$, let $B = A \times - + 1$ and $K = \mathbb{S} \times -^A$. Consider $\kappa \colon \mathcal{M}B \Rightarrow K\mathcal{M}$ defined as follows [12]: $\kappa_X(\varphi) = (\varphi(*), \lambda a.\lambda x.\varphi(a, x))$. This induces a determinization procedure $\mathcal{M}^\kappa$ as in (6), for weighted automata. Let $\alpha \circledcirc \rho$ be the forgetful logic for weighted automata introduced in Example 6, and recall that the logical semantics on a weighted automaton is the usual notion of acceptance of weighted languages. We use Corollary 1 to prove that the determinization procedure $\mathcal{M}^\kappa$ is correct with respect to $\alpha \circledcirc \rho$. To this end, consider the logic $\theta^\flat : \mathbb{S} \times (\mathbb{S}^-)^A \Rightarrow \mathbb{S}^{A \times - + 1}$ given by the isomorphism, similar to the logic in Example 4. Since $\theta^\flat$ is componentwise injective, θ is expressive. Moreover, $\alpha^\flat$ is an action (see Section 5). The only remaining condition is commutativity of the diagram in Theorem 1, which is a straightforward calculation. This proves correctness of the determinization $\mathcal{M}^\kappa$ with respect to the semantics of $\alpha \circledcirc \rho$.

Example 8. In [24] it is shown how to determinize non-deterministic automata of the form $B\mathcal{P}_\omega$, where $BX = 2 \times X^A$, based on $\kappa = \langle \kappa^o, \kappa^t \rangle \colon \mathcal{P}_\omega(2 \times -^A) \Rightarrow 2 \times (\mathcal{P}_\omega -)^A$ (note that $B = K$ in this example) where $\kappa^o_X(S) = \mathsf{tt}$ iff $\exists t.(\mathsf{tt}, t) \in S$, and $\kappa^t_X(a) = \{x \mid x \in t(a) \text{ for some } (o, t) \in S\}$. In Example 4 we have seen an expressive logic ρ and an α so that the logical semantics of $\rho \circledcirc \alpha$ yields the usual language semantics. It is now straightforward to check that the determinization κ together with the logics ρ, α above satisfies the condition of Theorem 1, where $\theta = \rho$. By Corollary 1 this shows the expected result that determinization of non-deterministic automata is correct with respect to language semantics.

Moreover, recall that the logic $\rho \circledcirc \beta$, where β is as defined in Example 4, yields a conjunctive semantics. Take the natural transformation $\tau = \langle \tau^o, \tau^t \rangle$ of the same type as κ, where $\tau^o(S) = \mathsf{tt}$ iff $o = \mathsf{tt}$ for every $(o, t) \in S$, and $\tau^t = \kappa^t$. Using Corollary 1 we can verify that this determinization procedure is correct.

One can also get the finite trace semantics of transition systems (Example 4) by turning them into non-deterministic automata (then, B and K are different).

Example 9. Alternating automata (Example 5) can be determinized into non-deterministic automata; we show that this determinization preserves language semantics, using Theorem 1. Notice that this does not involve final semantics.

Let ρ, α, β and τ be as in Example 8, and let $\chi \colon \mathcal{P}_\omega\mathcal{P}_\omega \Rightarrow \mathcal{P}_\omega\mathcal{P}_\omega$ be as follows: $\chi_X(S) = \{\overrightarrow{g}(S) \mid g \colon S \to X \text{ s.t. } g(U) \in U \text{ for each } U \in S\}$, that is, given a family of sets S, it returns all possible sets obtained by choosing one element from each set in S. Now the composition $B\chi \circ \tau\mathcal{P}_\omega : \mathcal{P}_\omega B\mathcal{P}_\omega \Rightarrow B\mathcal{P}_\omega\mathcal{P}_\omega$ yields a determinization procedure, turning an alternating automaton into a non-deterministic one over sets of states (to be interpreted as conjunctions).

We instantiate Theorem 1 by $T = \mathcal{P}_\omega$, the functor B from the theorem is $BT = 2 \times T^A$, the logics ρ and θ are instantiated respectively to ρ and $\rho \circledcirc \alpha$ from above. Then commutativity of the diagram in Theorem 1 boils down to the similar diagram for τ given in Example 8, and that χ distributes conjunction over disjunction. Finally, $\beta^\flat$ is an action of the powerset monad (Section 5). By Theorem 1 we obtain that for any alternating automaton: $s^\flat = s^\flat_{\rho \circledcirc \alpha} \circ \eta_X$ where X is the set of states, $s^\flat$ is the semantics and $s^\flat_{\rho \circledcirc \alpha}$ is the usual language semantics on the non-deterministic automaton obtained by determinization.

7 Logics Whose Mates are Isomorphisms

Corollary 1 provides a sufficient condition for a given determinization procedure to be correct with respect to a forgetful logic. However, in general there is no guarantee that a correct determinization procedure for a given logic exists. Indeed it would be quite surprising if it did: the language semantics of (weighted) tree automata (see Example 6) is an example of a forgetful logic, and such automata are well known not to determinize in a classical setting.

In this section we provide a sufficient condition for a correct determinization procedure to exist. Specifically, for an endofunctor B, we assume a logic ρ whose mate $\rho^\flat : BG \Rightarrow GL$ is a natural isomorphism. This condition holds, for instance, for ρ in Example 4 and for θ in Example 7. It has been studied before in the context of determinization constructions [12]. Its important consequence is that $s^\flat$ in (3) from Section 3 can be seen as a B-coalgebra morphism from (X, h) to $(G\Phi, (\rho^\flat_\Phi)^{-1} \circ Ga)$. Moreover, as shown in [12, Lemma 6] (see also [10]), the construction mapping any $g : LA \to A$ to $(\rho^\flat_A)^{-1} \circ Gg : GA \to BGA$ defines a functor $\hat{G}\colon \mathsf{Alg}(L) \to \mathsf{Coalg}(B)$, which is a contravariant adjoint to $\hat{F}$ (see (1) in Section 3). As a result, $\hat{G}$ maps initial objects to final ones, hence $(G\Phi, (\rho^\flat_\Phi)^{-1} \circ Ga)$ is a final B-coalgebra, therefore $s^\flat$ is a final coalgebra morphism from (X, h).

In the remainder of this section, due to space limitations we only deal with TB-coalgebras. However, a completely analogous development can be made for BT-coalgebras with little effort.

7.1 Canonical Determinization

The setting of a forgetful logic $\alpha \circledcirc \rho$ where the mate of ρ is a natural isomorphism gives rise to the following diagram:

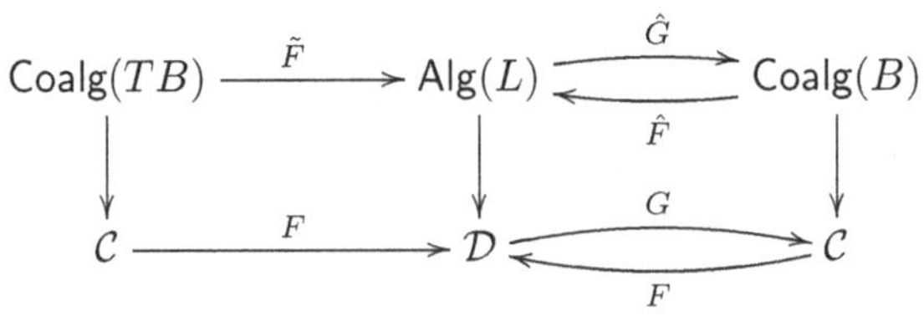

The functor $\tilde{F}$ arises from the logic $\alpha \circledcirc \rho$, the functor $\hat{F}$ arises from ρ and its contravariant adjoint $\hat{G}$ from the fact that $\rho^\flat$ is iso. Note that we make no assumptions on α; in particular, $\alpha^\flat$ need not be an action.

The composition $\hat{G}\tilde{F}$ is a determinization procedure, turning a coalgebra $f\colon X \to TBX$ into a B-coalgebra with carrier GFX. Explicitly, $\hat{G}\tilde{F}(X, f)$ is

$$GFX \xrightarrow{GFf} GFTBX \xrightarrow{G\alpha_{BX}} GFBX \xrightarrow{G\rho_X} GLFX \xrightarrow{(\rho^\flat)^{-1}_{FX}} BGFX \qquad (8)$$

This determinization procedure is correct with respect to $\alpha \circledcirc \rho$ in the following sense, much stronger then required by Definition 3:

Theorem 2. *For any TB-coalgebra (X, f), the logical semantics $s^\flat$ of $\alpha \circledcirc \rho$ on (X, f) coincides with the final semantics of the B-coalgebra $\hat{G}\tilde{F}(X, f)$ precomposed with $\iota\colon \mathsf{Id} \Rightarrow GF$.*

Strictly speaking, this is not an example of a determinization procedure as understood in [12]: the functor $\hat{G}\tilde{F}$ lifts GF rather than T, and the lifting does not arise from a distributive law κ as described in Section 6. However, it is *almost* an example: after an encoding of TB-coalgebras as GFB-coalgebras, it arises from a distributive law $\kappa\colon GFB \Rightarrow BGF$.

Indeed, define $\Gamma\colon \mathsf{Coalg}(TB) \to \mathsf{Coalg}(GFB)$ by:

$$\Gamma(X, f) = (X, \gamma_{BX} \circ f) \qquad \text{where} \qquad \gamma = \alpha^\flat F \circ T\iota : T \Rightarrow GF. \qquad (9)$$

GFB-coalgebras have a forgetful logic $\bar{\alpha} \circledcirc \rho$, where

$$\bar{\alpha} = \epsilon F : F \Rightarrow FGF, \qquad \text{equivalently,} \qquad \bar{\alpha}^\flat = G\epsilon : GFG \Rightarrow G.$$

(Note that $\bar{\alpha}^\flat$ is *always* a GF-action on G.) It is not difficult to calculate that for any TB-coalgebra (X, f), the logical semantics of $\bar{\alpha} \circledcirc \rho$ on $\Gamma(X, f)$ coincides with the logical semantics of $\alpha \circledcirc \rho$ on (X, f). Thus, encoding TB-coalgebras as GFB-coalgebras does not change their logical semantics.

Thanks to the mate $\rho^\flat\colon BG \Rightarrow GL$ being an isomorphism, the monad GF has a distributive law over B, denoted $\kappa\colon GFB \Rightarrow BGF$ and defined by:

$$GFB \xRightarrow{G\rho} GLF \xRightarrow{(\rho^\flat)^{-1}F} BGF \qquad (10)$$

Using κ we can apply the determinization construction from [12] as described in Section 6, putting $K = B$. Straightforward diagram chasing using Corollary 1 shows that the determinization procedure $(GF)^\kappa$ defined as in (6) is correct with respect to $\bar{\alpha} \circledcirc \rho$. Altogether, a two-step determinization procedure arises:

$$\begin{array}{ccccc}
\mathsf{Coalg}(TB) & \xrightarrow{\Gamma} & \mathsf{Coalg}(GFB) & \xrightarrow{(GF)^\kappa} & \mathsf{Coalg}(B) \\
\downarrow & & \downarrow & & \downarrow \\
\mathcal{C} & \xrightarrow{\qquad \mathsf{Id} \qquad} & \mathcal{C} & \xrightarrow{\qquad GF \qquad} & \mathcal{C}
\end{array}$$

and it is correct with respect to $\alpha \circledcirc \rho$. Correctness can also be proved without Corollary 1, since the procedure coincides with the construction from (8):

Theorem 3. $(GF)^\kappa \circ \Gamma = \hat{G} \circ \tilde{F}$.

7.2 A Connection to Brzozowski's Algorithm

Call a B-coalgebra *observable* if the morphism into a final coalgebra (assuming it exists) is mono [3]. The above canonical determinization procedure can be adapted to construct, for any TB-coalgebra, an observable B-coalgebra whose final semantics coincides with the logical semantics on the original one.

Indeed, suppose $\mathsf{Alg}(L)$ has an (epi,mono)-factorization system. Given a coalgebra $f\colon X \to TBX$, the algebra homomorphism $s\colon (\Phi, a) \to \tilde{F}(X, f)$ then decomposes as $s = m \circ e$, where m and e are mono and epi respectively; call the L-algebra in the middle (R, r). Recall that Gs is a coalgebra homomorphism into the final coalgebra. In the present situation it decomposes as follows:

$$\hat{G}\tilde{F}(X,f) \xrightarrow[Gm]{} \hat{G}(R,r) \xrightarrow[Ge]{} \hat{G}(\Phi,a) \qquad (Gs = Ge \circ Gm)$$

and recall that $\hat{G}(\Phi, a)$ is a final coalgebra. Because G is a right adjoint, it maps epis to monos, therefore Ge is mono and $\hat{G}(R, r)$ is observable. Moreover, thanks to Theorem 2 we have $s^\flat = Ge \circ Gm \circ \iota_X$, hence the final semantics Ge of $\hat{G}(R, r)$ coincides with the logical semantics on (X, f) along the mapping $Gm \circ \iota_X$.

Note that the construction of $\hat{G}(R, r)$ from (X, f) is not a determinization procedure itself according to Definition 2, as it does not lift any functor on $\mathcal{C}$.

The above refers to TB-coalgebras, but as everything else in this section, analogous reasoning works also for BT-coalgebras. For $T = \mathsf{Id}$ and $B = 2 \times -^A$, that (almost) corresponds to Brzozowski's algorithm for minimization of deterministic automata [4]. Applying $\tilde{F}$ to the given automaton corresponds to reversing transitions and turning final states into initial ones. Epi-mono factorization corresponds to taking the *reachable* part of this automaton. Then, applying $\hat{G}$ reverses transitions again, and turns initial states into final ones. Our abstract approach stops here; the original algorithm concludes by taking the reachable part again, which ensures minimality.

For a more detailed coalgebraic presentation of several concrete examples see [3]. Another approach, based on duality theory, is presented in [2]; this is related to the present development, but it uses dual equivalences rather than plain contravariant adjunctions. Another coalgebraic approach to minimization, based on factorization structures, is in [1]. A precise connection of these works to the present development is yet to be understood.

Notice that we only assume the mate of ρ to be iso; there are no requirements on α. The mate of ρ is iso for the logic from Example 4. Thus, we can instantiate α to obtain observable deterministic automata from non-deterministic automata or even alternating automata (by taking $T = \mathcal{P}_\omega\mathcal{P}_\omega$ and, for α, the composition of α and β from Example 5). The logic θ from Example 7 is covered as well, so one can treat Moore automata and weighted automata. However, the abstract construction of an observable automaton does not necessarily yield a concrete algorithm, as discussed for the case of weighted automata in [3].

Acknowledgments. We are grateful to Marcello Bonsangue, Helle Hvid Hansen, Ichiro Hasuo and Jan Rutten for discussions and suggestions, and to anonymous referees for their insightful comments.

References

1. Adámek, J., Bonchi, F., Hülsbusch, M., König, B., Milius, S., Silva, A.: A coalgebraic perspective on minimization and determinization. In: Birkedal, L. (ed.) FOSSACS 2012. LNCS, vol. 7213, pp. 58–73. Springer, Heidelberg (2012)
2. Bezhanishvili, N., Kupke, C., Panangaden, P.: Minimization via duality. In: Ong, L., de Queiroz, R. (eds.) WoLLIC 2012. LNCS, vol. 7456, pp. 191–205. Springer, Heidelberg (2012)
3. Bonchi, F., Bonsangue, M.M., Hansen, H.H., Panangaden, P., Rutten, J.J.M.M., Silva, A.: Algebra-coalgebra duality in Brzozowski's minimization algorithm. ACM Trans. Comput. Log. 15(1), 3 (2014)
4. Brzozowski, J.: Canonical regular expressions and minimal state graphs for definite events. Mathematical Theory of Automata 12, 529–561 (1962)
5. Cîrstea, C.: From branching to linear time, coalgebraically. In: Procs. FICS 2013. EPTCS, vol. 126, pp. 11–27 (2013)
6. Cîrstea, C.: A coalgebraic approach to linear-time logics. In: Muscholl, A. (ed.) FOSSACS 2014 (ETAPS). LNCS, vol. 8412, pp. 426–440. Springer, Heidelberg (2014)
7. Cîrstea, C., Pattinson, D.: Modular construction of modal logics. In: Gardner, P., Yoshida, N. (eds.) CONCUR 2004. LNCS, vol. 3170, pp. 258–275. Springer, Heidelberg (2004)
8. Goncharov, S.: Trace semantics via generic observations. In: Heckel, R., Milius, S. (eds.) CALCO 2013. LNCS, vol. 8089, pp. 158–174. Springer, Heidelberg (2013)
9. Hasuo, I., Jacobs, B., Sokolova, A.: Generic trace semantics via coinduction. Log. Meth. Comp. Sci. 3(4) (2007)
10. Hermida, C., Jacobs, B.: Structural induction and coinduction in a fibrational setting. Inf. and Comp. 145, 107–152 (1997)
11. Jacobs, B.: Introduction to coalgebra. Towards mathematics of states and observations, Draft (2014)
12. Jacobs, B., Silva, A., Sokolova, A.: Trace semantics via determinization. J. Comp. and Sys. Sci. (2014) (to appear)
13. Jacobs, B., Sokolova, A.: Exemplaric expressivity of modal logics. J. Log. and Comput. 20(5), 1041–1068 (2010)
14. Kissig, C., Kurz, A.: Generic trace logics. CoRR, abs/1103.3239 (2011)
15. Klin, B.: Coalgebraic modal logic beyond sets. ENTCS 173, 177–201 (2007)
16. Kupke, C., Pattinson, D.: Coalgebraic semantics of modal logics: An overview. Theor. Comput. Sci. 412(38), 5070–5094 (2011)
17. Kurz, A., Milius, S., Pattinson, D., Schröder, L.: Simplified coalgebraic trace equivalence. CoRR, abs/1410.2463 (2014)
18. Lenisa, M., Power, J., Watanabe, H.: Category theory for operational semantics. Theor. Comput. Sci. 327(1-2), 135–154 (2004)
19. Lane, S.M.: Categories for the working mathematician, vol. 5. Springer (1998)
20. Pavlovic, D., Mislove, M.W., Worrell, J.B.: Testing semantics: Connecting processes and process logics. In: Johnson, M., Vene, V. (eds.) AMAST 2006. LNCS, vol. 4019, pp. 308–322. Springer, Heidelberg (2006)

21. Power, J., Turi, D.: A coalgebraic foundation for linear time semantics. ENTCS 29, 259–274 (1999)
22. Rutten, J.J.M.M.: Universal coalgebra: A theory of systems. Theor. Comput. Sci. 249(1), 3–80 (2000)
23. Schröder, L., Pattinson, D.: Modular algorithms for heterogeneous modal logics via multi-sorted coalgebra. Math. Struct. in Comp. Sci. 21(2), 235–266 (2011)
24. Silva, A., Bonchi, F., Bonsangue, M.M., Rutten, J.J.M.M.: Generalizing determinization from automata to coalgebras. Log. Meth. Comp. Sci. 9(1) (2013)

Unifying Hyper and Epistemic Temporal Logics*

Laura Bozzelli[1], Bastien Maubert[2], and Sophie Pinchinat[3]

[1] UPM, Madrid, Spain
[2] LORIA - CNRS / Université de Lorraine, Nancy, France
[3] IRISA, Université de Rennes 1, France

Abstract. In the literature, two powerful temporal logic formalisms have been proposed for expressing information-flow security requirements, that in general, go beyond regular properties. One is classic, based on the knowledge modalities of epistemic logic. The other one, the so-called hyper logic, is more recent and subsumes many proposals from the literature. In an attempt to better understand how these logics compare with each other, we consider the logic KCTL^* (the extension of CTL^* with knowledge modalities and synchronous perfect recall semantics) and $\mathsf{HyperCTL}^*$. We first establish that KCTL^* and $\mathsf{HyperCTL}^*$ are expressively incomparable. Then, we introduce a natural linear past extension of $\mathsf{HyperCTL}^*$, called $\mathsf{HyperCTL}^*_{lp}$, that unifies KCTL^* and $\mathsf{HyperCTL}^*$. We show that the model-checking problem for $\mathsf{HyperCTL}^*_{lp}$ is decidable, and we provide its exact computational complexity in terms of a new measure of path quantifiers' alternation. For this, we settle open complexity issues for unrestricted quantified propositional temporal logic.

1 Introduction

Temporal logics provide a fundamental framework for the description of the dynamic behavior of reactive systems, and they usually support the successful model-checking approach to automatically verify complex finite-state systems.

Classic *regular* temporal logics, such as standard LTL [21] or the more expressive CTL^* [10], lack mechanisms to relate distinct paths or executions of a system. These mechanisms are required to formally express information-flow security properties which specify how information may propagate from inputs to outputs, such as non-interference [12] or opacity [5]. In the literature, two powerful temporal logic formalisms have been proposed for expressing such security requirements that, in general, go beyond regular properties.

One is classical and is based on the extension of temporal logic with the knowledge modalities of epistemic logic [11], which relate paths that are observationally equivalent for a given agent. A classic instance is KCTL^*, the extension of CTL^* with knowledge modalities under the synchronous perfect recall semantics (where an agent remembers the whole sequence of its observations, and observations are time-sensitive) [14,24,22,8]. This logic and its linear-time fragment,

* We acknowledge financial suppport from ERC project EPS 313360.

A. Pitts (Ed.): FOSSACS 2015, LNCS 9034, pp. 167–182, 2015.
DOI: 10.1007/978-3-662-46678-0_11

KLTL, have been used to specify secrecy policies that involve sets of execution traces sharing some similar information [1,13,3].

In the second, more recent, framework [7] one can express properties of sets of execution traces, known as *hyperproperties*; these are useful to formalize security policies, such as non-interference [12] and observational determinism [18]. The general hyper logical framework introduced in [7] is based on a second-order logic for which model-checking is undecidable. More recently, fragments of this logic have been introduced [6], namely the logics HyperCTL* and HyperLTL, for which model checking is decidable. These logics extend CTL* and LTL in a simple and natural way by allowing explicit and simultaneous quantification over multiple paths. In [6], an extension of the semantics of HyperCTL* and HyperLTL is also considered. In this setting, a formula can refer to propositions which extend the alphabet AP of the model K. Then, the path quantification ranges over all the traces on the augmented alphabet whose projections over AP correspond to the execution traces of K. Within this affected generalization, KLTL can be effectively expressed in HyperLTL [6]. The logic HyperCTL* also generalizes the temporal logic secLTL, introduced in [9]. Other logics for hyperproperties were introduced in [19] but no general approach to verifying such logics exists.

Contribution. Our first contribution in this paper is the comparison of the expressive power of hyper temporal logics and epistemic temporal logics. We establish by formal non-trivial arguments that HyperCTL* and KCTL* are expressively incomparable.

As a second contribution, we unify HyperCTL* and KCTL* by extending HyperCTL* with new logical features which provide very natural modeling facilities. The proposed extension is based on two important observations: first, HyperCTL* has no explicit mechanism to refer to the past which would be useful to relate histories of different executions (paths). This ability is partially supported in KCTL* by means of observational equivalences between path prefixes; however, such equivalences are not expressed in the logic itself but are given as separate input parameters in the model specification. On the other hand, it is well-known that temporal logics which combine both past and future temporal modalities make specifications easier to write and more natural. In particular, the *linear past* setting, where the history of the current situation increases with time and is never forgotten, especially suits the specification of dynamic behaviors. A relevant example is given by the logic CTL^*_{lp}, a well-known equi-expressive linear past extension of CTL* [15] obtained by adding past temporal modalities and where path quantification is 'memoryful': it ranges over paths that start at the root of the computation tree and visit the current node. The second observation is that HyperCTL* has no explicit mechanism to select, at a given non-initial instant, paths which do not visit the current node. This is clearly a strong limitation for expressing general information-flow requirements.

We remove the above two limitations of HyperCTL* by introducing both linear past modalities and the *general hyper quantifier*, where path quantification ranges over all the paths that start at the root of the computation tree. These new features yield a novel logic that we call $\mathsf{HyperCTL}^*_{lp}$. In fact, as we formally establish, the only addition of general path quantification to HyperCTL* makes the resulting logic already more expressive than HyperCTL*. However, it remains open whether both linear past and general quantification are necessary to capture all the KCTL* definable properties. Like for the logics KCTL* and HyperCTL*, the finite-state model-checking problem for HyperCTL^*_{lp} is non-elementarily decidable, and we provide the exact complexity in terms of a variant of the standard alternation depth of path quantifiers. For this, we settle complexity issues for satisfiability of full Quantified Propositional Temporal Logic (QPTL) [23]. The optimal upper bounds for full QPTL are obtained by a sophisticated generalization of the standard automata-theoretic approach for QPTL in prenex normal form [23], which exploits a subclass of parity two-way alternating word automata. Our results also improve in a meaningful way the upper bounds provided in [6] for model-checking of HyperCTL*. An extended version of this paper with all the proofs can be found in [4].

2 Preliminaries

Let $\mathbb{N}$ be the set of natural numbers and for all $i, j \in \mathbb{N}$, let $[i, j] := \{h \in \mathbb{N} \mid i \leq h \leq j\}$. We fix a *finite* set AP of atomic propositions. A *trace* is a finite or infinite word over 2^{AP}. For a word w over some alphabet, $|w|$ is the length of w ($|w| = \infty$ if w is infinite), and for each $0 \leq i < |w|$, $w(i)$ is the ith symbol of w. For a logic formalism $\mathcal{L}$ and an $\mathcal{L}$ formula φ, the size $|\varphi|$ of φ is the number of subformulas of φ.

Structures and Tree Structures. A *Kripke structure* (*over AP*) is a tuple $K = \langle S, s_0, E, V \rangle$, where S is a set of states, $s_0 \in S$ is the initial state, $E \subseteq S \times S$ is a transition relation such that for each $s \in S$, $(s, t) \in E$ for some $t \in S$, and $V : S \to 2^{\mathsf{AP}}$ is an *AP-valuation* assigning to each state s the set of propositions in AP which hold at s. A *path* $\pi = t_0, t_1, \ldots$ of K is an infinite word over S such that for all $i \geq 0$, $(t_i, t_{i+1}) \in E$. For each $i \geq 0$, $\pi[0, i]$ denotes the prefix of π leading to the ith state and $\pi[i, \infty]$ the suffix of π from the ith state. A finite path of K is a prefix of some path of K. An *initial path* of K is a path starting from the initial state. For a (finite) path $\pi = t_0, t_1, \ldots$, the *trace* $V(\pi)$ *of* π is $V(t_0), V(t_1), \ldots$. We say that $K = \langle S, s_0, E, V \rangle$ is a *tree structure* if S is a prefix-closed subset of $\mathbb{N}^*$, $s_0 = \varepsilon$ (the root of K), and $(\tau, \tau') \in E \Rightarrow \tau' = \tau \cdot i$ for some $i \in \mathbb{N}$. States of a tree structure are also called *nodes*. For a Kripke structure K, *Unw*(K) is the tree structure obtained by unwinding K from the initial state. A *tree structure* is *regular* if it is the unwinding of some finite Kripke structure.

2.1 Temporal Logics with Knowledge Modalities

We recall the *non-regular* extensions, denoted by KCTL* and KLTL, of standard CTL* and LTL obtained by adding the knowledge modalities of epistemic logic under the *synchronous* perfect recall semantics [14,24,22,8]. Unlike the asynchronous setting, the synchronous setting can be considered time sensitive in the sense that it can model an observer who knows that a transition has occurred even if the observation has not changed. We fix a finite set Agts of agents.

Formulas φ of KCTL^* over Agts and AP are defined as follows:

$$\varphi ::= \top \mid p \mid \neg\varphi \mid \varphi \vee \varphi \mid \mathsf{X}\varphi \mid \varphi \mathsf{U} \varphi \mid \exists\varphi \mid \mathsf{K}_a\varphi$$

where $p \in \mathsf{AP}$, $a \in \mathsf{Agts}$, X and U are the "next" and "until" temporal modalities, $\exists$ is the CTL^* existential path quantifier, and K_a is the knowledge modality for agent a. We also use standard shorthands: $\forall\varphi := \neg\exists\neg\varphi$ ("universal path quantifier"), $\mathsf{F}\varphi := \top\mathsf{U}\varphi$ ("eventually") and its dual $\mathsf{G}\varphi := \neg\mathsf{F}\neg\varphi$ ("always"). A formula φ is a *sentence* if each temporal/knowledge modality is in the scope of a path quantifier. The logic KLTL is the LTL-like fragment of KCTL^* consisting of sentences of the form $\forall\varphi$, where φ does not contain any path quantifier.

The logic KCTL^* is interpreted over *extended* Kripke structures (K, Obs), i.e., Kripke structures K equipped with an *observation map* $\mathit{Obs} : \mathsf{Agts} \to 2^{\mathsf{AP}}$ associating to each agent $a \in \mathsf{Agts}$, the set $\mathit{Obs}(a)$ of propositions which are observable by agent a. For an agent a and a finite trace $w \in (2^{\mathsf{AP}})^*$, the a-observable part $\mathit{Obs}_a(w)$ of w is the trace of length $|w|$ such that $\mathit{Obs}_a(w)(i) = w(i) \cap \mathit{Obs}(a)$ for all $0 \leq i < |w|$. Two finite traces w and w' are *(synchronously) Obs_a-equivalent* if $\mathit{Obs}_a(w) = \mathit{Obs}_a(w')$ (note that $|w| = |w'|$). Intuitively, an agent a does not distinguish prefixes of paths whose traces are Obs_a-equivalent.

For a KCTL^* formula φ, an extended Kripke structure $\Lambda = (K, \mathit{Obs})$, an *initial* path π of K, and a position i along π, the satisfaction relation $\pi, i \models_\Lambda \varphi$ for KCTL^* is defined as follows (we omit the clauses for the Boolean connectives):

$$\begin{array}{ll}
\pi, i \models_\Lambda p & \Leftrightarrow p \in V(\pi(i)) \\
\pi, i \models_\Lambda \mathsf{X}\varphi & \Leftrightarrow \pi, i+1 \models_\Lambda \varphi \\
\pi, i \models_\Lambda \varphi_1 \mathsf{U} \varphi_2 & \Leftrightarrow \text{for some } j \geq i : \pi, j \models_\Lambda \varphi_2 \text{ and } \pi, k \models_\Lambda \varphi_1 \text{ for all } i \leq k < j \\
\pi, i \models_\Lambda \exists\varphi & \Leftrightarrow \pi', i \models_\Lambda \varphi \text{ for some initial path } \pi' \text{ of } K \text{ s.t. } \pi'[0,i] = \pi[0,i] \\
\pi, i \models_\Lambda \mathsf{K}_a\varphi & \Leftrightarrow \text{for all initial paths } \pi' \text{ of } K \text{ such that} \\
& \quad V(\pi[0,i]) \text{ and } V(\pi'[0,i]) \text{ are } \mathit{Obs}_a\text{-equivalent, } \pi', i \models_\Lambda \varphi
\end{array}$$

We say that (K, Obs) *satisfies* φ, denoted $(K, \mathit{Obs}) \models \varphi$, if there is an initial path π of K s.t. $\pi, 0 \models_{(K,\mathit{Obs})} \varphi$. Note that if φ is a sentence, then the satisfaction relation $\pi, 0 \models_{(K,\mathit{Obs})} \varphi$ is independent of π. One can easily show that KCTL^* is bisimulation invariant and, in particular, $(K, \mathit{Obs}) \models \varphi$ iff $(\mathit{Unw}(K), \mathit{Obs}) \models \varphi$.

Example 1. Let us consider the KLTL sentence $\varphi_p := \forall\mathsf{X}\mathsf{F}\mathsf{K}_a\neg p$. For all observation maps Obs such that $\mathit{Obs}(a) = \emptyset$, $(K, \mathit{Obs}) \models \varphi_p$ means that there is some non-root level in the unwinding of K at which *no* node satisfies p. Property ϕ_p is a well-known non-regular context-free branching-time property (see e.g. [2]).

2.2 Hyper Logics

In this section, we first recall the logics $\mathsf{HyperCTL}^*$ and $\mathsf{HyperLTL}$ [6] which are non-regular extensions of CTL^* and LTL with a restricted form of explicit first-order quantification over paths. Intuitively, path variables are used to express linear-time properties simultaneously on multiple paths. Then, we introduce the novel logic $\mathsf{HyperCTL}^*_{lp}$, an extension of $\mathsf{HyperCTL}^*$ obtained by adding linear past and the general hyper path quantifier. In this logic, path quantification is 'memoryful', i.e., it ranges over paths that start at the root of the computation tree (the unwinding of the Kripke structure) and either visit the current node τ (*regular* path quantification), or visit a node τ' at the same level as τ (*non-regular* path quantification).

The Logic $\mathsf{HyperCTL}^*$ [6]. For a finite set VAR of *path variables*, the syntax of $\mathsf{HyperCTL}^*$ formulas φ over AP and VAR is defined as follows:

$$\varphi ::= \top \mid p[x] \mid \neg\varphi \mid \varphi \wedge \varphi \mid \mathsf{X}\varphi \mid \varphi \mathsf{U} \varphi \mid \exists x.\varphi$$

where $p \in \mathsf{AP}$, $x \in \mathsf{VAR}$, and $\exists x$ is the *hyper* existential path quantifier for variable x. Informally, formula $\exists x.\varphi$ requires that there is an initial path π such that φ holds when x is mapped to π, and $p[x]$ asserts that p holds at the current position of the path assigned to x. The hyper universal quantifier $\forall x$ is defined as: $\forall x.\varphi := \neg\exists x.\neg\varphi$. A $\mathsf{HyperCTL}^*$ formula φ is a *sentence* if each temporal modality occurs in the scope of a path quantifier and for each atomic formula $p[x]$, x is bound by a path quantifier. The logic $\mathsf{HyperLTL}$ is the fragment of $\mathsf{HyperCTL}^*$ consisting of formulas in prenex form, i.e., of the form $Q_1 x_1. \ldots .Q_n x_n.\varphi$, where $Q_1, \ldots, Q_n \in \{\exists, \forall\}$ and φ does not contain any path quantifier.

We give a semantics for $\mathsf{HyperCTL}^*$ that is equivalent to the one in [6] but more suitable for a linear-past generalization. $\mathsf{HyperCTL}^*$ formulas φ are interpreted over Kripke structures $K = \langle S, s_0, E, V\rangle$ equipped with a *path assignment* $\Pi : \mathsf{VAR} \to S^\omega$ associating to each variable $x \in \mathsf{VAR}$ an *initial path* of K, a variable $y \in \mathsf{VAR}$, and a position $i \geq 0$. Intuitively, $\Pi(y)$ is the current path and i is the current position along the paths in Π. The satisfaction relation $\Pi, y, i \models_K \varphi$ is defined as follows (we omit the clauses for the Boolean connectives):

$$\begin{array}{ll}
\Pi, y, i \models_K p[x] & \Leftrightarrow p \in V(\Pi(x)(i)) \\
\Pi, y, i \models_K \mathsf{X}\varphi & \Leftrightarrow \Pi, y, i+1 \models_K \varphi \\
\Pi, y, i \models_K \varphi_1 \mathsf{U} \varphi_2 & \Leftrightarrow \text{for some } j \geq i : \Pi, y, j \models_K \varphi_2 \text{ and} \\
& \quad\ \Pi, y, k \models_K \varphi_1 \text{ for all } i \leq k < j \\
\Pi, y, i \models_K \exists x.\varphi & \Leftrightarrow \text{for some initial path } \pi \text{ of } K \text{ such that } \pi[0,i] = \Pi(y)[0,i], \\
& \quad\ \Pi[x \leftarrow \pi], x, i \models \varphi
\end{array}$$

where $\Pi[x \leftarrow \pi](x) = \pi$ and $\Pi[x \leftarrow \pi](y) = \Pi(y)$ for all $y \neq x$. We say that K *satisfies* φ, written $K \models \varphi$, if there is a path assignment Π of K and $y \in \mathsf{VAR}$ such that $\Pi, y, 0 \models_K \varphi$. If φ is a *sentence*, then the satisfaction relation $\Pi, y, 0 \models_K \varphi$ is independent of y and Π.

Example 2. As an example of a formula expressing a non-regular requirement, we consider the $\mathsf{HyperLTL}$ sentence $\exists x.\exists y.\ p[x]\ \mathsf{U}\ \Big((p[x] \wedge \neg p[y]) \wedge \mathsf{XG}(p[x] \leftrightarrow p[y])\Big)$ which asserts that there are two distinct initial paths π and π' and $\ell > 0$ such that p always holds along the prefix $\pi[0,\ell]$, p does not hold at position ℓ of π', and the valuations of p along π and π' coincide for all positions $j > \ell$.

The Novel Logic $\mathsf{HyperCTL}^*_{lp}$. $\mathsf{HyperCTL}^*_{lp}$ formulas φ are defined as follows:

$$\varphi ::= \top \mid p[x] \mid \neg\varphi \mid \varphi \wedge \varphi \mid \mathsf{X}\varphi \mid \mathsf{X}^-\varphi \mid \varphi\mathsf{U}\varphi \mid \varphi\mathsf{U}^-\varphi \mid \exists x.\varphi \mid \exists^G x.\varphi$$

where X^- and U^- are the past-time counterparts of the temporal modalities X and U, respectively, and $\exists^G x$ is the *general* (hyper) existential quantifier for variable x. We also use some shorthands: $\forall^G x.\varphi := \neg\exists^G x.\neg\varphi$ ("general universal path quantifier"), $\mathsf{F}^-\varphi := \top\mathsf{U}^-\varphi$ ("sometime in the past") and its dual $\mathsf{G}^-\varphi := \neg\mathsf{F}^-\neg\varphi$ ("always in the past"). The notion of sentence is defined as for $\mathsf{HyperCTL}^*$. The semantics of the modalities X^-, U^-, and $\exists^G x$ is as follows.

$$\begin{array}{ll} \Pi, y, i \models_K \mathsf{X}^-\varphi & \Leftrightarrow i > 0 \text{ and } \Pi, y, i-1 \models_K \varphi \\ \Pi, y, i \models_K \varphi_1\mathsf{U}^-\varphi_2 & \Leftrightarrow \text{for some } j \leq i : \Pi, y, j \models_K \varphi_2 \text{ and} \\ & \quad\ \Pi, y, k \models_K \varphi_1 \text{ for all } j < k \leq i \\ \Pi, y, i \models_K \exists^G x.\varphi & \Leftrightarrow \text{for some initial path } \pi \text{ of } K,\ \Pi[x \leftarrow \pi], x, i \models \varphi \end{array}$$

Thus, general hyper quantification range over all the initial paths (not only the ones which visit the current node). The satisfaction relation $K \models \varphi$ is defined as for $\mathsf{HyperCTL}^*$. Note that while the one-variable fragment of $\mathsf{HyperCTL}^*$ corresponds to standard CTL^*, the $\exists^G$-free one-variable fragment of $\mathsf{HyperCTL}^*_{lp}$ corresponds to the well-known equi-expressive linear past memoryful extension CTL^*_{lp} of CTL^* [15]. The model-checking problem for $\mathsf{HyperCTL}^*_{lp}$ is checking given a *finite* Kripke structure K and a $\mathsf{HyperCTL}^*_{lp}$ sentence φ, whether $K \models \varphi$. It is plain to see that $\mathsf{HyperCTL}^*_{lp}$ is bisimulation invariant and, in particular, $K \models \varphi$ iff $Unw(K) \models \varphi$.

We consider now two relevant examples from the literature which demonstrate the expressive power of $\mathsf{HyperCTL}^*_{lp}$. Both examples rely on the ability to express observational equivalence in the logic. We fix an observation map *Obs*. For an agent $a \in \mathsf{Agts}$ and two paths variables x and y in VAR, define $\psi(a, x, y) := \mathsf{G}^-(\bigwedge_{p \in Obs(a)} p[x] \leftrightarrow p[y])$

The first example shows that the logic can express *distributed knowledge*, a notion extensively investigated in [11]. It is crucial for information-flow security requirements as it allows to reason about adversaries who can communicate to share their knowledge: a group of agents $A \subseteq \mathsf{Agts}$ has distributed knowledge of φ, which we will denote by $\mathsf{D}_A\varphi$, if the combined knowledge of the members of A implies φ. It is well known that the modality D_A cannot be expressed by means of modalities K_a [11]. Also, since $\mathsf{HyperCTL}^*$ cannot express the modality K_a (see Section 3.2) and K_a is $\mathsf{D}_{\{a\}}$, it cannot express either D_A. However, D_A is expressible in $\mathsf{HyperCTL}^*_{lp}$. Given a $\mathsf{HyperCTL}^*_{lp}$ formula φ, we have: $\mathsf{D}_A\varphi \equiv \forall^G y.\,[(\bigwedge_{a \in A} \psi(a, x, y)) \rightarrow \varphi]$. Observe that both distinctive features of $\mathsf{HyperCTL}^*_{lp}$ are used here: the linear past modalities to capture observational equivalence, and the general hyper quantifier to range over all the initial paths.

The second example, inspired by [1], is an opacity requirement that we conjecture can be expressed neither in $\mathsf{HyperCTL}^*$ nor in KCTL^*. Assume that agent a can observe the low-security (Boolean) variables p (i.e., $p \in Obs(a)$), but not the high-security variables q (i.e., $q \notin Obs(a)$). Consider the case of a secret represented by the value `true` of a high variable q_s. Then, the requirement $\forall x.\mathsf{G}(q_s \to \forall^G y.\psi(a, x, y))$ says that whenever q_s holds at some node in the computation tree, all the nodes at the same level have the same valuations of low variables. Hence, the observer a cannot infer that the secret has been revealed. Here again, both the linear past and the general hyper quantifier are required.

3 Expressiveness Issues

In this section, we establish that HyperCTL* and KCTL* are expressively incomparable, and $\mathsf{HyperCTL}^*_{lp}$ is more expressive than both HyperCTL* and KCTL*.

Let $\mathcal{L}$ be a logic interpreted over Kripke structures, $\mathcal{L}'$ be a logic interpreted over *extended* Kripke structures, and C be a class of Kripke structures. For a sentence φ of $\mathcal{L}$, a sentence φ' of $\mathcal{L}'$, and an observation map *Obs*, φ and φ' *are equivalent w.r.t.* C *and Obs*, written $\varphi \equiv_{C,Obs} \varphi'$ if for all Kripke structures $K \in C$, $K \models \varphi$ iff $(K, Obs) \models \varphi'$. $\mathcal{L}'$ is *at least as expressive as* $\mathcal{L}$ w.r.t. C, written $\mathcal{L} \leq_C \mathcal{L}'$, if for every sentence φ of $\mathcal{L}$, there is an observation map *Obs* and a sentence φ' of $\mathcal{L}'$ such that $\varphi \equiv_{C,Obs} \varphi'$. Conversely, $\mathcal{L}$ is *at least as expressive as* $\mathcal{L}'$ w.r.t. the class C, written $\mathcal{L}' \leq_C \mathcal{L}$, if for every sentence φ' of $\mathcal{L}'$ and for every observation map *Obs*, there is a sentence φ of $\mathcal{L}$ such that $\varphi \equiv_{C,Obs} \varphi'$. Note the obvious asymmetry in the above two definitions due to the fact that for evaluating a sentence in $\mathcal{L}'$, we need to fix an observation map. If $\mathcal{L} \not\leq_C \mathcal{L}'$ and $\mathcal{L}' \not\leq_C \mathcal{L}$, then $\mathcal{L}$ and $\mathcal{L}'$ are *expressively incomparable w.r.t.* C. We denote by *fin* the class of finite Kripke structures.

3.1 HyperCTL* is not Subsumed by KCTL*

In this section, we show that HyperCTL* and its fragment HyperLTL are not subsumed by KCTL* even if we restrict ourselves to *finite* Kripke structures.

Theorem 1. *HyperLTL* $\not\leq_{fin}$ *KCTL**.

The main intuition for Theorem 1 is that unlike HyperLTL, KCTL* does not allow to relate two initial paths at an unbounded number of positions. Thus, for example, there is no mechanism in KCTL* to select two distinct paths π and π' such that the evaluations of a given LTL formula along π and π' coincide at every position. Formally, in order to prove Theorem 1, we use the HyperLTL sentence of Example 2 given by $\varphi_p := \exists x.\exists y.\ p[x]\ \mathsf{U}\ \Big((p[x] \wedge \neg p[y]) \wedge \mathsf{XG}(p[x] \leftrightarrow p[y])\Big)$.

We exhibit two families of *regular* tree structures $(K_n)_{n>1}$ and $(M_n)_{n>1}$ over $2^{\{p\}}$ such that: (i) for all $n > 1$, φ_p distinguishes between K_n and M_n,[1] and (ii) for every KCTL* sentence ψ, there is $n > 1$ s.t. ψ does *not* distinguish between (K_n, Obs) and (M_n, Obs) for all observation maps *Obs*. Hence, Theorem 1 follows.

In the following, we fix $n > 1$. The regular tree structure K_n is illustrated in Fig. 1, where $\ell_n > 1$. Note that the root has label $\{p\}$ and $2n + 1$ successors

[1] i.e., φ_p evaluates to true on one strucutre and to false on the other one.

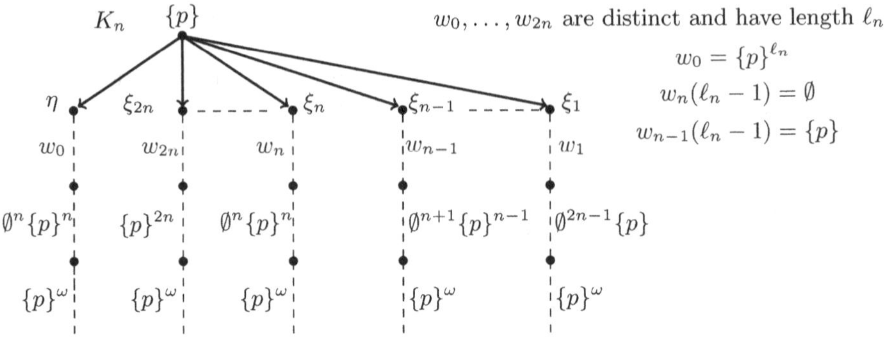

Fig. 1. The regular tree structure K_n for the witness HyperLTL formula φ_p

$\eta, \xi_1, \ldots, \xi_{2n}$, and there is a *unique* initial path visiting η (resp., ξ_k with $k \in [1, 2n]$). We denote this path by $\pi(\eta)$ (resp., $\pi(\xi_k)$). The tree structure M_n is obtained from K_n by replacing the label $\{p\}$ of node $\pi(\xi_n)(\ell_n + 1 + n)$ with $\emptyset$. Note that in M_n, the traces of $\pi(\xi_n)[\ell_n + 1, \infty]$ and $\pi(\xi_{n-1})[\ell_n + 1, \infty]$ coincide.

Proposition 1. *$K_n \models \varphi_p$ and $M_n \not\models \varphi_p$.*

Proof. In the structure K_n, the trace of the finite path $\pi(\eta)[0, \ell_n]$ is $\{p\}^{\ell_n+1}$, the label of $\pi(\xi_n)$ at position ℓ_n is $\emptyset$, and the traces of $\pi(\eta)[\ell_n + 1, \infty]$ and $\pi(\xi_n)[\ell_n + 1, \infty]$ coincide, which make $\pi(\eta)$ and $\pi(\xi_n)$ good candidates to fulfill φ_p. Hence, $K_n \models \varphi_p$. It remains to show that $M_n \not\models \varphi_p$.
By construction, for all distinct initial paths π and π' and $\ell \in [0, \ell_n]$, the traces of $\pi[\ell, \infty]$ and $\pi'[\ell, \infty]$ in M_n are distinct (recall that $\pi(\xi_n)(\ell_n)$ and $\pi(\xi_{n-1})(\ell_n)$ have distinct labels). Moreover, $\pi(\eta)$ is the unique initial path of M_n where p holds at every position in $[0, \ell_n]$. Thus, since $\pi(\eta)(\ell_n + 1)$ has label $\emptyset$ and there is no distinct initial path π'' of M_n such that the traces of $\pi(\eta)[\ell_n + 1, \infty]$ and $\pi''[\ell_n + 1, \infty]$ coincide, by construction of φ_p, $M_n \not\models \varphi_p$. □

A KCTL* formula ψ is *balanced* if for every until subformula $\psi_1 \mathsf{U} \psi_2$ of ψ, it holds that $|\psi_1| = |\psi_2|$. By using the atomic formula $\top$, it is trivial to convert a KCTL* sentence ψ into an *equivalent* balanced KCTL* sentence of size at most $|\psi|^2$. This observation together with Proposition 1, and the following non-trivial result provide a proof of Theorem 1.

Theorem 2. *Let ψ be a* balanced *KCTL* sentence such that $|\psi| < n$. Then, for all observation maps Obs, $(K_n, Obs) \models \psi \Leftrightarrow (M_n, Obs) \models \psi$.*

Proof. Given an observation map *Obs*, it suffices to show that for all initial paths π and positions $i \in [0, \ell_n]$, $\pi, i \models_{K_n, Obs} \psi$ iff $\pi, i \models_{M_n, Obs} \psi$. The key for obtaining this result is that since $|\psi| < n$, ψ cannot distinguish the nodes $\pi(\xi_n)(\ell_n + 1)$ and $\pi(\xi_{n-1})(\ell_n + 1)$ both in (K_n, Obs) and in (M_n, Obs). For M_n, this indistinguishability easily follows from the construction and is independent of the size of ψ. For K_n, the indistinguishability is non-trivial and is formally proved by defining equivalence relations on the set of nodes at distance $d \in [\ell_n + 1, \ell_n + 2n]$ from the root, which are parameterized by a natural number $h \in [1, n]$, where h intuitively represents the size of the current balanced subformula of ψ in the recursive evaluation of ψ on K_n. □

3.2 KCTL* is not Subsumed by HyperCTL*

In this section, we show that KCTL* and its fragment KLTL are not subsumed by HyperCTL* even with respect to finite Kripke structures. The intuitive insight is that unlike KLTL, HyperCTL* cannot express requirements which relate at some position an unbounded number of paths.

For $p \in \mathsf{AP}$, an observation map *Obs* is *p-blind* if for all agents a, $p \notin Obs(a)$.

Theorem 3. *KLTL* $\not\leq_{fin}$ *HyperCTL**.

As witness KLTL sentence for Theorem 3, we use the KLTL sentence of Example 1 given by $\varphi_p := \forall \mathsf{X}\mathsf{F}\mathsf{K}_a \neg p$. We exhibit two families of *regular* tree structures $(K_n)_{n>1}$ and $(M_n)_{n>1}$ over $2^{\{p\}}$ such that the following holds for all $n > 1$: (i) for each *p-blind* observation map *Obs*, φ_p distinguishes between (K_n, Obs) and (M_n, Obs), and (ii) no HyperCTL* formula ψ of size less than n distinguishes between K_n and M_n. Hence, Theorem 3 follows.

Fix $n > 1$. In order to define K_n and M_n, we need additional definitions.

An *n-block* is a word in $\{p\}\emptyset^*$ of length at least $n+2$. Given finite words $w_1, \ldots, w_k$ over $2^{\{p\}}$ having the same length ℓ, the join $join(w_1, \ldots, w_k)$ of $w_1, \ldots, w_k$ is the word of length ℓ such that $join(w_1, \ldots, w_k)(i) = w_1(i) \cup \ldots \cup w_k(i)$ for all $i \in [0, \ell - 1]$. For a finite word w over $2^{\{p\}}$, the *dual* $\widetilde{w}$ of w is the word over $2^{\{p\}}$ of length $|w|$ such that for all $i \in [0, |w| - 1]$, $p \in \widetilde{w}(i)$ iff $p \notin w(i)$.

Given n finite words $w_1, \ldots, w_n$ over $2^{\{p\}}$ of the same length, the tuple $\langle w_1, \ldots, w_n \rangle$ *satisfies the n-fractal requirement* if for all $k \in [1, n]$,

$$join(w_1, \ldots, w_k) \text{ is of the form } bl_1^k \ldots bl_{m_k}^k \cdot \{p\}$$

where $bl_1^k \ldots bl_{m_k}^k$ are n-blocks. Moreover, $m_1 = n + 4$, and the following holds: if $k < n$, then w_{k+1} is obtained from $join(w_1, \ldots, w_k)$ by replacing the last symbol with $\emptyset$, and by replacing each n-block bl_i^k of $join(w_1, \ldots, w_k)$ by a sequence of $n+4$ n-blocks preceded by a non-empty word in $\emptyset^*$ of length at least $n+2$.

Remark 1. Assume that $\langle w_1, \ldots, w_n \rangle$ satisfies the n-fractal requirement and let ℓ be the common length of $w_1, \ldots, w_n$. Then, for all $i \in [0, \ell - 1]$, there is at most one $k \in [1, n]$ such that $p \in w_k(i)$. Moreover, $p \in w_1(0)$ and $p \in w_1(\ell - 1)$.

Definition 1 (The Tree Structures K_n and M_n). *K_n is illustrated in Fig. 2 where $\ell_n > 1$. The unique initial path visiting node η (resp., ξ_k with $k \in [1, n]$) is denoted by $\pi(\eta)$ (resp., $\pi(\xi_k)$).*

A main position *is a position in $[1, \ell_n]$. Let i_{alert} be the* third *(in increasing order) main position i along $\pi(\xi_1)$ such that the label of $\pi(\xi_1)(i)$ in K_n is $\{p\}$ (note that i_{alert} exists). Then, the regular tree structure M_n is obtained from K_n by replacing the label $\{p\}$ of $\pi(\xi_1)$ at position i_{alert} with $\emptyset$.*

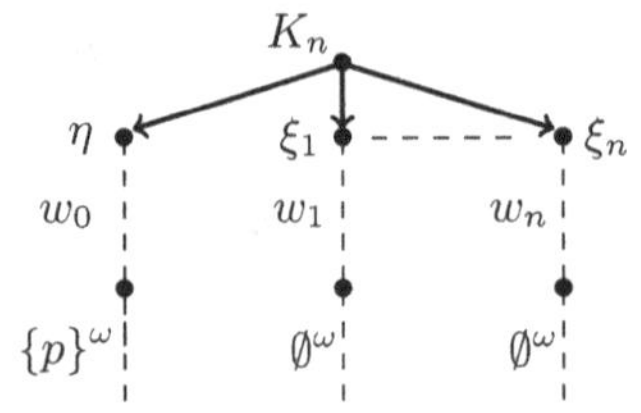

$|w_0| = |w_1| = \ldots = |w_n| = \ell_n$

$\langle w_1, \ldots, w_n \rangle$ satisfies the n-fractal requirement

w_0 is the dual of $join(w_1, \ldots, w_n)$

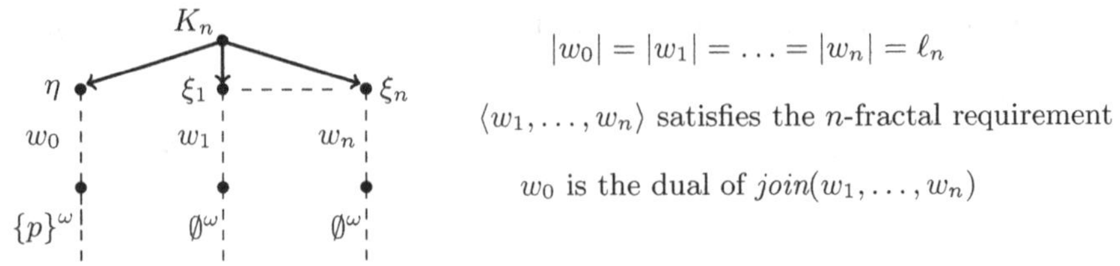

Fig. 2. The regular tree structure K_n for the witness KLTL formula $\varphi_p := \forall \mathsf{X} \mathsf{F} \mathsf{K}_a \neg p$

By construction, in the tree structure K_n, for each non-root level, there is a node where p holds and a node where p does not hold. Hence, $(K_n, Obs) \not\models \varphi_p$. By Remark 1, for each main position i, there is at most one $k \in [1, n]$ such that the label of $\pi(\xi_k)(i)$ in K_n is $\{p\}$. If such a k exists, we say that i is a *main p-position* and ξ_k is the *type* of i. Now, for the level of M_n at distance i_{alert} from the root, p *uniformly* does not hold (i.e., there is no node of M_n at distance i_{alert} from the root where p holds). Thus, we obtain the following result.

Proposition 2. *For each p-blind observation map Obs,* $(K_n, Obs) \not\models \varphi_p$ *and* $(M_n, Obs) \models \varphi_p$.

Theorem 3 directly follows from Proposition 2 and the following result.

Theorem 4. *For all HyperCTL* sentences* ψ *with* $|\psi| < n$, $K_n \models \psi \Leftrightarrow M_n \models \psi$.

Proof. The main idea is that for a HyperCTL* sentence ψ of size less than n, in the recursive evaluation of ψ on the tree structure M_n, there will be $h_* \in [2, n]$ such that the initial path $\pi(\xi_{h_*})$ is not bound by the current path assignment. Then, the n-fractal requirement ensures that in M_n, the main p-position i_{alert} (which in M_n has label $\emptyset$ along $\pi(\xi_1)$) is indistinguishable from the main p-positions j of type ξ_{h_*} which are sufficiently 'near' to i_{alert} (such positions j have label $\emptyset$ along the initial paths $\pi(\xi_k)$ with $k \neq h*$). We formalize this intuition by defining equivalence relations on the set of main positions which are parameterized by h_* and a natural number $\mathfrak{m} \in [0, n]$ and reflect the fractal structure of the main p-position displacement. Since the number of main p-positions of type ξ_1 following i_{alert} is at least n, we then deduce that in all the positions i such that $i \leq i_F$, where i_F is the main p-position of type ξ_1 preceding i_{alert}, no HyperCTL* formula ψ can distinguish M_n and K_n with respect to path assignments such that $|\Pi| + |\psi| < n$, where $|\Pi|$ is the number of initial paths bound by Π. Hence, the result follows. □

3.3 HyperCTL$^*_{lp}$ Unifies KCTL* and HyperCTL*

We show that KCTL* can be easily translated in linear time into the two-variable fragment of HyperCTL$^*_{lp}$. Intuitively, the knowledge modalities can be simulated by the general hyper path quantifiers combined with the temporal past modalities. Hence, we obtain the following result.

Theorem 5. *Given a* KCTL* *sentence* ψ *and an observation map Obs, one can construct in* linear time *a* $\mathsf{HyperCTL}^*_{lp}$ *sentence* φ *with just two path variables such that for each Kripke structure* K, $K \models \varphi \Leftrightarrow (K, Obs) \models \psi$.

Note that the KCTL* sentence $\forall \mathsf{XFK}_a \neg p$ used to prove Theorem 3 is equivalent w.r.t. p-blind observation maps to the $\mathsf{HyperCTL}^*_{lp}$ sentence $\forall x. \mathsf{XF}(\forall^G y. \neg p[y])$ which does not use past modalities. Thus, by Theorems 1, 3, and 5, we obtain:

Corollary 1. $\mathsf{HyperCTL}^*_{lp}$ *is more expressive than both* HyperCTL* *and* KCTL*. *Moreover, the* future *fragment of* $\mathsf{HyperCTL}^*_{lp}$ *(where past-time modalities are disallowed) is already more expressive than* HyperCTL*.

4 Model-Checking against $\mathsf{HyperCTL}^*_{lp}$

In this section, we address the model-checking problem for $\mathsf{HyperCTL}^*_{lp}$. Similarly to the proof given in [6] for the less expressive logic HyperCTL*, we show that the above problem is non-elementarily decidable by linear-time reductions from/to satisfiability of *full* Quantified Propositional Temporal Logic (QPTL, for short) [23], which extends LTL with past (PLTL) by quantification over propositions. As main contribution of this section, we address complexity issues for the considered problem by providing optimal complexity bounds in terms of a parameter of the given $\mathsf{HyperCTL}^*_{lp}$ formula, we call *strong alternation depth.* For this, we first provide similar optimal complexity bounds for satisfiability of QPTL. As a corollary of our results, we also obtain that for a relevant fragment of $\mathsf{HyperCTL}^*_{lp}$, model-checking is EXPSPACE-complete. With regard to QPTL, well-known optimal complexity bounds, in terms of the alternation depth of existential and universal quantifiers, concern the fragment of QPTL in prenex form (quantifiers cannot occur in the scope of temporal modalities) [23]. QPTL formulas can be translated in polynomial time into equisatisfiable QPTL formulas in prenex form, but in this conversion, the nesting depth of temporal modalities in the original formula (in particular, the alternation depth between always and eventually modalities and the nesting depth of until modalities) lead to an equal increasing in the quantifier alternation depth of the resulting formula. We show that this can be avoided by *directly* applying a non-trivial automatic theoretic approach to unrestricted QPTL formulas. Our results also improve in a meaningful way the upper bounds provided in [6] for model-checking of HyperCTL*; indeed, in [6], differently from our approach, occurrences of temporal modalities count as additional alternations.

The Logic QPTL [23]. QPTL formulas φ over AP are defined as follows:

$$\varphi ::= \top \mid p \mid \neg\varphi \mid \varphi \wedge \varphi \mid \mathsf{X}\varphi \mid \mathsf{X}^-\varphi \mid \varphi \mathsf{U} \varphi \mid \varphi \mathsf{U}^- \varphi \mid \exists p . \varphi$$

where $p \in \mathsf{AP}$. The *positive normal form* of a QPTL formula φ is obtained by pushing inward negations to propositional literals using De Morgan's laws and the duals R (release), R^- (past release), and $\forall p$ (propositional universal quantifier) of U, U^-, and $\exists p$, respectively. A formula is (*pure*) *existential* if its positive normal has no universal quantifier. Analogous notions apply to $\mathsf{HyperCTL}^*_{lp}$.

QPTL formulas are interpreted over (infinite) *pointed words* (w, i) over 2^{AP} consisting of an infinite word w over 2^{AP} and a position $i \geq 0$. The semantics of propositional quantification is as follows.

$$(w, i) \models \exists p.\varphi \;\Leftrightarrow\; \text{there is } w' \in (2^{\mathsf{AP}})^\omega \text{ such that } w =_{\mathsf{AP}\setminus\{p\}} w' \text{ and } (w', i) \models \varphi$$

where $w =_{\mathsf{AP}\setminus\{p\}} w'$ means that the projections of w and w' over $\mathsf{AP} \setminus \{p\}$ coincide. For a QPTL formula φ, let $\mathcal{L}_\wp(\varphi)$ be the set of pointed words satisfying φ, and $\mathcal{L}(\varphi)$ be the set $\{w \mid (w, 0) \in \mathcal{L}_\wp(\varphi)\}$; φ is satisfiable if $\mathcal{L}(\varphi) \neq \emptyset$.

Optimal Bounds for QPTL Satisfiability. First, we give a generalization of the standard notion of alternation depth between existential and universal quantifiers, we call *strong alternation depth.* This notion takes into account also the occurrence of temporal modalities between quantifier occurrences, but the nesting depth of temporal modalities is not considered (it is collapsed to one).

Definition 2. *Let* $\mathcal{O} = \{\exists, \forall, \mathsf{U}, \mathsf{U}^-, \mathsf{R}, \mathsf{R}^-, \mathsf{G}, \mathsf{G}^-, \mathsf{F}, \mathsf{F}^-\}$. *First, we define the* strong alternation length $\ell(\chi)$ *of finite sequences* $\chi \in \mathcal{O}^*$: $\ell(\varepsilon) = 0$, $\ell(O) = 1$ *for all* $O \in \mathcal{O}$, *and*

$$\ell(OO'\chi) = \begin{cases} \ell(O'\chi) & \text{if } O' \in \mathcal{O} \setminus \{\exists, \forall\} \\ \ell(O'\chi) & \text{if either } O, O' \in \{\exists, \mathsf{F}, \mathsf{F}^-\} \text{ or } O, O' \in \{\forall, \mathsf{G}, \mathsf{G}^-\} \\ 1 + \ell(O'\chi) & \text{otherwise} \end{cases}$$

[2]*Then, the* strong alternation depth $sad(\varphi)$ *of a QPTL formula* φ *is the maximum over the strong alternation lengths* $\ell(\chi)$, *where* χ *is the sequence of modalities in* $\mathcal{O}$ *along a path in the tree encoding of the positive normal form of* φ. *The* strong alternation depth $sad(\varphi)$ *of a* $\mathsf{HyperCTL}^*_{lp}$ *formula* φ *is defined similarly but we replace quantification over propositions with quantification over path variables. For a QPTL (resp.,* $\mathsf{HyperCTL}^*_{lp}$*) formula* φ, *if there is a subformula* ψ *of the positive normal form of* φ *whose root operator is a universal quantifier and such that* $sad(\psi) = sad(\varphi)$, *then we say that* φ *is a* first-level universal *formula; otherwise, we say that* φ *is a* first-level existential *formula.*

Note that for a QPTL formula φ in prenex form, the strong alternation depth corresponds to the alternation depth of existential and universal quantifiers plus one. For all $n, h \in \mathbb{N}$, $\mathsf{Tower}(h, n)$ denotes a tower of exponentials of height h and argument n: $\mathsf{Tower}(0, n) = n$ and $\mathsf{Tower}(h + 1, n) = 2^{\mathsf{Tower}(h,n)}$. We establish the following result, where h-EXPSPACE is the class of languages decided by deterministic Turing machines bounded in space by functions of n in $O(\mathsf{Tower}(h, n^c))$ for some constant $c \geq 1$.

Theorem 6. *For all* $h \geq 1$, *satisfiability of QPTL formulas* φ *with strong alternation depth at most* h *is* h-EXPSPACE-*complete, and* $(h - 1)$-EXPSPACE-*complete in case* φ *is* first-level existential *or* pure existential *(even if we only allow temporal modalities in* $\{\mathsf{X}, \mathsf{X}^-, \mathsf{F}, \mathsf{F}^-, \mathsf{G}, \mathsf{G}^-\}$*).*

[2] For example, $\ell(\exists\mathsf{G}\mathsf{U}\exists\mathsf{U}) = \ell(\mathsf{U}\exists\mathsf{U}) = 2$.

Here, we illustrate the upper bounds of Theorem 6. In the automata-theoretic approach for QPTL formulas φ in prenex form, first, one converts the quantifier-free part ψ of φ into an equivalent Büchi nondeterministic automaton (Büchi NWA) accepting $\mathcal{L}(\psi)$. Then, by using the closure of Büchi NWA definable languages under projection and complementation, one obtains a Büchi NWA accepting $\mathcal{L}(\varphi)$. This approach would not work for arbitrary QPTL formulas φ, where quantifiers can occur in the scope of temporal modalities. In this case, for a subformula φ' of φ, we need to keep track of the full set $\mathcal{L}_\wp(\varphi')$ of pointed words satisfying φ, and not simply $\mathcal{L}(\varphi')$. Thus, we resort to *two-way* automata $\mathcal{A}$ accepting languages $\mathcal{L}_\wp(\mathcal{A})$ of *pointed words*. In particular, the proposed approach is based on a compositional translation of QPTL formulas into a simple two-way extension of Büchi NWA, which we call Büchi SNWA. Essentially, given an input pointed word (w, i), a Büchi SNWA splits in two copies: the first one moves forward along the suffix $w[i, \infty]$ and the second one moves backward along the prefix $w[0, i]$.

Moreover, at each step of the translation into Büchi SNWA, we use as an intermediate formalism a two-way extension of the class of (one-way) *hesitant alternating automata* (HAA, for short) over infinite words introduced in [17]. Like one-way HAA, the set of states Q of a two-way HAA is partitioned into a set of components $Q_1, \ldots, Q_n$ such that moves from states in Q_i lead to states in components Q_j so that $j \leq i$. Moreover, each component is classified as either *past*, or *Büchi*, or *coBüchi*: in a past (resp., Büchi/coBüchi) component Q_i, the unique allowed moves from Q_i to Q_i itself are backward (resp., forward). These syntactical requirements ensure that in a run over a pointed word, every infinite path π of the run gets trapped in some Büchi or coBüchi component, and the path π eventually use only forward moves. Moreover, the acceptance condition of a two-way HAA encodes a particular kind of parity condition of index 2: a Büchi/coBüchi component Q_i has an associated subset $F_i \subseteq Q_i$ of accepting states. Then, a run is accepting if for every infinite path π, denoting with Q_i the Büchi/coBüchi component in which π gets trapped, π satisfies the Büchi/coBüchi acceptance condition associated with Q_i. For two-way HAA $\mathcal{A}$, we establish two crucial results. First, the *dual automaton* $\widetilde{\mathcal{A}}$ obtained from $\mathcal{A}$ by dualizing the transition function, and by converting a Büchi (resp., coBüchi) component into a coBüchi (resp., Büchi) component is still a two-way HAA. Thus, by standard arguments (see e.g. [25]), automaton $\widetilde{\mathcal{A}}$ accepts the complement of $\mathcal{L}_\wp(\mathcal{A})$. Second, by using the notion of odd ranking function for standard coBüchi alternating automata [16] (which allows to convert a coBüchi acceptance condition into a Büchi-like acceptance condition) and a non-trivial generalization of the Miyano-Hayashi construction [20], we show that two-way HAA can be converted in singly exponential time into equivalent Büchi SNWA.

Theorem 7. *Given a two-way HAA $\mathcal{A}$ with n states, the following holds:*
1. *the dual automaton $\widetilde{\mathcal{A}}$ of $\mathcal{A}$ is a two-way HAA accepting the complement of $\mathcal{L}_\wp(\mathcal{A})$;*
2. *one can build "on the fly" and in singly exponential time a Büchi SNWA accepting $\mathcal{L}_\wp(\mathcal{A})$ with $2^{O(n \cdot \log(n))}$ states.*

Finally, by using Theorem 7, we establish the following result from which the upper bounds of Theorem 6 directly follow (note that Büchi SNWA $\mathcal{A}$ can be trivially converted into Büchi NWA accepting the set of infinite words w such that $(w, 0) \in \mathcal{L}_\wp(\mathcal{A})$, and checking non-emptiness for Büchi NWA is in NLOGSPACE).

Theorem 8. *Let φ be a first-level existential (resp., first-level universal) QPTL formula and $h = sad(\varphi)$. Then, one can construct "on the fly" a Büchi SNWA $\mathcal{A}_\varphi$ accepting $\mathcal{L}_\wp(\varphi)$ in time $\mathsf{Tower}(h, O(|\varphi|))$ (resp., $\mathsf{Tower}(h+1, O(|\varphi|))$).*

Proof. By structural induction on the positive normal form φ_+ of φ. The relevant case is when the outermost operator of φ_+ is a temporal modality (the other cases easily follow from Theorem 7 and the closure of Büchi SNWA definable pointed languages under union, intersection, and projection). This case is handled by first building a two-way HAA $\mathcal{A}$ accepting $\mathcal{L}_\wp(\varphi)$ and then by applying Theorem 7(2). The construction of $\mathcal{A}$ is obtained by a generalization of the standard linear-time translation of LTL formulas into Büchi alternating automata which exploits the (inductively built) Büchi SNWA associated with the maximal quantified subformulas of φ_+. □

Optimal Bounds for Model-Checking of $\mathsf{HyperCTL}^*_{lp}$. By establishing linear-time reductions from/to satisfiability of QPTL and by exploiting Theorem 6, we provide optimal bounds on the complexity of model-checking for $\mathsf{HyperCTL}^*_{lp}$ in terms of the strong alternation depth of the formula. In particular, the linear-time reduction to satisfiability of QPTL generalizes the one given in [6] for the model checking of $\mathsf{HyperCTL}^*$.

Theorem 9. *For all $h \geq 1$ and $\mathsf{HyperCTL}^*_{lp}$ sentences φ with strong alternation depth at most h, model-checking against φ is h-EXPSPACE-complete, and $(h-1)$-EXPSPACE-complete in case φ is* first-level existential *or* pure existential *(even if we allow only temporal modalities in $\{X, X^-, F, F^-, G, G^-\}$).*

By Theorem 9, for the first-level existential fragment $\mathcal{F}$ of $\mathsf{HyperCTL}^*_{lp}$ where the strong alternation depth is at most 2, model-checking is EXPSPACE-complete. Notice that the $\mathsf{HyperCTL}^*$ fragment $\mathcal{F}'$ of $\mathcal{F}$ can express important classes of information-flow requirements as illustrated in [6], and that the model-checking algorithm in [6] applied to $\mathcal{F}'$ leads to a non-elementary upper bound.

5 Discussion

We plan to extend this work in many directions. First, we intend to identify tractable fragments of $\mathsf{HyperCTL}^*_{lp}$ and to investigate their synthesis problem; note that satisfiability of $\mathsf{HyperCTL}^*$ is already undecidable [6]. Second, we should extend the framework to deal with asynchronicity, as information flows are relevant for security in many asynchronous frameworks, such as distributed systems or cryptographic protocols. In the same line, we would like to investigate the possibility of extending the verification of information-flow requirements to relevant classes of infinite-state systems such as the class of pushdown systems, a model extensively investigated in software verification.

References

1. Alur, R., Černý, P., Chaudhuri, S.: Model checking on trees with path equivalences. In: Grumberg, O., Huth, M. (eds.) TACAS 2007. LNCS, vol. 4424, pp. 664–678. Springer, Heidelberg (2007)
2. Alur, R., Černý, P., Zdancewic, S.: Preserving secrecy under refinement. In: Bugliesi, M., Preneel, B., Sassone, V., Wegener, I. (eds.) ICALP 2006. LNCS, vol. 4052, pp. 107–118. Springer, Heidelberg (2006)
3. Balliu, M., Dam, M., Guernic, G.L.: Epistemic temporal logic for information flow security. In: Proc. PLAS, p. 6. ACM (2011)
4. Bozzelli, L., Maubert, B., Pinchinat, S.: Unifying hyper and epistemic temporal logic. CoRR, abs/1409.2711 (2014)
5. Bryans, J., Koutny, M., Mazaré, L., Ryan, P.Y.A.: Opacity generalised to transition systems. Int. J. Inf. Sec. 7(6), 421–435 (2008)
6. Clarkson, M.R., Finkbeiner, B., Koleini, M., Micinski, K.K., Rabe, M.N., Sánchez, C.: Temporal logics for hyperproperties. In: Abadi, M., Kremer, S. (eds.) POST 2014. LNCS, vol. 8414, pp. 265–284. Springer, Heidelberg (2014)
7. Clarkson, M., Schneider, F.: Hyperproperties. Journal of Computer Security 18(6), 1157–1210 (2010)
8. Dima, C.: Revisiting satisfiability and model-checking for CTLK with synchrony and perfect recall. In: Fisher, M., Sadri, F., Thielscher, M. (eds.) CLIMA IX. LNCS (LNAI), vol. 5405, pp. 117–131. Springer, Heidelberg (2009)
9. Dimitrova, R., Finkbeiner, B., Kovács, M., Rabe, M.N., Seidl, H.: Model checking information flow in reactive systems. In: Kuncak, V., Rybalchenko, A. (eds.) VMCAI 2012. LNCS, vol. 7148, pp. 169–185. Springer, Heidelberg (2012)
10. Emerson, E., Halpern, J.: "Sometimes" and "Not Never" revisited: On branching versus linear time temporal logic. J. ACM 33(1), 151–178 (1986)
11. Fagin, R., Halpern, J., Vardi, M.: Reasoning about knowledge, vol. 4. MIT Press, Cambridge (1995)
12. Goguen, J., Meseguer, J.: Security policies and security models. In: IEEE Symposium on Security and Privacy, vol. 12 (1982)
13. Halpern, J., O'Neill, K.: Secrecy in multiagent systems. ACM Trans. Inf. Syst. Secur. 12(1) (2008)
14. Halpern, J., van der Meyden, R., Vardi, M.: Complete Axiomatizations for Reasoning about Knowledge and Time. SIAM J. Comput. 33(3), 674–703 (2004)
15. Kupferman, O., Pnueli, A., Vardi, M.: Once and for all. J. Comput. Syst. Sci. 78(3), 981–996 (2012)
16. Kupferman, O., Vardi, M.: Weak alternating automata are not that weak. ACM Transactions on Computational Logic 2(3), 408–429 (2001)
17. Kupferman, O., Vardi, M., Wolper, P.: An Automata-Theoretic Approach to Branching-Time Model Checking. J. ACM 47(2), 312–360 (2000)
18. McLean, J.: Proving noninterference and functional correctness using traces. Journal of Computer Security 1(1), 37–58 (1992)
19. Milushev, D., Clarke, D.: Towards incrementalization of holistic hyperproperties. In: Degano, P., Guttman, J.D. (eds.) POST 2012. LNCS, vol. 7215, pp. 329–348. Springer, Heidelberg (2012)
20. Miyano, S., Hayashi, T.: Alternating finite automata on ω-words. Theoretical Computer Science 32, 321–330 (1984)
21. Pnueli, A.: The temporal logic of programs. In: Proc. 18th FOCS, pp. 46–57. IEEE Computer Society (1977)

22. Shilov, N.V., Garanina, N.O.: Model checking knowledge and fixpoints. In: Proc. FICS. BRICS Notes Series, pp. 25–39 (2002)
23. Sistla, A., Vardi, M., Wolper, P.: The complementation problem for Büchi automata with appplications to temporal logic. Theoretical Computer Science 49, 217–237 (1987)
24. van der Meyden, R., Shilov, N.V.: Model checking knowledge and time in systems with perfect recall (extended abstract). In: Pandu Rangan, C., Raman, V., Sarukkai, S. (eds.) FSTTCS 1999. LNCS, vol. 1738, pp. 432–445. Springer, Heidelberg (1999)
25. Zielonka, W.: Infinite games on finitely coloured graphs with applications to automata on infinite trees. Theoretical Computer Science 200(1-2), 135–183 (1998)

Concurrent, Probabilistic and Timed Systems

On the Total Variation Distance of Semi-Markov Chains*

Giorgio Bacci, Giovanni Bacci, Kim Guldstrand Larsen, and Radu Mardare

Department of Computer Science, Aalborg University, Denmark
{grbacci,giovbacci,kgl,mardare}@cs.aau.dk

Abstract. Semi-Markov chains (SMCs) are continuous-time probabilistic transition systems where the residence time on states is governed by generic distributions on the positive real line.

This paper shows the *tight* relation between the total variation distance on SMCs and their model checking problem over linear real-time specifications. Specifically, we prove that the total variation between two SMCs *coincides* with the maximal difference w.r.t. the likelihood of satisfying arbitrary MTL formulas or ω-languages recognized by timed automata.

Computing this distance (i.e., solving its threshold problem) is NP-hard and its decidability is an open problem. Nevertheless, we propose an algorithm for approximating it with arbitrary precision.

1 Introduction

The growing interest in quantitative aspects in real world applications motivated the introduction of quantitative models and formal methods for studying their behaviors. Classically, the behavior of two models is compared by means of an equivalence (e.g., bisimilarity, trace equivalence, logical equivalence, etc.). However, when the models depend on numerical values that are subject to error estimates or obtained from statistical samplings, any notion of equivalence is too strong a concept. This motivated the study of *behavioral distances.* The idea is to generalize the concept of equivalence with that of *pseudometric*, aiming at measuring the behavioral dissimilarities between nonequivalent models.

Given a suitably large set of properties Φ, containing all the properties of interest, the behavioral dissimilarities of two states s, s' of a quantitative model are naturally measured by the pseudometric $d(s,s') = \sup_{\phi \in \Phi} |\phi(s) - \phi(s')|$, where $\phi(s)$ denotes the value of ϕ at s. This has been the leading idea for several proposals of behavioral distances, the first one given by Desharnais et al. [12] on probabilistic systems, and further developed by De Alfaro, van Breugel, Worrell, and others [10,11,18,15].

* Work supported by the European Union 7th Framework Programme (FP7/2007-2013) under Grants Agreement nr. 318490 (SENSATION), nr. 601148 (CASSTING) and by the Sino-Danish Basic Research Center IDEA4CPS funded by the Danish National Research Foundation and the National Science Foundation China.

A. Pitts (Ed.): FOSSACS 2015, LNCS 9034, pp. 185–199, 2015.
DOI: 10.1007/978-3-662-46678-0_12

For probabilistic models $\phi(s)$ may represent the probability of satisfaction of a modal formula ϕ measured at s, hence relating the distance d to the *probabilistic model checking problem*. In this context an immediate application is that the probability $\phi(s)$ of satisfying the formula ϕ at s can be approximated by $\phi(s')$ with an error bounded by $d(s, s')$, for any $\phi \in \Phi$. This may lead to savings in the overall cost of model checking.

In this paper we study the total variation distance of probabilistic systems, a popular distance used in a number of domains such as networks security and artificial intelligence, that measures the maximal difference in the probabilities of two systems of realizing the same event. We show that it is a genuine behavioral distance in the above sense by relating it to the probabilistic model checking problem over linear real-time specifications. Specifically, we prove that the total variation distance on semi-Markov chains coincides with the maximal difference in the probability of satisfying the same property, expressed either as an MTL formula [2,3] or an ω-language accepted by a timed automaton (TA) [1].

Semi-Markov chains (SMCs) are continuous-time probabilistic transition systems where the residence time on states is governed by generic distributions on the positive real line. SMCs subsume many probabilistic models, e.g., Markov chains (MCs) and continuous-time Markov Chains (CTMCs). Our attention on linear real-time properties is motivated by applications where the system to be modeled cannot be internally accessed but only tested via observations performed over a set of random executions. For instance, this is mostly common in domains such as systems biology, modeling/testing and machine learning, where real-time features are important e.g. for performance evaluation of cyber-physical systems or dependability analysis.

The total variation distance was already known to be a bound for the maximal difference w.r.t. the probability of satisfying linear-time formulas; our result guarantees that it is the tightest one. Since SMCs and MTL subsume MCs and LTL, respectively, the result holds also in the discrete-time case.

This further motivates the study of efficient methods for computing the total variation. Unfortunately, in [14,9] the threshold problem for the total variation distance is proven to be NP-hard in the case of MCs, and to the best of our knowledge, its decidability is still an open problem. Nevertheless, we prove that the problem of approximating the total variation distance with arbitrary precision is computable. This is done providing two effective sequences that converge from below and above to the total variation distance. This result generalizes that of [9] to the real-time setting. Our approach, however, is different, as it is based on a duality that characterizes the total variation between two measures as the minimal discrepancy associated with their couplings.

The technical contributions of the paper can be summarized as follows.

1. We solved the open problem of how tight is the upper-bound given by the total variation distance w.r.t. the variational distance ranging over MTL formulas and TA specifications, respectively. This has been made possible due to a more general result (Theorem 6) that entails many other nontrivial characterizations of the total variation distance on SMCs.

2. We provided sufficient conditions to construct sequences that converge, from below and above, to the total variation distance. Differently from [9], these conditions are not specific to the probabilistic transition system at hand, but the results hold for probability measures on an arbitrary measurable space.

3. Lastly, we proved the computability of the converging sequences of the previous point. This yields a decidable procedure to approximate the total variation distance with arbitrary precision.

An extended version of the paper containing all the proofs is available at [5].

2 Preliminaries

The set of functions from X to Y is denoted by Y^X and for $f \in Y^X$, let $\equiv_f = \{(x, x') \mid f(x) = f(x')\}$. Given an equivalence relation $R \subseteq X \times X$, $X/_R$ denotes the set of R-equivalence classes and $[x]_R$ the equivalence class of $x \in X$.

Measure Theory. A *field* over a set X is a nonempty family $\Sigma \subseteq 2^X$ closed under complement and finite union. Σ is a σ-algebra if, in addition, it is closed under countable union; in this case (X, Σ) is called a *measurable space* and the elements of Σ *measurable sets*. The σ-algebra generated by $\Sigma \subseteq 2^X$, denoted by $\sigma(\Sigma)$, is the smallest σ-algebra containing Σ. Hereafter $(\mathbb{R}_+, \mathbb{B})$ denotes the measurable space of positive real numbers (including zero) with Borel algebra.

Given two measurable spaces (X, Σ) and (Y, Θ), a function $f \colon X \to Y$ is *measurable* if for all $E \in \Theta$, $f^{-1}(E) = \{x \mid f(x) \in E\} \in \Sigma$. The *product space*, $(X, \Sigma) \otimes (Y, \Theta)$, is the measurable space $(X \times Y, \Sigma \otimes \Theta)$, where $\Sigma \otimes \Theta$ is the σ-algebra generated by the *rectangles* $E \times F$ for $E \in \Sigma$ and $F \in \Theta$.

A *measure* on (X, Σ) is a function $\mu \colon \Sigma \to \mathbb{R}_+$ s.t. $\mu(\bigcup_{E \in \mathcal{F}} E) = \sum_{E \in \mathcal{F}} \mu(E)$ for all countable families $\mathcal{F}$ of pairwise disjoint measurable sets (σ*-additive*); it is a *probability measure* if, in addition, $\mu(X) = 1$. In what follows $\Delta(X, \Sigma)$ denotes the set of probability measures on (X, Σ) and let $\mathcal{D}(X) = \Delta(X, 2^X)$.

Given a measurable function $f \colon (X, \Sigma) \to (Y, \Theta)$, any measure μ on (X, Σ) defines a measure $\mu[f]$ on (Y, Θ) by $\mu[f](E) = \mu(f^{-1}(E))$, for all $E \in \Theta$; it is called the *push forward of μ under f*.

Given μ and ν measures on (X, Σ) and (Y, Θ), respectively, the *product measure* $\mu \times \nu$ on $(X, \Sigma) \otimes (Y, \Theta)$ is *uniquely* defined by $(\mu \times \nu)(E \times F) = \mu(E) \cdot \nu(E)$, for all $(E, F) \in \Sigma \times \Theta$.

A measure ω on $(X, \Sigma) \otimes (Y, \Theta)$ is a *coupling* for (μ, ν) if for all $E \in \Sigma$ and $F \in \Theta$, $\omega(E \times Y) = \mu(E)$ and $\omega(X \times F) = \nu(F)$ (μ is the *left* and ν the *right marginals* of ω). We denote by $\Omega(\mu, \nu)$ the set of couplings for (μ, ν).

Metric Spaces. Given a set X, $d \colon X \times X \to \mathbb{R}_+$ is a *pseudometric* on X if for arbitrary $x, y, z \in X$, $d(x, x) = 0$, $d(x, y) = d(y, x)$ and $d(x, y) + d(y, z) \geq d(x, z)$; d is a *metric* if, in addition, $d(x, y) = 0$ implies $x = y$. If d is a (pseudo)metric on X, (X, d) is called a *(pseudo)metric space.*

Given a measurable space (X, Σ), the set of measures $\Delta(X, \Sigma)$ is metrized by the *total variation distance*, defined by $\|\mu - \nu\| = \sup_{E \in \Sigma} |\mu(E) - \nu(E)|$.

The Space of Timed Paths. A *timed path* over a set X is an infinite sequence $\pi = x_0, t_0, x_1, t_1 \ldots$, where $x_i \in X$ and $t_i \in \mathbb{R}_+$; t_i are called *time*

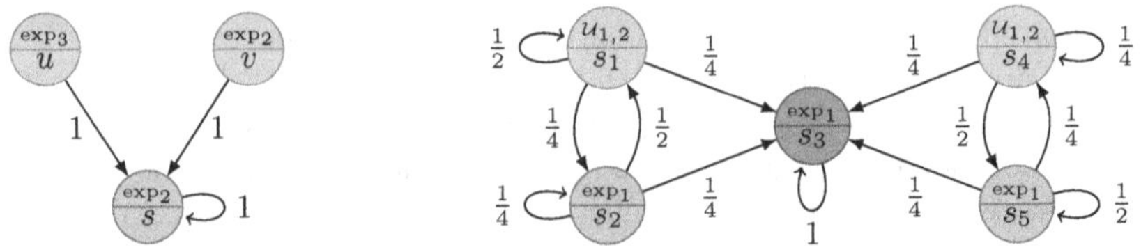

Fig. 1. Two SMCs. (left) the differences are only in the residence time distributions; (right) the behavioral differences arise only from their transition distributions.

delays. For any $i \in \mathbb{N}$, let $\pi[i] = x_i$, $\pi\langle i\rangle = t_i$, $\pi|^i = x_0, t_0, .., t_{i-1}, x_i$, and $\pi|_i = x_i, t_i, x_{i+1}, t_{i+1}, \dots$. Let $\Pi(X)$ denote the set of timed paths on X.

The *cylinder set* (of rank n) for $X_i \subseteq X$ and $R_i \subseteq \mathbb{R}_+$, $i = 0..n$ is the set $\mathfrak{C}(X_0, R_0, .., R_{n-1}, X_n) = \{\pi \in \Pi(X) \mid \pi|^n \in X_0 \times R_0 \times \cdots \times R_{n-1} \times X_n\}$. For $\mathcal{F} \subseteq 2^X$ and $\mathcal{I} \subseteq 2^{\mathbb{R}_+}$, let $\mathfrak{C}_n(\mathcal{F}, \mathcal{I}) = \{\mathfrak{C}(X_0, R_0, .., R_{n-1}, X_n) \mid X_i \in \mathcal{F}, R_i \in \mathcal{I}\}$, for $n \in \mathbb{N}$, and $\mathfrak{C}(\mathcal{F}, \mathcal{I}) = \bigcup_{n \in N} \mathfrak{C}_n(\mathcal{F}, \mathcal{I})$.

If (X, Σ) is a measurable space, $\Pi(X, \Sigma)$ denotes the measurable space of timed paths with σ-algebra generated by $\mathfrak{C}(\Sigma, \mathbb{B})$. If $\Sigma = \sigma(\mathcal{F})$ and $\mathbb{B} = \sigma(\mathcal{I})$, then $\sigma(\mathfrak{C}(\Sigma, \mathbb{B})) = \sigma(\mathfrak{C}(\mathcal{F}, \mathcal{I}))$. Moreover, if both $\mathcal{F}$ and $\mathcal{I}$ are fields, so is $\mathfrak{C}(\mathcal{F}, \mathcal{I})$.

Any function $f\colon X \to Y$ can be stepwise extended to $f^\omega\colon \Pi(X) \to \Pi(Y)$. Note that if f is measurable, so is f^ω.

3 Semi-Markov Chains and Trace Distance

In this section we recall labelled *semi-Markov chains* (SMCs), models that subsume most of the space-finite Markovian models including Markov chains (MCs) and continuous-time Markov chains (CTMCs). We define the total variation distance between SMCs, called *trace distance*, which measures the difference between two SMCs w.r.t. their probabilities of generating labelled timed traces.

In what follows we fix a countable set $\mathbb{A}$ of atomic properties.

Definition 1 (Semi-Markov Chains). *A labelled* semi-Markov chain *is a tuple $\mathcal{M} = (S, \tau, \rho, \ell)$ consisting of a finite set S of* states, *a* transition probability function $\tau\colon S \to \mathcal{D}(S)$, *a* residence-time probability function $\rho\colon S \to \Delta(\mathbb{R}_+)$, *and a* labelling function $\ell\colon S \to 2^{\mathbb{A}}$.

In what follows we use $\mathcal{M} = (S, \tau, \rho, \ell)$ to range over the class of SMCs.

Intuitively, if $\mathcal{M}$ is in the state s, it moves to an arbitrary $s' \in S$ within time $t \in \mathbb{R}_+$ with probability $\rho(s)([0,t]) \cdot \tau(s)(s')$. For example, in Fig. 1(right) the SMC moves from s_1 to s_2 before time $t > 0$ with probability $\frac{1}{4} \cdot U[1,2]([0,t))$, where $U[i,j]$ is the uniform distribution on $[i,j]$. An atomic proposition $p \in \mathbb{A}$ is said to hold in s if $p \in \ell(s)$.

Notice that MCs are the SMCs s.t. for all $s \in S$, $\rho(s)$ is the Dirac measure at 0 (transitions happen instantaneously); while CTMCs are the SMCs s.t. for all $s \in S$, $\rho(s) = \mathit{Exp}(\lambda)$ —the exponential distribution with rate $\lambda > 0$.

An SMC in an initial state is a stochastic process generating timed paths. They are distributed as in the next definition.

Definition 2. *Given $s \in S$ state in $\mathcal{M}$, let $\mathbb{P}_s$ be the unique probability measure*[1] *on $\Pi(S)$ such that for all $s_i \in S$ and $R_i \in \mathbb{B}$, $i = 0..n$,*

$$\mathbb{P}_s(\mathfrak{C}(\{s_0\}, R_0, \dots, R_{n-1}, \{s_n\})) = \mathbb{1}_{\{s\}}(s_0) \cdot \prod_{i=0}^{n-1} P(s_i, R_i, s_{i+1}),$$

where $\mathbb{1}_A$ is the indicator function of A and $P(u, R, v) = \rho(u)(R) \cdot \tau(u)(v)$.

Since the only things that we observe in a state are the atomic properties (labels), timed paths are considered up to label equivalence. This leads to the definition of *trace cylinders*, which are elements in $\mathfrak{C}(S/_{\equiv_\ell}, \mathbb{B})$, and to the following equivalence between states.

Definition 3 (Trace Equivalence). *For arbitrary $\mathcal{M} = (S, \tau, \rho, \ell)$, $s, s' \in S$ are* trace equivalent, *written $s \approx s'$, if for all $T \in \mathfrak{C}(S/_{\equiv_\ell}, \mathbb{B})$, $\mathbb{P}_s(T) = \mathbb{P}_{s'}(T)$.*

Hereafter, we use $\mathcal{T}$ to denote the set $\mathfrak{C}(S/_{\equiv_\ell}, \mathbb{B})$ of trace cylinders.

If two states of an SMCs are *not* trace equivalent, then their difference is usually measured by the total variation distance between their corresponding probabilities restricted to events generated by labelled traces.

Definition 4 (Trace Pseudometric). *Given $\mathcal{M} = (S, \tau, \rho, \ell)$, the* trace pseudometric *$\delta \colon S \times S \to [0, 1]$ is defined, for arbitrary $s, s' \in S$, by*

$$\delta(s, s') = \sup_{E \in \sigma(\mathcal{T})} |\mathbb{P}_s(E) - \mathbb{P}_{s'}(E)|.$$

It is not difficult to observe that two states $s, s' \in S$ are trace equivalent if and only if $\delta(s, s') = 0$. This demonstrates that the trace equivalence is a *behavioural distance*.

4 Trace Distance and Probabilistic Model Checking

In this section we investigate the connections between the trace distance and model checking SMCs over linear real-time specifications. We show that the variational distance over measurable sets expressed either as Metric Temporal Logic (MTL) formulas or as languages accepted by Timed Automata (TAs) coincides with the trace distance introduced in the previous section. Both these results are instances of a more general result (Theorem 6), which also entails other similar nontrivial characterizations of the trace distance.

A measure μ on (X, Σ) induces the so-called *Fréchet-Nikodym pseudometric* on Σ, $d_\mu \colon \Sigma \times \Sigma \to \mathbb{R}_+$ defined for arbitrary $E, F \in \Sigma$, by $d_\mu(E, F) = \mu(E \triangle F)$, where $E \triangle F := (E \setminus F) \cup (F \setminus E)$ is the symmetric difference between sets.

Recall that in a (pseudo)metric space a subset D is dense if its closure $\overline{D}$ (i.e., the set of all the points arbitrarily close to D) coincides with the entire space. In order to prove the aforementioned general result, we need firstly to provide a sufficient condition for a family of measurable sets to be dense w.r.t. the Fréchet-Nikodym pseudometric for some finite measure.

[1] Existence and uniqueness of $\mathbb{P}_s$ is guaranteed by the Hahn-Kolmogorov extension theorem and by the fact that, for all $s \in S$, $\tau(s)$ and $\rho(s)$ are finite measures.

Lemma 5. *Let (X, Σ) be a measurable space and μ be a measure on it. If Σ is generated by a field $\mathcal{F}$, then $\mathcal{F}$ is dense in the pseudometric space (Σ, d_μ).*

Proof (sketch). We show that $\overline{\mathcal{F}} := \{E \in \Sigma \mid \forall \varepsilon > 0.\ \exists F \in \mathcal{F}.\ d_\mu(E, F) < \varepsilon\} = \Sigma$. To prove $\Sigma \subseteq \overline{\mathcal{F}}$, it is sufficient to show that $\overline{\mathcal{F}}$ is a σ-algebra. The closure under complement follows from $E \triangle F = (X \setminus E) \triangle (X \setminus F)$. The closure under countable union follows from monotonicity, additivity and ω-continuity from below of μ given that for any $\{E_i \mid i \in \mathbb{N}\} \subseteq \overline{\mathcal{F}}$ and $\varepsilon > 0$ the following hold:

a) there exists $k \in \mathbb{N}$, such that $d_\mu(\bigcup_{i\in\mathbb{N}} E_i, \bigcup_{i=0}^{k} E_i) < \frac{\varepsilon}{2}$;
b) for all $n \in \mathbb{N}$, there exist $F_0, \dots, F_n \in \mathcal{F}$, such that $d_\mu(\bigcup_{i=0}^{n} E_i, \bigcup_{i=0}^{n} F_i) < \frac{\varepsilon}{2}$.

Indeed, by triangular inequality, for arbitrary $F_0, \dots, F_k \in \mathcal{F}$,

$$d_\mu(\textstyle\bigcup_{i\in\mathbb{N}} E_i, \bigcup_{i=0}^{k} F_i) \leq d_\mu(\bigcup_{i\in\mathbb{N}} E_i, \bigcup_{i=0}^{k} E_i) + d_\mu(\bigcup_{i=0}^{k} E_i, \bigcup_{i=0}^{k} F_i) < \varepsilon\,.$$

Then, the lemma follows since $\mathcal{F}$ is a field. □

With this result in hands we can state the main theorem of this section.

Theorem 6. *Let (X, Σ) be a measurable space and μ, ν be two finite measures on it. If Σ is generated by a field $\mathcal{F}$, then $\|\mu - \nu\| = \sup_{E\in\mathcal{F}} |\mu(E) - \nu(E)|$.*

Proof. For $Y \neq \emptyset$ and $f\colon Y \to \mathbb{R}$ bounded and continuous, if $D \subseteq Y$ is dense then $\sup f(D) = \sup f(Y)$. By Lemma 5, $\mathcal{F}$ is dense in $(\Sigma, d_{\mu+\nu})$. We show that $|\mu - \nu|\colon \Sigma \to \mathbb{R}$ is bounded and continuous. Boundedness follows since μ and ν are finite. By monotonicity, positivity, and additivity of the measures one can show that μ and ν are 1-Lipschitz continuous, so $|\mu - \nu|$ is continuous. □

4.1 Model Checking for MTL Formulas

Metric Temporal Logic [2] has been introduced as a formalism for reasoning on sequences of events in a real-time setting. The grammar of formulas is as follows

$$\varphi ::= p \mid \bot \mid \varphi \to \varphi \mid \mathsf{X}^{[t,t']}\varphi \mid \varphi\, \mathsf{U}^{[t,t']}\, \varphi\,,$$

where $p \in \mathbb{A}$ and $[t, t']$ are positive-reals intervals with rational boundaries.

The formal semantics[2] of MTL is given by means of a satisfiability relation defined, for an arbitrary SMC $\mathcal{M}$ and a timed path $\pi \in \Pi(S)$, as follows [16].

$$\begin{array}{ll}
\mathcal{M}, \pi \models p & \text{if } p \in \ell(\pi[0])\,, \\
\mathcal{M}, \pi \models \bot & \text{never}\,, \\
\mathcal{M}, \pi \models \varphi \to \psi & \text{if } \mathcal{M}, \pi \models \psi \text{ whenever } \mathcal{M}, \pi \models \varphi\,, \\
\mathcal{M}, \pi \models \mathsf{X}^{[t,t']}\varphi & \text{if } \pi\langle 0\rangle \in [t, t'], \text{ and } \mathcal{M}, \pi|_1 \models \varphi\,, \\
\mathcal{M}, \pi \models \varphi\, \mathsf{U}^{[t,t']}\, \psi & \text{if } \exists i > 0 \text{ such that } \sum_{k=0}^{i-1} \pi\langle k\rangle \in [t, t'],\ \mathcal{M}, \pi|_i \models \psi, \\
& \quad \text{and } \mathcal{M}, \pi|_j \models \varphi \text{ whenever } 0 \leq j < i\,.
\end{array}$$

[2] This is known as the *point-based* semantics, since the connectives quantify over a countable set of positions in the path; it differs from the *interval-based* semantics, adopted in [7,17], which associates a state with each point in the real line, and let the temporal connectives quantify over intervals with uncountable many points.

Having fixed an SMC $\mathcal{M}$, let $[\![\varphi]\!] = \{\pi \mid \mathcal{M}, \pi \models \varphi\}$ and $[\![\mathcal{L}]\!] = \{[\![\varphi]\!] \mid \varphi \in \mathcal{L}\}$, for any $\mathcal{L} \subseteq$ MTL. Let MTL$^-$ be the fragment of MTL without until operator.

Lemma 7. *(i)* $[\![\text{MTL}]\!] \subseteq \sigma(\mathcal{T})$ *and (ii)* $\mathcal{T} \subseteq \sigma([\![\text{MTL}^-]\!])$.

Lemma 7 states that (i) MTL formulas describe events in the σ-algebra generated by the trace cylinders; and (ii) the trace cylinders are measurable sets generated by MTL formulas without until operator. Consequently, the probabilistic model checking problem for SMC, which is to determine the probability $\mathbb{P}_s([\![\varphi]\!])$ given the initial state s of $\mathcal{M}$, is well defined. Moreover, for any $\mathcal{L} \subseteq$ MTL,

$$\delta_{\mathcal{L}}(s, s') = \sup_{\varphi \in \mathcal{L}} |\mathbb{P}_s([\![\varphi]\!]) - \mathbb{P}_{s'}([\![\varphi]\!])|$$

is a well-defined pseudometric that distinguishes states w.r.t. their maximal difference in the likelihood of satisfying formulas in $\mathcal{L}$.

Obviously, the trace distance δ is an upper bound of $\delta_{\mathcal{L}}$; however, Theorem 6 reveals a set of conditions on $\mathcal{L}$ guaranteeing that the two actually coincide.

Corollary 8 (Logical Characterization). *Let $\mathcal{L}$ be a Boolean-closed fragment of* MTL *s.t. $\mathcal{T} \subseteq \sigma([\![\mathcal{L}]\!])$. Then, $\delta_{\mathcal{L}} = \delta$. In particular, $\delta_{\text{MTL}} = \delta_{\text{MTL}^-} = \delta$.*

Remark 9. The supremum in the definition of δ_{MTL} is not a maximum. Fig.1 shows two examples. The SMC on the right is taken from [9, Example 1][3], where it is proven that $\delta(s_1, s_4)$ has a maximizing event that is not an ω-regular language, hence not describable by an LTL formula. As for the SMC on the left, the maximizing event corresponding to $\delta(u, v)$ should have the form $\mathsf{X}^I \top$ for $I = [0, \log(3) - \log(2)]$. However the previous is not an MTL formula since I has an irrational endpoint. ■

4.2 Model Checking for Timed Automata

Timed Automata (TAs) [1] have been introduced to model the behavior of real-time systems over time. Here we consider TAs without location invariants.

Let $\mathcal{X}$ be a finite set of variables (*clocks*) and $\mathcal{V}(\mathcal{X})$ the set of *valuations* $v \colon \mathcal{X} \to \mathbb{R}_+$. As usual, for $v \in \mathcal{V}(\mathcal{X})$, $t \in \mathbb{R}_+$ and $X \subseteq \mathcal{X}$, we denote by $\mathbf{0}$ the null valuation, by $v + t$ the t-delay of v and by $v[X := t]$ the update of X in v.

A *clock guard* $g \in \mathcal{G}(\mathcal{X})$ over $\mathcal{X}$ is a finite set of expressions of the form $x \bowtie q$, for $x \in \mathcal{X}$, $q \in \mathbb{Q}_+$ and $\bowtie \in \{<, \leq, >, \geq\}$. We say that a valuation $v \in \mathcal{V}(\mathcal{X})$ *satisfies* a clock guard $g \in \mathcal{G}(\mathcal{X})$, written $v \models g$, if $v(x) \bowtie n$ holds, for all $x \bowtie q \in g$. Two clock guards $g, g' \in \mathcal{G}(\mathcal{X})$ are *orthogonal* (or *non-overlapping*), written $g \perp g'$, if there is no $v \in \mathcal{V}(\mathcal{X})$ such that $v \models g$ and $v \models g'$.

Definition 10 (Timed Automaton). *A* timed (Muller) automaton *over a set of clocks $\mathcal{X}$ is a tuple $\mathcal{A} = (Q, L, q_0, F, \to)$ consisting of a finite set Q of* locations, *a set L of* input symbols, *an* initial location $q_0 \in Q$, *a family $F \subseteq 2^Q$ of* final sets of locations, *and a* transition relation $\to \subseteq Q \times L \times \mathcal{G}(\mathcal{X}) \times 2^{\mathcal{X}} \times Q$.

$\mathcal{A}$ is deterministic *if $(q, a, g, X, q'), (q, a, g', X', q'') \in \to$ and $g \neq g'$ implies $g \perp g'$; it is* resetting *if $(q, a, g, X, q') \in \to$ implies $X = \mathcal{X}$.*

[3] The SMC has been adapted to the current setting where the labels are in the state, instead of in the transitions.

A *run* of $\mathcal{A} = (Q, L, q_0, F, \rightarrow)$ over a timed path $\pi = a_0, t_0, a_1, t_1, \dots$ is an infinite sequence

$$(q_0, v_0) \xrightarrow{a_0, t_0} (q_1, v_1) \xrightarrow{a_1, t_1} (q_2, v_2) \xrightarrow{a_2, t_2} \cdots$$

with $q_i \in Q$ and $v_i \in \mathcal{V}(\mathcal{X})$ for all $i \geq 0$, satisfying the following requirements: (*initialization*) $v_0 = \mathbf{0}$; (*consecution*) for all $i \geq 0$, exists $(q_i, a_i, g_i, X_i, q_{i+1}) \in \rightarrow$ such that $v_{i+1} = (v_i + t_i)[X_i := 0]$ and $v_i + t_i \models g_i$.

A run over π is *accepting* (π is *accepted* by $\mathcal{A}$) if the set of locations visited infinitely often is in F. Let $\mathcal{L}(\mathcal{A})$ be the set of timed paths accepted by $\mathcal{A}$.

A deterministic TA (DTA) has at most one accepting run over a given timed path in $\Pi(L)$. With respect to TAs, which are only closed under finite union and intersection, DTAs are also closed under complement [1].

To relate TAs and SMCs, consider $\mathcal{M} = (S, \tau, \rho, \ell)$ and a TA $\mathcal{A}$ that uses the labels of $\mathcal{M}$ as input symbols. Let $[\![\mathcal{A}]\!] = \{\pi \mid \ell^\omega(\pi) \in \mathcal{L}(\mathcal{A})\}$ be the set of timed paths in $\mathcal{M}$ accepted by $\mathcal{A}$ and $[\![\mathcal{F}]\!] = \{[\![\mathcal{A}]\!] \mid \mathcal{A} \in \mathcal{F}\}$ for any set $\mathcal{F} \in \text{TA}$.

Lemma 11. *(i)* $[\![TA]\!] \subseteq \sigma(\mathcal{T})$ *and (ii)* $\mathcal{T} \subseteq \sigma([\![\text{DTA}]\!])$.

Lemma 11 states that the model checking problem of an SMC $\mathcal{M}$ against a TA $\mathcal{A}$, which is to determine the probability $\mathbb{P}_s([\![\mathcal{A}]\!])$ given the initial state s of $\mathcal{M}$, is well defined and for any $\Phi \subseteq \text{TA}$ we can define the pseudometric

$$\delta_\Phi(s, s') = \sup_{\mathcal{A} \in \Phi} |\mathbb{P}_s([\![\mathcal{A}]\!]) - \mathbb{P}_{s'}([\![\mathcal{A}]\!])|$$

that distinguishes states looking at a specific subclass Φ of TA specifications. For a generic $\Phi \subseteq \text{TA}$, the trace distance is an upper bound of δ_Φ. However, Theorem 6 provides conditions that guarantee the equality of the two distances.

Corollary 12. *Let* $\Phi \subseteq \text{TA}$ *be closed under Boolean operations and such that* $\mathcal{T} \subseteq \sigma([\![\Phi]\!])$. *Then,* $\delta_\Phi = \delta$. *In particular,* $\delta_{\text{TA}} = \delta_{\text{DTA}} = \delta$.

Single-Clock Resetting DTAs. The decidability of model checking CTMCs against TA specifications is open, even for the subclass of DTAs. Recently, Chen et al. [8] provided a decidable algorithm for the case of *single-clock* DTAs (1-DTAs). In this context, an alternative characterization of the trace distance in terms of 1-DTAs is appealing. Notice however that Corollary 12 cannot be applied, since 1-DTAs are not closed under union. We show that the *resetting* 1-DTAs (1-RDTA) satisfy the requirements, hence $\delta_{\text{1-DTA}} = \delta_{\text{1-RDTA}} = \delta$.

Lemma 13. *(i)* $[\![\text{1-RDTA}]\!]$ *is a field and (ii)* $\mathcal{T} \subseteq \sigma([\![\text{1-RDTA}]\!])$.

5 General Convergence Criteria

In this section we provide sufficient conditions to construct sequences that converge, from below and from above, to the total variation distance between a generic pair of probability measures. Eventually, we instantiate these results to the specific case of the trace distance on SMCs.

Convergence from Below. To define a converging sequence of under-approximations of the total variation distance we exploit Theorem 6 as follows.

Theorem 14. *Let (X, Σ) be a measurable space and μ, ν be probability measures on it. Let $\mathcal{F}_0 \subseteq \mathcal{F}_1 \subseteq \mathcal{F}_2 \subseteq \dots$ be a sequence s.t. $\mathcal{F} = \bigcup_{i \in \mathbb{N}} \mathcal{F}_i$ is a field that generates Σ and*

$$l_i = \sup \{ |\mu(E) - \nu(E)| \mid E \in \mathcal{F}_i \} .$$

Then, $l_i \leq l_{i+1}$ and $\sup_{i \in \mathbb{N}} l_i = \|\mu - \nu\|$, for all $i \in \mathbb{N}$.

Proof. $l_i \leq l_{i+1}$ follows from $\mathcal{F}_i \subseteq \mathcal{F}_{i+1}$. Because $\mathcal{F}$ is a field s.t. $\sigma(\mathcal{F}) = \Sigma$, μ and ν are finite measures and $\sup_{i \in \mathbb{N}} l_i = \sup_{E \in \mathcal{F}} |\mu(E) - \nu(E)|$, Theorem 6 concludes our proof. □

According to Theorem 14, to approximate the trace distance δ from below, we just need to find an increasing sequence of collections of measurable sets of timed paths whose union is a field generating $\sigma(\mathcal{T})$. We define it as follows.

For $k \in \mathbb{N}$, let $\mathcal{E}_k$ be the set of all finite unions of cylinders in $\mathfrak{C}_k(S/_{\equiv_\ell}, \mathfrak{R}_k)$, where $\mathfrak{R}_k = \left\{ \left[\frac{n}{2^k}, \frac{n+1}{2^k} \right) \mid 0 \leq n < k2^k \right\} \cup \{[k, \infty)\}$. Note that, these cylinders are pairwise disjoint and, in particular, they form a $\sigma(\mathcal{T})$-measurable partition of $\Pi(S)$. The choice is justified by the following result.

Lemma 15. *For all $k \in \mathbb{N}$, $\mathcal{E}_k \subseteq \mathcal{E}_{k+1}$ and $\bigcup_{k \in \mathbb{N}} \mathcal{E}_k$ is a field generating $\sigma(\mathcal{T})$.*

Given an SMC $\mathcal{M}$, a sequence of under-approximations of the trace distance δ is given, for $k \in \mathbb{N}$, by $\delta{\uparrow}_k \colon S \times S \to [0, 1]$ defined by

$$\delta{\uparrow}_k(s, s') = \sup \{ |\mathbb{P}_s(E) - \mathbb{P}_{s'}(E)| \mid E \in \mathcal{E}_k \} . \tag{1}$$

The next result is an immediate consequence of Lemma 15 and Theorem 14.

Corollary 16. *For all $k \in \mathbb{N}$, $\delta{\uparrow}_k \leq \delta{\uparrow}_{k+1}$ and $\delta = \sup_{k \in \mathbb{N}} \delta{\uparrow}_k$.*

Remark 17 (A logical convergence). Note that Theorem 14 suggests alternative constructions of convergent sequences. For example, as lower-approximations of δ one can use the pseudometrics $\delta_{\mathrm{MTL}_k^-}$, where MTL_k^- is the set of MTL^- formulas with *modal depth* at most $k \in \mathbb{N}$. ■

Convergence from Above. The construction of the converging sequence of over-approximations of the total variation is based on a classic duality result asserting that *the total variation of two measures corresponds to the minimal discrepancy measured among all their possible couplings* [13].

Recall that a coupling $\omega \in \Omega(\mu, \nu)$ for two probability measures μ, ν on (X, Σ) is a measure in the product space $(X, \Sigma) \otimes (X, \Sigma)$ whose left and right marginals are μ and ν, respectively. The *discrepancy* associated with ω is the value $\omega(\not\cong)$, where $\cong \; = \bigcap_{E \in \Sigma} \{(x, y) \mid x \in E \text{ iff } y \in E\}$ is the *inseparability relation* w.r.t. measurable sets in Σ. Then, the following duality holds.

Lemma 18 ([13, Th.5.2]). *Let μ, ν be probability measures on (X, Σ). Then, provided that $\not\cong$ is measurable in $\Sigma \otimes \Sigma$, $\|\mu - \nu\| = \min \{ \omega(\not\cong) \mid \omega \in \Omega(\mu, \nu) \}$.*

Given the above result, we can state a second general converging criterion to approach the total variation distance from above.

Theorem 19. *Let (X, Σ) be a measurable space s.t. $\cong \in \Sigma \otimes \Sigma$ and μ, ν be probability measures on it. Let $\Omega_0 \subseteq \Omega_1 \subseteq \Omega_2 \dots$ be an increasing sequence s.t. $\bigcup_{i \in \mathbb{N}} \Omega_i$ is dense in $\Omega(\mu, \nu)$ w.r.t. the total variation distance and define*

$$u_i = \inf \{\omega(\ncong) \mid \omega \in \Omega_i\} \ .$$

Then, $u_i \geq u_{i+1}$ and $\inf_{i \in \mathbb{N}} u_i = \|\mu - \nu\|$, for all $i \in \mathbb{N}$.

Proof. $u_i \geq u_{i+1}$ follows from $\Omega_i \subseteq \Omega_{i+1}$. To prove $\inf_{i \in \mathbb{N}} u_i = \|\mu - \nu\|$, recall that for $Y \neq \emptyset$ and $f \colon Y \to \mathbb{R}$ bounded and continuous, if $D \subseteq Y$ is dense then $\inf f(D) = \inf f(Y)$. By hypothesis $\bigcup_{i \in \mathbb{N}} \Omega_i \subseteq \Omega(\mu, \nu)$ is dense; moreover, $\mu \times \nu \in \Omega(\mu, \nu) \neq \emptyset$. We show that $ev_{\ncong} \colon \Omega(\mu, \nu) \to \mathbb{R}$, defined by $ev_{\ncong}(\omega) = \omega(\ncong)$ is bounded and continuous. It is bounded since all $\omega \in \Omega(\mu, \nu)$ are finite measures. It is continuous because $\|\omega - \omega'\| \geq |\omega(\ncong) - \omega'(\ncong)| = |ev_{\ncong}(\omega) - ev_{\ncong}(\omega')|$ (1-Lipschitz continuity). Now, applying Lemma 18, we derive our result. □

To conclude this section, we define a sequence of sets of couplings that, according to Theorem 19, characterizes the trace distance δ on SMCs.

Observe that the inseparability relation w.r.t. the σ-algebra generated by trace cylinders is measurable and it can be characterized as follows.

Lemma 20. $\equiv_{\ell^\omega} = \bigcap_{E \in \sigma(\mathcal{T})} \{(\pi, \pi') \mid \pi \in E \textit{ iff } \pi' \in E\} \in \sigma(\mathcal{T}) \otimes \sigma(\mathcal{T})$.

Next we introduce the notion of *coupling structure* for an SMC. Let $\Pi^k(S) = \{s_0, t_0, .., t_{k-1}, s_k \mid s_i \in S,\ t_i \in \mathbb{R}_+\}$ be the measurable space with σ-algebra generated by $\mathcal{R}_k = \{\{s_0\} \times R_0 \times .. \times R_{k-1} \times \{s_k\} \mid s_i \in S,\ R_i \in \mathbb{B}\}$. Note that, the prefix function $(\cdot)|^k \colon \Pi(S) \to \Pi^k(S)$ is measurable, hence, the push forward w.r.t. it on $\mu \in \Delta(\Pi(S))$, denoted by $\mu|^k$, is a measure in $\Pi^k(S)$.

Definition 21 (Coupling Structure). *A* coupling structure of rank $k \in \mathbb{N}$ *for an SMC $\mathcal{M}$ is a function $\mathcal{C} \colon S \times S \to \Delta(\Pi^k(S) \times \Pi^k(S))$ such that, for all states $s, s' \in S$, $\mathcal{C}(s, s') \in \Omega(\mathbb{P}_s|^k, \mathbb{P}_{s'}|^k)$.*

The set of coupling structures of rank k for $\mathcal{M}$ is denoted by $\mathbb{C}_k(\mathcal{M})$.

A coupling structure of rank k together with a distinguished initial pair of states, can be intuitively seen as a stochastic process generating pairs of timed paths divided in multi-steps of length k and distributed according to the following probability.

Definition 22. *For $k \in \mathbb{N}$, $s, s' \in S$ states in $\mathcal{M}$ and $\mathcal{C} \in \mathbb{C}_k(\mathcal{M})$, let $\mathbb{P}^{\mathcal{C}}_{s,s'}$ be the unique probability measure*[4] *on $\Pi(S) \otimes \Pi(S)$ such that, for all $n \in \mathbb{N}$ and $E = \{u_0\} \times R_0 \times .. \times R_{nk-1} \times \{u_{nk}\}, F = \{v_0\} \times H_0 \times .. \times H_{nk-1} \times \{v_{nk}\} \in \mathcal{R}_{nk}$*

$$\mathbb{P}^{\mathcal{C}}_{s,s'}(\mathfrak{C}(E) \times \mathfrak{C}(F)) = \mathbb{1}_{\{(s,s')\}}(u_0, v_0) \cdot \prod_{h=0}^{n-1} \mathcal{C}(u_{hk}, v_{hk})(E_h \times F_h)\,,$$

where $\mathfrak{C}(E)$ denotes the cylinder obtained as the pre-image under $(\cdot)|^{nk}$ of E and $E_h = \{u_{hk}\} \times R_{hk} \times .. \times R_{(h+1)k-1} \times \{u_{(h+1)k}\}$ (similarly for F).

[4] The existence and the uniqueness of this measure follow by Hahn-Kolmogorov extension theorem and the fact that any cylinder of rank k can always be represented as a disjoint union of cylinders of rank $k' \geq k$ (see e.g., [6, pp.29–32]).

The name "coupling structure" is justified by the following result.

Lemma 23. *Let $\mathcal{C}$ be a coupling structure for $\mathcal{M}$, then $\mathbb{P}^{\mathcal{C}}_{s,s'} \in \Omega(\mathbb{P}_s, \mathbb{P}_{s'})$.*

We are finally ready to describe a decreasing sequence that converges to the trace distance on SMCs. Given $\mathcal{M}$, let $\delta{\downarrow}_k \colon S \times S \to [0,1]$ for $k \in \mathbb{N}$, be

$$\delta{\downarrow}_k(s,s') = \min \left\{ \mathbb{P}^{\mathcal{C}}_{s,s'}(\not\equiv_{\ell^\omega}) \mid \mathcal{C} \in \mathbb{C}_{2^k}(\mathcal{M}) \right\} . \tag{2}$$

According to Theorem 14 the following suffices to prove the convergence.

Lemma 24. *Let $s, s' \in S$ be a pair of states of an SMC $\mathcal{M}$. Then,*
(i) for all $k \in \mathbb{N}$, $\{\mathbb{P}^{\mathcal{C}}_{s,s'} \mid \mathcal{C} \in \mathbb{C}_k(\mathcal{M})\} \subseteq \{\mathbb{P}^{\mathcal{C}}_{s,s'} \mid \mathcal{C} \in \mathbb{C}_{2k}(\mathcal{M})\}$;
(ii) $\bigcup_{k\in\mathbb{N}} \{\mathbb{P}^{\mathcal{C}}_{s,s'} \mid \mathcal{C} \in \mathbb{C}_{2^k}(\mathcal{M})\}$ is dense in $\Omega(\mathbb{P}_s, \mathbb{P}_{s'})$ w.r.t. the total variation.

Proof (sketch). (i) Let $k > 0$ and $\mathcal{C} \in \mathbb{C}_k(\mathcal{M})$. Define $\mathcal{D}(s,s')$ as the unique measure on $\Pi^{2k}(S) \otimes \Pi^{2k}(S)$ s.t., for all $E = \{u_0\} \times R_0 \times .. \times R_{2k-1} \times \{u_{2k}\}$ and $F = \{v_0\} \times H_0 \times .. \times H_{2k-1} \times \{v_{2k}\}$ in $\mathcal{R}_{2k}$

$$\mathcal{D}(s,s')(E \times F) = \mathcal{C}(s,s')(E' \times F') \cdot \mathcal{C}(u_k, v_k)(E'' \times F'') ,$$

where $E'=\{u_0\} \times R_0 \times .. \times R_{k-1} \times \{u_k\}$ and $E''=\{u_k\} \times R_k \times .. \times R_{2k-1} \times \{u_{2k}\}$ (similarly for F). One can check that $\mathcal{D} \in \mathbb{C}_{2k}(\mathcal{M})$ and $\mathbb{P}^{\mathcal{C}}_{s,s'} = \mathbb{P}^{\mathcal{D}}_{s,s'}$.

(ii) Let $\Omega = \bigcup_{k\in\mathbb{N}} \{\mathbb{P}^{\mathcal{C}}_{s,s'} \mid \mathcal{C} \in \mathbb{C}_{2^k}(\mathcal{M})\}$. Let $\mathcal{F}_k$ be the collection of all finite union of sets of the form $\mathfrak{C}(E) \times \mathfrak{C}(F)$, for $E, F \in \mathcal{R}_k$. Note that $\mathcal{F} = \bigcup_{k\in\mathbb{N}} \mathcal{F}_k$ is a field generating the σ-algebra of $\Pi(S) \otimes \Pi(S)$. By Lemma 5 and Definition 22, to prove that Ω is dense it suffices that for all $\mu \in \Omega(\mathbb{P}_s, \mathbb{P}_{s'})$, $k \in \mathbb{N}$ and $F \in \mathcal{F}_k$, there exists $\omega \in \Omega$ s.t. $\omega(F) = \mu(F)$. One can check that $\omega = \mathbb{P}^{\mathcal{C}}_{s,s'}$, where $\mathcal{C} \in \mathbb{C}_{2^k}(\mathcal{M})$ is s.t. $\mathcal{C}(s,s') = \mu[(\cdot)|^{2^k} \times (\cdot)|^{2^k}]$ (i.e., the push forward of μ along the function $(\pi, \pi') \mapsto (\pi|^{2^k}, \pi'|^{2^k})$) has the desired property. □

The following corollary derives from Lemma 24 and Theorem 19.

Corollary 25. *For all $k \in \mathbb{N}$, $\delta{\downarrow}_k \geq \delta{\downarrow}_{k+1}$ and $\delta = \inf_{k\in\mathbb{N}} \delta{\downarrow}_k$.*

6 An Approximation Algorithm

This section exploits the aforementioned results to propose a decidable procedure for approximating the trace distance δ on SMCs with arbitrary precision.

Let $\varepsilon > 0$ and consider the sequences $\{\delta{\uparrow}_k\}_{k\in\mathbb{N}}$ and $\{\delta{\downarrow}_k\}_{k\in\mathbb{N}}$ from Section 5. The procedure proceeds step-wise (increasing $k \geq 0$) by computing the point-wise difference $\delta{\downarrow}_k - \delta{\uparrow}_k$ until is smaller then ε. Termination and correctness is ensured by the convergence of the sequences from above and below to δ.

Theorem 26. *Let $\mathcal{M}$ be a SMC. There exists an algorithm that, given a rational number $\varepsilon > 0$, computes a function $d \colon S \times S \to [0,1] \cap \mathbb{Q}_+$ such that $|d - \delta| < \varepsilon$.*

We prove this theorem under two reasonable assumptions regarding SMCs:

A1. For all $s \in S$ and $q, q' \in \mathbb{Q}_+$, $\rho(s)([q, q'))$ is computable;
A2. For all $s, s' \in S$, $\|\rho(s) - \rho(s')\|$ is computable.

In the above $\rho(s)([q, q'))$ and $\|\rho(s) - \rho(s')\|$ may assume real values, and with the term "compute" we mean that there exists an effective Cauchy sequence of rationals that converges to the value.

Lemma 27. *Assuming A1, $\delta\!\uparrow_k$ is computable for all $k \in \mathbb{N}$.*

Proof (sketch). For each $k \in \mathbb{N}$, the set $\mathcal{E}_k$ is finite. Moreover, for each $s \in S$ and $E \in \mathcal{E}_k$, $\mathbb{P}_s(E)$ is computable thanks to its additivity and the hypothesis A1. □

The computability of the sequence $\{\delta\!\downarrow_k\}_{k \in \mathbb{N}}$ is less trivial. Equation (2) suggests to look for a coupling structure $\mathcal{C} \in \mathbb{C}_{2^k}(\mathcal{M})$ that minimizes the discrepancy $\mathbb{P}^{\mathcal{C}}_{s,s'}(\not\equiv_{\ell^\omega})$. This is done by following a searching strategy similar to the one in [4] and structured as follows: (i) we provide an alternative characterization of the discrepancy associated with a coupling structure (Section 6.1); (ii) we describe how to construct an optimal coupling structure and show that its associated discrepancy is computable (Section 6.2).

6.1 Fixed Point Characterization of the Discrepancy

We characterize the discrepancy associated with a coupling structure $\mathcal{C}$ by means of the least fixed point of a suitable operator parametric in $\mathcal{C}$. To define the fixed point operator it is convenient to split a coupling structure into two "projections": on discrete state transitions (regardless of time delays); and on residence times (given that a sequence of transitions has occurred). To this end define $\mathbb{S}^k \colon S \to \mathcal{D}(S^{k+1})$ and $\mathbb{T}^k \colon S^k \to \Delta(\mathbb{R}^k_+)$ as follows

$$\mathbb{S}^k(s)(u_0..u_k) = \mathbb{1}_s(u_0) \cdot \textstyle\prod_{i=0}^{k-1} \tau(u_i)(u_{i+1}), \quad \mathbb{T}^k(v_1..v_k) = \rho(v_1) \times \cdots \times \rho(v_k).$$

Lemma 28. *The set $\mathbb{C}_k(\mathcal{M})$ is in bijection with the set of pairs of functions $\tau_{\mathcal{C}} \colon S \times S \to \mathcal{D}(S^{k+1} \times S^{k+1})$ and $\rho_{\mathcal{C}} \colon S^k \times S^k \to \Delta(\mathbb{R}^k_+ \times \mathbb{R}^k_+)$ such that*

$$\tau_{\mathcal{C}}(u, v) \in \Omega(\mathbb{S}^k(u), \mathbb{S}^k(v)) \quad \textit{and} \quad \rho_{\mathcal{C}}(u_1..u_k, v_1..v_k) \in \Omega(\mathbb{T}^k(u_1..u_k), \mathbb{T}^k(v_1..v_k)).$$

Hereafter we identify the coupling structure $\mathcal{C}$ with its bijective image $(\tau_{\mathcal{C}}, \rho_{\mathcal{C}})$.

Intuitively, $\tau_{\mathcal{C}}(u, v)(u_0..u_k, v_0..v_k)$ is the probability that two copies of $\mathcal{M}$, scheduled according to $\mathcal{C}$, have respectively generated the sequences of states $u_0..u_k$ and $v_0..v_k$ starting from u and v; while $\rho(u_0..u_{k-1}, v_0..v_{k-1})(R \times R')$ is the probability that, having observed $u_0..u_{k-1}$ and $v_0..v_{k-1}$, the generated sequence of time delays are in $R, R' \subseteq \mathbb{R}^k_+$, respectively.

For a coupling structure $\mathcal{C} = (\tau_{\mathcal{C}}, \rho_{\mathcal{C}}) \in \mathbb{C}_k(\mathcal{M})$, define the self-map $\Gamma^{\mathcal{C}}$ over $[0, 1]$-valued functions on $S^{k+1} \times S^{k+1}$ as follows[5]

$$\Gamma^{\mathcal{C}}(d)(u_0..u_k, v_0..v_k) = \begin{cases} 0 & \text{if } \alpha = 0 \\ 1 & \text{if } \alpha \neq 0,\ \exists i.\ u_i \not\equiv_\ell v_i \\ \beta + (1 - \beta) \cdot \int d \, \mathrm{d}\tau_{\mathcal{C}}(u_k, v_k) & \text{otherwise} \end{cases}$$

[5] Since, for all $u, v \in S$, $\tau_{\mathcal{C}}(u, v)$ is a discrete measure on a finite space, the Lebesgue integral $\int d \, \mathrm{d}\tau_{\mathcal{C}}(u, v)$ in the definition of $\Gamma^{\mathcal{C}}$ is $\sum_{x,y \in S^{k+1}} d(x, y) \cdot \tau_{\mathcal{C}}(u, v)(x, y)$.

where $\beta = \rho_{\mathcal{C}}(u_0..u_{k-1}, v_0..v_{k-1})(\neq)$ and $\alpha = \tau_{\mathcal{C}}(u_0, v_0)(u_0..u_k, v_0..v_k)$.

The operator $\Gamma^{\mathcal{C}}$ is monotonic w.r.t. the point-wise order on $[0,1]$-valued functions. Hence, by Tarski's fixed point theorem, $\Gamma^{\mathcal{C}}$ has a least fixed point, which we denote by $\gamma^{\mathcal{C}}$. The next result shows that $\gamma^{\mathcal{C}}$ is closely related to the discrepancy associated with the coupling structure $\mathcal{C}$, and this will eventually be used to compute it.

Lemma 29. *For any coupling structure* $\mathcal{C}$, $\mathbb{P}^{\mathcal{C}}_{s,s'}(\not\equiv_{\ell^\omega}) = \int \gamma^{\mathcal{C}} \, \mathrm{d}\tau_{\mathcal{C}}(s, s')$.

6.2 Construction of an Optimal Coupling Structure

In this subsection we construct an optimal coupling structure by iterating successive updates of a given coupling structure. We provide necessary and sufficient conditions for a coupling structure $\mathcal{C}$ to ensure that $\delta{\downarrow_k}$ is obtained from $\gamma^{\mathcal{C}}$.

To this end, we first introduce the notion of update for a coupling structure.

Definition 30 (Update). *Let* $\mathcal{C} = (\tau_{\mathcal{C}}, \rho_{\mathcal{C}}) \in \mathbb{C}_k(\mathcal{M})$. *For* $\mu \in \Omega(\mathbb{S}^k(u), \mathbb{S}^k(v))$ *and* $\nu \in \Omega(\mathbb{T}^k(u_1..u_k), \mathbb{T}^k(v_1..v_k))$, *define*

- *transition update:* $\mathcal{C}[(u,v)/\mu] = (\tau_{\mathcal{C}}[(u,v) \mapsto \mu], \rho_{\mathcal{C}})$;
- *delay update:* $\mathcal{C}\langle(u_1..u_k, v_1..v_k)/\nu\rangle = (\tau_{\mathcal{C}}, \rho_{\mathcal{C}}[(u_1..u_k, v_1..v_k) \mapsto \nu])$.

where, for a function $f \colon X \to Y$, $f[x \mapsto y]$ *denotes the update of* f *at* x *with* y.

Our update strategy relies on the following result.

Lemma 31 (Update Criteria). *Let* $\mathcal{C} = (\tau_{\mathcal{C}}, \rho_{\mathcal{C}}) \in \mathbb{C}_k(\mathcal{M})$ *be a coupling structure and* $u_0..u_k, v_0..v_k \in S$ *such that* $\tau_{\mathcal{C}}(u_0..u_k, v_0..v_k) > 0$ *and, for all* $i \leq k$, $u_i \equiv_\ell v_i$. *Then, for* $\mu \in \Omega(\mathbb{S}^k(u_k), \mathbb{S}^k(v_k))$, $\nu \in \Omega(\mathbb{T}^k(u_0..u_{k-1}), \mathbb{T}^k(v_0..v_{k-1}))$ *and* $\mathcal{D} = \mathcal{C}[(u_k, v_k)/\mu]\langle(u_0..u_{k-1}, v_1..v_{k-1})/\nu\rangle$, *it holds* $\gamma^{\mathcal{D}} < \gamma^{\mathcal{C}}$ *whenever*

(i) $\nu(\neq) < \rho_{\mathcal{C}}(u_0..u_{k-1}, v_1..v_{k-1})(\neq)$ *and* $\int \gamma^{\mathcal{C}} \, \mathrm{d}\mu \leq \int \gamma^{\mathcal{C}} \, \mathrm{d}\tau_{\mathcal{C}}(u_k, v_k)$, *or*

(ii) $\nu(\neq) \leq \rho_{\mathcal{C}}(u_0..u_{k-1}, v_1..v_{k-1})(\neq)$ *and* $\int \gamma^{\mathcal{C}} \, \mathrm{d}\mu < \int \gamma^{\mathcal{C}} \, \mathrm{d}\tau_{\mathcal{C}}(u_k, v_k)$.

Condition (i) in Lemma 31 ensures that any $\mathcal{C} = (\tau_{\mathcal{C}}, \rho_{\mathcal{C}}) \in \mathbb{C}_k(\mathcal{M})$ is improved by replacing $\rho_{\mathcal{C}}$ with the function $\rho^* \colon S^k \times S^k \to \Delta(\mathbb{R}^k_+ \times \mathbb{R}^k_+)$ defined as

$$\begin{aligned} \rho^*(u_0..u_{k-1}, v_1..v_{k-1}) &= \min\left\{\nu(\neq) \mid \nu \in \Omega(\mathbb{T}^k(u_0..u_{k-1}), \mathbb{T}^k(v_0..v_{k-1}))\right\} \\ &= \|\mathbb{T}^k(u_0..u_{k-1}) - \mathbb{T}^k(v_0..v_{k-1})\| \qquad \text{(Lemma 18)} \\ &= 1 - \textstyle\prod_{i=0}^{k-1}(1 - \|\rho(u_i) - \rho(v_i)\|) = \beta^* , \end{aligned}$$

where the last equality follows by the definition of $\mathbb{T}^k(u_0..u_{k-1})$ and $\mathbb{T}^k(v_0..v_{k-1})$ as product measures. Notice that, assuming A2, the above is computable. By replacing β in the definition of $\Gamma^{\mathcal{C}}$ with β^*, $\gamma^{\mathcal{C}}$ can be computed as the least solution of the linear equation system induced by the definition of $\Gamma^{\mathcal{C}}$.

Condition (ii) of Lemma 31 suggests to improve $\mathcal{C}$ with $\mathcal{C}[(u_k, v_k)/\mu^*]$ where

$$\begin{aligned} \mu^* &= \arg\min\left\{\textstyle\int \gamma^{\mathcal{C}} \, \mathrm{d}\mu \mid \mu \in \Omega(\mathbb{S}^k(u_k), \mathbb{S}^k(v_k))\right\} \\ &= \arg\min\left\{\textstyle\sum_{x,y \in S^{k+1}} \gamma^{\mathcal{C}}(x,y) \cdot \mu(x,y) \mid \mu \in \Omega(\mathbb{S}^k(u_k), \mathbb{S}^k(v_k))\right\} . \end{aligned}$$

The above is a linear program (a.k.a. *transportation problem*), hence computable.
The sufficient conditions for termination is provided by the following lemma.

Lemma 32. *Let $\mathcal{C} = (\tau_{\mathcal{C}}, \rho^*) \in \mathbb{C}_{2^k}(\mathcal{M})$ be such that $\delta{\downarrow}_k(u,v) \neq \int \gamma^{\mathcal{C}} \, \mathrm{d}\tau_{\mathcal{C}}(u,v)$ for some $u, v \in S$. Then there exist $u', v' \in S$ and $\mu \in \Omega(\mathbb{S}^{2^k}(u'), \mathbb{S}^{2^k}(v'))$ such that $\int \gamma^{\mathcal{C}} \, \mathrm{d}\mu < \int \gamma^{\mathcal{C}} \, \mathrm{d}\tau_{\mathcal{C}}(u',v')$.*

Intuitively, the above ensures that, unless $\mathcal{C}$ is an optimal coupling structure, (ii) in Lemma 31 is satisfied, so that, we can further improve $\mathcal{C}$ as aforesaid.

Proposition 33. *Assuming A2, $\delta{\downarrow}_k$ is computable for all $k \in \mathbb{N}$.*

Proof (sketch). The aforementioned strategy ensures that the updated couplings are chosen from the vertices of the polytopes $\Omega(\mathbb{S}^k(u), \mathbb{S}^k(v))$, for $u, v \in S$. Since these polytopes have finitely many vertexes, the procedure eventually terminates. By Lemma 32, the last coupling describes $\delta{\downarrow}_k$. □

7 Conclusions and Future Work

In this paper we showed that the total variation distance of SMCs (i.e., the trace distance) is the appropriate behavioral distance to reason about linear real-time properties. This has been done by giving characterizations in terms of MTL formulas or timed ω-regular languages that arise naturally in the context of linear real-time probabilistic model checking. Notably, the technique that has been proposed to prove this result is more general and allows for many more interesting characterizations. We showed, for instance, that the distance can be characterized by considering strictly less expressive fragments of MTL, namely MTL$^-$; analogously, it suffices to consider only the subclass of ω-languages recognized by single-clock always resetting DTAs.

Moreover, we studied the problem of approximating the trace distance within any absolute error. We showed that the problem is computable by approximating the total variation distance both from above and below by means of the sequences $\{\delta{\downarrow}_k\}_k$ and $\{\delta{\uparrow}_k\}_k$, that are proved to be effective. This both extends the result of [9] to the real-time setting and gives an alternative way to approximate the total variation distance on MCs.

As a future work we consider to further explore the potentiality of the presented results by studying how fast the sequences converge to the total variation distance. Moreover, we would like to see if similar results can be used to link different behavioral distances, such as the Kantorovich-based bisimilarity distance and the total variation (for which the former is know to be an upper bound of the latter), opening for the possibility of "bridging the gap" between trace and branching-based behavioral distances.

From a computational perspective, also motivated by our previous work [4] on MCs, we would like to implement an on-the-fly algorithm for computing tight over-approximations of the trace distance.

References

1. Alur, R., Dill, D.: Automata for Modeling real-time Systems. In: Paterson, M. S. (ed.) ICALP 1990. LNCS, vol. 443, pp. 322–335. Springer, Heidelberg (1990)
2. Alur, R., Henzinger, T.A.: Real-Time Logics: Complexity and Expressiveness. Information and Computation 104(1), 35–77 (1993)
3. Alur, R., Henzinger, T.A.: A Really Temporal Logic. Journal of the ACM 41(1), 181–204 (1994)
4. Bacci, G., Bacci, G., Larsen, K.G., Mardare, R.: On-the-Fly Exact Computation of Bisimilarity Distances. In: Piterman, N., Smolka, S.A. (eds.) TACAS 2013. LNCS, vol. 7795, pp. 1–15. Springer, Heidelberg (2013)
5. Bacci, G., Bacci, G., Larsen, K.G., Mardare, R.: On the Total Variation Distance of Semi-Markov Chains. Technical report, AAU, DK (2014), `http://people.cs.aau.dk/~grbacci/Papers/tvsmc_ext.pdf`
6. Billingsley, P.: Probability and Measure, 3rd edn. Wiley, New York (1995)
7. Chen, T., Diciolla, M., Kwiatkowska, M., Mereacre, A.: Time-Bounded Verification of CTMCs against Real-Time Specifications. In: Fahrenberg, U., Tripakis, S. (eds.) FORMATS 2011. LNCS, vol. 6919, pp. 26–42. Springer, Heidelberg (2011)
8. Chen, T., Han, T., Katoen, J.-P., Mereacre, A.: Model checking of continuous-time markov chains against timed automata specifications. Logical Methods in Computer Science 7(1) (2011)
9. Chen, T., Kiefer, S.: On the Total Variation Distance of Labelled Markov Chains. In: Proc. of CSL-LICS 2014, p. 33:1–33:10. ACM, New York (2014)
10. de Alfaro, L., Faella, M., Stoelinga, M.: Linear and branching metrics for quantitative transition systems. In: Díaz, J., Karhumäki, J., Lepistö, A., Sannella, D. (eds.) ICALP 2004. LNCS, vol. 3142, pp. 97–109. Springer, Heidelberg (2004)
11. de Alfaro, L., Majumdar, R., Raman, V., Stoelinga, M.: Game Relations and Metrics. In: LICS, pp. 99–108 (July 2007)
12. Desharnais, J., Gupta, V., Jagadeesan, R., Panangaden, P.: Metrics for labelled Markov processes. Theoretical Compututer Science 318(3), 323–354 (2004)
13. Lindvall, T.: Lectures on the Coupling Method. Wiley Series in Probability and Mathematical Statistics. John Wiley, New York (1992)
14. Lyngsø, R.B., Pedersen, C.N.: The consensus string problem and the complexity of comparing hidden Markov models. Journal of Computer and System Sciences 65(3), 545–569 (2002), Special Issue on Computational Biology 2002
15. Mio, M.: Upper-Expectation Bisimilarity and Łukasiewicz μ-Calculus. In: Muscholl, A. (ed.) FOSSACS 2014. LNCS, vol. 8412, pp. 335–350. Springer, Heidelberg (2014)
16. Ouaknine, J., Worrell, J.: On the decidability and complexity of Metric Temporal Logic over finite words. Logical Methods in Computer Science 3(8) (2007)
17. Sharma, A., Katoen, J.-P.: Weighted Lumpability on Markov Chains. In: Clarke, E., Virbitskaite, I., Voronkov, A. (eds.) PSI 2011. LNCS, vol. 7162, pp. 322–339. Springer, Heidelberg (2012)
18. van Breugel, F., Worrell, J.: Approximating and computing behavioural distances in probabilistic transition systems. Theoretical Computer Science 360(3), 373–385 (2006)

Decidable and Expressive Classes of Probabilistic Automata

Rohit Chadha[1], A. Prasad Sistla[2], Mahesh Viswanathan[3], and Yue Ben[2]

[1] University of Missouri, USA
[2] Univ. of Illinois, Chicago, USA
[3] Univ. of Illinois, Urbana-Champaign, USA

Abstract. Hierarchical probabilistic automata (HPA) are probabilistic automata whose states are partitioned into levels such that for any state and input symbol, at most one transition with non-zero probability goes to a state at the same level, and all others go to states at a higher level. We present expressiveness and decidability results for 1-level HPAs that work on both finite and infinite length input strings; in a 1-level HPA states are divided into only two levels (0 and 1). Our first result shows that 1-level HPAs, with acceptance threshold $1/2$ (both in the finite and infinite word cases), can recognize non-regular languages. This result is surprising in the light of the following two facts. First, all earlier proofs demonstrating the recognition of non-regular languages by probabilistic automata employ either more complex automata or irrational acceptance thresholds or HPAs with more than two levels. Second, it has been previously shown that simple probabilistic automata (SPA), which are 1-level HPAs whose accepting states are all at level 0, recognize only regular languages. We show that even though 1-level HPAs with threshold $1/2$ are very expressive (in that they recognize non-regular languages), the non-emptiness and non-universality problems are both decidable in **EXPTIME**. To the best our knowledge, this is the first such decidability result for any subclass of probabilistic automata that accept non-regular languages. We prove that these decision problems are also **PSPACE**-hard. Next, we present a new sufficient condition when 1-level HPAs recognize regular languages (in both the finite and infinite cases). Finally, we show that the emptiness and universality problems for this special class of HPAs is **PSPACE**-complete.

1 Introduction

Probabilistic automata (PA) [13,12,1,10] are finite state machines that have probabilistic transitions on input symbols. Such machines can either recognize a language of finite words (probabilistic finite automata PFA [13,12]) or a language of infinite words (probabilistic Büchi/Rabin/Muller automata [1,10,6]) depending on the notion of accepting run; on finite input words, an accepting run is one that reaches a final state, while on an infinite input, an accepting run is one whose set of states visited infinitely often satisfy a Büchi, Rabin, or Muller acceptance condition. The set of accepting runs in all these cases can be shown to be measurable and the probability of this set is taken to be probability of accepting the input word. Given an acceptance threshold x, the language $\mathsf{L}_{>x}(\mathcal{A})$ ($\mathsf{L}_{\geq x}(\mathcal{A})$) of a PA $\mathcal{A}$ is the set of all inputs whose acceptance probability is $> x$ ($\geq x$). In this paper the threshold x is always a rational number in $(0, 1)$.

A. Pitts (Ed.): FOSSACS 2015, LNCS 9034, pp. 200–214, 2015.
DOI: 10.1007/978-3-662-46678-0_13

Hierarchical probabilistic automata (HPA) are a syntactic subclass of probabilistic automata that are computationally more tractable for extremal thresholds [5] — problems of emptiness and universality which are undecidable for PAs on infinite words with threshold 0 become decidable for HPAs. Over finite words, the problem of deciding whether the infimum of acceptance probabilities is 0 also becomes decidable for HPAs [8], even though it is undecidable for general PAs [9]. Intuitively, a HPA is a PA whose states are stratified into (totally) ordered levels with the property that from any state q, and input a, the machine can transition with non-zero probability to at most one state in the same level as q, and all other probabilistic successors belong to a higher level. Such automata arise naturally as models of *client-server systems*. Consider such a system where clients can request services of multiple servers that can fail (catastrophically) with some probability. The state of the automaton models the global state of all the servers and inputs to the machine correspond to requests from the client to the servers. The levels of the automaton correspond to the number of failed servers, with the lowest level modeling no failures. Since failed servers can't come back, the transitions in such a system satisfy the hierarchical nature. While HPAs are tractable with extremal thresholds, the emptiness and universality problems are undecidable for HPA with threshold $\frac{1}{2}$ [4]. In fact, solving these decision problems for 6-level HPAs is undecidable [4]. In this paper, we investigate how the landscape changes when we restrict our attention to 1-level HPAs.

1-level HPAs (henceforth simply called HPAs) are machines whose states are partitioned into two levels (0 and 1), with initial state in level 0, and transitions satisfying the hierarchical structure. These automata model client-server systems where only one server failure is allowed. Despite their extremely simple structure, we show that (1-level) HPAs turn out to be surprisingly powerful — they can recognize non-regular languages over finite and infinite words (even with threshold $\frac{1}{2}$). This result is significant because all earlier constructions of PFAs [12,13] and probabilistic Büchi automata [10,2] recognizing non-regular languages use either more complex automata or irrational acceptance thresholds or HPAs with more than two levels. Moreover, this result is also unexpected because it was previously shown that *simple probabilistic automata* only recognize regular languages [4,5]. The only difference between (1-level) HPAs and simple probabilistic automata is that all accepting states of a simple probabilistic automaton are required to be in level 0 (same level as the initial state).

Next, we consider the canonical decision problems of emptiness and universality for (1-level) HPAs with threshold x. Decision problems for PAs with non-extremal thresholds are often computationally harder than similar questions when the threshold is extremal (either 0 or 1), and the problems are always undecidable [7,5,2,12]. Even though 1-level HPAs are expressive, we show that both emptiness and universality problems for 1-level HPAs are decidable in **EXPTIME** and are **PSPACE**-hard. As far as we know, this is the first decidability result for any subclass of PAs with non-extremal thresholds that can recognize non-regular languages. Our decision procedure relies on observing that when the language of a HPA $\mathcal{A}$ is non-empty (or non-universal), then there is an input whose length is exponentially bounded in the size of the HPA that witnesses this fact.

Finally, we introduce a special subclass of (1-level) HPAs called *integer* HPAs. Integer HPA are HPAs where from any level 0 state q, on any input a, the probability of transitioning to a level 1 state is an integer multiple of the probability of the (unique) transition to a level 0 state on a from q. With this restriction, we can show that integer HPA with threshold x only recognize regular languages (over finite and infinite words). For integer HPAs, we show that the canonical decision decision problems of emptiness and universality are **PSPACE**-complete.

The rest of the paper is organized as follows. Section 2 has basic definitions, and introduces HPAs along with some useful propositions. The results characterizing the expressiveness and decidability of HPAs are presented in Section 3. The results on integer HPAs are presented in Section 4. Section 5 contains concluding remarks.

2 Preliminaries

We assume that the reader is familiar with finite state automata, regular languages, Büchi automata, Muller automata and ω-regular languages. The set of natural numbers will be denoted by $\mathbb{N}$, the closed unit interval by $[0, 1]$ and the open unit interval by $(0, 1)$. The power-set of a set X will be denoted by 2^X.

Sequences. Given a finite set S, $|S|$ denotes the cardinality of S. Given a sequence (finite or infinite) $\kappa = s_0 s_1 \ldots$ over S, $|\kappa|$ will denote the length of the sequence (for infinite sequence $|\kappa|$ will be ω), and $\kappa[i]$ will denote the ith element s_i of the sequence. As usual S^* will denote the set of all finite sequences/strings/words over S, S^+ will denote the set of all finite non-empty sequences/strings/words over S and S^ω will denote the set of all infinite sequences/strings/words over S. We will use u, v, w to range over elements of S^*, α, β, γ to range over infinite words over S^ω.

Given $\kappa \in S^* \cup S^\omega$, natural numbers $i, j \leq |\kappa|$, $\kappa[i : j]$ is the finite sequence $s_i \ldots s_j$ and $\kappa[i : \infty]$ is the infinite sequence $s_i s_{i+1} \ldots$, where $s_k = \kappa[k]$. The set of *finite prefixes* of κ is the set $\mathit{Pref}(\kappa) = \{\kappa[0 : j] \mid j \in \mathbb{N}, j \leq |\kappa|\}$. Given $u \in S^*$ and $\kappa \in S^* \cup S^\omega$, $u\kappa$ is the sequence obtained by concatenating the two sequences in order. Given $\mathsf{L}_1 \subseteq \Sigma^*$ and $\mathsf{L}_2 \subseteq S^* \cup \Sigma^\omega$, the set $\mathsf{L}_1\mathsf{L}_2$ is defined to be $\{u\kappa \mid u \in \mathsf{L}_1 \text{ and } \kappa \in \mathsf{L}_2\}$. Given $u \in S^+$, the word u^ω is the unique infinite sequence formed by repeating u infinitely often. An infinite word $\alpha \in S^\omega$ is said to be *ultimately* periodic if there are finite words $u \in S^*$ and $v \in S^+$ such that $\alpha = uv^\omega$. For an infinite word $\alpha \in S^\omega$, we write $\mathsf{inf}(\alpha) = \{s \in S \mid s = \alpha[i] \text{ for infinitely many } i\}$.

Languages. Given a finite alphabet Σ, a language L of finite words is a subset of Σ^*. A language L of infinite words over a finite alphabet Σ is a subset of Σ^ω. We restrict only to finite alphabets.

Probabilistic Automaton (PA). Informally, a PA is like a finite-state deterministic automaton except that the transition function from a state on a given input is described as a probability distribution which determines the probability of the next state.

Definition 1. A *finite state probabilistic automata* (PA) over a finite alphabet Σ is a tuple $\mathcal{A} = (Q, q_s, \delta, \mathsf{Acc})$ where Q is a finite set of *states*, $q_s \in Q$ is the *initial state*,

$\delta : Q \times \Sigma \times Q \to [0,1]$ is the *transition relation* such that for all $q \in Q$ and $a \in \Sigma$, $\delta(q,a,q')$ is a rational number and $\sum_{q' \in Q} \delta(q,a,q') = 1$, and Acc is an *acceptance condition*.

Notation: The transition function δ of PA $\mathcal{A}$ on input a can be seen as a square matrix δ_a of order $|Q|$ with the rows labeled by "current" state, columns labeled by "next state" and the entry $\delta_a(q,q')$ equal to $\delta(q,a,q')$. Given a word $u = a_0 a_1 \ldots a_n \in \Sigma^+$, δ_u is the matrix product $\delta_{a_0}\delta_{a_1}\ldots\delta_{a_n}$. For an empty word $\epsilon \in \Sigma^*$ we take δ_ϵ to be the identity matrix. Finally for any $Q_0 \subseteq Q$, we say that $\delta_u(q,Q_0) = \sum_{q' \in Q_0} \delta_u(q,q')$. Given a state $q \in Q$ and a word $u \in \Sigma^+$, $\mathsf{post}(q,u) = \{q' \mid \delta_u(q,q') > 0\}$. For a set $C \subseteq Q, post(C,u) = \cup_{q \in C}\, post(q,u)$.

Intuitively, the PA starts in the initial state q_s and if after reading $a_0, a_1 \ldots, a_i$ results in state q, then it moves to state q' with probability $\delta_{a_{i+1}}(q,q')$ on symbol a_{i+1}. A *run* of the PA $\mathcal{A}$ starting in a state $q \in Q$ on an input $\kappa \in \Sigma^* \cup \Sigma^\omega$ is a sequence $\rho \in Q^* \cup Q^\omega$ such that $|\rho| = 1 + |\kappa|$, $\rho[0] = q$ and for each $i \geq 0$, $\delta_{\kappa[i]}(\rho[i], \rho[i+1]) > 0$.

Given a word $\kappa \in \Sigma^* \cup \Sigma^\omega$, the PA $\mathcal{A}$ can be thought of as a (possibly infinite-state) (sub)-Markov chain. The set of states of this (sub)-Markov Chain is the set $\{(q,v) \mid q \in Q, v \in \mathit{Pref}(\kappa)\}$ and the probability of transitioning from (q,v) to (q',u) is $\delta_a(q,q')$ if $u = va$ for some $a \in \Sigma$ and 0 otherwise. This gives rise to the standard σ-algebra on Q^ω defined using cylinders and the standard probability measure on (sub)-Markov chains [14,11]. We shall henceforth denote the σ-algebra as $\mathcal{F}_{\mathcal{A},\kappa}$ and the probability measure as $\mu_{\mathcal{A},\kappa}$.

Acceptance Conditions and PA **Languages.** The language of a PA $\mathcal{A} = (Q, q_s, \delta, \mathsf{Acc})$ over an alphabet Σ is defined with respect to the acceptance condition Acc and a threshold $x \in [0,1]$. We consider three kinds of acceptance conditions.

Finite acceptance: When defining languages over finite words, the acceptance condition Acc is given in terms of a finite set $Q_f \subseteq Q$. In this case we call the PA $\mathcal{A}$, a probabilistic finite automaton (PFA). Given a finite acceptance condition $Q_f \subseteq Q$ and a finite word $u \in \Sigma^*$, a run ρ of $\mathcal{A}$ on u is said to be accepting if the last state of ρ is in Q_f. The set of accepting runs on $u \in \Sigma^*$ is measurable [14] and we shall denote its measure by $\mu^{acc,f}_{\mathcal{A},u}$. Note that $\mu^{acc,f}_{\mathcal{A},u} = \delta_u(q_s, Q_f)$. Given a rational threshold $x \in [0,1]$ and $\rhd \in \{\geq, >\}$, the language of finite words $\mathsf{L^f}_{\rhd x}(\mathcal{A}) = \{u \in \Sigma^* \mid \mu^{acc,f}_{\mathcal{A},u} \rhd x\}$ is the set of finite words accepted by $\mathcal{A}$ with probability $\rhd x$.

Büchi acceptance: Büchi acceptance condition defines languages over infinite words. For Büchi acceptance, the acceptance condition Acc is given in terms of a finite set $Q_f \subseteq Q$. In this case, we call the PA $\mathcal{A}$, a probabilistic Büchi automaton (PBA). Given a Büchi acceptance condition Q_f, a run ρ of $\mathcal{A}$ on an infinite word $\alpha \in \Sigma^\omega$ is said to be *accepting* if $\inf(\rho) \cap Q_f \neq \emptyset$. The set of accepting runs on $\alpha \in \Sigma^\omega$ is once again measurable [14] and we shall denote its measure by $\mu^{acc,b}_{\mathcal{A},\alpha}$. Given a rational threshold $x \in [0,1]$ and $\rhd \in \{\geq, >\}$, the language of infinite words $\mathsf{L^b}_{\rhd x}(\mathcal{A}) = \{\alpha \in \Sigma^\omega \mid \mu^{acc,b}_{\mathcal{A},\alpha} \rhd x\}$ is the set of infinite words accepted by PBA $\mathcal{A}$ with probability $\rhd x$.

Muller acceptance: For Muller acceptance, the acceptance condition Acc is given in terms of a finite set $F \subseteq 2^Q$. In this case, we call the PA $\mathcal{A}$, a probabilistic Muller

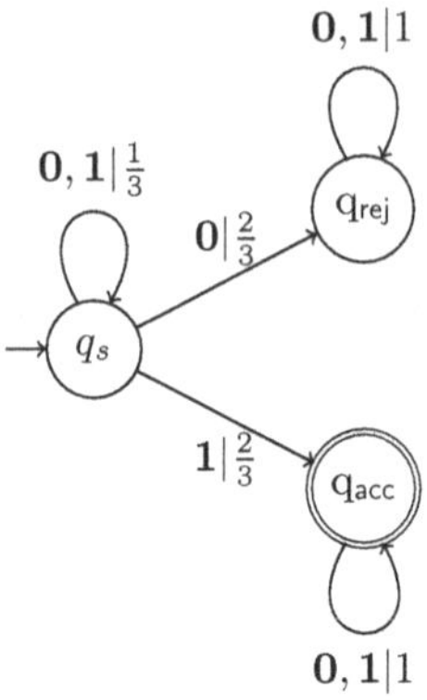

Fig. 1. PA $\mathcal{A}_{\mathsf{int}}$

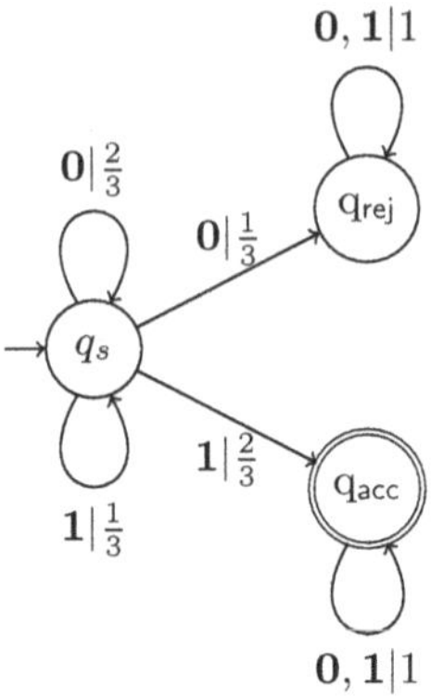

Fig. 2. PA $\mathcal{A}_{\frac{1}{3}}$

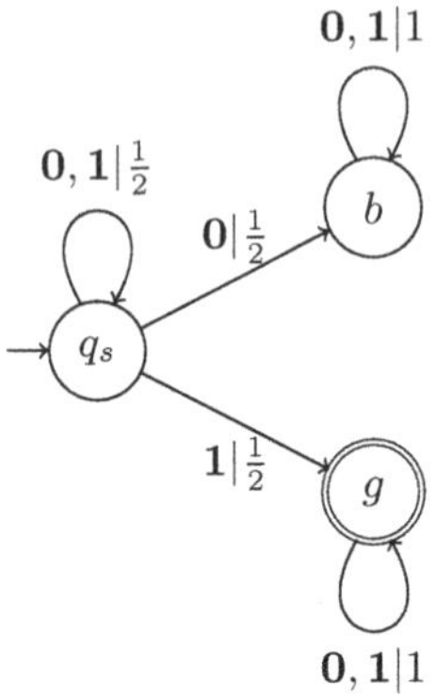

Fig. 3. PA $\mathcal{A}_{\text{Rabin}}$

automaton (PMA). Given a Muller acceptance condition $F \subseteq 2^Q$, a run ρ of $\mathcal{A}$ on an infinite word $\alpha \in \mathcal{A}$ is said to be *accepting* if $\mathsf{inf}(\rho) \in F$. Once again, the set of accepting runs are measurable [14]. Given a word α, the measure of the set of accepting runs is denoted by $\mu^{acc,m}_{\mathcal{A},\,\alpha}$. Given a a threshold $x \in [0,1]$ and $\rhd \in \{\geq, >\}$, the language of infinite words $\mathsf{L}^{\mathsf{m}}{}_{\rhd x}(\mathcal{A}) = \{\alpha \in \Sigma^\omega \,|\, \mu^{acc,m}_{\mathcal{A},\,\alpha} \rhd x\}$ is the set of infinite words accepted by PMA $\mathcal{A}$ with probability $\rhd x$.

2.1 Hierarchical Probabilistic Automata

Intuitively, a hierarchical probabilistic automaton is a PA such that the set of its states can be stratified into (totally) ordered levels. From a state q, for each letter a, the machine can transition with non-zero probability to at most one state in the same level as q, and all other probabilistic successors belong to a higher level. We define such automata for the special case when the states are partitioned into two levels (level 0 and level 1).

Definition 2. A 1-*level hierarchical probabilistic automaton* HPA is a probabilistic automaton $\mathcal{A} = (Q, q_s, \delta, \mathsf{Acc})$ over alphabet Σ such that Q can be partitioned into two sets Q_0 and Q_1 with the following properties.

- $q_s \in Q_0$,
- For every $q \in Q_0$ and $a \in \Sigma$, $|\mathsf{post}(q, a) \cap Q_0| \leq 1$
- For every $q \in Q_1$ and $a \in \Sigma$, $\mathsf{post}(q, a) \subseteq Q_1$ and $|\mathsf{post}(q, a)| = 1$.

Given a 1-level HPA $\mathcal{A}$, we will denote the level 0 and level 1 states by the sets Q_0 and Q_1 respectively.

Example 1. Consider the PAs $\mathcal{A}_{\mathsf{int}}$, $\mathcal{A}_{\frac{1}{3}}$, and $\mathcal{A}_{\mathsf{Rabin}}$ shown in Figs. 1, 2, and 3 respectively. All three automata have the same set of states ($\{q_s, \mathsf{q_{acc}}, \mathsf{q_{rej}}\}$), same initial state ($q_s$), same alphabet ($\{\mathbf{0}, \mathbf{1}\}$), the same acceptance condition ($Q_f = \{\mathsf{q_{acc}}\}$ if finite/Büchi, and $F = \{\{q_{acc}\}\}$ if Muller) and the same transition structure. The only difference is in the probability of transitions out of q_s. All three of these automata are (1-level) HPAs; we can take $Q_0 = \{q_s\}$, and $Q_1 = \{q_{acc}, q_{rej}\}$. Though all three are very similar automata, we will show that $\mathcal{A}_{int}$ and $\mathcal{A}_{Rabin}$ are symptomatic of automata that accept only regular languages (with rational thresholds), while the other ($\mathcal{A}_{\frac{1}{3}}$) accepts non-regular languages (with rational thresholds). The automata $\mathcal{A}_{Rabin}$ was originally presented in [13] and it is known to accept a non-regular language with an *irrational threshold* [13,3]. Similarly it can be shown that $\mathcal{A}_{int}$ also accepts a non-regular language with an irrational threshold.

Notation: For the rest of the paper, by a HPA we shall mean 1-level HPA, unless otherwise stated.

Let us fix a HPA $\mathcal{A} = (Q, q_s, \delta, \mathsf{Acc})$ over alphabet Σ with Q_0 and Q_1 being the level 0 and level 1 states. Observe that given any state $q \in Q_0$ and any word $\kappa \in \Sigma^* \cup \Sigma^\omega$, $\mathcal{A}$ has at most one run ρ on α where all states in ρ belong to Q_0. We now present a couple of useful definitions. A set $W \subseteq Q$ is said to be a *witness* set if W has at most one level 0 state, i.e., $|W \cap Q_0| \leq 1$. Observe that for any word $u \in \Sigma^*$, $\mathsf{post}(q_s, u)$ is a witness set, i.e., $|\mathsf{post}(q_s, u) \cap Q_0| \leq 1$. We will say a word $\kappa \in \Sigma^* \cup \Sigma^\omega$ (depending on whether $\mathcal{A}$ is an automaton on finite or infinite words) is *definitely accepted* from witness set W iff for every $q \in W$ with $q \in Q_i$ (for $i \in \{0, 1\}$) there is an accepting run ρ on κ starting from q such that for every j, $\rho[j] \in Q_i$ and $\delta_{\kappa[j]}(\rho[j], \rho[j+1]) = 1$. In other words, κ is definitely accepted from witness set W if and only if κ is accepted from every state q in W by a run where you stay in the same level as q, and all transitions in the run are taken with probability 1. Observe that the set of all words definitely accepted from a witness set W is regular.

Proposition 1. *For any* HPA $\mathcal{A}$ *and witness set* W*, the language*

$$\mathsf{L}_W = \{\kappa \mid \kappa \textit{ is definitely accepted by } \mathcal{A} \textit{ from } W\}$$

is regular.

Observe that $\mathsf{L}_W = \cap_{q \in W} \mathsf{L}_{\{q\}}$ and $\mathsf{L}_\emptyset$ (as defined above) is the set of all strings. Thus, the emptiness of L_W can be checked in **PSPACE**.

Proposition 2. *For any* HPA $\mathcal{A}$ *and witness set* W*, the problem of checking the emptiness of* L_W *(as defined in Proposition 1) is in* **PSPACE**.

For a set $C \subseteq Q_1$, a threshold $x \in (0, 1)$, and a word $u \in \Sigma^*$, we will find it useful to define the following quantity $\mathsf{val}(C, x, u)$ given as follows. If $\delta_u(q_s, Q_0) \neq 0$ then

$$\mathsf{val}(C, x, u) = \frac{x - \delta_u(q_s, C)}{\delta_u(q_s, Q_0)}.$$

On the other hand, if $\delta_u(q_s, Q_0) = 0$ then

$$\mathsf{val}(C, x, u) = \begin{cases} +\infty & \text{if } \delta_u(q_s, C) < x \\ 0 & \text{if } \delta_u(q_s, C) = x \\ -\infty & \text{if } \delta_u(q_s, C) > x \end{cases}.$$

The quantity $\mathsf{val}(C, x, u)$ measures the fraction of $\delta_u(q_s, Q_0)$ that still needs to move to C such that the probability of reaching C exceeds the threshold x. This intuition is captured by the following proposition whose proof follows immediately from the definition of $\mathsf{val}(C, x, u)$.

Proposition 3. *Consider a* HPA $\mathcal{A}$ *with threshold* x*, and words* $u, v \in \Sigma^*$*. Let* $C, D \subseteq Q_1$ *such that* $\mathsf{post}(C, v) = D$*. The following properties hold.*

- *If* $\mathsf{val}(C, x, u) < 0$ *then* $\delta_{uv}(q_s, D) > x$*.*
- *If* $\mathsf{val}(C, x, u) = 0$ *then* $\delta_u(q_s, C) = x$*.*

Witness sets and the value function play an important role in deciding whether a word κ is accepted by a HPA. In particular, κ is accepted iff κ can be divided into strings u, κ' such that $\mathcal{A}$ reaches a witness set W with "sufficient probability" on u, and κ' is definitely accepted from W. We state this intuition precisely next.

Proposition 4. *For a* HPA $\mathcal{A}$*, threshold* $x \in [0, 1]$*, and word* κ*,* $\kappa \in \mathsf{L}^{\mathsf{a}}{}_{>x}(\mathcal{A})$ *(where* $\mathsf{a} \in \{\mathsf{f}, \mathsf{b}, \mathsf{m}\}$*) if and only if there is a witness set* W*,* $u \in \Sigma^*$ *and* $\kappa' \in \Sigma^* \cup \Sigma^\omega$ *such that* $\kappa = u\kappa'$*,* κ' *is definitely accepted by* $\mathcal{A}$ *from* W*, and one of the following holds.*

- *Either* $W \subseteq Q_1$ *and* $\mathsf{val}(W, x, u) < 0$*, or*
- $W \cap Q_0 \neq \emptyset$ *and* $0 \leq \mathsf{val}(W \cap Q_1, x, u) < 1$*.*

3 Expressiveness and Decidability

One-level HPAs have a very simple transition structure. In spite of this, we will show that HPA can recognize non-regular languages (Section 3.1). Even though it has been shown before that PFAs [12,13] and PBAs [10,2] recognize non-regular languages, all the examples before, use either more complex automata or irrational acceptance thresholds or HPAs with more than two levels. We shall then show that even though HPAs can recognize non-regular languages, nevertheless the emptiness and universality problems of HPAs are decidable (Section 3.2).

3.1 Non-regular Languages Expressed by 1-level HPA

We will now show that HPA can recognize non-regular languages, under both finite acceptance and Büchi acceptance conditions. We consider a special type of HPA which we shall call *simple absorbing* HPA (SAHPA).

Definition 3. *Let* $\mathcal{A} = (Q, q_s, \delta, \mathsf{Acc})$ *be a* HPA *over an alphabet* Σ *with* Q_0 *and* Q_1 *as the sets of states at level* 0 *and* 1 *respectively.* $\mathcal{A}$ *is said to be a* simple absorbing HPA *(*SAHPA*) if*

- $Q_0 = \{q_s\}, Q_1 = \{\mathsf{q_{acc}}, \mathsf{q_{rej}}\}$*.*
- *The states* $\mathsf{q_{acc}}, \mathsf{q_{rej}}$ *are absorbing, i.e., for each* $a \in \Sigma$*,* $\delta_a(\mathsf{q_{acc}}, \mathsf{q_{acc}}) = 1$ *and* $\delta_a(\mathsf{q_{rej}}, \mathsf{q_{rej}}) = 1$*.*

For an $\kappa \in \Sigma^* \cup \Sigma^\omega$, $\text{GoodRuns}(\kappa)$ *is the set of runs* ρ *of* $\mathcal{A}$ *on* κ *such there is an* $i \geq 0$ *with* $\rho(j) = \mathsf{q}_{\mathsf{acc}}$ *for all* $i \leq j \leq |\kappa|$. *A word* $\alpha \in \Sigma^\omega$ *is said to be* always alive *for* $\mathcal{A}$ *iff for each* $i > 0$, $\delta_{\alpha[0:i]}(q_s, q_s) > 0$.

Example 2. All three automata $\mathcal{A}_{\mathsf{int}}$, $\mathcal{A}_{\frac{1}{3}}$ and $\mathcal{A}_{\mathsf{Rabin}}$ (Example 1) shown in Figs. 1, 2, and 3 are simple absorbing HPAs.

The following lemma states some important properties satisfied by SAHPA.

Lemma 1. *Let* $\mathcal{A} = (Q, q_s, \delta, \mathsf{Acc})$ *be a* SAHPA *over an alphabet* Σ *with* Q_0 *and* Q_1 *as the sets of states at level* 0 *and* 1 *respectively. For any always alive* $\alpha \in \Sigma^\omega$,

1. *if* α *is ultimately periodic and* $\mu_{\mathcal{A},\alpha}(\text{GoodRuns}(\alpha)) = x$ *then the set* $\{\mathsf{val}(\{\mathsf{q}_{\mathsf{acc}}\}, x, \alpha[0:i]) \mid i \in \mathbb{N}, i \geq 0\}$ *is a finite set,*
2. *if* $\lim_{i\to\infty} \delta_{\alpha[0:i]}(q_s, q_s) = 0$ *and* $x \in (0,1)$ *then* $\mu_{\mathcal{A},\alpha}(\text{GoodRuns}(\alpha)) = x \Leftrightarrow \forall i \geq 0, \mathsf{val}(\{\mathsf{q}_{\mathsf{acc}}\}, x, \alpha[0:i]) \in [0,1]$.

Now, we shall show that SAHPA can recognize non-regular languages. We start by recalling a result originally proved in [13]. Let $\Sigma = \{\mathbf{0}, \mathbf{1}\}$. Any word $\kappa \in \Sigma^* \cup \Sigma^\omega$ can be thought of as the binary representation of a number in the unit interval $[0, 1]$ by placing a decimal in front of it. Formally,

Definition 4. *Let* $\Sigma = \{\mathbf{0}, \mathbf{1}\}$. *The map* $\Sigma^* \cup \Sigma^\omega \to [0,1]$ *is the unique map such that* $\mathsf{bin}(\epsilon) = 0$ *and* $\mathsf{bin}(a\kappa_1) = \frac{\bar{a}}{2} + \frac{1}{2}\mathsf{bin}(\kappa_1)$, *where* $\bar{a} = 0$ *if* $a = \mathbf{0}$ *and* 1 *otherwise.*

Note that $\mathsf{bin}(\alpha)$ is irrational iff α is an infinite word which is not ultimately periodic. The following is shown in [13].

Theorem 1. $\Sigma = \{\mathbf{0}, \mathbf{1}\}$ *and* $\alpha \in \Sigma^\omega$ *be a word which is not ultimately periodic. Given* $\rhd \in \{>, \geq\}$,

- $\{u \in \Sigma^* \mid \mathsf{bin}(u) \rhd \mathsf{bin}(\alpha)\}$ *is not regular.*
- $\{\gamma \in \Sigma^\omega \mid \mathsf{bin}(\gamma) \rhd \mathsf{bin}(\alpha)\}$ *is not* ω*-regular.*

We make some observations about the automaton $\mathcal{A}_{\frac{1}{3}}$ shown in Fig. 2 in Lemma 2.

Lemma 2. *Let* $\mathcal{A}_{\frac{1}{3}}$ *be the* SAHPA *over the alphabet* $\Sigma = \{\mathbf{0}, \mathbf{1}\}$ *defined in Example 1. Let* $\alpha \in \Sigma^\omega$ *be such that* α *is not an ultimately periodic word. We have that for each* $\kappa \in \Sigma^* \cup \Sigma^\omega$,

$$\mathsf{bin}(\kappa) < \mathsf{bin}(\alpha) \Leftrightarrow \mu_{\mathcal{A},\kappa}(\text{GoodRuns}(\kappa)) < \mu_{\mathcal{A},\alpha}(\text{GoodRuns}(\alpha))$$

and

$$\mathsf{bin}(\kappa) > \mathsf{bin}(\alpha) \Leftrightarrow \mu_{\mathcal{A},\kappa}(\text{GoodRuns}(\kappa)) > \mu_{\mathcal{A},\alpha}(\text{GoodRuns}(\alpha)).$$

We have:

Theorem 2. *Consider the* SAHPA $\mathcal{A}_{\frac{1}{3}}$ *over the alphabet* $\Sigma = \{\mathbf{0}, \mathbf{1}\}$ *defined in Example 1. Consider the finite acceptance condition and the Büchi acceptance condition defined by setting* $\mathsf{Acc} = \{\mathsf{q}_{\mathsf{acc}}\}$. *Given* $\rhd \in \{>, \geq\}$, *we have that the language of finite words* $\mathsf{L^f}_{\rhd\frac{1}{2}}(\mathcal{A})$ *is not regular and the language of infinite words* $\mathsf{L^b}_{\rhd\frac{1}{2}}(\mathcal{A})$ *is not* ω*-regular.*

Proof. Given $u \in \Sigma^*$, we shall denote $\mathsf{val}(\{\mathsf{q_{acc}}\}, \frac{1}{2}, u)$ by val_u. We observe some properties of the value val_u.

Claim (A). For any $u \in \Sigma^*$,

- $\mathsf{val}_{u\mathbf{0}} = \frac{3}{2}\mathsf{val}_u$ and $\mathsf{val}_{u\mathbf{1}} = 3\mathsf{val}_u - 2$.
- If $\mathsf{val}_u \in [0,1]$ then it is of the form $\frac{p}{2^i}$ where p is an odd number and $i-1$ is the number of occurrences of $\mathbf{0}$ in u.
- $\mathsf{val}_u \notin \{0, 1, \frac{2}{3}\}$.

Proof. The first part of the claim follows from observing that $\delta_{u\mathbf{0}}(q_s, q_s) = \frac{2}{3}\delta_u(q_s, q_s)$, $\delta_{u\mathbf{0}}(q_s, \mathsf{q_{acc}}) = \delta_u(q_s, \mathsf{q_{acc}}), \delta_{u\mathbf{1}}(q_s, q_s) = \frac{1}{3}\delta_u(q_s, q_s)$ and that $\delta_{u\mathbf{1}}(q_s, \mathsf{q_{acc}}) = \delta_u(q_s, \mathsf{q_{acc}}) + \delta_u(q_s, q_s)\frac{2}{3}$. The second part can be shown easily by an induction on the length of u using the first part of the claim. (Observe that the base case is $\mathsf{bin}(\epsilon) = \frac{1}{2}$). The third part of the claim is an easy consequence of the second part. (End: Proof of Claim (A)) □

We now show that there is exactly one word $\beta \in \Sigma^\omega$ such that $\mu_{\mathcal{A},\beta}(\text{GoodRuns}(\beta)) = \frac{1}{2}$. As each $\alpha \in \Sigma^\omega$ is always alive and $\lim_{i\to\infty} \delta_{\alpha[0:i]}(q_s, q_s) = 0$, it follows from Lemma 1 and Claim (A) that it suffices to show that there is exactly one word $\beta \in \Sigma^\omega$ such that $\forall i \geq 0$, $\mathsf{val}_{\beta[0:i]} \in (0,1)$.

We prove this by constructing β, starting from the empty word and showing that it can be extended one letter at a time in exactly one way. Clearly, thanks to Claim (A), since $\mathsf{val}_{\mathbf{0}} = \frac{3}{4}$ and $\mathsf{val}_{\mathbf{1}} = -\frac{1}{2}$, $\beta[0]$ should be $\mathbf{0}$. Suppose we have constructed $\beta[0:i]$. Now, thanks to Claim (A) if $0 < \mathsf{val}_{\beta[0:i]} < \frac{2}{3}$ then $0 < \mathsf{val}_{\beta[0:i]\mathbf{0}} < \frac{3}{2}\frac{2}{3} = 1$ and $\mathsf{val}_{\beta[0:i]\mathbf{1}} < 3\frac{2}{3} - 2 < 0$. If $\frac{2}{3} < \mathsf{val}_{\beta[0:i]} < 1$ then $\mathsf{val}_{\beta[0:i]\mathbf{0}} > \frac{3}{2}\frac{2}{3} = 1$ and $0 = 3\frac{2}{3} - 2 < \mathsf{val}_{\beta[0:i]\mathbf{1}} < 3.1 - 2 = 1$. Thus if $\mathsf{val}_{\beta[0:i]} < \frac{2}{3}$ then $\beta[i+1]$ has to be $\mathbf{0}$, otherwise $\beta[i+1]$ has to be $\mathbf{1}$. Thus, we see that there is exactly one word $\beta \in \Sigma^\omega$ such that $\mu_{\mathcal{A},\beta}(\text{GoodRuns}(\beta)) = \frac{1}{2}$. We shall now show that the values $\mathsf{val}_{\beta[0:i]}$ are all distinct.

Claim (B). For each i, j such that $i \neq j$, $\mathsf{val}_{\beta[0:i]} \neq \mathsf{val}_{\beta[0:j]}$.

Proof. Fix i, j. Without loss of generality, we can assume that $j > i$. Note that thanks to Claim (A) that if there is an occurrence of $\mathbf{0}$ in $\beta[i+1:j]$ then $\mathsf{val}_{\beta[0:i]} \neq \mathsf{val}_{\beta[0:j]}$. If there is no occurrence of $\mathbf{0}$ in $\beta[i+1:j]$ then every letter of $\beta[i+1:j]$ must be a $\mathbf{1}$. Thus, the result will follow if we can show that for each $i+1 \leq k < j$, we have that $\mathsf{val}_{\beta[1:k]\mathbf{1}} < \mathsf{val}_{\beta[1:k]}$. Using Claim (A), we have that

$$\mathsf{val}_{\beta[1:k]\mathbf{1}} < \mathsf{val}_{\beta[1:k]} \Leftrightarrow 3\mathsf{val}_{\beta[1:k]} - 2 < \mathsf{val}_{\beta[1:k]} \Leftrightarrow \mathsf{val}_{\beta[1:k]} < 1.$$

Now $\mathsf{val}_{\beta[1:k]} < 1$ by construction of β. The claim follows. (End: Proof of Claim (B)) □

Now, thanks to Lemma 1 and Claim (B), we have that β is not ultimately periodic. The result follows from Lemma 2 and Theorem 1. □

Remark 1. Note that since any Büchi acceptance condition can be converted into an equivalent Muller acceptance condition, HPAs also recognize non-regular languages under Muller acceptance conditions.

3.2 Decision Problems for 1-level HPA

We now show that the problems of checking emptiness and universality for HPAs are decidable, more specifically, they are in **EXPTIME**. We start by considering emptiness for the language $\mathsf{L^a}_{>x}(\mathcal{A})$ for a HPA $\mathcal{A}$. In order to construct the decision procedure for this language, we need to consider special kinds of witness sets. We will say that a witness set W is *good* if the language L_W defined in Proposition 1 is non-empty. We have the following.

Proposition 5. *Give a* HPA $\mathcal{A} = (Q, q_s, \delta, \mathsf{Acc})$*, threshold* $x \in [0,1]$ *and* $\mathsf{a} \in \{\mathsf{f}, \mathsf{b}, \mathsf{m}\}$*, the language* $\mathsf{L^a}_{>x}(\mathcal{A}) \neq \emptyset$ *iff there is a word* $u \in \Sigma^*$ *and a good non-empty set* H *such that* $\delta_u(q_s, H) > x$*.*

The decision procedure for checking emptiness (or rather non-emptiness) will search for a word u as in Proposition 5. The following lemma shows that, it is enough to search for words of exponential length.

Lemma 3. *Let* $\mathcal{A} = (Q, q_s, \delta, \mathsf{Acc})$ *be an* HPA *with* n *states (i.e.,* $|Q| = n$*) such that all the transition probabilities of* $\mathcal{A}$ *have size at most* r [1]*. Let* $x \in [0,1]$ *be a rational threshold of size at most* r*. For any* $\mathsf{a} \in \{\mathsf{f}, \mathsf{b}, \mathsf{m}\}$*,* $\mathsf{L^a}_{>x}(\mathcal{A}) \neq \emptyset$ *iff there is a finite word* u *and a good non-empty set* H*, such that* $|u| \leq 4rn8^n$ *and* $\delta_u(q_s, H) > x$*.*

Proof. Observe that if there is a finite word u and a good non-empty set H such that $\delta_u(q_s, H) > x$ then by Proposition 5, $\mathsf{L^a}_{>x}(\mathcal{A}) \neq \emptyset$. Thus, we only need to prove that nonemptiness of $\mathsf{L^a}_{>x}(\mathcal{A})$ guarantees the existence of u and H as in the lemma.

Let $gwords = \{(s, G) \mid G \neq \emptyset, G \text{ is good and } \delta_s(q_s, G) > x\}$. By Proposition 5, $gwords$ is non-empty. Fix $(s, G) \in gwords$ such that for every $(s_1, G_1) \in gwords$, $|s| \leq |s_1|$, i.e., s is the shortest word appearing in a pair in $gwords$. Note if $|s| \leq 2^n$ then the lemma follows.

Let us consider the case when $|s| > 2^n$. Let $k_1 = |s| - 1$. Observe that by our notation, $s = s[0:k_1]$. Now, for any $0 \leq i \leq k_1$, let $Y_i = \mathsf{post}(q_s, s[0:i]) \cap Q_1$ and $X_i = \{q \in Y_i : \mathsf{post}(q, s[i+1:k_1]) \subseteq G\}$. Note that $X_i \subseteq Y_i$ and is good. Since $|s| > 2^n$ and $\mathcal{A}$ has n states, there must be i, j with $i < j \leq k_1$ such $X_i = X_j$ and $\mathsf{post}(q_s, s[0:i]) \cap Q_0 = \mathsf{post}(q_s, s[0:j]) \cap Q_0$. If $\mathsf{post}(q_s, s[0:i]) \cap Q_0 = \emptyset$ then it is easy to see that $(s[0:i]s[j+1:k_1], G) \in gwords$ contradicting the fact that s is the shortest such word. Hence, fix j to be the smallest integer such that for some $i < j$, $X_i = X_j$ and $\mathsf{post}(q_s, s[0:i]) \cap Q_0 = \mathsf{post}(q_s, s[0:j]) \cap Q_0 \neq \emptyset$. Let q be the unique state in $\mathsf{post}(q_s, s[0:i]) \cap Q_0$.

Let $s[0:i] = v, s[i+1:j] = w, s[j+1:k_1] = t$; thus, $s = vwt$. Now, let $z_1 = \delta_v(q_s, X_i)$ and $y_1 = \delta_v(q_s, Q_1)$. Similarly, let $z_2 = \delta_w(q, X_j)$, $y_2 = \delta_w(q, Q_1)$ and $z_3 = \delta_t(q, G)$. Since $X_i, X_j \subseteq Q_1$, $z_1 \leq y_1$ and $z_2 \leq y_2$. Also note that $|w| > 0$ by construction of j and that $y_2 = \delta_w(q, Q_1) > 0$ (by the minimality of length of s).

For any integer $\ell \geq 0$, let $u_\ell = vw^\ell$ and $s_\ell = u_\ell t$. Note that $u_0 = v$ and $s_1 = s$. Let $\ell > 0$. We observe that

$$\delta_{s_\ell}(q_s, G) = \delta_{u_{(\ell-1)}}(q_s, X_i) + (1 - \delta_{u_{(\ell-1)}}(q_s, Q_1)) \cdot z_2 + (1 - \delta_{u_\ell}(q_s, Q_1)) \cdot z_3$$

[1] We say a rational number s has size r iff there are integers m, n such that $s = \frac{m}{n}$ and the binary representation of m and n has at most r-bits.

and

$$\delta_{s_{(\ell-1)}}(q_s, G) = \delta_{u_{(\ell-1)}}(q_s, X_i) + (1 - \delta_{u_{(\ell-1)}}(q_s, Q_1)) \cdot z_3. \tag{1}$$

Therefore,

$$\delta_{s_\ell}(q_s, G) - \delta_{s_{(\ell-1)}}(q_s, G) = (1 - \delta_{u_{(\ell-1)}}(q_s, Q_1)) \cdot z_2 - \\ (\delta_{u_\ell}(q_s, Q_1) - \delta_{u_{(\ell-1)}}(q_s, Q_1)) \cdot z_3.$$

In addition, $\delta_{u_\ell}(q_s, Q_1) = \delta_{u_{(\ell-1)}}(q_s, Q_1) + (1 - \delta_{u_{(\ell-1)}}(q_s, Q_1)) \cdot y_2$ and hence $\delta_{u_\ell}(q_s, Q_1) - \delta_{u_{(\ell-1)}}(q_s, Q_1) = (1 - \delta_{u_{(\ell-1)}}(q_s, Q_1)) \cdot y_2$ Putting all the above together, we get for all $\ell > 0$,

$$\delta_{s_\ell}(q_s, G) - \delta_{s_{(\ell-1)}}(q_s, G) = (1 - \delta_{u_{(\ell-1)}}(q_s, Q_1)) \cdot (z_2 - y_2 \cdot z_3).$$

Since $s = s_1$ is the shortest word in $gwords$ and $s_0 = vt$ is a strictly smaller word than s_1, we must have that $\delta_{s_0}(q_s, G) \leq x$ and hence $\delta_{s_1}(q_s, G) > \delta_{s_0}(q_s, G)$. From this and the above equality, we see that $(1 - \delta_{u_0}(q_s, Q_1)) > 0$ and that $(z_2 - y_2 \cdot z_3) > 0$. This also means that, for all $\ell > 0$, $\delta_{s_\ell}(q_s, G) \geq \delta_{s_{(\ell-1)}}(q_s, G)$. Hence, $\lim_{\ell \to \infty} \delta_{s_\ell}(q_s, G)$ exists and is $\geq \delta_{s_1}(q_s, G)$. Since $s_1 = s$, we get that $\lim_{\ell \to \infty} \delta_{s_\ell}(q_s, G) > x$.

Observe that $\delta_w(q, Q_1) > 0$. Hence, one can show that $\lim_{\ell \to \infty} (1 - \delta_{u_{(\ell-1)}}(q_s, Q_1)) = 0$. This along with Equation (1) means that $\lim_{\ell \to \infty} \delta_{s_\ell}(q_s, G) = \lim_{\ell \to \infty} \delta_{u_\ell}(q_s, X_i)$. The right hand side of this equation is seen to be $z_1 + (1 - y_1) \cdot \frac{z_2}{y_2}$ and since $\lim_{\ell \to \infty} \delta_{s_\ell}(q_s, G) > x$, we get that $z_1 + (1 - y_1) \cdot \frac{z_2}{y_2} > x$. Observe that X_i is a good set. Let m be the minimum ℓ such that $\delta_{u_\ell}(q_s, X_i) > x$. Now, we show that the length of u_m is bounded by $4rn8^n$ and hence the lemma is satisfied by taking u to be u_m and H to be X_i. Observe that

$$\delta_{u_\ell}(q_s, X_i) = z_1 + (1 - y_1) \cdot (1 - (1 - y_2)^\ell) \cdot \frac{z_2}{y_2}.$$

From this, we see that m is the minimum ℓ such that

$$(1 - y_2)^\ell < 1 - \frac{(x - z_1)y_2}{(1 - y_1)z_2}.$$

That is, m is the minimum ℓ such that $\ell > \frac{\log(n_1)}{\log(n_2)}$, where

$$n_1 = \frac{(1-y_1)z_2}{(1-y_1)z_2-(x-z_1)y_2} \text{ and } n_2 = \frac{1}{(1-y_2)}.$$

Now, observe that the probability of a run ρ of $\mathcal{A}$ starting from any state, on an input string of length at most 2^n is a product of 2^n fractions of the form $\frac{m_1}{m_2}$ where m_i, for $i = 1, 2$, is an integer bounded by 2^r. Hence the probability of such a run is itself a fraction whose numerator and denominator are bounded by 2^{r2^n}. Second, in an HPA with n states, on any input of length k, there are at most kn different runs; this is because once the run reaches a state in Q_1 the future is deterministic, and for any prefix, there is at most one run in a state in Q_0. Hence, $\delta_v(q_s, Q_1)$ is the sum of at most $n2^n$ such fractions. Therefore, y_1 is a fraction whose numerator and denominator are integers bounded by 2^{rn4^n}. By a similar argument, we see that z_1, y_2, z_2 are also fractions whose numerators and denominators are similarly bounded. Now, it should be easy to see that n_1 is bounded by 2^{4rn4^n} and hence $m \leq 4rn4^n$. Now, the length of $u_m = |vw| + (m-1)|w|$ which is easily seen to be bounded $m2^n$ since $|vw|$ and $|w|$ are bounded by 2^n. Hence $u_m \leq 4rn8^n$. □

Now, we have the following theorem.

Theorem 3. *Given a* HPA $\mathcal{A} = (Q, q_s, \delta, \mathsf{Acc})$*, a rational threshold* $x \in [0,1]$ *and* $\mathsf{a} \in \{\mathsf{f}, \mathsf{b}, \mathsf{m}\}$*, the problem of determining if* $\mathsf{L^a}_{>x}(\mathcal{A}) = \emptyset$ *is in* **EXPTIME**.

Proof. It suffices to show that the problem of determining if $\mathsf{L^a}_{>x}(\mathcal{A}) \neq \emptyset$ is in **EXPTIME**. Let $\mathcal{X}$ be the collection of all witness sets U such that $U \cap Q_0 \neq \emptyset$ and $U \cap Q_1$ is a good set; for a witness set $U \in \mathcal{X}$, we will denote by q_U the unique state in $U \cap Q_0$. Let $\mathcal{Y}$ be the collection of good witness sets. For $U \in \mathcal{X}$ and natural number $i > 0$, let

$$\mathsf{Prob}(U, i) = \max\{\delta_u(q_U, W) \mid u \in \Sigma^*,\ W \in \mathcal{Y},\ \mathsf{post}(U \cap Q_1, u) \subseteq W,\ |u| \leq i\}.$$

In the above definition, we take the maximum of the empty set to be 0. Let k be the bound given by Lemma 3 for the length of the word u. Lemma 3 implies that $\mathsf{L^a}_{>x}(\mathcal{A}) \neq \emptyset$ iff $\mathsf{Prob}(\{q_s\}, k) > x$. This observation yields a simple algorithm to check non-emptiness: compute $\mathsf{Prob}(\{q_s\}, k)$ and check if it is greater than x.

$\mathsf{Prob}(\cdot,\cdot)$ can be computed by an iterative dynamic programming algorithm as follows.

$$\begin{aligned}\mathsf{Prob}(U, 1) &= \max\{\delta_a(q_U, W) \mid a \in \Sigma,\ W \in \mathcal{Y},\ \mathsf{post}(U \cap Q_1, a) \subseteq W\}\\ \mathsf{Prob}(U, i+1) &= \max\big(\{\mathsf{Prob}(U, i)\} \bigcup \\ &\qquad \{\delta_a(q_U, q_V)\mathsf{Prob}(V, i) + \delta_a(q_U, V \cap Q_1) \mid a \in \Sigma,\ V \in \mathcal{X},\\ &\qquad\qquad \mathsf{post}(U \cap Q_1, a) \subseteq V\}\big).\end{aligned}$$

Let us analyze the algorithm computing $\mathsf{Prob}(\cdot,\cdot)$. Let us assume that $\mathcal{A}$ has n states, and that $\delta_a(p, q)$ is of size at most r for any $a \in \Sigma$ and $p, q \in Q$. Thus, $\mathcal{X}$ and $\mathcal{Y}$ have cardinality at most 2^n, and by Proposition 2, the sets $\mathcal{X}$ and $\mathcal{Y}$ can be computed in **EXPTIME** (in fact, even in **PSPACE**). In addition, because $|\mathcal{X}|$, $|\mathcal{Y}| \leq 2^n$, the maximum in the above equations for computing Prob is over at most $O(2^n)$ terms. Thus, we would get an exponential time bound provided the arithmetic operations needed to compute Prob can also be carried out in exponential time. This requires us to bound the size of the numbers involved in computing $\mathsf{Prob}(U, i)$. Observe that for any witness set W and $q \in Q$, $\delta_a(q, W)$ is the sum of at most n rational numbers and so has size at most $r + n$. Hence, we can inductively show that the size of $\mathsf{Prob}(U, i)$ (for any U) is a rational number of size at most $2i(r+n)$. Since $i \leq k$ and k is at most exponential in n (by Lemma 3), the dynamic programming algorithm is in **EXPTIME**. □

The emptiness problem for the languages $\mathsf{L^a}_{\geq x}(\mathcal{A})$ can be shown to be decidable using similar methods.

Theorem 4. *Given a* HPA $\mathcal{A}$*, a rational threshold* $x \in [0,1]$ *and* $\mathsf{a} \in \{\mathsf{f}, \mathsf{b}, \mathsf{m}\}$*, the problem of determining if* $\mathsf{L^a}_{\geq x}(\mathcal{A}) = \emptyset$ *is in* **EXPTIME**.

Now, we give the following lower bound results for checking non-emptiness of the languages $\mathsf{L^a}_{\rhd x}(\mathcal{A}) \neq \emptyset$ for $\rhd \in \{>, \geq\}$.

Theorem 5. *Given a* HPA $\mathcal{A}$, $\mathsf{a} \in \{\mathsf{f}, \mathsf{b}, \mathsf{m}\}$, $\rhd \in \{>, \geq\}$, *the problem of determining if* $\mathsf{L^a}_{\rhd x}(\mathcal{A}) \neq \emptyset$ *is* **PSPACE**-*hard.*

Theorem 3 and Theorem 4 yield that checking non-universality is also decidable.

Theorem 6. *Given a* HPA $\mathcal{A}$, $\mathsf{a} \in \{\mathsf{f}, \mathsf{b}, \mathsf{m}\}$, $\rhd \in \{>, \geq\}$, *the problem of checking universality of the language* $\mathsf{L^a}_{\rhd x}(\mathcal{A})$ *is in* **EXPTIME** *and is* **PSPACE**-*hard.*

4 Integer HPAs

In the previous section we saw that even though (1-level) HPAs have a very simple transition structure, their ability to toss coins allows them to recognize non-regular languages. In this section, we will show that if we restrict the numbers that appear as transition probabilities in the automaton, then the HPA can only recognize regular languages (see Theorem 7). We will also show that the problems of checking emptiness and universality of this class of HPAs are **PSPACE**-complete (see Theorem 8). We will call this restricted class of HPAs, integer HPAs.

Definition 5. *An* integer HPA *is a (1-level)* HPA $\mathcal{A} = (Q, q_s, \delta, \mathsf{Acc})$ *over alphabet* Σ *with* Q_0 *and* Q_1 *being the level 0 and level 1 states, respectively, such that for every* $q \in Q_0$ *and* $a \in \Sigma$, *if* $\mathsf{post}(q, a) \cap Q_0$ *is non-empty and equal to* $\{q'\}$, *then for every* $q'' \in Q_1$, $\delta_a(q, q'')$ *is an integer multiple of* $\delta_a(q, q')$.

Example 3. Consider automata $\mathcal{A}_{\mathsf{int}}$, $\mathcal{A}_{\frac{1}{3}}$, and $\mathcal{A}_{\mathsf{Rabin}}$ from Example 1 that are shown in Figs. 1, 2, and 3. Observe that $\mathcal{A}_{\mathsf{int}}$ and $\mathcal{A}_{\mathsf{Rabin}}$ are integer automata. On the other hand, $\mathcal{A}_{\frac{1}{3}}$, which was shown to accept non-regular languages in Section 3.1, is not an integer automaton. The reason is because of the transition from q_s on symbol **0**; $\delta_0(q_s, \mathsf{q_{rej}}) = \frac{1}{3}$ is not an integer multiple of $\delta_0(q_s, q_s) = \frac{2}{3}$.

The main result of this section is that for any integer HPA $\mathcal{A}$, and rational x, the language $\mathsf{L^a}_{>x}(\mathcal{A})$ is regular (for $\mathsf{a} \in \{\mathsf{f}, \mathsf{b}, \mathsf{m}\}$). The proof of this result will rest on observations made in Proposition 4 that states that a word κ is accepted exactly when a prefix of κ reaches a witness set with sufficient probability, and the rest of the word κ is definitely accepted from the witness set. Proposition 1 states that the words definitely accepted from any witness set is regular. Thus, the crux of the proof will be to show that there is a way to maintain the $\mathsf{val}(\cdot, x, \cdot)$ function for each witness set using only finite memory. This observation will rest on a few special properties of integer HPAs.

Proposition 6. *Let* $\mathcal{A}$ *be an integer* HPA *over alphabet* Σ *with level 0 and level 1 sets* Q_0 *and* Q_1, $C \subseteq Q_1$, *and* x *be a rational number* $\frac{c}{d}$. *For any* $u \in \Sigma^*$, *if* $\mathsf{val}(C, x, u) \in [0, 1]$ *then there is* $e \in \{0, 1, 2, \ldots d\}$ *such that* $\mathsf{val}(C, x, u) = \frac{e}{d}$.

The above proposition makes a very important observation — the set of relevant values that the function val can take are finite. Proposition 3 in Section 2.1 essentially says that when the function val takes on values either below 0 or above 1, either all extensions of the current input will have sufficient probability among witness sets in Q_1 or no extension will have sufficient probability. Thus, when measuring the quantity val what matters is only whether it is strictly less than 0, strictly greater than 1 or its exact value when it is in $[0, 1]$. Proposition 6 above, guarantees that val is finite when it lies within $[0, 1]$. This allows us to keep track of val using finite memory. This is captured in the following Lemma.

Lemma 4. *Consider an integer* HPA $\mathcal{A}$ *over alphabet* Σ *with* Q_0 *and* Q_1 *as level 0 and level 1 states. Let* $x = \frac{c}{d}$ *be a rational threshold. For an arbitrary* $C \subseteq Q_1$, $q \in Q_0$, *and* $e \in \{0, 1, \ldots d\}$, *the following six languages*

$$\begin{aligned}
\mathsf{L}_{(q,C,e)} &= \{u \in \Sigma^* \mid \mathsf{post}(q_s, u) \cap Q_0 = \{q\} \textit{ and } \mathsf{val}(C, x, u) \leq \tfrac{e}{d}\} \\
\mathsf{L}_{(q,C,-)} &= \{u \in \Sigma^* \mid \mathsf{post}(q_s, u) \cap Q_0 = \{q\} \textit{ and } \mathsf{val}(C, x, u) < 0\} \\
\mathsf{L}_{(q,C,+)} &= \{u \in \Sigma^* \mid \mathsf{post}(q_s, u) \cap Q_0 = \{q\} \textit{ and } \mathsf{val}(C, x, u) > 1\} \\
\mathsf{L}_{(*,C,e)} &= \{u \in \Sigma^* \mid \mathsf{post}(q_s, u) \cap Q_0 = \emptyset \textit{ and } \mathsf{val}(C, x, u) \leq \tfrac{e}{d}\} \\
\mathsf{L}_{(*,C,-)} &= \{u \in \Sigma^* \mid \mathsf{post}(q_s, u) \cap Q_0 = \emptyset \textit{ and } \mathsf{val}(C, x, u) < 0\} \\
\mathsf{L}_{(*,C,+)} &= \{u \in \Sigma^* \mid \mathsf{post}(q_s, u) \cap Q_0 = \emptyset \textit{ and } \mathsf{val}(C, x, u) > 1\}
\end{aligned}$$

are all regular.

We are ready to present the main result of this section.

Theorem 7. *For any integer* HPA $\mathcal{A}$, *rational threshold* $x \in [0, 1]$, *the languages* $\mathsf{L}^{\mathsf{a}}{}_{>x}(\mathcal{A})$ *and* $\mathsf{L}^{\mathsf{a}}{}_{\geq x}(\mathcal{A})$ *are regular (where* $\mathsf{a} \in \{\mathsf{f}, \mathsf{b}, \mathsf{m}\}$*).*

Proof. From Proposition 4, we can conclude that

$$\mathsf{L}^{\mathsf{a}}{}_{>x}(\mathcal{A}) = \left(\bigcup_{C \subseteq Q_1,\ q \in Q_0 \cup \{*\}} \mathsf{L}_{(q,C,-)} \mathsf{L}_C \right) \cup \left(\bigcup_{C \subseteq Q_1,\ q \in Q_0, e \in [0,1)} \mathsf{L}_{(q,C,e)} \mathsf{L}_{C \cup \{q\}} \right)$$

where L_W is the set of words definitely accepted from witness set W, as defined in Proposition 1. From Proposition 1 and Lemma 4, we can conclude that each of the languages on the right hand side is regular, and therefore, $\mathsf{L}^{\mathsf{a}}{}_{>x}(\mathcal{A})$ is regular. The proof of regularity of $\mathsf{L}^{\mathsf{a}}{}_{\geq x}(\mathcal{A})$ is omitted for lack of space reasons. □

The following theorem shows that the problems of checking emptiness and universality are **PSPACE**-complete for integer HPAs, thus giving a tight upper bound.

Theorem 8. *Given an integer* HPA $\mathcal{A}$, $\mathsf{a} \in \{\mathsf{f}, \mathsf{b}, \mathsf{m}\}$, $\rhd \in \{>, \geq\}$, *the problem of determining if* $\mathsf{L}^{\mathsf{a}}{}_{\rhd x}(\mathcal{A}) = \emptyset$ *is* **PSPACE**-*complete. Similarly, the problem of checking universality is also* **PSPACE**-*complete.*

5 Conclusions

We investigated the expressiveness of (1-level) HPAs with non-extremal thresholds and showed, in spite of their very simple transition structure, they can recognize non-regular languages. Nevertheless, the canonical decision problems of emptiness and universality for HPAs turn out to be decidable in **EXPTIME** and are **PSPACE**-hard. Imposing a very simple restriction on the transition probabilities result in automata that we call integer HPAs which recognize only regular languages. For integer HPAs, the canonical decision problems turn out to be **PSPACE**-complete.

There are a few problems left open by our investigations. The first one is of course the gap in the complexity of deciding emptiness and universality for these problems. Our investigations in this paper were motivated by understanding the relationship between the number of levels in HPAs and the tractability of the model. The results in [4] suggest that problems become hard for 6-level HPAs and non-extremal thresholds. Our results here suggest that 1-level HPAs (with non-extremal thresholds) are tractable. Exactly where the boundary between decidability and undecidability lies is still open. Finally, as argued in the Introduction, HPAs arise naturally as models of client-server systems, and it would useful to apply the theoretical results here to such models.

Acknowledgements. Rohit Chadha was partially supported by NSF CNS 1314338. Mahesh Viswanathan was partially supported by NSF CNS 1314485. A. Prasad Sistla and Yue Ben were paritally supported by CNS 1035914, CCF 1319754 and CNS 1314485.

References

1. Baier, C., Größer, M.: Recognizing ω-regular languages with probabilistic automata. In: 20th IEEE Symp. on Logic in Computer Science, pp. 137–146 (2005)
2. Baier, C., Größer, M., Bertrand, N.: Probabilistic ω-automata. Journal of the ACM 59(1), 1–52 (2012)
3. Chadha, R., Sistla, A.P., Viswanathan, M.: On the expressiveness and complexity of randomization in finite state monitors. Journal of the ACM 56(5) (2009)
4. Chadha, R., Sistla, A.P., Viswanathan, M.: Probabilistic Büchi automata with non-extremal acceptance thresholds. In: Jhala, R., Schmidt, D. (eds.) VMCAI 2011. LNCS, vol. 6538, pp. 103–117. Springer, Heidelberg (2011)
5. Chadha, R., Sistla, A.P., Viswanathan, M.: Power of randomization in automata on infinite strings. Logical Methods in Computer Science 7(3), 1–22 (2011)
6. Chatterjee, K., Henzinger, T.A.: Probabilistic automata on infinite words: Decidability and undecidability results. In: Bouajjani, A., Chin, W.-N. (eds.) ATVA 2010. LNCS, vol. 6252, pp. 1–16. Springer, Heidelberg (2010)
7. Condon, A., Lipton, R.J.: On the complexity of space bounded interactive proofs (extended abstract). In: Symp. on Foundations of Computer Science, pp. 462–467 (1989)
8. Fijalkow, N., Gimbert, H., Oualhadj, Y.: Deciding the value 1 problem for probabilistic leak-tight automata. In: IEEE Symp. on Logic in Computer Science, pp. 295–304 (2012)
9. Gimbert, H., Oualhadj, Y.: Probabilistic automata on finite words: Decidable and undecidable problems. In: Abramsky, S., Gavoille, C., Kirchner, C., Meyer auf der Heide, F., Spirakis, P.G. (eds.) ICALP 2010, Part II. LNCS, vol. 6199, pp. 527–538. Springer, Heidelberg (2010)
10. Größer, M.: Reduction Methods for Probabilistic Model Checking. PhD thesis, TU Dresden (2008)
11. Kemeny, J., Snell, J.: Denumerable Markov Chains. Springer (1976)
12. Paz, A.: Introduction to Probabilistic Automata. Academic Press (1971)
13. Rabin, M.O.: Probabilistic automata. Inf. and Control 6(3), 230–245 (1963)
14. Vardi, M.: Automatic verification of probabilistic concurrent finite-state programs. In: Symp. on Foundations of Computer Science, pp. 327–338 (1985)

Knowledge = Observation + Memory + Computation*

Blaise Genest[1], Doron Peled[2], and Sven Schewe[3]

[1] CNRS, IRISA, Rennes, France
[2] Bar Ilan University, Israel
[3] University of Liverpool, UK

Abstract. We compare three notions of knowledge in concurrent system: memoryless knowledge, knowledge of perfect recall, and causal knowledge. Memoryless knowledge is based only on the current state of a process, knowledge of perfect recall can take into account the local history of a process, and causal knowledge depends on the causal past of a process, which comprises the information a process can obtain when all processes exchange the information they have when performing joint transitions. We compare these notions in terms of knowledge strength, number of bits required to store this information, and the complexity of checking if a given process has a given knowledge. We show that all three notions of knowledge can be implemented using finite memory. Causal knowledge proves to be strictly more powerful than knowledge with perfect recall, which in turn proves to be strictly more powerful than memoryless knowledge. We show that keeping track of causal knowledge is cheaper than keeping track of knowledge of perfect recall.

1 Introduction

Knowledge represents the information that processes can have about each other and, consequently, about the state of the entire system. In concurrency theory, there are multiple definitions of knowledge based on the specification of the system, a limited view of the other processes, and some information related to the observed history [11]. We study three types of knowledge for concurrent systems. According to the first type, *memoryless knowledge*, a process knows everything consistent with all executions that end in its current local state. For the second type, *knowledge of perfect recall* [3,11,12], a process knows everything consistent with all executions that share the same local history visible to this process. We define a third type of knowledge, *causal knowledge*, where a process knows everything consistent with all executions that have the same past, where the past of a process includes the past of other processes up to their last joint transition.

We are interested in the implementation of different kinds of knowledge as a transformation of the system under consideration. The transformation can use additional variables in order to collect information about history, and also to pass this information from process to process as part of the scheduled system synchronization. In particular, such a transformation can keep information related to the observable history in order to

* The work of the second author was partly supported by ISF grant 126-12 "Practical Synthesis of Control for Distributed Systems", and partly done while invited professor in University of Rennes 1.

A. Pitts (Ed.): FOSSACS 2015, LNCS 9034, pp. 215–229, 2015.
DOI: 10.1007/978-3-662-46678-0_14

obtain additional knowledge. This transformation cannot change the values of the original variables of the program (including program counters) or the enabledness condition of the transitions (operations) of the system. Thus, the executions of the original system are projections of the executions of the transformed system; only further information is collected in new variables. The different kinds of knowledge become memoryless knowledge after the transformation, which stores all information required in the processes' local states.

This transformation can be used to monitor the global behavior of a system by local processes. For example we may use it to control the system to force it to satisfy some global property by blocking transitions based on knowledge [1,8,16]. Another application is to perform some run time checking that a process satisfies some global properties when reaching particular local states.

Our study differs from the classical question of model-checking knowledge [11], as it does not attempt to provide algorithms for checking the knowledge of processes. Instead, we are interested in providing the run-time support to use knowledge. In particular we are interested in the implementing algorithms and their complexity. When comparing the commonly used memoryless knowledge and knowledge of perfect recall [1,11], there is a tradeoff between the amount of knowledge available to processes and the complexity of maintaining it. We can know more properties under perfect recall, but have to maintain some history related information for that. Quite surprisingly, the new definition of causal knowledge both improves our knowledge and reduces the time and space complexity required when compared to knowledge of perfect recall. The price to pay for this is increased communication: processes have to update each other, through communication, when performing joint transitions in order to achieve this type of knowledge. We show that implementing the third kind of knowledge, knowledge based on causality, can be obtained using a construction based on the "gossip" automata of Mukund and Sohoni [14], related to the Zielonka construction [17,7,5].

We establish complexity results for implementing the different types of knowledge. In particular, we show that causal knowledge requires less memory, thanks to the sharing of information during communication. It is, however, interesting to note the stark difference in cost between implementing causal knowledge and knowledge of perfect recall: communication does not only improve knowledge, it also saves resources.

2 Transition Systems

Definition 1. *A transition system is a tuple* $\mathsf{Tr} = \langle P, V, L_v, T, L_t, S, s_0, R\rangle$ *where*

- P *is a finite set of processes.*
- V *is a finite set of Boolean variables.*
- $L_v : V \to P$ *is a mapping from variables to processes, such that each variable* v *is local to the process* $L_v(p)$. *Let* $V_p = \{x \mid L_v(x) \in p\}$ *(the set of variables of process* p*).*
- T *is a finite set of transitions, where each transition* $\tau \in T$ *has an enabling condition* $\mathsf{en}_\tau \subseteq 2^V$, *which is a propositional property, and a transformation* $f_\tau : 2^V \to 2^V$ *over the set of variables. The enabledness condition and transformation have some constraints as described below.*

$L_t : T \to 2^P$ *maps each transition to the set of processes that execute it. The transition is executed synchronously by the processes in* $L_t(\tau)$. *Let* $\mathsf{var}(\tau) = \bigcup_{p \in L_t(\tau)} V_p$. *Then only the variables* $\mathsf{var}(\tau)$ *can be used in* en_τ, *and* f_τ *can use and change only these variables.*

$S \subseteq 2^V$ *is a finite set of states, where each state of* Tr *is a possible assignments of values to the variables of* V.

$s_0 \in S$ *is the* initial state.

$R \subseteq S \times S$ *is a relation over* S. *We have* $(s, s') \in R$ *exactly when there exists some transition* $\tau \in T$ *such that* $s \models \mathsf{en}_\tau$ *and* $s' = f_\tau(s)$. *We say that* τ *can be executed (is enabled) from* s, *producing* s'.

For some future constructions, it will be convenient to assume at times that the system is first executing some initial ("mythological") transition ℓ, shared by all the processes, i.e., $L_t(\ell) = P$, ending up with the initial state s_0 (starting with some ("mythological") initial state s_{-1}).

We assume that S is the set of states reachable from s_0, such that the global state space S and the global transition relation R over S are defined by the other components.

The size $|\mathsf{Tr}|$ of a transition system Tr is the number $|P|$ of processes plus the number $|V|$ of variables plus the number $|T|$ of transitions.

We define a *local state* $s|_p$ as the projection of global state $s \in S$ on the local variables V_p of process p. For a set of processes $P' \subseteq P$, the semi-local state $s|_{P'}$ is the projection of s to the variables in $\bigcup_{p \in P'} V_p$. In particular, we have $s|_P = s$.

Definition 2. *A* history *of a transition system* Tr *is an alternating sequence* $h = s_0\tau_1 s_1\tau_2 s_2 \ldots s_n$ *of states and transitions such that, for each* $i \geq 0$, $s_i \models \mathsf{en}_{\tau_{i+1}}$ *and* $s_{i+1} = f_{\tau_{i+1}}(s_i)$. *We denote by* $\mathsf{last}(h)$ *the last state* s_n *of* h, *and* $\mathsf{last}_p(h) = \mathsf{last}(h)|_p$.

A state s is *reachable* if $s = \mathsf{last}(h)$ for some history h. Note that it is PSPACE-complete to check whether a state is reachable in a transition system [13]. As the initial state is unique and the effect of transitions is deterministic, we sometimes use only the sequence of transitions $\tau_1\tau_2\tau_3\ldots$ to denote a history or execution $s_0\tau_1 s_1\tau_2 s_2\tau_3 s_3\ldots$ of a transition system.

3 Notions of Knowledge

In order to avoid using a specific logical formalism, we define state properties abstractly:

Definition 3. *A* (state) property φ *of a transition system* Tr *is a subset of its states. That is,* $\varphi \subseteq S$. *A state* s *satisfies* φ, *denoted* $s \models \varphi$, *if* $s \in \varphi$. *An history* h *satisfies* φ, *denoted* $h \models \varphi$, *if* $\mathsf{last}(h) \in \varphi$.

Note that properties can be defined compactly, using, for example, propositional logic. In order to define a general notion of knowledge of state properties, the different kinds of knowledge are abstracted as information available to a process. In order to define different kinds of knowledge, we define an equivalence relation between histories. Let Γ represent a type of knowledge. (The types of knowledge that we consider will be presented later.)

Definition 4. *Let $\equiv_p^\Gamma$ be an equivalence relation between histories with respect to process $p \in P$ in a transition system* Tr. *Process p in a transition system* Tr *knows a state property φ after history h, according to knowledge type Γ, denoted $h \models K_p^\Gamma \varphi$, if, for each history h' such $h \equiv_p^\Gamma h'$, $\mathsf{last}(h') \models \varphi$.*

We study three types of knowledge: memoryless, perfect recall, and causal knowledge. Accordingly, Γ is ML, PR and C, respectively.

Definition 5. *We say that the knowledge type Γ is* deeper[1] *than knowledge type Γ', denoted $\Gamma \rhd \Gamma'$, if, for each history h, process p and property φ, $h \models K_p^{\Gamma'} \varphi$ implies $h \models K_p^\Gamma \varphi$. If $\Gamma \rhd \Gamma'$, but $\Gamma' \not\rhd \Gamma$, then we call Γ* strictly deeper *than Γ', denoted $\Gamma \blacktriangleright \Gamma'$.*

A simple observation that follows immediately from the above definition can be used to show that one kind of knowledge is deeper than another:

Observation 1 *Let Γ and Γ' be two notions of knowledge with $\equiv_p^\Gamma \subseteq \equiv_p^{\Gamma'}$ for each p. Then $\Gamma \rhd \Gamma'$.*

Memoryless Knowledge. This is a conservative version of knowledge, where a property φ is known if it holds in all the states with the same local state of process p. That is, $h \equiv_p^{ML} h'$ if $\mathsf{last}_p(h) = \mathsf{last}_p(h')$.

Knowledge of Perfect Recall. In the epistemic community, knowledge of perfect recall [3,11,12] refers to the ability of process p to use local observation to distinguish between different histories. We can define, in fact, multiple different versions of knowledge of perfect recall:

- $PR(l)$ A process can view (and recall) its local states along the executions (this is the version that is used in [11]).
- $PR(t)$ A process can view the occurrences of transitions in which it participates.
- $PR(lt)$ A process can view both the local state and the executed transition.
- $PR(ct)$ A process can, when executing a transition, view the combined local state of the processes involved in this transition.

We choose $PR = PR(lt)$ as our canonical definition of knowledge of perfect recall. The observations in this case are sequences of $p-events$, as defined below.

Definition 6. *A $p-event$ is a pair $\langle \tau, r \rangle$, where $\tau \in T$, $p \in L_t(\tau)$, and r is a local state of p. A $p-event$ is obtained from a history by taking a transition τ that is executed and involves the process p and the local state just after its execution. We define the sequence of $p-events$ of a history h, $\mathsf{Ev}_p(h)$, inductively. For $h = s_0$, $\mathsf{Ev}_p(s_0) = \epsilon$, the empty word. Let $h' = h\,\tau\,s$ (that is, h' extends h with a transition τ, leading to state s). Now, if $p \in L_t(\tau)$, then $\mathsf{Ev}_p(h') = \mathsf{Ev}_p(h)\langle \tau, s|_p \rangle$, and otherwise $\mathsf{Ev}_p(h') = \mathsf{Ev}_p(h)$.*

For instance, for $p \in L_t(\tau)$, $p \notin L_t(\tau')$, and $h = s_0\,\tau\,s\,\tau'\,t\,\tau\,r$, we have $\mathsf{Ev}_p(h) = \langle \tau, s|_p \rangle \langle \tau, r|_p \rangle$.

[1] We use the term "deeper" instead of "stronger", as the latter is associated with an implication of the opposite direction: in logic, φ is stronger than φ' when $\varphi \rightarrow \varphi'$.

Definition 7. *Knowledge of perfect recall is based on the equivalence $\equiv_p^{PR}$ such that $h \equiv_p^{PR} h'$ exactly when $\mathsf{Ev}_p(h) = \mathsf{Ev}_p(h')$.*

Similarly, $PR(t)$ is defined based on the projection of $\mathsf{Ev}_p(h)$ on its first components, while $PR(l)$ is defined based on the projection of $\mathsf{Ev}_p(h)$ on its second components. Also, $PR(ct)$ is defined based on a sequence of extended events of the form $\langle \tau, s|_{L(\tau)} \rangle$, using the respective semi-local states (rather than the local states) in $\mathsf{Ev}_p(h)$. In the example above, this would be $\mathsf{Ev}_p(h) = \langle \tau, s|_{L_t(\tau)} \rangle \langle \tau, r|_{L_t(\tau)} \rangle$.

Notice that the sequence Ev_p can grow arbitrarily as the history grows. However, it has been shown [12,1] that a bounded implementation of $PR(l)$ is possible. We will give a uniform implementations for all versions of PR in the next section. We now compare ML and the different definitions of PR.

Lemma 1. *Knowledge of perfect recall is strictly deeper than memoryless knowledge. More precisely, $PR(ct) \blacktriangleright PR(lt) \blacktriangleright PR(l) \blacktriangleright ML$ and $PR(lt) \blacktriangleright PR(t)$. However, $PR(t)$ is incomparable (with respect to $\rhd$) with ML and with $PR(l)$.*

Proof. By definition, the relation $\equiv_p^{PR(ct)}$ refines $\equiv_p^{PR(lt)}$, which refines both $\equiv_p^{PR(l)}$ and $\equiv_p^{PR(t)}$, for all $p \in P$. Now, $\equiv_p^{PR(l)}$ keeps the sequence of states of p, and in particular the last one. Hence $h \equiv_p^{PR(l)} h'$ implies $\mathsf{last}_p(h) = \mathsf{last}_p(h')$, hence the relation $\equiv_p^{PR(l)}$ refines $\equiv_p^{ML}$. We now show that the implications are strict.

"$PR(ct)$ vs. $PR(lt)$": To show strictness, we consider the histories $h = ac$ and $h' = bc$ for the transition system from Figure 1. Obviously, $h \models \{2\}$ and $h \models K_{P_2}^{PR(ct)}\{2\}$, because, under $PR(ct)$, P_2 knows after executing the joint c transition that P_1 is in (the sink) state 2. At the same time, $h' \not\models \{2\}$, and under $PR(lt)$, P_2 sees the same sequence of $P_2-events$: $\mathsf{Ev}_{P_2}^{PR(lt)}(h) = \mathsf{Ev}_{P_2}^{PR(lt)}(h')$. Thus, $h \not\models K_{P_2}^{PR(lt)}\{2\}$.

"$PR(t)$ vs. $PR(l)$": Consider the histories $h = ad$ and $h' = bc$ for the transition system from Figure 1. Obviously, $h \models \{2\}$ and $h \models K_{P_2}^{PR(t)}\{2\}$, because, under $PR(t)$, P_2 knows after executing the joint d transition that P_1 is in (the sink) state 2. At the same time, $h' \not\models \{2\}$, but, under $PR(l)$, P_2 sees the same sequence of $P_2-events$: $\mathsf{Ev}_{P_2}^{PR(l)}(h) = \mathsf{Ev}_{P_2}^{PR(l)}(h')$. Thus, $h \not\models K_{P_2}^{PR(l)}\{2\}$. This also implies strictness for "$PR(lt)$ vs. $PR(l)$" and implies that ML is not deeper than $PR(t)$.

"$PR(l)$ vs. ML": We consider the histories $h = \varepsilon$ and $h' = bc$ for the transition system from Figure 1. Obviously, $h \models \{0,1,2,3\}$ and $h \models K_{P_2}^{PR(l)}\{0,1,2,3\}$, because, under $PR(l)$, P_2 knows after h that it has not taken part in any transition, and 4 is only reachable upon taking a c transition. At the same time, $h' \not\models \{0,1,2,3\}$, but $\mathsf{last}(h)|_{P_2} = \mathsf{last}(h')|_{P_2}$. Thus, $h \not\models K_{P_2}^{ML}\{0,1,2,3\}$.

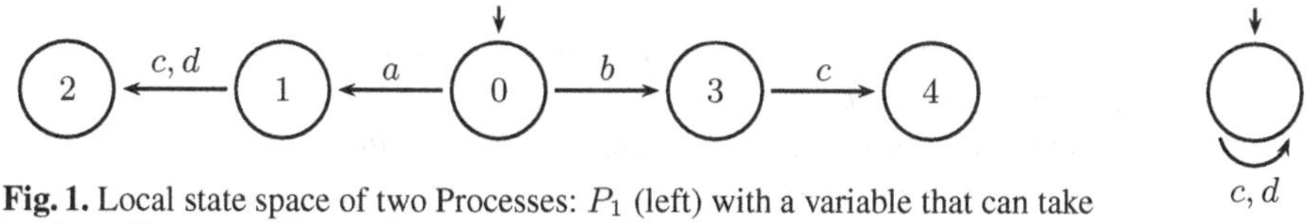

Fig. 1. Local state space of two Processes: P_1 (left) with a variable that can take 5 values $\{0,1,2,3,4\}$ and P_2 without variable. Transitions c, d are joint between P_1 and P_2

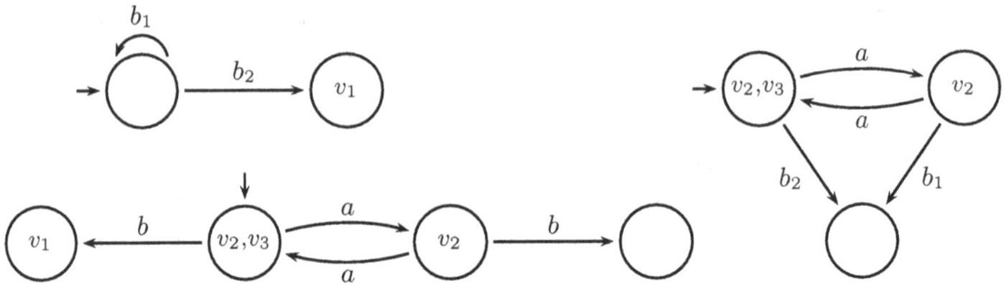

Fig. 2. The bottom left shows the global state space for two Processes P_1 (top left) and P_2 (right), with $V_{P_1} = \{v_1\}$ and $V_{P_2} = \{v_2, v_3\}$. Boolean variables represented in the states are those with value true. Transition a is local to P_2. It toggles the value of the variable v_3. Transition b is joint between P_1 and P_2. It first assigns v_1 the value of v_3 and then sets v_2 and v_3 to false. Both transitions are enabled if, and only if, v_2 is true. Initially, v_2 and v_3 are set to true and v_1 is set to false. Thus, the effect of b on the each process depends on the state of the other process. To reflect this, the action b is graphically 'split' into b_1 and b_2 in the graphic representation of the processes. Note, however, that b_1 and b_2 refer to the same action, b.

"ML vs. $PR(t)$": To show that $PR(t)$ is not deeper than ML, and thus not deeper than $PR(l)$ and $PR(lt)$, we consider the transition system from Figure 2. Consider the histories $h = b$ and $h' = ab$. Obviously, $h \models \{v_1\}$ and $h' \not\models \{v_1\}$. Under $PR(t)$, P_1 sees the same sequence of $P_1\!-\!events$ for h, h': $\mathsf{Ev}_{P_1}^{PR(t)}(h) = \mathsf{Ev}_{P_1}^{PR(t)}(h')$. Thus, $h \not\models K_{P_1}^{PR(t)}\{v_1\}$. However, $\mathsf{last}(h)|_{P_1} = \{v_1\}$, hence $h \models K_{P_1}^{ML}\{v_1\}$ holds.

Notice that $PR(t)$ is deeper than $PR(l)$ when, for all processes p and all transitions τ, the p-local state after the transition τ only depends on the p-local state before τ. In this case, the history of local states can be retrieved from the history of transitions. This is, for example, the case for products of finite state systems.

Causal Knowledge. This notion is related to partial order semantics [10], and has been used informally in distributed games [4,15,6]. However, as far as we know, it has not been used in an epistemic framework before. The assumption is that processes may exchange information each time they perform a joint transition.

We first define the chain of transitions that can affect the view of a process p in a given history. The exact ordering of transitions is not necessarily known to p, hence the information function is represented as a partial order. We now define the partial order associated with a history.

Definition 8. *The* partial order $PO(h)$ *associated with a history* $h = s_0\tau_1 s_1 \tau_2 s_2 \ldots \tau_n s_n$ *is a triple* $\langle E, \lambda, \prec\rangle$ *where*

- $E = \{e_0, e_1, \ldots, e_m\}$ *is the set of occurences of events in* h.
- $\lambda : E \to T$ *labels* $\lambda(e_i) = t_i$,
- $\prec \subseteq E \times E$ *is the smallest partial order relation (i.e., transitive, reflexive and asymmetric relation) satisfying the following: if* $e, e' \in E$ *with* $L_t(\lambda(e)) \cap L_t(\lambda(e')) \neq \emptyset$ *and* e *appearing before* e' *in* h *then* $e \prec e'$.

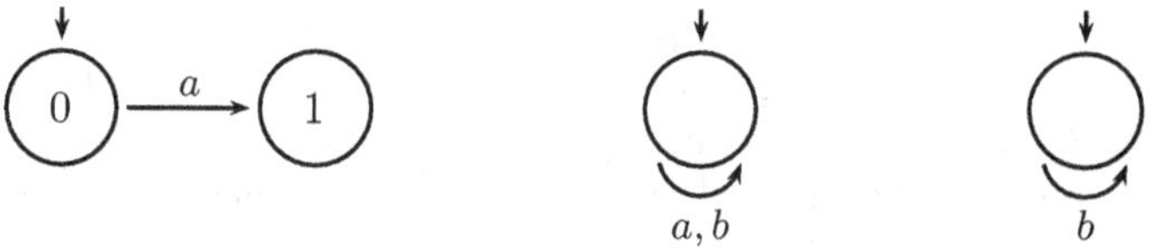

Fig. 3. Processes P_1 with a boolean variable (left), P_2 (middle) and P_3 (right) without variables

For instance, for three processes p, q, and r and three transitions a, b, and c with $L_t(a) = p$, $L_t(b) = q$, $L_t(c) = \{p, r\}$, we have $PO_p(abc)=PO_p(acb)=\langle\{e_a, e_b, e_c\}, \prec, \lambda\rangle$ with $\lambda(e_x)=x$ for all $x \in \{a, b, c\}$ and $e_a \prec e_c$. Process p sees transitions in the past (for $\prec$) of the last transition on p.

Definition 9. *The causal view $Ca_p(h)$ of process p in history h includes all the occurrences of events that precede its last occurrence according to the partial order $PO(h) = \langle E, \prec \lambda\rangle$. If e is the latest occurrence of h that involves p, then let $E' = \{e' \in E | e' \preceq e\}$. Then, $Ca_p(h) = \langle E', \prec \cap E' \times E', \lambda|_{E'}\rangle$.*

The equivalence $\equiv_p^C$ on histories, used to define causal knowledge, is based on $h \equiv_p^C h'$ iff $\mathsf{Ca}_p(h) = \mathsf{Ca}_p(h')$.

Lemma 2. *Causal knowledge is strictly deeper than knowledge of perfect recall.*

Proof (Sketch). We first prove $Ca \rhd PR(ct)$. By Lemma 1, this implies $Ca \rhd PR$ for all version of PR. Although the causal view $\mathsf{Ca}_p(h)$ of a process p in a history h is a partial order, it contains, according to Definition 9, in particular, all the occurrences of transitions of p. The occurrences of transitions in which p participates are totally ordered by $\prec$ in the causal view. Given the unique mythological event and the causal view, one can also construct the $p-events$ corresponding to the occurrences in E and, in particular, the occurrences in which p participates. To do this, one can complete the partial order $\prec$ into some total order that contains it, and start to calculate the global state after each occurrence, taking the relevant component of p for transitions involving this process. Although the global states generated in this way are not necessarily the ones appearing in h, one can show by induction over the length of the constructed sequence that the $p-events$ are the same. This is the case, because occurrences of h that are not in E do not affect the values of occurrences in E. Moreover, by the disjointness of the variables for each process, the order of occurrences not in E can be commuted with occurrences in E to appear at the end, without affecting the value of the p local states.

To show that causal knowledge is *strictly* deeper than knowledge of perfect recall, we consider the histories $h = ab$ and $h' = b$ in the transitions system from Figure 3. Obviously, $h \models \{1\}$ holds. Further, $h \models K_{P_3}^{Ca}\{1\}$: the partial order $PO(h)$ associated with h is the total order $\langle\{e_1, e_2\}, \lambda(e_1) = a, \lambda(e_2) = b, e_1 < e_2\}\rangle$, and we have $Ca_{P3}(h) = PO(h)$. That is, Process P_3 knows that P_1 is in 1.

At the same time, $h' \not\models \{1\}$, but, under $PR(ct)$, P_3 sees the same sequence of $P_3-events$: $\mathsf{Ev}_{P_3}^{PR(ct)}(h) = \mathsf{Ev}_{P_3}^{PR(ct)}(h')$. Thus, $h \not\models K_{P_3}^{PR(ct)}\{1\}$. □

Notice that the third process in the proof is necessary, because, for two process and $PR(ct)$, each process learns the global state of the transition system when executing a joint transition. Ca and $PR(lt)$ can be separated using the transition system with two processes from Figure 1. This indeed follows from the proof that $PR(lt)$ is not deeper than $PR(ct)$.

4 Application of Knowledge

Knowledge can be applied to control systems by blocking some transitions. The more is known about a transition system, the less restrictive the control needs to be. Consider the system with three processes arb, p, p' from Figure 4. Process p needs to access a critical section twice, and process p' needs to access it once. Process arb helps process p, p' to access the critical section in a mutually exclusive way.

Processes p and p' can try to enter the critical section using an e and e' transition, respectively, which they share with the arbiter, and leave it using the shared l and l' transition, respectively. The effect of transition e (resp. e') depends on the state of the arbiter. If arb has given permission to the other process to enter the critical section, and not yet received the respective 'leave' transition, transition e does not change the state. In Figure 4, e is therefore split into e_1 (the case where p progresses) and e_2 (the case where p stays in its previous state). Similarly, e' is split into e'_1 and e'_2.

Process p can also ignore the arbiter, and progress using an i transition.

Without control, the system is too permissive. For example, it allows for the history $h = e'i$ (with $h \models c \wedge c'$), where first p' enters the critical section through the e' transition, followed by p entering the critical section.

However, the following control can be written easily using knowledge: If $K_p(f')$, then allow the 'ignore' transition i. Else, disallow it. Clearly, this only allows p to ignore the arbiter if no future conflict is possible, as p' will remain in this sink state and does no longer compete for entering the critical section.

Now we compare different notions of knowledge. With memoryless knowledge, just looking at its local state, process p will never be able to ignore the arbiter, using i.

With perfect recall, consider the following history: $h = e'el'e$. After this history, process p knows under PR that p' had been in the critical section when it first requested

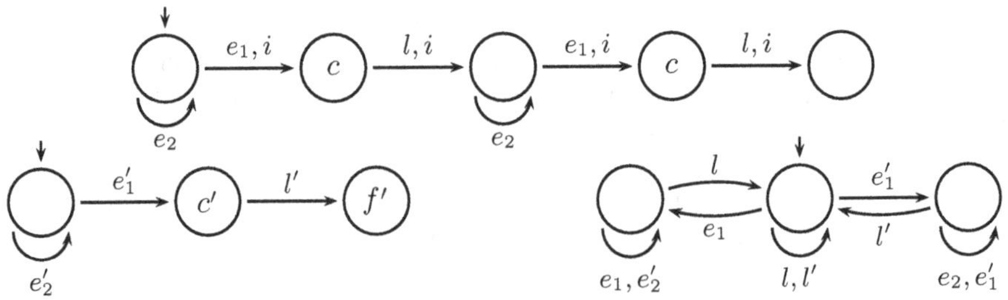

Fig. 4. Three Processes: p (top), p' (bottom left), and arb (bottom right). Only some local boolean variables are represented: c and c' (set to 1 for p and p' in critical section, respectively), and f' set to 1 for p' has finished. The remaining variables are omitted. Effect of the transitions e (resp. e') on process p (resp. p') depends on the arbiter state. It is therefore split into e_1, e_2 (resp. e'_1, e'_2).

entry, but has left it meanwhile. It thus knows that f' holds henceforth, and p can make use of i, ignoring the arbiter.

With causal recall, Process p can make even more use of i. Consider the history $h = e'l'e$.

With perfect recall, p cannot distinguish it from $h' = e$, and can make no use of i. With causal recall, the knowledge of the arbiter that p' is in its sink state (such that f' holds henceforth) is transferred to p through the shared transition e. It thus knows that f' holds henceforth, and p can make use of i, ignoring the arbiter.

5 Implementation of Knowledge Using Bounded Memory

The notions of knowledge discussed in this paper are quite abstract: they represent some mathematical definition based on the observation that the processes can have. These observations are not directly implemented by the processes. Except for theoretical reasoning about programs, knowledge can be used in order to control the program [8]. If the processes need to *use* such observations so that they can act based on their knowledge, they necessarily need to store the observation and act on it. If the observation information is stored and available to a process, it can decide, based on some precalculated knowledge table, to restrict its behavior accordingly.

The definitions of knowledge of perfect recall and knowledge with causal memory are based on unbounded observations. We are interested in transforming the transition system for these two kinds of knowledge, such that only a bounded amount of information is needed. The transformation will add variables and augment the transitions in such a way, that one can control the system based on the knowledge through a precalculated table. In essence, such transformations convert the original system into a new system, where the knowledge can be observed by a process from its most recent local state. We provide complexity measures for both the transformations.

5.1 Implementation of Memoryless Knowledge

The implementation of memoryless knowledge of a process is simple, as the observation that is used consists only of the local state of the process. To decide the current knowledge regarding a property φ from a p-local state s_p, we recall that p knows that φ holds if, and only if, for all *reachable* states s with $s|_p = s_p$, $s \models \varphi$ holds. It therefore suffices to check the existence of a global state s with $s|_p = s_p$ and $s \not\models \varphi$.

This is a simple reachability problem. An implementation of memoryless knowledge may or may not use an offline precomputation.

Online Only. The reachability problem can be solved in time $|\mathsf{Tr}| \cdot 2^{\mathcal{O}(|V|)}$ (or in PSPACE) by constructing all reachable states ending with the observed local state.

With an Offline Precomputation. Alternatively, for each p-local state, one can first compute the reachable states with this p-local state in a preprocessing step. One can then save this knowledge with respect to p-local states in a binary tree with $2^{|V_p|}$ entries. Accessing this tree at runtime only takes time linear in the number of variables local to p, that is, time $\mathcal{O}(|V_p|)$. The offline construction of the tree during the preprocessing step can be done in time $|\mathsf{Tr}| \cdot 2^{\mathcal{O}(|V|)}$.

5.2 Implementing Knowledge of Perfect Recall

We describe the transformation of knowledge for all version of perfect recall. The transformation was already known for $PR(l)$ [12,1]. The idea of the construction is that each process p can consult a global automaton, representing the transformation of the entire system. A process p is only aware of the occurrences of its own transitions. Hence, upon an occurrence of a transition τ with $p \in L_t(\tau)$, the automaton moves according to τ. However, process p is not aware of further moves of transitions not involving p. Thus, the actual global state of the system can further change through the firing of any sequence of such transitions. A subset construction can be used to encode the possible global states that can be reached without being distinguished by p after a transition τ.

Definition 10. *Let $\langle S, s_0, T, \delta\rangle$ be a global automaton for the system* Tr. *Recall the notation $\delta^*(S, \rho)$ that stands for the usual extension of δ from a single state and a single transition into a set of states and a finite (possibly empty) sequences of transitions. Let, for a process p,*

- *$T_p = \{\tau \in T \mid p \in L_t(\tau)\}$ be the set of transtitions executed by p (possibly joined by other processes) and*
- *$I_p = T \setminus T_p$ be the set of transitions that do not involve p.*

Then we construct a deterministic automaton $\mathcal{D}_p = \langle 2^S, S_0, p\text{−}events, \delta_p\rangle$ such that

- *$S_0 = \{\delta^*(\{s_0\}, \rho) \mid \rho \in {I_p}^*\}$,*
- *$\delta_p(S', \langle\tau, r\rangle) = \bigcup_{\rho\in I_p^*} \delta^*(\{s' \mid \exists s \in S'.\ \delta(s, \tau) = s' \wedge s'|_p = r\}, \rho)$.*

$\mathcal{D}_p$ reads a sequence $\tau \in {T_p}^*$ of $p\text{−}events$. Its state reflects, in which global state the system can be at a point in time, where process p has seen a sequence of $p\text{−}events$.

Lemma 3. *For a given transition system* Tr *with automaton $\langle S, s_0, T, \delta\rangle$, a process $p \in P$, and a sequence $h \in T^*$, we have that $s \in {\delta_p}^*\big(S_0, \mathsf{Ev}_p(h)\big)$ if, and only if, there is a sequence h' with $\mathsf{Ev}_p(h) = \mathsf{Ev}_p(h')$ such that $s \in \delta^*(s_0, h')$.*

This can be shown by induction over the length of $\mathsf{Ev}_p(h)$.

For each property φ, we equip $\mathcal{D}_p$ with an acceptance mechanism to obtain $\mathcal{D}_p^\varphi = \langle 2^S, S_0, p\text{−}events, \delta_p, F_\varphi\rangle$, where the set of final states is:

$$F_\varphi = \{S' \subseteq S \mid \forall s \in S'.\ s \models \varphi\}.$$

For D_p^φ, Lemma 3 provides the following corollary.

Corollary 1. *For a given transition system* Tr *with automaton $\langle S, s_0, T, \delta\rangle$, a process $p \in P$, and a sequence $h \in T^*$, we have that $\mathsf{Ev}_p(h)$ is accepted by $\mathcal{D}_p^\varphi$ iff $h \models K_p^{\mathrm{PR}}\varphi$.*

Thus, $\mathcal{D}_p^\varphi$ can be used to check whether or not process p knows φ. The complexity of this construction is quite high: as a subset automaton, $\mathcal{D}_p^\varphi$ can have $2^{|S|}$ states. However, subset automata like $\mathcal{D}_p^\varphi$ can be represented succinctly, such that the representation of a state requires 'only' S bits. As S can be exponential in the number of variables, this translates to $\mathcal{O}(2^{2^{|V|}})$ states, where each state is represented by $\mathcal{O}(2^{|V|})$ bits.

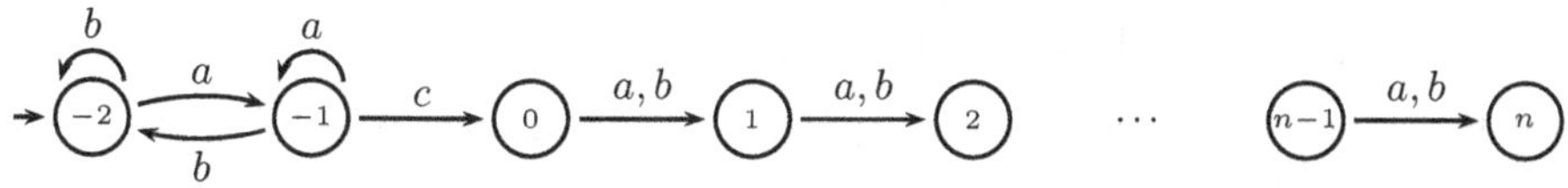

Fig. 5. Process 2 from the proof of Theorem 2

Consequently, we can transform Tr by including, for each process p, an implementation of the automaton $\mathcal{D}_p^{\varphi}$. This may require $|S|$ additional variables to represent the state of $\mathcal{D}_p^{\varphi}$, which will be variables local to p. They have no influence on the enabledness of transitions.

These new variables intuitively reflect the subset of the states, in which the system might be in, or, likewise, the set of assignments to its variables consistent with the sequence of $p-events$ observed. This representation can be improved: the valuation of the p-local variables V_p is already given by the p-local state, and storing this information again would be redundant. Thus, $\mathcal{O}(2^{|V \setminus V_p|})$ variables are sufficient to represent the additional information.

The above construction implements the $PR = PR(lt)$ knowledge. Similarly, we can implement the other notions of knowledge of perfect recall:

$PR(t)$ $\mathcal{D}_p^{\varphi} = \langle 2^S, S_0, T_p, \delta_p, F_\varphi \rangle$,
  $\delta_p(S', \tau) = \bigcup_{\rho \in I_p^*} \delta^*(\{s' \mid \exists s \in S'.\ \delta(s, \tau) = s'\}, \rho)$.
$PR(l)$ $\mathcal{D}_p^{\varphi} = \langle 2^S, S_0, S|_p, \delta_p, F_\varphi \rangle$,
  $\delta_p(S', r) = \bigcup_{\rho \in I_p^*} \delta^*(\{s' \mid \exists s \in S'.\ \exists \tau \in T_p\, \delta(s, \tau)|_p = r\}, \rho)$.
$PR(ct)$ $\mathcal{D}_p^{\varphi} = \langle 2^S, S_0, p-events, \delta_p, F_\varphi \rangle$,
  $\delta_p(S', \langle \tau, r \rangle) = \bigcup_{\rho \in I_p^*} \delta^*(\{s' \mid \exists s \in S'.\ \delta(s, \tau) = s' \wedge s'|_{L_t(\tau)} = r\}, \rho)$.
  (Note that the $p-events$ for $PR(ct)$ and $PR(lt)$ are different.)

5.3 Lower Bound on the Transformations for Perfect Recall

We show that the exponential memory blow-up for implementing PR is unavoidable.

Theorem 2. *There exists a family of systems $(\mathsf{Tr}_n)_{n \in \mathbb{N}}$ with 2 processes $\{1, 2\}$, one variable with $n + 3$ valuations (or equivalently $\lceil \log_2 n + 3 \rceil$ binary variables), four transitions, and $n + 3$ states and a family of assertion φ_n such that knowing with PR whether φ_n holds requires 2^n memory states.*

Notice that using $|V|$ binary variables, a counter up to $2^{|V|}$ can be encoded. Hence, Theorem 2 proves that one needs at least $2^{|V|} - 3$ bits of memory to implement PR, even when the description size of Tr_n is polynomial in $|V|$. For convenience, we use a variable with domain $\{-2, -1, 0, \ldots, n\}$ instead of encoding the values in binary. Process 2 is shown in Figure 5.

The proof uses the well-known family $(L_n)_{n \in \mathbb{N}} = \{w \in \{a, b\}^* \mid w = uav \text{ and } |v| = n\}$ of regular languages, accepted by a *non-deterministic* automaton with $n + 2$ states but not by any *deterministic* automaton with less than 2^n states.

Proof. The systems are defined as follows:

- there is only one variable v, it is on process 2, and its domain is $\{-2, -1, 0, \ldots, n\}$. Its initial value is -2.
- there are three transitions, $\{a, b, c\}$, with $L_t(a) = L_t(b) = \{1, 2\}$ and $L_t(c) = \{2\}$.
- transitions a, b are enabled in a state v iff $v < n$.
- a leads from -2 and -1 to -1, b leads from -2 and -1 to -2, such that the states -1 and -2 distinguish if the last transition seen has been an a (which is the case in -1 but not in -2),
- c is only enabled if $v = -1$ and updates the valuation of v to 0, and
- finally, for $0 \leq v < n$, transitions a, b increment the value of v by 1.

The state property φ_n is $v \neq n$. Let H_n be the set of histories h such that the suffix of h is bw with the number of a, b in w is n (w can have 0 or one c). We have that $\forall h \in H_n$, $last(h) \models \varphi_n$. The reason is that after a c, there are at most n letters a, b. Now, writing $h = ubw$, there cannot be a c in u, as there are $n + 1$ transition at least being done afterwards. That is, ub reached state -2. Now, it means that the first letter of w is not a c, and thus it is an a or a b. In any case, if c happens in w, there will be strictly less than n letters after it, and thus the valuation $v = n$ cannot be reached.

Notice now that $h \in H_n$ iff $\mathsf{Ev}_1(h) = ubw$ with $w \in \{a, b\}^n$ (process 1 has a unique state as it has no variable, hence we do not indicate it in the $p-events$). Thus for all h' such that $\mathsf{Ev}_1(h') = \mathsf{Ev}_1(h)$, we have $h' \in H_n$. Thus process 1 knows φ_n after any $h \in H_n$ using PR.

Assume by contradiction that there is an implementation of PR with less than 2^n memory states. Process 1 has no variables, such that its memory is updated only based on the sequence $Ev_1(h)$. As there are less than 2^n states, there exists 2 histories $u_1 \cdots u_n \neq u'_1 \cdots u'_n \in \{a, b\}^*$ leading to the same state s of the implementation. Let $u'_i \neq u_i$, let say $u_i = b$ and $u'_i = a$. Now, let us consider the histories $h = u_1 \cdots u_n a^{n-i}$ and $h' = u'_1 \cdots u'_i c u'_{i+1} \cdots u'_n a^{n-i}$. Clearly, $h \in H_n$, and thus process 1 knows φ_n after h using PR. However, the memory state after histories h, h' are the same, as a same sequence of 1-event is seen from state s. However, $last(h') = (v = n) \not\models \varphi_n$, hence 1 does not know φ_n after h using this implementation. A contradiction. $\square$

5.4 Implementation of Causal Knowledge

In order to provide a finite representation for causal knowledge we will adapt a construction by Mukund and Sohoni [14] for gossip automata.

Recall Definition 8 of a partial order $PO(h) = \langle E, \lambda, \prec \rangle$ associated with a history h and the causal view of a process p in h (Definition 9). We use the following notation:

- Recall that $\mathsf{last}_p(h) \in 2^{V_p}$ is the p-state reached by h (or equivalently by $PO(h)$),
- $\mathsf{latest}_p(h) = \max_\prec \{e \in E \mid p \in L_t(\lambda(e))\}$. This is the most recent occurrence of an event in h that is executed by p, and therefore the last occurrence of an event in $Ca_p(h)$. Notice that the p-state reached on $Ca_p(h)$ is also $\mathsf{last}_p(h)$,
- $\mathsf{latest}_{p \leftarrow q}(h) = \max_\prec \{e \in E \mid q \in L_t(\lambda(e))$ and $e \prec \mathsf{latest}_p(E)\}$. This is the most recent occurrence on q that precedes (or is the same as) the most recent occurrence of p. We denote by $\mathsf{last}_{p \leftarrow q}(h)$ the q-state reached on $Ca_p(h)$, which corresponds to the q-state reached by $\mathsf{latest}_{p \leftarrow q}(h)$.

The set $\mathsf{R}_p(h) = (\mathsf{last}_{p\leftarrow q}(h))_{q\in P}$ is the global state reached by $Ca_p(h)$. We can define the associated equivalence relation:

Definition 11. $h \approx_p h'$ *iff* $\mathsf{R}_p(h) = \mathsf{R}_p(h')$.

We can define a knowledge R based on this $\approx_p$. It is immediately clear that $\mathsf{Ca} \rhd \mathsf{R}$, since $\equiv_p^{\mathsf{C}}$ refines $\approx_p$. In fact, we have equality:

Lemma 4. R *is as deep as* Ca.

Proof. (Sketch) It is enough to show that for every history h, $\{\mathsf{last}(h') \mid Ca_p(h') = Ca_p(h)\} = \{\mathsf{last}(h') \mid R_p(h') = R_p(h)\}$.

We have trivially $\{h' \mid Ca_p(h') = Ca_p(h)\} \subseteq \{h' \mid R_p(h') = R_p(h)\}$ for every history h. Hence it suffices to prove that $\{\mathsf{last}(h') | R_p(h') = R_p(h)\} \subseteq \{\mathsf{last}(h') | Ca_p(h') = Ca_p(h)\}$ for every history h.

Let h' such that $R_p(h') = R_p(h)$. We thus have that the global state reached by $Ca_p(h)$ is the same as the global state reached by $Ca_p(h')$. By definition of $Ca_p(h')$, h' can be obtained from $Ca_p(h')$ by performing a sequence w of occurrences not on p. Now, consider doing this sequence w of occurrences from $Ca_p(h)$. It is possible as the global states reached by $Ca_p(h)$ and by $Ca_p(h')$ is the same. Hence we obtain a history $h'' = Ca_p(h)\,w$. Because the system is deterministic from a global state, $\mathsf{last}(h'') = \mathsf{last}(h')$ holds. We conclude by remarking that $Ca_p(h'') = Ca_p(hw) = Ca_p(h)$. □

This means that, for p, keeping $\mathsf{last}_{p\leftarrow q}(h)$ for all q is enough to implement Ca_p. Keeping this information is, however, not totally straightforward. Indeed, when performing transition a, all processes q involved in that transition a will have a value for $\mathsf{last}_{q\leftarrow r}(h)$ for all process r just before performing a. First, we have $\mathsf{last}_{p\leftarrow r}(ha) = \mathsf{last}_{q\leftarrow r}(ha)$ for all $p, q \in L_t(a)$ and all process r: each process will update the value in the same way. Let $state$ be the tuple $(\mathsf{last}_{s\leftarrow s}(h))_{s\in L_t(a)}$ aggregating all the latest s-state from all processes s involved in a. It is easy to see that, if $r \in L_t(a)$ is involved in a, then $\mathsf{last}_{q\leftarrow r}(ha) = \delta(state, a)_r$. That is, it suffices to deterministically perform a from $state$ and take the r-component. Now, the difficulties appear for $r \notin L_t(a)$, that is, if r is not involved in the transition. Then, it is easy to see that, for all $q \in L_t(a)$ involved in a (for which we need to update their state), $\mathsf{last}_{q\leftarrow r}(ha) = \mathsf{last}_{s\leftarrow r}(ha)$ for some process $s \in L_t(a)$. The question is, which one of all the process $s \in L_t(a)$ has the freshest information about r. If we know this, then every process p can keep accurately $\mathsf{last}_{p\leftarrow r}(h)$ for all r and implement Ca_p by the previous lemma.

It turns out that knowing which process among a set Q has the freshest information about any other process r is exactly what the gossip transformation of [14] does. Roughly speaking, the gossip transformation keeps a partial ordering regarding not only the occurrences $\mathsf{latest}_{p\leftarrow q}$ but also the occurrence $\mathsf{latest}_{p\leftarrow q\leftarrow r}$ (called the tertiary information), which corresponds to the latest occurrence on r before $\mathsf{latest}_{p\leftarrow q}$. Comparing these partial orders from every process $p \in L_t(a)$ involved in the transition a, one can determine who has the latest information on r for every process r [14]. As the number of processes is linear, the number of occurrences of the tertiary information is polynomial.

Keeping the partial order about occurrences of the tertiary information therefore only requires a polynomial number of bits. Notice that [9] (see also [17,2] for the original timestamping) gives a construction that uses only $O(P^2 \log P)$ bits of memory.

Table 1. Complexity of checking knowledge

Knowledge	additional bits of information	on-the-fly complexity	with precomputation
memoryless	0	PSPACE($\|V\|$)	$O(\|V_p\|)$
perfect recall	$2^{\|V\|}$	EXPTIME($\|V\|$)	$O(\|V\| \cdot 2^{\|V\|})$
causal	$\|P\|^2 \log(\|P\|) \log(\|\mathsf{Tr}\|) + \|V\|$	PSPACE($\|V\|$)	$O(\|V\|)$

We thus augment the program (the transitions, in our case) with variables that will implement the gossip automata construction, as well as the state $\mathsf{last}_{p \leftarrow q}$ for each process q. That is, the number of bits we need to implement Ca_p is $O(|V| + P^2 \log P)$.

There are again two alternative ways to check for a particular knowledge:

With Offline Precomputation: We precalculate a table that, for each $state = (\mathsf{last}_{p \leftarrow q})_{q \in P}$, tells whether every global state which can be reached from $state$ by performing only occurrences not on p models φ. If it is the case, then $s \models K_p^C \varphi$ holds. This can be held in a table of $\mathcal{O}(2^n)$ entries. The complexity to check on the fly using the table whether $state$ satisfies the property can then be done in PTIME.

Online Construction: If the table is not calculated in advance, we need to perform a search for a global state not satisfying φ and reachable from $state$ using only occurrences not on p. This may takes exponential time (or, alternatively, PSPACE).

The various complexity results we obtained are summed up in Table 1.

6 Conclusions

Knowledge is the foundation for reasoning about the correctness of concurrent systems. It is a prerequisite for enforcing some global coordination with minimal synchronization. While the most basic notion of knowledge, which only depends on the current local state, is essentially an invariant (given the current local state of a process, the global state satisfies some property), knowledge can also be defined based on the observable history: 'knowledge of perfect recall' takes the local observable history of a process into account [3]. We add another notion of knowledge, one that allows not only to memorize local history, but also to update it through communication. We provide a corresponding new definition of knowledge, based on causality.

Knowledge has proven to be useful for the construction of control in concurrent systems [1,8,16]: based on the knowledge calculation, the system can be controlled to satisfy additional imposed global properties. Such constructions are monotonic in the sense that they preserve the knowledge calculated before control was added. When memoryless knowledge is not sufficient, one may need to use constructions that exploit perfect recall or causal knowledge. The view we take in this paper is that using knowledge in this context amounts to a simple transformation of the system. Specifically, the construction we provide here for causal knowledge can be used for supporting such a control construction. It is interesting to observe that causal knowledge is cheaper than knowledge of perfect recall, both in terms of bits to remember and in terms of time complexity. Moreover, causal knowledge is stronger: it refines the knowledge available under perfect recall. However, the transformation, which is required for causal knowledge, is based on the ability to exchange information while performing a joint transition (by the observed or controlled system). If this is not allowed, one may revert to the weaker control through knowledge of perfect recall, where the controller may need to keep an expensive progress table that represents the reachable global states.

References

1. Basu, A., Bensalem, S., Peled, D., Sifakis, J.: Priority scheduling of distributed systems based on model checking. Formal Methods in System Design 39(3), 229–245 (2011)
2. Diekert, V., Rozenberg, G.: In particular. In: Diekert, V., Muscholl, A. (eds.) The Book of Traces, ch. 8, World Scientific, Singapore (1995)
3. Fagin, R., Halpern, J.Y., Moses, Y., Vardi, M.: Reasoning About Knowledge. MIT Press, Cambridge (1995)
4. Gastin, P., Lerman, B., Zeitoun, M.: Distributed Games with Causal Memory Are Decidable for Series-Parallel Systems. In: Lodaya, K., Mahajan, M. (eds.) FSTTCS 2004. LNCS, vol. 3328, pp. 275–286. Springer, Heidelberg (2004)
5. Genest, B., Gimbert, H., Muscholl, A., Walukiewicz, I.: Optimal zielonka-type construction of deterministic asynchronous automata. In: Abramsky, S., Gavoille, C., Kirchner, C., Meyer auf der Heide, F., Spirakis, P.G. (eds.) ICALP 2010, Part II. LNCS, vol. 6199, pp. 52–63. Springer, Heidelberg (2010)
6. Genest, B., Gimbert, H., Muscholl, A., Walukiewicz, I.: Asynchronous Games over Tree Architectures. In: Fomin, F.V., Freivalds, R., Kwiatkowska, M., Peleg, D. (eds.) ICALP 2013, Part II. LNCS, vol. 7966, pp. 275–286. Springer, Heidelberg (2013)
7. Genest, B., Muscholl, A.: Constructing Exponential-size Deterministic Zielonka Automata. In: Bugliesi, M., Preneel, B., Sassone, V., Wegener, I. (eds.) ICALP 2006, Part II. LNCS, vol. 4052, pp. 565–576. Springer, Heidelberg (2006)
8. Graf, S., Peled, D., Quinton, S.: Monitoring Distributed Systems Using Knowledge. In: Bruni, R., Dingel, J. (eds.) FORTE 2011 and FMOODS 2011. LNCS, vol. 6722, pp. 183–197. Springer, Heidelberg (2011)
9. Krishnan, R., Venkatesh, S.: Optimizing the gossip automaton, Report TCS-94-3, School of Mathematics, SPIC Science Foundation, Madras, India (1994)
10. Mazurkiewicz, A.: Concurrent program schemes and their interpretation. Technical report, DAIMI Report PB-78, Aarhus University (1977)
11. van der Meyden, R.: Common Knowledge and Update in Finite Environment. Information and Computation 140(2), 115–157 (1998)
12. van der Meyden, R., Shilov, N.V.: Model Checking Knowledge and Time in Systems with Perfect Recall. In: Pandu Rangan, C., Raman, V., Sarukkai, S. (eds.) FST TCS 1999. LNCS, vol. 1738, pp. 432–445. Springer, Heidelberg (1999)
13. Meyer, A.R., Stockmeyer, L.J.: The Equivalence Problem for Regular Expressions with Squaring Requires Exponential Space. In: Proc. of STOC 1973, pp. 1–9 (1973)
14. Mukund, M., Sohoni, M.: Keeping Track of the Latest Gossip in a Distributed System. Distr. Computing 10(3), 137–148 (1997)
15. Madhusudan, P., Thiagarajan, P.S., Yang, S.: The MSO Theory of Connectedly Communicating Processes. In: Sarukkai, S., Sen, S. (eds.) FSTTCS 2005. LNCS, vol. 3821, pp. 201–212. Springer, Heidelberg (2005)
16. Ricker, S.L., Rudie, K.: Know means no: Incorporating knowledge into discrete-event control systems. IEEE Trans. Automat. Contr. 45(9), 1656–1668 (2000)
17. Zielonka, W.: Notes on finite asynchronous automata. R.A.I.R.O. - Informatique Théorique et Applications 21, 99–135 (1987)

Compositional Metric Reasoning with Probabilistic Process Calculi

Daniel Gebler[1], Kim Guldstrand Larsen[2,⋆], and Simone Tini[3]

[1] VU University Amsterdam (NL)
[2] Aalborg University (DK)
[3] University of Insubria (IT)

Abstract. We study which standard operators of probabilistic process calculi allow for compositional reasoning with respect to bisimulation metric semantics. We argue that uniform continuity (generalizing the earlier proposed property of non-expansiveness) captures the essential nature of compositional reasoning and allows now also to reason compositionally about recursive processes. We characterize the distance between probabilistic processes composed by standard process algebra operators. Combining these results, we demonstrate how compositional reasoning about systems specified by continuous process algebra operators allows for metric assume-guarantee like performance validation.

1 Introduction

Probabilistic process algebras describe probabilistic concurrent communicating systems (probabilistic processes for short). In this paper we study compositional reasoning over probabilistic processes, specified by terms of probabilistic process algebras.

Behavioral equivalences equate processes that are indistinguishable to any external observer. The most prominent example is bisimulation equivalence [15], which provides a well-established theory of the behavior of probabilistic nondeterministic transition systems. However, bisimulation equivalence is too sensitive to the exact probabilities of transitions. The slightest perturbation of the probabilities can destroy bisimilarity. Bisimulation metric [3, 7, 8] provides a robust semantics for probabilistic processes. It is the quantitative analogue to bisimulation equivalence and assigns to each pair of processes a distance which measures the proximity of their quantitative properties. The distances form a pseudometric[1] where bisimilar processes are in distance 0.

In order to specify and verify systems in a compositional manner, it is necessary that the behavioral semantics is compatible with all operators of the language that describe these systems. For behavioral equivalence semantics there is common agreement that compositional reasoning requires that the considered behavioral equivalence is a congruence wrt. all operators. On the other hand, for behavioral metric semantics there are several proposals of properties that operators should satisfy in order to facilitate compositional reasoning. Most prominent examples are non-expansiveness [8]

⋆ This research is partially supported by the European FET projects SENSATION and CASSTING and the Sino-Danish Center IDEA4CPS.

[1] A bisimulation metric is in fact a pseudometric. For convenience we use the term bisimulation metric instead of bisimulation pseudometric.

A. Pitts (Ed.): FOSSACS 2015, LNCS 9034, pp. 230–245, 2015.
DOI: 10.1007/978-3-662-46678-0_15

and non-extensiveness [1]. We discuss these properties and propose uniform continuity as the most natural property of process operators to facilitate compositional reasoning wrt. behavioral metric semantics especially in presence of recursion. Uniform continuity generalizes non-extensiveness and non-expansiveness and captures the essential nature of compositional reasoning wrt. behavioral metric semantics. A uniformly continuous binary process operator f ensures that for any non-zero bisimulation distance ϵ (understood as the admissible tolerance from the operational behavior of the composed process $f(p_1, p_2)$) there are non-zero bisimulation distances δ_1 and δ_2 (understood as the admissible tolerances from the operational behavior of the processes p_1 and p_2) such that the distance between the composed processes $f(p_1, p_2)$ and $f(p'_1, p'_2)$ is at most ϵ whenever the component p'_1 (resp. p'_2) is in distance of at most δ_1 from p_1 (resp. at most δ_2 from p_2). Our key contributions are as follows:

1. We develop for many non-recursive and recursive process operators used in various probabilistic process algebras tight upper bounds on the distance between processes combined by those operators (Sec. 3.2 and 4.2).
2. We show that non-recursive process operators, esp. (nondeterministic and probabilistic variants of) sequential, alternative and parallel composition, allow for compositional reasoning wrt. the compositionality criteria of non-expansiveness and hence also wrt. uniform continuity (Sec. 3).
3. We show that recursive process operators, e.g. (nondeterministic and probabilistic variants of) Kleene-star iteration and π-calculus bang replication, allow for compositional reasoning wrt. the compositionality criterion of uniform continuity, but not wrt. non-expansiveness and non-extensiveness (Sec. 4).
4. We demonstrate the usefulness of compositional reasoning using a network protocol build from uniformly continuous operators. In particular, we show how it is possible to derive performance guarantees of the entire system from performance assumptions about individual components. Conversely, we show how it is also possible to derive performance requirements on individual components from performance requirements of the complete system (Sec. 5).

2 Preliminaries

We consider transition systems with process terms as states and a transition relation inductively defined by means of SOS rules. Process terms are inductively defined by the process combinators. The SOS rules are syntax-driven inference rules that define the behavior of complex processes in terms of the behavior of their components.

Probabilistic Transition Systems. A *signature* is a structure $\Sigma = (F, \mathsf{r})$, where F is a countable set of *operators*, or *process combinators*, and $\mathsf{r}\colon F \to \mathbb{N}$ is a *rank function*, which gives the arity of an operator. By $f \in \Sigma$ we mean $f \in F$. We assume an infinite set of *process variables* (or *state variables*) $\mathcal{V}_s$ disjoint from F. The set of *process terms* (or *state terms*) over a signature Σ and a set $V \subseteq \mathcal{V}_s$ of variables, notation $\mathsf{T}(\Sigma, V)$, is the least set satisfying: (i) $V \subseteq \mathsf{T}(\Sigma, V)$, and (ii) $f(t_1, \ldots, t_n) \in \mathsf{T}(\Sigma, V)$ whenever $f \in \Sigma$, $t_1, \ldots, t_n \in \mathsf{T}(\Sigma, V)$ and $n = \mathsf{r}(f)$. We will use n for $\mathsf{r}(f)$ if it is clear from the context. We write $\mathsf{T}(\Sigma)$ for $\mathsf{T}(\Sigma, \emptyset)$ (set of all *closed process terms*) and $\mathbb{T}(\Sigma)$ for $\mathsf{T}(\Sigma, \mathcal{V}_s)$ (set of all *open process terms*). We may refer to closed process terms as *processes*.

Probabilistic transition systems extend transition systems by allowing for probabilistic choices in the transitions. We consider probabilistic nondeterministic labelled transition systems [15]. The state space is defined as the set $\mathsf{T}(\Sigma)$ of all processes. Probability distributions over this state space are mappings $\pi\colon \mathsf{T}(\Sigma) \to [0,1]$ with $\sum_{t\in\mathsf{T}(\Sigma)} \pi(t) = 1$ that assign to each process t its respective probability $\pi(t)$. By $\Delta(\mathsf{T}(\Sigma))$ we denote the set of all probability distributions on $\mathsf{T}(\Sigma)$. We let π, π' range over $\Delta(\mathsf{T}(\Sigma))$.

Definition 1 (PTS). *A probabilistic nondeterministic labeled transition system (PTS) is given by a triple $(\mathsf{T}(\Sigma), A, \to)$, where Σ is a signature, A is a countable set of* actions, *and* $\to\, \subseteq \mathsf{T}(\Sigma) \times A \times \Delta(\mathsf{T}(\Sigma))$ *is a* transition relation. *We write $t \xrightarrow{a} \pi$ for $(t, a, \pi) \in\, \to$.*

Bisimulation Metric on PTS. We define now bisimulation metric as the quantitative analogue to bisimulation equivalence. A 1-*bounded pseudometric* on the set of processes $\mathsf{T}(\Sigma)$ is a function $d\colon \mathsf{T}(\Sigma) \times \mathsf{T}(\Sigma) \to [0,1]$ with $d(t,t) = 0$, $d(t,t') = d(t',t)$, and $d(t,t') \leq d(t,t'') + d(t'',t')$, for all $t,t',t'' \in \mathsf{T}(\Sigma)$. We will use 1-bounded pseudometrics to describe the behavioral distances between processes. We order 1-bounded pseudometrics by $d_1 \sqsubseteq d_2$ iff $d_1(t,t') \leq d_2(t,t')$ for all $t,t' \in \mathsf{T}(\Sigma)$.

A 1-bounded pseudometric on processes $\mathsf{T}(\Sigma)$ is lifted to a 1-bounded pseudometric on distributions $\Delta(\mathsf{T}(\Sigma))$ by means of the Kantorovich pseudometric. A *matching* for $(\pi,\pi') \in \Delta(\mathsf{T}(\Sigma)) \times \Delta(\mathsf{T}(\Sigma))$ is a distribution $\omega \in \Delta(\mathsf{T}(\Sigma) \times \mathsf{T}(\Sigma))$ with $\sum_{t'\in\mathsf{T}(\Sigma)} \omega(t,t') = \pi(t)$ and $\sum_{t\in\mathsf{T}(\Sigma)} \omega(t,t') = \pi'(t')$ for all $t,t' \in \mathsf{T}(\Sigma)$. Let $\Omega(\pi,\pi')$ be the set of all matchings for (π,π'). The *Kantorovich pseudometric* $\mathbf{K}(d)\colon \Delta(\mathsf{T}(\Sigma)) \times \Delta(\mathsf{T}(\Sigma)) \to [0,1]$ for a pseudometric $d\colon \mathsf{T}(\Sigma) \times \mathsf{T}(\Sigma) \to [0,1]$ is given by $\mathbf{K}(d)(\pi,\pi') = \min_{\omega\in\Omega(\pi,\pi')} \sum_{t,t'\in\mathsf{T}(\Sigma)} d(t,t') \cdot \omega(t,t')$ for all $\pi,\pi' \in \Delta(\mathsf{T}(\Sigma))$.

A 1-bounded pseudometric is a bisimulation metric if for all pairs of process terms t and t' each transition of t can be mimicked by a transition of t' with the same label and the distance between the accessible distributions does not exceed the distance between t and t'. By means of a *discount factor* $\lambda \in (0,1]$ we allow to specify how much the behavioral distance of future transitions is taken into account [6,8]. The discount factor $\lambda = 1$ expresses no discount, meaning that the differences in the behavior between t and t' are considered irrespective of after how many steps they can be observed.

Definition 2 (Bisimulation metric [8]). *A* 1*-bounded pseudometric d on $\mathsf{T}(\Sigma)$ is a λ-*bisimulation metric *for $\lambda \in (0,1]$ if for all process terms $t,t' \in \mathsf{T}(\Sigma)$ with $d(t,t') < 1$, if $t \xrightarrow{a} \pi$ then there exists a transition $t' \xrightarrow{a} \pi'$ such that $\lambda \cdot \mathbf{K}(d)(\pi,\pi') \leq d(t,t')$.*

The smallest λ-bisimulation metric, notation $\mathbf{d}_\lambda$, is called *λ-bisimilarity metric* [3,7,8]. By λ-bisimulation distance between t and t' we mean $\mathbf{d}_\lambda(t,t')$. Bisimilarity equivalence [15] is the kernel of $\mathbf{d}_\lambda$ [8], i.e. $\mathbf{d}_\lambda(t,t') = 0$ iff t and t' are bisimilar. We may write $\mathbf{d}$ for $\mathbf{d}_1$.

Remark 3. Clearly, $\mathbf{d}_\lambda(t,t') \in [0,\lambda] \cup \{1\}$ for all $t,t' \in \mathsf{T}(\Sigma)$. Let $\lambda < 1$. Then, $\mathbf{d}_\lambda(t,t') = 1$ iff t can perform an action which t' cannot (or vice versa), $\mathbf{d}_\lambda(t,t') = 0$ iff t and t' have the same reactive behavior, and $\mathbf{d}_\lambda(t,t') \in (0,\lambda]$ iff t and t' have different reactive behavior after performing the same initial action.

Algebra of Probability Distributions. We start with some notations and operations on probability distributions. We denote by $\delta(t)$ with $t \in \mathsf{T}(\Sigma)$ the *Dirac distribution* defined by $(\delta(t))(t) = 1$ and $(\delta(t))(t') = 0$ if $t \neq t'$. The convex combination $\sum_{i \in I} p_i \pi_i$ of a family $\{\pi_i\}_{i \in I}$ of probability distributions $\pi_i \in \Delta(\mathsf{T}(\Sigma))$ with $p_i \in (0, 1]$ and $\sum_{i \in I} p_i = 1$ is defined by $(\sum_{i \in I} p_i \pi_i)(t) = \sum_{i \in I}(p_i \pi_i(t))$ for all $t \in \mathsf{T}(\Sigma)$. The expression $f(\pi_1, \ldots, \pi_n)$ with $f \in \Sigma$ and $\pi_i \in \Delta(\mathsf{T}(\Sigma))$ denotes the product distribution of $\pi_1, \ldots, \pi_n$ defined by $f(\pi_1, \ldots, \pi_n)(f(t_1, \ldots, t_n)) = \prod_{i=1}^{n} \pi_i(t_i)$ and $f(\pi_1, \ldots, \pi_n)(t) = 0$ for all $t \in \mathsf{T}(\Sigma)$ not in the form $t = f(t_1, \ldots, t_n)$. For binary operators f we may write $\pi_1 \, f \, \pi_2$ for $f(\pi_1, \pi_2)$.

In order to describe probabilistic behavior, we need syntactic expressions that denote probability distributions. To be precise, each closed expression will denote some probability distribution, and each open expression instantiates by a closed substitution to some probability distribution. We assume an infinite set of *distribution variables* $\mathcal{V}_d$. We let μ, ν range over $\mathcal{V}_d$. We denote by $\mathcal{V}$ the set of process and distribution variables $\mathcal{V} = \mathcal{V}_s \cup \mathcal{V}_d$. The set of *distribution terms* over process variables $V_s \subseteq \mathcal{V}_s$ and distribution variables $V_d \subseteq \mathcal{V}_d$, notation $\mathsf{DT}(\Sigma, V_s, V_d)$, is the least set satisfying [12]: (i) $V_d \subseteq \mathsf{DT}(\Sigma, V_s, V_d)$, (ii) $\{\delta(t) \mid t \in \mathsf{T}(\Sigma, V_s)\} \subseteq \mathsf{DT}(\Sigma, V_s, V_d)$, (iii) $\sum_{i \in I} p_i \theta_i \in \mathsf{DT}(\Sigma, V_s, V_d)$ whenever $\theta_i \in \mathsf{DT}(\Sigma, V_s, V_d)$ and $p_i \in (0, 1]$ with $\sum_{i \in I} p_i = 1$, and (iv) $f(\theta_1, \ldots, \theta_n) \in \mathsf{DT}(\Sigma, V_s, V_d)$ whenever $f \in \Sigma$ and $\theta_i \in \mathsf{DT}(\Sigma, V_s, V_d)$. We write $\mathbb{DT}(\Sigma)$ for $\mathsf{DT}(\Sigma, \mathcal{V}_s, \mathcal{V}_d)$ (set of all *open distribution terms*), and $\mathsf{DT}(\Sigma)$ for $\mathsf{DT}(\Sigma, \emptyset, \emptyset)$ (set of all *closed distribution terms*).

Distribution terms have the following meaning. A *distribution variable* $\mu \in \mathcal{V}_d$ is a variable that takes values from $\Delta(\mathsf{T}(\Sigma))$. An *instantiable Dirac distribution* $\delta(t)$ is an expression that takes as value the Dirac distribution $\delta(t')$ when variables in t are substituted so that t becomes the closed term t'. Case iii allows to construct convex combinations of distributions. We write $\theta_1 \oplus_p \theta_2$ for $\sum_{i=1}^{2} p_i \theta_i$ with $p_1 = p$ and $p_2 = 1-p$. Case iv lifts the structural inductive construction of state terms to distribution terms.

A *substitution* is a mapping $\sigma \colon \mathcal{V} \to \mathbb{T}(\Sigma) \cup \mathbb{DT}(\Sigma)$ s.t. $\sigma(x) \in \mathbb{T}(\Sigma)$ if $x \in \mathcal{V}_s$ and $\sigma(\mu) \in \mathbb{DT}(\Sigma)$ if $\mu \in \mathcal{V}_d$. σ extends to a mapping from process terms to process terms as usual and to a mapping from distribution terms to distribution terms by $\sigma(\delta(t)) = \delta(\sigma(t))$, $\sigma(\sum_{i \in I} p_i \theta_i) = \sum_{i \in I} p_i \sigma(\theta_i)$, and $\sigma(f(\theta_1, \ldots, \theta_n)) = f(\sigma(\theta_1), \ldots, \sigma(\theta_n))$. A substitution σ is *closed* if $\sigma(x) \in \mathsf{T}(\Sigma)$ for all $x \in \mathcal{V}_s$ and $\sigma(\mu) \in \mathsf{DT}(\Sigma)$ for all $\mu \in \mathcal{V}_d$.

Specification of Process Combinators. We specify the operational semantics of process combinators by SOS rules in the probabilistic GSOS format [2,12]. The operational semantics of a process term is given by inductively applying the respective SOS rules.

Definition 4 (PGSOS rule [2, 12]). *A* PGSOS rule *has the form:*

$$\frac{\{x_i \xrightarrow{a_{i,k}} \mu_{i,k} \mid i \in I, k \in K_i\} \qquad \{x_i \stackrel{b_{i,l}}{\not\longrightarrow} \mid i \in I, l \in L_i\}}{f(x_1, \ldots, x_n) \xrightarrow{a} \theta}$$

with n the rank of operator $f \in \Sigma$, $I = \{1, \ldots, n\}$ the indices of the arguments of f, finite index sets K_i, L_i, actions $a_{i,k}, b_{i,l}, a \in A$, process variables $x_i \in \mathcal{V}_s$, distribution variables $\mu_{i,k} \in \mathcal{V}_d$, distribution term $\theta \in \mathbb{DT}(\Sigma)$, and constraints:

1. *all $\mu_{i,k}$ for $i \in I, k \in K_i$ are pairwise different;*
2. *all $x_1, \ldots, x_n$ are pairwise different;*
3. *$Var(\theta) \subseteq \{\mu_{i,k} \mid i \in I, k \in K_i\} \cup \{x_1 \ldots, x_n\}$.*

The expressions $x_i \xrightarrow{a_{i,k}} \mu_{i,k}$ and $x_i \stackrel{b_{i,l}}{\not\longrightarrow}$ above the line, and $f(x_1, \ldots, x_n) \xrightarrow{a} \theta$ below the line, are called, resp., *positive premises*, *negative premises* and *conclusion* of the rule.

Table 1. Standard non-recursive process combinators

$$\frac{}{\varepsilon \xrightarrow{\surd} \delta(0)} \qquad \frac{}{a.\bigoplus_{i=1}^{n}[p_i]x_i \xrightarrow{a} \sum_{i=1}^{n} p_i\delta(x_i)} \qquad \frac{x \xrightarrow{a} \mu \quad a \neq \surd}{x;y \xrightarrow{a} \mu;\delta(y)} \qquad \frac{x \xrightarrow{\surd} \mu \quad y \xrightarrow{a} \nu}{x;y \xrightarrow{a} \nu}$$

$$\frac{x \xrightarrow{a} \mu}{x+y \xrightarrow{a} \mu} \qquad \frac{y \xrightarrow{a} \nu}{x+y \xrightarrow{a} \nu} \qquad \frac{x \xrightarrow{a} \mu \quad y \xrightarrow{a} \nu}{x \mid y \xrightarrow{a} \mu \mid \nu} \qquad \frac{x \xrightarrow{a} \mu}{x \mathbin{|||} y \xrightarrow{a} \mu \mathbin{|||} \delta(y)} \qquad \frac{y \xrightarrow{a} \nu}{x \mathbin{|||} y \xrightarrow{a} \delta(x) \mathbin{|||} \nu}$$

$$\frac{x \xrightarrow{a} \mu \quad y \xrightarrow{a} \nu \quad a \in B\setminus\{\surd\}}{x \parallel_B y \xrightarrow{a} \mu \parallel_B \nu} \qquad \frac{x \xrightarrow{a} \mu \quad a \notin B\cup\{\surd\}}{x \parallel_B y \xrightarrow{a} \mu \parallel_B \delta(y)} \qquad \frac{y \xrightarrow{a} \nu \quad a \notin B\cup\{\surd\}}{x \parallel_B y \xrightarrow{a} \delta(x) \parallel_B \nu} \qquad \frac{x \xrightarrow{\surd} \mu \quad y \xrightarrow{\surd} \nu}{x \parallel_B y \xrightarrow{\surd} \delta(0)}$$

A *probabilistic transition system specification* (PTSS) in PGSOS format is a triple $P = (\Sigma, A, R)$, where Σ is a signature, A is a countable set of actions and R is a countable set of PGSOS rules. A *supported model* of P is a PTS $(\mathsf{T}(\Sigma), A, \rightarrow)$ such that the transition relation $\rightarrow$ contains all and only those transitions for which P offers a justification, i.e. $t \xrightarrow{a} \pi \in \rightarrow$ iff for some rule $r \in R$ and some closed substitution σ all premises of r hold, i.e. for all positive premises $x_i \xrightarrow{a_{i,k}} \mu_{i,k}$ we have $\sigma(x_i) \xrightarrow{a_{i,k}} \sigma(\mu_{i,k}) \in \rightarrow$ and for all negative premises $x_i \stackrel{b_{i,l}}{\not\longrightarrow}$ we have $\sigma(x_i) \xrightarrow{b_{i,l}} \pi \notin \rightarrow$ for all $\pi \in \Delta(\mathsf{T}(\Sigma))$, and the conclusion $f(x_1, \ldots, x_n) \xrightarrow{a} \theta$ instantiates to $\sigma(f(x_1, \ldots, x_n)) = t$ and $\sigma(\theta) = \pi$. Each PTSS in PGSOS format has a supported model which is moreover unique [2].

Intuitively, a term $f(t_1, \ldots, t_n)$ represents the composition of processes $t_1, \ldots, t_n$ by operator f. A rule r specifies some transition $f(t_1, \ldots, t_n) \xrightarrow{a} \pi$ that represents the evolution of the composed process $f(t_1, \ldots, t_n)$ by action a to the distribution π.

Definition 5 (Disjoint Extension). *Let $P = (\Sigma, A, R)$ and $P' = (\Sigma', A, R')$ be two PTSSs in PGSOS format. P' is a* disjoint extension *of P, notation $P \sqsubseteq P'$, iff $\Sigma \subseteq \Sigma'$, $R \subseteq R'$ and R' introduces no new rule for any operator in Σ.*

The disjoint extension of the specification of some process combinator allows to specify arbitrary processes while the operational semantics of the process combinator remains unchanged. This allows us to study the compositionality properties of concrete process combinators which hold for the composition of arbitrary processes.

3 Non-recursive Processes

We start by discussing compositional reasoning over probabilistic processes that are composed by non-recursive process combinators. First we introduce the most common non-recursive process combinators, then study the distance between composed processes, and conclude by analyzing their compositionality properties. Our study of compositionality properties generalizes earlier results of [7, 8] which considered only a small set of process combinators and only the property of non-expansiveness. The development of tight bounds on the distance between composed process (necessary for effective metric assume-guarantee performance validation) is novel.

3.1 Non-recursive Process Combinators

We introduce a probabilistic process algebra that comprises many of the probabilistic CCS [2] and CSP [4] process combinators. Let Σ_{PA} be a signature with the following

Table 2. Standard non-recursive probabilistic process combinators

$$\frac{x \xrightarrow{a} \mu \quad y \not\xrightarrow{a}}{x +_p y \xrightarrow{a} \mu} \qquad \frac{x \not\xrightarrow{a} \quad y \xrightarrow{a} \nu}{x +_p y \xrightarrow{a} \nu} \qquad \frac{x \xrightarrow{a} \mu \quad y \xrightarrow{a} \nu}{x +_p y \xrightarrow{a} \mu \oplus_p \nu}$$

$$\frac{x \xrightarrow{a} \mu \quad y \not\xrightarrow{a}}{x \mathbin{|||_p} y \xrightarrow{a} \mu \mathbin{|||_p} \delta(y)} \qquad \frac{x \not\xrightarrow{a} \quad y \xrightarrow{a} \nu}{x \mathbin{|||_p} y \xrightarrow{a} \delta(x) \mathbin{|||_p} \nu} \qquad \frac{x \xrightarrow{a} \mu \quad y \xrightarrow{a} \nu}{x \mathbin{|||_p} y \xrightarrow{a} \mu \mathbin{|||_p} \delta(y) \oplus_p \delta(x) \mathbin{|||_p} \nu}$$

operators: i) constants 0 (stop process) and ε (skip process); ii) a family of n-ary probabilistic prefix operators $a.([p_1]\_ \oplus \ldots \oplus [p_n]\_)$ with $a \in A$, $n \geq 1$, $p_1, \ldots, p_n \in (0, 1]$ and $\sum_{i=1}^{n} p_i = 1$; iii) binary operators $\_;\_$ (sequential composition), $\_ + \_$ (alternative composition), $\_ +_p \_$ (probabilistic alternative composition), $\_ \mid \_$ (synchronous parallel composition), $\_ ||| \_$ (asynchronous parallel composition), $\_ |||_p \_$ (probabilistic parallel composition), and $\_ \|_B \_$ for each for each $B \subseteq A$ (CSP parallel composition). The PTSS $P_{\mathrm{PA}} = (\Sigma_{\mathrm{PA}}, A, R_{\mathrm{PA}})$ is given by the rules R_{PA} in Tab. 1 and Tab. 2. We write $a.\bigoplus_{i=1}^{n}[p_i]\_$ for $a.([p_1]\_ \oplus \ldots \oplus [p_n]\_)$ and $a.\_$ for $a.([1]\_)$. Moreover, by process a we mean $a.0$.

3.2 Distance between Non-recursive Processes

We develop now tight bounds on the distance between processes combined by the non -recursive process combinators. This allows us later to derive the compositionality properties of those operators. As we will discuss two different compositionality properties for non-recursive processes, we split in this section the discussion on the distance bounds accordingly. We use disjoint extensions of the specification of the process combinators in order to reason over the composition of arbitrary processes.

We will express the bound on the distance between composed processes $f(s_1, \ldots, s_n)$ and $f(t_1, \ldots, t_n)$ in terms of the distance between their respective components s_i and t_i. Intuitively, given a probabilistic process $f(s_1, \ldots, s_n)$ we provide a bound on the distance to the respective probabilistic process $f(t_1, \ldots, t_n)$ where each component s_i is replaced by the component t_i. We start with those process combinators that satisfy the later discussed compositionality property of non-extensiveness (Def. 9).

Proposition 6. *Let $P = (\Sigma, A, R)$ be any PTSS with $P_{\mathrm{PA}} \sqsubseteq P$. For all $s_i, t_i \in T(\Sigma)$*

(a) $\mathbf{d}_\lambda(a.\bigoplus_{i=1}^{n}[p_i]s_i, a.\bigoplus_{i=1}^{n}[p_i]t_i) \leq \lambda \sum_{i=1}^{n} p_i \mathbf{d}_\lambda(s_i, t_i)$;
(b) $\mathbf{d}_\lambda(s_1 + s_2, t_1 + t_2) \leq \max(\mathbf{d}_\lambda(s_1, t_1), \mathbf{d}_\lambda(s_2, t_2))$;
(c) $\mathbf{d}_\lambda(s_1 +_p s_2, t_1 +_p t_2) \leq \max(\mathbf{d}_\lambda(s_1, t_1), \mathbf{d}_\lambda(s_2, t_2))$.

The distance between action prefixed processes (Prop. 6.a) is discounted by λ since the processes $a.\bigoplus_{i=1}^{n}[p_i]s_i$ and $a.\bigoplus_{i=1}^{n}[p_i]t_i$ perform first the action a before s_i and t_i may evolve. The distances between processes composed by either the nondeterministic alternative composition operator or by the probabilistic alternative composition are both bounded by the maximum of the distances between their respective arguments (Prop. 6.b and Prop. 6.c). The distance bounds for these operators coincide since the first two rules specifying the probabilistic alternative composition define the same operational behavior as the nondeterministic alternative composition and the third rule defines a convex combination of these transitions.

We proceed with those process combinators that satisfy the later discussed compositionality property of non-expansiveness (Def. 12).

Proposition 7. *Let $P = (\Sigma, A, R)$ be any PTSS with $P_{PA} \sqsubseteq P$. For all $s_i, t_i \in T(\Sigma)$*

(a) $\mathbf{d}_\lambda(s_1; s_2, t_1; t_2) \leq \begin{cases} 1 & \textit{if } \mathbf{d}_\lambda(s_1, t_1) = 1 \\ \max(d^a_{1,2}, \mathbf{d}_\lambda(s_2, t_2)) & \textit{if } \mathbf{d}_\lambda(s_1, t_1) \in [0, 1) \end{cases}$

(b) $\mathbf{d}_\lambda(s_1 \mid s_2, t_1 \mid t_2) \leq d^s$

(c) $\mathbf{d}_\lambda(s_1 \mid\mid\mid s_2, t_1 \mid\mid\mid t_2) \leq d^a$

(d) $\mathbf{d}_\lambda(s_1 \mid\mid_B s_2, t_1 \mid\mid_B t_2) \leq \begin{cases} d^s & \textit{if } B \setminus \{\surd\} \neq \emptyset \\ d^a & \textit{otherwise} \end{cases}$

(e) $\mathbf{d}_\lambda(s_1 \mid\mid\mid_p s_2, t_1 \mid\mid\mid_p t_2) \leq d^a$*, with*

$$d^s = \begin{cases} 1 & \textit{if } \mathbf{d}_\lambda(s_1, t_1) = 1 \textit{ or } \mathbf{d}_\lambda(s_2, t_2) = 1 \\ \mathbf{d}_\lambda(s_1, t_1) + (1 - \mathbf{d}_\lambda(s_1, t_1)/\lambda)\mathbf{d}_\lambda(s_2, t_2) & \textit{otherwise} \end{cases}$$

$$d^a = \begin{cases} 1 & \textit{if } \mathbf{d}_\lambda(s_1, t_1) = 1 \\ 1 & \textit{if } \mathbf{d}_\lambda(s_2, t_2) = 1 \\ \max(d^a_{1,2}, d^a_{2,1}) & \textit{otherwise} \end{cases} \qquad \begin{aligned} d^a_{1,2} &= \mathbf{d}_\lambda(s_1, t_1) + \lambda(1 - \mathbf{d}_\lambda(s_1, t_1)/\lambda)\mathbf{d}_\lambda(s_2, t_2) \\ d^a_{2,1} &= \mathbf{d}_\lambda(s_2, t_2) + \lambda(1 - \mathbf{d}_\lambda(s_2, t_2)/\lambda)\mathbf{d}_\lambda(s_1, t_1) \end{aligned}$$

The expression d^s captures the distance bound between the synchronously evolving processes s_1 and s_2 on the one hand and the synchronously evolving processes t_1 and t_2 on the other hand. We remark that distances $\mathbf{d}_\lambda(s_1, t_1)$ and $\mathbf{d}_\lambda(s_2, t_2)$ contribute symmetrically to d^s since $\mathbf{d}_\lambda(s_1, t_1) + (1 - \mathbf{d}_\lambda(s_1, t_1)/\lambda)\mathbf{d}_\lambda(s_2, t_2) = \mathbf{d}_\lambda(s_2, t_2) + (1 - \mathbf{d}_\lambda(s_2, t_2)/\lambda)\mathbf{d}_\lambda(s_1, t_1) = \mathbf{d}_\lambda(s_1, t_1) + \mathbf{d}_\lambda(s_2, t_2) - \mathbf{d}_\lambda(s_1, t_1)\mathbf{d}_\lambda(s_2, t_2)/\lambda$. The expressions $d^a_{1,2}, d^a_{2,1}, d^a$ cover different scenarios of the asynchronous evolution of those processes. The expression $d^a_{1,2}$ (resp. $d^a_{2,1}$) denotes the distance bound between the asynchronously evolving processes s_1 and s_2 on the one hand and the asynchronously evolving processes t_1 and t_2 on the other hand, at which the first transition is performed by the processes s_1 and t_1 (resp. the first transition is performed by processes s_2 and t_2). Hence, the distances of the asynchronously evolving processes $d^a_{1,2}$ and $d^a_{2,1}$ differ from the distance d^s of the synchronously evolving processes only by the discount factor λ that is applied to the delayed process. Finally, d^a captures the distance between asynchronously evolving processes independent of which of those processes moves first. If $\mathbf{d}_\lambda(s_i, t_i) = 1$ the processes may disagree on the initial actions they can perform and the composed processes have then also the maximal distance of 1 (cf. Rem. 3).

We consider now the process combinators in detail. The distance between sequentially composed processes $s_1; s_2$ and $t_1; t_2$ (Prop. 7.a) is given if $\mathbf{d}_\lambda(s_1, t_1) \in [0, 1)$ as the maximum of (i) the distance $d^a_{1,2}$ (which captures the case that first the processes s_1 and t_1 evolve followed by s_2 and t_2), and (ii) the distance $\mathbf{d}_\lambda(s_2, t_2)$ (which captures the case that the processes s_2 and t_2 evolve immediately because both s_1 and t_1 terminate successfully). The distance $d^a_{1,2}$ weights the distance between s_2 and t_2 by $\lambda(1 - \mathbf{d}_\lambda(s_1, t_1)/\lambda)$. The discount λ expresses that the distance between processes s_2 and t_2 is observable just after s_1 and t_1 have performed at least one step. Additionally, note that the difference between s_2 and t_2 can only be observed when s_1 and t_1 agree to terminate. When processes s_1 and t_1 evolve by one step, they disagree by $\mathbf{d}_\lambda(s_1, t_1)/\lambda$ on their behavior. Hence they agree by $1 - \mathbf{d}_\lambda(s_1, t_1)/\lambda$. Thus, the distance between processes s_2 and t_2 needs to be additionally weighted by $(1 - \mathbf{d}_\lambda(s_1, t_1)/\lambda)$. In case (ii) the distance between s_2 and t_2 is not discounted since both processes start immediately.

The distance between synchronous parallel composed processes $s_1 \mid s_2$ and $t_1 \mid t_2$ is $\mathbf{d}_\lambda(s_1,t_1)+(1-\mathbf{d}_\lambda(s_1,t_1)/\lambda)\mathbf{d}_\lambda(s_2,t_2) = \lambda(1-(1-\mathbf{d}_\lambda(s_1,t_1)/\lambda)(1-\mathbf{d}_\lambda(s_2,t_2)/\lambda))$. The distance between $s_1 \mid s_2$ and $t_1 \mid t_2$ is bounded by the sum of the distance between s_1 and t_1 (degree of dissimilarity between s_1 and t_1) and the distance between s_2 and t_2 weighted by the probability that s_1 and t_1 agree on their behavior (degree of dissimilarity between s_2 and t_2 under equal behavior of s_1 and t_1). Alternatively, the distance between $s_1 \mid s_2$ and $t_1 \mid t_2$ can be understood as composing processes on the behavior they agree upon, i.e. $s_1 \mid s_2$ and $t_1 \mid t_2$ agree on their behavior if s_1 and t_1 agree (probability of similarity $1 - \mathbf{d}_\lambda(s_1,t_1)/\lambda$) and if s_2 and t_2 agree (probability of similarity $1 - \mathbf{d}_\lambda(s_2,t_2)/\lambda$). The resulting distance is then the probability of dissimilarity of the respective behavior expressed by $1 - (1 - \mathbf{d}_\lambda(s_1,t_1)/\lambda)(1 - \mathbf{d}_\lambda(s_2,t_2)/\lambda)$ multiplied by the discount factor λ.

The distance between asynchronous parallel composed processes $s_1 \mid\mid\mid s_2$ and $t_1 \mid\mid\mid t_2$ is exactly the expression d^a. The distance between processes composed by the probabilistic parallel composition operator $s_1 \mid\mid\mid_p s_2$ and $t_1 \mid\mid\mid_p t_2$ is bounded by the same expression d^a since the first two rules specifying the probabilistic parallel composition define the same operational behavior as the nondeterministic parallel composition. The third rule defining a convex combination of these transitions applies only for those actions that can be performed by both processes s_1 and s_2 and resp. t_1 and t_2.

Processes that are composed by the CSP parallel composition operator $\_ \mid\mid_B \_$ evolve synchronously for actions in $B \setminus \{\surd\}$, evolve asynchronously for actions in $A \setminus (B \cup \{\surd\})$, and the action $\surd$ leads always to the stop process if both processes can perform $\surd$. Since $d^s \geq d^a$, the distance is bounded by d^s if there is at least one action $a \in B$ with $a \neq \surd$ for which the composed processes can evolve synchronously, and otherwise by d^a.

The distance bounds for non-recursive process combinators are tight.

Proposition 8. *Let $\epsilon_i \in [0,1]$. There are $s_i, t_i \in T(\Sigma_{PA})$ with $\mathbf{d}_\lambda(s_i,t_i) = \epsilon_i$ such that the inequalities in Prop. 6 and 7 become equalities.*

3.3 Compositional Reasoning Over Non-recursive Processes

In order to specify and verify systems in a compositional manner, it is necessary that the behavioral semantics is compatible with all operators of the language that describe these systems. There are multiple proposals which properties of process combinators facilitate compositional reasoning. In this section we discuss non-extensiveness [1] and non-expansiveness [7, 8]), which are compositionality properties based on the p-norm. They allow for compositional reasoning over probabilistic processes that are built of non-recursive process combinators. Non-extensiveness and non-expansiveness are very strong forms of uniform continuity. For instance, a non-expansive operator ensures that the distance between the composed processes is at most the sum of the distances between its parts. Later in Sec. 4.3 we will propose uniform continuity as generalization of these properties that allows also for compositional reasoning over recursive processes.

Definition 9 (Non-extensive Process Combinator). *A process combinator $f \in \Sigma$ is* non-extensive *wrt. λ-bisimulation metric $\mathbf{d}_\lambda$ if or all closed process terms $s_i, t_i \in T(\Sigma)$*

$$\mathbf{d}_\lambda(f(s_1,\ldots,s_n), f(t_1,\ldots,t_n)) \leq \max_{i=1}^{n} \mathbf{d}_\lambda(s_i,t_i)$$

Theorem 10. *The process combinators probabilistic action prefix* $a.\bigoplus_{i=1}^{n}[p_i]\_$, *non-deterministic alternative composition* $\_ + \_$ *and probabilistic alternative composition* $\_ +_p \_$ *are non-extensive wrt.* $\mathbf{d}_\lambda$ *for any* $\lambda \in (0, 1]$.

Proposition 11. *The process combinators sequential composition* $\_;\_$, *synchronous parallel composition* $\_ \mid \_$, *asynchronous parallel composition* $\_ \mid\mid\mid \_$, *CSP-like parallel composition* $\_ \|_B \_$ *and probabilistic parallel composition* $\_ \mid\mid\mid_p \_$ *are not non-extensive wrt.* $\mathbf{d}_\lambda$ *for any* $\lambda \in (0, 1]$.

Note that Thm. 10 follows from Prop. 6, and that Prop. 11 follows from Prop. 7 and Prop. 8. We proceed now with the compositionality property of non-expansiveness.

Definition 12 (Non-expansive Process Combinator). *A process combinator* $f \in \Sigma$ *is* non-expansive *wrt.* λ*-bisimulation metric* $\mathbf{d}_\lambda$ *if for all closed process terms* $s_i, t_i \in T(\Sigma)$

$$\mathbf{d}_\lambda(f(s_1, \ldots, s_n), f(t_1, \ldots, t_n)) \leq \sum_{i=1}^{n} \mathbf{d}_\lambda(s_i, t_i)$$

If f is non-extensive, then f is non-expansive.

Theorem 13. *All non-recursive process combinators of* Σ_{PA} *are non-expansive wrt.* $\mathbf{d}_\lambda$ *for any* $\lambda \in (0, 1]$.

Note that Thm. 13 follows from Prop. 6 and Prop. 7. Thm. 13 generalizes a similar result of [8] which considered only PTSs without nondeterministic branching and only a small set of combinators. The analysis which operators are non-extensive (Thm. 10) and the tight distance bounds (Prop. 6 and 7) are novel.

4 Recursive Processes

Recursion is necessary to express infinite behavior in terms of finite process expressions. Moreover, recursion allows to express repetitive finite behavior in a compact way. We will discuss now compositional reasoning over probabilistic processes that are composed by recursive process combinators. We will see that the compositionality properties used for non-recursive process combinators (Sec. 3.3) fall short for recursive process combinators. We will propose the more general property of uniform continuity (Sec. 4.3) that captures the inherent nature of compositional reasoning over probabilistic processes. In fact, it allows to reason compositionally over processes that are composed by both recursive and non-recursive process combinators. In the next section we apply these results to reason compositionally over a communication protocol and derive its respective performance properties. To the best of our knowledge this is the first study which explores systematically compositional reasoning over recursive processes in the context of bisimulation metric semantics.

4.1 Recursive Process Combinator

We define $P_{\mathrm{PA}^{\circlearrowleft}}$ as disjoint extension of P_{PA} with the operators finite iteration $\_^n$, infinite iteration $\_^\omega$, binary Kleene-star iteration $\_^*\_$, probabilistic Kleene-star iteration $\_^{*_p}\_$,

Table 3. Standard recursive process combinators

$$\frac{x \xrightarrow{a} \mu}{x^{n+1} \xrightarrow{a} \mu; \delta(x^n)} \qquad \frac{x \xrightarrow{a} \mu}{x^{\omega} \xrightarrow{a} \mu; \delta(x^{\omega})} \qquad \frac{x \xrightarrow{a} \mu}{x^{*}y \xrightarrow{a} \mu; \delta(x^{*}y)} \qquad \frac{y \xrightarrow{a} \nu}{x^{*}y \xrightarrow{a} \nu}$$

$$\frac{x \xrightarrow{a} \mu \quad y \xrightarrow{a} \nu}{x^{*p}y \xrightarrow{a} \nu \oplus_p \mu; \delta(x^{*p}y)} \qquad \frac{x \xrightarrow{a} \mu \quad y \stackrel{a}{\nrightarrow}}{x^{*p}y \xrightarrow{a} \mu; \delta(x^{*p}y)} \qquad \frac{x \stackrel{a}{\nrightarrow} \quad y \xrightarrow{a} \nu}{x^{*p}y \xrightarrow{a} \nu}$$

$$\frac{x \xrightarrow{a} \mu}{!^{n+1}x \xrightarrow{a} \mu \mathbin{|||} \delta(!^n x)} \qquad \frac{x \xrightarrow{a} \mu}{!x \xrightarrow{a} \mu \mathbin{|||} \delta(!x)} \qquad \frac{x \xrightarrow{a} \mu}{!_p x \xrightarrow{a} \mu \oplus_p (\mu \mathbin{|||} \delta(!_p x))}$$

finite replication $!^n\_$, infinite replication (bang) operator $!\_$, and probabilistic bang operator $!_p\_$. The operational semantics of these operators is specified by the rules in Tab. 3. The finite iteration t^n (resp. infinite iteration t^{ω}) of process t expresses that t is performed n times (resp. infinitely often) in sequel. The binary Kleene-star is as usual. The bang operator expresses for $!t$ (resp. finite replication $!^n t$) that infinitely many copies (resp. n copies) of t evolve asynchronously. The probabilistic variants of Kleene-star iteration [2, Sec. 5.2.4(vi)] and bang replication [14, Fig. 1] substitute the nondeterministic choice of the non-probabilistic variants by a respective probabilistic choice.

4.2 Distance between Recursive Processes

We develop now tight bounds for recursive process combinators.

Proposition 14. *Let $P = (\Sigma, A, R)$ be any PTSS with $P_{PA^{\circlearrowleft}} \sqsubseteq P$. For all $s, t \in T(\Sigma)$*

(a) $\mathbf{d}_\lambda(s^n, t^n) \le d^n$
(b) $\mathbf{d}_\lambda(!^n s, !^n t) \le d^n$
(c) $\mathbf{d}_\lambda(s^{\omega}, t^{\omega}) \le d^{\omega}$
(d) $\mathbf{d}_\lambda(!s, !t) \le d^{\omega}$
(e) $\mathbf{d}_\lambda(s_1{}^{*}s_2, t_1{}^{*}t_2) \le \max(\mathbf{d}_\lambda(s_1{}^{\omega}, t_1{}^{\omega}), \mathbf{d}_\lambda(s_2, t_2))$
(f) $\mathbf{d}_\lambda(s_1^{*p} s_2, t_1^{*p} t_2) \le \mathbf{d}_\lambda(s_1{}^{*}s_2, t_1{}^{*}t_2)$
(g) $\mathbf{d}_\lambda(!_p s, !_p t) \le \begin{cases} \mathbf{d}_\lambda(s,t)\frac{1}{1-(1-p)(\lambda - \mathbf{d}_\lambda(s,t))} & \text{if } \mathbf{d}_\lambda(s,t) \in (0,1) \\ \mathbf{d}_\lambda(s,t) & \text{if } \mathbf{d}_\lambda(s,t) \in \{0,1\} \end{cases}$, *with*

$$d^n = \begin{cases} \mathbf{d}_\lambda(s,t)\frac{1-(\lambda-\mathbf{d}_\lambda(s,t))^n}{1-(\lambda-\mathbf{d}_\lambda(s,t))} & \text{if } \mathbf{d}_\lambda(s,t) \in (0,1) \\ \mathbf{d}_\lambda(s,t) & \text{if } \mathbf{d}_\lambda(s,t) \in \{0,1\} \end{cases} \qquad d^{\omega} = \begin{cases} \mathbf{d}_\lambda(s,t)\frac{1}{1-(\lambda-\mathbf{d}_\lambda(s,t))} & \text{if } \mathbf{d}_\lambda(s,t) \in (0,1) \\ \mathbf{d}_\lambda(s,t) & \text{if } \mathbf{d}_\lambda(s,t) \in \{0,1\} \end{cases}$$

First we explain the distance bounds of the nondeterministic recursive process combinators. To understand the distance bound between processes that iterate finitely many times (Prop. 14.a), observe that s^n and $s;\ldots;s$ (where $s;\ldots;s$ denotes n sequentially composed instances of s) denote the same PTSs (up to renaming of states). Recursive application of the distance bound Prop. 7.a yields $\mathbf{d}_\lambda(s^n, t^n) = \mathbf{d}_\lambda(s;\ldots;s, t;\ldots;t) \le \mathbf{d}_\lambda(s,t)\sum_{k=0}^{n-1}(\lambda - \mathbf{d}_\lambda(s,t)) = d^n$. The same reasoning applies to the finite replication operator (Prop.14.b) by observing that $!^n s$ and $s \mathbin{|||} \ldots \mathbin{|||} s$ denote the same PTSs (up to renaming of states) and that the bounds in Prop. 7.a and 7.c coincide if $s_1 = s_2 = s$ and $t_1 = t_2 = t$. The distance between processes that may iterate infinitely many times

(Prop. 14.c), and the distance between processes that may spawn infinite many copies that evolve asynchronously (Prop. 14.d) are the limit of the respective finite iteration and replication bounds. The distance between the Kleene-star iterated processes $s_1{}^*s_2$ and $t_1{}^*t_2$ is bounded by the maximum of the distance $\mathbf{d}_\lambda(s_1{}^\omega, t_1{}^\omega)$ (infinite iteration of s_1 and t_1 s.t. s_2 and t_2 never evolve), and the distance $\mathbf{d}_\lambda(s_2, t_2)$ (s_2 and t_2 evolve immediately). The case where s_1 and t_1 iterate n-times and then s_2 and t_2 evolve leads always to a distance $\mathbf{d}_\lambda(s_1{}^n, t_1{}^n) + (\lambda - \mathbf{d}_\lambda(s_1, t_1))^n \mathbf{d}_\lambda(s_2, t_2) \leq \max(\mathbf{d}_\lambda(s_1{}^\omega, t_1{}^\omega), \mathbf{d}_\lambda(s_2, t_2))$.

Now we explain the bounds of the probabilistic recursive process combinators. The distance between processes composed by the probabilistic Kleene star is bounded by the distance between those processes composed by the nondeterministic Kleene star (Prop. 14.f), since the second and third rule specifying the probabilistic Kleene star define the same operational behavior as the nondeterministic Kleene star. The first rule which defines a convex combination of these transitions applies only for those actions that both of the combined processes can perform. In fact, $\mathbf{d}_\lambda(s_1{}^{*_p}s_2, t_1{}^{*_p}t_2) = \mathbf{d}_\lambda(s_1{}^*s_2, t_1{}^*t_2)$ if the initial actions that can be performed by processes s_1, t_1 are disjoint from the initial actions that can be performed by processes s_2, t_2 (and hence the first rule defining $\_{}^{*_p}\_$ cannot be applied). Thus, the distance bound of the probabilistic Kleene star coincides with the distance bound of the nondeterministic Kleene star. The bound on the distance of processes composed by the probabilistic bang operator can be understood by observing that $!_p s$ behaves as $!^{n+1}s$ with probability $p(1-p)^n$. Hence, by Prop. 14.b we get $\mathbf{d}_\lambda(!_p s, !_p t) \leq \sum_{n=0}^{\infty} p(1-p)^n \mathbf{d}_\lambda(!^{n+1}s, !^{n+1}t) \leq \sum_{n=0}^{\infty} p(1-p)^n d^{n+1} = \mathbf{d}_\lambda(s,t)/(1-(1-p)(\lambda - \mathbf{d}_\lambda(s,t)))$.

The distance bounds for recursive process combinators are tight.

Proposition 15. *Let $\epsilon_i \in [0,1]$. There are $s_i, t_i \in T(\Sigma_{PA})$ with $\mathbf{d}_\lambda(s_i, t_i) = \epsilon_i$ such that the inequalities in Prop. 14 become equalities.*

4.3 Compositional Reasoning Over Recursive Processes

From Prop. 14 and Prop. 15 it follows that none of the recursive process combinators discussed in this section satisfies the compositionality property of non-expansiveness.

Proposition 16. *All recursive process combinators of $\Sigma_{PA^{\circlearrowleft}}$ (unbounded recursion and bounded recursion with $n \geq 2$) are not non-expansive wrt. $\mathbf{d}_\lambda$ for any $\lambda \in (0,1]$.*

However, a weaker property suffices to facilitate compositional reasoning. To reason compositionally over probabilistic processes it is enough if the distance of the composed processes can be related to the distance of its parts. In essence, compositional reasoning over probabilistic processes is possible whenever a small variance in the behavior of the parts leads to a bounded small variance in the behavior of the composed processes.

We introduce uniform continuity as the compositionality property for both recursive and non-recursive process combinators. Uniform continuity generalizes the properties non-extensiveness and non-expansiveness for non-recursive process combinators.

Definition 17 (Uniformly Continuous Process Combinator). *A process combinator $f \in \Sigma$ is* uniformly continuous *wrt. λ-bisimulation metric $\mathbf{d}_\lambda$ if for all $\epsilon > 0$ there are $\delta_1, \ldots, \delta_n > 0$ such that for all closed process terms $s_i, t_i \in T(\Sigma)$*

$$\forall i = 1, \ldots, n.\ \mathbf{d}_\lambda(s_i, t_i) < \delta_i \implies \mathbf{d}_\lambda(f(s_1, \ldots, s_n), f(t_1, \ldots, t_n)) < \epsilon.$$

Note that by definition each non-expansive operator is also uniformly continuous (by $\delta_i = \epsilon/n$). A uniformly continuous combinator f ensures that for any non-zero bisimulation distance ϵ there are appropriate non-zero bisimulation distances δ_i s.t. for any composed process $f(s_1, \ldots, s_n)$ the distance to the composed process where each s_i is replaced by any t_i with $\mathbf{d}_\lambda(s_i, t_i) < \delta_i$ is $\mathbf{d}_\lambda(f(s_1, \ldots, s_n), f(t_1, \ldots, t_n)) < \epsilon$. We consider the uniform notion of continuity (technically, the δ_i depend only on ϵ and are independent of the concrete states s_i) because we aim at universal compositionality guarantees.

The distance bounds of Sec. 4.2 allow us to derive that finitely recursing process combinators are uniformly continuous wrt. both non-discounted and discounted bisimulation metric (Thm. 18). On the contrary, unbounded recursing process combinators are uniformly continuous only wrt. discounted bisimulation metric (Thm. 19 and Prop. 20).

Theorem 18. *The process combinators finite iteration* $\_^n$, *finite replication* $!^n\_$, *and probabilistic replication (bang)* $!_p\_$ *are uniformly continuous wrt.* $\mathbf{d}_\lambda$ *for any* $\lambda \in (0, 1]$.

Note that the probabilistic bang is uniformly continuous wrt. non-discounted bisimulation metric $\mathbf{d}_1$ because in each step there is a non-zero probability that the process is not copied. On contrary, the process $s_1 {}^{*_p} s_2$ applying the probabilistic Kleene star creates with probability 1 a copy of s_1 for actions that s_1 can and s_2 cannot perform. Hence, $\_^{*_p}\_$ is uniformly continuous only for discounted bisimulation metric $\mathbf{d}_\lambda$ with $\lambda < 1$.

Theorem 19. *The process combinators infinite iteration* $\_^\omega$, *nondeterministic Kleene-star iteration* $\_^*\_$, *probabilistic Kleene-star iteration* $\_^{*_p}\_$, *and infinite replication (bang)* $!\_$ *are uniformly continuous wrt.* $\mathbf{d}_\lambda$ *for any* $\lambda \in (0, 1)$.

Proposition 20. *The process combinators* $\_^\omega$, $\_^*\_$, $!\_$ *and* $\_^{*_p}\_$ *are not uniformly continuous wrt.* $\mathbf{d}_1$.

5 Application

To advocate both uniform continuity as adequate property for compositional reasoning as well as bisimulation metric semantics as a suitable distance measure for performance validation of communication protocols, we exemplify the discussed compositional reasoning method by analyzing the bounded retransmission protocol (BRP) as a case study.

The BRP allows to transfer streams of data from a sender (e.g. a remote control RC) to a receiver (e.g. a TV). The RC tries to send to the TV a stream of n data, $d_0, \ldots, d_{n-1}$, with each d_i a member of the finite data domain D. The length n of the stream is bounded by a given N. Each d_i is sent separately and has probability p to get lost. When the TV receives d_i, it sends back an acknowledgment message (ack), which may also get lost, with probability q. If the RC does not receive the ack for d_i within a given time, it assumes that d_i got lost and retries to transmit it. However, the maximal number of attempts is T. Since the ack may get lost, it may happen that the RC sends more than once the same datum d_i notwithstanding that it was correctly received by the TV. Therefore the RC attaches a control bit b to each datum d_i s.t. the TV can recognize if this datum is original or already received. Data items at even positions, i.e. d_{2k} for some $k \in \mathbb{N}$, get control bit 0 attached, and data items d_{2k+1} get control bit 1 attached.

$$BRP(N,T,p,q) = RC(N,T,p,q) \parallel_B TV, \text{ where } B = \{c(d,b) \mid d \in D, b \in \{0,1\}\} \cup \{ack, lost\}$$

$$RC(N,T,p,q) = \Bigg[\sum_{0 \le n \le N, n=2k} i(n).\Big(CH(0,T,p,q)\,;\, CH(1,T,p,q)\Big)^{\frac{n}{2}} +$$

$$\sum_{0 \le n \le N, n=2k+1} i(n).\bigg(\Big(CH(0,T,p,q)\,;\, CH(1,T,p,q)\Big)^{\frac{n-1}{2}}; CH(0,T,p,q)\bigg)\Bigg]; res(\mathrm{OK}).\surd$$

$$CH(b,t,p,q) = \sum_{d \in D} i(d).CH'(d,b,t,p,q)$$

$$CH'(d,b,t,p,q) = \begin{cases} (\bot.\, CH'(d,b,t-1,p,q)) \oplus_p (c(d,b).CH_2(d,b,t,p,q)) & \text{if } t > 0 \\ res(NOK) & \text{if } t = 0 \end{cases}$$

$$CH_2(d,b,t,p,q) = \begin{cases} (lost.CH'(d,b,t-1,p,q)) \oplus_q (ack.\surd) & \text{if } t > 0 \\ res(NOK) & \text{if } t = 0 \end{cases}$$

$$TV = \Bigg[\bigg(\Big(\sum_{d \in D} c(d,1).(ack.\surd + lost.\surd)\Big)^{*}\Big(\sum_{d \in D} c(d,0).o(d).(ack.\surd + lost.\surd)\Big)\bigg);$$

$$\bigg(\Big(\sum_{d \in D} c(d,0).(ack.\surd + lost.\surd)\Big)^{*}\Big(\sum_{d \in D} c(d,1).o(d).(ack.\surd + lost.\surd)\Big)\bigg)\Bigg]^{\omega}$$

Fig. 1. Specification of the Bounded Retransmission Protocol

The BRP is specified in Fig. 1. Our specification adapts the nondeterministic process algebra specification of [10] by refining the configuration of lossy channels. While in the nondeterministic setting a lossy channel (nondeterministically) either successfully transmits a datum or looses it, we attached a success and failure probability to this choice. The protocol specification $BRP(N,T,p,q)$ represents a system consisting of the RC modeled as process $RC(N,T,p,q)$, the TV modeled as process TV, and the channels $CH(b,t,p,q)$ for data transmission and $CH_2(d,b,t,p,q)$ for acknowledgment. The processes $RC(N,T,p,q)$ and TV synchronize over the actions: (i) $c(d,b)$, modeling the correct transmission of pair (d,b) from the RC to the TV; (ii) *ack*, modeling the correct transmission of the ack from the TV to the RC, and (iii) *lost*, used to model the timeout due to loss of the ack. Timeout due to the loss of pair (d,b) is modeled by action $\bot$ by the RC. $RC(N,T,p,q)$ starts by receiving the size $n \le N$ of the data stream, by means of action $i(n)$. Then, for n times it reads the datum d_i by means of action $i(d)$ and tries to send it to the TV. If all data are sent successfully, then the other RC components are notified by means of action $res(OK)$. In case of T failures for one datum, the whole transmission fails and emits $res(NOK)$. If TV receives a pair (d,b) by action $c(d,b)$ then, if d is original, namely b is the expected control bit, then d is sent to other TV components by $o(d)$, otherwise (d,b) is ignored.

To advocate bisimulation metric semantics as a suitable distance measure for performance validation of communication protocols we translate performance properties of a BRP implementation with lossy channels $BRP(N,T,p,q)$ to the bisimulation distance between this implementation and the specification with perfect channels $BRP(N,T,0,0)$.

Proposition 21. *Let $N, T \in \mathbb{N}$ and $p, q \in [0, 1]$.*

(a) Bisimulation distance $\mathbf{d}(BRP(N, T, 0, 0), BRP(N, T, p, q)) = \epsilon$ *relates as follows to the protocol performance properties:*
  - *The likelihood that N data items are sent and acknowledged without any retry (i.e. BRP(N, T, p, q) behaves as BRP(N, T, 0, 0)) is* $1 - \epsilon$.
  - *The likelihood that N data items are sent and acknowledged with at most* $k \leq N \cdot T$ *retries is* $(1 - \epsilon)\frac{1-(1-(1-\epsilon)^{1/N})^k}{(1-\epsilon)^{1/N}}$.
  - *The likelihood that N items are sent and acknowledged is* $(1 - \epsilon)\frac{1-(1-(1-\epsilon)^{1/N})^{N \cdot T}}{(1-\epsilon)^{1/N}}$.

(b) Bisimulation distance $\mathbf{d}(CH(b, T, 0, 0), CH(b, T, p, q)) = \delta$ *relates as follows to the channel performance properties:*
  - *The likelihood that one datum is sent and acknowledged without retry is* $1 - \delta$.
  - *The likelihood that one datum is sent and acknowledged with at most* $k \leq T$ *retries is* $1 - \delta^k$.

Now we show that by applying the compositionality results in Prop. 6, 7, 14 we can relate the bisimulation distance between the specification *BRP(N, T, 0, 0)* and some implementation *BRP(N, T, p, q)* of the entire protocol with the distances between the specification and some implementation of its respective components. On the one hand, this allows to derive from specified performance properties of the entire protocol individual performance requirements of its components (compositional verification). On the other hand, it allows to infer from performance properties of the protocol components suitable performance guarantees on the entire protocol (compositional specification).

Proposition 22. *Let $N, T \in \mathbb{N}$ and $p, q \in [0, 1]$. For all $d \in D$ and $b \in \{0, 1\}$*

(a) $\mathbf{d}(BRP(N, T, 0, 0), BRP(N, T, p, q)) \leq 1 - (1 - \mathbf{d}(CH(b, T, 0, 0), CH(b, T, p, q)))^N$
(b) $\mathbf{d}(CH(b, T, 0, 0), CH(b, T, p, q)) = 1 - (1 - p)(1 - q)$

Prop. 22.a follows from Props. 6, 7, 14 and Prop. 22.b from Props. 6, 7.

To advocate uniform continuity as adequate property for compositional reasoning, we show that the uniform continuity of process combinators in *BRP(N, T, p, q)* allows us to relate the distance between this implementation and the specification *BRP(N, T, 0, 0)* (which relates by Prop. 21 to performance properties of the entire protocol) to the concrete parameters p, q and N of the system. In detail, by Thm. 10, 13, 18 and Prop. 22 we get $\mathbf{d}(BRP(N, T, p, q), BRP(N, T, 0, 0)) \leq N/2 \cdot (\mathbf{d}(CH(0, T, p, q), CH(0, T, 0, 0)) + \mathbf{d}(CH(1, T, p, q), CH(1, T, 0, 0))) \leq N(1 - (1 - p)(1 - q))$. We infer the following result.

Proposition 23. *Let $N, T \in \mathbb{N}$ and $p, q \in [0, 1]$. For all $\epsilon \geq 0$, $p + q - pq < \epsilon/N$ ensures*

$$\mathbf{d}(BRP(N, T, p, q), BRP(N, T, 0, 0)) < \epsilon$$

Combining Prop. 21 – 23 allows us now to reason compositionally over a concrete scenario. We derive from a given performance requirement to transmit a stream of data the necessary performance properties of the channel components.

Example 24. Consider the following scenario. We want to transmit a data stream of $N = 20$ data items with at most $T = 1$ retry per data item. We want to build an implementation that should satisfy the performance property 'The likelihood that all 20 data items are successfully transmitted is at least 99%'. By Prop. 21.a we translate this performance property to the resp. bisimulation distance $\mathbf{d}(BRP(N,T,0,0), BRP(N,T,p,q)) \leq 0.01052$ on the entire system. By Prop. 22.a we derive the bisimulation distance for its channel component $\mathbf{d}(CH(b,T,0,0), CH(b,T,p,q) \leq 0.00053$. By Prop. 22.b this distance can be translated to appropriate parameters of the channel component, e.g. $p = 0.0002$ and $q = 0.00032$ or equivalently $p = 0.020\%$ and $q = 0.032\%$. Finally, Prop. 21.b allows to translate the distance between the specification and implementation of the channel component back to an appropriate performance requirement, e.g. 'The likelihood that one datum is successfully transmitted is at least 99.95%'. ■

6 Conclusion

We argued that uniform continuity is an appropriate property of process combinators to facilitate compositional reasoning wrt. bisimulation metric semantics. We showed that all standard (non-recursive and recursive) process algebra operators are uniformly continuous. In addition, we provided tight bounds on the distance between the composed processes. We exemplified how these results can be used to reason compositionally over protocols. In fact, they allow to derive from performance requirements on the entire system appropriate performance properties of the respective components, and in reverse to induce from performance assumptions on the system components performance guarantees on the entire system.

We will continue this line of research as follows. First, we generalize the analysis of concrete process algebra operators as discussed in this paper to general SOS rule and specification formats. Preliminary results show that in essence, a process combinator is uniformly continuous if the combined processes are copied only finitely many times along their evolution [11]. Then, we explore further (as initiated in Sec. 5) the relation between various behavioral distance measures, e.g. convex bisimulation metric [5], trace metric [9], and total-variation distance based metrics [13] with performance properties of communication and security protocols. This will provide further practical means to apply process algebraic methods and compositional metric reasoning wrt. uniformly continuous process combinators.

References

1. Bacci, G., Bacci, G., Larsen, K.G., Mardare, R.: Computing Behavioral Distances, Compositionally. In: Chatterjee, K., Sgall, J. (eds.) MFCS 2013. LNCS, vol. 8087, pp. 74–85. Springer, Heidelberg (2013)
2. Bartels, F.: On Generalised Coinduction and Probabilistic Specification Formats. Ph.D. thesis, VU University Amsterdam (2004)
3. van Breugel, F., Worrell, J.: A Behavioural Pseudometric for Probabilistic Transition Systems. TCS 331(1), 115–142 (2005)
4. D'Argenio, P.R., Lee, M.D.: Probabilistic Transition System Specification: Congruence and Full Abstraction of Bisimulation. In: Birkedal, L. (ed.) FOSSACS 2012. LNCS, vol. 7213, pp. 452–466. Springer, Heidelberg (2012)
5. De Alfaro, L., Majumdar, R., Raman, V., Stoelinga, M.: Game relations and metrics. In: Proc. LICS 2007, pp. 99–108. IEEE (2007)

6. De Alfaro, L., Henzinger, T.A., Majumdar, R.: Discounting the Future in Systems Theory. In: Baeten, J.C.M., Lenstra, J.K., Parrow, J., Woeginger, G.J. (eds.) ICALP 2003. LNCS, vol. 2719, pp. 1022–1037. Springer, Heidelberg (2003)
7. Deng, Y., Chothia, T., Palamidessi, C., Pang, J.: Metrics for Action-labelled Quantitative Transition Systems. ENTCS 153(2), 79–96 (2006)
8. Desharnais, J., Gupta, V., Jagadeesan, R., Panangaden, P.: Metrics for Labelled Markov Processes. TCS 318(3), 323–354 (2004)
9. Fahrenberg, U., Legay, A.: The quantitative linear-time-branching-time spectrum. TCS 538, 54–69 (2014)
10. Fokkink, W.: Modelling Distributed Systems. Springer (2007)
11. Gebler, D., Tini, S.: Fixed-point Characterization of Compositionality Properties of Probabilistic Processes Combinators. In: Proc. EXPRESS/SOS 2014. EPTCS, vol. 160, pp. 63–78 (2014)
12. Lee, M.D., Gebler, D., D'Argenio, P.R.: Tree Rules in Probabilistic Transition System Specifications with Negative and Quantitative Premises. In: Proc. EXPRESS/SOS 2012. EPTCS, vol. 89, pp. 115–130 (2012)
13. Mio, M.: Upper-Expectation Bisimilarity and Łukasiewicz μ-Calculus. In: Muscholl, A. (ed.) FOSSACS 2014. LNCS, vol. 8412, pp. 335–350. Springer, Heidelberg (2014)
14. Mio, M., Simpson, A.: A Proof System for Compositional Verification of Probabilistic Concurrent Processes. In: Pfenning, F. (ed.) FOSSACS 2013. LNCS, vol. 7794, pp. 161–176. Springer, Heidelberg (2013)
15. Segala, R.: Modeling and Verification of Randomized Distributed Real-Time Systems. Ph.D. thesis. MIT (1995)

Semantics of Programming Languages II

Fragments of ML Decidable by Nested Data Class Memory Automata

Conrad Cotton-Barratt[1,⋆], David Hopkins[1,⋆⋆], Andrzej S. Murawski[2,⋆⋆⋆], and C.-H. Luke Ong[1,†]

[1] Department of Computer Science, University of Oxford, UK
[2] Department of Computer Science, University of Warwick, UK

Abstract. The call-by-value language RML may be viewed as a canonical restriction of Standard ML to ground-type references, augmented by a "bad variable" construct in the sense of Reynolds. We consider the fragment of (finitary) RML terms of order at most 1 with free variables of order at most 2, and identify two subfragments of this for which we show observational equivalence to be decidable. The first subfragment, $\mathrm{RML}^{\text{P-Str}}_{2\vdash 1}$, consists of those terms in which the P-pointers in the game semantic representation are determined by the underlying sequence of moves. The second subfragment consists of terms in which the O-pointers of moves corresponding to free variables in the game semantic representation are determined by the underlying moves. These results are shown using a reduction to a form of automata over data words in which the data values have a tree-structure, reflecting the tree-structure of the threads in the game semantic plays. In addition we show that observational equivalence is undecidable at every third- or higher-order type, every second-order type which takes at least two first-order arguments, and every second-order type (of arity greater than one) that has a first-order argument which is not the final argument.

1 Introduction

RML is a call-by-value functional language with state [2]. It is similar to Reduced ML [17], the canonical restriction of Standard ML to ground-type references, except that it includes a "bad variable" constructor (in the absence of the constructor, the equality test is definable). This paper concerns the decidability of observational equivalence of finitary RML, RML_f. Our ultimate goal is to classify the decidable fragments of RML_f completely. In the case of finitary Idealized Algol (IA), the decidability of observational equivalence depends only on the type-theoretic order [13] of the type sequents. In contrast, the decidability of RML_f sequents is not so neatly characterised by order (see Figure 1): there are undecidable sequents of order as low as 2 [12], amidst interesting classes of decidable sequents at each of orders 1 to 4.

Following Ghica and McCusker [6], we use game semantics to decide observational equivalence of RML_f. Take a sequent $\Gamma \vdash M : \theta$ with $\Gamma = x_1 : \theta_1, \cdots, x_n : \theta_n$.

⋆ Supported by an EPSRC Doctoral Training Grant.
⋆⋆ Supported by Microsoft Research and Tony Hoare. Now at Ensoft Limited, UK.
⋆⋆⋆ Supported by EPSRC (EP/J019577/1).
† Partially supported by Merton College Research Fund.

A. Pitts (Ed.): FOSSACS 2015, LNCS 9034, pp. 249–263, 2015.
DOI: 10.1007/978-3-662-46678-0_16

In game semantics [7][10], the type sequent is interpreted as a P-strategy $[\![\Gamma \vdash M : \theta]\!]$ for playing (against O, who takes the environment's perspective) in the prearena $[\![\overline{\theta} \vdash \theta]\!]$. A play between P and O is a sequence of moves in which each non-initial move has a justification pointer to some earlier move – its justifier. Thanks to the fully abstract game semantics of RML, observational equivalence is characterised by *complete plays* i.e. $\Gamma \vdash M \cong N$ iff the P-strategies, $[\![\Gamma \vdash M]\!]$ and $[\![\Gamma \vdash N]\!]$, contain the same set of complete plays. Strategies may be viewed as highly constrained processes, and are amenable to automata-theoretic representations; the chief technical challenge lies in the encoding of pointers.

In [9] we introduced the *O-strict* fragment of $\mathrm{RML_f}$, $\mathrm{RML_{O\text{-}Str}}$, consisting of sequents $x_1 : \theta_1, \cdots, x_n : \theta_n \vdash M : \theta$ such that θ is *short* (i.e. order at most 2 and arity at most 1), and every argument type of every θ_i is short. Plays over prearenas denoted by O-strict sequents enjoy the property that the pointers from O-moves are uniquely determined by the underlying move sequence. The main result in [9] is that the set of complete plays of a $\mathrm{RML_{O\text{-}Str}}$-sequent is representable as a visibly pushdown automaton (VPA). A key idea is that it suffices to require each word of the representing VPA to encode the pointer from only *one* P-question. The point is that, when the full word language is analysed, it will be possible to uniquely place all justification pointers.

The simplest type that is not O-strict is $\beta \to \beta \to \beta$ where $\beta \in \{\mathsf{int}, \mathsf{unit}\}$. Encoding the pointers from O-moves is much harder because O-moves are controlled by the environment rather than the term. As observational equivalence is defined by a quantification over all contexts, the strategy for a term must consider *all* legal locations of pointer from an O-move, rather than just a single location in the case of pointer from a P-move. In this paper, we show that automata over data words can precisely capture strategies over a class of non-O-strict types.

Contributions. We identify two fragments of $\mathrm{RML_f}$ in which we can use deterministic weak nested data class memory automata [4] (equivalent to the locally prefix-closed nested data automata in [5]) to represent the set of complete plays of terms in these fragments. These automata operate over a data set which has a tree structure, and we use this structured data to encode O-pointers in words.

Both fragments are contained with the fragment $\mathrm{RML_{2\vdash 1}}$, which consists of terms-in-context $\Gamma \vdash M$ where every type in Γ is order at most 2, and the type of M is order at most 1. The first fragment, the *P-Strict subfragment*, consists of those terms in $\mathrm{RML_{2\vdash 1}}$ for which in the game semantic arenas have the property that the P-pointers in plays are uniquely determined by the underlying sequence of moves. This consists of terms-in-context $\Gamma \vdash M : \theta$ in which θ is any first order type, and each type in Γ has arity at most 1 and order at most 2. The second fragment, $\mathrm{RML^{res}_{2\vdash 1}}$, consists of terms-in-context $\Gamma \vdash M : \theta$ in which θ, again, is any first order type, and each type $\theta' \in \Gamma$ is at most order 2, such that each argument for θ' has arity at most 1. Although these two fragments are very similar, they use different encodings of data values, and we discuss the difficulties in extending these techniques to larger fragments of $\mathrm{RML_f}$.

Finally we show that observational equivalence is undecidable at every third- or higher-order type, every second-order type which takes at least two first-order arguments, and every second-order type (of arity greater than one) that has a first-order argument which is not the final argument. See Figure 1 for a summary.

Fragment	Representative Type Sequent	Recursion	Ref.
	Decidable		
O-Strict / RML$_{\text{O-Str}}$ (EXPTIME-Complete)	$((\beta \to \ldots \to \beta) \to \beta) \to \ldots \to \beta \vdash (\beta \to \ldots \to \beta) \to \beta$	**while**	[8,9]
O-Strict + Recursion (DPDA-Hard)	$((\beta \to \ldots \to \beta) \to \beta) \to \ldots \to \beta \vdash (\beta \to \ldots \to \beta) \to \beta$	$\beta \to \beta$	[8]
RML$^{\text{P-Str}}_{2\vdash 1}$	$(\beta \to \cdots \to \beta) \to \beta \vdash \beta \to \cdots \to \beta$	**while**	†
RML$^{\text{res}}_{2\vdash 1}$	$(\beta \to \beta) \to \cdots \to (\beta \to \beta) \to \beta \vdash \beta \to \cdots \to \beta$	**while**	†
	Undecidable		
Third-Order	$\vdash ((\beta \to \beta) \to \beta) \to \beta$ $(((\beta \to \beta) \to \beta) \to \beta) \to \beta \vdash \beta$	$\bot$	[8],†
Second-Order	$\vdash (\beta \to \beta) \to \beta \to \beta$ $((\beta \to \beta) \to \beta \to \beta) \to \beta \vdash \beta$	$\bot$	[8],†
Recursion	Any	$(\beta \to \beta) \to \beta$	[8],†
	Unknown		
RML$_{2\vdash 1}$	$(\beta \to \cdots \to \beta) \to \cdots \to (\beta \to \cdots \to \beta) \to \beta \vdash \beta \to \cdots \to \beta$	$\bot$	-
RML$_X$	$\vdash \beta \to (\beta \to \beta) \to \beta$ $((\beta \to \beta) \to \beta) \to \beta \vdash \beta \to \beta \to \beta$	$\bot$	-
FO RML + Recursion	$\vdash \beta \to \cdots \to \beta$	$\beta \to \beta \to \beta$	-

Fig. 1. Summary of RML Decidability Results. († marks new results presented here; $\beta \in \{\mathsf{int}, \mathsf{unit}\}$; we write $\bot$ to mean an undecidability result holds (or none is known) even if no recursion or loops are present, and the only source of non-termination is through the constant Ω).

Related Work. A related language with full ground references (i.e. with a int ref ref type) was studied in [15], and observational equivalence was shown to be undecidable even at types $\vdash$ unit $\to$ unit $\to$ unit. In contrast, for RML$_{\text{f}}$ terms, we show decidability at the same type. The key technical innovation of our work is the use of automata over infinite alphabets to encode justification pointers. Automata over infinite alphabets have already featured in papers on game semantics [14,15] but there they were used for a different purpose, namely, to model fresh-name generation. The nested data class memory automata we use in this paper are an alternative presentation of locally prefix-closed data automata [5].

2 Preliminaries

RML. We assume base types unit, for commands, int for a finite set of integers, and a integer variable type, int ref. Types are built from these in the usual way. The *order* of a type $\theta \to \theta'$ is given by $max(order(\theta) + 1, order(\theta'))$, where base types unit and int have order 0, and int ref has order 1. The *arity* of a type $\theta \to \theta'$ is $arity(\theta') + 1$ where unit and int have arity 0, and int ref has arity 1. A full syntax and set of typing rules for RML is given in Figure 2. Note though we include only the arithmetic operations $\mathbf{succ}(i)$ and $\mathbf{pred}(i)$, these are sufficient to define all the usual comparisons and operations. We will write $\mathbf{let}\, x = M \,\mathbf{in}\, N$ as syntactic sugar for $(\lambda x.N)M$, and $M; N$ for $(\lambda x.N)M$ where x is a fresh variable.

$$\frac{}{\Gamma \vdash () : \mathsf{unit}} \qquad \frac{i \in \mathbb{N}}{\Gamma \vdash i : \mathsf{int}} \qquad \frac{\Gamma \vdash M : \mathsf{int}}{\Gamma \vdash \mathbf{succ}(M) : \mathsf{int}} \qquad \frac{\Gamma \vdash M : \mathsf{int}}{\Gamma \vdash \mathbf{pred}(M) : \mathsf{int}}$$

$$\frac{\Gamma \vdash M : \mathsf{int} \qquad \Gamma \vdash M_0 : \theta \qquad \Gamma \vdash M_1 : \theta}{\Gamma \vdash \mathbf{if}\, M\, \mathbf{then}\, M_1\, \mathbf{else}\, M_0 : \theta} \qquad \frac{\Gamma \vdash M : \mathsf{int\ ref}}{\Gamma \vdash !M : \mathsf{int}}$$

$$\frac{\Gamma \vdash M : \mathsf{int\ ref} \qquad \Gamma \vdash N : \mathsf{int}}{\Gamma \vdash M := N : \mathsf{unit}} \qquad \frac{\Gamma \vdash M : \mathsf{int}}{\Gamma \vdash \mathbf{ref}\, M : \mathsf{int\ ref}} \qquad \frac{}{\Gamma, x : \theta \vdash x : \theta}$$

$$\frac{\Gamma \vdash M : \theta \to \theta' \qquad \Gamma \vdash N : \theta}{\Gamma \vdash MN : \theta'} \qquad \frac{\Gamma, x : \theta \vdash M : \theta'}{\Gamma \vdash \lambda x^{\theta}.M : \theta \to \theta'}$$

$$\frac{\Gamma \vdash M : \mathsf{int} \qquad \Gamma \vdash N : \mathsf{unit}}{\Gamma \vdash \mathbf{while}\, M\, \mathbf{do}\, N : \mathsf{unit}} \qquad \frac{\Gamma \vdash M : \mathsf{unit} \to \mathsf{int} \qquad \Gamma \vdash N : \mathsf{int} \to \mathsf{unit}}{\Gamma \vdash \mathbf{mkvar}(M, N) : \mathsf{int\ ref}}$$

Fig. 2. Syntax of RML

The operational semantics, defined in terms of a big-step relation, are standard [12]. For closed terms $\vdash M$ we write $M\Downarrow$ just if there exist s, V such that $\emptyset, M \Downarrow s, V$. Two terms $\Gamma \vdash M : \theta$ and $\Gamma \vdash N : \theta$ are *observationally equivalent* (or *contextually equivalent*) if for all (closing) contexts $C[-]$ such that $\emptyset \vdash C[M], C[N] : \mathsf{unit}$, $C[M]\Downarrow$ if and only if $C[N]\Downarrow$.

It can be shown that every RML term is effectively convertible to an equivalent term in *canonical form* [8, Prop. 3.3], defined by the following grammar ($\beta \in \{\mathsf{unit}, \mathsf{int}\}$).

$$\begin{aligned}\mathbb{C} ::= {} & () \mid i \mid x^{\beta} \mid \mathbf{succ}(x^{\beta}) \mid \mathbf{pred}(x^{\beta}) \mid \mathbf{if}\, x^{\beta}\, \mathbf{then}\, \mathbb{C}\, \mathbf{else}\, \mathbb{C} \mid x^{\mathsf{int\ ref}} := y^{\mathsf{int}} \mid !x^{\mathsf{int\ ref}} \mid \\ & \lambda x^{\theta}.\mathbb{C} \mid \mathbf{mkvar}(\lambda x^{\mathsf{unit}}.\mathbb{C}, \lambda y^{\mathsf{int}}.\mathbb{C}) \mid \mathbf{let}\, x = \mathbf{ref}\, 0\, \mathbf{in}\, \mathbb{C} \mid \mathbf{while}\, \mathbb{C}\, \mathbf{do}\, \mathbb{C} \mid \mathbf{let}\, x^{\beta} = \mathbb{C}\, \mathbf{in}\, \mathbb{C} \mid \\ & \mathbf{let}\, x = zy^{\beta}\, \mathbf{in}\, \mathbb{C} \mid \mathbf{let}\, x = z\, \mathbf{mkvar}(\lambda u^{\mathsf{unit}}.\mathbb{C}, \lambda v^{\mathsf{int}}.\mathbb{C})\, \mathbf{in}\, \mathbb{C} \mid \mathbf{let}\, x = z(\lambda x^{\theta}.\mathbb{C})\, \mathbf{in}\, \mathbb{C}\end{aligned}$$

Game Semantics. We use a presentation of call-by-value game semantics in the style of Honda and Yoshida [7], as opposed to Abramsky and McCusker's isomorphic model [2], as Honda and Yoshida's more concrete constructions lend themselves more easily to recognition by automata. We recall the following presentation of the game semantics for RML from [9].

An *arena* A is a triple $(M_A, \vdash_A, \lambda_A)$ where M_A is a set of *moves* where $I_A \subseteq M_A$ consists of *initial* moves, $\vdash_A \subseteq M_A \times (M_A \backslash I_A)$ is called the *justification relation*, and $\lambda_A : M_A \to \{O, P\} \times \{Q, A\}$ a labelling function such that for all $i_A \in I_A$ we have $\lambda_A(i_A) = (P, A)$ and if $m \vdash_A m'$ then $(\pi_1 \lambda_A)(m) \neq (\pi_1 \lambda_A)(m')$ and $(\pi_2 \lambda_A)(m') = A \Rightarrow (\pi_2 \lambda_A)(m) = Q$.

The function λ_A labels moves as belonging to either *Opponent* or *Proponent* and as being either a *Question* or an *Answer*. Note that answers are always justified by questions, but questions can be justified by either a question or an answer. We will use arenas to model types. However, the actual games will be played over *prearenas*, which are defined in the same way except that initial moves are O-questions.

Three basic arenas are 0, the empty arena, 1, the arena containing a single initial move $\bullet$, and $\mathbb{Z}$, which has the integers as its set of moves, all of which are initial P-answers. The constructions on arenas are defined in Figure 3. Here we use $\overline{I_A}$ as an abbreviation for $M_A \backslash I_A$, and $\overline{\lambda_A}$ for the O/P-complement of λ_A. Intuitively $A \otimes B$ is the union of the arenas A and B, but with the initial moves combined pairwise. $A \Rightarrow B$ is slightly more complex. First we add a new initial move, $\bullet$. We take the O/P-complement of A, change the initial moves into questions, and set them to now be justified by $\bullet$. Finally, we take B and set its initial moves to be justified by A's initial moves. The final construction, $A \to B$, takes two arenas A and B and produces a prearena, as shown below. This is essentially the same as $A \Rightarrow B$ without the initial move $\bullet$.

$$
\begin{aligned}
M_{A\Rightarrow B} &= \{\bullet\} \uplus M_A \uplus M_B \\
I_{A\Rightarrow B} &= \{\bullet\} \\
\lambda_{A\Rightarrow B} &= m \mapsto \begin{cases} PA & \text{if } m = \bullet \\ OQ & \text{if } m \in I_A \\ \overline{\lambda_A}(m) & \text{if } m \in \overline{I_A} \\ \lambda_B(m) & \text{if } m \in M_B \end{cases} \\
\vdash_{A\Rightarrow B} &= \{(\bullet, i_A) | i_A \in I_A\} \\
&\quad \cup \{(i_A, i_B) | i_A \in I_A, i_B \in I_B\} \\
&\quad \cup \vdash_A \cup \vdash_B
\end{aligned}
\qquad
\begin{aligned}
M_{A\otimes B} &= I_A \times I_B \uplus \overline{I_A} \uplus \overline{I_B} \\
I_{A\otimes B} &= I_A \times I_B \\
\lambda_{A\otimes B} &= m \mapsto \begin{cases} PA & \text{if } m \in I_A \times I_B \\ \lambda_A(m) & \text{if } m \in \overline{I_A} \\ \lambda_B(m) & \text{if } m \in \overline{I_B} \end{cases} \\
\vdash_{A\otimes B} &= \{((i_A, i_B), m) | i_A \in I_A \wedge i_B \in I_B \\
&\quad \wedge (i_A \vdash_A m \vee i_B \vdash_B m)\} \\
&\quad \cup (\vdash_A \cap (\overline{I_A} \times \overline{I_A})) \\
&\quad \cup (\vdash_B \cap (\overline{I_B} \times \overline{I_B}))
\end{aligned}
$$

$$
\begin{aligned}
M_{A\to B} &= M_A \uplus M_B & \lambda_{A\to B}(m) &= \begin{cases} OQ & \text{if } m \in I_A \\ \overline{\lambda_A}(m) & \text{if } m \in \overline{I_A} \\ \lambda_B(m) & \text{if } m \in M_B \end{cases} \\
I_{A\to B} &= I_A & \vdash_{A\to B} &= \{(i_A, i_B) | i_A \in I_A, i_B \in I_B\} \cup \vdash_A \cup \vdash_B
\end{aligned}
$$

Fig. 3. Constructions on Arenas

We intend arenas to represent types, in particular $[\![\mathsf{unit}]\!] = 1$, $[\![\mathsf{int}]\!] = \mathbb{Z}$ (or a finite subset of $\mathbb{Z}$ for RML$_\mathrm{f}$) and $[\![\theta_1 \to \theta_2]\!] = [\![\theta_1]\!] \Rightarrow [\![\theta_2]\!]$. A term $x_1 : \theta_1, \ldots, x_n : \theta_n \vdash M : \theta$ will be represented by a *strategy* for the prearena $[\![\theta_1]\!] \otimes \ldots \otimes [\![\theta_n]\!] \to [\![\theta]\!]$.

A *justified sequence* in a prearena A is a sequence of moves from A in which the first move is initial and all other moves m are equipped with a pointer to an earlier move m', such that $m' \vdash_A m$. A *play* s is a justified sequence which additionally satisfies the standard conditions of Alternation, Well-Bracketing, and Visibility.

A *strategy* σ for prearena A is a non-empty, even-prefix-closed set of plays from A, satisfying the determinism condition: if $s\,m_1, s\,m_2 \in \sigma$ then $s\,m_1 = s\,m_2$. We can think of a strategy as being a playbook telling P how to respond by mapping odd-length plays to moves. A play is *complete* if all questions have been answered. Note that (unlike in the call-by-name case) a complete play is not necessarily maximal. We denote the set of complete plays in strategy σ by $\mathbf{comp}(\sigma)$.

In the game model of RML, a term-in-context $x_1 : \theta_1, \ldots, x_n : \theta_n \vdash M : \theta$ is interpreted by a strategy of the prearena $[\![\theta_1]\!] \otimes \ldots \otimes [\![\theta_n]\!] \to [\![\theta]\!]$. These strategies are defined by recursion over the syntax of the term. Free identifiers $x : \theta \vdash x : \theta$ are interpreted as *copy-cat* strategies where P always copies O's move into the other copy of $[\![\theta]\!]$, $\lambda x.M$ allows multiple copies of $[\![M]\!]$ to be run, application MN requires a form of parallel composition plus hiding and the other constructions can be interpreted using special strategies. The game semantic model is fully abstract in the following sense.

Theorem 1 (Abramsky and McCusker [1,2]). *If $\Gamma \vdash M : \theta$ and $\Gamma \vdash N : \theta$ are* RML *type sequents, then $\Gamma \vdash M \cong N$ iff* $\mathbf{comp}(\llbracket \Gamma \vdash M \rrbracket) = \mathbf{comp}(\llbracket \Gamma \vdash N \rrbracket)$.

Nested Data Class Memory Automata. We will be using automata to recognise game semantic strategies as languages. Equality of strategies can then be reduced to equivalence of the corresponding automata. However, to represent strategies as languages we must encode pointers in the words. To do this we use data languages, in which every position in a word has an associated *data value*, which is drawn from an infinite set (which we call the *data set*). Pointers between positions in a play can thus be encoded in the word by the relevant positions having suitably related data values. Reflecting the hierarchical structure of the game semantic prearenas, we use a data set with a tree-structure.

Recall a *tree* is a simple directed graph $\langle D, pred \rangle$ where $pred : D \rightharpoonup D$ is the predecessor map defined on every node of the tree except the root, such that every node has a unique path to the root. A node n has level l just if $pred^l(n)$ is the root (thus the root has level 0). A tree is of level l just if every node in it has level $\leq l$. We define a *nested data set* of level l to be a tree of level l such that each data value of level strictly less than l has infinitely many children. We fix a nested data set of level l, $\mathcal{D}$, and a finite alphabet Σ, to give a data alphabet $\mathbb{D} = \Sigma \times \mathcal{D}$.

We will use a form of automaton over these data sets based on class memory automata [3]. Class memory automata operate over an unstructured data set, and on reading an input letter (a, d), the transitions available depend both on the state the automaton is currently in, and the state the automaton was in after it last read an input letter with data value d. We will be extending a weaker variant of these automata, in which the only acceptance condition is reaching an accepting state. The variant of class memory automata we will be using, nested data class memory automata [4], works similarly: on reading input (a, d) the transitions available depend on the current state of the automaton, the state the automaton was in when it last read a descendant (under the *pred* function) of d, and the states the automaton was in when it last read a descendant of each of d's ancestors. We also add some syntactic sugar (not presented in [4]) to this formalism, allowing each transition to determine the automaton's memory of where it last saw the read data value and each of its ancestors: this does not extend the power of the automaton, but will make the constructions we make in this paper easier to define.

Formally, a Weak Nested Data Class Memory Automaton (WNDCMA) of level l is a tuple $\langle Q, \Sigma, \Delta, q_0, F \rangle$ where Q is the set of states, $q_0 \in Q$ is the initial state, $F \subseteq Q$ is the set of accepting states, and the transition function $\delta = \bigcup_{i=0}^{l} \delta_i$ where each δ_i is a function:

$$\delta_i : Q \times \Sigma \times (\{i\} \times (Q \uplus \{\bot\})^{i+1}) \to \mathcal{P}(Q \times Q^{i+1})$$

We write $Q_\bot$ for the set $Q \uplus \{\bot\}$, and may refer to the $Q_\bot^j$ part of a transition as its *signature*. The automaton is *deterministic* if each set in the image of δ is a singleton. A configuration is a pair (q, f) where $q \in Q$, and $f : \mathcal{D} \to Q_\bot$ is a class memory function (i.e. $f(d) = \bot$ for all but finitely many $d \in \mathcal{D}$). The initial configuration is (q_0, f_0) where f_0 is the class memory function mapping every data value to $\bot$. The automaton can transition from configuration (q, f) to configuration (q', f') on reading input (a, d) just if d is of level-i, $(q', (t_0, t_1, \ldots, t_i)) \in \delta(q, a, (i, f(pred^i(d), \ldots, f(pred(d)), f(d))),$

and $f' = f[d \mapsto t_i, pred(d) \mapsto t_{i-1}, \ldots, pred^{i-1}(d) \mapsto t_1, pred^i(d) \mapsto t_0]$. A run is defined in the usual way, and is accepting if the last configuration (q_n, f_n) in the run is such that $q_n \in F$. We say $w \in L(\mathcal{A})$ if there is an accepting run of $\mathcal{A}$ on w.

Weak nested data class memory automata have a decidable emptiness problem, reducible to coverability in a well-structured transition system [4,5], and are closed under union and intersection by the standard automata product constructions. Further, Deterministic WNDCMA are closed under complementation again by the standard method of complementing the final states. Hence they have a decidable equivalence problem.

3 P-Strict $\mathrm{RML}_{2\vdash 1}$

In [9], the authors identify a fragment of RML, the O-strict fragment, for which the plays in the game-semantic strategies representing terms have the property that the justification pointers of O-moves are uniquely reconstructible from the underlying moves. Analogously, we define the P-strict fragment of RML to consist of typed terms in which the pointers for P-moves are uniquely determined by the underlying sequence of moves. Then our encoding of strategies for this fragment will only need to encode the O-pointers: for which we will use data values.

3.1 Characterising P-Strict RML

In working out which type sequents for RML lead to prearenas which are P-strict, it is natural to ask for a general characterisation of such prearenas. The following lemma, which provides exactly that, is straightforward to prove:

Lemma 1. *A prearena is P-strict iff there is no enabling sequence $q \vdash \cdots \vdash q'$ in which both q and q' are P-questions.*

Which type sequents lead to a P-question hereditarily justifying another P-question? It is clear, from the construction of the prearena from the type sequent, that if a free variable in the sequent has arity > 1 or order > 2, the resulting prearena will have a such an enabling sequence, so not be P-strict. Conversely, if a free variable is of a type of order at most 2 and arity at most 1, it will not break P-strictness. On the RHS of the type sequent, things are a little more complex: there will be a "first" P-question whenever the type has an argument of order ≥ 1. To prevent this P-question hereditarily justifying another P-question, the argument must be of arity 1 and order ≤ 2. Hence the P-strict fragment consists of type sequents of the following form:

$$(\beta \to \cdots \to \beta) \to \beta \vdash ((\beta \to \cdots \to \beta) \to \beta) \to \cdots \to ((\beta \to \cdots \to \beta) \to \beta) \to \beta$$

(where $\beta \in \{\mathsf{unit}, \mathsf{int}\}$.)

From results shown here and in [8], we know that observational equivalence of all type sequents with an order 3 type or order 2 type with order 1 non-final argument on the RHS are undecidable. Hence the only P-strict types for which observational equivalence may be decidable are of the form: $(\beta \to \cdots \to \beta) \to \beta \vdash \beta \to \cdots \to \beta$ or $(\beta \to \cdots \to \beta) \to \beta \vdash \beta \to \cdots \to \beta \to (\beta \to \beta) \to \beta$. In this section we show that the first of these, which is the intersection of the P-strict fragment and $\mathrm{RML}_{2\vdash 1}$, does lead to decidability.

Definition 1. *The P-Strict fragment of* $\mathrm{RML}_{2\vdash 1}$*, which we denote* $\mathrm{RML}^{\text{P-Str}}_{2\vdash 1}$*, consists of typed terms of the form* $x_1 : \widehat{\Theta_1}, \dots, x_n : \widehat{\Theta_1} \vdash M : \Theta_1$ *where the type classes* Θ_i *are as described below:*

$$\Theta_0 ::= \mathsf{unit} \mid \mathsf{int} \qquad \Theta_1 ::= \Theta_0 \mid \Theta_0 \to \Theta_1 \mid \mathsf{int\ ref} \qquad \widehat{\Theta_1} ::= \Theta_0 \mid \Theta_1 \to \Theta_0 \mid \mathsf{int\ ref}$$

This means we allow types of the form $(\beta \to \cdots \to \beta) \to \beta \vdash \beta \to \cdots \to \beta$ where $\beta \in \{\mathsf{unit}, \mathsf{int}\}$.

3.2 Deciding Observational Equivalence of $\mathrm{RML}^{\text{P-Str}}_{2\vdash 1}$

Our aim is to decide observational equivalence by constructing, from a term M, an automaton that recognises a language representing $[\![M]\!]$. As $[\![M]\!]$ is a set of plays, the language representing $[\![M]\!]$ must encode both the moves and the pointers in the play. Since answer moves' pointers are always determined by well-bracketing, we only represent the pointers of question moves, and we do this with the nested data values. The idea is simple: if a play s is in $[\![M]\!]$ the language $L([\![M]\!])$ will contain a word, w, such that the string projection of w is the underlying sequence of moves of s, and such that:

- The initial move takes the (unique) level-0 data value; and
- Answer moves take the same data value as that of the question they are answering; and
- Other question moves take a fresh data value whose predecessor is the data value taken by the justifying move.

Of course, the languages recognised by nested data automata are closed under automorphisms of the data set, so in fact each play s will be represented by an infinite set of data words, all equivalent to one another by automorphism of the data set.

Theorem 2. *For every typed term* $\Gamma \vdash M : \theta$ *in* $\mathrm{RML}^{\text{P-Str}}_{2\vdash 1}$ *that is in canonical form we can effectively construct a deterministic weak nested data class memory automata,* $\mathcal{A}^M$*, recognising the complete plays of* $L([\![\Gamma \vdash M]\!])$*.*

Proof. We prove this by induction over the canonical forms. We note that for each canonical form construction, if the construction is in $\mathrm{RML}^{\text{P-Str}}_{2\vdash 1}$ then each constituent canonical form must also be. For convenience of the inductive constructions, we in fact construct automata $\mathcal{A}^M_\gamma$ recognising $[\![\Gamma \vdash M]\!]$ restricted to the initial move γ. Here we sketch two illustrative cases.

$\boldsymbol{\lambda x^\beta.M : \beta \to \theta}$**.** The prearenas for $[\![M]\!]$ and $[\![\lambda x^\beta.M]\!]$ are shown in Figure 4. Note that in this case we must have that $\Gamma, x : \beta \vdash M : \theta$, and so the initial moves in $[\![M]\!]$ contain an x-component. We therefore write these initial moves as (γ, i_x) where γ is the Γ-component and i_x is the x-component.

P's strategy $[\![\lambda x^\beta.M]\!]$ is as follows: after an initial move γ, P plays the unique a_0-move $\bullet$, and waits for a q_1-move. Once O plays a q_1-move i_x, P plays as in $[\![\Gamma, x \vdash M]\!]$ when given an initial move (γ, i_x). However, as the q_1-moves are not initial, it is possible that O will play another q_1-move, i'_x. Each time O does this it opens a new thread which P plays as per $[\![\Gamma, x \vdash M]\!]$ when given initial move (γ, i'_x). Only O may switch

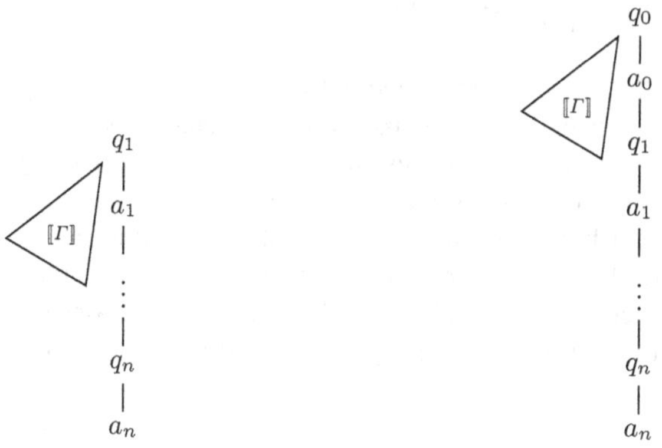

(a) $[\![\Gamma, \beta \vdash \theta]\!]$ (b) $[\![\Gamma \vdash \beta \to \theta]\!]$

Fig. 4. Prearenas for $[\![\Gamma, x : \beta \vdash M : \theta]\!]$ and $[\![\Gamma \vdash \lambda x^{\beta}.M : \beta \to \theta]\!]$

between threads, and this can only happen immediately after P plays an a_j-move (for any j).

By our inductive hypothesis, for each initial move (γ, i_x) of $[\![\Gamma, x : \beta \vdash \theta]\!]$ we have an automaton $\mathcal{A}^M_{\gamma,i_x}$ recognising the complete plays of $[\![\Gamma, x : \beta \vdash M : \theta]\!]$ starting with the initial move (γ, i_x). We construct the automaton $\mathcal{A}^{\lambda x.M}_{\gamma}$ by taking a copy of each $\mathcal{A}^M_{\gamma,i_x}$, and quotient together the initial states of these automata to one state, p, (which by conditions on the constituent automata we can assume has no incoming transitions). This state p will hold the unique level-0 data value for the run, and states and transitions are added to have initial transitions labelled with q_0 and a_0, ending in state p. The final states will be the new initial state, the quotient state p, and the states which are final in the constituent automata. The transitions inside the constituent automata fall into two categories: those labelled with moves corresponding to the RHS of the term in context $\Gamma \vdash M$, and those labelled with moves corresponding to the LHS. Those transitions corresponding to moves on the RHS are altered to have their level increased by 1, with their signature correspondingly altered by requiring a level-0 data value in state p. Those transitions corresponding to moves on the LHS retain the same level, but have the top value of their data value signature replaced with the state p. Finally, transitions are added between the constituent automata to allow switching between threads: whenever there is a transition out of a final state in one of the automata, copies of the transition are added from every final state (though keeping the data-value signature the same). Note that the final states correspond to precisely the points in the run where the environment is able to switch threads.

let $x^{\beta} = M$ in N. Here we assume we have automata recognising $[\![M]\!]$ and $[\![N]\!]$. The strategy $[\![\mathbf{let}\ x^{\beta} = M\ \mathbf{in}\ N]\!]$ essentially consists of a concatenation of $[\![M]\!]$ and $[\![N]\!]$, with the result of playing $[\![M]\!]$ determining the value of x to use in $[\![N]\!]$. Hence the automata construction is very similar to the standard finite automata construction for concatenation of languages, though branching on the different results for $[\![M]\!]$ to different automata for $[\![N]\!]$.

Corollary 1. *Observational equivalence of terms in* $\mathrm{RML}^{\text{P-Str}}_{2\vdash 1}$ *is decidable.*

4 A Restricted Fragment of $\mathrm{RML}_{2\vdash 1}$

It is important, for the reduction to nested data automata for $\mathrm{RML}^{\text{P-Str}}_{2\vdash 1}$, that variables cannot be partially evaluated: in prearenas where variables have only one argument, once a variable is evaluated those moves cannot be used to justify any future moves. If we could later return to them we would need ensure that they were accessed only in ways which did not break visibility. We now show that this can be done, using a slightly different encoding of pointers, for a fragment in which variables have unlimited arity, but each argument for the variable must be evaluated all at once. This means that the variables have their O-moves uniquely determined by the underlying sequence of moves.

4.1 Fragment Definition

Definition 2. *The fragment we consider in this section, which we denote* $\mathrm{RML}^{\text{res}}_{2\vdash 1}$, *consists of typed terms of the form* $x_1 : \Theta^1_2, \ldots, x_n : \Theta^1_2 \vdash M : \Theta_1$ *where the type classes* Θ_i *are as described below:*

$$\Theta_0 ::= \mathsf{unit} \mid \mathsf{int} \qquad \Theta^1_1 ::= \Theta_0 \mid \Theta_0 \to \Theta_0 \mid \mathsf{int\ ref}$$

$$\Theta_1 ::= \Theta_0 \mid \Theta_0 \to \Theta_1 \mid \mathsf{int\ ref} \qquad \Theta^1_2 ::= \Theta_1 \mid \Theta^1_1 \to \Theta^1_2$$

This allows types of the form $(\beta \to \beta) \to \cdots \to (\beta \to \beta) \to \beta \vdash \beta \to \cdots \to \beta$ where $\beta \in \{\mathsf{unit}, \mathsf{int}\}$. The shape of the prearenas for this fragment is shown in Figure 5. Note that moves in section A of the prearena (marked in Figure 5) relate to the type Θ_1 on the RHS of the typing judgement, and that we need only represent O-pointers for this section, since the P-moves are all answers so have their pointers uniquely determined by well-bracketing. Moves in sections B and C of the prearena correspond to the types on the LHS of the typing judgement. Moves in section B need only have their P-pointers represented, since the O-moves are all answer moves. Moves in section C have both their O- and P-pointers represented by the underlying sequence of moves: the P-pointers because all P-moves in this section are answer moves, the O-pointers by the visibility condition.

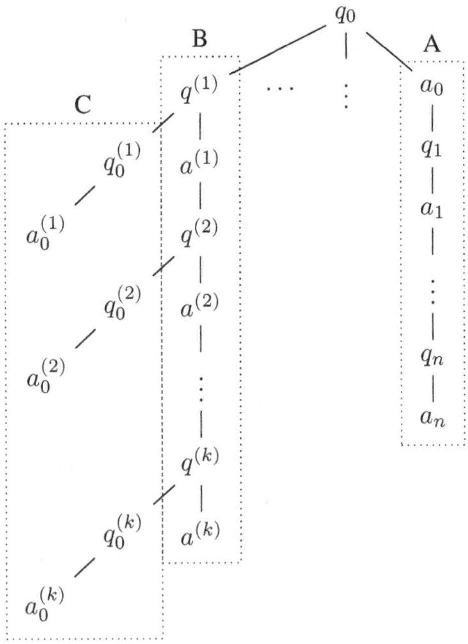

Fig. 5. Shape of arenas in $\mathrm{RML}^{\text{res}}_{2\vdash 1}$

4.2 Deciding Observation Equivalence

Similarly to the P-Strict case, we provide a reduction to weak nested data class memory automata that uses data values to encode O-pointers. However, this time we do not need to represent any O-pointers on the LHS of the typing judgement, so use data values only to represent pointers of the questions on the RHS. We do, though, need to represent P-pointers of moves on the LHS. This we do using the same technique used for representing P-pointers in [9]: in each word in the language we represent only one pointer by using a "tagging" of moves: the string $s \overset{\circ}{m} s' \overset{\bullet}{m'}$ is used to represent the pointer $s\ \overset{\frown}{m\ s'\ m'}$. Because P's strategy is deterministic, representing one pointer in each word is enough to uniquely reconstruct all P-pointers in the plays from the entire language. Due to space constraints we do not provide a full explanation of this technique in this paper: for a detailed discussion see [8,9]. Hence for a term $[\![\Gamma \vdash M : \theta]\!]$ the data language we seek to recognise, $L([\![\Gamma \vdash M]\!])$ represents pointers in the following manner:

- The initial move takes the (unique) level-0 data value;
- Moves in $[\![\Gamma]\!]$ (i.e. in section B or C of the prearena) take the data value of the previous move;
- Answer moves in $[\![\theta]\!]$ (i.e. in section A of the prearena) take the data value of the question they are answering; and
- Non-initial question moves in $[\![\theta]\!]$ (i.e. in section A of the prearena) take a fresh data value nested under the data value of the justifying answer move.

Theorem 3. *For every typed term $\Gamma \vdash M : \theta$ in $\mathrm{RML}^{\mathrm{res}}_{2\vdash 1}$ that is in canonical form we can effectively construct a deterministic weak nested data class memory automaton, $\mathcal{A}_M$, recognising the complete plays of $L([\![\Gamma \vdash M]\!])$.*

Proof. This proof takes a similar form to that of Theorem 2: by induction over canonical forms. We here sketch the λ-abstraction case.

$\boldsymbol{\lambda x^{\beta}.M : \beta \to \theta}$**.** This construction is almost identical to that in the proof of Theorem 2: again the strategy for P is interleavings of P's strategy for $M : \theta$. The only difference in the construction is that where in the encoding for Theorem 2 the moves in each $\mathcal{A}^{M}_{\gamma,i_x}$ corresponding to the LHS and RHS of the prearena needed to be treated separately, in this case they can be treated identically: all being nested under the new level-0 data value. We demonstrate this construction in Example 1

Example 1. Figure 6 shows two weak nested data class memory automata. We draw a transition $p, a, (j, \begin{pmatrix} s_0 \\ \vdots \\ s_j \end{pmatrix}) \to p', \begin{pmatrix} s'_0 \\ \vdots \\ s'_j \end{pmatrix} \in \delta$ as an arrow from state p to p' labelled with "$a, \begin{pmatrix} s_0 \\ \vdots \\ s_j \end{pmatrix} \to \begin{pmatrix} s'_0 \\ \vdots \\ s'_j \end{pmatrix}$". We omit the "$\to \begin{pmatrix} s'_0 \\ \vdots \\ s'_j \end{pmatrix}$" part of the label if $s'_j = p'$ and $s_i = s'_i$ for all $i \in \{0, 1, \ldots, j-1\}$.

The automaton obtained by the constructions in Theorem 3 for the term-in-context $[\![\vdash \mathbf{let}\, c = \mathbf{ref}\, 0\, \mathbf{in}\, \lambda y^{\mathsf{unit}}.\mathbf{if}\, !c = 0\, \mathbf{then}\, c := 1\, \mathbf{else}\, \Omega]\!]$ is shown in Figure 6a (to aid readability, we have removed most of the dead and unreachable states and transitions).

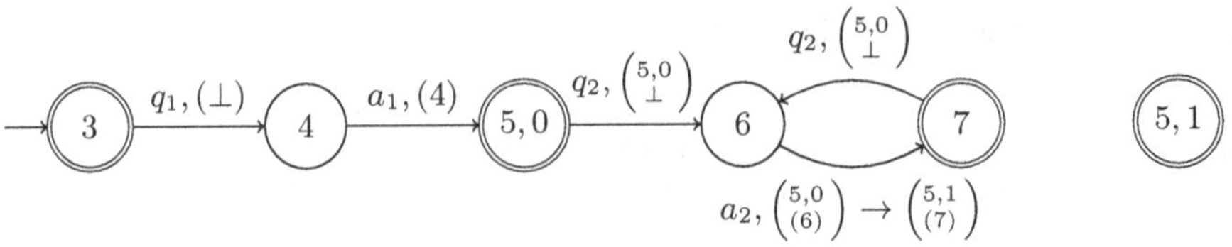

(a) Automaton for $[\![\vdash \mathbf{let}\, c = \mathbf{ref}\, 0\, \mathbf{in}\, \lambda y^{\mathsf{unit}}.\mathbf{if}\, !c = 0\, \mathbf{then}\, c := 1\, \mathbf{else}\, \Omega]\!]$

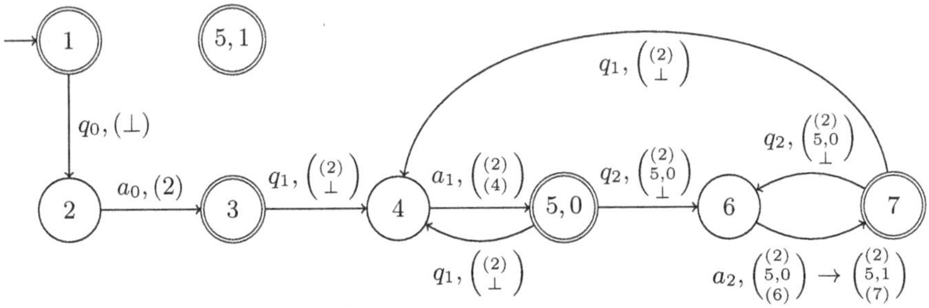

(b) Automaton for $[\![\vdash \lambda x^{\mathsf{unit}}.\mathbf{let}\, c = \mathbf{ref}\, 0\, \mathbf{in}\, \lambda y^{\mathsf{unit}}.\mathbf{if}\, !c = 0\, \mathbf{then}\, c := 1\, \mathbf{else}\, \Omega]\!]$

Fig. 6. Automata recognising strategies

Note that we have the states $(5, 0)$ and $(5, 1)$ - here the second part of the state label is the value of the variable c: the top-level data value will remain in one of these two states, and by doing so store the value of c at that point in the run. The move q_2 in this example corresponds to the environment providing an argument y: note that in a run of the automaton the first time a y argument is passed, the automaton proceeds to reach an accepting state, but in doing so sets the top level data value to the state $(5, 1)$. This means the outgoing transition shown from state 7 cannot fire.

The automaton for $[\![\vdash \lambda x^{\mathsf{unit}}.\mathbf{let}\, c = \mathbf{ref}\, 0\, \mathbf{in}\, \lambda y^{\mathsf{unit}}.\mathbf{if}\, !c = 0\, \mathbf{then}\, c := 1\, \mathbf{else}\, \Omega]\!]$ is shown in Figure 6b (again, cleaned of dead/unreachable transitions for clarity). Note that this contains the first automaton as a sub-automaton, though with a new top-level data value added to the transitions. The q_1 move now corresponds to providing a new argument for x, thus starting a thread. Transitions have been added from the accepting states (5) and (7), allowing a new x-thread to be started from either of these locations. Note that the transition from (7) to (6), which could not fire before, now can fire because several data values (corresponding to different x-threads) can be generated and left in the state $(5, 0)$.

5 Undecidable Fragments

In this section we consider which type sequents and forms of recursion are expressive enough to prove undecidability. The proofs of the results this section proceed by identifying terms such that the induced complete plays correspond to runs of Turing-complete machine models.

On the Right of the Turnstile. In [11] it is shown that observational equivalence is undecidable for 5th-order terms. The proof takes the strategy that was used to show undecidability for 4th-order IA and finds an equivalent call-by-value strategy. It is relatively straightforward to adapt the proof to show that observational equivalence is undecidable at 3rd-order types, e.g. $((\mathsf{unit} \to \mathsf{unit}) \to \mathsf{unit}) \to \mathsf{unit}$. A further result in [12] showed that the problem is undecidable at the type $(\mathsf{unit} \to \mathsf{unit}) \to (\mathsf{unit} \to \mathsf{unit}) \to \mathsf{unit}$. Both results easily generalise to show that the problem is undecidable at *every* 3rd-order type and *every* 2nd-order type which takes at least two 1st-order arguments. We modify the second of these proofs to show undecidability at $(\mathsf{unit} \to \mathsf{unit}) \to \mathsf{unit} \to \mathsf{unit}$. Our proof of this easily adapts to a proof of the following.

Theorem 4. *Observational equivalence is undecidable at every 2nd-order type (of arity at least two) which contains a 1st-order argument that is not the final argument.*

On the Left of the Turnstile. Note that $\vdash M \cong N : \theta$ if, and only if, $f : \theta \to \mathsf{unit} \vdash fM \cong fN : \mathsf{unit}$. Thus, for any sequent $\vdash \theta$ at which observational equivalence is undecidable, the sequent $\theta \to \mathsf{unit} \vdash \mathsf{unit}$ is also undecidable. So the problem is undecidable if, on the left of the turnstile, we have a fourth-order type or a (third-order) type which has a second-order argument whose first-order argument is not the last.

Recursion. In IA, observational equivalence becomes undecidable if we add recursive first-order functions [16]. The analogous results for RML with recursion also hold:

Theorem 5. *Observational equivalence is undecidable in* $\mathrm{RML}_{\text{O-Str}}$ *equipped with recursive functions* $(\mathsf{unit} \to \mathsf{unit}) \to \mathsf{unit}$

6 Conclusion

We have used two related encodings of pointers to data values to decide two related fragments of $\mathrm{RML}_{2\vdash 1}$: $\mathrm{RML}^{\text{P-Str}}_{2\vdash 1}$, in which the free variables were limited to arity 1, and $\mathrm{RML}^{\text{res}}_{2\vdash 1}$, in which the free variables were unlimited in arity but each argument of the free variable was limited to arity 1. It is natural to ask whether we can extend or combine these approaches to decide the whole of $\mathrm{RML}_{2\vdash 1}$. Here we discuss why this seems likely to be impossible with the current machinery used.

In deciding $\mathrm{RML}^{\text{P-Str}}_{2\vdash 1}$ we used the nested data value tree-structure to mirror the shape of the prearenas. These data values can be seen as names for different threads, with the sub-thread relation captured by the nested structure. What happens if we attempt to use this approach to recognise strategies on types where the free variables have arity greater than 1? With free variables having arity 1, whenever they are interrogated by P, they are entirely evaluated immediately: they cannot be partially evaluated. With arity greater than 1, this partial evaluation can happen: P may provide the first argument at some stage, and then at later points evaluate the variable possibly several times with different second arguments. P will only do this subject to visibility conditions though: if P partially evaluates a variable x while in a thread T, it can only continue that partial evaluation of x in T or a sub-thread of T. This leads to problems when our automata recognise interleavings of similar threads using the same part of the automaton. If P's strategy for the thread T is the strategy $[\![M]\!]$ for a term M, and recognised by an automaton $\mathcal{A}^M$, then $[\![\lambda y.M]\!]$ will consist of interleavings of $[\![M]\!]$. The automaton $\mathcal{A}^{\lambda y.M}$ will use a copy of $\mathcal{A}^M$ to simulate an unbounded number of M-threads. If T is one such thread, which performs a partial evaluation of x, this partial evaluation will be represented by input letters with data values unrelated to the data value of T. If a sibling of T, T', does the same, the internal state of the automaton will have no way of telling which of these partial evaluations was performed by T and which by T'. Hence it may recognise data words which represent plays that break the visibility condition.

Therefore, to recognise strategies for terms with free variables of arity greater than 1, the natural approach to take is to have the data value of free-variable moves be related to the thread we are in. This is the approach we took in deciding $\mathrm{RML}^{\mathrm{res}}_{2\vdash 1}$: the free variable moves precisely took the data value of the part of the thread they were in. Then information about the partial evaluation was stored by the thread's data value. This worked when the arguments to the free variables had arity at most 1: however if we allow the arity of this to increase we need to start representing O-pointers in the evaluation of these arguments. For this to be done in a way that makes an inductive construction work for **let** $x = (\lambda y.M)$ **in** N, we must use some kind of nesting of data values for the different M-threads. The naïve approach to take is to allow the M-thread data values to be nested under the data value of whatever part of the N-thread they are in. However, the M-thread may be started and partially evaluated in one part of the N-thread, and then picked up and continued in a descendant part of that N-thread. The data values used in continuing the M-thread must therefore be related to the data values used to represent the partial evaluation of the M-thread, but also to the part of the N-thread the play is currently in. This would break the tree-structure of the data values, and so seem to require a richer structure on the data values.

Further Work. A natural direction for further work, therefore, is to investigate richer data structures and automata models over them that may provide a way to decide $\mathrm{RML}_{2\vdash 1}$.

The automata we used have a non-primitive recursive emptiness problem, and hence the resulting algorithms both have non-primitive recursive complexity also. Although work in [8] shows that this is not the best possible result in the simplest cases, the exact complexities of the observational equivalence problems are still unknown.

To complete the classification of $\mathrm{RML_f}$ also requires deciding (or showing undecidable) the fragment containing order 2 types (on the RHS) with one order 1 argument, which is the last argument. A first step to deciding this would be the fragment labelled RML_X in figure 1. Deciding this fragment via automata reductions similar to those in this paper would seem to require both data values to represent O-pointers, and some kind of visible stack to nest copies of the body of the function, as used in [9]. In particular, recognising strategies of second-order terms such as $\lambda f.f()$ requires the ability to recognise data languages (roughly) of the form $\{d_1 d_2 ... d_n d_n ... d_2 d_1 \mid n \in N, \text{each } d_i \text{ is distinct}\}$. A simple pumping argument shows such languages cannot be recognised by nested data class memory automata, and so some kind of additional stack would seem to be required.

References

1. Abramsky, S., McCusker, G.: Linearity, sharing and state: a fully abstract game semantics for idealized algol with active expressions. Electr. Notes Theor. Comput. Sci. 3, 2–14 (1996)
2. Abramsky, S., McCusker, G.: Call-by-value games. In: Nielsen, M., Thomas, W. (eds.) CSL 1997. LNCS, vol. 1414, pp. 1–17. Springer, Heidelberg (1998)
3. Björklund, H., Schwentick, T.: On notions of regularity for data languages. Theor. Comput. Sci. 411(4-5), 702–715 (2010)
4. Cotton-Barratt, C., Murawski, A.S., Ong, C.-H.L.: Weak and nested class memory automata. In: Proceedings of LATA 2015 (to appear, 2015)
5. Decker, N., Habermehl, P., Leucker, M., Thoma, D.: Ordered navigation on multi-attributed data words. In: Baldan, P., Gorla, D. (eds.) CONCUR 2014. LNCS, vol. 8704, pp. 497–511. Springer, Heidelberg (2014)
6. Ghica, D.R., McCusker, G.: The regular-language semantics of second-order idealized algol. Theor. Comput. Sci. 309(1-3), 469–502 (2003)
7. Honda, K., Yoshida, N.: Game-theoretic analysis of call-by-value computation. Theor. Comput. Sci. 221(1-2), 393–456 (1999)
8. Hopkins, D.: Game Semantics Based Equivalence Checking of Higher-Order Programs. PhD thesis, Department of Computer Science, University of Oxford (2012)
9. Hopkins, D., Murawski, A.S., Ong, C.-H.L.: A fragment of ML decidable by visibly push-down automata. In: Aceto, L., Henzinger, M., Sgall, J. (eds.) ICALP 2011, Part II. LNCS, vol. 6756, pp. 149–161. Springer, Heidelberg (2011)
10. Hyland, J.M.E., Luke Ong, C.-H.: On full abstraction for PCF: i, ii, and III. Inf. Comput. 163(2), 285–408 (2000)
11. Murawski, A.S.: On program equivalence in languages with ground-type references. In: 18th IEEE Symposium on Logic in Computer Science (LICS 2003), p. 108. IEEE Computer Society (2003)
12. Murawski, A.S.: Functions with local state: Regularity and undecidability. Theor. Comput. Sci. 338(1-3), 315–349 (2005)
13. Murawski, A.S., Ong, C.-H.L., Walukiewicz, I.: Idealized algol with ground recursion, and DPDA equivalence. In: Caires, L., Italiano, G.F., Monteiro, L., Palamidessi, C., Yung, M. (eds.) ICALP 2005. LNCS, vol. 3580, pp. 917–929. Springer, Heidelberg (2005)
14. Murawski, A.S., Tzevelekos, N.: Algorithmic nominal game semantics. In: Barthe, G. (ed.) ESOP 2011. LNCS, vol. 6602, pp. 419–438. Springer, Heidelberg (2011)
15. Murawski, A.S., Tzevelekos, N.: Algorithmic games for full ground references. In: Czumaj, A., Mehlhorn, K., Pitts, A., Wattenhofer, R. (eds.) ICALP 2012, Part II. LNCS, vol. 7392, pp. 312–324. Springer, Heidelberg (2012)
16. Luke Ong, C.-H.: An approach to deciding the observational equivalence of algol-like languages. Ann. Pure Appl. Logic 130(1-3), 125–171 (2004)
17. Pitts, A.M., Stark, I.D.B.: Operational reasoning for functions with local state. In: Higher Order Operational Techniques in Semantics, pp. 227–273 (1998)

Operational Nominal Game Semantics

Guilhem Jaber

Queen Mary University of London, UK

Abstract. We present a formal correspondence between Laird's trace semantics and the nominal game model of Murawski and Tzevelekos for RefML, a call-by-value language with higher-order references. This gives an operational flavor to game semantics, where denotation of terms is generated via an interactive reduction, which allows to reduce terms with free functional variables, and where pointer structure is represented with name pointers. It also leads to transferring the categorical structure defined on the game model to the trace model. Then, representing the notion of view from game semantics in terms of available name pointers, we restrict our trace semantics to GroundML, a language with first-order references and show its full abstraction using a correspondence with visible strategies. This gives the first fully abstract trace model for this language.

1 Introduction

Game Semantics [6,3] is a powerful theory to build fully abstract denotational models of various programming languages. The denotation of a term is represented as a *strategy*, a set of *plays* between that term and any context in a *game arena*, which sets the rules the plays have to satisfy. One of its most important contributions, the so-called "Abramsky Cube", is the characterization of the absence of various impure effects in terms of extra conditions on the denotation of terms, namely *well-bracketing* for the absence of control operators, *visibility* for the absence of higher-order store, *innocence* for pure terms. In recent years, game semantics has been developed to deal with languages with nominal aspects, from the ν-calculus [1], an extension with storage cells [10], to ML-like languages with higher-order nominal references [13].

The starting point of this article is the nominal game semantics of Murawski and Tzevelekos [13], which is fully abstract for RefML, but also for GroundML as soon as one adds a visibility condition to strategies [14]. As opposed to previous games models for languages with stores, initiated by Abramsky, Honda and McCusker [2], it uses nominal techniques [5], to avoid the problem of *bad variables*. In a more operational setting, Laird [9] has introduced a trace semantics for a variant of RefML, and has proven its full abstraction. This model marries a trace representation inspired by game semantics with an operational definition, *i.e.* denotations of terms are computed via a rewriting system rather than defined by induction on their typing judgment.

In this article, we introduce a trace semantics for RefML, whose definition is a typed variant to the one introduced by Laird. Traces are generated by an *interactive reduction*, which can be seen as an extension of the usual operational semantics to open terms with free functional variables. Then, the denotation of terms is defined via *trace-strategies*, *i.e.* sets of traces that terms generate using this reduction. In fact, traces can be seen

A. Pitts (Ed.): FOSSACS 2015, LNCS 9034, pp. 264–278, 2015.
DOI: 10.1007/978-3-662-46678-0_17

$$\begin{array}{lll}
\tau,\sigma & \overset{def}{=} & \text{Int} \mid \text{ref}\,\tau \mid \tau \to \sigma \\
v & \overset{def}{=} & () \mid \widehat{n} \mid x \mid l \mid \lambda x:\tau.M \mid \Omega_\tau \qquad \text{(where } n \in \mathbb{Z}, l \in \text{Loc)} \\
M,N & \overset{def}{=} & v \mid MN \mid M+N \mid \mathtt{case_z}(M_1)(M_2,M_3) \mid M == N \mid \\
& & \text{ref}\,M \mid !M \mid M := N \\
K & \overset{def}{=} & \bullet \mid KM \mid vK \mid K+M \mid v+K \mid \mathtt{case_z}(K)(M,M') \mid \text{ref}\,K \mid \\
& & !K \mid K := M \mid v := K \mid K == M \mid v == K
\end{array}$$

Fig. 1. Definition of RefML

as a representation of plays used in game semantics where the usual pointer structure, which represents the causality between the different moves, is encoded with variables. Such variables that are of functional type are called *name pointers*.

Following this idea, we build a correspondence between the trace and the game model of RefML. To do so, we impose on trace-strategies a categorical apparatus that capture call-by-value languages, namely a *closed-Freyd category* [16]. To build such a structure on traces, we recast the definitions of game semantics from [10,13] in the setting of trace semantics. The main difficulty is that the pointer structure of traces is no more defined explicitly, but need to be rebuilt from a study of freshness of name pointers (*i.e.* functional variables). Finally, we answer a question asked by Laird at the end of [9] about a possible trace semantics for a language with restricted references, rephrasing the usual notion of *visibility* which characterizes this restriction in the setting of trace semantics.

All missing definitions and proofs can be found in Chapter 4 of the PhD thesis of the author [7].

2 RefML and GroundML

Let us first introduce RefML, a call-by-value λ-calculus with *higher-order references*. The syntax of types τ, values v, terms M and evaluation contexts K of RefML is given in Figure 1.A type is said to be *ground* if it is not equal to $\tau \to \sigma$. So for example $\text{ref}\,(\tau \to \sigma)$ is ground. As usual, `let` x `=` N `in` M is defined as $(\lambda x.M)N$ and $M; N$ is defined as $(\lambda x.M)N$ with x fresh in M.

Locations live in sets Loc_τ where τ is the type of values they are storing. We define Loc as $\biguplus_\tau \text{Loc}_\tau$ and Loc_ϕ as $\biguplus_{\sigma,\tau} \text{Loc}_{\sigma\to\tau}$. Heaps h are defined as finite partial maps $\text{Loc} \rightharpoonup \text{Val}$ respecting types, *i.e.* $h(l)$ is a closed value of type τ when $l \in \text{Loc}_\tau$. The empty heap is written ε. Adding a new element to a partial map h is written $h \cdot [l \hookrightarrow v]$, and is defined only if $l \notin \text{dom}(h)$. We also define $h[l \hookrightarrow v]$, for $l \in \text{dom}(h)$, as the partial function h' which satisfies $h'(l') = h(l')$ when $l' \neq l$, and $h'(l) = v$. The restriction of a heap h to a set of locations L is written $h_{|L}$. We write h_{fn} for the subheap of h which stores higher-order values A heap is said to be *closed* when, for all $l \in \text{dom}(h)$, if $h(l)$ is itself a location l' then $l' \in \text{dom}(h)$. Taking a set L of locations and h a heap, we define the image of L by h, written $h^*(L)$ as $h^*(L) \overset{def}{=} \bigcup_{j\leq 0} h^j(L)$ with $h^0(L) = L$, $h^{j+1}(L) = h(h^j(L)) \cap \text{Loc}$. Using it, we define $\mathbf{Cl}(L)$, the set of minimal closed heaps whose domain contains L, as $\mathbf{Cl}(L) \overset{def}{=} \{h \mid h \text{ closed}, \text{dom}(h) = h^*(L)\}$.

$$\begin{array}{llll}(K[(\lambda x.M)v],h) \mapsto (K[M\{v/x\}],h) & & (K[\text{ref } v],h) & \mapsto (K[l],h\cdot[l\hookrightarrow v]) \\ (K[!l],h) & \mapsto (K[h(l)],h) & (K[l:=v],h) & \mapsto (K[()],h[l\hookrightarrow v]) \\ (K[l==l],h) & \mapsto (K[\widehat{1}],h) & (K[l==l'],h) & \mapsto (K[\widehat{0}],h) \\ (K[\mathtt{case_z}(\widehat{n})(M_1,M_2)],h) \mapsto (K[M_i],h) & & (i=1 \text{ if } n=0, \text{otherwise } i=2) & \end{array}$$

Fig. 2. Operational Semantics of RefML

The small step operational semantics of RefML is defined in Figure 2. We write $M\{v/x\}$ to represent the (capture-free) substitution of x by v in M. This reduction is deterministic, so we suppose that the reduction $(K[\text{ref } v],h) \mapsto (K[l],h\cdot[l\hookrightarrow v])$ chooses a location $l \notin \text{dom}(h)$. We also consider the non-deterministic reduction $\mapsto_{nd}$, defined in the same way but for the rule of allocation, which is *s.t.* $(K[\text{ref } v],h) \mapsto_{nd} (K[l],h\cdot[l\hookrightarrow v])$ for any $l \notin \text{dom}(h)$.

Then typing judgments are of the form $\Sigma;\Gamma \vdash M : \tau$, where Γ is a variable context and $\Sigma = (l_1,\dots,l_n)$ is a location context. Notice that we do not need to indicate the types of locations of l in Σ, since the membership $l \in \text{Loc}_\tau$ already gives its type.

In the following, we make a clear distinction between variables of ground types and variables of functional types. Such variable of functional types are called name pointers, which live in the set $\mathbb{P} \subseteq \text{Var}$. Indeed, we deal abstractly with variables of functional types, so we write $\Sigma;\Gamma_g,\Gamma_f \vdash M : \tau$ to distinguish between typing contexts Γ_g,Γ_f containing respectively ground type variables and functional type variables.

From a typing context Γ and a function $\gamma : \text{Var} \rightharpoonup \text{Val}$, we say that γ is a *substitution* on Γ—written $\gamma : \Gamma$—if γ is defined exactly on all the variables occurring in Γ, and $\gamma(x)$ is a value of type τ whenever $(x,\tau) \in \Gamma$. Then, the action of the substitution γ on a term M, defined as $M\{\overrightarrow{\gamma(x_i)/x_i}\}$ with x_i ranging over Γ, is written $\gamma(M)$.

In this article, we also consider GroundML, a restriction of RefML with only full ground references, *i.e.* references which can store integers or other full ground references. It is formally defined as the set of terms of RefML whose type do not contain any subtypes ref $(\tau \to \sigma)$, and which do not contain any subterms of the form ref M with M functional. In GroundML, we cannot define diverging terms anymore via higher-order references, so we rely on special terms Ω_τ for each type τ that always diverge. It is important to have such diverging terms when studying contextual equivalence.

To reason abstractly over name pointers and locations, we use the framework of *nominal sets* [5] over a set of names $\mathbb{A}$. More precisely, all the objects we consider in this article can be seen as nominal sets which is either the set of locations or name pointers, so $\mathbb{A}$ will either be Loc or $\mathbb{P}$. Then two elements t,u of a ($\mathbb{A}$-) nominal set X are said to be *nominally-equivalent*, written $t \sim_{\mathbb{A}} u$ if there exists a finite permutation π over $\mathbb{A}$ *s.t.* $t = \pi \cdot u$ holds. Then a subset X of a nominal set is *nominally closed* if for all $t \in X$ and permutation π over $\mathbb{A}$, $\pi \cdot t \in X$. We write $\nu_{\mathbb{A}}(t)$ for the *support* of an element t of a nominal set X.

3 Trace Semantics

We now introduce a semantics for RefML where denotations of terms are sets of *traces*. It is a variant of the work of Laird [9] more amenable to a comparison with game semantics by taking track of type informations. Traces are used to represent all possible interactions of terms with contexts. They are generated by an *interactive reduction*, defined as a *labeled transition system*, which generalizes the small-step reduction of Figure 2 by producing *actions* to deal with free functional variables.

To be able to generate all possible executions, we need to keep track of values disclosed to contexts, namely location—so that a context can set arbitrary values in it—or λ-abstraction—so that a context can call it at any time when it takes control back.

Notice that this reduction is history-independent, *i.e.* the reduction of a callback $K[f\ v]$ does not depend on the possible previous occurrences of $K'[f\ v]$ in the reduction. This is due to the fact that our language has references, so that contexts can keep track of the number of times their functional arguments provided to the term are called, and thus give each time a different answer. This corresponds to the fact that strategies for RefML are not innocent.

3.1 Game-Like Definitions

We start introducing traces following the usual presentation of game semantics, mimicking the definitions of the previous section. The notion corresponding to a game move is called here an *action*. Actions are formed over ground values and variables, used to represent higher-order values. These variables, of functional type, are called *opponent* and *player* name pointers. opponent name pointers represent higher-order values provided by contexts (*i.e.* opponent) to terms (*i.e.* player), while it is the opposite for player name pointers. There are four kinds of *basic* actions:

- a question of the term (resp. context) via a name pointer x with argument v (with $x \neq v$), represented by the action $\bar{x}\langle v\rangle$ (resp. $x\langle v\rangle$),
- an answer by the term (resp. context) of the value v, represented by the action $\langle\bar{v}\rangle$ (resp. $\langle v\rangle$).

A name pointer y appearing as an argument of a player (resp. opponent) question $\bar{x}\langle y\rangle$ (resp. $x\langle y\rangle$) or in a player (resp. opponent) answer $\langle\bar{y}\rangle$ (resp. $\langle y\rangle$) is called a *player name pointer* (resp. *opponent name pointer*). This means that being an opponent or a player name pointer depends on the action, and is not inherent to the name pointer. The sets of player and opponent name pointers (*i.e.* their supports) of an element X formed by actions are respectively written $\nu_{\mathbb{P}}^{P}(X)$ and $\nu_{\mathbb{P}}^{O}(X)$.

Actions a are defined as pairs (a, ξ) of a basic action a and a tag ξ. Tags are words over the alphabet $\{\ell, r, s\}$, where the concatenation is written $\xi \cdot \xi'$ and the empty word is written ε. Such tags are used to indicate to which set (*i.e.* arena) a basic action belongs to. This is useful to avoid the use of disjoint unions (as coproduct) and the corresponding injections $\mathbf{in}_{\mathrm{l}}, \mathbf{in}_{\mathrm{r}}$ which are usually used in game semantics. In our setting, such injections are represented respectively by tags beginning with ℓ and r, while s is used to represent actions corresponding to functions stored in heaps.

Player, Opponent and initial actions are respectively written p, o and i. The labeling of actions (*i.e.* the fact they are *player* or *opponent* and *question* or *answer* actions) is hard-wired, while labeling of moves in game semantics depends on the underlying arena. As we will see, this complicates some definitions (arrow arenas and restrictions of traces to a given arena) where we need to change the labeling of actions.

We define the operation $a^{\perp}$ as the operation which simply transforms an opponent action into the corresponding player action, and vice-versa (leaving the tag unchanged).

$$
\begin{aligned}
&\mathfrak{I}_{\mathfrak{A}\otimes\mathfrak{B}} \stackrel{def}{=} \ell \cdot \mathfrak{I}_{\mathfrak{A}} \times r \cdot \mathfrak{I}_{\mathfrak{B}} \qquad \mathfrak{M}_{\mathfrak{A}\otimes\mathfrak{B}} \stackrel{def}{=} \mathfrak{I}_{\mathfrak{A}\otimes\mathfrak{B}} \uplus \ell \cdot (\mathfrak{M}_{\mathfrak{A}} \backslash \mathfrak{I}_{\mathfrak{A}}) \uplus r \cdot (\mathfrak{M}_{\mathfrak{B}} \backslash \mathfrak{I}_{\mathfrak{B}})\\
&\vdash_{\mathfrak{A}\otimes\mathfrak{B}} \stackrel{def}{=} \{((\ell \cdot \mathrm{i}_{\mathfrak{A}}, r \cdot \mathrm{i}_{\mathfrak{B}}), \ell \cdot a) \mid \mathrm{i}_{\mathfrak{A}} \vdash_{\mathfrak{A}} a\} \uplus \{((\ell \cdot \mathrm{i}_{\mathfrak{A}}, r \cdot \mathrm{i}_{\mathfrak{B}}), r \cdot a) \mid \mathrm{i}_{\mathfrak{B}} \vdash_{\mathfrak{B}} a\}\\
&\qquad \uplus (\ell \cdot \vdash_{\mathfrak{A}|(\mathfrak{M}_{\mathfrak{A}} \backslash \mathfrak{I}_{\mathfrak{A}})^2}) \uplus (r \cdot \vdash_{\mathfrak{B}|(\mathfrak{M}_{\mathfrak{B}} \backslash \mathfrak{I}_{\mathfrak{B}})^2})\\
&\mathfrak{I}_{\mathfrak{A}\Rightarrow\mathfrak{B}} \stackrel{def}{=} \{\langle \bar{x} \rangle \mid x \in \mathbb{P}\}\\
&\mathfrak{M}_{\mathfrak{A}\Rightarrow\mathfrak{B}} \stackrel{def}{=} \mathfrak{I}_{\mathfrak{A}\Rightarrow\mathfrak{B}} \uplus \ell \cdot (\mathfrak{M}_{\mathfrak{A}} \backslash \mathfrak{I}_{\mathfrak{A}})^{\perp} \uplus \{(x\langle u \rangle, \ell \cdot \xi) \mid x \in \mathbb{P}, (\langle \bar{u} \rangle, \xi) \in \mathfrak{I}_{\mathfrak{A}}\} \uplus r \cdot \mathfrak{M}_{\mathfrak{B}}\\
&\vdash_{\mathfrak{A}\Rightarrow\mathfrak{B}} \stackrel{def}{=} \{(\langle \bar{x} \rangle, (x\langle u \rangle, \ell \cdot \xi)) \mid x \in \mathbb{P}, (\langle \bar{u} \rangle, \xi) \in \mathfrak{I}_{\mathfrak{A}}\}\\
&\qquad \uplus \{((x\langle u \rangle, \ell \cdot \xi), \ell \cdot a) \mid x \in \mathbb{P}, (\langle \bar{u} \rangle, \xi) \in \mathfrak{I}_{\mathfrak{A}}, a \in \mathfrak{M}_{\mathfrak{A}}, (\langle \bar{u} \rangle, \xi) \vdash_{\mathfrak{A}} a\}\\
&\qquad \uplus \{((x\langle u \rangle, \ell \cdot \xi), r \cdot \mathrm{i}_{\mathfrak{B}}) \mid x \in \mathbb{P}, (\langle \bar{u} \rangle, \xi) \in \mathfrak{I}_{\mathfrak{A}}\} \uplus (\ell \cdot \vdash_{\mathfrak{A}|(\mathfrak{M}_{\mathfrak{A}} \backslash \mathfrak{I}_{\mathfrak{A}})^2})^{\perp} \uplus (r \cdot \vdash_{\mathfrak{B}})\\
&\mathfrak{I}_{\mathfrak{A}\to\mathfrak{B}} \stackrel{def}{=} \{(?\langle u \rangle, \ell \cdot \xi) \mid (\langle \bar{u} \rangle, \xi) \in \mathfrak{I}_{\mathfrak{A}}\} \qquad \mathfrak{M}_{\mathfrak{A}\to\mathfrak{B}} \stackrel{def}{=} \mathfrak{I}_{\mathfrak{A}\to\mathfrak{B}} \uplus \ell \cdot (\mathfrak{M}_{\mathfrak{A}} \backslash \mathfrak{I}_{\mathfrak{A}})^{\perp} \uplus r \cdot \mathfrak{M}_{\mathfrak{B}}\\
&\vdash_{\mathfrak{A}\to\mathfrak{B}} \stackrel{def}{=} \{((?\langle u \rangle, \ell \cdot \xi), r \cdot \mathrm{i}_{\mathfrak{B}}) \mid (\langle \bar{u} \rangle, \xi) \in \mathfrak{I}_{\mathfrak{A}}, \mathrm{i}_{\mathfrak{B}} \in \mathfrak{I}_{\mathfrak{B}}\} \uplus (\ell \cdot \vdash_{\mathfrak{A}|(\mathfrak{M}_{\mathfrak{A}} \backslash \mathfrak{I}_{\mathfrak{A}})^2})^{\perp} \uplus (r \cdot \vdash_{\mathfrak{B}})\\
&\qquad \uplus \{((?\langle u \rangle, \ell \cdot \xi), \ell \cdot a) \mid (\langle \bar{u} \rangle, \xi) \in \mathfrak{I}_{\mathfrak{A}}, a \in \mathfrak{M}_{\mathfrak{A}}, (\langle \bar{u} \rangle, \xi) \vdash_{\mathfrak{A}} a\}
\end{aligned}
$$

Fig. 3. Definition of compound arenas

It is extended to sets and relations of actions. Then, we introduce the notion of *arenas*, which are simply triples $(\mathfrak{M}, \mathfrak{I}, \vdash)$ of a set of actions $\mathfrak{M}$, a set of initial actions $\mathfrak{I} \subseteq \mathfrak{M}$ and a justification relation $\vdash \subseteq \mathfrak{M} \times \mathfrak{M} \backslash \mathfrak{I}$. Following the correspondence with game semantics, we define: *value-arenas* (resp. *term-arenas*) as arenas whose initial actions are player answers (resp. opponent question).

From two trace value-arenas $\mathfrak{A}, \mathfrak{B}$ we construct the value arenas $\mathfrak{A} \otimes \mathfrak{B}$ and $\mathfrak{A} \Rightarrow \mathfrak{B}$ and the term arena $\mathfrak{A} \to \mathfrak{B}$ in Figure 3. In the definition of $\mathfrak{A} \to \mathfrak{B}$, the symbol ? is used as a distinguished name pointer to represent what is interrogated by the initial opponent question. To each type τ, we associate a trace value-arena $\lceil \tau \rceil$ as:

- $\lceil \iota \rceil \stackrel{def}{=} (\mathfrak{M}_{\iota}, \mathfrak{M}_{\iota}, \varnothing)$ where $\mathfrak{M}_{\iota} \stackrel{def}{=} \{\langle \bar{v} \rangle \mid v$ a value of type $\iota\}$, $\iota = \mathrm{Unit}, \mathrm{Int}, \mathrm{ref}\ \tau$
- $\lceil \sigma \to \tau \rceil \stackrel{def}{=} \lceil \sigma \rceil \Rightarrow \lceil \tau \rceil$.

To relate actions to the evolution of the heap, we introduce *actions-with-heap* on an arena $\mathfrak{A}$, *i.e.* pairs (a, h) of an action $a \in \mathfrak{M}_{\mathfrak{A}}$ and a *functional-free heap* h, that is a heap where stored higher-order values are represented by distinct name pointers. An action-with-heap (a, ξ, h) is said to introduce the name pointer x if either a is of the form $\bar{y}\langle x \rangle, y\langle x \rangle, \langle \bar{x} \rangle$ or $\langle x \rangle$, or if x is in the co-domain of h (written $\mathrm{codom}(h)$). In the latter case, we say that x is l-introduced when $h(l) = x$.

Such actions which l-introduce name pointers, called *ϕ-actions*, correspond to call-backs coming from disclosed locations storing functions. They belong to the set $\mathfrak{M}_{\phi}$ defined as $\bigcup_{\tau,\tau'} \mathfrak{M}_{\lceil \tau \to \tau' \rceil}$. Using it, we define the set $\mathrm{Trace}_{\mathfrak{A}}$ over an arena $\mathfrak{A}$ as the set of sequences T of actions-with-heap on $\mathfrak{M}_{\mathfrak{A}} \uplus (s \cdot \mathfrak{M}_{\phi})$ *s.t.* for each name pointer x in T, x is introduced by at most one action-with-heap in T. $\mathrm{Trace}_{\mathfrak{A}}$ can be seen as a nominal set over Loc and $\mathbb{P}$. We write $T' \sqsubseteq T$ when T' is a prefix of T.

We say that a trace $T \in \mathrm{Trace}_{\mathfrak{A}}$ is *justified* if every name pointer x in T is introduced by a previous action in T. Then, we define the *depth* of an action (a, h) in a trace T, written $\mathbf{depth}_T(a, h)$ as the difference between the number of questions and the number of answers of T_1, where $T = T_1 \cdot (a, h) \cdot T_2$.

Definition 1. *Let* $(a_1, h_1), (a_2, h_2)$ *two actions-with-heap* s.t. (a_1, h_1) *appears before* (a_2, h_2) *in a trace* T. *We say that* (a_1, h_1) *justifies* (a_2, h_2) *when:*

- a_2 *is an answer and* a_1 *is the latest question of* T *appearing before* a_2 s.t. $\mathbf{depth}_T(a_2, h_2) = \mathbf{depth}_T(a_1, h_1) + 1$,

– *or a_2 is a question $\bar{x}\langle u\rangle$ or $x\langle u\rangle$, and (a_1, h_1) is the first action introducing x, so a_1 is either equal to $\langle\bar{x}\rangle, \langle x\rangle, \bar{y}\langle x\rangle, y\langle x\rangle$ or $x \in \text{codom}(h_1)$.*

In the latter case, we say that x is l-justified when $h_1(l) = x$. A question of T which does not justify any answer is said to be pending.

We define the set of *available locations* of a trace T, written $\mathbf{Av}(T)$, as $\mathbf{Av}(\varepsilon) \stackrel{def}{=} \varnothing$ and $\mathbf{Av}(T \cdot (a,h)) \stackrel{def}{=} h^*(\mathbf{Av}(T) \cup \nu_L(a))$. A justified trace over $\mathfrak{A}$ is said to be *legal* if only its first action-with-heap is in $\mathfrak{I}_{\mathfrak{A}}$ and it alternates between player and opponent actions, and is said to be a *play* if it is furthermore *frugal, i.e.* for all $T' \cdot (a,h) \sqsubseteq T$, $\text{dom}(h) = \mathbf{Av}(T' \cdot (a,h))$. Using all these definitions, we can finally introduce the notion of *trace-strategy* used to define the denotation of terms.

Definition 2. *A* trace-strategy $\mathfrak{s}$ *over an arena $\mathfrak{A}$ is a non-empty set of even-length plays on $\mathfrak{A}$* s.t.*:*

– *If $T \cdot (o,h) \cdot (p,h') \in \mathfrak{s}$ then $T \in \mathfrak{s}$.*
– *If $T \in \sigma$ and $T \sim T'$ then $T' \in \mathfrak{s}$.*
– *If $T_1 \cdot (p_1, h_1)$ and $T_2 \cdot (p_2, h_2)$ are in $\mathfrak{s}$ and $T_1 \sim T_2$, then $T_1 \cdot (p_1, h_1) \sim T_2 \cdot (p_2, h_2)$.*

3.2 A Correspondence between Traces and Plays

There is a direct correspondence between actions introduced in this paper and moves in game semantics defined in [13], where we suppose that injections coming from coproducts are also represented by tags. It is obtained by transforming questions $\bar{x}\langle v\rangle$ and $x\langle v\rangle$ into v, transforming answers $\langle\bar{v}\rangle$ and $\langle v\rangle$ into v, and then transforming all remaining name pointers into $\star$, the initial move of game arenas for functional types[1]. The function θ, which performs this two-step translation, transforms actions from an arena $\mathfrak{A}$ to moves to the corresponding game-arena A, leaving tags unchanged. The labeling function is then defined straightforwardly.

We extend this correspondence to justified traces and *well-bracketed* justified sequences of game semantics. More precisely, we first extend the function θ to actions-with-heaps, transforming name pointers stored in heaps into the move $\star$, and then pointwisely from traces to sequences of moves. So we define a function Θ which transforms a justified trace T on an arena $\mathfrak{A}$ to a sequence of moves $\theta(T)$ on the corresponding arena A, and *s.t.* for two actions-with-heaps (a_1, h_1), (a_2, h_2) of T, there is a pointer from $\theta(a_2, h_2)$ to $\theta(a_1, h_1)$ when (a_2, h_2) is justified by (a_1, h_1). Notice that two traces which are $\mathbb{P}$-nominal equivalent give rise to the same sequence of moves.

Extending Θ to sets of traces, it is direct that $\Theta(\mathfrak{s})$ is a game-strategy on an arena A when $\mathfrak{s}$ is a trace-strategy on the corresponding arena $\mathfrak{A}$.

3.3 Interactive Reduction

We now introduce an *interactive reduction* which generates traces from terms, representing their interactions with any possible applicative contexts $K[\bullet_{\tau,\xi}]$, where the

[1] We do not need to transform the symbol "?" since it is automatically removed, appearing only in $?\langle v\rangle$.

Intern $\langle (M,\tau,\xi)\cdot\overrightarrow{K_i},\gamma,\mathcal{I},h,D\rangle \longrightarrow \langle (M',\tau,\xi)\cdot\overrightarrow{K_i},\gamma,\mathcal{I},h',D\rangle$
(when $(M,h)\mapsto_{nd}(M',h')$)

P-AnsG $\langle (v,\iota,\xi)\cdot\overrightarrow{K_i},\gamma,\mathcal{I},h,D\rangle \xrightarrow{(\langle\bar{v}\rangle,r\cdot\xi,h'_{|D'})} \langle\overrightarrow{K_i},\gamma',\mathcal{I},h',D'\rangle$
(v of type ι, $\gamma'=\gamma\cdot\overrightarrow{[x_i\hookrightarrow(h(l_i),\tau_i,s)]}$)

P-Ans $\langle (v,\tau,\xi)\cdot\overrightarrow{K_i},\gamma,\mathcal{I},h,D\rangle \xrightarrow{(\langle\bar{x}\rangle,r\cdot\xi,h'_{|D'})} \langle\overrightarrow{K_i},\gamma',\mathcal{I},h',D'\rangle$
(x fresh, $\gamma'=\gamma\cdot[x\hookrightarrow(v,\tau,r\cdot\xi)]\cdot\overrightarrow{[x_i\hookrightarrow(h(l_i),\tau_i,s)]}$)

P-QuestG $\langle (K[x\,v],\tau,\xi)\cdot\overrightarrow{K_i},\gamma,\mathcal{I},h,D\rangle \xrightarrow{(\bar{x}\langle v\rangle,f\cdot\xi',h'_{|D'})} \langle (K[\bullet_{\iota,\xi'}],\tau,\xi)\cdot\overrightarrow{K_i},\gamma',\mathcal{I},h',D'\rangle$
($(x,\iota\to\sigma,\xi')\in\mathcal{I}$, v of type ι, $\gamma'=\gamma\cdot\overrightarrow{[x_i\hookrightarrow(h(l_i),\tau_i,s)]}$)

P-Quest $\langle (K[x\,v],\tau,\xi)\cdot\overrightarrow{K_i},\gamma,\mathcal{I},h,D\rangle \xrightarrow{(\bar{x}\langle y\rangle,f\cdot\xi',h'_{|D'})} \langle (K[\bullet_{\sigma',\xi'}],\tau,\xi)\cdot\overrightarrow{K_i},\gamma',\mathcal{I},h',D'\rangle$
($(x,\sigma\to\sigma',\xi')\in\mathcal{I}$, y fresh, $\gamma'=\gamma\cdot[y\hookrightarrow(v,\sigma,f\cdot\xi')]\cdot\overrightarrow{[x_i\hookrightarrow(h(l_i),\tau_i,s)]}$)
in all P-rules: $D'=\mathrm{discl}(v,h,D)$ and $h'=h\overrightarrow{[l_i\hookrightarrow x_i]}$ with the x_i fresh
where l_i ranges over $\mathrm{dom}(h_{\mathrm{fn}})\cap D'$ with $l_i\in\mathrm{Loc}_{\tau_i}$)

O-AnsG $\langle (K[\bullet_{\iota,\xi'}],\tau,\xi)\cdot\overrightarrow{K_i},\gamma,\mathcal{I},h,D\rangle \xrightarrow{(\langle v\rangle,r\cdot\xi',h'_{|D'})} \langle (K[v],\tau,\xi)\cdot\overrightarrow{K_i},\gamma,\mathcal{I}',h',D'\rangle$
(v of type ι, $v\notin\mathrm{dom}(h)\cap\overline{D}$, $D'=\mathrm{discl}(v,h',D)$, $\mathcal{I}'=\mathcal{I}\cdot\overrightarrow{(h(l_i),\tau_i,s)}$)

O-Ans $\langle (K[\bullet_{\sigma,\xi'}],\tau,\xi)\cdot\overrightarrow{K_i},\gamma,\mathcal{I},h,D\rangle \xrightarrow{(\langle y\rangle,r\cdot\xi',h'_{|D'})} \langle (K[y],\tau,\xi)\cdot\overrightarrow{K_i},\gamma,\mathcal{I}',h',D'\rangle$
($D'=\mathrm{discl}(h',D)$, $\mathcal{I}'=\mathcal{I}\cdot(y,\sigma,r\cdot\xi')\cdot\overrightarrow{(h(l_i),\tau_i,s)}$)

O-QuestG $\langle\overrightarrow{K_i},\gamma,\mathcal{I},h,D\rangle \xrightarrow{(x\langle v\rangle,f\cdot\xi,h'_{|D'})} \langle (u\,v,\tau,\xi)\cdot\overrightarrow{K_i},\gamma,\mathcal{I}',h',D'\rangle$
($\gamma(x)=(u,\iota\to\tau,\xi)$, v of type ι, $v\notin\mathrm{dom}(h)\cap\overline{D}$, $D'=\mathrm{discl}(v,h',D)$, $\mathcal{I}'=\mathcal{I}\cdot\overrightarrow{(h'(l_i),\tau_i,s)}$)

O-Quest $\langle\overrightarrow{K_i},\gamma,\mathcal{I},h,D\rangle \xrightarrow{(x\langle y\rangle,f\cdot\xi,h'_{|D'})} \langle (u\,y,\tau,\xi)\cdot\overrightarrow{K_i},\gamma,\mathcal{I}',h',D'\rangle$
($\gamma(x)=(u,\sigma\to\tau,\xi)$, $D'=\mathrm{discl}(h',D)$, $\mathcal{I}'=\mathcal{I}\cdot(y,\tau,f\cdot\xi))\cdot\overrightarrow{(h'(l_i),\tau_i,s)}$)
in all O-Rules: l_i ranges over $\mathrm{dom}(h'_{\mathrm{fn}})\cap\mathcal{D}'$ *s.t.* $l_i\in\mathrm{Loc}_{\tau_i}$, y and $h'(l_i)$ fresh,
$h'_{|\overline{D'}}=h_{|\overline{D}}$ and $h'_{|D'}$ is closed and functional-free)

Fig. 4. Definition of the interaction semantics

symbol $\bullet$, representing a "hole" (*i.e.* a pending question), is tagged with a type τ and a tag ξ, representing the type and the arena of the expected answer which will fill the hole. This reduction is defined on "stacks" $(M,\tau,\xi)\cdot\overrightarrow{(K_i,\tau_i,\xi_i)}$ formed by a term M and contexts $\overrightarrow{K_i}$ for *player configurations*, or on stacks $\overrightarrow{(K_i,\tau_i,\xi_i)}$ for *opponent configurations*. Such elements of the stacks comes also with a type τ and a tag ξ. The empty stack is simply written $\Diamond$. When Player provides a higher-order value to Opponent, either via a callback (*i.e.* a question) or directly when reducing to a λ-abstraction (*i.e.* an answer), it is stored in an environment γ, which is a partial map from $\mathbb{P}$ to Val. Then Opponent can interrogate what is stored in γ, by asking a question. Opponent only provides opponent name pointers to represent higher-order values. They are stored in a set $\mathcal{I}\subseteq\mathbb{P}$. They can also be interrogated by Player.

To represent disclosure of locations, we use a set D which grows as the term or the context discloses new locations. To determine which locations are disclosed when a value v is played with a heap h, we define a function $\mathrm{discl}(v,h,D)$ as $h^*(D\cup\{l\})$ if v is a location l, $h^*(D)$ otherwise. We simply write $\mathrm{discl}(h,D)$ for $h^*(D)$.

The interactive reduction is defined in Figure 4 between player and opponent configurations. The rule **Intern** allows us to perform the usual (operational) reduction of terms. Notice that it uses the non-deterministic reduction $\mapsto_{nd}$ rather than the usual $\mapsto$, in order to be exhaustive w.r.t. names of locations created. The rules **P-AnsG** and **P-Ans** represent player answers. If the answer is a ground value, then if it is a location it is put in D', otherwise it is simply forgotten by Opponent since it has no meaning to interrogate it. Otherwise, it is a higher-order value, which is thus stored in γ'. The rules **P-QuestG** and **P-Quest** represent player questions. That is, Player interrogates an opponent name pointer of $\mathcal{I}$ with a value. Player can also disclose indirectly either new locations or new higher-order values via the already disclosed locations. The new disclosed locations are caught via $\mathrm{discl}(v, h, D)$, while disclosed higher-order values live in $\mathrm{dom}(h_{\mathrm{fn}}) \cap \mathcal{D}'$ (recall that h_{fn} is the subheap of h which stores higher-order values), so that they are replaced by fresh player name pointers in h' and γ is updated consequently. The rules **O-AnsG** and **O-Ans** represent opponent answers. When Opponent answers a location, it cannot be one which is private to Player. This explain the condition "v is ground and not in $\mathrm{dom}(h) \cap \overline{D}$" (where $\overline{D}$ is the complement of D) in the definition of **O-AnsG**. And when it should be a higher-order value, it is simply represented by a *fresh* opponent name pointer. the rules **O-QuestG** and **O-Quest** represent opponent questions. In that case, Opponent adds to the current execution stack a new thread, corresponding to the higher-order values stored in γ. Opponent can also provide new name pointers via the disclosed part of the heap. Those ones live in the disclosed part of h'_{fn}, *i.e.* in $\mathrm{codom}(h'_{\mathrm{fn}|\mathcal{D}'})$. An important point here is that the context can also disclose *indirectly* new locations via the already disclosed ones. This explain the great liberty Opponent has when it extends h to h' with new disclosed locations. It must however satisfy the equation $D' = \mathrm{discl}(v, h', D)$, so that it cannot add as many new (necessarily disclosed) locations as it wants.

This reduction is highly non-deterministic, since we consider the interactions with all possible contexts. Moreover, the choice of name pointers and locations is also non-deterministic (even in the rule **P-Intern** with the use of $\mapsto_{nd}$).

We say that a trace T is *generated* by a configuration C if it can be written as a sequence $(a_1, h_1) \cdots (a_n, h_n)$ of actions-with-heap *s.t.* $C \xrightarrow{(a_1,h_1)} C_1 \xrightarrow{(a_2,h_2)} \ldots \xrightarrow{(a_n,h_n)} C_n$, and we write $C \xrightarrow{T} C_n$. We can see that it is indeed a trace due to the freshness conditions in the rules P-Ans, P-Quest, O-Ans and O-Quest. The set of traces generated by C is written $\mathbf{Tr}(C)$. Notice that such traces are not in general justified, since name-pointers of C are not introduced. As we will see, the initial (opponent question) action is missing. Moreover, $\mathbf{Tr}(C)$ is not nominally-closed: if π is a permutation *s.t.* $\pi(a) \neq a$ for $a \in \nu_{\mathbb{A}}(C)$, then taking $T \in \mathbf{Tr}(C)$, $\pi * T$ is not in general in $\mathbf{Tr}(C)$. This is useful to distinguish sets $\mathbf{Tr}\langle x, \gamma, \mathcal{I}, h, D\rangle$ and $\mathbf{Tr}\langle x', \gamma, \mathcal{I}, h, D\rangle$ for different opponent name pointers $x, x' \in \mathcal{I}$, or to distinguish $\mathbf{Tr}\langle l, \gamma, \mathcal{I}, h, D\rangle$ and $\mathbf{Tr}\langle l', \gamma, \mathcal{I}, h, D\rangle$ for locations $l, l' \in \mathrm{dom}(h)$.

Example. Let us consider the term M_{inc} defined as

$$\mathtt{let\ x} = \mathrm{ref}\,0\ \mathtt{in\ let\ f} = \mathrm{ref}\,(\lambda\_.\mathtt{x} := !\mathtt{x} + 1)\ \mathtt{in}\ \lambda \mathtt{g}.\mathtt{g\ f}; !\mathtt{f}(); !\mathtt{x}$$

The reader can check that one possible trace of this term starting from the initial configuration $\langle M_{inc}, \varepsilon, \varepsilon, \varepsilon, \varepsilon\rangle$ is

$$(\langle\bar{a}\rangle, \varepsilon) \cdot (a\,\langle b\rangle, \varepsilon) \cdot (\bar{b}\,\langle l\rangle, [l \hookrightarrow c]) \cdot (c\,\langle()\rangle, [l \hookrightarrow c]) \cdot (\langle\bar{()}\rangle, [l \hookrightarrow c]) \cdot$$
$$(\langle()\rangle, [l \hookrightarrow d]) \cdot (\bar{c}\,\langle()\rangle, [l \hookrightarrow d]) \cdot (\langle()\rangle, [l \hookrightarrow d]) \cdot (\langle\bar{1}\rangle, [l \hookrightarrow d]).$$

Intuitively, this trace corresponds to the interaction with the context defined as $\bullet(\lambda \mathtt{c}.!\mathtt{c}(); \mathtt{c} := \lambda\_.())$. Notice that the value stored in x is incremented not by the call to $!\mathtt{f}()$ in M_{inc}, but by the call made by the context after the disclosure of f via g.

Indeed, the call to !f() corresponds to the call to $\lambda\_.()$ since the context has modified the function stored in f.

An important point to notice is that the tags of actions of traces generated by the interactive reduction can be inferred knowing just the tags of initial actions:

Lemma 1. *Let (a_1, ξ_1, h_1) an action justified by (a_2, ξ_2, h_2) in a trace T. Then:*
- *If a_2 is an answers, then $\xi_1 = \mathfrak{l} \cdot \xi$ and $\xi_2 = r \cdot \xi$,*
- *If a_2 is a question, then if a_2 is l-justified by a_1, $\xi_2 = \mathfrak{l} \cdot s \cdot \xi_1$, otherwise $\xi_2 = \mathfrak{l} \cdot \xi_1$.*

So in the following, we often omit tags when considering actions and traces.

3.4 Copycat Behavior

When a term provides to the context an opponent name pointer x (*i.e.* a functional variable), the environment γ is extended with $[y \mapsto x]$, with y a fresh player name pointer. Then, when the context interrogates y, this gives rise to a *copycat* behavior. Following [13], a pair of consecutive actions $(a_1, h_1), (a_2, h_2)$ of a trace T is a *copycat pair* when:
- $\theta((a_1, h_1)) = \theta((a_2, h_2))$,
- if (a_1, h_1) is justified by (a'_1, h'_1) then (a_2, h_2) is justified by (a'_2, h'_2) *s.t.* (a'_2, h'_2), (a'_1, h'_1) are consecutive in T, and moreover if (a_1, h_1) is l-justified with $l \in \mathrm{dom}(h'_1)$, then (a_2, h_2) is l-justified so $l \in \mathrm{dom}(h'_2)$.

Notice that a copycat pair $((\langle u_1 \rangle, h_1) \cdot (\langle \bar{u_2} \rangle, h_2))$ will not satisfy $u_1 = u_2$ nor $h_1 = h_2$ when the u_i are name pointers and when the h_i store name pointers, due to the freshness condition of name pointers in the rules of the interactive reduction. This justifies the use of θ in the definition. Such copycat pairs occur frequently in the heap, when the term does not modify a higher-order value stored in a disclosed location. Indeed, only name pointers are stored in disclosed functional part of heaps. And even if what is stored in a location is not modified, the interaction rule refreshes this name pointer. We use the following definition to control this refreshing.

Definition 3. *Let T a legal trace and $T' \sqsubseteq T$, with T' ending with $(a_1, h_1) \cdot (a_2, h_2)$ and $l \in \mathrm{dom}(h_1) \cap \mathrm{dom}(h_2) \cap \mathrm{Loc}_\phi$ a location of functional type, we say that (T, T', l) is a* copycat triple *if for all ϕ-actions (a'_1, h'_1) of T which are hereditarily l-justified by (a_1, h_1) or (a_2, h_2), there exists an action (a'_2, h'_2)* s.t.*:*
- *if a'_1 has the same player as a_1, then $(a'_1, h'_1) \cdot (a'_2, h'_2)$ is a copycat pair of T,*
- *if a'_1 has the same player as a_2, then $(a'_2, h'_2) \cdot (a'_1, h'_1)$ is a copycat pair of T.*

3.5 Interpretation of Terms

Given a term M *s.t.* $\Sigma; \Gamma_g, \Gamma_f \vdash M : \tau$, we define an associated trace strategy. It is generated using the interactive reduction. To do so, we first define the list of opponent name pointers $\mathcal{I}_\xi^{\Gamma_f}$ as $\mathcal{I}_\xi^{\varepsilon} = \varepsilon$ and $\mathcal{I}_\xi^{(x:\tau),\Gamma} \stackrel{def}{=} (x, \tau, \mathfrak{l} \cdot \xi) \cdot \mathcal{I}_{r \cdot \xi}^{\Gamma}$.

Definition 4 (Trace Semantics). *Let M a term* s.t. *$\Sigma; \Gamma_g, \Gamma_f \vdash M : \tau$. We define $[\Sigma; \Gamma_g, \Gamma_f \vdash M : \tau]$ as the set of even-length traces belonging to the nominal closure over* Loc *and* $\mathbb{P}$ *of*

$$\left\{ \left(? \left\langle \Sigma, \overrightarrow{\gamma_g(x_i)}, \mathcal{I} \right\rangle, \iota, h\right) \cdot \mathbf{Tr}\langle(\gamma_g(M), \tau, \varepsilon), \varepsilon, \mathcal{I}, h, D\rangle \;\middle|\; \begin{array}{l} \gamma_g : \Gamma_g \\ h \in \mathbf{Cl}(\Sigma, \mathrm{codom}(\gamma_g)) \\ \mathrm{codom}(h_{\mathrm{fn}}) \subseteq \mathbb{P} \end{array} \right\}$$

where $\overrightarrow{x_i}$ *ranges overs the variables of* Γ_g*,* $D = \mathrm{dom}(h)$ *and* $\mathcal{I} = \mathcal{I}_\xi^{\Gamma_f} \cdot \overrightarrow{(h(l_i), \tau_i, s)}$ s.t. l_i *ranges over* $\mathrm{dom}(h_{\mathrm{fn}})$ *and* $l_i \in \mathrm{Loc}_{\tau_i}$.

Recall that h_{fn} is the subheap of h formed by higher-order references. We reason up to nominal equivalence of $\nu_{\mathrm{Loc}}(M)$ (*i.e.* Σ) and $\nu_{\mathbb{P}}(M)$ (*i.e.* Γ_f) so that $[\Sigma; \Gamma_g, \Gamma_f \vdash M : \tau]$ is nominally closed. Moreover, the substitution γ_g of ground variables of M introduces new locations for variables of type ref τ, so we must consider them in h to have a closed heap. Finally, h is functional-free (*i.e.* $\mathrm{codom}(h_{\mathrm{fn}}) \subseteq \mathbb{P}$), so that for any location $l \in \mathrm{Loc}_\phi$, if $h(l)$ or $h'(l)$ is defined, it has to store an opponent name pointer.

Let us define $[\Gamma]$ as $[\tau_1] \otimes \ldots \otimes [\tau_m]$ when $\Gamma = (x_1 : \tau_1) \ldots (x_m : \tau_m)$ and $[\Sigma]$ is defined as $[\mathrm{ref}\,\tau_1] \otimes \ldots \otimes [\mathrm{ref}\,\tau_n]$ when $\Sigma = (l_1, \ldots, l_n : \tau_n)$ with $l_i \in \mathrm{Loc}_{\tau_i}$.

Theorem 1. *Let* M *a term* s.t. $\Sigma; \Gamma_g, \Gamma_f \vdash M : \tau$, *then* $[\Sigma; \Gamma_g, \Gamma_f \vdash M : \tau]$ *is a trace-strategy over the arena* $[\Sigma] \otimes [\Gamma_g, \Gamma_f] \to [\tau]$.

A trace $T \in \mathbf{Tr}\langle M \cdot \overrightarrow{K_i}, \gamma, \mathcal{I}, h, D\rangle$ is said to be *complete* if the number of answers occurring in the trace is greater than its number of questions plus the length of the sequence $\overrightarrow{K_i}$. The set of complete traces of a configuration C is written $\mathbf{comp}(\mathbf{Tr}(C))$.

4 A Correspondence between Trace and Game Denotations

We now prove a formal link between the denotation of a term in trace semantics and in game semantics. The problem is that the definition of $[\Sigma; \Gamma \vdash M : \tau]$ is done operationally, while $[\![\Sigma; \Gamma \vdash M : \tau]\!]$—the game interpretation of terms defined in [13]—is given denotationally, by induction on the typing judgment $\Sigma; \Gamma \vdash M : \tau$. To fill this gap, we show in this section that $[\Sigma; \Gamma \vdash M : \tau]$ can actually be decomposed by similar induction steps on the typing judgment. Using the definition of Θ, which transforms a trace strategy on a $\mathfrak{A}$ into a game strategy of the corresponding game arena A, introduced in Section 3.1, we can state a correspondence between the two semantics.

Theorem 2 (Equivalence of the trace and the game semantics). *Let* M *a term of RefML* s.t. $\Sigma; \Gamma \vdash M : \tau$, *then* $[\![\Sigma; \Gamma \vdash M : \tau]\!]$ *is equal to* $\Theta([\Sigma; \Gamma \vdash M : \tau])$.

Using this correspondence with game semantics, we can import the full abstraction result of [13] to trace semantics. Notice that Laird has already proven this result directly [9], where he needed a complex proof of definability of trace strategy to achieve it. The proof of Theorem 2 goes in four steps:

- we build a category $\mathcal{T}$ whose objects are arenas and morphisms are trace strategies,
- we equip $\mathcal{T}$ with a structure of closed-Freyd category, that is a symmetric premonoidal structure $(\mathcal{T}, I, \otimes)$, a lluf subcategory $\mathcal{T}_{sst}$ of $\mathcal{T}$ for which $\otimes$ is cartesian, and a premonoidal functor $(.)^\dagger$ between $\mathcal{T}_{sst}$ and $\mathcal{T}$, which is identity on objects, *s.t.* for every object $\mathfrak{A}$ of $\mathcal{T}$, the functor $(\_ \otimes \mathfrak{A})^\dagger : \mathcal{T}_{sst} \to \mathcal{T}$ has a right adjoint,
- we show that Θ is a functor from $\mathcal{T}$ to the game category $\mathcal{G}$ which conserve the closed-Freyd structure,

– we prove that the canonical interpretation of terms derived from the closed-Freyd structure is equal to the interpretation of terms, built using the interactive reduction, of Definition 4.

In the following, we sketch the main points of these four steps. Let us first define a composition between trace strategy, as parallel composition plus hidden like in game semantics. following the definition from game semantics, we introduce *interaction traces* over a term-arena $\mathfrak{A} \to \mathfrak{B} \to \mathfrak{C}$ formed from three trace value-arenas $\mathfrak{A}, \mathfrak{B}, \mathfrak{C}$. Given a trace T on $\mathfrak{A} \to \mathfrak{B} \to \mathfrak{C}$, we reason on the restricted traces $T_{|(\mathfrak{A},\mathfrak{B})}$, $T_{|(\mathfrak{B},\mathfrak{C})}$ and $T_{|(\mathfrak{A},\mathfrak{C})}$ which are not in general frugal. So we introduce a function **Frug** which removes part of the heap which has not been disclosed in traces, imposing frugality.

Definition 5. *A justified trace T on $\mathfrak{A} \to \mathfrak{B} \to \mathfrak{C}$ is an* interaction trace *if*

- *it is frugal,*
- *$T_{|(\mathfrak{A},\mathfrak{B})}, T_{|(\mathfrak{B},\mathfrak{C})}$ and $T_{|(\mathfrak{A},\mathfrak{C})}$ are legal,*
- *$\mathbf{P}(\mathbf{Frug}(T_{|(\mathfrak{A},\mathfrak{B})})), \mathbf{P}(\mathbf{Frug}(T_{|(\mathfrak{B},\mathfrak{C})})), \mathbf{O}(\mathbf{Frug}(T_{|(\mathfrak{A},\mathfrak{C})}))$ are two by two disjoint, where $\mathbf{P}(T)$ (resp. $\mathbf{O}(T)$) is the set of locations introduced by Player (resp. Opponent),*
- *for each $T' \sqsubseteq T$ ending in $(a, h) \cdot (a', h')$ and $l \in \mathrm{dom}(h')$,*
  - *if a is a player action in X and $l \notin \mathbf{Av}(T_{|X})$ with $X \in \{(\mathfrak{A},\mathfrak{B}), (\mathfrak{B},\mathfrak{C})\}$,*
  - *or a is an opponent action in $(\mathfrak{A},\mathfrak{C})$ and $l \notin \mathbf{Av}(T_{|(\mathfrak{A},\mathfrak{C})})$,*

  then $\theta(h(l)) = \theta(h'(l))$ and, moreover, if $l \in \mathrm{Loc}_\phi$ then $(T_{|X}, T'_{|X}, l)$ are a copycat triple, where X is the respective element of $\{(\mathfrak{A},\mathfrak{B}), (\mathfrak{B},\mathfrak{C}), (\mathfrak{A},\mathfrak{C})\}$.

We now define the parallel composition of two trace strategies $\mathfrak{s}, \mathfrak{t}$, written $\mathfrak{s}||\mathfrak{t}$ as the set of interaction traces $T \in \mathfrak{A} \to \mathfrak{B} \to \mathfrak{C}$ *s.t.* $T_{|\mathbf{F}(\mathfrak{A},\mathfrak{B})} \in \mathfrak{s}$ and $T_{|\mathbf{F}(\mathfrak{B},\mathfrak{C})} \in \mathfrak{t}$.

Definition 6. *Given $\mathfrak{s}, \mathfrak{t}$ two trace-strategies defined respectively on $\mathfrak{A} \to \mathfrak{B}$ and $\mathfrak{B} \to \mathfrak{C}$, we define their* composition, *written $\mathfrak{s}; \mathfrak{t}$, as the trace-strategy on $\mathfrak{A} \to \mathfrak{C}$ formed by plays T on $\mathfrak{A} \to \mathfrak{C}$* s.t. *there exists $T' \in \mathfrak{s}||\mathfrak{t}$ with $T = T'_{|\mathbf{F}(\mathfrak{A},\mathfrak{C})}$.*

This composition can be shown to be associative, so that we can define a category $\mathcal{T}$ whose objects are arenas and whose morphisms are trace strategies. It is straightforward to see that Θ is a functor between $\mathcal{T}$ and the game category $\mathcal{G}$ from [13]. Moreover, this composition corresponds to the one coming from the interactive reduction.

Theorem 3. $[\Gamma \vdash N : \sigma] ; [x : \sigma \vdash M : \tau] = [\Gamma \vdash \texttt{let } x = N \texttt{ in } M : \tau]$.

Next, we build a lluf category $\mathcal{T}_{sst}$ of $\mathcal{T}$, in order to get a closed-Freyd category. Morphisms of $\mathcal{T}_{sst}$ are formed by *strongly single threaded* strategies. To define them, we first introduce the notion of *total* strategies, for which traces begin with an opponent question $(? \langle u_1 \rangle, h_1)$ followed by a player answer $(\langle \bar{u_2} \rangle, h_2)$, without modifying the heap (this last point is controlled using copycat triples from Section 3.4).

For such total strategies, we define the notion of *threads*, which are subtraces which are generated by the opponent questions of the player answer $(\langle \bar{u_1} \rangle, h_1)$. Total strategies which are formed by such frugal threads can be characterized, they are called *strongly single-threaded* strategies Then, we define a function $\mathfrak{L}^{\mathfrak{B}}_{\mathfrak{A},\mathfrak{C}}$ which maps trace-strategies of $(\mathfrak{A} \otimes \mathfrak{B}) \to \mathfrak{C}$ into strongly single-threaded trace-strategy of $\mathfrak{A} \to (\mathfrak{B} \Rightarrow \mathfrak{C})$. From this, we can define the notion of *thread-independent* trace plays. They correspond to plays where there is no interaction between their threads. Thus, following [13], we can define a "shuffle" operation $(\cdot)^\dagger$ which transforms a strongly single-threaded strategy $\mathfrak{s}$ on $\mathfrak{A}$ into a thread-independent strategy $\mathfrak{s}^\dagger$. This shuffle operation satisfies that for any thread-independent trace strategy $\mathfrak{s}$, $(\gamma(\mathbf{thr}(\mathfrak{s})))^\dagger = \mathfrak{s}$. Then, we can easily check that $[\Sigma; \Gamma \vdash \lambda x.M : \sigma \to \tau]$ is thread-independent. Using it, we can decompose the denotation of λ-abstraction exactly as it is done in game semantics:

Theorem 4. $[\Sigma; \Gamma \vdash \lambda x.M : \sigma \to \tau] = (\mathfrak{L}^{[\sigma]}_{[\Sigma;\Gamma],[\tau]}([\Sigma; \Gamma, x : \sigma \vdash M : \tau]))^\dagger$.

5 Trace Semantics for GroundML

In this section, we refine our trace semantics to handle GroundML, importing the characterizations of terms of this language, in terms of visible strategies [14], into trace semantics.

Definition 7 (View and Visibility). *The* view $\ulcorner T \urcorner$ *of a legal trace* T *on* $\mathfrak{A}$ *is a subsequence of* T *defined by induction:*

- $\ulcorner \varepsilon \urcorner = \varepsilon$ *and* $\ulcorner (\mathrm{i}_\mathfrak{A}, h) \urcorner = (\mathrm{i}_\mathfrak{A}, h)$,
- $\ulcorner T' \cdot (a,h) \cdot T'' \cdot (a',h') \urcorner = \ulcorner T' \urcorner \cdot (a,h) \cdot (a',h')$ *when* (a',h') *is justified by* (a,h).

A trace T *is* P-visible *(resp.* O-visible*) iff for all* $T' \cdot (a,h) \sqsubseteq^{\text{even}} T$ *(resp.* $T' \cdot (a,h) \sqsubseteq^{\text{odd}} T$ *with* (a,h) *a* player *(resp.* opponent*) action, the justifier of* (a,h) *is in* $\ulcorner T' \urcorner$. *A trace strategy is said to be* X-visible *if all its traces are X-visible, for* $X \in \{P, O\}$.

In our setting, justification is defined using freshness of name pointers, so we introduce the notion of *available X-name pointers*, for $X \in \{P, O\}$, to reason on the view.

Definition 8 (Available Name-Pointers). *We define the set of* available opponent *or* player name pointers $\mathbf{Av_X}(T)$ *(*$X \in \{O, P\}$*) inductively as*

- $\mathbf{Av_X}(\varepsilon) \stackrel{def}{=} \varnothing$ *and* $\mathbf{Av_X}((\mathrm{i}, h)) \stackrel{def}{=} \nu^X_{\mathbb{P}}(\mathrm{i})$,
- $\mathbf{Av_X}(T \cdot (a_1,h_1) \cdot T' \cdot (a_2,h_2)) \stackrel{def}{=} \mathbf{Av_X}(T) \cup \nu^X_{\mathbb{P}}(a_2)$ *when* (a_1,h_1) *is justified by* (a_2,h_2).

Notice in the previous definition that we do not need to consider name pointers in heaps, since we consider terms of GroundML, which do not store any functions in heaps, and for which contexts cannot disclose higher-order references. Moreover, in the last clause above, we do not need to consider the name pointers of a_1 since its polarity is opposed as the one of a_2. Next, we link available name pointers to the notion of view:

Lemma 2. *Let* T *a justified trace, then for all name pointers* $x \in \mathbf{Av_X}(T)$ *(*$X \in \{P, O\}$*),* x *is introduced by an action* (a,h) *which appears in* $\ulcorner T \urcorner$.

5.1 Ground-refererences Terms of RefML and P-visible Strategies

The characterization of trace-strategies coming from terms of GroundML is given by the following theorem.

Theorem 5. *Let* M *a term of GroundML* s.t. $\Sigma; \Gamma \vdash M : \tau$. *Then* $[\Sigma; \Gamma \vdash M : \tau]$ *is a P-visible trace strategy.*

Intern $\langle (M,\tau,\xi,\mathcal{A})\cdot\overrightarrow{K_i},\gamma,\mathcal{I},h,D\rangle \xrightarrow{\qquad} \langle (M',\tau,\xi,\mathcal{A})\cdot\overrightarrow{K_i},\gamma,\mathcal{I},h',D\rangle$
(when $(M,h)\mapsto_{nd}(M',h')$)

P-AnsG $\langle (v,\iota,\xi,\mathcal{A})\cdot\overrightarrow{K_i},\gamma,\mathcal{I},h,D\rangle \xrightarrow{(\langle\bar{v}\rangle,r\cdot\xi,h'_{|D})} \langle\overrightarrow{K_i},\gamma',\mathcal{I},h,D',\mathcal{A}\rangle$
(v of type ι, $D'=\mathrm{discl}(v,h,D)$)

P-Ans $\langle (v,\tau,\xi,\mathcal{A})\cdot\overrightarrow{K_i},\gamma,\mathcal{I},h,D\rangle \xrightarrow{(\langle\bar{x}\rangle,r\cdot\xi,h_{|D})} \langle\overrightarrow{K_i},\gamma',\mathcal{I},h,D,x\cdot\mathcal{A}\rangle$
(x fresh, $\gamma'=\gamma\cdot[x\hookrightarrow(v,\tau,r\cdot\xi)]$)

P-QuestG $\langle (K[x\,v],\tau,\xi,\mathcal{A})\cdot\overrightarrow{K_i},\gamma,\mathcal{I},h,D\rangle \xrightarrow{(\bar{x}\langle v\rangle,\ell\cdot\xi',h_{|D'})} \langle (K[\bullet_{\iota,\xi'}],\tau,\xi,\mathcal{A})\cdot\overrightarrow{K_i},\gamma,\mathcal{I},h,D',\mathcal{A}'\rangle$
($(x,\iota\to\sigma,\xi',\mathcal{A}')\in\mathcal{I}$, v of type ι, $D'=\mathrm{discl}(v,h,D)$)

P-Quest $\langle (K[x\,v],\tau,\xi,\mathcal{A})\cdot\overrightarrow{K_i},\gamma,\mathcal{I},h,D\rangle \xrightarrow{(\bar{x}\langle y\rangle,\ell\cdot\xi',h_{|D})} \langle (K[\bullet_{\sigma',\xi'}],\tau,\xi,\mathcal{A})\cdot\overrightarrow{K_i},\gamma',\mathcal{I},h,D,y\cdot\mathcal{A}'\rangle$
($(x,\sigma\to\sigma',\xi',\mathcal{A}')\in\mathcal{I}$, y fresh, $\gamma'=\gamma\cdot[y\hookrightarrow(v,\sigma,\ell\cdot\xi')]$)

O-AnsG $\langle (K[\bullet_{\iota,\xi'}],\tau,\xi,\mathcal{A})\cdot\overrightarrow{K_i},\gamma,\mathcal{I},h,D,\mathcal{A}'\rangle \xrightarrow{(\langle v\rangle,r\cdot\xi',h'_{|D'})} \langle (K[v],\tau,\xi,\mathcal{A})\cdot\overrightarrow{K_i},\gamma,\mathcal{I},h',D'\rangle$
(v of type ι, $v\notin\mathrm{dom}(h)\cap\overline{D}$)

O-Ans $\langle (K[\bullet_{\sigma,\xi'}],\tau,\xi,\mathcal{A})\cdot\overrightarrow{K_i},\gamma,\mathcal{I},h,D,\mathcal{A}'\rangle \xrightarrow{(\langle x\rangle,r\cdot\xi',h'_{|D'})} \langle (K[x],\tau,\xi,\mathcal{A})\cdot\overrightarrow{K_i},\gamma,\mathcal{I}',h',D'\rangle$
(x fresh, $\mathcal{I}'=\mathcal{I}\cdot(x,\sigma,r\cdot\xi',\mathcal{A}')$)

O-QuestG $\langle\overrightarrow{K_i},\gamma,\mathcal{I},h,D,\mathcal{A}\rangle \xrightarrow{(x\langle v\rangle,\ell\cdot\xi,h'_{|D'})} \langle (u\,v,\tau,\xi,\mathcal{A})\cdot\overrightarrow{K_i},\gamma,\mathcal{I}',h',D'\rangle$
($x\in\mathcal{A}$, $\gamma(x)=(u,\iota\to\tau,\xi)$, v of type ι and not in $\mathrm{dom}(h)\cap\overline{D}$)

O-Quest $\langle\overrightarrow{K_i},\gamma,\mathcal{I},h,D,\mathcal{A}\rangle \xrightarrow{(x\langle y\rangle,\ell\cdot\xi,h'_{|D'})} \langle (u\,y,\tau,\xi)\cdot\overrightarrow{K_i},\gamma,\mathcal{I}',h',D'\rangle$
($x\in\mathcal{A}$, $\gamma(x)=(u,\sigma\to\tau,\xi)$, y fresh, $\mathcal{I}'=\mathcal{I}\cdot(y,\tau,\ell\cdot\xi,\mathcal{A})$)
in all O-Rules: $D'=\mathrm{discl}(v,h',D)$, $h'_{|\overline{D'}}=h_{|\overline{D}}$ and $h'_{|D'}$ is closed)

Fig. 5. Definition of the interaction semantics for GroundML

To conduct the proof, we need to analyze the structure of traces more closely. We first notice a crucial property of the interactive reduction of such terms, that when reducing (M,h) to (M',h'), we know that the name pointers contained in M' are also in M. Using this property, we prove that a term M' appearing in the interactive reduction of M via a trace T only contains name pointers from $\mathbf{Av}_{\mathrm{O}}(T)$.

Lemma 3. *Let M a term of GroundML* s.t. $\Sigma;\Gamma\vdash M:\tau$, *and* $((a_0,h_0)\cdot T\cdot(a,h))\in[\Sigma;\Gamma\vdash M:\tau]$ s.t. $\langle M,\gamma,\mathcal{I},h_0,D\rangle\xrightarrow{T}\langle M'\cdot\overrightarrow{K_i},\gamma',\mathcal{I}',h',D'\rangle$ *Then* $\nu^{O}_{\mathbb{P}}(M')\subseteq\mathbf{Av}_{\mathrm{O}}((a_0,h_0)\cdot T)$.

From this lemma we get directly the following corollary:

Corollary 1. *Let M a term of GroundML* s.t. $\Sigma;\Gamma\vdash M:\tau$, *and* $T\cdot(\bar{x}\langle u\rangle,h)\in[\Sigma;\Gamma\vdash M:\tau]$. *Then* $x\in\mathbf{Av}_{\mathrm{O}}(T)$.

We can finally prove Theorem 5 using the conjunction of Lemma 2 and Corollary 1.

5.2 Full Abstraction for GroundML

We have seen in Section 5.1 that terms of GroundML give rise to P-visible traces. However, the trace semantics of Section 3.3 is not fully abstract, since there are still traces which are not generated by an interaction between contexts and terms of GroundML. To get full abstraction, we need to constrain traces to be O-visible by modifying the interactive reduction to control the scope of name pointers *s.t.* only pointers appearing in the view of an action are available. We present the modified interactive reduction in Figure 5. First notice that, since we do not have higher-order references in our language, we do not need to extend $\mathcal{I}$ and γ with pointers representing functions stored in the disclosed part of the heap. Then, we keep track of available player name pointers, represented by a set $\mathcal{A}$, in different places of the configuration:

- in opponent configurations $\langle \overrightarrow{K_i}, \gamma, \mathcal{I}, h, D, \mathcal{A} \rangle$, representing the current available player name pointers;
- within each element $(M, \tau, \xi, \mathcal{A})$ or $(K[\bullet_{\tau,\xi}], \sigma, \xi', \mathcal{A})$ of the execution stack, representing the player name pointers available when Opponent add this element to the execution stack via a question;
- within each opponent name pointers $x \in \mathcal{I}$, representing the player name pointers available when x has been introduced by an opponent action.

Using this set of available player name pointers, we can control the questions Opponent can interrogate, as shown by the condition $x \in \mathcal{A}$ in the rules **O-QuestG** and **O-Quest**. This idea is formalized in the following lemma:

Lemma 4. *For* $(\mathrm{i}, h_0) \cdot T \in [\Sigma; \Gamma_f \vdash M : \tau]$ s.t. $\langle (M, \tau, \xi, \varnothing), \gamma, \mathcal{I}, h, \mathcal{D} \rangle \xrightarrow{T} \langle \overrightarrow{K_i}, \gamma', , \mathcal{I}', h', \mathcal{D}' \rangle \mathcal{A}$ *we have* $\mathbf{Av_P}(T) = \mathcal{A}$.

Using our restricted interactive reduction, we define the ground interpretation of a judgment $[\Sigma; \Gamma \vdash M : \tau]_G$ in the same way than in Definition 4, with the empty set of pointers associated to M in the execution stack. From Lemma 4, we can deduce that the ground interpretation always gives rise to visible strategies.

Theorem 6. *Let M a term of GroundML* s.t. $\Sigma; \Gamma \vdash M : \tau$. *Then* $[\Sigma; \Gamma \vdash M : \tau]_G$ *is a visible strategy* (i.e. *both P-visible and O-visible).*

It is straightforward to see that the notion of visibility introduced here corresponds exactly to the usual notion of visibility of game semantics. So we can import the full abstraction result of [14] into our trace semantics of GroundML.

6 Discussion and Future Work

We would like to extend our trace semantics to a polymorphic language, where the mechanism to represent the arenas an action belongs to in terms of tags would become crucial, as in [11]. It would also be interesting to extend the characterization of fragments of RefML in trace semantics by dealing with the restriction to integer references, namely RedML, as in [15]. We believe that our interactive reduction defined for GroundML can be restricted to give a fully abstract model of RedML, using similar restrictions on the use of name pointers in locations.

As we have said, the well-bracketing condition is hard-wired in the definition of justified traces. To remove it, we would need to specify which question an answer is answering. One possibility to do that would be to use the work of Gabbay and Ghica [4], which uses nominal sets to represent strategies. In fact, our work is halfway to them: the way they name questions, and the freshness condition they impose, seems similar to our use of name-pointers and the nominal reasoning we perform on them. It should thus be possible to use their work to also give fresh name to answers actions. This would allow us to study languages where we need semantically to remove the well-bracketing condition, namely languages with control operators like `call/cc` or exceptions.

Finally, a correspondence between trace and game models has been previously built by Laird [8] in a different setting, the asynchronous π-calculus (so without references). Levy and Staton [12] have also recently build an abstract categorical setting to study such correspondences. It would be interesting if our work could be spelt out in their framework, and therefore give a high-level categorical meaning to our construction.

References

1. Abramsky, S., Ghica, D., Murawski, A., Ong, L., Stark, I.: Nominal games and full abstraction for the nu-calculus. In: Proceedings of LICS 2004, pp. 150–159. IEEE (2004)
2. Abramsky, S., Honda, K., McCusker, G.: A fully abstract game semantics for general references. In: Proceedings of LICS 1998, pp. 334–344. IEEE (1998)
3. Abramsky, S., Jagadeesan, R., Malacaria, P.: Full abstraction for PCF. Information and Computation 163(2), 409–470 (2000)
4. Gabbay, M., Ghica, D.: Game semantics in the nominal model. In: Proceedings of the 28th Conference on the Mathematical Foundations of Programming Semantics (MFPS 2012). Electronic Notes in Theoretical Computer Science, vol. 286, pp. 173–189. Elsevier (2012)
5. Gabbay, M., Pitts, A.: A new approach to abstract syntax with variable binding. Formal Aspects of computing 13(3-5), 341–363 (2002)
6. Hyland, M., Ong, L.: On full abstraction for PCF: I, II and III. Information and Computation 163(2), 285–408 (2000)
7. Jaber, G.: A Logical Study of Program Equivalence. PhD thesis, École des Mines de Nantes (2014)
8. Laird, J.: A game semantics of the asynchronous p-calculus. In: Abadi, M., de Alfaro, L. (eds.) CONCUR 2005. LNCS, vol. 3653, pp. 51–65. Springer, Heidelberg (2005)
9. Laird, J.: A fully abstract trace semantics for general references. In: Arge, L., Cachin, C., Jurdziński, T., Tarlecki, A. (eds.) ICALP 2007. LNCS, vol. 4596, pp. 667–679. Springer, Heidelberg (2007)
10. Laird, J.: A game semantics of names and pointers. Annals of Pure and Applied Logic 151(2), 151–169 (2008)
11. Laird, J.: Game semantics for call-by-value polymorphism. In: Abramsky, S., Gavoille, C., Kirchner, C., Meyer auf der Heide, F., Spirakis, P.G. (eds.) ICALP 2010. LNCS, vol. 6199, pp. 187–198. Springer, Heidelberg (2010)
12. Levy, P., Staton, S.: Transition systems over games. In: Proceedings of LICS 2014, pp. 64:1–64:10 (2014)
13. Murawski, A., Tzevelekos, N.: Game semantics for good general references. In: Proceedings of LICS 2011, pp. 75–84. IEEE (2011)
14. Murawski, A., Tzevelekos, N.: Algorithmic games for full ground references. In: Czumaj, A., Mehlhorn, K., Pitts, A., Wattenhofer, R. (eds.) ICALP 2012, Part II. LNCS, vol. 7392, pp. 312–324. Springer, Heidelberg (2012)
15. Murawski, A., Tzevelekos, N.: Full abstraction for reduced ml. Annals of Pure and Applied Logic (2013)
16. Power, J., Thielecke, H.: Closed freyd- and κ-categories. In: Wiedermann, J., Van Emde Boas, P., Nielsen, M. (eds.) ICALP 1999. LNCS, vol. 1644, pp. 625–634. Springer, Heidelberg (1999)

Step-Indexed Logical Relations for Probability

Aleš Bizjak and Lars Birkedal

Aarhus University
{abizjak,birkedal}@cs.au.dk

Abstract. It is well-known that constructing models of higher-order probabilistic programming languages is challenging. We show how to construct step-indexed logical relations for a probabilistic extension of a higher-order programming language with impredicative polymorphism and recursive types. We show that the resulting logical relation is sound and complete with respect to the contextual preorder and, moreover, that it is convenient for reasoning about concrete program equivalences. Finally, we extend the language with dynamically allocated first-order references and show how to extend the logical relation to this language. We show that the resulting relation remains useful for reasoning about examples involving both state and probabilistic choice.

1 Introduction

It is well known that it is challenging to develop techniques for reasoning about programs written in probabilistic higher-order programming languages. A probabilistic program evaluates to a distribution of values, as opposed to a set of values in the case of nondeterminism or a single value in the case of deterministic computation. Probability distributions form a monad. This observation has been used as a basis for several denotational domain-theoretic models of probabilistic languages and also as a guide for designing probabilistic languages with monadic types [15,21,20]. Game semantics has also been used to give models of probabilistic programming languages [9,12] and a fully abstract model using coherence spaces for PCF with probabilistic choice was recently presented [13].

The majority of models of probabilistic programming languages have been developed using denotational semantics. However, Johann et.al. [14] developed operationally-based logical relations for a polymorphic programming language with effects. Two of the effects they considered were probabilistic choice and *global* ground store. However, as pointed out by the authors [14], extending their construction to local store and, in particular, higher-order local store, is likely to be problematic. Recently, operationally-based bisimulation techniques have been extended to probabilistic extensions of PCF [7,8]. The operational semantics of probabilistic higher-order programming languages has been investigated in [16].

Step-indexed logical relations [2,3] have proved to be a successful method for proving contextual approximation and equivalence for programming languages with a wide range of features, including computational effects.

In this paper we show how to extend the method of step-indexed logical relations to reason about contextual approximation and equivalence of probabilistic

A. Pitts (Ed.): FOSSACS 2015, LNCS 9034, pp. 279–294, 2015.
DOI: 10.1007/978-3-662-46678-0_18

higher-order programs. To define the logical relation we employ biorthogonality [17,19] and step-indexing. Biorthogonality is used to ensure completeness of the logical relation with respect to contextual equivalence, but it also makes it possible to keep the value relations simple, see Fig. 1. Moreover, the definition using biorthogonality makes it possible to "externalize" the reasoning in many cases when proving example equivalences. By this we mean that the reasoning reduces to algebraic manipulations of probabilities. This way, the quantitative aspects do not complicate the reasoning much, compared to the usual reasoning with step-indexed logical relations. To define the biorthogonal lifting we use two notions of observation; the termination probability and its stratified version approximating it. We define these and prove the required properties in Section 3.

We develop our step-indexed logical relations for the call-by-value language $\mathbf{F}^{\mu,\oplus}$. This is system **F** with recursive types, extended with a single probabilistic choice primitive `rand`. The primitive `rand` takes a natural number n and reduces with uniform probability to one of $1, 2, \ldots, n$. Thus `rand` n represents the uniform probability distribution on the set $\{1, 2, \ldots, n\}$. We choose to add `rand` instead of just a single coin flip primitive to make the examples easier to write.

To show that the model is useful we use it to prove some example equivalences in Section 5. We show two examples based on parametricity. In the first example, we characterize elements of the universal type $\forall\alpha.\alpha \to \alpha$. In a deterministic language, and even in a language with nondeterministic choice, the only interesting element of this type is the identity function. However, since in a probabilistic language we not only observe the end result, but also the likelihood with which it is returned, it turns out that there are many more elements. Concretely, we show that the elements of the type $\forall\alpha.\alpha \to \alpha$ that are of the form $\Lambda\alpha.\lambda x.e$, correspond precisely to *left-computable* real numbers in the interval $[0, 1]$. In the second example we show a free theorem involving functions on lists. We show additional equivalences in the Appendix, including the correctness of von Neumann's procedure for generating a fair sequence of coin tosses from an unfair coin, and equivalences from the recent papers using bisimulations [7,8].

We add dynamically allocated references to the language and extend the logical relation to the new language in Section 6. For simplicity we only sketch how to extend the construction with first-order state. This already suggests that an extension with general references can be done in the usual way for step-indexed logical relations. We conclude the section by proving a representation independence result involving both state and probabilistic choice.

All the references to the Appendix in this paper refer to appendix in the online long version [6].

2 The Language $\mathbf{F}^{\mu,\oplus}$

The language is a standard pure functional language with recursive, universal and existential types with an additional choice primitive `rand`. The base types include the type of natural numbers `nat` with some primitive operations.

The grammar of terms e is

$$e ::= x \mid \langle\rangle \mid \texttt{rand}\,e \mid \underline{n} \mid \texttt{if}_1\ e\ \texttt{then}\ e_1\ \texttt{else}\ e_2 \mid \texttt{P}\,e \mid \texttt{S}\,e \mid \langle e_1, e_2\rangle \mid \texttt{proj}_i\,e$$
$$\mid \lambda x.e \mid e_1\,e_2 \mid \texttt{inl}\ e \mid \texttt{inr}\ e \mid \texttt{match}(e, x_1.e_1, x_2.e_2) \mid \Lambda.e \mid e[]$$
$$\mid \texttt{pack}\,e \mid \texttt{unpack}\ e_1\ \texttt{as}\ x\ \texttt{in}\ e_2 \mid \texttt{fold}\,e \mid \texttt{unfold}\,e$$

We write $\underline{n}$ for the numeral representing the natural number n and S and P are the successor and predecessor functions, respectively. For convenience, numerals start at $\underline{1}$. Given a numeral $\underline{n}$, the term $\texttt{rand}\,\underline{n}$ evaluates to one of the numerals $\underline{1}, \dots, \underline{n}$ with uniform probability. There are no types in the syntax of terms, e.g., instead of $\Lambda\alpha.e$ and $e\,\tau$ we have $\Lambda.e$ and $e[]$. This is for convenience only.

We write $\alpha, \beta, \dots$ for *type variables* and $x, y, \dots$ for *term variables.* The notation $\tau[\vec{\tau}/\vec{\alpha}]$ denotes the simultaneous capture-avoiding substitution of types $\vec{\tau}$ for the free type variables $\vec{\alpha}$ in the type τ; $e[\vec{v}/\vec{x}]$ denotes simultaneous capture-avoiding substitution of values $\vec{v}$ for the free term variables $\vec{x}$ in the term e.

We write **Stk** for the set of evaluation contexts given by the call-by-value reduction strategy. Given two evaluation contexts E, E' we define their composition $E \circ E'$ by induction on E in the natural way. Given an evaluation context E and expression e we write $E[e]$ for the term obtained by plugging e into E. For any two evaluation contexts E and E' and a term e we have $E[E'[e]] = (E \circ E')[e]$.

For a type variable context Δ, the judgment $\Delta \vdash \tau$ expresses that the free type variables in τ are included in Δ. The typing judgments are entirely standard with the addition of the typing of `rand` which is given by the rule

$$\frac{\Delta \mid \Gamma \vdash e : \texttt{nat}}{\Delta \mid \Gamma \vdash \texttt{rand}\ e : \texttt{nat}}.$$

The complete set of typing rules are in the Appendix. We write $\mathfrak{T}(\Delta)$ for the set of types well-formed in context Δ, and $\mathfrak{T}$ for the set of *closed* types τ. We write $\mathbf{Val}(\tau)$ and $\mathbf{Tm}(\tau)$ for the sets of *closed* values and terms of type τ, respectively. We write **Val** and **Tm** for the set of *all*[1] *closed* values and closed terms, respectively. $\mathbf{Stk}(\tau)$ denotes the set of τ-accepting evaluation contexts, i.e., evaluation contexts E, such that given any closed term e of type τ, $E[e]$ is a typeable term. **Stk** denotes the set of all evaluation contexts.

For a typing context $\Gamma = x_1{:}\tau_1, \dots, x_n{:}\tau_n$ with $\tau_1, \dots, \tau_n \in \mathfrak{T}$, let $\mathbf{Subst}(\Gamma)$ denote the set of type-respecting value substitutions, i.e. for all i, $\gamma(x_i) \in \mathbf{Val}(\tau_i)$. In particular, if $\Delta \mid \Gamma \vdash e : \tau$ then $\varnothing \mid \varnothing \vdash e\gamma : \tau\delta$ for any $\delta \in \mathfrak{T}^{\Delta}$ and $\gamma \in \mathbf{Subst}(\Gamma\delta)$, and the type system satisfies standard properties of progress and preservation and a canonical forms lemma.

The operational semantics of the language is a standard call-by-value semantics but weighted with $p \in [0, 1]$ which denotes the likelihood of that reduction. We write $\overset{p}{\leadsto}$ for the one-step reduction relation. All the usual β reductions have weight equal to 1 and the reduction from $\texttt{rand}\,\underline{n}$ is

$$\texttt{rand}\,\underline{n} \overset{\frac{1}{n}}{\leadsto} \underline{k} \qquad \text{for } k \in \{1, 2, \dots, n\}.$$

[1] In particular, we do not require them to be typeable.

The rest of the rules are given in Fig. 5 in the Appendix. The operational semantics thus gives rise to a Markov chain with closed terms as states. In particular for each term e we have $\sum_{e' \mid e \overset{p}{\rightsquigarrow} e'} p \leq 1$.

3 Observations and Biorthogonality

We will use biorthogonality to define the logical relation. This section provides the necessary observation predicates used in the definition of the biorthogonal lifting of value relations to expression relations. Because of the use of biorthogonality the value relations (see Fig. 1) remain as simple as for a language without probabilistic choice. The new quantitative aspects only appear in the definition of the biorthogonal lifting (⊤⊤-closure) defined in Section 4. Two kinds of observations are used. The probability of termination, $\mathfrak{P}^{\Downarrow}(e)$, which is the actual probability that e terminates, and its approximation, the *stratified* termination probability $\mathfrak{P}_k^{\Downarrow}(e)$, where $k \in \mathbb{N}$ denotes, intuitively, the number of computation steps. The stratified termination probability provides the link between steps in the operational semantics and the indexing in the definition of the interpretation of types.

The probability of termination, $\mathfrak{P}^{\Downarrow}(\cdot)$, is a function of type $\mathbf{Tm} \to \mathcal{I}$ where $\mathcal{I}$ is the unit interval $[0,1]$. Since $\mathcal{I}$ is a pointed ω-cpo for the usual order, so is the space of all functions $\mathbf{Tm} \to \mathcal{I}$ with pointwise ordering. We define $\mathfrak{P}^{\Downarrow}(\cdot)$ as a fixed point of the continuous function Φ on this ω-cpo: Let $\mathcal{F} = \mathbf{Tm} \to \mathcal{I}$ and define $\Phi : \mathcal{F} \to \mathcal{F}$ as

$$\Phi(f)(e) = \begin{cases} 1 & \text{if } e \in \mathbf{Val} \\ \sum\limits_{e \overset{p}{\rightsquigarrow} e'} p \cdot f(e') & \text{otherwise} \end{cases}$$

Note that if e is stuck then $\Phi(f)(e) = 0$ since the empty sum is 0.

The function Φ is monotone and preserves suprema of ω-chains. The proof is straightforward and can be found in the Appendix. Thus Φ has a least fixed point in $\mathcal{F}$ and we denote this fixed point by $\mathfrak{P}^{\Downarrow}(\cdot)$, i.e., $\mathfrak{P}^{\Downarrow}(e) = \sup_{n\in\omega} \Phi^n(\bot)(e)$.

To define the stratified observations we need the notion of a path. Given terms e and e' a path π from e to e', written $\pi : e \rightsquigarrow^* e'$, is a sequence $e \overset{p_1}{\rightsquigarrow} e_1 \overset{p_2}{\rightsquigarrow} e_2 \overset{p_3}{\rightsquigarrow} \cdots \overset{p_n}{\rightsquigarrow} e'$. The *weight* $\mathfrak{W}(\pi)$ of a path π is the product of the weights of reductions in π. We write $\mathfrak{R}$ for the set of all paths and $\cdot$ for their concatenation (when defined). For a non-empty path $\pi \in \mathfrak{R}$ we write $\ell(\pi)$ for its last expression.

We call reductions of the form $\texttt{unfold}(\texttt{fold}\, v) \overset{1}{\rightsquigarrow} v$ *unfold-fold* reductions and reductions of the form $\texttt{rand}\, \underline{n} \overset{\frac{1}{n}}{\rightsquigarrow} \underline{k}$ *choice* reductions. If *none* of the reductions in a path π is a choice reduction we call π *choice-free* and similarly if none of the reductions in π is an unfold-fold reductions we call π *unfold-fold free.*

We define the following types of multi-step reductions which we use in the definition of the logical relation.

– $e \overset{\text{cf}}{\Longrightarrow} e'$ if there is a *choice-free* path from e to e'

- $e \overset{\text{uff}}{\Longrightarrow} e'$ if there is an *unfold-fold* free path from e to e'.
- $e \overset{\text{cuff}}{\Longrightarrow} e'$ if $e \overset{\text{cf}}{\Longrightarrow} e'$ and $e \overset{\text{uff}}{\Longrightarrow} e'$.

The following useful lemma states that all but choice reductions preserve the probability of termination. As a consequence, we will see that all but choice reductions preserve equivalence.

Lemma 3.1. *Let $e, e' \in \mathbf{Tm}$ and $e \overset{cf}{\Longrightarrow} e'$. Then $\mathfrak{P}^{\Downarrow}(e) = \mathfrak{P}^{\Downarrow}(e')$.*

The proof proceeds on the length of the reduction path with the strengthened induction hypothesis stating that the probabilities of termination of all elements on the path are the same. To define the stratified probability of termination that approximates $\mathfrak{P}^{\Downarrow}(\cdot)$ we need an auxiliary notion.

Definition 3.2. *For a closed expression $e \in \mathbf{Tm}$ we define $\mathbf{Red}(e)$ as the (unique) set of paths containing* exactly one *unfold-fold or choice reduction and* ending *with such a reduction. More precisely, we define the function $\mathbf{Red}: \mathbf{Tm} \to \mathcal{P}(\mathfrak{R})$ as the least function satisfying*

$$\mathbf{Red}(e) = \begin{cases} \{e \overset{1}{\rightsquigarrow} e'\} & \textit{if } e = E[\mathtt{unfold}\,(\mathtt{fold}\, v)] \\ \{e \overset{p}{\rightsquigarrow} E[\underline{k}] \mid p = \frac{1}{n}, k \in \{1,2,\ldots,n\}\} & \textit{if } e = E[\mathtt{rand}\,\underline{n}] \\ \left\{(e \overset{1}{\rightsquigarrow} e') \cdot \pi \mid \pi \in \mathbf{Red}(e')\right\} & \textit{if } e \overset{1}{\rightsquigarrow} e' \textit{ and } e \overset{cuff}{\Longrightarrow} e' \\ \emptyset & \textit{otherwise} \end{cases}$$

where we order the power set $\mathcal{P}(\mathfrak{R})$ by subset inclusion.

Using $\mathbf{Red}(\cdot)$ we define a monotone map $\Psi : \mathcal{F} \to \mathcal{F}$ that preserves ω-chains.

$$\Psi(f)(e) = \begin{cases} 1 & \text{if } \exists v \in \mathbf{Val}, e \overset{\text{cuff}}{\Longrightarrow} v \\ \sum_{\pi \in \mathbf{Red}(e)} \mathfrak{W}(\pi) \cdot f(\ell(\pi)) & \text{otherwise} \end{cases}$$

and then define $\mathfrak{P}_k^{\Downarrow}(e) = \Psi^k(\bot)(e)$. The intended meaning of $\mathfrak{P}_k^{\Downarrow}(e)$ is the probability that e terminates within k unfold-fold and choice reductions. Since Ψ is monotone we have that $\mathfrak{P}_k^{\Downarrow}(e) \leq \mathfrak{P}_{k+1}^{\Downarrow}(e)$ for any k and e.

The following lemma is the reason for counting only certain reductions, cf. [10]. It allows us to stay at the same step-index even when taking steps in the operational semantics. As a consequence we will get a more extensional logical relation. The proof is by case analysis and can be found in the Appendix.

Lemma 3.3. *Let $e, e' \in \mathbf{Tm}$. If $e \overset{cuff}{\Longrightarrow} e'$ then for all k, $\mathfrak{P}_k^{\Downarrow}(e) = \mathfrak{P}_k^{\Downarrow}(e')$.*

The following is immediate from the definition of the chain $\left\{\mathfrak{P}_k^{\Downarrow}(e)\right\}_{k=0}^{\infty}$ and the fact that $\mathtt{rand}\,\underline{n}$ reduces with uniform probability.

Lemma 3.4. *Let e be a closed term. If $e \overset{1}{\rightsquigarrow} e'$ and the reduction is an unfold-fold reduction then $\mathfrak{P}_{k+1}^{\Downarrow}(e) = \mathfrak{P}_k^{\Downarrow}(e')$. If the reduction from e is a choice reduction, then $\mathfrak{P}_{k+1}^{\Downarrow}(e) = \frac{1}{|\mathbf{Red}(e)|} \sum_{\pi \in \mathbf{Red}(e)} \mathfrak{P}_k^{\Downarrow}(\ell(\pi))$.*

The following proposition is needed to prove adequacy of the logical relation with respect to contextual equivalence. It is analogous to the property used to prove adequacy of step-indexed logical relations for deterministic and nondeterministic languages. Consider the case of may-equivalence. To prove adequacy in this case (cf. [4, Theorem 4.8]) we use the fact that if e may-terminates, then there is a natural number n such that e terminates in n steps. This property does not hold in the probabilistic case, but the property analogous to it that is sufficient to prove adequacy still holds.

Proposition 3.5. *For each* $e \in \mathbf{Tm}$ *we have* $\mathfrak{P}^{\Downarrow}(e) \leq \sup_{k\in\omega}\left(\mathfrak{P}^{\Downarrow}_{k}(e)\right)$.

Proof. We only give a sketch; the full proof can be found in the Appendix. We use Scott induction on the set $\mathcal{S} = \left\{f \in \mathcal{F} \mid \forall e, f(e) \leq \sup_{k\in\omega}\left(\mathfrak{P}^{\Downarrow}_{k}(e)\right)\right\}$. It is easy to see that $\mathcal{S}$ is closed under limits of ω-chains and that $\bot \in \mathcal{S}$ so we only need to show that $\mathcal{S}$ is closed under Φ. We can do this by considering the kinds of reductions from e when considering $\Phi(f)(e)$ for $f \in \mathcal{S}$.

4 Logical, CIU and Contextual Approximation Relations

The contextual and CIU (closed instantiations of uses [18]) approximations are defined in a way analogous to the one for deterministic programming languages. We require some auxiliary notions. A *type-indexed relation* $\mathcal{R}$ is a set of tuples $(\Delta, \Gamma, e, e', \tau)$ such that $\Delta \vdash \Gamma$ and $\Delta \vdash \tau$ and $\Delta \mid \Gamma \vdash e : \tau$ and $\Delta \mid \Gamma \vdash e' : \tau$. We write $\Delta \mid \Gamma \vdash e \mathrel{\mathcal{R}} e' : \tau$ for $(\Delta, \Gamma, e, e', \tau) \in \mathcal{R}$.

Definition 4.1 (Precongruence). *A type-indexed relation* $\mathcal{R}$ *is* reflexive *if* $\Delta \mid \Gamma \vdash e : \tau$ *implies* $\Delta \mid \Gamma \vdash e \mathrel{\mathcal{R}} e : \tau$. *It is* transitive *if* $\Delta \mid \Gamma \vdash e \mathrel{\mathcal{R}} e' : \tau$ *and* $\Delta \mid \Gamma \vdash e' \mathrel{\mathcal{R}} e'' : \tau$ *implies* $\Delta \mid \Gamma \vdash e \mathrel{\mathcal{R}} e'' : \tau$. *It is* compatible *if it is closed under the term forming rules, e.g.,*[2]

$$\frac{\Delta \mid \Gamma, x{:}\tau_1 \vdash e \mathrel{\mathcal{R}} e' : \tau_2}{\Delta \mid \Gamma \vdash \lambda x.e \mathrel{\mathcal{R}} \lambda x.e' : \tau_1 \to \tau_2} \qquad \frac{\Delta \mid \Gamma \vdash e \mathrel{\mathcal{R}} e' : \mathtt{nat}}{\Delta \mid \Gamma \vdash \mathtt{rand}\, e \mathrel{\mathcal{R}} \mathtt{rand}\, e' : \mathtt{nat}}$$

A precongruence *is a reflexive, transitive and compatible type-indexed relation.*

The compatibility rules guarantee that a compatible relation is sufficiently big, i.e., at least reflexive. In contrast, the notion of adequacy, which relates the operational semantics with the relation, guarantees that it is not too big. In the deterministic case, a relation $\mathcal{R}$ is adequate if when $e \mathrel{\mathcal{R}} e'$ are two related closed terms, then if e terminates so does e'. Here we need to compare probabilities of termination instead, since these are our observations.

Definition 4.2. *A type-indexed relation* $\mathcal{R}$ *is* adequate *if for all* e, e' *such that* $\varnothing \mid \varnothing \vdash e \mathrel{\mathcal{R}} e' : \tau$ *we have* $\mathfrak{P}^{\Downarrow}(e) \leq \mathfrak{P}^{\Downarrow}(e')$.

[2] We only show a few rules, the rest are analogous and can be found in the Appendix.

The *contextual approximation relation*, written $\Delta \mid \Gamma \vdash e \lesssim^{ctx} e' : \tau$, is defined as the *largest adequate precongruence* and the *CIU approximation relation*, written $\Delta \mid \Gamma \vdash e \lesssim^{CIU} e' : \tau$, is defined using evaluation contexts in the usual way, e.g. [18], using $\mathfrak{P}^{\Downarrow}(\cdot)$ for observations. The fact that the largest adequate precongruence exists is proved as in [18].

Logical Relation. We now define the step-indexed logical relation. We present the construction in the elementary way with explicit indexing instead of using a logic with guarded recursion as in [10] to remain self-contained.

Interpretations of types will be defined as decreasing sequences of relations on *typeable* values. For *closed types* τ and σ we define the sets $\mathbf{VRel}(\tau, \sigma)$, $\mathbf{SRel}(\tau, \sigma)$ and $\mathbf{TRel}(\tau, \sigma)$ to be the sets of decreasing sequences of relations on typeable values, evaluation contexts and expressions respectively. The types τ and σ denote the types of the left-hand side and the right-hand side respectively, i.e. if $(v, u) \in \varphi(n)$ for $\varphi \in \mathbf{VRel}(\tau, \sigma)$ then v has type τ and u has type σ. The order relation $\leq$ on these sets is defined pointwise, e.g. for $\varphi, \psi \in \mathbf{VRel}(\tau, \sigma)$ we write $\varphi \leq \psi$ if $\forall n \in \mathbb{N}, \varphi(n) \subseteq \psi(n)$. We implicitly use the inclusion from $\mathbf{VRel}(\tau, \sigma)$ to $\mathbf{TRel}(\tau, \sigma)$. The reason for having relations on values and terms of different types on the left and right-hand sides is so we are able to prove parametricity properties in Section 5.

We define maps $\cdot^{\top}_{\tau,\sigma} : \mathbf{VRel}(\tau, \sigma) \to \mathbf{SRel}(\tau, \sigma)$ and $\cdot^{\perp}_{\tau,\sigma} : \mathbf{SRel}(\tau, \sigma) \to \mathbf{TRel}(\tau, \sigma)$. We usually omit the type indices when they can be inferred from the context. The maps are defined as follows

$$r^{\top}_{\tau,\sigma}(n) = \left\{(E, E') \mid \forall k \leq n, \forall (v, v') \in r(k), \mathfrak{P}^{\Downarrow}_{k}(E[v]) \leq \mathfrak{P}^{\Downarrow}(E'[v'])\right\}$$

and $r^{\perp}_{\tau,\sigma}(n) = \left\{(e, e') \mid \forall k \leq n, \forall (E, E') \in r(k), \mathfrak{P}^{\Downarrow}_{k}(E[e]) \leq \mathfrak{P}^{\Downarrow}(E'[e'])\right\}$. Note that we only count steps evaluating the left term in defining $r^{\top}$ and $r^{\perp}$. We write $r^{\top\top} = r^{\top\perp}$ for their composition from $\mathbf{VRel}(\tau, \sigma)$ to $\mathbf{TRel}(\tau, \sigma)$. The function $\cdot^{\top}$ is order-reversing and $\cdot^{\top\top}$ is order-preserving and inflationary.

Lemma 4.3. *Let τ, σ be closed types and $r, s \in \mathbf{VRel}(\tau, \sigma)$. Then $r \leq r^{\top\top}$ and if $r \leq s$ then $s^{\top} \leq r^{\top}$ and $r^{\top\top} \leq s^{\top\top}$.*

For a type-variable context Δ we define $\mathbf{VRel}(\Delta)$ using $\mathbf{VRel}(\cdot, \cdot)$ as

$$\mathbf{VRel}(\Delta) = \left\{(\varphi_1, \varphi_2, \varphi_r) \mid \varphi_1, \varphi_2 \in \mathfrak{T}^{\Delta}, \forall \alpha \in \Delta, \varphi_r(\alpha) \in \mathbf{VRel}(\varphi_1(\alpha), \varphi_2(\alpha))\right\}$$

where the first two components give syntactic types for the left and right hand sides of the relation and the third component is a relation between those types.

The interpretation of types, $[\![\cdot \vdash \cdot]\!]$ is by induction on the judgement $\Delta \vdash \tau$. For a judgment $\Delta \vdash \tau$ and $\varphi \in \mathbf{VRel}(\Delta)$ we have $[\![\Delta \vdash \tau]\!](\varphi) \in \mathbf{VRel}(\varphi_1(\tau), \varphi_2(\tau))$ where the φ_1 and φ_2 are the first two components of φ and $\varphi_1(\tau)$ denotes substitution. Moreover $[\![\cdot]\!]$ is *non-expansive* in the sense that $[\![\Delta \vdash \tau]\!](\varphi)(n)$ can depend only on the values of $\varphi_r(\alpha)(k)$ for $k \leq n$, see [5] for this metric view of step-indexing. The interpretation of types is defined in Fig. 1. Observe that the value relations are as simple as for a language without probabilistic choice. The crucial difference is hidden in the $\top\top$-closure of value relations.

$$\begin{aligned}
\llbracket \Delta \vdash \mathtt{nat} \rrbracket (\varphi)(n) &= \{(\underline{k}, \underline{k}) \mid k \in \mathbb{N}, k > 0\} \\
\llbracket \Delta \vdash \tau \to \sigma \rrbracket (\varphi)(n) &= \{(\lambda x.e, \lambda y.e') \mid \forall j \leq n, \forall (v, v') \in \llbracket \Delta \vdash \tau \rrbracket (\varphi)(j), \\
&\qquad ((\lambda x.e)\, v, (\lambda y.e')\, v') \in \llbracket \Delta \vdash \sigma \rrbracket (\varphi)^{\top\top}(j)\} \\
\llbracket \Delta \vdash \forall \alpha.\tau \rrbracket (\varphi)(n) &= \{(\Lambda.e, \Lambda.e') \mid \forall \sigma, \sigma' \in \mathfrak{T}, \forall r \in \mathbf{VRel}(\sigma, \sigma'), \\
&\qquad (e, e') \in \llbracket \Delta, \alpha \vdash \tau \rrbracket (\varphi[\alpha \mapsto r])^{\top\top}(n)\} \\
\llbracket \Delta \vdash \exists \alpha.\tau \rrbracket (\varphi)(n) &= \{(\mathtt{pack}\, v, \mathtt{pack}\, v') \mid \exists \sigma, \sigma' \in \mathfrak{T}, \exists r \in \mathbf{VRel}(\sigma, \sigma'), \\
&\qquad (v, v') \in \llbracket \Delta, \alpha \vdash \tau \rrbracket (\varphi[\alpha \mapsto r])(n)\} \\
\llbracket \Delta \vdash \mu\alpha.\tau \rrbracket (\varphi)(0) &= \mathbf{Val}(\varphi_1(\mu\alpha.\tau)) \times \mathbf{Val}(\varphi_2(\mu\alpha.\tau)) \\
\llbracket \Delta \vdash \mu\alpha.\tau \rrbracket (\varphi)(n+1) &= \{(\mathtt{fold}\, v, \mathtt{fold}\, v') \mid \\
&\qquad (v, v') \in \llbracket \Delta, \alpha \vdash \tau \rrbracket (\varphi[\alpha \mapsto \llbracket \Delta \vdash \mu\alpha.\tau \rrbracket (\varphi)])(n)\}
\end{aligned}$$

Fig. 1. Interpretation of types. The cases for sum and product types are in Appendix.

Context extension lemmas. To prove soundness and completeness we need lemmas stating how extending evaluation contexts preserves relatedness. We only show the case for `rand`. The rest are similarly simple.

Lemma 4.4. *Let $n \in \mathbb{N}$. If $(E, E') \in \llbracket \Delta \vdash \mathtt{nat} \rrbracket (\varphi)^{\top}(n)$ are related evaluation contexts then $(E \circ (\mathtt{rand}\,[]), E' \circ (\mathtt{rand}\,[])) \in \llbracket \Delta \vdash \mathtt{nat} \rrbracket (\varphi)^{\top}(n)$.*

Proof. Let $n \in \mathbb{N}$ and $(v, v') \in \llbracket \Delta \vdash \tau \rrbracket (\varphi)(n)$. By construction we have $v = v' = \underline{m}$ for some $m \in \mathbb{N}$, $m \geq 1$. Let $k \leq n$. If $k = 0$ the result is immediate, so assume $k = \ell + 1$. Using Lemma 3.4 we have $\mathfrak{P}^{\Downarrow}_{k}(E[\mathtt{rand}\,\underline{m}]) = \frac{1}{m}\sum_{i=1}^{m} \mathfrak{P}^{\Downarrow}_{\ell}(E[\underline{i}])$ and using the assumption $(E, E') \in \llbracket \Delta \vdash \mathtt{nat} \rrbracket (\varphi)^{\top}(n)$, the fact that $k \leq n$ and monotonicity in the step-index the latter term is less than $\frac{1}{m}\sum_{i=1}^{m} \mathfrak{P}^{\Downarrow}(E'[\underline{i}])$ which by definition of $\mathfrak{P}^{\Downarrow}(\cdot)$ is equal to $\mathfrak{P}^{\Downarrow}(E'[\mathtt{rand}\,\underline{m}])$.

We define the logical approximation relation for open terms given the interpretations of types in Fig. 1. We define $\Delta \mid \Gamma \vdash e \lesssim^{log} e' : \tau$ to mean

$$\forall n \in \mathbb{N}, \forall \varphi \in \mathbf{VRel}(\Delta), \forall (\gamma, \gamma') \in \llbracket \Delta \vdash \Gamma \rrbracket (\varphi)(n), (e\gamma, e'\gamma) \in \llbracket \Delta \vdash \tau \rrbracket \varphi^{\top\top}(n)$$

Here $\llbracket \Delta \vdash \Gamma \rrbracket$ is the obvious extension of interpretation of types to interpretation of contexts which relates substitutions, mapping variables to values. We have

Proposition 4.5 (Fundamental Property). *The logical approximation relation $\lesssim^{log}$ is compatible. In particular it is reflexive.*

Proof. The proof is a simple consequence of the context extension lemmas. We show the case for `rand`. We have to show that $\Delta \mid \Gamma \vdash e \lesssim^{log} e' : \mathtt{nat}$ implies $\Delta \mid \Gamma \vdash \mathtt{rand}\, e \lesssim^{log} \mathtt{rand}\, e' : \mathtt{nat}$. Let $n \in \mathbb{N}$, $\varphi \in \mathbf{VRel}(\Delta)$ and $(\gamma, \gamma') \in \llbracket \Delta \vdash \Gamma \rrbracket (\varphi)(n)$. Let $f = e\gamma$ and $f' = e'\gamma'$. Then our assumption gives us $(f, f') \in \llbracket \Delta \vdash \mathtt{nat} \rrbracket (\varphi)^{\top\top}(n)$ and we are to show $(\mathtt{rand}\, f, \mathtt{rand}\, f') \in \llbracket \Delta \vdash \mathtt{nat} \rrbracket (\varphi)^{\top\top}(n)$. Let $j \leq n$ and $(E, E') \in \llbracket \Delta \vdash \mathtt{nat} \rrbracket (\varphi)^{\top}(j)$. Then from Lemma 4.4 we have $(E \circ (\mathtt{rand}\,[]), E' \circ (\mathtt{rand}\,[])) \in \llbracket \Delta \vdash \mathtt{nat} \rrbracket (\varphi)^{\top}(j)$ which suffices by the definition of the orthogonality relation and the assumption $(f, f') \in \llbracket \Delta \vdash \mathtt{nat} \rrbracket (\varphi)^{\top\top}(n)$.

We now want to relate logical, CIU and contextual approximation relations.

Corollary 4.6. *Logical approximation relation $\lesssim^{log}$ is adequate.*

Proof. Assume $\varnothing \mid \varnothing \vdash e \lesssim^{log} e' : \tau$. We are to show that $\mathfrak{P}^{\Downarrow}(e) \leq \mathfrak{P}^{\Downarrow}(e')$. Straight from the definition we have $\forall n \in \mathbb{N}, (e, e') \in [\![\varnothing \vdash \tau]\!]^{\top\top}(n)$. The empty evaluation context is always related to itself (at any type). This implies $\forall n \in \mathbb{N}, \mathfrak{P}^{\Downarrow}_n(e) \leq \mathfrak{P}^{\Downarrow}(e')$ which further implies (since the right-hand side is independent of n) that $\sup_{n\in\omega}(\mathfrak{P}^{\Downarrow}_n(e)) \leq \mathfrak{P}^{\Downarrow}(e')$. Using Proposition 3.5 we thus have $\mathfrak{P}^{\Downarrow}(e) \leq \sup_{n\in\omega}(\mathfrak{P}^{\Downarrow}_n(e)) \leq \mathfrak{P}^{\Downarrow}(e')$ concluding the proof.

We now have that the logical relation is adequate and compatible. This does not immediately imply that it is contained in the contextual approximation relation, since we do not know that it is transitive. However we have the following lemma where by transitive closure we mean that for each Δ, Γ and τ we take the transitive closure of the relation $\{(e, e') \mid \Delta \mid \Gamma \vdash e \lesssim^{log} e' : \tau\}$. This is another type-indexed relation.

Lemma 4.7. *The transitive closure of $\lesssim^{log}$ is compatible and adequate.*

Proof. Transitive closure of an adequate relation is adequate. Similarly the transitive closure of a compatible and *reflexive* relation (in the sense of Definition 4.1) is again compatible (and reflexive).

Theorem 4.8 (CIU Theorem). *The relations $\lesssim^{log}$, $\lesssim^{CIU}$ and $\lesssim^{ctx}$ coincide.*

Proof. It is standard (e.g. [18]) that $\lesssim^{ctx}$ is included in $\lesssim^{CIU}$. We show that the logical approximation relation is contained in the CIU approximation relation in the standard way for biorthogonal step-indexed logical relations. To see that $\lesssim^{log}$ is included in $\lesssim^{ctx}$ we have by Lemma 4.7 that the transitive closure of $\lesssim^{log}$ is an adequate precongruence, thus included in $\lesssim^{ctx}$. And $\lesssim^{log}$ is included in the transitive closure of $\lesssim^{log}$. Corollary A.13 in the appendix completes the cycle of inclusions.

Using the logical relation and Theorem 4.8 we can prove some extensionality properties. The proofs are standard and can be found in the Appendix.

Lemma 4.9 (Functional Extensionality for Values). *Suppose $\tau, \sigma \in \mathfrak{T}(\Delta)$ and let f and f' be two* values *of type $\tau \to \sigma$ in context $\Delta \mid \Gamma$. If for all $u \in \mathbf{Val}(\tau)$ we have $\Delta \mid \Gamma \vdash f\,u \lesssim^{ctx} f'\,u : \sigma$ then $\Delta \mid \Gamma \vdash f \lesssim^{ctx} f' : \tau \to \sigma$.*

The extensionality for *expressions*, as opposed to only *values*, of function type does not hold in general due to the presence of choice reductions. See Remark 5.2 for an example. We also have extensionality for *values* of universal types.

Lemma 4.10 (Extensionality for the Universal Type). *Let $\tau \in \mathfrak{T}(\Delta, \alpha)$ be a type. Let f, f' be two* values *of type $\forall\alpha.\tau$ in context $\Delta \mid \Gamma$. If for all closed types σ we have $\Delta \mid \Gamma \vdash f[] \lesssim^{ctx} f'[] : \tau[\sigma/\alpha]$ then $\Delta \mid \Gamma \vdash f \lesssim^{ctx} f' : \forall\alpha.\tau$.*

5 Examples

We now use our logical relation to prove some example equivalences. We show two examples involving polymorphism. In the Appendix we show additional examples. In particular we show the correctness of von Neumann's procedure for generating a fair sequence of coin tosses from an unfair coin. That example in particular shows how the use of biorthogonality allows us to "externalize" the reasoning to arithmetic manipulations.

We first define $\texttt{fix} : \forall \alpha, \beta.((\alpha \to \beta) \to (\alpha \to \beta)) \to (\alpha \to \beta)$ be the term $\Lambda.\Lambda.\lambda f.\lambda z.\delta_f(\texttt{fold}\,\delta_f)\,z$ where δ_f is the term $\lambda y.\texttt{let}\,y' = \texttt{unfold}\,y\,\texttt{in}\,f\,(\lambda x.y'\,y\,x)$. This is a call-by-value fixed-point combinator. We also write $e_1 \oplus e_2$ for the term $\texttt{if}_1\,\texttt{rand}\,\underline{2}\,\texttt{then}\,e_1\,\texttt{else}\,e_2$. Note that the choice is made before evaluating e_i's.

We characterize inhabitants of a polymorphic type and show a free theorem. For the former, we need to know which real numbers can be probabilities of termination of programs. Recall that a real number r is *left-computable* if there exists a *computable* increasing (not necessarily strictly) sequence $\{q_n\}_{n\in\omega}$ of *rational numbers* such that $r = \sup_{n\in\omega} q_n$. In Appendix B we prove

Proposition 5.1. *For any expression e, $\mathfrak{P}^{\Downarrow}(e)$ is a left-computable real number and for any left-computable real number r in the interval $[0,1]$ there is a closed term e_r of type $\mathbf{1} \to \mathbf{1}$ such that $\mathfrak{P}^{\Downarrow}(e_r\,\langle\rangle) = r$.*

Inhabitants of the Type $\forall\alpha.\alpha \to \alpha$. In this section we use further syntactic sugar for sequencing. When $e, e' \in \mathbf{Tm}$ are closed terms we write $e; e'$ for $(\lambda\_.e')\,e$, i.e. first run e, ignore the result and then run e'. We will need the property that for all terms $e, e' \in \mathbf{Tm}$, $\mathfrak{P}^{\Downarrow}(e; e') = \mathfrak{P}^{\Downarrow}(e) \cdot \mathfrak{P}^{\Downarrow}(e')$. The proof is by Scott induction and can be found in the Appendix.

Using Proposition 5.1 we have for each left-computable real r in the interval $[0,1]$ an inhabitant t_r of the type $\forall\alpha.\alpha \to \alpha$ given by $\Lambda.\lambda x.e_r\,\langle\rangle; x$.

We now show that these are the only inhabitants of $\forall\alpha.\alpha \to \alpha$ of the form $\Lambda.\lambda x.e$. Given such an inhabitant let $r = \mathfrak{P}^{\Downarrow}(e[\langle\rangle/x])$. We know from Proposition 5.1 that r is left-computable.

Given a value v of type τ and $n \in \mathbb{N}$ we define relations $R(n) = \{(\langle\rangle, v)\}$ and $S(n) = \{(v, \langle\rangle)\}$. Note that the relations are independent of n, i.e. R and S are constant relations. By reflexivity of the logical relation and the relational actions of types we have

$$\forall n, (e[\langle\rangle/x], e[v/x]) \in R^{\top\top}(n) \qquad \text{and} \qquad \forall n, (e[v/x], e[\langle\rangle/x]) \in S^{\top\top}(n) \tag{1}$$

from which we conclude that $\mathfrak{P}^{\Downarrow}(e[\langle\rangle/x]) = \mathfrak{P}^{\Downarrow}(e[v/x])$. We now show that v and $e[v/x]$ are CIU-equivalent. Let $E \in \mathbf{Stk}(\tau)$ be an evaluation context. Let $q = \mathfrak{P}^{\Downarrow}(E[v])$. Define the evaluation context $E' = -; e_q\,\langle\rangle$. Then $(E, E') \in S^{\top}(n)$ for all n which then means, using (1) and Proposition 3.5, that $\mathfrak{P}^{\Downarrow}(E[e[v/x]]) \leq \mathfrak{P}^{\Downarrow}(E'[e[\langle\rangle/x]])$. We then have

$$\mathfrak{P}^{\Downarrow}(E'[e[\langle\rangle/x]]) = \mathfrak{P}^{\Downarrow}(e[\langle\rangle/x]) \cdot \mathfrak{P}^{\Downarrow}(e_q\,\langle\rangle) = r \cdot \mathfrak{P}^{\Downarrow}(E[v])$$

and so $\mathfrak{P}^{\Downarrow}(E[e[v/x]]) \leq r \cdot \mathfrak{P}^{\Downarrow}(E[v])$.

Similarly we have $(E', E) \in R^{\top}(n)$ for all n which implies $\mathfrak{P}^{\Downarrow}(E[e[v/x]]) \geq \mathfrak{P}^{\Downarrow}(E'[e[\langle\rangle/x]])$. We also have $\mathfrak{P}^{\Downarrow}(E'[e[\langle\rangle/x]]) = r \cdot \mathfrak{P}^{\Downarrow}(E[v])$.

So we have proved $\mathfrak{P}^{\Downarrow}(E[e[v/x]]) = r \cdot \mathfrak{P}^{\Downarrow}(E[v]) = \mathfrak{P}^{\Downarrow}(e[v/x]) \cdot \mathfrak{P}^{\Downarrow}(E[v])$. It is easy to show by Scott induction, that $\mathfrak{P}^{\Downarrow}(E[t_r[]\, v]) = \mathfrak{P}^{\Downarrow}(e_r\,\langle\rangle) \cdot \mathfrak{P}^{\Downarrow}(E[v])$. We have thus shown that for any value v, the terms $e[v/x]$ and $\mathfrak{P}^{\Downarrow}(t_r[]\, v)$ are CIU-equivalent. Using Theorem 4.8 and Lemmas 4.10 and 4.9 we conclude that the terms $\forall\alpha.\lambda x.e$ and t_r are contextually equivalent.

Remark 5.2. Unfortunately we cannot so easily characterize general values of the type $\forall\alpha.\alpha \to \alpha$, that is, those not of the form $\Lambda.v$ for a value v. Consider the term $\Lambda.t_{\frac{1}{2}} \oplus t_{\frac{1}{3}}$. It is a straightforward calculation that for any evaluation context E and value v, $\mathfrak{P}^{\Downarrow}\left(E\left[\left(t_{\frac{1}{2}} \oplus t_{\frac{1}{3}}\right) v\right]\right) = \frac{5}{12}\mathfrak{P}^{\Downarrow}(E[v]) = \mathfrak{P}^{\Downarrow}\left(E\left[t_{\frac{5}{12}}\, v\right]\right)$ thus if $\Lambda.t_{\frac{1}{2}} \oplus t_{\frac{1}{3}}$ is equivalent to any $\Lambda.t_r$ it must be $\Lambda.t_{\frac{5}{12}}$.

Let E be the evaluation context $E = \texttt{let}\ f\ = -[]\ \texttt{in}\ \texttt{let}\ x\ = f\,\langle\rangle\ \texttt{in}\ f\,\langle\rangle$. We compute $\mathfrak{P}^{\Downarrow}\left(E\left[\Lambda.t_{\frac{1}{2}} \oplus t_{\frac{1}{3}}\right]\right) = \frac{13}{72}$ and $\mathfrak{P}^{\Downarrow}\left(E\left[\Lambda.t_{\frac{5}{12}}\right]\right) = \frac{25}{144}$ showing that $\Lambda.t_{\frac{1}{2}} \oplus t_{\frac{1}{3}}$ is *not* equivalent to $\Lambda.t_{\frac{5}{12}}$.

This example also shows that extensionality for *expressions*, as opposed to *values*, of function type does not hold. The reason is that probabilistic choice is a computational effect and so it matters how many times we evaluate the term and this is what the constructed evaluation context uses to distinguish the terms.

A Free Theorem for Lists. Let τ be a type and α not free in τ. We write $[\tau]$ for the type of lists $\mu\alpha.(\mathbf{1}+\tau\times\alpha)$, $\texttt{nil}$ for the empty list and $\texttt{cons} : \forall\alpha.\alpha \to [\alpha] \to [\alpha]$ for the other constructor $\texttt{cons} = \Lambda.\lambda x.\lambda xs.\texttt{fold}\,(\texttt{inr}\,\langle x, xs\rangle)$. The function $\texttt{map}$ of type $\forall\alpha.\forall\beta.(\alpha \to \beta) \to [\alpha] \to [\beta]$ is the function applying the given function to all elements of the list in order. Additionally, we define composition of terms $f \circ g$ as the term $\lambda x.f(g(x))$ (for x not free in f and g).

We will now show that any term m of type $\forall\alpha.\forall\beta.(\alpha \to \beta) \to [\alpha] \to [\beta]$ equivalent to a term of the form $\Lambda.\Lambda.\lambda x.e$ satisfies $m[][]\,(f \circ g) =^{ctx} m[][]f \circ \texttt{map}[][]\,g$ for all *values* f and all *deterministic and terminating* g. By this we mean that for each value v in the domain of g, there exists a *value* u in the codomain of g, such that $g\,v =^{ctx} u$. For instance, if g reduces without using choice reductions and is terminating, then g is deterministic. There are other functions that are also deterministic and terminating, though, for instance $\lambda x.\langle\rangle \oplus \langle\rangle$. In the Appendix we show that these restrictions are not superfluous.

So let m be a closed term of type $\forall\alpha.\forall\beta.(\alpha \to \beta) \to [\alpha] \to [\beta]$ and suppose further that m is equivalent to a term of the form $\Lambda.\Lambda.\lambda x.e$. Let $\tau, \sigma, \rho \in \mathfrak{T}$ be closed types and $f \in \mathbf{Val}\,(\sigma \to \rho)$ and $g \in \mathbf{Tm}\,(\tau \to \sigma)$ be a deterministic and terminating function. Then

$$\varnothing \mid \varnothing \vdash m[][](f \circ g) =^{ctx} m[][]f \circ \texttt{map}[][]g : [\tau] \to [\rho].$$

We prove two approximations separately, starting with $\lesssim^{ctx}$. We use Theorem 4.8 multiple times. We have $\alpha, \beta \mid \varnothing \vdash m[][] : (\alpha \to \beta) \to [\alpha] \to [\beta]$. Let $R = \lambda n.\{(v,u) \mid g\,v =^{ctx} u\}$ be a member of $\mathbf{VRel}(\tau,\sigma)$ and $S \in \mathbf{VRel}(\rho,\rho)$ be the constant identity relation on $\mathbf{Val}(\rho)$. Let φ map α to R and β to S. Proposition 4.5 gives $(m[][], m[][]) \in [\![(\alpha \to \beta) \to [\alpha] \to [\beta]]\!](\varphi)^{\top\top}(n)$ for all $n \in \mathbb{N}$.

We first claim that $(f \circ g, f) \in [\![\alpha \to \beta]\!](\varphi)(n)$ for all $n \in \mathbb{N}$. Since f is a value and has a type, it must be of the form $\lambda x.e$ for some x and e. Take $j \in \mathbb{N}$, related values $(v,u) \in r(j)$, $k \leq j$ and $(E, E') \in S^{\top}(k)$ two related evaluation contexts. We then have $\mathfrak{P}^{\Downarrow}(E'[f\,u]) = \mathfrak{P}^{\Downarrow}(E'[f(g\,v)])$ by Theorem 4.8 and the definition of relation R. Using the results about $\mathfrak{P}^{\Downarrow}_{k}(\cdot)$ and $\mathfrak{P}^{\Downarrow}(\cdot)$ proved in Section C in the Appendix this gives us

$$\mathfrak{P}^{\Downarrow}_{k}(E[f(g(v))]) \leq \sum_{\pi : f(g(v)) \rightsquigarrow^{*} w} \mathfrak{W}(\pi)\,\mathfrak{P}^{\Downarrow}_{k}(E[w]) \leq \sum_{\pi : f(g(v)) \rightsquigarrow^{*} w} \mathfrak{W}(\pi)\,\mathfrak{P}^{\Downarrow}(E'[w])$$

and the last term is equal to $\mathfrak{P}^{\Downarrow}(E'[f(g\,v)])$ which is equal to $\mathfrak{P}^{\Downarrow}(E'[f\,u])$.

From this we can conclude $(m[][]\,(f \circ g), m[][]\,f) \in [\![[\alpha] \to [\beta]]\!](\varphi)^{\top\top}(n)$ for all $n \in \mathbb{N}$. Note that we have *not yet* used the fact that g is deterministic and terminating. We do so now.

Let xs be a list of elements of type τ. Then induction on the length of xs, using the assumption on g, we can derive that there exists a list ys of elements of type σ, such that $\mathtt{map}[][]\,g\,xs =^{ctx} ys$ and $(xs, ys) \in [\![[\alpha]]\!](\varphi)(n)$ for all n.

This gives us $(m[][]\,(f \circ g)\,xs, m[][]\,f\,ys) \in [\![[\beta]]\!](\varphi)^{\top\top}(n)$ for all $n \in \mathbb{N}$. Since the relation S is the identity relation we have for all evaluation contexts E of a suitable type, $(E, E) \in S^{\top}(n)$ for all n, which gives

$$m[][]\,(f \circ g)\,xs \lesssim^{CIU} m[][]\,f\,ys =^{ctx} m[][]\,f\,(\mathtt{map}[][]\,g\,xs) =^{ctx} (m[][]\,f \circ \mathtt{map}[][]\,g)\,xs$$

where the last equality holds because β-reduction is an equivalence.

We now conclude by using the fact that m is (equivalent to) a term of the form $\Lambda.\Lambda.\lambda x.e$ and use Lemma 4.9 to conclude $m[][]\,(f \circ g) \lesssim^{ctx} m[][]\,f \circ \mathtt{map}[][]\,g$.

For the other direction, we proceed analogously. The relation for β remains the identity relation, and the relation for R for α is $\{(v,u) \mid v =^{ctx} g\,u\}$.

6 Extension to References

We now sketch the extension of $\mathbf{F}^{\mu,\oplus}$ to include dynamically allocated references. For simplicity we add ground store only, so we do not have to solve a domain equation giving us the space of semantic types and worlds [1]. We show an equivalence using state and probabilistic choice which shows that the addition of references to the language is orthogonal to the addition of probabilistic choice. We conjecture that the extension with *higher-order* dynamically allocated references can be done as in earlier work on step-indexed logical relations [11].

We extend the language by adding the type $\mathtt{ref\,nat}$ and extend the grammar of terms with $\ell \mid \mathtt{ref}\,e \mid e_1 := e_2 \mid\, !e$ with ℓ being locations.

To model allocation we need to index the interpretation of types by worlds. To keep things simple a world $w \in \mathcal{W}$ is partial bijection f on locations together with, for each pair of locations $(\ell_1, \ell_2) \in f$, a relation R on numerals. We write $(\ell_1, \ell_2, R) \in w$ when the partial bijection in w relates ℓ_1 and ℓ_2 and R is the relation assigned to the pair (ℓ_1, ℓ_2). Technically, worlds are relations of type $\mathtt{Loc}^2 \times \mathcal{P}(\{\underline{n} \mid n \in \mathbb{N}\})$ satisfying the conditions described above.

The operational semantics has to be extended to include heaps, which are modeled as finite maps from locations to numerals. A pair of heaps (h_1, h_2) satisfies the world w, written $(h_1, h_2) \in \lfloor w \rfloor$, when $\forall (\ell_1, \ell_2, R) \in w, (h_1(\ell_1), h_2(\ell_2)) \in R$. The interpretation of types is then extended to include worlds. The denotation of a type is now an element of $\mathcal{W} \stackrel{mon}{\to} \mathbf{VRel}(\cdot, \cdot)$ where the order on $\mathcal{W}$ is inclusion. Let $\mathbf{WRel}(\tau, \tau') = \mathcal{W} \stackrel{mon}{\to} \mathbf{VRel}(\tau, \tau')$. We define $[\![\Delta \vdash \mathtt{ref\ nat}]\!](\varphi)(n)$ as $\lambda w. \{(\ell_1, \ell_2) \mid (\ell_1, \ell_2, =) \in w\}$ where $=$ is the equality relation on numerals.

The rest of the interpretation stays the same, apart from some quantification over "future worlds" in the function case to maintain monotonicity. We also need to change the definition of the $\top\top$-closure to use the world satisfaction relation. For $r \in \mathbf{WRel}(\tau, \tau')$ we define an indexed relation (indexed by worlds) $r^{\top}$ as

$$r^{\top}(w)(n) \left\{ (E, E') \;\middle|\; \begin{array}{c} \forall w' \geq w, \forall k \leq n, \forall (h_1, h_2) \in \lfloor w' \rfloor, \forall v_1, v_2 \in r(w')(k), \\ \mathfrak{P}_k^{\Downarrow}(\langle h_1, E[v_1] \rangle) \leq \mathfrak{P}^{\Downarrow}(\langle h_2, E[v_2] \rangle) \end{array} \right\}$$

and analogously for $\cdot^{\perp}$.

We now sketch a proof that two modules, each implementing a counter by using a single internal location, are contextually equivalent. The increment method is special. When called, it chooses, uniformly, whether to increment the counter or not. The two modules differ in the way they increment the counter. One module increments the counter by 1, the other by 2. Concretely, we show that the two counters $\mathtt{pack}\,(\lambda - .\mathtt{ref}\,\underline{1}, \lambda x.!x, \lambda x.\langle\rangle \oplus (x := \mathtt{S}\,!x))$ and $\mathtt{pack}\,(\lambda - .\mathtt{ref}\,\underline{2}, \lambda x.!x\ \mathtt{div}\ \underline{2}, \lambda x.\langle\rangle \oplus (x := \mathtt{S}\,(\mathtt{S}\,!x)))$ are contextually equivalent at type $\exists \alpha.(\mathbf{1} \to \alpha) \times (\alpha \to \mathtt{nat}) \times (\alpha \to \mathbf{1})$. We have used $\mathtt{div}$ for the division function on numerals which can easily be implemented.

The interpretation of existentials $[\![\Delta \vdash \exists \alpha.\tau]\!](\varphi)(n)$ now maps world w to

$$\left\{ (\mathtt{pack}\,v, \mathtt{pack}\,v') \;\middle|\; \begin{array}{l} \exists \sigma, \sigma' \in \mathfrak{T}, \exists r \in \mathbf{WRel}(\sigma, \sigma'), \\ (v, v') \in [\![\Delta, \alpha \vdash \tau]\!](\varphi[\alpha \mapsto r])(w)(n) \end{array} \right\}$$

To prove the counters are contextually equivalent we show them directly related in the value relation. We choose the types σ and σ' to be $\mathtt{ref\,nat}$ and the relation r to be $\lambda w. \{(\ell_1, \ell_2) \mid (\ell_1, \ell_2, \{(\underline{n}, \underline{2 \cdot n}) \mid n \in \mathbb{N}\}) \in w\}$. We now need to check all three functions to be related at the value relation.

First, the allocation functions. We only show one approximation, the other is completely analogous. Concretely, we show that for any $n \in \mathbb{N}$ and any world $w \in \mathcal{W}$ we have $(\lambda - .\mathtt{ref}\ \underline{1}, \lambda - .\mathtt{ref}\ \underline{2}) \in [\![\mathbf{1} \to \alpha]\!](r)(w)(n)$. Let $n \in \mathbb{N}$ and $w \in \mathcal{W}$. Take $w' \geq w$ and related arguments v, v' at type $\mathbf{1}$. We know by construction that $v = v' = \langle\rangle$ so we have to show that $(\mathtt{ref}\ \underline{1}, \mathtt{ref}\ \underline{2}) \in [\![\alpha]\!](r)^{\top\top}(w')(n)$.

Let $w'' \geq w'$ and $j \leq n$ and take two related evaluation contexts (E, E') at $[\![\alpha]\!]\,(r)^{\top}(w'')(j)$ and $(h, h') \in \lfloor w'' \rfloor$. Let $\ell \notin \mathrm{dom}\,(h)$ and $\ell' \notin \mathrm{dom}\,(h')$. We have

$$\mathfrak{P}_j^{\Downarrow}\,(\langle h, E[\texttt{ref}\ \underline{1}]\rangle) = \mathfrak{P}_j^{\Downarrow}\,(\langle h\,[\ell \mapsto \underline{1}], E[\ell]\rangle)$$

and $\mathfrak{P}^{\Downarrow}\,(\langle h', E'[\texttt{ref}\ \underline{2}]\rangle) = \mathfrak{P}^{\Downarrow}\,(\langle h'\,[\ell' \mapsto \underline{2}], E'[\ell']\rangle)$.

Let w''' be w'' extended with (ℓ, ℓ', r). Then the extended heaps are in $\lfloor w''' \rfloor$ and $w''' \geq w''$. Thus E and E' are also related at w''' by monotonicity. Similarly we can prove that $(\ell, \ell') \in [\![\alpha]\!]\,(r)(j)(w''')$. This then allows us to conclude $\mathfrak{P}_j^{\Downarrow}\,(\langle h\,[\ell \mapsto \underline{1}], E[\ell]\rangle) \leq \mathfrak{P}^{\Downarrow}\,(\langle h'\,[\ell' \mapsto \underline{2}], E'[\ell']\rangle)$ which concludes the proof.

Lookup is simple so we omit it. Update is more interesting. Let $n \in \mathbb{N}$ and $w \in \mathcal{W}$. Let ℓ and ℓ' be related at $[\![\alpha]\!]\,(r)(w)(n)$. We need to show that $(\langle\rangle \oplus (\ell := \mathtt{S}\,!\ell), \langle\rangle \oplus (\ell' := \mathtt{S}\,(\mathtt{S}\,!\ell'))) \in [\![\mathbf{1}]\!]\,(r)^{\top\top}(w)(n)$. Take $w' \geq w$, $j \leq n$ and $(h, h') \in \lfloor w' \rfloor$. Take related evaluation contexts E and E' at w' and j. We have

$$\mathfrak{P}_j^{\Downarrow}\,(\langle h, E\,[\langle\rangle \oplus (\ell := \mathtt{S}\,!\ell)]\rangle) = \tfrac{1}{2}\mathfrak{P}_j^{\Downarrow}\,(\langle h, E\,[\langle\rangle]\rangle) + \tfrac{1}{2}\mathfrak{P}_j^{\Downarrow}\,(\langle h, E\,[\ell := \mathtt{S}\,!\ell]\rangle)$$
$$\mathfrak{P}^{\Downarrow}\,(\langle h', E'\,[\langle\rangle \oplus (\ell' := \mathtt{S}\,\mathtt{S}\,!\ell')]\rangle) = \tfrac{1}{2}\mathfrak{P}^{\Downarrow}\,(\langle h', E'\,[\langle\rangle]\rangle) + \tfrac{1}{2}\mathfrak{P}^{\Downarrow}\,(\langle h', E'\,[\ell' := \mathtt{S}\,\mathtt{S}\,!\ell']\rangle)$$

Since ℓ and ℓ' are related at $[\![\alpha]\!]\,(r)(w)(n)$ and $w' \geq w$ and $(h, h') \in \lfloor w' \rfloor$ we know that $h(\ell) = \underline{m}$ and $h'(\ell') = \underline{2 \cdot m}$ for some $m \in \mathbb{N}$.

Thus $\mathfrak{P}_j^{\Downarrow}\,(\langle h, E\,[\ell := \mathtt{S}\,!\ell]\rangle) = \mathfrak{P}_j^{\Downarrow}\,(\langle h_1, E[\langle\rangle]\rangle)$ where $h_1 = h\,[\ell \mapsto \underline{m+1}]$. Also $\mathfrak{P}^{\Downarrow}\,(\langle h', E'\,[\ell' := \mathtt{S}\,\mathtt{S}\,!\ell']\rangle) = \mathfrak{P}^{\Downarrow}\,(\langle h_2, E'[\langle\rangle]\rangle)$ where $h_2 = h'\left[\ell' \mapsto \underline{2 \cdot (m+1)}\right]$. The fact that h_1 and h_2 are still related concludes the proof.

The above proof shows that reasoning about examples involving state and choice is possible and that the two features are largely orthogonal.

7 Conclusion

We have constructed a step-indexed logical relation for a higher-order language with probabilistic choice. In contrast to earlier work, our language also features impredicative polymorphism and recursive types. We also show how to extend our logical relation to a language with dynamically allocated local state. In future work, we will explore whether the step-indexed technique can be used for developing models of program logics for probabilistic computation that support reasoning about more properties than just contextual equivalence. We are also interested in including primitives for continuous probability distributions.

Acknowledgments. We thank Filip Sieczkowski, Kasper Svendsen and Thomas Dinsdale-Young for discussions of various aspects of this work and the reviewers for their comments.

This research was supported in part by the ModuRes Sapere Aude Advanced Grant from The Danish Council for Independent Research for the Natural Sciences (FNU) and in part by Microsoft Research through its PhD Scholarship Programme.

References

1. Ahmed, A.: Semantics of Types for Mutable State. Ph.D. thesis, Princeton University (2004)
2. Ahmed, A.: Step-indexed syntactic logical relations for recursive and quantified types. In: Sestoft, P. (ed.) ESOP 2006. LNCS, vol. 3924, pp. 69–83. Springer, Heidelberg (2006)
3. Appel, A.W., McAllester, D.: An indexed model of recursive types for foundational proof-carrying code. ACM Transactions on Programming Languages and Systems 23(5) (2001)
4. Birkedal, L., Bizjak, A., Schwinghammer, J.: Step-indexed relational reasoning for countable nondeterminism. Logical Methods in Computer Science 9(4) (2013)
5. Birkedal, L., Reus, B., Schwinghammer, J., Støvring, K., Thamsborg, J., Yang, H.: Step-indexed kripke models over recursive worlds. In: Proceedings of the 38th Symposium on Principles of Programming Languages, pp. 119–132. ACM (2011)
6. Bizjak, A., Birkedal, L.: Step-indexed logical relations for probability. arXiv:1501.02623 [cs.LO] (2015), long version of this paper
7. Crubillé, R., Dal Lago, U.: On probabilistic applicative bisimulation and call-by-value λ-calculi. In: Shao, Z. (ed.) ESOP 2014 (ETAPS). LNCS, vol. 8410, pp. 209–228. Springer, Heidelberg (2014)
8. Dal Lago, U., Sangiorgi, D., Alberti, M.: On coinductive equivalences for higher-order probabilistic functional programs. In: Proceedings of 41st Symposium on Principles of Programming Languages, pp. 297–308. ACM (2014)
9. Danos, V., Harmer, R.S.: Probabilistic game semantics. ACM Transactions on Computational Logic 3(3) (2002)
10. Dreyer, D., Ahmed, A., Birkedal, L.: Logical step-indexed logical relations. Logical Methods in Computer Science 7(2) (2011)
11. Dreyer, D., Neis, G., Birkedal, L.: The impact of higher-order state and control effects on local relational reasoning. Journal of Functional Programming 22(4-5 special issue), 477–528 (2012)
12. Ehrhard, T., Pagani, M., Tasson, C.: The computational meaning of probabilistic coherence spaces. In: Proceedings of the 26th IEEE Symposium on Logic in Computer Science, pp. 87–96. IEEE (2011)
13. Ehrhard, T., Tasson, C., Pagani, M.: Probabilistic coherence spaces are fully abstract for probabilistic pcf. In: Proceedings of 41st Symposium on Principles of Programming Languages, pp. 309–320. ACM (2014)
14. Johann, P., Simpson, A., Voigtländer, J.: A generic operational metatheory for algebraic effects. In: Proceedings of the 25th Annual IEEE Symposium on Logic in Computer Science, pp. 209–218. IEEE (2010)
15. Jones, C., Plotkin, G.: A probabilistic powerdomain of evaluations. In: Proceedings of the 4th Symposium on Logic in Computer Science, pp. 186–195. IEEE (1989)
16. Lago, U.D., Zorzi, M.: Probabilistic operational semantics for the lambda calculus. RAIRO - Theoretical Informatics and Applications 46 (2012)
17. Pitts, A.M.: Parametric polymorphism and operational equivalence. Mathematical Structures in Computer Science 10(3) (2000)
18. Pitts, A.M.: Typed operational reasoning. In: Pierce, B.C. (ed.) Advanced Topics in Types and Programming Languages, ch. 7. MIT Press (2005)
19. Pitts, A.M.: Step-indexed biorthogonality: a tutorial example. In: Ahmed, A., Benton, N., Birkedal, L., Hofmann, M. (eds.) Modelling, Controlling and Reasoning About State. No. 10351 in Dagstuhl Seminar Proceedings (2010)

20. Ramsey, N., Pfeffer, A.: Stochastic lambda calculus and monads of probability distributions. In: Proceedings of the 29th Symposium on Principles of Programming Languages, pp. 154–165. ACM (2002)
21. Saheb-Djahromi, N.: Cpo's of measures for nondeterminism. Theoretical Computer Science 12(1) (1980)

Automata, Games, Verification

Minimisation of Multiplicity Tree Automata

Stefan Kiefer, Ines Marusic, and James Worrell

University of Oxford, UK

Abstract. We consider the problem of minimising the number of states in a multiplicity tree automaton over the field of rational numbers. We give a minimisation algorithm that runs in polynomial time assuming unit-cost arithmetic. We also show that a polynomial bound in the standard Turing model would require a breakthrough in the complexity of polynomial identity testing by proving that the latter problem is logspace equivalent to the decision version of minimisation. The developed techniques also improve the state of the art in multiplicity word automata: we give an NC algorithm for minimising multiplicity word automata. Finally, we consider the minimal consistency problem: does there exist an automaton with n states that is consistent with a given finite sample of weight-labelled words or trees? We show that this decision problem is complete for the existential theory of the rationals, both for words and for trees of a fixed alphabet rank.

1 Introduction

Minimisation is a fundamental problem in automata theory that is closely related to both learning and equivalence testing. In this work we analyse the complexity of minimisation for multiplicity automata, i.e., weighted automata over a field. We take a comprehensive view, looking at multiplicity automata over both words and trees and considering both function and decision problems. We also look at the closely related problem of obtaining a minimal automaton consistent with a given finite set of observations. We characterise the complexity of these problems in terms of arithmetic and Boolean circuit classes. In particular, we give relationships to longstanding open problems in arithmetic complexity theory.

Multiplicity tree automata were first introduced by Berstel and Reutenauer [1] under the terminology of linear representations of a tree series. They generalise multiplicity word automata, introduced by Schützenberger [25], which can be viewed as multiplicity tree automata on unary trees. The minimisation problem for multiplicity word automata has long been known to be solvable in polynomial time [25].

In this work, we give a new procedure for computing minimal word automata and thereby place minimisation in NC improving also on a randomised NC procedure in [22]. (Recall that NL $\subseteq$ NC $\subseteq$ P, where NC comprises those languages having L-uniform Boolean circuits of polylogarithmic depth and polynomial size, or, equivalently, those problems solvable in polylogarithmic time on

A. Pitts (Ed.): FOSSACS 2015, LNCS 9034, pp. 297–311, 2015.
DOI: 10.1007/978-3-662-46678-0_19

parallel random-access machines with polynomially many processors.) By comparison, minimising deterministic word automata is NL-complete [12], while minimising non-deterministic word automata is PSPACE-complete [20].

Over trees, we give what is (to the best of our knowledge) the first complexity analysis of the problem of minimising multiplicity automata. We present an algorithm that minimises a given tree automaton $\mathcal{A}$ in time $O\left(|\mathcal{A}|^2 \cdot r\right)$ where r is the maximum alphabet rank, assuming unit-cost arithmetic. This procedure can be viewed as a concrete version of the construction of a syntactic algebra of a recognisable tree series in [4]. We thus place the problem within PSPACE in the conventional Turing model. We are moreover able to precisely characterise the complexity of the decision version of the minimisation problem as being logspace equivalent to the arithmetic circuit identity testing (ACIT) problem, commonly also called the polynomial identity testing problem. The latter problem is very well studied, with a variety of randomised polynomial-time algorithms, but, as yet, no deterministic polynomial-time procedure. In previous work we have reduced equivalence testing of multiplicity tree automata to ACIT [24]; the advance here is to reduce the more general problem of minimisation also to ACIT.

Finally, we consider the problem of computing a minimal multiplicity automaton consistent with a finite set of input-output behaviours. This is a natural learning problem whose complexity for non-deterministic finite automata was studied by Gold [17]. For multiplicity word automata over a field $\mathbb{F}$, we show that the decision version of this problem is logspace equivalent to the problem of deciding the truth of existential first-order sentences over the field $(\mathbb{F}, +, \cdot, 0, 1)$, a long-standing open problem in case $\mathbb{F} = \mathbb{Q}$. Furthermore we show that the same result holds for multiplicity tree automata of a fixed alphabet rank, but we leave open the complexity of the problem for general multiplicity tree automata.

The full version of this paper is available as [21].

Further Related Work. Based on a generalisation of the Myhill-Nerode theorem to trees, one obtains a procedure for minimising deterministic tree automata that runs in time quadratic in the size of the input automaton [7,11]. There have also been several works on minimising deterministic tree automata with weights in a semi-field (that is, a semi-ring with multiplicative inverses). In particular, Maletti [23] gives a polynomial-time algorithm in this setting, assuming unit cost for arithmetic in the semi-field. In the non-deterministic case, Carme et al. [10] define the subclass of *residual finite* non-deterministic tree automata. They show that this class expresses the class of regular tree languages and admits a polynomial-space minimisation procedure.

2 Preliminaries

Let $\mathbb{N}$ and $\mathbb{N}_0$ denote the set of all positive and non-negative integers, respectively. For every $n \in \mathbb{N}$, we write $[n]$ for the set $\{1, 2, \ldots, n\}$.

Matrices and Vectors. Let $n \in \mathbb{N}$. We write I_n for the identity matrix of order n. For every $i \in [n]$, we write e_i for the ith n-dimensional coordinate row vector. For any matrix A, we write A_i for its ith row, A^j for its jth column, and $A_{i,j}$ for its $(i,j)^{\text{th}}$ entry. Given nonempty subsets I and J of the rows and columns of A, respectively, we write $A_{I,J}$ for the submatrix $(A_{i,j})_{i\in I, j\in J}$ of A.

Let A be an $m \times n$ matrix with entries in a field $\mathbb{F}$. The *row space* of A, written $RS(A)$, is the subspace of $\mathbb{F}^n$ spanned by the rows of A. The *column space* of A, written $CS(A)$, is the subspace of $\mathbb{F}^m$ spanned by the columns of A.

Given a set $S \subseteq \mathbb{F}^n$, we use $\langle S \rangle$ to denote the vector subspace of $\mathbb{F}^n$ that is spanned by S, where we often omit the braces when denoting S.

Kronecker Product. Let A be an $m_1 \times n_1$ matrix and B an $m_2 \times n_2$ matrix. The *Kronecker product* of A by B, written as $A \otimes B$, is an $m_1 m_2 \times n_1 n_2$ matrix where $(A \otimes B)_{(i_1-1)m_2+i_2,(j_1-1)n_2+j_2} = A_{i_1,j_1} \cdot B_{i_2,j_2}$ for every $i_1 \in [m_1]$, $i_2 \in [m_2]$, $j_1 \in [n_1]$, $j_2 \in [n_2]$.

The Kronecker product is bilinear, associative, and has the following *mixed-product property*: For any matrices A, B, C, D such that products $A \cdot C$ and $B \cdot D$ are defined, it holds that $(A \otimes B) \cdot (C \otimes D) = (A \cdot C) \otimes (B \cdot D)$.

For every $k \in \mathbb{N}_0$ we define the *k-fold Kronecker power* of a matrix A, written as $A^{\otimes k}$, inductively by $A^{\otimes 0} = I_1$ and $A^{\otimes k} = A^{\otimes(k-1)} \otimes A$ for $k \geq 1$.

Multiplicity Word Automata. Let Σ be a finite alphabet and ε be the empty word. The set of all words over Σ is denoted by Σ^*, and the length of a word $w \in \Sigma^*$ is denoted by $|w|$. For any $n \in \mathbb{N}_0$ we write $\Sigma^n := \{w \in \Sigma^* : |w| = n\}$, $\Sigma^{\leq n} := \bigcup_{l=0}^{n} \Sigma^l$, and $\Sigma^{<n} := \Sigma^{\leq n} \setminus \Sigma^n$. Given two words $x, y \in \Sigma^*$, we denote by xy the concatenation of x and y. Given two sets $X, Y \subseteq \Sigma^*$, we define $XY := \{xy : x \in X, y \in Y\}$.

Let $\mathbb{F}$ be a field. A *word series* over Σ with coefficients in $\mathbb{F}$ is a mapping $f : \Sigma^* \to \mathbb{F}$. The *Hankel matrix* of f is the matrix $H : \Sigma^* \times \Sigma^* \to \mathbb{F}$ such that $H_{x,y} = f(xy)$ for all $x, y \in \Sigma^*$.

An $\mathbb{F}$-*multiplicity word automaton* ($\mathbb{F}$-*MWA*) is a 5-tuple $\mathcal{A} = (n, \Sigma, \mu, \alpha, \gamma)$ which consists of the *dimension* $n \in \mathbb{N}_0$ representing the number of states, a finite alphabet Σ, a function $\mu : \Sigma \to \mathbb{F}^{n\times n}$ assigning a *transition matrix* $\mu(\sigma)$ to each $\sigma \in \Sigma$, the *initial weight vector* $\alpha \in \mathbb{F}^{1\times n}$, and the *final weight vector* $\gamma \in \mathbb{F}^{n\times 1}$. We extend the function μ from Σ to Σ^* by $\mu(\varepsilon) := I_n$ and $\mu(\sigma_1 \ldots \sigma_k) := \mu(\sigma_1) \cdot \ldots \cdot \mu(\sigma_k)$ for any $\sigma_1, \ldots, \sigma_k \in \Sigma$. It is easy to see that $\mu(xy) = \mu(x) \cdot \mu(y)$ for any $x, y \in \Sigma^*$. Automaton $\mathcal{A}$ *recognises* the word series $\|\mathcal{A}\| : \Sigma^* \to \mathbb{F}$ where $\|\mathcal{A}\|(w) = \alpha \cdot \mu(w) \cdot \gamma$ for every $w \in \Sigma^*$.

Finite Trees. A *ranked alphabet* is a tuple (Σ, rk) where Σ is a nonempty finite set of symbols and $rk : \Sigma \to \mathbb{N}_0$ is a function. Ranked alphabet (Σ, rk) is often written Σ for short. For every $k \in \mathbb{N}_0$, we define the set of all *k-ary* symbols $\Sigma_k := rk^{-1}(\{k\})$. We say that Σ has *rank* r if $r = \max\{rk(\sigma) : \sigma \in \Sigma\}$.

The set of Σ-*trees* (*trees* for short), written T_Σ, is the smallest set T satisfying (i) $\Sigma_0 \subseteq T$, and (ii) if $\sigma \in \Sigma_k$, $t_1, \ldots, t_k \in T$ then $\sigma(t_1, \ldots, t_k) \in T$. The *height* of a tree t, $height(t)$, is defined by $height(t) = 0$ if $t \in \Sigma_0$, and $height(t) = 1 + \max_{i\in[k]} height(t_i)$ if $t = \sigma(t_1, \ldots, t_k)$ for some $k \geq 1$. For any $n \in \mathbb{N}_0$ we write $T_\Sigma^n := \{t \in T_\Sigma : height(t) = n\}$, $T_\Sigma^{\leq n} := \bigcup_{l=0}^{n} T_\Sigma^l$, and $T_\Sigma^{<n} := T_\Sigma^{\leq n} \setminus T_\Sigma^n$.

Let $\Box$ be a nullary symbol not contained in Σ. The set C_Σ of *Σ-contexts* (*contexts* for short) is the set of $(\{\Box\} \cup \Sigma)$-trees in which $\Box$ occurs exactly once. Let $n \in \mathbb{N}_0$. We denote by C^n_Σ the set of all contexts $c \in C_\Sigma$ where the distance between the root and the $\Box$-labelled node of c is equal to n. Moreover, we write $C^{\leq n}_\Sigma := \bigcup_{l=0}^{n} C^l_\Sigma$ and $C^{<n}_\Sigma := C^{\leq n}_\Sigma \setminus C^n_\Sigma$. A *subtree* of $c \in C_\Sigma$ is a Σ-tree consisting of a node in c and all of its descendants. Given a set $S \subseteq T_\Sigma$, we denote by $C^n_{\Sigma,S}$ the set of all contexts $c \in C^n_\Sigma$ where every subtree of c is an element of S; we moreover write $C^{\leq n}_{\Sigma,S} := \bigcup_{l=0}^{n} C^l_{\Sigma,S}$ and $C^{<n}_{\Sigma,S} := C^{\leq n}_{\Sigma,S} \setminus C^n_{\Sigma,S}$.

Given $c \in C_\Sigma$ and $t \in T_\Sigma \dot\cup C_\Sigma$, we write $c[t]$ for the tree obtained by substituting t for $\Box$ in c. Let $\mathbb{F}$ be a field. A *tree series* over Σ with coefficients in $\mathbb{F}$ is a mapping $f : T_\Sigma \to \mathbb{F}$. The *Hankel matrix* of $f : T_\Sigma \to \mathbb{F}$ is the matrix $H : T_\Sigma \times C_\Sigma \to \mathbb{F}$ such that $H_{t,c} = f(c[t])$ for every $t \in T_\Sigma$ and $c \in C_\Sigma$.

Multiplicity Tree Automata. Let $\mathbb{F}$ be a field. An *$\mathbb{F}$-multiplicity tree automaton* (*$\mathbb{F}$-MTA*) is a 4-tuple $\mathcal{A} = (n, \Sigma, \mu, \gamma)$ which consists of the *dimension* $n \in \mathbb{N}_0$ representing the number of states, a ranked alphabet Σ, the *tree representation* $\mu = \{\mu(\sigma) : \sigma \in \Sigma\}$ where for every symbol $\sigma \in \Sigma$, $\mu(\sigma) \in \mathbb{F}^{n^{rk(\sigma)} \times n}$ represents the *transition matrix* associated to σ, and the *final weight vector* $\gamma \in \mathbb{F}^{n \times 1}$. We speak of an MTA if the field $\mathbb{F}$ is clear from the context or irrelevant. The *size* of $\mathcal{A}$, written as $|\mathcal{A}|$, is the total number of entries in all transition matrices and the final weight vector of $\mathcal{A}$, i.e., $|\mathcal{A}| := \sum_{\sigma \in \Sigma} n^{rk(\sigma)+1} + n$.

We extend the tree representation μ from Σ to T_Σ by $\mu(\sigma(t_1, \ldots, t_k)) := (\mu(t_1) \otimes \cdots \otimes \mu(t_k)) \cdot \mu(\sigma)$ for every $\sigma \in \Sigma_k$ and $t_1, \ldots, t_k \in T_\Sigma$. Automaton $\mathcal{A}$ *recognises* the tree series $\|\mathcal{A}\| : T_\Sigma \to \mathbb{F}$ where $\|\mathcal{A}\|(t) = \mu(t) \cdot \gamma$ for every $t \in T_\Sigma$.

We further extend μ from T_Σ to C_Σ by treating $\Box$ as a unary symbol and defining $\mu(\Box) := I_n$. This allows to define $\mu(c) \in \mathbb{F}^{n \times n}$ for every $c = \sigma(t_1, \ldots, t_k) \in C_\Sigma$ inductively as $\mu(c) := (\mu(t_1) \otimes \cdots \otimes \mu(t_k)) \cdot \mu(\sigma)$. It is easy to see that for every $t \in T_\Sigma \dot\cup C_\Sigma$ and $c \in C_\Sigma$, $\mu(c[t]) = \mu(t) \cdot \mu(c)$.

MWAs can be seen as a special case of MTAs: An MWA $(n, \Sigma, \mu, \alpha, \gamma)$ "is" the MTA $(n, \Sigma \dot\cup \{\sigma_0\}, \mu, \gamma)$ where the symbols in Σ are unary, symbol σ_0 is nullary, and $\mu(\sigma_0) = \alpha$. That is, we view $(\Sigma \dot\cup \{\sigma_0\})$-trees as words over Σ by omitting the leaf symbol σ_0. Hence if a result holds for MTAs, it also holds for MWAs. Some concepts, such as contexts, would formally need adaptation, however we omit such adaptations as they are straightforward. Therefore, we freely view MWAs as MTAs whenever convenient.

Two MTAs $\mathcal{A}_1, \mathcal{A}_2$ are said to be *equivalent* if $\|\mathcal{A}_1\| = \|\mathcal{A}_2\|$. An MTA is said to be *minimal* if no equivalent automaton has strictly smaller dimension. The following result was first shown by Habrard and Oncina [18], although a closely related result was given by Bozapalidis and Louscou-Bozapalidou [6].

Theorem 1 ([6,18]). *Let Σ be a ranked alphabet, $\mathbb{F}$ be a field, and $f : T_\Sigma \to \mathbb{F}$. Let H be the Hankel matrix of f. Then, f is recognised by some MTA if and only if H has finite rank over $\mathbb{F}$. In case H has finite rank over $\mathbb{F}$, the dimension of a minimal MTA recognising f is rank(H) over $\mathbb{F}$.*

It follows from Theorem 1 that an $\mathbb{F}$-MTA $\mathcal{A}$ of dimension n is minimal if and only if the Hankel matrix of $\|\mathcal{A}\|$ has rank n over $\mathbb{F}$.

Remark 2. Theorem 1 specialised to word automata was proved by Carlyle and Paz [9] and Fliess [16]. Their proofs show that if $X, Y \subseteq \Sigma^*$ are such that $rank(H_{X,Y}) = rank(H)$, then f is uniquely determined by $H_{X,Y}$ and $H_{X\Sigma,Y}$.

The following closure properties for MTAs can be found in [1,3]; see also [21].

Proposition 3. *Let $\mathcal{A}_1 = (n_1, \Sigma, \mu_1, \gamma_1)$, $\mathcal{A}_2 = (n_2, \Sigma, \mu_2, \gamma_2)$ be two $\mathbb{F}$-MTAs. One can construct an $\mathbb{F}$-MTA $\mathcal{A}_1 - \mathcal{A}_2$, called the* difference *of $\mathcal{A}_1$ and $\mathcal{A}_2$, such that $\|\mathcal{A}_1 - \mathcal{A}_2\| = \|\mathcal{A}_1\| - \|\mathcal{A}_2\|$. Secondly, one can construct an $\mathbb{F}$-MTA $\mathcal{A}_1 \times \mathcal{A}_2 = (n_1 \cdot n_2, \Sigma, \mu, \gamma_1 \otimes \gamma_2)$, called the* product *of $\mathcal{A}_1$ by $\mathcal{A}_2$, such that $\mu(t) = \mu_1(t) \otimes \mu_2(t)$ for every $t \in T_\Sigma$, $\mu(c) = \mu_1(c) \otimes \mu_2(c)$ for every $c \in C_\Sigma$, and $\|\mathcal{A}_1 \times \mathcal{A}_2\| = \|\mathcal{A}_1\| \cdot \|\mathcal{A}_2\|$. When $\mathbb{F} = \mathbb{Q}$, both automata $\mathcal{A}_1 - \mathcal{A}_2$ and $\mathcal{A}_1 \times \mathcal{A}_2$ can be computed from $\mathcal{A}_1$ and $\mathcal{A}_2$ in logarithmic space.*

3 Fundamentals of Minimisation

In this section we prepare the ground for minimisation algorithms. Let us fix a field $\mathbb{F}$ for the rest of this section and assume that all automata are over $\mathbb{F}$. We also fix an MTA $\mathcal{A} = (n, \Sigma, \mu, \gamma)$ for the rest of the section. We will construct from $\mathcal{A}$ another MTA $\tilde{\mathcal{A}}$ which we show to be equivalent to $\mathcal{A}$ and minimal. A crucial ingredient for this construction are special vector spaces induced by $\mathcal{A}$, called the forward space and backward space.

3.1 Forward and Backward Space

The *forward space* $\mathcal{F}$ of $\mathcal{A}$ is the (row) vector space $\mathcal{F} := \langle \mu(t) : t \in T_\Sigma \rangle$ over $\mathbb{F}$. The *backward space* $\mathcal{B}$ of $\mathcal{A}$ is the (column) vector space $\mathcal{B} := \langle \mu(c) \cdot \gamma : c \in C_\Sigma \rangle$ over $\mathbb{F}$. The following Propositions 4 and 5, proved in [21], provide fundamental characterisations of $\mathcal{F}$ and $\mathcal{B}$, respectively.

Proposition 4. *The forward space $\mathcal{F}$ has the following properties:*

(a) The space $\mathcal{F}$ is the smallest vector space V over $\mathbb{F}$ such that for all $k \in \mathbb{N}_0$, $v_1, \ldots, v_k \in V$, and $\sigma \in \Sigma_k$ it holds that $(v_1 \otimes \cdots \otimes v_k) \cdot \mu(\sigma) \in V$.
(b) The set of row vectors $\{\mu(t) : t \in T_\Sigma^{<n}\}$ spans $\mathcal{F}$.

Proposition 5. *Let S be a set of Σ-trees such that $\{\mu(t) : t \in S\}$ spans $\mathcal{F}$. The backward space $\mathcal{B}$ has the following properties:*

(a) The space $\mathcal{B}$ is the smallest vector space V over $\mathbb{F}$ such that $\gamma \in V$, and for every $v \in V$ and $c \in C^1_{\Sigma,S}$ it holds that $\mu(c) \cdot v \in V$.
(b) The set of column vectors $\{\mu(c) \cdot \gamma : c \in C^{<n}_{\Sigma,S}\}$ spans $\mathcal{B}$.

3.2 A Minimal Automaton

Let F and B be matrices whose rows and columns span $\mathcal{F}$ and $\mathcal{B}$, respectively. That is, $RS(F) = \mathcal{F}$ and $CS(B) = \mathcal{B}$. We discuss later (Section 4.1) how to efficiently compute F and B. The following lemma states that $rank(F \cdot B)$ is the dimension of a minimal automaton equivalent to $\mathcal{A}$.

Lemma 6. *A minimal automaton equivalent to $\mathcal{A}$ has $m := rank(F \cdot B)$ states.*

Proof. Let H be the Hankel matrix of $\|\mathcal{A}\|$. Define the matrix $\overline{F} \in \mathbb{F}^{T_\Sigma \times [n]}$ where $\overline{F}_t = \mu(t)$ for every $t \in T_\Sigma$. Define the matrix $\overline{B} \in \mathbb{F}^{[n] \times C_\Sigma}$ where $\overline{B}^c = \mu(c) \cdot \gamma$ for every $c \in C_\Sigma$. For every $t \in T_\Sigma$ and $c \in C_\Sigma$ we have by the definitions that

$$H_{t,c} = \|\mathcal{A}\|(c[t]) = \mu(c[t]) \cdot \gamma = \mu(t) \cdot \mu(c) \cdot \gamma = \overline{F}_t \cdot \overline{B}^c ,$$

hence $H = \overline{F} \cdot \overline{B}$. Note that

$$RS(\overline{F}) = \mathcal{F} = RS(F) \qquad \text{and} \qquad CS(\overline{B}) = \mathcal{B} = CS(B) . \tag{1}$$

We now have $m = rank(H) = rank(\overline{F} \cdot \overline{B}) = rank(F \cdot B)$, where the first equality is by Theorem 1, and the last equality is by (1) and a general linear-algebra argument, see [21]. ∎

By definition, there exist m rows of $F \cdot B$ that span $RS(F \cdot B)$. The corresponding m rows of F form a matrix $\tilde{F} \in \mathbb{F}^{m \times n}$ with $RS(\tilde{F} \cdot B) = RS(F \cdot B)$. Define a multiplicity tree automaton $\tilde{\mathcal{A}} = (m, \Sigma, \tilde{\mu}, \tilde{\gamma})$ with $\tilde{\gamma} = \tilde{F} \cdot \gamma$ and

$$\tilde{\mu}(\sigma) \cdot \tilde{F} \cdot B = \tilde{F}^{\otimes k} \cdot \mu(\sigma) \cdot B \qquad \text{for every } \sigma \in \Sigma_k. \tag{2}$$

We show that $\tilde{\mathcal{A}}$ minimises $\mathcal{A}$:

Proposition 7. *The MTA $\tilde{\mathcal{A}}$ is well defined and is a minimal automaton equivalent to $\mathcal{A}$.*

We provide a proof in [21]. Due to the importance of Proposition 7, we sketch its proof in the rest of this subsection. We do this by proving Proposition 7 for multiplicity *word* automata. The main arguments are similar for the tree case.

Let $\mathcal{A} = (n, \Sigma, \mu, \alpha, \gamma)$ be an MWA. The forward and backward space can then be written as $\mathcal{F} = \langle \alpha \cdot \mu(w) : w \in \Sigma^* \rangle$ and $\mathcal{B} = \langle \mu(w) \cdot \gamma : w \in \Sigma^* \rangle$, respectively. The MWA $\tilde{\mathcal{A}}$ can be written as $\tilde{\mathcal{A}} = (m, \Sigma, \tilde{\mu}, \tilde{\alpha}, \tilde{\gamma})$ with $\tilde{\gamma} = \tilde{F} \cdot \gamma$,

$$\tilde{\alpha} \cdot \tilde{F} \cdot B = \alpha \cdot B \qquad \text{and} \tag{3}$$

$$\tilde{\mu}(\sigma) \cdot \tilde{F} \cdot B = \tilde{F} \cdot \mu(\sigma) \cdot B \qquad \text{for every } \sigma \in \Sigma. \tag{4}$$

First, we show that $\tilde{\mathcal{A}}$ is a well-defined automaton:

Lemma 8. *There exists a unique vector $\tilde{\alpha}$ satisfying Equation (3). For every symbol $\sigma \in \Sigma$, there exists a unique matrix $\tilde{\mu}(\sigma)$ satisfying Equation (4).*

Proof. Since the rows of $\tilde{F} \cdot B$ form a basis of $RS(F \cdot B)$, it suffices to prove that $\alpha \cdot B \in RS(F \cdot B)$ and $RS(\tilde{F} \cdot \mu(\sigma) \cdot B) \subseteq RS(F \cdot B)$ for every $\sigma \in \Sigma$. By a general linear-algebra argument (see [21]), it further suffices to prove that $\alpha \in RS(F)$ and $RS(\tilde{F} \cdot \mu(\sigma)) \subseteq RS(F)$ for every $\sigma \in \Sigma$.

We have $\alpha = \alpha \cdot \mu(\varepsilon) \in \mathcal{F} = RS(F)$. Let $i \in [m]$. Since $\tilde{F}_i \in RS(F) = \mathcal{F}$, it follows from Proposition 4 (a) that $(\tilde{F} \cdot \mu(\sigma))_i = \tilde{F}_i \cdot \mu(\sigma) \in \mathcal{F}$ for all $\sigma \in \Sigma$. ■

We now show that the automaton $\tilde{\mathcal{A}}$ minimises $\mathcal{A}$:

Lemma 9. *Automaton $\tilde{\mathcal{A}}$ is a minimal MWA equivalent to $\mathcal{A}$.*

Proof. First, we show that $\tilde{\alpha}\tilde{\mu}(w)\tilde{F}B = \alpha\mu(w)B$ for every $w \in \Sigma^*$. Our proof is by induction on the length of w. For the base case, we have $w = \varepsilon$ and by definition of $\tilde{\mathcal{A}}$ it holds that $\tilde{\alpha}\tilde{\mu}(\varepsilon)\tilde{F}B = \tilde{\alpha}\tilde{F}B = \alpha B = \alpha\mu(\varepsilon)B$.

For the induction step, let $l \in \mathbb{N}_0$ and assume that $\tilde{\alpha}\tilde{\mu}(w)\tilde{F}B = \alpha\mu(w)B$ holds for every $w \in \Sigma^l$. Take any $w \in \Sigma^l$ and $\sigma \in \Sigma$. For every $b \in \mathcal{B}$ we have by Proposition 5 (a) that $\mu(\sigma)b \in \mathcal{B}$, and thus by the induction hypothesis

$$\tilde{\alpha}\tilde{\mu}(w\sigma)\tilde{F}b = \tilde{\alpha}\tilde{\mu}(w)\tilde{\mu}(\sigma)\tilde{F}b \overset{\text{Eq. (4)}}{=} \tilde{\alpha}\tilde{\mu}(w)\tilde{F}\mu(\sigma)b = \alpha\mu(w)\mu(\sigma)b = \alpha\mu(w\sigma)b,$$

which completes the induction. Now for any $w \in \Sigma^*$, since $\gamma \in \mathcal{B}$ we have

$$\|\tilde{\mathcal{A}}\|(w) = \tilde{\alpha} \cdot \tilde{\mu}(w) \cdot \tilde{\gamma} = \tilde{\alpha} \cdot \tilde{\mu}(w) \cdot \tilde{F} \cdot \gamma = \alpha \cdot \mu(w) \cdot \gamma = \|\mathcal{A}\|(w).$$

Hence, automata $\tilde{\mathcal{A}}$ and $\mathcal{A}$ are equivalent. Minimality follows from Lemma 6. ■

By a result of Bozapalidis and Alexandrakis [5, Proposition 4], all equivalent minimal MTAs are equal up to a change of basis. Thus the MTA $\tilde{\mathcal{A}}$ is "canonical" in the sense that any minimal MTA equivalent to $\mathcal{A}$ can be obtained from $\tilde{\mathcal{A}}$ via a linear transformation: any m-dimensional MTA $\tilde{\mathcal{A}}' = (m, \Sigma, \tilde{\mu}', \tilde{\gamma}')$ is equivalent to $\mathcal{A}$ if and only if there exists an invertible matrix $U \in \mathbb{F}^{m \times m}$ such that $\tilde{\gamma}' = U \cdot \tilde{\gamma}$ and $\tilde{\mu}'(\sigma) = U^{\otimes rk(\sigma)} \cdot \tilde{\mu}(\sigma) \cdot U^{-1}$ for every $\sigma \in \Sigma$.

3.3 Spanning Sets for the Forward and Backward Spaces

The minimal automaton $\tilde{\mathcal{A}}$ from Section 3.2 is defined in terms of matrices F and B whose rows and columns span the forward space $\mathcal{F}$ and the backward space $\mathcal{B}$, respectively. In fact, the central algorithmic challenge for minimisation lies in the efficient computation of those matrices. In this section we prove a key proposition, Proposition 10 below, suggesting a way to compute F and B, which we exploit in Sections 4.2 and 5.

Propositions 4 and 5 and their proofs already suggest an efficient algorithm for iteratively computing bases of $\mathcal{F}$ and $\mathcal{B}$. We make this algorithm more explicit and analyse its unit-cost complexity in Section 4.1. The drawback of the resulting algorithm will be the use of "if-conditionals": the algorithm branches according to whether certain sets of vectors are linearly independent. Such conditionals are ill-suited for efficient *parallel* algorithms and also for many-one reductions. Thus it cannot be used for an NC-algorithm nor for a reduction to ACIT.

The following proposition exhibits polynomial-size sets of spanning vectors for $\mathcal{F}$ and $\mathcal{B}$, which, as we will see later, can be computed efficiently without branching. The proposition is based on the *product* automaton $\mathcal{A} \times \mathcal{A}$ defined in Proposition 3. It defines a sequence $(f(l))_{l\in\mathbb{N}}$ of row vectors and a sequence $(b(l))_{l\in\mathbb{N}}$ of square matrices. Part (a) states that the vector $f(n)$ and the matrix $b(n)$ determine matrices F and B, whose rows and columns span $\mathcal{F}$ and $\mathcal{B}$, respectively. Part (b) gives a recursive characterization of the sequences $(f(l))_{l\in\mathbb{N}}$ and $(b(l))_{l\in\mathbb{N}}$. This allows for an efficient computation of $f(n)$ and $b(n)$.

Proposition 10. *Let Σ have rank r. Let MTA $\mathcal{A}\times\mathcal{A} = (n^2, \Sigma, \mu', \gamma^{\otimes 2})$ be the product of $\mathcal{A}$ by $\mathcal{A}$. For every $l \in \mathbb{N}$, define $f(l) := \sum_{t\in T_\Sigma^{<l}} \mu'(t) \in \mathbb{F}^{1\times n^2}$ and $b(l) := \sum_{c\in C^{<l}_{\Sigma,T_\Sigma^{<n}}} \mu'(c) \in \mathbb{F}^{n^2\times n^2}$.*

(a) Let $F \in \mathbb{F}^{n\times n}$ be the matrix with $F_{i,j} = f(n)\cdot(e_i\otimes e_j)^\top$. Let $B \in \mathbb{F}^{n\times n}$ be the matrix with $B_{i,j} = (e_i\otimes e_j)\cdot b(n)\cdot\gamma^{\otimes 2}$. Then, $RS(F) = \mathcal{F}$ and $CS(B) = \mathcal{B}$.
(b) We have $f(1) = \sum_{\sigma\in\Sigma_0}\mu'(\sigma)$, $b(1) = I_{n^2}$, and for all $l \in \mathbb{N}$:

$$f(l+1) = \sum_{k=0}^{r} f(l)^{\otimes k} \sum_{\sigma\in\Sigma_k} \mu'(\sigma)$$

$$b(l+1) = I_{n^2} + \sum_{k=1}^{r}\sum_{j=1}^{k} \left(f(n)^{\otimes(j-1)} \otimes b(l) \otimes f(n)^{\otimes(k-j)}\right) \sum_{\sigma\in\Sigma_k} \mu'(\sigma)$$

Proof (sketch). We provide a proof in [21]. Here we only prove the statement $RS(F) = \mathcal{F}$ from part (a). Let $\widehat{F} \in \mathbb{F}^{T_\Sigma^{<n}\times[n]}$ be the matrix such that $\widehat{F}_t = \mu(t)$ for every $t \in T_\Sigma^{<n}$. From Proposition 4 (b) it follows that $RS(\widehat{F}) = \mathcal{F}$. By a general linear-algebra argument (see [21]) we have $RS(\widehat{F}^\top\widehat{F}) = RS(\widehat{F})$ and hence $RS(\widehat{F}^\top\widehat{F}) = \mathcal{F}$. Thus in order to prove that $RS(F) = \mathcal{F}$, it suffices to show that $\widehat{F}^\top\widehat{F} = F$. Indeed, using the mixed-product property of the Kronecker product, we have for all $i, j \in [n]$:

$$\begin{aligned}(\widehat{F}^\top\widehat{F})_{i,j} = (\widehat{F}^\top)_i\cdot(\widehat{F})^j &= \sum_{t\in T_\Sigma^{<n}} \mu(t)_i\cdot\mu(t)_j = \sum_{t\in T_\Sigma^{<n}} (\mu(t)\cdot e_i^\top)\otimes(\mu(t)\cdot e_j^\top)\\ &= \left(\sum_{t\in T_\Sigma^{<n}} (\mu(t)\otimes\mu(t))\right)(e_i\otimes e_j)^\top \overset{\text{Prop. 3}}{=} \left(\sum_{t\in T_\Sigma^{<n}} \mu'(t)\right)(e_i\otimes e_j)^\top\\ &= f(n)\cdot(e_i\otimes e_j)^\top.\end{aligned}$$

■

Loosely speaking, Proposition 10 says that the sum over a small subset of the forward space of the product automaton encodes a spanning set of the whole forward space of the original automaton, and similarly for the backward space.

4 Minimisation Algorithms

In this section we devise algorithms for minimising a given multiplicity automaton: Section 4.1 considers general MTAs, while Section 4.2 considers MWAs. For the sake of a complexity analysis in standard models, we fix the field $\mathbb{F} = \mathbb{Q}$.

4.1 Minimisation of Multiplicity Tree Automata

In this section we describe an implementation of the algorithm implicit in Section 3.2, and analyse the number of operations. We denote by r the rank of Σ.

Step 1 "Forward". The first step is to compute a matrix F whose rows form a basis of $\mathcal{F}$. Seidl [26] outlines a saturation-based algorithm for that and proves that the algorithm takes polynomial time assuming unit-cost arithmetic. Based on Proposition 4 (a) we give in [21] an explicit version of Seidl's algorithm. This allows for the following lemma:

Lemma 11. *There is an algorithm that, given a $\mathbb{Q}$-MTA (n, Σ, μ, γ), computes a matrix F whose rows span the forward space $\mathcal{F}$. Each row of F equals $\mu(t)$ for some tree $t \in T_\Sigma^{<n}$. The algorithm executes $O\left(\sum_{k=0}^{r} |\Sigma_k| \cdot n^{2k+1}\right)$ operations.*

Step 2 "Backward". The next step suggested in Section 3.2 is to compute a matrix B whose columns form a basis of $\mathcal{B}$. Each row of the matrix F computed by the algorithm from Lemma 11 equals $\mu(t)$ for some tree $t \in T_\Sigma^{<n}$. Let S denote the set of those trees. By Proposition 5 (a) we have that $\mathcal{B}$ is the smallest vector space $V \subseteq \mathbb{Q}^n$ such that $\gamma \in V$ and $M \cdot v \in V$ for all $M \in \mathcal{M} := \{\mu(c) : c \in C_{\Sigma,S}^1\}$ and $v \in V$. Tzeng [27] shows, for an arbitrary column vector $\gamma \in \mathbb{Q}^n$ and an arbitrary finite set of matrices $\mathcal{M} \subseteq \mathbb{Q}^{n \times n}$, how to compute a basis of V in time $O(|\mathcal{M}| \cdot n^4)$. This can be improved to $O(|\mathcal{M}| \cdot n^3)$ (see, e.g., [14]). This leads to the following lemma (full proof in [21]):

Lemma 12. *Given the matrix F from Lemma 11, a matrix B whose columns span $\mathcal{B}$ can be computed with $O\left(\sum_{k=1}^{r} |\Sigma_k| \cdot (kn^{2k} + kn^{k+2})\right)$ operations.*

Step 3 "Solve". The final step suggested in Section 3.2 has two substeps. The first substep is to compute a matrix $\tilde{F} \in \mathbb{Q}^{m \times n}$, where $m = \mathit{rank}(F \cdot B)$ and $RS(\tilde{F} \cdot B) = RS(F \cdot B)$. Matrix $\tilde{F}$ can be computed from F by going through the rows of F one by one and including only those rows that are linearly independent of the previous rows when multiplied by B. This can be done in time $O(n^3)$, e.g., by transforming matrix $F \cdot B$ into a triangular form using Gaussian elimination.

The second substep is to compute the minimal MTA $\tilde{\mathcal{A}}$. The vector $\tilde{\gamma} = \tilde{F} \cdot \gamma$ is easy to compute. Solving Equation (2) for each $\tilde{\mu}(\sigma)$ can be done via Gaussian elimination in time $O(n^3)$, however, the bottleneck is the computation of $\tilde{F}^{\otimes k} \cdot \mu(\sigma)$ for every $\sigma \in \Sigma_k$, which takes $O\left(\sum_{k=0}^{r} |\Sigma_k| \cdot n^k \cdot n^k \cdot n\right) = O\left(\sum_{k=0}^{r} |\Sigma_k| \cdot n^{2k+1}\right)$ operations. Combining the results of this section, we get:

Theorem 13. *There is an algorithm that transforms a given $\mathbb{Q}$-MTA $\mathcal{A}$ into an equivalent minimal $\mathbb{Q}$-MTA. Assuming unit-cost arithmetic, the algorithm takes time $O\left(\sum_{k=0}^{r} |\Sigma_k| \cdot (n^{2k+1} + kn^{2k} + kn^{k+2})\right)$, which is $O\left(|\mathcal{A}|^2 \cdot r\right)$.*

4.2 Minimisation of Multiplicity Word Automata in NC

In this section we consider the problem of minimising a given $\mathbb{Q}$-MWA $\mathcal{A} = (n, \Sigma, \mu, \alpha, \gamma)$. We prove the following result:

Theorem 14. *There is an* NC *algorithm that transforms a given $\mathbb{Q}$-MWA into an equivalent minimal $\mathbb{Q}$-MWA. In particular, given a $\mathbb{Q}$-MWA and a number $d \in \mathbb{N}_0$, one can decide in* NC *whether there exists an equivalent $\mathbb{Q}$-MWA of dimension at most d.*

Theorem 14 improves on two results of [22]. First, [22, Theorem 4.2] states that deciding whether a $\mathbb{Q}$-MWA is minimal is in NC. Second, [22, Theorem 4.5] states the same thing as our Theorem 14, but with NC replaced with *randomised* NC.

Proof (of Theorem 14). The algorithm relies on Propositions 7 and 10. Let $\mathcal{A} = (n, \Sigma, \mu, \alpha, \gamma)$ be the given $\mathbb{Q}$-MWA. In the notation of Proposition 10, we have for all $l \in \mathbb{N}$ that $b(l+1) = I_{n^2} + b(l) \cdot \sum_{\sigma \in \Sigma} \mu'(\sigma)$. From here one can easily show, using an induction on l, that $b(n) = \sum_{k=0}^{n-1} \left(\sum_{\sigma\in\Sigma} \mu'(\sigma)\right)^k$. It follows for the matrix $B \in \mathbb{Q}^{n \times n}$ from Proposition 10 that for all $i, j \in [n]$:

$$B_{i,j} = (e_i \otimes e_j) \cdot \left(\sum_{k=0}^{n-1} \Big(\sum_{\sigma \in \Sigma} \mu'(\sigma) \Big)^k \right) \cdot \gamma^{\otimes 2}$$

Similarly, we have for the matrix $F \in \mathbb{Q}^{n \times n}$ from Proposition 10 and all $i, j \in [n]$:

$$F_{i,j} = \alpha^{\otimes 2} \cdot \left(\sum_{k=0}^{n-1} \Big(\sum_{\sigma \in \Sigma} \mu'(\sigma) \Big)^k \right) \cdot (e_i \otimes e_j)^\top .$$

The matrices F, B can be computed in NC since sums and matrix powers can be computed in NC [13]. Next we show how to compute in NC the matrix $\tilde{F}$, which is needed to compute the minimal $\mathbb{Q}$-MWA $\tilde{\mathcal{A}}$ from Section 3.2. Our NC algorithm includes the ith row of F (i.e., F_i) in $\tilde{F}$ if and only if $\mathit{rank}(F_{[i],[n]} \cdot B) > \mathit{rank}(F_{[i-1],[n]} \cdot B)$. This can be done in NC since the rank of a matrix can be computed in NC [19]. It remains to compute $\tilde{\gamma} := \tilde{F}\gamma$ and solve Equations (3) and (4) for $\tilde{\alpha}$ and $\tilde{\mu}(\sigma)$, respectively. Both are easily done in NC. ■

5 Decision Problem

In this section we characterise the complexity of the following decision problem: Given a $\mathbb{Q}$-MTA and a number $d \in \mathbb{N}_0$, the *minimisation* problem asks whether there is an equivalent $\mathbb{Q}$-MTA of dimension at most d. We show, in Theorem 15 below, that this problem is interreducible with the ACIT problem.

The latter problem can be defined as follows. An *arithmetic circuit* is a finite directed acyclic vertex-labelled multigraph whose vertices, called *gates*, have indegree 0 or 2. Vertices of indegree 0, called *input gates*, are labelled with a non-negative integer or a variable from the set $\{x_i : i \in \mathbb{N}\}$. Vertices of indegree 2 are labelled with one of the arithmetic operations $+$, $\times$, or $-$. One can associate, in a straightforward inductive way, each gate with the polynomial it computes. The *Arithmetic Circuit Identity Testing (*ACIT*)* problem asks, given an arithmetic circuit and a gate, whether the polynomial computed by the gate is equal to the zero polynomial. We show:

Theorem 15. *Minimisation is logspace interreducible with* ACIT.

We consider the lower and the upper bound separately.

Lower Bound. Given a $\mathbb{Q}$-MTA $\mathcal{A}$, the *zeroness* problem asks whether $\|\mathcal{A}\|(t) = 0$ for all trees t. Observe that $\|\mathcal{A}\|(t) = 0$ for all trees t if and only if there exists an equivalent automaton of dimension 0. Therefore, zeroness is a special case of minimisation. We prove:

Proposition 16. *There is a logspace reduction from* ACIT *to zeroness.*

This implies ACIT-hardness of minimisation.

Proof (of Proposition 16). It is shown in [24] that the *equivalence* problem for $\mathbb{Q}$-MTAs is logspace equivalent to ACIT. This problems asks, given two $\mathbb{Q}$-MTAs $\mathcal{A}_1$ and $\mathcal{A}_2$, whether $\|\mathcal{A}_1\|(t) = \|\mathcal{A}_2\|(t)$ holds for all trees t. By Proposition 3 one can reduce this problem to zeroness in logarithmic space. ■

Upper Bound. We prove:

Proposition 17. *There is a logspace reduction from minimisation to* ACIT.

Proof. Let $\mathcal{A} = (n, \Sigma, \mu, \gamma)$ be the $\mathbb{Q}$-MTA, and $d \in \mathbb{N}_0$ the given number. In our reduction to ACIT we allow input gates with rational labels as well as division gates. Rational numbers and division gates can be eliminated in a standard way by constructing separate gates for the numerators and denominators of the rational numbers computed by the original gates.

By Lemma 6, the dimension of a minimal automaton equivalent to $\mathcal{A}$ is $m := \mathit{rank}(F \cdot B)$ where F, B are matrices with $\mathit{RS}(F) = \mathcal{F}$ and $\mathit{CS}(B) = \mathcal{B}$. Thus we have $m \leq d$ if and only if $\mathit{rank}(F \cdot B) \leq d$. The recursive characterisation of F and B from Proposition 10 allows us to compute in logarithmic space an arithmetic circuit for $F \cdot B$. Thus, the result follows from Lemma 18 below. ■

The following lemma follows easily from the well-known NC procedure for computing matrix rank [15].

Lemma 18. *Let $M \in \mathbb{Q}^{m \times n}$. Let $d \in \mathbb{N}_0$. The problem of deciding whether $\mathit{rank}(M) \leq d$ is logspace reducible to* ACIT.

Proof. We have $\mathit{rank}(M) \leq d$ if and only if $\dim \mathit{ker}(M) \geq n - d$. As $\mathit{ker}(M) = \mathit{ker}(M^T M)$, this is equivalent to $\dim \mathit{ker}(M^T M) \geq n - d$. Now $M^T M$ is Hermitian, so $\dim \mathit{ker}(M^T M) \geq n - d$ if and only if the $n - d$ lowest-order coefficients of the characteristic polynomial of $M^T M$ are all zero [19]. But these coefficients are representable by arithmetic circuits with inputs from M (see [15]). ■

We emphasise that our reduction to ACIT is a many-one reduction, thanks to Proposition 10: our reduction computes only a single instance of ACIT; there are no if-conditionals.

6 Minimal Consistent Multiplicity Automaton

Fix a field $\mathbb{F}$ of characteristic 0. A natural computational problem is to compute an $\mathbb{F}$-MWA $\mathcal{A}$ of minimal dimension that is consistent with a given finite set of $\mathbb{F}$-weighted words $S = \{(w_1, r_1), \ldots, (w_m, r_m)\}$, where $w_i \in \Sigma^*$ and $r_i \in \mathbb{F}$ for every $i \in [m]$. Here *consistency* means that $\|\mathcal{A}\|(w_i) = r_i$ for every $i \in [m]$.

The above problem can be studied in the Blum-Shub-Smale model [2] of computation over a field $\mathbb{F}$. Since we wish to stay within the conventional Turing model, we consider instead a decision version of the problem, which we call *minimal consistency problem*, in which the output weights r_i are all rational numbers and we ask whether there exists an $\mathbb{F}$-MWA consistent with the set of input-output behaviours S that has dimension at most some non-negative integer bound n. We show that the minimal consistency problem is logspace equivalent to the problem of deciding the truth of first-order sentences over the field $(\mathbb{F}, +, \cdot, 0, 1)$. In case $\mathbb{F} = \mathbb{R}$ the latter problem is in PSPACE [8], whereas over $\mathbb{Q}$ decidability is open. This should be compared with the result that the problem of finding the smallest deterministic automaton consistent with a set of accepted or rejected strings is NP-complete [17].

The reduction of the minimal consistency problem to the decision problem for existential sentences is immediate. The idea is to represent an $\mathbb{F}$-MWA $\mathcal{A} = (n, \Sigma, \mu, \alpha, \gamma)$ "symbolically" by introducing separate variables for each entry of the initial weight vector α, final weight vector γ, and each transition matrix $\mu(\sigma)$, $\sigma \in \Sigma$. Then, consistency of automaton $\mathcal{A}$ with a given finite sample $S \subseteq \Sigma^* \times \mathbb{Q}$ can directly be written as an existential sentence.

Conversely, we reduce the decision problem for sentences of the form

$$\exists x_1 \ldots \exists x_n \bigwedge_{i=1}^{m} f_i(x_1, \ldots, x_n) = 0\,, \tag{5}$$

where $f_i(x_1, \ldots, x_n) = \sum_{j=1}^{l_i} c_{i,j} x_1^{k_{i,j,1}} \cdots x_n^{k_{i,j,n}}$ is a polynomial with rational coefficients, to the minimal consistency problem. It suffices to consider conjunctions of positive atoms in the matrix of (5) since $f = 0 \vee g = 0$ is equivalent to $\exists x\,(x^2 - x = 0 \wedge xf = 0 \wedge (1-x)g = 0)$ and $f \neq 0$ is equivalent to $\exists x\,(fx = 1)$ for polynomials f and g.

Define an alphabet $\Sigma = \{s, t\} \cup \{\#_i, \bar{c}_{i,j}, \bar{x}_k : i \in [m], j \in [l_i], k \in [n]\}$, including symbols $\bar{c}_{i,j}$ and $\bar{x}_k$ for each coefficient $c_{i,j}$ and variable x_k respectively. Over alphabet Σ we consider the 3-dimensional $\mathbb{F}$-MWA $\mathcal{A}$, depicted in Figure 1 (b). The transitions in this automaton are annotated by label-weight pairs in $\Sigma \times \mathbb{F}$ or simply by labels from Σ, in which case the weight is assumed to be 1. Recall that the weights $c_{i,j}$ are coefficients of the polynomials f_i. For each $k \in [n]$, the weight a_k is a fixed but arbitrary element of $\mathbb{F}$.

	st	t	ε
ε	1	0	0
s	0	1	0
st	0	0	1
$\#_i$	1	1	0
$s\#_i$	0	0	1
$st\#_i$	0	0	1
$\bar{c}_{i,j}$	1	0	0
$s\bar{c}_{i,j}$	0	$c_{i,j}$	0
$st\bar{c}_{i,j}$	0	0	1
$\bar{x}_k$	1	0	0
$s\bar{x}_k$	0	a_k	0
$st\bar{x}_k$	0	0	1
t	0	0	0
stt	0	0	0
ss	0	0	0
sts	0	0	0

(a)

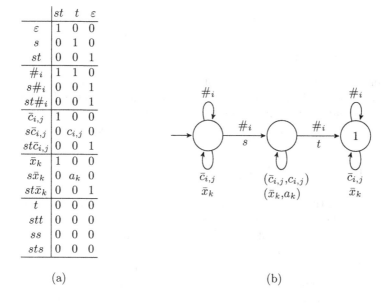

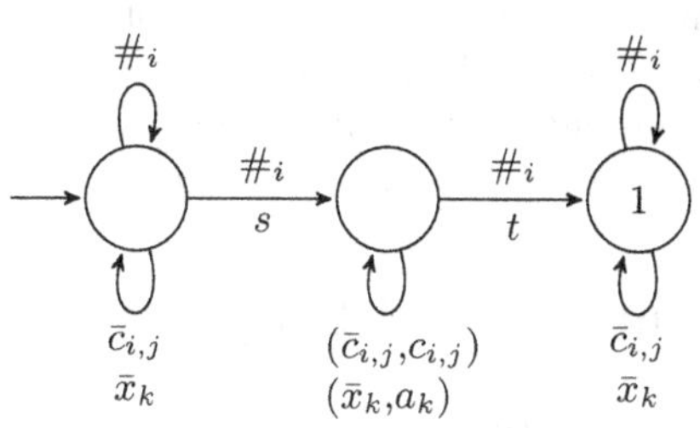

(b)

Fig. 1. The left figure (a) shows a Hankel-matrix fragment $\tilde{H}$, where $i \in [m]$, $j \in [l_i]$, $k \in [n]$. The right figure (b) shows a graph representation of the automaton $\mathcal{A}$.

Define $X, Y \subseteq \Sigma^*$ by $X = \{\varepsilon, s, st\}$ and $Y = \{st, t, \varepsilon\}$, and consider the fragment $\tilde{H} = H_{X \cup X\Sigma, Y}$, shown in Figure 1 (a), of the Hankel matrix H of $\mathcal{A}$. Since $rank(\tilde{H}) = 3 = rank(H)$, from Remark 2 it follows that any 3-dimensional $\mathbb{F}$-MWA $\mathcal{A}'$ that is consistent with $\tilde{H}$ is equivalent to $\mathcal{A}$.

Now for every $i \in [m]$, we encode polynomial f_i by the word

$$w_i := \#_i \bar{c}_{i,1} \bar{x}_1^{k_{i,1,1}} \ldots \bar{x}_n^{k_{i,1,n}} \ldots \#_i \bar{c}_{i,l_i} \bar{x}_1^{k_{i,l_i,1}} \ldots \bar{x}_n^{k_{i,l_i,n}} \#_i$$

over alphabet Σ. Note that w_i comprises l_i 'blocks' of symbols, corresponding to the l_i monomials in f_i, with each block enclosed by two $\#_i$ symbols. From the definition of w_i it follows that $\|\mathcal{A}\|(w_i) = f_i(a_1, \ldots, a_n)$.

Define the set $S \subseteq \Sigma^* \times \mathbb{Q}$ of weighted words as $S := S_1 \cup S_2$, where S_1 is the set of all pairs $(uv, \tilde{H}_{u,v})$ with $u \in X \cup X\Sigma$, $v \in Y$, and $uv \notin \{s\bar{x}_k t : k \in [n]\}$, and $S_2 := \{(w_i, 0) : i \in [m]\}$.

Any 3-dimensional $\mathbb{F}$-MWA $\mathcal{A}'$ consistent with S_1 is equivalent to an automaton of the form $\mathcal{A}$ for some $a_1, \ldots, a_n \in \mathbb{F}$. If $\mathcal{A}'$ is moreover consistent with S_2, then $f_i(a_1, \ldots, a_n) = 0$ for every $i \in [m]$. From this observation we have the following proposition (proof in [21]).

Proposition 19. *The sample S is consistent with a 3-dimensional $\mathbb{F}$-MWA if and only if the sentence (5) is true in $\mathbb{F}$.*

From Proposition 19 we derive the main result of this section:

Theorem 20. *The minimal consistency problem for $\mathbb{F}$-MWAs is logspace equivalent to the decision problem for existential first-order sentences over $\mathbb{F}$.*

Theorem 20 also holds for $\mathbb{F}$-MTAs of a fixed alphabet rank, because the minimal consistency problem can be reduced to the decision problem for existential first-order sentences over $\mathbb{F}$ in similar manner to the case for words. Here, fixing the alphabet rank keeps the reduction in polynomial time.

7 Conclusions and Future Work

We have looked at the problem of minimising a given multiplicity tree automaton from several angles. Specifically, we have analysed the complexity of *computing* a minimal automaton in the unit-cost model, of the minimisation *decision problem*, and of the *minimal consistency problem*. One of the key technical contributions of our work is Proposition 10, which, based on the product of a given automaton by itself, provides small spanning sets for forward space $\mathcal{F}$ and backward space $\mathcal{B}$. This technology also led us to an NC algorithm for minimising multiplicity *word* automata, thus improving the best previous algorithms (polynomial time and randomised NC).

It is an open question whether the complexity of the minimal consistency problem for $\mathbb{F}$-MTAs is higher if the alphabet rank is not fixed. We also plan to investigate *probabilistic* tree automata, a class that lies strictly between deterministic and multiplicity tree automata.

Acknowledgements. The authors would like to thank Michael Benedikt for stimulating discussions, and anonymous referees for their helpful suggestions. Kiefer is supported by a University Research Fellowship of the Royal Society. Marusic and Worrell gratefully acknowledge the support of the EPSRC.

References

1. Berstel, J., Reutenauer, C.: Recognizable formal power series on trees. Theoretical Computer Science 18(2), 115–148 (1982)
2. Blum, L., Cucker, F., Shub, M., Smale, S.: Complexity and real computation. Springer (1997)
3. Borchardt, B.: A pumping lemma and decidability problems for recognizable tree series. Acta Cybern. 16(4), 509–544 (2004)
4. Bozapalidis, S.: Effective construction of the syntactic algebra of a recognizable series on trees. Acta Inf. 28(4), 351–363 (1991)
5. Bozapalidis, S., Alexandrakis, A.: Représentations matricielles des séries d'arbre reconnaissables. RAIRO-Theoretical Informatics and Applications-Informatique Théorique et Applications 23(4), 449–459 (1989)
6. Bozapalidis, S., Louscou-Bozapalidou, O.: The rank of a formal tree power series. Theoretical Computer Science 27(1), 211–215 (1983)

7. Brainerd, W.S.: The minimalization of tree automata. Information and Control 13(5), 484–491 (1968)
8. Canny, J.: Some algebraic and geometric computations in PSPACE. In: Proceedings of STOC 1988, pp. 460–467. ACM (1988)
9. Carlyle, J.W., Paz, A.: Realizations by stochastic finite automata. Journal of Computer and System Sciences 5(1), 26–40 (1971)
10. Carme, J., Gilleron, R., Lemay, A., Terlutte, A., Tommasi, M.: Residual finite tree automata. In: Ésik, Z., Fülöp, Z. (eds.) DLT 2003. LNCS, vol. 2710, pp. 171–182. Springer, Heidelberg (2003)
11. Carrasco, R.C., Daciuk, J., Forcada, M.L.: An implementation of deterministic tree automata minimization. In: Holub, J., Žďárek, J. (eds.) CIAA 2007. LNCS, vol. 4783, pp. 122–129. Springer, Heidelberg (2007)
12. Cho, S., Huynh, D.T.: The parallel complexity of finite-state automata problems. Inf. Comput. 97(1), 1–22 (1992)
13. Cook, S.A.: A taxonomy of problems with fast parallel algorithms. Information and Control 64(1-3), 2–22 (1985)
14. Cortes, C., Mohri, M., Rastogi, A.: On the computation of some standard distances between probabilistic automata. In: Ibarra, O.H., Yen, H.-C. (eds.) CIAA 2006. LNCS, vol. 4094, pp. 137–149. Springer, Heidelberg (2006)
15. Csanky, L.: Fast parallel matrix inversion algorithms. SIAM J. Comput. 5(4), 618–623 (1976)
16. Fliess, M.: Matrices de Hankel. Journal de Mathématiques Pures et Appliquées 53, 197–222 (1974)
17. Gold, E.M.: Complexity of automaton identification from given data. Information and Control 37(3), 302–320 (1978)
18. Habrard, A., Oncina, J.: Learning multiplicity tree automata. In: Sakakibara, Y., Kobayashi, S., Sato, K., Nishino, T., Tomita, E. (eds.) ICGI 2006. LNCS (LNAI), vol. 4201, pp. 268–280. Springer, Heidelberg (2006)
19. Ibarra, O.H., Moran, S., Rosier, L.E.: A note on the parallel complexity of computing the rank of order n matrices. Information Processing Letters 11(4/5), 162 (1980)
20. Jiang, T., Ravikumar, B.: Minimal NFA problems are hard. SIAM J. Comput. 22(6), 1117–1141 (1993)
21. Kiefer, S., Marusic, I., Worrell, J.: Minimisation of multiplicity tree automata. Technical report, arxiv.org (2014), `http://arxiv.org/abs/1410.535`
22. Kiefer, S., Murawski, A., Ouaknine, J., Wachter, B., Worrell, J.: On the complexity of equivalence and minimisation for $\mathbb{Q}$-weighted automata. Logical Methods in Computer Science 9(1) (2013)
23. Maletti, A.: Minimizing deterministic weighted tree automata. Inf. Comput. 207(11), 1284–1299 (2009)
24. Marusic, I., Worrell, J.: Complexity of equivalence and learning for multiplicity tree automata. In: Csuhaj-Varjú, E., Dietzfelbinger, M., Ésik, Z. (eds.) MFCS 2014, Part I. LNCS, vol. 8634, pp. 414–425. Springer, Heidelberg (2014)
25. Schützenberger, M.P.: On the definition of a family of automata. Information and Control 4(2-3), 245–270 (1961)
26. Seidl, H.: Deciding equivalence of finite tree automata. SIAM J. Comput. 19(3), 424–437 (1990)
27. Tzeng, W.-G.: A polynomial-time algorithm for the equivalence of probabilistic automata. SIAM J. Comput. 21(2), 216–227 (1992)

Robust Multidimensional Mean-Payoff Games are Undecidable

Yaron Velner*

The Blavatnik School of Computer Science, Tel Aviv University, Israel

Abstract. Mean-payoff games play a central role in quantitative synthesis and verification. In a single-dimensional game a weight is assigned to every transition and the objective of the protagonist is to assure a non-negative limit-average weight. In the multidimensional setting, a weight vector is assigned to every transition and the objective of the protagonist is to satisfy a boolean condition over the limit-average weight of each dimension, e.g., $LimAvg(x_1) \leq 0 \vee LimAvg(x_2) \geq 0 \wedge LimAvg(x_3) \geq 0$. We recently proved that when one of the players is restricted to finite-memory strategies then the decidability of determining the winner is inter-reducible with Hilbert's Tenth problem over rationals (a fundamental long-standing open problem). In this work we consider arbitrary (infinite-memory) strategies for both players and show that the problem is undecidable.

1 Introduction

Two-player games on graphs provide the mathematical foundation for the study of reactive systems. In these games, the set of vertices is partitioned into player-1 and player-2 vertices; initially, a pebble is placed on an initial vertex, and in every round, the player who owns the vertex that the pebble resides in, advances the pebble to an adjacent vertex. This process is repeated forever and give rise to a *play* that induces an infinite sequence of edges. In the quantitative framework, an objective assigns a value to every play, and the goal of player 1 is to assure a value of at least ν to the objective. In order to have robust quantitative specifications, it is necessary to investigate games on graphs with multiple (and possibly conflicting) objectives. Typically, multiple objectives are modeled by multidimensional weight functions (e.g., [4,5,7,1]), and the outcome of a *play* is a vector of values $(r_1, r_2, \ldots, r_k)$. A *robust specification* is a boolean formula over the atoms $r_i \sim \nu_i$, for $\sim \in \{\leq, <, \geq, >\}, i \in \{1, \ldots, k\}$ and $\nu_i \in \mathbb{Q}$. For example, $\varphi = ((r_1 \geq 9 \vee r_2 \leq 9) \wedge r_3 < 0 \wedge r_4 > 9)$. The most well studied quantitative metric is the mean-payoff objective, which assigns the limit-average (long-run average) weight to an infinite sequence of weights (and if the limit does not exist, then we consider the limit infimum of the sequence). In this setting, r_i is the limit-average of dimension i of the weight function, and the goal of player 1 is to satisfy the boolean condition. In this work we prove that determining whether player 1 can satisfy such a condition is undecidable.

* The author was funded by the European Research Council under the European Unions Seventh Framework Program (FP7/20072013) / ERC grant agreement no. [321174-VSSC].

A. Pitts (Ed.): FOSSACS 2015, LNCS 9034, pp. 312–327, 2015.
DOI: 10.1007/978-3-662-46678-0_20

Related Work. The model checking problem (one-player game) for such objectives (with some extensions) was considered in [1,6,3,12,13] and decidability was established. Two-player games for restricted subclasses that contain only conjunction of atoms were studied in [15,7,2,9] and tight complexity bounds were obtained (and in particular, the problem was proved to be decidable). In [16] a subclass that contains disjunction and conjunction of atoms of the form $r_i \sim \nu_i$ for $\sim \in \{\geq, >\}$ was studied and decidability was shown. In [14] we considered a similar objective but restricted player-1 to play only with finite-memory strategies. We showed that the problem is provably hard to solve and its decidability is inter-reducible with Hilbert's tenth problem over rationals — a fundamental long standing open problem. In this work we consider for the first time games with robust quantitative class of specifications that is closed under boolean union, intersection and complement with arbitrary (infinite-memory) strategies.

Undecidability for (single-dimensional) mean-payoff games was proved for partial information mean-payoff games [10] and for mean-payoff games that are played over infinite-state pushdown automata [8]. These works did not exploit the different properties of the $\geq$ and $\leq$ operators (which correspond to the different properties of limit-infimum-average and limit-supremum-average). To the best of our knowledge, the undecidability proof in the paper is the first to exploit these properties. (As we mentioned before, when we consider only the $\geq$ and $>$ operators, the problem is decidable.)

Robust multidimensional mean-payoff games were independently suggested as a subject to future research by Alur et al [1], by us [16], and by Doyen [11].

Structure of this Paper. In the next section we give the formal definitions for robust multidimensional mean-payoff games. We prove undecidability by a reduction from the halting problem of a two-counter machine. For this purpose we first present a reduction from the halting problem of a one-counter machine and then we extend it to two-counter machine. In Section 3 we present the reduction and give an intuition about its correctness. In Section 4 we give a formal proof for the correctness of the reduction and extend the reduction to two-counter machine. Due to lack of space, some of the proof are omitted. Full proofs are available in the technical report [17].

2 Robust Multidimensional Mean-Payoff Games

Game Graphs. A *game graph* $G = ((V, E), (V_1, V_2))$ consists of a *finite* directed graph (V, E) with a set of vertices V a set of edges E, and a partition (V_1, V_2) of V into two sets. The vertices in V_1 are *player-1 vertices*, where player 1 chooses the outgoing edges, and the vertices in V_2 are *player 2 vertices*, where player 2 (the adversary to player 1) chooses the outgoing edges. We assume that every vertex has at least one out-going edge.

Plays. A game is played by two players: player 1 and player 2, who form an infinite path in the game graph by moving a token along edges. They start by placing the token on an initial vertex, and then they take moves indefinitely in the following way. If the token is on a vertex in V_1, then player 1 moves the token along one of the edges going out of the vertex. If the token is on a vertex in V_2, then player 2 does likewise. The result is an infinite path in the game graph, called *plays*. Formally, a *play* is an infinite sequence of vertices such that $(v_k, v_{k+1}) \in E$ for all $k \geq 0$.

Strategies. A strategy for a player is a rule that specifies how to extend plays. Formally, a *strategy* τ for player 1 is a function $\tau \colon V^* \cdot V_1 \to V$ that, given a finite sequence of vertices (representing the history of the play so far) which ends in a player 1 vertex, chooses the next vertex. The strategy must choose only available successors. The strategies for player 2 are defined analogously. A winning objective is a subset of V^ω and a strategy is a winning strategy if it assures that every formed play is in the winning objective.

Multidimensional Mean-Payoff Objectives. For multidimensional mean-payoff objectives we will consider game graphs along with a weight function $w : E \to \mathbb{Q}^k$ that maps each edge to a vector of rational weights. For a finite path π, we denote by $w(\pi)$ the sum of the weight vectors of the edges in π and $avg(\pi) = \frac{w(\pi)}{|\pi|}$, where $|\pi|$ is the length of π, denote the average vector of the weights. We denote by $avg_i(\pi)$ the projection of $avg(\pi)$ to the i-th dimension. For an infinite path π, let π_i denote the finite prefix of length i of π; and we define $LimInfAvg_i(\pi) = \liminf_{i\to\infty} avg(\rho_i)$ and analogously $LimSupAvg_i(\pi)$ with lim inf replaced by lim sup. For an infinite path π, we denote by $LimInfAvg(\pi) = (LimInfAvg_1(\pi), \ldots, LimInfAvg_k(\pi))$ (resp. $LimSupAvg(\pi) = (LimSupAvg_1(\pi), \ldots, LimSupAvg_k(\pi))$) the limit-inf (resp. limit-sup) vector of the averages (long-run average or mean-payoff objectives). A multidimensional mean-payoff condition is a boolean formula over the atoms $LimInfAvg_i \sim \nu_i$ for $\sim \in \{\geq, >, \leq, >\}$. For example, the formula $LimInfAvg_1 > 8 \vee LimInfAvg_2 \leq -10 \wedge LimInfAvg < 9$ is a possible condition and a path π satisfies the formula if $LimInfAvg_1(\pi) > 8 \vee LimInfAvg_2(\pi) \leq -10 \wedge LimInfAvg(\pi) < 9$. We note that we may always assume that the boolean formula is positive (i.e., without negation), as, for example, we can always replace $\neg(r \geq \nu)$ with $r < \nu$.

For a given multidimensional weighted graph and a multidimensional mean-payoff condition, we say that player 1 is the winner of the game if he has a winning strategy that satisfy the condition against any player-2 strategy.

For an infinite sequence or reals $x_1, x_2, x_3, \ldots$ we have $LimInfAvg(x_1, x_2, \ldots) = -LimSupAvg(-x_1, -x_2, \ldots)$. Hence, an equivalent formulation for multidimensional mean-payoff condition is a positive boolean formula over the atoms $LimInfAvg_i \sim \nu_i$ and $LimSupAvg_i \sim \nu_i$ for $\sim \in \{\geq, >\}$. For positive formulas in which only the $LimInfAvg_i \sim \nu_i$ occur, determining the winner is decidable by [16]. In the sequel we abbreviate $LimInfAvg_i$ with $\underline{i}$ and $LimSupAvg_i$ with $\bar{i}$. In this work we prove undecidability for the general case and for this purpose it is enough to consider only the $\geq$ operator and thresholds 0. Hence, in the sequel, whenever it is clear that the threshold is 0, we abbreviate the condition $\underline{i} \geq 0$ with $\underline{i}$ and $\bar{i} \geq 0$ with $\bar{i}$. For example, $\underline{i} \vee \bar{j} \wedge \underline{\ell}$ stands for $LimInfAvg_i \geq 0 \vee LimSupAvg_j \geq 0 \wedge LimInfAvg_\ell \geq 0$. By further abuse of notation we abbreviate the current total weight in dimension i by i (and make sure that the meaning of i is always clear from the context) and the absolute value of the total weight by $|i|$.

3 Reduction from the Halting Problem and Informal Proof of Correctness

In this chapter we prove the undecidability of determining the winner in games over general multidimensional mean-payoff condition by a reduction from the halting problem of two-counter machine. For this purpose we will first show a reduction from the halting problem of a one-counter machine to multidimensional mean-payoff games, and the reduction from two-counter machines relies on similar techniques. We first give a formal definition for a one-counter machine, and in order to simplify the proofs we give a non-standard definition that is tailored for our needs. A *two-sided one-counter machine* M consists of two finite set of control states, namely Q (*left states*) and P (*right states*), an initial state $q_0 \in Q$, a final state $q_f \in Q$, a finite set of *left to right* instructions $\delta_{\ell \to r}$ and a finite set of *right to left* instructions $\delta_{r \to \ell}$. An instruction determines the next state and manipulates the value of the counter c (and initially the value of c is 0). A left to right instruction is of the form of either:

- $q : \mathit{if}\, c = 0\ \mathit{goto}\ p\ \mathit{else}\ c := c - 1\ \mathit{goto}\ p'$, for $q \in Q$ and $p, p' \in P$; or
- $q : \mathit{goto}\ p$, for $q \in Q$ and $p \in P$ (the value of c does not change).

A right to left instruction is of the form of either

- $p : c := c + 1\ \mathit{goto}\ q$, for $p \in P$ and $q \in Q$; or
- $p : \mathit{goto}\ q$, for a state $p \in P$ and a state $q \in Q$ (the value of c does not change).

We observe that in our model, decrement operations are allowed only in left to right instructions and increment operations are allowed only in right to left instructions. However, since the model allows state transitions that do not change the value of the counter (*nop transitions*), it is trivial to simulate a standard one-counter machine by a two-sided counter machine.

For the reduction we use the states of the game graph to simulate the states of the counter machine and we use two dimensions to simulate the value of the one counter. In the most high level view our reduction consists of three main gadgets, namely, reset, sim and blame (see Figure 1), and a state q_f that represents the final state of the counter machine. Intuitively, in the sim gadget player 1 simulates the counter machine, and if the final state q_f is reached then player 1 loses. If player 2 detects that player 1 does not simulate the machine correctly, then the play goes to the blame gadget. From the blame gadget the play will eventually arrive to the reset gadget. This gadget assigns proper values for all the dimensions of the game that are suited for an honest simulation in the sim gadget. When a play leaves the reset gadget, it goes to the first state of the simulation gadget which represent the first state of the counter machine.

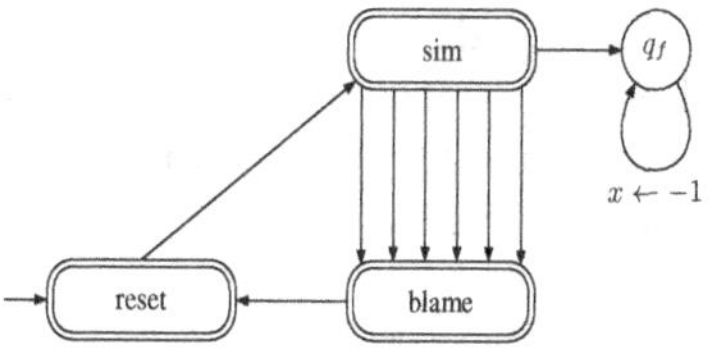

Fig. 1. Overview

We now describe the construction with more details. We first present the winning objective and then we describe each of the three gadgets. For a two-sided counter machine M we construct a game graph with 8 dimensions denoted by $\ell, r, g_s, c_+, c_-, g_c, x$ and y and the objective $[(\underline{\ell} \wedge \underline{r} \vee \overline{g_s}) \wedge (\underline{c_+} \wedge \underline{c_-} \vee \overline{g_c}) \wedge \overline{x} \wedge \overline{y}$.

The Sim Gadget. In the sim gadget player 1 suppose to simulate the run of M, and if the simulation is not honest, then player 2 activates a blame gadget. The simulation of the states is straight forward (since the game graph has states), and the difficulty is to simulate the counter value, more specifically, to simulate the zero testing of the counter. For this purpose we use the dimensions r, ℓ, g_s and c_+, c_-, g_c.

We first describe the role of r, ℓ and g_s. The reset gadget makes sure that in every invocation of the sim gadget, we have $avg(g_s) \approx -1, avg(r) \approx 1$ and $avg(\ell) \approx 0$. (The reader should read $a \approx b$ as "the value of a is *very close* to the value of b". Precise definitions are given in Section 4.) Then, during the simulation the value of g_s is always negative, and the blame gadget makes sure that player 1 must play in such a way that whenever the machine M is in a right state, $r \approx |g_s|$ and $\ell \approx 0$, and whenever the machine is in a left state, then $r \approx 0$ and $\ell \approx |g_s|$. Intuitively, the role of ℓ and r is to make sure that every left to right or right to left transition is simulated by a *significant* number of rounds in the sim gadget, and g_s is a *guard* dimension that makes sure that the above assumptions on r and ℓ are satisfied.

We now describe the role of c_+, c_- and g_c. In the beginning of each simulation (i.e., every time that the sim gadget is invoked), we have $avg(c_+) \approx avg(c_-) \approx 1$ and $avg(g_c) \approx -1$. During the entire simulation we have $avg(g_c) \approx -1$ and if c is the value of the counter in the current simulation (i.e., since the sim gadget was invoked), then $c_+ \approx |g_c| + |g_s|c$ and $c_- \approx |g_c| - |g_s|c$. Intuitively, whenever $c > 0$, then $c_- \ll |g_c|$, and if $c < 0$ (this can happen only if player 1 is dishonest), then $c_+ \ll |g_c|$ (the reader should read $a \ll b$ as "a is much smaller than b").

We now describe the gadgets that simulate the operations of inc, dec and nop. The gadgets are illustrated in Figures 2-5 and the following conventions are used: (i) Player 1 owns the ○ vertices, player 2 owns the □ vertices, and the ⧈ vertex stands for a gadget; (ii) A transition is labeled either with $a \leftarrow b$ symbol or with a text (e.g., blame). For a transition e the label $a \leftarrow b$ stands for $w_a(e) = b$. Whenever the weight of a dimension is not explicitly presented, then the weight is 0. We use text labels only to give intuition on the role of the transition. In such transitions the weights of all dimensions are 0.

In order to satisfy the invariants, in the first state of every inc, dec or nop gadget, in a left to right transition, player 1 always moves to the state below (namely, to $\ell \ll 0$?) until $\ell \approx 0$ and $r \approx |g_s|$, and in a right to left transition he always moves to the state below (namely, to $r \ll 0$?) loops until $r \approx 0$ and $\ell \approx |g_s|$. If in a left to right gadget the loop is followed too many times, then ℓ is decremented too many times and player 2 has an incentive invokes the $\ell \ll 0$ gadget. If the loop was not followed enough times, then r was not incremented enough times and player 2 invokes the $r \ll |g_s|$ blame gadget. Hence, the blame gadgets allows player 2 to blame player 1 for violating the assumptions about the values of ℓ, r and g_s.

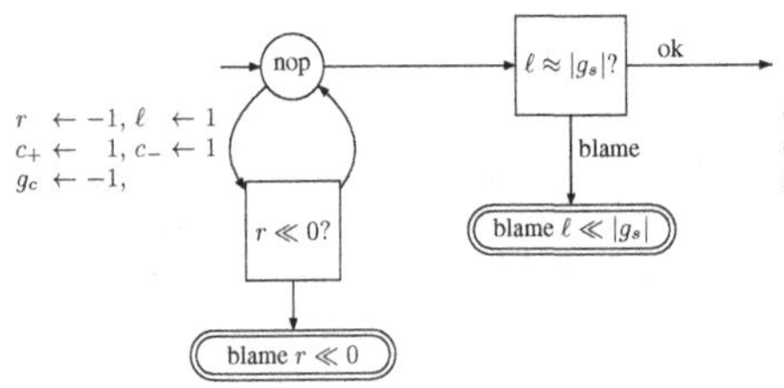

Fig. 2. nop $r \to \ell$ gadget

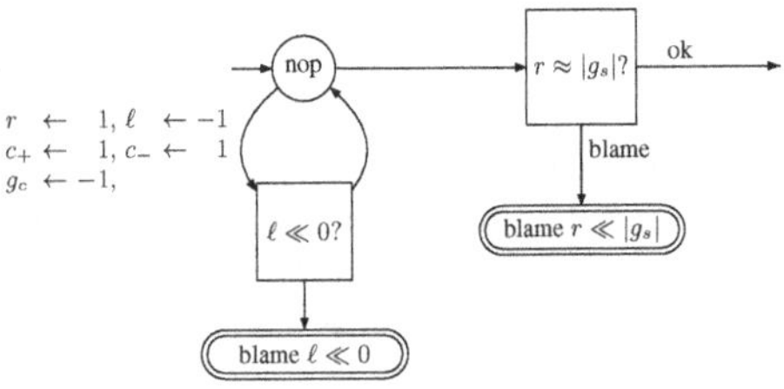

Fig. 3. nop $\ell \to r$ gadget

A transition q : *if* $c = 0$ *goto* p *else* $c := c - 1$ *goto* p', for $q \in Q$ and $p, p' \in P$ is described in Figure 6.

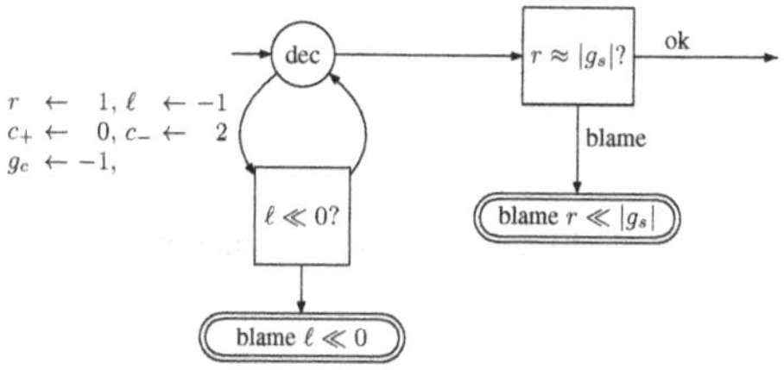

Fig. 4. dec $\ell \to r$ gadget

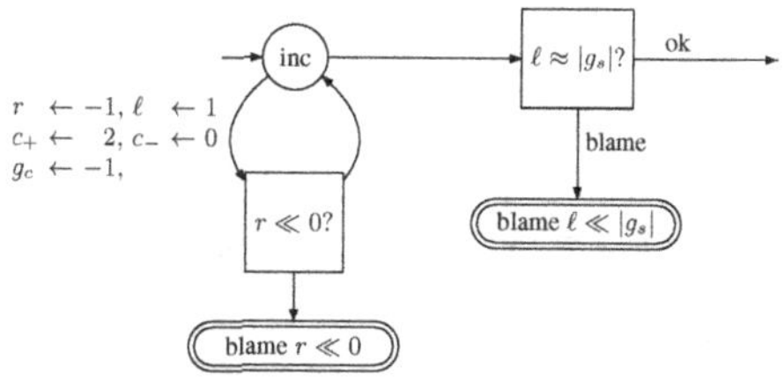

Fig. 5. inc $r \to \ell$ gadget

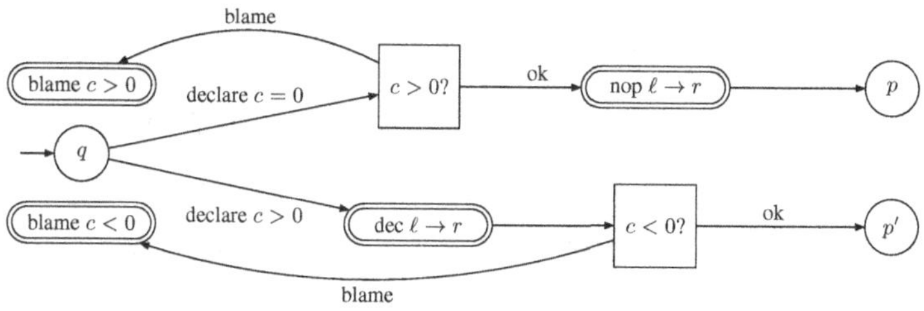

Fig. 6. q : if $c = 0$ then goto p else $c := c - 1$ goto p'

The Blame Gadgets. The role of the blame gadgets is to make sure that the assumptions on ℓ, r and g_s are kept in the simulation and to make sure that the zero testing is honestly simulated. There are six blame gadgets. Four for the honest simulation of r, ℓ and g_s, and two for the zero testing (one for $c > 0$ and one for $c < 0$). The gadgets are described in Figures 7-12. In the blame $r \ll 0$ and blame $\ell \ll 0$ gadgets the play immediately continues to the reset gadget. The concept of the other four gadgets is similar and hence we describe only the blame $r \ll |g_s|$ gadget. We note that in an honest simulation we have $avg(r), avg(\ell), avg(c_+), avg(c_-) \gtrapprox 0$ in every round. Hence, if player 1 honestly simulates M and M does not halt, then the winning condition is satisfied. The $r \ll |g_s|$ blame gadget is described in Figure 12. If the gadget is invoked and $r \ll |g_s|$, then player 2 can loop on the first state until $r \ll 0$ and still have $g_s \ll 0$. If $r \approx g_s$, then whenever we have $r \ll 0$ we will also have $g_s \gtrapprox 0$, and thus the winning objective is still satisfied. We note that player 2 should eventually exit the blame gadget, since otherwise he will lose the game.

The Reset Gadget. The role of the reset gadget is to assign the following values for the dimensions: $avg(\ell) \approx 0, avg(r) \approx 1, avg(g_s) \approx -1, avg(c_-) \approx avg(c_+) \approx 1, avg(g_c) \approx -1$. The gadget is described in Figure 13. We construct the gadget is such way that each of the players can enforce the above values (player 2 by looping enough times on the first state, player 1 by looping enough time on his two states). But the construction only gives this option to the players and it does not *punish* a player if he acts differently. However, the game graph is constructed in such way that if:

- M does not halt and in the reset gadget, at least one of the players, correctly resets the values, then player 1 wins.

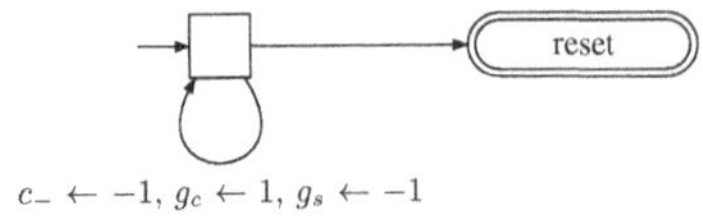

Fig. 7. blame $c > 0$ gadget

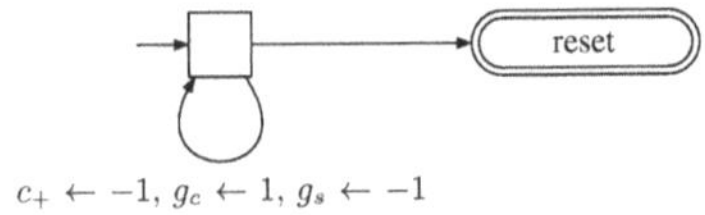

Fig. 8. blame $c < 0$ gadget

Fig. 9. blame $\ell \ll 0$ gadget

Fig. 10. blame $r \ll 0$ gadget

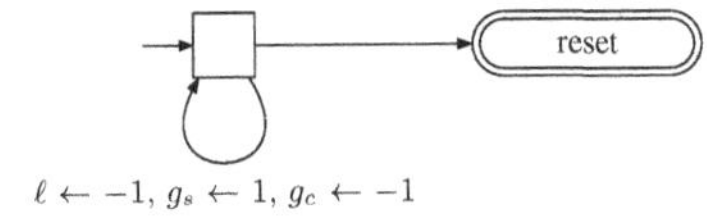

Fig. 11. blame $\ell \ll |g_s|$ gadget

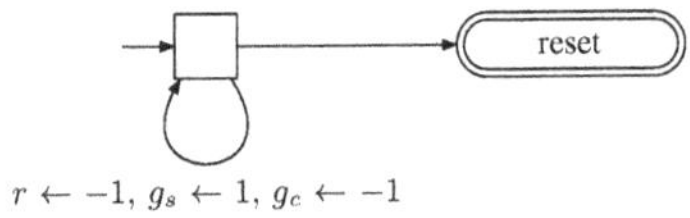

Fig. 12. blame $r \ll |g_s|$ gadget

- M halts and in the reset gadget (at least one of the players) correctly reset the values, then player 2 wins.

Hence, if M does halts, then player 2 winning strategy will make sure that the reset assigns correct values, and if M does not halt, then we can rely on player 1 to reset the values. We note that player 2 will not stay forever in his state (otherwise he will lose). In order to make sure that player 1 will not stay forever in one of his states we introduce two *liveness dimensions*, namely x and y. In the simulation and blame gadgets they get 0 values. But if player 1 remains forever in one of his two states in the reset gadget, then either x or y will have negative lim-sup value and player 1 will lose. Hence, in the reset gadget, player 1 should not only reset the values, but also assign a positive value for y and then a positive value for x.

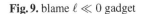

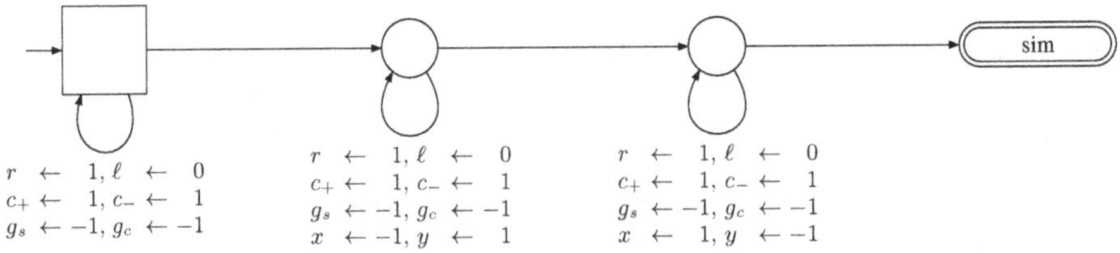

Fig. 13. Reset gadget

Correctness of the Reduction. We claim that player 1 has a winning strategy if and only if the machine M does not halt. We first summarize the (informal) invariants that we described in the construction of the reduction. Then, we prove that if M halts, then player 2 has a winning strategy, and then we prove the converse direction (the proofs are informal, and formal proofs are given in Section 4).

Summary of Invariants. We first describe the *reset invariants* that hold each time the play leaves the reset gadget (or equivalently, each time the sim gadget is invoked). The reset invariants for the side dimensions are: $avg(g_s) \approx -1$, $avg(r) \approx 1$, $avg(\ell) \approx 0$, and for the counter dimensions the invariants are: $avg(c_+) \approx 1, avg(c_-) \approx 1, avg(g_c) \approx -1$. We now describe the *sim invariants* that hold whenever the play is in the sim gadget (in all rounds that are played in the sim gadget and also before the first round that is played in the sim gadget). The sim invariants for the side dimensions are: When the play is in a right state (i.e., in a state of Q) then $r \approx |g_s|$ and $\ell \approx 0$. When the play is in a left state (i.e., in a state of P) then $\ell \approx |g_s|$ and $r \approx 0$.

The next claim follows from the sim invariants: whenever the play is in a state from Q or P (i.e., after the machine step was simulated), then $c_+ \approx |g_c| + |g_s|c$ and $c_- \approx |g_c| - |g_s|c$, where c is the current value of the counter according to the simulation steps (i.e., c is the value of the number of times the increment gadget was invoked minus the number of times that the decrement gadget was invoked from the beginning of the current invocation of the sim gadget). Informally, the proof of the claim follows by the fact that according to the sim invariants every step of the machine is simulated by a sub-play of length $|g_s|$ and by the fact that in the increment gadget the dimension c_+ is incremented by 2 while $|g_c|$ is incremented by 1 (and similar arguments can be applied for the decrement gadget and for dimension c_-). We formally prove the claim in Section 4.

Another simple consequence of the sim invariants is that $r + \ell \approx |g_s|$ in every round in the sim gadget. Indeed, whenever in a right or left state the equality holds directly from the invariants, and in every transition of the sim gadget the sum of weights of dimension ℓ and r is zero.

If M Halts, Then Player 2 Wins. The winning strategy for player 2 is as follows: In the reset gadget make sure that the *reset invariants* are satisfied. This is done by looping the first state of the reset gadget for enough rounds. In the sim gadget, whenever the *sim invariants* are not fulfilled or whenever player 1 cheats a zero-test, then player 2 invokes a blame gadget. If the sim invariants are fulfilled and player 1 does not cheat a zero test, then it must be the case that the game reaches state q_f, and in that case player 2 wins. Otherwise, we claim the player 2 wins.

We first prove that if player 1 violates the sim invariants infinitely often, then the winning condition is violated. W.l.o.g we assume that the first sim invariant is violated infinitely often and the proof for the second invariant is similar. By the assumption infinitely often the play is in a right state and either $r \gg |g_s|$ and $\ell \ll 0$ or $r \ll |g_s|$ and $\ell \gg 0$. If $r \gg |g_s|$, then $\ell \ll 0$ and it follows that in the last round that the state $\ell \ll 0$? was visited, the value of ℓ was much smaller than 0. Hence, player 2 invoked the $\ell \ll 0$ blame gadget and the play immediately continued to the reset gadget. If this happens infinitely often then $\underline{\ell} < 0$ while $\overline{g_s} < 0$ (as g_s remains negative in the blame $\ell \ll 0$ gadget and never increases in the sim and reset gadgets) and the winning condition is violated. If $r \ll |g_s|$, then player 2 invokes the blame gadget and loop the first state until $r \ll 0$. As $r \ll |g_s|$ we still have $g_s \ll 0$, and thus $\underline{r} < 0$ while $\overline{g_s} < 0$ and the condition is violated.

We now assume that the sim invariants are violated only finitely often (for simplicity we assume that they are never violated) and we assume that infinitely often player 1 cheats the zero-test before the play reaches q_f. W.l.o.g we assume that player 1 infinitely often declares $c = 0$ while the actual value of c is positive (and the proof for the second cheat is similar). In this case, as $c_- \approx |g_c| - |g_s|c$, we have $c_- \ll |g_c|$. Hence, in the blame $c > 0$ gadget player 2 loops the first state until $c_- \ll 0$. As $c_- \ll |g_c|$ it still holds that $g_c \ll 0$. Hence, $\underline{c_-} < 0$ while $\overline{g_c} < 0$ and the condition is violated.

To conclude, if the invariants are not maintained or player 1 does not honestly simulate the zero-tests, then in each simulation, the guard dimensions have negative average weights, while at least one of the dimensions ℓ, r, c_+ or c_- has a negative average weight in the blame gadget. Hence, we get that $\overline{g_s}, \overline{g_c} < 0$ and $\underline{\ell} < 0$ or $\underline{r} < 0$ or $\overline{c_-} < 0$ or $\underline{c_+} < 0$. Hence, the winning condition is not satisfied and player 2 is the winner.

If M does not Halt, Then Player 1 Wins. The winning strategy is to honestly simulate M while maintaining the *sim invariants* and the *reset invariants*. If player 2 never invokes the blame gadget, namely, the play stays forever in the sim gadget, then the winning condition is satisfied. Indeed, in the sim gadget g_s, c_+, c_-, x and y are never decremented, thus their mean-payoff value is at least zero and the winning condition is satisfied. Otherwise, after every invocation of the blame gadget, if a *side blame gadget* was invoked, then either the average value of r and ℓ is non-negative or the value of the guard dimension g_s is non-negative. Indeed, if the sim invariants are maintained, then before a blame $\ell \ll |g_s|$ gadget is invoked we have $\ell \approx |g_s|$. Hence, if in the gadget we have $\ell < 0$, then it must be the case that $g_s \geq 0$. Thus, eventually, we get that $\underline{r}, \underline{\ell} \geq 0$ or $\overline{g_s} \geq 0$. Similarly, when a $c > 0$ gadget is invokes, we have $c = 0$ and thus $c_- \approx |g_c|$, and thus in the gadget either c_- is non-negative or g_c is non-negative (and similar arguments hold for the $c < 0$ gadget and for c_+). Hence, we get that $\underline{c_+}, \overline{c_-} \geq 0$ or $\overline{g_c} \geq 0$. Thus, the winning condition is satisfied, and player 1 is the winner.

4 Detailed Proof

In the previous section we accurately described the reduction, and only the proof of the correctness was informal. In this section we give a precise proof for the correctness of the reduction, namely, we formally describe player-2 winning strategy in the case that M halts (Subsection 4.1), and player-1 winning strategy in the case that M does not halt (Subsection 4.2). In Subsection 4.3 we extend the reduction to two-counter machine.

Terminology. In the next subsections we use the next terminology and definitions:

A *round* is a round in the game graph (i.e., either player-1 or player-2 move).

A *simulation step* denotes all the rounds that are played in a transition gadget (i.e., in a *nop*,*inc* or *dec* gadget). Formally, a simulation step is a sub-play that begins and ends in a node from $P \cup Q$ (i.e., a left or a right state) and visits exactly one time in a left state and exactly one time in a right state.

A *simulation session* is a sub-play that begins in an invocation of the sim gadget and ends before (or exactly when) the play leaves the sim gadget. The *first i simulation steps* of a simulation session is a sub-play that begins in an invocation of the sim gadget and ends after i simulation steps were played.

A *loop* in a transition gadget is a two round sub-play in the gadget that consists of the loop that is formed by the first state and the state beneath it.

The *total number of rounds* is the total number of rounds (moves) from the beginning of the play. We say that the average weight of dimension d in round i is a, and we denote $avg(d) = a$, if the value of dimension d in round i is $a \cdot i$ (i.e., the average weight of d from the beginning of the play up to round i is a). Given a play prefix of length i, we say player-2 can achieve $avg(d_1) \leq a_1$ while maintaining $avg(d_2) \leq a_2$, for dimensions d_1, d_2 and thresholds a_1, a_2, if player 2 has a strategy to extend the play prefix in such way that in some round $j \geq i$ it holds that $avg(d_1) \leq a_1$ and in every round k such that $i \leq k \leq j$ it holds that $avg(d_2) \leq a_2$.

4.1 If M Halts, Then Player 2 is the Winner

In this subsection we assume that M halts. We denote by N the number of steps after which M halts (for initial counter value 0) and we denote $\epsilon = \frac{1}{(N+1)^2}$. WLOG we assume that $N > 10$. The strategy of player 2 in the reset gadget is to achieve the following *reset invariants* (after the play leaves the gadget):

- $avg(g_s), avg(g_c) \leq -\frac{1}{2}$
- $(1 - \frac{\epsilon}{4})|g_s| \leq r \leq (1 + \frac{\epsilon}{4})|g_s|$
- $-\frac{\epsilon}{4}|g_s| \leq \ell \leq \frac{\epsilon}{4}|g_s|$
- $(1 - \frac{\epsilon}{4})|g_c| \leq c_+, c_- \leq (1 + \frac{\epsilon}{4})|g_c|$

We note that player 2 can maintain the above by looping sufficiently long time in the first state, and once the invariants are reached, player 1 cannot violate them in his states in the reset gadget (since the average value of g_s and g_c can only get closer to -1, the value of $\frac{\ell}{|g_s|}$ only gets closer to 0 and $\frac{r}{|g_s|}$, $\frac{c_-}{|g_c|}$ and $\frac{c_+}{|g_c|}$ only gets closer to 1).

The strategy of player 2 in the sim gadget is to maintain, in every step of the simulation session, the next three invariants, which we denote by the *left right invariants*:

- (Left state invariant) If the machine is in a left state, then $(1 - \epsilon)|g_s| \leq \ell \leq (1 + \epsilon)|g_s|$ and $-\epsilon|g_s| \leq r \leq \epsilon|g_s|$.
- (Right state invariant) If the machine is in a right state, then $(1 - \epsilon)|g_s| \leq r \leq (1 + \epsilon)|g_s|$ and $-\epsilon|g_s| \leq \ell \leq +\epsilon|g_s|$.
- (Minimal value invariant) In every round of a simulation session $r, \ell \geq -\epsilon|g_s|$.

We denote $\delta = \frac{1}{\frac{1}{2}+2N(1+2\epsilon)}$. We first prove that under these invariants $avg(g_s) \leq -\delta$ in every round of the play. Then we use this fact to show that if player 1 violates these invariants, then player 2 can violate $(\underline{\ell} \wedge \underline{r} \vee \overline{g_s})$, and therefore he wins.

Lemma 1. *Assume that for a given simulation session: (i) in the beginning of the session $avg(g_s) \leq -\frac{1}{2}$; (ii) no more that N steps are played in the simulation session; and (iii) the left-right invariants are maintained in the session. Then for every round in the session $avg(g_s) \leq -\delta$.*

Proof. We denote by R the number of rounds that were played before the current invocation of the simulation gadget. We claim that after simulating i steps of the machine (in the current invocation of the sim gadget), the **total** number of rounds in the play (i.e., number of rounds from the beginning of the play, not from the beginning of the current invocation) is at most $R + 2i \cdot |g_s|(1 + 2\epsilon)$. The proof is by a simple induction, and for the base case $i = 0$ the proof is trivial. For $i > 0$, we assume WLOG that the i-th transition is a left-to-right transition. Hence, before the last simulation step we had $r \geq -\epsilon|g_s|$ and after the i-th step was completed we had $r \leq (1 + \epsilon)|g_s|$. Since in every odd round of a step gadget the value of r is incremented by 1, we get that at most $2(1 + 2\epsilon)|g_s|$ rounds were played and the proof of the claim follows (and the proof for a right-to-left transition is symmetric).

Hence, after N simulation steps we have $avg(g_s) \leq \frac{g_s}{R+2N|g_s|(1+2\epsilon)}$. Since in the beginning of the sim gadget we had $avg(g_s) \leq -\frac{1}{2}$, then $R \leq \frac{|g_s|}{2}$. Hence, and since $g_s < 0$ we get $avg(g_s) \leq \frac{g_s}{\frac{|g_s|}{2}+2N|g_s|(1+2\epsilon)} = -\frac{1}{\frac{1}{2}+2N(1+2\epsilon)} = -\delta$.

We note that in every transition of a simulation session the value of g_s is not changed. Hence, $avg(g_s)$ gets the maximal value after the N-th step and the proof is complete. □

Lemma 2. *Let* $\gamma = \min(\frac{\epsilon\delta}{4}, \frac{\frac{\epsilon}{4}}{1+\frac{1}{2\delta}-\frac{\epsilon}{4}})$*. If player 1 violates the left-right invariants in the first* N *steps of a session, then player 2 can achieve in the blame gadget either* $avg(r) \leq -\gamma$ *or* $avg(\ell) \leq -\gamma$ *(or both) while maintaining* $avg(g_s), avg(g_c) \leq -\gamma$*.*

Proof. We first prove the assertion over the value of g_c. It is an easy observation that if at the invocation of the sim gadget $avg(g_c) \leq -\frac{1}{2}$, then it remains at most $-\frac{1}{2}$ as it gets a value of -1 in every round in a blame gadget and -1 in every odd round in a step gadget.

Next, we prove the assertion for the left-state and minimal value invariants and the proof for the right-state invariant is symmetric. Recall that the invariant consistences of four assumptions, namely, (i) $(1-\epsilon)|g_s| \leq \ell$ after a right to left transition; (ii) $\ell \leq (1+\epsilon)|g_s|$ after a right to left transition; (iii) $-\epsilon|g_s| \leq r$ in every round; and (iv) $r \leq \epsilon|g_s|$ after a right to left transition. We first prove the assertion when the first condition is violated, i.e., we assume that $\ell < (1-\epsilon)|g_s|$. If this is the case after a right-to-left transition, then player 2 will invoke the blame $\ell \ll |g_s|$ gadget after the transition ends. In the blame gadget he will traverse the self-loop for $X \cdot (1-\frac{\epsilon}{2})$ times, where X is the value of $|g_s|$ before the invocation of the blame gadget, and then he will go to the reset gadget. As a result (since in every loop ℓ is decremented by 1 and g_s is incremented by 1) we get that the value of ℓ and g_s is at most $-X \cdot \frac{\epsilon}{2}$. Before the last simulation step the left-right invariants were maintained. Hence, before the last step we had $\ell \geq -\epsilon|g_s|$ (by the left-right invariants) and thus the last step had at most $|g_s|$ rounds (as we assume that after the last step $\ell < (1-\epsilon)|g_s|$). In addition, as the invariants were maintained, by Lemma 1 we get that before the last step we had $avg(g_s) \leq -\delta$ and thus after the last step we have $avg(g_s) \leq -\frac{\delta}{2}$ (as the value of g_s is not changed in simulation steps). Hence, if R is the number of rounds before the invocation of the blame gadget, then $R \leq \frac{X}{2\delta}$. Hence, after the blame gadget ends, we have $avg(\ell), avg(g_s) \leq -\frac{X\cdot\frac{\epsilon}{2}}{R+X\cdot(1-\frac{\epsilon}{2})} \leq -\frac{X\cdot\frac{\epsilon}{2}}{\frac{X}{2\delta}+X\cdot(1-\frac{\epsilon}{2})} = -\frac{\frac{\epsilon}{2}}{1+\frac{1}{2\delta}-\frac{\epsilon}{2}}$. In addition, the value of g_s is incremented in every round of the blame gadget. Thus, if after the gadget ends we have $avg(g_s) \leq -\gamma$, then in every round in the blame gadget we also have $avg(g_s) \leq -\gamma$.

If the second condition is violated, namely, if $\ell > (1+\epsilon)|g_s|$, then we claim that it must be the case that $r < -\frac{\epsilon|g_s|}{2}$. Indeed, when the sim gadget is invoked we have $r \leq |g_s|(1+\frac{\epsilon}{4})$ and $\ell \leq |g_s|\frac{\epsilon}{4}$. In the sim gadget the value of the sum $r+\ell$ is not changed (since r is incremented only when ℓ is decremented and vice versa). Hence, the sum never exceeds $|g_s|(1+\frac{\epsilon}{2})$. Thus, if $\ell > (1+\epsilon)|g_s|$, then it must be the case that $r < -\frac{\epsilon|g_s|}{2}$. Hence, in the first round that $avg(r) \leq -\frac{\epsilon}{2}|g_s|$ player 2 can invoke the blame $r \ll 0$ gadget which leads the play to the reset gadget after exactly one move. We note that in this scenario the left-right invariants are satisfied and thus, after leaving the blame gadget by Lemma 1 we have $avg(g_s) \leq -\delta$ and as $r \leq -\frac{\epsilon|g_s|}{2}$ we get that $avg(r) \leq -\frac{\epsilon\delta}{2}$.

If the third condition is violated, namely, if $r < -\epsilon|g_s|$, then it must be the case that the condition is first violated in a left to right transition (since in a right to left transition

r is incremented) and the proof follows by the same arguments as in the proof of the second case.

Finally, if the fourth condition is violated, namely, if $r > \epsilon|g_s|$, then by analyzing the sum $r + \ell$ we get that $\ell \leq (1 - \frac{\epsilon}{2})|g_s|$. We repeat the same analysis as in the case where the first invariant is violated (i.e., when $\ell \leq (1 - \epsilon)|g_s|$) and get that $avg(g_s), avg(r) \leq -\frac{\frac{\epsilon}{4}}{1+\frac{1}{2\delta}-\frac{\epsilon}{4}}$. The proof is complete. □

By Lemma 2, if player 2 maintains the reset invariant in the reset gadget, then other than finitely many simulation sessions, in every simulation session player 1 must satisfy the left-right invariants. Otherwise, we get that infinitely often the average value of either r or ℓ is at most $-\gamma$ while the average value of g_s is always at most $-\gamma$. Hence $\overline{g_s} < 0$ and either $\underline{r} < 0$ or $\underline{\ell} < 0$ and thus the condition $(\underline{\ell} \wedge \underline{r} \vee \overline{g_s})$ is violated and therefore player 1 is losing.

In the next three lemmas we prove that player 1 must honestly simulates the zero-testing. The first lemma is a simple corollary of the left-right invariants.

Lemma 3. *Under the left-right invariants, in the dec, inc and nop gadgets, player 1 follows the loop of the first state at most $|g_s|(1 + 2\epsilon)$ times and at least $|g_s|(1 - 2\epsilon)$ times.*

The next lemma shows the correlation between g_c and c_+ and c_-.

Lemma 4. *Let $\#inc$ (resp., $\#dec$) be the number of times that the inc (dec) gadget was visited (in the current simulation session), and we denote $c = \#inc - \#dec$ (namely, c is the actual value of the counter in the counter machine M). Then under the left-right invariants, in the first N steps of the simulation session we always have $c_+ \leq |g_c|(1 + \epsilon) + c|g_s| + \frac{|g_s|}{2}$ and $c_- \leq |g_c|(1 + \epsilon) - c|g_s| + \frac{|g_s|}{2}$.*

Proof. We prove the claim of the lemma for c_+ and the proof for c_- is symmetric. Let X be the value of $|g_c|$ when the sim gadget is invoked. By the reset invariants we get that $c_+ \leq X(1 + \frac{\epsilon}{4})$. By Lemma 3 we get that every visit in the inc gadget contributes at most $|g_s|(1 + 2\epsilon)$ more to c_+ than its contribution to $|g_c|$ and every visit in the dec contributes at least $|g_s|(1 - 2\epsilon)$ more to $|g_c|$ than its contribution to c_+. Hence,

$$\begin{aligned} c_+ &\leq X(1 + \tfrac{\epsilon}{4}) + (|g_c| - X) + \#inc \cdot |g_s|(1 + 2\epsilon) - \#dec \cdot |g_s|(1 - 2\epsilon) = \\ &|g_c| + \epsilon X + (\#inc - \#dec)|g_s|(1 + 2\epsilon) + 4\epsilon|g_s| \cdot \#dec \end{aligned}$$

We recall that $c = (\#inc - \#dec)$, and observe that $X \leq |g_c|$, and that $\#dec \leq N$ and thus $\epsilon \cdot \#dec < \frac{1}{10}$. Hence, we get that $c_+ \leq |g_c|(1 + \epsilon) + c|g_s| + \frac{|g_s|}{2}$. □

The next lemma suggests that player 1 must honestly simulate the zero-tests.

Lemma 5. *If the reset and left-right invariants hold, then for $\gamma = \min(\frac{1}{20N}, \frac{\delta}{8})$ the following hold: (i) if the blame $c < 0$ gadget is invoked and $c < 0$ then player 2 can achieve $avg(c_+) \leq -\gamma$ while maintaining $avg(g_s), avg(g_c) \leq -\gamma$; and (ii) if the blame $c > 0$ gadget is invoked and $c > 0$ then player 2 can achieve $avg(c_-) \leq -\gamma$ while maintaining $avg(g_s), avg(g_c) \leq -\gamma$.*

Proof. We prove the first item of the lemma and the proof for the second item is symmetric. Suppose that $c < 0$ (i.e., $c \leq -1$) when blame $c < 0$ gadget is invoked. Let X and Y be the values of $|g_c|$ and $|g_s|$ before the invocation of the blame gadget. Then by

Lemma 4, before the invocation we have $c_+ \leq X(1+\epsilon) - \frac{Y}{2}$. Hence, by traversing the loop of the first state of the blame $c < 0$ gadget for $X(1+\epsilon) - \frac{Y}{4}$ times we get $c_+ \leq -\frac{Y}{4}$ and $g_c \leq \epsilon X - \frac{Y}{4}$. Let R be the number of rounds that were played from the beginning of the play (and not just from the beginning of the current invocation of the sim gadget). Since g_c is decremented by at most 1 in every round we get that $X(1+\epsilon) - \frac{Y}{4} \leq 2X \leq 2R$. By lemma 1 we have $\frac{Y}{R} \leq -\delta$. Hence, $avg(c_+) \leq \frac{c_+}{2R} \leq -\frac{Y}{8R} \leq -\frac{\delta}{8}$. Similarly, since $\frac{X}{R}$ is bounded by 1, we have $avg(g_c) \leq \frac{\epsilon X}{2R} - \frac{\delta}{8} \leq \frac{\epsilon}{2} - \frac{\delta}{8}$. Recall that $\delta = \frac{1}{\frac{1}{2}+2N(1+2\epsilon)}$. Hence, $avg(g_c) \leq \frac{2\epsilon+4N\epsilon+8\epsilon^2-1}{8(\frac{1}{2}+N(1+2\epsilon))}$ and since $\epsilon = \frac{1}{(N+1)^2}$ and $N > 10$ we get that $avg(g_c) \leq -\frac{1}{20N}$. Note that g_c is only incremented in the blame gadget. Thus, as $avg(g_c) \leq -\gamma$ after the last round of the blame gadget we get that $avg(g_c) \leq -\gamma$ in all the rounds that are played in the blame gadget. The value of g_s was at most $-\delta R$ before the blame gadget, and in the blame gadget g_s is decreased by 1 in every round. Hence $avg(g_s) \leq -\delta$ in every round of the blame gadget and the proof follows by taking $\gamma = \min(\frac{1}{20N}, \frac{\delta}{8})$. □

We are now ready to prove one side of the reduction.

Proposition 1. *If the counter machine M halts, then player 2 has a winning strategy for violating $(\underline{\ell} \wedge \underline{r} \vee \overline{g_s}) \wedge (\underline{c_+} \wedge \underline{c_-} \vee \overline{g_c}) \wedge \overline{x} \wedge \overline{y}$. Moreover, if M halts then there exists a constant $\zeta > 0$ that depends only on M such that player 2 has a winning strategy for violating $(\underline{\ell} \geq -\zeta \wedge \underline{r} \geq -\zeta \vee \overline{g_s} \geq -\zeta) \wedge (\underline{c_+} \geq -\zeta \wedge \underline{c_-} \geq -\zeta \vee \overline{g_c} \geq -\zeta) \wedge \overline{x} \geq -\zeta \wedge \overline{y} \geq -\zeta$.*

Proof. Suppose that M halts and let N be the number of steps that M runs before it halts (for an initial counter value 0). Player-2 strategy is to (i) maintain the reset-invariants; (ii) whenever the left-right invariants are violated, he invokes a side blame gadget; (iii) whenever the zero-testing is dishonest, he activates the corresponding blame gadget (either $c > 0$ or $c < 0$); and (iv) if q_f is reached, he stays there forever. The correctness of the construction is immediate by the lemmas above. We first observe that it is possible for player 2 to satisfy the reset-invariants and that if player 1 stays in the reset gadget forever, then he loses.

Whenever the left-right invariant is violated, then the average weight of r and/or ℓ is negative, while the average weight of g_s and g_c remains negative. Hence, if in every simulation session player 1 violates the left-right invariants in the first N steps we get that the condition is violated since $\overline{g_s} \leq -\gamma$ and either $\underline{r} \leq -\gamma$ or $\underline{\ell} \leq -\gamma$. Hence, we may assume that these invariants are kept in every simulation session.

Whenever the zero-testing is dishonest (while the left-right invariants are satisfied), then by Lemma 5, player 2 can invoke a counter blame gadget and achieve negative average for either c_+ or c_- while maintaining g_c and g_s negative. If in every simulation session player 1 is dishonest in zero-testing, then we get that either $\underline{c_-} \leq -\gamma$ or $\underline{c_+} \leq -\gamma$ while $\overline{g_c} \leq -\gamma$ and the condition is violated. Hence, we may assume that player 1 honestly simulates the zero-tests. Finally, if the transitions of M are properly simulated, then it must be the case the state q_f is reached and when looping this state forever player 1 loses (since $\overline{x} \leq -1 < 0$). □

4.2 If M does not Halt, Then Player 1 is the Winner

Suppose that M does not halt. A winning strategy of player 1 in the reset gadget is as following: Let i be the number of times that the reset gadget was visited, and we denote $\epsilon_i = \frac{1}{i+10}$. Similarly to player-2 strategy in Subsection 4.1, player-1 strategy in the reset gadget is to achieve the following invariants (after the play leaves the gadget): (i) $avg(g_s), avg(g_c) \leq -\frac{1}{2}$; (ii) $(1 - \frac{\epsilon_i}{4})|g_s| \leq r \leq (1 + \frac{\epsilon_i}{4})|g_s|$; (iii) $-\frac{\epsilon_i|g_s|}{4} \leq \ell \leq \frac{\epsilon_i|g_s|}{4}$; and (iv) $(1 - \frac{\epsilon_i}{4})|g_c| \leq c_+, c_- \leq (1 + \frac{\epsilon_i}{4})|g_c|$. To satisfy these invariants, he follows the self-loop of his first state until $avg(y) \geq 0$ and then follows the self-loop of the second state until the invariants are fulfilled and $avg(x) \geq 0$. In the sim gadget, player-1 strategy is to simulate every *nop*,*inc* and *dec* step by following the self-loop in the corresponding gadget for $|g_s|$ rounds, and to honestly simulate the zero-tests..

We denote the above player-1 strategy by τ. The next two lemmas show the basic properties of a play according to τ, and that player 2 loses if he invokes the blame gadgets infinitely often.

Lemma 6. *In any play according to τ, after the reset gadget was visited for i times, in the sim gadget we always have: (i) in a right state: $r \geq -\epsilon_i|g_s|, \ell \geq (1-\epsilon_i)|g_s|$ and in a left state $\ell \geq -\epsilon_i|g_s|, r \geq (1-\epsilon_i)|g_s|$; (ii) in every round of the simulation session $r, \ell \geq -\epsilon_i|g_s|$; and (iii) $c_+ \geq (1-\epsilon_i)|g_c| + c|g_s|$ and $c_- \geq (1-\epsilon_i)|g_c| - c|g_s|$, where $c = \#inc - \#dec$ in the current invocation of the sim gadget.*

Lemma 7. *In a play prefix consistent with τ, in every round that is played in a blame gadget: (1) In the blame $\ell \ll 0$ and blame $r \ll 0$ gadgets: $avg(\ell), avg(r) \geq -\epsilon_i$. (2) In blame $\ell \ll \| g_s|$ gadget: if $avg(\ell) \leq -\epsilon_i$, then $avg(g_s) \geq -\epsilon_i$. (3) In blame $r \ll |g_s|$ gadget: if $avg(r) \leq -\epsilon_i$, then $avg(g_s) \geq -\epsilon_i$. (4) In the blame $c < 0$ gadget: if $avg(c_+) \leq -\epsilon_i$, then $avg(g_c) \geq -\epsilon_i$. (5) In the blame $c > 0$ gadget: if $avg(c_-) \leq -\epsilon_i$, then $avg(g_c) \geq -\epsilon_i$. Where i is the number of times that the reset gadget was visited.*

We are now ready to prove the τ is a winning strategy.

Proposition 2. *If M does not halt, then τ is a winning strategy.*

Proof. In order to prove that τ satisfies the condition $(\underline{\ell} \wedge \underline{r} \vee \overline{g_s}) \wedge (\underline{c_+} \wedge \underline{c_-} \vee \overline{g_c}) \wedge \overline{x} \wedge \overline{y}$ it is enough to prove that when playing according to τ, for any constant $\delta > 0$ the condition $(\underline{\ell} \geq -\delta \wedge \underline{r} \geq -\delta \vee \overline{g_s} \geq -\delta) \wedge (\underline{c_+} \geq -\delta \wedge \underline{c_-} \geq -\delta \vee \overline{g_c} \geq -\delta) \wedge \overline{x} \wedge \overline{y}$ is satisfied.

Let $\delta > 0$ be an arbitrary constant and in order to prove the claim we consider two distinct cases: In the first case, player 2 strategy will invoke the blame gadgets only finitely many times. Hence, there is an infinite suffix that is played only in either a blame gadget, the reset gadget or the sim gadget and in such suffix player 2 loses.

In the second case we consider, player 2 always eventually invokes a blame gadget. Since a blame gadget is invoked infinitely many times we get that the reset gadget is invoked infinitely often, and thus $\overline{x}, \overline{y} \geq 0$. In addition, the sim gadget is invoked infinitely often. Let i be the minimal index for which $\epsilon_i \leq \delta$. By Lemmas 6 and 7 we get that after the i-th invocation of the sim gadget, in every round (i) either $avg(\ell) \geq -\epsilon_i \wedge avg(r) \geq -\epsilon_i$ or $avg(g_s) \geq -\epsilon_i$; and (ii) either $avg(c_+) \geq -\epsilon_i \wedge avg(c_-) \geq -\epsilon_i$ or $avg(g_c) \geq -\epsilon_i$. (A detailed proof is given in the technical report.) Thus, as of certain round, either $avg(\ell)$ and $avg(r)$ are always at least $-\epsilon_i$, or infinitely often $avg(g_s) \geq -\epsilon_i$. Hence, $(\underline{\ell} \geq -\epsilon_i \wedge \underline{r} \geq -\epsilon_i \vee \overline{g_s} \geq -\epsilon_i)$ is satisfied and similarly $(\underline{c_+} \geq -\epsilon_i \wedge \underline{c_-} \geq -\epsilon_i \vee \overline{g_c} \geq -\epsilon_i)$ is satisfied. The proof is complete. □

4.3 Extending the Reduction to Two-counter Machine

When M is a two-counter machine, we use 4 dimensions for the counters, namely $c_+^1, c_-^1, c_+^2, c_-^2$ and one guard dimension g_c. The winning condition is $(\underline{\ell} \wedge \underline{r} \vee \overline{g_s}) \wedge (\underline{c_+^1} \wedge \underline{c_-^1} \wedge \underline{c_+^2} \wedge \underline{c_-^2} \vee \overline{g_c}) \wedge \overline{x} \wedge \overline{y}$. In a nop gadget all four dimensions $c_+^1, c_-^1, c_+^2, c_-^2$ get a value of 1 in the self-loop. When a counter c_i (for $i = 1, 2$) is incremented (resp., decremented), then counter c_+^i and c_-^i are assigned with weights according to the weights of c_+ and c_- in the inc (dec) gadget that we described in the reduction for a one counter machine, and c_+^{3-i}, c_-^{3-i} are assigned with weights according to a nop gadget.

The proofs of Proposition 1 and Proposition 2 easily scale to a two-counter machine. Hence, the undecidability result is obtained.

Theorem 1. *The problem of deciding who is the winner in a multidimensional mean-payoff game with ten dimensions is undecidable.*

The winning condition that we use in the reduction can be encoded also by mean-payoff expressions [6]. Hence, games over mean-payoff expressions are also undecidable.

References

1. Alur, R., Degorre, A., Maler, O., Weiss, G.: On omega-languages defined by mean-payoff conditions. In: de Alfaro, L. (ed.) FOSSACS 2009. LNCS, vol. 5504, pp. 333–347. Springer, Heidelberg (2009)
2. Bohy, A., Bruyère, V., Filiot, E., Raskin, J.-F.: Synthesis from LTL specifications with mean-payoff objectives. In: Piterman, N., Smolka, S.A. (eds.) TACAS 2013 (ETAPS 2013). LNCS, vol. 7795, pp. 169–184. Springer, Heidelberg (2013)
3. Boker, U., Chatterjee, K., Henzinger, T.A., Kupferman, O.: Temporal specifications with accumulative values. In: LICS (2011)
4. Brázdil, T., Brozek, V., Chatterjee, K., Forejt, V., Kucera, A.: Two views on multiple mean-payoff objectives in markov decision processes. In: LICS (2011)
5. Brázdil, T., Chatterjee, K., Kučera, A., Novotný, P.: Efficient controller synthesis for consumption games with multiple resource types. In: Madhusudan, P., Seshia, S.A. (eds.) CAV 2012. LNCS, vol. 7358, pp. 23–38. Springer, Heidelberg (2012)
6. Chatterjee, K., Doyen, L., Edelsbrunner, H., Henzinger, T.A., Rannou, P.: Mean-payoff automaton expressions. In: Gastin, P., Laroussinie, F. (eds.) CONCUR 2010. LNCS, vol. 6269, pp. 269–283. Springer, Heidelberg (2010)
7. Chatterjee, K., Randour, M., Raskin, J.-F.: Strategy synthesis for multi-dimensional quantitative objectives. In: Koutny, M., Ulidowski, I. (eds.) CONCUR 2012. LNCS, vol. 7454, pp. 115–131. Springer, Heidelberg (2012)
8. Chatterjee, K., Velner, Y.: Mean-payoff pushdown games. In: LICS (2012)
9. Chatterjee, K., Velner, Y.: Hyperplane separation technique for multidimensional mean-payoff games. In: D'Argenio, P.R., Melgratti, H. (eds.) CONCUR 2013 – Concurrency Theory. LNCS, vol. 8052, pp. 500–515. Springer, Heidelberg (2013)
10. Degorre, A., Doyen, L., Gentilini, R., Raskin, J.-F., Toruńczyk, S.: Energy and mean-payoff games with imperfect information. In: Dawar, A., Veith, H. (eds.) CSL 2010. LNCS, vol. 6247, pp. 260–274. Springer, Heidelberg (2010)
11. Doyen, L.: Games and automata: From boolean to quantitative verification. Memoire d'habilitation, ENS Cachan, France (2012)
12. Tomita, T., Hiura, S., Hagihara, S., Yonezaki, N.: A temporal logic with mean-payoff constraints. In: Aoki, T., Taguchi, K. (eds.) ICFEM 2012. LNCS, vol. 7635, pp. 249–265. Springer, Heidelberg (2012)

13. Velner, Y.: The complexity of mean-payoff automaton expression. In: Czumaj, A., Mehlhorn, K., Pitts, A., Wattenhofer, R. (eds.) ICALP 2012, Part II. LNCS, vol. 7392, pp. 390–402. Springer, Heidelberg (2012)
14. Velner, Y.: Finite-memory strategy synthesis for robust multidimensional mean-payoff objectives. In: CSL-LICS (2014)
15. Velner, Y., Chatterjee, K., Doyen, L., Henzinger, T.A., Rabinovich, A., Raskin, J.-F.: The complexity of multi-mean-payoff and multi-energy games. CoRR (2012)
16. Velner, Y., Rabinovich, A.: Church synthesis problem for noisy input. In: Hofmann, M. (ed.) FOSSACS 2011. LNCS, vol. 6604, pp. 275–289. Springer, Heidelberg (2011)
17. Yaron Velner. Robust multidimensional mean-payoff games are undecidable. CoRR (2015)

The Cyclic-Routing UAV Problem is PSPACE-Complete

Hsi-Ming Ho and Joël Ouaknine

Department of Computer Science, University of Oxford
Wolfson Building, Parks Road, Oxford, OX1 3QD, UK

Abstract. Consider a finite set of targets, with each target assigned a *relative deadline*, and each pair of targets assigned a fixed transit *flight time*. Given a flock of identical UAVs, can one ensure that every target is repeatedly visited by some UAV at intervals of duration at most the target's relative deadline? The ***Cyclic-Routing UAV Problem*** (CR-UAV) is the question of whether this task has a solution.

This problem can straightforwardly be solved in PSPACE by modelling it as a network of timed automata. The special case of there being a single UAV is claimed to be NP-complete in the literature. In this paper, we show that the CR-UAV Problem is in fact PSPACE-complete even in the single-UAV case.

1 Introduction

Unmanned aerial vehicles (UAVs) have many uses, ranging from civilian to military operations. Like other autonomous systems, they are particularly well-suited to 'dull, dirty, and/or dangerous' missions [21]. A common scenario in such missions is that a set of targets have to be visited by a limited number of UAVs. This has given rise to a large body of research on *path planning* for UAVs.[1] Depending on the specific application at hand, paths of UAVs may be subject to various complex constraints, e.g., related to kinematics or fuel (see, e.g., [1, 17, 19, 23]).

In this work, we consider the *Cyclic-Routing UAV Problem* (CR-UAV) [7]: the decision version of a simple *recurrent* UAV path-planning problem in which each target must be visited not only once but repeatedly, i.e., at intervals of prescribed maximal duration. Problems of this type have long been considered in many other fields such as transportation [16, 22] and robotics [6, 12]. More recently, a number of game-theoretic frameworks have been developed to study similar problems in the context of security [4, 11, 20].

A special case of the problem (with a single UAV) is considered in [3, 4, 13], and is claimed to be NP-complete in [4]. However, the proof of NP-membership in [4] is not detailed.[2] The main result of the present paper is that the CR-UAV Problem is in fact PSPACE-complete, even in the single-UAV case. We note that this problem can be seen as a recurrent variant of the decision version

[1] `http://scholar.google.com/` lists thousands of papers on the subject.

[2] A counterexample to a crucial claim in [4] is given in the full version of this paper [10].

A. Pitts (Ed.): FOSSACS 2015, LNCS 9034, pp. 328–342, 2015.
DOI: 10.1007/978-3-662-46678-0_21

of the *Travelling Salesman Problem with Time Windows* (TSPTW) with upper bounds only (or *TSP with Deadlines* [5]). Its PSPACE-hardness hence stems from recurrence: the decision version of the (non-recurrent) TSPTW Problem is NP-complete [18].

PSPACE-membership of the (general) CR-UAV Problem follows straightforwardly by encoding the problem as the existence of infinite paths in a network of timed automata; we briefly sketch the argument in the next section. The bulk of the paper is then devoted to establishing PSPACE-hardness of the single-UAV case. This is accomplished by reduction from the PERIODIC SAT Problem, known to be PSPACE-complete [15].

2 Preliminaries

2.1 Scenario

Let there be a set of targets and a number of identical UAVs. Each target has a ***relative deadline***: an upper bound requirement on the time between successive visits by UAVs. The UAVs are allowed to fly freely between targets, with a ***flight time*** given for each pair of targets: the amount of time required for a UAV to fly from one of the targets to the other. We assume that flight times are symmetric, that they obey the triangle inequality, and that the flight time from target v to target v' is zero iff v and v' denote the same target. In other words, flight times are a metric on the set of targets. The goal is to decide whether there is a way to coordinate UAVs such that no relative deadline is ever violated. We make a few further assumptions:

- Initially, each UAV starts at some target; there may be more than one UAV at the same target.
- The first visit to each target must take place at the latest by the expiration time of its relative deadline.
- The UAVs are allowed to 'wait' as long as they wish at any given target.
- Time units are chosen so that all relative deadlines and flight times are integers, and moreover all relative deadlines are interpreted as closed constraints (i.e., using non-strict inequalities).

2.2 Modelling via Networks of Timed Automata

We briefly sketch how to model the CR-UAV Problem as the existence of infinite non-Zeno paths in a network of Büchi timed automata, following the notation and results of [2], from which PSPACE-membership immediately follows.

Intuitively, one ascribes a particular timed automaton to each UAV and to each target. Each UAV-automaton keeps track of the location of its associated UAV, and enforces flight times by means of a single clock, which is reset the instant the UAV leaves a given target. Each target-automaton is likewise equipped with a single clock, keeping track of time elapsed since the last visit by some UAV. The action of a UAV visiting a target is modelled by synchronising on a particular event; when this takes place, provided the target's relative deadline has not been violated, the target resets its internal clock and instantaneously visits a Büchi location. Similarly, the action of a UAV leaving a target is modelled by event synchronisation. Finally, since multiple UAVs may visit a given target simultaneously, each target is in addition equipped with a counter to keep track at any time of whether or not it is currently being visited by some UAV.

The given instance of the CR-UAV Problem therefore has a solution iff there exists a non-Zeno run of the resulting network of timed automata in which each Büchi accepting location is visited infinitely often. By Thm. 7 of [2], this can be decided in PSPACE.

It is worth noting that, since all timing constraints are closed by assumption, standard digitisation results apply (cf. [9]) and it is sufficient to consider integer (i.e., discrete) time. In the next section, we therefore present a discrete graph-based (and timed-automaton independent) formulation of the problem specialised to a single UAV, in order to establish PSPACE-hardness.

2.3 Weighted Graph Formulation

The solution to a single-UAV instance of the CR-UAV Problem consists of an infinite path from target to target in which each target is visited infinitely often, at time intervals never greater than the target's relative deadline. One may clearly assume that the UAV never 'lingers' at any given target, i.e., targets are visited instantaneously. Formally, a single-UAV instance of the CR-UAV Problem can be described as follows. Let V be a set of $n \geq 2$ vertices, with each vertex $v \in V$ assigned a strictly positive integer weight $RD(v)$ (intuitively, the relative deadline of target v). Consider a weighted undirected clique over V, i.e., to each pair of vertices (v, v') with $v \neq v'$, one assigns a strictly positive integer weight $FT(v, v')$ (intuitively, the flight time from v to v'). In addition we require that FT be symmetric and satisfy the triangle inequality.

Let $G = \langle V, RD, FT \rangle$ be an instance of the above data. Given a finite path u in (the clique associated with) G, the ***duration*** $dur(u)$ of u is defined to be the sum of the weights of the edges in u. A ***solution*** to G is an infinite path s through G with the following properties:

- s visits every vertex in V infinitely often;
- Any finite subpath of s that starts and ends at consecutive occurrences of a given vertex v must have duration at most $RD(v)$.

Definition 1 (The CR-UAV Problem with a Single UAV). *Given G as described above, does G have a solution?*

As pointed out in [13], if a solution exists at all then a *periodic* solution can be found, i.e., an infinite path in which the targets are visited repeatedly in the same order.

2.4 The PERIODIC SAT Problem

PERIODIC SAT is one of the many PSPACE-complete problems introduced in [15]. In the following definition (and in the rest of this paper), let $\overline{x}$ be a finite set of variables and let $\overline{x}^j$ be the set of variables obtained from $\overline{x}$ by adding a superscript j to each variable.

Definition 2 (The PERIODIC SAT Problem [15]). *Consider a CNF formula $\varphi(0)$ over $\overline{x}^0 \cup \overline{x}^1$. Let $\varphi(j)$ be the formula obtained from $\varphi(0)$ by replacing all variables $x_i^0 \in \overline{x}^0$ by x_i^j and all variables $x_i^1 \in \overline{x}^1$ by x_i^{j+1}. Is there an assignment of $\bigcup_{j\geq 0} \overline{x}^j$ such that $\bigwedge_{j\geq 0} \varphi(j)$ is satisfied?*

3 PSPACE-Hardness

In this section, we give a reduction from the PERIODIC SAT Problem to the CR-UAV Problem with a single UAV. Consider a CNF formula $\varphi(0) = c_1 \wedge \cdots \wedge c_h$ over $\overline{x}^0 = \{x_1^0, \ldots, x_m^0\}$ and $\overline{x}^1 = \{x_1^1, \ldots, x_m^1\}$. Without loss of generality, we assume that each clause c_j of $\varphi(0)$ is non-trivial (i.e., c_j does not contain both positive and negative occurrences of a variable) and $m > 2$, $h > 0$. We can construct an instance G of the CR-UAV Problem (with the largest constant having magnitude $O(m^2 h)$ and $|V| = O(mh)$) such that $\bigwedge_{j\geq 0} \varphi(j)$ is satisfiable if and only if G has a solution.

The general idea of the reduction can be described as follows. We construct *variable gadgets* that can be traversed in two 'directions' (corresponding to assignments **true** and **false** to variables). A *clause vertex* is visited if the corresponding clause is satisfied by the assignment. Crucially, we use *consistency gadgets*, in which we set the relative deadlines of the vertices carefully to ensure that the directions of traversals of the variable gadgets for $\overline{x}^1$ (corresponding to a particular assignment of variables) in a given iteration is consistent with the directions of traversals of the variable gadgets for $\overline{x}^0$ in the next iteration.

3.1 The Construction

We describe and explain each part of G in detail. The reader is advised to glance ahead to Figure 5 to form an impression of G. Note that for ease of presentation, we temporarily relax the requirement that FT be a metric and describe G as an incomplete graph.[3] In what follows, let $l = 24h + 34$ and

$$T = 2\Big(m(2(3m+1)l + l) + m(2(3m+2)l + l) + l + 2h\Big).$$

[3] In the single-UAV case, if the FT of some edge is greater than any value in RD, that edge can simply be seen as non-existent.

Variable Gadgets. For each variable x_i^0, we construct (as a subgraph of G) a *variable gadget*. It consists of the following vertices (see Figure 1):

- Three vertices on the left side ($LS_i = \{v_i^{t,L}, v_i^{m,L}, v_i^{b,L}\}$)
- Three vertices on the right side ($RS_i = \{v_i^{t,R}, v_i^{m,R}, v_i^{b,R}\}$)
- A '*clause box*' ($CB_i^j = \{v_i^{a,j}, v_i^{b,j}, v_i^{c,j}, v_i^{d,j}, v_i^{e,j}, v_i^{f,j}\}$) for each $j \in \{1, \dots, h\}$
- A '*separator box*' ($SB_i^j=\{v_i^{\bar{a},j}, v_i^{\bar{b},j}, v_i^{\bar{c},j}, v_i^{\bar{d},j}, v_i^{\bar{e},j}, v_i^{\bar{f},j}\}$) for each $j\in\{0, \dots, h\}$
- A vertex at the top (v_{top} if $i = 0$, v_{i-1} otherwise)
- A vertex at the bottom (v_i).

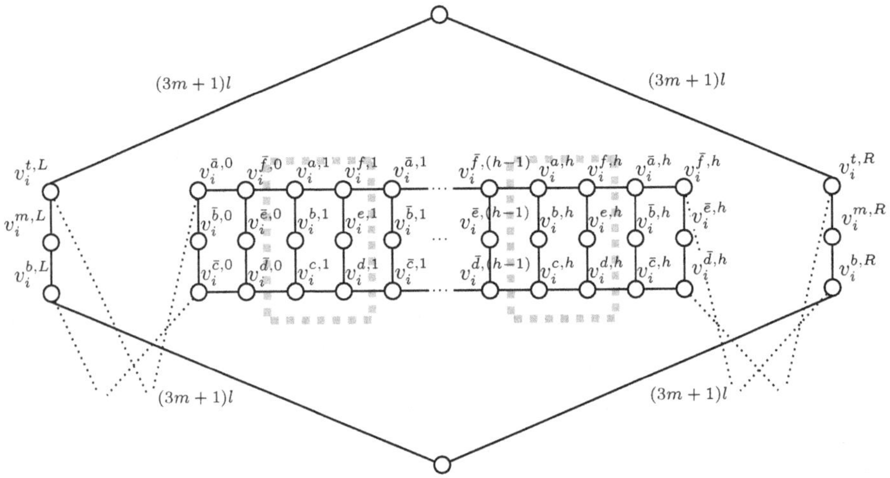

Fig. 1. The variable gadget for x_i^0

The clause boxes for $j \in \{1, \dots, h\}$ are aligned horizontally in the figure. A separator box is laid between each adjacent pair of clause boxes and at both ends. This row of boxes ($Row_i = \bigcup_{j\in\{1,\dots,h\}} CB_i^j \cup \bigcup_{j\in\{0,\dots,h\}} SB_i^j$) is then put between LS_i and RS_i. The RD of all vertices $v \in LS_i \cup RS_i \cup Row_i$ are set to $T + l + 2h$.

The vertices are connected as indicated by solid lines in the figure. The four 'long' edges in the figure have their FT set to $(3m + 1)l$ while all other edges have FT equal to 2, e.g., $FT(v_{top}, v_1^{t,L}) = (3m + 1)l$ and $FT(v_1^{b,1}, v_1^{c,1}) = 2$. There is an exception though: $FT(v_m^{b,L}, v_m)$ and $FT(v_m^{b,R}, v_m)$ (in the variable gadget for x_m^0) are equal to $(3m + 2)l$.

The variable gadgets for variables x_i^1 are constructed almost identically. The three vertices on the left and right side are now LS_{i+m} and RS_{i+m}. The set of vertices in the row is now $Row_{i+m} = \bigcup_{j\in\{1,\dots,h\}} CB_{i+m}^j \cup \bigcup_{j\in\{0,\dots,h\}} SB_{i+m}^j$. The vertex at the top is v_{i+m-1} and the vertex at the bottom is v_{i+m} ($i \neq m$) or v_{bot} ($i = m$). The RD of vertices in $LS_{i+m} \cup RS_{i+m} \cup Row_{i+m}$ are set to

$T + l + 2h$, and the FT of the edges are set as before, except that all the 'long' edges now have FT equal to $(3m + 2)l$.

Now consider the following ordering of variables:

$$x_1^0, x_2^0, \ldots, x_m^0, x_1^1, x_2^1, \ldots, x_m^1 .$$

Observe that the variable gadgets for two 'neighbouring' variables (with respect to this ordering) have a vertex in common. To be precise, the set of shared vertices is $S = \{v_1, \ldots, v_{2m-1}\}$. We set the RD of all vertices in S to $T + 2h$ and the RD of v_{top} and v_{bot} to T.

Clause Vertices. For each clause c_j in $\varphi(0)$, there is a *clause vertex* v^{c_j} with RD set to $\frac{3}{2}T$. If x_i^0 occurs in c_j as a literal, we connect the j-th clause box in the variable gadget for x_i^0 to v^{c_j} as shown in Figure 2 and set the FT of these new edges to 2 (e.g., $FT(v^{c_j}, v_i^{c,j}) = FT(v^{c_j}, v_i^{d,j}) = 2$). If instead $\neg x_i^0$ occurs in c_j, then v^{c_j} is connected to $v_i^{a,j}$ and $v_i^{f,j}$ (with FT equal to 2). Likewise, the variable gadget for x_i^1 may be connected to v^{c_j} via $\{v_{i+m}^{c,j}, v_{i+m}^{d,j}\}$ (if x_i^1 occurs in c_j) or $\{v_{i+m}^{a,j}, v_{i+m}^{f,j}\}$ (if $\neg x_i^1$ occurs in c_j).

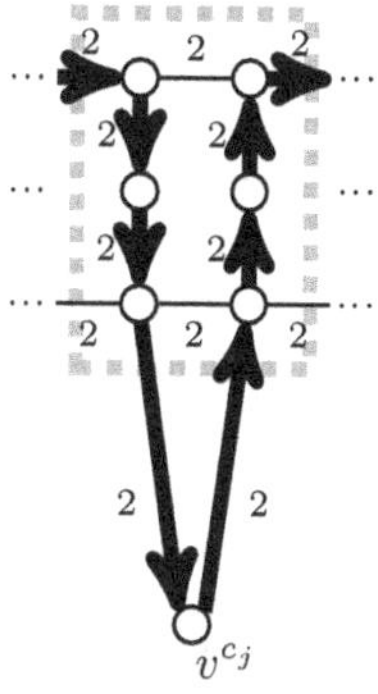

Fig. 2. The variable occurs positively in c_j

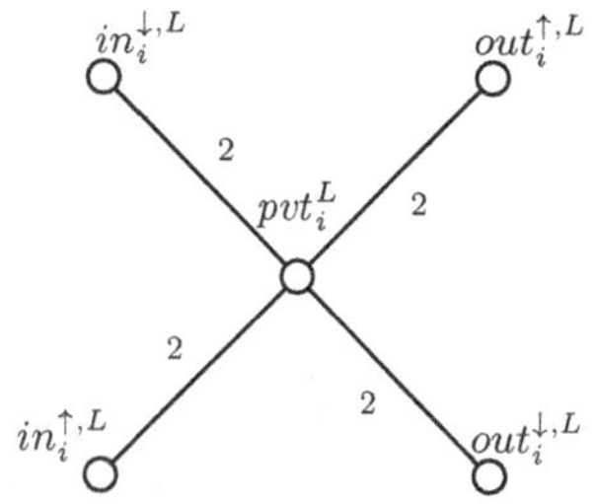

Fig. 3. A consistency gadget LCG_i

Consistency Gadgets. For each $i \in \{1, \ldots, m\}$, we construct two *consistency gadgets* LCG_i (see Figure 3) and RCG_i. In LCG_i, the vertex at the centre ($pvt_i^{t,L}$) has RD equal to $\frac{1}{2}T + m(2(3m+2)l + l) - (2i-1)l + 4h$. The other four vertices ($in_i^{\downarrow,L}$, $out_i^{\uparrow,L}$, $in_i^{\uparrow,L}$ and $out_i^{\downarrow,L}$) have RD equal to $\frac{3}{2}T$. The FT from $pvt_i^{t,L}$ to any of the other four vertices is 2. RCG_i is identical except that the subscripts on the vertices change from L to R.

LCG_i and RCG_i are connected to the variable gadgets for x_i^0 and x_i^1 as in Figure 4. The vertices $in_i^{\downarrow,L}, out_i^{\uparrow,L}, in_i^{\downarrow,R}, out_i^{\uparrow,R}$ are connected to certain vertices in the variable gadget for x_i^0—this allows pvt_i^L and pvt_i^R to be traversed 'from above'. Similarly, the edges connected to $in_i^{\uparrow,L}, out_i^{\downarrow,L}, in_i^{\uparrow,L}, out_i^{\downarrow,L}$ allow pvt_i^L and pvt_i^R to be traversed 'from below'. Formally, $FT(v, v') = 2$ if

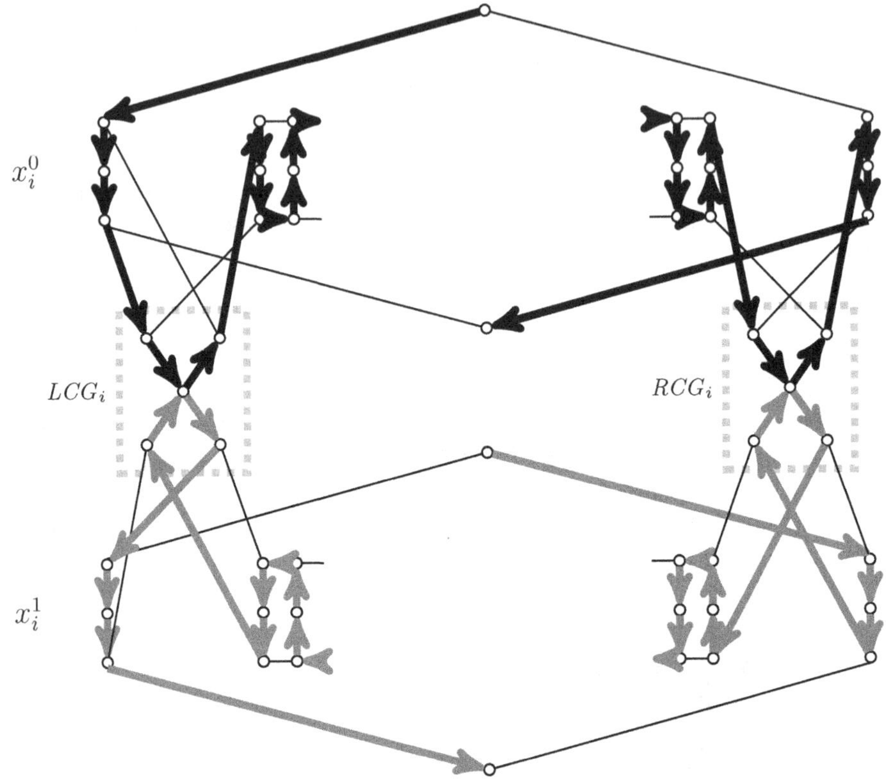

Fig. 4. Connecting the variable gadgets for x_i^0 and x_i^1 to LCG_i and RCG_i

- $v = in_i^{\downarrow,L}, v' \in \{v_i^{b,L}, v_i^{\bar{c},0}\}$ or $v = in_i^{\downarrow,R}, v' \in \{v_i^{\bar{f},h}, v_i^{b,R}\}$
- $v = out_i^{\uparrow,L}, v' \in \{v_i^{t,L}, v_i^{\bar{a},0}\}$ or $v = out_i^{\uparrow,R}, v' \in \{v_i^{\bar{d},h}, v_i^{t,R}\}$
- $v = in_i^{\uparrow,L}, v' \in \{v_{(i+m)}^{b,L}, v_{(i+m)}^{\bar{c},0}\}$ or $v = in_i^{\uparrow,R}, v' \in \{v_{(i+m)}^{\bar{f},h}, v_{(i+m)}^{b,R}\}$
- $v = out_i^{\downarrow,L}, v' \in \{v_{(i+m)}^{t,L}, v_{(i+m)}^{\bar{a},0}\}$ or $v = out_i^{\downarrow,R}, v' \in \{v_{(i+m)}^{\bar{d},h}, v_{(i+m)}^{t,R}\}$.

Two parts of an intended path, which we will explain in more detail later, is also illustrated in Figure 4.

Finally, there is a vertex v_{mid} with $RD(v_{mid}) = T$ connected to v_{bot} and v_{top} with two edges, both with FT equal to $\frac{1}{4}T$. The FT of all the missing edges are $2T$ (note that the largest value in RD is less than $2T$, so these edges can never be taken). This completes the construction of G. An example with $m = 3$ is given in Figure 5, where vertices in S (shared by two variable gadgets) are depicted as solid circles.

The rest of this section is devoted to the proof of the following proposition.

Proposition 3. *$\bigwedge_{j \geq 0} \varphi(j)$ is satisfiable iff G has a solution.*

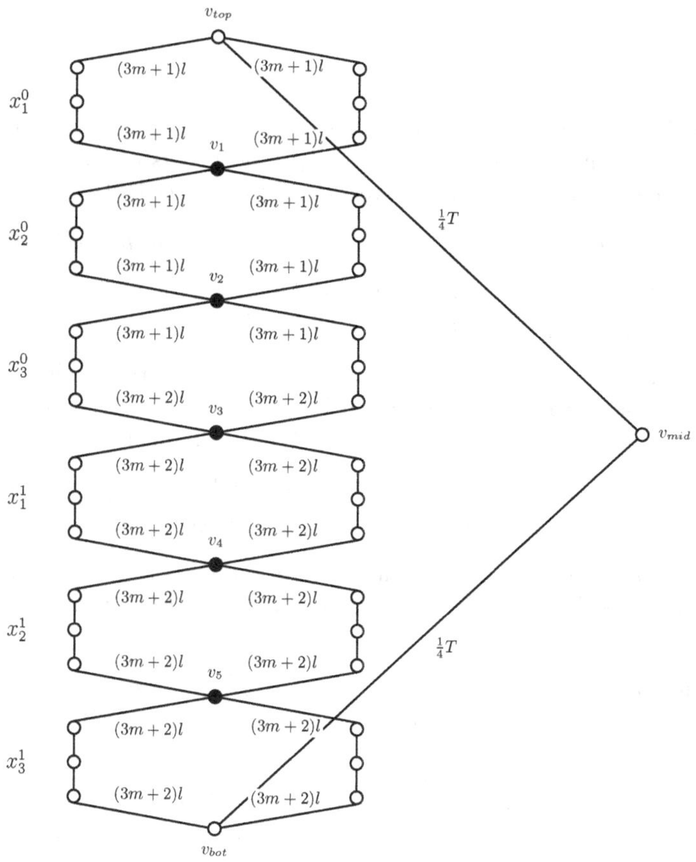

Fig. 5. An example with $m = 3$. Solid circles denote shared vertices $S = \{v_1, \ldots, v_5\}$.

3.2 The Proof of Proposition 3

We first prove the forward direction. Given a satisfying assignment of $\bigwedge_{j \geq 0} \varphi(j)$, we construct a solution s as follows: s starts from v_{top} and goes through the variable gadgets for $x_1^0, x_2^0, \ldots, x_m^0, x_1^1, x_2^1, \ldots, x_m^1$ in order, eventually reaching v_{bot}. Each variable gadget is traversed according to the truth value assigned to its corresponding variable. In such a traversal, both pvt_i^L and pvt_i^R are visited once (see the thick arrows in Figure 4 for the situation when x_i^0 is assigned **true** and x_i^1 is assigned **false**). Along the way from v_{top} to v_{bot}, s detours at certain times and 'hits' each clause vertex exactly once as illustrated by the thick arrows in Figure 2 (this can be done as $\varphi(0)$ is satisfied by the assignment). Then s goes back to v_{top} through v_{mid} and starts over again, this time following the truth values assigned to variables in $\overline{x}^1 \cup \overline{x}^2$, and so on. One can verify that this describes a solution to G.

Now consider the other direction. Let

$$s = (v_{mid}s_1v_{mid} \dots v_{mid}s_p)^\omega$$

be a periodic solution to G where each *segment* s_j, $j \in \{1, \dots, p\}$ is a finite subpath visiting only vertices in $V \setminus \{v_{mid}\}$. The proofs of the following two propositions can be found in the full version of this paper [10].

Proposition 4. *In* $s = (v_{mid}s_1v_{mid} \dots v_{mid}s_p)^\omega$*, either of the following holds:*

- *All* s_j*,* $j \in \{1, \dots, p\}$ *starts with* v_{top} *and ends with* v_{bot}
- *All* s_j*,* $j \in \{1, \dots, p\}$ *starts with* v_{bot} *and ends with* v_{top}*.*

We therefore further assume that s satisfies the first case of the proposition above (this is sound as a periodic solution can be 'reversed' while remaining a valid solution). We argue that s 'witnesses' a satisfying assignment of $\bigwedge_{j \geq 0} \varphi(j)$.

Proposition 5. *In each segment* s_j*, each vertex in* $\bigcup_{i \in \{1,\dots,m\}} \{pvt_i^L, pvt_i^R\}$ *appears twice whereas other vertices in* $V \setminus \{v_{mid}\}$ *appear once.*

Based on this proposition, we show that s cannot 'jump' between variable gadgets via clause vertices. It follows that the traversal of each Row_i must be done in a single pass.

Proposition 6. *In each segment* s_j*, if* v^{c_k} *is entered from a clause box (in some variable gadget), the edge that immediately follows must go back to the same clause box.*

Proof. Consider a 3×3 'box' formed by a separator box and (the left- or right-) half of a clause box. Note that except for the four vertices at the corners, no vertex in this 3×3 box is connected to the rest of the graph. Recall that if each vertex in this 3×3 box is to be visited only once (as enforced by Proposition 5), it must be traversed in the patterns illustrated in Figures 6 and 7.

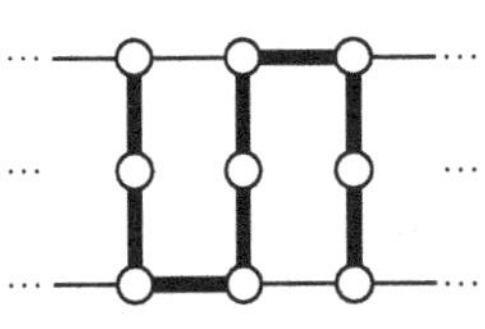

Fig. 6. Pattern '⊔⊓'

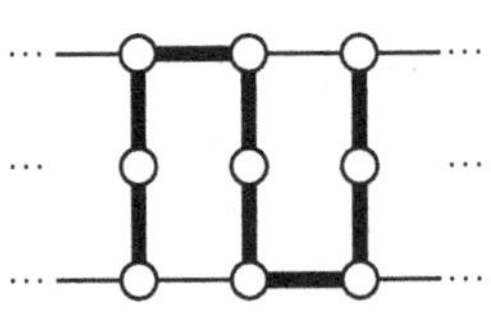

Fig. 7. Pattern '⊓⊔'

Now consider the situation in Figure 8 where s_j goes from v_z to v^{c_k}. The 3×3 box with v_z at its lower-right must be traversed in Pattern '⊔⊓' (as otherwise v_z will be visited twice). Assume that s_j does not visit v_x immediately after v^{c_k}. As v_x cannot be entered or left via v_z and v^{c_k}, the 3×3 box with v_x at its lower-left must also be traversed in Pattern '⊔⊓'. However, there is then no way to enter or leave v_y. This is a contradiction. □

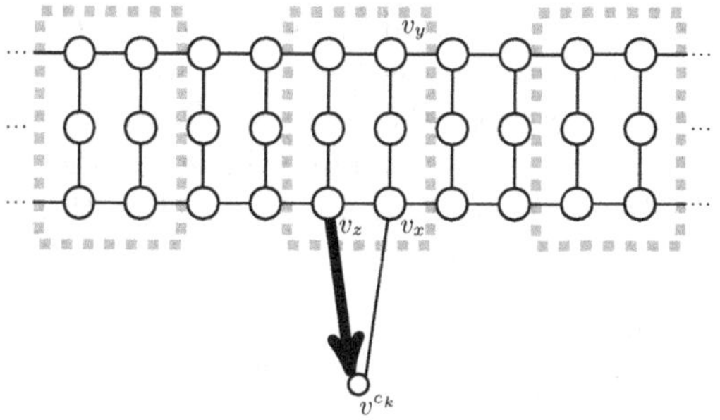

Fig. 8. x_i^0 occurs positively in c_k

Note that in Figure 8, the three clause boxes (framed by dotted lines) are all traversed in Pattern '⊓' or they are all traversed in Pattern '⊔'. More generally, we have the following proposition.

Proposition 7. *In each segment s_j, clause boxes in a given variable gadget are all traversed in Pattern '⊓' or they are all traversed in Pattern '⊔' (with possible detours via clause vertices).*

Write $v \to v'$ for the edge from v to v' and $v \rightsquigarrow v'$ for a finite path that starts with v and ends with v'. By Proposition 5, each segment s_j can be written as $v_{top} \rightsquigarrow v_{b_1} \rightsquigarrow \cdots \rightsquigarrow v_{b_{2m-1}} \rightsquigarrow v_{bot}$ where $b_1, \ldots, b_{2m-1}$ is a permutation of $1, \ldots, 2m-1$. We show that each subpath $v \rightsquigarrow v'$ of s_j with distinct $v, v' \in S \cup \{v_{top}, v_{bot}\}$ and no $v'' \in S \cup \{v_{top}, v_{bot}\}$ in between must be of a very restricted form. For convenience, we call such a subpath $v \rightsquigarrow v'$ a *fragment.*

Proposition 8. *In each segment $s_j = v_{top} \rightsquigarrow v_{b_1} \rightsquigarrow \cdots \rightsquigarrow v_{b_{2m-1}} \rightsquigarrow v_{bot}$, a fragment $v \rightsquigarrow v'$ visits pvt_i^L and pvt_i^R (once for each) for some $i \in \{1, \ldots, m\}$. Moreover, each fragment $v \rightsquigarrow v'$ in $v_{top} \rightsquigarrow v_{b_1} \rightsquigarrow \cdots \rightsquigarrow v_{b_m}$ visits a different set $\{pvt_i^L, pvt_i^R\}$. The same holds for $v_{b_m} \rightsquigarrow v_{b_{m+1}} \rightsquigarrow \cdots \rightsquigarrow v_{bot}$.*

Proof. It is clear that $dur(v \rightsquigarrow v') \geq 2(3m+1)l$, and hence $dur(v_{top} \rightsquigarrow v_{b_1} \rightsquigarrow \cdots v_{b_m}) \geq m\big(2(3m+1)l\big)$. Let there be a vertex $v \in \bigcup_{i \in \{1,\ldots,m\}} \{pvt_i^L, pvt_i^R\}$ missing in $v_{top} \rightsquigarrow v_{b_1} \rightsquigarrow \cdots v_{b_m}$. Since the time needed from v_{b_m} to v is greater than $(3m+1)l$, even if s_j visits v as soon as possible after v_{b_m}, the duration from v_{bot} in s_{j-1} to v in s_j will still be greater than $\frac{1}{2}T + m\big(2(3m+1)l\big) + (3m+1)l > RD(v)$, which is a contradiction. Therefore, all vertices in $\bigcup_{i \in \{1,\ldots,m\}} \{pvt_i^L, pvt_i^R\}$ must appear in the subpath from v_{top} to v_{b_m}. The same holds for the subpath from v_{b_m} to v_{bot} by similar arguments. Now note that by Proposition 6, a fragment $v \rightsquigarrow v'$ may visit at most two vertices—$\{pvt_i^L, pvt_i^R\}$ for some $i \in \{1, \ldots, m\}$. The proposition then follows from Proposition 5. □

Proposition 9. *In each segment s_j, a fragment $v \rightsquigarrow v'$ visits all vertices in either Row_i or Row_{i+m} for some $i \in \{1, \ldots, m\}$ but not a single vertex in $\bigcup_{\substack{j \neq i \\ j \in \{1,\ldots,m\}}} (Row_j \cup Row_{j+m})$.*

Now consider a fragment $v \rightsquigarrow v'$ that visits pvt_i^L and pvt_i^R (by Proposition 8). By Proposition 5, $v \rightsquigarrow v'$ must also visit exactly two vertices other than pvt_i^L in LCG_i and exactly two vertices other than pvt_i^R in RCG_i (once for each). It is not hard to see that $v \rightsquigarrow v'$ must contain, in order, the following subpaths (together with some obvious choices of edges connecting these subpaths):

(i). A long edge, e.g., $v_i \rightarrow v_i^{b,R}$.
(ii). A 'side', e.g., $v_i^{b,R} \rightarrow v_i^{m,R} \rightarrow v_i^{t,R}$.
(iii). A subpath consisting of a *pvt* vertex and two other vertices in the relevant consistency gadget, e.g., $out_i^{\uparrow,R} \rightarrow pvt_i^R \rightarrow in_i^{\downarrow,R}$.
(iv). A traversal of a row with detours.
(v). A subpath consisting of a *pvt* vertex and two other vertices in the relevant consistency gadget.
(vi). A side.
(vii). A long edge.

The following proposition is then immediate. In particular, the exact value of $dur(v \rightsquigarrow v')$ is decided by:

- FT of the long edges taken in (i) and (vii)
- detours to clause vertices in (iv).

Proposition 10. *In each segment s_j, the following holds for all fragments $v \rightsquigarrow v'$:*

$$2(3m+1)l + l \leq dur(v \rightsquigarrow v') \leq 2(3m+2)l + l + 2h.$$

Proposition 11. *The order the sets $\{pvt_i^L, pvt_i^R\}$ are visited (regardless of which vertex in the set is first visited) in the first m fragments of each segment s_j is identical to the order they are visited in the last m fragments of s_{j-1}.*

Proof. By Proposition 10, if this does not hold then there must be a *pvt* vertex having two occurrences in s separated by more than $\frac{1}{2}T + m\big(2(3m+1)l + l\big) + 2(3m+1)l$. This is a contradiction. □

For each segment s_j, we denote by $first(s_j)$ the 'first half' of s_j, i.e., the subpath of s_j that consists of the first m fragments of s_j and by $second(s_j)$ the 'second half' of s_j. Write $\exists(v \rightsquigarrow v') \subseteq u$ if u has a subpath of the form $v \rightsquigarrow v'$.

Proposition 12. *In each segment $s_j = v_{top} \rightsquigarrow v_{b_1} \rightsquigarrow \cdots \rightsquigarrow v_{b_{2m-1}} \rightsquigarrow v_{bot}$, we have $b_i = i$ for all $i \in \{1, \ldots, 2m-1\}$.*

Proof. First note that by construction and Proposition 8, $\{pvt_m^L, pvt_m^R\}$ must be the last set of *pvt* vertices visited in $second(s_{j-1})$. By Proposition 11, it must also be the last set of *pvt* vertices visited in $first(s_j)$. Now assume that a long edge of flight time $(3m+2)l$ is taken before pvt_m^L and pvt_m^R are visited in $first(s_j)$. Consider the following cases:

- $\exists(pvt_m^L \rightsquigarrow pvt_m^R) \subseteq second(s_{j-1})$ and $\exists(pvt_m^R \rightsquigarrow pvt_m^L) \subseteq first(s_j)$: Note that the last edge taken in s_{j-1} is a long edge of flight time $(3m+2)l$, and hence there are two occurrences of pvt_m^L in s separated by at least $\frac{1}{2}T + m(2(3m+1)l+l)+2l > \frac{1}{2}T + m(2(3m+1)l+l)+l+4h = RD(pvt_m^L)$.
- $\exists(pvt_m^R \rightsquigarrow pvt_m^L) \subseteq second(s_{j-1})$ and $\exists(pvt_m^L \rightsquigarrow pvt_m^R) \subseteq first(s_j)$: The same argument shows that pvt_m^R must miss its relative deadline.
- $\exists(pvt_m^L \rightsquigarrow pvt_m^R) \subseteq second(s_{j-1})$ and $\exists(pvt_m^L \rightsquigarrow pvt_m^R) \subseteq first(s_j)$: The same argument shows that both pvt_m^L and pvt_m^R must miss their relative deadlines.
- $\exists(pvt_m^R \rightsquigarrow pvt_m^L) \subseteq second(s_{j-1})$ and $\exists(pvt_m^R \rightsquigarrow pvt_m^L) \subseteq first(s_j)$: The same argument shows that both pvt_m^L and pvt_m^R must miss their relative deadlines.

We therefore conclude that in $first(s_j)$, all long edges taken before pvt_m^L and pvt_m^R are visited must have FT equal to $(3m+1)l$. Furthermore, all such long edges must be traversed 'downwards' (by Proposition 5). It follows that $b_i = i$ for $i \in \{1, \ldots, m-1\}$. By Proposition 11, Proposition 5 and $m > 2$, we easily derive that $b_m = m$ and then $b_i = i$ for $i \in \{m+1, \ldots, 2m-1\}$. □

By Proposition 12, the long edges in each variable gadget must be traversed in the ways shown in Figures 9 and 10.

Fig. 9. The variable is assigned to **true**

Fig. 10. The variable is assigned to **false**

Proposition 13. *For each segment s_j, the ways in which the long edges are traversed in the last m fragments of s_j are consistent with the ways in which the long edges are traversed in the first m fragments of s_{j+1}.*

Proof. Without loss of generality, consider the case that $\exists(pvt_i^L \rightsquigarrow pvt_i^R) \subseteq second(s_j)$ and $\exists(pvt_i^R \rightsquigarrow pvt_i^L) \subseteq first(s_{j+1})$. By Proposition 12, these two occurrences of pvt_i^L in s are separated by, at least, the sum of $\frac{1}{2}T + m(2(3m+2)l+l) - (2i-1)l$ and the duration of the actual subpath $pvt_i^R \rightsquigarrow pvt_i^L$ in $first(s_{j+1})$. It is clear that pvt_i^L must miss its relative deadline. □

Proposition 14. *In each segment s_j, if a variable gadget is traversed as in Figure 9 (Figure 10), then all of its clause boxes are traversed in Pattern '⊔' (Pattern '⊓').*

Consider a segment s_j. As each clause vertex is visited once in s_j (by Proposition 5), the ways in which the long edges are traversed in all fragments $v \rightsquigarrow v'$

of s_j (i.e., as in Figure 9 or Figure 10) can be seen as a satisfying assignment of $\varphi(0)$ (by construction and Proposition 14). By the same argument, the ways in which the long edges are traversed in all fragments of s_{j+1} can be seen as a satisfying assignment of $\varphi(1)$. Now by Proposition 13, the assignment of variables $\overline{x}^1$ is consistent in both segments. By IH, s witnesses a (periodic) satisfying assignment of $\bigwedge_{j\geq 0} \varphi(j)$. Proposition 3 is hence proved.

Finally, note that FT can easily be modified into a metric over V by replacing each entry of value $2T$ with the 'shortest distance' between the two relevant vertices. It is easy to see that Proposition 3 still holds. Our main result, which holds for the metric case, follows immediately from Section 2.2.

Theorem 15. *The* CR-UAV *Problem is* PSPACE-*complete.*[4]

4 Conclusion

We have proved that the CR-UAV Problem is PSPACE-complete even in the single-UAV case. The proof reveals a connection between a periodically specified problem and a recurrent path-planning problem (which is not *succinctly specified* in the sense of [14]). We list below some possible directions for future work:

1. A number of crucial problems in other domains, e.g., the generalised pinwheel scheduling problem [8] and the message ferrying problem [24], share similarities with the CR-UAV Problem—namely, they have relative deadlines and therefore 'contexts'. Most of these problems are only known to be NP-hard. It would be interesting to investigate whether our construction can be adapted to establish PSPACE-hardness of these problems.
2. It is claimed in [13] that the restricted case in which vertices can be realised as points in a two-dimensional plane (with discretised distances between points) is NP-complete (with a single UAV). A natural question is the relationship with the problem studied in the present paper.
3. Current approaches to solving the CR-UAV Problem often formulate it as a Mixed-Integer Linear Program (MILP) and then invoke an off-the-shelf solver (see, e.g., [4]). Yet as implied by Proposition 3, the length of a solution can however be exponential in the size of the problem instance. We are currently investigating alternative implementations which would overcome such difficulties.

References

1. Alighanbari, M., Kuwata, Y., How, J.: Coordination and control of multiple uavs with timing constraints and loitering. In: Proceedings of ACC 2003, vol. 6, pp. 5311–5316. IEEE Press (2003)
2. Alur, R.: Timed automata. In: NATO-ASI Summer School on Verification of Digital and Hybrid Systems. Springer (1998), `http://www.cis.upenn.edu/~alur/Nato97.ps`

[4] Our result holds irrespective of whether the numbers are encoded in unary or binary.

3. Basilico, N., Gatti, N., Amigoni, F.: Developing a deterministic patrolling strategy for security agents. In: Proceedings of WI-IAT 2009, pp. 565–572. IEEE Computer Society Press (2009)
4. Basilico, N., Gatti, N., Amigoni, F.: Patrolling security games: Definition and algorithms for solving large instances with single patroller and single intruder. Artificial Intelligence 184-185, 78–123 (2012)
5. Böckenhauer, H.J., Hromkovic, J., Kneis, J., Kupke, J.: The parameterized approximability of TSP with deadlines. Theory Comput. Syst 41(3), 431–444 (2007), `http://dx.doi.org/10.1007/s00224-007-1347-x`
6. Crama, Y., Van De Klundert, J.: Cyclic scheduling of identical parts in a robotic cell. Operations Research 45(6), 952–965 (1997)
7. Drucker, N., Penn, M., Strichman, O.: Cyclic routing of unmanned air vehicles. Tech. Rep. IE/IS-2014-02, Faculty of Industrial Engineering and Management, Technion (2010), `http://ie.technion.ac.il/tech_reports/1393234936_AUVSI-Abstract-31Aug2010-submitted.pdf`
8. Feinberg, E.A., Curry, M.T.: Generalized pinwheel problem. Mathematical Methods of Operations Research 62(1), 99–122 (2005)
9. Henzinger, T.A., Manna, Z., Pnueli, A.: What good are digital clocks? In: Kuich, W. (ed.) ICALP 1992. LNCS, vol. 623, pp. 545–558. Springer, Heidelberg (1992)
10. Ho, H.M., Ouaknine, J.: The cyclic-routing UAV problem is PSPACE-complete. CoRR abs/1411.2874 (2014), `http://arxiv.org/abs/1411.2874`
11. Jain, M., Kardes, E., Kiekintveld, C., Ordóñez, F., Tambe, M.: Security games with arbitrary schedules: A branch and price approach. In: Proceedings of AAAI 2010, pp. 792–797. AAAI Press (2010)
12. Kats, V., Levner, E.: Minimizing the number of robots to meet a given cyclic schedule. Annals of Operations Research 69, 209–226 (1997)
13. Las Fargeas, J., Hyun, B., Kabamba, P., Girard, A.: Persistent visitation under revisit constraints. In: Proceedings of ICUAS 2013, pp. 952–957. IEEE Press (2013)
14. Marathe, M.V., Hunt III, H.B., Stearns, R.E., Radkakrishnan, V.: Complexity of hierarchically and 1-dimensional periodically specified problems. In: Satisfiability Problem: Theory and Applications. DIMACS Series in Discrete Mathematics and Theoretical Computer Science, vol. 35, pp. 225–260. DIMACS (1997)
15. Orlin, J.B.: The complexity of dynamic languages and dynamic optimization problems. In: Proceedings of STOC 1981, pp. 218–227. ACM Press (1981)
16. Orlin, J.B.: Minimizing the number of vehicles to meet a fixed periodic schedule: An application of periodic posets. Operations Research 30(4), 760–776 (1982)
17. Richards, A., How, J.P.: Aircraft trajectory planning with collision avoidance using mixed integer linear programming. In: Proceedings of ACC 2002, vol. 3, pp. 1936–1941. IEEE Press (2002)
18. Savelsbergh, M.W.: Local search in routing problems with time windows. Annals of Operations Research 4(1), 285–305 (1985)
19. Sundar, K., Rathinam, S.: Route planning algorithms for unmanned aerial vehicles with refueling constraints. In: Proceedings of ACC 2012, pp. 3266–3271. IEEE Press (2012)
20. Tsai, J., Kiekintveld, C., Ordonez, F., Tambe, M., Rathi, S.: IRIS—a tool for strategic security allocation in transportation networks. In: Tambe, M. (ed.) Security and Game Theory: Algorithms, Deployed Systems, Lessons Learned. Cambridge University Press (2009)
21. Unmanned air vehicle systems association, `http://www.uavs.org/`
22. Wollmer, R.D.: An airline tail routing algorithm for periodic schedules. Networks 20(1), 49–54 (1990)

23. Yang, G., Kapila, V.: Optimal path planning for unmanned air vehicles with kinematic and tactical constraints. In: Proceedings of CDC 2002, vol. 2, pp. 1301–1306. IEEE Press (2002)
24. Zhao, W., Ammar, M.H., Zegura, E.W.: A message ferrying approach for data delivery in sparse mobile ad hoc networks. In: Proceedings of MobiHoc 2004, pp. 187–198. ACM Press (2004)

Typing Weak MSOL Properties

Sylvain Salvati and Igor Walukiewicz

CNRS, Université de Bordeaux, INRIA

Abstract. We consider λY-calculus as a non-interpreted functional programming language: the result of the execution of a program is its normal form that can be seen as the tree of calls to built-in operations. Weak monadic second-order logic (wMSO) is well suited to express properties of such trees. We give a type system for ensuring that the result of the execution of a λY-program satisfies a given wMSO property. In order to prove soundness and completeness of the system we construct a denotational semantics of λY-calculus that is capable of computing properties expressed in wMSO.

1 Introduction

Higher-order functional programs are more and more often used to write interactive applications. In this context it is important to reason about behavioral properties of programs. We present a kind of type and effect discipline [22] where a well-typed program will satisfy behavioral properties expressed in weak monadic second-order logic (wMSO).

We consider the class of programs written in the simply-typed calculus with recursion and finite base types: the λY-calculus. This calculus offers an abstraction of higher-order programs that faithfully represents higher-order control. The dynamics of an interaction of a program with its environment is represented by the Böhm tree of a λY-term that is a tree reflecting the control flow of the program. For example, the Böhm tree of the term $Yx.ax$ is the infinite sequence of a's, representing that the program does an infinite sequence of a actions without ever terminating. Another example is presented in Figure 1. A functional program for the factorial function is written as a λY-term Fct and the value of Fct applied to a constant c is calculated. Observe that all constants in Fct are non-interpreted. The Böhm tree semantics means call-by-name evaluation strategy. Nevertheless, call-by-value evaluation can be encoded, so can be finite data domains, and conditionals over them [18,13]. The approach is then to translate a functional program to a λY-term and to examine the Böhm tree it generates.

Since the dynamics of the program is represented by a potentially infinite tree, monadic second-order logic (MSOL) is a natural candidate for the language to formulate properties in. This logic is an extension of first-order logic with quantification over sets. MSOL captures precisely regular properties of trees [25], and it is decidable if the Böhm tree generated by a given λY-term satisfies a given property [23]. In this paper we will restrict to weak monadic second-order logic (wMSO). The difference is that in wMSO quantification is restricted to range

A. Pitts (Ed.): FOSSACS 2015, LNCS 9034, pp. 343–357, 2015.
DOI: 10.1007/978-3-662-46678-0_22

$$
\begin{aligned}
\mathit{Factorial}(x) &\equiv \textbf{if } x = 0 \textbf{ then } 1 \textbf{ else } x \cdot \mathit{Factorial}(x-1) \\
\mathit{Fct} &\equiv YF.\ \lambda x.\ \textbf{if } (z\ x)\ 1\ (m\ x\ (F(-\ x\ 1)))
\end{aligned}
$$

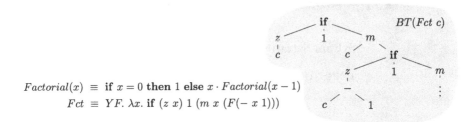

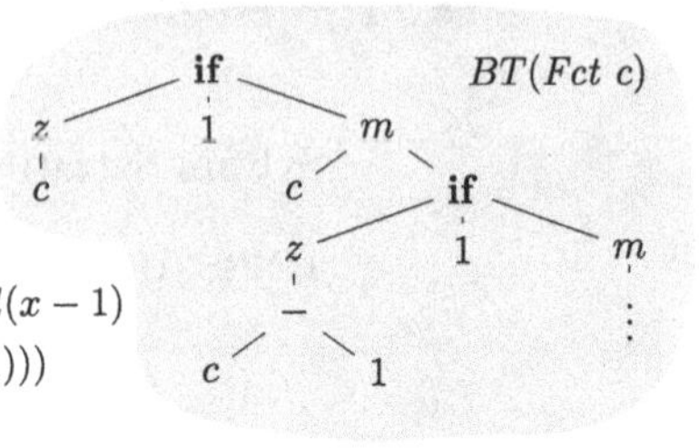

Fig. 1. Böhm tree of the factorial function

over finite sets. While wMSO is a proper fragment of MSO, it is sufficiently strong to express safety, reachability, and many liveness properties. Over sequences, that is degenerated trees where every node has one successor, wMSO is equivalent to full MSO.

The basic judgments we are interested in are of the form $BT(M) \vDash \alpha$ meaning that the result of the evaluation of M, i.e. the Böhm tree of M, has the property α formulated in wMSO. Going back to the example of the factorial function from Figure 1, we can consider a property: all computations that eventually take the "if" branch of the conditional are finite. This property holds in $BT(\mathit{Fct}\ c)$. Observe by the way that $BT(\mathit{Fct}\ c)$ is not regular – it has infinitely many non-isomorphic subtrees as the number of subtractions is growing. In general the interest of judgments of the form $BT(M) \vDash \alpha$ is to be able to express liveness and fairness properties of executions, like: "every *open* action is eventually followed by a *close* action", or that "there are infinitely many read actions". Various other verification problems for functional programs can be reduced to this problem [18,20,24,32,12].

Technically, the judgment $BT(M) \vDash \alpha$ is equivalent to determining whether a Böhm tree of a given λY-term is accepted by a given weak alternating automaton. This problem is known to be decidable thanks to the result of Ong [23], but here we present a denotational approach. Our two main contributions are:

- A construction of a finitary model for a given weak alternating automaton. The value of a term in this model determines if the Böhm tree of the term is accepted by the automaton. So verification is reduced to evaluation.
- Two type systems. A typing system deriving statements of the form "the value of a term M is bigger than an element d of the model"; and a typing system for dual properties. These typing systems use standard fixpoint rules and follow the methodology coined as *Domains in Logical Form* [1]. Thanks to the first item, these typing systems can directly talk about acceptance/rejection of the Böhm tree of a term by an automaton. These type systems are decidable, and every term has a "best" type that simply represents its value in the model.

Having a model and a type system has several advantages over having just a decision procedure. First, it makes verification compositional: the result for a term is calculated from the results for its subterms. In particular, it opens possibilities for a modular approach to the verification of large programs. Next, it enables semantic based program transformations as for example reflection of a given property in a given term [8,29,13]. It also implies the transfer theorem for wMSO [28] with a number of consequences offered by this theorem. Finally, models open a way to novel verification algorithms be it through evaluation, type system, or through hybrid algorithms using typing and evaluation at the same time [31]. We come back to these points in the conclusions.

Historically, Ong [23] has shown the decidability of the MSO theory of Böhm trees for all λY-terms. This result has been revisited in several different ways. Some approaches take a term of the base type, and unroll it to some infinite object: tree with pointers [23], computation of a higher-order pushdown automaton with collapse [14], a collection of typing judgments that are used to define a game [19], a computation of a Krivine machine [27]. Very recently Tsukada and Ong [33] have presented a compositional approach: a typing system is used to reduce the verification problem to a series of game solving problems. Another recent advance is given by Hofmann and Chen who provide a type system for verifying path properties of trees generated by first-order λY-terms [11]. In other words, this last result gives a typing system for verifying path properties of trees generated by deterministic pushdown automata. Compared to this last work, we consider the whole λY-calculus and an incomparable set of properties.

Already some time ago, Aehligh [2] has discovered an easy way to prove Ong's theorem restricted to properties expressed by tree automata with trivial acceptance conditions (TAC automata). The core of his approach can be formulated by saying that the verification problem for such properties can be reduced to evaluation in a specially constructed and simple model. Later, Kobayashi proposed a type system for such properties and constructed a tool based on it [18]. This in turn opened a way to an active ongoing research resulting in the steady improvement of the capacities of the verification tools [17,9,10,26]. TAC automata can express only safety properties. Our model and typing systems set the stage for practical verification of wMSO properties.

The model approach to verification of λY-calculus is quite recent. In [29] it is shown that simple models with greatest fixpoints capture exactly properties expressed with TAC automata. An extension is then proposed to allow one to detect divergence. The simplicity offered by models is exemplified by Haddad's recent work [13] giving simple semantic based transformations of λY-terms.

We would also like to mention two other quite different approaches to integrate properties of infinite behaviors into typing. Naik and Palsberg [21] make a connection between model-checking and typing. They consider only safety properties, and since their setting is much more general than ours, their type system is more complex too. Jeffrey [15,16] has shown how to incorporate Linear Temporal Logic into types using a much richer dependent types paradigm. The calculus is intended to talk about control and data in functional reactive programming framework, and aims at using SMT solvers.

In the next section we introduce the main objects of our study: λY-calculus, and weak alternating automata. Section 3 presents the type system. Its soundness and completeness can be straightforwardly formulated for closed terms of atomic type. For the proof though we need a statement about all terms. This is where the model based approach helps. Section 4 describes how to construct models for wMSO properties. In Section 5 we come back to our type systems. The general soundness and completeness property we prove says that types can denote every element of the model, and the type systems can derive precisely the judgments that hold in the model (Theorem 3). In the conclusion section we mention other applications of our model. All proofs can be found in a long version of the paper [30].

2 Preliminaries

We quickly fix notations related to the simply typed λY-calculus and to Böhm trees. We then recall the definition of weak alternating automata on ranked trees. These will be used to specify properties of Böhm trees.

λY-calculus. The *set of types* $\mathcal{T}$ is constructed from a unique *basic type* o using a binary operation $\to$ that associates to the right. Thus o is a type and if A, B are types, so is $(A \to B)$. The order of a type is defined by: $order(o) = 0$, and $order(A \to B) = max(1 + order(A), order(B))$. We work with *tree signatures* that are finite sets of *typed constants of order at most* 1. Types of order 1 are of the form $o \to \cdots \to o \to o$ that we abbreviate $o^i \to o$ when they contain $i+1$ occurrences of o. For convenience we assume that $o^0 \to o$ is just o. If Σ is a signature, we write $\Sigma^{(i)}$ for the set of constants of type $o^i \to o$. In examples we will often use constants of type $o \to o$ as this makes the examples more succinct. At certain times, we will restrict to the types o and $o^2 \to o$ that are representative for all the cases.

Simply typed λY-terms are built from the constants in the signature, and constants Y^A, Ω^A for every type A. These stand for the *fixpoint combinator* and *undefined term*, respectively. Apart from constants, for each type A there is a countable set of variables $x^A, y^A, \dots$. Terms are built from these constants and variables using typed application and λ-abstraction. We shall write sequences of λ-abstractions $\lambda x_1. \dots \lambda x_n.\ M$ with only one λ: either $\lambda x_1 \dots x_n.\ M$, or even shorter $\lambda \boldsymbol{x}.\ M$. We will often write $Yx.M$ instead of $Y(\lambda x.M)$. Every λY-term can be written in this notation since YN has the same Böhm tree as $Y(\lambda x.Nx)$, and the latter term is $Yx.(Nx)$. We take for granted the operational semantics of the calculus given by β and δ reductions. The *Böhm tree* of a term M is obtained by reducing it until one reaches a term of the form $\lambda \boldsymbol{x}.N_0 N_1 \dots N_k$ with N_0 a variable or a constant. Then $BT(M)$ is a tree having its root labeled by $\lambda \boldsymbol{x}.N_0$ and having $BT(N_1), \dots, BT(N_k)$ as subtrees. Otherwise $BT(M) = \Omega^A$, where A is the type of M. Böhm trees are infinite normal forms of λY-terms. A Böhm tree of a closed term of type o over a tree signature is a potentially infinite ranked tree: a node labeled by a constant a of type $o^i \to o$ has i successors (c.f. Figure 1).

Example. As an example take $(YF.\ N)a$ where $N = \lambda g.g(b(F(\lambda x.g(g\,x))))$. Both a and b have the type $o \to o$; while F has type $(o \to o) \to o$, and so does N. Observe that we are using a more convenient notation YF here. The Böhm tree of $(YF.N)a$ is $BT((YF.N)a) = aba^2ba^4b \dots a^{2^n}b \dots$ after every consecutive occurrence of b the number of occurrences of a doubles because of the double application of g inside N.

wMSO and Weak Alternating Automata. We will be interested in properties of trees expressed in weak monadic second-order logic. This is an extension of first-order logic with quantification over finite sets of elements. The interplay of negation and quantification allows the logic to express many infinitary properties. The logic is closed for example under constructs: "for infinitely many vertices a given property holds", "every path consisting of vertices having a given property is finite". From the automata point of view, the expressive power of the logic is captured by weak alternating automata. A *weak alternating automaton* accepts trees over a fixed tree signature Σ.

A *weak alternating tree automaton* over the signature Σ is:

$$\mathcal{A} = \langle Q, \Sigma, q^0 \in Q, \{\delta_i\}_{i \in \mathcal{N}}, \rho : Q \to \mathcal{N} \rangle$$

where Q is a finite set of states, $q^0 \in Q$ is the initial state, ρ is the *rank function*, and $\delta_i : Q \times \Sigma^{(i)} \to \mathcal{P}(\mathcal{P}(Q)^i)$ is the transition function. For q in Q, we call $\rho(q)$ *its rank.* The automaton is *weak* in the sense that when $(S_1, \dots, S_i)$ is in $\delta_i(q, a)$, then the rank of every q' in $\bigcup_{1 \le j \le i} S_j$ is not bigger than the rank of q, $\rho(q') \le \rho(q)$.

Observe that since Σ is finite, only finitely many δ_i are nontrivial. From the definition it follows that $\delta_2 : Q \times \Sigma^{(2)} \to \mathcal{P}(\mathcal{P}(Q) \times \mathcal{P}(Q))$ and $\delta_0 : Q \times \Sigma^{(0)} \to \{0, 1\}$. We will simply write δ without a subscript when this causes no ambiguity.

Automata will work on Σ-labeled binary trees that are partial functions $t : \mathcal{N}^* \to \Sigma \cup \{\Omega\}$ such that the number successors of a node is determined by the label of the node. In particular, if $t(u) \in \Sigma^{(0)} \cup \{\Omega\}$ then u is a leaf.

The acceptance of a tree is defined in terms of *games* between two players that we call Eve and Adam. A *play* between Eve and Adam from some node v of a tree t and some state $q \in Q$ proceeds as follows. If v is a leaf and is labeled by some $c \in \Sigma^{(0)}$ then Eve wins iff $\delta_0(q, c)$ holds. If the node is labeled by Ω then Eve wins iff the rank of q is even. Otherwise, v is an internal node; Eve chooses a tuple of sets of states $(S_1, \dots, S_i) \in \delta(q, t(v))$. Then Adam chooses S_j (for $j = 1, \dots, i$) and a state $q' \in S_j$. The play continues from the j-th son of v and state q'. When a player is not able to play any move, he/she looses. If the play is infinite then the winner is decided by looking at ranks of states appearing on the play. Due to the weakness of $\mathcal{A}$ the rank of states in a play can never increase, so it eventually stabilizes at some value. Eve wins if this value is even. A tree t is *accepted* by $\mathcal{A}$ from a state $q \in Q$ if Eve has a winning strategy in the game started from the root of t and from q.

Automata with *trivial acceptance conditions*, as considered by Kobayashi [17], are obtained by requiring that all states have rank 0. Automata with co-trivial are just those whose all states have rank 1.

Observe that without a loss of generality we can assume that δ is monotone, i.e. if $(S_1,\dots,S_i) \in \delta(q,a)$ then for every $(S'_1,\dots,S'_i)$ such that $S_j \subseteq S'_j \subseteq \{q' : \rho(q') \leq \rho(q)\}$ we have $(S'_1,\dots,S'_i) \in \delta(q,a)$. Indeed, adding the transitions needed to satisfy the monotonicity condition does not give Eve more winning possibilities.

An automaton defines a language of closed terms of type o whose Böhm trees it accepts from its initial state q^0:

$$L(\mathcal{A}) = \{M \,:\, M \text{ is closed term of type } o,\ BT(M) \text{ is accepted by } \mathcal{A} \text{ from } q^0\}$$

3 Type Systems for wMSOL

In this section we describe the main result of the paper. We present a type system to reason about wMSO properties of Böhm trees of terms (a dual type system is presented in the appendix). We will rely on the equivalence of wMSO and weak alternating automata, and construct a type system for an automaton. For a fixed weak alternating automaton $\mathcal{A}$ we want to characterize the terms whose Böhm trees are accepted by $\mathcal{A}$, i.e. the set $L(\mathcal{A})$. The characterization will be purely type theoretic (cf. Theorem 1).

Fix an automaton $\mathcal{A} = \langle Q, \Sigma, q^0, \{\delta_i\}_{i\in\mathcal{N}}, \rho\rangle$. Let m be the maximal rank, i.e., the maximal value ρ takes on Q. For every $0 \leq k \leq m$ we write $Q_k = \{q \in Q : \rho(q) = k\}$ and $Q_{\leq k} = \{q \in Q : \rho(q) \leq k\}$.

The type system we propose is obtained by allowing the use of intersections inside simple types. This idea has been used by Kobayashi [18] to give a typing characterization for languages of automata with trivial acceptance conditions. We work with, more general, weak acceptance conditions, and this will be reflected in the stratification of types, and two fixpoint rules: greatest fixpoint rule for even strata, and the least fixpoint rule for odd strata.

First, we define the sets of intersection types. They are indexed by a rank of the automaton and by a simple type. Note that every intersection type will have a corresponding simple type; this is a crucial difference with intersection types characterizing strongly normalizing terms [4]. Letting $\mathrm{Types}^k_A = \bigcup_{0\leq l\leq k} \mathrm{types}^l_A$ we define:

$$\mathrm{types}^k_o = \{q \in Q : \rho(q) = k\},\ \mathrm{types}^k_{A\to B} = \{T \to s : T \subseteq \mathrm{Types}^k_A \text{ and } s \in \mathrm{types}^k_B\}\ .$$

The difference with simple types is that now we have a set constructor that will be interpreted as the intersection of its elements.

When we write types_A or Types_A we mean types^m_A and Types^m_A respectively; where m is the maximal rank used by the automaton $\mathcal{A}$.

For $S \subseteq \mathrm{Types}^k_A$ and $T \subseteq \mathrm{types}^k_B$ we write $S \to T$ for $\{S \to t : t \in T\}$. Notice that $S \to T$ is included in $\mathrm{types}^k_{A\to B}$.

We now give subsumption rules that express the intuitive dependence between types. So as to make the connection with the model construction later, we have adopted an ordering of intersection types that is dual to the usual one.

$$\frac{S \subseteq T \subseteq Q}{S \sqsubseteq_0 T} \qquad \frac{\forall s \in S, \exists t \in T, s \sqsubseteq_A t}{S \sqsubseteq_A T} \qquad \frac{s = t}{s \sqsubseteq_0 t} \qquad \frac{T \sqsubseteq_A S \quad s \sqsubseteq_B t}{S \to s \sqsubseteq_{A \to B} T \to t}$$

Given $S \subseteq \mathrm{Types}_{A \to B}$ and $T \subseteq \mathrm{Types}_A$ we write $S(T)$ for the set $\{t : (U \to t) \in S \wedge U \sqsubseteq T\}$.

The typing system presented in Figure 2 derives judgments of the form $\Gamma \vdash M \geq S$ where Γ is an environment containing all the free variables of the term M, and $S \subseteq \mathrm{Types}_A$ with A the type of M. As usual, an environment Γ is a finite list $x_1 \geq S_1, \ldots, x_n \geq S_n$ where $x_1, \ldots, x_n$ are pairwise distinct variables of type A_i, and $S_i \subseteq \mathrm{Types}_{A_i}$. We will use a functional notation and write $\Gamma(x_i)$ for S_i. We shall also write $\Gamma, x \geq S$ with its usual meaning.

The rules in the first row of Figure 2 express standard intersection types dependencies: the axiom, the intersection rule and the subsumption rule. The rules in the second line are specific to our fixed automaton. The third line contains the usual rules for application and abstraction. The least fixpoint rule in the next line is standard. The greatest fixpoint rule in the last line is more intricate. It is allowed only on even strata. If taken for $k = 0$ the rule becomes the standard rule for the greatest fixpoint as the set T must be the empty set. For $k > 0$ the rule permits to incorporate T that is the result of the fixpoint computation on the lower stratum.

$$\frac{}{\Gamma, x \geq S \vdash x \geq S} \qquad \frac{\Gamma \vdash M \geq S \quad \Gamma \vdash M \geq T}{\Gamma \vdash M \geq S \cup T} \qquad \frac{\Gamma \vdash M \geq S \quad T \sqsubseteq S}{\Gamma \vdash M \geq T}$$

$$\frac{}{\Gamma \vdash c \geq \{q : \delta_o(q, c) \text{ holds}\}} \qquad \frac{(S_1, \ldots, S_i) \in \delta(a, q)}{\Gamma \vdash a \geq \{S_1 \to \cdots \to S_i \to q\}}$$

$$\frac{\Gamma \vdash M \geq S \quad \Gamma \vdash N \geq T}{\Gamma \vdash MN \geq S(T)} \qquad \frac{S \subseteq \mathrm{Types}^k,\ T \subseteq \mathrm{types}^k \quad \Gamma, x \geq S \vdash M \geq T}{\Gamma \vdash \lambda x.M \geq S \to T}$$

$$\frac{\Gamma \vdash (\lambda x.M) \geq S \quad \Gamma \vdash (Yx.M) \geq T}{\Gamma \vdash Yx.M \geq S(T)}\ Y \text{ odd}$$

$$\frac{S \subseteq \mathrm{types}_A^{2k}, \quad T \subseteq \mathrm{Types}_A^{2k-1}, \quad \Gamma \vdash \lambda x.M \geq (S \cup T) \to S \quad \Gamma \vdash Yx.M \geq T}{\Gamma \vdash Yx.M \geq S \cup T}\ Y \text{ even}$$

Fig. 2. Type system

The main result of the paper says that the typing in this system is equivalent to accepting with our fixed weak alternating automaton.

Theorem 1. *For every closed term M of type o and every state q of $\mathcal{A}$: the judgment $\vdash M \geq q$ is derivable iff $\mathcal{A}$ accepts $BT(M)$ from q.*

Since there are finitely many types, this typing system is decidable. As we will see in the following example, this type system allows us to prove in a rather simple manner properties of Böhm trees that are beyond the reach of trivial automata. Compared to Kobayashi and Ong type system [19], the fixpoint typing rules we propose avoid the use of an external solver for a parity game. Our type system makes it also evident what is the meaning of higher-order terms with free variables. In the example below we use fixpoint rules on terms of order 2.

Example 2. Consider the term $M = (YF.N)a$ where $N = \lambda g.g(b(F(\lambda x.g(g\,x))))$. As we have seen on page 347, $BT(M) = aba^2ba^4b\ldots a^{2^n}b\ldots$. We show with typing that there are infinitely many occurrences of b in $BT(M)$. To this end we take an automaton has states $Q = \{q_1, q_2\}$, and works over the signature that contains a and b. The transitions of the automaton are:

$$\delta(q_1, a) = \{q_1\} \quad \delta(q_2, a) = \{q_1, q_2\} \quad \delta(q_1, b) = \emptyset \quad \delta(q_2, b) = q_2$$

The ranks of states are indicated by their subscripts. Starting with state q_2, the automaton only accepts sequences that contain infinitely many b's. So our goal is to derive $\vdash (YF.N)a \geq q_2$. First observe that from the definition of the transitions of the automaton we get axioms:

$$\frac{}{\vdash a \geq q_1 \to q_1} \quad \frac{}{\vdash a \geq \{q_1, q_2\} \to q_2} \quad \frac{}{\vdash b \geq \emptyset \to q_1} \quad \frac{}{\vdash b \geq q_2 \to q_2}$$

Looking at the typings of a, we can see that we will get our desired judgment from the application rule if we prove:

$$\vdash YF.N \geq S \qquad \text{where } S \text{ is } \{q_1 \to q_1, \{q_1, q_2\} \to q_2\} \to q_2.$$

To this end, we apply subsumption rule and the greatest fixpoint rule:

$$\dfrac{\dfrac{\vdash \lambda F.N \geq (S \cup T) \to S \quad \vdash YF.N \geq T}{\vdash YF.N \geq S \cup T}\,Y\ even}{\vdash YF.N \geq S} \qquad \text{where } T = \{(q_1 \to q_1) \to q_1\}$$

The derivation of the top right judgment uses the least fixpoint rule:

$$\dfrac{\dfrac{\dfrac{\dfrac{}{g \geq q_1 \to q_1 \vdash g \geq q_1 \to q_1} \quad g \geq q_1 \to q_1 \vdash b(F(\lambda x.g(g\,x))) \geq q_1}{g \geq q_1 \to q_1 \vdash g(b(F(\lambda x.g(g\,x)))) \geq q_1}}{\vdash \lambda F \lambda g.g(b(F(\lambda x.g(gx)))) \geq \emptyset \to (q_1 \to q_1) \to q_1}\,Y\ odd}{\vdash YF.N \geq (q_1 \to q_1) \to q_1}$$

We have displayed only one of the two premises of the $Y odd$ rule since the other is of the form $\geq \emptyset$ so it is vacuously true. The top right judgment is derivable directly from the axiom on b. The derivation of the remaining judgment $\vdash \lambda F.N \geq (S \cup T) \to S$ is as follows.

$$\dfrac{\dfrac{\overline{\Gamma \vdash g \geq \{q_1, q_2\} \to q_2} \qquad \Gamma \vdash b(F(\lambda x.g(g\,x))) \geq q_1, q_2}{\Gamma \vdash g(b(F(\lambda x.g(g\,x)))) \geq q_2}}{\vdash \lambda F \lambda g.g(b(F(\lambda x.g(g\,x)))) \geq (S \cup T) \to S}$$

where Γ is $F \geq S \cup T, g \geq \{q_1 \to q_1, \{q_1, q_2\} \to q_2\}$. So the upper left judgment is an axiom. The other judgment on the top is an abbreviation of two judgments: one to show $\geq q_1$ and the other one to show $\geq q_2$. These two judgments are proven directly using application and intersection rules.

4 Models for Weak Automata

This section presents the model that captures wMSO properties. We assume basic knowledge about domain theory. More specifically, we shall work with (finite) complete lattices and with monotone functions between complete lattices. Given two complete lattices $\mathcal{L}_1$ and $\mathcal{L}_2$ we write $\mathrm{mon}[\mathcal{L}_1 \mapsto \mathcal{L}_2]$ for the complete lattice of monotone functions between $\mathcal{L}_1$ and $\mathcal{L}_2$. We construct a model that captures the language defined by a weak automaton: this model depends only on the states of the automaton and their ranks. The transitions of the automaton will be encoded in the interpretation of constants.

The challenge in this construction comes from the fact that simply using the least or greatest fixpoints is not sufficient. Indeed, we have shown in [29] that extremal fixpoints in finitary models of λY-calculus capture precisely boolean combinations of properties expressed by automata with trivial acceptance conditions. The structure of a weak automaton will help us here. For the sake of the discussion let us fix an automaton $\mathcal{A}$, and let $\mathcal{A}_{\leq k}$ stand for $\mathcal{A}$ restricted to states of rank at most k. Ranks stratify the automaton: transitions for states of rank k depend only on states of rank at most k. We will find this stratification in our model too. The interpretation of a term at stratum k will give us the complete information about the behaviour of the term with respect to $\mathcal{A}_{\leq k}$. Stratum $k+1$ will refine this information. Since in a run the ranks cannot increase, the information calculated at stratum $k+1$ does not change what we already know about $\mathcal{A}_{\leq k}$. Abstract interpretation tells us that refinements of models are obtained via Galois connections which are instrumental in our construction. In our model, every element in the stratum k is refined into a complete lattice in the stratum $k+1$ (cf. Figure 3). Therefore we will be able to define the interpretations of fixpoints by taking at stratum k the least or the greatest fixpoint depending on the parity of k. In the whole model, the fixpoint computation will perform a sort of zig-zag as represented in Figure 4.

We fix a finite set of states Q and a ranking function $\rho : Q \to \mathcal{N}$. Let m be the maximal rank, i.e., the maximal value ρ takes on Q. Recall that for every $0 \leq k \leq m$ we let $Q_k = \{q \in Q : \rho(q) = k\}$ and $Q_{\leq k} = \{q \in Q : \rho(q) \leq k\}$.

We define by induction on $k \leq m$ an applicative structure $\mathcal{D}^k = (\mathcal{D}^k_A)_{A \in \mathrm{types}}$ and a logical relation $\mathcal{L}^k$ (for $0 < k$) between $\mathcal{D}^{k-1}$ and $\mathcal{D}^k$. For $k = 0$, the model $\mathcal{D}^0$ is just the model of monotone functions over the powerset of Q_0 with

$\mathcal{D}_o^0 = \mathcal{P}(Q_0)$ and $\mathcal{D}_{A\to B}^0 = \text{mon}[\mathcal{D}_A^0 \mapsto \mathcal{D}_B^0]$. For $k > 0$, we define $\mathcal{D}^k$ by means of $\mathcal{D}^{k-1}$ and a logical relation $\mathcal{L}^k$:

$$\mathcal{D}_o^k = \mathcal{P}(Q_{\leq k}) \quad \mathcal{L}_o^k = \{(R, P) \in \mathcal{D}_o^{k-1} \times \mathcal{D}_o^k \ : \ R = P \cap Q_{\leq (k-1)}\},$$

$$\mathcal{L}_{A\to B}^k = \{(f_1, f_2) \in \mathcal{D}_{A\to B}^{k-1} \times \text{mon}[\mathcal{D}_A^k \mapsto \mathcal{D}_B^k] : \forall (g_1, g_2) \in \mathcal{L}_A^k.\ (f_1(g_1), f_2(g_2)) \in \mathcal{L}_B^k\}$$

$$\mathcal{D}_{A\to B}^k = \{f_2 \ : \ \exists f_1 \in \mathcal{D}_{A\to B}^{k-1}.\ (f_1, f_2) \in \mathcal{L}_{A\to B}^k\}$$

Observe that $\mathcal{D}_A^k$ is defined by a double induction: the outermost on k and the auxiliary induction on the size of the type. Since $\mathcal{L}^k$ is a logical relation between $\mathcal{D}^{k-1}$ and $\mathcal{D}^k$, each $\mathcal{D}^k$ is an applicative structure. As $\mathcal{D}_o^{k-1} = \mathcal{P}(Q_{\leq (k-1)})$, the refinements of elements R in $\mathcal{D}_o^{k-1}$ are simply the sets P in $\mathcal{P}(Q_{\leq k})$ so that $R = P \cap Q_{\leq (k-1)}$. This explains the definition of $\mathcal{L}_o^k$. For higher types, $\mathcal{L}^k$ is defined as it is usual for logical relations. Notice that $\mathcal{D}_{A\to B}^k$ is the subset of the monotone functions e from $\mathcal{D}_A^k$ to $\mathcal{D}_B^k$ for which there exist an element d in $\mathcal{D}_{A\to B}^{k-1}$ so that (d, e) is in $\mathcal{L}_{A\to B}^k$; that is we only keep those monotone functions that correspond to refinements of elements in $\mathcal{D}_{A\to B}^{k-1}$.

Remarkably this construction puts a lot of structure on $\mathcal{D}_A^k$. The first thing to notice is that for each type A, $\mathcal{D}_A^k$ is a complete lattice. Given d in $\mathcal{D}_A^{k-1}$, we write $\mathcal{L}_A^k(d)$ for the set $\{e \in \mathcal{D}_A^k : (d, e) \in \mathcal{L}_A^k\}$. For each d, we have that $\mathcal{L}_A^k(d)$ is a complete lattice and that moreover, for d_1 and d_2 in $\mathcal{D}_A^{k-1}$, $\mathcal{L}_A^k(d_1)$ and $\mathcal{L}_A^k(d_2)$ are isomorphic complete lattices. We write $d^{\uparrow\vee}$ and $d^{\uparrow\wedge}$ respectively for the greatest and the least elements of $\mathcal{L}_A^k(d)$. Finally, for each element e in $\mathcal{D}_A^k$, there is a unique d so that (d, e) is in $\mathcal{L}_A^k$, we write $e^{\downarrow}$ for that element. Figure 3 represents schematically the essential properties of $\mathcal{D}_A^k$.

The formalization of the intuition that $\mathcal{D}_A^k$ is a refinement of $\mathcal{D}_A^{k-1}$ is given by the fact that the mappings $(\cdot)^{\downarrow}$ and $(\cdot)^{\uparrow\vee}$ form a Galois connection between $\mathcal{D}_A^k$ and $\mathcal{D}_A^{k-1}$ and that $(\cdot)^{\downarrow}$ and $(\cdot)^{\uparrow\wedge}$ form a Galois connection between $\mathcal{D}_A^{k-1}$ and $\mathcal{D}_A^k$.

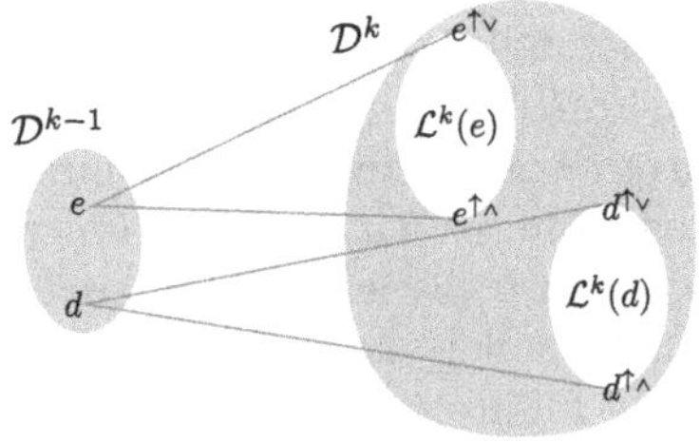

Fig. 3. Relation between models $\mathcal{D}^{k-1}$ and $\mathcal{D}^k$. Every element in $\mathcal{D}^{k-1}$ is related to a sub-lattice of elements in $\mathcal{D}^k$.

We can now define fixpoint operators in every applicative structure $\mathcal{D}^k$.

Definition 1. *For $f \in \mathcal{D}^0_{A \to A}$ we define $\mathrm{fix}^0_A(f) = \bigwedge\{f^n(\top^0) : n \geq 0\}$. For $0 < 2k \leq m$ and $f \in \mathcal{D}^{2k}_{A \to A}$ we define*

$$\mathrm{fix}^{2k}_A(f) = \bigwedge\{f^n(e) : n \geq 0\} \text{ where } e = (\mathrm{fix}^{2k-1}_A(f^{\downarrow}))^{\uparrow\vee}$$

For $0 < 2k+1 \leq m$ and $f \in \mathcal{D}^{2k+1}_{A \to A}$ we define

$$\mathrm{fix}^{2k+1}_A(f) = \bigvee\{f^n(d) : n \geq 0\} \text{ where } d = (\mathrm{fix}^{2k}_A(f^{\downarrow}))^{\uparrow\wedge}$$

Observe that, for even k, e is obtained with $(\cdot)^{\uparrow\vee}$; while for odd k, $(\cdot)^{\uparrow\wedge}$ is used.

The intuitive idea behind the definition of the fixpoint is presented in Figure 4. On stratum 0 it is just the greatest fixpoint. Then this greatest fixpoint is lifted to stratum 1, and the least fixpoint computation is started from it. The result is then lifted to stratum 2, and once again the greatest fixpoint computation is started, and so on. The Galois connections between strata guarantee that this process makes sense.

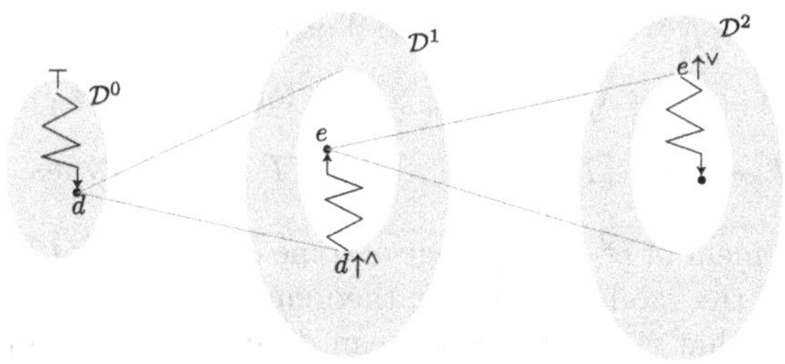

Fig. 4. A computation of a fixpoint: it starts in $\mathcal{D}^0$, and then the least and the greatest fixpoints alternate

Equipped with the interpretation of fixpoints given by Definition 1 the applicative structure $\mathcal{D}^k$ is a model of the λY-calculus. In particular, two terms that are $\beta\delta$-convertible have the same interpretation in that model. A constant c in $\Sigma^{(i)}$, is then interpreted as the function $f_{k,c}$ of $\mathcal{D}^k_{o^i \to o}$ so that for every $S_1, \ldots, S_i \subseteq \mathcal{D}^k_o$, $f_{k,c}(S_1, \ldots, S_i) = \{q \in \mathcal{D}^k_o : (S_1, \ldots, S_i) \in \delta(c, q)\}$. Observe that the identity $(f_{k+1,c})^{\downarrow} = f_{k,c}$ holds. Moreover if we let $\mathcal{A}(M) = \{q \in Q : \mathcal{A}$ accepts $BT(M)$ from $q\}$ be the set of states from which $\mathcal{A}$ accepts the tree $BT(M)$, then we have that:

Theorem 2. *For every closed term M of type 0, and for every $0 \leq k \leq m$ we have: $[\![M]\!]^k = \mathcal{A}(M) \cap Q_{\leq k}$.*

The two directions of Theorem 2 are proved using different techniques. The left to right inclusion uses a rather simple unrolling. The other inclusion is proved using a standard technique based on logical relations.

5 From Models to Type Systems

We are now in a position to show that our type system from Figure 2 can reason about the values of λY-terms in a stratified model (Theorem 3). Thanks to Theorem 2 this means that the type system can talk about the acceptance of the Böhm tree of a term by the automaton. This implies soundness and completeness of our type system, Theorem 1.

Throughout this section we work with a fixed signature Σ and a fixed weak alternating automaton $\mathcal{A} = \langle Q, \Sigma, q^0, \delta_o, \delta_{o^2 \to o}, \rho \rangle$. As in the previous section, for simplicity of notations we will assume that the constants in the signature are of type o or $o \to o \to o$. We will also prefer the notation $Yx.M$ to $Y(\lambda x.M)$.

The arrow constructor in types will be interpreted as a step function in the model. Step functions are particular monotone functions from a lattice $\mathcal{L}_1$ to a lattice $\mathcal{L}_2$. For d in $\mathcal{L}_1$ and e in $\mathcal{L}_2$, the *step function* $d \rightharpoondown e$ is defined by:

$$(d \rightharpoondown e)(h) = e \text{ when } d \leq h \quad \bot \text{ otherwise}$$

Types can be meaningfully interpreted at every level of the model. So $[\![t]\!]^l$ will denote the interpretation of t in $\mathcal{D}^l$ defined as follows.

$$[\![q]\!]^l = \{q\} \text{ if } \rho(q) \leq l, \emptyset \text{ otherwise}$$

$$[\![S]\!]^l = \bigvee\{[\![t]\!]^l : t \in S\} \qquad \text{for } S \subseteq \text{Types}_A$$

$$[\![T \to s]\!]^l = [\![T]\!]^l \rightharpoondown [\![s]\!]^l \qquad \text{for } (T \to s) \in \text{Types}_A$$

Actually every element of $\mathcal{D}^l$ is the image of some type via $[\![\cdot]\!]^l$: types are syntactic representations of the model. The next theorem is the main technical result of the paper. It says that the type system can derive all lower-approximations of the meanings of terms in the model. For an environment Γ, we write $[\![\Gamma]\!]^k$ for the valuation such that $[\![\Gamma]\!]^k(x) = [\![\Gamma(x)]\!]^k$.

Theorem 3. *For* $k = 0, \ldots, m$ *and* $S \subseteq \text{Types}^k$*:* $[\![M]\!]^k_{[\![\Gamma]\!]^k} \geq [\![S]\!]^k$ *iff* $\Gamma \vdash M \geq S$ *is derivable.*

The above theorem implies Theorem 1 stating soundness and completeness of the type system. Indeed, let us take a closed term M of type o, and a state q of our fixed automaton $\mathcal{A}$. Theorem 2 tells us that $[\![M]\!] = \mathcal{A}(M)$; where $\mathcal{A}(M)$ is the set of states from which $\mathcal{A}$ accepts $BT(M)$. So $\vdash M \geq q$ is derivable iff $[\![M]\!] \supseteq \{q\}$ iff $q \in \mathcal{A}(M)$.

One may ask if it is also possible to reason about over-approximations of the value of a term, i.e. about statements of the form $[\![M]\!]^k_{[\![\Gamma]\!]^k} \leq d$. This is indeed possible thanks to the dualities of the model. It is enough to dualize the type system: restricting the rule for greatest fixpoint on odd ranks instead of even ones, taking the dual subsumption order for the types, and typing constant with the transitions of the dual weak alternating automaton. This dual system is presented in the appendix. It derives judgments of the form: $\Gamma \vdash M \not\geq S$ since the interpretation of S is also dualized. Without going into details of this dualization we can state the following theorem.

Theorem 4. *For every closed term M of type o and every state q of $\mathcal{A}$: the judgment $\vdash M \ngeq q$ is derivable iff $\mathcal{A}$ does not accept $BT(M)$ from q.*

Together the type system and its dual give a precise characterization of $[\![M]\!] = L(\mathcal{A})$ that is the set of states from which our fixed automaton $\mathcal{A}$ accepts $BT(M)$.

Corollary 1. *For a closed term M of type o, $[\![M]\!] = [\![S]\!]$ iff both $\vdash M \geq S$ and $\vdash M \ngeq (Q - S)$.*

6 Conclusions

We have shown how to construct a model for a given weak alternating tree automaton so that the value of a term in the model determines if the Böhm tree of the term is accepted by the automaton. Our construction builds on ideas from [29] but requires to bring out the modular structure of the model. This structure is very rich, as testified by Galois connections. This structure allows us to derive type systems for wMSO properties following the "domains in logical form" approach.

The type systems are relatively streamlined: the novelty is the stratification of types used to restrict applicability of the greatest fixpoint rule. In comparison, Kobayashi and Ong [19] use a type system only as an intermediate formalism to obtain a game whose solution answers the model-checking problem. Their type system handles only closed terms of type o. It does not have a rule for lambda-abstraction, nor for fixpoints (that are handled via games). Tsukada and Ong have recently proposed a higher-order analogue of this system [33]. Even in this new approach the fixpoint is still handled by games, and the algorithmic properties of the model behind their system are not investigated. While our approach applies only to wMSO, our model is simply based on functions over finite sets with standard application operation.

Typing in our system is decidable, actually the height of the derivation is bounded by the size of the term. Yet the width can be large, that is unavoidable given that the typability is n-EXPTIME hard for terms of order n [31]. Due to the correspondence of the typing with semantics, every term has a "best" type.

While the paper focuses on typing, our model construction can be also used in other contexts. It allows us to immediately deduce reflection [8] and transfer [28] theorems for wMSO. Our techniques used to construct models and prove their correctness rely on usual techniques of domain theory [3], offering an alternative, and arguably simpler, point of view to techniques based on unrolling.

The idea behind the reflection construction is to transform a given term so that at every moment of its evaluation every subterm "knows" its meaning in the model. In [8] this property is formulated slightly differently and is proved using a detour to higher-order pushdown automata. Recently Haddad [13] has given a direct proof for all MSO properties. The proof is based on some notion of applicative structure that is less constrained than a model of the λY-calculus. One could apply his construction, or take the one from [29].

The transfer theorem says that for a fixed finite vocabulary of terms, an MSOL formula φ can be effectively transformed into an MSOL formula $\widehat{\varphi}$ such that for every term M of type 0 over the fixed vocabulary: M satisfies $\widehat{\varphi}$ iff the Böhm tree of M satisfies φ. Since the MSO theory of a term, that is a finite graph, is decidable, the transfer theorem implies decidability of MSO theory of Böhm trees of λY-terms. As shown in [28] it gives also a number of other results.

A transfer theorem for wMSO can be deduced from our model construction. For every wMSO formula φ we need to find a formula $\widehat{\varphi}$ as above. For this we transform φ into a weak alternating automaton $\mathcal{A}$, and construct a model $\mathcal{D}_\varphi$ based on $\mathcal{A}$. Thanks to the restriction on the vocabulary, it is quite easy to write for every element d of the model $\mathcal{D}_\varphi$ a wMSO formula α_d such that for every term M of type 0 in the restricted vocabulary: $M \vDash \alpha_d$ iff $[\![M]\!]^{\mathcal{D}_\varphi} = d$. The formula $\widehat{\varphi}$ is then just a disjunction $\bigvee_{d\in F} \alpha_d$, where F is the set elements of $\mathcal{D}_\varphi$ characterizing terms whose Böhm tree satisfies φ.

The fixpoints in our models are non-extremal: they are neither the least nor the greatest fixpoints. From [29] we know that this is unavoidable. We are aware of very few works considering such cases. Our models are an instance of cartesian closed categories with internal fixpoint operation as studied by Bloom and Esik [6]. Our model satisfies not only Conway identities but also a generalization of the *commutative axioms* of iteration theories [5]. Thus it is possible to give semantics to the infinitary λ-calculus in our models. It is an essential step towards obtaining an algebraic framework for weak regular languages [7].

References

1. Abramsky, S.: Domain theory in logical form. Ann. Pure Appl. Logic 51(1-2), 1–77 (1991)
2. Aehlig, K.: A finite semantics of simply-typed lambda terms for infinite runs of automata. Logical Methods in Computer Science 3(1), 1–23 (2007)
3. Amadio, R.M., Curien, P.-L.: *Domains and Lambda-Calculi.* Cambridge Tracts in Theoretical Computer Science, vol. 46. Cambridge University Press (1998)
4. Barendregt, H., Coppo, M., Dezani-Ciancaglini, M.: A filter lambda model and the completeness of type assignment. J. Symb. Log. 4, 931–940 (1983)
5. Bloom, S.L., Ésik, Z.: Iteration Theories: The Equational Logic of Iterative Processes. EATCS Monographs in Theoretical Computer Science. Springer (1993)
6. Bloom, S.L., Ésik, Z.: Fixed-point operations on CCC's. part I. Theoretical Computer Science 155, 1–38 (1996)
7. Blumensath, A.: An algebraic proof of Rabin's tree theorem. Theor. Comput. Sci. 478, 1–21 (2013)
8. Broadbent, C., Carayol, A., Ong, L., Serre, O.: Recursion schemes and logical reflection. In: LICS, pp. 120–129 (2010)
9. Broadbent, C.H., Carayol, A., Hague, M., Serre, O.: C-shore: a collapsible approach to higher-order verification. In: ICFP, pp. 13–24. ACM (2013)
10. Broadbent, C.H., Kobayashi, N.: Saturation-based model checking of higher-order recursion schemes. In: CSL. LIPIcs, vol. 23, pp. 129–148. Schloss Dagstuhl (2013)
11. Chen, W., Hofmann, M.: Buchi abstraction. In: LICS (2014) (to appear)
12. Grabowski, R., Hofmann, M., Li, K.: Type-based enforcement of secure programming guidelines — code injection prevention at SAP. In: Barthe, G., Datta, A., Etalle, S. (eds.) FAST 2011. LNCS, vol. 7140, pp. 182–197. Springer, Heidelberg (2012)

13. Haddad, A.: Model checking and functional program transformations. In: FSTTCS. LIPIcs, vol. 24, pp. 115–126 (2013)
14. Hague, M., Murawski, A.S., Ong, C.-H.L., Serre, O.: Collapsible pushdown automata and recursion schemes. In: LICS, pp. 452–461. IEEE Computer Society (2008)
15. Jeffrey, A.S.A.: LTL types FRP: Linear-time Temporal Logic propositions as types, proofs as functional reactive programs. In: ACM Workshop Programming Languages meets Program Verification (2012)
16. Jeffrey, A.S.A.: Functional reactive types. In: LICS (2014) (to appear)
17. Kobayashi, N.: Types and higher-order recursion schemes for verification of higher-order programs. In: POPL, pp. 416–428 (2009)
18. Kobayashi, N.: Model checking higher-order programs. J. ACM 60(3), 20–89 (2013)
19. Kobayashi, N., Ong, L.: A type system equivalent to modal mu-calculus model checking of recursion schemes. In: LICS, pp. 179–188 (2009)
20. Kobayashi, N., Tabuchi, N., Unno, H.: Higher-order multi-parameter tree transducers and recursion schemes for program verification. In: POPL, pp. 495–508 (2010)
21. Naik, M., Palsberg, J.: A type system equivalent to a model checker. ACM Trans. Program. Lang. Syst. 30(5) (2008)
22. Nielson, F., Riis Nielson, H.: Type and effect systems. In: Olderog, E.-R., Steffen, B. (eds.) Correct System Design. LNCS, vol. 1710, pp. 114–136. Springer, Heidelberg (1999)
23. Ong, C.-H.L.: On model-checking trees generated by higher-order recursion schemes. In: LICS, pp. 81–90 (2006)
24. Ong, C.-H.L., Ramsay, S.: Verifying higher-order programs with pattern-matching algebraic data types. In: POPL, pp. 587–598 (2011)
25. Rabin, M.O.: Decidability of second-order theories and automata on infinite trees. Transactions of the AMS 141, 1–23 (1969)
26. Ramsay, S.J., Neatherway, R.P., Ong, C.-H.L.: A type-directed abstraction refinement approach to higher-order model checking. In: POPL, pp. 61–72. ACM (2014)
27. Salvati, S., Walukiewicz, I.: Krivine machines and higher-order schemes. In: Aceto, L., Henzinger, M., Sgall, J. (eds.) ICALP 2011, Part II. LNCS, vol. 6756, pp. 162–173. Springer, Heidelberg (2011)
28. Salvati, S., Walukiewicz, I.: Evaluation is MSOL-compatible. In: FSTTCS. LIPIcs, vol. 24, pp. 103–114 (2013)
29. Salvati, S., Walukiewicz, I.: Using models to model-check recursive schemes. In: Hasegawa, M. (ed.) TLCA 2013. LNCS, vol. 7941, pp. 189–204. Springer, Heidelberg (2013)
30. alvati, S., Walukiewicz, I.: Typing weak MSOL properties (2014), `https://hal.archives-ouvertes.fr/hal-01061202`
31. Terui, K.: Semantic evaluation, intersection types and complexity of simply typed lambda calculus. In: RTA. LIPIcs, vol. 15, pp. 323–338. Schloss Dagstuhl (2012)
32. Tobita, Y., Tsukada, T., Kobayashi, N.: Exact flow analysis by higher-order model checking. In: Schrijvers, T., Thiemann, P. (eds.) FLOPS 2012. LNCS, vol. 7294, pp. 275–289. Springer, Heidelberg (2012)
33. Tsukada, T., Ong, C.-H.L.: Compositional higher-order model checking via ω-regular games over Böhm trees. In: LICS (to appear, 2014)

Logical Aspects of Computational Complexity

Three Variables Suffice for Real-Time Logic

Timos Antonopoulos[1], Paul Hunter[2], Shahab Raza[1], and James Worrell[1]

[1] Department of Computer Science, Oxford University, UK
{timos,shahab,jbw}@cs.ox.ac.uk
[2] Département d'Informatique, Université Libre de Bruxelles, Belgium
paul.hunter@ulb.ac.be

Abstract. A natural framework for real-time specification is monadic first-order logic over the structure $(\mathbb{R}, <, +1)$—the ordered real line with unary $+1$ function. Our main result is that $(\mathbb{R}, <, +1)$ has the 3-variable property: every monadic first-order formula with at most 3 free variables is equivalent over this structure to one that uses 3 variables in total. As a corollary we obtain also the 3-variable property for the structure $(\mathbb{R}, <, f)$ for any fixed linear function $f : \mathbb{R} \to \mathbb{R}$. On the other hand, we exhibit a countable dense linear order $(E, <)$ and a bijection $f : E \to E$ such that $(E, <, f)$ does not have the k-variable property for any k.

1 Introduction

Monadic first-order logic is an expansion of first-order logic by infinitely many unary predicate variables. In this setting a class of structures $\mathcal{C}$ is said to have the *k-variable property* if every formula with at most k free first-order variables is equivalent over $\mathcal{C}$ to a formula with at most k first-order variables in total (allowing multiple binding occurrences of the same variable). The k-variable property for monadic first-order logic over linearly ordered structures has been studied in [1,2,4,8,12,14,15], among others. In finite model theory the k-variable property plays an important role in descriptive complexity. Over infinite models it is closely connected with expressive completeness of temporal logics.

It is well known that Linear Temporal Logic (LTL) with Stavi modalities is expressively complete for monadic first-order logic over the class of linear orders [3,13]. More precisely, LTL is expressively complete for the class of monadic first-order formulas with one free variable (corresponding to the fact that LTL formulas are evaluated at a single point of a linear order). The translation from LTL to first-order logic is a straightforward inductive construction that maps into the 3-variable fragment of first-order logic. It follows that every monadic first-order formula with at most one free variable is equivalent to a 3-variable formula over linear orders. However this is a strictly weaker condition than the 3-variable property in general: Hodkinson and Simon [8] give a class of partial orders over which every monadic first-order formula with at most one free variable is equivalent to a 3-variable formula, but which does not have the k-variable property for any k. Nevertheless the 3-variable property *does* hold over linear orders, as shown by Poizat [14] and Immerman and Kozen [12], using Ehrenfeucht-Fraïssé games.

A. Pitts (Ed.): FOSSACS 2015, LNCS 9034, pp. 361–374, 2015.
DOI: 10.1007/978-3-662-46678-0_23

Going beyond pure linear orders, Venema [16] gives a dense linear order with a single equivalence relation over which monadic first-order logic does not have the k-variable property for any k. A more powerful result by Rossman [15] shows that the class of finite linearly ordered graphs does not have the k-variable property for any k, resolving a longstanding conjecture of Immerman [11].

In this paper we are concerned with monadic first-order logic over the ordered reals with unary $+1$ function $(\mathbb{R}, <, +1)$. This logic has been extensively studied in the context of real-time verification. An expansion of $(\mathbb{R}, <, +1)$ with interpretations of the unary predicate variables can be seen as a real-time signal, with the unary predicates denoting propositions that may or may not hold at any given time. First-order logic over signals can express both metric and order-theoretic temporal properties and is an expressive meta-language into which many different real-time logics can directly be translated [5,6]. In particular, first-order logic over signals is expressively equivalent with Metric Temporal Logic (MTL) [9,10].

Our main result is that $(\mathbb{R}, <, +1)$ has the 3-variable property. For example, the property

$$\forall x_1 \exists x_2 \exists x_3 \exists x_4 \left(x_4 < x_1 + 1 \wedge \bigwedge_{1 \le i \le 3} x_i < x_{i+1} \wedge \bigwedge_{2 \le i \le 4} P(x_i) \right)$$

that P is true at least 3 times in every unit interval can equivalently be written

$$\forall x \exists y (x < y \wedge P(y) \wedge \exists z (y < z \wedge P(z) \wedge \exists y (z < y < x + 1 \wedge P(y)))) .$$

From the expressive completeness of MTL it follows that every monadic first-order formula with at most one free variable is equivalent to a 3-variable formula over $(\mathbb{R}, <, +1)$. However, as remarked above, this condition is weaker than the 3-variable property in general. Moreover the proof of expressive completeness of MTL combines intricate syntactic manipulations of MTL formulas together with technically involved results of [3] for LTL. On the other hand, the model-theoretic argument given here, using Ehrenfeucht-Fraïssé games, is self-contained and exposes a novel two-level compositional technique that can potentially be applied in more general settings and to other ends (see the Conclusion).

As a corollary of our main result we straightforwardly derive the 3-variable property for each structure $(\mathbb{R}, <, f)$ with $f : \mathbb{R} \to \mathbb{R}$ a linear function $f(x) = ax + b$. We believe that the result can be generalised to other linear orders and suitably well-behaved functions. However, unsurprisingly, the property fails for sufficiently 'wild' functions. Adapting Venema's construction [16], we give an example of a countable dense linear order E and a (far from monotone) bijection $f : E \to E$ such that $(E, <, f)$ does not have the k-variable property for any k.

The paper naturally divides into two parts. Sections 3 to 4 are exclusively concerned with the structure $(\mathbb{R}, <, +1)$, while Sections 5 and 6 consider other unary functions in place of $+1$.

2 Background

2.1 Ehrenfeucht-Fraïssé Games

Throughout the paper we work with a first-order signature σ with a binary relation symbol $<$ and a unary function symbol f. The monadic first-order language over σ is defined as follows:

- There is an infinite collection of monadic predicate variables $P_1, P_2, \ldots$.
- The atomic formulas are $x = y$, $x < y$, $P_n(x)$, and $x = f(y)$ for first-order variables x and y and $n \in \mathbb{N}$.
- If φ_1 and φ_2 are formulas and x is a variable then $\neg\varphi_1$, $\varphi_1 \wedge \varphi_2$ and $\exists x\, \varphi_1$ are also formulas.

Referring to the restricted use of the function symbol f in atomic formulas, we say that the formulas above are *unnested*. The unnesting assumption essentially amounts to treating the function symbol f as a binary relation symbol. We make this assumption as an alternative to restricting to a purely relational signature. The unnesting assumption does not affect expressiveness since we can translate an arbitrary formula to an equivalent unnested formula by successively replacing atomic formulas $f^m(x) = f^n(y)$ with $m > 0$ by $\exists z\, (z = f(x) \wedge f^{m-1}(z) = f^n(y))$, and similarly for $f^m(x) < f^n(y)$. While this transformation may increase the quantifier depth, it preserves the subclass of 3-variable formulas.

Let $\mathbf{A} = (A, <^{\mathbf{A}}, f^{\mathbf{A}}, \overline{P}^{\mathbf{A}})$ denote a σ-structure expanded with interpretations of the monadic predicate variables $P_1, P_2, \ldots$. We call $\mathbf{A}$ a *labelled σ-structure*. Given first-order variables $x_1, \ldots, x_k$, an *assignment* in $\mathbf{A}$ with domain $\{x_1, \ldots, x_k\}$ is a tuple $\overline{u} = u_1 \ldots u_k$ in A^k. Given another assignment $\overline{v}$ with the same domain in a labelled σ-structure $\mathbf{B}$, we say that $(\overline{u}, \overline{v})$ is a *partial isomorphism* between $\mathbf{A}$ and $\mathbf{B}$ if $\mathbf{A} \models \varphi[\overline{u}]$ iff $\mathbf{B} \models \varphi[\overline{v}]$ for all atomic formulas $\varphi(x_1, \ldots, x_k)$.

The *Ehrenfeucht-Fraïssé* (EF) game on structures $\mathbf{A}$ and $\mathbf{B}$ is played by two players—*Spoiler* and *Duplicator*.[1] Each player has a collection of pebbles, respectively labelled $x_1, x_2, \ldots$. The game is played over a fixed number of rounds. In each round Spoiler chooses a structure and places a pebble on an element of the structure (either an unused pebble or one that has already been placed); Duplicator responds by placing a pebble with the same label on some element of the other structure. A placement of k pebbles on each structure naturally determines a pair of assignments $(\overline{u}, \overline{v})$, called a *$k$-configuration*. (Our notation for k-configurations leaves the structures $\mathbf{A}$ and $\mathbf{B}$ implicit.) If the configuration after each round is a partial isomorphism then Duplicator wins, otherwise Spoiler wins. For each configuration $(\overline{u}, \overline{v})$ and number of rounds n, exactly one of the players has a winning strategy in the n-round game starting from $(\overline{u}, \overline{v})$ (see [12] for more details).

A natural restriction on Ehrenfeucht-Fraïssé games is to limit each player to a fixed number of pebbles. In the *k-pebble game* both Spoiler and Duplicator

[1] By convention, Spoiler is male and Duplicator is female.

possess only k pebbles, respectively labelled $x_1, \ldots, x_k$. The following theorem shows how Ehrenfeucht-Fraïssé games can be used to characterise the expressiveness of first-order logic according to the number of variables.

Theorem 2.1 ([12]). *Let C be a class of σ-structures such that for all n there exists m such that if Spoiler wins the n-round Ehrenfeucht-Fraïssé game on a pair of labelled structures from C starting in a k-configuration $(\overline{u}, \overline{v})$, then he also wins the m-round k-pebble game starting in $(\overline{u}, \overline{v})$. Then C has the k-variable property.*

In the remainder of this section we specialise our attention to the σ-structure $(\mathbb{R}, <, +1)$. In this case we call a labelled σ-structure a *signal*.

In addition to k-pebble games, on signals we introduce another restriction of Ehrenfeucht-Fraïssé games. Given an assignment $\overline{u} \in \mathbb{R}^k$ with domain $\{x_1, \ldots, x_k\}$, the *diameter* of $\overline{u}$ is $diam(\overline{u}) = \max\{|u_i - u_j| : 1 \leq i, j \leq k\}$. Given $D \in \mathbb{R}$, the *D-local game* on a pair of signals is such that Spoiler and Duplicator must maintain the invariant that all assignments have diameter at most D.

We will always explicitly indicate any restrictions on the number of pebbles or the diameter of configurations in games: thus the default notion of Ehrenfeucht-Fraïssé game is without restriction on the number of pebbles or the diameter.

Recall that our main result is that $(\mathbb{R}, <, +1)$ has the 3-variable property. The main conceptual insight underlying the proof is that one should first prove the 3-variable property for "local" formulas. We treat locality semantically through the notion of local EF games, as defined above, but intuitively a local formula is one that asserts properties of elements at a bounded distance from one another. For example, $\exists x \exists y\, (P(x) \wedge Q(y) \wedge x, < y < x + 1)$ is local but $\exists x \exists y\, (P(x) \wedge Q(y))$ is not local.

We prove the 3-variable property for local formulas by a compositional argument based on the fractional-part preorder on $\mathbb{R}$. We then extend the 3-variable property to all formulas by adapting the well-known composition lemma for sums of linear orders to the structure $(\mathbb{R}, <, +1)$. Roughly speaking, this second compositional lemma shows that Duplicator strategies on summands can be composed provided that there is sufficient distance between pebbles in different summands. However this precondition is not always met and here it is crucial that we have already established the 3-variable property for local formulas.

2.2 Interpretations

In this section we briefly deviate from the setting of linear orders and unary functions to recall from [7, Chapter 4.3] the notion of an interpretation of one first-order structure in another.

Let σ_1 and σ_2 be signatures, $\mathbf{A}$ a σ_1-structure with domain A, $\mathbf{B}$ a σ_2-structure with domain B, and n a positive integer. An n-dimensional *interpretation* Γ of $\mathbf{B}$ in $\mathbf{A}$ consists of three items:

- a σ_1-formula $\partial_\Gamma(x_1, \ldots, x_n)$ denoting the *domain* of the interpretation, which is the set $\partial_\Gamma(A^n) := \{\overline{a} \in A^n : \mathbf{A} \models \partial_\Gamma[\overline{a}]\}$.

- for each unnested atomic σ_2-formula $\varphi(x_1,\ldots,x_m)$, a σ_1-formula $\varphi_\Gamma(\overline{x}_1,\ldots,\overline{x}_m)$ in which the $\overline{x}_i$ are disjoint n-tuples of distinct variables,
- a surjective *coding map* $f_\Gamma : \partial_\Gamma(A^n) \to B$ such that for all unnested atomic σ_2-formulas φ and all $\overline{a}_i \in \partial_\Gamma(A^n)$,

$$\mathbf{B} \models \varphi[f_\Gamma\overline{a}_1,\ldots,f_\Gamma\overline{a}_m] \text{ iff } \mathbf{A} \models \varphi_\Gamma[\overline{a}_1,\ldots,\overline{a}_m].$$

3 From Local Games to 3-Pebble Games

In this section we consider an Ehrenfeucht-Fraïssé game on two signals **A** and **B**. Here $\overline{u} = u_1\ldots u_s$ will always denote an assignment in **A** and $\overline{v} = v_1\ldots v_s$ will always denote an assignment in **B**.

Write $\overline{u} \equiv \overline{v}$ if $\overline{u}$ and $\overline{v}$ are indistinguishable by difference constraints, that is, $u_i - u_j < c \Leftrightarrow v_i - v_j < c$ and $u_i - u_j = c \Leftrightarrow v_i - v_j = c$ for all constants $c \in \mathbb{Z}$ and indices $1 \le i,j \le s$. Equivalently, $\overline{u} \equiv \overline{v}$ if and only if $\lfloor u_i - u_j \rfloor = \lfloor v_i - v_j \rfloor$ for all indices $1 \le i,j \le s$.[2] Assignments that are indistinguishable by difference constraints are, in particular, ordered the same way.

Define the *fractional part* of $u \in \mathbb{R}$ by $\mathrm{frac}(u) = u - \lfloor u \rfloor$. The proof of the following proposition can be found in the Appendix.

Proposition 3.1. *Let $\overline{u} = u_1\ldots u_s$ and $\overline{v} = v_1\ldots v_s$ be two assignments with $\overline{u} \equiv \overline{v}$. Then*

$$\mathrm{frac}(u_i - u_k) < \mathrm{frac}(u_j - u_k) \ \Leftrightarrow\ \mathrm{frac}(v_i - v_k) < \mathrm{frac}(v_j - v_k)$$

for all indices $i,j,k \in \{1,\ldots,s\}$.

We say that $u_1\ldots u_s$ is in *increasing order* if $\mathrm{frac}(u_i - u_1) \le \mathrm{frac}(u_{i+1} - u_1)$ for $i = 1,\ldots,s-1$. Intuitively $u_1\ldots u_s$ is in increasing order if it is listed in increasing order of fractional parts relative to u_1. Note that if $u_1\ldots u_s$ is in increasing order then any cyclic permutation is also in increasing order. By Proposition 3.1, if $\overline{u} \equiv \overline{v}$ then $\overline{u}$ and $\overline{v}$ can both be brought into increasing order by a common permutation.

The following proposition can be seen as a compositional lemma for $\equiv$. The proof can be found in the Appendix.

Proposition 3.2. *Suppose that $u_1\ldots u_s$ and $v_1\ldots v_s$ are both increasing and that $u_1\ldots u_m \equiv v_1\ldots v_m$ and $u_m\ldots u_s \equiv v_m\ldots v_s$ for some m, $1 \le m \le s$. Then $u_1\ldots u_s \equiv v_1\ldots v_s$.*

Proposition 3.3 and Corollary 3.4 show that three pebbles suffice to determine equivalence of configurations under the relation $\equiv$.

Proposition 3.3. *Let $n \in \mathbb{N}$. Consider a 2-configuration (u_1u_2, v_1v_2) such that either (i) $u_1 - u_2 < c$ and $v_1 - v_2 \not< c$ for some non-negative integer $c < 2^n$ or (ii) $u_1 - u_2 = c$ and $v_1 - v_2 \neq c$ for some non-negative integer $c \le 2^n$. Then Spoiler wins the n-round 3-pebble game from (u_1u_2, v_1v_2).*

[2] Note that $\lceil u_i - u_j \rceil = \lceil v_i - v_j \rceil$ if and only if $\lfloor u_j - u_i \rfloor = \lfloor v_j - v_i \rfloor$, so there is no need to add a separate clause for ceiling in the characterisation of $\equiv$.

Proof. The proof is by induction on n.

Base case ($n = 0$). Under either assumption (i) or (ii) the configuration (u_1u_2, v_1v_2) is not a partial isomorphism, and is therefore immediately winning for Spoiler in the 3-pebble game.

Induction step ($n \geq 1$). Suppose $u_1 - u_2 < c$ but $v_1 - v_2 \not< c$, where $c < 2^n$. Write $c' = \lfloor c/2 \rfloor$, so that $c' < 2^{n-1}$ and $c - c' \leq 2^{n-1}$. Suppose that Spoiler places a pebble on u_3 such that $u_1 - u_3 = c - c'$ and $u_3 - u_2 < c'$. Since $v_1 - v_2 \not< c$, for any response v_3 of Duplicator we either have $v_1 - v_3 \neq c - c'$ or $v_3 - v_2 \not< c'$. In the first case, by the induction hypothesis, (u_1u_3, v_1v_3) is winning in $n-1$ rounds for Spoiler; likewise in the second case (u_2u_3, v_2v_3) is winning in $n-1$ rounds for Spoiler. Thus in either case $(u_1u_2u_3, v_1v_2v_3)$ is winning in $n-1$ rounds for Spoiler. We conclude that (u_1u_2, v_1v_2) is winning in n rounds for Spoiler. This handles (i); Case (ii) is almost identical. □

Corollary 3.4. *Let $(\overline{u}, \overline{v})$ be a 3-configuration such that $\overline{u} \not\equiv \overline{v}$ and at least one of $\overline{u}$ and $\overline{v}$ has diameter at most 2^m. Then Spoiler wins the m-round 3-pebble game from $(\overline{u}, \overline{v})$.*

Proof. Since $\overline{u} \not\equiv \overline{v}$, there are indices i, j such that $u_i - u_j \sim c$ and $v_i - v_j \not\sim c$ for some non-negative integer constant c and comparison operator $\sim \in \{<, =\}$. Moreover, since at least one of $\overline{u}$ and $\overline{v}$ has diameter at most 2^m, we can assume that $c \leq 2^m$. But then Spoiler wins the m-round 3-pebble game from $(\overline{u}, \overline{v})$ by Proposition 3.3. □

One can think of following proposition as showing the 3-variable property for local formulas. The proof uses the compositional principle in Proposition 3.2.

Proposition 3.5. *Let $(\overline{u}, \overline{v})$ be a 3-configuration of diameter at most 2^m. If Spoiler wins the n-round 2^m-local game from $(\overline{u}, \overline{v})$ then he wins the $(m+n)$-round 3-pebble game from $(\overline{u}, \overline{v})$.*

Proof. If $\overline{u} \not\equiv \overline{v}$ then the result follows from Corollary 3.4. Thus it suffices to prove the proposition under the assumption $\overline{u} \equiv \overline{v}$.

Without loss of generality assume that $\overline{u}$ and $\overline{v}$ are both increasing. The proof is by induction on n, with the following induction hypothesis.

Induction Hypothesis: Let assignments $u_1 \dots u_s \equiv v_1 \dots v_s$ be increasing and have diameter at most 2^m. If Spoiler wins the n-round 2^m-local game from $(\overline{u}, \overline{v})$, then he wins the $(m+n)$-round 3-pebble game from a 2-configuration of the form (u_iu_{i+1}, v_iv_{i+1}), $1 \leq i \leq s-1$, or (u_su_1, v_sv_1).

Base case ($n = 0$). By assumption $(\overline{u}, \overline{v})$ is immediately winning for Spoiler in the local game. Since $\overline{u} \equiv \overline{v}$, u_i and v_i must disagree on a unary predicate for some index i. Then (u_i, v_i) is immediately winning for Spoiler in the 3-pebble game. Clearly the position remains immediately winning for Spoiler if we add an extra pebble to each assignment. Thus the base case of the induction is established.

Induction step ($n \geq 1$). Pick a Spoiler move according to his winning strategy in the local game in configuration $(\overline{u}, \overline{v})$. Without loss of generality, assume that this move, say u', is in structure **A**. Since any cyclic permutation of an increasing configuration is also increasing, we may assume without loss of generality that $u_1 \ldots u_s u'$ is increasing.

If $(u_1 u_s, v_1 v_s)$ is winning for Spoiler in the $(m+n)$-round 3-pebble game then we are done, so suppose that this is not the case. Then there exists a Duplicator move v' such that $(u_1 u_s u', v_1 v_s v')$ is winning for Duplicator in the $(m+n-1)$-round 3-pebble game. Since $\mathrm{diam}(u_1 u_s u') \leq 2^m$, by Corollary 3.4 we must have $u_1 u_s u' \equiv v_1 v_s v'$. It follows that $v_1 \ldots v_s v'$ is increasing.

Since $u_1 \ldots u_s u'$ and $v_1 \ldots v_s v'$ are increasing, $u_1 \ldots u_s \equiv v_1 \ldots v_s$, and $u_s u' \equiv v_s v'$, by Proposition 3.2 we have

$$u_1 \ldots u_s u' \equiv v_1 \ldots v_s v' . \tag{1}$$

Since the pair of assignments in (1) is winning for Spoiler in the $(n-1)$-round local game, by the induction hypothesis there exists a sub-configuration (comprising two consecutive pebbles in each assignment) from which Spoiler wins the $(m+n-1)$-round 3-pebble game. This 2-configuration cannot be $(u_s u', v_s v')$ nor $(u_1 u', v_1 v')$, since $(u_1 u_s u', v_1 v_s v')$ is winning for Duplicator in the $(m+n-1)$-round 3-pebble game. Thus Spoiler must win the $(m+n-1)$-round 3-pebble game from a 2-configuration $(u_i u_{i+1}, v_i v_{i+1})$ for some $i \in \{1, \ldots, s-1\}$. *A fortiori* Spoiler also wins the $(m+n)$-round 3-pebble game from this configuration. □

4 Main Results

4.1 Composition Lemma

In this section we consider an Ehrenfeucht-Fraïssé game on two signals **A** and **B**. We will prove a Composition Lemma that allows us to compose winning Duplicator strategies under certain assumptions. From this we obtain our main result, that monadic first-order logic over signals has the 3-variable property.

Assume assignments $\overline{u} = u_1 \ldots u_s$ in **A** and $\overline{v} = v_1 \ldots v_s$ in **B** with $u_1 < \ldots < u_s$ and $v_1 < \ldots < v_s$. The Composition Lemma is predicated on a decomposition of $\overline{u}$ into a *left part* $\overline{u}_{\triangleleft} = u_1 \ldots u_l$, *middle part* $\overline{u}_{\diamond} = u_l \ldots u_r$, and *right part* $\overline{u}_{\triangleright} = u_r \ldots u_s$, where $1 \leq l \leq r \leq s$. We call u_l the *left boundary* and u_r the *right boundary*. The *left margin* is defined to be $margin(\overline{u}_{\triangleleft}) = u_l - u_{l-1}$, where $u_0 = -\infty$ by convention. Likewise the *right margin* is defined to be $margin(\overline{u}_{\triangleright}) = u_{r+1} - u_r$, where $u_{s+1} = \infty$ by convention. We consider a corresponding decomposition of $\overline{v}$ into $\overline{v}_{\triangleleft} = v_1 \ldots v_l$, $\overline{v}_{\diamond} = v_l \ldots v_r$, and $\overline{v}_{\triangleright} = v_r \ldots v_s$, for the same values of l and r.

The Composition Lemma gives conditions under which we can obtain a winning strategy for Duplicator in a configuration $(\overline{u}, \overline{v})$ by composing winning Duplicator strategies in the *left configuration* $(\overline{u}_{\triangleleft}, \overline{v}_{\triangleleft})$, the *middle configuration* $(\overline{u}_{\diamond}, \overline{v}_{\diamond})$, and *right configuration* $(\overline{u}_{\triangleright}, \overline{v}_{\triangleright})$, see Figure 1. The main idea behind the proof is to maintain adequate separation between pebbles played by the left and middle Duplicator strategies, and likewise between pebbles played by the middle and right strategies. We do this by maintaining the left and right margins

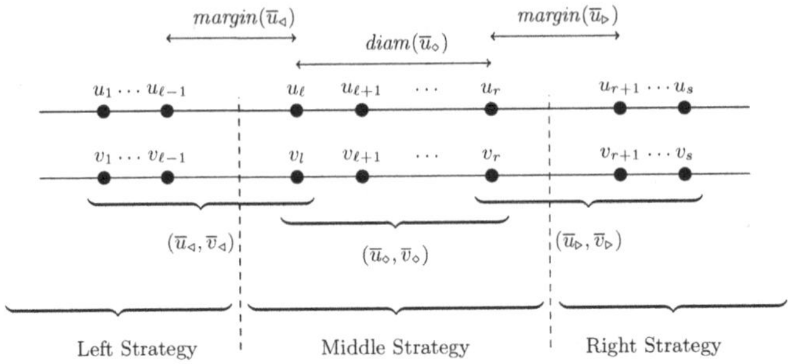

Fig. 1. Situation of the Composition Lemma

appropriately. Importantly for later use, we need only assume that Duplicator has a local winning strategy in the middle configuration.

Lemma 4.1 (Composition Lemma). *Suppose that Duplicator wins the n-round games from configurations* $(\overline{u}_\triangleleft, \overline{v}_\triangleleft)$ *and* $(\overline{u}_\triangleright, \overline{v}_\triangleright)$ *respectively, and let D be such that Duplicator wins the* $3n$*-round D-local game from configuration* $(\overline{u}_\diamond, \overline{v}_\diamond)$*. If* $margin(\overline{u}_\triangleleft) > 2^n$, $margin(\overline{u}_\triangleright) > 2^n$, $D \geq diam(\overline{u}_\diamond)+2^{n+1}$*, and the corresponding three conditions also hold for* $\overline{v}$*, then Duplicator wins the n-round game from configuration* $(\overline{u}, \overline{v})$.

Proof. We show that configuration $(\overline{u}, \overline{v})$ is winning for Duplicator in the n-round game. The proof is by induction on n.

Base case ($n = 0$). Note that $(\overline{u}, \overline{v})$ is a partial isomorphism since $(\overline{u}_\triangleleft, \overline{v}_\triangleleft)$, $(\overline{u}_\diamond, \overline{v}_\diamond)$, and $(\overline{u}_\triangleright, \overline{v}_\triangleright)$ are all partial isomorphisms, $margin(\overline{u}_\triangleleft)$ and $margin(\overline{v}_\triangleleft)$ are both greater than one, and likewise for $margin(\overline{u}_\triangleright)$ and $margin(\overline{v}_\triangleright)$.

Induction step ($n > 0$). Without loss of generality assume that Spoiler plays a move u' in structure **A**. We consider three cases.

Case (i). Suppose that $u' < u_l - 2^{n-1}$. Then Duplicator's winning strategy in configuration $(\overline{u}_\triangleleft, \overline{v}_\triangleleft)$ yields a response v' such that $(\overline{u}_\triangleleft u', \overline{v}_\triangleleft v')$ is winning for Duplicator in the $(n-1)$-round game. In particular, applying Proposition 3.3, we have $v' < v_l - 2^{n-1}$. Applying the induction hypothesis to $(\overline{u}_\triangleleft u', \overline{v}_\triangleleft v')$, $(\overline{u}_\diamond, \overline{v}_\diamond)$, and $(\overline{u}_\triangleright, \overline{v}_\triangleright)$ we get that $(\overline{u}u', \overline{v}v')$ is winning for Duplicator in the $(n-1)$-round game.

Case (ii). Suppose that $u' > u_r + 2^{n-1}$. This case is entirely analogous to Case (i), except that Duplicator's response to u' is generated from her winning strategy in configuration $(\overline{u}_\triangleright, \overline{v}_\triangleright)$.

Case (iii). Suppose that $u_l - 2^{n-1} \leq u' \leq u_r + 2^{n-1}$. Then Duplicator's winning strategy in configuration $(\overline{u}_\diamond, \overline{v}_\diamond)$ yields a response v' such that Duplicator wins the $(3n-1)$-round D-local game from $(\overline{u}_\diamond u', \overline{v}_\diamond v')$. By Proposition 3.3 we must have $v_l - 2^{n-1} \leq v' \leq v_r + 2^{n-1}$.

To apply the induction hypothesis, the idea is to "expand the middle configuration" by adding new left and right boundary pebbles u'_l, u'_r and v'_l, v'_r respectively. Formally, Spoiler moves $u'_l := u_l - 2^{n-1}$ and $u'_r := u_r + 2^{n-1}$ in the D-local game in position $(\overline{u}_\diamond u', \overline{v}_\diamond v')$ force Duplicator responses $v'_l := v_l - 2^{n-1}$ and $v'_r := v_r + 2^{n-1}$ such that $(u'_l \overline{u}_\diamond u' u'_r, v'_l \overline{v}_\diamond v' v'_r)$ is winning for Duplicator in the $3(n-1)$-round D-local game. By the same reasoning, $(\overline{u}_\triangleleft u'_l, \overline{v}_\triangleleft v'_l)$ and $(u'_r \overline{u}_\triangleright, v'_r \overline{v}_\triangleright)$ are both winning positions for Duplicator in the $(n-1)$-round game. *A fortiori* $(u_1 \dots u_{l-1} u'_l, v_1 \dots v_{l-1} v'_l)$ and $(u'_r u_{r+1} \dots u_s, v'_r v_{r+1} \dots v_s)$ are also both winning for Duplicator in the $(n-1)$-round game. Finally, applying the induction hypothesis with left configuration $(u_1 \dots u_{l-1} u'_l, v_1 \dots v_{l-1} v'_l)$, middle configuration $(u'_l \overline{u}_\diamond u' u'_r, v'_l \overline{v}_\diamond v' v'_r)$, and right configuration $(u'_r u_{r+1} \dots u_s, v'_r v_{r+1} \dots v_s)$, we conclude that $(\overline{u} u', \overline{v} v')$ is winning for Duplicator in $n-1$ rounds. □

4.2 3-Variable Theorem

Proposition 4.2. *Suppose that Duplicator wins the $(4n+2)$-round 3-pebble game from a configuration $(\overline{u}, \overline{v})$ with $|\overline{u}| = |\overline{v}| \leq 3$. Then she also wins the n-round (unrestricted-pebble) game from configuration $(\overline{u}, \overline{v})$.*

Proof. The proof is by induction on n. The base case ($n = 0$) is immediate, and the induction step ($n > 0$) is as follows. Suppose that $|\overline{u}| = |\overline{v}| < 3$. Then for any Spoiler move, Duplicator replies using her 3-pebble strategy, leading to a 3-configuration $(\overline{u}', \overline{v}')$. Duplicator now has a winning strategy for the $(4n+1)$-round 3-pebble game starting from the configuration $(\overline{u}', \overline{v}')$, and therefore she also has a winning strategy for the $(4(n-1)+2)$-round 3-pebble game from $(\overline{u}', \overline{v}')$. By the induction hypothesis, she has a winning strategy for the $(n-1)$-round unrestricted game from $(\overline{u}', \overline{v}')$, and therefore a winning strategy for the n-round game from $(\overline{u}, \overline{v})$.

Now suppose that $|\overline{u}| = |\overline{v}| = 3$. We claim that given any 3-configuration $(\overline{u}, \overline{v})$, we can decompose it into a left part $(\overline{u}_\triangleleft, \overline{v}_\triangleleft)$, a middle part $(\overline{u}_\diamond, \overline{v}_\diamond)$ and a right part $(\overline{u}_\triangleright, \overline{v}_\triangleright)$, satisfying the following desiderata:

1. $\mathit{diam}(\overline{u}_\diamond) \leq 2^{n+1}$,
2. $\mathit{margin}(\overline{u}_\triangleleft) > 2^n$ and $\mathit{margin}(\overline{u}_\triangleright) > 2^n$,
3. $|\overline{u}_\triangleleft| \leq 2$ and $|\overline{u}_\triangleright| \leq 2$,
4. Conditions 1–3 hold for $\overline{v}_\triangleleft$, $\overline{v}_\diamond$, and $\overline{v}_\triangleright$.

By Proposition 3.5, if the above four conditions hold, we obtain that Duplicator has a winning strategy for the $3n$-round 2^{n+2}-local game from the configuration $(\overline{u}_\diamond, \overline{v}_\diamond)$. Furthermore, by (3) and the case described above for configurations of size strictly less than 3, it follows that Duplicator has a winning strategy for the n-round games from the configurations $(\overline{u}_\triangleleft, \overline{v}_\triangleleft)$ and $(\overline{u}_\triangleright, \overline{v}_\triangleright)$. Thus, by applying the Composition Lemma 4.1, Duplicator has a winning strategy for the n-round game from the configuration $(\overline{u}, \overline{v})$.

It remains to show that given any 3-configuration $(\overline{u}, \overline{v})$, we can always find a decomposition that satisfies the above conditions. We show this by the following case analysis. Without loss of generality, assume that $u_1 \leq u_2 \leq u_3$ and $v_1 \leq v_2 \leq v_3$.

Case(i). Suppose that $u_2 - u_1 \leq 2^n$ and $u_3 - u_2 \leq 2^n$. Then it is also the case that $v_2 - v_1 \leq 2^n$ and $v_3 - v_2 \leq 2^n$, since otherwise Spoiler would have a n-round 3-pebble winning strategy by the contraposition of Corollary 3.4. Then let

$\overline{u}_{\triangleleft} = u_1$, $\overline{u}_{\triangleright} = u_3$ and $\overline{u}_{\diamond} = u_1u_2u_3$, and assume a corresponding decomposition of $\overline{v}$.

Case(ii). Suppose that $u_3 - u_2 > 2^n$ and $u_2 - u_1 > 2^n$. Then it is also the case that $v_3 - v_2 > 2^n$ and $v_2 - v_1 > 2^n$ by Corollary 3.4. Let then $\overline{u}_{\diamond} = u_2$, $\overline{u}_{\triangleleft} = u_1u_2$, $\overline{u}_{\triangleright} = u_2u_3$, and consider the corresponding decomposition for $\overline{v}$.

Case(iii). Suppose finally that $u_3 - u_2 > 2^n$ and $u_2 - u_1 \leq 2^n$. By Corollary 3.4, we also have that $v_3 - v_2 > 2^n$ and $v_2 - v_1 \leq 2^n$. Let $\overline{u}_{\triangleleft} = u_1$, $\overline{u}_{\diamond} = u_1u_2$, $\overline{u}_{\triangleright} = u_2u_3$ and consider the corresponding decomposition of $\overline{v}$.

The case where $u_3 - u_2 \leq 2^n$ and $u_2 - u_1 > 2^n$ is symmetric. □

From Proposition 4.2 and Theorem 2.1 we immediately obtain our main result:

Theorem 4.3. $(\mathbb{R}, <, +1)$ *has the 3-variable property.*

5 Linear Functions

In this section we show the 3-variable property for the σ-structure $(\mathbb{R}, <, f)$ with $f : \mathbb{R} \to \mathbb{R}$ a linear function $f(x) = ax + b$. This follows fairly straightforwardly from our main result, Theorem 4.3, using the classical compositional method for sums of ordered structures.

5.1 Monotone Linear Functions

Consider $f : \mathbb{R} \to \mathbb{R}$ given by $f(x) = ax + b$, where $a, b \in \mathbb{R}$ and $a > 0$. We prove that $(\mathbb{R}, <, f)$ has the 3-variable property.

Suppose that $a = 1$, that is, $f(x) = x + b$. If $b > 0$ then $(\mathbb{R}, <, f)$ is isomorphic to $(\mathbb{R}, <, +1)$. If $b < 0$ then $(\mathbb{R}, <, f)$ is isomorphic to $(\mathbb{R}, <^{\mathrm{op}}, +1)$, where $<^{\mathrm{op}}$ is the opposite order on $\mathbb{R}$. In either case $(\mathbb{R}, <, f)$ inherits the 3-variable property from $(\mathbb{R}, <, +1)$.

Assume now that $a \neq 1$. Notice that f has a unique fixed point $x^* = \frac{b}{1-a}$. Moreover, considering the intervals $I_0 = (-\infty, x^*)$ and $I_1 = (x^*, \infty)$, f restricts to bijections $f_i : I_i \to I_i$ for $i = 0, 1$. Now the map $\Phi_0(x) = -\log(x^* - x)$ defines an isomorphism of σ-structures from $(I_0, <, f_0)$ to $(\mathbb{R}, <, +a)$. Likewise the map $\Phi_1(x) = \log(x - x^*)$ defines an isomorphism from $(I_1, <, f_1)$ to $(\mathbb{R}, <, +a)$. It follows that $(I_0, <, f_0)$ and $(I_1, <, f_1)$ both have the 3-variable property.

We argue that $(\mathbb{R}, <, f)$ has the 3-variable property as follows. Let $\mathbf{A}$ and $\mathbf{B}$ be expansions of $(\mathbb{R}, <, f)$ with interpretations of the monadic predicate variables. Let $\mathbf{A}_0$ be the sub-structure of $\mathbf{A}$ with domain I_0 and let $\mathbf{A}_1$ be the sub-structure of $\mathbf{A}$ with domain I_1. Define $\mathbf{B}_0$ and $\mathbf{B}_1$ likewise. Then if Spoiler wins the n-round EF game on $\mathbf{A}$ and $\mathbf{B}$ he also wins the n-round game on the substructures $\mathbf{A}_0$ and $\mathbf{B}_0$ and the n-round game on $\mathbf{A}_1$ and $\mathbf{B}_1$. Thus there exists m, depending only on n, such that Spoiler wins the m-round 3-pebble EF games on $\mathbf{A}_0$ and $\mathbf{B}_0$ and on $\mathbf{A}_1$ and $\mathbf{B}_1$. Then by the usual composition argument on sums of ordered structures [12], we can show that Spoiler wins the m-round 3-pebble game on $\mathbf{A}$ and $\mathbf{B}$.

5.2 Antitone Linear Functions

Consider a linear function $f(x) = ax + b$, where $a < 0$. Note that the map $f^2 := f \circ f : \mathbb{R} \to \mathbb{R}$ is monotone and linear. The idea is to exploit the fact that $(\mathbb{R}, <, f^2)$ has the 3-variable property to rewrite a given monadic first-order σ-sentence φ to a 3-variable sentence φ'' that is equivalent to φ over $(\mathbb{R}, <, f)$. In this rewriting it is convenient to use x^* as an additional constant symbol in intermediate forms, where x^* is the unique fixed point of f. We also allow nested applications of f in intermediate formulas.

We obtain φ'' as follows. Motivated by the fact that f maps the open interval (x^*, ∞) onto $(-\infty, x^*)$ and *vice versa*, working bottom-up, replace each subformula $\exists x\, \psi$ by

$$\exists x\, (x > x^* \wedge (\psi \vee \psi[f(x)/x] \vee \psi[x^*/x]))\,.$$

Now simplify the atomic subformulas as follows, bearing in mind that all variables range over (x^*, ∞). Replace every term $f^n(x^*)$ with x^*. Replace $f^n(x) = x^*$ with **false**. Replace $f^n(x) = f^m(y)$ with $f^{n-1}(x) = f^{m-1}(y)$ if n and m are both odd, and with **false** if n and m have different parity. If n is odd then replace $x^* < f^n(x)$ with **false** and $f^n(x) < x^*$ with **true**. Replace $f^n(x) < f^m(y)$ by $f^{n-1}(x) < f^{m-1}(y)$ if n and m are both odd, by **true** if n is odd and m is even, and by **false** if n is even and m is odd. Finally eliminate the constant symbol x^* using the fact that it is definable in terms of f^2, e.g., replace each subformula $P(x^*)$ with $\exists y\, (y = f^2(y) \wedge P(y))$.

Let φ' denote the sentence arising from the above transformation. Treating the atomic formulas $P(f(x))$ as unary predicate variables, we can interpret φ' as a monadic first-order sentence over the structure $(\mathbb{R}, <, f^2)$. Since f^2 is monotone we can use the result of Section 5.1 to transform φ' to an equivalent 3-variable sentence φ'' over $(\mathbb{R}, <, f^2)$. Then φ'' is equivalent to φ considered as a formula over the structure $(\mathbb{R}, <, f)$.

6 Counterexample

In this section we exhibit a countable dense linear order E and function $g : E \to E$ such that $(E, <, g)$ does not have the k-variable property for any k.

Let $(S, <)$ be the set of non-empty finite sequences of integers under the lexicographic order, and let E be the equivalence relation on S that relates any two such sequences that end with the same element. Since the integers have no greatest or least element, any non-empty interval in S contains an element of each E-equivalence class. Venema [16] has shown that the structure $(S, <, E)$ does not have the k-variable property for any k. For example, one can express the property *"predicate P holds on at least $k+1$ E-inequivalent elements"* with $k+1$ variables but not k variables. Indeed it is not hard to see that in the k-pebble EF game (over any number of rounds) Spoiler cannot distinguish the cases that predicate P is a union of k E-equivalence classes and that P is a union of $k+1$ E-equivalence classes.

We next translate this example to the setting of linear orders with unary functions. Consider the equivalence relation E above as an ordered set under the lexicographic order on $S \times S$. Define $g : E \to E$ by $g(s,t) = (t,s)$ and consider the σ-structure $\mathbf{E} = (E, <, g)$ (where σ is the signature for linear orders and unary functions, defined in Section 2.1). Note that g is very far from being monotone.

To each labelled expansion $\mathbf{S}$ of $(S, <, E)$ we associate a labelled expansion $\mathbf{E}$ of $(E, <, g)$, where $P^{\mathbf{E}} = \{(s,s) : s \in P^{\mathbf{S}}\}$ for each monadic predicate symbol P. There is moreover a one-dimensional interpretation Γ (cf. Section 2.2) of $\mathbf{S}$ in $\mathbf{E}$. The domain formula $\partial_\Gamma(x)$ of Γ is $x = g(x)$ so that $\partial_\Gamma(E) = \{(s,t) \in E : s = t\}$. The coding map $f_\Gamma : \partial_\Gamma(E) \to S$ is given by $f_\Gamma(s,s) = s$. The interpretation also specifies for each atomic formula $\varphi(x_1, \ldots, x_m)$ over $\mathbf{S}$ a corresponding formula $\varphi_\Gamma(x_1, \ldots, x_m)$ over $\mathbf{E}$, with $\mathbf{S} \models \varphi[s_1, \ldots, s_m]$ if and only if $\mathbf{E} \models \varphi_\Gamma[(s_1,s_1), \ldots, (s_m,s_m)]$ for all $s_1, \ldots, s_m \in S$. This correspondence sends $x < y$ and $P(x)$ to themselves and $E(x,y)$ to the formula $\psi(x,y) \vee \psi(y,x)$, where

$$\begin{aligned}\psi(x,y) := \exists u\, (x < u < g(u) < y \wedge \\ \forall v(x < v < u \vee g(u) < v < y \to g(v) \neq v))\,.\end{aligned}$$

Conversely there is a natural two-dimensional first-order interpretation Γ of $\mathbf{E}$ in $\mathbf{S}$. The domain formula is $\partial_\Gamma(x,y) = E(x,y)$, and thus $\partial_\Gamma(S^2) = \{(s,t) \in S \times S : (s,t) \in E\}$. The coding map $f_\Gamma : \partial_\Gamma(S^2) \to E$ is given by $f_\Gamma(s,t) = (s,t)$. The translation of atomic formulas over $\mathbf{E}$ to corresponding formulas over $\mathbf{S}$ is similarly straightforward, e.g., $x < y$ is mapped to $x_1 < y_1 \vee (x_1 = y_1 \wedge x_2 < y_2)$.

As observed in Dawar [1, Section 3] in a similar context, the existence of such a two-way interpretation entails that if $(E, <, g)$ has the k-variable property for some k then $(S, <, E)$ has the k'-variable property for some k'. It follows that $(E, <, g)$ does not have the k-variable property for any k.

7 Conclusion and Future Work

We have shown that the structure $(\mathbb{R}, <, f)$ has the 3-variable property for linear functions $f : \mathbb{R} \to \mathbb{R}$. In future work it would be natural to consider whether the k-variable property holds, for some k, for richer classes of functions, e.g., classes of polynomials.

Moving beyond the reals, we would like to explore whether the results in this paper generalise to arbitrary linear orders and families of monotone functions thereon. More generally, there is the problem, raised by Immerman and Kozen in the conclusion of [12], of finding a model-theoretic characterisation of those classes of structures possessing the k-variable property for some k.

In those settings in which the k-variable property holds, following [4], it is natural to consider how the number of variables affects the succinctness of formulas and, in view of [2], also to seek expressively complete temporal logics.

References

1. Dawar, A.: How many first-order variables are needed on finite ordered structures? In: We Will Show Them! Essays in Honour of Dov Gabbay, vol. 1, pp. 489–520. College Publications (2005)
2. Gabbay, D.M.: Expressive functional completeness in tense logic. In: Mönnich, U. (ed.) Aspects of Philosophical Logic, pp. 91–117. Reidel, Dordrecht (1981)
3. Gabbay, D.M., Pnueli, A., Shelah, S., Stavi, J.: On the temporal basis of fairness. In: POPL, pp. 163–173. ACM Press (1980)
4. Grohe, M., Schweikardt, N.: The succinctness of first-order logic on linear orders. Logical Methods in Computer Science 1(1) (2005)
5. Hirshfeld, Y., Rabinovich, A.: Continuous time temporal logic with counting. Inf. Comput. 214, 1–9 (2012)
6. Hirshfeld, Y., Rabinovich, A.M.: Timer formulas and decidable metric temporal logic. Inf. Comput. 198(2), 148–178 (2005)
7. Hodges, W.: A Shorter Model Theory. Cambridge University Press, New York (1997)
8. Hodkinson, I., Simon, A.: The k-variable property is stronger than H-dimension k. Journal of Philosophical Logic 26(1), 81–101 (1997)
9. Hunter, P.: When is metric temporal logic expressively complete? In: CSL. LIPIcs, vol. 23, pp. 380–394. Schloss Dagstuhl (2013)
10. Hunter, P., Ouaknine, J., Worrell, J.: Expressive completeness for metric temporal logic. In: LICS, pp. 349–357. IEEE Computer Society Press (2013)
11. Immerman, N.: Upper and lower bounds for first order expressibility. J. Comput. Syst. Sci. 25(1), 76–98 (1982)
12. Immerman, N., Kozen, D.: Definability with bounded number of bound variables. Inf. Comput. 83(2), 121–139 (1989)
13. Kamp, H.: Tense Logic and the Theory of Linear Order. PhD thesis, University of California (1968)
14. Poizat, B.: Deux ou trois choses que je sais de L_n. J. Symb. Log. 47(3), 641–658 (1982)
15. Rossman, B.: On the constant-depth complexity of k-clique. In: STOC, pp. 721–730. ACM (2008)
16. Venema, Y.: Expressiveness and completeness of an interval tense logic. Notre Dame Journal of Formal Logic 31(4), 529–547 (1990)

A Appendix

A.1 Missing Proofs from Section 3

Proposition 3.1. *Let $u_1 \dots u_s \equiv v_1 \dots v_s$ be two assignments. Then*

$$\mathrm{frac}(u_i - u_k) < \mathrm{frac}(u_j - u_k) \Leftrightarrow \mathrm{frac}(v_i - v_k) < \mathrm{frac}(v_j - v_k)$$

for all indices $i, j, k \in \{1, \dots, s\}$.

Proof. Fix $i, j, k \in \{1, \dots, s\}$. From the assumption $u_1 \dots u_s \equiv v_1 \dots v_s$ we have the following chain of equivalences:

$$\begin{aligned}
\mathrm{frac}(u_i - u_k) < \mathrm{frac}(u_j - u_k) &\Leftrightarrow u_i - u_k - \lfloor u_i - u_k \rfloor < u_j - u_k - \lfloor u_j - u_k \rfloor \\
&\Leftrightarrow u_i - u_j < \lfloor u_i - u_k \rfloor - \lfloor u_j - u_k \rfloor \\
&\Leftrightarrow v_i - v_j < \lfloor u_i - u_k \rfloor - \lfloor u_j - u_k \rfloor \\
&\Leftrightarrow v_i - v_j < \lfloor v_i - v_k \rfloor - \lfloor v_j - v_k \rfloor \\
&\Leftrightarrow v_i - v_k - \lfloor v_i - v_k \rfloor < v_j - v_k - \lfloor v_j - v_k \rfloor \\
&\Leftrightarrow \mathrm{frac}(v_i - v_k) < \mathrm{frac}(v_j - v_k) .
\end{aligned}$$

□

Proposition 3.2. *Suppose that $u_1 \dots u_s$ and $v_1 \dots v_s$ are both increasing and that $u_1 \dots u_m \equiv v_1 \dots v_m$ and $u_m \dots u_s \equiv v_m \dots v_s$ for some m, $1 \leq m \leq s$. Then $u_1 \dots u_s \equiv v_1 \dots v_s$.*

Proof. We must show that $\lfloor u_j - u_i \rfloor = \lfloor v_j - v_i \rfloor$ for all $i \leq m < j$. To this end, we observe that since $u_1 \dots u_s$ is increasing,

$$\begin{aligned}
\mathrm{frac}(u_j - u_i) &= \mathrm{frac}(u_j - u_m + (u_m - u_i)) \\
&= \mathrm{frac}(u_j - u_m) + \mathrm{frac}(u_m - u_i) .
\end{aligned}$$

It follows that

$$\begin{aligned}
\lfloor u_j - u_i \rfloor &= u_j - u_i - \mathrm{frac}(u_j - u_i) \\
&= (u_j - u_m) + (u_m - u_i) - (\mathrm{frac}(u_j - u_m) + \mathrm{frac}(u_m - u_i)) \\
&= (u_j - u_m) - \mathrm{frac}(u_j - u_m) + (u_m - u_i) - \mathrm{frac}(u_m - u_i) \\
&= \lfloor u_j - u_m \rfloor + \lfloor u_m - u_i \rfloor .
\end{aligned}$$

We can similarly show that

$$\lfloor v_j - v_i \rfloor = \lfloor v_j - v_m \rfloor + \lfloor v_m - v_i \rfloor .$$

But $\lfloor u_j - u_m \rfloor = \lfloor v_j - v_m \rfloor$ since $u_m \dots u_s \equiv v_m \dots v_s$. Likewise $\lfloor u_m - u_i \rfloor = \lfloor v_m - v_i \rfloor$ since $u_1 \dots u_m \equiv v_1 \dots v_m$. We conclude that $\lfloor u_j - u_i \rfloor = \lfloor v_j - v_i \rfloor$. □

On Presburger Arithmetic Extended with Modulo Counting Quantifiers*

Peter Habermehl[1] and Dietrich Kuske[2]

[1] LIAFA, University Paris Diderot, France
[2] TU Ilmenau, Germany

Abstract. We consider Presburger arithmetic (PA) extended with modulo counting quantifiers. We show that its complexity is essentially the same as that of PA, i.e., we give a doubly exponential space bound. This is done by giving and analysing a quantifier elimination procedure similar to Reddy and Loveland's procedure for PA. We also show that the complexity of the automata-based decision procedure for PA with modulo counting quantifiers has the same triple-exponential time complexity as the one for PA when using least significant bit first encoding.

1 Introduction

Presburger arithmetic is the first-order theory of the structure $\mathcal{Z}$, i.e., the integers with addition and comparision. More precisely, we also allow the binary relations $\equiv_k$ (standing for equality modulo k) for $k \geqslant 2$, and all constants $c \in \mathbb{Z}$ to appear in formulas. This theory was shown to be decidable by Presburger [17], upper bounds on the complexity of (fragments of) Presburger arithmetic can, e.g., be found in [16,18,7,2,8,20,9]. Coding integers in binary, we know since the 60's that every definable relation can be accepted by a synchronous multi-tape automaton. The basic idea is that a synchronous three-tape automaton can verify the equation $k + \ell = m$ (in terms of the codings of the numbers k, ℓ, and m) and synchronously rational relations are effectively closed under Boolean operations and projection. At first glance, this translation results in automata of non-elementary size since complementation of automata comes with an exponential blow-up. From Klaedtke's results [13], it follows that automata of triply-exponential size suffice and that they can be constructed in four-fold exponential time using purely automata-theoretic methods. This result was improved by Durand-Gasselin and Habermehl who showed that "small" automata can be constructed efficiently, i.e., in triply-exponential time. Their first proof [6] uses an *ad hoc* construction of automata, their second proof [5] is more uniform in the sense that it applies to the structure $\mathcal{Z}$ and to automatic structures [10,11,3] of bounded degree (improving a result from [14]). Thus, Presburger arithmetic can be decided using automata-theoretic methods in triply exponential time.

More generally, these automata-theoretic methods rely on the fact that $\mathcal{Z}$ is an automatic structure. The motivating result on automatic structures is that their

* This work was partially supported by EGIDE/DAAD-Procope TAMTV.

A. Pitts (Ed.): FOSSACS 2015, LNCS 9034, pp. 375–389, 2015.
DOI: 10.1007/978-3-662-46678-0_24

first-order theory is decidable [10,11,3]. One line of research on automatic structures concentrated on the extension of this result to more powerful logics. One can, for instance, extend first-order logic by a modulo-counting quantifier $\exists^{(p',p)}$ saying "modulo p, there are p' elements satisfying ...". The reason is that, as in the case of $\mathcal{Z}$ and first-order logic, one can construct from a formula in this extended logic a synchronous n-tape automaton that accepts all satisfying assignments of the formula [12] (see [19] for more quantifiers with this property).[1] Since $\mathcal{Z}$ is an automatic structure, this also holds here independent of whether we code integers in base 2 or 3. Consequently, by the Cobham-Semenov theorem [4,22], any relation in $\mathcal{Z}$ definable in this extended logic is effectively semilinear and therefore definable in first-order logic not using the modulo-counting quantifier (this claim also follows from [1] that presents a quantifier elimination for Härtig's quantifier "the number of witnesses for φ equals that for ψ", see also [21]).

This paper determines the complexity of the set of all formulas in the extended logic that hold in $\mathcal{Z}$. To this aim, we first present a procedure that eliminates modulo-counting quantifiers (see the beginning of Section 3.3 for a comparision with Apelt's [1] and Schweikardt's [21] procedures). This procedure is inspired by the classical one by Reddy and Loveland [18]. As in [18], we do not analyse the complexity of this procedure, but the resulting quantifier-free formula. We obtain that every formula in the extended logic has an equivalent quantifier-free formula that uses coefficients and moduli of doubly exponential size and constants of triply exponential size. Based on this finding and classical results on solutions of linear Diophantine equations [23], we show that the theory of the structure $\mathcal{Z}$ in the extended logic can be decided in doubly exponential space. Based on the quantifier elimination, we can also show that the construction of automata from formulas using the algorithms known from the theory of automatic structures can be done in triply exponential time. Thus, the theory of the structure $\mathcal{Z}$ in the extended logic can be decided in triply exponential time using automata-theoretic methods. In summary, we obtain that adding modulo-counting quantifiers does not increase the complexity of the theory of integer addition. Proof details can be found in the full version of the paper.

2 Preliminaries

The structure. The universe of the structure $\mathcal{Z}$ is the set of integers $\mathbb{Z}$. On this set, we consider the constants $c \in \mathbb{Z}$, the binary function $+$, the binary relation $<$ and the binary relations $\equiv_k$ for $k \geqslant 2$ (with $m \equiv_k n$ iff $k \mid m - n$).

The language. We will use a sequence $\bar{x} = (x_i)_{i \in \mathbb{N}}$ of variables. A *term* is an expression $\bar{a}\,\bar{x} + c$ where $\bar{a} = (a_i)_{i \in \mathbb{N}}$ is a sequence of integers with $a_i \neq 0$ for finitely many $i \in \mathbb{N}$ and $c \in \mathbb{Z}$. Let P be an arbitrary but fixed natural number. Then *formulas* of $\mathcal{L}_P$, *Presburger's logic with modulo-counting quantifiers*, are defined by recursion:

[1] In the complete version of this extended abstract, we show that the theory of an automatic structure using *only* modulo-counting quantifiers can be non-elementary.

- If s and t are terms, then $s < t$ (also written $t > s$) and $s \equiv_k t$ are (atomic) formulas (for $k \geqslant 2$).
- If φ and ψ are formulas, then so are $\neg\varphi$, $\varphi \wedge \psi$, $\varphi \vee \psi$, and $\varphi \leftrightarrow \psi$.
- If φ is a formula, x is a variable, and $0 \leqslant p' < p$, $2 \leqslant p \leqslant P$ are natural numbers[2], then $\exists x \colon \varphi$ and $\exists^{(p',p)} x \colon \varphi$ are formulas.

An *evaluation* is a function f that assigns integers to variables. For x a variable and $a \in \mathbb{Z}$, we let $f[x/a]$ be the evaluation with $f[x/a](x) = a$ and $f[x/a](y) = f(y)$ for all variables $y \neq x$. We can extend in a standard way an evaluation f to a function (also denoted f) that maps terms into $\mathbb{Z}$ and formulas to the truth values $\mathtt{tt}$ and $\mathtt{ff}$. In particular, if s and t are terms, then $f(s \equiv_k t) = \mathtt{tt}$ iff $f(s) - f(t)$ is a multiple of k. Furthermore, if φ and ψ are formulas, x a variable, and $0 \leqslant p' < p$ natural numbers, then $f(\exists^{(p',p)} x \colon \varphi) = \mathtt{tt}$ iff the set $\{a \in \mathbb{Z} \mid f[x/a](\varphi) = \mathtt{tt}\}$ is finite and $|\{a \in \mathbb{Z} \mid f[x/a](\varphi) = \mathtt{tt}\}| \equiv_p p'$.

A formula φ is *valid* if $f(\varphi) = tt$ for all evaluations f. *Presburger arithmetic with modulo-counting quantifiers* is the set of all valid formulas of $\mathcal{L}_P$. For two formulas F and G, we write $F \Leftrightarrow G$ for "$f(F) = f(G)$ for all evaluations f". We define as usual addition of terms as well as multiplication of a term with an integer.

For a term $t = \bar{a}\,\bar{x} + c$ and a variable x_i, we call a_i the *coefficient* of x_i in t. If the coefficient of x_i in t is 0, then we call t an *x_i-free term*.

Let x be a variable. Then an atomic formula φ is *x-separated* if there are an x-free term t and a non-negative integer $a \in \mathbb{N}$ such that φ is of the form $ax < t$, $t < ax$, or $ax \equiv_k t$. If t is an x-free term, then, e.g., the formula $0 \equiv_k t$ is x-separated since we identified the terms $0x$ and 0.

An atomic formula is *constant separated* if it is of the form $c < s$ or $s \equiv_k c$ where s is a term and c a constant.

A formula φ with a vector of k free variables $\boldsymbol{x} = (x_1, \ldots, x_k)$ is also written as $\varphi(\boldsymbol{x})$. Then we define $[\![\varphi(\boldsymbol{x})]\!] = \{(f(x_1), \ldots, f(x_k)) \mid f$ is an evaluation such that $f(\varphi) = \mathtt{tt}\}$. We also write $\boldsymbol{a}.\boldsymbol{x} > c$ (resp. $\boldsymbol{a}.\boldsymbol{x} \equiv_k c$) for constant separated formulas with free variables $\boldsymbol{x}$.

Next, let φ be a formula. Then $\textsc{Coeff}(\varphi) \subseteq \mathbb{Z}$ is the set of integers $-1, 0, 1$ and $\pm a$ such that there is an atomic formula $s < t$ in φ such that a is a coefficient appearing in the term $s - t$. Similarly, $\textsc{Const}(\varphi) \subseteq \mathbb{Z}$ is the set of integers $-1, 0, 1$ and $\pm c$ such that there is an atomic formula $s < t$ in φ such that c is the constant term in $s - t$. The set $\textsc{Mod}(\varphi) \subseteq \mathbb{N}$ contains all integers $k \geqslant 2$ such that an atomic formula of the form $s \equiv_k t$ appears in φ. Finally, $\mathbf{P}(\varphi) = \textsc{Coeff}(\varphi) \cup \textsc{Mod}(\varphi)$.

Note that $\textsc{Coeff}(\varphi)$ and $\textsc{Const}(\varphi)$ depend on subformulas of the form $s < t$, but not on subformulas of the form $s \equiv_k t$. On the other hand, $\textsc{Mod}(\varphi)$ only depends on subformulas of the form $s \equiv_k t$.

---

[2] This insures that we have only finitely many quantifiers.

3 Quantifier Elimination and a Decision Procedure

3.1 Elimination of ∃

In this section, we will eliminate the quantifier from a formula of the form $\exists x\colon \beta$ where β is a Boolean combination of atomic formulas. Our main concern is the "size" of the resulting formula, more precisely, of the coefficients, constants, and moduli appearing in it. Neither the result (Proposition 3.3) nor the method presented here is new, but this section is meant to simplify reading and to allow the reader to grasp the new results concerning the modulo-counting quantifier.

To this aim, we define the following sets (that will turn out to overapproximate the corresponding sets of the resulting quantifier-free formula):

$$\begin{aligned}
\textsc{Coeff}'(\beta) &= \{a_1a_2 - a_3a_4 \mid a_1, a_2, a_3, a_4 \in \textsc{Coeff}(\beta)\} \\
\textsc{Const}'(\beta) &= \left\{ a_1c_1 - a_2(c_2 + c) \;\middle|\; \begin{array}{l} a_1, a_2 \in \textsc{Coeff}(\beta), c_1, c_2 \in \textsc{Const}(\beta) \\ |c| \leqslant \max \textsc{Coeff}(\beta) \cdot \operatorname{lcm} \textsc{Mod}(\beta) \end{array} \right\} \\
\textsc{Mod}'(\beta) &= \{a_1a_2kp \mid a_1a_2 \in \textsc{Coeff}(\beta), k \in \textsc{Mod}(\beta), 1 \leqslant p \leqslant P\}
\end{aligned}$$

Using these sets, we formulate the following condition on the pair of formulas (β, γ):

$$\textsc{Coeff}(\gamma) \subseteq \textsc{Coeff}'(\beta)\,,\ \textsc{Const}(\gamma) \subseteq \textsc{Const}'(\beta)\,, \textsc{Mod}(\gamma) \subseteq \textsc{Mod}'(\beta) \quad (1)$$

Lemma 3.1. *Let β be a Boolean combination of x-separated atomic formulas, $ax < t$ or $t < ax$ some atomic formula from β with $a > 0$ and $-aN \leqslant c \leqslant aN$ where $N = \operatorname{lcm} \textsc{Mod}(\beta)$. There exists a Boolean combination $\beta_{a,t+c}$ of x-free atomic formulas such that $(\beta, \beta_{a,t+c})$ satisfies* (1) *and, for all evaluations f,*

$$f(ax) = f(t + c) \Longrightarrow f(\beta) = f(\beta_{a,t+c})\,.$$

Proof. The formula $\beta_{a,t+c}$ is obtained from β by the following replacements (where s is some x-free term and $k \geqslant 2$):

$$\begin{aligned}
a'x < s &\text{ is replaced by } a't + a'c < as \\
s < a'x &\text{ is replaced by } as < a't + a'c \\
a'x \equiv_k s &\text{ is replaced by } a't + a'c \equiv_{ak} as
\end{aligned}$$

□

Lemma 3.2. *Let x be a variable and β a Boolean combination of x-separated atomic formulas. Then there exists a Boolean combination γ of x-free atomic formulas such that (β, γ) satisfies* (1) *and* $(\exists x\colon \beta) \Leftrightarrow \gamma$.

Proof. Let T be the set of all pairs (a, t) such that β contains an atomic formula of the form $ax < t$ or $t < ax$ with $a > 0$ (or $T = \{(1, 0)\}$ if no such atomic formula exists). Let furthermore $N = \operatorname{lcm}(\textsc{Mod}(\beta))$ such that N is a multiple of every integer k such that an atomic formula of the form $ax \equiv_k t$ appears in β. Then $\exists x\colon \beta$ is equivalent with the formula $\gamma := \bigvee_{(a,t)\in T} \bigvee_{-aN\leqslant c\leqslant aN} (\beta_{a,t+c} \wedge 0 \equiv_a t + c)$.

□

Proposition 3.3. *Let x be a variable and α a Boolean combination of atomic formulas. Then there exists a Boolean combination γ of x-free atomic formulas such that (β, γ) satisfies (1) and $(\exists x \colon \alpha) \Leftrightarrow \gamma$.*

Proof. Without changing the sets COEFF etc., we can transform α into an equivalent Boolean combination β of x-separated atomic formulas. Then γ is the formula obtained from Lemma 3.2. □

3.2 Elimination of $\exists^{(p',p)}$

In this section, we want to prove a proposition analogous to Prop. 3.3, where $\exists x \colon \alpha$ is replaced by $\exists^{(p',p)} x \colon \alpha$. The crucial point is to prove the analogue of Lemma 3.2.

Lemma 3.4. *Let x be a variable, β a Boolean combination of x-separated atomic formulas, and $0 \leqslant p' < p \leqslant P$ natural numbers. Then there exists a Boolean combination of atomic formulas γ such that (β, γ) satisfies (1) and $(\exists^{(p',p)} x \colon \beta) \Leftrightarrow \gamma$.*

The proof of this lemma requires several claims and definitions that we demonstrate first, the actual proof of Lemma 3.4 can be found on page 381.

Let T be the set of all pairs (a, t) such that β contains an atomic formula of the form $ax < t$ or $t < ax$ with $a > 0$ (if no such formula exists, set $T = \{(1, 0)\}$).

Let S be some non-empty subset of T and let $\prec$ be a strict linear order on S. We call an evaluation f *consistent* with $\prec$ if the following hold:

- $\frac{f(s_1)}{a_1} < \frac{f(s_2)}{a_2} \iff (a_1, s_1) \prec (a_2, s_2)$ for all $(a_1, s_1), (a_2, s_2) \in S$
- for all $(a_1, t_1) \in T$, there exists $(a_2, s_2) \in S$ with $\frac{f(t_1)}{a_1} = \frac{f(s_2)}{a_2}$.

In the following, let $S = \{(a_1, s_1), (a_2, s_2), \ldots, (a_n, s_n)\}$ with $(a_1, s_1) \prec (a_2, s_2) \prec \cdots \prec (a_n, s_n)$. Consider the following formulas for $0 \leqslant r < p$ and $1 \leqslant i < n$:

$$\beta_{0,r} = \exists^{(r,p)} x \colon (a_1 x < s_1 \wedge \beta) \qquad \beta_{n,r} = \exists^{(r,p)} x \colon (s_n < a_n x \wedge \beta)$$

$$\beta_{i,r} = \exists^{(r,p)} x \colon (s_i < a_i x \wedge a_{i+1} x < s_{i+1} \wedge \beta) \qquad \beta'_{i,r} = \exists^{(r,p)} x \colon (x = s_i \wedge \beta)$$

If f is an evaluation, then $\beta_{0,r}$ expresses that (modulo p) there are r integers b with $f[x/b](\beta) = \mathrm{tt}$ and $b < \frac{f(s_1)}{a_1}$. Similarly, $\beta_{i,r}$ holds under f if and only if there are (modulo p) r integers b in the open interval $\left(\frac{f(s_i)}{a_i}, \frac{f(s_{i+1})}{a_{i+1}}\right)$ with $f[x/b](\beta) = \mathrm{tt}$ etc. Now consider the formula

$$\varphi^{\prec} = \bigvee \left(\bigwedge_{0 \leqslant i \leqslant n} \beta_{r_i, p} \wedge \bigwedge_{1 \leqslant i \leqslant n} \beta'_{r'_i, p} \right)$$

where the disjunction extends over all tuples $(r_0, r_1, \ldots, r_n, r'_1, r'_2 \ldots, r'_n)$ of integers from $\{0, 1, \ldots, p-1\}$ that, modulo p, sum up to p'. For any evaluation f consistent with $\prec$, we therefore get $f(\exists^{(p',p)} x \colon \beta) = f(\varphi^{\prec})$. In order to construct γ as claimed in Lemma 3.4, it therefore suffices to eliminate the counting quantifiers from the formulas $\beta_{i,r}$ and $\beta'_{i,r}$. In this elimination procedure (detailed in the following claims), we will assume the evaluation to be consistent with $\prec$.

Claim 3.4.1. *Let $0 \leqslant r < p$. There exist Boolean combinations $\gamma_{0,r}^{\prec}$ and $\gamma_{n,r}^{\prec}$ of atomic formulas such that $(\beta, \gamma_{0,r}^{\prec})$ and $(\beta, \gamma_{n,r}^{\prec})$ satisfy (1) and $f(\beta_{0,r}) = f(\gamma_{0,r}^{\prec})$ as well as $f(\beta_{n,r}) = f(\gamma_{n,r}^{\prec})$ for all evaluations f that are consistent with $\prec$.*

We next want to eliminate the quantifier from $\beta_{i,r}$ for $1 \leqslant i < n$, i.e., we consider the integers in the open interval $\left(\frac{f(s_i)}{a_i}, \frac{f(s_{i+1})}{a_{i+1}}\right)$. It turns out to be convenient to split the set of these integers b according to $(a_i b - f(s_i)) \bmod a_i N$.

Claim 3.4.2. *For $1 \leqslant i < n$, $1 \leqslant c \leqslant a_i N$, and $0 \leqslant r < p$, set*

$$\beta_{i,r,c} = \exists^{(r,p)} c\colon (s_i < a_i x \wedge a_{i+1} x < s_{i+1} \wedge a_i x \equiv_{a_i N} s_i + c \wedge \beta)\,.$$

There exists a Boolean combination $\gamma_{i,r,c}^{\prec}$ of atomic formulas such that $(\beta, \gamma_{i,r,c}^{\prec})$ satisfies (1) and $f(\beta_{i,r,c}) = f(\gamma_{i,r,c}^{\prec})$ for all evaluations f consistent with $\prec$.

Proof. Let f be any evaluation that is consistent with $\prec$. We consider the following two sets $X \supseteq Y$:

$$X = \left\{ b \in \mathbb{Z} \;\middle|\; \frac{f(s_i)}{a_i} < b < \frac{f(s_{i+1})}{a_{i+1}}, a_i b \equiv_{a_i N} f(s_i) + c \right\} \text{ and}$$
$$Y = \{ b \in X \mid f[x/b](\beta) = \mathtt{tt} \}$$

Our aim is to construct a formula $\gamma_{i,r,c}^{\prec}$ that holds under the evaluation f if and only if $|Y| \equiv_p r$. Since the formula we construct is independent from f, this will prove the claim.

Let b be an integer from the open interval $\left(\frac{f(s_i)}{a_i}, \frac{f(s_{i+1})}{a_{i+1}}\right)$. Then $b \in X$ iff $a_i b \equiv_{a_i N} f(s_i) + c$. But this is the case iff $b \equiv_N \frac{f(s_i)+c}{a_i}$ (which, in particular, means $\frac{f(s_i)+c}{a_i} \in \mathbb{Z}$). Hence X is the set of integers of the form $\frac{f(s_i)+c}{a_i} + N \cdot k$ for some $k \in \mathbb{N}$ from the above open interval.

Next let $b_1 \in Y \subseteq X$ and $b_2 \in X$. Then $b_1 \equiv_N b_2$ and $f[x/b_1](\beta) = \mathtt{tt}$. Since N is a multiple of all moduli appearing in β, we get $f[x/b_2](\beta) = \mathtt{tt}$ and therefore $b_2 \in Y$. Hence $Y \in \{\emptyset, X\}$. Since $\frac{f(s_i)+c}{a_i} \in X$ if and only if $X \neq \emptyset$, we have $Y = X$ if $\frac{f(s_i)+c}{a_i} \in Y$ and $Y = \emptyset$ otherwise. Note that the first case occurs if and only if $f(\theta) = \mathtt{tt}$ where

$$\theta = \exists x (a_i x = s_i + c \wedge a_{i+1} x < s_{i+1} \wedge \beta)\,.$$

Now assume $\frac{f(s_i)+c}{a_i} \in Y$ which in particular implies that a_i divides $f(s_i) + c$. Then the size $|X|$ of the set X is the maximal natural number k with $\frac{f(s_i)+c}{a_i} + N \cdot k < \frac{f(s_{i+1})}{a_{i+1}}$, i.e., $|X| = k$ if and only if

$$a_{i+1}(f(s_i) + c + a_i N \cdot k) < a_i f(s_{i+1}) \leqslant a_{i+1}(f(s_i) + c + a_i N \cdot (k+1))\,.$$

Consequently, we have in this case $|Y| \equiv_p r$ if and only if $|X| \equiv_p r$ if and only if the following formula ν holds under f:

$$\nu = \exists y\colon \begin{pmatrix} a_i a_{i+1} N y < a_i s_{i+1} - a_{i+1} s_i - a_{i+1} c \\ \wedge\, a_i s_{i+1} - a_{i+1} s_i - a_{i+1} c - a_i a_{i+1} N \leqslant a_i a_{i+1} N y \\ \wedge\, y \equiv_p r \end{pmatrix}$$

So far, we showed that $f(\beta_{i,r,c}) = \mathtt{tt}$ if and only if

$$f(\theta \wedge \nu) = \mathtt{tt} \text{ or } (r = 0 \text{ and } f(\nu) = \mathtt{ff}). \tag{2}$$

Now, we can construct quantifier-free formulas $\bar{\theta}$ and $\bar{\nu}$ that can be shown to be equivalent to θ and ν, respectively, and to satisfy (1). □

Claim 3.4.3. *Let $1 \leqslant i < n$ and $0 \leqslant r < p$. There exists a Boolean combination $\gamma_{i,r}^{\prec}$ of atomic formulas such that $(\beta, \gamma_{i,r}^{\prec})$ satisfies* (1) *and $f(\beta_{i,r}) = f(\gamma_{i,r}^{\prec})$ for all evaluations f consistent with $\prec$.*

Proof. Note that the formulas $s_i < a_i x \wedge a_{i+1} x < s_{i+1} \wedge \beta$ and

$$\bigvee_{1 \leqslant c \leqslant a_i N} (s_i < a_i x \wedge a_{i+1} x < s_{i+1} \wedge a_i x \equiv_{a_i N} s_i + c \wedge \beta)$$

are equivalent and the disjunction in this formula is exclusive (i.e., every x satisfies at most one conjunct). Therefore, we can set

$$\gamma_{i,r}^{\prec} = \bigvee \bigwedge_{1 \leqslant c \leqslant a_i N} \gamma_{i,c,r_c}^{\prec}$$

where the disjunction extends over all tuples $(r_1, r_2, \ldots, r_{a_i N})$ of integers from $\{0, 1, \ldots, p-1\}$ with $\sum_{1 \leqslant c \leqslant a_i N} r_c \equiv_p r$. Now the claim follows from Claim 3.4.2. □

Claim 3.4.4. *Let $1 \leqslant i \leqslant n$ and $0 \leqslant r < p$. There exists a Boolean combination $\delta_{i,r}^{\prec}$ of atomic formulas such that $(\beta, \delta_{i,r}^{\prec})$ satisfies* (1) *and, for all evaluations f (even those that are not consistent with $\prec$),*

$$f(\beta'_{i,r}) = f(\delta_{i,r}^{\prec}).$$

Proof. By Lemma 3.1, the formulas $a_i x = s_i \wedge \beta$ and $a_i x = s_i \wedge \beta_{a_i, s_i}$ are equivalent. Hence the formula

$$\delta_{i,r}^{\prec} = \begin{cases} \neg \beta_{a_i, s_i} & \text{if } r = 0 \\ \beta_{a_i, s_i} & \text{if } r = 1 \\ 0 < 0 & \text{if } r > 1 \end{cases}$$

is equivalent with $\beta'_{i,r}$. Since $\delta_{i,r}^{\prec}$ is a Boolean combination of the formulas β_{a_i, s_i} and $0 < 0$, the pair $(\beta, \delta_{i,r}^{\prec})$ satisfies (1) by Lemma 3.1. □

Having shown all these claims, we now use them to finally prove Lemma 3.4.

Proof (of Lemma 3.4). Let $S \subseteq T$ be some non-empty subset of T and let $\prec$ be a strict linear order on S. As above, we let $S = \{(a_1, s_1), \ldots, (a_n, s_n)\}$ with $(a_1, s_1) \prec (a_2, s_2) \prec \cdots \prec (a_n, s_n)$. Then set

$$\gamma^{\prec} = \bigvee \left(\bigwedge_{0 \leqslant i \leqslant n+1} \gamma_{i,r_i}^{\prec} \wedge \bigwedge_{1 \leqslant i \leqslant n} \delta_{i,r'_i}^{\prec} \right)$$

where the disjunction extends over all tuples $(r_0, r_1, \ldots, r_{n+1}, r'_1, r'_2 \ldots, r'_n)$ of natural numbers from $\{0, 1, \ldots, p-1\}$ with $\sum_{0 \leqslant i \leqslant n+1} r_i + \sum_{1 \leqslant i \leqslant n} r'_i \equiv_p p'$. Then $f(\varphi^{\prec}) = f(\gamma^{\prec})$ for all evaluations f that are consistent with $\prec$. Furthermore, $\gamma^{\prec}$ is a Boolean combination of atomic formulas and $(\beta, \gamma^{\prec})$ satisfies (1).

Next consider the formla

$$\alpha^{\prec} = \bigwedge_{1 \leqslant i < n} a_{i+1} s_i < a_i s_{i+1} \wedge \bigwedge_{(a,t) \in T} \bigvee_{1 \leqslant i \leqslant n} a_i t = a s_i \,.$$

Then, for any evaluation f, we have $f(\alpha^{\prec}) = \mathrm{tt}$ if and only if f is consistent with $\prec$. Since $\alpha^{\prec}$ is a Boolean combination of formulas of the form $a's < at$ with $(a, s), (a', t) \in T$, the pair $(\beta, \alpha^{\prec})$ satisfies (1).

Finally, let

$$\gamma = \bigwedge_{(*)} (\alpha^{\prec} \to \gamma^{\prec})$$

where the conjunction $(*)$ extends over all strict linear orders $\prec$ on some non-empty subset of T. □

Proposition 3.5. *Let x be a variable and α a Boolean combination of atomic formulas. Let furthermore $E = \exists$ or $E = \exists^{(p',p)}$ for some $0 \leqslant p' < p$ and $2 \leqslant p \leqslant P$. Then there exists a Boolean combination γ of atomic formulas such that $(Ex\colon \alpha) \Leftrightarrow \gamma$. Furthermore, we have the following:*

$$\max \mathbf{P}(\gamma) \leqslant \max \mathbf{P}(\alpha)^3 \cdot P$$

$$\max \textsc{Const}(\gamma) \leqslant \max \textsc{Const}(\alpha) \cdot 2^{\max \mathbf{P}(\alpha)^3}$$

3.3 An Efficient Decision Procedure

Now, by induction on the quantifier depth we can obtain the following theorem.

Theorem 3.6. *Let $\varphi \in \mathcal{L}_P$ be a formula of quantifier-depth d. There exists an equivalent Boolean combination γ of atomic formulas with*

$$\max \mathbf{P}(\gamma) \leqslant (P \cdot \max \mathbf{P}(\varphi))^{4^d} \text{ and}$$

$$\max \textsc{Const}(\gamma) \leqslant 2^{(P \cdot \max \mathbf{P}(\varphi))^{4^d}} \cdot \max \textsc{Const}(\varphi) \,.$$

Comparison with Apelt's and with Schweikardt's elimination procedure. In the structure $\mathcal{Z}$, the modulo counting quantifier is a special case of Härtig's quantifier. Apelt [1] and Schweikardt [21] presented quantifier elimination procedures for Härtig's quantifier and therefore for its special case, the modulo counting quantifier. Differently from Schweikardt, we do not transform φ into disjunctive normal form, we do not normalize terms, and we do not replace a counting quantifier by many existential quantifiers. While we are not able to handle Härtig's quantifer this way, these differences allow to obtain the elementary bounds described in the theorem above. These elementary bounds are the basis for the following decision procedure.

Let $\varphi(x)$ be a Boolean combination of atomic formulas (note that x is the only free variable) and $A = \max(\mathbf{P}(\varphi) \cup \{6\})$. If φ is satisfiable, then results from [23] imply that φ has a witness of absolute value at most $A^{A^5} \cdot \max \text{Const}(\varphi)$. Using Theorem 3.6, we can infer a similar result for arbitrary formulas $\varphi(x)$ with one free variable. If φ has ℓ additional variables, instantiated by integers of absolute value $\leqslant N$, we can prove the following:

Corollary 3.7. *There exists $\kappa \geqslant 1$ with the following property. Consider a formula $\varphi(x, y_1, \ldots, y_\ell)$ from $\mathcal{L}_P$ of quantifier-depth d. Let $n_1, \ldots, n_\ell \in \mathbb{Z}$ with $|n_i| \leqslant N$. Then the formula $\exists x\colon \varphi(x, n_1, \ldots, n_\ell)$ is true if and only if there exists $n \in \mathbb{Z}$ such that $\varphi(n, n_1, \ldots, n_\ell)$ is true with*

$$|n| \leqslant 2^{(P \cdot \max \mathbf{P}(\varphi))^{\kappa^d}} \cdot \max \text{Const}(\varphi) \cdot N \cdot \max(1, \ell).$$

Next, we want to prove a similar result for the modulo-counting quantifier. Recall that $\exists^{(p',p)}x\colon \varphi(x)$ can only be true if φ has only finitely many witnesses, i.e., if the formula $\exists y \forall x\colon (\varphi(x) \to |x| \leqslant y)$ is true. Applying the above corollary, one finds a finite interval such that φ has infinitely many witnesses iff it has at least one witness in this interval. In case φ has only finitely many witnesses, then all of them are of bounded absolute value. More precisely, we get the following

Corollary 3.8. *Let κ be the constant from Corollary 3.7 and*

$$C = 2^{(P \cdot \max \mathbf{P}(\varphi))^{\kappa^{d+1}}} \cdot \max \text{Const}(\varphi) \cdot N \cdot \max(1, \ell).$$

Let $\varphi = \varphi(x, y_1, \ldots, y_\ell) \in \mathcal{L}_P$ be a formula of quantifier-depth d, let $n_1, \ldots, n_\ell \in \mathbb{Z}$ with $|n_i| \leqslant N$. Then $\exists^{(p',p)}x\colon \varphi(x, n_1, \ldots, n_\ell)$ is true if and only if the following hold:

(1) no integer n with $C < |n| \leqslant C^2$ makes $\varphi(n, n_1, \ldots, n_\ell)$ true and
(2) $|\{n \in \mathbb{Z} \mid |n| \leqslant C$ and $\varphi(n, n_1, \ldots, n_\ell)$ is true$\}| \equiv_p p'$.

Corollaries 3.7 and 3.8 allow to evaluate the truth value of a sentence φ by, recursively, evaluating the truth value of subformulas ψ of φ with arguments of bounded size. Analysing this size carefully, one obtains

Theorem 3.9. *Presburger arithmetic with modulo-counting quantifiers is decidable in doubly exponential space.*

Note that this complexity matches the best known upper bound for Presburger arithmetic without modulo-counting quantifiers from [7].

4 Automata Based Decision Procedure

In this section we show that an automaton accepting all solutions of a formula of $\mathcal{L}_P$ can be constructed in triply exponential time. We follow the same ideas as in [6] where the same result was given for Presburger's logic.

4.1 Encoding

We represent integer vectors as finite words. We use a vectorial least significant bit first coding. For $h > 0$ we define $\Sigma_h = \{0,1\}^h$. Moreover we use the separate sign alphabet $S_h = \{+,-\}^h$ (indicating if the corresponding integer is positive or negative). Given any letter a in Σ_h or S_h we write $\pi_i(a)$ with $1 \leq i \leq h$ for its i-th component. Similarly, the i-th component of a h dimensional vector $\boldsymbol{x} \in \mathbb{Z}^h$ is denoted by $\pi_i(\boldsymbol{x})$. The symbol $+$ corresponds to 0 and $-$ corresponds to 1. In this way, to each letter $a \in \Sigma_h$ corresponds a letter $s(a) \in S_h$. Similarly to each letter $s \in S_h$ corresponds a letter $a(s) \in \Sigma_h$. Words of $\Sigma_h^* S_h$ represent h-dimensional integer vectors. A word $w_0 \dots w_n s \in \Sigma_h^* S_h$ represents the integer vector denoted by $\langle w_0 \dots w_n s\rangle$ whose i^{th} component (with $1 \leq i \leq h$) is computed as: If $s_i = +$, then $\pi_i(\langle w_0 \dots w_n s\rangle) = \sum_{j=0}^{n} 2^j.\pi_i(w_j)$ and if $s_i = -$, then $\pi_i(\langle w_0 \dots w_n s\rangle) = -2^{n+1} + \sum_{j=0}^{n} 2^j.\pi_i(w_j)$. For example, $\langle (0,1)(1,1)(1,0)(+,-)\rangle = \langle (0,1)(1,1)(1,0)\ (0,1)(+,-)\rangle = (6,-5)$. In particular, $\langle + \rangle = 0$ and $\langle - \rangle = -1$. We also define the notation $\langle . \rangle_+$ over Σ_h^* as $\langle w \rangle_+ = \langle w(+,\dots,+)\rangle$.

Remark 4.1. Let $w', w \in \Sigma_h^*, s \in S_h$. We have $\langle w'ws \rangle = \langle w' \rangle_+ + 2^{|w'|}\langle ws \rangle$.

Each vector has an infinite number of representations. Indeed for each word $w_0 \dots w_n s \in \Sigma_h^* S_h$, any word in $w_0 \dots w_n (a(s))^* s$ represents the same vector. To get a unique representation for each vector, we can take the shortest word representing it.

Given a Presburger formula $\varphi(\boldsymbol{x})$ with h free variables, we say that it defines the language $L_\varphi = \{w \in \Sigma_h^* S_h \mid \langle w \rangle \in [\![\varphi(\boldsymbol{x})]\!]\}$. Such languages are regular, called Presburger-definable and meet the following saturation property: If a representation of a vector is in the language then any other representation of that vector is also in the language. Our coding satisfies the following property [15].

Property 4.2. Any residual of a Presburger-definable language is either a Presburger-definable language, or the empty word language.

A *deterministic automaton* (DFA) is a tuple $(\Sigma, Q, q_0, Q_f, \delta)$ where Σ is the finite alphabet, Q the set of states, q_0 the initial state, $Q_f \subseteq Q$ the set of final states and δ the transition function from $Q \times \Sigma$ to Q. We suppose DFA to be complete (containing a sink state, if necessary). In a DFA accepting all solutions of a Presburger formula $\varphi(\boldsymbol{x})$ with h free variables, a word $w \in \Sigma_h^*$ leads from the initial state to a state accepting exactly all solutions of $\varphi(2^{|w|}\boldsymbol{x} + \langle w \rangle_+)$. Therefore, we can consider states (except final ones) of such automata as being Presburger formulas.

Given any Presburger-definable language L, the corresponding *uniformised Presburger-definable language* is defined by taking only one word (the shortest) representing the given vector. We obtain it by intersecting L (or the corresponding automaton) with a regular language ($\subseteq \Sigma_h^* S_h$) which forbids that words end with $a(s)s \in \Sigma_h S_h$ for some $s \in S_h$. We call this operation *uniformisation.*

4.2 Complexity of the Automata Based Decision Procedure

The well-known decision procedure for Presburger arithmetic using automata is based on recursively constructing an automaton accepting solutions of a Presburger formula by using automata constructions for handling logical connectives and quantifiers. Automata for constant separated formulas can be easily constructed. The following lemmas are from [6]. Let $||\boldsymbol{a}||_+ = \Sigma_{\{i \mid a_i \geq 0\}} a_i$ and $||\boldsymbol{a}||_- = \Sigma_{\{i \mid a_i \leq 0\}} |a_i|$. Let $\perp$ be the formula $0 < 0$.

Lemma 4.3. *The minimal DFA accepting the Presburger definable language corresponding to the formula* $\boldsymbol{a}.\boldsymbol{x} > c$ *has at most* $2 \cdot max(||\boldsymbol{a}||, |c|) + 1$ *states. Each non-final state accepts languages corresponding to formulas of the form* $\perp$ *or* $\boldsymbol{a}.\boldsymbol{x} > c'$ *with* $c' = c$ *or* $\min(c, -||a||_+) \leq c' < \max(c, ||a||_-)$

Lemma 4.4. *The minimal DFA accepting the Presburger definable language corresponding to the formula* $\boldsymbol{a}.\boldsymbol{x} \equiv_{2^m(2n+1)} c$ *with* $0 \leq c < 2^m(2n+1)$ *and* $m, n \geq 0$ *has at most* $2^m(2n+1)+1$ *states. Each non-final state accepts languages corresponding to formulas of the form* $\boldsymbol{a}.\boldsymbol{x} \equiv_{2n+1} c'$ *with* $c' \in [0, 2n]$ *(this type of states is reached after* m *transitions) and* $\boldsymbol{a}.\boldsymbol{x} \equiv_{2^{m_1}(2n+1)} c'$ *where* $(m_1 = m \wedge c' = c) \vee (m_1 < m \wedge \gamma \in [0, 2^{m_1}(2n+1) - 1]$ *and* $m_1 < m$.

Each logical connective ($\wedge$, $\vee$, $\leftrightarrow$, $\neg$) corresponds then naturally to operations on automata (For $\neg$ it is of course crucial to have a deterministic automaton). Furthermore to get an automaton for $\exists y\colon \varphi(y, \boldsymbol{x})$ given an automaton for $\varphi(y, \boldsymbol{x})$ one *projects away* [3] the component for y and obtains a *non-deterministic* automaton. Then, to be able to continue the recursive construction, the automaton is determinised, uniformised and minimised. Starting from an automaton of triple-exponential size, determinisation might lead to an automaton of quadruple-exponential size. However, for Presburger's logic the size of the automata during the construction is at most triple-exponential in the size of the formula [6]. We refine this analysis here to get the same upper bound for formula containing also $\exists^{(p',p)}$ quantifiers. For that we first detail the corresponding automata construction before analysing the size of the (intermediate) automata.

Automata Construction for the Modulo-Counting Quantifier. We adapt the construction of [12,19] for our particular encoding. Here it is crucial to have uniformised automata.

Lemma 4.5. *Given a DFA* $\mathcal{A}_\varphi$ *accepting the uniformised Presburger language* L_φ *defined by a formula* $\varphi(y, \boldsymbol{x})$ *of* $\mathcal{L}_P$ *one can construct a DFA* $\mathcal{A}_\psi$ *accepting the uniformised Presburger definable language* L_ψ *defined by* $\psi = \exists^{(p',p)} y\colon \varphi(y, \boldsymbol{x})$.

Proof. Without loss of generality we suppose that the value of y is given by the first component of letters of $\mathcal{A}_\varphi$. We need first some definitions. A *max-V*

[3] As the automaton should accept shortest encodings, additional transitions with a sign letter going to the final state have to be added before uniformisation.

multiset wrt. a natural number $max \geq 1$ and a set V is a multiset of elements of V such that each element appears at most max times. We denote all of these multisets by $\mathcal{M}_{max}(V)$. A *max-V* multiset can be seen as a multiplicity function mapping elements from V to $\{0, 1, 2, \ldots, max\}$. For positive natural numbers x and y with $y > 1$, we define $x\ mod_1\ y = x\ mod\ y$ if $x\ mod\ y \neq 0$, $x\ mod_1\ y = 0$ if $x = 0$ and $x\ mod_1\ y = y$ else. Given two *max-V* multisets m_1, m_2 their union $m_1 \cup m_2$ is defined as $(m_1 \cup m_2)(v) = (m_1(v) + m_2(v))\ mod_1\ max$ for all $v \in V$.

Since $\mathcal{A}_\varphi$ is uniformised, we can suppose that $\mathcal{A}_\varphi$ has exactly one accepting state which has outgoing transitions only to the sink state. Let $\mathcal{A}_\varphi = (\Sigma_h \cup S_h, Q \cup \{F\}, q_0, \{F\}, \delta)$ with $L(\mathcal{A}) \subseteq \Sigma_h^* S_h$. We construct a DFA $\mathcal{A}_\psi = (\Sigma_{h-1} \cup S_{h-1}, Q' \cup \{F'\}, q_0', \{F'\}, \delta')$ with $L(\mathcal{A}_\psi) \subseteq \Sigma_{h-1}^* S_{h-1}$ as follows: The idea is to count modulo p how often a state can be reached (0 means unreachable) from the initial state using transitions where the first component of letters is arbitrary.

Formally, we have $Q' \subseteq \mathcal{M}_p(Q)$. Furthermore, we construct Q' starting from the multiset $q_0' = \{q_0\}$ with a modified on the fly subset construction. That means that Q' only contains *reachable p-Q* multisets of states. For each letter $a \in \Sigma_{h-1}$ and each state m (a p-Q multiset) of Q' we define a successor state $m' = \delta(m, a)$ by setting for all $q \in Q$, $m'(q) = (\sum_{q_1 \in Q} m(q_1) \cdot |\{(q_1, b) \mid \delta(q_1, (b, a)) = q$ and $b \in \{0, 1\}\}|)\ mod_1\ p$. Now, we describe how to determine the transitions going to the final state F'. Here we have to take into account the number of times (which can be infinite) a vector corresponding to a word from Σ_{h-1}^* obtained by projection from a word w of $L(\mathcal{A}_\varphi)$ can be obtained by projection from other longer words of $L(\mathcal{A}_\varphi)$ with same prefix w. Since the automaton $\mathcal{A}_\varphi$ is uniformised each such word is only counted once. For each sign letter $s \in S_h$ with $s = (s_1, \ldots, s_h)$ we first define $s^+ = (+, s_2, \ldots, s_h)$ and $s^- = (-, s_2, \ldots, s_h)$. For each sign letter $s \in S_h$ and each state $q \in Q$, we compute then $m_{s,q}$, the (possible infinite) number of paths from q in $\mathcal{A}$ to the final state F labeled by a word from the language $(a(s^+) + a(s^-))^* s$. Then, for each sign letter $s \in S_{h-1}$ there is a transition from a state $m \in Q'$ to the final state F' iff (1) $m_{(+,s),q}$ and $m_{(-,s),q}$ are both not infinite for all $q \in Q$ with $m(q) \neq 0$ and (2) $(\sum_{q \in Q \wedge \delta(q,(+,s))=F} m(q) m_{(+,s),q} + \sum_{q \in Q \wedge \delta(q,(-,s))=F} m(q) m_{(-,s),q})\ mod\ p = p'$. The obtained automaton is then uniformised and completed to obtain $\mathcal{A}_\psi$. □

Our analysis relies on building automata for Boolean combinations of constant separated formulas. A Boolean combination of formulas $\varphi_1, \ldots, \varphi_n$ is a formula generated by $\top, \bot, \varphi_1, \ldots, \varphi_n, \neg, \vee, \wedge$ or $\leftrightarrow$. We denote by $\mathcal{C}(\varphi_1, \ldots, \varphi_n)$ such a Boolean combination. We build (on the fly) a product automaton whose states are Presburger formulas (not tuples of formulas).

Definition 4.6. *Given a Boolean combination of constant separated formulas $\mathcal{C}(\varphi_1(\boldsymbol{x}), \ldots, \varphi_n(\boldsymbol{x}))$ containing h free variables we define the product automaton $A_{\mathcal{C}(\varphi_1(\boldsymbol{x}), \ldots, \varphi_n(\boldsymbol{x}))} = (\Sigma_h \cup S_h, Q \cup \{F\}, q_0, \{F\}, \delta)$ by: Q is the set of Presburger formulas, F the designated final state, $q_0 = \mathcal{C}(\varphi_1(\boldsymbol{x}), \ldots, \varphi_n(\boldsymbol{x}))$ and for all $a \in \Sigma_h$, $\delta(\mathcal{C}(\psi_1(\boldsymbol{x}), \ldots, \psi_n(\boldsymbol{x})), a) = \mathcal{C}(\psi_1'(\boldsymbol{x}), \ldots, \psi_n'(\boldsymbol{x}))$ each $\psi_i(\boldsymbol{x})$ being a state, possibly $\bot$ (equivalent to $0 < 0$), of $\mathcal{A}_{\varphi_i}$ (the automaton of φ_i), and $\psi_i'(\boldsymbol{x}) = \delta_{\varphi_i}(\psi_i(\boldsymbol{x}), a)$. If $s \in S_h$, then $\delta(\mathcal{C}(\psi_1(\boldsymbol{x}), \ldots, \psi_n(\boldsymbol{x})),\ s) = F$, when $\langle s \rangle \in [\![\mathcal{C}(\psi_1(\boldsymbol{x}), \ldots, \psi_n(\boldsymbol{x}))]\!]$ and $\delta(\mathcal{C}(\psi_1(\boldsymbol{x}), \ldots, \psi_n(\boldsymbol{x})), s) = \bot$ otherwise.*

The following theorem gives a bound on the automata size for a formula in Presburger's logic with modulo-counting quantifiers. A corresponding theorem for classical Presburger's logic was given in [6] (using results from [13] where a most significant digit first encoding is used). Its proof is basically the same, as we can also eliminate all quantifiers and construct an automaton from the resulting atomic formulas. We will need the construction of the automaton later to handle the $\exists^{(p',p)}$ quantifier. We use the abbreviations $exp2(x) = 2^{2^x}$ and $exp3(x) = 2^{2^{2^x}}$. Notice that in [6] the size of the DFA was bounded by $exp3(\kappa n \log n)$.

Theorem 4.7. *The size of the minimal DFA accepting solutions of a formula $\varphi(\boldsymbol{x})$ from $\mathcal{L}_P$ with h free variables and length n is at most $exp3(\kappa n)$ for some constant κ.*

Proof. Let $d < n$ be the quantifier depth of φ. Let $\gamma(\boldsymbol{x})$ be the equivalent quantifier free formula obtained from φ using Theorem 3.6. We have $\max \mathbf{P}(\gamma) \leqslant (P \cdot \max \mathbf{P}(\varphi))^{4^d}$ and $\max \textsc{Const}(\gamma) \leqslant 2^{(P \cdot \max \mathbf{P}(\varphi))^{4^d}} \cdot \max \textsc{Const}(\varphi)$. Clearly, $\max \textsc{Const}(\gamma) \leq exp3(\kappa_1 n)$ for some constant κ_1. If we build the product automaton for γ according to Definition 4.6, a naive analysis of its size gives a quadruple-exponential, as there are possibly a quadruple exponential number of distinct inequations in γ. We give a slightly different construction of the automaton A_γ accepting solutions of γ. Let $\boldsymbol{a}_1, \ldots, \boldsymbol{a}_{t_\gamma}$ be an enumeration of all different vectors $\boldsymbol{a}$ corresponding to coefficients of variables of $\boldsymbol{x} = (x_1, \ldots, x_h)$ appearing in constant separated inequations of γ. Let $\gamma_1, \ldots, \gamma_{t'_\gamma}$ be an enumeration of all atomic formulas of the form $\boldsymbol{a}_i.\boldsymbol{x} > c_j$ with $1 \leq i \leq t_\gamma$ and c_j such that $|c_j| \in [-\|\boldsymbol{a}_i\|_+ - 1, \|\boldsymbol{a}_i\|_-]$. Due to the bound on $\max \mathbf{P}(\gamma)$ we have $t'_\gamma \leqslant exp2(\kappa_2 n)$ for some constant κ_2. Let $(\boldsymbol{b}_1, k_1), \ldots, (\boldsymbol{b}_{d_\gamma}, k_{d_\gamma})$ be an enumeration of all different vectors $\boldsymbol{b}$ corresponding to coefficients of variables of $\boldsymbol{x} = (x_1, \ldots, x_h)$ together with its modulus appearing in constant separated modulo constraints of γ. Each k_i can be written as $k_i = k'_i \cdot k''_i$ where k'_i is the biggest possible power of 2 and k''_i odd. Let $\phi_1, \ldots, \phi_{d'_\gamma}$ be an enumeration of all modulo constraints of the form $\boldsymbol{b}_i \boldsymbol{x} \equiv_{k''_i} c_j$ with $1 \leq i \leq d_\gamma$ and $c_j < k''_i$. Again due to the bound on $\max \mathbf{P}(\gamma)$ we have $d'_\gamma \leqslant exp2(\kappa_3 n)$ for some constant κ_3.

We define $\mathcal{BC}$ to be the set of all Boolean combinations having the form $\mathcal{C}(\gamma_1, \ldots, \gamma_{t'_\gamma}, \phi_1, \ldots, \phi_{d'_\gamma})$. For each member of $\mathcal{BC}$ an automaton can be built with the product construction of Definition 4.6. All these automata are the same except for transitions leading to the final and sink states.

We describe now informally the automaton A_γ which we construct from γ. It has first the form of a complete tree starting at the initial state. Its branching factor is the size of the alphabet Σ_h and its depth is $exp2(\kappa_1 n)$. Each of the states in the tree recognises the solutions of the formula $\gamma(2^{|w|}\boldsymbol{x} + \langle w \rangle_+)$ where $w \in \Sigma_h^*$ with $|w| \leq exp2(\kappa_1 n)$ is the word leading to the state from the initial state. Then, at level $exp2(\kappa_1 n)$ there are separate automata accepting solutions of the corresponding formulas reached after reading the word leading to them. All these automata correspond to Boolean combinations of $\mathcal{BC}$. Indeed, for any constant separated formula $\zeta(\boldsymbol{x}) = \boldsymbol{a}.\boldsymbol{x} > c$ of γ and any word $w \in \Sigma_h^*$ with $|w| = exp2(\kappa_1 n)$ we have $\zeta(2^{|w|}\boldsymbol{x} + \langle w \rangle_+) \Leftrightarrow \boldsymbol{a}.\boldsymbol{x} > c'$ for some $c' \in [-\|a\|_+ - 1, \|a\|_-]$. Therefore, for any atomic inequation $\zeta(\boldsymbol{x})$ of γ, $\zeta(2^{|w|}\boldsymbol{x} + \langle w \rangle_+)$ is equivalent to some γ_i. The same is true for modulo constraints, i.e. each modulo constraint reached after w is equivalent to some ϕ_i. So, $\gamma(2^{|w|}\boldsymbol{x} + \langle w \rangle_+)$ is equivalent to a formula of $\mathcal{BC}$. Notice that in any member of $\mathcal{BC}$ *all* atomic formulas of a given form appear. That is not a restriction, since we can just expand each Boolean combination to be of this form. Let $W = \{w \in \Sigma_h^* \mid |w| = exp2(\kappa_1 n)\}$. For any $w \in W$, let $\mathcal{C}_w \in \mathcal{BC}$ be the Boolean combination equivalent to $\gamma(2^{|w|}\boldsymbol{x} + \langle w \rangle_+)$. For each $\mathcal{C}_w$ we can construct an automaton $A_{\mathcal{C}_w} = (\Sigma_h \cup S_h, Q_w \cup \{F\}, q_{w,0}, \{F\}, \delta_w)$ according to Definition 4.6. Notice that the automata $A_{\mathcal{C}_w}$ only differ in the transitions going to the final state, since the atomic formulas composing them are all the same. The final state F is the same in each automaton.

We can now give the definition of the automaton for the formula γ formally, i.e. $A_\gamma = (\Sigma_h \cup S_h, Q, q_\epsilon, \{F\}, \delta)$ where $Q = Q_1 \cup Q_2 \cup \{F\}$ with $Q_1 = \{q_w \mid w \in \Sigma_h^* \wedge |w| < exp2(\kappa_1 n)\}$ and $Q_2 = \bigcup_{w \in W} Q_w$. Furthermore, $\delta(q_w, b) = \{q_{wb}\}$ for all $b \in \Sigma_h$ and $|w| < exp2(\kappa_1 n) - 1$, $\delta(q_w, b) = \{q_{wb,0}\}$ for all $b \in \Sigma_h$ and $|w| = exp2(\kappa_1 n) - 1$ and $\delta(q, b) = \delta_w(q, b)$ for all $b \in \Sigma_h$ and $q \in Q_2$. Clearly, the number of states (and also the size) of the automaton A_γ is smaller than $exp3(\kappa n)$ for some constant κ. □

When applying the construction of Lemma 4.5 to eliminate a modulo-counting quantifier, one could have a potential exponential blow-up which could lead to a quadruple exponential automaton. We can show that this is not the case by analysing the structure of the constructed automaton (similarly as in [6] for the existential quantifier) and obtain the following theorem.

Theorem 4.8. *Let $\exists y^{(p',p)} : \varphi(y, \boldsymbol{x})$ be a formula from $\mathcal{L}_P$ of size n, A the minimal DFA accepting the uniform Presburger definable language corresponding to $\varphi(y, \boldsymbol{x})$ and A' the automaton obtained for $\exists y^{(p',p)} : \varphi(y, \boldsymbol{x})$ using the construction of Lemma 4.5. Then A' is of size at most $exp3(\kappa n)$ for some constant κ.*

Corollary 4.9. *The automata based decision procedure for Presburger arithmetic with modulo-counting quantifiers takes triple-exponential time in the size of the formula.*

In [5] the complexity of the automata based construction for Presburger's logic is analysed using Ehrenfeucht-Fraïssé relations. There a most significant bit first encoding is used. An open question is to know if this approach can be also applied for modulo-counting quantifiers.

References

1. Apelt, H.: Axiomatische Untersuchungen über einige mit der Presburgerschen Arithmetik verwandten Systeme. Z. Math. Logik Grundlagen Math. 12, 131–168 (1966)
2. Berman, L.: The complexity of logical theories. Theor. Comput. Sci. 11, 71–77 (1980)

3. Blumensath, A., Grädel, E.: Finite presentations of infinite structures: Automata and interpretations. Theory of Computing Systems 37(6), 641–674 (2004)
4. Cobham, A.: On the base-dependence of sets of numbers recognizable by finite automata. Mathematical Systems Theory 3(2), 186–192 (1969)
5. Durand-Gasselin, A., Habermehl, P.: Ehrenfeucht-Fraïssé goes elementarily automatic for structures of bounded degree. In: STACS 2012, pp. 242–253. Dagstuhl Publishing (2012)
6. Durand-Gasselin, A., Habermehl, P.: On the use of non-deterministic automata for Presburger arithmetic. In: Gastin, P., Laroussinie, F. (eds.) CONCUR 2010. LNCS, vol. 6269, pp. 373–387. Springer, Heidelberg (2010)
7. Ferrante, J., Rackoff, C.W.: The computational complexity of logical theories.. Lecture Notes in Mathematics, vol. 718, 243 p. Springer, Heidelberg (1979)
8. Grädel, E.: Subclasses of Presburger arithmetic and the polynomial-time hierarchy. Theor. Comput. Sci. 56, 289–301 (1988)
9. Haase, C.: Subclasses of Presburger arithmetic and the weak EXP hierarchy. In: CSL-LICS 2014, paper no. 47, 10 pages. ACM (2014)
10. Hodgson, B.R.: On direct products of automaton decidable theories. Theoretical Computer Science 19, 331–335 (1982)
11. Khoussainov, B., Nerode, A.: Automatic presentations of structures. In: Leivant, D. (ed.) LCC 1994. LNCS, vol. 960, pp. 367–392. Springer, Heidelberg (1995)
12. Khoussainov, B., Rubin, S., Stephan, F.: Definability and regularity in automatic structures. In: Diekert, V., Habib, M. (eds.) STACS 2004. LNCS, vol. 2996, pp. 440–451. Springer, Heidelberg (2004)
13. Klaedtke, F.: Bounds on the Automata Size for Presburger Arithmetic. ACM Trans. Comput. Logic 9(2), 1–34 (2008)
14. Kuske, D., Lohrey, M.: Automatic structures of bounded degree revisited. Journal of Symbolic Logic 76(4), 1352–1380 (2011)
15. Leroux, J.: Structural Presburger Digit Vector Automata. Theoretical Computer Science 409(3), 549–556 (2008)
16. Oppen, D.C.: A $2^{2^{2^{pn}}}$ Upper Bound on the Complexity of Presburger Arithmetic. J. Comput. Syst. Sci. 16(3), 323–332 (1978)
17. Presburger, M.: Über die Vollständigkeit eines gewissen Systems der Arithmetik ganzer Zahlen, in welchem die Addition als einzige Operation hervortritt. In: Sprawozdanie z 1 Kongresu Matematyków Krajow Slowiańskich, Ksiaznica Atlas, pp. 92–101. Warzaw (1930)
18. Reddy, C.R., Loveland, D.W.: Presburger Arithmetic with Bounded Quantifier Alternation. In: ACM Symposium on Theory of Computing, pp. 320–325 (1978)
19. Rubin, S.: Automata presenting structures: A survey of the finite string case. Bulletin of Symbolic Logic 14, 169–209 (2008)
20. Schöning, U.: Complexity of Presburger arithmetic with fixed quantifier dimension. Theory Comput. Syst. 30(4), 423–428 (1997)
21. Schweikardt, N.: Arithmetic, first-order logic, and counting quantifiers. ACM Trans. Comput. Log. 6(3), 634–671 (2005)
22. Semenov, A.L.: Presburgerness of predicates regular in two number systems. Sib. Math. J. 18, 289–300 (1977)
23. Von Zur Gathen, J., Sieveking, M.: A bound on solutions of linear integer equalities and inequalities. Proc. AMS 72, 155–158 (1978)

Parity Games of Bounded Tree- and Clique-Width

Moses Ganardi

University of Siegen, Germany
ganardi@eti.uni-siegen.de

Abstract. In this paper it is shown that deciding the winner of a parity game is in LogCFL, if the underlying graph has bounded tree-width, and in LogDCFL, if the tree-width is at most 2. It is also proven that parity games of bounded clique-width can be solved in LogCFL via a log-space reduction to the bounded tree-width case, assuming that a k-expression for the parity game is part of the input.

1 Introduction

Parity games are two-player graph games of infinite duration. The central question in the study of parity games is to determine the winner of a given game. This problem is motivated by its close connection to the μ-calculus model-checking problem [1] but also from a complexity theoretical perspective the problem has an interesting status: The best known upper bound is NP $\cap$ coNP (to be precise, UP $\cap$ coUP [2]) and no polynomial time algorithm is known.

In this paper we study the parallel complexity of parity games of bounded tree- and clique-width. It was shown by Obdržálek that on such classes parity games become polynomial time solvable [3,4]. Recently, Fearnley and Schewe presented an efficient parallel algorithm for parity games of bounded tree-width; more precisely, they proved that the problem belongs to NC^2 [5].

We improve the complexity bounds for parity games of bounded tree- and clique-width to LogCFL, a subclass of NC^2 containing those languages which are log-space reducible to a context-free language [6]. In the tree-width case the LogCFL bound follows from the observation that the polynomial time algorithm by Obdržálek can be simulated by a bottom-up tree automaton reading the tree decomposition. For the sake of completeness we present a new proof inspired by [7], in which hierarchically defined parity games are treated. For parity games of tree-width ≤ 2 we can improve the bound further to LogDCFL, containing those languages which are log-space reducible to a deterministic context-free language. Graphs of tree-width ≤ 2 are also known as series-parallel graphs. Finally, we prove that parity games of bounded clique-width can be log-space reduced to parity games of bounded tree-width if we assume that a k-expression for the input game is given. This yields an alternative proof for Obdržálek's clique-width result with an improved complexity bound.

A. Pitts (Ed.): FOSSACS 2015, LNCS 9034, pp. 390–404, 2015.
DOI: 10.1007/978-3-662-46678-0_25

2 Preliminaries

For $k \in \mathbb{N}$ we abbreviate $\{1, \ldots, k\}$ by $[k]$. For a function f we write $\mathrm{dom}(f)$ for the domain of f. We denote by $[a \mapsto b]$ the function which maps a to b, and by $f[a \mapsto b]$ the function which maps a to b and is otherwise defined as f. All graphs considered in this paper are directed graphs. We assume familiarity with the basic concepts of log-space reductions, in particular the fact that the composition of two log-space computable functions is log-space computable again. We refer to [8] for more details on parallel complexity theory.

2.1 Parity Games

A *parity game* $\mathcal{G} = (V_0, V_1, E, \lambda)$ consists of a directed graph (V, E) where $V = V_0 \cup V_1$ is partitioned into vertices, or *positions*, of Player 0 and 1, and a *priority function* $\lambda : V \to \mathbb{N}$. We only consider finite parity games and define the *size* of $\mathcal{G}$ is the number of positions $|V|$. The two players move a token from a starting position along the edges forming a path π, also called *play*: if the token is currently in position $v \in V_s$ then Player s moves the token to a successor position of v. If a position $v \in V_s$ without successors is reached, then Player $1-s$ wins the play. Otherwise the play $\pi = v_0 v_1 \ldots$ is infinite and is won by Player 0 if and only if the maximal priority occurring infinitely often in $\lambda(v_0)\lambda(v_1)\ldots$ is even.

A *strategy* σ for Player s is a partial function $\sigma : V^* V_s \to V$ which maps a finite sequence $v_0 \ldots v_n$ to a successor of v_n. A play $\pi = v_0 v_1 \ldots$ is *conform* with σ if $\sigma(v_0 \ldots v_i) = v_{i+1}$ for all $i < |\pi|$ where $v_i \in V_s$. A strategy σ for Player s is *winning* from $v_0 \in V$ if Player s wins every play which is conform with σ; we also say that Player s *wins* $\mathcal{G}$ from v_0. The *winning region* of Player s is the set of all positions from which Player s wins $\mathcal{G}$. A *positional strategy* σ for Player s depends only on the current position and can be represented by a partial function $\sigma : V_s \to V$ where $(v, \sigma(v)) \in E$ for all $v \in \mathrm{dom}(\sigma)$. It is known that every parity game $\mathcal{G}$ is *positionally determined*, i.e. from every position either Player 0 or 1 has a positional winning strategy [9]. Solving parity games is formulated as the decision problem: Given a parity game $\mathcal{G}$ and a starting position $v_0 \in V$, does Player 0 win $\mathcal{G}$ from v_0?

An important parameter of a parity game $\mathcal{G}$ is the maximal priority d occurring in $\mathcal{G}$ because the running times of many algorithms for solving parity games are polynomial in the size of $\mathcal{G}$ but exponential in d. It is also known that the winning regions of parity games where the maximal priority is bounded can be defined by a fixed MSO-formula [10]. Hence, by the log-space version of Courcelle's Theorem [11] parity games whose tree-width and maximal priority are bounded by constants can be solved in log-space. For our purposes it is important that the maximal priority of a parity game can be assumed to be linear in the number of vertices by a *compression* of the priority function, see [12].

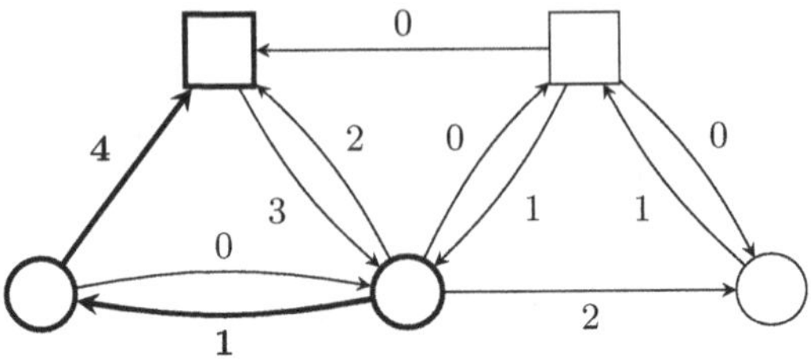

Fig. 1. An edge-labeled parity game where circles belong to Player 0 and squares belong to Player 1

2.2 Edge-Labeled Parity Games

For the tree-width result it is useful to convert the given parity game into a different form where priorities are assigned to edges instead of vertices. Further we allow multiple (finitely many) edges between two vertices, which is convenient for gluing together two parity games. Formally, an *edge-labeled parity game* has the form $\mathcal{G} = (V_0, V_1, E)$ where $E \subseteq V \times \mathbb{N} \times V$ is a finite set of labeled edges. In this context, a play $\pi = (v_0, p_0, v_1)(v_1, p_1, v_2)\ldots$ is a finite or infinite sequence of edges, which is won by Player 0 if and only if the maximal priority occurring infinitely often in $p_0 p_1 \ldots$ is even. A strategy for Player s is a partial function $\rho : V^* V_s \to E$ which maps a finite sequence $v_0 \ldots v_n$ to an outgoing edge (v_n, p, v_{n+1}) of v_n. A positional strategy is a partial function $\rho : V_s \to E$, where $\rho(v)$ is an outgoing edge of v for all $v \in \mathrm{dom}(\rho)$. Winning strategies and winning regions are defined similarly as for standard parity games. Figure 1 depicts an edge-labeled parity game where the marked positions and edges form the winning region and a positional winning strategy of Player 0.

Lemma 1. *For every parity game there is an edge-labeled parity game with the same winning regions, and vice versa. In particular, edge-labeled parity games are positionally determined.*

Proof. Given a parity game, assign to each edge the priority of its starting vertex. Conversely, given an edge-labeled parity game, subdivide every edge and assign its priority to its new vertex; all other vertices have priority 0. □

We will mainly deal with edge-labeled parity games $\mathcal{G}$ without multiple edges, i.e. $(u, p, v), (u, q, v) \in E$ implies $p = q$, which we call *simple (edge-labeled) parity games*. Whenever an edge-labeled parity game contains exactly one edge between a pair of positions u and v, we sometimes denote the edge by (u, v) without the priority and we write $\lambda(u, v) = p$. Every edge-labeled parity game can be made simple as witnessed by the following lemma.

Lemma 2. *For every edge-labeled parity game one can compute in log-space a simple edge-labeled parity game with the same winning regions.*

Proof. Consider the *reward order* $\sqsubseteq$ on $\mathbb{N}$, which intuitively sorts the priorities according to their attractivity to Player 0: We define $p \sqsubseteq q$ if p and q are even and $p \leq q$, or p and q are odd and $p \geq q$, or p is odd and q is even.

For an edge-labeled parity game $\mathcal{G} = (V_0, V_1, E)$ we define the *simplified* edge-labeled parity game $\mathsf{simple}(\mathcal{G})$ by combining multiple edges between two endpoints (u, v) into a single one with the following priority:

$$\lambda(u,v) = \begin{cases} \max_{\sqsubseteq}\{p \in \mathbb{N} : (u,p,v) \in E\}, & \text{if } u \in V_0, \\ \min_{\sqsubseteq}\{p \in \mathbb{N} : (u,p,v) \in E\}, & \text{if } u \in V_1. \end{cases}$$

It can be verified that winning regions are preserved. □

2.3 Tree-Width

In the following we define two well-known graph decompositions and the corresponding graph measures, tree-width and clique-width. Many NP-complete problems become solvable in log-space or linear time on classes of bounded tree- or clique-width, see [11,13,14].

A *tree decomposition* $\mathcal{T} = (T, \{X_i\}_{i \in I})$ of a graph $G = (V, E)$ consists of a rooted tree T with node set I and a family of *bags* $X_i \subseteq V$ for $i \in I$ such that for all $(u, v) \in E$ there exists $i \in I$ with $u, v \in X_i$, and for all $v \in V$ the set $\{i \in I : v \in X_i\}$ is non-empty and connected in T. The *width* of $\mathcal{T}$ is $\max_{i \in I} |X_i| - 1$ and the *tree-width* of a graph G is the minimum width of a tree decomposition of G. The tree-width of a parity game is the tree-width of its underlying graph. Deciding whether the tree-width of a given graph is at most a given parameter $k \in \mathbb{N}$ is NP-complete [15]; however, for every fixed $k \in \mathbb{N}$ there exists a log-space algorithm which decides whether a given graph has tree-width $\leq k$ and in that case computes a width-k tree decomposition for it [11]. We call a width-k tree decomposition $\mathcal{T} = (T, \{X_i\}_{i \in I})$ *smooth* if

(a) $|X_i| = k + 1$ for all $i \in I$,
(b) $|X_i \cap X_j| = k$ for all edges (i, j) in T.

It is known that tree decompositions can be made smooth in linear time, see [16, Chapter 6]. For our purposes we devise a space efficient algorithm:

Lemma 3. *For every fixed $k \in \mathbb{N}$ there exists a log-space algorithm which, given a width-k tree decomposition $\mathcal{T}$ of G, computes a smooth width-k tree decomposition of G.*

Proof. Let $\mathcal{T} = (T, \{X_i\}_{i \in I})$ be a tree decomposition of width k. First of all, we root T at some node $i \in I$ such that $|X_i| = k + 1$, which is computable in log-space.

For property (a) we present a procedure which adds a vertex to each bag X_i which does not have maximal size. Let $I_0 = \{i \in I : |X_i| = k + 1\}$. For each $i \in I \setminus I_0$ independently we add a vertex to X_i as follows: Let j be the lowest ancestor of i in I_0 and let j' be the unique child of j on the path from j to i.

We add the lexicographically smallest vertex in $X_j \setminus X_{j'}$ to X_i. This procedure preserves the tree decomposition properties and can be performed in log-space. After at most $k+1$ iterations of this procedure, all bags have uniform size.

For property (b) consider an inclusion maximal set $J \subseteq I$ where $X_i = X_j$ for all $i, j \in J$, which forms a connected subtree of T. All such sets J can be found in log-space and can be merged into single nodes such that all bags are pairwise distinct. Now assume $|X_i \cap X_j| < k$ for some tree edge (i, j). Let $X_i \setminus X_j = \{u_1, \dots, u_m\}$ and $X_j \setminus X_i = \{v_1, \dots, v_m\}$. We replace the edge (i, j) by a path $(i_0, \dots, i_m)$ where $X_{i_\ell} = (X_i \cap X_j) \cup \{v_1, \dots, v_\ell, u_{\ell+1}, \dots, u_m\}$. □

2.4 Clique-Width

To define clique-width we need to consider *colored graphs* $G = (V, E, \gamma)$ where $\gamma : V \to [k]$ is a *coloring function.* A *k-expression* is a term built up from constants $i \in [k]$, unary symbols ρ_β and $\alpha_{i,j}$ where $\beta : [k] \to [k]$ and $i, j \in [k]$, and a binary symbol $\oplus$. Every k-expression t defines a colored graph $\text{val}(t)$ up to isomorphism as follows:

- $\text{val}(i) = (\{v\}, \emptyset, [v \mapsto i])$ where v is a fresh symbol.
- $\text{val}(t_1 \oplus t_2)$ is the disjoint union of $\text{val}(t_1)$ and $\text{val}(t_2)$.
- If $\text{val}(t) = (V, E, \gamma)$, we set $\text{val}(\rho_\beta(t)) = (V, E, \beta \circ \gamma)$.
- If $\text{val}(t) = (V, E, \gamma)$, we set $\text{val}(\alpha_{i,j}(t)) = (V, E', \gamma)$ where

$$E' = E \cup \{(v, w) \in V^2 : \gamma(v) = i, \gamma(w) = j\}.$$

The *clique-width* of a graph G is the minimal number $k \in \mathbb{N}$ such that there is a k-expression t and a coloring function γ of G with $\text{val}(t) = (G, \gamma)$. We remark that the standard definition of k-expressions uses operations of the form $\rho_{i \to j}$ which recolors all vertices with color i to j; this does not affect the definition of clique-width. To define the clique-width of parity games we modify the form of k-expressions to define *colored parity games* $(\mathcal{G}, \gamma)$. In this context a k-expression is built up from constants $(i, s, p) \in [k] \times \{0, 1\} \times \mathbb{N}$, which defines a parity game with a single vertex of Player s with color i and priority p, and the unary and binary symbols as before.

It is known that every graph class of bounded tree-width has also bounded clique-width but not vice versa [17]. In that sense clique-width is a more general graph measure than tree-width. As with tree-width, deciding whether the clique-width of a given graph is at most a given parameter is NP-complete [18]. Unlike tree-width it is open whether for fixed $k \geq 4$ the question, does a given graph have clique-width $\leq k$, is solvable in polynomial time. In Section 5 we will assume that a k-expression for the parity game is already part of the input.

2.5 Tree Automata

We consider terms (or *trees*) over a *ranked alphabet* Σ, i.e. a finite set of function symbols where every symbol has an arity. A *(bottom-up) tree automaton*

$\mathcal{A} = (Q, \Delta, F)$ over Σ consists of a finite set of *states* Q, a set Δ of *transition rules* of the form $a(q_1, \dots, q_n) \to q$ where $a \in \Sigma$ is n-ary and $q_1, \dots, q_n, q \in Q$, and a set of *final states* $F \subseteq Q$. We call $\mathcal{A}$ *deterministic* if there are no two rules in Δ with the same left-hand side, otherwise $\mathcal{A}$ is called *nondeterministic*. A tree t is *accepted* by $\mathcal{A}$ if $t \xrightarrow{*}_\Delta q$ for some $q \in F$ where $\to_\Delta$ is the *one-step rewriting relation* defined by Δ. The uniform membership problem for (non)deterministic tree automata asks: Does a given (non)deterministic tree automaton accept a given tree? It is known that the uniform membership problem is LogCFL-complete in the nondeterministic case and in LogDCFL in the deterministic case [19].

3 Parse Trees

Instead of working directly with tree decompositions our algorithm for parity games of bounded tree-width uses an equivalent notion from [16, Chapter 6], called *parse trees*, which describe how a graph or a parity game of bounded tree-width can be constructed using simple operations.

3.1 Parse Trees for Graphs

A *k-graph* (V, E, τ) is a graph together with an injective function $\tau : [k] \to V$, which distinguishes k vertices, called *boundary vertices*. Vertices which are not boundary are called *internal*. Given k-graphs $G = (V, E, \tau)$, $G' = (V', E', \tau')$ we define the following *parsing operators*:

- $\mathsf{rename}_\beta(G) = (V, E, \tau \circ \beta^{-1})$ where β is a permutation of $[k]$,
- $\mathsf{push}(G) = (V \cup \{v\}, E, \tau[1 \mapsto v])$ where v is a fresh symbol,
- $\mathsf{glue}(G, G')$ takes the disjoint union of two k-graphs, and identifies $\tau(i)$ and $\tau'(i)$ for all $i \in [k]$.

If $\mathsf{glue}(G, G') = (V'', E'', \tau'')$, we assume for simplified notation that $V \cup V' = V''$ and $\tau = \tau' = \tau''$, i.e. a boundary vertex in $\mathsf{glue}(G, G')$ has the same name in G and in G'. We will consider graphs constructed by combining *atomic* k-graphs, which are k-graphs of size k, with the parsing operators. A *parse tree* t of width k is the representation of such a construction as a labeled tree. A parse tree t *defines* a k-graph G if G is isomorphic to the k-graph obtained by evaluating t bottom-up; we also simply say that G is *definable* if the parse tree is irrelevant. A parse tree t *defines* a graph G if t defines (G, τ) for some τ.

It was shown in [16] that a graph has tree-width $\leq k$ if and only if it is definable by a parse tree of width $\leq k+1$. Their proof shows that the conversion from tree decompositions to parse trees can be carried out in linear time. Using smooth tree decompositions we prove that parse trees can be computed in log-space for graphs of bounded tree-width.

Lemma 4. *For every fixed $k \in \mathbb{N}$, there exists a log-space algorithm which, given a graph G of tree-width $\leq k$, computes a parse tree of width $\leq k+1$ defining G.*

Proof. Let $\mathcal{T} = (T, \{X_i\}_{i \in I})$ be a width-k tree decomposition of G computed by the log-space algorithm from [11]. By Lemma 3 we can make $\mathcal{T}$ smooth in log-space. For each $i \in I$ we fix a numbering of the $k + 1$ vertices in X_i. Let G_i be the $(k + 1)$-graph induced by the subtree of T rooted in i where the j-th boundary vertex of G_i is the j-th vertex in X_i.

We present a bottom-up construction for the $(k + 1)$-graphs G_i. If $i \in I$ is a leaf node, then G_i is atomic. If $i \in I$ is an inner node, for each child $j \in I$ of i we apply the following operations to G_j to obtain G'_j: Assume $X_j \setminus X_i = \{v\}$ and $X_i \setminus X_j = \{w\}$. Permute v to be the first boundary vertex, introduce w using push, add existing edges between w and the other boundary vertices by gluing with a suitable atomic $(k + 1)$-graph and permute the boundary vertices according to the order on X_i. By gluing all such graphs G'_j we obtain a $(k + 1)$-graph isomorphic to G_i. This construction gives rise to a parse tree, which can be computed in log-space from $\mathcal{T}$. □

3.2 Parse Trees for Parity Games

We want to transfer the notion of parse trees to parity games. For that we consider *k-games*, i.e. edge-labeled parity games $\mathcal{G} = (V_0, V_1, E, \tau)$ with k *boundary positions* given by an injective function $\tau : [k] \to V$. The operator rename_β is defined as previously. The operator push_s carries a parameter $s \in \{0, 1\}$ which specifies that the new position belongs to Player s. Finally $\mathsf{glue}(\mathcal{G}_1, \mathcal{G}_2)$ is only defined if $\mathcal{G}_1$ and $\mathcal{G}_2$ are *compatible*, i.e. corresponding boundary positions belong to the same player. Parse trees for k-games are defined in an analogous manner. Here the leaf nodes are labeled by *atomic k-games*, i.e. k-games of size k.

As a precomputation step of the algorithms in the next section we compute for a given parity game $\mathcal{G}$ and a starting position v_0 a parse tree t of width k which defines a k-game in which v_0 is a boundary position. This can be done in log-space by an adaption of Lemma 4: First we compute in log-space a smooth tree decomposition of the underlying graph of $\mathcal{G}$. Then we root the tree decomposition at some bag containing v_0 before converting it into a parse tree. In the conversion phase we label the leaf nodes of the parse tree by the atomic k-games induced by the leaf bags. Whenever a new position v is introduced by push, we annotate the push-operator by the parameter $s \in \{0, 1\}$ depending on the owner of v.

4 Parity Games of Bounded Tree-Width

In this section by parity games we always mean edge-labeled parity games. Consider the construction of a definable k-game $\mathcal{G}$ from atomic k-games using the parsing operators, as described by a parse tree. We reduce the problem of determining the winner of $\mathcal{G}$ from some boundary position to the evaluation of a tree automaton reading the parse tree. One possible approach is to compute in a bottom-up manner for each tree node a small k-game which is equivalent in a certain sense to the k-game defined by the subtree rooted in that node. In the end it remains to solve a small parity game in the root node. In fact, every definable 3-game has an equivalent simple atomic 3-game. Simple parity games of constant size can be stored in space $\mathcal{O}(\log d)$ where d is the maximal priority. However, this approach fails for definable k-games where $k > 3$, i.e. parity games with tree-width > 2. Instead, with the help of a nondeterministic tree automaton we guess and fix a positional strategy for Player 0, and obtain a parity game in which only Player 1 makes non-trivial moves. So called solitaire k-games can again be compressed to size k. In both approaches the tree automata can be constructed using only logarithmic space. Since the uniform membership problems for the corresponding tree automata can be solved in LogCFL and LogDCFL, respectively, parity games of bounded tree-width can be solved in LogCFL and parity games of tree-width ≤ 2 can be solved in LogDCFL.

4.1 Equivalent k-Games and Valid Reduction Rules

We start by defining the following Myhill-Nerode type equivalence: Two compatible k-games $\mathcal{G}_1, \mathcal{G}_2$ are called *equivalent*, denoted by $\mathcal{G}_1 \approx \mathcal{G}_2$, if for all k-games $\mathcal{H}$ compatible with $\mathcal{G}_1$ and $\mathcal{G}_2$ and all positions v in $\mathcal{H}$ we have

$$\text{Player 0 wins } \mathsf{glue}(\mathcal{G}_1, \mathcal{H}) \text{ from } v \iff \text{Player 0 wins } \mathsf{glue}(\mathcal{G}_2, \mathcal{H}) \text{ from } v.$$

In fact, $\approx$ is a congruence with respect to the parsing operators, i.e. $\mathcal{G}_1 \approx \mathcal{G}_2$ implies $\mathsf{rename}_\beta(\mathcal{G}_1) \approx \mathsf{rename}_\beta(\mathcal{G}_2)$, $\mathsf{push}_s(\mathcal{G}_1) \approx \mathsf{push}_s(\mathcal{G}_2)$ and $\mathsf{glue}(\mathcal{G}_1, \mathcal{H}) \approx \mathsf{glue}(\mathcal{G}_2, \mathcal{H})$ for all k-games $\mathcal{H}$ compatible with $\mathcal{G}_1$ and $\mathcal{G}_2$.

We introduce *valid reduction rules*, which compute in log-space to a given k-game $\mathcal{G}$ an equivalent k-game $\mathcal{G}'$. For example, the operation simple from Lemma 2, which removes multiple edges, is valid, which can be shown by a very similar proof. We will always append the application of simple to valid reduction rules without mentioning it. In the following let $\mathcal{G} = (V_0, V_1, E, \tau)$ be a simple k-game. For the sake of easier proofs we can assume that each player uses a *uniform* positional winning strategy, which is winning from all positions in his winning region [20, Chapter 6]. A positional strategy ρ *uses* an edge $(u, p, v) \in E$ if $\rho(u) = (u, p, v)$. One can also assume that a positional winning strategy ρ for Player s is *minimal*, i.e. $\mathrm{dom}(\rho)$ is contained in the winning region of Player s. In the following, if we mention winning strategies, we always mean uniform minimal positional winning strategies.

Lemma 5. *Let $u \in V_s$ be an internal position where $(u, p, u) \in E$.*

1. *If $p \equiv s \pmod 2$, it is valid to add loops with priority s to all predecessors of u in V_s and then to remove u.*
2. *If $p \not\equiv s \pmod 2$, it is valid to remove the loop (u, p, u).*

Proof. Let $\mathcal{H}$ be a k-game compatible with $\mathcal{G}$ and let $\mathcal{G}'$ be the modified k-game.

1. If a winning strategy for Player s in $\mathsf{glue}(\mathcal{G}, \mathcal{H})$ uses an edge leading to u, Player s can instead use the new loops with priority s in $\mathsf{glue}(\mathcal{G}', \mathcal{H})$. On the other hand no winning strategy for Player $1 - s$ in $\mathsf{glue}(\mathcal{G}, \mathcal{H})$ can use one of the edges leading to u.

2. The loop (u, p, u) cannot be used by any winning strategy for Player s in $\mathsf{glue}(\mathcal{G}, \mathcal{H})$. Hence, $\mathsf{glue}(\mathcal{G}, \mathcal{H})$ and $\mathsf{glue}(\mathcal{G}', \mathcal{H})$ have the same winning regions. □

Lemma 6. *Let $u, v \in V_s$ where $(v, u) \in E$. It is valid to add edges (v, p, w) where $p = \max(\lambda(v, u), \lambda(u, w))$ for each successor w of u, and then to remove the edge (v, u).*

Proof. Let $\mathcal{H}$ be a k-game compatible with $\mathcal{G}$, let $\mathcal{G}'$ be the modified k-game and let ρ be a winning strategy for Player s in $\mathsf{glue}(\mathcal{G}, \mathcal{H})$. If $\rho(v) = (v, u)$, then $\rho(u)$ must be defined, say $\rho(u) = (u, w)$. In $\mathsf{glue}(\mathcal{G}', \mathcal{H})$ Player s can win from the same winning region by moving from v directly to w and otherwise playing according to ρ. Conversely, if ρ is a winning strategy for Player s in $\mathsf{glue}(\mathcal{G}', \mathcal{H})$ which uses one of the new edges (v, p, w), then Player s can win from the same winning region by moving from v via u to w, and otherwise playing according to ρ. □

Lemma 7. *Let $(u, p, v), (v, q, u) \in E$ where u and v belong to different players and let $s = \max(p, q) \bmod 2$. It is valid to remove the edge from the cycle whose starting point belongs to Player $1 - s$.*

Proof. Let $\mathcal{H}$ be a k-game compatible with $\mathcal{G}$. No winning strategy for Player $1 - s$ in $\mathsf{glue}(\mathcal{G}, \mathcal{H})$ can use the edge which is to be removed because Player s could win by responding with the other edge. □

Let $\mathcal{C}$ be a class of k-games and let f be an n-ary partial operation mapping n-tuples $\overline{\mathcal{G}} = (\mathcal{G}_1, \ldots, \mathcal{G}_n)$ of k-games to a k-game $f(\overline{\mathcal{G}})$. A partial operation $f' : \mathcal{C}^n \to \mathcal{C}$ *implements* f *on* $\mathcal{C}$ if $f(\overline{\mathcal{G}}) \approx f'(\overline{\mathcal{G}})$ for all $\overline{\mathcal{G}} \in \mathrm{dom}(f) \cap \mathcal{C}^n$. With the help of the previous lemmata we can prove the following main ingredient for solving parity games of tree-width at most 2 using deterministic tree automata.

Lemma 8. *All parsing operators have log-space computable implementations on the class of all simple atomic 3-games.*

Proof. On the class of all simple atomic k-games rename_β implements itself and $\mathsf{simple} \circ \mathsf{glue}$ implements glue. It remains to treat the parsing operator push_s.

If $\mathcal{G}$ is an atomic 3-game, then $\mathsf{push}_s(\mathcal{G})$ is the disjoint union of a 2-game of size 3 and a boundary position belonging to Player s. Since the addition of an isolated boundary position respects $\approx$, it suffices to show that for each simple 2-game of size 3 one can compute in log-space an equivalent 2-game of size 2.

So let $\mathcal{G} = (V_0, V_1, E, \tau)$ be a simple 2-game of size 3. Let $v_i = \tau(i)$ for $i \in \{1, 2\}$ and let $u \in V_s$ be the unique internal position. By applying the reduction rules from Lemma 5, 6 and 7 to u, we can eliminate all cycles of length at most 2 in $\mathcal{G}$ which contain u. Hence, between u and each v_i there exists at most one edge in one direction. We can eliminate u using the following valid reduction rules:

1. If u has no incoming edge, remove u.

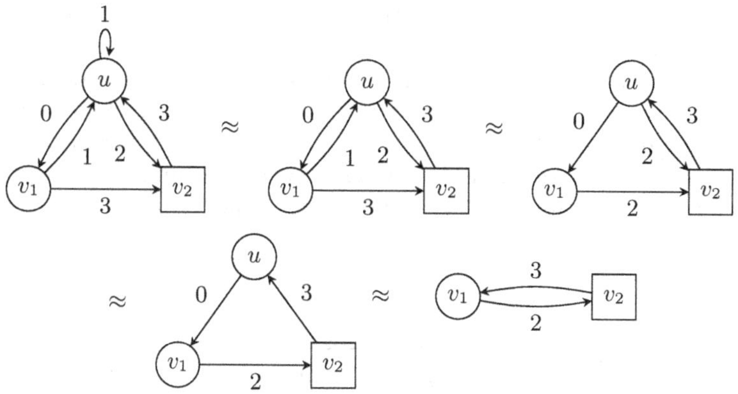

Fig. 2. Applying valid reduction rules to a 2-game

2. If u has no outgoing edge, add loops with priority $1-s$ to all predecessors of u in V_{1-s} and remove u.
3. Otherwise the only edges incident to u are $(v_i, u), (u, v_j) \in E$ for $i \neq j$. Add an edge (v_i, v_j) with priority $\max(\lambda(v_i, u), \lambda(u, v_j))$ and remove u. □

Later we will see that Lemma 8 cannot be extended to k-games for $k > 3$. However, if we fix a positional strategy of Player 0 it suffices to consider parity games in which Player 1 makes non-trivial moves. A *solitaire game* for Player s is a parity game where all positions belong to Player s.

Lemma 9. *For every $k \in \mathbb{N}$ and $s \in \{0,1\}$, all parsing operators except for* push_{1-s} *have log-space computable implementations on the class of all simple atomic solitaire k-games for Player s.*

Proof. As in Lemma 8 we only need to show that every simple atomic solitaire k-game $\mathcal{G}$ of size $k+1$ can be compressed to size k in log-space. Using Lemma 5 and 6 we can eliminate all incoming edges of the unique internal position u in $\mathcal{G}$. Then u can be removed. □

4.2 Construction of the Tree Automata

We fix the following (arbitrary) encoding of isomorphism classes of k-games. An atomic k-game $\mathcal{G} = (V_0, V_1, E, \tau)$ is in *normal form* if $V = [k]$ and $\tau(i) = i$ for all $i \in [k]$. Given an atomic k-game $\mathcal{G}$, we denote by $[\mathcal{G}]$ the unique k-game in normal form isomorphic to $\mathcal{G}$.

Theorem 10. *Parity games of tree-width ≤ 2 can be solved in LogDCFL.*

Proof. Let $\mathcal{G}_0$ be a parity game of tree-width ≤ 2 with maximal priority d and let v_0 be a given starting position. We apply simple to $\mathcal{G}_0$ and compute a parse tree t of width 3 as explained in Section 3.2 such that v_0 is the i-th boundary position of the 3-game defined by t. We assume that the atomic 3-games in the leaf nodes of t are in normal form.

Let $\mathcal{C}$ be the set of simple atomic 3-games in normal form with maximal priority $\leq d$. We can encode the elements $\mathcal{G} \in \mathcal{C}$ using $\mathcal{O}(\log d)$ bits where d was assumed to be linear in the size of $\mathcal{G}$. We compute from the parameters d and i a deterministic tree automaton $\mathcal{A} = (\mathcal{C}, \Delta, F)$ over the alphabet of t, where Δ contains for all compatible $\mathcal{G}, \mathcal{H} \in \mathcal{C}$ transitions of the form

$$\begin{aligned} \mathcal{G} &\to \mathcal{G}, \\ \mathsf{rename}_\beta(\mathcal{G}) &\to [\mathsf{rename}'_\beta(\mathcal{G})], \\ \mathsf{push}_s(\mathcal{G}) &\to [\mathsf{push}'_s(\mathcal{G})], \\ \mathsf{glue}(\mathcal{G}, \mathcal{H}) &\to [\mathsf{glue}'(\mathcal{G}, \mathcal{H})]. \end{aligned}$$

Here f' denotes the implementation of f from Lemma 8. A state $\mathcal{G}$ is contained in F if and only if Player 0 wins $\mathcal{G}$ from the i-th boundary position, which can be easily computed in log-space. Player 0 wins $\mathcal{G}_0$ from v_0 if and only if $\mathcal{A}$ accepts t, which can be decided in LogDCFL [19]. □

For our approach to solve parity games with tree-width > 2 it is convenient to assume that every position has at least one successor, which can be established by adding to each position of Player s a loop with priority $1 - s$. Let ρ be a positional strategy for Player 0 in an edge-labeled parity game $\mathcal{G} = (V_0, V_1, E)$. We define $\mathcal{G}_\rho = (\emptyset, V_0 \cup V_1, E_\rho)$ where

$$E_\rho = \{\rho(v) : v \in \mathrm{dom}(\rho)\} \cup \{(v, p, w) \in E : v \in V_1\},$$

which is a solitaire game for Player 1. It is easy to see that Player 0 wins $\mathcal{G}$ from v if and only if there exists a positional strategy ρ for Player 0 with $\mathrm{dom}(\rho) = V_0$ such that Player 0 wins $\mathcal{G}_\rho$ from v. A nondeterministic automaton reading a parse tree can guess and fix positional strategies for Player 0 on the atomic k-games in the leaf nodes and verify whether they together form a positional strategy ρ in the whole game such that $\mathrm{dom}(\rho) = V_0$.

Theorem 11. *Parity games of bounded tree-width can be solved in LogCFL.*

Proof. We adapt the proof of Theorem 10 where $\mathcal{G}_0$ now has tree-width $\leq k$. We compute in log-space a parse tree t which defines a $(k+1)$-game $(\mathcal{G}_0, \tau)$ such that $\tau(i) = v_0$. Let $M = \{j \in [k+1] : \tau(j) \in V_0\}$ and let $\mathcal{C}$ be the set of simple atomic solitaire $(k+1)$-games for Player 1 in normal form with maximal priority $\leq d$. We define $\mathcal{A} = (\mathcal{C} \times 2^{[k+1]}, \Delta, F)$ over the alphabet of t, where Δ contains for all compatible $\mathcal{G}, \mathcal{H} \in \mathcal{C}$, subsets $U, W \subseteq [k+1]$ and positional strategies ρ for Player 0 on $\mathcal{G}$, transitions of the form

$$\begin{aligned} \mathcal{G} &\to (\mathcal{G}_\rho, \mathrm{dom}(\rho)), \\ \mathsf{rename}_\beta((\mathcal{G}, U)) &\to ([\mathsf{rename}'_\beta(\mathcal{G})], \beta(U)), \\ \mathsf{push}_s((\mathcal{G}, U)) &\to ([\mathsf{push}'_1(\mathcal{G})], U \setminus \{1\}), \\ \mathsf{glue}((\mathcal{G}, U), (\mathcal{H}, W)) &\to ([\mathsf{glue}'(\mathcal{G}, \mathcal{H})], U \cup W), \quad \text{if } U \cap W = \emptyset. \end{aligned}$$

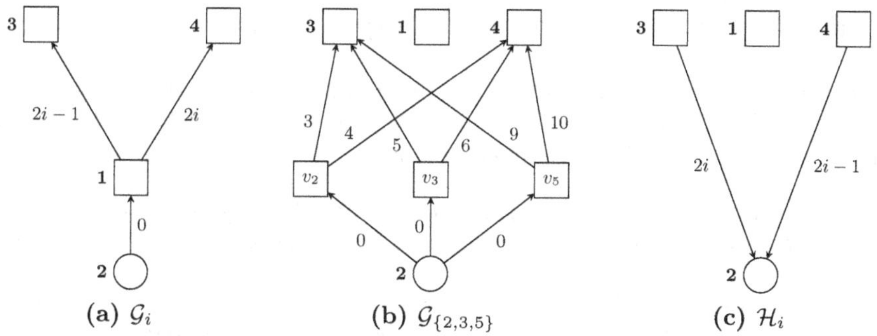

Fig. 3. 4-games for the separation of $\approx$-classes

Here f' denotes the implementation of f from Lemma 9. A state $(\mathcal{G}, U)$ is in F if and only if Player 0 wins $\mathcal{G}$ from the i-th boundary position and $U = M$. We can encode all states using $\mathcal{O}(\log d)$ bits and compute Δ and F in log-space. Player 0 wins $\mathcal{G}_0$ from v_0 if and only if $\mathcal{A}$ accepts t, which can be decided in LogCFL. □

4.3 A Lower Bound

We conclude this section with a proof that parity games of tree-width 3 cannot be solved in LogDCFL using the deterministic tree automata approach as in Theorem 10.

Theorem 12. *For each $d \in \mathbb{N}$ there exist $2^d - 1$ many definable 4-games which have maximal priority $\leq 2d$ and are pairwise inequivalent.*

Proof. Consider the atomic 4-games $\mathcal{G}_i$ and $\mathcal{H}_i$ depicted in Figure 3. For every non-empty subset $I \subseteq [d]$ we construct a 4-game $\mathcal{G}_I$ by gluing all 4-games $\mathsf{push}_1(\mathcal{G}_i)$ for $i \in I$ together. In $\mathsf{glue}(\mathcal{G}_I, \mathcal{H}_i)$ we denote by u the unique position of Player 0 and by v_k the position whose outgoing edges are labeled by $2k - 1$ and $2k$ for all $k \in I$.

We claim that for all $i \in [d]$ and non-empty $I \subseteq [d]$, Player 0 wins $\mathsf{glue}(\mathcal{G}_I, \mathcal{H}_i)$ from u if and only if $i \in I$, which proves that all 4-games $\mathcal{G}_I$ are pairwise inequivalent. If $i \in I$, Player 0 wins $\mathsf{glue}(\mathcal{G}_I, \mathcal{H}_i)$ by always moving from u to v_i. If $i \notin I$, Player 1 wins $\mathsf{glue}(\mathcal{G}_I, \mathcal{H}_i)$ as follows. From a position v_k Player 1 moves along the edge labeled by $2k - 1$ if $k > i$, and along the edge labeled by $2k$ if $k < i$. □

For numbers $k, d \in \mathbb{N}$ and $i \in [k]$, consider the tree language of all parse trees which define k-games with maximal priority $\leq d$ won by Player 0 from the i-th boundary position. This tree language is regular by Theorem 11 but already for $k = 4$ it cannot be recognized by a deterministic tree automaton with a polynomial number of states in d according to Theorem 12. It remains open whether the presented complexity bounds for parity games of bounded tree-width can be improved.

5 Parity Games of Bounded Clique-Width

In this final section we present a log-space reduction which transforms parity games given by k-expressions into parity games of tree-width $\leq 8k-1$ and preserves the winners. As a corollary we obtain the following theorem:

Theorem 13. *For every $k \in \mathbb{N}$, parity games of clique-width $\leq k$ can be solved in LogCFL, assuming that a k-expression for the parity game is part of the input.*

Let $t_\mathcal{G}$ be a k-expression which defines a parity game $\mathcal{G} = (V_0, V_1, E, \lambda)$. We view $t_\mathcal{G}$ as a labeled tree and define T to be the set of all tree nodes, i.e. all subterms of $t_\mathcal{G}$. For each $v \in V$ we denote by $t_v \in T$ the unique leaf node which introduces v. Recall that t_v specifies the color of v when first introduced, which we denote by $\gamma(v)$, the owner of v and its priority $\lambda(v)$.

We simulate $\mathcal{G}$ by the *tree game* $\mathcal{G}^*$, which is basically played on the tree $t_\mathcal{G}$. During a play in the tree game we need to memorize additional information, which is why we have multiple copies of each tree node. The positions in the tree game $\mathcal{G}^*$ are of the form (t, i, m, s) where

- $t \in T$ is a tree node,
- $i \in [k]$ is the current color,
- $m \in \{\uparrow, \downarrow\}$ specifies the current direction and
- $s \in \{0, 1\}$ indicates that the position (t, i, m, s) belongs to Player s.

For every position $v \in V_s$ in $\mathcal{G}$ we define the corresponding position $v^\uparrow = (t_v, \gamma(v), \uparrow, s)$ in $\mathcal{G}^*$. The edges of $\mathcal{G}^*$ are defined in the following: Player s can draw from a position $(t, i, \uparrow, s)$ to $(t', j, \uparrow, s)$ where t' is the father node of t and, if $t' = \rho_\beta(t)$, then $\beta(i) = j$, otherwise $i = j$. In a position of the form $(\alpha_{i,j}(t), i, \uparrow, s)$ Player s can decide to draw to $(\alpha_{i,j}(t), j, \downarrow, s)$. Then, Player s can draw from a position $(t, i, \downarrow, s)$ to $(t', j, \downarrow, s)$ where t' is a child node of t and, if $t = \rho_\beta(t')$ then $\beta(j) = i$, otherwise $i = j$. From a position of the form $(t_w, \gamma(w), \downarrow, s)$ Player s has to draw to $w^\uparrow$ from where the owner of w continues to play. Note that there are positions without outgoing edges in the tree game, for example positions $(t_v, i, \downarrow, s)$ where $i \neq \gamma(v)$ or positions $(\alpha_{i,j}(t), k, \uparrow, s)$ where $i \neq k$ and $\alpha_{i,j}(t)$ is the root of $t_\mathcal{G}$. For all $v \in V$ we assign the priority $\lambda(v)$ to the position $v^\uparrow$ and to all other positions priority 0. Clearly, $\mathcal{G}^*$ can be computed in log-space from $t_\mathcal{G}$. The following lemma shows how plays in $\mathcal{G}$ can be simulated in the tree game.

Lemma 14. *Player 0 wins $\mathcal{G}$ from $v_0 \in V$ if and only if she wins the tree game $\mathcal{G}^*$ from $v_0^\uparrow$.*

Proof. A move from $v \in V_s$ to a successor w in $\mathcal{G}$ can be simulated by a finite path π_{vw} in $\mathcal{G}^*$ from $v^\uparrow$ to $w^\uparrow$. Let $\alpha_{i,j}(t)$ be a tree node that introduces the edge (v, w). Player s moves "upwards" to $(\alpha_{i,j}(t), i, \uparrow, s)$, then to $(\alpha_{i,j}(t), j, \downarrow, s)$. After that Player s moves "downwards" to $(t_w, \gamma(w), \downarrow, s)$ and finally to $w^\uparrow$. In this way, every positional strategy σ for Player s in $\mathcal{G}$ defines a strategy σ^* for Player s in $\mathcal{G}^*$, which in general is not positional. The maximal priority of a position in π_{vw} is $\max(\lambda(v), \lambda(w))$. Also notice that $v \in V_s$ has no outgoing

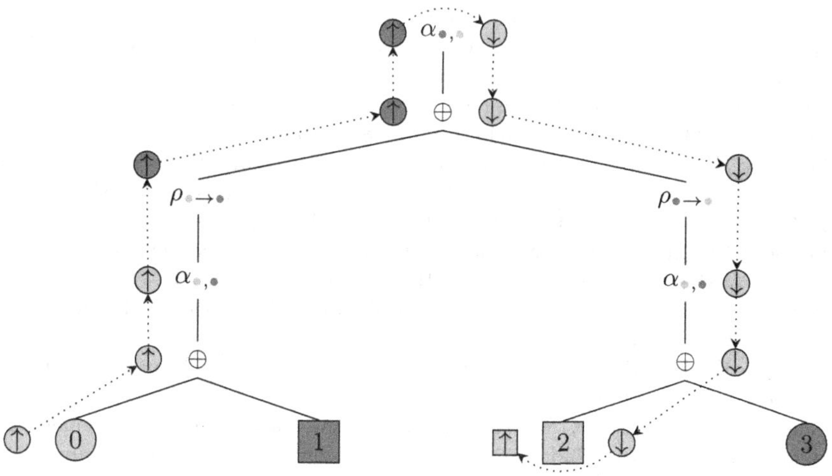

Fig. 4. A 2-expression and a finite play in the tree game

edges in $\mathcal{G}$ if and only if no other position of the form $w^{\uparrow}$ is reachable from $v^{\uparrow}$ in $\mathcal{G}^*$, i.e. Player s loses $\mathcal{G}^*$ from $v^{\uparrow}$.

Consider a positional strategy σ of Player s in $\mathcal{G}$ and a play π^* in $\mathcal{G}^*$ from $v_0^{\uparrow}$ which is conform with σ^*. If π^* is infinite, it is of the form $\pi^* = \pi_{v_0 v_1} \pi_{v_1 v_2} \cdots$ where $\pi = v_0 v_1 \ldots$ is a play in $\mathcal{G}$ conform with σ and both plays have the same winner. If π^* is finite, it can be decomposed as $\pi^* = \pi_{v_0 v_1} \pi_{v_1 v_2} \cdots \pi_{v_{n-1} v_n} \pi'$ where π' has no prefix of the form π_{vw}. In this case $v_0 \ldots v_n$ is a finite play in $\mathcal{G}$ conform with σ and both plays are lost by the owner of v_n. Hence, if σ is winning from v_0, then σ^* is winning from $v_0^{\uparrow}$. □

The simulation is illustrated in Figure 4 using two colors. Using the notion from [21] we can state that $\mathcal{G}^*$ has *strong tree-width* $\leq 4k$, which implies a tree-width bound of $8k-1$. This proves that parity games of clique-width $\leq k$ are log-space reducible to parity games of tree-width $\leq 8k-1$, under the assumption that a k-expression is provided, and hence Theorem 13 follows.

The algorithm by Obdržálek for parity games of bounded clique-width in [4] uses the fact that every winning strategy can be transformed into an equivalent t-*strategy*, which is a simple corollary of Lemma 14: By the positional determinacy theorem we can assume that Player 0 uses a positional strategy in the tree game $\mathcal{G}^*$, which indeed defines a t-strategy in $\mathcal{G}$.

References

1. Stirling, C.: Local model checking games. In: Lee, I., Smolka, S.A. (eds.) CONCUR 1995. LNCS, vol. 962, pp. 1–11. Springer, Heidelberg (1995)
2. Jurdziński, M.: Deciding the winner in parity games is in UP ∩ co-UP. Information Processing Letters 68(3), 119–124 (1998)

3. Obdržálek, J.: Fast mu-calculus model checking when tree-width is bounded. In: Hunt Jr., W.A., Somenzi, F. (eds.) CAV 2003. LNCS, vol. 2725, pp. 80–92. Springer, Heidelberg (2003)
4. Obdržálek, J.: Clique-width and parity games. In: Duparc, J., Henzinger, T.A. (eds.) CSL 2007. LNCS, vol. 4646, pp. 54–68. Springer, Heidelberg (2007)
5. Fearnley, J., Schewe, S.: Time and parallelizability results for parity games with bounded treewidth. In: Czumaj, A., Mehlhorn, K., Pitts, A., Wattenhofer, R. (eds.) ICALP 2012, Part II. LNCS, vol. 7392, pp. 189–200. Springer, Heidelberg (2012)
6. Sudborough, I.H.: On the tape complexity of deterministic context-free languages. Journal of the Association for Computing Machinery 25(3), 405–414 (1978)
7. Göller, S., Lohrey, M.: Fixpoint logics over hierarchical structures. Theory Comput. Syst. 48(1), 93–131 (2011)
8. Vollmer, H.: Introduction to Circuit Complexity. Texts in Theoretical Computer Science. Springer (1999)
9. Emerson, E.A., Jutla, C.S.: Tree automata, mu-calculus and determinacy (extended abstract). In: 32nd Annual Symposium on Foundations of Computer Science, pp. 368–377. IEEE Computer Society (1991)
10. Walukiewicz, I.: Monadic second order logic on tree-like structures. In: Puech, C., Reischuk, R. (eds.) STACS 1996. LNCS, vol. 1046, pp. 401–413. Springer, Heidelberg (1996)
11. Elberfeld, M., Jakoby, A., Tantau, T.: Logspace versions of the theorems of Bodlaender and Courcelle. In: 51st Annual IEEE Symposium on Foundations of Computer Science, pp. 143–152 (2010)
12. Friedmann, O., Lange, M.: Solving parity games in practice. In: Liu, Z., Ravn, A.P. (eds.) ATVA 2009. LNCS, vol. 5799, pp. 182–196. Springer, Heidelberg (2009)
13. Courcelle, B.: Graphs as relational structures: An algebraic and logical approach. In: Ehrig, H., Kreowski, H.-J., Rozenberg, G. (eds.) Graph Grammars 1990. LNCS, vol. 532, pp. 238–252. Springer, Heidelberg (1991)
14. Courcelle, B., Makowsky, J.A., Rotics, U.: Linear time solvable optimization problems on graphs of bounded clique-width. Theory Comput. Syst. 33(2), 125–150 (2000)
15. Arnborg, S., Corneil, D.G., Proskurowski, A.: Complexity of finding embeddings in a k-tree. SIAM J. Algebraic Discrete Methods 8(2), 277–284 (1987)
16. Downey, M.R.R.G., Fellows: Parameterized Complexity. Monographs in Computer Science. Springer (1999)
17. Courcelle, B., Olariu, S.: Upper bounds to the clique width of graphs. Discrete Applied Mathematics 101(1-3), 77–114 (2000)
18. Fellows, M.R., Rosamond, F.A., Rotics, U., Szeider, S.: Clique-width is NP-complete. SIAM J. Discrete Math. 23(2), 909–939 (2009)
19. Lohrey, M.: On the parallel complexity of tree automata. In: Middeldorp, A. (ed.) RTA 2001. LNCS, vol. 2051, pp. 201–215. Springer, Heidelberg (2001)
20. Grädel, E., Thomas, W., Wilke, T. (eds.): Automata, Logics, and Infinite Games: A Guide to Current Research. LNCS, vol. 2500. Springer, Heidelberg (2002)
21. Seese, D.: Tree-partite graphs and the complexity of algorithms. In: Budach, L. (ed.) FCT 1985. LNCS, vol. 199, pp. 412–421. Springer, Heidelberg (1985)

Type Theory, Proof Theory and Implicit Computational Complexity

Programming and Reasoning with Guarded Recursion for Coinductive Types

Ranald Clouston, Aleš Bizjak, Hans Bugge Grathwohl, and Lars Birkedal

Department of Computer Science, Aarhus University, Denmark
{ranald.clouston,abizjak,hbugge,birkedal}@cs.au.dk

Abstract. We present the guarded lambda-calculus, an extension of the simply typed lambda-calculus with guarded recursive and coinductive types. The use of guarded recursive types ensures the productivity of well-typed programs. Guarded recursive types may be transformed into coinductive types by a type-former inspired by modal logic and Atkey-McBride clock quantification, allowing the typing of acausal functions. We give a call-by-name operational semantics for the calculus, and define adequate denotational semantics in the topos of trees. The adequacy proof entails that the evaluation of a program always terminates. We demonstrate the expressiveness of the calculus by showing the definability of solutions to Rutten's behavioural differential equations. We introduce a program logic with Löb induction for reasoning about the contextual equivalence of programs.

1 Introduction

The problem of ensuring that functions on coinductive types are well-defined has prompted a wide variety of work into productivity checking, and rule formats for coalgebra. *Guarded recursion* [11] guarantees productivity and unique solutions by requiring that recursive calls be nested under a constructor, such as cons (written ::) for streams. This can sometimes be established by a simple syntactic check, as for the stream toggle and binary stream function interleave below:

toggle = 1 :: 0 :: toggle
interleave (x :: xs) ys = x :: interleave ys xs

Such syntactic checks, however, are often too blunt and exclude many valid definitions. For example the *regular paperfolding sequence*, the sequence of left and right turns (encoded as 1 and 0) generated by repeatedly folding a piece of paper in half, can be defined via the function interleave as follows [12]:

paperfolds = interleave toggle paperfolds

This definition is productive, but the putative definition below, which also applies interleave to two streams and so apparently is just as well-typed, is not:

paperfolds' = interleave paperfolds' toggle

A. Pitts (Ed.): FOSSACS 2015, LNCS 9034, pp. 407–421, 2015.
DOI: 10.1007/978-3-662-46678-0_26

This equation is satisfied by any stream whose *tail* is the regular paperfolding sequence, so lacks a unique solution. Unfortunately the syntactic productivity checker of the proof assistant Coq [13] will reject both definitions.

A more flexible approach, first suggested by Nakano [19], is to guarantee productivity via *types*. A new modality, for which we follow Appel et al. [3] by writing $\blacktriangleright$ and using the name 'later', allows us to distinguish between data we have access to now, and data which we have only later. This $\blacktriangleright$ must be used to guard self-reference in type definitions, so for example *guarded streams* of natural numbers are defined by the guarded recursive equation

$$\mathsf{Str}^{\mathsf{g}} \triangleq \mathbf{N} \times \blacktriangleright \mathsf{Str}^{\mathsf{g}}$$

asserting that stream heads are available now, but tails only later. The type of $\mathsf{interleave}$ will be $\mathsf{Str}^{\mathsf{g}} \to \blacktriangleright \mathsf{Str}^{\mathsf{g}} \to \mathsf{Str}^{\mathsf{g}}$, capturing the fact the (head of the) first argument is needed immediately, but the second argument is needed only later. In term definitions the types of self-references will then be guarded by $\blacktriangleright$ also. For example $\mathsf{interleave}\,\mathsf{paperfolds}'\,\mathsf{toggle}$ becomes ill-formed, as the $\mathsf{paperfolds}'$ self-reference has type $\blacktriangleright \mathsf{Str}^{\mathsf{g}}$, rather than $\mathsf{Str}^{\mathsf{g}}$, but $\mathsf{interleave}\,\mathsf{toggle}\,\mathsf{paperfolds}$ will be well-formed.

Adding $\blacktriangleright$ alone to the simply typed λ-calculus enforces a discipline more rigid than productivity. For example the obviously productive stream function

$$\mathsf{every2nd}\ (\mathsf{x} :: \mathsf{x}' :: \mathsf{xs}) = \mathsf{x} :: \mathsf{every2nd}\ \mathsf{xs}$$

cannot be typed because it violates *causality* [15]: elements of the result stream depend on deeper elements of the argument stream. In some settings, such as reactive programming, this is a desirable property, but for productivity guarantees alone it is too restrictive. We need the ability to remove $\blacktriangleright$ in a controlled way. This is provided by the *clock quantifiers* of Atkey and McBride [4], which assert that all data is available now. This does not trivialise the guardedness requirements because there are side-conditions controlling when clock quantifiers may be introduced. Moreover clock quantifiers transform guarded recursive types into first-class *coinductive* types, with guarded recursion defining the rule format for their manipulation.

Our presentation departs from Atkey and McBride's [4] by regarding the 'everything now' operator as a unary type-former, written $\blacksquare$ and called 'constant', rather than a quantifier. Observing that the types $\blacksquare A \to A$ and $\blacksquare A \to \blacksquare\blacksquare A$ are always inhabited allows us to see the type-former, via the Curry-Howard isomorphism, as an *S4* modality, and hence base our operational semantics on the established typed calculi for intuitionistic S4 (IS4) of Bierman and de Paiva [5]. This is sufficient to capture all examples in the literature, which use only one clock; for examples that require multiple clocks we suggest extending our calculus to a *multimodal* logic.

In this paper we present the guarded λ-calculus, $\mathsf{g}\lambda$, extending the simply typed λ-calculus with coinductive and guarded recursive types. We define call-by-name operational semantics, which blocks non-termination via recursive definitions unfolding indefinitely. We define adequate denotational semantics in the topos of trees [6] and as a consequence prove normalisation. We introduce a program logic $Lg\lambda$ for reasoning about the denotations of gλ-programs; given adequacy this permits proofs about the operational behaviour of terms. The logic is based on the internal logic of the topos of trees, with modalities $\triangleright, \square$ on predicates, and Löb induction for reasoning about functions on both guarded recursive and coinductive types. We demonstrate the expressiveness of the calculus by showing the definability of solutions to Rutten's behavioural differential equations [21], and show that $Lg\lambda$ can be used to reason about them, as an alternative to standard bisimulation-based arguments.

We have implemented the gλ-calculus in Agda, a process we found helpful when fine-tuning the design of our calculus. The implementation, with many examples, is available at `http://cs.au.dk/~hbugge/gl-agda.zip`.

2 Guarded λ-calculus

This section presents the guarded λ-calculus, written gλ, its call-by-name operational semantics, and its types, then gives some examples.

Definition 2.1. gλ-terms *are given by the grammar*

$$t ::= x \mid \langle\rangle \mid \mathsf{zero} \mid \mathsf{succ}\, t \mid \langle t, t\rangle \mid \pi_d t \mid \lambda x.t \mid tt \mid \mathsf{fold}\, t \mid \mathsf{unfold}\, t \\ \mid \mathsf{next}\, t \mid \mathsf{prev}\, \sigma.t \mid \mathsf{box}\, \sigma.t \mid \mathsf{unbox}\, t \mid t \circledast t$$

where $d \in \{1,2\}$, x is a variable and $\sigma = [x_1 \leftarrow t_1, \ldots, x_n \leftarrow t_n]$, usually abbreviated $[\vec{x} \leftarrow \vec{t}]$, is a list of variables paired with terms.

$\mathsf{prev}[\vec{x} \leftarrow \vec{t}].t$ *and* $\mathsf{box}[\vec{x} \leftarrow \vec{t}].t$ *bind all variables of $\vec{x}$ in t, but* not *in $\vec{t}$. We write* $\mathsf{prev}\,\iota.t$ *for* $\mathsf{prev}[\vec{x} \leftarrow \vec{x}].t$ *where $\vec{x}$ is a list of all free variables of t. If furthermore t is closed we simply write* $\mathsf{prev}\, t$*. We will similarly write* $\mathsf{box}\,\iota.t$ *and* $\mathsf{box}\, t$*. We adopt the convention that* prev *and* box *have highest precedence.*

We may extend gλ with sums; for space reasons these appear only in the extended version of this paper [9].

Definition 2.2. *The* reduction rules *on closed* gλ*-terms are*

$$\begin{aligned}
\pi_d\langle t_1, t_2\rangle &\mapsto t_d && (d \in \{1,2\}) \\
(\lambda x.t_1)t_2 &\mapsto t_1[t_2/x] \\
\mathsf{unfold}\,\mathsf{fold}\, t &\mapsto t \\
\mathsf{prev}[\vec{x} \leftarrow \vec{t}].t &\mapsto \mathsf{prev}\, t[\vec{t}/\vec{x}] && (\vec{x} \text{ non-empty}) \\
\mathsf{prev}\,\mathsf{next}\, t &\mapsto t \\
\mathsf{unbox}(\mathsf{box}[\vec{x} \leftarrow \vec{t}].t) &\mapsto t[\vec{t}/\vec{x}] \\
\mathsf{next}\, t_1 \circledast \mathsf{next}\, t_2 &\mapsto \mathsf{next}(t_1 t_2)
\end{aligned}$$

The rules above look like standard β-reduction, removing 'roundabouts' of introduction then elimination, with the exception of those regarding prev and next. An apparently more conventional β-rule for these term-formers would be

$$\mathsf{prev}[\vec{x} \leftarrow \vec{t}].(\mathsf{next}\, t) \;\mapsto\; t[\vec{t}/\vec{x}]$$

but where $\vec{x}$ is non-empty this would require us to reduce an open term to derive $\mathsf{next}\, t$. We take the view that reduction of open terms is undesirable within a call-by-name discipline, so first apply the substitution without eliminating prev.

The final rule is not a true β-rule, as $\circledast$ is neither introduction nor elimination, but is necessary to enable function application under a next and hence allow, for example, manipulation of the tail of a stream. It corresponds to the 'homomorphism' equality for applicative functors [16].

We next impose our call-by-name strategy on these reductions.

Definition 2.3. Values *are terms of the form*

$$\langle\rangle \mid \mathsf{succ}^n\,\mathsf{zero} \mid \langle t, t\rangle \mid \lambda x.t \mid \mathsf{fold}\, t \mid \mathsf{box}\,\sigma.t \mid \mathsf{next}\, t$$

where succ^n *is a list of zero or more* succ *operators, and* t *is any term.*

Definition 2.4. Evaluation contexts *are defined by the grammar*

$$E ::= \cdot \mid \mathsf{succ}\, E \mid \pi_d E \mid Et \mid \mathsf{unfold}\, E \mid \mathsf{prev}\, E \mid \mathsf{unbox}\, E \mid E \circledast t \mid v \circledast E$$

If we regard $\circledast$ as a variant of function application, it is surprising in a call-by-name setting to reduce on both its sides. However both sides must be reduced until they have main connective next before the reduction rule for $\circledast$ may be applied. Thus the order of reductions of gλ-terms cannot be identified with the call-by-name reductions of the corresponding λ-calculus term with the novel connectives erased.

Definition 2.5. Call-by-name reduction *has format* $E[t] \mapsto E[u]$, *where* $t \mapsto u$ *is a reduction rule. From now the symbol* $\mapsto$ *will be reserved to refer to call-by-name reduction. We use* $\rightsquigarrow$ *for the reflexive transitive closure of* $\mapsto$.

Lemma 2.6. *The call-by-name reduction relation* $\mapsto$ *is deterministic.*

Definition 2.7. gλ-types *are defined inductively by the rules of Fig. 1.* ∇ *is a finite set of* type variables. *A variable* α *is* guarded in *a type* A *if all occurrences of* α *are beneath an occurrence of* $\blacktriangleright$ *in the syntax tree. We adopt the convention that unary type-formers bind closer than binary type-formers.*

$$\frac{}{\nabla, \alpha \vdash \alpha} \qquad \frac{}{\nabla \vdash \mathbf{1}} \qquad \frac{}{\nabla \vdash \mathbf{N}} \qquad \frac{\nabla \vdash A_1 \qquad \nabla \vdash A_2}{\nabla \vdash A_1 \times A_2} \qquad \frac{\nabla \vdash A_1 \qquad \nabla \vdash A_2}{\nabla \vdash A_1 \to A_2}$$

$$\frac{\nabla, \alpha \vdash A}{\nabla \vdash \mu\alpha.A}\ \alpha\ \text{guarded in}\ A \qquad \frac{\nabla \vdash A}{\nabla \vdash \blacktriangleright A} \qquad \frac{\cdot \vdash A}{\nabla \vdash \blacksquare A}$$

Fig. 1. Type formation for the gλ-calculus

Note the side condition on the μ type-former, and the prohibition on $\blacksquare A$ for open A, which can also be understood as a prohibition on applying $\mu\alpha$ to any α with $\blacksquare$ above it. The intuition for these restrictions is that unique fixed points exist only where the variable is displaced in time by a $\blacktriangleright$, but $\blacksquare$ cancels out this displacement by giving 'everything now'.

Definition 2.8. *The* typing judgments *are given in Fig. 2. There $d \in \{1, 2\}$, and the* typing contexts *Γ are finite sets of pairs $x : A$ where x is a variable and A a closed type. Closed types are* constant *if all occurrences of $\blacktriangleright$ are beneath an occurrence of $\blacksquare$ in their syntax tree.*

$$\frac{}{\Gamma, x : A \vdash x : A} \qquad \frac{}{\Gamma \vdash \langle\rangle : \mathbf{1}} \qquad \frac{}{\Gamma \vdash \mathsf{zero} : \mathbf{N}} \qquad \frac{\Gamma \vdash t : \mathbf{N}}{\Gamma \vdash \mathsf{succ}\, t : \mathbf{N}}$$

$$\frac{\Gamma \vdash t_1 : A \qquad \Gamma \vdash t_2 : B}{\Gamma \vdash \langle t_1, t_2 \rangle : A \times B} \qquad \frac{\Gamma \vdash t : A_1 \times A_2}{\Gamma \vdash \pi_d t : A_d} \qquad \frac{\Gamma, x : A \vdash t : B}{\Gamma \vdash \lambda x.t : A \to B}$$

$$\frac{\Gamma \vdash t_1 : A \to B \qquad \Gamma \vdash t_2 : A}{\Gamma \vdash t_1 t_2 : B} \qquad \frac{\Gamma \vdash t : A[\mu\alpha.A/\alpha]}{\Gamma \vdash \mathsf{fold}\, t : \mu\alpha.A} \qquad \frac{\Gamma \vdash t : \mu\alpha.A}{\Gamma \vdash \mathsf{unfold}\, t : A[\mu\alpha.A/\alpha]}$$

$$\frac{\Gamma \vdash t : A}{\Gamma \vdash \mathsf{next}\, t : \blacktriangleright A} \qquad \frac{\begin{array}{c} x_1 : A_1, \ldots, x_n : A_n \vdash t : \blacktriangleright A \\ \Gamma \vdash t_1 : A_1 \quad \cdots \quad \Gamma \vdash t_n : A_n \end{array}}{\Gamma \vdash \mathsf{prev}[x_1 \leftarrow t_1, \ldots, x_n \leftarrow t_n].t : A} \; A_1, \ldots, A_n \text{ constant}$$

$$\frac{\begin{array}{c} x_1 : A_1, \ldots, x_n : A_n \vdash t : A \\ \Gamma \vdash t_1 : A_1 \quad \cdots \quad \Gamma \vdash t_n : A_n \end{array}}{\Gamma \vdash \mathsf{box}[x_1 \leftarrow t_1, \ldots, x_n \leftarrow t_n].t : \blacksquare A} \; A_1, \ldots, A_n \text{ constant} \qquad \frac{\Gamma \vdash t : \blacksquare A}{\Gamma \vdash \mathsf{unbox}\, t : A}$$

$$\frac{\Gamma \vdash t_1 : \blacktriangleright(A \to B) \qquad \Gamma \vdash t_2 : \blacktriangleright A}{\Gamma \vdash t_1 \circledast t_2 : \blacktriangleright B}$$

Fig. 2. Typing rules for the gλ-calculus

The *constant* types exist 'all at once', due to the absence of $\blacktriangleright$ or presence of $\blacksquare$; this condition corresponds to the freeness of the clock variable in Atkey and McBride [4] (recalling that we use only one clock in this work). Its use as a side-condition to $\blacksquare$-introduction in Fig. 2 recalls (but is more general than) the 'essentially modal' condition for natural deduction for IS4 of Prawitz [20]. The term calculus for IS4 of Bierman and de Paiva [5], on which this calculus is most closely based, uses the still more restrictive requirement that $\blacksquare$ be the main connective. This would preclude some functions that seem desirable, such as the isomorphism $\lambda n.\, \mathsf{box}\, \iota.n : \mathbf{N} \to \blacksquare\mathbf{N}$.

In examples prev usually appears in its syntactic sugar forms

$$\frac{x_1 : A_1, \ldots, x_n : A_n \vdash t : \blacktriangleright A}{\Gamma, x_1 : A_1, \ldots, x_n : A_n \vdash \mathsf{prev}\,\iota.t : A} \; A_1, \ldots, A_n \; \mathsf{constant} \qquad \frac{\vdash t : \blacktriangleright A}{\Gamma \vdash \mathsf{prev}\, t : A}$$

and similarly for box; the more general form is nonetheless necessary because $(\mathsf{prev}\,\iota.t)[\vec{u}/\vec{x}] = \mathsf{prev}[\vec{x} \leftarrow \vec{u}].t$. Getting substitution right in this setting is somewhat delicate. For example our reduction rule $\mathsf{prev}[\vec{x} \leftarrow \vec{t}].t \mapsto \mathsf{prev}\, t[\vec{t}/\vec{x}]$ breaches subject reduction on open terms (but not for closed terms). See Bierman and de Paiva [5] for more discussion of substitution with respect to IS4.

Lemma 2.9 (Subject Reduction). *$\vdash t : A$ and $t \rightsquigarrow u$ implies $\vdash u : A$.*

Example 2.10. (i) The type of guarded recursive streams of natural numbers, $\mathsf{Str}^{\mathsf{g}}$, is defined as $\mu\alpha.\, \mathbf{N} \times \blacktriangleright\alpha$. These provide the setting for all examples below, but other definable types include infinite binary trees, as $\mu\alpha.\, \mathbf{N} \times \blacktriangleright\alpha \times \blacktriangleright\alpha$, and potentially infinite lists, as $\mu\alpha.\, \mathbf{1} + (\mathbf{N} \times \blacktriangleright\alpha)$.

(ii) We define guarded versions of the standard stream functions cons (written infix as ::), head, and tail as obvious:

$$:: \triangleq \lambda n.\lambda s.\, \mathsf{fold}\langle n, s\rangle : \mathbf{N} \to \blacktriangleright\mathsf{Str}^{\mathsf{g}} \to \mathsf{Str}^{\mathsf{g}}$$
$$\mathsf{hd}^{\mathsf{g}} \triangleq \lambda s.\pi_1\, \mathsf{unfold}\, s : \mathsf{Str}^{\mathsf{g}} \to \mathbf{N} \qquad \mathsf{tl}^{\mathsf{g}} \triangleq \lambda s.\pi_2\, \mathsf{unfold}\, s :: \mathsf{Str}^{\mathsf{g}} \to \blacktriangleright\mathsf{Str}^{\mathsf{g}}$$

then use the $\circledast$ term-former for observations deeper into the stream:

$$\mathsf{2nd}^{\mathsf{g}} \triangleq \lambda s.(\mathsf{next}\,\mathsf{hd}^{\mathsf{g}}) \circledast (\mathsf{tl}^{\mathsf{g}}\, s) : \mathsf{Str}^{\mathsf{g}} \to \blacktriangleright \mathbf{N}$$
$$\mathsf{3rd}^{\mathsf{g}} \triangleq \lambda s.(\mathsf{next}\,\mathsf{2nd}^{\mathsf{g}}) \circledast (\mathsf{tl}^{\mathsf{g}}\, s) : \mathsf{Str}^{\mathsf{g}} \to \blacktriangleright\blacktriangleright \mathbf{N} \;\cdots$$

(iii) Following Abel and Vezzosi [2, Sec. 3.4] we may define a fixed point combinator fix with type $(\blacktriangleright A \to A) \to A$ for any A. We use this to define a stream by iteration of a function: iterate takes as arguments a natural number and a function, but the function is not used until the 'next' step of computation, so we may reflect this with our typing:

$$\mathsf{iterate} \triangleq \lambda f.\, \mathsf{fix}\, \lambda g.\lambda n.n :: (g \circledast (f \circledast \mathsf{next}\, n)) : \blacktriangleright(\mathbf{N} \to \mathbf{N}) \to \mathbf{N} \to \mathsf{Str}^{\mathsf{g}}$$

We may hence define the guarded stream of natural numbers

$$\mathsf{nats} \triangleq \mathsf{iterate}\, (\mathsf{next}\, \lambda n.\, \mathsf{succ}\, n)\, \mathsf{zero}\,.$$

(iv) With interleave, following our discussion in the introduction, we again may reflect in our type that one of our arguments is not required until the next step, defining the term interleave as:

$$\mathsf{fix}\, \lambda g.\lambda s.\lambda t.(\mathsf{hd}^{\mathsf{g}}\, s) :: (g \circledast t \circledast \mathsf{next}(\mathsf{tl}^{\mathsf{g}}\, s)) : \mathsf{Str}^{\mathsf{g}} \to \blacktriangleright\mathsf{Str}^{\mathsf{g}} \to \mathsf{Str}^{\mathsf{g}}$$

This typing decision is essential to define the paper folding stream:

$$\mathsf{toggle} \triangleq \mathsf{fix}\, \lambda s.(\mathsf{succ}\, \mathsf{zero}) :: (\mathsf{next}(\mathsf{zero} :: s))$$
$$\mathsf{paperfolds} \triangleq \mathsf{fix}\, \lambda s.\, \mathsf{interleave}\, \mathsf{toggle}\; s$$

Note that the unproductive definition with $\mathsf{interleave}\, s\ \mathsf{toggle}$ cannot be made to type check: informally, $s : \blacktriangleright\mathsf{Str}^{\mathsf{g}}$ cannot be converted into a $\mathsf{Str}^{\mathsf{g}}$ by prev, as it is in the scope of a variable s whose type $\mathsf{Str}^{\mathsf{g}}$ is not constant. To see a less artificial non-example, try to define a filter function on streams which eliminates elements that fail some boolean test.

(v) μ-types are in fact *unique* fixed points, so carry both final coalgebra and initial algebra structure. To see the latter, observe that we can define

$$\mathsf{foldr} \triangleq \mathsf{fix}\,\lambda g \lambda f.\lambda s.f\langle \mathsf{hd}^{\mathsf{g}}\, s, g \circledast \mathsf{next}\, f \circledast \mathsf{tl}^{\mathsf{g}}\, s\rangle : ((\mathbf{N} \times \blacktriangleright A) \to A) \to \mathsf{Str}^{\mathsf{g}} \to A$$

and hence for example $\mathsf{map}^{\mathsf{g}}\, h : \mathsf{Str}^{\mathsf{g}} \to \mathsf{Str}^{\mathsf{g}}$ is $\mathsf{foldr}\,\lambda x.(h\pi_1 x) :: (\pi_2 x)$.

(vi) The $\blacksquare$ type-former lifts guarded recursive streams to coinductive streams, as we will make precise in Ex. 3.4. Let $\mathsf{Str} \triangleq \blacksquare\mathsf{Str}^{\mathsf{g}}$. We define $\mathsf{hd} : \mathsf{Str} \to \mathbf{N}$ and $\mathsf{tl} : \mathsf{Str} \to \mathsf{Str}$ by $\mathsf{hd} = \lambda s.\, \mathsf{hd}^{\mathsf{g}}(\mathsf{unbox}\, s)$ and $\mathsf{tl} = \lambda s.\, \mathsf{box}\,\iota.\, \mathsf{prev}\,\iota.\, \mathsf{tl}^{\mathsf{g}}(\mathsf{unbox}\, s)$, and hence define observations deep into streams whose results bear no trace of $\blacktriangleright$, for example $\mathsf{2nd} \triangleq \lambda s.\, \mathsf{hd}(\mathsf{tl}\, s) : \mathsf{Str} \to \mathbf{N}$.
In general boxed functions lift to functions on boxed types by

$$\mathsf{lim} \triangleq \lambda f.\lambda x.\, \mathsf{box}\,\iota.(\mathsf{unbox}\, f)(\mathsf{unbox}\, x) : \blacksquare(A \to B) \to \blacksquare A \to \blacksquare B$$

(vii) The more sophisticated acausal function $\mathsf{every2nd} : \mathsf{Str} \to \mathsf{Str}^{\mathsf{g}}$ is

$$\mathsf{fix}\,\lambda g.\lambda s.(\mathsf{hd}\, s) :: (g \circledast (\mathsf{next}(\mathsf{tl}(\mathsf{tl}\, s)))).$$

Note that it must take a *coinductive* stream Str as argument. The function with coinductive result type is then $\lambda s.\, \mathsf{box}\,\iota.\, \mathsf{every2nd}\, s : \mathsf{Str} \to \mathsf{Str}$.

3 Denotational Semantics and Normalisation

This section gives denotational semantics for $\mathsf{g}\lambda$-types and terms, as objects and arrows in the topos of trees [6], the presheaf category over the first infinite ordinal ω (we give a concrete definition below). These semantics are shown to be sound and, by a logical relations argument, adequate with respect to the operational semantics. Normalisation follows as a corollary of this argument. Note that for space reasons many proofs, and some lemmas, appear only in the extended version of this paper [9].

Definition 3.1. *The* topos of trees $\mathcal{S}$ *has, as objects* X*, families of sets* $X_1, X_2, \ldots$ *indexed by the positive integers, equipped with families of* restriction functions $r_i^X : X_{i+1} \to X_i$ *indexed similarly. Arrows* $f : X \to Y$ *are families of functions* $f_i : X_i \to Y_i$ *indexed similarly obeying the naturality condition* $f_i \circ r_i^X = r_i^Y \circ f_{i+1}$.

$\mathcal{S}$ is a cartesian closed category with products defined pointwise. Its exponential A^B has, as its component sets $(A^B)_i$, the set of i-tuples $(f_1 : A_1 \to B_1, \ldots, f_i : A_i \to B_i)$ obeying the naturality condition, and projections as restriction functions.

Definition 3.2. – *The category of sets* **Set** *is a full subcategory of* $\mathcal{S}$ *via the functor* $\Delta : \mathbf{Set} \to \mathcal{S}$ *with* $(\Delta Z)_i = Z$, $r_i^{\Delta Z} = id_Z$, *and* $(\Delta f)_i = f$. *Objects in this subcategory are called* constant objects. *In particular the terminal object* 1 *of* $\mathcal{S}$ *is* $\Delta\{*\}$ *and the* natural numbers object *is* $\Delta\mathbb{N}$;

- Δ *is left adjoint to* $hom_{\mathcal{S}}(1, \text{-})$; *write* $\blacksquare$ *for* $\Delta \circ hom_{\mathcal{S}}(1, \text{-}) : \mathcal{S} \to \mathcal{S}$. $\mathsf{unbox} : \blacksquare \dot{\to} id_{\mathcal{S}}$ *is the counit of the resulting comonad. Concretely* $\mathsf{unbox}_i(x) = x_i$, *i.e. the i'th component of* $x : 1 \to X$ *applied to* $*$;
- $\blacktriangleright : \mathcal{S} \to \mathcal{S}$ *is defined by* $(\blacktriangleright X)_1 = \{*\}$ *and* $(\blacktriangleright X)_{i+1} = X_i$, *with* $r_1^{\blacktriangleright X}$ *defined uniquely and* $r_{i+1}^{\blacktriangleright X} = r_i^X$. *Its action on arrows* $f : X \to Y$ *is* $(\blacktriangleright f)_1 = id_{\{*\}}$ *and* $(\blacktriangleright f)_{i+1} = f_i$. *The natural transformation* $\mathsf{next} : id_{\mathcal{S}} \dot{\to} \blacktriangleright$ *has* next_1 *unique and* $\mathsf{next}_{i+1} = r_i^X$ *for any* X.

Definition 3.3. *We interpet types in context* $\nabla \vdash A$, *where* ∇ *contains n free variables, as functors* $[\![\nabla \vdash A]\!] : (\mathcal{S}^{op} \times \mathcal{S})^n \to \mathcal{S}$, *usually written* $[\![A]\!]$. *This mixed variance definition is necessary as variables may appear negatively or positively.*

- $[\![\nabla, \alpha \vdash \alpha]\!]$ *is the projection of the objects or arrows corresponding to* positive *occurrences of* α, *e.g.* $[\![\alpha]\!](\vec{W}, X, Y) = Y$;
- $[\![\mathbf{1}]\!]$ *and* $[\![\mathbf{N}]\!]$ *are the constant functors* $\Delta\{*\}$ *and* $\Delta\mathbb{N}$ *respectively;*
- $[\![A_1 \times A_2]\!](\vec{W}) = [\![A_1]\!](\vec{W}) \times [\![A_2]\!](\vec{W})$ *and likewise for* $\mathcal{S}$*-arrows;*
- $[\![A_1 \to A_2]\!](\vec{W}) = [\![A_2]\!](\vec{W})^{[\![A_2]\!](\vec{W}')}$ *where* $\vec{W}'$ *is* $\vec{W}$ *with odd and even elements switched to reflect change in polarity, i.e.* $(X_1, Y_1, \ldots)' = (Y_1, X_1, \ldots)$;
- $[\![\blacktriangleright A]\!], [\![\blacksquare A]\!]$ *are defined by composition with the functors* $\blacktriangleright, \blacksquare$ *(Def. 3.2).*
- $[\![\mu\alpha.A]\!](\vec{W}) = \mathsf{Fix}(F)$, *where* $F : (\mathcal{S}^{op} \times \mathcal{S}) \to \mathcal{S}$ *is the functor given by* $F(X, Y) = [\![A]\!](\vec{W}, X, Y)$ *and* $\mathsf{Fix}(F)$ *is the unique (up to isomorphism)* X *such that* $F(X, X) \cong X$. *The existence of such* X *relies on* F *being a suitably locally contractive functor, which follows by Birkedal et al [6, Sec. 4.5] and the fact that* $\blacksquare$ *is only ever applied to closed types. This restriction on* $\blacksquare$ *is necessary because the functor* $\blacksquare$ *is not strong.*

Example 3.4. $[\![\mathsf{Str}^{\mathsf{g}}]\!]_i = \mathbb{N}^i$, with projections as restriction functions, so is an object of *approximations* of streams – first the head, then the first two elements, and so forth. $[\![\mathsf{Str}]\!]_i = \mathbb{N}^\omega$ at all levels, so is the constant object of streams. More generally, any polynomial functor F on **Set** can be assigned a $\mathsf{g}\lambda$-type A_F with a free type variable α that occurs guarded. The denotation of $\blacksquare\mu\alpha.A_F$ is the constant object of the carrier of the final coalgebra for F [18, Thm. 2].

Lemma 3.5. *The interpretation of a recursive type is isomorphic to the interpretation of its unfolding:* $[\![\mu\alpha.A]\!](\vec{W}) \cong [\![A[\mu\alpha.A/\alpha]]\!](\vec{W})$.

Lemma 3.6. *Closed constant types denote constant objects in* $\mathcal{S}$.

Note that the converse does not apply; for example $[\![\blacktriangleright 1]\!]$ is a constant object.

Definition 3.7. *We interpret typing contexts* $\Gamma = x_1 : A_1, \ldots, x_n : A_n$ *as* $\mathcal{S}$*-objects* $[\![\Gamma]\!] \triangleq [\![A_1]\!] \times \cdots \times [\![A_n]\!]$ *and hence interpret typed terms-in-context* $\Gamma \vdash t : A$ *as* $\mathcal{S}$*-arrows* $[\![\Gamma \vdash t : A]\!] : [\![\Gamma]\!] \to [\![A]\!]$ *(usually written* $[\![t]\!]$*) as follows.*

$[\![x]\!]$ is the projection $[\![\Gamma]\!] \times [\![A]\!] \to [\![A]\!]$. $[\![\mathsf{zero}]\!]$ and $[\![\mathsf{succ}\, t]\!]$ are as obvious. Term-formers for products and function spaces are interpreted via the cartesian closed structure of $\mathcal{S}$. Exponentials are not pointwise, so we give explicitly:

- *$[\![\lambda x.t]\!]_i(\gamma)_j$ maps $a \mapsto [\![\Gamma, x : A \vdash t : B]\!]_j(\gamma\restriction_j, a)$, where $\gamma\restriction_j$ is the result of applying restriction functions to $\gamma \in [\![\Gamma]\!]_i$ to get an element of $[\![\Gamma]\!]_j$;*
- *$[\![t_1 t_2]\!]_i(\gamma) = ([\![t_1]\!]_i(\gamma)_i) \circ [\![t_2]\!]_i(\gamma)$;*

$[\![\mathsf{fold}\, t]\!]$ and $[\![\mathsf{unfold}\, t]\!]$ are defined via composition with the isomorphisms of Lem. 3.5. $[\![\mathsf{next}\, t]\!]$ and $[\![\mathsf{unbox}\, t]\!]$ are defined by composition with the natural transformations introduced in Def. 3.2. The final three cases are

- *$[\![\mathsf{prev}[x_1 \leftarrow t_1, \ldots].t]\!]_i(\gamma) \triangleq [\![t]\!]_{i+1}([\![t_1]\!]_i(\gamma), \ldots)$, where $[\![t_1]\!]_i(\gamma) \in [\![A_1]\!]_i$ is also in $[\![A_1]\!]_{i+1}$ by Lem. 3.6;*
- *$[\![\mathsf{box}[x_1 \leftarrow t_1, \ldots].t]\!]_i(\gamma)_j = [\![t]\!]_j([\![t_1]\!]_i(\gamma), \ldots)$, again using Lem. 3.6;*
- *$[\![t_1 \circledast t_2]\!]_1$ is defined uniquely; $[\![t_1 \circledast t_2]\!]_{i+1}(\gamma) \triangleq ([\![t_1]\!]_{i+1}(\gamma)_i) \circ [\![t_2]\!]_{i+1}(\gamma)$.*

Lemma 3.8. *Given typed terms in context $x_1 : A_1, \ldots, x_m : A_m \vdash t : A$ and $\Gamma \vdash t_k : A_k$ for $1 \le k \le m$, $[\![t[\vec{t}/\vec{x}]]\!]_i(\gamma) = [\![t]\!]_i([\![t_1]\!]_i(\gamma), \ldots, [\![t_m]\!]_i(\gamma))$.*

Theorem 3.9 (Soundness). *If $t \rightsquigarrow u$ then $[\![t]\!] = [\![u]\!]$.*

We now define a logical relation between our denotational semantics and terms, from which both normalisation and adequacy will follow. Doing this inductively proves rather delicate, because induction on size will not support reasoning about our values, as fold refers to a larger type in its premise. This motivates a notion of *unguarded size* under which $A[\mu\alpha.A/\alpha]$ is 'smaller' than $\mu\alpha.A$. But under this metric $\blacktriangleright A$ is smaller than A, so next now poses a problem. But the meaning of $\blacktriangleright A$ at index $i+1$ is determined by A at index i, and so, as in Birkedal et al [7], our relation will also induct on index. This in turn creates problems with box, whose meaning refers to all indexes simultaneously, motivating a notion of *box depth*, allowing us finally to attain well-defined induction.

Definition 3.10. *The* unguarded size us *of an open type follows the obvious definition for type size, except that* $\mathsf{us}(\blacktriangleright A) = 0$.

The box depth bd *of an open type is*

- $\mathsf{bd}(A) = 0$ *for* $A \in \{\alpha, \mathbf{0}, \mathbf{1}, \mathbf{N}\}$;
- $\mathsf{bd}(A \times B) = \mathsf{min}(\mathsf{bd}(A), \mathsf{bd}(B))$, *and similarly for* $\mathsf{bd}(A \to B)$;
- $\mathsf{bd}(\mu\alpha.A) = \mathsf{bd}(A)$, *and similarly for* $\mathsf{bd}(\blacktriangleright A)$;
- $\mathsf{bd}(\blacksquare A) = \mathsf{bd}(A) + 1$.

Lemma 3.11. *(i) α guarded in A implies* $\mathsf{us}(A[B/\alpha]) \le \mathsf{us}(A)$.
(ii) $\mathsf{bd}(B) \le \mathsf{bd}(A)$ *implies* $\mathsf{bd}(A[B/\alpha]) \le \mathsf{bd}(A)$

Definition 3.12. *The family of relations R_i^A, indexed by closed types A and positive integers i, relates elements of the semantics $a \in [\![A]\!]_i$ and closed typed terms $t : A$ and is defined as*

- $*R_i^{\mathbf{1}} t$ *iff* $t \rightsquigarrow \langle\rangle$;
- $nR_i^{\mathbf{N}} t$ *iff* $t \rightsquigarrow \mathsf{succ}^n\, \mathsf{zero}$;
- $(a_1, a_2)R_i^{A_1 \times A_2} t$ *iff* $t \rightsquigarrow \langle t_1, t_2\rangle$ *and* $a_d R_i^{A_d} t_d$ *for* $d \in \{1, 2\}$;
- $fR_i^{A \to B} t$ *iff* $t \rightsquigarrow \lambda x.s$ *and for all* $j \le i$, $aR_j^A u$ *implies* $f_j(a)R_j^B s[u/x]$;
- $aR_i^{\mu\alpha.A} t$ *iff* $t \rightsquigarrow \mathsf{fold}\, u$ *and* $h_i(a)R_i^{A[\mu\alpha.A/\alpha]} u$, *where* h *is the "unfold" isomorphism for the recursive type (ref. Lem. 3.5)*;
- $aR_i^{\blacktriangleright A} t$ *iff* $t \rightsquigarrow \mathsf{next}\, u$ *and, where* $i > 1$, $aR_{i-1}^A u$.
- $aR_i^{\blacksquare A} t$ *iff* $t \rightsquigarrow \mathsf{box}\, u$ *and for all* j, $a_j R_j^A u$;

This is well-defined by induction on the lexicographic ordering on box depth, then index, then unguarded size. First the $\blacksquare$ *case strictly decreases box depth, and no other case increases it (ref. Lem. 3.11.(ii) for* μ*-types). Second the* $\blacktriangleright$ *case strictly decreases index, and no other case increases it (disregarding* $\blacksquare$*). Finally all other cases strictly decrease unguarded size, as seen via Lem. 3.11.(i) for* μ*-types.*

Lemma 3.13 (Fundamental Lemma). *Take* $\Gamma = (x_1 : A_1, \ldots, x_m : A_m)$, $\Gamma \vdash t : A$, *and* $\vdash t_k : A_k$ *for* $1 \le k \le m$. *Then for all* i, *if* $a_k R_i^{A_k} t_k$ *for all* k, *then*

$$[\![\Gamma \vdash t : A]\!]_i(\vec{a})\, R_i^A\, t[\vec{t}/\vec{x}].$$

Theorem 3.14 (Adequacy and Normalisation).

(i) For all closed terms $\vdash t : A$ *it holds that* $[\![t]\!]_i R_i^A t$;
(ii) $[\![\vdash t : \mathbf{N}]\!]_i = n$ *implies* $t \rightsquigarrow \mathsf{succ}^n\, \mathsf{zero}$;
(iii) All closed typed terms evaluate to a value.

Proof. (i) specialises Lem. 3.13 to closed types. $(ii), (iii)$ hold by (i) and inspection of Def. 3.12.

Definition 3.15. *Typed* contexts *with typed holes are defined as obvious. Two terms* $\Gamma \vdash t : A, \Gamma \vdash u : A$ *are* contextually equivalent, *written* $t \simeq_{\mathsf{ctx}} u$, *if for all* closing *contexts* C *of type* $\mathbf{N}$, *the terms* $C[t]$ *and* $C[u]$ *reduce to the same value.*

Corollary 3.16. $[\![t]\!] = [\![u]\!]$ *implies* $t \simeq_{\mathsf{ctx}} u$.

Proof. $[\![C[t]]\!] = [\![C[u]]\!]$ by compositionality of the denotational semantics . Then by Thm. 3.14.(ii) they reduce to the same value.

4 Logic for Guarded Lambda Calculus

This section presents our program logic $Lg\lambda$ for the guarded λ-calculus. The logic is an extension of the internal language of $\mathcal{S}$ [6,10]. Thus it extends multi-sorted intuitionistic higher-order logic with two propositional modalities $\triangleright$ and $\Box$, pronounced later and always respectively. The term language of $Lg\lambda$ includes the terms of $\mathsf{g}\lambda$, and the types of $Lg\lambda$ include types definable in $\mathsf{g}\lambda$. We write Ω for the type of propositions, and also for the subobject classifier of $\mathcal{S}$.

The rules for *definitional equality* extend the usual $\beta\eta$-laws for functions and products with new equations for the new $\mathsf{g}\lambda$ constructs, listed in Fig. 3.

$$\frac{\Gamma \vdash t : A\,[\mu\alpha.A/\alpha]}{\Gamma \vdash \mathsf{unfold}(\mathsf{fold}\,t) = t} \qquad \frac{\Gamma \vdash t : \mu\alpha.A}{\Gamma \vdash \mathsf{fold}(\mathsf{unfold}\,t) = t} \qquad \frac{\Gamma \vdash t_1 : A \to B \qquad \Gamma \vdash t_2 : A}{\Gamma \vdash \mathsf{next}\,t_1 \circledast \mathsf{next}\,t_2 = \mathsf{next}(t_1 t_2)}$$

$$\frac{\Gamma_{\blacksquare} \vdash t : A \qquad \Gamma \vdash \vec{t} : \Gamma_{\blacksquare}}{\Gamma \vdash \mathsf{prev}[\vec{x} \leftarrow \vec{t}].(\mathsf{next}\,t) = t\,[\vec{t}/\vec{x}]} \qquad \frac{\Gamma_{\blacksquare} \vdash t : \blacktriangleright A \qquad \Gamma \vdash \vec{t} : \Gamma_{\blacksquare}}{\Gamma \vdash \mathsf{next}\left(\mathsf{prev}[\vec{x} \leftarrow \vec{t}].t\right) = t\,[\vec{t}/\vec{x}]}$$

$$\frac{\Gamma_{\blacksquare} \vdash t : A \qquad \Gamma \vdash \vec{t} : \Gamma_{\blacksquare}}{\Gamma \vdash \mathsf{unbox}(\mathsf{box}[\vec{x} \leftarrow \vec{t}].t) = t\,[\vec{t}/\vec{x}]} \qquad \frac{\Gamma_{\blacksquare} \vdash t : \blacksquare A \qquad \Gamma \vdash \vec{t} : \Gamma_{\blacksquare}}{\Gamma \vdash \mathsf{box}[\vec{x} \leftarrow \vec{t}].\,\mathsf{unbox}\,t = t\,[\vec{t}/\vec{x}]}$$

Fig. 3. Additional equations. The context $\Gamma_{\blacksquare}$ is assumed constant.

Definition 4.1. *A type X is* total and inhabited *if the formula* $\mathrm{Total}(X) \equiv \forall x : \blacktriangleright X, \exists x' : X, \mathbf{next}(x') =_{\blacktriangleright X} x$ *is valid.*

All of the gλ-types defined in Sec. 2 are total and inhabited (see the extended version [9] for a proof using the semantics of the logic), but that is not the case when we include sum types as the empty type is not inhabited.

Corresponding to the modalities $\blacktriangleright$ and $\blacksquare$ on types, we have modalities $\triangleright$ and $\Box$ on formulas. The modality $\triangleright$ is used to express that a formula holds only "later", that is, after a time step. It is given by a function symbol $\triangleright : \Omega \to \Omega$. The $\Box$ modality is used to express that a formula holds for all time steps. Unlike the $\triangleright$ modality, $\Box$ on formulas does not arise from a function on Ω [8]. As with box, it is only well-behaved in constant contexts, so we will only allow $\Box$ in such contexts. The rules for $\triangleright$ and $\Box$ are listed in Fig. 4.

$$\frac{}{\Gamma \mid \Xi, (\triangleright\phi \Rightarrow \phi) \vdash \phi}\ \text{LÖB} \qquad \frac{}{\Gamma, x : X \mid \exists y : Y, \triangleright\phi(x,y) \vdash \triangleright(\exists y : Y, \phi(x,y))}\ \exists\triangleright$$

$$\frac{}{\Gamma, x : X \mid \triangleright(\forall y : Y, \phi(x,y)) \vdash \forall y : Y, \triangleright\phi(x,y)}\ \forall\triangleright \qquad \frac{}{\Gamma \mid \Xi, \phi \vdash \triangleright\phi}$$

$$\frac{\star \in \{\wedge, \vee, \Rightarrow\}}{\Gamma \mid \triangleright(\phi \star \psi) \dashv\vdash \triangleright\phi \star \triangleright\psi} \qquad \frac{\Gamma \mid \neg\neg\phi \vdash \psi}{\Gamma \mid \phi \vdash \Box\psi} \qquad \frac{\Gamma \mid \phi \vdash \Box\psi}{\Gamma \mid \neg\neg\phi \vdash \psi} \qquad \frac{\Gamma \mid \phi \vdash \psi}{\Gamma \mid \Box\phi \vdash \Box\psi}$$

$$\frac{}{\Gamma \mid \Box\phi \vdash \phi} \qquad \frac{}{\Gamma \mid \Box\phi \vdash \Box\Box\phi} \qquad \frac{}{\forall x, y : X.\, \triangleright(x =_X y) \Leftrightarrow \mathsf{next}\,x =_{\blacktriangleright X} \mathsf{next}\,y}\ \mathrm{EQ}^{\triangleright}_{\mathsf{next}}$$

Fig. 4. Rules for $\triangleright$ and $\Box$. The judgement $\Gamma \mid \Xi \vdash \phi$ expresses that in typing context Γ, hypotheses in Ξ prove ϕ. The converse entailment in $\forall\triangleright$ and $\exists\triangleright$ rules holds if Y is *total and inhabited*. In all rules involving the $\Box$ the context Γ is assumed constant.

The $\triangleright$ modality can in fact be defined in terms of $\mathsf{lift} : \blacktriangleright\Omega \to \Omega$ (called *succ* by Birkedal et al [6]) as $\triangleright = \mathsf{lift} \circ \mathsf{next}$. The lift function will be useful since it allows us to define predicates over guarded types, such as predicates on $\mathsf{Str}^{\mathsf{g}}$.

The semantics of the logic is given in $\mathcal{S}$; terms are interpreted as morphisms of $\mathcal{S}$ and formulas are interpreted via the subobject classifier. We do not present the semantics here; except for the new terms of $\mathsf{g}\lambda$, whose semantics are defined in Sec. 3, the semantics are as in [6,8].

Later we will come to the problem of proving $x =_{\blacksquare A} y$ from $\mathsf{unbox}\, x =_A \mathsf{unbox}\, y$, where x, y have type $\blacksquare A$. This in general does not hold, but using the semantics of $L\mathsf{g}\lambda$ we can prove the proposition below.

Proposition 4.2. *The formula* $\square(\mathsf{unbox}\, x =_A \mathsf{unbox}\, y) \Rightarrow x =_{\blacksquare A} y$ *is valid.*

There exists a fixed-point combinator of type $(\blacktriangleright A \to A) \to A$ for all types A in the logic (not only those of in $\mathsf{g}\lambda$) [6, Thm. 2.4]; we also write fix for it.

Proposition 4.3. *For any term* $f : \blacktriangleright A \to A$ *we have* $\mathsf{fix}\, f =_A f\,(\mathsf{next}(\mathsf{fix}\, f))$ *and, if* u *is any other term such that* $f(\mathsf{next}\, u) =_A u$*, then* $u =_A \mathsf{fix}\, f$.

In particular this can be used for recursive definitions of predicates. For instance if $P : \mathbf{N} \to \Omega$ is a predicate on natural numbers we can define a predicate $P_{\mathsf{Str}^{\mathsf{g}}}$ on $\mathsf{Str}^{\mathsf{g}}$ expressing that P holds for all elements of the stream:

$$P_{\mathsf{Str}^{\mathsf{g}}} \triangleq \mathsf{fix}\, \lambda r.\lambda xs.P(\mathsf{hd}^{\mathsf{g}}\, xs) \wedge \mathsf{lift}\,(r \circledast (\mathsf{tl}^{\mathsf{g}}\, xs)) : \mathsf{Str}^{\mathsf{g}} \to \Omega.$$

The logic may be used to prove contextual equivalence of programs:

Theorem 4.4. *Let* t_1 *and* t_2 *be two* $\mathsf{g}\lambda$ *terms of type* A *in context* Γ*. If the sequent* $\Gamma \mid \emptyset \vdash t_1 =_A t_2$ *is provable then* t_1 *and* t_2 *are contextually equivalent.*

Proof. Recall that equality in the internal logic of a topos is just equality of morphisms. Hence t_1 and t_2 denote same morphism from Γ to A. Adequacy (Cor. 3.16) then implies that t_1 and t_2 are contextually equivalent.

Example 4.5. We list some properties provable using the logic. Except for the first property all proof details are in the extended version [9].

(i) For any $f : A \to B$ and $g : B \to C$ we have

$$(\mathsf{map}^{\mathsf{g}}\, f) \circ (\mathsf{map}^{\mathsf{g}}\, g) =_{\mathsf{Str}^{\mathsf{g}} \to \mathsf{Str}^{\mathsf{g}}} \mathsf{map}^{\mathsf{g}}(f \circ g).$$

Unfolding the definition of $\mathsf{map}^{\mathsf{g}}$ from Ex. 2.10(vi) and using β-rules and Prop. 4.3 we have $\mathsf{map}^{\mathsf{g}}\, f\, xs = f\,(\mathsf{hd}^{\mathsf{g}}\, xs) :: (\mathsf{next}(\mathsf{map}^{\mathsf{g}}\, f) \circledast (\mathsf{tl}^{\mathsf{g}}\, xs))$. Equality of functions is extensional so we have to prove

$$\Phi \triangleq \forall xs : \mathsf{Str}^{\mathsf{g}}, \mathsf{map}^{\mathsf{g}}\, f\,(\mathsf{map}^{\mathsf{g}}\, g\, xs) =_{\mathsf{Str}^{\mathsf{g}}} \mathsf{map}^{\mathsf{g}}(f \circ g)\, xs.$$

The proof is by Löb induction, so we assume $\triangleright \Phi$ and take $xs : \mathsf{Str}^{\mathsf{g}}$. Using the above property of $\mathsf{map}^{\mathsf{g}}$ we unfold $\mathsf{map}^{\mathsf{g}}\, f\,(\mathsf{map}^{\mathsf{g}}\, g\, xs)$ to

$$f\,(g\,(\mathsf{hd}^{\mathsf{g}}\, xs)) :: (\mathsf{next}(\mathsf{map}^{\mathsf{g}}\, f) \circledast ((\mathsf{next}(\mathsf{map}^{\mathsf{g}}\, g)) \circledast \mathsf{tl}^{\mathsf{g}}\, xs))$$

and we unfold $\mathsf{map}^{\mathsf{g}}(f \circ g)\, xs$ to $f\,(g\,(\mathsf{hd}^{\mathsf{g}}\, xs)) :: (\mathsf{next}(\mathsf{map}^{\mathsf{g}}(f \circ g)) \circledast \mathsf{tl}^{\mathsf{g}}\, xs)$. Since $\mathsf{Str}^{\mathsf{g}}$ is a total type there is a $xs' : \mathsf{Str}^{\mathsf{g}}$ such that $\mathsf{next}\, xs' = \mathsf{tl}^{\mathsf{g}}\, xs$. Using this and the rule for $\circledast$ we have

$$\mathsf{next}(\mathsf{map}^{\mathsf{g}}\, f) \circledast ((\mathsf{next}(\mathsf{map}^{\mathsf{g}}\, g)) \circledast \mathsf{tl}^{\mathsf{g}}\, xs) =_{\blacktriangleright \mathsf{Str}^{\mathsf{g}}} \mathsf{next}(\mathsf{map}^{\mathsf{g}}\, f(\mathsf{map}^{\mathsf{g}}\, g\, xs'))$$

and $\mathsf{next}(\mathsf{map}^{\mathsf{g}}(f \circ g)) \circledast \mathsf{tl}^{\mathsf{g}}\, xs =_{\blacktriangleright \mathsf{Str}^{\mathsf{g}}} \mathsf{next}(\mathsf{map}^{\mathsf{g}}(f \circ g)\, xs')$. From the induction hypothesis $\triangleright \Phi$ we have $\triangleright(\mathsf{map}^{\mathsf{g}}(f \circ g)\, xs' =_{\mathsf{Str}^{\mathsf{g}}} \mathsf{map}^{\mathsf{g}}\, f\,(\mathsf{map}^{\mathsf{g}}\, g\, xs'))$ and so rule $\mathrm{EQ}^{\triangleright}_{\mathsf{next}}$ concludes the proof.

(ii) We can also reason about acausal functions. For any $n : \mathbf{N}, f : \mathbf{N} \to \mathbf{N}$,

$$\mathsf{every2nd}(\mathsf{box}\,\iota.\,\mathsf{iterate}\,(\mathsf{next}\,f)\,n) =_{\mathsf{Str^g}} \mathsf{iterate}\,(\mathsf{next}\,f^2)\,n,$$

where f^2 is $\lambda m.f\,(f\,m)$. The proof again uses Löb induction.

(iii) Since our logic is higher-order we can state and prove very general properties, for instance the following general property of map

$$\forall P, Q : (\mathbf{N} \to \Omega), \forall f : \mathbf{N} \to \mathbf{N}, (\forall x : \mathbf{N}, P(x) \Rightarrow Q(f(x)))$$
$$\Rightarrow \forall xs : \mathsf{Str^g}, P_{\mathsf{Str^g}}(xs) \Rightarrow Q_{\mathsf{Str^g}}(\mathsf{map^g}\,f\,xs).$$

The proof illustrates the use of the property $\mathsf{lift} \circ \mathsf{next} = \triangleright$.

(iv) Given a closed term (we can generalise to terms in constant contexts) f of type $A \to B$ we have $\mathsf{box}\,f$ of type $\blacksquare(A \to B)$. Define $\mathcal{L}(f) = \mathsf{lim}(\mathsf{box}\,f)$ of type $\blacksquare A \to \blacksquare B$. For any closed term $f : A \to B$ and $x : \blacksquare A$ we can then prove $\mathsf{unbox}(\mathcal{L}(f)\,x) =_B f\,(\mathsf{unbox}\,x)$. Then using Prop. 4.2 we can, for instance, prove $\mathcal{L}(f \circ g) = \mathcal{L}(f) \circ \mathcal{L}(g)$.
For functions of arity k we define $\mathcal{L}_k$ using $\mathcal{L}$, and analogous properties hold, e.g. we have $\mathsf{unbox}(\mathcal{L}_2(f)\,x\,y) = f\,(\mathsf{unbox}\,x)\,(\mathsf{unbox}\,y)$, which allows us to transfer equalities proved for functions on guarded types to functions on $\blacksquare$'d types; see Sec. 5 for an example.

5 Behavioural Differential Equations in gλ

In this section we demonstrate the expressivity of our approach by showing how to construct solutions to behavioural differential equations [21] in gλ, and how to reason about such functions in Lgλ, rather than with bisimulation as is more traditional. These ideas are best explained via a simple example.

Supposing addition $+ : \mathbf{N} \to \mathbf{N} \to \mathbf{N}$ is given, then pointwise addition of streams, plus, can be defined by the following behavioural differential equation

$$\mathsf{hd}(\mathsf{plus}\,\sigma_1\,\sigma_2) = \mathsf{hd}\,\sigma_1 + \mathsf{hd}\,\sigma_2 \qquad \mathsf{tl}(\mathsf{plus}\,\sigma_1\,\sigma_2) = \mathsf{plus}(\mathsf{tl}\,\sigma_1)\,(\mathsf{tl}\,\sigma_2).$$

To define the solution to this behavioural differential equation in gλ, we first translate it to a function on guarded streams $\mathsf{plus^g} : \mathsf{Str^g} \to \mathsf{Str^g} \to \mathsf{Str^g}$, as

$$\mathsf{plus^g} \triangleq \mathsf{fix}\,\lambda f.\lambda s_1.\lambda s_2.(\mathsf{hd^g}\,s_1 + \mathsf{hd^g}\,s_2) :: (f \circledast (\mathsf{tl^g}\,s_1) \circledast (\mathsf{tl^g}\,s_2))$$

then define $\mathsf{plus} : \mathsf{Str} \to \mathsf{Str} \to \mathsf{Str}$ by $\mathsf{plus} = \mathcal{L}_2(\mathsf{plus^g})$. By Prop. 4.3 we have

$$\mathsf{plus^g} = \lambda s_1.\lambda s_2.(\mathsf{hd^g}\,s_1 + \mathsf{hd^g}\,s_2) :: ((\mathsf{next}\,\mathsf{plus^g}) \circledast (\mathsf{tl^g}\,s_1) \circledast (\mathsf{tl^g}\,s_2)). \qquad (1)$$

This definition of plus satisfies the specification given by the behavioural differential equation above. Let $\sigma_1, \sigma_2 : \mathsf{Str}$ and recall that $\mathsf{hd} = \mathsf{hd^g} \circ \lambda s.\,\mathsf{unbox}\,s$. Then use Ex. 4.5.(iv) and equality (1) to get $\mathsf{hd}(\mathsf{plus}\,\sigma_1\sigma_2) = \mathsf{hd}\,\sigma_1 + \mathsf{hd}\,\sigma_2$.

For tl we proceed similarly, also using that $\mathsf{tl^g}(\mathsf{unbox}\,\sigma) = \mathsf{next}(\mathsf{unbox}(\mathsf{tl}\,\sigma))$ which can be proved using the β-rule for box and the η-rule for next.

Since $\mathsf{plus}^{\mathsf{g}}$ is defined via guarded recursion we can reason about it with Löb induction, for example to prove that it is commutative. Ex. 4.5.(iv) and Prop. 4.2 then immediately give that plus on *coinductive* streams Str is commutative.

Once we have defined $\mathsf{plus}^{\mathsf{g}}$ we can use it when defining other functions on streams, for instance stream multiplication $\otimes$ which is specified by equations

$$\mathsf{hd}(\sigma_1 \otimes \sigma_2) = (\mathsf{hd}\,\sigma_1) \cdot (\mathsf{hd}\,\sigma_2) \quad \mathsf{tl}(\sigma_1 \otimes \sigma_2) = (\rho(\mathsf{hd}\,\sigma_1) \otimes (\mathsf{tl}\,\sigma_2)) \oplus ((\mathsf{tl}\,\sigma_1) \otimes \sigma_2)$$

where $\rho(n)$ is a stream with head n and tail a stream of zeros, and $\cdot$ is multiplication of natural numbers, and using $\oplus$ as infix notation for plus. We can define $\otimes^{\mathsf{g}} : \mathsf{Str}^{\mathsf{g}} \to \mathsf{Str}^{\mathsf{g}} \to \mathsf{Str}^{\mathsf{g}}$ by $\otimes^{\mathsf{g}} \triangleq$

$$\begin{aligned}&\mathsf{fix}\,\lambda f.\lambda s_1.\lambda s_2.\,((\mathsf{hd}^{\mathsf{g}}\,s_1) \cdot (\mathsf{hd}^{\mathsf{g}}\,s_2)) :: \\ &\qquad (\mathsf{next}\,\mathsf{plus}^{\mathsf{g}} \circledast (f \circledast \mathsf{next}\,\iota^{\mathsf{g}}(\mathsf{hd}^{\mathsf{g}}\,s_1) \circledast \mathsf{tl}^{\mathsf{g}}\,s_2) \circledast (f \circledast \mathsf{tl}^{\mathsf{g}}\,s_1 \circledast \mathsf{next}\,s_2))\end{aligned}$$

then define $\otimes = \mathcal{L}_2\,(\otimes^{\mathsf{g}})$. It can be shown that the function $\otimes$ so defined satisfies the two defining equations above. Note that the guarded $\mathsf{plus}^{\mathsf{g}}$ is used to define $\otimes^{\mathsf{g}}$, so our approach is *modular* in the sense of [17].

The example above generalises, as we can show that any solution to a behavioural differential equation in **Set** can be obtained via guarded recursion together with $\mathcal{L}_k$. The formal statement is somewhat technical and can be found in the extended version [9].

6 Discussion

Following Nakano [19], the ► modality has been used as type-former for a number of λ-calculi for guarded recursion. Nakano's calculus and some successors [15,22,2] permit only *causal* functions. The closest such work to ours is that of Abel and Vezzosi [2], but due to a lack of destructor for ► their (strong) normalisation result relies on a somewhat artificial operational semantics where the number of nexts that can be reduced under is bounded by some fixed natural number.

Atkey and McBride's extension of such calculi to acausal functions [4] forms the basis of this paper. We build on their work by (aside from various minor changes such as eliminating the need to work modulo first-class type isomorphisms) introducing normalising operational semantics, an adequacy proof with respect to the topos of trees, and a program logic.

An alterative approach to type-based productivity guarantees are *sized types*, introduced by Hughes et al [14] and now extensively developed, for example integrated into a variant of System F_ω [1]. Our approach offers some advantages, such as adequate denotational semantics, and a notion of program proof without appeal to dependent types, but extensions with realistic language features (e.g. following Møgelberg [18]) clearly need to be investigated.

Acknowledgements. We gratefully acknowledge our discussions with Andreas Abel, Tadeusz Litak, Stefan Milius, Rasmus Møgelberg, Filip Sieczkowski, and Andrea Vezzosi, and the comments of the reviewers. This research was supported in part by the ModuRes Sapere Aude Advanced Grant from The Danish

Council for Independent Research for the Natural Sciences (FNU). Aleš Bizjak is supported in part by a Microsoft Research PhD grant.

References

1. Abel, A., Pientka, B.: Wellfounded recursion with copatterns: A unified approach to termination and productivity. In: ICFP, pp. 185–196 (2013)
2. Abel, A., Vezzosi, A.: A formalized proof of strong normalization for guarded recursive types. In: APLAS, pp. 140–158 (2014)
3. Appel, A.W., Melliès, P.A., Richards, C.D., Vouillon, J.: A very modal model of a modern, major, general type system. In: POPL, pp. 109–122 (2007)
4. Atkey, R., McBride, C.: Productive coprogramming with guarded recursion. In: ICFP, pp. 197–208 (2013)
5. Bierman, G.M., de Paiva, V.C.: On an intuitionistic modal logic. Studia Logica 65(3), 383–416 (2000)
6. Birkedal, L., Møgelberg, R.E., Schwinghammer, J., Støvring, K.: First steps in synthetic guarded domain theory: step-indexing in the topos of trees. LMCS 8(4) (2012)
7. Birkedal, L., Schwinghammer, J., Støvring, K.: A metric model of lambda calculus with guarded recursion. In: FICS, pp. 19–25 (2010)
8. Bizjak, A., Birkedal, L., Miculan, M.: A model of countable nondeterminism in guarded type theory. In: Dowek, G. (ed.) RTA-TLCA 2014. LNCS, vol. 8560, pp. 108–123. Springer, Heidelberg (2014)
9. Clouston, R., Bizjak, A., Grathwohl, H.B., Birkedal, L.: Programming and reasoning with guarded recursion for coinductive types. arXiv:1501.02925 (2015)
10. Clouston, R., Goré, R.: Sequent calculus in the topos of trees. In: Pitts, A. (ed.) FoSSaCS 2015. LNCS, vol. 9034, pp. 133–147. Springer, Heidelberg (2015)
11. Coquand, T.: Infinite objects in type theory. In: Barendregt, H., Nipkow, T. (eds.) TYPES 1993. LNCS, vol. 806, pp. 62–78. Springer, Heidelberg (1994)
12. Endrullis, J., Grabmayer, C., Hendriks, D.: Mix-automatic sequences. In: Fields Workshop on Combinatorics on Words, contributed talk (2013)
13. Giménez, E.: Codifying guarded definitions with recursive schemes. In: Smith, J., Dybjer, P., Nordström, B. (eds.) TYPES 1994. LNCS, vol. 996, pp. 39–59. Springer, Heidelberg (1995)
14. Hughes, J., Pareto, L., Sabry, A.: Proving the correctness of reactive systems using sized types. In: POPL, pp. 410–423 (1996)
15. Krishnaswami, N.R., Benton, N.: Ultrametric semantics of reactive programs. In: LICS, pp. 257–266 (2011)
16. McBride, C., Paterson, R.: Applicative programming with effects. J. Funct. Programming 18(1), 1–13 (2008)
17. Milius, S., Moss, L.S., Schwencke, D.: Abstract GSOS rules and a modular treatment of recursive definitions. LMCS 9(3) (2013)
18. Møgelberg, R.E.: A type theory for productive coprogramming via guarded recursion. In: CSL-LICS (2014)
19. Nakano, H.: A modality for recursion. In: LICS, pp. 255–266 (2000)
20. Prawitz, D.: Natural Deduction: A Proof-Theoretical Study. Dover Publ. (1965)
21. Rutten, J.J.M.M.: Behavioural differential equations: A coinductive calculus of streams, automata, and power series. Theor. Comput. Sci. 308(1-3), 1–53 (2003)
22. Severi, P.G., de Vries, F.J.J.: Pure type systems with corecursion on streams: from finite to infinitary normalisation. In: ICFP, pp. 141–152 (2012)

The Computational Contents of Ramified Corecurrence

Daniel Leivant[1] and Ramyaa Ramyaa[2]

[1] Indiana University Bloomington
leivant@indiana.edu
[2] Wesleyan University
ramyaa@wesleyan.edu

Abstract. The vast power of iterated recurrence is tamed by data ramification: if a function over words is definable by ramified recurrence and composition, then it is feasible, i.e. computable in polynomial time, i.e. any computation using the first n input symbols can have at most $p(n)$ distinct configurations, for some polynomial p. Here we prove a dual result for coinductive data: if a function over streams is definable by ramified *corecurrence,* then any computation to obtain the first n symbols of the output can have at most $p(n)$ distinct configurations, for some polynomial p. The latter computation is by multi-cursor finite state transducer on streams.

A consequence is that a function over *finite* streams is definable by ramified corecurrence *iff* it is Turing-computable in logarithmic space. Such corecursive definitions over finite streams are of practical interest, because large finite data is normally used as a knowledge base to be consumed, rather than as recurrence template. Thus, we relate a syntactically restricted computation model, amenable to static analysis, to a major complexity class for streaming algorithms.

1 Introduction

Implicit computational complexity relates resource-based complexity classes of functions and languages to declarative paradigms, restricted along various conceptual parameters, such as functionality, linearity, repetition, and flow control. The theoretical and practical benefits of this research abound, notably in leading to static analysis of the computational complexity of declarative programs.

A well known approach along these lines is *data ramification*, also known as *tiering*. Here one construes data as coming in varying computational strengths. For instance, querying a large database might be feasible, but using it to drive a recurrence would not. This is reflected in a requirement that a function's recurrence argument should be computationally stronger than its output, i.e. at a higher tier. This approach was used to characterize major complexity classes such as PTime [1,9], and PSpace [13].

In [14] we initiated an exploration of ramified declarative programming over coinductive data, such as streams, rather than inductive data, such as words.

A. Pitts (Ed.): FOSSACS 2015, LNCS 9034, pp. 422–435, 2015.
DOI: 10.1007/978-3-662-46678-0_27

We showed that functions defined by ramified corecurrence and composition using just *two tiers* are feasible, in the sense of being computable by finite state transducers (with cursor jump). Moreover, such transducers can be simulated by Turing-transducers over streams that operate in logarithmic space with respect to the *output,* that is: to compute the n-th entry of the output requires auxiliary computation space of size $O(\log n)$.

The analysis of corecurrence ramified into an arbitrary number of tiers requires a more foundational approach. We introduce here notions of locality, weak-locality and continuity for machines over streams, and show that a function defined by ramified corecurrence and composition, with output tier t, is computable by a finite-state transducer (with jumps) which is continuous (with polynomial moduli of continuity) in arguments of tiers $< t$, weakly-local in arguments of tier t, and local in arguments of tiers $> t$. These properties are used to show that if a function f is defined by corecurrence from step-functions that are so defined, then f is computable by a continuous finite-state transducer (with jump).

Our results reveal a striking duality between ramified recurrence and ramified corecurrence. If a function f over words is definable by ramified recurrence then it is polynomial time or — equivalently — any computation of f that uses the first n input symbols has at most $p(n)$ distinct configurations (p a polynomial). Dually, if a function over streams is definable by ramified *corecurrence,* then any computation to obtain the first n symbols of the output can have at most $p(n)$ distinct configurations (p a polynomial). There is, however, an asymmetry: read-only inputs are given, whereas write-only outputs are not. corecurrence the configurations must, in addition, be of size logarithmic in the n, because the input is given, $p(n)$ entries input entries that might occur in configurations are determined merely by their address. This contrasts with recurrence: the output is not given, and so the $p(n)$ output entries that might occur in configurations may well be different.

These results have further consequences for functions over *finite* streams: such a function is definable by ramified corecurrence (in any number of tiers) iff it is Turing-computable (as a function over words) in logarithmic space, in the usual sense. Referring to finite streams may seem at first blush to be an oxymoron. Indeed, finite data is commonly identified with textual data, or more generally data generated inductively from constant values by iterating finite closure rules. A salient property of inductive data of that sort is their use to drive the recurrence schema associated with the corresponding generative process; for example, the recurrence (i.e. "primitive recursive") schema for the natural numbers. However, the increasing relevance of finite, but very large data, suggests an alternative viewpoint of finite data, that emphasizes access to data-elements. Viewed from that angle, it becomes relevant and interesting to consider finite instances of coinductive data. In particular, *finite boolean streams,* are extensionally similar to words, but their computational behavior is coinductive: while a computation over words gets as input complete words and produces complete words as output, a computation over streams produces its output piecemeal, using pieces of its input(s). Indeed, important applications that involve computing over very large data are modeled better by streams than by words (see for example [15,6]). Thus, ramified corecurrence lends credence to the importance and stability of log-space computing over large data, which is what all of us do daily in our use of the internet.

In summary, our results elucidate the foundational inter-relations between coinductive data, ramification, finite-state stream-transducers, and log-space computing, while providing a static-analysis method for establishing the feasibility of functional programs over streams.

2 Finite Transducers on Streams

2.1 Jumping Finite Transducers

Fix a finite alphabet $\Sigma = \{a_0, a_1, \ldots, a_\ell\}$ ($\ell \geq 2$). The set of *streams over* Σ, denoted $S(\Sigma)$ or simply S when Σ is clear, is defined coinductively by the closure condition:

$$\sigma \in S \implies (\exists a \in \Sigma)\ (\exists \tau \in S)\ \sigma = a : \tau$$

The basic machine model for computing functions from streams to streams is the *finite stream transducer (FT)* over an alphabet Σ. A FT reads its input stream one-way at multiple cursors ("heads") and writes its output stream one-way forward. The read is optional (i.e. read ε is possible), and so is the write. We also consider a less restrictive variant of FTs, the *jumping finite transducer (JFT)*. Here a cursor that scans the input may be re-positioned ("jump") to the current position of another cursor. Neither FTs nor JFTs can detect coincidence between two cursors. Using such detection, JFTs could simulate two-way cursors on the input, and consequently be Turing complete (on infinite streams).

Formally, an *r-ary JFT over Σ-streams* F consists of a finite set Q of states, a distinguished *start state* $s \in Q$, a finite set $C = \{c_1, \ldots, c_k\}$ of *cursors*, an initial *cursor configuration* $\gamma : C \to \{1, .., r\}$, a *transition* partial-function, and an *output* partial function. The transition partial-function

$$\delta : Q \times (C \to \Sigma) \quad \rightharpoonup \quad Q \times (C \to M)$$

refers to the set of *moves* $M = C \cup \{+\}$. When $\delta(q, \kappa) = \langle p, \alpha \rangle$ we also write $q \xrightarrow{\kappa(\alpha)} p$. The intent is: an argument $\kappa : C \to \Sigma$ gives the source values of the cursors; an action $\alpha : C \to M$ instructs each cursor c to jump to the position of cursor $\alpha(c)$, if $\alpha(c) \in C$, or to step forward if $\alpha(c) = +$.

The output partial-function

$$\mathcal{O} : Q \times (C \to \Sigma) \quad \rightharpoonup \quad \Sigma$$

indicates the output symbol, if any, that F emits.

To give the formal semantics of JFTs we refer to *configurations*, each consisting of a state and a mapping $\pi : C \to [1..r] \times \mathbb{N}$, that assigns to each cursor c a stream index $i \in [1..r]$ and an address (in binary) on that stream. Note that configurations are finite objects, and do not refer to input or output stream as a whole.

Let *Cfg* be the set of configurations. The *initial configuration* is $\beta_0 = \langle s, \pi_0 \rangle$, where $\pi_0(c) = \langle \gamma(c), 0 \rangle$.

Given infinite streams $\sigma_1, \dots, \sigma_r$ as inputs, δ determines a partial *Yield* function

$$Yld_{F,\tilde{\sigma}} : Cfg \rightharpoonup Cfg$$

that maps a configuration to its successor configuration, as described informally above.[1] When $\beta' = Yld_{F,\tilde{\sigma}}(\beta)$ we also write $\beta \Longrightarrow_{F,\tilde{\sigma}} \beta'$. Thus, each configuration β generates a (finite or infinite) stream of configurations,

$$T(\beta) = \beta_1 : \beta_2 : \cdots$$

dubbed the *trace for* β, where β_1 is β and $\beta_i \Longrightarrow_{F,\tilde{\sigma}} \beta_{i+1}$. The trace $T(\beta)$ is finite when δ is undefined for its last configuration.

The output function $\mathcal{O}$ determines, for input streams $\tilde{\sigma}$, a *partial* function

$$Outbit_{F,\tilde{\sigma}} : Cfg \rightharpoonup \Sigma$$

that maps some configuration to symbols $a \in \Sigma$. The *output stream* of F for inputs $\tilde{\sigma}$ is obtained from collecting into a stream the output symbols emitted by $Outbit_{F,\tilde{\sigma}}$ for the trace of F for $\tilde{\sigma}$.

2.2 Composition of JFTs

We consider functions over the two base type Σ (the alphabet symbols) and S (streams over Σ). Consider the schema of typed composition of functions. $f(\tilde{x}) = d(e_1(\tilde{x}), \dots, e_k(\tilde{x}))$. Using auxiliary variables, this can be reduced to the schema $f(\tilde{x}) = d(e(\tilde{x}), \tilde{x})$.

Theorem 1. *If d, e are JFT-computable functions over Σ and S, then so is $f(x_1, \dots x_r) = d(e(\tilde{x}), \tilde{x})$.*

Proof. Suppose $d : S \times \tau_1 \times \cdots \times \tau_r \to S$ is computed by a JFT D, and $e : \tau_1 \cdots \times \tau_r \to S$ is computed by a JFT E, where the τ_i's are S or Σ.

We construct a JFT F to compute f, using a copy of D, as well as a copy E_c of E for each cursor c that D maintains on its first (i.e. composition-) argument, which we take to be x_0. Each such copy is intended to represent E producing the n-th entry of $e(\tilde{x})$, where n is the current position of the cursor c. Accordingly, F also maintains internally the value $\sigma_c \in \Sigma$ at that position.

F starts by initializing each σ_c to the first output symbol of E. It then moves on to simulate D. Where D would step forward a cursor c on D's first argument F runs E_c until the next output symbol σ is produced, leaves the internal configuration of E_c as reached, and updates σ_c to σ. Where D would read the value at c of its i-th input, F supplies σ_c as that value. Where D would relocate cursor c to the position of cursor c', F sets the configuration of E_c (internal states, cursor positions, and σ_c) to the configuration of $E_{c'}$. □

[1] We use tilde for vectors.

2.3 Locality and Continuity Properties of JFTs

Equational computing systems, such as the primitive corecursive functions, permit effortless copying of an input to the output, an operation which a JFT must carry out by an infinite entry-by-entry transfer. To better reflect the ease of equational copying we consider a variant of JFTs with an added operation $\mathbf{Go}_c$, whose semantics is: *The output from this point on is the stream starting with the current position of cursor c.* No computation power is added, of course, since each invocation of $\mathbf{Go}_c$ can be replaced by a trivial loop.

We say that a JFT F is *local* on an argument (i.e. input) x if there is a bound b (uniform with respect to all remaining inputs) such that F does not move cursors beyond x's b-th entry, and does not invoke a $\mathbf{Go}_c$ operation for any cursor c residing on x. F is *weakly-local* on x if it is local as above, except that F's output is obtained by a **Go** for some cursor on x (necessarily abiding by the locality condition, i.e. at a position $\leq b$). Note that this violates locality: sufficiently far-out entries of the output will depend on far-out entries of x, but in a very simple way: by identity. In either case, we refer to b as the *bound* of F on x.

We say that F is *continuous on x, with modulus $\omega : \mathbb{N} \rightarrow \mathbb{N}$*, if for each $n \geq 1$, while calculating its n-th output symbol F does not move cursors beyond the $\omega(n)$-th entry of x. We say that F *has degree k on argument y* if it has a modulus ω of order $O(n^k)$. F is *polynomial* on argument y if it has degree k on y for some k.

The next Lemma shows how the locality and continuity properties of functions determine those properties for their composition.

Lemma 1. *Assume the premises of Theorem 1, and let F be the JFT defined in its proof. Let y be one of the variables $x_1, \ldots, x_r$.*

1. *If D is local on x_0, or E is local on y, then F has the same property on y as D on y: local, weakly-local, or continuous with modulus ω.*
2. *If D has modulus ω_0 on x_0 and ω_1 on y, whereas E has modulus ω_E on y, then F has modulus $\max(\omega_0 \circ \omega_E, \omega_1)$ on y.*
   In particular, if ω_E and ω_0 are both constants, i.e. D is weakly-local on x_0 and E is weakly-local on y, and if D has modulus ω on y, then F has a modulus of order $O(\omega)$ on y.

Proof.

1. If D is local on z then F needs to access y via E only for a fixed finite set of entries of E's output, and since E is continuous, that means a fixed number of positions of y. On the other hand, if E is local on y, then F access y via E only for a fixed finite set of entries, regardless of D's queries for the output of E. In either case, the use of y by F is dominated by the direct access of D to y.
2. To calculate its n-th output symbol F reads $\omega_y(n)$ symbols of y when accessing y directly. It also needs to identify the first $\omega_z(n)$ symbols of the output of E, which calls for reading $\omega_E(\omega_z(n))$ entries of y.

□

3 Corecurrence

3.1 Stream Functions Defined by Corecurrence

We continue to refer to an alphabet $\Sigma = \{a_0, a_1, \ldots, a_\ell\}$ and to the set S of streams over Σ. The scheme of corecurrence over streams provides a definition of a function $f : S^r \to S$ from given functions $h : S^r \to \Sigma$ and $g_i : S^r \to S^r$ $(i = 1..r)$:

$$f(\tilde{x}) = h(\tilde{x}) : f(\tilde{g}(\tilde{x})) \qquad (1)$$

More generally, a function-vector $\tilde{f} = (f_1, \ldots, f_m)$ is defined from functions $\tilde{h}$, $\tilde{g}_1, \ldots, \tilde{g}_m$:

$$f_i(\tilde{x}) = h_i(\tilde{x}) : f_{j_i}(\tilde{g}_i(\tilde{x})) \qquad (2)$$

The functions $\tilde{h}$ are the *head-functions*, and $\tilde{g}_i$ $(i = 1..r)$ the *step-functions.*

If $p : \{1..m\} \to \{1..m\}$ is defined by $p(i) = j_i$, then Equation (2) can be written $f_{p(i)}(\tilde{g}_i(\tilde{x}))$. In most cases of interest p is a permutation, but it need not be. For $\tilde{h} : S^r \to \Sigma$, $\tilde{g}_i : S^r \to S^r$, and p as above we write $\mathbf{corec}^{r,m,p}[\tilde{h}, \tilde{g}_1, \ldots, \tilde{g}_m]$ for the function tuple $\tilde{f} : S^r \to S^r$ defined as above. We omit the indices r, m, p when in no danger of confusion.

Note that the schema (2) requires that each cycle generate an output symbol. This is natural, because the focus of coinductive computing is generating the output, rather than consuming the input as in the scheme of recurrence (i.e. primitive-recursion). Just as recurrence consumes one input element at each computation cycle, thereby guaranteeing termination of the computation with a finite output, the scheme of corecurrence generates one output element in each cycle, thereby guaranteeing a productive (i.e. infinite) output. We comment below on an alternative, "lazy," variant of corecurrence, where the production of an output symbol is optional.

3.2 Primitive Corecursive Stream Functions

Definition 1. *The* initial stream-valued functions *are:*

- *Projections functions* $P^n_i : S^n \to S$ $(1 \leq i \leq n)$, *defined by* $P^n_i(x_1, \ldots, x_n) = x_i$.
- *The tail function* $tl : S \to S$, *defined by* $tl(a : \sigma) = \sigma$.
- *The branching function* $B : \Sigma \times S^\ell \to S$, *defined by* $B(a, y_1, \ldots, y_\ell) =$ **if** $a = a_i$ **then** y_i.

The initial symbol-valued functions *are:*

- *Projection functions* $Q^n_i : \Sigma^n \to \Sigma$ $(1 \leq i \leq n)$, *defined by* $Q^n_i(x_1, \ldots, x_n) = x_i$.
- *For each* $a \in \Sigma$ *a nullary function* a.
- *The head function* $hd : S \to \Sigma$.
- *The branching function* $L : \Sigma^{\ell+1} \to \Sigma$, *defined by* $L(a, z_1, \ldots, z_\ell) =$ **if** $a = a_i$ **then** z_i.

The primitive corecursive (p.c.) stream functions *are generated from the initial functions above using type-correct composition and the scheme of corecurrence 2. That is, a function over streams and letters is p.c. when it is the denotation of a term of the typed-lambda calculus with base types Σ and S, and constants for the initial functions and the corecursion operator above.*

3.3 Locality and Continuity Under Corecurrence

Suppose

$$f(x_1 \ldots, x_r) = h(\tilde{x}) : f(g_1(\tilde{x}), \ldots, g_r(\tilde{x})) \tag{3}$$

with each g_i computed by a JFT G_i and h by H. In general we cannot expect f to be computed by a JFT: if it were, then it would be Turing-computable in logspace [14], but Example [14, §2.3(vi)] shows that it need not be.

However, our next Lemma shows that if the arguments $x_1, \ldots, x_r$ are such that G_j is weakly local on x_j and local on $x_{j+1}, \ldots, x_r$, then a finite amount of information about $\tilde{g}^{[n]}(\tilde{x})$,[2] of the same size for all n, permits the computation of $\tilde{g}^{[n+1]}(\tilde{x})$. This makes it possible to define a JFT which is continuous on all arguments.

Lemma 2. *Suppose $f = \mathbf{corec}[h, \tilde{g}, \tilde{y}]$, as in 3. Suppose the corecursive arguments fall into q disjoint sub-lists $\tilde{x}_i$, where $\tilde{x}_i = \langle x_{i1}, \ldots, x_{ir_i} \rangle$, and that g_{ij} is computed by a JFT G_{ij} and h is computed by a JFT H so that:*

1. *Each G_{ij} is continuous on $\tilde{x}_m$ for $m < i$, with modulus ω_{ij} of order $n^{d_{ij}}$;*
2. *each G_{ij} is weakly-local on arguments $\tilde{x}_i$ (with bound b_i);*
3. *each G_{ij} is local on $\tilde{x}_m$ where $m > i$ (with bound b_i);*
4. *all cursor jumps and* **Go** *operations are within the same group: when G_{ij} jumps a cursor or fires a* **Go***, it must involve cursors on arguments of group i.*

Then f is computed by a JFT F which is continuous on all corecursive arguments, with as modulus a finite composition of depth $\leq r$ of the moduli ω_{im}.

Proof. Without loss of generality we assume that all b_i's are identical (and denoted b), and that $q = r$, with each group A_i consisting just of x_i. We can thus write G_i for G_{i1}. We also assume that $\omega_{i,i+p} = \omega_{i,i+1} \circ \omega_{i+1,i+2} \circ \cdots \circ \omega_{i+p-1,i+p}$, that is, the modulus of G_i on the $i+p$-th input is the composition of the one-step moduli. The proof of the general case only requires more tedious detail.

Define the *i-th cache* for a stream $\tilde{g}^{[n]}(\tilde{x})$ to be the list C_i of the first $\omega_{ir}(b)$ entries of $(\tilde{g}^{[n]}(\tilde{x}))_i$. The *cache* for $\tilde{g}[n]n(\tilde{x})$ is the list $C_1; \cdots; C_r$, $i = 1, \ldots, r$.

We now describe a JFT F that computes f, and is continuous on all its input. By assumption (4) of the Lemma, if an update of the cache invokes a **Go** by some G_i, then it must be on its i-th argument, and since G_i is weakly-local on that argument, it is invoked to generate a tail of x_i. When this operation is

[2] We write $\tilde{g}^{[n]}$ for the n-th iteration of $\tilde{g}$.

iterated, it therefore remains true that a **Go** is triggered by G_i to generate a tail of x_i.

G_i is weakly-local on its i-th argument; so when applied to $\tilde{g}^{[n]}(\tilde{x})$, G_i triggers a **Go** on $(\tilde{g}^{[n]}(\tilde{x}))_i$. By induction on n it follows that every such **Go** yields a stream which is a tail of the original i-th input x_1. F will use a reserved cursor on x_i to record that position. We refer to that cursor as the *i-th pointer.*

F calculates successively for $n = 1, 2, \ldots$ the caches and pointers for $\tilde{g}^{[n]}(\tilde{x})$. Each cycle concludes with F invoking H to calculate $h(\tilde{g}^{[n]}(\tilde{x}))$: since H needs only the first b entries of each of its inputs, and $\omega_{iq}(n) \geq n$ for all i, H needs only use the cache for that calculation.

F starts by initializing the cache for i to the first $\omega_{ir}(b)$ entries of x_i, and the pointer for i to the head entry of x_i.

F then proceeds to calculate the caches and pointers for $\tilde{g}^{[n+1]}(\tilde{x})$, from the caches and pointers for $\tilde{g}^{[n]}(\tilde{x})$, as follows. To calculate the first ω_{ir} entries of $(\tilde{g}^{[n+1]}(\tilde{x}))_i$ F invokes G_i. This calculation uses up to $\omega_{ji}(b)$ entries of $(\tilde{g}^{[n]}(\tilde{x}))_j$ for $j < i$, and up to b entries of $(\tilde{g}^{[n]}(\tilde{x}))_j$ for $j \geq i$. These are all available in caches for $\tilde{g}^{[n]}(\tilde{x})$, by our assumptions about the moduli $\omega_{\ldots}$. As noted, G_i finally triggers a **Go** on its i-th argument, namely $(\tilde{g}^{[n]}(\tilde{x}))_j$, by a cursor at position $p \leq b$. F thus steps its i-th pointer p times.

Clearly, the JFT F is continuous on its corecurrence arguments. □

4 Ramified Corecurrence

4.1 Computing with Ramified Data

Ramified recurrence [2,9] is based on a distinction between tiers (i.e. operational levels) of data. Inductive data of tiers t supports recurrence of (possibly parametrized) functions between data of lower tier. A consequence is that a function defined by recurrence on data of tier t has output of tier $< t$, thereby blocking the self-feeding of the output into the recurrence position, as would be the case in defining the iterate of a tier-lowering function g, $f(n) = g^{[[n]]}(\mathtt{0})$ by the recurrence $f(\mathtt{s}(x)) = g(f(x))$. Intuitively, the generative process leading up to the recurrence argument has a higher "energy level" than the function's output.

Dually, *ramified corecurrence,* requires that the output tier of a corecursive function is higher than the tiers of its inputs. Intuitively, this is because the decomposition of the output requires greater energy than the decomposition of the arguments. The duality between inductive and coinductive data is brought out in ramified second order logic [16]. Here one ramifies set variables, and restrict the instantiation of a universal set quantifiers: if X is a set variable of tier t, then formula $\forall X^t\ \varphi[X]$ can be instantiated to a set-definition $\lambda z.\varphi$ only when the formula φ does not refer to quantified set-variables of tier $\geq t$ or to free set variables of tier $> t$. In particular, this restriction blocks impredicative set-existence (Comprehension).

Referring in the ramified context to second-order definitions of inductive data using $\forall$ over sets, it follows that recurrence is admissible only if it is ramified. Dually, given that coinductive data is definable using $\exists$ over sets, corecurrence is admissible only if it is ramified in the sense above. See e.g. [14] for a more detailed discussion.

4.2 Ramified Corecurrence

To formally convey the notion of ramified corecurrence, we posit copies S_i $(i \geq 0)$ of the set S of Σ-streams, dubbed *tiers*. We can construe these as disjoint base types, in addition to the base type Σ.

As usual, we give rules for typing judgments of the form $\Gamma \vdash e : \tau$, where Γ is a type environment, e an expression and τ a type. We write Γ, Γ' for the union $\Gamma \cup \Gamma'$, which is implicitly assumed to be legal (i.e. without multiple types assigned to the same variable). Arrows associate to the right. Since we do not deal with higher types, our type environments will refer only to arrow-free types. The type system is given in the following table. The main points to keep in mind are these:

1. Each stream comes with a *tier*, which conveys its computational strength as input for a corecursive definition. Symbols $a \in \Sigma$ are not classified into tiers.
2. Ramified corecurrence defines a function from inputs of various tiers, to an output at a tier that majorizes them all. As explained above, a higher tier means here weaker computation power, so ramified corecurrence degrades the computation power of its arguments, by using them.
3. Composition is typed as usual, which implies here that it respects tiers.

Type system RC for the primitive corecursive functions

Underlying alphabet: $\Sigma = \{a_0, a_1, \ldots, a_\ell\}$.

Generic lambda rules

$$\frac{}{\Gamma \vdash x : \tau} \; (x : \tau \text{ in } \Gamma)$$

$$\frac{\Gamma, x : \tau \vdash E : \sigma}{\Gamma \vdash \lambda x.E : \tau \to \sigma} \qquad \frac{\Gamma \vdash E : \tau \to \sigma \quad \Gamma' \vdash F : \tau}{\Gamma, \Gamma' \vdash E(F) : \sigma}$$

$$\frac{\Gamma_j \vdash E_j : \tau_j \;\; (j = 0, 1)}{\Gamma_0, \Gamma_1 \vdash \langle E_0, E_1 \rangle : \tau_0 \times \tau_1} \qquad \frac{\Gamma \vdash E : \tau_0 \times \tau_1}{\Gamma \vdash \pi_j(E) : \tau_j} \; (j = 0, 1)$$

Initial functions

$$\overline{\vdash P^n_k : S_{i_1} \times \cdots \times S_{i_n} \rightarrow S_{i_k}}$$

$$\overline{\vdash \boldsymbol{\varepsilon} : S_j}$$

$$\overline{\vdash tl : S_j \rightarrow S_j}$$

$$\overline{\vdash B : \Sigma \times S_j^{\ell} \rightarrow S_j}$$

$$\overline{\vdash a : \Sigma} \qquad (a \in \Sigma)$$

$$\overline{\vdash hd : S_j \rightarrow \Sigma}$$

$$\overline{\vdash L : \Sigma^{\ell+1} \rightarrow \Sigma}$$

Corecurrence

If τ is a product of r base types,
and is of tier $i > 0$ where $i < j$, then

$$\frac{\Gamma \vdash h : \tau \rightarrow \Sigma^m \quad \Gamma' \vdash g : (\tau \rightarrow \tau)^m}{\Gamma, \Gamma' \vdash \mathbf{corec}^{r,m,p}[h, g] : \tau \rightarrow S_j^m}$$

4.3 The Computational Contents of Ramified Corecurrence

Theorem 2. *If a primitive-corecursive function f is defined by a term $\mathbf{t} : S_{i_1} \times \cdots \times S_{i_r} \rightarrow S_j$ in the type system* **RT***, then f is computable by a JFT F. Moreover, F is local on each argument of tier $> j$, weakly-local on each argument of tier S_j, and continuous with a polynomial modulus on each argument of tier $< j$.*

Also, if a symbol-valued function is definable by a term $\mathbf{t} : S_{i_1} \times \cdots \times S_{i_r} \rightarrow \Sigma$, then it is local on all arguments.

Proof. The proof proceeds by induction on the typing derivation of $\mathbf{t}$ in **RT**. The base cases are straightforward. The induction step for composition is given by Lemma 1, and the step for ramified corecurrence by Lemma 2. □

4.4 Characterization of Ramified Corecurrence

The schema (1) requires that each computation cycle generate an output symbol. The schema of *lazy corecurrence* relaxes this requirement, using *test functions* k_i to indicate whether or not it is triggered:

$$f_i(\tilde{x}) = \begin{cases} f_i(\tilde{x}) & \text{if } hd(k(\tilde{x})) = \varepsilon \\ f_j(\tilde{g}_i(\tilde{x})) & \text{otherwise} \end{cases} \tag{4}$$

This relaxation is useful for simulation of machine models, such as JFT, where computation steps need not always emit an output symbol. Indeed,

Theorem 3. [14, Proposition 4.1] *If a function over streams is computed by a JFT then it is definable from the initial functions using composition and lazy corecurrence.*

However, lazy corecurrence goes counter the very rationale of corecurrence. The point of the schema of recurrence (i.e. primitive recursion) is that it consumes its input, thereby guaranteeing termination. Dually, the point of corecurrence is that it builds its output, thereby guaranteeing productiveness. We might, for instance, consider a schema of "lazy recurrence", where the consumption of the input is optional; the result would simply be equational programs in the style of Herbrand-Gödel [8], i.e. a Turing-complete computation model. Lazy corecurrence has a similar effect for computing over streams: it captures Turing computability over functions of type $\mathbb{N} \to \Sigma$.

A drastic ramification of the definition into two tiers, reduces the computational power to that of a JFT [14], but the class of functions definable this way is not closed under composition.

Lazy corecurrence can be represented by our standard ("strict") corecurrence, by fixing a reserved symbol, say e, to stand for the "empty" output-symbol of a lazy-corecurrence. The intended output stream σ is then obtained from the actual output τ by a *collapse* operation, that erases all occurrences of e in τ. This representation is less trifling than may first seem: it keeps a record of computational resources, which is useful for function composition.

Theorem 4. *Let f be a function over streams. The following are equivalent.*

1. *f is definable by 2-tier ramified lazy corecurrence.*
2. *f is the collapse of a function definable by (all tier) ramified corecurrence.*
3. *f is computable by a JFT.*

Proof. <u>(1) implies (2)</u> trivially.

<u>(2) implies (3)</u>: Suppose f is the collapse of a function g defined by ramified corecurrence. By Theorem 2 g is computed by some JFT M, and so f is computed by the composition of M with a finite state transducer that erases all occurrences of e. By Theorem 1 it follows that f is computed by a JFT.

<u>(3) implies (1)</u> by [14]. □

5 Log-Space Computation over Finite Streams

5.1 Computing over Finite and Regular Streams

We have commented in the introduction about the practical significance of computing coinductively on very large (but finite) data. Several representations of finite streams are possible; the best suited to our purpose is the use of a symbol e as an end-marker. That is, a word $w \in \Sigma^*$ is represented by the stream that extends w with an indefinite repetition of e. (Recall that $\mathsf{e} \notin \Sigma$.)[3] We refer to w as the *significant portion* of the stream $w : \mathsf{e}^\omega \equiv w : \mathsf{e} : \mathsf{e} : \cdots$ representing w.

[3] A more principled representation uses of a nullary constructor for the empty word, yielding a coinductive type for both finite and infinite streams. That would call, though, for a restatement of the corecurrence schemas, and would not mesh well with the regular streams discussed below.

This representation of finite streams also agrees with a natural representation of *regular streams,* in the sense of [5], i.e. eventually-periodic streams. The salient property of such streams is that they have only finitely many distinct sub-streams.

Of course, we are particularly interested in the finite streams. Given a function $f : S^r \to S$ let f^{fin} denote the partial-function on Σ^* obtained by restricting f to finite streams, that is:

$$f^{fin}(\tilde{w}) = \text{the significant portion of the collapse of } f(\tilde{w})$$

Proposition 1. *If a function $f : S^r \to S$ is computed by a JFT M, then it maps (vectors of) regular streams to regular streams.*

More precisely, suppose that M has d states and k cursors. If $\tilde{\sigma} = (\sigma_1, \ldots, \sigma_r)$ is such that each σ_i has at most n distinct sub-streams, then $f(\tilde{\sigma})$ has at most $d \cdot n^{rk}$ distinct sub-streams.

Proof. The number of possible configurations of M for input $\tilde{\sigma}$ is $d \cdot n^{rk}$. □

Virtually the same argument establishes:

Corollary 1. *If $f : S^r \to S$ is computed by a JFT M, then f^{fin} is computable in logarithmic space.* □

5.2 Simulation of Log-Space by JFTs

In [14] we considered Turing transducers over streams. Such transducers are similar to JFT's, except that they have an auxiliary read/write memory. Note that we allow such machines to have several cursors on each input stream. We say that a Turing stream-transducer is *log-space* if the work-tape is restricted to size $O(\log n)$ when computing the n'the entry of the *output.*

A well-known simulation of log-space computation by multi-cursor two-way automata [7] is based on the representation of configurations of log-space size by cursors on the input. Our Turing transducers on streams can similarly be simulated by JFT's, provided the latter can place cursors on some word of length n when calculating the n'th output entry. That proviso is no longer needed when the inputs are finite streams. Indeed, if $f : S^r \to S$ is computed by a logspace Turing stream-transducer, then there is a JFT G which computes a function g that agrees with f on all finite input. Here we are interested in the following restricted case of that observation:

Proposition 2. *If $g : (\Sigma^*)^r \to \Sigma^*$ is computable by a log-space Turing transducer M, then there is a JFT F computing a function $f : S^r \to S$ such that $g = f^{fin}$.*

Proof. F simulates the work-tape of M using additional cursors on (the significant portion of) the input, whose end is detected by M by the first occurrence of e. Once M completes emitting output symbols for the given inputs, F proceeds to emit e indefinitely. □

Combining Corollary 1, Proposition 2, and Theorem 4 we obtain

Theorem 5. *Let $g : (\Sigma^*)^r \to \Sigma$. The following are equivalent:*

1. *g is log-space computable.*
2. *$g = f^{fin}$ for some $f : S^r \to S$ which is computable by a JFT, or equivalently definable by ramified lazy corecurrence, or equivalently is the collapse of a function definable by corecurrence.*

□

6 Conclusion and Research Directions

This paper is a contribution to the broad project of using ramification methods in Implicit Computational Complexity. We have settled here the status of the computational contents of ramified corecurrence in all tiers, and showed that it is captured by jumping finite transducers, and for finite streams by log-space Turing transducers. (The case of two tiers only was settled in [14] using the very strong limitations imposed on two tier corecurrence, due to the fact that the step functions must in that case be unary.) The converse holds, in a slightly modified form, by our previous work [14].

The methods developed here seem promising in tackling several more general or related questions. An obvious one is the generic extension of our treatment to arbitrary coinductive data, such as finite/infinite trees. We would expect that the extension of JFTs to such data,[4] might answer this question. Moreover, we would like to characterize the computational nature of ramified computing over data generated by both inductive and coinductive, for example in the framework of [12].

The effect of ramification in such a broad context can be brought to bear on more general forms of recurrence and corecurrence, in particular using higher type functionals. In [10] it was shown that the functions over inductive data defined by ramified recurrence in all finite types are precisely the Kalmar-elementary functions (as opposed to the ε_0-recursive functions in the un-ramified case), and [11] shows that the type-2 functionals defined by ramified recurrence (on base type) form precisely the Cook-Urquhart's class **BFF** of Basic Feasible Functionals. Our aim is to explore such results in the broader context of inductive/coinductive data-types.

Closer to home, we would like to better understand the nature of computational complexity over coinductive types in general, and streams in particular, e.g. the status of the "size yardsticks" that we used in the JFT simulation of logspace stream-transducers in [14].

Last but not least, there are intriguing and promising questions on the use of ramified corecurrence in the analysis and understanding of practical algorithms on streams and other coinductive data.

References

1. Bellantoni, S.: Predicative recursion and computational complexity. PhD thesis, University of Toronto (1992)
2. Bellantoni, S., Cook, S.: A new recursion-theoretic characterization of the poly-time functions (1992)
3. Comon, H., Dauchet, M., Gilleron, R., Löding, C., Jacquemard, F., Lugiez, D., Tison, S., Tommasi, M.: Tree automata techniques and applications (2007), `http://www.grappa.univ-lille3.fr/tata`
4. Cook, S.A., Rackoff, C.: Space lower bounds for maze threadability on restricted machines. SIAM J. Comput. 9(3), 636–652 (1980)
5. Cousineau, G.: An algebraic definition for control structures. Theoretical Computer Science 12, 175–192 (1980)

[4] Tree automata have been studied extensively [3]; jumping automata on *finite* graphs, i.e. regular trees, were considered in [4].

6. Czumaj, A., Muthukrishnan, S.M., Rubinfeld, R., Sohler, C. (eds.): Sublinear Algorithms, July 17-22, 2005. Dagstuhl Seminar Proceedings, vol. 05291. Internationales Begegnungs- und Forschungszentrum für Informatik (IBFI), Schloss Dagstuhl, Germany (2006)
7. Hartmanis, J.: On non-determinancy in simple computing devices. Acta Inf. 1, 336–344 (1972)
8. Kleene, S.C.: Introduction to Metamathematics. Wolters-Noordhof, Groningen (1952)
9. Leivant, D.: Ramified recurrence and computational complexity I: Word recurrence and poly-time. In: Clote, P., Remmel, J. (eds.) Feasible Mathematics II. Perspectives in Computer Science, pp. 320–343. Birkhauser-Boston, New York (1994)
10. Leivant, D.: Ramified recurrence and computational complexity III: higher type recurrence and elementary complexity. Ann. Pure Appl. Logic 96(1-3), 209–229 (1999)
11. Leivant, D.: Intrinsic reasoning about functional programs I: first order theories. Ann. Pure Appl. Logic 114(1-3), 117–153 (2002)
12. Leivant, D.: Global semantic typing for inductive and coinductive computing. Logical Methods in Computer Science 10(4) (2014)
13. Leivant, D., Marion, J.-Y.: Ramified recurrence and computational complexity II: Substitution and poly-space. In: Pacholski, L., Tiuryn, J. (eds.) CSL 1994. LNCS, vol. 933, pp. 486–500. Springer, Heidelberg (1995)
14. Ramyaa, R., Leivant, D.: Ramified corecurrence and logspace. Electronic Notes in Theorerical Computer Science 276, 247–261 (2011)
15. Rubinfeld, R., Shapira, A.: Sublinear time algorithms. Electronic Colloquium on Computational Complexity (ECCC) 18, 13 (2011)
16. Schütte, K.: Proof Theory. Springer, Berlin (1977)

On the Dependencies of Logical Rules

Marc Bagnol[1], Amina Doumane[2], and Alexis Saurin[2,⋆]

[1] IML, Université d'Aix-Marseille
bagnol@iml.univ-mrs.fr
[2] PPS, CNRS, Université Paris Diderot & INRIA
{amina.doumane,alexis.saurin}@pps.univ-paris-diderot.fr

Abstract. Many correctness criteria have been proposed since linear logic was introduced and it is not clear how they relate to each other. In this paper, we study proof-nets and their correctness criteria from the perspective of *dependency*, as introduced by Mogbil and Jacobé de Naurois. We introduce a new correctness criterion, called DepGraph, and show that together with Danos' contractibility criterion and Mogbil and Naurois criterion, they form the three faces of a notion of dependency which is crucial for correctness of proof-structures. Finally, we study the logical meaning of the dependency relation and show that it allows to recover and characterize some constraints on the ordering of inferences which are implicit in the proof-net.

Keywords: Linear logic, MLL, Proof nets, Correctness criterion, Contractibility, Mogbil-Naurois Criterion, Permutability of inferences.

1 Introduction

The benefits of Curry-Howard. Since the discovery of Curry-Howard correspondence [2], that is of the deep connections between logical proofs and computer programs, programming language theory and proof theory have been tightly intertwined.

Among the numerous and fruitful back-and-forths between proofs and programs, linear logic [3] certainly stands as exemplary.

While working on second-order arithmetics, Girard introduced system F [4,5], a polymorphic λ-calculus. Studying the semantics of system F, he later introduced the coherent semantics [6] which led to the linear decomposition of implication ($A \Rightarrow B = {!}\,A \multimap B$), the cornerstone of linear logic [3] since this semantical observation turns to be syntactically reflected in a well-behaved proof system. With linear logic came a very canonical representation of proofs (for fragments) of linear logic: proof nets [3,7,8] are a graphical notation for proofs, resulting in very canonical proof objects (contrarily to sequent proofs) in which cut-elimination is very elegant, and simple. As such, they are certainly one of the most original innovations of linear logic. The beauty of proof-nets is especially striking in the multiplicative fragment with no logical constant (also said unit-free multiplicative logic) to which most of the paper will be dedicated.

⋆ An extended version with supporting proofs can be found in [1] at `http://www.pps.univ-paris-diderot.fr/ saurin/Publi/DepGraphLong.pdf`

A. Pitts (Ed.): FOSSACS 2015, LNCS 9034, pp. 436–450, 2015.
DOI: 10.1007/978-3-662-46678-0_28

Proof-nets and logical correctness. By moving from inductive objects (*e.g.* sequent calculus proof trees) to more geometrical objects (proof structures), correctness becomes a global property contrarily to sequent proofs where correctness was local (a proof is correct if every step in the argument is correct). To give a status to those (possibly incorrect) objects, one speaks of *proof structures*, reserving the term *proof nets* to those objects which actually come from a sequent calculus proof. From this comes the need for conditions to ensure the logical correctness of proof structures. Several correctness criteria have been introduced in the literature. Among the best-known criteria, one can refer to the original long-trip criterion (LT) [3], Danos-Regnier criterion (DR) [8], counter-proofs criterion (CP) [9,10], contractibility (C) [11], graph-parsing criterion (GP) [12,13], Dominator Tree (DT) [14] and more recently Mogbil-Naurois criterion (MN) [15].

Relating correctness criteria. Actually, correctness criteria usually provide us with some specific viewpoints on the proof-theoretical or computational properties of proofs. For instance, they can (i) provide precise means to sequentialize a proof-net into a sequent proof, or (ii) tell us about the complexity of the correctness problem, or even (iii) say something about the structure of proofs.

Although correctness of proof-nets is now well-studied and understood, the question of comparing and relating those criteria attracted much less attention.

Contributions of the paper. The present paper is a contribution in this direction: we investigate a notion of dependency between inferences of a proof structure and use it to compare three correctness criteria (C, MN and DepGraph, a new criterion we introduce here) showing that they constitute three faces of this dependency relation.

We reformulate Contractibility in a big-step version from which arises the notion of dependency that one finds in MN criterion. This leads us to introduce a new criterion, DepGraph. We then show that these three criteria, arising from the notion of dependency, meet the three categories given above: we show that Contractibility gives actually a sequentialization of a proof-net, MN is a criterion with efficiency purposes and DepGraph emphasizes the structural properties of logic since (i) it deals separately with positive and negative inferences, suggesting possible connections with focusing, (ii) it is switching-independent, contrarily to MN, (iv) it makes use of a well-known necessary condition for correctness following from Euler-Poincaré property [10] and finally (iv) we use its notion of dependency in order to characterize constraints on the order of introduction of inferences which are shared by all sequentializations of a given proof-net.

We focus on multiplicative and unit-free linear logic. Rather than a restriction of the results, this is a matter of presentation: DepGraph criterion can easily be extended to MELL, thus capturing typed lambda-calculus

Organization of the paper. In Section 2, we recall the basics of proof nets and correctness criteria and dedicate Section 3 to analyzing and comparing the three criteria mentioned above by (i) showing how contractibility is related with sequentialization, (ii) formulating a big-step notion of contractibility, (iii) justifying the occurrence of a dependency relation in proof-nets, (iv) introducing a new correctness criterion, DepGraph and (iv) comparing DepGraph with MN-criterion. We finally focus in Section 4 on the logical meaning of dependency graphs. Due to lack of space, proofs are omitted but can be found in an extended version with supporting proofs and more material, available online in [1].

2 Correctness Problem of Proof Structures in Linear Logic

2.1 Linear Logic and Proof Nets

MLL. In this paper, we will deal with multiplicative linear logic (MLL), which is a fragment of linear logic. MLL formulas are built from the following grammar:

$$\boxed{A, B := X \mid X^{\perp} \mid A \otimes B \mid A \parr B \quad (X \in \mathcal{V})}$$

MLL is usually presented via a sequent calculus: an MLL sequent is a finite unordered list of MLL formulas, written $\vdash \Gamma$ and a proof is a tree with nodes labelled by $(ax), (cut), (\otimes), (\parr)$ and edges are labelled by sequents as follows:

Identity Group: $\dfrac{}{\vdash A, A^{\perp}}\,(ax) \qquad \dfrac{\vdash A, \Gamma \quad \vdash A^{\perp}, \Delta}{\vdash \Gamma, \Delta}\,(cut)$

Multiplicative Group: $\dfrac{\vdash A, \Gamma \quad \vdash B, \Delta}{\vdash A \otimes B, \Gamma, \Delta}\,(\otimes) \qquad \dfrac{\vdash A, B, \Gamma}{\vdash A \parr B, \Gamma}\,(\parr)$

Sequent calculus induces a sometimes irrelevant order between inferences. This is evidenced by possible permutations between inferences of a sequent proof. We recall in figure 1 the main cases of these permutations, the other cases are much alike, included the permutations involving the cut inference.

$$\dfrac{\dfrac{\vdash A, C, \Gamma \quad \vdash D, \Delta}{\vdash A, C \otimes D, \Gamma, \Delta}\,(\otimes) \quad \vdash B, \Sigma}{\vdash A \otimes B, C \otimes D, \Gamma, \Delta, \Sigma}\,(\otimes) \quad \leftrightarrow \quad \dfrac{\dfrac{\vdash A, C, \Gamma \quad \vdash B, \Sigma}{\vdash A \otimes B, C, \Gamma, \Sigma}\,(\otimes) \quad \vdash D, \Delta}{\vdash A \otimes B, C \otimes D, \Gamma, \Delta, \Sigma}\,(\otimes)$$

$$\dfrac{\dfrac{\vdash A, B, C, D, \Gamma}{\vdash A \parr B, C, D, \Gamma}\,(\parr)}{\vdash A \parr B, C \parr D, \Gamma}\,(\parr) \quad \leftrightarrow \quad \dfrac{\dfrac{\vdash A, B, C, D, \Gamma}{\vdash A, B, C \parr D, \Gamma}\,(\parr)}{\vdash A \parr B, C \parr D, \Gamma}\,(\parr)$$

$$\dfrac{\vdash A, \Gamma \quad \dfrac{\vdash B, C, D, \Delta}{\vdash B, C \parr D, \Delta}\,(\parr)}{\vdash A \otimes B, C \parr D, \Gamma, \Delta}\,(\otimes) \quad \leftrightarrow \quad \dfrac{\dfrac{\vdash A, \Gamma \quad \vdash B, C, D, \Delta}{\vdash A \otimes B, C, D, \Gamma, \Delta}\,(\otimes)}{\vdash A \otimes B, C \parr D, \Gamma, \Delta}\,(\parr)$$

Fig. 1. Key cases of inference permutations in the sequent calculus

Proof structures and proof nets. Proof nets are canonical representations of MLL sequent proofs quotienting them by the previous permutation rules, resulting in a confluent cut-elimination and other very good properties. Proof structures allow to present MLL proofs in a non-sequential way and therefore those objects are not inductively presented anymore which makes the checking of the logical correctness of those object challenging, calling for correctness criteria.

In the following, we shall consider only cut-free proof structures. Indeed, cut behaves exactly as $\otimes$ from the view point of correctness and therefore introduces no difficulty nor interesting aspects in our developments.

Definition 1 (Proof structure). *A proof structure is a finite undirected graph where vertices are labelled by the names of MLL inference rules or the special label* **c** *(for the conclusions of the proof) and edges are labelled with formulas of MLL. Moreover, edges which are adjacent to a vertex are partitioned into premises and conclusions according to the following rules:*

- *Nodes of label $\otimes$ (resp. $⅋$) have two premises and one conclusion. If A is the label of the first premise and B the label of the second premise, then the conclusion is labelled $A \otimes B$ (resp. $A ⅋ B$);*
- *Nodes of label* ***ax*** *have no premise and two conclusions. If the label of the first conclusion is A, the label of the second conclusion is $A^{\perp}$;*
- *Nodes labelled* **c** *have one premise and no conclusion*[1]*.*
- *Every edge is premise of one of its endpoints and conclusion of the other.*

Definition 2 (Desequentialization). *To any MLL proof π, one associates a proof structure $[\pi]$, its desequentialization, by forgetting the order of the inference rules and keeping only the subformula ordering together with the axiom links.*

Definition 3 (Proof net). *A* **proof net** *is any proof-structure which is the desequentialization of some sequent proof.*

By the previous definition, one immediately gets an inductive characterization of proof nets. Proof nets are those proof structures which can be obtained inductively as in figure 2

Remark 1. In the graphical representation of proof nets, we put arrows on edges to represent the information on premise/conclusion, but we consider the graph as undirected, in particular with respect to any notion such as paths, cycles, ...

2.2 Correctness Criteria

The graph in figure 3 is indeed a proof structure but it cannot be associated with a MLL proof. A proof structure therefore does not necessarily correspond to a sequent calculus proof; such a proof structure is called non-sequentializable. There is a number of methods to distinguish sequentializable proof structures – proof nets – from non sequentializable ones; such methods are called *correctness criteria.*

[1] We shall often omit those nodes in the graphical representation of nets: they will be depicted as pending edges.

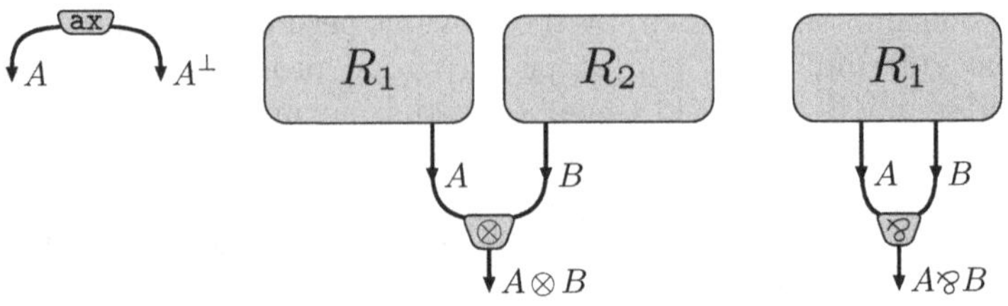

Fig. 2. Inductive characterization of proof nets

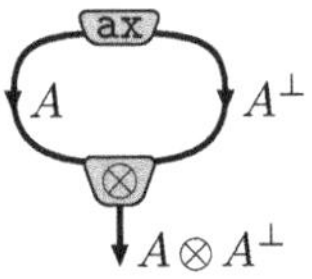

Fig. 3. A proof structure which is not a proof net

Several correctness criteria have been introduced in the literature. In the rest of this section, we shall present the Danos-Regnier (DR) criterion which is one of the most popular criteria; then we present Contractibility and Mogbil-Naurois (MN) criterion which we will compare in the next section.

2.3 Danos-Regnier Criterion

Definition 4 (Switching). *A* **switching** *of a proof structure R is the choice, for every ⅋ node of the graph, of one of its premises. More formally, a switching of R is a map from the ⅋ nodes of R to $\{l, r\}$.*

Given a switching s of a proof structure R, a ⅋ node n will be said to be switched to the right (resp. to the left) if the right premise (resp. left) has been selected, that is if $s(n) = l$ (resp. r).

Definition 5 (Correction Graph). *A* **Correction graph** *of a proof structure $R = (V_R, E_R)$ and a switching $\mathcal{S}$ of R is the undirected graph $\mathcal{S}(R) = (V_{\mathcal{S}(R)}, E_{\mathcal{S}(R)})$ defined as $V_{\mathcal{S}(R)} = V_R$ and $E_{\mathcal{S}(R)}$ is the subset of edges of R containing all edges from R but for the left (resp. right) premise of a ⅋ node n when $\mathcal{S}(n) = r$ (resp. l) and such that the labels are the inherited from R.*

Definition 6 (Danos-Regnier Criterion (DR)). *A proof structure satisfies the Danos-Regnier criterion if every correction graph is connected and acyclic; in that case, it is said to be DR-correct.*

Theorem 1 ([8]). *A proof structure is a proof net if, and only if, it is DR-correct.*

2.4 Contractibility

The contractibility criterion expresses a topological property of the proof structure, more precisely of an underlying graph structure, the paired graph which contains just enough information to distinguish premises of a ⅋ from the other edges.

Definition 7 (Paired Graph). *A* **paired graph** *is given by a graph $G = (V, E)$ together with a set $P(G)$ of* **paired edges**, *that are unordered pairs of edges which share at least one endpoint.*

Definition 8 ($C(R)$). *To a proof structure R, one associates a paired graph, written $C(R)$, which is simply R together with the set of paired edges given as the set of pairs of edges which are premises of a ⅋ node.*

Example. *We show below the unique proof net $R_{a⅋a^\perp}$ for the sequent $\vdash a⅋a^\perp$ and the paired graph $C(R_{a⅋a^\perp})$ which is associated to $R_{a⅋a^\perp}$ (paired edges are distinguished by a $\frown$):*

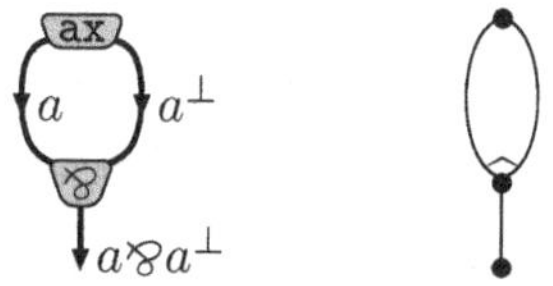

Definition 9 (Contraction rules). *One defines two graph-rewriting rules on paired graphs as follows (note that in both rules the two nodes shall be distinct and, in R_2, the contracted edge is not paired with any other edge):*

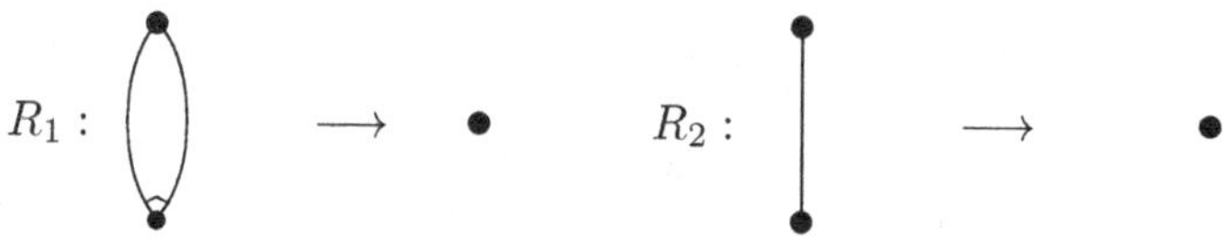

Definition 10 (Contractibility). *A proof structure R is* **contractible** *if*

$$C(R) \to^* \bullet.$$

Contractibility characterizes proof nets, it provides a correctness criterion:

Theorem 2 ([11]). *A proof structure is a proof net if, and only if, it is contractible.*

2.5 Mogbil-Naurois Criterion

We shall first present Mogbil-Naurois criterion, one of the most recent correctness criteria which characterized the space-complexity of the correctness problem.

Definition 11 (Elementary path). *A path in a undirected graph is* **elementary** *when it does not enter twice the same edge.*

Definition 12 (Dependency graph of a correction graph). *Given R a proof structure and $\mathcal{S}$ a switching of R, the dependency graph of $\mathcal{S}(R)$, written $D(\mathcal{S}, R)$ is an oriented graph (V, E) defined as follows:*

- *The set of nodes V consists in the set of conclusions of $\parr$ nodes of R together with an additional node s.*
- *Let x be a $\parr$ node in R, x_r (resp. x_l) the other endpoint of its right (resp. left) premise in R.*
  - *There is an edge $(s \to x)$ in E if there exists an elementary path $x_l, \ldots, x_r$ in $\mathcal{S}(R)$ which goes through no $\parr$ node.*
  - *Let y be another $\parr$ node in R. There is an edge $(y \to x)$ if there exists an elementary path $x_l, \ldots, x_r$ in $\mathcal{S}(R)$ containing y.*

Definition 13 (*SDAG* graphs). *A graph G is SDAG if: it is acyclic and it contains a node s, the source, such that all nodes of G are accessible from s.*

Definition 14 (Mogbil-Naurois Criterion). *A proof structure satisfies the Mogbil-Naurois criterion (MN) if there exists a connected and acyclic switching $\mathcal{S}$ such that $D(\mathcal{S}, R)$ is SDAG. Such a proof structure is said* **MN-correct**.

Theorem 3. *A proof structure is a proof net if, and only if, it is MN-correct.*

One notices that dependency graphs are defined on correction graphs and thus they depend on the switching. Compared to Danos-Regnier, the use of switchings in (MN)-criterion is quite odd: it only requires to analyze one switching and the corresponding correction graph. Moreover, the choice of this switching is itself arbitrary. It is therefore natural to wonder what is the exact role of this switching: is it really necessary? We answer this question in the following by going back to the origin of the idea of dependence, which was already present in the contractibility criterion as we shall see in section 3. From that point, we state a dependency-graph based criterion which does not rely on any switching.

3 On the Three Faces of Contractibility

Despite the wide diversity of correctness criteria, their relationship remains poorly studied in the literature. In this section, we shall investigate the connections between three criteria: Mogbil-Naurois, Contractibility and DepGraph which is a new criterion that we introduce in the remainder.

3.1 Contractibilty and Sequentialization

Before relating contractibility with the other two criteria, we make clear that it gives a genuine sequentialization. To do this, we simply label nodes of the paired graph of the proof structures with open proofs containing context variables. These open proofs correspond to partial sequentializations, which become larger and larger as contraction progresses, until reaching a full MLL proof. More precisely, these open proofs are constructed on sequents with context variables, generated by the following syntax (F is a formula and $\Gamma^?$ is a context variable):

$$S := \quad \emptyset \quad | \quad S, F \quad | \quad S, \Gamma^?$$

We consider these sequents up to commutativity. Open proofs are constructed by the following syntax:

$$\frac{}{\vdash A \parr A^\perp}(ax) \qquad \vdash S \qquad \frac{\vdash S_1, A \quad \vdash S_2, B}{\vdash S_1, S_2, A \otimes B}(\otimes) \qquad \frac{\vdash S, A, B}{\vdash S, A \parr B}(\parr)$$

Given a proof structure R, the labelled paired graph $C_l(R)$ is obtained by applying the following rules:

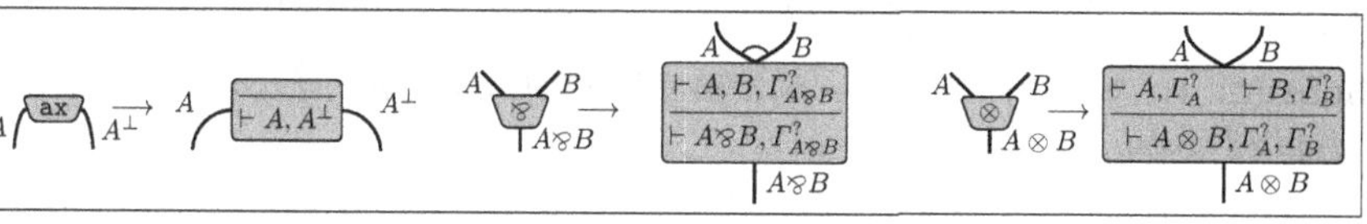

Labeled contractibility rules become:

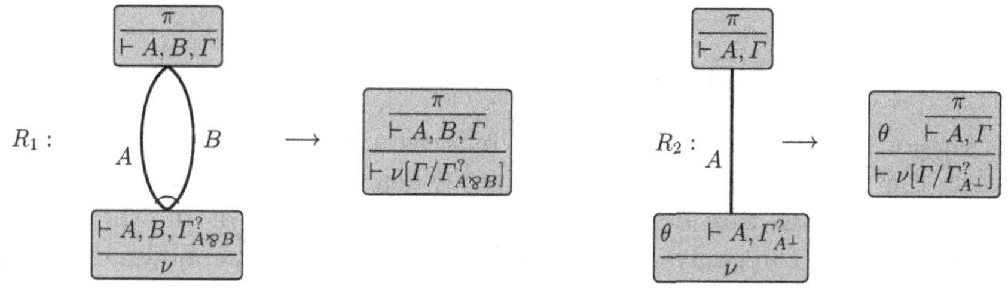

If R is actually a proof net, the node at which its paired graph contracts is labeled by one of its sequentializations:

Proposition 1. *Let R be a proof structure. If $C(R)$ contracts (by rules R_1 and R_2) to a point, then by following the same contraction path, $C_l(R)$ contracts to a point whose label is a sequentialization of R.*

Proof and examples are provided in the long version.Notice that two different contraction paths may lead to different sequentializations of a proof net.

Remark 2. Similar sequetialization processes directly based on a correctness criterion already exist in the literature. This ranges from the first naive correctness criterion to the so-called graph-parsing criterion. For instance, the naive criterion induces a bottom-up sequentialization, triggered by the conclusion of the proof, while the graph-parsing criterion induces a top-down sequentialization, triggered by the axioms. Compared to those, the above sequentialization can be triggered by "any" part of the proof-net.

3.2 Big-step Contractibility

We reformulate Contractibility in a big-step fashion to highlight the intrinsic notion of dependency present in this criterion.

One defines a new graph-rewriting rule R as follows:

Definition 15 (Big-step Contraction R). *An elementary cycle can be contracted to a point if it contains exactly two paired edges that are paired together that are adjacent in the cycle.*

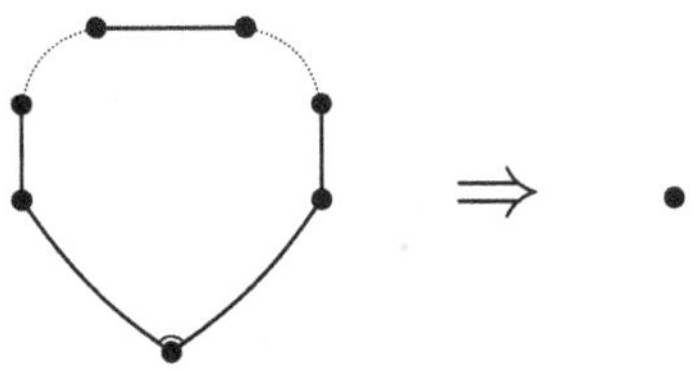

This new notion of contractibility is easily seen to correspond to usual contractibility and thus induces a correctness criterion expressed as:

Theorem 4. *A proof structure is a proof net if, and only if, contraction R can be applied until:*

- *no paired edges are left and*
- *it leads to a tree of unpaired edges.*

3.3 Towards Dependency Graphs

This version of contractibility criterion induces a natural dependency relation between the ⅋ nodes of the proof structure: when the premises of a ⅋ node are connected by a path that does not go through any premise of an other ⅋ node (see figure 4), one can contract directly this path; these are the nodes connected at the source in the dependency graph of MN-criterion. When, on the contrary, the path from the premises of a ⅋ node ($⅋_1$) goes through one of the premises of another ⅋ node ($⅋_2$) (see figure 4), we say that $⅋_1$ depends on $⅋_2$ because $⅋_1$ can only be contracted if $⅋_2$ is contracted before. In this way, we can construct a dependency graph which looks like the dependency graph of MN criterion, but this one is built directly on the proof structure rather than on a correction graph. The first condition of big-step contractibilty criterion says simply that this graph is SDAG. We will see how to transform the second condition in order to get a full correctness criterion. Before moving to the study of this new criterion, let us simply remark that one can actually define a dependency relation between ⅋ nodes of a proof structure R and any set of nodes of R as follows:

Definition 16 (Dependency graph of a proof structure, relatively to a set of nodes). *Let R be a proof structure and N a set of nodes of R. We denote by P the set of ⅋ nodes of R. The dependency graph of R relatively to N, $D_N(R)$, is the oriented graph (V, E) defined as follows:*

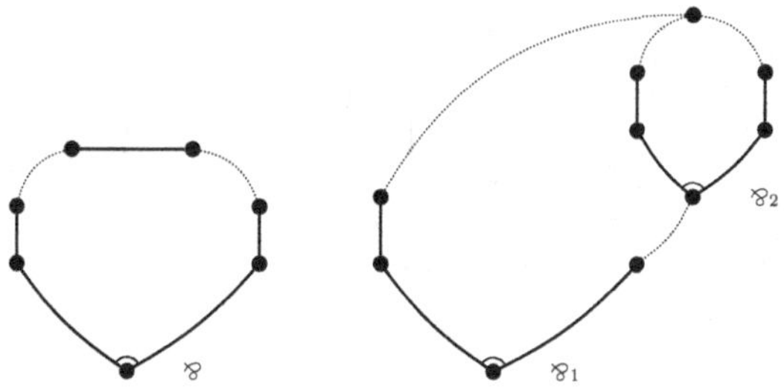

Fig. 4. VARIOUS DEPENDENCY CONFIGURATIONS

- *$V = N \cup P \cup \{s\}$ where s is an additional node.*
- *Let p be an element of P.*
  - *There is an edge $(s \to p)$ in E if the premises of p are connected by an elementary path in R which goes through no ⅋ node.*
  - *Let q be an element of V. There is an edge $(q \to p)$ if the premises of p are connected by an elementary path containing q which does not go successively through the two premises of a ⅋ node.*

Remark 3. The intuition underlying this extended notion of dependency graph is that in big-step contractibility, the contraction of the paired graph depends not only on dependencies between paired edges, but also on the fact that the $\otimes$ nodes on the cycles actually can be contracted to a point (with no loop), thus making a ⅋ node depend on a $\otimes$ node.

Notation. *The previous definition has two natural instances: when we take N to be the set of the ⅋ nodes of a proof structure R, $D_N(R)$ is a graph which expresses the dependency relation between ⅋ nodes only. We note it by $D_{⅋}(R)$; an example is given in figure 5. When N is taken to be the set of all ⅋ and $\otimes$ nodes of a proof structure, $D_N(R)$ is a graph which expresses the dependency relations between the ⅋ nodes and the other ⅋ and $\otimes$ nodes; we write it $D_{⅋,\otimes}(R)$. In the following we shall consider only $D_{⅋}(R)$ until section 4 where $D_{⅋,\otimes}(R)$ will be considered. When there is no ambiguity will shall omit the subscript.*

3.4 DepGraph Criterion

As said before, the first condition of big-step contractibility expresses that $D_{⅋}(R)$ is SDAG: the existence of a contractibility sequence ensures that there is some ⅋ node having a cycle that does not contain any paired edges which is the condition to be connected to the source, while the acyclicity condition ensures that we will always find a ⅋ node with a cycle that can be contracted.

To get a full correctness criterion, we will make use of a graph-theoretic property called Euler-Poincaré lemma, as suggested by Girard in [10].

Definition 17. *Let G be an undirected graph and n, e be its numbers of nodes and edges. We set $\chi_G = n - e$ and call this quantity the* **characteristic** *of G.*

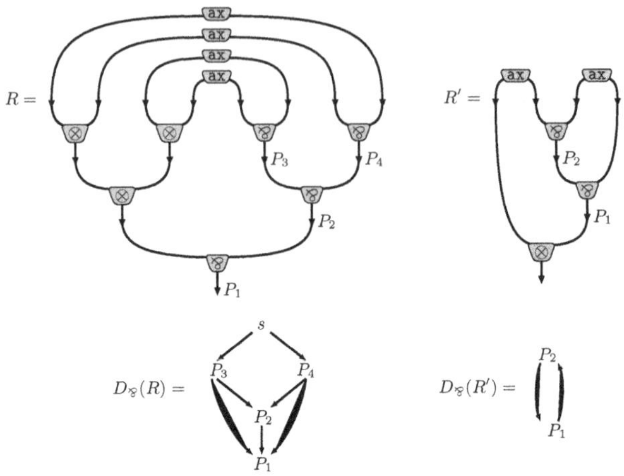

Fig. 5. Examples of dependency graphs

Theorem 5 (Euler-Poincaré Lemma). *Let G be an undirected acyclic graph and c_G be its number of connected components. The following equality holds:*

$$\chi_G = c_G.$$

Proposition 2. *For every correction graph G of a proof net, one has $\chi_G = 1$.*

Proposition 3. *Every correction graph G of a proof structure R satisfies:*

$$\chi_G = \#ax - \#\otimes.$$

Putting the two previous propositions together, a sequentializable proof structure must have one more axiom link than it has tensor links: $\#ax - \#\otimes = 1$.

Remark 4. When a structure contains cuts, one has $\chi_G = \#ax - \#\otimes - \#cut$ for every correction graph G. The condition above becomes $\#ax - \#\otimes - \#cut = 1$.

We can finally state our new criterion, *DepGraph*:

Definition 18 (DepGraph criterion). *A proof structure R is $D_⅋$-correct (or satisfies DepGraph criterion) if*

(1) $D_⅋(R)$ is a SDAG, (2) R is connected and (3) $\#ax - \#\otimes = 1$.

Theorem 6. *A proof structure is a proof net if, and only if, it is $D_⅋$-correct.*

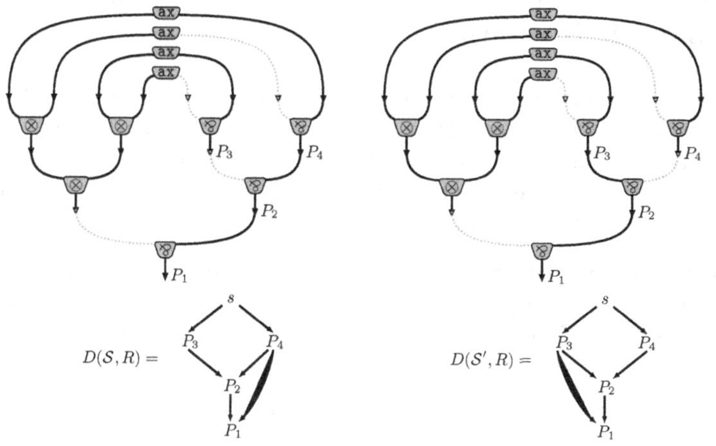

Fig. 6. SWITCHINGS $\mathcal{S}$ $\mathcal{S}'$ OF NET R, THE ASSOCIATED DEPENDENCY GRAPHS

3.5 Comparing the Two Notions of Dependency Graphs

Example in figure 6 shows that Mogbil-Naurois dependency graphs are switching-dependent, developing on example of figure 5. We will show that, for proof nets, they are almost invariant: the transitive closure of the dependency graphs induced by different switchings are all equal and are equal to the transitive closure of the dependency graph we introduced in the previous section.

Notations. *If $\mathcal{S}$ is a switching for a proof structure R and a a $\parr$-link in R, we note $\mathcal{S}_a$ the switching $\mathcal{S}$ in which we have toggled the switching for a.*

Given a graph D, $D^\star$ is its transitive closure.

Lemma 1. *Let z and a be two $\parr$ links of a proof net R and $\mathcal{S}$ be a switching.*

- *if $(z \to a) \in D(\mathcal{S}, R)$, then $(z \to a) \in D(\mathcal{S}_a, R)$*
- *if $(a \to z) \in D(\mathcal{S}, R)$, then $(a \to z) \in D(\mathcal{S}_a, R)$*

Theorem 7. *Let R be a proof net and $\mathcal{S}, \mathcal{S}'$ be switchings of R. Then we have*

$$D(\mathcal{S}, R)^\star = D(\mathcal{S}', R)^\star.$$

Remark 5. The proof relies strongly on the fact that in a connected acyclic graph, there always exists a single elementary path between two nodes. The result would not hold if the structure were not correct.

Finally, we have:

Theorem 8. *Let R be a proof net and $\mathcal{S}$ a switching for R. Then: $D_{\parr}(R)^\star = D(\mathcal{S}, R)^\star$.*

4 On the Order of Introduction of Connectives in Sequentializations

In this section, we will investigate the logical meaning of the notion of dependency introduced for DepGraph criterion. A crucial step in proving that a proof net satisfies DepGraph is to show that if π is a sequentialization of proof net R, every dependence in the dependency graph is also present in the order of introduction graph, more precisely:

Definition 19 (Order of introduction). *Let π be an MLL proof. For every $⅋$ or $\otimes$ rule $\mathbf{r}_F$ introducing formula F, we note π_F the sub-tree of π rooted in the conclusion of $\mathbf{r}_F$. We define a partial order on the (occurrences of) formulas introduced by $⅋$ or $\otimes$ inferences in π, that will be noted $<_\pi$ as follows:*

$$F <_\pi G \text{ if } \mathbf{r}_F \in \pi_G \text{ and } F \neq G$$

It formalizes the relation "to be introduced above".

The graph of this relation is noted $O^-(\pi)$ and one defines $O(\pi)$ as $O^-(\pi)$ augmented by adding a vertex s and, for all vertice e in $O^-(\pi)$, an edge $s \to e$.

To show that every proof net is $D_⅋$-correct, we established the following:

Lemma 2. *Let π be an MLL proof and R its desequentialization. Then*

$$D_⅋(R) \subseteq O(\pi).$$

As a consequence, $D_⅋(R) \subseteq O(R) := \cap_{\pi,[\pi]=R} O(\pi)$ where $O(R)$ can be seen as the essence of the sequentalizations of R. It is natural to wonder whether this inclusion can be sharpened in a characterization of $O(R)$ relying on our notion of dependency. Actually, $D_⅋$ expresses only the relationship betweep $⅋$ nodes, and it is not enough to characterize $O(R)$. We will use instead the dependency graph $D_{⅋,\otimes}(R)$ to take in account also the dependency relation between $⅋$ and $\otimes$ nodes.

Definition 20 (Subformula graph of a proof net). *Let R be a proof net. The subformula graph of R, $SF(R)$, is the directed graph (V, E) defined as follows:*

- *$V = P \cup T$ where P and T are respectively the set of $⅋$ nodes and $\otimes$ nodes.*
- *Let n and m be two elements of V. There is an edge $(m \to n)$ in E if the formula of the conclusion of m is a subformula of the formula of the conclusion of n.*

Theorem 9. *Let R be a proof net. Then $(D_{⅋,\otimes}(R) \cup SF(R))^\star = O(R)$.*

The result is proved by double inclusion.

Proposition 4. *Let π be an MLL proof and R its desequentialization. Then:*

$$D_{⅋,\otimes}(R) \subseteq O(\pi).$$

Corollary 1. *Let R be a proof net. One has $(D_{⅋,\otimes}(R) \cup SF(R))^\star \subseteq O(R)$.*

Proposition 5. *Let R be a proof net. One has $O(R) \subseteq (D_{⅋,\otimes}(R) \cup SF(R))^\star$.*

Proof. (Sketch, see [1] for details.) We prove the result by induction on the minimal distance between two inferences in any sequentialization of R. If this distance is zero, then we prove that if $(F_1 \to F_2) \in O(R)$ then either F_1 is a subformula of F_2 and then $(F_1 \to F_2) \in SF(R)$, or $(F_1 \to F_2) \in D_{⅋,\otimes}(R)$. In the inductive case, minimality ensures the existence of an F such that $(F_1 \to F) \in O(R)$ and $(F \to F_2) \in O(R)$ on which induction hypothesis applies. □

5 Conclusion

Comparing correctness criteria. We have seen that Contractibility, Mogbil and Naurois' criterion and DepGraph are three faces of the same notion, dependency. More precisely, those three criteria can be understood as different concrete implementations of a *proto-criterion* related with dependency relation, along the different points of view developed in the introduction: we showed that (i) Contractibility gives actually a sequentialization of a proof-net from which arises dependency, (ii) MN is a criterion with efficiency purposes (working on the generalized dependency graph, it is not clear how to stay in NL since it requires to remember which premise of a ⅋ node has been visited, thus justifying the seemingly odd choice of a switching) while (iii) DepGraph emphasizes structural properties of logic by clearly separating conditions on ⅋ inferences from other inferences and by unveiling the meaning of its dependency graph which corresponds (when considered together with the subformula relation) to the order of introduction of inferences common to all sequentializations of a given proof-net.

This last point actually evidences an interesting fact. While they are completely parallel proof objects, proof-nets contain enough logical dependency to allow for the retrieval of inherently sequential information. Indeed, computing the dependency relation extracts the true logical causality of sequential proofs.

Future works. The present work suggests three main directions for future works:

- The separation between positive and negative inferences which is the cornerstone of DepGraph criterion suggests connections with focusing. While proof-nets and focalized proofs are the results of diverging choices of proof-theoretical design (parallelism versus hypersequentiality), this suggests that they actually may be different aspects of the same phenomenon as already advocated in the study of multi-focusing [16].
- We plan to investigate connections between dependency graphs on the one hand, kingdoms and empires on the other. Indeed, the dependency graph $D_{⅋,\otimes}(R)$ corresponds to a characterization of kingdoms given in [17] for correct proof structures. We plan to focus on complexity issues and to study notions of kingdoms for incorrect proof structures.
- Another direction concerns the development and the validation of our comparative study of proof-nets. Indeed, the prototypical classification we suggested is mainly built on empirical considerations and we plan to investigate it more systematically in the future, in particular by considering connections

with other criteria which seems to be related with the notion of dependency such as Di Giamberardino and Faggian's work on jumps [18], Murawski and Ong's work on dominator's trees [14] or even earlier, with Banach sweepline sequentialization [19].

Acknowledgements. The authors wish to thank Claudia Faggian, Roberto Maieli and Virgile Mogbil for helpful discussions regarding this work.

References

1. Bagnol, M., Doumane, A., Saurin, A.: On the dependencies of logical rules. long version at `http://www.pps.univ-paris-diderot.fr/~saurin/Publi/DepGraphLong.pdf`
2. Howard, W.A.: The formulae-as-type notion of construction. In: Seldin, J.P., Hindley, R. (eds.) To H. B. Curry: Essays in Combinatory Logic, Lambda Calculus, and Formalism, pp. 479–490. Academic Press, New York (1980)
3. Girard, J.Y.: Linear logic. Theoretical Computer Science 50(1), 1–101 (1987)
4. Girard, J.Y.: Interprétation fonctionnelle et élimination des coupures de l'arithmétique d'ordre supérieur. Thèse de doctorat, Université Paris VII (1972)
5. Reynolds, J.C.: Towards a theory of type structure. In: Robinet, B. (ed.) Programming Symposium. LNCS, vol. 19, pp. 408–423. Springer, Heidelberg (1974)
6. Girard, J.Y.: The system F of variable types, fifteen years later. Theoretical Computer Science 45, 159–192 (1986)
7. Girard, J.Y.: Proof-nets: the parallel syntax for proof-theory. In: Ursini, A., Agliano, P. (eds.) Logic and Algebra. Lecture Notes In Pure and Applied Mathematics, vol. 180, pp. 97–124. Marcel Dekker, New York (1996)
8. Danos, V., Regnier, L.: The structure of multiplicatives 28, 181–203 (1989)
9. Curien, P.L.: Introduction to linear logic and ludics, part ii (2006)
10. Girard, J.Y.: Le Point Aveugle: Cours de logique. Tome 1, Vers la perfection; Tome 2, Vers l'imperfection. Hermann (2006)
11. Danos, V.: Une application de la logique linéaire à l'ètude des processus de normalisation. (principalement du λ-calcul). Thèse de doctorat, Université Denis Diderot, Paris 7 (1990)
12. Guerrini, S.: Correctness of multiplicative proof nets is linear. In: LICS, pp. 454–463. IEEE Computer Society (1999)
13. Guerrini, S.: A linear algorithm for MLL proof net correctness and sequentialization. Theor. Comput. Sci. 412(20), 1958–1978 (2011)
14. Murawski, A.S., Ong, C.H.L.: Fast verification of mll proof nets via imll. ACM Trans. Comput. Logic 7(3), 473–498 (2006)
15. de Naurois, P.J., Mogbil, V.: Correctness of linear logic proof structures is NL-complete. Theor. Comput. Sci. 412(20), 1941–1957 (2011)
16. Chaudhuri, K., Miller, D., Saurin, A.: Canonical sequent proofs via multi-focusing. In: Ausiello, G., Karhumäki, J., Mauri, G., Ong, L. (eds.) TCS 2008. IFIP, vol. 273, pp. 383–396. Springer, Boston (2008)
17. Bellin, G., van de Wiele, J.: Subnets of proof-nets in MLL^-. In: Girard, Lafont, Regnier (eds.) Advances in Linear Logic, vol. 222, pp. 249–270. CUP (1995)
18. Di Giamberardino, P., Faggian, C.: Jump from parallel to sequential proofs: Multiplicatives. In: Ésik, Z. (ed.) CSL 2006. LNCS, vol. 4207, pp. 319–333. Springer, Heidelberg (2006)
19. Banach, R.: Sequent reconstruction in LLM - A sweepline proof. Ann. Pure Appl. Logic 73(3), 277–295 (1995)

On the Mints Hierarchy in First-Order Intuitionistic Logic*

Aleksy Schubert[1], Paweł Urzyczyn[1], and Konrad Zdanowski[2]

[1] Institute of Informatics, University of Warsaw
ul. S. Banacha 2, 02–097 Warsaw, Poland
{alx,urzy}@mimuw.edu.pl
[2] Cardinal Stefan Wyszyński University in Warsaw
ul. Dewajtis 5, 01-815 Warsaw, Poland
k.zdanowski@uksw.edu.pl

Abstract. We study the decidability and complexity of fragments of intuitionistic first-order logic over $(\forall, \to)$ determined by the alternation of positive and negative occurrences of quantifiers (Mints hierarchy). We prove that fragments Π_2 and Σ_2 are undecidable and that Σ_1 is EXPSPACE-complete.

1 Introduction

The leading proof assistants such as Coq [6], Agda [3] or Isabelle/HOL [15] are founded on constructive logics. Still, the complexity behind proof search in constructive reasoning systems is not well understood even for their basic and crucial fragments where the implication and universal quantification are used. This situation is caused partly by the difficulty of the field and partly by the lack of a systematic approach, especially in the case of quantifiers.

Quantifiers are present in logic at least from the time of Aristotle but a modern theory of quantification was probably initiated by Ch.S. Peirce [1]. The systematic approach to quantifiers through their grouping at the beginning of a logical formulas was implicit in the work of Peirce, and made explicit by A. Church [5], who first used the term "prenex normal form". Since then classifying formulas according to the quantifier prefix remains a standard stratification tool in modern logic, just to mention Ehrenfeucht-Fraïssé games [11, Chapter 6] or the arithmetical hierarchy of Kleene and Mostowski [9, Chapter 7].

While the prenex normal form is useful for classification of formulas, which was demonstrated in full strength by Börger, Grädel, and Gurevich in their influential book [2], it is rarely used in practice. The structure of formulas arising from actual reasoning (in particular proof formalization) usually involves quantification in arbitrary positions. For instance this happens when a quantified definition is expanded in a formula.

In addition, the prenex normal form theorem applies to *classical* logic only. Things become quite different for constructive logic (aka intuitionistic logic), because the prenex fragment of intuitionistic logic is decidable [18]. This contrasts

* Project supported through NCN grant DEC-2012/07/B/ST6/01532.

A. Pitts (Ed.): FOSSACS 2015, LNCS 9034, pp. 451–465, 2015.
DOI: 10.1007/978-3-662-46678-0_29

with the undecidability of the general case (see e.g. [22]) and that makes this form of stratification unsuitable in the constructive context.

Can we replace the prenex classification by something adequate for intuitionistic logic? Yes, we can: as observed by Grigori Mints [14], the principal issue is the alternation of positive and negative occurrences of quantifiers in a formula. This yields the *Mints hierarchy* of formulas:

Π_1 – All quantifiers at positive positions.
Σ_1 – All quantifiers at negative positions.
Π_2 – Up to one alternation: no positive quantifier in scope of a negative one.
Σ_2 – Up to one alternation: no negative quantifier in scope of a positive one.

And so on. (This can be generalised to cover existential quantifiers.) In a classical reduction to a prenex form, all the quantifiers on positive positions become universal and those at negative positions become existential. But a formula can be classified as a Π_n or a Σ_n formula without actually reducing it to a prenex form. Therefore, Mints hierarchy makes perfect sense for intuitionistic logic.

As for the existing knowledge, Mints proved that the fragment Π_1 of the constructive logic with all connectives and quantifiers is decidable [14]. An alternative proof of Mints' result (for the calculus with $\forall$ and $\to$ only) was given by Dowek and Jiang [8]. A similar decidability result was also obtained by Rummelhoff [19] for the positive fragment of second-order propositional intuitionistic logic (system F). The 2-co-NEXPTIME lower bound for Π_1 was proved by Schubert, Urzyczyn and Walukiewicz-Chrząszcz [20], but the problem is conjectured to be non-elementary [21]. The undecidability of Σ_2 with all connectives and quantifiers can be derived from the undecidability of the classical satisfiability problem for $\forall^*\exists^*$ using a result of Kreisel [12, Thm. 7]. This would not work for Π_2 because the Ramsey class $\exists^*\forall^*$ is decidable. Undecidability for Π_2 (for the full language with one unary predicate) is implied by a result of Orevkov [16].

There are other forms of quantifier-oriented hierarchical stratifications of intuitionistic formulas. For instance, the classical prenex hierarchy can be embedded in a fragment of the intuitionistic logic: a negation of a prenex formula is classically provable if and only if it is provable intuitionistically [12]. A similar, but more general class of formulas in so called pseudoprenex form, where quantifiers may be separated by double negation $\neg\neg$, was studied in depth by Orevkov who gave a full characterisation of decidable cases [17]. Also a full characterization of decidable cases was given for the logic with equality and function symbols [7]. Other hierarchies of intuitionistic formulas were proposed e.g., by Fleischmann [10] and Burr [4] (the latter for arithmetic). However, we are not aware of any complexity-oriented results for those hierarchies.

In this paper we initiate a systematic study of the decision problem in Mints hierarchy. We restrict attention to the fragment where only the implication and the universal quantifier may occur. Our main results are as follows:

A. The decision problems for classes Σ_2 and Π_2 are undecidable;
B. The decision problem for the class Σ_1 is EXPSPACE-complete.

These results are supplemented by the 2-CO-NEXPTIME lower bound for Π_1 obtained in [20]. Observe that, because of conservativity, part A applies directly to the full intuitionistic logic, and the same holds for the lower bound in B. The upper bound in B also extends to the general case at the cost of some additional complication. This issue is deferred to the full version of this paper.

The undecidabilities in A are shown for the monadic fragment of minimal logic (i.e., the language with only unary predicate symbols). It is slightly different with B, where we conjecture that the monadic case is CO-NEXPTIME complete.

The paper is organized as follows. Section 2 introduces some basics, in particular the undecidable tiling puzzles. Those are encoded in Section 3 into Σ_2 and Π_2 formulas. In Section 3.3 we use a syntactic translation to obtain the undecidability results for the monadic fragments of Σ_2 and Π_2. In Section 4 we show EXPSPACE-completeness for Σ_1 using the decision problem of bus machines [23].

2 Preliminaries

We consider first-order intuitionistic logic without function symbols and without equality. That is, the only individual terms are *object variables*, written in lower case, e.g., $x, y, \ldots$ We also restrict attention to formulas built only from implication and the universal quantifier. A formula is therefore either an atom $\mathrm{P}(x_1, \ldots, x_n)$, where $n \geq 0$, or an implication $\varphi \to \psi$, or it has the form $\forall x\, \varphi$.

We use standard parentheses-avoiding conventions, in particular we take the implication to be right-associative, i.e., $\varphi \to \psi \to \vartheta$ stands for $\varphi \to (\psi \to \vartheta)$.

Mints hierarchy: We define classes of formulas Σ_n and Π_n by induction, beginning with $\Sigma_0 = \Pi_0$ being the set of open formulas. The induction step can be expressed by the following "grammar":

- $\Sigma_{n+1} ::= \Sigma_n \mid \Pi_n \mid \Pi_{n+1} \to \Sigma_{n+1}$;
- $\Pi_{n+1} ::= \Sigma_n \mid \Pi_n \mid \Sigma_{n+1} \to \Pi_{n+1} \mid \forall x\, \Pi_{n+1}$.

Our proof notation is an extended lambda-calculus of *proof terms* or simply *proofs* or *terms*. Types assigned to proof terms are formulas. In addition to object variables, in proof terms there are also *proof variables*, written as uppercase letters, like X, Y, Z. An *environment* is a set of declarations $(X : \varphi)$, where X is a proof variable and φ is a formula. The following type-assignment rules infer judgements of the form $\Gamma \vdash M : \varphi$, where Γ is an environment, M is a term, and φ is a formula. In $(\forall \mathrm{I})$ we require $x \notin FV(\Gamma)$ and y in $(\forall \mathrm{E})$ is an arbitrary object variable.

$$\Gamma, X : \varphi \vdash X : \varphi \quad \text{(Axiom)}$$

$$\frac{\Gamma, X : \varphi \vdash M : \psi}{\Gamma \vdash \lambda X^{\varphi} M : \varphi \to \psi}\,(\to \mathrm{I}) \qquad \frac{\Gamma \vdash M : \varphi \to \psi \quad \Gamma \vdash N : \varphi}{\Gamma \vdash MN : \psi}\,(\to \mathrm{E})$$

$$\frac{\Gamma \vdash M : \varphi}{\Gamma \vdash \lambda x\, M : \forall x \varphi}\,(\forall \mathrm{I}) \qquad \frac{\Gamma \vdash M : \forall x \varphi}{\Gamma \vdash My : \varphi[x := y]}\,(\forall \mathrm{E})$$

As we can see there are two kinds of lambda-abstraction here: the proof abstraction $\lambda X^\varphi\, M$ and the object abstraction $\lambda x\, M$. There are also two forms of application: the proof application MN, where N is a proof term, and the object application My, where y is an object variable. We use the common conventions, e.g., unnecessary parentheses are omitted and the application is left-associative. Terms and formulas are taken up to alpha-conversion.

The formalism is used liberally. For instance, we often say that "a term M has type α" leaving the environment implicit. Also we often identify environments with sets of formulas, as well as we write $\Gamma \vdash \varphi$ when $\Gamma \vdash M : \varphi$ and M is not relevant at the moment. Sometimes for convenience we drop φ from $\lambda X^\varphi\, M$ when it can be deduced from the context.

Free (object) variables $\mathrm{FV}(\varphi)$ in a formula φ are as usual. For proofs we define $\mathrm{FV}(X) = \varnothing$, $\mathrm{FV}(\lambda X^\varphi\, M) = \mathrm{FV}(\varphi) \cup \mathrm{FV}(M)$, $\mathrm{FV}(MN) = \mathrm{FV}(M) \cup \mathrm{FV}(N)$, $\mathrm{FV}(\lambda x\, M) = \mathrm{FV}(M) - \{x\}$, $\mathrm{FV}(My) = \mathrm{FV}(M) \cup \{y\}$. The notation $M[\vec{x} := \vec{y}]$ stands for the simultaneous substitution of variables $\vec{y}$ for free occurrences of (pairwise different) variables $\vec{x}$.

A term is in *normal form* when it contains no redex, i.e., no subterm such as $(\lambda X^\varphi.\, M)N$ or $(\lambda x\, M)y$. We also define the notion of a proof term in *long normal form*, abbreviated as *lnf*.

- If N is an lnf of type α then $\lambda x\, N$ is an lnf of type $\forall x\, \alpha$.
- If N is an lnf of type β then $\lambda X^\alpha.\, N$ is an lnf of type $\alpha \to \beta$.
- If $N_1, \ldots, N_n$ are lnf or object variables and $X N_1 \ldots N_n$ is of an atom type then $X N_1 \ldots N_n$ is an lnf.

Normalization for our proofs follows e.g., from [21]:

Lemma 1. *If σ is intuitionistically derivable from Γ then $\Gamma \vdash N : \sigma$, for some long normal form N.*

The *target* of a formula is the relation symbol at the end of it. The following observation is essential in long normal proof search.

Lemma 2. *If $\Gamma \vdash N : \mathrm{P}(\vec{x})$, where $\mathrm{P}(\vec{x})$ is an atomic formula and N is an lnf, then $N = X\vec{D}$, where $(X : \psi) \in \Gamma$ with target* P, *and $\vec{D}$ is a sequence of terms and object variables.*

2.1 Machines and Tilings

To give a concise account of our lower bound results, we disguise Turing Machines as tiling problems, cf. [2, Chapter 3.1.1]. While the masquerade is quite obvious to unveil, it is still useful: some formulas become simpler. Our *tiling puzzle* is defined as a tuple of the form $\mathcal{G} = \langle \mathcal{T}, \mathcal{R}, \mathrm{E}, \mathrm{OK} \rangle$, where $\mathcal{T}$ is a finite set of *tiles*, $\mathcal{R} : \mathcal{T}^4 \to \mathcal{T}$ is a *tiling function*, and E, OK are different elements of $\mathcal{T}$. Such $\mathcal{G}$ defines a unique *tiling* $T_{\mathcal{G}} : \mathbb{N} \times \mathbb{N} \to \mathcal{T}$:

- $T_{\mathcal{G}}(m, n) = \mathrm{E}$, when $n = 0$ or $m = 0$;
- $T_{\mathcal{G}}(m{+}1, n{+}1) = \mathcal{R}(\mathrm{K}, \mathrm{L}, \mathrm{M}, \mathrm{N})$, where $\mathrm{K} = T_{\mathcal{G}}(m, n{+}1)$, $\mathrm{L} = T_{\mathcal{G}}(m, n)$, $\mathrm{M} = T_{\mathcal{G}}(m{+}1, n)$, and $\mathrm{N} = T_{\mathcal{G}}(m{+}2, n)$.

That is, the tile E is placed along the horizontal and vertical edges of the grid $\mathbb{N} \times \mathbb{N}$ and every other tile is determined by its neighbourhood consisting of four tiles: one tile to the left and three tiles below. This is illustrated by Fig. 1, where $\mathrm{T} = \mathcal{R}(\mathrm{K}, \mathrm{L}, \mathrm{M}, \mathrm{N})$. We say that $\mathcal{G}$ is *solvable* when $T_{\mathcal{G}}(m, n) = \textsc{ok}$, for some numbers m, n. The following is unavoidable:

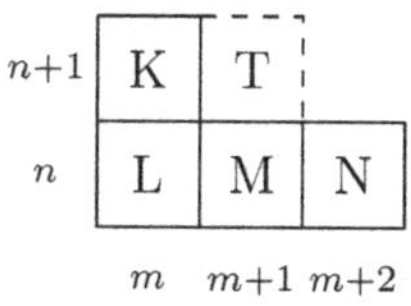

Fig. 1. Result tile

Lemma 3. *It is undecidable to determine if a given tiling puzzle is solvable.*

Proof. A routine reduction of the following problem:

Does a deterministic Turing Machine accept the empty input?

Row n in the tiling corresponds to the n-th step of a computation. □

Locations in tilings: To place a tile at a location (m, n) we must tile all locations in the set $\mathcal{L}(m, n) = \{(k, l) \mid l \leq n \wedge k \leq m + n - l\}$, as illustrated in Fig. 2, where the gray square is the location (m, n). Define $(m, n) \preceq (k, l)$ when $\mathcal{L}(m, n) \subseteq \mathcal{L}(k, l)$. This inherits the properties of inclusion, in particular the relation $\preceq$ is a well-founded partial order.

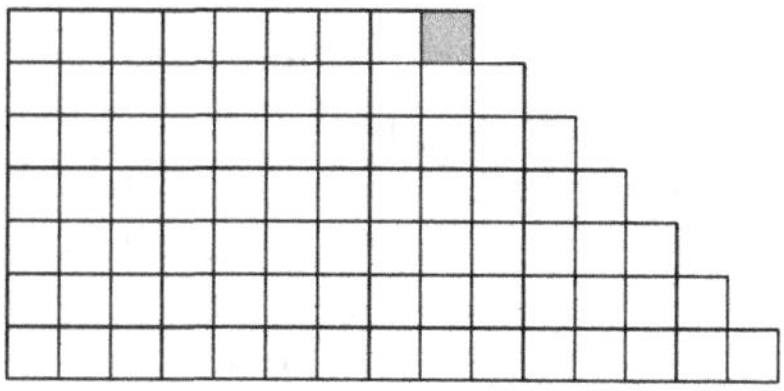

Fig. 2. Dependency of locations

3 Classes Σ_2 and Π_2

Our undecidability results are shown by a reduction from the tiling puzzle problem. The reader has to be aware that the argument to follow is proof-theoretical rather than semantical. We are not concerned with the interpretation of our formulas in any model, but in their formal structure and in the mechanism of proof construction. The construction of the tiling is encoded by expanding the proof environment: adding new tiles corresponds to adding more assumptions.

3.1 Undecidability for Σ_2

We encode a tiling puzzle $\mathcal{G} = \langle \mathcal{T}, \mathcal{R}, \mathrm{E}, \textsc{ok} \rangle$ as a Σ_2 formula over the signature:

- Nullary relation symbols: *start*, *loop*, for global control;
- Unary relation symbols T, for each tile $\mathrm{T} \in \mathcal{T}$, including E;
- Unary relation symbols A, B, representing border positions;
- Binary relation symbols H, V, for horizontal and vertical neighbourhood.

Technically, it is convenient to define a finite set $\Gamma_{\mathcal{G}}$ of Π_2 formulas, and consider the entailment problem $\Gamma_{\mathcal{G}} \vdash \mathit{start}$ rather than a single Σ_2 formula. For every "rule" of the form $\mathcal{R}(\mathrm{K}, \mathrm{L}, \mathrm{M}, \mathrm{N}) = \mathrm{X}$, the set $\Gamma_{\mathcal{G}}$ contains the formula:

$$(0)\ \forall yzuv\, (\mathrm{K}(y) \to \mathrm{L}(z) \to \mathrm{M}(u) \to \mathrm{N}(v) \to \mathrm{V}(z, y) \to \mathrm{H}(z, u) \to \mathrm{H}(u, v) \to \\ \forall x\, (\mathrm{T}(x) \to \mathrm{H}(y, x) \to \mathrm{V}(u, x) \to \mathit{loop}) \to \mathit{loop}).$$

Observe that quantifiers $\forall yzuv$ are positive in the formula (0), and $\forall x$ is negative. This is reversed in the judgement $\Gamma_{\mathcal{G}} \vdash start$. The intended meaning of the formula is illustrated by Fig. 3. Variables $yzuv$ represent tile positions, the assumptions $\mathrm{K}(y), \ldots, \mathrm{H}(u, v)$ describe the situation of the tiling before placing tile T at x. The predicates $\mathrm{T}(x), \mathrm{H}(y, x), \mathrm{V}(u, x)$ extend the proof environment to account for the new tile. The other formulas in $\Gamma_{\mathcal{G}}$ are the following:

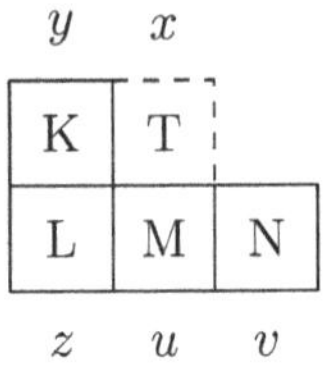

Fig. 3. Formula (0)

(1) $\forall y\,(\mathrm{E}(y) \to \mathrm{A}(y) \to \mathrm{B}(y) \to loop) \to start$;
(2) $\forall y\,(\mathrm{E}(y) \to \mathrm{A}(y) \to \forall x\,(\mathrm{H}(y, x) \to \mathrm{E}(x) \to \mathrm{A}(x) \to loop) \to loop)$;
(3) $\forall y\,(\mathrm{E}(y) \to \mathrm{B}(y) \to \forall x\,(\mathrm{V}(y, x) \to \mathrm{E}(x) \to \mathrm{B}(x) \to loop) \to loop)$;
(4) $\forall x\,(\mathrm{OK}(x) \to loop)$.

Let Δ be a set of formulas in the above signature. Object variables occurring in Δ may be interpreted as tile locations, and predicates H and V are used to determine these locations. A variable x may have one or more pairs of *coordinates* in Δ. This is defined by induction:

- If $\mathrm{A}(x), \mathrm{B}(x) \in \Delta$ then x has coordinates $(0, 0)$;
- If $\mathrm{H}(x, y) \in \Delta$ and x has coordinates (m, n) then y has coordinates $(m+1, n)$;
- If $\mathrm{V}(x, y) \in \Delta$ and x has coordinates (m, n) then y has coordinates $(m, n+1)$.

A set of formulas (i.e., an environment) Δ is *good* when all formulas in Δ are of the forms $\mathrm{A}(x)$, $\mathrm{B}(x)$, $\mathrm{H}(x, y)$, $\mathrm{V}(x, y)$, or $\mathrm{T}(x)$, where $\mathrm{T} \in \mathcal{T}$, and in addition:

- Each $x \in \mathrm{FV}(\Delta)$ has exactly one pair of coordinates.
- For each $x \in \mathrm{FV}(\Delta)$ with coordinates (m, n), and every $\mathrm{T} \in \mathcal{T}$,
  - $\mathrm{T}(x) \in \Delta$ if and only if $T_{\mathcal{G}}(m, n) = \mathrm{T}$;
  - $\mathrm{B}(x) \in \Delta$ if and only if $m = 0$;
  - $\mathrm{A}(x) \in \Delta$, if and only if $n = 0$.

The intuition is that a good environment consistently represents partial information about $T_{\mathcal{G}}$, with possible redundancy: several variables may have the same coordinates. Good environments consist only of atoms, and targets of non-atomic formulas in $\Gamma_{\mathcal{G}}$ are nullary. Therefore, for good Δ, and for a unary or binary atom α, it follows from Lemma 2 that $\Gamma_{\mathcal{G}}, \Delta \vdash \alpha$ is only possible when α actually belongs to Δ.

Lemma 4. *If $\Gamma_{\mathcal{G}}, \Delta \vdash F : loop$, for some good Δ, and some long normal proof F, then $\mathcal{G}$ is solvable.*

Proof. We proceed by induction with respect to the length of F. Since *loop* is an atom, the long normal proof F must begin with a proof variable Z declared in $\Gamma_{\mathcal{G}}, \Delta$ so that its type ends with *loop* (cf. Lemma 2).

If the variable Z is of type (4) then $F = Zx'D$, where x' is an object variable and $\Gamma_{\mathcal{G}}, \Delta \vdash D : \mathrm{OK}(x')$. Then $\mathrm{OK}(x')$ must actually be in Δ. Hence $T_{\mathcal{G}}(m, n) = \mathrm{OK}$, for some m, n.

Now suppose that Z is of type (2). Then $F = Zy'D_E D_A(\lambda x'\lambda Z_1 Z_2 Z_3.\, D)$, where D_E and D_A are, respectively, of type $\mathrm{E}(y')$ and $\mathrm{A}(y')$, and

$$\Gamma_{\mathcal{G}}, \Delta, Z_1 : \mathrm{H}(y', x'), Z_2 : \mathrm{E}(x'), Z_3 : \mathrm{A}(x') \ \vdash D : \mathit{loop}.$$

As in the previous case, the atoms $\mathrm{E}(y')$ and $\mathrm{A}(y')$ must occur in Δ. To apply induction to D, it suffices to prove that the environment

$$\Delta' = \Delta, Z_1 : \mathrm{H}(y', x'), Z_2 : \mathrm{E}(x'), Z_3 : \mathrm{A}(x')$$

is good. Since Δ is good, the variable y' has exactly one pair of coordinates $(m, 0)$ in Δ'. The new variable x' has the coordinates $(m+1, 0)$ and this is its only pair of coordinates. We conclude that Δ' is good.

If Z is of type (3) then the argument is similar as in case (2). If it is of type (0) then $F = Zy'z'u'v'D_{\mathrm{K}}D_{\mathrm{L}}D_{\mathrm{M}}D_{\mathrm{N}}D_{\mathrm{V}}D^1_{\mathrm{H}}D^2_{\mathrm{H}}(\lambda x'\lambda Z_1 Z_2 Z_3.\, D)$, where:

- Terms D_{K}, D_{L}, D_{M}, D_{N}, D_{V}, D^1_{H}, D^2_{H} are respectively of types $\mathrm{K}(y')$, $\mathrm{L}(z')$, $\mathrm{M}(u')$, $\mathrm{N}(v')$, $\mathrm{V}(z', y')$, $\mathrm{H}(z', u')$, $\mathrm{H}(u', v')$ in the environment $\Gamma_{\mathcal{G}}, \Delta$;
- $\Gamma_{\mathcal{G}}, \Delta, Z_1 : \mathrm{T}(x'), Z_2 : \mathrm{H}(y', x'), Z_3 : \mathrm{V}(u', x') \ \vdash D : \mathit{loop}$;
- $\mathrm{T} = \mathcal{R}(\mathrm{K}, \mathrm{L}, \mathrm{M}, \mathrm{N})$.

But if a long normal form has type $\mathrm{K}(y')$ in $\Gamma_{\mathcal{G}}, \Delta$ then it must be a proof variable. The same holds for all the proofs mentioned in the first item above: these atoms must simply belong to Δ.

Let $\Delta' = \Delta, \mathrm{T}(x'), \mathrm{H}(y', x'), \mathrm{V}(u', x')$. The environment Δ is good, so the variables y', z', v', and u' have exactly one pair of coordinates each. In addition, the presence of assumptions $\mathrm{V}(z', y')$ and $\mathrm{H}(z', u')$ forces that the coordinates of y', z', u' are of the form $(m, n+1)$, (m, n), and $(m+1, n)$, respectively. Since $\mathrm{H}(y', x'), \mathrm{V}(u', x') \in \Delta'$, the added variable x' has coordinates $(m+1, n+1)$ in Δ', and it is the only such pair. In addition, v' has coordinates $(m+2, n)$, because $\mathrm{H}(y', x') \in \Delta'$. Since Δ is good, and contains $\mathrm{K}(y')$, $\mathrm{L}(z')$, $\mathrm{M}(u')$, and $\mathrm{N}(v')$, we have $T_{\mathcal{G}}(m+1, n+1) = \mathrm{T}$.

It follows that Δ' is a good environment, and we can apply induction to D because it is a proof of *loop* shorter than F. □

Lemma 5. *If $\Gamma_{\mathcal{G}} \vdash$ start then $\mathcal{G}$ is solvable.*

Proof. A long normal proof of *start* must be of the form $D = Z(\lambda x\lambda XYV.\, D')$, for some variable Z of type (1) and some D' with

$$\Gamma_{\mathcal{G}}, X : \mathrm{E}(x), Y : \mathrm{A}(x), V : \mathrm{B}(x) \vdash D' : \mathit{loop}.$$

The set $\Delta = \{\mathrm{E}(x), \mathrm{A}(x), \mathrm{B}(x)\}$ is good and we apply Lemma 4. □

Our next aim is to show the converse to Lemma 5. For the rest of this section we assume that $\mathcal{G}$ is solvable with $T_{\mathcal{G}}(m_0, n_0) = \mathrm{OK}$. For a good set Δ define

$$S_\Delta = \{(m, n) \mid \text{some } x \in \mathrm{FV}(\Delta) \text{ has coordinates } (m, n)\}.$$

We say that a set Δ of formulas is *very good* when Δ is good and:

- The set S_Δ is a subset of $\mathcal{L}(m_0, n_0)$;
- For every $(m, n) \in S_\Delta$, exactly one $x \in \mathrm{FV}(\Delta)$ has coordinates (m, n);
- If $x \in \mathrm{FV}(\Delta)$ has coordinates $(m+1, n)$ then some $\mathrm{H}(y, x)$ is in Δ;
- If $x \in \mathrm{FV}(\Delta)$ has coordinates $(m, n+1)$ then some $\mathrm{V}(y, x)$ is in Δ.

Intuitively, in a very good set there is no redundancy and every location is "fully justified".

Lemma 6. *If $\Delta \neq \varnothing$ is very good then $\Gamma_{\mathcal{G}}, \Delta \vdash loop$.*

Proof. Induction with respect to the cardinality of the difference $\mathcal{L}(m_0, n_0) - S_\Delta$. In the base case we have $(m_0, n_0) \in S_\Delta$, whence $\mathrm{OK}(x) \in \Delta$, for some x. We use the assumption (4) to derive *loop*.

For the induction step, let $(m', n') \in \mathcal{L}(m_0, n_0) - S_\Delta$ be minimal with respect to $\preceq$. It exists because the relation $\preceq$ is well-founded. Suppose for example that $m' = m + 1$ and $n' = 0$. By the minimality of (m', n'), there is a unique variable $y \in \mathrm{FV}(\Delta)$ with coordinates $(m, 0)$ and with $\mathrm{E}(y), \mathrm{A}(y) \in \Delta$. Then $\Delta' = \Delta \cup \{\mathrm{H}(y, x), \mathrm{E}(x), \mathrm{A}(x)\}$ is very good, for a fresh x, whence $\Gamma_{\mathcal{G}}, \Delta' \vdash loop$. That is, we have $\Gamma_{\mathcal{G}}, \Delta \vdash \mathrm{H}(y, x) \to \mathrm{E}(x) \to \mathrm{A}(x) \to loop$. Since $x \notin \mathrm{FV}(\Delta)$, we generalize over x and use the assumption (2) to obtain $\Gamma_{\mathcal{G}}, \Delta \vdash loop$. □

Lemma 7. *If $\mathcal{G}$ is solvable then $\Gamma_{\mathcal{G}} \vdash start$.*

Proof. The set $\Delta = \{\mathrm{E}(x), \mathrm{A}(x), \mathrm{B}(x)\}$ is very good, so by Lemma 6 we have $\Gamma_{\mathcal{G}}, \mathrm{E}(x), \mathrm{A}(x), \mathrm{B}(x) \vdash loop$. Hence $\Gamma_{\mathcal{G}} \vdash \mathrm{E}(x) \to \mathrm{A}(x) \to \mathrm{B}(x) \to loop$. Using axiom (1) one derives $\Gamma_{\mathcal{G}} \vdash start$. □

Theorem 8. *Provability in Σ_2 is undecidable.*

Proof. By Lemma 3, solvability of tiling puzzles is undecidable. Lemmas 5 and 7 give an effective reduction from the tiling puzzle problem to provability. □

3.2 Undecidability for Π_2

The undecidability proof for Π_2 formulas follows a similar pattern as the proof for Σ_2. Given a tiling puzzle $\mathcal{G}$, we define a set $\Gamma_{\mathcal{G}}$ of Σ_2 formulas, where formulas (1) and (4) remain unchanged, while formulas (0), (2), and (3) are replaced by formulas (0'), (2'), and (3') using new unary predicates R, Rh, and Rv. Those serve as intermediate proof goals or "internal states" in proof construction.

(0') $\forall x\,[\forall yzuv\,(\mathrm{K}(y) \to \mathrm{L}(z) \to \mathrm{M}(u) \to \mathrm{N}(v) \to \mathrm{V}(z, y) \to \mathrm{H}(z, u) \to \mathrm{H}(u, v) \to (\mathrm{T}(x) \to \mathrm{H}(y, x) \to \mathrm{V}(u, x) \to loop) \to \mathrm{R}(x)) \to \mathrm{R}(x)] \to loop$;

(2') $\forall x[\mathrm{E}(x) \to \mathrm{A}(x) \to \forall y(\mathrm{E}(y) \to \mathrm{A}(y) \to (\mathrm{H}(y, x) \to loop) \to \mathrm{Rh}(x)) \to \mathrm{Rh}(x)] \to loop$;

(3') $\forall x[\mathrm{E}(x) \to \mathrm{B}(x) \to \forall y(\mathrm{E}(y) \to \mathrm{B}(y) \to (\mathrm{V}(y, x) \to loop) \to \mathrm{Rv}(x)) \to \mathrm{Rv}(x)] \to loop$.

Theorem 9. *Provability in Π_2 is undecidable.*

Proof. The proof is similar to that of Theorem 8. Lemmas 4–7 need some adjustments. We say that a set Σ of formulas is *neutral*, when it consists exclusively of formulas of the following shapes:

– $\forall yzuv\,[\mathrm{K}(y) \to \mathrm{L}(z) \to \mathrm{M}(u) \to \mathrm{N}(v) \to \mathrm{V}(z, y) \to \mathrm{H}(z, u) \to \mathrm{H}(u, v) \to (\mathrm{T}(x) \to \mathrm{H}(y, x) \to \mathrm{V}(u, x) \to loop) \to \mathrm{R}(x)]$;

- $\mathrm{E}(y) \to \mathrm{A}(y) \to (\mathrm{H}(y,x) \to loop) \to \mathrm{Rh}(x)$;
- $\mathrm{E}(y) \to \mathrm{B}(y) \to (\mathrm{V}(y,x) \to loop) \to \mathrm{Rv}(x)$,

where x and y may be any individual variables. We first show the following analogue of Lemma 4:

If $\Gamma_{\mathcal{G}}, \Delta, \Sigma \vdash F : loop$, for some good Δ, some neutral Σ, and some long normal proof F, then $\mathcal{G}$ is solvable.

The proof is quite similar to that of Lemma 4, but there are some alterations. For instance, a normal proof of *loop* using assumption Z of type (0′) may now take the form $Z(\lambda x' \lambda U. G)$, where U is a proof variable of type

$$\forall yzuv\, (\mathrm{K}(y) \to \mathrm{L}(z) \to \mathrm{M}(u) \to \cdots \to \mathrm{R}(x')),$$

and G is a proof of $\mathrm{R}(x')$, possibly using U. Now, since x' is a new eigenvariable, not occurring in $\Gamma_{\mathcal{G}}, \Delta, \Sigma$, the only way to define G is this:

$$G = Uy'z'u'v' D_{\mathrm{K}} D_{\mathrm{L}} D_{\mathrm{M}} D_{\mathrm{N}} D_{\mathrm{V}} D^1_{\mathrm{H}} D^2_{\mathrm{H}} (\lambda Z_1 Z_2 Z_3.\, D),$$

with D being a shorter proof of *loop* in an environment extended by the declarations of variables Z_1, Z_2, Z_3 (as in the proof of Lemma 4), but also by the declaration of U. However, adding Z_1, Z_2, and Z_3 to Δ preserves the goodness of Δ, and also adding U to Σ preserves the neutrality of Σ. We can thus use the induction hypothesis.

An analogue of Lemma 5 is easily derived from the above. For the converse we need to reprove the statement of Lemma 6:

If $\Delta \neq \varnothing$ is very good then $\Gamma_{\mathcal{G}}, \Delta \vdash loop$,

in the new setting, and this requires only minor adjustments. For example, in case $m' = m+1$ and $n' = n+1$, we have a very good $\Delta' = \Delta \cup \{\mathrm{T}(x), \mathrm{H}(y,x), \mathrm{V}(u,x)\}$, where x is a fresh variable. From the induction hypothesis we have $\Gamma_{\mathcal{G}}, \Delta' \vdash loop$, whence $\Gamma_{\mathcal{G}}, \Delta \vdash \mathrm{T}(x) \to \mathrm{H}(y,x) \to \mathrm{V}(u,x) \to loop$. So if $\vartheta(x)$ denotes

$$\forall yzuv\, (\mathrm{K}(y) \to \cdots \to \mathrm{H}(u,v) \to (\mathrm{T}(x) \to \mathrm{H}(y,x) \to \mathrm{V}(u,x) \to loop) \to \mathrm{R}(x)),$$

then we can derive $\Gamma_{\mathcal{G}}, \Delta, \vartheta(x) \vdash \mathrm{R}(x)$. This yields $\Gamma_{\mathcal{G}}, \Delta \vdash \forall x\, [\vartheta(x) \to \mathrm{R}(x)]$, because x is not free in $\Gamma_{\mathcal{G}}, \Delta$. It remains to apply (0’) to derive *loop*. □

3.3 Monadic Σ_2 and Π_2

Our proofs of Theorems 8 and 9 used binary relation symbols. We now show how to eliminate them by a syntactic translation.

Let **1** and **2** be fresh unary relation symbols (i.e., not occurring in the source language). With every binary relation symbol P we associate another fresh nullary symbol **p**. We define $\overline{\mathrm{P}(x,y)} = \mathbf{1}(x) \to \mathbf{2}(y) \to \mathbf{p}$, for binary P, and $\overline{\mathrm{P}(x)} = \mathrm{P}(x)$, $\overline{\mathrm{P}} = \mathrm{P}$, when P is unary or nullary. Then, by induction, define $\overline{\forall x\, \varphi} = \forall x\, \overline{\varphi}$, and $\overline{\varphi \to \psi} = \overline{\varphi} \to \overline{\psi}$.

Lemma 10. *Let Σ consist of binary atoms and let targets of all formulas in Γ be nullary or unary. Then $\overline{\Gamma}, \overline{\Sigma} \vdash \overline{\mathrm{P}(x,y)}$ implies $\mathrm{P}(x,y) \in \Sigma$.*

Proof. We have $\overline{\Gamma}, \overline{\Sigma}, \mathbf{1}(x), \mathbf{2}(y) \vdash \mathbf{p}$. No formula in $\overline{\Gamma}$ may end with $\mathbf{p}$, thus a long normal proof of $\mathbf{p}$ must begin with an element of $\overline{\Sigma}$: a variable of type $\overline{\mathrm{Q}(u,v)} = \mathbf{1}(u) \to \mathbf{2}(v) \to \mathbf{q}$. Then $\mathbf{q} = \mathbf{p}$, i.e., $\mathrm{P} = \mathrm{Q}$, and we have $\overline{\Gamma}, \overline{\Sigma}, \mathbf{1}(x), \mathbf{2}(y) \vdash \mathbf{1}(u)$ and $\overline{\Gamma}, \overline{\Sigma}, \mathbf{1}(x), \mathbf{2}(y) \vdash \mathbf{2}(v)$. There is no other way to prove $\mathbf{1}(u)$ but to use the assumption $\mathbf{1}(x)$. Hence, $x = u$, and similarly we also obtain $y = v$. Thus, $\mathrm{P}(x,y) = \mathrm{Q}(u,v) \in \Sigma$. □

We say that a formula is *easy* when it is either an atom, or has the form

– $\forall x\, \varphi$, where φ is easy and it is not an atom, or
– $\varphi \to \psi$, where φ and ψ are easy, and the target of ψ is unary or nullary.

Observe that the sets $\Gamma_{\mathcal{G}}$ in Section 3 and 3.2 consist of easy formulas.

Lemma 11. *If $\overline{\Gamma} \vdash \overline{\varphi}$, where φ and all formulas in Γ are easy, then $\Gamma \vdash \varphi$.*

Proof. A *quasi-long eliminator* is a term of the form $XE_1 \ldots E_m$, where X is a proof variable and every E_i is either a lnf or an object variable. Observe that if $\overline{\Gamma} \vdash M : \tau$, where M is a quasi-long eliminator, then either $\tau = \overline{\varphi}$, for some φ, or $\tau = \mathbf{2}(y) \to \mathbf{p}$, or $\tau = \mathbf{p}$, for some $\mathbf{p}$ and y. In the last two cases, we have $M = M'N_1$ or $M = M'N_1N_2$, with $M' : \overline{\mathrm{P}(x,y)}$, and $N_1 : \mathbf{1}(x)$, and $N_2 : \mathbf{2}(y)$, for some x.

Let now $\overline{\Gamma} \vdash M : \overline{\varphi}$, where M is an lnf or a quasi-long eliminator. We prove that $\Gamma \vdash \varphi$, by induction with respect to M. The case of a variable is obvious.

Let $M = \lambda Z.\, N$. The case of $\varphi = \mathrm{P}(x,y)$ follows from Lemma 10, because the only easy formulas with binary targets are atoms. So we can assume that $\varphi = \psi \to \vartheta$, and we have $\overline{\Gamma}, Z : \overline{\psi} \vdash N : \overline{\vartheta}$. By the induction hypothesis for N we have $\Gamma, \psi \vdash \vartheta$, whence $\Gamma \vdash \varphi$.

If $M = \lambda y\, N$ (where we can assume y fresh) then $\overline{\varphi} = \forall y\, \tau$, which means that $\varphi = \forall y\, \psi$ with $\overline{\psi} = \tau$. We have $\overline{\Gamma} \vdash N : \overline{\psi}$, so $\Gamma \vdash \psi$ and thus $\Gamma \vdash \varphi$ by generalization.

If $\overline{\Gamma} \vdash X\vec{E}N : \overline{\varphi}$ then the type of $X\vec{E}$ must be of the form $\overline{\psi} \to \overline{\varphi}$, because $\overline{\varphi}$ is neither of the form $\mathbf{2}(y) \to \mathbf{p}$ nor $\mathbf{p}$. By the induction hypothesis, both $\psi \to \varphi$ and ψ are provable, and so must be φ.

If $\overline{\Gamma} \vdash X\vec{E}y : \overline{\varphi}$, where y is an object variable, then $\overline{\Gamma} \vdash X\vec{E} : \forall x\, \tau$, for some τ with $\overline{\varphi} = \tau[y/x]$. Since $X\vec{E}$ is a quasi-long eliminator, we must have $\forall x\, \tau = \overline{\forall x\, \psi}$, and $\varphi = \psi[y/x]$. We apply induction to $X\vec{E}$. □

The converse to Lemma 11 is obvious. Since all formulas used in our coding are easy, we can restate Lemmas 5 and 7 using $\overline{\Gamma}_{\mathcal{G}}$ instead of $\Gamma_{\mathcal{G}}$.

Theorem 12. *It is undecidable whether a given Σ_2 (resp. Π_2) formula with unary predicates is provable.*

4 EXPSPACE-completeness for Σ_1

The lower bound is obtained by encoding the halting problem for bus machines [23] into the inhabitation problem. A bus machine is an alternating computing device operating on a finite word (bus) of a fixed length. At every step the whole content of the bus is updated according to one of the instructions of the machine. In addition new instructions may be created each time and those can be used in later steps. A precise definition is as follows.

A *simple switch* over a finite alphabet $\mathcal{A}$ is a pair of elements of $\mathcal{A}$, written $a \rhd b$. A *labeled switch* is a quadruple, written $a \rhd b(c \rhd d)$, where the simple switch $c \rhd d$ is the *label*. Finally, a *universal switch* is a triple, written $a \rhd b \times c$.

Formally, a *bus machine* is a tuple $\mathcal{M} = \langle \mathcal{A}, m, w_0, w_1, \mathcal{I} \rangle$, where $\mathcal{A}$ is a finite alphabet, $m > 0$ is the *bus length* of $\mathcal{M}$ (the length of the words processed), w_0 and w_1 are words of length m over $\mathcal{A}$, called the *initial* and *final word*, respectively, and $\mathcal{I}$ is a set of *global instructions*.

Every global instruction is an m-tuple $\mathbb{I} = \langle I_1, \ldots, I_m \rangle$ of sets of switches. Switches in I_i are meant to act on the i-th symbol of the bus. It is required that all switches in a given instruction $\mathbb{I}$ are of the same kind: either all are simple, or all are labeled, or all are universal. Therefore we classify instructions as simple, labeled, and universal. A *local instruction* is a special case of a simple instruction with singleton sets at all coordinates.

A *configuration* of $\mathcal{M}$ is a pair $\langle w, \mathcal{J} \rangle$, where w is a word over $\mathcal{A}$ of length m, and $\mathcal{J}$ is a set of local instructions. The *initial* configuration is $\langle w_0, \varnothing \rangle$, and any configuration of the form $\langle w_1, \mathcal{J} \rangle$ is called *final*.

Let $\mathbb{I} = \langle I_1, \ldots, I_m \rangle$, $w = a_1 \ldots a_m$, and $w' = b_1 \ldots b_m$, $w'' = c_1 \ldots c_m$. Transitions of $\mathcal{M}$ according to $\mathbb{I}$ are defined as follows:

- If $\mathbb{I}$ is a simple instruction, and for every $i \leq m$ the switch $a_i \rhd b_i$ belongs to I_i, then $\langle w, \mathcal{J} \rangle \Rightarrow^{\mathbb{I}}_{\mathcal{M}} \langle w', \mathcal{J} \rangle$;
- If $\mathbb{I}$ is a labeled instruction and $a_i \rhd b_i(c_i \rhd d_i)$ is in I_i, for every $i \leq m$, then $\langle w, \mathcal{J} \rangle \Rightarrow^{\mathbb{I}}_{\mathcal{M}} \langle w', \mathcal{J}' \rangle$, where $\mathcal{J}' = \mathcal{J} \cup \{\langle \{c_1 \rhd d_1\}, \ldots, \{c_m \rhd d_m\} \rangle\}$;
- If $\mathbb{I}$ is universal and $a_i \rhd b_i \times c_i$ is in I_i, for all $i \leq m$, then $\langle w, \mathcal{J} \rangle \Rightarrow^{\mathbb{I}}_{M} \langle w', \mathcal{J} \rangle$, and also $\langle w, \mathcal{J} \rangle \Rightarrow^{\mathbb{I}}_{M} \langle w'', \mathcal{J} \rangle$.

A configuration $\langle w, \mathcal{J} \rangle$ is *accepting* iff it is either a final configuration, or

- There is a non-universal instruction $\mathbb{I} \in \mathcal{I} \cup \mathcal{J}$, with $\langle w, \mathcal{J} \rangle \Rightarrow^{\mathbb{I}}_{\mathcal{M}} \langle w', \mathcal{J}' \rangle$, where $\langle w', \mathcal{J}' \rangle$ is accepting, or
- There is a universal $\mathbb{I} \in \mathcal{I} \cup \mathcal{J}$ such that we have $\langle w, \mathcal{J} \rangle \Rightarrow^{\mathbb{I}}_{\mathcal{M}} \langle w', \mathcal{J} \rangle$ and $\langle w, \mathcal{J} \rangle \Rightarrow^{\mathbb{I}}_{\mathcal{M}} \langle w'', \mathcal{J} \rangle$, where both $\langle w', \mathcal{J} \rangle$ and $\langle w'', \mathcal{J} \rangle$ are accepting.

The machine $\mathcal{M}$ *halts* iff the initial configuration is accepting. As usual with alternating machines, an accepting computation of a bus machine should be imagined as a tree with final configurations at all leaves and universal transitions at branching nodes.

Example 13. This example is based on [13]. Let $\mathcal{A} = \{0, 1, 2, 3\}$, and let

$$I^+ = \{0 \rhd 1(2 \rhd 3)\}, \quad I^- = \{1 \rhd 0(3 \rhd 2)\},$$
$$I = \{0 \rhd 0(2 \rhd 2), 1 \rhd 1(3 \rhd 3)\}, \quad I^* = \{1 \rhd 2\}.$$

Consider $\mathcal{M} = \langle \mathcal{A}, 4, 0000, 3333, \mathcal{I} \rangle$, where $\mathcal{I}$ consists of the following tuples:

$$\langle I, I, I, I^+ \rangle, \langle I, I, I^+, I^- \rangle, \langle I, I^+, I^-, I^- \rangle, \langle I^+, I^-, I^-, I^- \rangle, \langle I^*, I^*, I^*, I^* \rangle.$$

The machine $\mathcal{M}$ behaves in a deterministic way, for example the only instruction applicable in the initial configuration $\langle 0000, \varnothing \rangle$ is $\langle I, I, I, I^+ \rangle$. Executing it yields $\langle\, 0001, \{I_0\}\,\rangle$, where I_0 is $\langle\, \{2\rhd 2\}, \{2\rhd 2\}, \{2\rhd 2\}, \{2\rhd 3\}\,\rangle$. The latter can be used later to change a configuration of the form $\langle\, 2222, \mathcal{J}\,\rangle$ into $\langle\, 2223, \mathcal{J}\,\rangle$. But now the machine must execute $\langle\, I, I, I^+, I^-\,\rangle$ and enter $\langle\, 0010, \{I_0, I_1\}\,\rangle$, where $I_1 = \langle\, \{2 \rhd 2\}, \{2 \rhd 2\}, \{2 \rhd 3\}, \{3 \rhd 2\}\,\rangle$.

In the first phase of computation only global instructions are executed and all words over $\{0, 1\}$ appear on the bus in the lexicographic order. Every application of a global instruction creates a new unique local instruction. After arriving at 1111, the machine rewrites the bus to 2222 using $\langle\, I^*, I^*, I^*, I^*\,\rangle$ and then executes one by one all the local instructions, eventually reaching the final 3333.

Theorem 14 ([23]). *The bus machine halting problem is* EXPSPACE*-complete.*

Given a bus machine $\mathcal{M} = \langle\, \mathcal{A}, m, w_0, w_1, \mathcal{I}\,\rangle$, we construct (in LOGSPACE) a set of universal formulas $\Gamma_{\mathcal{M}}$ and an open formula $\alpha_{\mathcal{M}}$ such that $\Gamma_{\mathcal{M}} \vdash \alpha_{\mathcal{M}}$ if and only if $\mathcal{M}$ halts. The free variables in $\Gamma_{\mathcal{M}}$ and $\alpha_{\mathcal{M}}$ are identified with the symbols in $\mathcal{A}$ and the number, as well as arity, of relation symbols in our formulas also depend on $\mathcal{M}$. The main relation symbol Bus is m-ary and it is intended to represent the content of the bus. The obvious convention is to write $\mathsf{Bus}(w)$ for $\mathsf{Bus}(a_1, \ldots, a_m)$, when $w = a_1 \ldots a_m$ and to write $\vec{a}$ for $a_1 a_2 \ldots a_m$.

The formula α_M is $\mathsf{Bus}(w_0)$, and $\mathsf{Bus}(w_1)$ is a member of $\Gamma_{\mathcal{M}}$. The idea is that a proof of $\mathsf{Bus}(w_0)$ succeeds when every branch of a computation can terminate by calling the axiom $\mathsf{Bus}(w_1)$.

We associate binary (resp. ternary, quaternary) predicate symbols I with sets I of simple (resp. universal, labeled) switches occurring in the instructions of $\mathcal{M}$. Then for every simple switch $a \rhd b$ in I, the atomic formula $I(a, b)$ is placed in $\Gamma_{\mathcal{M}}$, and similarly for universal and labeled switches. For example, the set I in Example 13 yields two assumptions $I(0, 0, 2, 2)$ and $I(1, 1, 3, 3)$.

In $\Gamma_{\mathcal{M}}$ there are also formulas $\psi_{\mathbb{I}}$ for all global instructions $\mathbb{I}$ in $\mathcal{I}$. In case of a simple instruction $\mathbb{I} = \langle\, I_1, \ldots, I_m\,\rangle$, the formula takes the form:

(1) $\psi_{\mathbb{I}} = \forall \vec{x}\vec{y}\, (I_1(x_1, y_1) \to \cdots \to I_m(x_m, y_m) \to \mathsf{Bus}(\vec{y}) \to \mathsf{Bus}(\vec{x}))$.

If $\mathbb{I} = \langle\, I_1, \ldots, I_m\,\rangle$ is labeled, then:

$$(2)\ \psi_{\mathbb{I}} = \forall \vec{x}\vec{y}\vec{z}\vec{u}\, (I_1(x_1, y_1, z_1, u_1) \to \cdots \to I_m(x_m, y_m, z_m, u_m) \\ \to ((\mathsf{Bus}(\vec{u}) \to \mathsf{Bus}(\vec{z})) \to \mathsf{Bus}(\vec{y})) \to \mathsf{Bus}(\vec{x})).$$

Finally, for a universal instruction $\mathbb{I} = \langle\, I_1, \ldots, I_m\,\rangle$, we take:

$$(3)\ \psi_{\mathbb{I}} = \forall \vec{x}\vec{y}\vec{z}\, (I_1(x_1, y_1, z_1) \to \cdots \to I_m(x_m, y_m, z_m) \\ \to \mathsf{Bus}(\vec{z}) \to \mathsf{Bus}(\vec{y}) \to \mathsf{Bus}(\vec{x})).$$

A local instruction J may be identified with a rewrite rule of the form $w \Rightarrow v$. Such a rule will be represented as a formula φ_J of the form $\mathsf{Bus}(v) \to \mathsf{Bus}(w)$. We define $\Gamma_{\mathcal{J}} = \{\varphi_J \mid J \in \mathcal{J}\}$.

To see the motivation, suppose we want to derive $\Gamma_{\mathcal{M}} \vdash \mathsf{Bus}(1111)$, where $\mathcal{M}$ is as in Example 13. We use the formula $\psi_{\langle\, I^*, I^*, I^*, I^*\,\rangle}$:

$$\forall \vec{x}\vec{y}(I^*(x_1, y_1) \to I^*(x_2, y_2) \to I^*(x_3, y_3) \to I^*(x_4, y_4) \to \mathsf{Bus}(\vec{y}) \to \mathsf{Bus}(\vec{x}),$$

instantiated by substituting 1 for x_i and 2 for y_i. Since the assumption $I^*(1, 2)$ is in $\Gamma_{\mathcal{M}}$, the task of proving $\mathsf{Bus}(1111)$ is reduced to proving $\mathsf{Bus}(2222)$.

Lemma 15. *A configuration* $\langle w, \mathcal{J} \rangle$ *is accepting if and only if the judgement* $\Gamma_{\mathcal{M}}, \Gamma_{\mathcal{J}} \vdash \mathsf{Bus}(w)$ *is derivable.*

Proof. From left to right the proof is by induction with respect to the definition of an accepting configuration. Let $\langle w, \mathcal{J} \rangle$ be accepting. If it is final, the proof is trivial, because $\mathsf{Bus}(w_1) \in \Gamma_{\mathcal{M}}$. Otherwise, assume for example that $\langle w, \mathcal{J} \rangle \Rightarrow^{\mathbb{I}}_{\mathcal{M}} \langle w', \mathcal{J}' \rangle$, where $\langle w', \mathcal{J}' \rangle$ is accepting, by an application of a labeled instruction $\mathbb{I} = \langle I_1, \ldots, I_m \rangle$. Then $\mathcal{J}' = \mathcal{J} \cup \{J\}$, where J is a new local instruction. By the induction hypothesis we have $\Gamma_{\mathcal{M}}, \Gamma_{\mathcal{J}}, \varphi_J \vdash \mathsf{Bus}(w')$. It follows that $\Gamma_{\mathcal{M}}, \Gamma_{\mathcal{J}} \vdash \varphi_J \to \mathsf{Bus}(w')$. For $j = 1, \ldots, m$, let $a_j \rhd b_j(c_j \rhd d_j)$ be the switches used in this step. Then $w = a_1 \ldots a_m$, $w' = b_1 \ldots b_m$, and the formula φ_J is $\mathsf{Bus}(d_1 \ldots d_m) \to \mathsf{Bus}(c_1 \ldots c_m)$. Hence $\Gamma_{\mathcal{M}}, \Gamma_{\mathcal{J}} \vdash (\mathsf{Bus}(\vec{d}) \to \mathsf{Bus}(\vec{c})) \to \mathsf{Bus}(\vec{b})$. We have all the $I_j(a_j, b_j, c_j, d_j)$ in $\Gamma_{\mathcal{M}}$, so we prove $\mathsf{Bus}(\vec{a})$ using the appropriate axiom (2) instantiated with $\vec{x} := \vec{a}$, $\vec{y} := \vec{b}$, $\vec{z} := \vec{c}$, $\vec{u} := \vec{d}$.

The proof in the direction from right to left is by induction with respect to the length of long normal proofs. Assume that $\Gamma_{\mathcal{M}}, \Gamma_{\mathcal{J}} \vdash \mathsf{Bus}(w)$. If w is not final then a long normal proof must begin with a variable of type (2), (1), or (3). Suppose for example that (3) is the case. For some instantiation $\vec{x} := \vec{a} = w$, $\vec{y} := \vec{b}$, $\vec{z} := \vec{c}$, there are proofs of $I_i(a_i, b_i, c_i)$ and of $\mathsf{Bus}(\vec{b})$ and $\mathsf{Bus}(\vec{c})$. A proof of $I_i(a_i, b_i, c_i)$ is only possible when $I_i(a_i, b_i, c_i)$ actually occurs in $\Gamma_{\mathcal{M}}$. This is because there are no other assumptions with target I_i. In particular this proves that variables b_i, c_i do correspond to actual bus symbols. Since $\mathsf{Bus}(\vec{b})$ and $\mathsf{Bus}(\vec{c})$ are provable, it follows from the induction hypothesis that $\langle \vec{b}, \mathcal{J} \rangle$ and $\langle \vec{c}, \mathcal{J} \rangle$ are accepting. Therefore also $\langle w, \mathcal{J} \rangle$ is accepting. □

Upper bound for Σ_1: A judgement of the form $\Gamma \vdash \varphi$, where φ is a Σ_1 formula and all assumptions in Γ are Π_1 formulas, is called a *Σ_1 judgement*. Observe that normal proofs of Σ_1 judgements are of the form $\Gamma \vdash \lambda X\!:\!\alpha.\, M : \alpha \to \beta$ or $\Gamma \vdash X M_1 \ldots M_r : \beta$, where each M_i, for $i = 1, \ldots, r$, is a proof term or an object variable. Proofs of the latter shape are called *eliminators*. We say that N' is an *instance* of N when $N' = N[\vec{x} := \vec{y}]$ for some object variables $\vec{x}, \vec{y}$.

Lemma 16. *Fix an object variable* x_0. *If* $\Gamma \vdash N : \varphi$ *then* $\Gamma \vdash N' : \varphi$, *for some instance* N' *of* N *such that* $\mathrm{FV}(N') \subseteq \mathcal{W} = \mathrm{FV}(\Gamma) \cup \mathrm{FV}(\varphi) \cup \{x_0\}$.

Proof. If $x \notin \mathcal{W}$ then replacing x by x_0 in N does not affect Γ and φ. □

Lemma 17. *Let* $\Gamma \vdash N : \varphi$, *where* Γ *is a* Π_1 *environment and* N *is normal. Assume in addition that either* N *is an eliminator or* φ *is a* Σ_1 *formula. Then the term* N *contains no occurrences of object abstraction. In addition, if* N *is an eliminator then* φ *is in* Π_1.

Proof. Induction with respect to N. If $N = X$ then the type of X is in Π_1, because X is declared in Γ.

If $N = \lambda X\!:\!\psi.\, P$ then ψ is in Π_1 and $\Gamma, X\!:\!\psi \vdash P : \vartheta$, for some $\vartheta \in \Sigma_1$. We use the induction hypothesis for P. Case $N = \lambda x\, N'$ is impossible.

If $N = X\vec{N}M$, where M is a proof term, then we have $\Gamma \vdash X\vec{N} : \psi \to \varphi$ and $\Gamma \vdash M : \psi$, for some ψ. Since $X\vec{N}$ is an eliminator, the formula $\psi \to \varphi$ is in Π_1 and so must be φ, while ψ is in Σ_1. We apply induction to $X\vec{N}$ and M.

If $N = X\vec{N}y$, where y is an object variable, we apply induction to $X\vec{N}$. □

Let $\mathcal{W}$ be a set of variables. If $\mathrm{FV}(\Gamma) \cup \mathrm{FV}(\varphi) \cup \mathrm{FV}(M) \subseteq \mathcal{W}$ then we say that $\Gamma \vdash M : \varphi$ is a *$\mathcal{W}$-judgement.* A judgement is *$\mathcal{W}$-derivable* when it is derivable using only $\mathcal{W}$-judgements. We have the following easy lemma:

Lemma 18. *Let $\Gamma \vdash M : \varphi$ and let $\mathrm{FV}(\Gamma) \cup \mathrm{FV}(M) \cup \mathrm{FV}(\varphi) \subseteq \mathcal{W}$. If M contains no object abstraction then the judgement $\Gamma \vdash M : \varphi$ is $\mathcal{W}$-derivable.*

Lemma 19. *The decision problem for Σ_1 formulas is solvable in* EXPSPACE.

Proof. To find a proof of a given Σ_1 formula φ one uses an obvious generalization of the Ben-Yelles algorithm [22] for simple types. It follows from Lemma 17 that a normal inhabitant N of a Σ_1 formula φ must not contain any object abstraction. In addition, by Lemma 16 one can assume that free variables of N are all in the set $\mathcal{W} = \mathrm{FV}(\varphi) \cup \{x_0\}$. (The variable x_0 is added to make sure that the set is not empty.) By Lemma18, the judgement $\vdash N : \varphi$ is $\mathcal{W}$-derivable. Therefore the algorithm needs only to consider judgements $\Gamma' \vdash M : \psi$ where all object variables are in $\mathcal{W}$. The number of different formulas in Γ' is thus at most exponential in the size of φ. (With at most n variables, every subformula of φ has at most n^n instances.) Using the same argument as for simple types we therefore obtain an alternating exponential time algorithm. □

Theorem 20. *The decision problem for Σ_1 is* EXPSPACE*-complete.*

Proof. Lemma 15 reduces the halting problem for bus machines to provability in Σ_1. The upper bound is provided by Lemma 19. □

5 Conclusion

We proved that derivability of universally-implicational formulas for classes Σ_2 and Π_2 of Mints hierarchy is undecidable even for unary predicate symbols. In case of Σ_1 we proved EXPSPACE-completeness of the problem in the polyadic case. These results combined with an earlier analysis [20] give the picture of complexity of provability in Mints hierarchy in which the level of a formula φ is determined by the level of a prenex formula classically equivalent to φ. What is also important methodologically, the whole development uses purely proof-theoretical methods.

All the hardness results were obtained for formulas with a fixed depth of quantifiers. This suggests an interesting question to investigate: can all formulas be effectively reduced to ones with a fixed quantifier depth. Two other issues demanding future work are the exact complexity of the class Π_1 and monadic Σ_1.

References

1. Bonevac, D.: A history of quantification. In: Logic: A History of its Central Concepts. Handbook of the History of Logic, vol. 11, North Holland (2012)
2. Börger, E., Grädel, E., Gurevich, Y.: The Classical Decision Problem. Perspectives in Mathematical Logic (1997)
3. Bove, A., Dybjer, P., Norell, U.: A brief overview of Agda – A functional language with dependent types. In: Berghofer, S., Nipkow, T., Urban, C., Wenzel, M. (eds.) TPHOLs 2009. LNCS, vol. 5674, pp. 73–78. Springer, Heidelberg (2009)
4. Burr, W.: The intuitionistic arithmetical hierarchy. In: Logic Colloquium 1999. Lecture Notes in Logic, vol. 17, pp. 51–59. ASL (1999)
5. Church, A.: Introduction to Mathematical Logic. Princeton (1944)
6. Coq Development Team. The Coq Proof Assistant Reference Manual V8.4 (March 2012), `http://coq.inria.fr/distrib/V8.4/refman/`
7. Degtyarev, A., Gurevich, Y., Narendran, P., Veanes, M., Voronkov, A.: Decidability and complexity of simultaneous rigid E-unification with one variable and related results. Theoretical Computer Science 243(1-2), 167–184 (2000)
8. Dowek, G., Jiang, Y.: Eigenvariables, bracketing and the decidability of positive minimal predicate logic. Theoretical Computer Science 360(1-3), 193–208 (2006)
9. Fitting, M.: Fundamentals of Generalized Recursion Theory. Elsevier (1981)
10. Fleischmann, J.: Syntactic preservation theorems for intuitionistic predicate logic. Notre Dame Journal of Formal Logic 51(2), 225–245 (2010)
11. Immerman, N.: Descriptive Complexity. Springer (1999)
12. Kreisel, G.: Elementary completeness properties of intuitionistic logic with a note on negations of prenex formulae. J. Symbolic Logic 23(3), 317–330 (1958)
13. Kuśmierek, D.: The inhabitation problem for rank two intersection types. In: Della Rocca, S.R. (ed.) TLCA 2007. LNCS, vol. 4583, pp. 240–254. Springer, Heidelberg (2007)
14. Mints, G.E.: Solvability of the problem of deducibility in LJ for a class of formulas not containing negative occurrences of quantifiers. Steklov Inst. 98, 135–145 (1968)
15. Nipkow, T., Paulson, L.C., Wenzel, M.: Isabelle/HOL. A Proof Assistant for Higher-Order Logic. Springer (2002)
16. Orevkov, V.P.: The undecidability in the constructive predicate calculus of the class of formulas of the form $\neg\neg\forall\exists$. Doklady AN SSSR 163(3), 581–583 (1965)
17. Orevkov, V.P.: Solvable classes of pseudoprenex formulas. Zapiski nauchnyh Seminarov LOMI 60, 109–170 (1976)
18. Rasiowa, H., Sikorski, R.: On existential theorems in non-classical functional calculi. Fundamenta Mathematicae 41, 21–28 (1954)
19. Rummelhoff, I.: Polymorphic $\Pi 1$ Types and a Simple Approach to Propositions, Types and Sets. PhD thesis, University of Oslo (2007)
20. Schubert, A., Urzyczyn, P., Walukiewicz-Chrząszcz, D.: How hard is positive quantification? (2014), `http://www.mimuw.edu.pl/~alx/positive2conexp.pdf`
21. Schubert, A., Urzyczyn, P., Walukiewicz-Chrząszcz, D.: Positive quantification is not elementary (with restricted instantiation) (2014), `http://www.mimuw.edu.pl/~alx/positivenonelem.pdf`
22. Sørensen, M.H., Urzyczyn, P.: Lectures on the Curry-Howard Isomorphism. Elsevier (2006)
23. Urzyczyn, P.: Inhabitation of low-rank intersection types. In: Curien, P.-L. (ed.) TLCA 2009. LNCS, vol. 5608, pp. 356–370. Springer, Heidelberg (2009)

Author Index

Printed in the United States
By Bookmasters